AN

ECCLESIASTICAL HISTORY,

ANCIENT AND MODERN;

IN WHICH

THE RISE, PROGRESS, AND VARIATIONS OF CHURCH POWER, ARE CONSIDERED IN THEIR CONNEXION WITH THE STATE OF LEARNING AND PHILOSOPHY, AND THE POLITICAL HISTORY OF EUROPE DURING THAT PERIOD;

BY THE LATE LEARNED

JOHN LAURENCE MOSHEIM, D. D.

CHANCELLOR OF THE UNIVERSITY OF GOTTINGEN;

TRANSLATED FROM THE ORIGINAL LATIN,

AND ILLUSTRATED WITH NOTES, CHRONOLOGICAL TABLES, AND AN APPENDIX

BY ARCHIBALD MACLAINE, D. D.

A NEW EDITION—IN TWO VOLUMES,

CONTINUED TO THE YEAR 1826.

BY CHARLES COOTE, L. L. D.

AND FURNISHED WITH

A DISSERTATION ON THE STATE OF THE PRIMITIVE CHURCH

BY THE RIGHT REV.

DR. GEORGE GLEIG, OF STIRLING.

VOL. II.

NEW YORK:

HARPER & BROTHERS, PUBLISHERS,

329 & 331 PEARL STREET,

FRANKLIN SQUARE

1871.

AN

ECCLESIASTICAL HISTORY;

BOOK THE FOURTH,

CONTAINING THE

HISTORY OF THE CHURCH

FROM

THE BEGINNING OF THE REFORMATION BY LUTHER

TO

THE PRESENT TIMES

INTRODUCTION.

I. The order and method, that have been followed in the former part of this work, cannot be continued, without the greatest inconvenience, in this fourth book, which relates to the modern history of the church. From the commencement of the sixteenth century, the face of religion was remarkably changed; the divisions, that had formerly perplexed the church, increased considerably; and the Christian societies, that relinquished the established forms of divine worship, and erected themselves into separate assemblies, upon principles different from those of the Roman hierarchy, rapidly multiplied. This circumstance renders it impossible to present in one connected series, or, as it were, in one continued tablature, the events, vicissitudes, and revolutions, which happened in the church, divided its members, and enfeebled the dominion of its tyrants. From the period on which we now enter, the bond of union among Christians, that had been formed by a blind obedience to the Roman pontiff, was in almost every country, either dissolved, or at least relaxed; and consequently this period of our history must be divided into a multitude of branches, into as many parts, as there were famous sects that arose in this century.

II. It is however proper to observe here, that many of the events, which distinguished this century, had a manifest relation to the church in general, and not to any Christian society in particular; and, as these events deserve to be mentioned separately, on account of their remarkable tendency to throw a light upon the state of Christianity in general, as well as upon the history of each Christian society, we shall divide this fourth book into two main and principal parts, of which the one will contain the *General* and the other the *Particular History of the Christian Religion.*

III. To the *General History* belong all those events which relate to the state of Christianity, considered in itself and in its utmost extent, to the Christian church viewed in the general, and abstracted from the miserable and multiplied divisions into which it was rent by the passions of men. Under this head we shall take notice of the advancement and progress of Christianity in general, without any regard to the particular sects that were thus instrumental in promoting its interests; nor shall we omit the consideration of certain doctrines, rites, and institutions, which appeared worthy of admission to all, or at least to the greatest part of the Christian sects, and which consequently produced, in various countries, improvements or changes of greater or less importance.

IV. In the *Particular History* of this century, we propose reviewing, in their proper order, the various sects into which the church was divided. This part of our work, for the sake of method and precision, we shall subdivide into two. In the first we shall comprehend what relates to the more ancient Christian sects, both in the eastern and western hemispheres; while the second will be confined to the history of those more modern societies, the date of whose origin is posterior to the Reformation in Germany. In the accounts that are here to be given of the circumstances, fate, and doctrines of each sect, the method laid down in the introduction to this work shall be rigorously observed, as far as is possible, since it seems best calculated to lead us to an accurate knowledge of the nature, progress, and tenets of every Christian society, that arose in those times of discord.

V. The most momentous event that distinguished the church after the fifteenth century, and we may add, the most glorious of all the revolutions that happened in the state of Christianity since the time of its divine and immortal Founder, was that happy change introduced into religion, which is known by the title of the *Blessed Reformation.* This grand revolution, which arose in Saxony from small beginnings, not only spread itself with the utmost rapidity through all the European provinces, but also extended its efficacy to the most distant parts of the globe, and may be justly considered as the main spring which has moved the nations from that illustrious period, and occasioned the greatest part both of those civil and religious revolutions that fill the annals of history down to our times. The face of Europe was, in a more especial manner, changed by this great event. The present age feels yet, in a sensible manner, and ages to come will continue to perceive, the inestimable advantages produced by it, and the inconveniences of which it has been the innocent occasion. The history, therefore, of such an important revolution, from which so many others have derived their origin, and whose relations and connexions are so extensive and so general, demands a peculiar degree of attention, and has an unquestionable right to a distinguished place in such a work as this. We now proceed to give a compendious view of the modern history of the Christian church, according to the intimated plan and method

AN

ECCLESIASTICAL HISTORY.

THE SIXTEENTH CENTURY.

SECTION I.

THE HISTORY OF THE REFORMATION.

I. The History of the Reformation is too ample and extensive to be comprehended, without some degree of confusion, in the uninterrupted narrative of one Section: we shall therefore divide it into Four Parts.

The first will contain an account of the state of Christianity before the commencement of the Reformation;

The second will give the history of the Reformation from its beginning until the date of the Confession of Augsburg;

The third will exhibit a view of the same history, from this latter period to the commencement of the war of Smalcald; and

The fourth will carry it down to the peace that was concluded with the advocates of the Reformation in the year 1555.* This division is natural; it arises spontaneously from the events themselves.

CHAPTER I.

Concerning the State of the Christian Church before the Reformation.

I. About the commencement of this century, the Roman pontiffs lived in the utmost tranquillity; nor had they, as things seemed to be situated, the least reason to apprehend any opposition to their pretensions, or rebellion against their authority; since those dreadful commotions, which had been excited in the preceding ages by the Waldenses, Albigenses, and Beghards, and more recently by the Bohemians, were entirely suppressed, and had yielded to the united powers of counsel and the sword. Such of the Waldenses as yet remained, lived contented under the difficulties of extreme poverty in the valleys of Piedmont, and proposed to themselves no higher earthly felicity, than that of leaving to their descendants that wretched and obscure corner of Europe, which separates the Alps from the Pyrenean mountains; while the handful of Bohemians, that survived the ruin of their faction, and still persevered in their opposition to the Roman yoke, had neither strength nor knowledge adequate to any new attempt, and therefore, instead of inspiring terror, became objects of contempt.

II. We must not, however, conclude from this apparent tranquillity and security of the pontiffs and their adherents, that their measures were applauded, or that their chains were worn without reluctance; for not only private persons, but also the most powerful princes and sovereign states, exclaimed loudly against the despotic dominion of the pontiffs, the fraud, violence, avarice, and injustice that prevailed in their counsels, the arrogance, tyranny, and extortion of their legates, the unbridled licentiousness and enormous crimes of the clergy and monks of all denominations, the inordinate severity and partiality of the Roman laws; and demanded publicly, as their ancestors had done before them, a *reformation* of the church, in its head and in its members, and a general council to accomplish that necessary and happy purpose.* But these complaints and demands were not carried so far as to produce any good effect, since they came from persons who did not entertain the least doubt about the supreme authority of the pope in religious matters, and who, of consequence, instead of attempting, themselves, to bring about that reformation which was so ardently desired, remained entirely inactive, and looked for redress to the

* The writers of the history of the Reformation, of every rank and order, are enumerated by the very learned Philip Fred. Hane (who himself deserves a most eminent rank in this class) in his Historia Sacrorum a Luthero emendatorum, part i. and by Jo. Alb. Fabricius, in his Centifolium Lutheranum, part ii. cap. clxxxvii. The greatest part, or at least the most eminent, of this list of authors must be consulted by such as desire a farther confirmation or illustration of the matters which I propose to relate briefly in the course of this history. The illustrious names of Sleidan and Seckendorff, and others, who have distinguished themselves in this kind of erudition, are too well known to render it necessary to recommend their works to the perusal of the curious reader.

* These complaints and accusations have been largely enumerated by several writers. See, among many others, Val. Ern. Loescherus, in Actis et Documentis Reformationis, tom. i. cap. v. ix. et Ern Salom. Cyprian. Præfat. ad Wilk. Ern. Tenzelii Historiam Reformat. published at Leipsic in 1717.—The grievances complained of by the Germans in particular, are amply mentioned by J. F. Georgius in his Gravamina Imperator. et Nationis German. adversus Sedem Romanam, cap. vii. Nor do the wiser and more learned among the modern Romanists pretend to deny that the church and clergy, before the time of Luther, were corrupt in a very high degree

court of Rome, or to a general council. As long as the authority of the pontiff was deemed sacred, and his jurisdiction supreme, there could be no reason to expect any considerable reformation either of the corruptions of the church or of the manners of the clergy.

III. If any thing seemed proper to destroy the gloomy empire of superstition, and to alarm the security of the lordly pontiffs, it was the restoration of learning in Europe, and the number of men of genius that suddenly arose, under the benign influence of that auspicious revolution. But even this new scene was insufficient to terrify the lords of the church, or to make them apprehend the decline of their power. It is true, that this happy revolution in the republic of letters dispelled the gloom of ignorance, and kindled in the minds of many the love of truth and of sacred liberty. It is also certain that many of these great men, such as Erasmus and others, pointed the delicacy of their wit, or levelled the fury of their indignation, at the superstitions of the times, the corruptions of the priesthood, the abuses that reigned in the court of Rome, and the brutish manners of the monastic orders. But this was not sufficient, since none had the courage to strike at the root of the evil, to attack the papal jurisdiction and statutes, which were absurdly, yet artfully, sanctified by the title of *canon-law*, or to call in question the ancient and most pernicious opinion, that Christ had established a vicegerent at Rome, clothed with his supreme and unlimited authority. Entrenched within these strong holds, the pontiffs looked upon their own authority and the peace of the church as beyond the reach of danger, and treated with indifference the threats and invectives of their enemies. Armed with power to punish, and abundantly furnished with the means of rewarding in the most alluring manner, they were ready, on every commotion, to crush the obstinate, and to gain over the mercenary to their cause; and this indeed could not but contribute considerably to the stability of their dominion.

IV. Hence it was, that the bishops of Rome lived in the utmost security and ease, and, being free from apprehensions and cares of every kind, followed without reluctance, and gratified without any limitation or restraint, the various demands of their lusts and passions. Alexander VI., whom humanity disowns, and who is rather to be considered as a monster than as a man, whose deeds excite horror, and whose enormities place him on a level with the most execrable tyrants of ancient times, stained the commencement of this century by the most atrocious crimes. The world was delivered from this papal fiend in the year 1503, by the poisonous draught which he had prepared for others, as is generally believed, though there are historians who attribute his death to sickness and old age.* He was succeeded in the pontificate by Pius III., who, in less than a month, was deprived by death of that high dignity. The vacant chair was obtained, by fraud and bribery, by Julian de la Rovere, who assumed the denomination of Julius II.

V. To the odious list of vices with which Julius II. dishonoured the pontificate, we may add the most savage ferocity, the most audacious arrogance, the most despotic vehemence of temper, and the most extravagant and phrenetic passion for war and bloodshed. He began his military enterprises by entering into a war with the Venetians, after having strengthened his cause by an alliance with the emperor and the king of France.* He afterwards laid siege to Ferrara, and at length turned his arms against his former ally, the French monarch, in conjunction with the Venetians, Spaniards, and Swiss, whom he had drawn into this war, and engaged in his cause by an offensive league. His whole pontificate, in short, was one continued scene of military tumult; nor did he suffer Europe to enjoy a moment's tranquillity as long as he lived. We may easily imagine the miserable condition of the church under a *vicar* of Christ, who lived in camps, amidst the din of arms, and who was ambitious of no other fame than that which arose from battles won and cities desolated. Under such a pontiff all things must have gone to ruin; the laws must have been subverted, the discipline of the church destroyed, and the genuine lustre of true religion entirely effaced.

VI. Nevertheless, from this dreadful cloud that hung over Europe, some rays of light seemed to break forth, that promised a better state of things, and gave some reason to expect that reformation in the church which was so generally and so ardently desired. Louis XII., king of France, provoked by the insults he had received from this arrogant pontiff, meditated revenge, and even caused a medal to be stricken with a menacing inscription, expressing his resolution to overturn the power of Rome, which was represented on this coin by the title of Babylon.† Several cardinals also, encouraged by the protection of this monarch and the emperor Maximilian I.; assembled, in 1511, a council at Pisa, with an intention to set bounds to the tyranny of this furious pontiff, and to correct and reform the errors and corruptions of a superstitious church. Julius, on the other hand, relying on his own strength, and on the power of his allies, beheld these threatening appearances without the least concern, and even treated them with mockery and laughter. He did not, however, neglect the methods of rendering ineffectual the efforts of his enemies, that prudence dictated, and therefore gave orders for a council to meet in the Lateran palace in 1512,‡ in which the decrees of the council of Pisa were condemned and annulled in the most injurious and insulting terms. This condemnation would, undoubtedly, have been followed by

* See Cent. XV. part ii. chap. ii. sect. xviii. note (a.)

* See Du Bos, Histoire de la Ligue de Cambray.

† See B. Christ. Sigismund. Liebii Commentatio de Nummis Ludovici XII., Epigraphe, 'Perdam Babylonis nomen,' insignibus, Leipsic, 1717.—See also Thes. Epis. Crozianus, tom. i.—Colonia. His. Liter. de la Ville de Lyon, tom. ii.—The authenticity and occasion of this medal have been much disputed, and as is well known, have afforded matter of keen debate.

‡ Harduini Concil, t. ix. p. 1559.

the most dire and formidable anathemas against Louis and other princes, had not death carried off this audacious pontiff in 1512, in the midst of his ambitious and vindictive projects.

VII. He was succeeded, in 1513, by Leo X., of the family of Medicis, who, though of a milder disposition than his predecessor, was equally indifferent about the interests of religion and the advancement of true piety. He was a protector of men of learning, and was himself learned, as far as the darkness of the age would admit. His time was divided between conversation with men of letters and pleasure, though it must be observed that the greatest part of it was consecrated to the latter. He had an invincible aversion to whatever was accompanied with solicitude and care, and discovered the greatest impatience under events of that nature. He was remarkable for his prodigality, luxury, and imprudence, and has even been charged with impiety, if not atheism. He did not, however, lose sight of the grand object which the generality of his predecessors had so much at heart,—that of promoting and advancing the opulence and grandeur of the Roman see; for he took the utmost care that nothing should be transacted in the Lateran council, (which Julius had assembled and left sitting,) that had the least tendency to favour the reformation of the church; and, in a conference which he had with Francis I., king of France, at Bologna, he engaged that monarch to abrogate the Pragmatic Sanction,* which had been so long odious to the popes, and to substitute in its place another body of laws, more advantageous to the papacy; which he accordingly imposed upon his subjects under the title of the *Concordat*, but not without their utmost indignation and reluctance.†

VIII. The raging thirst of dominion that inflamed these pontiffs, and their arrogant endeavours to crush and oppress all who came within the reach of their power, were accompanied with the most insatiable avarice. All the provinces of Europe were, in a manner, drained to enrich these spiritual tyrants, who were perpetually gaping after new accessions of wealth, in order to augment the number of their friends and the stability of their dominion. And, indeed, according to the notions commonly entertained, the rulers of the church seemed, from the nature of their character, to have a fair pretence for demanding a sort of tribute from their flock; for none can deny to the supreme governors of any state (and such was the character assumed by the popes) the privilege of levying tribute from those over whom they bear rule. But, as the name of *tribute* obviously tended to alarm the jealousy and excite the indignation of the civil magistrate, the pontiffs were too cunning to employ it, and had recourse to various stratagems and contrivances to rob the subject without shocking the sovereign, and to levy taxes under the specious mask of religion. Among these contrivances, the distribution of *indulgences*, which enabled the wealthy to purchase impunity for their crimes by certain sums applied to religious uses, held an eminent rank. This traffic was renewed whenever the coffers of the church were exhausted. On these occasions, indulgences were warmly recommended to the ignorant multitude under some new and specious, yet fallacious pretext, and were greedily sought, to the great detriment both of individuals and of the community.

IX. Notwithstanding the veneration and homage that were paid to the Roman pontiffs, they were far from being universally reputed infallible in their decisions, or unlimited in their authority. The wiser part of the German, French, Flemish, and British nations, considered them as liable to error, and bounded

* We have mentioned this Pragmatic Sanction, Cent. XV. part ii. chap. ii. sect. xvi. note (c,) and given there some account of its nature and design. This important edict is published at large in the eighth volume of the Concilia Harduini. as is the Concordat in the ninth volume, and in Leibnitz' Mantissa Codicis Diplomat. part i. ii. The history of these two pieces is given in an ample and accurate manner by Bishop Burnet, in his History of the Reformation, vol. iii.—See also, on the same subject, Boulay's Hist. Acad. Paris, tom. vi.—Du Clos, Histoire de Louis XI.—Histoire du Droit Ecclesiastique Francois, tom. i. Diss. ix.—Menagiana, tom. iii.

☞ † The king went in person to the parliament to offer the Concordat to be registered; and letters patent were made out, requiring all the judges and courts of justice to observe this act, and see it executed. The parliament, after deliberating a month upon this important matter, concluded not to register the Concordat, but to observe still the Pragmatic Sanction, unless the new edict should be received and established in as great an assembly as that was, which published the other in the reign of Charles VII.; and when by violence and force they were obliged to publish the Concordat, they joined to this publication a solemn protest, and an appeal from the pope to the next general council; into both which measures the university and the clergy entered with the greatest alacrity and zeal. But royal and papal despotism at length prevailed.

The chancellor Du-Prat, who was principally concerned in promoting the Concordat, has been generally regarded as an enemy to the liberties of the Gallican church. The illustrious and learned president Henault has not, however, hesitated to defend his memory against this accusation, and to justify the Concordat as an equitable contract and as a measure attended with less inconvenience than the Pragmatic Sanction. He observes, that by the king's being invested, by the Concordat, with the privilege of nominating to the bishoprics and vacant benefices of the first class, many corruptions and abuses were prevented, which arose from the simoniacal practices that prevailed almost every where, while, according to the Pragmatic Sanction, every church chose its bishop, and every monastery its abbot. He observes, moreover, that this nomination was the natural right of the crown, as the most considerable part of the great benefices had been created by the kings of France; and he insists particularly on this consideration, that the right which Christian communities have to choose their leaders, cannot be exercised by such large bodies without much confusion and many inconveniences; and that the subjects, by entrusting their sovereign with the government of the state, invest him, *ipso facto*, with an authority over the church, which is a part of the state, and its noblest branch. See Henault's Abrege Chronologique de l'Histoire de France, in the particular remarks that are placed at the end of the reign of Louis XIV.

The most specious objection that was made to the Concordat was this: that, in return for the nomination to the vacant benefices, the king granted to the popes the *annates*, or first-fruits, which had so long been complained of as an intolerable grievance. There is, however, no mention of this equivalent in the Concordat; and it was by a papal bull that succeeded this compact, that the pontiffs claimed the payment of the first-fruits, of which they had put themselves in possession in 1316, and which had been suspended by the Pragmatic Sanction

by law. The councils of Constance and Basil had contributed extremely to rectify the notions of the people in that respect; and from that period all Christians, except the superstitious monks and parasites of Rome, were persuaded that the pope was subordinate to a general council, that his decrees were not infallible, and that the council had a right to depose him, whenever he was convicted of gross errors or enormous crimes. Thus were the people, in some measure, prepared for the reformation of the church; and hence arose that ardent desire, that earnest expectation of a general council, which filled the minds of the wisest and best Christians in this century. Hence also the frequent appeals which were made to this approaching council, when the court of Rome issued any new edict, or made any new attempt repugnant to the dictates of piety and justice.

X. The licentious examples of the pontiffs were zealously imitated in the lives and manners of the subordinate rulers and ministers of the church. The greatest part of the bishops and canons passed their days in dissolute mirth and luxury, and squandered away, in the gratification of their lusts and passions, the wealth that had been set apart for religious and charitable purposes. Nor were they less tyrannical than voluptuous; for the most despotic princes never treated their vassals with more rigour and severity, than these spiritual rulers employed toward all who were under their jurisdiction. The decline of virtue among the clergy was attended with the loss of the public esteem; and the most considerable part of that once respected body became, by their sloth and avarice, their voluptuousness and impurity, their ignorance and levity, contemptible and infamous, not only in the eyes of the wise and good, but also in the general judgment of the multitude.* Nor could the case be otherwise as matters were now constituted; for, as all the offices and dignities of the church had become *venal*, the way of preferment was inaccessible to merit, and the wicked and licentious were rendered capable of rising to the highest ecclesiastical honours.

XI. The prodigious swarms of monks that overspread Europe were justly considered as burthens to society, and occasioned frequent murmurs and complaints. Nevertheless, such was the genius of the age, of an age that was emerging from the thickest gloom of ignorance, and was suspended, as it were, in a dubious situation between darkness and light, that these monastic drones would have remained undisturbed, had they taken the least pains to preserve any remains even of the external air of decency and religion, that used to distinguish them in former times. But the Benedictine and other monkish fraternities, who were invested with the privilege of possessing certain lands and revenues, broke through all restraint, made the worst possible use of their opulence, and, forgetful of the gravity of their character and of the laws of their order, rushed headlong into the shameless practice of vice in all its various kinds and degrees. On the other hand, the Mendicant orders, and especially those who followed the rules of St. Dominic and St. Francis, though they were not carried away with the torrent of licentiousness that was overwhelming the church, lost their credit in a different way; for their rustic impudence, their ridiculous superstitions, their ignorance, cruelty, and brutish manners, tended to alienate from them the minds of the people, and gradually diminished their reputation. They had the most barbarous aversion to the arts and sciences, and expressed a like abhorrence of certain eminent and learned men, who, being eagerly desirous of opening the paths of science to the pursuit of the studious youth, recommended the culture of the mind, and attacked the barbarism of the age in their writings and in their discourse. This is sufficiently evident from what happened to Reuchlinus, Erasmus, and other learned men.

XII. Among all the monastic orders, none enjoyed a higher degree of power and authority than the Dominican friars, whose credit was great, and whose influence was very widely extended. This will not appear surprising, when we consider that they filled very eminent stations in the church, presided every where over the terrible tribunal of the inquisition, and had the care of souls, with the function of confessors, in all the courts of Europe; a circumstance which, in those times of ignorance and superstition, manifestly tended to put most of the European princes in their power. But, notwithstanding all this credit and authority, the Dominicans had their enemies; and about this time their influence began to decline. Several marks of perfidy, that appeared in the measures they employed to extend their authority, justly exposed them to the public indignation. Nothing could be more infamous than the frauds they practised to accomplish their purposes, as may be seen, among other examples, by the tragedy which they acted at Bern in 1509.* They

* See Cornelii Aurelii Gaudani Apocalypsis, seu Visio Mirabilis super miserabili Statu Matris Ecclesiæ, in Casp. Burmanni Analect Hist. de Iadriano VI. p. 245, printed at Utrecht in 1727.

☞ * This most impious fraud is recorded at length by Ruchat, at the end of the sixth volume of his Histoire de la Reformation en Suisse; and also by Hottinger, in his Histor. Eccles. Helvet. tom. i. There is also a compendious, but distinct, narration of this infernal stratagem, in bishop Burnet's Travels through France, Italy, Germany, and Switzerland. The stratagem in question was the consequence of a rivalry between the Franciscans and Dominicans, and more especially of their controversy concerning the immaculate conception of the Virgin Mary. The former maintained that she was born without the blemish of original sin; the latter asserted the contrary. The doctrine of the Franciscans, in an age of darkness and superstition, could not but be popular; and hence the Dominicans lost ground from day to day. To support the credit of their order, they resolved, at a chapter holden at Wimpfen in 1504, to have recourse to fictitious visions and dreams, in which the people at that time had an easy faith; and they determined to make Bern the scene of their operations. A person named Jetzer, who was extremely simple, and much inclined to austerities, and who had taken their habit as a lay-brother, was chosen as the instrument of the delusions they were contriving. One of the four Dominicans, who had undertaken the management of this plot, conveyed himself secretly into Jetzer's cell, and about midnight appeared to him in a horrid figure, surrounded with howling dogs, and seeming to blow fire from his nostrils, by the means of a box of

were perpetually employed in stigmatizing, with the opprobious mark of heresy, numbers of learned and pious men, in encroaching upon the rights and property of others to augment their possessions, and in contriving the most iniquitous snares and stratagems for the destruction of their adversaries;* and they were the principal counsellors by whose instigation and advice Leo X. was determined to that most rash and imprudent measure, even the public condemnation of Luther.

XIII. The principal places in the public schools of learning were filled very frequently by monks of the mendicant orders. This unhappy circumstance prevented their emerging from that ignorance and darkness which had so long enveloped them; and it also rendered

combustibles which he held near his mouth. In this frightful form he approached Jetzer's bed, told him that he was the ghost of a Dominican, who had been killed at Paris, as a judgment of Heaven for laying aside his monastic habit; that he was condemned to purgatory for this crime; adding, at the same time, that, by his means, he might be rescued from his misery, which was beyond expression. This story, accompanied with horrible cries and howlings, terribly alarmed poor Jetzer, and engaged him to promise to do all that was in his power to deliver the Dominican from his torment. Upon this the impostor told him, that nothing but the most extraordinary mortifications, such as the discipline of the whip, performed during eight days by the whole monastery, and Jetzer's lying prostrate in the form of one crucified in the chapel during mass, could contribute to his deliverance. He added, that the performance of these mortifications would draw down upon Jetzer the peculiar protection of the Blessed Virgin; and concluded by saying, that he would appear to him again, accompanied with two other spirits. Morning was no sooner come, than Jetzer gave an account of this apparition to the rest of the convent, who unanimously advised him to undergo the discipline that was enjoined him; and every one consented to bear his share of the task imposed. The deluded simpleton obeyed, and was admired as a saint by the multitudes that crowded about the convent, while the four friars who managed the imposture, magnified, in the most pompous manner, the miracle of this apparition, in their sermons and in their conversation. The night after, the apparition was renewed with the addition of two friars, dressed like devils; and Jetzer's faith was augmented by hearing from the spectre all the secrets of his life and thoughts, which the impostors had learned from his confessor. In this and some subsequent scenes, the impostor talked much of the Dominican order, which he said was peculiarly dear to the Blessed Virgin; he added, that the Virgin knew herself to be conceived in original sin; that the doctors who taught the contrary were in purgatory; that the blessed Virgin abhorred the Franciscans for making her equal with her son; and that the town of Bern would be destroyed for harbouring such plagues within its walls. In one of these apparitions, Jetzer imagined that the voice of the spectre resembled that of the prior of the convent, and this was not a mistake; but, not suspecting a fraud, he gave little attention to this. The prior appeared in various forms, sometimes in that of St. Barbara, at others in that of St. Bernard; at length he assumed that of the Virgin Mary, and, for that purpose, clothed himself in the habits that were employed to adorn her statue on the great festivals; the little images, that on these days are set on the altars, were used for angels, which, being tied to a cord that passed through a pulley over Jetzer's head, rose up and down, and danced about the pretended virgin to increase the delusion. The Virgin, thus equipped, addressed a long discourse to Jetzer, in which, among other things, she told him that she was conceived in original sin, though she had remained but a short time under that blemish. She gave him, as a miraculous proof of her presence, a *host*, or consecrated wafer, which turned from white to red in a moment; and after various visits, in which the greatest enormities were transacted, the *Virgin-prior* told Jetzer, that she would give him the most affecting and undoubted marks of her Son's love, by imprinting on him the five wounds tha pierced Jesus on the cross, as she had done before to St. Lucia and St. Catharine. Accordingly, she took his hand by force, and struck a large nail through it, which threw the poor dupe into the greatest torment. The next night this masculine virgin brought, as she pretended, some of the linen, in which Christ had been buried, to soften the wound, and gave Jetzer a soporofic draught, which had in it the blood of an unbaptized child, some grains of incense and of consecrated salt, some quicksilver, the hairs of the eye-brows of a child, all which, with some stupifying and poisonous ingredients, were mingled by the prior with magic ceremonies. and a solemn dedication of himself to the devil in hope of his succour. This draught threw the poor wretch into a sort of lethargy, during which the monks imprinted on his body the other four wounds of Christ in such a manner that he felt no pain. When he awoke, he found, to his unspeakable joy, these impressions on his body, and came at last to fancy himself a representative of Christ in the various parts of his passion. He was, in this state, exposed to the admiring multitude on the principal altar of the convent, to the great mortification of the Franciscans. The Dominicans gave him some other draughts, that threw him into convulsions, which were followed by a voice conveyed through a pipe into the mouths of two images, one of Mary, the other of the child Jesus; the former of which had tears painted upon its cheeks in a lively manner. The little Jesus asked his mother, by means of this voice, (which was that of the prior,) why she wept; and she answered, that her tears were occasioned by the impious manner in which the Franciscans attributed to *her* the honour that was due to *him*, in saying that she was conceived and born without sin.

The apparitions, false prodigies, and abominable stratagems of these Dominicans, were repeated every night; and the matter was at length so grossly overacted, that, simple as Jetzer was, he at last discovered it, and had almost killed the prior, who appeared to him one night in the form of the Virgin with a crown on her head, The Dominicans, fearing, by this discovery, to lose the fruits of their imposture, thought the best method would be to own the whole matter to Jetzer, and to engage him, by the most seducing promises of opulence and glory, to carry on the delusion. He was persuaded, or at least appeared to be so. But the Dominicans, suspecting that he was not entirely gained over, resolved to poison him His constitution was so vigorous, that though they gave him poison five times, he was not destroyed by it. One day they sent him a loaf prepared with some spices, which growing green in a day or two, he threw a piece of it to a wolf's whelps that were in the monastery, and it killed them immediately. At another time they poisoned the host; but as he vomited it soon after he had taken it, he escaped once more. In short, there were no means of securing him, which the most detestable impiety and barbarity could invent, that they did not put in practice, till, finding at last an opportunity of getting out of the convent, he threw himself into the hands of the magistrates, to whom he made a full discovery of this infernal plot. This intelligence being sent to Rome, commissaries were ordered to examine the affair; and the whole imposture being fully proved, the four friars were solemnly degraded from their priesthood, and were burned alive on the last day of May, 1509. Jetzer died some time after at Constance, having poisoned himself, as was believed by some. Had his life been taken away before he had found an opportunity of making the discovery already mentioned, this execrable and horrid plot, which, in many of its circumstances, was conducted with art, would have been handed down to posterity as a stupendous miracle. T is is a very brief account of the matter: such as are desirous of a more circumstantial relation of this famous imposture, may consult the authors mentioned in the beginning of this note.

* See Bilib. Pirkheimeri Epistola ad Hadrianum Pontif. Maxim. de Dominicanorum flagitiis, in operibus ejus, p. 372. This letter is also to be found in Gerdesii Intr. ad Hist. Renov. Evangel. t. i. p. 170. Append.

them inaccessible to that auspicious light of improved science, whose salutary beams had already been felt in several of the European countries. The instructors of youth, dignified with the *venerable* titles of *artists, grammarians, philosophers*, and *dialecticians*, loaded the memories of their laborious pupils with a certain quantity of barbarous terms, arid and senseless distinctions, and scholastic precepts, delivered in the most inelegant style; and all such as could repeat this jargon with readiness and rapidity, were considered as men of uncommon eloquence and erudition. The whole body of the philosophers extolled Aristotle beyond measure, while scarcely any studied him, and none understood him; for what was now exhibited, as the philosophy of that celebrated sage, was really nothing more than a confused and motley heap of obscure notions, sentences, and divisions, which even the public doctors and heads of schools were unable to comprehend; and if, among these thorns of scholastic wisdom, there was any thing that had the appearance of fruit, it was crushed and blasted by the furious wranglings and disputes of the Scotists and Thomists, the Realists and Nominalists, whose clamours and contentions were unhappily heard in all the European colleges.

XIV. The wretched and senseless manner of teaching theology in this century, may be learned from many books yet extant, which were written by the divines of that period, and which, in reality, have no other merit than their enormous bulk. There were very few expositors of the Scriptures during this century; and scarcely any of the Christian doctors had a critical acquaintance with the sacred oracles. This kind of knowledge was so rare, that, when Luther arose, there could not be found, even in the university of Paris, which was regarded as the first and most famous of all the public schools of learning, a single person qualified to dispute with him, or oppose his doctrine upon a scriptural foundation. Any commentators, that were at this time to be found, were such as, laying aside all attention to the true meaning and force of the words of Scripture, which their profound ignorance of the original languages and of the rules of criticism rendered them incapable of investigating, gave a loose to their vain and irregular fancies, in the pursuit of mysterious significations. The greatest part of the public teachers belonged to the classes of divines, already mentioned under the titles of *Positivi* and *Sententiarii*, who were extremely fond, the former of loading their accounts, both of the truths and precepts of religion, with multiplied quotations and authorities from the writings of the ancient doctors; the latter of explaining the doctrines of the Gospel by the rules of a subtile and intricate philosophy.

XV. It must at the same time be observed, that the divines of this century disputed with great freedom upon religious subjects, even upon those which were looked upon as most essential to salvation. There were several points of doctrine, which had not yet been determined by the authority of the church; nor did the pontiffs, without some very urgent reason, restrain the right of private judgment, or force the consciences of men, except in those cases where doctrines were adopted that seemed detrimental to the supremacy of the apostolic see, or to the temporal interests of the sacerdotal and monastic orders. Hence it is, that we could mention many Christian doctors before Luther, who inculcated not only with impunity, but even with applause, the very same tenets that afterwards drew upon him such heavy accusations and such bitter reproaches; and it is beyond all doubt, that this great reformer might have propagated these opinions without any danger of molestation, had he not pointed his warm remonstrances against the opulence of Rome, the overgrown fortunes of the bishops, the majesty of the pontiffs, and the towering ambition of the Dominicans.

XVI. The public worship of the Deity was now no more than a pompous round of external ceremonies, the greatest part of which were insignificant and senseless, and much more adapted to dazzle the eyes than to touch the heart. Of those who were at all qualified to administer public instruction to the people, the number was not very considerable; and their discourses, which contained little beside fictitious reports of miracles and prodigies, insipid fables, wretched quibbles, and illiterate jargon, deceived instead of instructing the multitude. Several of these sermons are yet extant, which it is impossible to read without the highest indignation and contempt. Those who, on account of their gravity of manners, or their supposed superiority in point of wisdom and knowledge, held the most distinguished rank among these vain declaimers, had a common-place set of subjects allotted to them, on which they were constantly exercising the force of their lungs and the power of their eloquence. These subjects were, the authority of the holy mother church, and the obligation of obedience to her decisions; the virtues and merits of the saints, and their credit in the court of heaven; the dignity, glory, and love of the blessed Virgin; the efficacy of relics; the duty of adorning churches, and endowing monasteries; the necessity of good works (as that phrase was then understood) to salvation; the intolerable burnings of purgatory, and the utility of indulgences. Such were the topics that employed the zeal and labours of the most eminent doctors of this century; and they were, indeed, the only subjects that could tend to fill the coffers of the *good old mother church*, and advance her temporal interests. Ministers who would have taken it into their heads to inculcate the doctrines and precepts of the Gospel, to exhibit the example of its divine author, and the efficacy of his mediation, as the most powerful motives to righteousness and virtue, and to represent the love of God and mankind as the great duties of the Christian life, would have been very unprofitable servants to the church and to the papacy, however they might have promoted the cause of virtue and the salvation of souls.

XVII. From this state of affairs we may draw conclusions respecting the true causes of that incredible ignorance in religious matters, which reigned in all countries, and among all ranks and orders of men; an ignorance accom panied with the vilest forms of superstition, and the greatest corruption of manners. The clergy were far from showing the least disposition to enlighten the ignorance, or to check the superstition of the times; which, indeed, they even nourished and promoted, as conducive to their safety, and favourable to their interests. Nor was there more zeal shown in stemming the torrent of immorality and licentiousness, than in dispelling the clouds of superstition and ignorance; for the prudence of the church had easily foreseen, that the traffic of indulgences could not but suffer from a diminution of the crimes and vices of mankind, and that, in proportion as virtue gained an ascendency upon the manners of the multitude, the profits arising from expiations, satisfactions, and the like ecclesiastical contrivances, would necessarily decrease.

XVIII. Such was the dismal condition of the church. Its corruption was complete, and the abuses which its rulers permitted had reached the greatest height of enormity. Proportioned to the greatness of this corruption was the impatient ardour with which all, who were endowed with any tolerable portion of solid learning, genuine piety, or even good sense, desired to see the church reformed and purged from these shocking abuses; and the number of those who were affected in this manner was very considerable in all parts of the western world. The greatest part of them, indeed, were perhaps over-moderate in their demands. They did not extend their views to a change in the form of ecclesiastical government, a suppression of those doctrines, which, however absurd, had acquired a high degree of credit by their antiquity, or even to an abrogation of those rites and ceremonies, which had been multiplied in such an extravagant manner, to the great detriment of true religion and rational piety. All they aimed at was, to set limits to the overgrown power of the pontiffs, reform the corrupt manners of the clergy, and prevent the frauds that were too commonly practised by that order of men; to dispel the ignorance and correct the errors of the blinded multitude, and to deliver them from the heavy and insupportable burthens which were imposed upon them under religious pretexts. But as it was impossible to obtain any of these salutary purposes without the suppression of various absurd and impious opinions, from which the grievances complained of sprang, or, indeed, without a general reformation of the religion that was publicly professed, this was supposed to be ardently, though silently wished for, by all those who openly demanded the 'reformation of the church in its head and in its members.'

XIX. If any sparks of real piety subsisted under this despotic empire of superstition, they were only to be found among the Mystics; for this sect, renouncing the subtlety of the schools, the vain contentions of the learned, and all the acts and ceremonies of external worship, exhorted their followers to aim at nothing but internal sanctity of heart, and communion with God, the centre and source of holiness and perfection. Hence they were loved and respected by many persons, who had a serious sense of religion and a devotional frame of mind. Yet, as they were not entirely free from the reigning superstitions, but associated many vulgar errors with their practical precepts and directions;—and as their excessive passion for contemplation led them into chimerical notions, and sometimes into a degree of fanaticism that approached to madness—more effectual succours than theirs were necessary to combat the inveterate errors of the times, and to bring about the reformation that was expected with such impatience.

CHAPTER II.

The History of the Reformation, from its Commencement to the Confession of Augsburg.

I. WHILE the Roman pontiff slumbered in security at the head of the church, and saw nothing throughout the vast extent of his dominion but tranquillity and submission; and while the worthy and pious professors of genuine Christianity almost despaired of seeing that reformation on which their most ardent desires and expectations were bent; an obscure and inconsiderable person suddenly offered himself to public view in the year 1517, and laid the foundation of this long-expected change, by opposing, with undaunted resolution, his single force to the torrent of papal ambition and despotism. This extraordinary man was Martin Luther, a native of Eisleben in Saxony, a monk of the Augustinian *Eremites*, (one of the Mendicant orders,) and, at the same time, professor of divinity in the university which had been erected at Wittenberg, a few years before this period, by Frederic the Wise. The papal chair was, at that time, filled by Leo X.; Maximilian I., a prince of the house of Austria, was king of the Romans and emperor of Germany; and Frederic, already mentioned, was elector of Saxony. The bold efforts of this new adversary of the pontiffs were honoured with the applause of many; but few or none entertained confident hopes of his success. It seemed scarcely possible that this puny David could hurt a Goliah, whom so many heroes had opposed in vain.

II. The qualities or talents that distinguished Luther were not of a common or ordinary kind. His genius was truly great and unparalleled; his memory vast and tenacious; his patience in supporting trials, difficulties, and labour, incredible; his magnanimity invincible, and unshaken by the vicissitudes of human affairs; and his learning most extensive, considering the age in which he lived. All this will be acknowledged, even by his enemies, at least by such of them as are not totally blinded by a spirit of partiality and faction. He was deeply versed in the theology and philosophy that were in vogue in the schools during this century, and he taught them both with great reputation and success in the university of Wittenberg. As a philosopher, he embraced the doctrine of the Nominalists, which was the system adopted by his order; while, in divinity, he followed chiefly the sentiments of Augustin; but in both he preferred the decisions of Scripture, and the dictates of right reason, to the authority and opinions of fallible men. It would be equally rash and absurd to represent this great man as exempt from error, and free from infirmities and defects; yet, if we except the contagious effects of the age in which he lived, and of the religion in which he had been brought up, we shall perhaps find few points of his character that render him liable to reproach.*

III. The first opportunity that this great man had of unfolding, to the view of a blinded and deluded age, the truth which struck his astonished sight, was offered by a Dominican, whose name was John Tetzel.† This bold and enterprising monk had been chosen on account of his uncommon impudence, by Albert, archbishop of Mentz and Magdeburg, to preach and proclaim, in Germany, those famous *indulgences* of Leo X., which administered the remission of all sins, past, present, and to come, however enormous their nature, to those who were rich enough to purchase them. The frontless monk executed this iniquitous commission not only with matchless insolence, indecency,‡ and fraud, but even carried his impiety so far as to derogate from the all-sufficient power and influence of the merits of Christ. At this, Luther, unable to repress his just indignation, raised his warning voice, and in ninety-five propositions, (maintained publicly at Wittenberg, on the 30th of September, 1517.) censured the extravagant extortion of these quæstors, and plainly pointed out the pontiff as a partaker of their guilt, since he suffered the people to be seduced, by such delusions, from placing their principal confidence in Christ, the only proper object of their trust. This was the commencement and foundation of that memorable rupture and revolution in the church, which humbled the grandeur of the lordly pontiffs, and eclipsed so great a part of their glory.§

IV. This debate between Luther and Tetzel was, at first, a matter of no great moment, and might have been determined with the utmost facility, had Leo been disposed to follow

* The writers who have given a circumstantial account of Luther and his transactions, are accurately enumerated by Jo. Alb. Fabricius, in his Centifolium Lutheranum.

† The historians who have particularly mentioned Tetzel, and his odious methods of deluding the multitude, are enumerated in the work quoted in the preceding note, part i. p. 47; part ii. p. 530.—What is said of this vile deceiver by Echard and Quetif, (Scriptores Ordin. Prædicator. tom. ii.) discovers the blindest zeal and the meanest partiality.

☞ ‡ In describing the efficacy of these indulgences, Tetzel said, among other enormities, that "even had any one ravished the mother of God, he (Tetzel) had wherewithal to efface his guilt." He also boasted that "he had saved more souls from hell by these indulgences, than St. Peter had converted to Christianity by his preaching."

☞ § Dr. Mosheim has taken no notice of the calumnies invented and propagated by some late authors, in order to make Luther's zealous opposition to the publication of indulgences appear to be the effect of selfish and ignoble motives. It may not, therefore, be improper to set that point in a true light; not that the cause of the reformation (which must stand by its own intrinsic dignity, and is in no way affected by the views or characters of its instruments) can derive any strength from this inquiry; but as it may tend to vindicate the personal character of a man, who has done eminent service to the cause of religion.

Mr. Hume, in his history of the reign of Henry VIII., has thought proper to repeat what the enemies of the reformation, and some of its dubious or ill-informed friends, have advanced, with respect to the motives that engaged Luther to oppose the doctrine of indulgences. This elegant historian affirms, that the "Augustin friars had *usually* been employed in Saxony to preach indulgences, and from this trust had derived both profit and consideration; that Arcemboldi gave this occupation to the Dominicans; that Martin Luther, an Augustin friar, professor in the university of Wittenberg, *resenting the affront put upon his order*, began to preach against the abuses that were committed in the sale of indulgences, and being provoked by opposition, proceeded even to decry indulgences themselves." It is to be wished, that Mr. Hume's candour had engaged him to examine this accusation better, before he had ventured to repeat it. In the first place, it is not true, that the Augustin friars had been usually employed in Saxony to preach indulgences. It is well known, that the commission had been offered alternately, and sometimes jointly, to all the Mendicants, whether Augustin friars, Dominicans, Franciscans, or Carmelites. From the year 1229, that lucrative commission was principally entrusted to the Dominicans;* and in the records which relate to indulgences, we rarely meet with the name of an Augustin friar, and not a single act by which it appears, that the Roman pontiff ever named the friars of that order to the office under consideration. More particularly it is remarkable, that for half a century before Luther, (i. e. from 1450 to 1517,) during which period indulgences were sold with the most scandalous marks of avaricious extortion and impudence, we scarcely find an Augustin friar mentioned as being employed in that service; if we except a monk named Baluzius, who was no more than an underling of the papal quæstor Raymond Peraldus; so far is it from being true, that the Augustin monks were exclusively, or even usually, engaged in that service.† Mr. Hume has built his assertion upon the sole authority of a single expression of Paul Sarpi, which has been abundantly refuted by De Priero, Pallavicini, and Graweson, the mortal enemies of Luther.—But it may be alleged, that, even supposing it was not usual to employ the Augustin friars alone in the propagation of indulgences, yet Luther might be offended at seeing such an important commission given to the Dominicans exclusively, and that, consequently, this was his motive in opposing the propagation of indulgences. To show the injustice of this allegation, I observe, secondly, that, in the time of Luther, the preaching of indulgences had become very odious and unpopular; and it is therefore far from being probable, that Luther would have been solicitous about obtaining such a commission, either for himself or for his order. The princes of Europe, with many bishops, and multitudes of learned and pious men, had opened their eyes upon the turpitude of this infamous traffick; and even the Franciscans and Dominicans, toward the conclusion of the fifteenth century, opposed it publicly, both in their discourses and in their writings.‡ The very commission, which is supposed to have excited the envy of Luther, was offered by Leo to the general of the Franciscans, and was refused both by him and his order,§ who gave it over entirely to Albert, bishop of Mentz and Magdeburg. Is it then to be imagined, that either Luther, or the other Augustin friars, aspired after a commission of which the Franciscans were ashamed? Besides, it is a mistake to affirm, that this office was given to the Dominicans in general; for it was given to Tetzel alone, an individual member of that order, who had been notorious for his extortion, profligacy, and barbarity.

But that neither resentment nor envy were the motives that led Luther to oppose the doctrine and publication of indulgences, will appear with the utmost evidence, if we consider, in the third place that he was never accused of any such motives,

* See Weismanni Memorabilia Historiæ Sacræ N. T. p. 1051, 1115.

† See Harpii Dissertat. de Nonnullis Indulgentiarum (Sæc. XIV. et XV.) Quæstoribus, p. 384, 387.

‡ See Walch. op. Lutheri, tom. xv. p. 114, 283, 312 349.—Seckendorf. Hist. Lutheranismi, lib. i. sect. vi p. 13.

§ See Walch. loc. cit. p. 371.

the healing method which common prudence must have naturally pointed out on such an occasion; for, after all, this was no more than the private dispute of two monks, concerning the extent of the pope's power with respect to the remission of sin. Luther confessed that the Roman pontiff was invested with the power of remitting the *human* punishments denounced against transgressors, i. e. the punishments ordained by the church, and its visible head, the bishop of Rome; but he strenuously denied that his power extended to the remission of the *divine* punishments allotted to offenders, either in the present or in a future state; affirming, on the contrary, that these punishments could only be removed by the merits of Christ, or by voluntary acts of mortification and penance, undertaken and performed by the transgressor. The doctrine of Tetzel was directly opposite to the sentiments of Luther; for that senseless and designing monk asserted, that all punishments, present and future, human and divine, were submitted to the authority of the pope, and came within the reach of his absolving power. This matter had often been debated before the present period; but the popes had always been prudent enough to leave it undecided. These debates, however, being sometimes treated with neglect, and at others carried on without wisdom, the seeds of discord imperceptibly gained new accessions of strength and vigour, and from small beginnings produced, at length, events of the most momentous nature.

---

either in the edicts of the pontiffs of his time, or amidst the other reproaches of the contemporary writers, who defended the cause of Rome, and who were generally very prodigal of their invectives and calumnies. All the contemporary adversaries of Luther are absolutely silent on this head. From the year 1517 to 1546, when the dispute about indulgences was carried on with the greatest warmth and animosity, not one writer ever ventured to reproach Luther with these ignoble motives of opposition now under consideration. I speak not of Erasmus, Sleidan, De Thou, Guicciardini, and others, whose testimony might be perhaps suspected of partiality in his favour; but I speak of Caietan, Hoogstrat, De Priero. Emser, and even the infamous John Tetzel, whom Luther opposed with such vehemence and bitterness. Even Cochlæus was silent on this head during the life of Luther, though, after the death of that great reformer, he broached the calumny I am here refuting. But such was the scandalous character of this man, who was notorious for fraud, calumny, lying, and their sister vices,* that Pallavicini, Bossuet, and other enemies of Luther, were ashamed to make use either of his name or testimony. Now may it not be fairly presumed, that the contemporaries of Luther were better judges of his character, and of the principles from which he acted, than those who lived in after-times? Can it be imagined, that motives to action, which escaped their prying eyes, should have discovered themselves to us who live at such a distance of time from the scene of action, to M. Bossuet, to Mr. Hume, and to other abettors of this ill-contrived and foolish story. Either there are no rules of moral evidence, or Mr. Hume's assertion is entirely groundless.

I might add many other considerations to show the unreasonableness of supposing that Luther exposed himself to the rage of the pontiff, to the persecutions of an exasperated clergy, to the severity of such a potent and despotic prince as Charles V., and to the risk of death itself, from a principle of avarice and ambition. But I have said enough to satisfy every candid mind.

* Sleidan de Statu Rel. et Reip. in Dedic. Epist. ad August. Electorem

V. The sentiments of Luther were received with applause by the greatest part of Germany, which had long groaned under the avarice of the pontiffs, and the extortions of their taxgatherers, and had murmured grievously against the various stratagems that were daily put in practice, with the most shameless impudence, to fleece the rich, and to grind the faces of the poor. But the votaries of Rome were filled with horror, when they were informed of the opinions propagated by the Saxon reformer; more especially the Dominicans, who looked upon their order as insulted and attacked in the person of Tetzel. The alarm of controversy was therefore sounded, and Tetzel himself appeared immediately in the field against Luther, whose sentiments he pretended to refute in two academical discourses, which he pronounced on occasion of his promotion to the degree of doctor in divinity. In the year following (1511) two famous Dominicans, Sylvester de Priero and Hoogstrat, the former a native of Italy, and the latter a German, rose up also against the adventurous reformer, and attacked him at Cologne with the utmost vehemence and ardour. Their example was soon followed by another formidable champion, named Eckius, a celebrated professor of divinity at Ingolstadt and one of the most zealous supporters of the Dominican order. Luther stood firm against these united adversaries, and was neither vanquished by their arguments, nor daunted by their talents and reputation; but answered their objections, and refuted their reasonings with the greatest strength of evidence, and a becoming spirit of resolution and perseverance. At the same time, he addressed letters, in the most submissive and respectful terms, to the pope, and to several of the bishops, showing them the uprightness of his intentions, as well as the justice of his cause, and declaring his readiness to change his sentiments, as soon as he should see them fairly proved to be erroneous

VI. At first, Leo beheld this controversy with indifference and contempt; but, being informed by the emperor Maximilian not only of its importance, but also of the fatal divisions it was likely to produce in Germany, he summoned Luther to appear before him at Rome, and there to plead the cause which he had undertaken to maintain. This papal citation was superseded by Frederic the Wise, elector of Saxony, who pretended, that the cause of Luther belonged to the jurisdiction of a German tribunal, and that it was to be decided by the ecclesiastical laws of the empire. The pontiff yielded to the remonstrances of this prudent and magnanimous prince, and ordered Luther to justify his intentions and doctrines before cardinal Caietan, who was at this time legate at the diet of Augsburg. In this first step the court of Rome gave a specimen of that temerity and imprudence with which all its negotiations, in this weighty affair, were afterwards conducted; for, instead of reconciling, nothing could tend more to inflame the dispute than the choice of Caietan, a Dominican, and, consequently, the declared enemy of Luther and friend of Tetzel, as judge and arbitrator in this nice and perilous controversy.

VII. Luther, however, repaired to Augsburg in October, 1518, and conferred, at three meetings, with Caietan himself,* concerning the points in debate. But had he even been disposed to yield to the court of Rome, this imperious legate was, of all others, the most unfit person to be employed in procuring from him any act or mark of submission. The high spirit of Luther was not to be tamed by the arrogant dictates of mere authority; such, however, were the only methods of persuasion adopted by the haughty cardinal. He, in an overbearing tone, desired Luther to renounce his opinions, without even attempting to prove them erroneous, and insisted, with importunity, on his confessing humbly his fault, and submitting respectfully to the judgment of the Roman pontiff.† The Saxon reformer could not think of yielding to terms so unreasonable in themselves, and so despotically proposed; so that the conferences were absolutely without effect. Luther, finding his adversary and judge inaccessible to reason and argument, suddenly left Augsburg, after having appealed from the pope's present decision to that which he should pronounce when better informed; and, in this step, he seemed yet to respect the dignity and authority of the bishop of Rome.‡ Leo, on the other hand, let loose the reins to ambition and despotism, and carried things to extremities; for he published an edict, *commanding* his spiritual subjects to acknowledge his power of delivering from all the punishments due to sin and transgression. As soon as Luther received information of this inconsiderate and violent measure, he perceived, plainly, that it would be impossible for him to bring the court of Rome to any reasonable terms; he therefore repaired to Wittenberg, and appealed from the pontiff to a general council.

VIII. In the mean time the pope became sensible of his imprudence in entrusting Caietan with such a commission, and therefore resolved to employ a man of more candour and impartiality, and better acquainted with business, in order to suppress the rebellion of Luther, and to engage that reformer to submission and obedience. This new legate was Charles Miltitz, a Saxon knight, who belonged to the court of Leo, and whose laic character exposed him less to the prejudices which arise from a spirit of party, than if he had been clothed with the splendid purple, or the monastic frock. He was also a person of great prudence, penetration, and dexterity, and every way qualified for the execution of such a nice and critical commission as this was. Leo sent him into Saxony to present to Frederic the golden consecrated rose, (which the pontiffs are accustomed to bestow, as a peculiar mark of distinction, on those princes for whom they have, or think proper to profess, an uncommon friendship and esteem,) and to treat with Luther, not only about finishing his controversy with Tetzel, but also with regard to the methods of bringing about a reconciliation between him and the court of Rome Nor, indeed, were the negotiations of this prudent minister entirely unsuccessful; for, in his first conference with Luther, at Altenburg, in 1519, he carried matters so far as to persuade him to write a submissive letter to Leo, promising to observe a profound silence upon the points in debate, provided that the same obligation should be imposed upon his adversaries. This same year, in the month of October, Miltitz had a second conference with Luther in the castle of Liebenwerd, and a third, the year following, at Lichtenberg.* These meetings, which were reciprocally conducted with moderation and decency, gave great hopes of an approaching reconciliation; nor were these hopes altogether ill-founded.† But the violent proceedings of the enemies of Luther, and the arrogant spirit, as well as unaccountable imprudence, of the court of Rome, blasted these fair expectations, and rekindled the flames of discord.

IX.‡ It is sufficient barely to mention the measures taken by Caietan to draw Luther anew under the papal yoke, because these were, indeed, nothing more than the wild suggestions of superstition and tyranny, maintained and avowed with the most shameless impudence. A man who began by commanding the reformer to renounce his errors, and to believe, upon the dictates of mere authority, that "one drop of Christ's blood being sufficient to redeem the whole human race, the remaining quantity, which was shed in the garden and on the cross, was left as a legacy to the church, to be a treasure whence indulgences were to be drawn and administered by the Roman pontiffs;"§ such a man was not to be reasoned with. But Miltitz proceeded in quite another manner, and his conferences with the Saxon reformer are worthy of attention. He was ordered, indeed, to demand of the elector, that

* There is an ample account of this cardinal given by Quetif and Echard, Scriptor. Ordin. Prædicator. tom. ii.

† The imperious and imprudent manner in which Caietan behaved toward Luther was highly disapproved, even at the court of Rome, as appears, among other testimonies, from Paolo Sarpi's History of the Council of Trent, book i. p. 22. The conduct of Caietan is defended by Echard, but with little prudence and less argument. The truth is, that the court of Rome, and its unthinking sovereign, were not less culpable than Caietan in the whole of this transaction, since they might easily foresee, that a Dominican legate was of all others the most unlikely to treat Luther with moderation and impartiality, and consequently the most improper to reconcile matters.

‡ See B. Ch. Fr. Borner. Diss. de Coll. Luth. cum Caietano, Leips. 1722. Val. Ern. Losch. Act. et Doc. Ref. t. ii. c xi. p. 435, op Luth. t. xxiv. p. 409.

* See Borneri Dissert. The records relating to the embassy of Miltitz, were first published by Cyprianus, in Addit. ad Tenzelii Histor. Reformat. tom. i. ii.,—as also by Loscherus, in his Acta Reformat. tom. ii. c. xvi. and tom. iii. cap. ii.

† In 1519, Leo wrote to Luther in the softest and most pacific terms. From this remarkable letter, (which was published in 1742, by Loscherus, in a German work entitled Unschuld Nachricht,) it appears that at the court of Rome, they looked upon a reconciliation between Luther and the pontiff as certain and near at hand.

☞ ‡ This whole ninth section is added to Dr. Mosheim's work by the translator, who thought that this part of Luther's history deserved to be related in a more circumstantial manner, than it is in the original.

☞ § Such, among others still more absurd, were the expressions of Caietan, which he borrowed from one of the Decretals of Clement VI. called (and that justly for more than one reason) *Extravagants*

he would either oblige Luther to renounce the doctrines he had hitherto maintained, or that he would withdraw from him his protection and favour. But, perceiving that he was received by the elector with a degree of coldness that bordered upon contempt, and that Luther's credit and cause were too far advanced to be destroyed by the efforts of mere authority, he had recourse to gentler methods. He loaded Tetzel with the bitterest reproaches, on account of the irregular and superstitious means he had employed for promoting the sale of indulgences, and attributed to this miserable wretch all the abuses that Luther had complained of. Tetzel, on the other hand, burthened with the iniquities of Rome, tormented with a consciousness of his own injustice and extortions, stung with the opprobrious censures of the new legate, and seeing himself equally despised and abhorred by both parties, died of grief and despair.* This incendiary being sacrificed as a victim to cover the Roman pontiff from reproach, Miltitz entered into a particular conversation with Luther at Altenburg, and, without pretending to justify the scandalous traffick in question, required only, that he would acknowledge the four following points: "1st, That the people had been seduced by false notions of indulgences: 2dly, That he (Luther) had been the cause of that seduction, by representing indulgences as much more heinous than they really were: 3dly, That the odious conduct of Tetzel alone had given occasion to these representations: and, 4thly, That, though the avarice of Albert, archbishop of Mentz, had set on Tetzel, this rapacious tax-gatherer had far exceeded the bounds of his commission." These proposals were accompanied with many soothing words, with pompous encomiums on Luther's character, capacity, and talents, and with the softest and most pathetic expostulations in favour of union and concord in an afflicted and divided church; all which Miltitz combined with the greatest dexterity and address, in order to touch and disarm the reformer. Nor were his mild and insinuating methods of negotiating without effect; and it was upon this occasion that Luther made submissions which showed that his views were not, as yet, very extensive, his former prejudices entirely expelled, or his reforming principles steadily fixed; for he not only offered to observe a profound silence for the future with respect to indulgences, provided that the same condition should be imposed on his adversaries; he went much farther; he proposed writing an humble and submissive letter to the pope, acknowledging that he had carried his zeal and animosity too far; and such a letter he wrote soon after the conference at Altenburg.† He even consented to publish a circular letter, exhorting all his disciples and followers to reverence and obey the dictates of the holy Roman church. He declared that his only intention, in the writings he had composed, was to brand with infamy those emissaries who abused his authority, and employed its protection as a mask to cover their abominable and impious frauds. It is true, indeed, that amidst those weak submissions which the impartial demands of historical truth oblige us to relate, there was, properly speaking, no retraction of his former tenets, nor the smallest degree of respect shown to the infamous traffick of indulgences. Nevertheless, the pretended majesty of the Roman church, and the authority of the Roman pontiff, were treated by Luther in this transaction, and in his letter to Leo, in a manner that could not naturally have been expected from a man who had already appealed from the pope to a general council.

Had the pope been so prudent as to accept the submission of Luther, he would have almost nipped in the bud the cause of the reformation, or would, at least, have considerably retarded its growth and progress. When he had gained over the head, the members would, with greater facility, have been reduced to obedience. But the flaming and excessive zeal of some inconsiderate bigots renewed (happily for the truth) the divisions, which were so near being healed, and, by animating both Luther and his followers to inspect more closely the enormities that prevailed in the papal hierarchy, promoted the principles, and augmented the spirit, which ultimately produced the blessed* reformation.

X. One of the circumstances that contributed principally, at least by its consequences, to render the embassy of Miltitz ineffectual for the restoration of peace, was a famous controversy of an incidental nature that was carried on at Leipsic, for some weeks successively, in 1519.† Eckius, the celebrated theologian, happened to differ widely from Carlostadt, the colleague and companion of Luther, in his sentiments concerning free will. The result of this variety in opinion was easy to be foreseen. The military genius of our ancestors had so far infected the schools of learning, that differences in points of religion and literature, when they grew to a certain degree of warmth and animosity, were decided, like the quarrels of valiant knights, by a single combat. Some famous university was pitched upon as the field of battle, while the rector and professors

☞ * Luther was so affected by the agonies of despair under which Tetzel laboured, that he wrote to him a pathetic letter of consolation, which, however, produced no effect. His infamy was perpetuated by a picture placed in the church of Pirna, in which he is represented sitting on an ass and selling indulgences.

☞ † This letter was dated the 13th of March, 1519, about two months after that conference.

☞ * See, for an ample account of Luther's conference with Miltitz, the incomparable work of Seckendorff, entitled Commentar. Histor. Apologet. de Lutheranismo, sive de Reformatione Religionis, &c. in which the facts relating to Luther and the Reformation are deduced from the most valuable and authentic manuscripts and records, contained in the library of Saxe-Gotha, and in other learned and princely collections: and in which the frauds and falsehoods of Maimbourg's History of Lutheranism are fully detected and refuted.—As to Miltitz, his fate was unhappy. His moderation (which nothing but the blind zeal of some furious monks could have prevented from being eminently serviceable to the cause of Rome) was represented by Eckius, as something worse than indifference about the success of his commission; and, after several marks of neglect received from the pontiff, he had the misfortune to lose his life in passing the Rhine, at Mentz.

† These disputes commenced on the 27th of June and ended on the 15th of July.

beheld the contest, and proclaimed the victory. Eckius, therefore, in compliance with the spirit of this fighting age, challenged Carlostadt, and even Luther himself, against whom he had already drawn his pen, to try the force of his theological arms. The challenge was accepted, the day appointed, and the three champions, appeared in the field. The first conflict was between Carlostadt and Eckius, respecting the powers and freedom of the human will;* it was carried on in the castle of Pleissenburg, before a numerous and splendid auditory, and was followed by a dispute between Luther and Eckius concerning the authority and supremacy of the Roman pontiff. This latter controversy, which the present situation of affairs rendered singularly nice and critical, was left undecided. Huffman, at that time rector of the university of Leipsic, and who had been also appointed judge of the arguments alleged on both sides, refused to declare to whom the victory belonged, so that the decision of the case was referred to the universities of Paris and Erfurt.† In the mean time, one of the immediate effects of this dispute was a visible increase of the bitterness and enmity which Eckius had conceived against Luther; for from this very period he breathed nothing but fury against the reformer,‡ whom he marked out as a victim to his vengeance, without considering, that the measures he took for the destruction of Luther, must have a most pernicious influence upon the cause of the pontiff, by fomenting the present divisions, and thus contributing to the progress of the reformation, as was really the case.§

☞ * This controversy turned upon *liberty*, considered not in a philosophical, but in a theological sense. It was rather a dispute concerning *power* than concerning *liberty*. Carlostadt maintained, that, since the fall of man, our natural liberty is not strong enough to conduct us to what is good, without the intervention of divine grace. Eckius asserted, on the contrary, that our natural liberty co-operates with divine grace, and that it is in the power of man to consent to the divine impulse, or to resist it. The former attributed all to God; the latter divided the merit of virtue between God and the creature. The modern Lutherans have almost universally abandoned the sentiments of Carlostadt.

† There is an ample account of this dispute at Leipsic, given by Loscherus, in his Acta et Documenta Reformationis.

☞ ‡ This was one proof that the issue of the controversy was not in his favour. The victor, in any combat, is generally too full of satisfaction and self-complacency, to feel the emotions of fury and vengeance, which seldom arise but from disappointment and defeat. There is even an insolent kind of clemency that arises from an eminent and palpable superiority. This indeed Eckius had no opportunity of exercising.—Luther demonstrated, in this conference, that the church of Rome, in the earlier ages, had never been acknowledged as superior to other churches; and he combated the pretensions of that church and its bishop, from the testimony of Scripture, the authority of the fathers, and the best ecclesiastical historians, and even from the decrees of the council of Nice; while all the arguments of Eckius were derived from the spurious and insipid Decretals, which were scarcely of 400 years' standing. See Seckendorff's History of Lutheranism.

☞ § It may be observed here, that, before Luther's attack upon the store-house of indulgences, Eckius was his intimate friend. The latter must certainly have been uncommonly unworthy, since even the mild and gentle Melancthon represents him as an inhuman persecutor, a sophist, and a knave, who maintained doctrines contrary to his belief, and against his conscience. See the learned Dr. Jortin's Life of Erasmus, vol. ii. p. 713; also Vitus' account of the death of Eckius in Seckendorff, lib. iii. p. 468.

XI. Among the spectators of this ecclesiastical combat, was Philip Melancthon, at that time professor of Greek at Wittenberg, who had not yet been involved in these divisions, (for the mildness of his temper, and his elegant taste for polite literature, rendered him averse from disputes of this nature,) though he was the intimate friend of Luther, and approved his design of delivering the pure and primitive science of theology from the darkness and subtlety of scholastic jargon.* As this eminent man was one of those whom the dispute with Eckius convinced of the excellence of Luther's cause; as he was, moreover, one of the illustrious and respectable instruments of the Reformation; it may not be improper to give some account of the talents and virtues that rendered his name immortal. His greatest enemies have borne testimony to his merit. They have been forced to acknowledge, that the annals of antiquity exhibit very few worthies that may be compared with him, whether we consider the extent of his knowledge in things human and divine, the fertility and elegance of his genius, the facility and quickness of his comprehension, or the uninterrupted industry that attended his learned and theological labours. He rendered to philosophy and the liberal arts the same eminent service that Luther had done to religion, by purging them from the dross with which they had been corrupted, and by recommending them, in a powerful and persuasive manner, to the study of the Germans. He had the rare talent of discerning truth in its most intricate connexions and combinations, of comprehending at once the most abstract notions, and expressing them with the utmost ease and perspicuity. And he applied this happy talent in religious disquisitions with such unparalleled success, that it may safely be affirmed, that the cause of true Christianity derived from the learning and genius of Melancthon more signal advantages, and a more effectual support, than it received from any of the other doctors of the age. His love of peace and concord, which partly arose from the sweetness of his natural temper, made him desire with ardour that a reformation might be effected without producing a schism in the church, and that the external communion of the contending parties might be preserved uninterrupted and entire. This spirit of mildness and charity, carried perhaps too far, led him sometimes to make concessions that were neither consistent with prudence, nor advantageous to the cause in which he was engaged. It is however certain, that he gave no quarter to those more dangerous and momentous errors that reigned in the church of Rome, but maintained on the contrary that their extirpation was essentially necessary, in order to the restoration of true religion. In the natural complexion of this great man there was something soft, timid, and yielding. Hence originated a certain diffidence of himself, that not only made him examine things with the great-

* See Melancthon's letter concerning the conference at Leipsic, in Loscherus' Acta et Documenta Reformationis, tom. iii.

est attention and care, before he resolved upon any measure, but also filled him with uneasy apprehensions where there was no danger, and made him fear even things that, in reality, could never happen. And yet, on the other hand, when the hour of real danger approached, when things bore a formidable aspect, and the cause of religion was in imminent peril, then this timorous man was at once converted into an intrepid hero, looked danger in the face with unshaken constancy, and opposed his adversaries with invincible fortitude. All this shows, that the force of truth and the power of principle had diminished the weaknesses and defects of Melancthon's natural character, without entirely removing them. Had his fortitude been more uniform and steady, his desire of reconciling all interests and pleasing all parties less vehement and excessive, his triumph over the superstitions imbibed in his infancy more complete,* he must deservedly have been considered as one of the greatest among men.†

XII. While the credit and authority of the pontiff were thus upon the decline in Germany, they received a mortal wound in Switzerland from Ulric Zuingle, a canon of Zurich, whose extensive learning and uncommon sagacity were accompanied with the most heroic intrepidity and resolution.‡ It must even be acknowledged,§ that this eminent man had perceived some rays of the truth before Luther came to an open rupture with the church of Rome. He was, however, afterwards still farther animated by the example, and instructed by the writings of the Saxon reformer; and thus his zeal for the good cause acquired new strength and vigour; for he not only explained the sacred writings in his public discourses to the people,* but also gave, in 1519, a signal proof of his courage, by opposing, with the greatest resolution and success, the ministry of a certain Italian monk, named Bernardine Samson, who was carrying on, in Switzerland, the impious traffick of indulgences with the same impudence that Tetzel had done in Germany.† This was the first remarkable event that prepared the way for the reformation among the Helvetic cantons. In process of time, Zuingle pursued with steadiness and resolution the design that he had begun with such courage and success; and some other learned men, educated in Germany, acting with zeal as his colleagues, succeeded so far in removing the credulity of a deluded people, that the pope's supremacy was rejected and denied in the greatest part of Switzerland. It is indeed to be observed, that he did not always use the same methods of conversion that were employed by Luther; nor, upon particular occasions, did he discountenance the use of violent measures against such as adhered with obstinacy to the superstitions of their ancestors. He is also said to have attributed, to the civil magistrate, such an extensive power in ecclesiastical affairs, as is quite inconsistent with the essence and genius of religion. But, upon the whole, even envy itself must acknowledge, that his intentions were upright, and his designs worthy of high approbation.

XIII. In the mean time, the religious dissensions in Germany increased, instead of diminishing; for, while Miltitz was treating with Luther in such a mild and prudent manner as offered the fairest prospect of an approaching accommodation, Eckius, inflamed with resentment and fury on account of his defeat, repaired with the utmost precipitation to Rome, to accomplish, as he imagined, the ruin of the bold reformer. There, entering into a league with the Dominicans, who were still in high credit at the papal court, and more especially with their two zealous patrons, De Priero and Caietan, he earnestly entreated Leo to level the thunder of his *anathemas* at the head of the delinquent, and to exclude him from the communion of the church. The Dominicans, desirous of revenging the affront which, in their opinion, their whole order had received by Luther's treatment of their brother Tetzel and

☞ * By this, no doubt, Dr. Mosheim means the credulity this great man discovered with respect to prodigies and dreams, and his having been somewhat addicted to the pretended science of astrology. See Schelhornii Amœnit. Hist. Eccles. et Lit. vol. ii. p. 609.

† We have a life of Melancthon, written by Joachim Camerarius; but a more accurate account of this illustrious reformer, composed by a prudent, impartial, and well-informed biographer, as also a complete collection of his works, would be an inestimable present to the republic of letters.

☞ ‡ The translator has added, to the portrait of Zuingle, the quality of *heroic intrepidity*, because it was a predominant and remarkable part of the character of this illustrious reformer, whose learning and fortitude, tempered by the greatest moderation, rendered him, perhaps beyond comparison, the brightest ornament of the protestant cause.

☞ § Our learned historian does not seem to acknowledge this with pleasure, as the Germans and Swiss contend for the honour of having given the first overtures toward the reformation. If, however, truth has obliged him to make this acknowledgment, he has accompanied it with some modifications which are more artful than accurate. He says, that Zuingle "had perceived some rays of the truth before Luther came to an open rupture," &c. to make us imagine that Luther might have seen the truth long before that rupture happened, and consequently as soon as Zuingle. But it is well known, that the latter, from his early years, had been shocked at several of the superstitious practices of the church of Rome; that, so early as the year 1516,* he had begun to explain the Scriptures to the people, and to censure, though with great prudence and moderation, the errors of a corrupt church; and that he had very noble and extensive ideas of a general reformation, at the very time that Luther retained almost the whole system of popery, indulgences excepted. Luther proceeded very slowly to exempt himself from those prejudices of education, which Zuingle, by the force of an adventurous genius, and an uncommon degree of knowledge and penetration, easily shook off.

* Ruchart, Hist. de la Reformation en Suisse, Zuinglii op. tom. i. p. 7. Nouveau Diction. vol. iv. p. 866. Durand, Hist. du xvi. Siecle, tom. ii. p. 8, &c. Jurieu, Apologie pour les Reformateurs, &c. partie i. p 119.

☞* This again is inaccurate. It appears from the preceding note, and from the most authentic records, that Zuingle had explained the Scriptures to the people, and called in question the authority and supremacy of the pope, before the name of Luther was known in Switzerland. Besides, instead of receiving instruction from the German reformer, he was much his superior in learning, capacity, and judgment, and was much fitter to be his master than his disciple, as the four volumes in folio which we have of his works abundantly testify.

† See Jo. Henr. Hottingeri Hist. Eccles. Helvet. tom. ii. lib. vi.—Ruchart, Histoire de la Reformation en Suisse, tom i. liv i.—Gerdes, Histor. Renovat. Evangelii, tom. ii.

their patron Caietan, seconded the furious efforts of Eckius; and the pontiff, overcome by the importunity of these pernicious counsellors, imprudently issued* a bull on the 15th of June, 1520, in which forty-one pretended heresies, extracted from the writings of Luther, were solemnly condemned, his works ordered to be publicly burned, and in which he was again summoned, on pain of excommunication, to confess and retract his pretended errors within the space of sixty days, and to throw himself upon the clemency of the pontiff.

XIV. As soon as the account of this rash sentence was communicated to Luther, he thought it was high time to consult both his present defence and his future security; and the first step he took for this purpose, was the renewal of his appeal from the sentence of the pontiff, to the more respectable decision of a general council. But as he foresaw that this appeal would be treated with contempt, and that, when the time prescribed for his recantation should have elapsed, the thunder of excommunication would be levelled at his devoted head, he judged it prudent to withdraw himself voluntarily from the communion of the church of Rome, before he was obliged to leave it by force; and thus to render this new bull of ejection a blow in the air, an exercise of authority without any object to act upon. At the same time, he resolved to execute this wise determination in a public manner, that his voluntary retreat from the communion of a corrupt and superstitious church might be universally known, before the lordly pontiff had prepared his ghostly thunder. With this view, on the 10th of December, 1520, he had a pile of wood erected without the walls of the city;† and there, in presence of a prodigious multitude of people of all ranks and orders, he committed to the flames both the bull that had been published against him, and the decretals and canons relating to the pope's supreme jurisdiction. By this he declared to the world, that he was no longer a subject of the pontiff, and that, consequently, the sentence of excommunication against him, which was daily expected from Rome, was entirely superfluous and insignificant; for the man who publicly commits to the flames the code that contains the laws of his sovereign, shows thereby that he has no longer any respect for his government, nor any intention of submitting to his authority; and the man who voluntarily withdraws himself from a society, cannot, with any appearance of reason or common sense, be afterwards forcibly and authoritatively excluded from it. It is not improbable, that Luther was directed, in this critical measure, by persons well skilled in the law, who are generally dexterous in furnishing a perplexed client with nice distinctions and plausible evasions. Be that as it may, he separated himself only from the church of Rome, which considers the pope as infallible, and not from the church considered in a more extensive sense; for he submitted to the decision of the universal church, when that decision should be given in a general council lawfully assembled. When this judicious distinction is considered, it will not appear at all surprising, that many, even of the Roman Catholics, who weighed matters with a certain degree of impartiality and wisdom, and were zealous for the maintenance of the liberties of Germany, justified this bold resolution of Luther.* In less than a month after he had taken this noble and important step, a second bull was issued against him, on the 6th of January, 1521, by which he was expelled from the communion of the church, for having insulted the majesty and disowned the supremacy of the pope.†

XV. Such iniquitous laws, enacted against the person and doctrine of Luther, produced an effect different from what was expected by the imperious pontiff. Instead of intimidating this bold reformer, they led him to form the project of founding a church upon principles opposite to those of Rome, and to establish, in it, a system of doctrine and ecclesiastical discipline agreeable to the spirit and precepts of the Gospel of truth. This, indeed, was the only resource left to him; for, to submit to the orders of a cruel and insolent enemy, would have been the greatest degree of imprudence imaginable; and to embrace, anew, errors which he had rejected with a just indignation, and exposed with the clearest evidence, would have discovered a want of integrity and principle, worthy only of the most abandoned profligate. From this time, therefore, he applied himself to the pursuit of the truth with increased assiduity and fervour; nor did he only review with attention, and confirm by new arguments, what he had hitherto taught, but went far beyond it, and made vigorous attacks upon the principal fortress of popery, the power and jurisdiction of the Roman pontiff, which he overturned from its very foundation. In this noble undertaking he was seconded by many learned and pious men, in various parts of Europe; by those professors of the university of Witten-

* The wisest and best part of the Roman catholics acknowledge, that Leo was chargeable with the most culpable imprudence in this rash and violent method of proceeding. See a Dissertation of the learned John Frederic Mayer, de Pontificis Leonis X. processum adversus Lutherum improbantibus, which is part of a work published at Hamburg, in 1698, under this singular title: Ecclesia Romana Reformationis Lutheranæ patrona et cliens. There were several wise and thinking persons at this time about the pontiff, who declared openly, without the least ceremony, their disapprobation of the violent counsels of Eckius and the Dominicans, and gave it as their opinion, that it was both prudent and just to wait for the issue of the conferences of Miltitz with Luther, before such forcible measures should be employed.

† Of Wittenberg.

☞ * This judicious distinction has not been sufficiently attended to; and the Romanists, some through artifice, others through ignorance, have confounded the *papacy* with the *catholic church*, though they are, in reality, two different things. The papacy, indeed, by the ambitious dexterity of the Roman pontiffs, incorporated itself by degrees into the church; but it was a preposterous supplement, and was really as foreign to its genuine constitution, as a new *citadel, erected* by a successful usurper, would be to an *ancient city*. Luther set out and acted upon this distinction; he went out of the citadel, but he intended to remain in the city, and, like a good patriot, hoped to reform its corrupted government.

† Both these bulls are to be found in the Bullarium Romanum, and also in the learned Pfaff's Histor Theol. Literar.

berg, who had adopted his principles; and in a more especial manner by the celebrated Melancthon; and, as the fame of Luther's wisdom and Melancthon's learning had filled that academy with an incredible number of students, who flocked to it from all parts, this happy circumstance propagated the principles of the Reformation with an amazing rapidity through all the countries of Europe.*

XVI. Not long after the commencement of these divisions, Maximilian I. had resigned his breath; and his grandson, Charles I. of Spain and V. of Austria, had succeeded him in the empire in 1519. Leo seized this new occasion of venting and executing his vengeance, by putting the new emperor in mind of his character as 'advocate and defender of the church,' and demanding the exemplary punishment of Luther, who had rebelled against its sacred laws and institutions. On the other hand, Frederic the Wise employed his credit with Charles to prevent the publication of any unjust edict against this reformer, and to have his cause tried by the canons of the Germanic church, and the laws of the empire. This request was so much the more likely to be granted, as Charles was under much greater obligations to Frederic than to any other of the German princes; for it was chiefly by his zealous and important services that he had been raised to the empire, in opposition to the pretensions of such a formidable rival as Francis I. king of France. The emperor was sensible of his obligations to the worthy elector, and was disposed to satisfy his demands. That, however, he might do this without displeasing the Roman pontiff, he resolved that Luther should be called before the council which was to be assembled at Worms in 1521, and that his cause should be there publicly heard, before any definitive sentence should be pronounced against him. It may perhaps appear strange, and even inconsistent with the laws of the church, that a cause of a religious nature should be examined and decided in the public diet. But it must be considered that these diets, in which the archbishops, bishops, and even some abbots, had their places, as well as the princes of the empire, were not only political assemblies, but also provincial councils for Germany, to whose jurisdiction, by the canon law, such causes as that of Luther properly belonged.

XVII. Luther, therefore, appeared at Worms, secured against the violence of his enemies by a safe-conduct from the emperor, and, on the 17th of April, pleaded his cause before that grand assembly with the utmost resolution and presence of mind. Menaces and entreaties were alternately employed to conquer the firmness of his purpose, to engage him to renounce the propositions he had hitherto maintained, and to bend him to a submission to the Roman pontiff. But he opposed all these attempts with a noble obstinacy, and peremptorily declared that he would never abandon his opinions, or change his conduct, unless he should be convinced by the word of God, or the dictates of right reason, that his opinions were erroneous, and his conduct unlawful. When therefore neither promises nor threats could shake the constancy of this magnanimous reformer, he obtained, indeed, from the emperor, the liberty of returning unmolested to his home: but, after his departure from the diet, he was condemned by the unanimous suffrages both of the emperor and the princes, and was declared an enemy to the holy Roman empire.* Frederic, who saw the storm rising against Luther, used the best precautions to secure him from its violence. For this purpose he sent three or four persons in whom he could confide, to meet him on his return from the diet, in order to conduct him to a place of safety. These emissaries, disguised by masks, executed their commission with the utmost secrecy and success. Meeting with Luther near Eisenach, they seized him, and carried him into the castle of Wartenberg; nor, as some have imagined upon probable grounds, was this done without the knowledge of his imperial majesty. In this retreat, which he called his Patmos, the reformer lay concealed for ten months, and employed this involuntary leisure in compositions that were afterwards very useful to the world.†

* There is a particular account of the rapid progress of the reformation in Germany, given by the learned Daniel Gerdes, professor at Groningen, in his Historia renovati Evangelii.

☞ * This sentence, which was dated the 8th of May, 1521, was excessively severe; and Charles, whether through sincere zeal or political cunning, showed himself in this affair an ardent abettor of the papal authority; for in this edict the pope is declared the only true judge of the controversy, in which he was evidently a party concerned; Luther is declared a member cut off from the church, a schismatic, a notorious and obstinate heretic; the severest punishments are denounced against those who shall receive, entertain, maintain, or countenance him, either by acts of hospitality, by conversation or writing; and all his disciples, adherents, and followers, are involved in the same condemnation. This edict was, however, received with the highest disapprobation by all wise and thinking persons, 1st, because Luther had been condemned without being heard, at Rome, by the college of cardinals, and afterwards at Worms, where, without any discussion or refutation of his doctrine, he was only despotically ordered to abandon and renounce it; 2dly, because Charles V., as emperor, had not a right to give an authoritative sentence against the doctrine of Luther, or to take for granted the infallibility of the Roman pontiff, before these matters were discussed and decided by a general council; and, 3dly, because a considerable number of the German princes, who were immediately interested in this affair, such as the electors of Cologne, Saxony, and the Palatinate, and other sovereign princes, had neither been present at the diet, nor examined and approved the edict; and, therefore, at best, it could only have force in the territories belonging to the house of Austria, and to such of the princes as had given their consent to its publication. But, after all, this edict produced scarcely any effect, not only for the reasons now mentioned, but also because Charles, whose presence, authority, and zeal, were necessary to render it respectable, was involved in other affairs of a civil nature which he had more at heart. Obliged to pass successively into Flanders, England, and Spain, to quell the seditions of his subjects, and to form new alliances against his great enemy and rival Francis, he lost sight of the edict, while it was treated with the highest indignation or the utmost contempt by all who had any regard for the liberties of the empire and the rights of the Germanic church.

☞ † This precaution of the humane and excellent elector being put in execution, on the 3d of May, five days before the solemn publication of the edict of Worms, the pope missed his blow; and the adversaries of Luther became doubly odious to the people of Germany, who, unacquainted with the scheme of

XVIII. His active spirit could not, however, long bear this confinement; he therefore left his Patmos in March, 1522, without the consent or even the knowledge of his patron and protector Frederic, and repaired to Wittenberg. One of the principal motives that engaged him to take this bold step, was the information he had received of the inconsiderate conduct of Carlostadt, and some other friends of the Reformation, who had already excited tumults in Saxony, and were acting in a manner equally prejudicial to the tranquillity of the state, and the true interests of the church. Carlostadt, professor at Wittenberg, was a man of considerable learning, who had pierced the veil, with which papal artifice and superstition had covered the truth, and, at the instigation of Eckius, had been excluded with Luther from the communion of the church. His zeal, however, was intemperate; his plans were laid with temerity, and executed without moderation. During Luther's absence, he threw down and broke the images of the saints that were placed in the churches, and instead of restraining the vehemence of a fanatical multitude, who had already begun in some places to abuse the precious liberty that was dawning upon them, he encouraged their ill-timed violence, and led them on to sedition and mutiny. Luther opposed the impetuosity of this imprudent reformer with the utmost fortitude and dignity, and wisely exhorted him and his adherents to eradicate error from the minds of the people, before they made war upon its external ensigns in the churches and public places; since, the former being once removed, the latter must fall of course,* and since the destruction of the latter alone could be attended with no lasting fruits. To these prudent admonitions this excellent reformer added the influence of example, by applying himself, with redoubled industry and zeal, to his German translation of the Holy Scriptures, which he carried on with expedition and success,† with the assistance of some learned and pious men whom he consulted in this important undertaking. The event abundantly showed the wisdom of Luther's advice; for the different parts of this translation, being successively and gradually spread abroad among the people, produced sudden and almost incredible effects, and extirpated, root and branch, the erroneous principles and superstitious doctrine of the church of Rome from the minds of a prodigious number of persons.

XIX. During these transactions, Leo died, and was succeeded in the pontificate by Adrian VI., a native of Utrecht. This pope, who had formerly been preceptor to Charles V., and who owed his new dignity to the good offices of that prince, was a man of probity and candour, who acknowledged ingenuously that the church laboured under the most fatal disorders, and declared his willingness to apply the remedies that should be judged the most adapted to heal them.‡ He began his pontificate by sending a legate to the diet, which was as-

Frederic, and not knowing what was become of their favourite reformer, imagined that he was imprisoned, or perhaps destroyed, by the emissaries of Rome. In the mean time, Luther lived in peace and quiet in the castle of Wartenberg, where he translated a great part of the New Testament into the German language, and wrote frequent letters to his trusty friends and intimates to comfort them under his absence. Nor was his confinement here inconsistent with amusement and relaxation; for he frequently enjoyed the pleasure of hunting in company with his keepers, passing for a country gentleman, under the appellation of *Younker George*.

☞ If we cast an eye upon the conduct of Luther, in this first scene of his trials, we shall find a true spirit of rational zeal, generous probity, and Christian fortitude, animating this reformer. In his behaviour, before and at the diet of Worms, we observe these qualities shining with a peculiar lustre, and tempered, notwithstanding the warmth of his complexion, with an unexpected degree of moderation and decent respect both for his civil and ecclesiastical superiors. When some of his friends, informed of the violent designs of the Roman court, and alarmed by the bull that had been published against him by the rash pontiff, advised him not to expose his person at the diet, notwithstanding the imperial safe-conduct, (which, in a similar case, had not been sufficient to protect John Huss and Jerome of Prague from the perfidy and cruelty of their enemies,) he answered with his usual intrepidity, that "were he obliged to encounter at Worms as many devils as there were tiles upon the houses of that city, this would not deter him from his fixed purpose of appearing there; that fear, in this case, could be only a suggestion of Satan, who apprehended the approaching ruin of his kingdom, and who was willing to avoid a public defeat before such a grand assembly." The fire and obstinacy that appeared in this answer seemed to prognosticate much warmth and vehemence in his conduct at the assembly. But it was quite otherwise. He exposed with decency and dignity the superstitious doctrines and practices of the church of Rome, and the grievances that arose from the over-grown power of its pontiff, and the abuse that was made of it. He acknowledged the writings with which he was charged, and offered, both with moderation and humility, to defend their contents. He desired the pope's legates and their adherents to hear him, to inform him, to reason with him; and solemnly offered, in presence of the assembled princes and bishops, to renounce his doctrines, if they were shown to be erroneous. But to all these expostulations he received no other answer, than the despotic dictates of mere authority, attended with injurious and provoking language.

* Dr. Mosheim's account of this matter is perhaps more advantageous to Luther than the rigorous demands of historical impartiality will admit; at least the defects of the great reformer are here shaded with art. It is evident from several passages in the writings of Luther, that he was by no means averse to the use of images, but that, on the contrary, he looked upon them as adapted to excite and animate the devotion of the people. But, perhaps, the true reason of his displeasure at the proceedings of Carlostadt, was, that he could not bear to see another crowned with the glory of executing a plan which he had formed, and that he was ambitious of appearing the principal, if not the only, conductor of this great work. This is not a mere conjecture. Luther himself has not taken the least pains to conceal this instance of his ambition: and it appears evidently in several of his letters. On the other hand, it must be owned, that Carlostadt was rash, violent, and prone to enthusiasm, as appears by the connexions he formed afterwards with the fanatical anabaptists headed by Munzer. His contest with Luther about the eucharist, in which he manifestly maintained the truth, shall be mentioned in its proper place.

† Of this German translation of the Bible, which contributed more than all other causes, taken together, to strengthen the foundations of the Lutheran church, we have an interesting history composed by Jo. Fred. Mayer, and published at Hamburg in 1701. A more ample one was expected from the labours of the learned J. Melchior Kraft; but his death disappointed the hopes of the learned. See Jo. Alb. Fabricii Centifolium Lutheranum, part i. p. 117, and part ii. p. 617.

‡ See Caspar. Burmanni Adrianus VI. sive Analecta Historica de Adriano VI. Papa Romano, published at Utrecht in 1727.

sembled at Nuremberg in 1522. Francis Cheregato, the person who was intrusted with this commission, had positive orders to demand the speedy and vigorous execution of the sentence that had been pronounced against Luther and his followers at the diet of Worms; but, at the same time, he was authorised to declare that the pontiff was ready to remove the abuses and grievances that had armed such a formidable enemy against the see of Rome. The princes of the empire, encouraged by this declaration, and also by the absence of the emperor, who at this time resided in Spain, seized this opportunity of proposing the convocation of a general council in Germany, in order to deliberate upon the proper methods of bringing about a universal reformation of the church. They exhibited, at the same time, a hundred articles, containing the heaviest complaints of the injurious treatment which the Germans had hitherto received from the court of Rome, and, by a public law, prohibited all innovation in religious matters, until a general council should decide what ought to be done in an affair of such high importance.* As long as the German princes were unacquainted with, or inattentive to, the measures that were taken in Saxony for founding a new church in direct opposition to that of Rome, they were zealously unanimous in their endeavours to set bounds to the papal authority and jurisdiction, which they all looked upon as overgrown and enormous; nor were they at all offended at Luther's contest with the pontiff, which they considered as a dispute of a private and personal nature.

XX. The good pope Adrian did not long enjoy the pleasure of sitting at the head of the church. He died in 1523, and was succeeded by Clement VII., a man of a reserved character, and prone to artifice.† This pontiff sent to the imperial diet at Nuremberg, in 1524, a cardinal legate, named Campeggio, whose orders, with respect to the affairs of Luther, breathed nothing but severity and violence, and who inveighed against the lenity of the German princes in delaying the execution of the decree of Worms, while he carefully avoided the smallest mention of Adrian's promise of reforming the corruptions of a superstitious church. The emperor seconded the demands of Campeggio, by the orders he sent to his minister to insist upon the execution of the decree. The princes of the empire, tired out by these importunities and remonstrances, changed in appearance the law they had passed, but confirming it in reality; for, while they promised to observe the edict, as far as it was possible, they renewed their demand of a general council, and left all other disputed points to be examined and decided at the diet that was soon to be assembled at Spire. The pope's legate, on the other hand, perceiving by these proceedings, that the German princes in general were no enemies to the Reformation, retired to Ratisbon, with the bishops and those princes who adhered to the cause of Rome, and there drew from them a new declaration, by which they engaged themselves to execute the edict with rigour in their respective dominions.

XXI. While the efforts of Luther toward the reformation of the church were so far successful, and almost all the nations seemed disposed to open their eyes upon the light, two unhappy occurrences, one of a foreign, and the other of a domestic nature, contributed greatly to retard the progress of this salutary and glorious work. The domestic, or internal incident, was a controversy concerning the *manner* in which the body and blood of Christ were present in the eucharist, that arose among those whom the pope had publicly excluded from the communion of the church, and unhappily produced among the friends of the good cause the most deplorable animosities and divisions. Luther and his followers, though they had rejected the monstrous doctrine of the church of Rome with respect to transubstantiation, or the change of the bread and wine into the body and blood of Christ, were nevertheless of opinion, that the partakers of the Lord's supper received, with the bread and wine, the real body and blood of Christ. This, in their judgment, was a mystery, which they did not pretend to explain.* Carlostadt, who was Luther's colleague, understood the matter otherwise; and his doctrine, which was afterwards more fully illustrated and confirmed by Zuingle, amounted to this: "That the body and blood of Christ were not *really* present in the eucharist; and that the bread and wine were no more than external *signs*, or *symbols*, designed to excite in the minds of Christians the remembrance of the sufferings and death of the divine Saviour, and of the benefits which arise from it."† This opinion was embraced by all the friends of the Reformation in Switzerland, and by a considerable number of its votaries in Germany. On the other hand, Luther maintained his doctrine, in relation to this point, with the utmost obstinacy; and hence arose, in 1524, a tedious and vehement controversy, which, notwithstanding the zealous endeavours that were used to reconcile the contending parties, terminated, at length, in a mischievous division between those who had embarked together in the sacred cause of religion and liberty.

* See Jac. Fred. Georgii Gravamina Germanorum adversus Sedem Romanam, lib. ii. p. 327.

† See Jac. Zeigleri Historia Clementis VII. in Jo. Georgii Schelhornii Amœnit. Histor. Eccles. tom. ii p. 210

☞ * Luther was not so modest as Dr. Mosheim here represents him. He pretended to explain his doctrine of the real presence, absurd and contradictory as it was, and uttered much senseless jargon on this subject. As in a red-hot iron, said he, two distinct substances, namely, iron and fire, are united, so is the body of Christ joined with the bread in the eucharist. I mention this miserable comparison to show into what absurdities the towering pride of system will often betray men of deep sense and true genius.

† See Val. Ern. Loscheri Historia Motuum inter Lutheranos et Reformatos, part i. lib. ii. cap. i.—See, on the other side of the question, Scultet's Annales Evangelii, published by Vonder Hardt in his Historia Liter. Reformat.; also Rud. Hospinianus, and other reformed writers, who have treated of the origin and progress of this dispute.—☞ It appears from this representation (which is a just one) of the sentiments of Zuingle concerning the holy sacrament of the Lord's supper, that they were the same with those maintained by bishop Hoadly, in his Plain Account of the Nature and Design of the Sacrament of the Lord's Supper

XXII. To these intestine divisions were added the horrors of a civil war, which was the fatal effect of oppression on the one hand, and of enthusiasm on the other, and, by its unhappy consequences, proved prejudicial to the cause and progress of the Reformation. In 1525, a prodigious multitude of seditious fanatics suddenly arose, like a whirlwind, in different parts of Germany, took arms, united their forces, waged war against the laws, the magistrates, and the empire in general, ravaged the country with fire and sword, and exhibited daily the most horrid spectacles of unrelenting barbarity. The greatest part of this furious and formidable mob was composed of peasants and vassals, who groaned under heavy burthens, and declared they were no longer able to bear the despotic severity of their chiefs; and hence the sedition was called the *Rustic war*, or the war of the peasants.* But it is also certain, that this motley crowd was intermixed with numbers, who joined in this sedition from different motives, some being impelled by the suggestions of enthusiasm, and others by the profligate and odious views of rapine and plunder, of repairing fortunes ruined by extravagant and dissolute living. At the first breaking out of this war, it seemed to have been kindled only by civil and political views; and agreeable to this is the general tenour of the Declarations and Manifestoes that were published by these rioters. The claims they made in these papers related to nothing farther than the diminution of the tasks imposed upon the peasants, and to their obtaining a greater measure of liberty than they had hitherto enjoyed. Religion seemed to be out of the question; at least, it was not the object of deliberation or debate. But no sooner had the enthusiast Munzer† put himself at the head of this outrageous rabble, than the face of things changed entirely; and, by the instigation of this man, who had deceived numbers before this time by his pretended visions and inspirations, the civil commotions in Saxony and Thuringia were soon directed toward a new object, and were turned into a religious war. The sentiments, however, of this seditious and dissolute multitude were greatly divided, and their demands were very different. One part of their number pleaded for an exemption from all laws, a licentious immunity from every sort of government; another, less outrageous and extravagant, confined their demands to a diminution of the taxes they were forced to pay, and of burthens under which they groaned;‡ another insisted upon a new form of religious doctrine, government, and worship, upon the establishment of a pure and unspotted church, and to add weight to this requisition, pretended, that it was suggested by the Holy Ghost, with which they were divinely and miraculously inspired; while a very considerable proportion of this furious rabble were without any distinct view or fixed purpose, and, being infected with the contagious spirit of sedition, and exasperated by the severity of their magistrates and rulers, went on headlong without reflection or foresight into every act of violence and cruelty which rebellion and enthusiasm could suggest: so that, if it cannot be denied that many of these rioters perversely misunderstood the doctrine of Luther concerning Christian liberty, and thence took occasion to commit the disorders that rendered them so justly odious, yet it would be a most absurd instance of partiality and injustice to charge that doctrine with the blame of those extravagant outrages which arose only from the manifest abuse of it. Luther himself, indeed, sufficiently defended both his principles and his cause against any such imputations, by the books he wrote against the riotous sect, and the advice he addressed to the princes of the empire to take arms against them. Accordingly, in 1525, the turbulent malcontents were defeated in a pitched battle fought at Mulhausen; and Munzer, their ringleader, was put to death.*

XXIII. While this fanatical insurrection raged in Germany, Frederic the Wise, elector of Saxony, departed this life. This excellent prince, whose character was distinguished by an uncommon degree of prudence and moderation, had, during his life, been a sort of mediator between the Roman pontiff and the reformer of Wittenberg, and had always entertained the pleasing hope of restoring peace in the church, and of so reconciling the contending parties as to prevent a separation either in point of ecclesiastical jurisdiction or religious communion. Hence it was, that while he made no opposition to Luther's design of reforming a corrupt and superstitious church, but rather encouraged him in the execution of this pious purpose, yet he was at no pains to introduce any change into the churches which were established in his own dominions, or to subject them to his jurisdiction. The elector John, his brother and successor, acted in a very different manner. Convinced of the truth of Luther's doctrine, and persuaded, that it must lose ground and be soon suppressed if the despotic authority of the Roman pontiff remained undisputed and entire, he, without hesitation or delay, assumed to himself that supremacy in ecclesiastical matters which every lawful sovereign may claim as his natural right, and founded and established a church in his dominions, very different from the church of Rome, in doctrine, discipline, and government. To bring this new and happy establishment to as great a degree of perfection as

* These kinds of wars or commotions, arising from the impatience of the peasants, under the heavy burthens that were imposed on them, were very common long before the time of Luther. Hence the author of the Danish Chronicle (published by the learned Ludewig in his Reliq. MSotrum) calls these insurrections a *common evil*. This will not appear surprising to such as consider, that, in most places, the condition of the peasants was much more intolerable and grievous before the Reformation, than it is in our times; and that the tyranny and cruelty of the nobility, before that happy period, were excessive and insupportable.

† Or Munster, as some call him.

‡ These burthens were the duties of vassalage or feudal services, which, in many respects, were truly grievous

* "Petri Gnodalii Historia de Seditione repentina Vulgi, præcipue Rusticorum, anno 1525, tempore verno per universam fere Germaniam exorta, *Basil*, 1570."—See also B. Tenzelii Histor. Reform. tom. ii. p. 331, and the observations of Ernest Cypriar upon that work

was possible, this resolute and active prince ordered a body of laws, relating to the form of ecclesiastical government, the method of public worship, the rank, offices, and revenues of the priesthood, and other matters of that nature, to be drawn up by Luther and Melancthon, and promulgated by heralds throughout his dominions in 1527. He also took care that all the churches should be supplied with pious and learned ministers, and that such of the clergy as dishonoured religion by their bad morals, or were incapable, from their want of talents, of promoting its influence, should be removed from the sacred function. The illustrious example of this elector was followed by all the princes and states of Germany that were unfriendly to the papal supremacy and jurisdiction; and similar forms of worship, discipline, and government, were thus introduced into all the churches which dissented from that of Rome. Thus may the elector John be considered as the second parent and founder of the Lutheran church, which he alone rendered a complete and independent body, distinct from the superstitious church of Rome, and fenced about with salutary laws, with a wise and well-balanced constitution. But as the best blessings may, through the influence of human corruption, become the innocent occasions of great inconveniences, such particularly was the fate of those wise and vigorous measures which this elector took for the reformation of the church; for, from that time the religious differences between the German princes, which had been hitherto kept within the bounds of moderation, broke out into a violent and lasting flame. The prudence, or rather timidity, of Frederic the Wise, who avoided every resolute measure that might tend to kindle the fire of discord, had preserved a sort of external union and concord among these princes, notwithstanding their differences in opinion. But as soon as his successor, by the open and undisguised steps he took, made it glaringly evident, that he designed to withdraw the churches in his dominions from the jurisdiction of Rome, and to reform the doctrine, discipline, and worship that had been hitherto established, then indeed the scene changed. The union, which was more specious than solid, and which was far from being well cemented, was suddenly dissolved: the spirits were heated and divided, and an open rupture ensued among the German princes, of whom one party embraced the Reformation, while the other adhered to the superstitions of their forefathers.

XXIV. Affairs being reduced to this violent and troubled state, the patrons of popery gave intimations that were far from being ambiguous, of their intention to make *war* upon the Lutheran party, and to suppress by *force* the doctrines which they were incapable of overturning by *argument;* and this design would certainly have been put in execution, had not the troubles of Europe disconcerted their measures. The Lutherans, informed of these hostile intentions, began to deliberate upon the most effectual methods of defending themselves against superstition armed with violence, and formed the plan of a confederacy that might answer this prudent purpose. In the mean time the diet, assembled at Spire in 1526, at which Ferdinand, the emperor's brother, presided, ended in a manner more favourable to the friends of the Reformation, than they could naturally expect. The emperor's ambassadors at this diet were ordered to use their most earnest endeavours for the suppression of all farther disputes concerning religion, and to insist upon the rigorous execution of the edict of Worms. The greatest part of the German princes strongly opposed this motion, declaring, that they could not execute that sentence, nor come to any determination with respect to the doctrines by which it had been occasioned, before the whole matter should be submitted to the cognizance of a general council lawfully assembled; alleging farther, that the decision of controversies of this nature belonged properly to such a council, and to it alone. This opinion, after long and warm debates, was adopted by a great majority, and, at length, consented to by the whole assembly; for it was unanimously agreed to present a solemn address to the emperor, beseeching him to assemble, without delay, a free and general council: and it was also agreed, that, in the mean time, the princes and states of the empire should, in their respective dominions, be at liberty to manage ecclesiastical matters in the manner which they might deem the most expedient, yet so as to be able to give to God and to the emperor an account of their administration, when it should be demanded of them.

XXV. Nothing could be more favourable to those who had the cause of pure and genuine Christianity at heart, than a resolution of this nature. For the emperor was, at this time, so entirely taken up in regulating the troubled state of his dominions in France, Spain, and Italy, which exhibited, from day to day, new scenes of perplexity, that, for some years, it was not in his power to turn his attention to the affairs of Germany in general, and still less to the state of religion in particular, which was beset with difficulties that, to a reflecting politician like Charles, must have appeared peculiarly critical and dangerous. Besides, had he really possessed leisure to form, or power to execute, a plan that might terminate, in favour of the Roman pontiff, the religious disputes which prevailed in Germany, it is evident that the inclination was wanting, and that Clement VII., who now sat in the papal chair, had nothing to expect from the good offices of Charles; for this pontiff, after the defeat of Francis at the battle of Pavia, filled with uneasy apprehensions of the growing power of the emperor in Italy, entered into a confederacy with the French and the Venetians against that prince. This measure inflamed the resentment and indignation of Charles to such a degree, that he abolished the papal authority in his Spanish dominions, made war upon the pope, laid siege to Rome in 1527, blocked up Clement in the castle of St. Angelo, and exposed him to the most severe and contumelious treatment. These critical events, together with the liberty granted by the diet of Spire, were prudently and industriously improved, by the friends of the Reformation, to the advantage of their cause, and to the augmentation of their number. Several princes, whom the fear of persecution and punishment had hitherto prevented from lending a hand to the good work, being delivered now from their restraint, publicly renounced the superstition of Rome, and introduced among their subjects the same forms of religious worship, and the same system of doctrine, that had been received in Saxony. Others, though placed in such circumstances as discouraged them from acting in an open manner against the interests of the pope, were far from manifesting any intention of opposing those who withdrew the people from his despotic yoke; nor did they molest the private assemblies of those who had separated themselves from the church of Rome. And all the Germans who, before the resolutions of the diet of Spire, had rejected the papal discipline and doctrine, were now, in consequence of the liberty they enjoyed by these resolutions, wholly employed in bringing their schemes and plans to a certain degree of consistency, and in adding vigour and firmness to the glorious cause in which they were engaged. In the mean time, Luther and his fellow-labourers, particularly those who were with him at Wittenberg, by their writings, their instructions, their admonitions and counsels, inspired the timorous with fortitude, dispelled the doubts of the ignorant, fixed the principles and resolution of the floating and inconstant, and animated all the friends of genuine Christianity with a spirit suitable to the grandeur of their undertaking.

XXVI. But the tranquillity and liberty they enjoyed, in consequence of the resolutions taken in the first diet of Spire, were not of long duration. They were interrupted by a new diet assembled, in 1529, in the same place, by the emperor, after he had appeased the commotions and troubles which had employed his attention in several parts of Europe, and concluded a treaty of peace with Clement. This prince, having now, in a great measure, shaken off the burthen that had for some time overwhelmed him, had leisure to direct the affairs of the church; and this the reformers soon felt by a disagreeable experience. For the power, which had been granted by the former diet to every prince of managing ecclesiastical matters as he thought proper, until the meeting of a general council, was now revoked by a majority of votes, and not only so, but every change was declared unlawful that should be introduced into the doctrine, discipline or worship of the established religion, before the determination of the approaching council was known.* This decree was justly considered as iniquitous and intolerable by the elector of Saxony, the landgrave of Hesse, and such other members of the diet, as were persuaded of the necessity of a reformation in the church. Nor was any one so simple, or so little acquainted with the politics of Rome, as to look upon the promise of assembling speedily a general council, in any other light than as an artifice to quiet the minds of the people; since it was easy to perceive, that a lawful council, free from the despotic influence of Rome, was the very last thing that a pope would grant in such a critical state of affairs. Therefore, when the princes and members now mentioned found that all their arguments and remonstrances against this unjust decree made no impression upon Ferdinand,* or upon the abettors of the ancient superstitions, (whom the pope's legate animated by his presence and exhortations,) they entered a solemn *protest* against this decree, on the 19th of April, and appealed to the emperor and to a future council.† Hence arose the denomination of *Protestants*, given from this period to those who renounce the superstitious communion of the church of Rome.

XXVII. The dissenting princes, who were the protectors and heads of the reformed churches, had no sooner entered their protest, than they sent proper persons to the emperor, who was then upon his passage from Spain to Italy, to acquaint him with their proceedings in this affair The ministers employed in this commission, executed the orders they had received with the greatest resolution and presence of mind, and behaved with the spirit and firmness of the princes, whose sentiments and conduct they were sent to justify and explain. The emperor, whose pride was wounded by this fortitude in persons that dared to oppose his designs, ordered the ambassadors to be apprehended, and detained for several days. Intelligence of this violent step was soon brought to the protestant princes, and made them conclude that their personal safety, and the success of their cause, depended entirely upon their courage and concord, the one animated, and the other cemented by a solemn confederacy. They, therefore, held several meetings at Nuremberg, Smalcald, and other places, in order to deliberate upon the means of forming such a powerful league as might enable them to repel the violence of their enemies.‡ But so different were their opinions and views of things, that they could come to no satisfactory conclusion.

XXVIII. Among the incidents that promoted animosity and discord between the friends of the Reformation, and prevented that union which was so much to be desired among persons embarked in the same good cause,

☞ * The resolution of the first diet of Spire, which had been taken unanimously, was revoked in the second, and another substituted in its place by a plurality of voices, which, as several of the princes then present observed, could not give to any decree the force of a law throughout the empire.

☞ * As the emperor was at Barcelona, while this diet was held at Spire, his brother Ferdinand was president in his place.

☞ † The princes of the empire, who entered this protest, and are consequently to be considered as the first protestant princes, were John, elector of Saxony, George, elector of Brandenburg, for Franconia, Ernest and Francis, dukes of Lunenburg, the landgrave of Hesse, and the prince of Anhalt. These princes were supported by thirteen imperial towns, viz. Strasburg, Ulm, Nuremberg, Constance, Rottingen, Windsheim, Memmingeu, Nordlingen, Lindaw, Kempten, Heilbron, Weissenburg, and St. Gall.

‡ See the history of the confession of Augsburg, written in German by the learned Christ. Aug. Salig, tom. i. book ii. ch. i. p. 128, and more especially an important work by Dr. Joachim Muller, entitled Historie von der Evangelischen Stande Protestation gegen den Speyerschen Reichs-Abscheid von 1529, Appellation, &c. published at Jena in 1705.

the principal one was the dispute that had arisen between the divines of Saxony and Switzerland, concerning the manner of Christ's presence in the *eucharist*. To terminate this controversy, Philip, landgrave of Hesse, invited, in 1529, to a conference at Marpurg, Luther and Zuingle, with some of the most eminent doctors who adhered to the respective parties of these contending chiefs. This expedient, which was designed by that truly magnanimous prince, not so much to end the matter by keen debate, as to accommodate differences by the conciliatory spirit of charity and prudence, was not attended with the salutary fruits that were expected from it. The divines that were assembled for this pacific purpose disputed, during four days, in presence of the landgrave. The principal champions in these debates were Luther, who attacked Œcolampadius, and Melancthon, who disputed against Zuingle; and the controversy turned upon several points of theology, in relation to which the Swiss doctors were supposed to entertain erroneous sentiments. For Zuingle was accused of heresy, not only on account of his explication of the nature and design of the Lord's Supper, but also in consequence of the false notions which he was supposed to have adopted, relating to the divinity of Christ, the efficacy of the divine word, original sin, and some other parts of the Christian doctrine. This illustrious reformer cleared himself, however, from the greatest part of these accusations, with the most triumphant evidence, and in such a manner as appeared entirely satisfactory, even to Luther himself. The dissension concerning the manner of Christ's presence in the eucharist still remained; nor could either of the contending parties be persuaded to abandon, or even to modify, their opinion of that matter.* The only advantage, therefore, that resulted from this conference, was, that the jarring doctors formed a sort of truce, by agreeing to a mutual toleration of their respective sentiments, and leaving the cure of their divisions to the disposal of Providence, and the effect of time, which sometimes cools the rage of party.

XXIX. The ministers of the churches which had embraced the sentiments of Luther, were preparing a new embassy to the emperor, when an account was received of the intention of that prince to come into Germany, with a view of terminating, in the approaching diet at Augsburg, the religious disputes which had produced such animosities and divisions in the empire. Charles, though long absent from Germany, and engaged in affairs that left him little leisure for theological disquisitions, was nevertheless attentive to these disputes, and foresaw their consequences. He had also, to his own deliberate reflections upon these disputes, added the counsels of men of wisdom, sagacity, and experience, and was thus, at certain seasons, rendered more cool in his proceedings, and more moderate and impartial in his opinion both of the contending parties and of the merits of the cause. He therefore, in an interview with the pope at Bologna, insisted, in the most serious and urgent manner, upon the necessity of assembling a general council. His remonstrances and expostulations could not, however, move Clement, who maintained with zeal the papal prerogatives, imputed to the emperor an ill-judged clemency, and alleged that it was the duty of that prince to support the church, and to execute speedy vengeance upon the obstinate *heretical* faction, who dared to call in question the authority of Rome and its pontiff. The imperial potentate was as little affected by this haughty discourse, as the pope had been by his wise remonstrances, and looked upon it as a most iniquitous thing, a measure also in direct opposition to the laws of the empire, to condemn, unheard, and to destroy, without any evidence of their demerit, a set of men, who had always approved themselves good citizens, and had in various respects deserved well of their country. Hitherto, indeed, it was not easy for Charles to form a clear idea of the matters in debate, since no regular system had yet been composed of the doctrines embraced by Luther and his followers, by which their real opinions, and the true causes of their opposition to the Roman pontiff, might be known with certainty. As, therefore, it was impossible, without some declaration of this nature, to examine with accuracy, or decide with equity, a matter of such high importance as that which gave rise to the divisions between the votaries of Rome and the friends of the Reformation, the elector of Saxony ordered Luther, and other eminent divines, to commit to writing, the chief articles of their religious system, and the principal points in which they differed from the church of Rome. Luther, in compliance with this order, delivered to the elector, at Torgaw, the seventeen articles which had been drawn up and voted in the conference at Sultzbach in 1529; and hence they were called the *articles of Torgaw*.* Though these articles were deemed by Luther a sufficient declaration of the sentiments of the reformers, yet it was judged proper to enlarge them; and, by a judicious detail, to give perspicuity to the arguments, and thereby strength to the cause. It was this consideration that engaged the protestant princes, assembled at Coburg and Augsburg, to employ Melancthon in extending these articles, in which important work he showed a due regard to the counsels of Luther, and expressed his sentiments and doctrine with the greatest elegance and perspicuity. And thus came forth to public view the famous *confession of Augsburg*, which did such honour to the acute judgment and the eloquent pen of Melancthon.

* Val. Ern. Loscheri Historia Motuum inter Lutheranos et Reformatos, tom. i. lib. i. cap. vi. p. 143.—Henr. Bullingeri Historia Colloquii Marpurgensis, in Jo. Conr. Fuesslin's Beytrægen zur Schweizer Reformat. Geschichte, tom. iii.—Abr. Sculteti Annal. Reformat. ad annum 1529.—Rudolphi Hospinani Histor. Sacramentor. part ii.

* See Chr. Aug. Heumanni Diss. de Lenitate Augustannæ Confess. in Sylloge Dissert Theologicar. tom. i. p. 14.—Jo. Joach. Muller's Historia Protestationis; and the other writers who have treated, either of the Reformation in general, or of the confession of Augsburg in particular.

XXX. During these transactions in Germany, the dawn of truth arose upon other nations. The light of the reformation spread itself far and wide; and almost all the European states welcomed its salutary beams, and exulted in the prospect of an approaching deliverance from the yoke of superstition and spiritual despotism. Some of the most considerable provinces of Europe had already broken their chains, and openly withdrawn themselves from the discipline of Rome and the jurisdiction of its pontiff. And thus it appears that Clement was not impelled by a false alarm to demand of the emperor the speedy extirpation of the reformers, since he had the strongest reasons to apprehend the destruction of his spiritual empire. The reformed religion was propagated in Sweden, soon after Luther's rupture with Rome, by one of his disciples, whose name was Olaus Petri, and who was the first herald of religious liberty in that kingdom. The zealous efforts of this missionary were powerfully seconded by that valiant and public-spirited prince, Gustavus Vasa Ericson, whom the Swedes had raised to the throne in the place of Christiern, king of Denmark, whose horrid barbarity lost him the sceptre that he had perfidiously usurped. This generous and patriotic hero had been in exile and in prison, while the brutal usurper, now mentioned, was involving his country in desolation and misery; but, having escaped from his confinement, and taken refuge at Lubeck, he was there instructed in the principles of the Reformation, and looked upon the doctrine of Luther, not only as agreeable to the genius and spirit of the Gospel, but also as favourable to the temporal state and political constitution of the Swedish dominions. The prudence, however, of this excellent prince was equal to his zeal, and always accompanied it: and, as the religious opinions of the Swedes were in a fluctuating state, and their minds divided between their ancient superstitions, recommended by custom, and the doctrine of Luther, which attracted their assent by the power of conviction and truth, Gustavus wisely avoided all vehemence and precipitation in spreading the new doctrine, and proceeded in this important undertaking with circumspection, and by degrees, in a manner suitable to the principles of the reformation, which are diametrically opposite to compulsion and violence.* Accordingly, the first object of his attention was the instruction of his people in the sacred doctrines of the Scriptures, for which purpose he invited into his dominions several learned Germans, and spread abroad through the kingdom Petri's Swedish translation of the Bible.* Some time after this, in 1526, he appointed a conference, at Upsal, between this eminent reformer and Peter Gallius, a zealous defender of the ancient superstition, in which these two champions were to plead publicly in behalf of their respective opinions, that it might thus be seen on which side the truth lay. The dispute, in which Olaus obtained a signal victory, contributed much to confirm Gustavus in his persuasion of the truth of Luther's doctrine, and to promote its progress in Sweden. In the following year, another event gave the finishing stroke to its propagation and success; and this was the assembly of the states at Westeraas, where the king recommended the doctrine of the reformers with such zeal, wisdom, and piety, that, after warm debates fomented by the clergy in general, and much opposition on the part of the bishops in particular, it was voted that the plan of reformation proposed by Luther should have free admittance among the Swedes.† This resolution was principally owing to the firmness and magnanimity of Gustavus, who declared publicly, that he would lay down his sceptre, and retire from his kingdom, rather than rule a people enslaved to the orders and authority of the pope, and more controlled by the tyranny of their bishops, than by the laws of their monarch.‡ Thus the papal empire in Sweden was overturned, and the king acted thenceforward as head of the church.

XXXI. The light of the reformation was

☞ * This incomparable model of princes gave many proofs of his wisdom and moderation. Once, while he was absent from Stockholm, a great number of German anabaptists, probably the riotous disciples of Munzer, arrived in that city, carried their fanaticism to extremities, and pulled down with fury the images and other ornaments of the churches, while the Lutherans dissembled their sentiments of this riot in expectation that the storm would turn to their advantage. But Gustavus no sooner returned to Stockholm, than he ordered the leaders of these fanatics to be seized and punished, and assailed the Lutherans with bitter reproaches for not having opposed them in time.

☞ * It is very remarkable, and shows the equity and candour of Gustavus in the most striking point of light, that while he ordered Olaus Petri to publish his literal translation of the sacred writings, he gave permission at the same time to the archbishop of Upsal, to prepare another version suited to the doctrine of the church of Rome; that, by a careful comparison of both translations with the original, an easier access might be opened to the truth. The bishops at first opposed this order, but were at length obliged to submit.

☞ † It was no wonder, indeed, that the bishops opposed warmly the proposal of Gustavus, since there was no country in Europe where that order and the clergy in general drew greater temporal advantages from the superstition of the times than in Sweden and Denmark. Most of the bishops had revenues superior to those of the sovereign; they possessed castles and fortresses that rendered them independent of the crown, enabled them to excite commotions in the kingdom, and gave them a degree of power that was dangerous to the state. They lived in the most dissolute luxury and overgrown opulence, while many of the nobles were in misery and want. The resolution formed by the states assembled at Westeraas, did not so much tend to regulate points of doctrine, as to reform the discipline of the church, to reduce the opulence and authority of the bishops within proper bounds, to restore to the impoverished nobility the lands and possessions which their superstitious ancestors had given to an all-devouring clergy, to exclude the prelates from the senate, to take from them their castles, and things of that nature. It was however resolved, at the same time, that the church should be provided with able pastors, who should explain the pure word of God to the people in their native tongue; and that no ecclesiastical preferments should be granted without the king's permission. This was a tacit and gentle method of promoting the Reformation.

‡ Bazii Inventarium Eccles. Sueco-Gothor. published at Lincoping in 1642. Sculteti Annales Evangelii Renovati, in Von-der-Hardt's Histor. Liter. Reformat. part v. p. 83, and 110. Raynal, Anecdotes Hist. Politiques et Militaires, tom. i. part ii.

also received in Denmark, in consequence of the ardent desire discovered by Christian or Christiern II. of having his subjects instructed in the principles and doctrines of Luther. This monarch, whose savage and infernal cruelty (either the effect of natural temper, or of bad counsels) rendered his name odious and his memory execrable, was nevertheless desirous of delivering his dominions from the superstition and tyranny of Rome. For this purpose, in 1520, he sent for Martin Reinard, one of the disciples of Carlostadt, out of Saxony, and appointed him professor of divinity at Copenhagen; and after his death, which happened in the following year, he invited Carlostadt himself to fill that important place, which he accepted indeed, but, after a short residence in Denmark, returned into Germany. These disappointments did not abate the reforming spirit of the Danish monarch, who used his utmost endeavours, though in vain, to engage Luther to visit his dominions, and took several steps that tended to the diminution, and, indeed, to the suppression of the jurisdiction, exercised over his subjects by the Roman pontiff.

It is, however, proper to observe, that in all these proceedings, Christiern was animated by no other motive than that of ambition. It was the prospect of extending his authority, and not a zeal for the advancement of true religion, that gave life and vigour to his reformative projects.

His very actions, independently of what may be concluded from his known character, evidently show, that he protected the religion of Luther with no other view than to rise by it to supremacy, both in church and state, and to find a pretext for depriving the bishops of that overgrown authority, and those ample possessions which they had gradually usurped,* and which he wished to appropriate to himself. A revolution produced by his avarice, tyranny, and cruelty, prevented the execution of this bold enterprise. The states of the kingdom, being exasperated, some by his schemes for destroying the liberty of Denmark, others by his attempts to abolish the superstition of their ancestors,† and all by his savage and barbarous treatment of those who dared to oppose his avarice or ambition, formed a conspiracy against him in 1523, by which he was deposed and banished from his dominions, and his uncle Frederic, duke of Holstein, placed on the Danish throne.

XXXII. This prince conducted matters with much more equity, prudence, and moderation, than his predecessor had done. He permitted the protestant doctors to preach publicly the opinions of Luther,* but did not venture so far as to change the established government and discipline of the church. He contributed, however, greatly to the progress of the reformation, by his successful attempts in favour of religious liberty, in the assembly of the states holden at Odensee in 1527; for it was here that he procured the publication of that famous edict, which declared every subject of Denmark free, either to adhere to the tenets of the church of Rome, or to embrace the doctrine of Luther.† Encouraged by this resolution, the protestant divines exercised the functions of their ministry with such zeal and success, that the greatest part of the Danes opened their eyes upon the auspicious beams of sacred liberty, and abandoned gradually both the doctrines and jurisdiction of the church of Rome. But the honour of finishing this glorious work, of destroying entirely the reign of superstition, and breaking asunder the bonds of papal tyranny, was reserved for Christiern III., a prince equally distinguished by his piety and prudence. He began by suppressing the despotic authority of the bishops, and by restoring to their lawful owners a great part of the wealth and possessions which the church had acquired by the artful stratagems of the crafty and designing clergy. This step was followed by a wise and well-judged settlement of religious doctrine, discipline, and worship, throughout the kingdom, according to a plan laid down by Bugenhagius, whom the king had invited from Wittenberg to perform that arduous task, for which his eminent piety, learning, and moderation, rendered him peculiarly proper. The assembly of the states at Odensee, in 1539, gave a solemn sanction to all these transactions; and thus the work of the reformation was brought to perfection in Denmark.‡

XXXIII. It is however to be observed, that, in the history of the reformation of Sweden and Denmark, we must carefully distinguish between the reformation of religious opinions, and that of the episcopal order; for, though these two things may appear to be closely connected, yet, in reality, they are so far distinct, that one might have been completely transacted without the other. A reform of doctrine might have been effected, without diminishing the authority of the bishops, or suppressing their order; and, on the other hand, the opulence and power of the bishops might

* See Jo. Gramii Diss. de Reformatione Daniæ a Christierno tentata, in the third volume of the Scriptor. Societ. Scientiarum Hafniens, p. 1—90.

† See, for a confirmation of this part of the accusation, a curious piece, containing the reasons that induced the states of Denmark to renounce their allegiance to Christiern. This piece is to be found in the fifth volume of Ludewig's compilation, entitled, Reliquiæ Manuscriptorum, in which the states of Denmark express their displeasure at the royal favour shown to the Lutherans, in the following terms: "Lutheranæ hæresis pullulatores, contra jus pietatemque, in regnum nostrum catholicum introduxit; doctorem Carolostadium, fortissimum Lutheri athletam, enutrivit."

* See Jo. Molleri Cimbria Literata, tom. ii. p. 883.—Christ. Olivarii Vita Pauli Eliæ, p. 108.—Erici Pontoppidani Annales Ecclesiæ Danicæ, tom. iii. p. 139.

☞ † It was farther provided by this edict, that no person should be molested on account of his religion; that a royal protection should be granted to the Lutherans to defend them from the insults and malignity of their enemies, and that ecclesiastics, of whatever rank or order, should be permitted to enter into the married state, and to fix their residence wherever they thought proper, without any regard to monasteries, or other religious societies.

‡ See a German work of the learned Eric Pontoppidan, entitled, A Compendious View of the History of the Reformation in Denmark; as also the Annales Ecclesiæ Danicæ, of the same author, tom ii. iii.—See also the work of Henry Muhl, de Reformat. Religionis in vicinis Daniæ Regionibus e potissimum in Cimbria, in ejus Dissertationibus Historico-Theologicis.

have been reduced within proper bounds, without introducing any change into the system of doctrine that had been so long established, and which was generally received.* In the measures taken in these northern kingdoms, for the reformation of a corrupt doctrine and a superstitious discipline, there was nothing that deserved the smallest censure: neither fraud nor violence were employed for this purpose; on the contrary, all things were conducted with wisdom and moderation, in a manner suitable to the dictates of equity and the spirit of Christianity. The same judgment cannot easily be pronounced with respect to the methods of proceeding in the reformation of the clergy, and more especially of the episcopal order. For here, certainly, violence was used, and the bishops were deprived of their honours, privileges, and possessions, without their consent; indeed, notwithstanding the greatest struggles and the warmest opposition.† The truth is, that so far as the reformation in Sweden and Denmark regarded the privileges and possessions of the bishops, it was rather a matter of political expediency than of religious obligation; for a change here had become so necessary, that, had Luther and his doctrine never appeared in the world, it must have been nevertheless attempted by a wise legislator; for the bishops, by a variety of perfidious stratagems, had gotten into their hands such enormous treasures, such ample possessions, so many castles and fortified towns, and had assumed such an unlimited and despotic authority, that they were in a condition to give law to the sovereign himself, to rule the nation as they thought proper, and, in effect, they already abused their power so far as to appropriate to themselves a considerable part of the royal patrimony, and of the public revenues of the kingdom. Such, therefore, was the critical state of these northern kingdoms, in the time of Luther, that it became absolutely necessary, either to degrade the bishops from that rank which they dishonoured, and to deprive them of the greatest part of those possessions and prerogatives which they had so unjustly acquired and so licentiously abused, or to see, tamely, royalty rendered contemptible by its weakness, the sovereign deprived of the means of protecting and succouring his people, and the state exposed to rebellion, misery, and ruin.

XXXIV. The kingdom of France was not inaccessible to the light of the Reformation. Margaret queen of Navarre, sister to Francis I., the implacable enemy and perpetual rival of Charles V., was inclined to favour the new doctrine, which delivered pure and genuine Christianity from a great part of the superstitions under which it had so long lain disguised. The auspicious patronage of this illustrious princess encouraged several pious and learned men, whose religious sentiments were the same with her's, to propagate the principles of the Reformation in France, and even to erect several protestant churches in that kingdom. It is manifest from the most authentic records, that, so early as the year 1523, there were, in several of the provinces of that country, multitudes of persons, who had conceived the utmost disgust to the doctrine and tyranny of Rome; and among these were many persons of rank and dignity, and even some of the episcopal order. As their numbers increased from day to day, and troubles and commotions were excited in several places on account of religious differences, the authority of the monarch and the cruelty of his officers intervened, to support the doctrine of Rome, by the edge of the sword and the terrors of the gibbet; and on this occasion many persons, eminent for their piety and virtue, were put to death with the most unrelenting barbarity.* Although this cruelty, instead of retarding, accelerated the progress of the Reformation, yet, in the reign of Francis, the restorers of genuine Christianity were not always equally successful and happy. Their situation was extremely uncertain, and it was perpetually changing. Sometimes they seemed to enjoy the auspicious shade of royal protection; at others they groaned under the weight of persecution, and at certain seasons they were forgotten, which oblivion rendered their condition tolerable. Francis, who had either no religion at all, or, at best, no fixed and consistent system of religious principles, conducted himself toward the protestants in such a manner as answered his private and personal views, or as reasons of policy and the public interest seemed to re-

☞ * This observation is not worthy of Dr. Mosheim's sagacity. The strong connexion between superstitious ignorance among the people, and influence and power in their spiritual rulers, is too evident to stand in need of any proof. A good clergy will, or ought to have an influence, in consequence of a respectable office, adorned with learning, piety, and morals; but the power of a licentious and despotic clergy can be only supported by the blind and superstitous credulity of their flock.

☞ † What does Dr. Mosheim mean here? Did ever an usurper give up his unjust possessions without reluctance? Does rapine constitute a right, when it is maintained by force? Is it unlawful to use violence against extortioners? The question here is, whether the bishops deserved the severe treatment they received from Christiern III.; and our author seems to answer this question in the affirmative, and to declare this treatment both just and necessary, in the following part of this section. Certain it is, that the bishops were treated with great severity, deposed from their sees, imprisoned on account of their resistance; all the church lands, towns, and fortresses, were annexed to the crown, and the temporal power of the clergy abolished. It is also certain, that Luther himself looked upon these measures as violent and excessive, and even wrote a letter to Christiern, exhorting him to use the clergy with more lenity. It is therefore proper to decide with moderation on this subject, and to grant, that, if the insolence and licentiousness of the clergy were enormous, the resentment of the Danish monarch may have been excessive. Nor indeed was his political prudence here so great as Dr. Mosheim seems to represent it; for the equipoise of government was hurt, by a total suppression of the power of the bishops. The nobility acquired by this a prodigious degree of influence, and the crown lost an order, which, under proper regulations, might have been rendered one of the strongest supports of its prerogative. But disquisitions of this nature are foreign to our purpose. It is only proper to observe, that, in the room of the bishops, Christiern created an order of men, with the denomination of *Superintendants*, who performed the spiritual part of the episcopal office without the least shadow of temporal authority.

* See Beza, Histoire des Eglises Reformees de France, tom. i.—Benoit, Histoire de l'Edit de Nantes, liv. i.—Christ. Aug. Salig. Histor. Augus. Confessionis, vol. ii.

quire. When it became necessary to engage in his cause the German protestants, in order to foment sedition and rebellion against his mortal enemy Charles V., he treated the protestants in France with the utmost equity, humanity, and gentleness; but, so soon as he had gained his point, and had no more occasion for their services, he threw off the mask, and appeared to them in the aspect of an implacable and persecuting tyrant.*

About this time the famous Calvin, upon whose character, talents, and religious exploits, we shall have occasion to dwell more amply in the course of this history, began to draw the attention of the public, but more especially of the queen of Navarre. He was born at Noyon in Picardy, on the 10th of July, 1509, and was bred to the law,† in which, as well as in all the other branches of literature, then known, his studies were attended with the most rapid and amazing success. Having acquired the knowledge of religion, by a diligent perusal of the holy scriptures, he began early to perceive the necessity of reforming the established system of doctrine and worship. His zeal exposed him to various perils; and the connexions he had formed with the friends of the Reformation, whom Francis was frequently committing to the flames, placed him more than once in imminent danger, from which he was delivered by the good offices of the excellent queen of Navarre. To escape the impending storm, he retired to Basil, where he published his Christian Institutions; and prefixed to them that famous dedication to Francis, which has attracted the admiration of succeeding ages, and which was designed to soften the unrelenting fury of that prince against the protestants.‡

XXXV. The instances of an opposition to the doctrine and discipline of Rome, in the other European states, were few in number, before the diet of Augsburg, and were too faint, imperfect, and ambiguous, to make much noise in the world. It, however, appears from the most authentic testimonies, that, even before that period, the doctrine of Luther had made a considerable, though perhaps a secret, progress in Spain, Hungary, Bohemia, Britain, Poland, and the Netherlands, and had, in all these countries, many friends, of whom several repaired to Wittenberg, to improve their knowledge and enlarge their views under such an eminent master. Some of these countries openly broke asunder the chains of superstition, and withdrew themselves, in a public and constitutional manner, from the jurisdiction of the Roman pontiff. In others, a prodigious number of families received the light of the blessed Reformation; rejected the doctrines and authority of Rome; and notwithstanding the calamities and persecutions they have suffered on account of their sentiments, under the sceptre of bigotry and superstition, continue still in the profession of the pure doctrines of Christianity; while in other, still more unhappy, lands, the most barbarous tortures, the most infernal spirit of cruelty, together with penal laws adapted to strike terror into the firmest minds, have extinguished, almost totally, the light of religious truth. It is, indeed, certain, and the Roman catholics themselves acknowledge it without hesitation, that the papal doctrines, jurisdiction, and authority, would have fallen into ruin in all parts of the world, had not the force of the secular arm been employed to support this tottering edifice, and fire and sword been let loose upon those who were assailing it only with reason and argument.

CHAPTER III.

The History of the Reformation, from the Time when the Confession of Augsburg was presented to Charles V., until the Commencement of the War which succeeded the League of Smalcald.

I. THE diet was opened at Augsburg on the 20th day of June, 1530; and, as it was unanimously agreed, that the affairs of religion should be discussed before the deliberations relating to the intended war with the Turks, the protestant members of this great assembly received from the emperor a formal permission to present to the diet an account of their religious principles and tenets. In consequence of this, Christian Bayer, chancellor of Saxony, read, in the German language, in presence of the emperor and the assembled princes, the famous confession which has been since distinguished by the denomination of the *Confession of Augsburg*. The princes heard it with the deepest attention and recollection of mind; it confirmed some in the principles they had embraced, surprised others; and many, who, before this time, had little or no idea of the religious sentiments of Luther, were now not only convinced of their innocence, but were, moreover, delighted with their purity and simplicity. The copies of this confession, which, after being read, were delivered to the emperor, were signed and subscribed by John, elector of Saxony, by four princes of the em

☞ * The inconsistency and contradiction that were visible in the conduct of Francis I. may be attributed to various causes. At one time, we see him resolved to invite Melancthon into France, probably with a view to please his sister the queen of Navarre, whom he loved tenderly, and who had strongly imbibed the principles of the protestants. At another time, we behold him exercising the most infernal cruelty toward the friends of the Reformation, and hear him making that mad declaration that, "if he thought the blood in his arm was tainted with the Lutheran heresy, he would order it to be cut off; and that he would not spare even his own children, if they entertained sentiments contrary to those of the catholic church." See Flor. de Remond, Hist. de la Naissance et du Progres de l'Heresie.

☞ † He was originally designed for the church, and had actually obtained a benefice; but the light that broke in upon his religious sentiments, as well as the preference given by his father to the profession of the law, induced him to give up his ecclesiastic vocation, which he afterwards resumed in a purer church.

☞ ‡ This paragraph relating to Calvin, is added to Dr. Mosheim's text by the translator, who was surprised to find, in a History of the Reformation, such late mention made of one of its most distinguished and remarkable instruments; a man whose extensive genius, flowing eloquence, immense learning, extraordinary penetration, indefatigable industry, and fervent piety, placed him at the head of the Reformers; all of whom he surpassed, at least, in learning and parts, as he also did the greater part of them in obstinacy, asperity, and turbulence.

pire, namely, George, marquis of Brandenburg; Ernest, duke of Lunenburg; Philip, landgrave of Hesse; Wolfgang, prince of Anhalt; and by the imperial cities of Nuremberg and Reutlingen; who all thereby solemnly declared their assent to the doctrines contained in it.*

II. The tenor and contents of the confession of Augsburg are well known; at least, by all who have the smallest acquaintance with ecclesiastical history; since that confession was adopted by the whole body of the protestants as the rule of their faith. The style that reigns in it is plain, elegant, grave, and perspicuous, such as becomes the nature of the subject, and such as might be expected from the admirable pen of Melancthon. The *matter* was, undoubtedly, supplied by Luther, who, during the diet, resided at Coburg, a town in the neighbourhood of Augsburg; and even the form it received from the eloquent pen of his colleague, was authorised by his approbation and advice. This confession contains twenty-eight chapters, of which the greatest part† are employed in representing, with perspicuity and truth, the religious opinions of the protestants, and the rest in pointing out the errors and abuses that occasioned their separation from the church of Rome.‡

III. The creatures of the Roman pontiff, who were present at this diet, employed John Faber, afterwards bishop of Vienne in Dauphinè, together with Eckius, and another doctor named Cochlæus, to draw up a refutation of this famous confession. This pretended refutation having been read publicly in the assembly, the emperor required of the protestant members that they would acquiesce in it, and put an end to their religious debates by an unlimited submission to the doctrines and opinions contained in this answer. But this demand was far from being complied with. The protestants declared, on the contrary, that they were by no means satisfied with the reply of their adversaries, and earnestly desired a copy of it, that they might demonstrate more fully its extreme insufficiency and weakness. This reasonable request was refused by the emperor, who, on this occasion, as well as on several others, showed more regard to the importunity of the pope's legate and his party, than to the demands of equity, candour, and justice. He even interposed his supreme authority to suspend any farther proceeding in this matter and solemnly prohibited the publication of any new writings or declarations that might contribute to lengthen out these religious debates. This, however, did not reduce the protestants to silence. The divines of that community, who had been present at the diet, endeavoured to recollect the arguments and objections employed by Faber, and again had recourse to the pen of Melancthon, who refuted them in an ample and satisfactory manner, in a learned piece that was presented to the emperor, but which that prince refused to receive. This answer was afterwards enlarged by Melancthon, when he had obtained a copy of Faber's reply, and was published in 1531, with the other pieces that related to the doctrine and discipline of the Lutheran church, under the title of 'A Defence of the Confession of Augsburg.'

IV. There were only three ways left of bringing to a conclusion these religious differences, which it was, in reality, most difficult to reconcile. The first and the most rational method was to grant, to those who refused to submit to the doctrine and jurisdiction of Rome, the liberty of following their private judgment in matters of a religious nature, and the privilege of serving God according to the dictates of their consciences, with a proviso that the public tranquillity should not be disturbed The second, and, at the same time, the shortest and most iniquitous expedient, was to end these dissensions by military apostles, who, sword in hand, should force the protestants to return to the bosom of the church, and to court the papal yoke, which they had so magnanimously thrown off. Some thought of a middle way, which was equally remote from the difficulties that attended the two methods now mentioned, and proposed that a reconciliation should be made upon fair, candid, and equitable terms, by engaging each of the contending parties to temper their zeal with moderation, to abate reciprocally the rigour of their pretensions, and to remit some of their respective claims. The first method, which seemed agreeable to the dictates of reason, charity, and justice, was highly approved by several wise and good men, on both sides; but it was ill-suited to the arrogant ambition of the pontiff, and the superstitious ignorance of the times, which beheld with horror whatever tended to introduce the sweets of religious liberty, or the exercise of private judgment. The second method, being violent and inhuman, was more agreeable to the spirit and sentiments of the age, and was peculiarly suited to the despotic genius and sanguinary zeal of the court of Rome: but the emperor had sufficient prudence and equity to induce him to

* There is a very voluminous history of the diet, which was published in 1577, at Frankfort on the Oder, by the laborious George Celestine. The history of the Confession of Augsburg was composed in Latin by David Chytræus, and more recently in German, by Ern. Solom. Cyprian and Christopher Aug. Salig. The performance of the latter is rather, indeed, a history of the Reformation in general, than of the Confession of Augsburg in particular. That of Cyprian is more concise and elegant, and is confirmed by original pieces which are equally authentic and curious.

† Twenty-one chapters were so employed. the other seven contained a detail of the errors and superstitions of the Romish church.

☞ ‡ It is proper to observe here, that, while the Lutherans presented their confession to the diet, another excellent remonstrance of the same nature was addressed to this august assembly by the cities of Strasburg, Constance, Memmingen, and Lindaw, which had rejected the errors and jurisdiction of Rome, but did not enter into the Lutheran league, because they had adopted the opinions of Zuingle in relation to the eucharist. The declaration of these four towns (called for that reason the *Tetrapolitan Confession*) was drawn up by the excellent Martin Bucer, and was considered as a master-piece of reasoning and eloquence, not only by the protestants, but even by several of the Roman catholics; and among others by M. Du-Pin. Zuingle also sent to this diet a private confession of his religious opinions. It is, however, remarkable, that though Bucer composed a separate remonstrance, his name appears among the subscribers at Smalcald, in 1537, to the confession of Augsburg, and to Melancthon's defence of it.

reject it; and it appeared shocking to those who were not lost to all sentiments of justice or moderation. The third expedient was therefore most generally approved: it was peculiarly agreeable to all who were zealous for the interests and tranquillity of the empire; nor did the pope seem to look upon it either with aversion or contempt. Hence various conferences ensued between persons of eminence, piety, and learning, who were chosen for that purpose from both sides; and nothing was omitted that might have the least tendency to calm the animosity, heal the divisions, and unite the hearts of the contending parties;* but all endeavours proved fruitless, since the difference of opinion was too considerable and too important to admit a reconciliation. It was in these conferences that the spirit and character of Melancthon appeared in their true and genuine colours; and it was here that the votaries of Rome exhausted their efforts to gain over to their party this pillar of the Reformation, whose abilities and virtues added such a lustre to the protestant cause. This humane and gentle spirit was apt to sink into a kind of yielding softness under the influence of mild and generous treatment. And, accordingly, while his adversaries soothed him with fair words and flattering promises, he seemed to melt as they spoke, and, in some measure, to comply with their demands; but, when they so far forgot themselves as to make use of imperious language and menacing terms, then did he appear in a very different point of light; then a spirit of intrepidity, ardour, and independence, animated all his words and actions, and he looked down with contempt on the threats of power, the frowns of fortune, and the fear of death. The truth is, that, in this great and good man, a soft and yielding temper was joined with the most inviolable fidelity, and the most invincible attachment to the truth.

V. As this method of terminating the religious debates between the friends of liberty and the votaries of Rome, proved ineffectual, the latter had recourse to other measures, which were suited to the iniquity of the times, though they were disavowed by the dictates of reason and the precepts of the Gospel. These measures were, the force of the secular arm, and the authority of imperial edicts. On the 19th day of November, a severe decree was issued, by the express order of the emperor, during the absence of the Hessian and Saxon princes, who were the chief supporters of the protestant cause; and, in this decree, every thing was manifestly calculated to deject the friends of religious liberty, if we except a faint and dubious promise of engaging the pope to assemble (in about six months after the separation of the diet) a general council. The dignity and excellence of the papal religion are extolled, beyond measure, in this partial decree; new degrees of severity and force were added to the edict of Worms; the changes that had been introduced into the doctrine and discipline of the protestant churches, were severely censured; and a solemn order was addressed to the princes, states, and cities, that had thrown off the papal yoke, to return to their duty and their allegiance to Rome, on pain of incurring the indignation and vengeance of the emperor, as the patron and protector of the church.*

VI. No sooner were the elector of Saxony and the confederate princes informed of this deplorable issue of the diet, than they assembled in order to deliberate upon the measures that were proper to be taken on this critical occasion. In 1530, and the following year, they met, first at Smalcald, afterwards at Frankfort, and formed a solemn alliance, with the intention of defending vigorously their religion and liberties against the dangers and encroachments with which they were menaced by the edict of Augsburg, without attempting, however, any thing positively offensive against the votaries of Rome. Into this confederacy they invited the kings of England, France, and Denmark, with several other republics and states, and left no means unemployed that might tend to corroborate and cement this important alliance.† Amidst these intrigues

☞ * As in the confession of Augsburg there were three sorts of articles; one sort orthodox, and adopted by both sides; another that consisted of certain propositions, which the papal party considered as ambiguous and obscure; and a third, in which the doctrine of Luther was entirely opposite to that of Rome; this gave some reason to hope, that by the means of certain concessions and modifications, conducted mutually by a spirit of candour and charity, matters might at last be accommodated. For this purpose, select persons were appointed to carry on this salutary work, at first seven from each party, consisting of princes, lawyers, and divines; which number was afterwards reduced to three. As Luther's obstinate, stubborn, and violent temper, rendered him unfit for healing divisions, he was not employed in these conferences; but he was constantly consulted by the Protestant party, and it was with a view to this that he resided at Coburg.

☞ * To give the greater degree of weight to this edict, it was resolved, that no judge who refused to approve and subscribe its contents, should be admitted into the imperial chamber of Spire, which was the supreme court in Germany. The emperor also, and the popish princes, engaged themselves to employ their united forces in order to maintain its authority, and to promote its execution.

☞ † Luther, who at first seemed averse to this confederacy, from an apprehension of the calamities and troubles it might produce, at length perceived its necessity, and consented to it; but, uncharitably, as well as imprudently, refused to comprehend in it the followers of Zuingle among the Swiss, together with the German states or cities, which had adopted the sentiments and confession of Bucer. And yet we find that the cities of Ulm and Augsburg had embraced the Reformation on the principles of Zuingle. In the invitation addressed to Henry VIII. whom the associated princes were willing to declare the head and protector of their league, the following points were expressly stipulated among several others: viz. That the king should encourage, promote, and maintain the true doctrine of Christ, as it was contained in the confession of Augsburg, and defend the same at the next general council;—that he should not agree to any council summoned by the bishop of Rome, but protest against it, and neither submit to its decrees, nor suffer them to be respected in his dominions;—that he should never allow the pontiff to have any pre-eminence or jurisdiction in his dominions;—that he should advance 100,000 crowns for the use of the confederacy, and double that sum if it should appear to be necessary; all which articles the confederate princes were obliged equally to observe on their parts. To these demands the king answered, immediately, in a manner that was not satisfactory. He declared, that he would maintain and promote the true doctrine of Christ; but, at the same time as the true ground of that doctrine lay

and preparations, which portended an approaching rupture, the electors of Mentz and of the Palatinate offered their mediation, and endeavoured to reconcile the contending princes. With respect to the emperor, various reasons united to turn his views towards peace. For, on the one hand, he stood in need of succours against the Turks, which the protestant princes refused to grant while the edicts of Worms and Augsburg remained in force; and, on the other, the election of his brother Ferdinand to the dignity of king of the Romans, which had been concluded by a majority of votes, at the diet of Cologne in 1531, was contested by the same princes as contrary to the fundamental laws of the empire.

VII. In this troubled state of affairs, many projects of reconciliation were proposed; and, after various negotiations, a treaty of peace was concluded at Nuremberg, in 1532, between the emperor and the protestant princes, on the following conditions: that the latter should furnish a subsidy for carrying on the war against the Turks, and acknowledge Ferdinand as lawful king of the Romans; and that the emperor should annul the edicts of Worms and Augsburg, and allow the Lutherans the free and unmolested exercise of their religious doctrine and discipline, until a rule of faith should be fixed, either in the free general council that was to be assembled in the space of six months, or in a diet of the empire. The apprehension of an approaching rupture was scarcely removed by this agreement, when John, elector of Saxony, died, and was succeeded by his son John Frederic, a prince of invincible fortitude and magnanimity, whose reign, however, was little better than a continued scene of disappointments and calamities.

VIII. The religious truce, concluded at Nuremberg, inspired with new vigour and resolution all the friends of the reformation. It gave strength to the feeble, and perseverance to the bold. Encouraged by it, those who had been hitherto only secret enemies to the Roman pontiff, now spurned his yoke publicly, and refused to submit to his imperious jurisdiction. This appears from the various cities and provinces in Germany, which, about this time, boldly enlisted themselves under the religious standard of Luther. On the other hand, as all hopes of terminating the religious debates that divided Europe were founded in the meeting of a general and independent council, so solemnly promised, Charles renewed his earnest request to Clement, that he would hasten an event that was expected and desired with so much impatience. The pontiff, whom the history of past councils filled with the most uneasy and discouraging apprehensions, endeavoured to retard what he could not, with any decency, absolutely refuse.* He formed innumerable pretexts to put off the evil day; and his whole conduct evidently showed, that he was more desirous of having these religious differences decided by the force of arms, than by the power of argument. He indeed, in 1533, made a proposal by his legate, to assemble a council at Mantua, Placentia, or Bologna; but the protestants refused their consent to the nomination of an Italian council, and insisted, that a controversy, which had its rise in the heart of Germany, should be decided within the limits of the empire. The pope, by his usual artifices, eluded his own promise, disappointed their expectations, and was cut off by death, in 1534, in the midst of his stratagems.†

IX. His successor Paul III. seemed to show less reluctance to the convocation of a general council, and even appeared disposed to comply with the desire of the emperor in that respect. Accordingly, in 1535, he expressed his inclination to convoke one at Mantua; and, in the following year, he actually sent circular letters for that purpose through all the kingdoms and states under his jurisdiction.‡ The protestants, on the other hand, fully persuaded, that, in such a council,§ all things would be carried by the votaries of Rome, and nothing concluded but what might be agreeable to the sentiments and ambition of the pontiff, assembled at Smalcald in 1537; and there they protested solemnly against such a partial and corrupt council as that which was convoked by Paul, but, at the same time, had a new summary of their doctrine drawn up by Luther, in order to present it to the assembled bishops, if it should be required of them. This summary, which was distinguished by the title of the *Articles of Smalcald*, is generally joined with the creeds and confessions of the Lutheran church.

only in the Holy Scriptures, he would not accept, at any one's hand, what should be his faith, or that of his kingdoms, and therefore desired they would send over learned men to confer with him, in order to promote a religious union between him and the confederates. He moreover declared himself of their opinion with respect to the meeting of a free general council, and promised to join with them, in all such councils, for the defence of the true doctrine; but thought the regulation of the ceremonial part of religion, being a matter of indifference, ought to be left to the choice of each sovereign for his own dominions. After this, he gave them a second answer more full and satisfactory; but, upon the fall of Anne Boleyn, this negotiation proved abortive. On the one hand, the king grew cold, when he perceived that the confederates could no longer be of service to him in supporting the validity of his marriage; and, on the other, the German princes were sensible that they could never succeed with Henry, unless they would allow him an absolute dictatorship in matters of religion.

☞ * Beside the fear of seeing his authority diminished by a general council, another reason engaged Clement to avoid an assembly of that nature; for, being conscious of the illegitimacy of his birth, as Father Paul observes, he had ground to fear that the Colonnas, or his other enemies, might plead this circumstance before the council, as a reason for his exclusion from the pontificate, since it might be well questioned whether a *bastard* could be a pope, though it is known, from many instances, that a *profligate* may.

† See an ample account of every thing relative to this council in Father Paul's History of the Council of Trent, book i.

☞ ‡ This council was summoned by Paul III. to assemble at Mantua, on the 23d of May, 1537, but several obstacles prevented its meeting. Frederic, duke of Mantua, was not much inclined to receive at once so many guests, some of whom might be very turbulent, into the place of his residence.

☞ § That is, in a council assembled by the authority of the pope alone, and that also in Italy; two circumstances that must have greatly contributed to give Paul an undue influence in that assembly. The protestants maintained, that the emperor and the other Christian princes of Europe had a right to be *authoritatively* concerned in calling a general council; so much the more, as the pontiff was evidently one of the parties in the present debate.

X. During these transactions, two remarkable events happened, of which the one was most detrimental to the cause of religion in general, to that of the Reformation in particular, and produced, in Germany, civil tumults and commotions of the most horrid kind; while the other was more salutary in its consequences and effects, and struck at the very root of the papal authority and dominion. The former event was a new sedition, excited by a fanatical and outrageous mob of the Anabaptists; and the latter, the rupture between Henry VIII. and the Roman pontiff, whose jurisdiction and spiritual supremacy were publicly renounced by that rough and resolute monarch.

In 1533, there came to Munster, a city in Westphalia, a certain number of Anabaptists, who surpassed the rest of that fanatical tribe in the extravagance of their proceedings, the phrensy of their disordered brains, and the madness of their pretensions and projects. They gave themselves out for the messengers of Heaven, invested with a divine commission to lay the foundations of a new government, a holy and spiritual empire, and to destroy and overturn all temporal rule and authority, all human and political institutions. Having turned all things into confusion and uproar at Munster by this seditious and extravagant declaration, they began to erect a new republic,* conformable to their absurd and chimerical notions of religion, and committed the administration of it to John Bockholt, a tailor by profession, and a native of Leyden. Their reign, however, was of a short duration; for, in 1535, the city was beseiged, and taken by the bishop of Munster, assisted by other German princes; this fanatical king and his wrong-headed associates were put to death in the most terrible and ignominious manner, and the new hierarchy destroyed with its furious and extravagant founders. This outrageous conduct of a handful of Anabaptists drew upon the whole body heavy marks of displeasure from the greatest part of the European princes. The severest laws were enacted against them for the second time, in consequence of which the innocent and the guilty were involved in the same terrible fate, and prodigious numbers were devoted to death in the most dreadful forms.†

XI. The pillars of papal despotism were at this time shaken in England, by an event, which, at first, did not seem to promise such important consequences. Henry VIII., a prince who, in vices and in abilities, was surpassed by none who swayed the sceptre in this age, and who, in the beginning of these religious troubles, had opposed the doctrine and views of Luther with the utmost vehemence, was the principal agent in this great revolution.‡ Bound in the chains of matrimony to Catharine of Arragon, aunt to Charles V., but at the same time captivated by the charms of an illustrious virgin, whose name was Anne Boleyn, he ardently desired to be divorced from the former, that he might render lawful his passion for the latter.* For this purpose, he addressed himself to Clement VII. in order to obtain a dissolution of his marriage with Catharine, alleging, that a principle of religion restrained him from enjoying any longer the sweets of connubial love with that princess, as she had been previously married to his elder brother Arthur, and as it was repugnant to the divine law to contract wedlock with a brother's widow. The pope was greatly perplexed upon this occasion, by the apprehension of incurring the indignation of the emperor, if his decision should be favourable to Henry; and therefore he contrived various pretexts to evade a positive answer, and exhausted all his policy and artifice to cajole and deceive the English monarch. Tired with the pretexts, apologies, vain promises, and tardy proceedings of the pontiff, Henry had recourse, for the accomplishment of his purposes, to an expedient which was suggested by the famous Thomas Cranmer, who was a secret friend to Luther and his cause, and who was afterwards raised to the see of Canterbury. This expedient was, to demand the opinions of the most learned European universities concerning the subject of his scruples. The result of this measure was favourable to his views. The greatest part of the universities declared the marriage with a brother's widow unlawful. Catharine was consequently divorced; Anne was conducted by a formal marriage into the royal bed, notwithstanding the remonstrances of Clement; and the English nation delivered from the tyranny of Rome, by Henry's renouncing the jurisdiction and supremacy of its imperious pontiff. Soon after this, the king was declared by the

* This fanatical establishment they distinguished by the title of the *New Jerusalem*.

† Hermanni Hamelmanni Historia Eccles. renati Evangelii per inferiorem Saxoniam et Westphal. part ii.—De Printz, Specimen Historiæ Anabapt. c. x. xi. xii.

☞ This sect was, in process of time, considerably reformed by the ministry of two Friselanders, Ubbo and Mennon, who purified it from the enthusiastic, seditious, and atrocious principles of its first founders, as will be seen in the progress of this history.

☞ ‡ Among the various portraits that have been given by historians of Henry VIII., there is not one that equals the masterly one drawn by Mr. Hume. This great painter, whose colouring, in other subjects, is sometimes more artful than accurate, has caught from nature the striking lines of Henry's motley character, and thrown them into a composition, in which they appear with the greatest truth, set out with all the powers of expression.

☞ * From Dr. Mosheim's manner of expressing himself, an uninformed reader might be led to conclude, that the charms of Anne Boleyn were the only motive that engaged Henry to dissolve his marriage with Catharine. But this representation of the matter is not accurate. The king had entertained scruples concerning the legitimacy of that marriage, before his acquaintance with the beautiful and unfortunate Anne. Conversant in the writings of Thomas Aquinas and other schoolmen, who looked upon the Levitical law as of moral and permanent obligation, and attentive to the remonstrances of the bishops, who declared his marriage unlawful he was filled with anxious doubts, which had made him break off all conjugal commerce with the queen, before his affections had been engaged by any other. This appears by cardinal Wolsey's proposing a marriage between his majesty and the sister of Francis I., which that pliant courtier would never have done had he known that the king's affections were other wise engaged. After all, it is very possible, that the age and infirmities of Catharine, together with the blooming charms of Anne Boleyn, tended much to animate Henry's remorse, and to render his conscience more scrupulous. See Burnet's History of the Reformation, and Hume's History of Great Britain

parliament and people supreme head, on earth, of the church of England; the monasteries were suppressed, and their revenues applied to other purposes; and the power and authority of the pope were abrogated and entirely overturned.*

XII. It is however carefully to be observed here, that Henry's subversion of the papal authority in England was not productive of much benefit, either to the friends or to the cause of the reformation; for the same monarch, who had so resolutely withdrawn himself from the dominion of Rome, yet superstitiously retained the greatest part of its errors, with its imperious and persecuting spirit. He still adhered to several of the most monstrous doctrines of popery, and frequently presented the terrors of death to those who differed from him in their religious sentiments. Besides, he considered the title of Head of the English Church, as if it transferred to him the enormous power which had been claimed, and indeed usurped, by the Roman pontiffs; and, in consequence of this interpretation of his title, he looked upon himself as master of the religious sentiments of his subjects, and as authorized to prescribe modes of faith according to his fancy. Hence it came to pass, that, during the life and reign of this prince, the face of religion was constantly changing, and thus resembled the capricious and unsteady character of its new chief. The prudence, learning, and activity of archbishop Cranmer, who was the favourite of the king, and the friend of the Reformation, counteracted, however, in many instances, the humour and vehemence of this inconstant and turbulent monarch. The pious productions and wise counsels of that venerable prelate diminished daily the influence of the ancient superstitions, dispelled by degrees the mists of ignorance that blinded the people in favour of popery, and considerably increased the number of those who wished well to the Reformation.†

XIII. After the meeting of the council of Mantua was prevented, various measures were taken, and many schemes proposed, by the emperor on the one hand, and the protestant princes on the other, for the restoration of concord and union, both civil and religious. But these measures and projects were unattended with any solid or salutary fruit, and were generally disconcerted by the intrigues and artifice of the court of Rome, whose legates and creatures were always lying in wait to blow the flame of discord in all those councils which seemed unfavourable to the ambition of its pontiffs. In 1541, the emperor, regardless of the pope's authority, appointed a conference at Worms, on the subject of religion, between persons of piety and learning chosen from each party. It was here that Melancthon and Eckius disputed for three days.* This conference was, for certain reasons, removed to the diet holden at Ratisbon in the same year, in which the principal subject of deliberation was a memorial, presented by a person unknown, containing a project of peace, with the terms of accommodation that were proper to terminate these religious differences.† This conference, however, produced no other effect, than a mutual agreement of the contending parties to refer the decision of their pretensions and debates to a general council; or, if the meeting of such a council should be prevented by any unforeseen obstacles, to the next German diet.

XIV. This resolution was rendered ineffectual by the period of perplexity and trouble that succeeded the diet of Ratisbon, and by various incidents that widened the breach, and delayed the deliberations which were designed to heal it. It is true, the pontiff ordered his legate to declare in the diet, which was assembled at Spire in 1542, that he would, according to the promise he had already made, assemble a general council, and that Trent should be the place of its meeting, if the diet had no objection to that city. Ferdinand, king of the Romans, and the princes who adhered to the papal cause, gave their consent to this proposal; while the protestant members of the diet objected both to a council summoned by the papal authority alone, and also to the place appointed for its meeting, and demanded a free and lawful council, which should not be influenced by the dictates, or awed by the proximity of the pontiff. This protestation produced no effect; Paul persisted in his purpose, and issued his circular letters for the convocation of the council,‡ with the approbation of the

* Beside the full and accurate account of this and other important events, that may be found in bishop Burnet's excellent History of the Reformation of the Church of England, the curious reader will do well to consult the records of this memorable revolution in Wilkins' Concil. Magnæ Britanniæ et Hiberniæ, tom. iii.—Raynal's Anecdotes Historiques, Politiques, et Militaires, tom. i.—Gen. Dictionary at the article Boleyn.

† Beside Burnet's History of the Reformation, see Neal's History of the Puritans, vol. i.

* See Jo. And. Roederi Libellus de Colloquio Wormatiensi. Norimb. 1744.

† See Jo. Erdmanni Bieckii Triplex Interim, cap. i.

☞ ‡ It is proper to observe here, that having summoned successively a council at Mantua, Vicenza, and Venice, without any effect, (for the council did not meet,) this pontiff thought it necessary to show the protestants that he was not averse to every kind of reformation; and therefore appointed four cardinals and five other persons eminent for their learning, to draw up a plan for the reformation of the church in general, and of the church of Rome in particular, well knowing, by the spirit which reigned in the conclave, that the project would come to nothing. A plan, however, was drawn up by the persons appointed for that purpose. The reformation proposed in this plan was indeed extremely superficial and partial; yet it contained some particulars, which scarcely could have been expected from the pens of those who composed it. They complained, for instance, of the pride and ignorance of the bishops, and proposed that none should receive orders but learned and pious men; and that, therefore, care should be taken to have proper masters to instruct the youth. They condemned translations from one benefice to another, grants of reservation, non-residence, and pluralities. They proposed that some convents should be abolished; that the liberty of the press should be restrained and limited; that the colloquies of Erasmus should be suppressed; that no ecclesiastic should enjoy a benefice out of his own country; that no cardinal should have a bishopric; that the questors of St. Antony, and several other saints, should be abolished; and (which was the best of all their proposals) that the effects and personal estate of ecclesiastics should be given to the poor. They concluded with complaining of the prodigious number of indigent and ragged priests that frequented St. Peter's church; and declared, that it was a great scandal to see the prostitutes lodged so magn-

emperor; while this prince endeavoured, at the diet of Worms, in 1545, to persuade the protestants to consent to the meeting of this council at Trent. But they were fixed in their resolution, and the efforts of Charles were vain; upon which the emperor, who had hitherto disapproved the violent measures which were incessantly suggested by the court of Rome, departed from his usual prudence and moderation, and, listening to the sanguinary counsels of Paul, formed, in conjunction with that artful pontiff, the design of terminating religious debates by the force of arms. The landgrave of Hesse, and the elector of Saxony, the chief protectors of the protestant cause, were no sooner informed of this, than they took the proper measures to prevent themselves from being surprised and overwhelmed by a superior force, and, accordingly, raised an army for their defence. While this terrible storm was rising, Luther, whose aversion to all violence in matters of religion was well known, and who recommended prayer and patience as the only arms worthy of those who had the cause of genuine Christianity at heart, was removed by Providence from this scene of tumult, and from the calamities that threatened his country. He died in peace, on the 18th of February, 1546, at Eisleben, the place of his birth.

CHAPTER IV.

The History of the Reformation, from the Commencement of the War of Smalcald, to the famous Pacification, commonly called the Peace of Religion, concluded at Augsburg.

I. CHARLES and the pontiff had determined upon the ruin of all who should dare to oppose the council of Trent. The meeting of that assembly was to serve as a signal for their taking arms; and accordingly, its deliberations were scarcely begun, in 1546, when the protestants perceived undoubted marks of the approaching storm, and of a formidable union of their chief adversaries to overwhelm and crush them by a sudden blow. There had been, it is true, a new conference in this very year, at the diet of Ratisbon, between some eminent doctors of both parties, with a view to the accommodation of their religious differences; but it appeared sufficiently, both from the nature of this dispute, the manner in which it was carried on, and its issue and result, that the matters in debate would sooner or later be decided in the field of battle. In the mean time, the fathers, assembled in the council of Trent, promulgated their decrees; while the protestant princes in the diet protested against their authority, and were, in consequence of this conduct, proscribed by the emperor, who raised an army to reduce them to obedience.

II. The elector of Saxony and the landgrave of Hesse led their forces into Bavaria against the emperor, and cannonaded his camp at Ingolstadt with great spirit. It was supposed that this would bring the two armies to a general action; but several circumstances prevented a battle, which was expected by most of the confederates, and, probably, would have been advantageous to their cause. Among these we may reckon, principally, the perfidy of Maurice, duke of Saxony, who, seduced by the promises of the emperor, and by his own ambition and avarice, invaded the electoral dominions of his uncle John Frederic, while that worthy prince was maintaining against the emperor the sacred cause of religion and liberty. Add to this the divisions that were fomented by the dissimulation of the emperor among the confederate princes, the failure of France in furnishing the subsidy that had been promised by its monarch, and some incidents of less moment. All these things so discouraged the heads of the protestant party, that their troops were soon dispersed, and the elector of Saxony directed his march homewards. But he was pursued by the emperor, who made several forced marches, with a view of subduing his enemy, before he should have time to recover his vigour; in which design he was assisted by the ill-grounded security of the elector, and, as there is too much reason to think, by the treachery of his officers. The two armies drew up in order of battle near Muhlberg on the Elbe, on the 24th of April, 1547, and, after a fierce conflict, that of the elector, being inferior in number, was entirely defeated, and himself made prisoner. Philip, landgrave of Hesse, the other chief of the protestants, was persuaded by the entreaties of his son-in-law, Maurice, now declared elector of Saxony,* to throw himself upon the mercy of the emperor, and to implore his pardon. To this he consented, relying on the promise of Charles for obtaining forgiveness, and being restored to liberty; but, notwithstanding these expectations, he was unjustly detained prisoner by a scandalous violation of the most solemn convention. It is said, that the emperor retracted his promise, and deluded this unhappy prince by the ambiguity of two German words, which resemble each other;† but this point of

ficently at Rome, and riding through the streets on fine mules, while the cardinals and other ecclesiastics accompanied them in a most courteous and familiar manner. The several articles of this plan of reformation (which Luther and Sturmius of Strasburg turned into ridicule, and which indeed left unredressed the most intolerable grievances of which the protestants complained) were published at Antwerp in or about the year 1539, with the answer of Cochlæus to the objections of Sturmius. They are likewise prefixed to the History of the Council of Trent, by Crabre, and were afterwards published at Paris in 1612.

☞* In the room of John Frederic, whom he had so basely betrayed.

☞† There is scarcely in history an instance of such mean, perfidious, and despotic behaviour, as that of the emperor to the landgrave in the case now before us. After having received in public the humble submissions of that unhappy prince, made upon his knees, in the most respectful and affecting terms, and after having set him at liberty by a solemn treaty, he ordered him to be again arrested, without alleging any reason, or even any pretext, and kept him for several years in a close and severe confinement. When Maurice remonstrated to the emperor against this new imprisonment, Charles answered, that he had never promised that the landgrave should not be imprisoned anew, but only that he should be exempted from perpetual imprisonment and, to support this assertion, he produced the treaty in which his ministers, in order to elude the true meaning of the accommodation, had perfidiously foisted in *ewiger gefangnis*, which signifies a *perpetual prison*, instead of *einiger gefangnis*, which

history has not been hitherto so far cleared up, as to enable us to judge with certainty of the confinement of this prince, and the real causes to which it may be ascribed.*

III. This revolution seemed to threaten ruin to the protestant cause, and to crown the efforts of the pontiff with the most triumphant success. In the diet of Augsburg, which was assembled soon after, with an imperial army at hand to promote union and despatch, the emperor required of the protestants, that they would leave the decision of these religious contests to the wisdom of the council that was to meet at Trent. The greatest part of the members consented to this proposal; and, among others, Maurice, the new elector of Saxony, who owed both his electorate and his dominions to the emperor, and who was ardently desirous of obtaining the liberty of his father-in-law the landgrave of Hesse. This general submission to the will of Charles, did not, however, produce the fruits that were expected from such a solemn and almost universal approbation of the council of Trent. A plague, which manifested itself (or was said to do so) in that city, induced the greatest part of the assembled fathers to retire to Bologna, and thereby the council was, in effect, dissolved; nor could all the entreaties and remonstrances of the emperor prevail upon the pope to reassemble it without delay. While affairs were in this situation, and the prospect of seeing a council assembled was obscured, the emperor judged it necessary, during this *interval*, to devise some method of maintaining peace in religious matters, until the decision, so long expected, should be finally obtained. It was with this view that he ordered Julius Pflugius, bishop of Naumburg, Michael Sidonius, a creature of the pontiff, and John Agricola, a native of Eisleben, to draw up a *formulary*, which might serve as a rule of faith and worship to both parties, until a council should begin to act. As this was only a temporary appointment, and had not the force of a permanent or perpetual institution, the rule in question was called the *Interim*.†

IV. This temporary rule of faith and discipline, though it was extremely favourable to the interests and pretensions of the court of Rome, had yet the fate to which schemes of reconciliation are often exposed; it pleased neither party, but was equally offensive to the followers of Luther and to the Roman pontiff. It was, however, promulgated with solemnity, by the emperor, at the diet of Augsburg; and the elector of Mentz, without even deigning to ask the opinions of the assembled princes and states, rose with an air of authority, and, as if he had been commissioned to represent the whole diet, gave a formal and public approbation to this famous *Interim*.* Thus were many princes of the empire, whose silence, though it proceeded from want of courage, was interpreted as the mark of a tacit consent, engaged against their will to receive this *book* as a body of ecclesiastical law. The major part of those, who had the resolution to dispute the authority of this imperial creed, were obliged to submit to it by the force of arms; and hence arose deplorable scenes of violence and bloodshed, which involved the empire in the greatest calamities. Maurice, elector of Saxony, who, for some time, had affected to be neutral, and neither declared himself for those who rejected, nor for those who had adopted the formulary, assembled, in 1548, the Saxon nobility and clergy, with Melancthon at the head of the latter, and, in several conferences at Leipsic and other places, took counsel concerning what was to be done in this critical affair. The deliberations, on this occasion, were long and tedious, and their result was ambiguous; for Melancthon, whose opinion was respected as a law by the reformed doctors, fearing the emperor on the one hand, and attentive to the sentiments of his sovereign on the other, pronounced a sort of conciliatory sentence which, he hoped, would be offensive to no party. He gave it as his opinion, that the whole of the book called *Interim* could not, by any means, be adopted by the friends of the Reformation; but he declared, at the same time, that he saw no reason, why this book might not be approved, adopted, and received, as an authoritative rule, in things that did not relate to the essential parts of religion, or in points which might be considered as accessory or *indifferent*.†

---

means *any prison*. This point, however, is contested by some historians.

* See a German work entitled, Benj. Grosch Vertheidigung der Evangelischen Kirche gegen Gottfr. Arnold.

☞ † This project of Charles was formed, partly to vent his resentment against the pope, and partly to answer other purposes of a more political kind. Be that as it may, the *Formula ad Interim*, or temporary rule of faith and worship here mentioned, contained all the essential doctrines of the church of Rome, though considerably softened and mitigated by the moderate, prudent, and artful terms in which they were expressed; terms quite different from those that were employed, before and after this period, by the council of Trent. There was even an affected ambiguity in many expressions, which rendered them susceptible of different senses, applicable to the sentiments of both communions, and therefore disagreeable to both. The *Interim* was composed with that fraudulent, specious, and seducing dexterity, which in aftertimes appeared in the deceitful exposition of the Catholic faith, by M. Bossuet, bishop of Meaux; and it was almost equally rejected by the Protestants and Roman Catholics. The cup was allowed, by this imperial creed, to the protestants in the administration of the Lord's supper, and priests and clerks were permitted by it to enter into the married state. These grants were however accompanied with the two following conditions: "1. That every one should be at liberty to use the cup, or to abstain from it, and to choose a state of marriage or a state of celibacy, as he should judge most fit or convenient: 2. That these grants should remain in force no longer than the happy period when a general council should terminate all religious differences." This second condition tended to produce the greatest disorder and confusion in case the future council should think proper to enjoin celibacy on the clergy, and declare, as it did in effect, their marriage unchristian and unlawful.

* See Jo. Erdm. Bieck, Triplex Interim.—Luc. Osianders Cent. XVI. Histor. Eccles. lib. ii. cap. lxviii. p. 425.—For an account of the authors and editions of the book called *Interim*, see Die Danische Biblioth. part v. and vi.

☞ † By things *indifferent*, Melancthon understood particularly the ceremonies of the popish worship which, superstitious as they were, that reformer yielding to the softness and flexibility of his natural temper, treated with a singular and excessive indulgence upon this occasion.

This decision, instead of pacifying matters, produced, on the contrary, new divisions, and formed, among the followers of Luther, a schism which placed the cause of the Reformation in the most perilous and critical circumstances, and might have contributed either to ruin it entirely, or to retard considerably its progress, had the pope and the emperor been dexterous enough to make the proper use of these divisions, and to seize the favourable occasion that was presented to them, of turning the force of the protestants against themselves.

V. Amidst these contests Paul III. was obliged to quit this life in the year 1549, and was succeeded, in the following year, by Julius III., who, yielding to the repeated and importunate solicitations of the emperor, consented to convoke a council at Trent. Accordingly, in the diet of Augsburg, which was again holden under the formidable artillery of an imperial army, Charles laid this matter before the states and princes of the empire. The majority of the princes gave their consent to the convocation of this council, to which also the elector Maurice submitted upon certain conditions.* The emperor then concluded the diet in 1551, desiring the assembled princes and states to prepare all things for the approaching council, and promising that he would use his most zealous endeavours to promote moderation and harmony, impartiality and charity, in the deliberations and transactions of that assembly. When the diet broke up, the protestants took the steps they judged most prudent to prepare themselves for what was to happen. The Saxons employed the pen of Melancthon, and the Wirtembergers that of Brentius, to draw up confessions of their faith, which were to be laid before the new council. Beside the ambassadors of the duke of Wirtemberg, several doctors of that city repaired to Trent. The Saxon divines, with Melancthon at their head, set out also for that place, but proceeded in their journey no farther than Nuremberg. They had received secret orders to stop there; for Maurice had no intention of submitting to the emperor's views: on the contrary, he hoped to reduce that prince to a compliance with his own projects. He therefore yielded in appearance, that he might carry his point, and thus command in reality.

VI. The real views of Charles, amidst the divisions and troubles in Germany, (which he fomented by negotiations that carried the outward aspect of a reconciling spirit,) will appear evidently to such as consider attentively the nature of the times, and compare the transactions of this prince, one with another. Relying on the extent of his power, and the success that frequently accompanied his enterprises, with a degree of confidence that was highly imprudent, he proposed to turn these religious commotions and dissensions to the confirmation and increase of his dominion in Germany, and, by sowing the seeds of discord among the princes of the empire, to weaken their power, and thereby the more easily to encroach upon their rights and privileges. On the other hand, ardently desirous of reducing within narrower limits the jurisdiction and dominion of the Roman pontiffs, that they might not set bounds to his ambition, or prevent the execution of his aspiring views, he flattered himself that this would be the natural effect of the approaching council. He was confirmed in this pleasing hope, by reflecting on what had happened in the assemblies of Constance and of Basil, in which the lust of papal ambition had been opposed with spirit, and restrained within certain limits. He also persuaded himself, that, by the dexterity of his agents, and the number of the Spanish and German bishops devoted to his interests, he should be able to influence and direct the deliberations of the council in such a manner, as to make its decisions answer his expectations, and contribute effectually to the accomplishment of his views. Such were the specious dreams of ambition that filled the imagination of this restless prince; but his views and projects were disconcerted by that very individual, that supposed friend, who had been one of the principal instruments of the violence and oppression which he had exercised against the protestant princes, and of the injury he had done to the protestant cause.

VII. The most considerable princes, not only of Germany, but even of all Europe, had, for a long time, addressed to the emperor their united entreaties for the deliverance of Philip, landgrave of Hesse, and John Frederic, elector of Saxony, from their confinement; and Maurice had solicited, with peculiar warmth and assiduity, the liberty of the former, who was his father-in-law. But all these solicitations produced no effect. Perceiving at length that he was duped by the emperor, and also convinced that this ambitious monarch was forming insidious designs upon the liberties of Germany, and the jurisdiction of its princes, the elector entered, with the utmost secrecy and expedition, into an alliance with the king of France and several of the German princes, for the maintenance of the rights and liberties of the empire. Encouraged by this respectable confederacy, the active Saxon led a powerful army against the emperor in 1552, with such astonishing valour and rapidity, that he surprised Charles at Inspruck, where he lay with a small force in the utmost security, and without the least apprehension of danger. This unforeseen event alarmed and dejected the emperor to such a degree, that he was willing to make peace on almost any conditions; and, consequently, he not only concluded, at Passau, the famous treaty of pacification with the

☞* Maurice (who was desirous of regaining the esteem of the protestants of Saxony, which he had lost by his perfidious behaviour to the late elector John Frederic, his benefactor and friend) gave his consent to the renewal of the council of Trent on the following conditions:—1st. That the points of doctrine, which had been already decided there, should be examined and discussed anew; 2dly, That this examination should be made in presence of the protestant divines, or their deputies; 3dly, That the Saxon protestants should have a liberty of *voting*, as well as of *deliberating*, in the council; and, 4thly, That the pope should not pretend to preside in that assembly, either in person or by his legates. This declaration was read in the diet, and the elector's deputies insisted upon its being registered, which the archbishop of Mentz, however, obstinately refused.

protestants,* but also promised to assemble, within the space of six months, a diet, in which all the tumults and dissensions that had been occasioned by a diversity of sentiment in religious matters should be entirely removed. Thus did the same prince, who stands foremost in the list of those that oppressed the protestants, and reduced their affairs to extremities, restore their expiring hopes, support and render triumphant their desperate cause, and procure for them that bulwark of peace and of liberty which still remains. Maurice, however, did not live to see this happy issue of his glorious expedition; for he lost his life in the following year, by a wound received at the battle of Siverhausen, while he was fighting against Albert of Brandenburg.†

VIII. The troubles of Germany, with several other incidents, rendered it impossible to assemble the diet, which the emperor had promised at the pacification of Passau, so soon as the period mentioned in the articles of that treaty. This famous diet met, however, at Augsburg, in 1555, was opened by Ferdinand in the name of the emperor, and terminated those deplorable scenes of bloodshed, desolation, and discord, that had so long afflicted both church and state, by that *religious peace* (as it is commonly called) which secured to the protestants the free exercise of their religion, and established this inestimable liberty upon the firmest foundations; for, after various debates, the following memorable acts were passed, on the 25th of September; that the protestants who followed the confession of Augsburg, should be for the future considered as entirely exempt from the jurisdiction of the Roman pontiff, and from the authority and superintendence of the bishops; that they were left at perfect liberty to enact laws for themselves, relating to their religious sentiments, discipline, and worship; that all the inhabitants of the German empire should be allowed to judge for themselves in religious matters, and to join themselves to that church whose doctrine and worship they thought the purest, and the most consonant to the spirit of true Christianity; and that all those who should injure or persecute any person under religious pretexts, and on account of opinions and belief, should be declared and proceeded against as public enemies of the empire, invaders of its liberty, and disturbers of its peace.* The difficulties that were to be surmounted before this equitable decision could be procured, the tedious deliberations, the warm debates, the violent animosities, and bloody wars, that were necessary to engage the greatest part of the German states to consent to conditions so agreeable to the dictates of right reason, as well as to the sacred injunctions of the Gospel, show us, in a shocking and glaring point of light, the ignorance and superstition of these miserable times, and stand upon record, as one of the most evident proofs of the necessity of religious reform.

IX. During these transactions in Germany, the friends of genuine Christianity in England deplored the gloomy reign of superstition, and the almost total extinction of true religion; and, seeing before their eyes the cause of popery maintained by the terrors of bloody persecution, and daily victims brought to the stake, to expiate the pretended crime of preferring the dictates of the Gospel to the despotic laws of Rome, they deemed the Germans happy, in having thrown off the yoke of an imperious and superstitious church. Henry VIII., whose personal vices, and whose arbitrary and capricious conduct, had greatly retarded the progress of the Reformation, was now no more. He died in 1547, and was succeeded by his only son, Edward VI. This amiable prince, whose early youth was crowned with that wisdom, sagacity, and virtue, that would have done honour to advanced years, gave new spirit and vigour to the protestant cause, and was its brightest ornament, as well as its most effectual support. He encouraged learned and pious men of foreign countries to settle in England, and addressed a particular invitation to Martin Bucer and Paul Fagius, whose moderation added a lustre to their other virtues, that, by the ministry and labours of these eminent men, in concert with those of the friends of the reformation in England, he might purge his dominions from the vile fictions of popery, and establish the pure doctrines of Christianity in their place. For this purpose he issued the wisest orders for the restoration of true religion; but his reign was too short to accomplish fully such a glorious purpose. In 1553, he was taken from his loving and afflicted subjects, whose sorrow was inexpressible, and suited to their loss. His sister Mary, (the daughter of Catharine of Arragon, from whom Henry had been separated by the famous divorce,) a furious bigot to the church of Rome, and a princess whose natural character, like the spirit of her religion, was despotic and cruel, succeeded him on the English throne, and imposed anew the arbitrary laws and the tyrannical yoke of Rome upon her reluctant subjects. Nor were

☞ * As this treaty is deemed by the German protestants the basis of their religious liberty, it will not be amiss to insert here some of its principal articles. By the three first articles it was stipulated, that Maurice and the confederates should lay down their arms, and should lend their troops to Ferdinand to defend Germany against the Turks, and that the landgrave of Hesse should be set at liberty. By the fourth it was agreed that the rule of faith, called *Interim*, should be considered as null and void; that the contending parties should enjoy the free and undisturbed exercise of their religion, until a diet should be assembled to determine amicably the present disputes (which diet was to meet in the space of six months;) and that this religious liberty should continue always, if it should be found impossible to come to an uniformity in doctrine and worship. It was also resolved, that all those who had suffered banishment, or any other calamity, on account of their having been concerned in the league or war of Smalcald, should be reinstated in their privileges, possessions, and employments; that the Imperial chamber at Spire should be open to the protestants as well as to the catholics; and that there should be always a certain number of the Lutheran persuasion in that high court.

☞ † Albert, marquis of Brandenburg, after the pacification of Passau, to which he refused to subscribe, continued the war against the Roman catholics; and afterwards committed such ravages in the empire, that a confederacy was formed against him, at the head of which Maurice was placed.

* Jo. Schilteri Liber de Pace Religiosa.—Christ. Lehmanni Acta Publica et Originalia de Pace Religiosa.

the methods she employed, in the cause of superstition, better than the cause itself, or tempered by any sentiments of equity or compassion. Barbarous tortures, and death in the most shocking forms, awaited those who opposed her will, or made the least stand against the restoration of popery. And, among many other victims, the learned and pious Cranmer, archbishop of Canterbury, who had been one of the most illustrious instruments of the Reformation in England, fell a sacrifice to her fury.* This odious scene of persecution was happily concluded, in 1558, by the death of the queen, who left no issue; and, as soon as her successor, the lady Elizabeth, ascended the throne, all things assumed a new and a pleasing aspect. This illustrious princess, whose sentiments, counsels, and projects, breathed a spirit superior to the natural softness and delicacy of her sex, exerted this vigorous and manly spirit in the defence of oppressed conscience and expiring liberty, broke anew the despotic yoke of papal authority and superstition, and delivering her people from the bondage of Rome, established that form of religious doctrine and ecclesiastical government which England still enjoys. This religious establishment differs, in some respects, from the plan formed by those whom Edward VI. had employed for promoting the cause of the reformation, and approaches nearer to the rites and discipline of former times, though it is widely different from, and in the most important points entirely opposite to, the principles of the Roman hierarchy.

X. The seeds of the reformation were very early sown in Scotland, by several noblemen of that nation, who had resided in Germany during the religious disputes that divided the empire. But the power of the Roman pontiff, supported and seconded by inhuman laws and barbarous executions, choked, for many years, these tender seeds, and prevented their taking root. The first and most eminent opposer of the papal jurisdiction was John Knox,† a disciple of Calvin, whose eloquence was persuasive, and whose fortitude was invincible.* This resolute reformer set out from Geneva for Scotland, in 1559, and, in a very short time inspired the people, by his private exhortations and his public discourses, with such a violent aversion to the superstitions of Rome, that the greatest part of the Scottish nation abandoned them entirely, and aimed at nothing less than the total extirpation of popery.† From this period to the present times, the doctrine, worship, and discipline that had been established at Geneva by the ministry of Calvin, have been maintained in Scotland with invincible obstinacy and zeal; and every attempt to introduce into that kingdom the rites and government of the church of England, has proved impotent and unsuccessful.‡

* This prelate was the less entitled to compassion, as, when in power, he followed the execrable example of the Romanists, by committing to the flames, against the will of the young king, two supposed heretics, two unfortunate foreigners, whom, one would think, every humane Briton would have spared, and whose destruction nothing could justify.—EDIT.

☞ † It will not be improper to insert here the character of this famous Scottish reformer, as it is drawn by the spirited, accurate, and impartial pen of Dr. Robertson, in his History of Scotland, book vi. "Zeal, intrepidity, disinterestedness, (says that incomparable writer,) were virtues which he possessed in an eminent degree. He was acquainted, too, with the learning cultivated in that age, and excelled in that species of eloquence which is calculated to rouse and to inflame. His maxims, however, were often too severe, and the impetuosity of his temper excessive. Rigid and uncomplying himself, he showed no indulgence to the infirmities of others. Regardless of the distinctions of rank and character, he uttered his admonitions with an acrimony and vehemence, more apt to irritate than to reclaim; and this often betrayed him into indecent and undutiful expressions with respect to the queen's person and conduct. Those very qualities, however, which now render his character less amiable, fitted him to be the instrument of Providence for advancing the reformation among a fierce people, and enabled him to face dangers, and to surmount opposition, from which a person of a more gentle spirit would have been apt to shrink back. By an unwearied application to study and to business, as well as by the frequency and fervour of his public discourses, he had worn out a constitution naturally strong. During a lingering illness, he discovered the utmost fortitude, and met the approaches of death with a magnanimity inseparable from his character. He was constantly employed in acts of devotion, and comforted himself with those prospects of immortality, which not only preserve good men from desponding, but fill them with exultation in their last moments."

☞ * The earl of Morton, who was present at his funeral, pronounced his eulogium in a few words, the more honourable for Knox, as they came from one whom he had often censured with peculiar severity: "There lies he who never feared the face of man."

† See Neal's History of the Puritans, vol. i. - Calderwood's History of Scotland's Reformation.—Georg. Buchanani Rerum Scoticar. Hist.—Melvil's Memoirs, vol. i.

☞ ‡ The indignation of the people, which has been excited by the *vices* of the clergy, was soon transferred to their *persons*, and settled at last, by a transition not unusual, upon the offices they enjoyed; and thus the effects of the reformation extended, not only to the doctrine, but also to the government of the popish church. But in Germany, England, and the northern kingdoms, its operations were checked by the power and policy of their princes, and episcopal hierarchy (which appears to be the most conformable to the practice of the church, since Christianity became the established religion of the Roman empire) was still continued in these countries, under certain limitations. The ecclesiastical government was in a great measure borrowed from the civil; and the dioceses and jurisdiction of patriarchs, archbishops, and bishops, corresponded with the division and constitution of the empire. In Switzerland and the Low Countries, the nature and spirit of a republican policy gave fuller scope to the reformers; and thus all pre-eminence of order in the church was destroyed, and that form of ecclesiastical government established, which has been since called Presbyterian. The situation of the primitive church (oppressed by continued persecutions, and obliged by its sufferings to be contented with a form of government extremely simple, and with a parity of rank for want of ambition to propose, or power to support, a subordination) suggested, without doubt, the idea of this latter system; though it would be unfair to allege this consideration as a victorious argument in favour of Presbyterianism, because a change of circumstances will sometimes justify a change in the methods and plans of government. Be that as it may, the church of Geneva, which received the decisions of Calvin with an amazing docility, restored this presbyterian or republican form of ecclesiastical policy; Knox studied, admired, and recommended it to his countrymen, and he was seconded by many of the Scottish nobles, of whom some hated the persons, while many others coveted the wealth of the dignified clergy. But, in introducing this system, that reformer did not deem it expedient to depart altogether from the ancient form; for, instead of bishops, he proposed the establishment of ten superintendents, to inspect the lives and doctrines of the other clergy, and preside in the inferior judicatories of the church,

XI. The cause of the reformation underwent, in Ireland, the same vicissitudes and revolutions that had attended it in England. When Henry VIII., after the abolition of the papal authority, was declared 'supreme head, upon earth, of the church of England,' George Brown, a monk of the Augustine order, whom that monarch had created, in 1535, archbishop of Dublin, began to act with the utmost vigour in consequence of this change in the hierarchy. He purged the churches of his diocese from superstition in all its various forms, pulled down images, destroyed relics, abolished absurd and idolatrous rites, and by the influence as well as authority which he possessed in Ireland, caused the king's supremacy to be acknowledged by that nation.* Henry showed soon after, that this supremacy was not a vain title; for he banished the monks out of that kingdom, confiscated their revenues, and secularized or suppressed their convents. In the reign of Edward VI. farther progress was made in the removal of popish superstitions, by the zealous labours of archbishop Brown, and the auspicious encouragement he granted to all who exerted themselves in the cause of the reformation. But the death of this excellent prince, and the accession of his sister to the throne, changed the face of affairs in Ireland,† as it had done in England. Mary pursued with fire and sword, and all the marks of unrelenting vengeance, the promoters of a pure and rational religion, and deprived Brown and other protestant bishops of their dignities in the church. But the reign of Elizabeth gave a new and a deadly blow to popery, which was recovering its force, and arming itself anew with the authority of the throne; and the Irish were obliged again to submit to the form of worship and discipline established in England.*

XII. The reformation had not been long established in Britain, when seven of the Netherland provinces, united by a respectable confederacy, renounced their spiritual allegiance to the Roman pontiff. Philip II. king of Spain, apprehending the danger to which the religion of Rome was exposed from that spirit of liberty and independence which reigned among the inhabitants of the Low-Countries, took the most violent measures to dispel it. For this purpose he augmented the number of the bishops, enacted the most severe and barbarous laws against all innovators in matters of religion, and erected that unjust and inhuman tribunal of the inquisition, which would

without pretending to claim either a seat in parliament, or the revenues and dignity of the former bishops. This proposal was drawn up, and presented to a convention of estates in 1561; and what it contained, in relation to ecclesiastical jurisdiction and discipline, would have easily obtained the sanction of that assembly, had not a design to recover the patrimony of the church, in order to apply it to the advancement of religion and learning, been insinuated in it. After this, at certain periods, the name of bishop was revived, but without the prerogatives, jurisdiction, or revenues, that were formerly appropriated to that order. They were made subject to the general assemblies of the clergy, and their power was gradually diminished, until their name and order were abolished at the revolution in 1688, when presbyterianism was established in Scotland by the laws of the state. See Robertson's History of Scotland.

☞ * The learned and pious primate Usher, in his Memoirs of the Ecclesiastical Affairs of Ireland, speaks of archbishop Brown in the following manner: "George Brown was a man of a cheerful countenance, in his acts and deeds plain down right; to the poor merciful and compassionate, pitying the state and condition of the souls of the people, and advising them, when he was provincial of the Augustine order in England, to make their application solely to Christ; which advice coming to the ears of Henry VIII., he became a favourite, and was made archbishop of Dublin. Within five years after he enjoyed that see, he caused all superstitious relics and images to be removed out of the two cathedrals in Dublin, and out of all the churches in his diocese; and caused the Ten Commandments, the Lord's Prayer, and the Creed, to be placed in gilded frames about the altars. He was the first that turned from the Romish religion of the clergy here in Ireland, to embrace the reformation of the church of England." See a very curious pamphlet in the fifth volume of the Harleian Miscellany, entitled Historical Collections of the Church of Ireland.

☞ † Here Dr. Mosheim has fallen into a mistake, by not distinguishing between the designs of the queen, which were indeed cruel, and their execution, which was happily and providentially prevented. This appears from a very singular and comical adventure, of which the account, as it has been copied from the papers of Richard, earl of Cork, and is to be found among the manuscripts of Sir James Ware, is as follows:

"Queen Mary, having dealt severely with the protestants in England, about the latter end of her reign signed a commission to take the same course with them in Ireland; and, to execute the same with greater force, she nominates Dr. Cole one of the commissioners. This doctor coming with the commission to Chester on his journey, the mayor of that city, hearing that her majesty was sending a messenger into Ireland, and he being a churchman, waited on the doctor, who, in discourse with the mayor, taketh out of a cloak-bag a leather box, saying unto him, 'Here is a commission that shall lash the *heretics* of Ireland,' (calling the protestants by that title.) The good woman of the house, being well affected to the protestant religion, and also having a brother named John Edmonds, of the same, then a citizen in Dublin, was much troubled at the doctor's words; but watching her convenient time, while the mayor took his leave, and the doctor complimented him down the stairs, she opens the box, takes the commission out, and places in lieu thereof a sheet of paper, with a pack of cards wrapped up therein, the knave of clubs being placed uppermost The doctor coming up to his chamber, suspecting nothing of what had been done, put up the box as formerly. The next day, going to the water-side, wind and weather serving him, he sails towards Ireland, and landed on the 7th of October, 1558, at Dublin. Then coming to the castle, the lord Fitz-Walter, being lord-deputy, sent for him to come before him and the privy council; who, coming in, after he made a speech relating upon what account he came over, presents the box unto the lord-deputy, who causing it to be opened, that the secretary might read the commission, there was nothing save a pack of cards with the knave of clubs uppermost; which not only startled the lord-deputy and council, but the doctor, who assured them he had a commission, but knew not how it was gone. Then the lord-deputy made answer, 'Let us have another commission, and we will shuffle the cards in the mean while.' The doctor, being troubled in his mind, went away, and returned into England; and coming to the court, obtained another commission, but staying for a wind on the water-side, news came to him that the queen was dead; and thus God preserved the protestants of Ireland."

Queen Elizabeth was so delighted with this story which was related to her by Lord Fitz-Walter on his return to England, that she sent for Elizabeth Edmonds, and gave her a pension of forty pounds during her life. See Cox, Hibernia Anglicana, or History of Ireland, vol. ii.—Harleian Miscellany, vol. v.

* See the life of Dr. George Brown, Archbishop of Dublin, published at London in 1681, and reprinted in the Harleian Miscellany.

intimidate and tame, as he thought, the manly spirit of an oppressed and persecuted people. But his measures, in this respect, were as unsuccessful as they were absurd; his furious and intemperate zeal for the superstitions of Rome accelerated their destruction; and the papal authority, which had only been in a critical state, was reduced to a desperate one, by the very steps that were designed to support it. The nobility formed themselves into an association, in 1566, with a view to procure the repeal of these tyrannical edicts; and, when their solicitations and requests were treated with contempt, they resolved to obtain, by force, what they hoped to have gained from clemency and justice. They addressed themselves to a free and an abused people, spurned the authority of a cruel yoke, and, with an impetuosity and vehemence that were perhaps excessive, trampled upon whatever was deemed sacred or respectable by the church of Rome.* To quell these tumults, a powerful army was sent from Spain, under the command of the duke of Alva, whose horrid barbarity and sanguinary proceedings kindled that long and bloody war from which the powerful republic of the United Provinces derived its origin, consistence, and grandeur. It was the heroic conduct of William of Nassau, prince of Orange, seconded by the succours of England and France, that delivered this state from the Spanish yoke; and no sooner was this deliverance obtained, than the reformed religion, as it was professed in Switzerland, was established in the United Provinces;† and, at the same time, an universal toleration was granted to those whose religious sentiments were of a different nature, whether they retained the faith of Rome, or embraced the reformation in another form,‡ provided that they made no attempts against the authority of the government, or the tranquillity of the public.*

XIII. The reformation made a considerable progress in Spain and Italy, soon after the rupture between Luther and the Roman pontiff. In all the provinces of Italy, but more especially in the territories of Venice, Tuscany, and Naples, the religion of Rome lost ground, and great numbers of persons, of all ranks and orders, expressed an aversion to the papal yoke. This gave rise to violent and dangerous commotions in the kingdom of Naples in 1536, of which the principal authors were Bernardo Ochino and Peter Martyr, who, in their public discourses from the pulpit, exhausted all the force of their irresistible eloquence in exposing the enormity of the reigning superstition. These tumults were appeased with much difficulty by the united efforts of Charles V. and his viceroy don Pedro de Toledo.† In several places the popes put a stop to the progress of the reformation, by letting loose, upon the pretended heretics, their bloody inquisitors, who spread the marks of their usual barbarity through the greatest part of Italy. These formidable ministers of superstition put such a number of supposed heretics to death, and perpetrated, on the friends of religious liberty, such horrid acts of cruelty and oppression, that most of the reformists consulted their safety by a voluntary exile, while others returned to the religion of Rome, at least in external appearance. But the terrors of the inquisition, which frightened back into the profession of popery many protestants in other parts of Italy, could not penetrate into the kingdom of Naples; nor could either the authority or entreaties of the Roman pontiffs engage the Neapolitans to admit within their territories either a court of inquisition, or even visiting inquisitors.‡

☞ * Dr. Mosheim seems here to distinguish too little between the spirit of the nobility and that of the multitude. Nothing was more temperate and decent than the conduct of the former; and nothing could be more tumultuous and irregular than the behaviour of the latter. While the multitude destroyed churches, pulled down monasteries, broke the images used in public worship, abused the officers of the inquisition, and committed a thousand enormities, the effects of furious resentment and brutish rage, the nobility and opulent citizens kept within the bounds of moderation and prudence. Though justly exasperated against a despotic and cruel government, they dreaded the consequences of popular tumults as the greatest of misfortunes. Many of them even united their counsels and forces with those of the governess, (the duchess of Parma,) to restrain the seditious and turbulent spirit of the people. The prince of Orange and count Egmont (whose memories will live for ever in the grateful remembrance of the Dutch nation, and be dear to all the lovers of heroic patriotism and sacred liberty throughout the world) signalized their moderation upon this occasion, and were the chief instruments of the repose that ensued. Their opposition to the government proceeded from the dictates of humanity and justice, and not from a spirit of licentiousness and rebellion; and their merit and respectability had secured to them such influence and authority among the people, that, had the imperious court of Spain condescended to make any reasonable concessions, the public tranquillity might have been restored, and the affections of the people entirely regained. See Le Clerc, Histoire des Prov. Un.

† In the year 1573.

☞ ‡ It is necessary to distinguish between the toleration that was granted to the Roman catholics, and that which the Anabaptists, Lutherans, &c. other protestant sects, enjoyed. They were all indiscriminately excluded from the civil employments of the state; but though they were equally allowed the exercise of their religion, the latter were permitted to enjoy their religious worship in a more open and public manner than the former, from whom the churches were taken, and whose religious assemblies were confined to private conventicles, which had no external resemblance to the edifices usually set apart for divine worship.

* See a farther account of this affair in Gerard Brandt's History of the Reformation in the Netherlands.

† See Giannone, Historia di Napoli, tom. iv.—Vita Galeacii in Museo Helvetico, tom. ii.

☞ ‡ It was an attempt to introduce a Roman inquisitor into the city of Naples, that, properly speaking, produced the tumult and sedition which Dr. Mosheim attributes in this section to the pulpit discourses of Ochino and Martyr; for these famous preachers, particularly the former, taught the doctrines of the reformation with great art, prudence, and caution, and secretly converted many, without giving public offence. The emperor himself, who heard him at Naples, declared that "he preached with such spirit and devotion as might almost make the very stones weep." After Ochino's departure from Naples, the disciples he had formed gave private instructions to others, among whom were some eminent ecclesiastics and persons of distinction, who began to form congregations and conventicles. This awakened the jealousy of the viceroy Toledo, who published a severe edict against heretical books, ordered some productions of Melancthon and Erasmus to be publicly burned, looked with a suspicious

The eyes of many persons in Spain were opened upon the truth, not only by the spirit of inquiry, which the controversies between Luther and Rome had excited in Europe, but even by the efforts of those divines whom Charles V. had brought with him into Germany, to combat the pretended heresy of the reformers; for these Spanish doctors imbibed this heresy instead of refuting it, and propagated it more or less, on their return home, as evidently appears from several circumstances.* But the inquisition, which could not gain any footing in the kingdom of Naples, reigned triumphant in Spain; and by racks, gibbets, stakes, and other formidable instruments of its method of persuading, soon terrified the people back into popery, and suppressed the vehement desire they had of changing a superstitious worship for a rational religion.*

XIV. I shall not enter into a contest with those writers, whatever their secret intentions may be, who observe, that many unjustifiable proceedings may be imputed to some of the most eminent promoters of this great change in the state of religion. For every impartial and attentive observer of the rise and progress of this reformation will ingenuously acknowledge, that wisdom and prudence did not always attend the transactions of those who were concerned in the glorious cause; that many things were done with violence, temerity, and precipitation; and, what is still worse, that several of the principal agents in this great revolution were actuated more by the impulse of passion and views of interest, than by a zeal for the advancement of true religion. But, on the other hand, the wise and candid observer of human affairs will own, as a most evident and incontestable truth, that many things which, when stripped of the circumstances and motives that attended them, appear to us, at this time, as real crimes, will be deprived of their enormity, and even acquire the aspect of noble deeds, if they be considered in one point of view with the times and places in which they were transacted, and with the frauds and crimes of the Roman pontiffs and their creatures, by which they were occasioned. But, after all, in defending the cause of the reformation, we are under no obligation to defend, in every respect, the moral characters of its promoters and instruments. These two objects are entirely distinct. The most just and excellent cause may be promoted with low views, and from sinister motives, without losing its nature, or ceasing to be just and excellent.

The true state of the question is, whether the opposition of Luther and other reformers to the Roman pontiff arose from just and solid reasons; and this question is entirely independent of the virtues or vices of particular persons.† Let many of these individuals be supposed as odious as, or still more detestable than, they are represented by their adversaries, provided that the cause which they supported be allowed to have been just and good.

---

eye on all kinds of literature, suppressed several academies, which had been erected about this time by the nobility for the advancement of learning; and, having received orders from the emperor to introduce the inquisition, desired pope Paul III. to send from Rome to Naples a deputy of that formidable tribunal. It was this that excited the people to take up arms in order to defend themselves against this branch of spiritual tyranny, which the Neapolitans never were patient enough to suffer, and which, on many occasions, they had opposed with vigour and success. Hostilities ensued, which were followed by an accommodation and a general pardon; while the emperor and viceroy, by this resolute opposition, were deterred from their design of introducing this despotic tribunal into the kingdom of Naples. Several other attempts were afterwards made, during the reigns of Philip II., III., IV., and Charles II. to establish the inquisition in Naples; but, by the jealousy and vigilance of the people, they all proved ineffectual. At length the emperor Charles VI., early in the eighteenth century, published an edict, expressly prohibiting all causes, relating to the holy faith, from being tried by any persons except the archbishop and bishops as ordinaries. See Giannone, lib. xxxii. and the Modern Univ. History.

☞ * This appears from the unhappy end of all the ecclesiastics who had attended Charles, and followed him into his retirement. No sooner was that monarch dead, than they were seized by order of the court of inquisition, and were afterwards committed to the flames, or sent to death in other forms equally terrible. Such was the fate of Augustin Casal, the emperor's preacher; of Constantine Pontius, his confessor; of the learned Egidius, whom he had nominated to the bishopric of Tortosa; of Bartholomew de Caranza, a Dominican, who had been confessor to king Philip and queen Mary, with above twenty more of less note. All this gave reason to presume that Charles died a protestant. Certain it is, that he knew well the corruptions and frauds of the church of Rome, and the grounds and reasons of the protestant faith, though business, ambition, interest, and the prejudices of education, may have blinded him for a while, until leisure, retirement, the absence of worldly temptations, and the approach of death, removed the veil, and led him to wise and serious reflections. See Burnet's History of the Reformation.

* See Geddes' Spanish Protestant Martyrology, in his Miscellaneous Tracts, tom. i.

† The *translator* has here added some paragraphs, to render more perspicuous the important observation of the learned author; and the *continuator* takes the opportunity of remarking, as an excuse for the intemperance and vehemence of Luther, that the mildness of a Melancthon, and the timidity of an Erasmus, would never have produced the desired reformation

SECTION II.

THE GENERAL HISTORY OF THE CHURCH.

I. The Spaniards and Portuguese, if we may give credit to their historians, exerted themselves, with the greatest vigour and success, in the propagation of the gospel, among the darkened nations;* and it must, indeed, be allowed, that they communicated some notions, such as they were, of the Christian religion to the inhabitants of America, to those parts of Africa where they carried their arms, and to the islands and maritime provinces of Asia, which they reduced under their dominion. It is also true, that considerable numbers of these savage people, who had hitherto lived, either under the bondage of the most extravagant superstitions, or in a total ignorance of any object of religious worship, embraced, at least in outward appearance, the doctrines of the Gospel. But when we reflect on the methods of conversion which were employed by the Spanish missionaries among these wretched nations, on the barbarous laws and inhuman tortures that were used to force them into the profession of Christianity; when it is considered, farther, that the denomination of a Christian was conferred upon every poor wretch who discovered a blind and excessive veneration for his stupid instructors, and who could by certain gestures, and the repetition of a little jargon, perform a few superstitious rites and ceremonies; then, instead of rejoicing at, we shall be tempted to lament, such a propagation of the Gospel, and to behold the labours of such miserable apostles with indignation and contempt. Such is the judgment passed upon these missionaries, not only by those whom the church of Rome placed in the list of heretics, but also by many of the most pious and eminent of her own doctors, in France, Germany, Spain, and Italy.

II. When the pontiffs saw their ambition checked by the progress of the Reformation, which deprived them of a great part of their spiritual dominion in Europe, they turned their lordly views toward the other parts of the globe, and became more solicitous than ever about the propagation of the Gospel among the nations that were yet involved in the darkness of paganism. This they considered as the best method of making amends for the loss they had sustained in Europe, and the most specious pretext for assuming to themselves, with some appearance of justice, the title of heads or parents of the universal church. The famous society, which, in 1540, took the denomination of *Jesuits*, or the *Company of Jesus*, seemed every way proper to assist the court of Rome in the execution of this extensive design. And accordingly, from their rise, this peculiar charge was given to them, that they should form a certain number of their order for the propagation of Christianity among the unenlightened nations, and that these missionaries should be at the absolute disposal of the pope, and always ready, at a moment's warning, to repair to whatever part of the world he should fix for the exercise of their ministry.* The many histories and relations which mention the labours, perils, and exploits of that prodigious multitude of Jesuits, who were employed in the conversion of the African, American, and Indian infidels, abundantly show, with what fidelity and zeal the members of this society executed the orders of the successive pontiffs.† And their labours would have undoubtedly crowned them with immortal glory, had it not appeared evident, from the most authentic records, that the greatest part of these new apostles had more in view the promotion of the ambitious views of Rome, and the advancement of the interests of their own society, than the propagation of the Christian religion, or the honour of its divine author.‡ It may also be affirmed, from records of the highest credit and authority, that the inquisition erected by the Jesuites at Goa, and the penal laws, whose terrors they employed so freely in the propagation of the Gospel, contributed much more than their arguments and exhortations, which were but sparingly used, to engage the Indians to embrace Christianity.§ The converting zeal of the Franciscans and Dominicans, which had, for a long time, been not only cooled, but almost totally extinguished, was animated anew by the example of the Jesuits; and several other religious orders, that slum-

* See Lafitau's Histoire des Decouvertes et Conquetes des Portugais dans le nouveau Monde, tom. iii. p. 420. All the relations given by this eloquent writer (who was afterwards created bishop of Sisteron) are taken from the Portuguese historians.—The other writers who have thrown light upon this part of ecclesiastical history, are enumerated by Fabricius, in his Lux Salutar. Evangelii toti Orbi exoriens.

☞* When the fanatic Ignatius first solicited the confirmation of his order by pope Paul III., the learned and worthy cardinal Guidiccioni opposed his request with great vehemence. But this opposition was vanquished by the dexterity of Ignatius, who changing the articles of his institution, in which he had promised obedience to the pope with certain restrictions, turned it in such a manner as to bind his order by a solemn vow of implicit, blind, and unlimited submission and obedience to the Roman pontiff. This change produced the desired effect, and made the popes look upon the Jesuits as the chief support of their authority. Hence arose the zeal which Rome has ever shown for that order. It is remarkable, that Ignatius and his company, in the very same charter in which they declared their implicit and blind allegiance to the court of Rome, promised a like implicit and unlimited allegiance to the general of their society, notwithstanding the impossibility of serving two absolute masters, whose commands might be often contradictory. See Histoire des Religieux de la Compagnie de Jesus, printed at Utrecht in 1741.

† See Jo. Alb. Fabricii Lux Evangelii toti Orbi exoriens, cap. xxxii. p. 550.

‡ B. Christ. Eberh. Weismanni Oratio de Virtutibus et Vitiis Mission. Roman. in Orat. ejus Academ.

§ See the Hist. de la Compagnie de Jesus, tom. ii

bered in their cells, were roused from their lethargy, if not by a principle of envy, at least by a spirit of emulation.

III. Of all the Jesuits who distinguished themselves by their zealous and laborious attempts to extend the limits of the church, none acquired a more shining reputation than Francis Xavier, who is commonly called the Apostle of the Indies.* An undaunted resolution, and no small degree of genius and sagacity, rendered this famous missionary one of the most proper persons that could be employed in such an arduous task. Accordingly, in 1522, he set sail for the Portuguese settlements in India, and, in a short time, spread the knowledge of the Christian religion, or, to speak more properly, of the Romish system, over a great part of the continent, and in several of the islands of that remote region. Thence, in 1529, he passed into Japan, and laid there, with amazing rapidity, the foundations of the famous church, which flourished during so many years in that vast empire. His indefatigable zeal prompted him to attempt the conversion of the Chinese; and with this view he embarked for that extensive and powerful kingdom, in sight of which he ended his days, in 1552.† After his death, other members of his insinuating order penetrated into China. Of these missionaries the chief was Matthew Ricci, an Italian, who, by his skill in the mathematics, became so acceptable to the Chinese nobility, and even to their emperor, that he obtained, both for himself and his associates, the liberty of explaining to the people the doctrines of the Gospel.‡ He may, therefore, be considered as the parent and founder of the Christian churches, which, though often dispersed, and tossed to and fro by the storms of persecution, still subsist in China.§

IV. The jurisdiction and territories of those princes, who first threw off the papal yoke, being confined within the limits of Europe, the churches that were under their protection could contribute little to the propagation of the Gospel in those distant regions of which we have been speaking. It is, however, recorded in history, that, in 1556, fourteen protestant missionaries were sent from Geneva to convert the Americans,‖ though it is not well known who was the promoter of this pious design, or with what success it was carried into execution. The English also, who, toward the conclusion of this century, sent colonies into the northern parts of America, transplanted with them the reformed religion, which they themselves professed; and, as their possessions were extended and multiplied from time to time, their religion also made a considerable progress among that rough and uncivilized people. We learn, moreover, that about this time the Swedes exerted their religious zeal in converting to Christianity many of the inhabitants of Finland and Lapland, of whom a considerable number had hitherto retained the impious and extravagant superstitions of their pagan ancestors.

V. It does not appear, from authentic records, that the sword of persecution was drawn against the Gospel, or any public opposition made to the progress of Christianity during this century; and it would betray a great ignorance, both of the situation, opinions, and maxims of the Turks, to imagine, that the war they waged against the Christians was carried on upon religious principles, or with a view to maintain and promote the doctrines of Mohammed. On the other hand, it is certain, that there lay concealed, in different parts of Europe, not a few persons who entertained a virulent enmity against religion in general, and, in a more especial manner, against the religion of the Gospel; and who, both in their writings and in private conversation, sowed the seeds of impiety and error, and instilled their odious principles into weak, unsteady, and credulous minds. In this pernicious and unhappy class are generally placed some of the Peripatetic philosophers, who adorned Italy by their erudition, and particularly Pomponatius; several French wits and philosophers, such as Bodin, Rabelais, Montagne, Bonaventure des Perieres, Dolet, Charron; some Italians, at whose head appears Leo X., followed by Bembo, Politian, Jordano Bruno, Ochino; and a few Germans, such as Theophrastus Paracelsus, Nicolas Taurellus, and others.* It is even reported, that, in certain provinces of France and Italy, schools were erected, whence whole swarms of these impious doctors soon issued to deceive the simple and unwary. This accusation will not be wholly rejected by such as are acquainted with the spirit and genius of these times; nor can it be said with truth, that all the persons charged with this heavy reproach were entirely guiltless. It is nevertheless certain, on the other hand, that, upon an accurate and impartial examination of this matter, the accusation brought against many of them will appear to be entirely groundless; and that, with respect to several who may deserve censure in a certain degree, their errors are less pernicious

* The late king of Portugal, in 1747, obtained for Xavier, or rather for his memory, the title of Protector of the Indies, from Benedict XIV. See the Lettres Edifiantes et Curieuses des Missions Etrangeres, tom. xliii. The body of this sainted missionary lies interred at Goa, where it is worshipped with the highest marks of devotion. There is also a magnificent church at Cotati dedicated to Xavier, to whom the inhabitants of that Portuguese settlement pay the most devout tribute of veneration and worship.

† See the writers enumerated by Fabricius, in his Lux Evangelii, &c. cap. xxxix. p. 677. Add to these Lafitau's Histoire des Decouvertes des Portugais dans le nouveau Monde, tom. iii. iv.—Histoire de la compagnie de Jesus, tom. i.

‡ J. B. Du-Halde, Description de l'Empire de la Chine, tom. iii.

§ It appears, however, that before the arrival of Ricci in China, some of the Dominicans had already been there, though to little purpose. See Le Quien, Oriens Christianus, tom. iii.

‖ Picteti Oratio de Trophæis Christi, in Orat. ejus, p. 570 There is no doubt that the divines here mentioned were those whom the illustrious admiral Coligni invited into France, when, in 1555, he had formed the project of sending a colony of Protestants into Brazil and other provinces of America See Charlevoix, Histoire de la Nouvelle France tom. i.

* See Reimanni Historia Atheismi et Atheorum.—Jo. Franc. Buddeus, Theses de Atheismo et Superstitione —Dictionnaire de Bayle.

and criminal, than they are uncharitably or rashly represented to be.

VI. It is, at the same time, evident, that, in this century, the arts and sciences were carried to a degree of perfection unknown to preceding ages; and, from this happy renovation of learning, the European churches derived the most signal and inestimable advantages, which they also transmitted to the most remote nations. The benign influence of true science, and its tendency to improve both the form of religion and the institutions of civil policy, were perceived by many of the states and princes of Europe: hence large sums were expended, and great zeal and industry employed, in promoting the progress of knowledge, by founding and encouraging literary societies, by protecting and exciting a spirit of emulation among men of genius, and by annexing distinguished honours and advantages to the culture of the sciences. And it is particularly worthy of observation, that this was the period, when the wise and salutary law, which excludes ignorant and illiterate persons from the sacred functions of the ministry, acquired, at length, that force which it still retains in the greatest part of the Christian world. There still remained, however, some seeds of that ancient discord between religion and philosophy, which had been sown and fomented by ignorance and fanaticism; and there were found, both among the friends and enemies of the reformation, several well-meaning, but inconsiderate men, who, in spite of common sense, maintained, with more vehemence and animosity than ever, that vital religion and piety could never flourish without being totally separated from learning and science, and nourished by the holy simplicity that reigned in the primitive ages of the church.

VII. The first rank in the literary world was now enjoyed by those who consecrated their studious hours, and their critical sagacity, to the publication, correction, and illustration, of the most famous Greek and Latin authors of ancient times, to the study of antiquity and the languages, and to the culture of eloquence and poetry. We see by the productions of this age (which yet remain, and continue to excite the admiration of the learned,) that in all the provinces of Europe these branches of literature were cultivated with a kind of enthusiasm, by such as were most distinguished by their taste and genius; and, what is still more extraordinary, (and perhaps not a little extravagant,) the welfare of the church, and the prosperity of the state, were supposed to depend upon the improvement of these branches of erudition, which were considered as the very essence of true and solid knowledge. If such encomiums were swelled beyond the bounds of truth and wisdom by enthusiastical philologists, it is nevertheless certain, that the species of learning here under consideration, was of the highest importance, as it opened the way that led to the treasures of solid wisdom, to the improvement of genius, and thus undoubtedly contributed, in a great measure, to deliver both reason and religion from the prepossessions of ignorance and the servitude of superstition.* And, therefore, we ought not to be surprised, when we meet with persons who exaggerate the merit, and dwell beyond measure on the praises of those who were our first guides from the regions of darkness and error, into the luminous paths of evidence and truth.

VIII. Though the lovers of philology and the *belles lettres* were much superior in number to those who turned their principal views to the study of philosophy, yet the latter were far from being contemptible either in point of number or capacity. The philosophers were divided into two classes: some were wholly absorbed in contemplation, while others were employed in the investigation of truth, and endeavoured by experience, as well as by reasoning, to trace out the laws and operations of nature. The former were subdivided into two sects, one of which followed certain leaders, while the other, unrestrained by the dictates of authority, struck out a new way for themselves, following freely their own inventions. Those who submitted to the direction of philosophical guides, enlisted themselves under the standard of Aristotle, or that of Plato, who continued still to have many admirers, especially in Italy. Nor were the followers of Aristotle agreed among themselves; they all acknowledged the Stagirite as their chief, but they followed him through very different paths. Some were for retaining the ancient method of proceeding in philosophical pursuits, which their doctors falsely called the Peripatetic system. Others pleaded for the pure and unmixed philosophy of Aristotle, and recommended his writings as the source of wisdom, and as the system which was most adapted, when properly illustrated and explained, to the instruction of youth. A third sort of Aristotelians, who differed equally from these now mentioned, and of whom the celebrated Melancthon was the chief, pursued another method. They extracted the marrow out of the lucubrations of the Grecian sage, illustrated it by the aids of genuine literature and the rules of good criticism, and corrected it by the dictates of right reason and the doctrines and principles of true religion.

Of those who struck out a path to themselves in the regions of philosophy, without any regard to that which had been opened by ancient sages, and pursued by their followers,

☞ * Many vehement debates have been carried on concerning the respective merit of literature and philosophy; but these debates are almost as absurd as a comparison that should be made between the means and the end, the instrument and its effect. Literature is the key by which we often open the treasures of wisdom, both human and divine. But, as the sordid miser absurdly converts the means into an end, and acquires a passion for the shining metal, considered abstractedly from the purposes which it was calculated to serve, so the pedantic philologist erects literature into an independent science, and contemns the divine treasures of philosophy, which it was designed both to discover and to illustrate. Hence arose that wretched tribe of "word-catchers that live on syllables," (as Pope, I think, happily expresses their tasteless pursuits,) who made the republic of letters groan under their commentaries, annotations, various readings, &c., and who forget that an acquaintance with language was intended

Cardan,* Telesius,† and Campanella,‡ deservedly hold the first rank, as they were undoubtedly men of superior genius, though too much addicted to the suggestions and visions of an irregular fancy. To these may be added Peter Ramus, that ingenious French philosopher, who, by attempting to substitute, in the place of Aristotle's logic, a method of reasoning more adapted to the use of rhetoric and the improvement of eloquence, excited such a terrible uproar in the Gallic schools. Nor must we omit here the mention of Theophrastus Paracelsus, who, by an assiduous observation of nature, by a great number of experiments indefatigably repeated, and by applying the penetrating force of fire* to discover the first principles or elements of bodies, endeavoured to throw new light and evidence on the important science of natural philosophy. As the researches of this industrious inquirer into nature excited the admiration of all, his example was consequently followed by many; and hence arose a new sect of philosophers, who assumed the denomination of *Theosophists*,† and who, placing little confidence in the decisions of human reason, or the efforts of speculation, attributed all to divine illumination and repeated experience.

IX. This revolution in philosophy and literature, together with the spirit of emulation that animated the different sects or classes into which the learned men of this age were divided, produced many happy effects of various kinds. It, in a more particular manner, brought into disrepute, though it could not at once utterly eradicate, that intricate, barbarous, and insipid method of teaching theology, which had hitherto prevailed in all the schools and pulpits of Christendom. The sacred writings, which, in the preceding ages, had been either entirely neglected, or very absurdly explained, were now much more consulted and respected in the debates and writings of the Christian doctors than they had formerly been; the sense and language of the inspired writers were more carefully studied and more accurately developed; the doctrines and precepts of religion taught in a more methodical manner, and with greater connexion and perspicuity; and that dry, barren, and vapid language, which the ancient schoolmen affected so much in their theological compositions, was wholly exploded by the wiser part of the divines of this century. It must not, however, be imagined, that this reformation of the schools was so perfect, as to leave no room for improvement in succeeding ages; this, indeed, was far from be-

to lead us to the improvement of the mind and to the knowledge of things.

☞ * Cardan was a man of a bold, irregular, enterprising genius, who by a wild imagination, was led into the study of astrology and magic, by which he excited the astonishment and attracted the veneration of the multitude, while his real merit as a philosopher was little known. He was accused of atheism, but seems much rather chargeable with superstition. His life and character seem to have formed an amazing mixture of wisdom and folly; and nothing can give a more unfavourable idea of his temper and principles, than the hideous portrait he has drawn of himself in his book De Genituris. His knowledge of physic and of mathematics was considerable, and his notions of natural philosophy may be seen in his famous book De Subtilitate et Veritate Rerum, in which some important truths and discoveries are mixed with the most fanatical visions, and the most extravagant and delirious effusions of mystical folly. See the ample and judicious account that has been given of the character and philosophy of this writer (whose voyage to Britain is well known) by the learned Brucker, in his Historia Critica Philosophiæ, tom. iv.

☞ † This philosopher, less known than the former, was born in 1508, at Cosenza, in the kingdom of Naples, and was the restorer of the philosophy formerly taught by Parmenides, upon whose principles he built a new system, or at least, a system which appeared new, by the elegant connexion which he gave to its various parts, and the arguments used to maintain and support it against the philosophy of Aristotle. It was the vague and uncertain method of reasoning which the Stagirite had introduced into natural philosophy, that engaged Telesius to compose his famous book De Principiis Rerum Naturalium. In this work, after having refuted the visionary principles of the Aristotelian philosophy, he substitutes in their place such as are immediately derived from the testimony of the senses, even heat and cold, from which, like Parmenides, he deduces the nature, origin, qualities, and changes, of all material beings. To these two principles he adds a third, namely, matter; and on these three he builds with some dexterity his physical system, for a part of which he seems also to have been indebted to a book of Plutarch, De Primo Frigido. It will be entertaining to the philosophical reader, to compare this work of Telesius with lord Bacon's physical account of the story of Cupid and Cœlus, in his book de Principiis et Originibus, &c.

☞ ‡ Campanella, a native of Calabria, made a great noise in the seventeenth century, by his innovations in philosophy. Shocked at the atheism and absurdities of the Aristotelian system, he early acquired a contempt of it, and turned his pursuits toward something more solid, perusing the writings of all the ancient sages, and comparing them with the great volume of nature, to see whether the pretended copies resembled the original. The sufferings that this man endured are almost incredible; but they were said to be inflicted on him in consequence of the treasonable practices which were imputed to him, partly against the court of Spain, and partly against the kingdom of Naples, which (it was supposed) he had formed the design of delivering into the hands of the Turks. He was freed from his prison and tortures by the interposition of pope Urban VIII., who gave him particular marks of his favour and esteem, and, finding that he was not safe at Rome, had him conveyed to Paris, where he was honoured with the protection of Louis XIII. and cardinal Richelieu, and ended his days in peace. As to the writings and philosophy of this great man, they are tinged, indeed, with the colour of the times, and bear, in many places, the marks of a chimerical and undisciplined imagination; but, among a few visionary notions, they contain a great number of important truths. He undertook an entire reformation of philosophy, but was unequal to the task. For an account of his principles of logic, ethics, and natural philosophy, see Brucker's Hist. Critica Philosophiæ, tom. iv. He was accused of atheism, but unjustly; he was also accused of suggesting cruel measures against the protestants, and not without reason.

☞ * The principal merit of Paracelsus consisted in inventing, or at least restoring from oblivion and darkness, the important science of chemistry, giving it a regular form, reducing it into a connected system, and applying it most successfully to the art of healing, which was the peculiar profession of this philosopher, whose friends and enemies have drawn him in the falsest colours. His application to the study of magic, of which he treats in the tenth volume of his works, under the denomination of the Sagacious Philosophy, is a circumstance dishonourable to his memory, and nothing can discover a more total absence of common sense and reasoning than his discourses on that subject. As to his philosophical system, it is so obscure, and so contradictory, that we shall not pretend to delineate it here.

† See, for an ample account of the lives, transactions, and systems of these philosophers, Brucker's Historia Critica Philosophiæ

ing the case. Much imperfection yet remained in the method of treating theology; and many things, which had great need of a correcting hand, were left untouched. It would, nevertheless, be either an instance of ingratitude, or a mark of great ignorance, to deny to this age the honour of having begun what was afterwards more happily finished, and of having laid the foundations of that striking superiority, which the divines of succeeding ages obtained over those of ancient times.

X. The improvements, which have been now mentioned, as proceeding from the restoration of letters and philosophy, not only extended to the method of conveying theological instruction, but also purified the science of theology itself. For the true nature, genius, and design of the Christian religion, which even the most learned and pious doctors of antiquity had but imperfectly comprehended, were now unfolded with evidence and precision, and drawn, like truth, from an abyss in which they had hitherto lain concealed. It is true, the influence of error was far from being totally suppressed, and many false and absurd doctrines are still maintained and propagated in the Christian world. But it may nevertheless be affirmed, that the Christian societies, whose errors at this day are the most numerous and extravagant, have much less absurd and perverse notions of the nature and design of the Gospel, and the duties and obligations of its votaries, than were entertained by those doctors of antiquity, who ruled the church with an absolute authority, and were considered as the chief oracles of theology. It may farther be observed, that the reformation contributed much to soften and civilize the manners of many nations, who, before that happy period, were sunk in the most savage stupidity, and carried the most rude and insocial aspect. It must indeed be confessed, that a variety of circumstances, not immediately connected with religion, combined to produce that lenity of character, and that milder temperature of manners, maxims, and actions, which gradually appeared in the greatest part of the European nations, after the period that was signalized by the reformative exertions of Luther. It is nevertheless evident, beyond all contradiction, that the disputes concerning religion, and the accurate and rational inquiries into the doctrines and duties of Christianity to which those disputes gave rise, had a great tendency to eradicate from the minds of men the ferocity that had been so long nourished by the barbarous suggestions of unmanly superstition. It is also certain, that at the very dawn of this happy revolution in the state of Christianity, and even before its salutary effects were manifested in all their extent, pure religion had many sincere and fervent votaries, though they were concealed from public view by the multitudes of fanatics with which they were surrounded.

SECTION III.

THE PARTICULAR HISTORY OF THE CHURCH.

PART I.

THE HISTORY OF THE ANCIENT CHURCHES.

CHAPTER I.

History of the Roman or Latin Church.

I. THE Roman or Latin church is a system of government, whose jurisdiction extends over a great part of the known world, though its authority has been circumscribed within narrower limits since the happy revolution that, in many countries, delivered Christianity from the yoke of superstition and spiritual tyranny. This system of ecclesiastical policy, extensive as it is, is under the direction of the bishop of Rome alone, who, by virtue of a sort of hereditary succession, claims the authority, prerogatives, and rights, of St. Peter, the supposed prince of the apostles, and gives himself out for the supreme head of the universal church, the vicegerent of Christ upon earth. This lordly ruler of the church is, at this time, elected to his high office, by the chosen members of the Roman clergy, who bear the ancient denomination of cardinals. Of these, six are bishops, within the precincts of Rome; fifty are ministers of the Roman churches, and are called priests or presbyters; and fourteen are inspectors of the hospitals and charitable foundations, and are called deacons. These cardinals (while the papal chair is vacant, and they are employed in the choice of a successor to the deceased pontiff) are closely confined in a sort of prison, called the Conclave, that they may thus be induced to bring this difficult matter to a speedy conclusion. No person, except one who is an Italian by descent, and who has already obtained a place in the college of cardinals, is capable of being raised to the supremacy of the church: nor have all the Italian cardinals the privilege of aspiring to this high office.* Some are rendered incapable of filling the papal chair by the place of their birth,

* See J. F. Mayer's Comment. de Electione Pontif. Romani, published at Hamburg in 1691. The ceremonies observed in the election and installation are amply described by Meuschen, in a work published at Frankfort in 1732, under the following title, Ceremoniale Electionis et Coronationis Pontificis Romani

others by the manner of their life, and a few by other reasons.* It is also to be observed, that the emperor and the kings of France and Spain have acquired, either expressly by stipulation, or imperceptibly through custom, the privilege of excluding, from the number of the candidates for this high office, such as they dislike or think proper to oppose. Hence it often happens, that, in the numerous college of cardinals, a very small number are permitted, upon a vacancy, to aspire to the papacy; the greatest part being generally prevented by their birth, their characters, their circumstances, and by the force of political intrigues, from flattering themselves with the pleasing hope of ascending that towering summit of ecclesiastical power and dominion.

II. It must not be imagined that the personal power and authority of the Roman pontiff are circumscribed by no limits, since it is well known, that in all his decisions relating to the government of the church, he previously consults the *brethren*, i. e. the cardinals, who compose his ministry or privy council. In matters of religious controversy and doctrine, he is even obliged to ask the advice and opinion of eminent divines, in order to secure his pretended infallibility from the suggestions of error. Besides this, all affairs that are not of the highest moment and importance, are divided into classes according to their respective nature, and left to the management of certain colleges, called *Congregations*,† in every one of which, one or more cardinals preside.* The decisions of these societies are generally approved by the pontiff, who has not a right, without alleging the most weighty and evident reasons,

☞ * The great obstacle that prevents several cardinals from aspiring to the pontificate, is what they call at Rome, *il peccato originale*, or *original sin*. This mark of exclusion belongs to those who are born subjects of some crown or republic which are beyond the bounds of Italy, or are upon a footing of jealousy with the court of Rome. Those also who were made cardinals by the nomination of the kings of France or Spain, or their adherents, are also included in this imputation of original sin, which excludes from the papal chair. The accidental circumstances that excludes certain cardinals from the pontificate, are their being born princes or independent sovereigns, or their declaring themselves openly in favour of certain courts, or their family's being too numerous, or their morals being irregular. Even youth, and a good complexion and figure, are considered as obstacles. But all these maxims and rules vary and change according to the inconstant and precarious impulse of policy and faction.

For an account of the different methods of electing the pope, whether by compromise, inspiration, scrutiny, or access, (by which last is meant a second election, employed when the other methods fail,) see Aymon's Tableau de la Cour de Rome.

☞ † These congregations are as follow: I. The congregation of the pope, instituted first by Sixtus V. to prepare the matters that were to be brought before the consistory, at which the pontiff is always present. Hence this is called the Consistorial Congregation, and in it are treated all affairs relative to the erection of bishoprics and cathedral churches, the reunion or suppression of episcopal fees, the alienation of church goods, and the taxes and annates that are imposed upon all benefices in the pope's gift. The cardinal dean presides in this assembly. II. The congregation of the inquisition, or (as it is otherwise called) of the Holy Office, instituted by Paul III., which takes cognizance of heresies, apostasy, magic, and profane writings. The office of Grand Inquisitor, which encroached upon the prerogatives of the pontiff, has been long suppressed, or rather distributed among the cardinals who belong to this congregation, and whose decisions come under the supreme cognizance of his holiness. III. The congregation for the propagation of the Roman catholic faith, founded under the pontificate of Gregory XV. composed of eighteen cardinals, one of the secretaries of state, a protonotary, a secretary of the inquisition, and other members of less rank. Here it is that the deliberations are carried on, which relate to the extirpation of heresy, the appointment of missionaries, &c. This congregation has built a most beautiful and magnificent palace in one of the most agreeable situations that could be chosen at Rome where proselytes to popery from foreign countries are lodged and nourished *gratis*, in a manner suitable to their rank and condition, and instructed in those branches of knowledge to which the bent of their genius points. The prelates, curates, and vicars also, who are obliged, without any fault of theirs, to abandon the places of their residence, are entertained charitably in this noble edifice in a manner proportioned to their station in the church. IV. The congregation designed to explain the decisions of the council of Trent. V. The congregation of the Index, whose principal business is to examine manuscripts and books that are designed for publication, to decide whether the people may be permitted to read them, to correct those books whose errors are not numerous, and which contain useful and salutary truths, to condemn those whose principles are heretical and pernicious, and to grant to certain individuals the peculiar privilege of perusing heretical books. This congregation, which is sometimes held in the presence of the pope, but generally in the palace of the cardinal-president, has a more extensive jurisdiction than that of the inquisition, as it not only takes cognizance of books that contain doctrines contrary to the Roman catholic faith, but of those also which concern the duties of morality, the discipline of the church, and the interests of society Its name is derived from the alphabetical tables, or indexes of heretical books and authors, which have been composed by its appointment. VI. The congregation for maintaining the rights and immunities of the clergy, and of the knights of Malta. This congregation was formed by Urban VIII. to decide the disputes, and remove the difficulties and inconveniences that arose from the trials of ecclesiastics, before princes, or other lay-judges. VII. The congregations relating to the bishops and regular clergy, instituted by Sixtus V. to decide the debates which arise between the bishops and their diocesans, and to compose all differences that occur among the monastic orders. VIII. The congregation appointed by Gregory XIV. for examining the capacity and learning of the bishops. IX. Another for inquiring into their lives and morals. X. A third, for obliging them to reside in their dioceses, or to dispense them from that obligation. XI. The congregation for suppressing monasteries, i. e. such whose revenues are exhausted, and who thereby become a charge upon the public. XII. The congregation of the Apostolic Visitation, which names the visitors, who perform the duties and visitations of the churches and convents within the district of Rome. XIII. The congregation of relics, authorized to examine the marks, and to augment the number of these instruments of superstition. XIV. The congregation of indulgences, designed to examine the cases of those who have recourse to this method of quieting the conscience. XV. The congregation of rites, which Sixtus V. appointed to regulate and invent the religious ceremonies that are to be observed in the worship of each new saint that is added to the calendar.

These are the congregations of cardinals, set apart for administering the spiritual affairs of the church; and they are undoubtedly, in some respects, a check upon the power of the pontiff, enormous as it may be. There are six more, which relate to the temporal government of the papal territories. In these congregations, all things are transacted which relate to the execution of public justice in civil or criminal matters, the levying of taxes, the providing of the cities and each of the provinces with good governors, the relieving of those who are unjustly oppressed by subordinate magistrates, the coinage, the care of the rivers, aqueducts, bridges, roads, churches, and public edifices.

* The court of Rome is very particularly and accurately described by Aymon (who had been, before his conversion to the protestant religion, domestic

to reverse what they pronounce to be just and expedient. This form of ecclesiastical government is, doubtless, a check to the authority of the pope; and hence it is, that many things are transacted at Rome in a manner that is in direct opposition to the sentiments of its spiritual ruler. This may serve to show us, that those persons are little acquainted with the nature and limits of the papal hierarchy, who pretend, that all the iniquitous proceedings of the court of Rome, the calamities it has occasioned, the contentions, rebellions, and tumults it has excited, are entirely imputable to the pontiff himself.*

III. The power of the pope hath excited debates even among those who are under the papal hierarchy; and the spiritual subjects of this pretended head of the church, are very far from agreeing with respect to the extent of his authority and jurisdiction. Hence it happens, that this authority and dominion are not the same in all places, having a larger scope in some provinces, and being reduced within narrower bounds in others. If, indeed, we consider only the pretensions of the pontiff, we shall find that his power is unlimited and supreme; for there are no prerogatives that can flatter ambition, which he does not claim for himself and his court. He not only pretends, that the whole power and majesty of the church reside in his person, and are transmitted, in certain portions, from him to the inferior bishops, but moreover asserts the absolute infallibility of all decisions and decrees which he pronounces from his lordly tribunal. These arrogant pretensions are, however, opposed by many, and chiefly by the French, who expressly maintain, that every bishop receives immediately from Christ himself a portion of that spiritual power which is imparted to the church; that the collective sum, or whole of this power, is lodged in the aggregate body of its pastors, or (which is the same thing) in a general council lawfully assembled; and that the pontiff, considered personally, and as distinct from the church, is liable to error. This complicated and important controversy may be easily brought within narrower bounds, and may be reduced to the following plain question;—'Is the Roman pontiff, properly speaking, the Legislator of the church, or, is he no more than the Guardian and Depositary of the laws enacted by Christ and the church?' There is no prospect of seeing this question decided, or the debates terminated to which it has given rise, since the contending parties do not even agree about the proper and lawful judge of this important controversy.* Some great revolution alone can effect the decision of this matter.

IV. The church of Rome lost much of its ancient splendour and majesty, as soon as Luther, and the other luminaries of the reformation, had exhibited to the view of the European nations the Christian religion restored, at least to a considerable part of its native purity, and delivered from many of the superstitions under which it had lain so long disfigured. Among the most opulent states of Europe, several withdrew entirely from the jurisdiction of Rome; in others, certain provinces threw off the yoke of papal tyranny; and, upon the whole, this defection produced a striking diminutión both of the wealth and power of the Roman pontiffs. It must also be observed, that even the kings, princes, and sovereign states, who adhered to the religion of Rome, yet changed their sentiments with respect to the claims and pretensions of its bishop. If they were not persuaded by the writings of the protestants to renounce the superstitions of popery, yet they received most useful instructions from them in other matters of very great moment. They drew from these writings important discoveries of the groundless claims and unlawful usurpations of the Roman pontiffs, and came, at length, to perceive, that, if the jurisdiction and authority of Rome should continue the same as before the rise of Luther, the rights of temporal princes, and the majesty of civil government, would, sooner or later, be absorbed in the gulph of papal avarice and ambition. Hence it was, that most of the sovereign states of Europe, partly by secret and prudent measures, partly by public negociations and remonstrances, set bounds to the daring ambition of Rome, which aimed at nothing less than universal dominion both in ecclesiastical and civil affairs; nor did the pontiff think it either safe or expedient to have recourse to the ancient arms of the church, *war* and *excommunication*, in order to repel these attacks upon his authority. Even those very kingdoms, which acknowledged the Roman pontiff as the lawgiver of the church, and an infallible guide, confined his power of enacting laws within narrow limits.

V. In this declining state of their affairs, it was natural for the humble pontiffs to look about for some method of repairing their losses; and, for this purpose, they exerted much more zeal and industry, than had been shown by their predecessors, in extending the limits of

chaplain to Innocent XI.) in a book entitled Tableau de la Cour de Rome. See also Relation de la Cour de Rome, et des Ceremonies qui s'y observent, which Father Labat translated into French from the Italian of Jerome Limadoro, and subjoined to his Voyages en Espagne et Italie, tom. viii.—For an account of the Roman congregations, &c. see Doroth. Ascian. de Montibus Pietatis Romanis, p. 510, as also Hunold. Plettenberg, Notitia Tribunalium et Congregationum Curiæ Romanæ.

* Hence arises that important distinction, frequently employed by the French and other nations in their debates with the pope; I mean the distinction between his holiness and the court of Rome. The latter is often loaded with the bitterest reproaches and the heaviest accusations, while the former is spared, and in some measure excused. Nor is this distinction by any means groundless, since the cardinals and congregations, whose rights and privileges are deemed sacred, undertake and execute many projects without the knowledge, and sometimes against the will and consent, of the pontiff himself

* The arguments employed by the pontiff's creatures in defence of his unlimited authority, may be seen in the words of Bellarmine and other writers, of which a voluminous collection has been made by Roccaberti; and what is not a little extraordinary, a French writer, named Petitdier, appeared in defence of the pope's pretensions, in a book published at Luxemburg, in 1724, sur l' Autorite et l' Infallibilite des Papes. The sentiments of the Gallican church, and the arguments by which it opposes the pretensions of Rome, may be seen in the writings of Richer and Launoy.

their spiritual dominion beyond Europe, and left no means unemployed of gaining proselytes and adherents in the Indies and in Africa, both among the pagan nations and the Christian sects. The Jesuits, as we have already had occasion to observe, were the first missionaries who were employed for this purpose in those distant parts of the world; but able men, selected from the other monastic orders, were afterwards entrusted with this arduous undertaking. If, however, we except the exploits of Francis Xavier and his companions in India, China, and Japan, of which notice has been already taken, there were no great matters effected in this century; as, generally speaking, the persons who were appointed to execute this grand project, were not endowed with that experience and dexterity which it necessarily required, and entered upon the work with more zeal than prudence and knowledge.

The Portuguese had, in the preceding century, opened a passage into the country of the Abyssinians, who professed the doctrine, and observed the religious rites of the Monophysites; and hence arose a favourable occasion of reducing that people under the papal yoke. Accordingly John Bermudez was sent into Ethiopia for this purpose; and, that he might appear with a certain degree of dignity, he was invested with the title of Patriarch of the Abyssinians. The same important commission was afterwards given to Ignatius Loyola, and the companions of his labours;* and, at the commencement of their undertaking, several circumstances, and particularly a war with a neighbouring prince, which the Abyssinian monarch was desirous of terminating by the powerful succours of the Portuguese, seemed to promise them a successful and happy ministry. But the event did not answer this fond expectation; and, in some time, it appeared plainly, that the Abyssinians stood too firm in the faith of their ancestors, to be easily engaged to abandon and forsake it; so that, toward the conclusion of this century, the Jesuits had almost lost all hopes of succeeding in their attempts.†

VI. The Egyptians, or Copts, who were closely connected with the Abyssinians in their religious sentiments, and also in their external forms of worship, became the next objects of Rome's ambitious zeal; and, in 1562, Christopher Roderic, a Jesuit of note, was sent, by the express order of pope Pius IV., to propagate the cause of popery among that people. This ecclesiastic, notwithstanding the rich presents and ingenious arguments by which he attempted to change the sentiments and shake the constancy of Gabriel,‡ who was at that time patriarch of Alexandria, returned to Rome with no other effect of his embassy, than fair words and a few compliments.* It is, however, true, that, in 1594, during the pontificate of Clement VIII., an envoy from another patriarch of Alexandria, whose name was also Gabriel, appeared at Rome, and this circumstance was considered as a subject of triumph and boasting by the creatures of the pope.† But the more candid and sensible, even among the Roman catholics, looked upon this embassy, and not without reason, as a stratagem of the Jesuits to persuade the Abyssinians (who were so prone to follow the example of their brethren of Alexandria) to join themselves to the communion of Rome, and submit to the authority and jurisdiction of its pontiff.‡ It is at least certain, that we do not subsequently find the smallest token of a propensity in the Copts to embrace the doctrine or discipline of Rome.

Many years before this period, a considerable sect of the Armenians had been accustomed to treat the pope with particular marks of veneration and respect, without departing, however, from the religious doctrine, discipline, or worship of their ancestors. Of this a farther account shall be given in the history of the Eastern Churches: it may, however, be proper to observe here, that the attachment of this sect to the pontiff was greatly increased, and his votaries were considerably multiplied, by the zeal of Serapion, an opulent man, who was entirely devoted to the court of Rome, and who, by engaging himself to discharge the debts under which the Armenians groaned, obtained, in 1593, the title and dignity of Patriarch, though there were already two patriarchs at the head of the Armenian church. He did not, however, long enjoy this dignity; for, soon after his promotion, he was sent into exile by the Persian monarch, at the desire of those Armenians who adhered to the ecclesiastical discipline of their ancestors; and thus the boasting and exultation of the Romans suddenly subsided, and their hopes vanished.§

VII. The ambitious views of the Roman pontiffs sowed the pestilential seeds of animosity and discord among all the eastern churches;

☞* It is certainly by mistake that Dr. Mosheim mentions Loyola as having made a voyage into Abyssinia. Jesuits were sent at different periods to that country, and with little success; but their founder was never there in person.

† See Ludolfi Histor. Ethiopica et Comm.—Geddes, Church History of Ethiopia, p. 120.—Le Grand, Dissertation de la Conversation des Abyssins, which is to be found in the Voyage Historique d'Abyssinie du R. P. Jerome Lobo.—La Croze, Hist. du Christianisme en Ethiopie, liv. ii.

‡ Franc. Sacchini, Histor. Societat. Jesu. pars ii. lib. v.—Euseb. Renaudot, Historia Patriarchar. Alexandrin. p. 611 Hist de la Compagnie de Jesus, tom. iii.

☞* This patriarch offered to send one of his bishops to the council of Trent, in order to get rid of the importunity of these Jesuits; but he positively refused to send any of his young students to be educated among their order, and declared plainly, that he owed no obedience or submission to the bishop of Rome, who had no more dignity or authority than any other prelate, except within the bounds of his own diocese. See Histoire des Religieux de la Compagnie de Jesus, tom. ii.

† The transactions of this embassy, adorned with an ample and pompous preface, are subjoined to the sixth vol. of the Ann. Eccl. of Baronius.

‡ Renaudot, in his Hist. Patriarch. Alexandrin., endeavours to maintain the credit and importance of this mission, of which Baronius has given such a pompous account. He is, however, in an error when he asserts, that father Simon, relying upon the fallacious testimony of George Douza, was the only person who ever considered this embassy as a stratagem, since it is evident, that Thomas a Jesu, a Carmelite, in his treatise de Conversione omnium Gentium procuranda, has considered it in the same light, as well as several other writers. See Geddes, Church History of Ethiopia.

§ See Nouv. Mem. des Mis. de la Com. de Jesus dans le Levant. t. iii.

and the Nestorian Christians, who are also known by the denomination of Chaldeans, felt early the effects of their imperious counsels. In 1551, a warm dispute arose among that people about the creation of a new patriarch, Simeon Barmamas being proposed by one party, and Sulaka earnestly desired by the other. The latter, to support his pretensions the more effectually, repaired to Rome, and was consecrated patriarch, in 1553, by pope Julius III., whose jurisdiction he had acknowledged, and to whose commands he had promised unlimited submission and obedience. Julius gave the name of John to the new Chaldean patriarch, and, upon his return to his own country, sent with him several persons, skilled in the Syriac language, to assist him in establishing and extending the papal empire among the Nestorians. From this time that unhappy people were divided into two factions, and were often involved in the greatest dangers and difficulties by the jarring sentiments and perpetual quarrels of their patriarchs.*

The Nestorians, or as they are more commonly called, the Christians of St. Thomas, who inhabited a part of the coast of India, suffered much from the methods employed by the Portuguese to engage them to embrace the doctrine and discipline of the church of Rome, and to abandon the religion of their ancestors, which was much more simple and infinitely less absurd.† The finishing stroke was put to the violence and brutality of these attempts by don Alexis de Menezes, bishop of Goa, who, about the conclusion of this century, calling the Jesuits to his assistance, obliged this unhappy and reluctant people to embrace the religion of Rome, and to acknowledge the pope's supreme jurisdiction; against both of which acts they had always expressed the utmost abhorrence. These violent counsels and arrogant proceedings of Menezes, and his associates, were condemned by such of the Roman catholics as were most remarkable for their equity and wisdom.‡

VIII. The greatest part of the first legates and missionaries of the court of Rome treated with much severity and injustice the Christians whom they were desirous of gaining over to their communion. For they not only required that these Christians should renounce the particular opinions that separated them from the Greek and Latin churches, and that they should acknowledge the pontiff as Christ's sole vicegerent upon earth: their demands went still farther; they opposed some opinions that were at least worthy of toleration, and others which were highly agreeable to the dictates both of reason and Scripture; they insisted upon the suppression and abolition of several customs, rites, and institutions, which had been handed down from successive ancestors, and which were perfectly innocent in their nature and tendency; in a word, they would be satisfied with nothing less than an entire and minute conformity of the religious rites and opinions of the people, with the doctrine and worship of the church of Rome. The papal court, however, rendered wise by experience, perceived, at length, that this manner of proceeding was highly imprudent, and very unlikely to extend the limits of the papal empire in the East. It was therefore determined to treat with more artifice and moderation a matter of such moment and importance, and the missionaries were, consequently, ordered to change the plan of their operations, and confine their views to the two following points; namely, the subjection of these Christians to the jurisdiction of the pope, and their renouncing, or at least professing to renounce, the opinions that had been condemned in the general councils of the church. In all other matters, the Roman envoys were commanded to allow a perfect toleration, and to let the people remain unmolested in following the sentiments, and observing the institutions, which they had derived from their ancestors. To give the greater credit and plausibility to this new method of conversion, certain learned doctors of the church endeavoured to demonstrate, that the religious tenets of Rome, when explained according to the simplicity of truth, and not by the subtleties and definitions of the schools, differed very little from the opinions received in the Greek and the other eastern churches. But this demonstration was very far from being satisfactory, and it discovered less of an ingenuous spirit, than a disposition to gain proselytes by all sorts of means, and at all events. Be that as it may, the cause of Rome received much more advantage from this plan of moderation, than it had derived from the severity of its former counsels, though much less than the authors of this reconciling plan fondly expected.

IX. While the pontiffs were using their utmost efforts to extend their dominion abroad, they did not neglect the means that were proper to strengthen and maintain it at home. On the contrary, from the dawn of the reformation, they began to redouble their diligence in defending the internal form and constitution of their church against the dexterity and force of its adversaries. They could no more have recourse to the expedient of crusades, by which they had so often diminished the power and influence of their enemies. The revolutions which had happened in the affairs of Rome, and in the state of Europe, rendered any such method of subduing heretics visionary and impracticable. Other methods were, therefore, to be found out, and all the resources of prudence were to be exhausted in support of a declining church. Hence the laws and proceedings of the inquisition were revised and corrected in those countries where that formidable court was permitted to exert its dreadful power. Colleges and schools of learning were erected in various places, in which the studious youth were trained up, by perpetual exercise, in the art of disputing, that thus they might wield, with more dexterity and success, the arms of controversy against the enemies

* Jos. Sim. Assemani, Bib. Orient. Clementino-Vaticana, t. iii. pars ii.

☞ † For an account of the doctrines and worship of these, and the other eastern Christians, see the following chapter; as also two learned books of La Croze; one entitled, Histoire du Christianisme des Indes, and the other, Histoire du Christianisme en Ethiopie.

‡ La Croze, Hist. du Christ. des Indes, liv. i. p. 88.

of Rome. The circulation of such books as were supposed to have a pernicious tendency, was either entirely prevented, or at least much obstructed, by certain lists or indexes, composed by men of learning and sagacity, and published by authority, in which these books were marked with a note of infamy, and their perusal prohibited, though with certain restrictions. The pursuit of knowledge was earnestly recommended to the clergy, and honourable marks of distinction, as well as ample rewards, were bestowed on those who made the most remarkable progress in the cultivation of letters. And, to enlarge no farther on this head, the youth, in general, were more carefully instructed in the principles and precepts of their religion, than they had formerly been. Thus it happens, that signal advantages are frequently derived from what are looked upon as the greatest evils, and much wisdom and improvement are daily acquired in the school of opposition and adversity. It is more than probable, that the church of Rome would never have been enriched with the acquisitions we have now been mentioning, had it continued in that state of uninterrupted ease and undisputed authority, which nourish a spirit of indolence and luxury, and had not the pretended heretics attacked its territories, trampled upon its jurisdiction, and eclipsed a great part of its ancient majesty and splendour.

X. The monastic orders and religious societies have been always considered by the Roman pontiffs as the principal support of their authority and dominion. It is chiefly by them that they rule the church, maintain their influence on the minds of the people, and augment the number of their votaries. And, indeed, various causes contribute to render the connexion between the pontiff and these religious communities much more intimate, than that which subsists between him and the other clergy, of whatever rank or order we may suppose them to be. It was therefore judged necessary, when the success of Luther and the progress of the reformation had effaced such a considerable part of the majesty of Rome, to found some new religious fraternity, that should, in a particular manner, be devoted to the interests of the Roman pontiff, and the very express end of whose institution should be to renew the vigour of a declining hierarchy, to heal the deep wound it had received, to preserve those parts of the papal dominions that remained yet entire, and to augment them by new accessions. This was so much the more necessary, as the two famous *Mendicant* societies,* by whose ministry the popes had chiefly governed, during many ages, with success and glory, had now lost, on several accounts, a considerable part of their influence and authority, and were thereby less capable of serving the church with efficacy and vigour than they had formerly been. What the pontiff sought in this declining state of his affairs, was found in that famous and most powerful society, which, from the name of Jesus, derived the appellation of *Jesuits*, while its members were styled by their enemies *Loyolites* from *Loyola*, and sometimes *Inighists*,* from the Spanish name of their founder.† This zealot was Ignatius Loyola, a Spanish knight, who, from an illiterate soldier, became an unparalleled fanatic; a fanatic, indeed, of a fertile and enterprising genius,‡ who, after having passed through various scenes of life, repaired to Rome, and, being there directed by the prudent counsels of persons much wiser than himself, was rendered capable of instituting such an order as the state of the church at that time essentially required.§

XI. The Jesuits hold a middle rank between the monks and the secular clerks, and, with respect to the nature of their institute, approach nearer to the regular canons than to any other order; for, though they resemble the monks in this, that they live separate from the multitude, and are bound by religious vows, yet they are exempt from stated hours of worship, and other numerous and burthensome services, which lie heavy upon the monastic orders, that they may have more time to employ in the education of youth, in directing the consciences of the faithful, in edifying the church by their pious and learned productions, and in transacting other matters that relate to the prosperity of the papal hierarchy. Their whole order is divided into three classes. The first comprehends the *professed*

☞ * These two orders were the Franciscans and the Dominicans.

☞ * The Spanish name of the founder of this order was Don Inigo de Guipuscoa.

† The writers who have given the most particular and circumstantial accounts of the order of the Jesuits, are enumerated by Christoph. Aug. Salig, in his Historia August. Confessionis, tom. ii. p. 73.

‡ Many Jesuits have written the life of this extraordinary man: but the greatest part of these biographers seem more intent upon advancing the glory of their founder, than solicitous about the truth and fidelity of their relations; and hence the most common events, and the most trivial actions that concern Ignatius, are converted into prodigies and miracles. The history of this enterprising fanatic has been composed with equal truth and ingenuity, though seasoned with a very large portion of wit and pleasantry, by a French writer, who calls himself Hercules Rasiel de Selve.* This work, which is divided into two volumes, is entitled, Histoire de l'admirable Don Inigo de Guipuscoa, Chevalier de la Vierge, et Fondateur de la Monarchie des Inighistes.

§ Not only the Protestants, but also a great number of the more learned and judicious Roman catholics, have unanimously denied, that Ignatius Loyola had either learning sufficient to compose the writings of which he is said to be the author, or genius enough to form the society of which he is considered as the founder. They maintain, on the contrary, that he was no more than a flexible instrument in the hands of able and ingenious men, who made use of his fortitude and fanaticism to answer their purposes; and that persons much more learned than he, were employed to compose the writings which bear his name. See Geddes' Miscellaneous Tracts, vol. iii.—The greatest part of his works are supposed to have proceeded from the pen of his secretary John de Palanco; see La Croze, Histoire du Christianisme en Ethiopie, p. 55, 271. The Benedictines affirm, that his book of Spiritual Exercises is copied from the work of a Spanish Benedictine monk, whose name was Cisneros (see La Vie de M. de la Croze par Jordan;) and the constitutions of the society were probably the work of Lainez and Salmeron, two learned men who were among its first members See Histoire des Religieux de la Compagnie de Jesus tom. i.

☞ * This is a feigned name; the real author was Le Vier, an ingenious bookseller, who lived formerly at the Hague.

members, who live in what are called the professed houses; the second contains the *scholars*, who instruct the youth in the colleges; and to the third belong the *novices*, who live in the houses of probation.* The professed members, beside the three ordinary vows of poverty, chastity, and obedience, common to all the monastic tribes, are obliged to take a fourth, by which they solemnly bind themselves to go without deliberation or delay wherever the pope shall think fit to send them; they are also a kind of Mendicants, being without any fixed subsistence, and living upon the liberality of pious and well-disposed persons. The other Jesuits, and more particularly the scholars, possess large revenues, and are obliged, in case of urgent necessity, to contribute to the support of the professed members. The latter, who are few in number, in comparison with the other classes, are, in general, men of prudence and learning, deeply skilled in the affairs of the world, and dexterous in transacting all kinds of business from long experience, added to their natural penetration and sagacity; in a word, they are the true and perfect Jesuits. The rest have, indeed, the title, but are rather the companions and assistants of the Jesuits, than real members of that mysterious order; and it is only in a very vague and general sense, that the denomination of Jesuits can be applied to them. What is still more remarkable, the secrets of the society are not revealed even to all the professed members. It is only a small number of this class, whom old age has enriched with thorough experience, and whom long trial has declared to be worthy of such an important trust, that are instructed in the mysteries of the order.

XII. The church and court of Rome, since the remarkable period when so many kingdoms and provinces withdrew from their jurisdiction, have derived more influence and support from the labours of this single order than from all their other emissaries and ministers, and all the various exertions of their power and opulence. It was this famous company which, spreading itself with an astonishing rapidity over the greatest part of the habitable world, confirmed the wavering nations in the faith of Rome, restrained the progress of the rising sects, gained over a prodigious number of Pagans in the most barbarous and remote parts of the globe to the profession of popery, and attacked the pretended heretics of all denominations; appearing almost alone in the field of controversy, sustaining with fortitude and resolution the whole burthen of this religious war, and far surpassing the champions of antiquity, both in the subtlety of their reasonings, and the eloquence of their discourses. Nor was this all; for, by the affected softness and complying spirit which reigned in their conversation and manners, by their consummate skill and prudence in civil transactions, by their acquaintance with the arts and sciences, and a variety of other qualities and accomplishments, they insinuated themselves into the peculiar favour and protection of statesmen, persons of the first distinction, and even of crowned heads. Nor did any thing contribute more to give them a general ascendancy, than the cunning and dexterity with which they relaxed and modified their system of morality, accommodating it artfully to the propensities of mankind, and depriving it, on certain occasions, of the severity that rendered it burthensome to the sensual and voluptuous. By this they supplanted, in the palaces of the great, and in the courts of princes, the Dominicans and other rigid doctors, who formerly held there the tribunal of confession and the direction of consciences; and engrossed to themselves an exclusive and irresistible influence in those retreats of royal grandeur, whence issue the counsels that govern mankind.* An order of this nature could not but be highly adapted to promote the interests of the court of Rome; and this, indeed, was its great end, and the leading purpose of which it never lost sight, employing every where its utmost vigilance and art to support the authority of the pontiffs, and to save them from the contempt, of which they must have been naturally apprehensive, in consequence of a revolution that opened the eyes of a great part of mankind.

All these circumstances placed the order of Jesuits in a conspicuous point of light. Their capacity, their influence, and their zeal for the papacy, had a very advantageous retrospect upon themselves, as it swelled the sources of their opulence, and procured to their society an uncommon, and indeed an excessive degree of respect and veneration. But it is also true, that these signal honours and advantages exposed them, at the same time, to the envy of other religious orders; that their enemies multiplied from day to day; and that they were often involved in the greatest perplexities and perils. Monks, courtiers, civil magistrates, public schools, united their efforts to crush this rising fabric of ambition and policy; and a prodigious number of books were published to prove, that nothing could be more detrimental to the interests of religion, and the well-being of society, than the institution of the Jesuits. In France, Poland, and other countries, they were declared public enemies to their country, traitors, and parricides, and were even banished with ignominy.† But the prudence, or rather the craft and artifice, of the disciples of Loyola, calmed this storm of opposition, and, by gentle and imperceptible methods, restored the credit and authority of their order, delivered it from the perils with which it had been threatened,

☞ * Other writers add a fourth class, consisting of the spiritual and temporal coadjutors, who assist the professed members, and perform the same functions, without being bound by any more than the three *simple* vows; though, after a long and approved exercise of their employment, the spiritual coadjutors are admitted to the fourth vow, and thus become *professed* members.

* Before this order was instituted, the Dominicans alone directed the consciences of all the European kings and princes; and it was by the Jesuits that the Dominicans were deprived of a privilege so precious to spiritual ambition. See Peyrat's Antiquites de la Chapelle de France.

† See the Histoire des Religieux de la Compagnie de Jesus, tom. iii. p. 48, &c.—Boulay, Hist. Academ. Paris. tom. vi. p. 559—648—as well as almost all the writers (but more particularly the Jansenists,) who have given accounts of the sixteenth century.

and even put it in a state of defence against the future attempts of its adversaries.*

XIII. The pontiffs of this century, after Alexander VI., were Pius III., Julius II.,† Leo X., Adrian VI., whose characters and transactions have been already noticed; Clement VII., of the house of Medici; Paul III.,‡ of the illustrious family of Farnese, Julius III.,§ whose name was John Maria Giocci; Marcellus II.; Paul IV.,* whose name, before his elevation to the pontificate, was John Peter Caraffa; Pius IV., who was ambitious of being looked upon as a branch of the house of Medici, and who had been known, before his promotion, by the name of John Angelo de Medicis; Pius V., a Dominican, called Michael Ghisleri, a man of an austere and melancholy turn of mind, by which, and other similar qualities, he obtained a place in the calendar; Gregory XIII., who was previously known by the name of Hugo Buoncompagno;† Sixtus V., otherwise named Felix Peretti di Montalto, who, in pride, magnificence, intrepidity, and strength of mind, and in other great virtues and vices, far surpassed all his predecessors' Urban VII., Gregory XIV., Innocent IX., the shortness of whose reigns prevented them from acquiring reputation, or incurring reproach.

Among these pontiffs there were better and worse;‡ but they were all men of decent and even exemplary characters, when compared with the greatest part of those who governed the church before the reformation. For the number of adversaries, both foreign and domestic, that arose to set limits to the despotism of Rome, and to call in question the authority and jurisdiction of its pontiff, rendered the college of cardinals, and the Roman nobility, more cautious and circumspect in the choice of a spiritual ruler; nor did they dare, in these critical circumstances of opposition and danger, to entrust such an important dignity to any ecclesiastic, whose bare-faced licentiousness shameless arrogance, or inconsiderate youth,

* The character and spirit of the Jesuits were admirably described, and their transactions and fate foretold, with a sagacity almost prophetic, so early as the year 1551, in a sermon preached in Christ Church, Dublin, by Dr. George Brown, archbishop of that see; a copy of which was given to Sir James Ware, and may be found in the Harleian Miscellany, vol. v. p. 566. The remarkable passage relating to that order, is as follows: "There are a new fraternity of late sprung up, who call themselves *Jesuits*, which will deceive many, who are much after the Scribes' and Pharisees' manner. Amongst the Jews they shall strive to abolish the truth, and shall come very near to do it. For these sorts will turn themselves into several forms; with the heathens a heathenist, with the atheist an atheist, with the Jews a Jew, with the Reformers a Reformade, purposely to know your intentions, your minds, your hearts, and your inclinations, and thereby bring you at last to be like the fool that said in his heart, 'There was no God.' These shall spread over the whole world, shall be admitted into the councils of princes, and they never the wiser; charming of them, yea, making your princes reveal their hearts and the secrets therein, and yet they not perceive it; which will happen from falling from the law of God, by neglect of fulfilling the law of God, and by winking at their sins; yet, in the end, God, to justify his law, shall suddenly cut off this society, even by the hands of those who have most succoured them, and made use of them; so that, at the end, they shall become odious to all nations. They shall be worse than Jews, having no resting-place upon earth; and then shall a Jew have more favour than a Jesuit."—This singular passage, I had almost said prediction, seems to be accomplished in part, by the present suppression of the Jesuits in France, (I write this note in the year 1762,) and by the great indignation which the perfidious stratagems, iniquitous avarice, and ambitious views of that society, have excited among all orders of the French nation, from the throne to the cottage.

☞ † It was from a foolish ambition of resembling Cæsar, (a very singular model for a Christian pontiff,) that this pope, whose name was Rovere, assumed the denomination of Julius II. It may indeed be said, that Cæsar was sovereign pontiff, (*pontifex maximus*,) and that the bishop of Rome enjoyed the same dignity, though with some change in the title.

‡ The sentiments and character of Paul III. have given rise to much debate, even in our time, especially between the late cardinal Quirini, and Keisling, Schelhorn, and some other writers. The cardinal has used his utmost efforts to defend the probity and merit of this pontiff, while the two learned men above mentioned represent him as a perfidious politician, whose predominant qualities were dissimulation and fraud. See Quirini's work de Gestis Pauli III. Farnesii. ☞ Among the *resgestæ* of Paul III. were two bastards, whose offspring, Farnese and Sforza, were made cardinals in their infancy. See Keislingii Epist. de Gestis Pauli III.—Schelhorn Amœnitates His. Eccles. et Liter. But the licentious exploits of this pope do not end here. He was reproached, in a book published before his death under the name of Ochino, with having poisoned his mother and his nephew, with having ravished a young virgin at Ancona, with an incestuous and adulterous commerce with his daughter Constantia, who died of poison administered by him, to prevent any interruption in his odious amours. It is said, in the same book, that, being caught in bed with his niece, Laura Farnese, who was the wife of Nic. Quercei, he received from this incensed husband a stab of a dagger, of which he bore the marks to his death. See Sleidan's Comment. de Statu Relig. et Reipublicæ, Carolo Quinto Cæsare, lib. xxi.

☞ § This was the worthy pontiff, who was scarcely seated in the papal chair, when he bestowed the cardinal's hat on the keeper of the monkeys, a boy chosen from among the lowest of the populace, and who was also the infamous object of his unnatural pleasures. See Thuan. lib. vi. et xv.—Hoffin. His Eccl. t. v. p. 572—and more especially Sleidan's Histor. lib. xxi.—When Julius was reproached by the cardinals for introducing such an unworthy member into the sacred college, a person who had neither learning, nor virtue, nor merit of any kind, he impudently replied by asking them, "What virtue or merit they had found in him, that could induce them to place him (Julius) in the papal chair?"

☞ * Nothing could exceed the arrogance and ambition of this violent and impetuous pontiff, as appears from his treatment of Queen Elizabeth. See Burnet's History of the Reformation.—It was he who, by a bull, pretended to raise Ireland to the privilege and quality of an independent kingdom; and it was he also who first instituted the Index of prohibited books, mentioned above, in the first note, sect. iii.

† See Jo. Petr. Maffei Annales Gregorii XIII.

‡ Pius V. and Sixtus V. made a much greater figure in the annals of fame, than the other pontiffs here mentioned; the former on account of his excessive severity against heretics, and the famous bull *In Cæna Domini*, which is read publicly at Rome every year on the Festival of the Holy Sacrament; and the latter, in consequence of many services rendered to the church, and numberless attempts, carried on with spirit, fortitude, generosity, and perseverance, to promote its glory, and maintain its authority.—Several modern writers employed their pens in describing the life and actions of Pius V. as soon as they saw him canonised, in 1712, by Clement XI. Of the bull to which we have alluded, and the tumults it occasioned, there is an ample account in Giannone's Historia di Napoli, vol. iv The life of Sixtus V. was written by Gregorio Leti, and the work has been translated into several languages; it is, however, a very indifferent performance, and the relations which it contains are, in many places, inaccurate and unfaithful.

might render him peculiarly obnoxious to reproach, and furnish new matter of censure to their adversaries. It is also worthy of observation, that from this period of opposition, occasioned by the ministry of the Reformers, the pontiffs have never pretended to such an exclusive authority, as they had formerly usurped; nor could they, indeed, make good such pretensions, were they so presumptuous as to avow them. They claim, therefore, no longer a power of deciding, by their single authority, matters of the highest moment and importance; but, for the most part, pronounce according to the sentiments that prevail in the college of cardinals, and in the different congregations, which are entrusted with their respective parts in the government of the church; and they rarely venture to excite serious divisions in foreign states, to arm subjects against their rulers, or to level the thunder of their excommunications at the heads of princes. All such proceedings, which were formerly so frequent at the court of Rome, have been in a great measure suspended, in consequence of the gradual decline of that ignorance and superstition which prescribed a blind obedience to the pontiff, and of the new degrees of power and authority that monarchs and other civil rulers have gained by the revolutions that have shaken the papal throne. In a word, imperious necessity has produced prudence and moderation even at Rome.

XIV. That part of the body of the clergy, which was more peculiarly devoted to the pope, seemed to undergo no change during this century. As to the bishops, it is certain that they made several zealous attempts, and some even in the council of Trent, for the recovery of the ancient rights and privileges, of which they had been forcibly deprived by the pontiffs. They were even persuaded that his holiness might be lawfully obliged to acknowledge, that the episcopal dignity was of divine original, and that the bishops received their authority immediately from Christ himself.* But all these attempts were successfully opposed by the artifice and dexterity of the court of Rome, which did not cease to propagate and enforce this despotic maxim: "That the bishops are no more than the legates or ministers of Christ's vicar; and that the authority which they exercise is entirely derived from the munificence and *favour of the apostolic see*:" a maxim, however, that several bishops, and more especially those of France, treated with little respect. Some advantages, however, and those not inconsiderable, were obtained for the clergy at the expense of the pontiffs; for those *reservations*, *provisions*, *exemptions*, and *expectatives*, (as they are termed by the Roman lawyers,) which before the Reformation had excited such heavy and bitter complaints throughout Europe, and exhibited the clearest proofs of papal avarice and tyranny, were now almost totally suppressed.

XV. Among the subjects of deliberation in the council of Trent, the reformation of the lives and manners of the clergy, and the suppression of the scandalous vices that had too long reigned in that order, were not forgotten; and several wise and prudent laws were enacted with a view to that important object. But those who had the cause of virtue at heart, complained (and the reason of such complaint still subsists) that these laws were no more than feeble precepts, without any avenging arm to maintain their authority; and that they were transgressed, with impunity, by the clergy of all ranks, and particularly by those who filled the highest stations and dignities of the church. In reality, if we cast our eyes upon the Romish clergy, even in the present time, these complaints will appear as well founded now, as they were in the sixteenth century. In Germany, as is notorious to daily observation, the bishops, if we except their habit, their title, and a few ceremonies that distinguish them, have nothing in their manner of living that is, in the least, adapted to point out the nature of their sacred office. In other countries, a great part of the episcopal order, unmolested by the remonstrances or reproofs of the Roman pontiff, pass their days amidst the pleasures and cabals of courts, and appear rather the slaves of temporal princes, than the servants of Him *whose kingdom is not of this world.* They court glory; they aspire after riches, while very few employ their time and labours in edifying the people, or in promoting among them the vital spirit of practical religion and substantial virtue; and (what is still more deplorable) those bishops, who, sensible of the sanctity of their character and the duties of their office, distinguish themselves by their zeal in the cause of virtue and good morals, are frequently exposed to the malicious efforts of envy, often loaded with false accusations, and involved in perplexities of various kinds. It may, indeed, be partly in consequence of the examples they have received, and still too often receive, from the heads of the church, that so many of the bishops live dissolved in the arms of luxury, or toiling in the service of ambition. Many of them, perhaps, would have been more attentive to their vocation, and more exemplary in their manners, if they had not been corrupted by the models exhibited to them by the bishops of Rome, and if they had not constantly before their eyes a splendid succession of popes and cardinals, remarkable only for their luxury and avarice, their arrogance and vindictive spirit, their voluptuousness and vanity.

Those ecclesiastics who go under the denomination of canons, continue, almost every where, their ancient course of life, and consume, in a manner far remote from piety and virtue, the treasures which the religious zeal and liberality of their ancestors had consecrated to the uses of the church and the relief of the poor.

It must not, however, be imagined, that all the other orders of the clergy are at liberty to follow such corrupt models, or, indeed, that their inclinations and reigning habits tend toward such a loose and voluptuous manner of living: for it is certain, that the Reformation had a manifest influence even upon the Roman catholic clergy, by rendering them, at

* See Paolo Sarpi's History of the Council of Trent.

least, more circumspect and cautious in their external conduct, that they might be thus less obnoxious to the censures of their adversaries; and it is accordingly well known, that since that period the clergy of the inferior orders have been more attentive than they formerly were to the rules of outward decency, and have given less offence by open and scandalous vices and excesses.

XVI. The same observation holds good with respect to the monastic orders. There are, indeed, several things, worthy of the severest animadversion, chargeable upon many of the heads and rulers of these societies; nor are these societies themselves entirely exempt from that indolence, intemperance, ignorance, artifice, discord, and voluptuousness, which were formerly the common and reigning vices in the monastic retreats. It would be, nevertheless, an instance of great partiality and injustice to deny, that in many countries the manner of living, among these religious orders, has been considerably reformed, severe rules have been employed to restrain licentiousness, and much pains taken to conceal, at least, such vestiges of ancient corruption and irregularity as may yet remain. In some places, the austerity of the ancient rules of discipline, which had been so shamefully relaxed, was restored by several zealous patrons of monastic devotion; while others, animated with the same zeal, instituted new communities, in order to promote, as they piously imagined, a spirit of religion, and thus to contribute to the well-being of the church.

Of this latter number was Matthew de Bassi, a native of Italy, the extent of whose capacity was much inferior to the goodness of his intentions. He was a Franciscan of the rigid class,* one of those who were zealous in observing rigorously the primitive rules of their institution. This honest enthusiast seriously persuaded himself, that he was divinely inspired with the zeal which impelled him to restore the rules of the Franciscan order to their primitive austerity; and, looking upon this violent and irresistible impulse as a celestial commission, attended with sufficient authority, he commenced this work of monastic reformation with the most devout assiduity and ardour.† His enterprise was honoured, in 1525, with the solemn approbation of Clement VII.; and this was the origin of the order of *Capuchins*. The vows of this order implied the greatest contempt of the world and its enjoyments, and the most profound humility, accompanied with the most austere and sullen gravity of external aspect;‡ and its reputation and success excited, in the other Franciscans, the most bitter feelings of indignation and envy.* The Capuchins were so called from the sharp-pointed *capuche*, or cowl,† which they added to the ordinary Franciscan habit, and which is supposed to have been used by St. Francis himself.‡

Another branch of the Franciscan order formed a new community, under the denomination of Recollets in France, Reformed Franciscans in Italy, and Barefooted Franciscans in Spain; these were erected into a separate order, with their respective laws and rules of discipline, in 1532, by the authority of Clement VII. They differed from the other Franciscans in this only, that they professed to follow, with greater zeal and exactness, the austere institute of their common founder and chief; whence they were sometimes called Friars Minors of the strict observance.§

St. Theresa, a Spanish lady of an illustrious family, undertook the difficult task of reforming the Carmelite order,‖ which had departed much from its primitive sanctity, and of restoring its neglected and violated laws to their original credit and authority. Her associate, in this arduous attempt, was Juan de Santa-Cruz; and her enterprise was not wholly unsuccessful, although the greater part of the Carmelites opposed her aims. Hence the order was, during a period of ten years, divided into two branches, of which one followed a milder rule of discipline, while the other embraced an institute of the most severe and self-denying kind.¶ But, as these different rules of life among the members of the same community were a perpetual source of animosity and discord, the more austere, or bare-footed Carmelites, were separated from the others, and formed into a distinct body, in 1580, by Gregory XIII. at the particular desire of Philip II. king of Spain. This separation was confirmed, in 1587, by Sixtus V. and completed, in 1593, by Clement VIII. who allowed the bare-footed Carmelites to have their own chief, or general. But, after having withdrawn themselves from the others, these austere friars quarrelled among themselves, and in a few years their dissensions

☞* The dispute that arose among the Franciscans by Innocent the Fourth's relaxing so far their institute as to allow property and possessions in their community, produced a division of the order into two classes, of which the more considerable, who adopted the papal relaxation, were denominated Conventuals, and the other, who rejected it, Brethren of the Observance. The latter professed to observe and follow rigorously the primitive laws and institute of their founder.

☞† The Brethren of the Observance, mentioned in the preceding note, had degenerated, in process of time, from their primitive self-denial; and hence arose the reforming spirit that animated Bassi.

‡ See Luc. Waddingi Annales Ordinis Minorum, tom. xvi.—Helyot, Histoire des Ordres Monastiques, tom. vii. ch. xxiv. and, above all, Zach. Boverii Annales Capucinorum.

☞* One of the circumstances that exasperated most the Franciscans, was the innovation made in their habit by the Capuchins. Whatever was the cause of their choler, true it is, that their provincial persecuted the new monks, and obliged them to fly from place to place, until they at last took refuge in the palace of the duke of Camerino, by whose credit they were received under the obedience of the Conventuals, in the quality of hermits minors, in 1527 The next year the pope approved this union, and confirmed to them the privilege of wearing the square capuche; and thus the order was established in 1528.

☞† I know not on what authority the learned Michael Geddes attributes the erection and denomination of this order to one Francis Puchine.

‡ See Du Fresne, Glossarium Latinitat. Medii Ævi, tom. ii.

§ See the Annales of Wadding, tom. xvi.—Helyot Histoire des Ordres Monast. tom. vii. ch. xviii.

‖ Otherwise called the White-Friars.

☞¶ The former, who were the Carmelites of the ancient observance, were called the moderate or mitigated, while the latter, who were of the strict observance, were distinguished by the denomination of bare-footed Carmelites.

grew to an intolerable height: hence they were divided anew, by the last mentioned pontiff, into two communities, each of which had its governor or general.*

XVII. Of all the new orders instituted in this century, the most eminent, beyond all doubt, was that of the Jesuits, which we have already had occasion to mention, in speaking of the chief pillars of the church of Rome, and the principal supports of the declining authority of its pontiffs. Compared with this aspiring and formidable society, all the other religious orders appear inconsiderable and obscure. The Reformation, among the other changes which it occasioned, even in the Romish church, by exciting the circumspection and emulation of those who still remained addicted to popery, gave rise to various communities, which were all comprehended under the general denomination of Regular Clerks; and as all these communities were, according to their own solemn declarations, formed with a design of imitating that sanctity of manners, and reviving that spirit of piety and virtue, which had distinguished the sacred order in the primitive times, this was a plain, though tacit confession of the present corruption of the clergy, and consequently of the indispensable necessity of the reformation.

The first society of these regular clerks arose in 1524, under the denomination of *Theatins*, which they derived from their principal founder John Peter Caraffa, (then bishop of Theate, or Chieti, in the kingdom of Naples, and afterwards pope, under the title of Paul IV.,) who was assisted in this pious undertaking by Caietan, or Gaetan, and other devout associates. These monks, being by their vows destitute of all possessions and revenues, and even precluded from the resource of begging, subsist entirely upon the voluntary liberality of pious persons. They are called by their profession and institute to revive a spirit of devotion, to purify and reform the eloquence of the pulpit, to assist the sick and the dying by their spiritual instructions and counsels, and to combat heretics of all denominations with zeal and assiduity.† There are also some female convents established under the rule and title of this order.

This establishment was followed by that of the *Regular Clerks of St. Paul*, so called from their having chosen that apostle for their patron; though they are more commonly known under the denomination of *Barnabites*, from the church of St. Barnabas, at Milan, which was bestowed upon them in 1545. This order, which was approved in 1532 by Clement VII., and confirmed about three years after by Paul III., was originally founded by Antonio Mavia Zacharias of Cremona, and Bartholomew Ferrari, and Ant. Morigia, noblemen of Milan. Its members were at first obliged to live after the manner of the Theatins, renouncing all worldly goods and possessions, and depending upon the spontaneous donations of the liberal for their daily subsistence. But they soon became weary of this precarious method of living from hand to mouth, and therefore took the liberty, in process of time, of securing to their community certain possessions and stated revenues. Their principal function is to go from place to place, like the apostles, in order to convert sinners, and bring back transgressors into the paths of repentance and obedience.*

The Regular Clerks of St. Maieul, who are also called the fathers of Somasquo, from the place where their community was first established, and which was also the residence of their founder, were erected into a distinct society by Jerome Æmiliani, a noble Venetian, and were afterwards successively confirmed, in the years 1540 and 1543, by the Roman pontiffs Paul III. and Pius IV.† Their chief occupation was to instruct the ignorant, and particularly young persons, in the principles and precepts of the Christian religion, and to procure assistance for those who were reduced to the unhappy condition of orphans. The same important ministry was committed to the Fathers of the Christian doctrine in France and Italy. The order that bore this title in France was instituted by Cæsar de Bus, and confirmed in 1597 by Clement VIII., while that which is known in Italy under the same denomination, derived its origin from Mark Cusani, a Milanese knight, and was established by the approbation and authority of Pius V. and Gregory XIII.

XVIII. It would be an endless, and, indeed, an unprofitable labour to enumerate particularly the prodigious multitude of less considerable orders and religious associations, that were instituted in Germany and other countries, from an apprehension of the pretended heretics, who disturbed by their innovations the peace, or rather the lethargy, of the church; for certainly no age produced such a swarm of monks, and such a number of convents, as that in which Luther and other reformers opposed the divine light and power of the Gospel to ignorance, superstition, and papal tyranny. We therefore pass over in silence these less important establishments, of which many have been long buried in oblivion, because they were erected on unstable foundations, while numbers were suppressed by the wisdom of certain pontiffs, who considered the multitude of these communities rather as prejudicial than advantageous to the church. Nor can we take particular notice of the female convents, or nunneries, among which the Ursulines shone forth with a superior lustre both in point of number and dignity.—The *Priests of the Oratory*, founded in Italy by Philip Neri, a native of Florence, and publicly honoured with the protection of Gregory XIII. in 1577, must, however, be excepted from this general silence, on account of the eminent figure they made in the republic of letters. It was this community that produced Baronius, Raynaldus, and

* Helyot, Histoire des Ordres, tom. i. ch. xlvii. p. 340.

† Helyot, tom. iv. ch. xii.

* Helvot, tom. iv. ch. xvi. p. 100.—In the same volume of his incomparable history, this learned author gives a most accurate, ample, and interesting account of the other religious orders, which are here, for the sake of brevity, barely mentioned.

† Acta San[illegible] or. Februar. tom. ii. p. 217.

Ladurchius, who hold so high a rank among the ecclesiastical historians of the sixteenth and following centuries; and there are still to be found in it men of considerable erudition and capacity. The name of this religious society was derived from an apartment, accommodated in the form of an *Oratory*,* or cabinet for devotion, which St. Philip Neri built at Florence for himself, and in which, for many years, he held spiritual conferences with his more intimate companions.†

XIX. It is too evident to admit the least dispute, that all kinds of erudition, whether sacred or profane, were held in much higher esteem in the western world since the time of Luther, than they had been before that auspicious period. The Jesuits, more especially, boast, and perhaps not without reason, that their society contributed more, at least in this century, to the culture of the languages, the improvement of the arts, and the advancement of true science, than all the rest of the religious orders. It is certain that the directors of schools and academies, either through indolence or design, persisted obstinately in their ancient method of teaching, though that method was intricate and disagreeable in many respects; nor would they suffer themselves to be better informed, or permit the least change in their uncouth and disgusting systems. The monks were not more remarkable than the academic teachers for their compliance with the growing taste for polished literature, nor did they seem at all disposed to admit, into the retreats of their gloomy cloisters, a more solid and elegant method of instruction than they had been formerly accustomed to. These facts furnish a rational account of the surprising variety that appears in the style and manner of the writers of this age, of whom several express their sentiments with elegance, perspicuity, and order, while the diction and style of a great number of their contemporaries are barbarous, perplexed, obscure, and insipid

Cæsar Baronius, already mentioned, undertook to throw light on the history of religion by his annals of the Christian church; but this pretended light was scarcely any thing better than perplexity and darkness.‡ His example, however, excited many to enterprises of the same nature. The attempts of the persons whom the Romanists called heretics, rendered indeed such enterprises necessary: for these heretics, with the learned Flacius and Chemnitz at their head,* demonstrated with the utmost evidence, that not only the declarations of Scripture, but also the testimony of ancient history and the records of the primitive church, were in direct opposition both to the doctrines and pretensions of the church of Rome. This was wounding popery with its own arms, and attacking it in its pretended strong-holds. It was, therefore, incumbent upon the friends of Rome to employ, while it was time, their most zealous efforts in maintaining the credit of those ancient fables, on which the greatest part of the papal authority reposed, as its only foundation and support.

XX. Several men of genius in France and Italy, who have been already mentioned with the esteem that is due to their valuable labours,† used their most zealous endeavours to reform the barbarous philosophy of the times. But the excessive attachment of the scholastic doctors to the Aristotelian philosophy on one hand, and, on the other, the timorous prudence of many weak-minded persons, who were apprehensive that the liberty of striking out new discoveries and ways of thinking might be prejudicial to the church, and open a new source of division and discord, crushed all these generous efforts. The throne of the Stagirite, remained therefore unshaken; and his philosophy, whose very obscurity afforded a certain gloomy kind of pleasure, and flattered the pride of such as were implicitly supposed to understand it, reigned unrivalled in the schools and monasteries. It even acquired new credit and authority from the Jesuits, who taught it in their colleges, and made use of it in their writings and disputes. By this, however, these artful ecclesiastics showed evidently, that the captious jargon and subtleties of that intricate philosophy were much more adapted to puzzle heretics, and to give the popish doctors at least the appearance of carrying on the controversy with success, than the plain and obvious method of disputing, which is pointed out by the genuine dictates of right reason.

XXI. The church of Rome produced in this century, a prodigious number of theological writers. The most eminent of these, in point of reputation and merit, were the following: Thomas de Vio, otherwise named cardinal Caietan, Eckius, Cochlæus, Emser, Surius, Hosius, Faber, Sadolet, Pighius, Vatable, Canus, D'Esperce, Caranza, Maldonatus, Turrianus, Arias Montanus, Catharinus, Reginald Pole, Sixtus Senensis, Cassander, Paya d'Andrada, Baius, Pamelius, and others.‡

XXII. The religion of Rome, which the pontiffs are so desirous of imposing upon the faith of all that bear the Christian name, is derived, according to the unanimous accounts of its doctors, from two sources, the written word of God, and the unwritten; or, in other words, from Scripture and tradition. But, as the most eminent divines of that church are

* Helyot, tom. viii. ch. iv. p 12.

☞ † He was peculiarly assisted in these conferences by Baronius, author of the Ecclesiastical Annals, who also succeeded him as general of the order, and whose annals, on account of his imperfect knowledge of the Greek language, are remarkably full of gross faults, misrepresentations, and blunders.

☞ ‡ The learned Isaac Casaubon undertook a refutation of the Annals of Baronius, in an excellent work, entitled, Exercitationes, &c. and though he carried it no farther down than the 34th year of the Christian æra, yet he pointed out a prodigious number of palpable, and (many of them) shameful errors, into which the Romish annalist has fallen during that short space. Even the Roman catholic *literati* acknowledge the inaccuracies and faults of Baronius; hence many learned men, such as Pagi, Noris, and Tillemont, employed themselves in the task of correction; and accordingly a new edition of the work, with their emendations, appeared at Lucca.

* The former in the Centuriæ Magdeburgenses; the latter in his Examen Concilii Tridentini.

† See above, Sect. II.

‡ For an ample account of the literary characters, rank, and writings of these learned men, and of several others whose names are here omitted, see Louis El. Du-Pin, Bibliotheque des Auteurs Ecclesiastiques, tom. xiv. and xvi.

far from being agreed concerning the persons who are authorized to interpret the declarations of these two oracles, and to determine their sense; so it may be asserted, with truth, that there is, as yet, no possibility of knowing with certainty what are the real doctrines of the church of Rome, or where, in that communion, the judge of religious controversy is to be found. It is true, the court of Rome, and all who favour the despotic pretensions of its pontiff, maintain, that he alone, who governs the church as Christ's vicegerent, is authorized to explain and determine the sense of Scripture and tradition in matters pertaining to salvation, and that, in consequence, a devout and unlimited obedience is due to his decisions. To give weight to this opinion, Pius IV. formed the plan of a council, which was afterwards instituted and confirmed by Sixtus V., and called the Congregation for interpreting the decrees of the Council of Trent. This congregation was authorized to examine and decide, in the name of the pope, all matters of small moment relating to ecclesiastical discipline, while every debate of importance, and particularly all disquisitions concerning points of faith and doctrine, were left to the decision of the pontiff alone, as the great oracle of the church.* Notwithstanding all this, it was impossible to persuade the wiser part of the Roman catholic body to acknowledge this exclusive authority in their head. And accordingly, the greatest part of the Gallican church, and a considerable number of very learned men of the popish religion in other countries, think very differently from the court of Rome on this subject. They maintain, that all bishops and doctors have a right to consult the sacred fountains of Scripture and tradition, and to draw thence the rules of faith and manners for themselves and their flock; and that all difficult points and debates of consequence are to be referred to the cognizance and decision of general councils. Such is the difference of opinion (with respect to the adjustment of doctrine and controversy) that still divides the church of Rome; and, as no judge has been (and perhaps none can be) found to compose it, we may reasonably despair of seeing the religion of Rome acquire a permanent, stable, and determinate form.

XXIII. The council of Trent was assembled, as was pretended, to correct, illustrate, and fix with perspicuity, the doctrine of the church, to restore the vigour of its discipline, and to reform the lives of its ministers. But, in the opinion of those who examine things with impartiality, this assembly, instead of reforming ancient abuses, rather gave rise to new enormities; and many transactions of this council have excited the just complaints of the wisest men in both communions. They complain that many of the opinions of the scholastic doctors on intricate points (that had formerly been left undecided, and had been wisely permitted as subjects of free debate) were, by this council, absurdly adopted as articles of faith, were recommended as such, and even imposed with violence upon the consciences of the people, under pain of excommunication. They complain of the ambiguity that prevails in the decrees and declarations of that council, by which the disputes and dissensions that had formerly rent the church, instead of being removed by clear definitions and wise and temperate decisions, were rendered, on the contrary, more perplexed and intricate, and were, in reality, propagated and multiplied, instead of being suppressed or diminished. Nor were these the only reasons of complaint; for it must have been afflicting to those who had the cause of true religion and Christian liberty at heart, to see all things decided, in that assembly, according to the despotic will of the pope, without any regard to the dictates of truth, or the authority of Scripture, its genuine and authentic source, and to see the assembled fathers reduced to silence by the arrogance of the Roman legates, and deprived of that influence and credit which might have rendered them capable of healing the wounds of the church. It was moreover a grievance justly to be complained of, that the few wise and pious regulations that were made in that council, were never supported by the authority of the church, but were suffered to degenerate into a mere lifeless form, or shadow of law, which was treated with indifference, and transgressed with impunity. To sum up all in one short sentence, the most candid and impartial observers of things consider the council of Trent as an assembly that was more attentive to what might maintain the despotic authority of the pontiff, than solicitous about entering into the measures that were necessary to promote the good of the church. It will not, therefore, appear surprising, that certain doctors of the Romish church, instead of submitting to the decisions of the council of Trent, as an ultimate rule of faith, maintain, that these decisions are to be explained by the dictates of Scripture and the language of tradition; nor, when all these things are duly considered, shall we have reason to wonder, that this council has not throughout the same degree of credit and authority, even in those countries which profess the Roman catholic religion.*

Some countries, indeed, such as Germany, Poland, and Italy, have adopted implicitly and absolutely the decrees of this assembly, without the smallest restriction of any kind. But in other regions it has been received and acknowledged on certain conditions, which modify not a little its pretended authority. Among the latter we may reckon the Spanish dominions, which disputed, during many years, the authority of this council, and acknowledged it at length only so far as it could be adopted without any prejudice to the rights and prerogatives of the king of Spain.† In

* See Aymon, Tableau de la Cour de Rome, part v. chap. iv. ☞ Hence it was, that the approbation of Innocent XI. was refused to the artful and insidious work of Bossuet, bishop of Meaux, entitled, 'An Exposition of the Doctrine of the Catholic Church,' until the author had suppressed the first edition of that work, and made corrections and alterations in the second.

☞ * The translator has here inserted in the text the note [h] of the original, and has thrown the citations it contains into different notes.

† See Giannone, Historia di Napoli, vol. iv

other countries, such as France* and Hungary,† it never has been solemnly received, or publicly acknowledged. It is true, indeed, that, in the former of these kingdoms, such decrees of Trent as relate to points of religious doctrine, have, tacitly and imperceptibly, through the power of custom, acquired the force and authority of rules of faith; but those which regard external discipline, spiritual power, and ecclesiastical government, have been constantly rejected, both in a public and private manner, as inconsistent with the authority and prerogatives of the throne, and prejudicial to the rights and liberties of the Gallican church.‡

XXIV. Notwithstanding all this, such as are desirous of forming some notion of the religion of Rome, will do well to consult the decrees of the council of Trent, together with the compendious confession of faith, which was drawn up by the order of Pius IV. Those, however, who expect to derive, from these sources, a clear, complete, and perfect knowledge of the Romish faith, will be greatly disappointed. To evince the truth of this assertion, it might be observed, as has been already hinted, that both in the decrees of Trent, and in this papal confession, many things are expressed, *designedly*, in a vague and ambiguous manner, on account of the intestine divisions and warm debates that then reigned in the church. Another singular circumstance might also be added, that several tenets are omitted in both, which no Roman catholic is allowed to deny, or even to call in question. But, waving both these considerations, let it only be observed, that in these decrees and in this confession several doctrines and rules of worship are inculcated in a much more rational and decent manner, than that in which they appear in the daily service of the church, and in the public practice of its members.§ Hence we may conclude, that the justest notion of the doctrine of Rome is not to be derived so much from the *terms* used in the decrees of that council, as from the *real signification* of these terms, which must be drawn from the customs, institutions, and observances, that prevail in the Romish church. Add, to all this, another consideration, which is, that, in the bulls issued out from the papal throne in these latter times, certain doctrines which were obscurely proposed in the council of Trent, have been explained with sufficient perspicuity, and avowed without either hesitation or reserve. Of this Clement XI. gave a notorious example, in the famous bull called Unigenitus, which was an enterprise as audacious it proved unsuccessful.

XXV. As soon as the popes perceived the remarkable detriment which their authority had suffered from the accurate interpretations of the Scriptures that had been given by the learned, and from the perusal of these divine oracles, which were now very frequently consulted by the people, they left no methods unemployed that might discourage the culture of this most important branch of sacred erudition. While the tide of resentment ran high, they forgot themselves in a most unaccountable manner. They permitted their champions to indulge themselves openly in reflections injurious to the indignity of the sacred writings, and by an excess of blasphemy almost incredible (if the passions of men did not render them capable of the greatest enormities) to declare publicly, that the edicts of the pontiffs, and the records of oral tradition, were superior, in point of authority, to the express language of the Scriptures. As it was impossible, however, to bring the sacred writings wholly into disrepute, they took the most effectual methods in their power to render them obscure and useless. For this purpose the ancient Latin translation of the Bible, commonly called the Vulgate, though it abounds with innumerable gross errors, and, in a great number of places, exhibits the most shocking barbarity of style, and the most impenetrable obscurity with respect to the sense of the inspired writers, was declared, by a solemn decree of the council of Trent, an authentic, i. e. a faithful, accurate, and perfect* translation, and was consequently recommended as a production beyond the reach of criticism or censure. It was easy to foresee that such a declaration was calculated only to keep the people in ignorance, and to veil from their understandings the true meaning of the sacred writings. In the same council, farther steps were taken to execute, with suc-

* See Hect. Godofr. Masii Diss. de Contemptu Concilii Tridentini in Gallia; and also the excellent discourse which Dr. Courayer has annexed to his French translation of Father Paul's History of the Council of Trent.

† See Lorand. Samuelof, Vita Andr. Dudithii.

‡ See Du-Pin, Biblioth. des Auteurs Ecclesiastiques, tom. xv. p. 380.

☞ For what relates to the literary history of the council of Trent, to the historians who have transmitted accounts of it, and other circumstances of that nature, see Jo. Chr Kocheri Bibliotheca Theol. Symbolicæ, and Salig's History of the Council of Trent, in German.

☞ § This is true, in a more especial manner, with respect to the canons of the council of Trent, relating to the doctrine of purgatory, the invocation of saints, the worship of images and relics. The terms employed in these canons are artfully chosen, so as to avoid the imputation of idolatry, in the philosophical sense of that word; for, in the scriptural sense, they cannot avoid it, as all use of images in religious worship is expressly forbidden in various parts of the sacred writings. But this circumspection does not appear in the worship of the Roman Catholics, which is notoriously idolatrous in both senses of that word.

☞ * If we consult the canons of the council of Trent we shall find that the word *authentic* is there explained in terms less positive and offensive than those used by Dr. Mosheim. Nor is it strictly true, that the Vulgate was declared by this council to be a production beyond the reach of criticism or censure, since, as we learn from Fra. Paolo, it was determined that this version should be corrected, and a new edition of it published by persons appointed for that purpose.* There was, indeed, something highly ridiculous in the proceedings of the council in relation to this point; for, if the natural order of things had been observed, the revisal and correction of the Vulgate would have preceded the pompous approbation with which the council honoured, and, as it were, consecrated that ancient version. For how, with any shadow of good sense, could the assembled fathers set the seal of their approbation to a work which they acknowledged to stand in need of correction, and that before they knew whether or not the correction would answer their views, and merit their approbation?

* See Father Paul's History of the Council of Trent, book ii. part liii. and Dr. Courayer's French translation of this History, vol. i. p. 284, note 29.

cess, the designs of Rome. A severe and intolerable law was enacted, with respect to all interpreters and expositors of the Scriptures, by which they were forbidden to explain the sense of these divine books, in matters relating to faith and practice, in such a manner as to make them speak a different language from that of the church and the ancient doctors.* The same law farther declared, that the church alone (i. e. its ruler) had the right of determining the true meaning and signification of Scripture. To fill up the measure of these tyrannical and iniquitous proceedings, the church persisted obstinately in affirming, though not always with the same impudence and plainness of speech, that the Scriptures were not composed for the use of the multitude, but only for that of their spiritual teachers; and, in consequence, ordered these divine records to be taken from the people in all places where it was allowed to execute its imperious demands.†

XXVI. These circumstances had a visible influence upon the spirit and productions of the commentators and expositors of Scripture, which the example of Luther and his followers had rendered, through emulation, extremely numerous. The popish doctors, who vied with the protestants in this branch of sacred erudition, were insipid, timorous, servilely attached to the glory and interests of the court of Rome, and betrayed, in their explications, all the marks of slavish dependence and constraint. They seem to have been in constant apprehension that some expressions might escape from their pens that savoured of opinions different from what were commonly received; they appeal every moment to the declarations and authority of the holy *fathers*, as they usually styled them; nor do they appear to have so much consulted the real doctrines taught by the sacred writers, as the language and sentiments which the church of Rome has taken the liberty to put into their mouths. Several of these commentators rack their imaginations in order to force out of each passage of Scripture the four kinds of significations, called *Literal*, *Allegorical*, *Topological*, and *Anagogical*, which ignorance and superstition had first invented, and afterwards held so sacred, in the explication of the inspired writings. Nor was their attachment to this manner of interpretation unskilfully managed, since it enabled them to make the sacred writers speak the language that was favourable to the views of the church, and to draw out of the Bible, with the help of a little subtlety, whatever doctrine they wished to impose upon the credulity of the multitude.

It must, however, be acknowledged, that, beside these miserable commentators whose efforts dishonour the church, there were some in its communion, who had wisdom enough to despise such senseless methods of interpretation, and who, avoiding all mysterious significations and fancies, followed the plain, natural, and literal sense of the expressions used in the holy Scriptures. In this class the most eminent were, Erasmus of Rotterdam, who translated into Latin, with an elegant and faithful simplicity, the books of the New Testament, and explained them with judgment in a paraphrase which is deservedly esteemed; cardinal Caietan, who disputed with Luther at Augsburg, and who gave a brief, but judicious exposition of almost all the books of the Old and New Testament; Francis Titelman, Isidorus Clarius, and John Maldonat, beside Benedict Justinian, who acquired no mean reputation by his commentaries on the Epistles of St. Paul. To these may be added Gagny, D'Espence, and other expositors.* But these eminent men, whose example was so adapted to excite emulation, had very few followers; and, in a short time, their influence was gone, and their labours were forgotten; for, toward the conclusion of this century, Edmund Richer, that strenuous opposer of the encroachments made by the pontiffs on the liberties of the Gallican church, was the only doctor in the university of Paris who followed the literal sense and the plain and natural signification of the words of Scripture, while all the other commentators and interpreters, imitating the pernicious example of several ancient expositors, were always racking their brains for mysterious and sublime significations, where none such either were, or could be, designed by the sacred writers.†

XXVII. The seminaries of learning were filled, before the Reformation, with that subtle kind of theological doctors, commonly known under the denomination of *schoolmen;* so that even at Paris, which was considered as the principal seat of sacred erudition, no doctors were to be found who were capable of disputing with the protestant divines in the method they generally pursued, which was that of proving the doctrines they maintained by arguments drawn from the Scriptures and the writings of the fathers. This uncommon scarcity of didactic and scriptural divines produced much confusion and perplexity, on many occasions, even in the council of Trent, where the scholastic doctors fatigued some, and almost turned the heads of others, by examining and explaining the doctrines that were there proposed, according to the intricate and ambiguous rules of their captious philosophy. Hence it became absolutely necessary to reform the methods of proceeding in theological disquisitions, and to restore to its former credit that practice which drew the truths of religion more from the dictates of the sacred writings, and from the sentiments of the ancient doctors, than from the uncertain suggestions of human reason, and the ingenious conjectures of philosophy.‡ It was, however, impossible to deprive

☞ * It is remarkable, that this prohibition extends even to such interpretations as were not designed for public view: "Etiamsi hujusmodi interpretationes nullo unquam tempore in lucem edendæ forent." Sessio 4ta. tit. cap. ii.

† The papal emissaries were not suffered to execute this despotic order in all countries that acknowledged the jurisdiction of the church of Rome. The French and some other nations have the Bible in their mother-tongue, in which they peruse it, though much against the will of the pope's creatures.

* See Simon's Hist. Critique du Vieux et du Nouv. Testament.

† See Baillet's Vie d'Edmund Richer, p. 9. 10

‡ See Du-Boulay's account of the reformation of

entirely the scholastic divines of the ascendancy which they had acquired in the seminaries of learning, and had so long maintained almost without opposition; for, after having been threatened with a diminution of their authority, they seemed to resume new vigour from the time that the Jesuits adopted their philosophy, and made use of their subtle dialectic, as a more effectual armour against the attacks of the heretics, than either the language of Scripture, or the authority of the fathers. And, indeed, the scholastic jargon was every way proper to answer the purposes of a set of men, who found it necessary to puzzle and perplex, where they could neither refute with perspicuity, nor prove with evidence. Thus they artfully concealed their defeat, and retreated, in the dazzled eyes of the multitude, with the appearance of victory.*

The Mystics lost almost all their credit in the church of Rome after the Reformation, partly on account of the favourable reception they found among the protestants, and partly in consequence of their pacific system, which, giving them an aversion to controversy in general, rendered them little disposed to defend the papal cause against its numerous and formidable adversaries. These enthusiasts, however, were, in some measure, tolerated, and allowed to indulge themselves in their philosophical speculations, on certain conditions, which obliged them to abstain from censuring either the laws or the corruptions of the church, and from declaiming, with their usual freedom and vehemence, against the vanity of external worship, and the dissensions of jarring and contentious divines.

XXVIII. There was no successful attempt made, in this century, to correct or improve the practical or moral system of doctrine that was followed in the church of Rome; nor, indeed, could any one make such an attempt without drawing upon himself the displeasure, and perhaps the fury, of the papal hierarchy; for, in reality, such a project of reformation seemed in no wise conducive to the *interests* of the church, as these interests were understood by its ambitious and rapacious rulers; and it is undoubtedly certain, that many doctrines and regulations, on which the power, opulence, and grandeur of that church essentially depended, would have run the risk of falling into discredit and contempt, if the pure and rational system of morality, contained in the Gospel, had been exhibited in its native beauty and simplicity, to the view and perusal of all Christians without distinction. Little or no zeal was therefore exerted in amending or improving the doctrines that immediately relate to practice. On the contrary, many persons of eminent piety and integrity, in the communion of Rome, have grievously complained (with what justice shall be shown in its proper place,*) that, as soon as the Jesuits had gained an ascendancy in the courts of princes, and in the schools of learning, the cause of virtue began visibly to decline. It has been alleged, more particularly, that this artful order employed all the force of subtle distinctions to sap the foundations of morality, and, in process of time, opened a door to all sorts of licentiousness and iniquity, by the loose and dissolute rules of conduct which they propagated as far as their influence extended. This poisonous doctrine spread, indeed, its contagion, in a latent manner, during the sixteenth century; but, in the following age, its abettors ventured to expose some specimens of its turpitude to public view, and thus gave occasion to great commotions in several parts of Europe.

All the moral writers of the church, in this century, may be distinguished into three classes, the *Schoolmen*, the *Dogmatists*,† and the *Mystics*. The first explained, or rather obscured, the virtues and duties of the Christian life, by knotty distinctions and unintelligible forms of speech, and buried them under an enormous load of arguments and demonstrations: the second illustrated them from the declarations of Scripture and the opinions of the ancient doctors; while the third placed the whole of morality in the tranquillity of a mind withdrawn from all sensible objects, and habitually employed in the contemplation of the divine nature.

XXIX. The number of combatants brought by the pontiffs into the field of controversy, during this century, was prodigious, and their glaring defects are abundantly known. It may be said, with truth, of the greater part of them, that, like many warriors of another class, they generally lost sight of all considerations, except those of victory and plunder. The disputants, whom the order of Jesuits sent forth in great numbers against the adversaries of the church of Rome, surpassed all the rest in subtlety, impudence, and invective. The

the theological faculty at Paris, in his Hist. Acad. Paris. tom. vi. In this reform the bachelors of divinity, called *Sententiarii* and *Biblici*, are particularly distinguished; and (what is extremely remarkable) he Augustine monks, who were Luther's fraternity, are ordered to furnish the college of divinity once a year with a scriptural bachelor (Baccalaureum Biblicum præsentare;) whence we may conclude, that the monks of the Augustine order were much more conversant in the study of the Scriptures than any of the other monastic societies which then existed. But this academical law deserves to be quoted here at length, so much the more, as Du-Boulay's History is in few hands. It is as follows: "Augustinenses quolibet anno Biblicum præsentabunt, secundum statutum fol. 21, quod sequitur: Quilibet ordo Mendicantium et Collegium S. Bernardi habeant quolibet anno Biblicum qui legat ordinarie, alioqui priventur pro illo anno Baccalaureo sententiario." It appears by this law, that each mendicant order was, by a decree of the theological faculty, obliged to furnish, yearly, a scriptural bachelor; (such was Luther;) and yet we see, that, in the reformation already mentioned, this obligation is imposed upon none but the Augustine monks. We may therefore presume that the Dominicans, Franciscans, and the other mendicants, had entirely neglected the study of the Scriptures, and consequently had among them no scriptural bachelors; and that the Augustine monks alone were in a condition to satisfy the demands of the theological faculty.

☞ * The translator has added the two last sentences of this paragraph, to illustrate more fully the sense of the author.

☞ * See cent. xvii. sect. ii. part i. chap. i. sect. xxxiv.

☞ † The reader will easily perceive, by the short account of these three classes, given by Dr. Mosheim, that the word *Dogmatist* must not be taken in that magisterial sense which it bears in modern language.

principal leader and champion of the polemic tribe was Robert Bellarmine, a Jesuit, and a member of the college of cardinals, who treated, in several bulky volumes, of all the controversies that subsisted between the protestants and the church of Rome, and whose merit as a writer consisted, principally, in clearness of style, and a certain copiousness of argument, which showed a rich and fruitful imagination. This eminent defender of the church of Rome arose about the conclusion of this century, and, on his first appearance, all the force and attacks of the most illustrious protestant doctors were turned against him alone. His candour and plain dealing exposed him, however, to the censures of several divines of his own communion; for he collected, with diligence, the reasons and objections of his adversaries, and proposed them, for the most part, in their full force, with integrity and exactness. Had he been less remarkable for his fidelity and industry; had he taken care to select the weakest arguments of his antagonists, and to render them still weaker, by proposing them in an imperfect and unfaithful light, his fame would have been much greater among the friends of Rome than it actually is.*

XXX. If we turn our view to the internal state of the church of Rome, and consider the respective sentiments, opinions, and manners of its different members, we shall find that, notwithstanding its boasted unity of faith, and its ostentatious pretensions to harmony and concord, it was, in the sixteenth century, and is, at this day, divided and distracted with dissensions and contests of various kinds. The Franciscans and the Dominicans contend with vehemence about several points of doctrine and discipline. The Scotists and Thomists are at eternal war. The bishops have never ceased disputing with the pope (and with the congregations that he has instituted to maintain his pretensions) upon the origin and precise limits of his authority and jurisdiction. The French and Flemings, with the inhabitants of other countries, openly oppose the pontiff on many occasions, and refuse to acknowledge his supreme and unlimited dominion in the church; while, on the other hand, he still continues to encroach upon their privileges, sometimes with violence and resolution, when he can do so with impunity, at other times with circumspection and prudence, when vigorous measures appear dangerous or unnecessary. The Jesuits, who, on their first appearance, had formed the project of diminishing the credit and influence of all the other religious orders, used their warmest endeavours to share with the Benedictine and other monasteries, which were richly endowed, a part of their opulence; and their endeavours were crowned with success. Thus they drew upon their society the indignation and vengeance of the other religious communities, and armed against it the monks of every other denomination; and, in a more especial manner, the Benedictines and Dominicans, who surpassed all its enemies in the keenness and bitterness of their resentment. The rage of the Benedictines is animated by reflecting on the possessions of which they have been deprived, while the Dominicans contend for the honour of their order, the privileges annexed to it, and the religious tenets by which it is distinguished. Nor are the theological colleges and seminaries of learning more exempt from the flame of controversy than the clerical and monastic orders: on the contrary, debates concerning almost all the doctrines of Christianity are multiplied in them, and conducted with little moderation. It is true, indeed, that all these contests are tempered and managed, by the prudence and authority of the pontiffs, in such a manner as to prevent their being carried to an excessive height, to a length that might prove fatal to the church, by destroying that phantom of external unity which is the source of its consistence as an ecclesiastical body: I say, *tempered* and *managed;* for, to heal entirely these divisions, and calm these animosities, however it may be judged an undertaking worthy of one who calls himself the Vicar of Christ, is, nevertheless, a work beyond his power, and contrary to his intention.

XXXI. Beside these debates of inferior moment, which made only a slight breach in the tranquillity and union of the Romish church, there arose, after the period in which the council of Trent was assembled, controversies of much greater importance, which deservedly attracted the attention of Christians of all denominations. These controversies were set on foot by the Jesuits, and from small beginnings have increased gradually, and gathered strength; so that the flame they produced has been transmitted even to our times, and continues, at this very day, to divide the members of the church in a manner that does not a little endanger its stability. While the pontiffs foment, perhaps, instead of endeavouring to extinguish, the less momentous disputes mentioned above, they observe a different conduct with respect to those now under consideration. The most zealous efforts of artifice and authority are constantly employed to calm the contending parties (since it appears impossible to unite and reconcile them,) and to diminish the violence of commotion, which they can scarcely ever hope entirely to suppress. All their exertions, however, have hitherto been ineffectual. They have not been able to calm the agitation and vehemence with which these debates are carried on, or to inspire any sentiments of moderation and mutual forbearance into minds, which are less animated by the love of truth, than by the spirit of faction.

XXXII. Whoever will look with attention and impartiality into these controversies may easily perceive that there are two parties in the Romish church, whose notions with respect both to doctrine and discipline are extremely different. The Jesuits, considered as a body,*

* See Mayer's Ecloga de fide Baronii et Bellarmini ipsis Pontificiis dubia, published at Amsterdam in 1698.

☞ * The Jesuits are here taken in the general and collective sense of that denomination, because there are several individuals of that order, whose sentiments differ from those which generally prevail in their community.

maintain with the greatest zeal and obstinacy, the ancient system of doctrine and manners, which pervaded the church before the rise of Luther, and which, though absurd and ill-digested, the zealots have constantly considered as highly favourable to the views of Rome, and the grandeur of its pontiffs. These sagacious ecclesiastics, whose peculiar office it is to watch for the security and defence of the papal throne, are fully persuaded that the authority of the pontiffs, the opulence, pomp, and grandeur of the clergy, depend entirely upon the preservation of the ancient forms of doctrine; and that every project which tends either to remove these forms, or even to correct them, must be, in the highest degree, detrimental to what they call the interests of the church, and gradually bring on its ruin. On the other hand, there are within the pale of the Romish church, especially since the dawn of the reformation, many pious and well-meaning men, whose eyes have been opened, by the perusal of the inspired and primitive writers, upon the corruptions and defects of the received forms of doctrine and discipline. Comparing the dictates of primitive Christianity with the vulgar system of popery, they have found the latter full of enormities, and have always been desirous of a reform (though indeed a partial one, according to their particular fancies,) that thus the church may be purified from those unhappy abuses which have given rise to such mischievous divisions, and still draw upon it the censures and reproaches of the heretics.

From these opposite ways of thinking, arose naturally the warmest contentions and debates, between the Jesuits and many doctors of the church. These debates may be reduced under the six following heads:

The first subject of debate concerns the limits and extent of the papal power and jurisdiction. The Jesuits, with their numerous tribe of followers and dependents, maintain, that the pontiff is infallible; that he is the only visible source of that universal and unlimited power which Christ has granted to the church; that all bishops and subordinate rulers derive from him alone the authority and jurisdiction with which they are invested; that he is not bound by any laws of the church, nor by any decrees of the councils that compose it; that he alone is the supreme legislator of that sacred community, and that it is in the highest degree criminal to oppose or disobey his edicts and commands. Such are the strange sentiments of the Jesuits; but they are very far from being universally adopted; for other members of the church hold, on the contrary, that the pope is liable to error; that his authority is inferior to that of a general council; that he is bound to obey the commands of the church, and its laws, as they are enacted in the councils that represent it; that these councils have a right to depose him from the papal chair, when he abuses, in a flagrant manner, the dignity and prerogatives with which he is intrusted; and that, in consequence of these principles, the bishops and inferior rulers and doctors derive the authority that is annexed to their respective dignities, not from the pontiff, but from Christ himself.

XXXIII. The extent and prerogatives of the church form the second subject of debate The Jesuits and their adherents stretch out its borders far and wide. They not only comprehend, within its large circuit, many who live separate from the communion of Rome,* but even extend the inheritance of eternal salvation to nations that have not the least knowledge of the Christian religion, or of its divine Author, and consider as true members of the church open transgressors, who outwardly profess its doctrines. But the adversaries of the Jesuits reduce within narrower limits the kingdom of Christ, and not only exclude from all hope of salvation those who are not within the pale of the church of Rome, but also those who, though they live within its external communion, yet dishonour their profession by a vicious and profligate course of life. The Jesuits moreover (not to mention differences of less moment) assert, that the church can never pronounce an erroneous or unjust decision, either relating to matters of fact, or points of doctrine;† while the adverse party declare, that, in judging of matters of fact, it is not secured against all possibility of erring.

XXXIV. In the third class of controversies, that divide the church, are comprehended the debates relating to the nature, efficacy, and necessity of divine grace, together with those which concern original sin, the natural power of man to obey the laws of God, and the nature and foundation of those eternal decrees that have for their object the salvation of men. The Dominicans, Augustinians, and Jansenists, with several other doctors of the church, adopt the following propositions: that the impulse of divine grace cannot be opposed or resisted; that there are no remains of purity or goodness in human nature since its fall; that the eternal decrees of God, relating to the salvation of men, are neither founded upon, nor attended with, any condition whatsoever; that God wills the salvation of all mankind: and they hold several other tenets connected with these. The Jesuits maintain, on the contrary, that the natural dominion of sin in the human mind, and the hidden corruption it has produced in our internal frame, are less general and dreadful than they are represented by the doctors now mentioned; that human nature is far from being deprived of all power of doing good; that the succours of grace are administered to all mankind in a measure sufficient to lead them to eternal life and salvation; that the operations of grace offer no violence to the faculties and powers of nature, and therefore

☞ * They were accused at Spoleto, in 1653, of having maintained, in their public instructions, the probability of the salvation of many heretics. See Le Clerc, Biblioth. Univers. et Historique, tom. xiv.

☞ † This distinction, with respect to the objects of infallibility, chiefly arose from the following historical circumstance. Pope Innocent X. condemned five propositions, drawn from the famous book of Jansenius, entitled *Augustinus;* and this condemnation occasioned the two following questions: 1st, Whether these propositions were erroneous? This was the question *de jure*, i. e. as the translator has rendered it, respecting doctrine. 2d, Whether these propositions were really taught by Jansenius? This was the question *de facto*, i. e. relating to the matter of fact. The church was supposed, by some, infallible only in deciding questions of the former kind

may be resisted; and that God from all eternity has appointed everlasting rewards and punishments, as the portion of men in a future world, not by an absolute, arbitrary, and unconditional decree, but in consequence of that divine and unlimited prescience, by which he foresaw the actions, merit, and character, of every individual.

XXXV. The fourth head, in this division of the controversies that destroy the pretended unity of the church, contains various subjects of debate, relative to doctrines of morality and rules of practice, which it would be both tedious and foreign from our purpose to enumerate in a circumstantial manner, though it may not be improper to touch lightly the first principles of this endless controversy.*

The Jesuits and their followers have inculcated a very strange doctrine with respect to the motives that determine the moral conduct and actions of men. They represent it as a matter of perfect indifference from what motives men obey the laws of God, provided that these laws be really obeyed; and maintain, that the service of those who obey from the fear of punishment is as agreeable to the Deity, as are those actions which proceed from a principle of love to him and to his laws. This decision excites the horror of the greatest part of the doctors of the Roman church, who affirm, that no acts of obedience, when they do not proceed from the love of God, can be acceptable to that pure and holy Being. Nor is the doctrine of the Jesuits only chargeable with the corrupt tenets already mentioned. They maintain farther, that a man never sins, properly speaking, but when he transgresses a divine law that is fully known to him, which is present to his mind while he acts, and of which he understands the true meaning and intent. And they hence conclude, that, in strict justice, the conduct of that transgressor cannot be looked upon as criminal, who is either ignorant of the law, or is in doubt about its true signification, or loses sight of it, through forgetfulness, at the time that he violates it. From these propositions they deduce the famous doctrines of probability and philosophical sin, which have cast an eternal reproach upon the schools of the Jesuits.† Their adversaries behold these pernicious tenets with the utmost abhorrence, and assert that neither ignorance, nor forgetfulness of the law, nor the doubts that may be entertained with respect to its signification, will be admitted as sufficient to justify transgressors before the tribunal of God. This contest, about the main and fundamental points of morality, has given rise to a great variety of debates concerning the duties we owe to God, our neighbour, and ourselves; and has produced two sects of moral teachers, whose animosities and divisions have miserably rent the Romish church in all parts of the world, and involved it in the greatest perplexities.

XXXVI. The administration of the sacraments, especially those of penance and the eucharist, forms the fifth subject of controversy. The Jesuits and many other doctors are of opinion, that the salutary effects of the sacraments are produced by their intrinsic virtue and immediate operation* upon the mind at the time when they are administered, and that consequently it requires little preparation to receive them to edification and comfort; nor do they think that God requires a mind adorned with inward purity, and a heart animated with divine love, in order to the obtaining of the ends and purposes of these religious institutions. And hence it is, that, according to their doctrine, the priests are empowered to give immediate absolution to all such as confess their transgressions and crimes, and afterwards to admit them to the use of the sacraments. But such sentiments are rejected with indignation by all those of the Romish communion who have the progress of vital and practical religion truly at heart. These look upon it as the duty of the clergy to use the greatest diligence and assiduity in examining the characters, tempers, and actions of those who demand absolution and the use of the sacraments, before they grant their requests; since, in their sense of things, the real benefits of these institutions can extend to those only whose hearts are care-

* No author has given a more accurate, precise, and clear enumeration of the objections that have been made to the moral doctrine of the Jesuits, and the reproaches which have been cast on their rules of life; and no one at the same time has defended their cause with more art and dexterity than the eloquent and ingenious Gabriel Daniel (a famous member of their order,) in a piece, entitled, Entretiens de Cleandre et d'Eudoxe. This dialogue was intended as an answer to the celebrated Provincial Letters of Pascal, which did more real prejudice to the society of the Jesuits than many would imagine, and exposed their loose and perfidious system of morals with the greatest fidelity and perspicuity, embellished by the most exquisite strokes of humour and irony. Father Daniel, in the piece above mentioned, treats with great acuteness the famous doctrine of probability, the method of directing our intentions, equivocation and mental reservation, sins of ignorance and oblivion; and it must be acknowledged, that, if the cause and pretensions of the Jesuits were susceptible of defence or plausibility, they have found in this writer an able and dexterous champion.

☞ † The doctrine of probability consists in this: That an opinion or precept may be followed with a good conscience, when it is inculcated by four, or three, or two, or even by one doctor of considerable reputation, even though it be contrary to the judgment of the person who follows it, and even of him that recommends it.' This doctrine rendered the Jesuits capable of accommodating themselves to all the different passions of men, and to persons of all tempers and characters, from the most austere to the most licentious. Philosophical sin (according to the Jesuits' doctrine) is an action, or course of actions, repugnant to the dictates of reason, and yet not offensive to the Deity. See a more particular account of these two odious doctrines in the following part of this work, cent. xvii. sect. ii. part i. chap. i. sect. xxxv. and in the author's and translator's notes.

☞ * This is the only expression that occurred to the translator, as proper to render the true sense of that phrase of the scholastic divines, who say, that the sacraments produce their effect *opere operato.* The Jesuits and Dominicans maintain that the sacraments have in themselves an instrumental and efficient power, by virtue of which they work in the soul (independently of its previous preparation or propensities) a disposition to receive the divine grace; and this is what is commonly called the *opus operatum* of the sacraments. Thus, according to their doctrine, neither knowledge, wisdom, humility, faith, nor devotion, are necessary to the efficacy of the sacraments, whose victorious energy no thing but a mortal sin can resist. See Dr. Courayer 's Translation of Paul Sarpi's History of the Council of Trent.

fully purged from the corruptions of iniquity, and filled with that divine love which 'casteth out fear.' Hence arose that famous dispute concerning a frequent approach to the holy communion, which was carried on with such warmth in the last (*the seventeenth*) century, between the Jesuits and the Jansenists, with Arnauld* at the head of the latter, and has been renewed in our times by the Jesuit Pichon, who thereby incurred the indignation of the greatest part of the French Bishops.† The frequent celebration of the Lord's supper is one of the main duties, which the Jesuits recommend with peculiar earnestness to all who are under their spiritual direction, representing it as the most certain and infallible method of appeasing the Deity, and obtaining from him the entire remission of their sins and transgressions. This manner of proceeding the Jansenists censure with their usual severity; and it is also condemned by many other learned and pious doctors of the Romish communion, who reject the intrinsic virtue and efficient operation which are attributed to the sacraments, and wisely maintain, that the sacrament of the Lord's supper can be profitable to those only whose minds are prepared, by faith, repentance, and the love of God, for that solemn service.

XXXVII. The sixth (or last) controversy turns upon the proper method of instructing Christians in the truths and precepts of religion. Some of the Romish doctors, who have the progress of religion truly at heart, deem it expedient and even necessary to sow the seeds of divine truth in the mind, in the tender and flexible state of infancy, when it is most susceptive of good impressions, and to give it, by degrees, according to the measure of its capacity, a full and accurate knowledge of the doctrines and duties of religion. Others, who have a greater zeal for the interests of the church than the improvement of its members, recommend a devout ignorance to such as submit to their direction, and think a Christian sufficiently instructed when he has learned to yield a blind and unlimited obedience to the orders of the church. The former are of opinion, that nothing can be so profitable and instructive to Christians as the study of the Scriptures, and consequently judge it highly expedient that they should be translated into the vulgar tongue of each country. The latter exclude the people from the satisfaction of consulting the sacred oracles of truth, and look upon all vernacular translations of the Bible as dangerous, and even of a pernicious tendency. They accordingly maintain, that it ought only to be published in a learned language to prevent its instructions from becoming familiar to the multitude. The former compose pious and instructive books to nourish a spirit of devotion in the minds of Christians, to enlighten their ignorance, and dispel their errors; they illustrate and explain the public prayers and the solemn acts of religion in the language of the people, and exhort all, who attend to their instructions, to peruse constantly these pious productions, in order to improve their knowledge, purify their affections, and learn the method of worshipping the Deity in a rational and acceptable manner. All this, however, is highly displeasing to the latter kind of doctors, who are always apprehensive, that the blind obedience and implicit submission of the people will diminish in proportion as their views are enlarged, and their knowledge increased.*

XXXVIII. All the controversies that have been here mentioned did not break out at the same time. The disputes concerning divine grace, the natural power of man to perform good actions, original sin, and predestination, which have been ranged under the third class, were publicly carried on in the century of which we are now writing. The others were conducted with more secrecy and reserve, and did not come forth to public view before the following age. Nor will this appear at all surprising to those who consider that the controversies concerning grace and free-will, which had been set in motion by Luther, were neither accurately examined, nor peremptorily decided in the church of Rome, but were rather artfully suspended and hushed into silence. The sentiments of Luther were indeed condemned; but no fixed and perspicuous rule of faith, with respect to these disputed points, was substituted in their place. The decisions of St. Augustin were solemnly approved; but the points of dissimilitude, between these decisions and the sentiments of Luther, were never clearly explained. This fatal controversy originated in the zeal of Michael Baius, a doctor in the university of Louvain, equally remarkable on account of the warmth of his piety and the extent of his learning. This

* Arnauld published, on this occasion, his famous book concerning the practice of communicating frequently. The French title is, 'Traite de la frequente Communion.'

† See Journal Universel, tom xiii xv. xvi

* The account here given of the more momentous controversies that divide the church of Rome, may be confirmed, illustrated and enlarged, by consulting a multitude of books published in the last and present centuries, especially in France and Flanders, by Jansenists, Dominicans, Jesuits, and others. All the productions, in which the doctrine and precepts of the Jesuits, and the other creatures of the pontiff, are opposed and refuted, are enumerated by Dominic Colonia, a French Jesuit, in a work published in 1735, under the following title: "Bibliotheque Janseniste, ou Catalogue Alphabetique des principaux livres Jansenistes, ou suspects de Jansenisme, avec des notes critiques." This writer is led into many absurdities by his extravagant attachment to the pope, and to the cause and tenets of his order. His book, however, is of use in pointing out the various controversies that perplex and divide the church. It was condemned by pope Benedict XIV. but was republished in a new form, with some change in the title, and a great enlargement of its contents. This new edition appeared at Antwerp in 1752, under the following title: "Dictionaire des livres Jansenistes, ou qui favorisent le Jansenisme, a Anvers, chez J. B. Verdussen." And it must be acknowledged, that it is extremely useful, in showing the intestine divisions of the church, the particular contests that divide its doctors, the religious tenets of the Jesuits, and the numerous productions that relate to the six heads of controversy here mentioned. It must be observed, at the same time, that this work abounds with the most malignant invectives against many persons of eminent learning and piety, and with the most notorious instances of partiality and injustice.*

☞ * See a particular account of this learned and scandalous work in the "Bibliotheque des Sciences et des Beaux Arts," printed at the Hague.

eminent divine, like the other followers of Augustin, had an invincible aversion to that contentious, subtle, and intricate manner of teaching theology, which had long prevailed in the schools; and under the auspicious name of that famous prelate, who was his admired guide, he had the courage or temerity to condemn and censure, in an open and public manner, the tenets commonly received in the church, in relation to the natural powers of man and the merit of good works. This bold step drew upon Baius the indignation of some of his academical colleagues, and the heavy censures of several Franciscan monks. Whether the Jesuits immediately joined in this opposition, and may be reckoned among the first accusers of Baius, is a point unknown, or uncertain; but it is unquestionably evident, that, even at the rise of this controversy, they abhorred the principal tenets of Baius, which he had taken from Augustin, and adopted as his own. In 1567, this doctor was accused at the court of Rome; and seventy-six propositions, drawn from his writings, were condemned by Pius V. in a circular letter expressly composed for that purpose. This condemnation, however, was issued in an artful and insidious manner, without any mention of the name of the author; for the fatal consequences that had arisen from the rash and inconsiderate measures employed by the court of Rome against Luther, were too fresh in the remembrance of the prudent pontiff to permit his falling into new blunders of the same nature. The thunder of excommunication was therefore suppressed by the dictates of prudence, and the person and functions of Baius were spared, while his tenets were censured. About thirteen years after this transaction, Gregory XIII. complied so far with the importunate solicitations of a Jesuit, named Francis Tolet, as to reinforce the sentence of Pius V. by a new condemnation of the opinions of the Flemish doctor. Baius submitted to this new sentence, either from an apprehension that it would be followed by more severe proceedings in case of resistance, or, which is more probable, on account of the ambiguity of the papal edict, and the vague and confused manner in which the obnoxious propositions were therein expressed. But his example, in this respect, was not followed by the other doctors who had formed their theological system upon that of Augustin;* and, even at this day, many divines of the Romish communion, and particularly the Jansenists, declare openly that Baius was unjustly treated, and that the two edicts of Pius and Gregory are absolutely destitute of all authority, and have never been received as laws of the church.†

XXXIX. Be that as it may, it is at least certain, that the doctrine of Augustin, with respect to the nature and operations of divine grace, lost none of its credit in consequence of these edicts, but was embraced and propagated, with the same zeal as formerly, throughout all the Belgic provinces, and more especially in the two flourishing universities of Louvain and Douay. This appeared very soon after, when two Jesuits, named Lessius and Hamelius, ventured to represent the doctrine of predestination in a manner different from that in which it appears in the writings of Augustin; for the sentiments of these Jesuits were publicly condemned by the doctors of Louvain in 1587, and by those of Douay in the following year. The bishops of the Low Countries were disposed to follow the example of these two universities, and had already deliberated about assembling a provincial council for this purpose, when pope Sixtus V. suspended the proceedings by the interposition of his authority, and declared, that the cognizance and decision of religious controversies belonged only to the vicar of Christ, residing at Rome. But this politic vicar, whose sagacity, prudence, and knowledge of men and things, never failed him in transactions of this nature, wisely avoided making use of the privilege he claimed with such confidence, that he might not inflame the divisions and animosities which already subsisted. And, accordingly, in 1588, this contest was finished, and the storm allayed in such a manner, that the contending parties were left in the quiet possession of their respective opinions, and solemnly prohibited from disputing, either in public or in private, upon the intricate points that had excited their divisions. Had the succeeding pontiffs, instead of assuming the character of judges in this ambiguous and difficult controversy, imitated the prudence of Sixtus, and imposed silence on the litigious doctors, who renewed afterwards the debates concerning divine grace, the tranquillity and unity of the church would not have been interrupted by such violent divisions as rage at present in its bosom.*

XL. The church had scarcely perceived the fruits of that calm, which the prudence of Sixtus had restored, by suppressing, instead of deciding the late controversies, when new commotions, of the same nature, but of a much more terrible aspect, arose to disturb its tranquillity. These were occasioned by the Jesuit Molina,† professor of divinity in the universi-

---

* See, for an account of the disputes relating to Baius, the works of that author, published at Cologne in 1696, particularly the second part, or appendix, entitled, "Baiana, seu scripta, quæ controversias spectant occasione Sententiarum Baii exortas." See also Bayle's Dict., in which there is an ample and circumstantial account of these disputes;—Du-Pin, Bibliotheque des Auteurs Ecclesiastiques, tom. xvi.—Histoire de la Compagnie de Jesus, tom. iii.

† This is demonstrated fully by an anonymous writer in a piece entitled. "Dissertation sur les Bulles contre Baius, ou l'on montre qu'elles ne sont pas reçues par l'Eglise," published at Utrecht in 1737.

* See Apologie Historique des deux Censures de Louvain et de Douay, par M. Gery. The famous Pasquier Quesnel was the author of this apology, if we may give credit to the writer of a book entitled, "Catechisme Historique et Dogmatique sur les Contestations de l'Eglise," tom. i. See an account of this controversy in the "Memoires pour servir a l'Histoire des Controversies dans l'Eglise Romaine sur la Predestination et sur la Grace." This curious piece is to be found in the fourteenth tome of Le Clerc's Bibliotheque Universelle Historique.

† From the name of this Spanish doctor proceeded the well-known denomination of Molinists, by which those Roman Catholics are distinguished, who seem to incline to the doctrines of grace and

ty of Ebora in Portugal, who, in 1588, published a book to show that the operations of divine grace were entirely consistent with the freedom of human will,* and who introduced a new kind of hypothesis, to remove the difficulties attending the doctrines of predestination and liberty, and to reconcile the jarring opinions of Augustinians, Thomists, Semi-Pelagians, and other contentious divines.† This attempt of the subtle Spanish doctor was so offensive to the Dominicans, who followed St. Thomas as their theological guide, that they sounded throughout Spain and Portugal the alarm of heresy, and accused the Jesuits of endeavouring to renew the errors of Pelagius. This alarm was followed by great commotions, and all things seemed to prognosticate a general flame, when Clement VIII., in 1594, imposed silence on the contending parties, promising that he himself would examine with care and diligence every thing relating to this new debate, in order to decide it in such a manner as might tend to promote the cause of truth, and the peace of the church.

XLI. The pontiff was persuaded that these gentle remedies would soon remove the disease, and that, through length of time, these heats and animosities would undoubtedly subside. But the event was far from being answerable to such pleasing hopes. The Dominicans, who had long fostered a deep-rooted and invincible hatred against the Jesuits, having now an opportunity of venting their indignation, exhausted their furious zeal against the doctrine of Molina, notwithstanding the pacific injunctions of the papal edict. They incessantly fatigued Philip II. of Spain, and pope Clement VIII., with their importunate clamours, until at length the latter found himself under a necessity of assembling at Rome a sort of council for the decision of this controversy. And thus commenced, about the beginning of the year 1598, those famous deliberations concerning the contest of the Jesuits and Dominicans, which took place in what was called the congregation *de auxiliis*, or of aids. This congregation was so denominated on account of the principal point in debate, which was the efficacy of the aids and succours of divine grace; and its consultations were directed by Louis Madrusi, bishop of Trent, and one of the college of cardinals, who sat as president in this assembly, which was composed besides of three bishops and seven divines chosen out of so many different orders. The remaining part of this century was wholly employed by these spiritual judges in hearing and weighing the arguments alleged in favour of their respective opinions by the contending parties.* The Dominicans maintained, with the greatest obstinacy, the doctrine of their patron St. Thomas, as alone conformable to truth. The Jesuits, on the other hand, though they did not adopt the religious tenets of Molina, thought the honour of their order concerned in this controversy, on account of the opposition so publicly made to one of its members, and consequently used their utmost endeavours to have the Spanish doctor acquitted of the charge of Pelagianism, and declared free from any errors of moment. In this they acted according to the true monastic spirit, which leads each order to resent the affronts that are offered to any of its members, as if they had been cast upon the whole community, and to maintain, at all adventures, the cause of every individual monk, as if the interests of the whole society were involved in it.

XLII. Notwithstanding the zealous attempts that were made, by several persons of eminent piety, to restore the institutions of public worship to their primitive simplicity, a multitude of vain and useless ceremonies still remained in the church; nor did the pontiffs judge it proper to diminish that pomp and show, which gave the ministers of religion a great, though ill-acquired, influence on the minds of the people. Beside these ceremonies, many popular customs and inventions, which were multiplied

---

free-will, maintained in opposition to those of Augustin. Many, however, who differ widely from the sentiments of Molina, are unjustly ranked in the class of Molinists.

* The title of this famous book is as follows: "Liberi Arbitrii Concordia cum Gratiæ donis, divina Præscientia, Providentia, Prædestinatione, et Reprobatione, Auctore Lud. Molina." This book was first published at Lisbon, in 1588; afterwards, with additions, at Antwerp, Lyons, Venice, and other places, in 1595. A third edition, still farther augmented, appeared at Antwerp in 1609.

☞ † Molina affirmed, that the decree of predestination to eternal glory was founded upon a previous knowledge and consideration of the merits of the elect; that the grace, from whose operation these merits are derived, is not efficacious by its own intrinsic power only, but also by the consent of our own will, and because it is administered in those circumstances in which the Deity, by that branch of his knowledge which is called *Scientia Media*, foresees that it will be efficacious. The kind of prescience denominated in the schools *Scientia Media*, is that fore-knowledge of future contingencies, that arises from an acquaintance with the nature and faculties of rational beings, the circumstances in which they shall be placed, the objects that shall be presented to them, and the influence that these circumstances and objects must have on their actions.

* The history and transactions of this Congregation are related and illustrated by several writers of different complexions, by Jesuits, Dominicans, and Jansenists. Hyacinth Serri, a Dominican, published, under the feigned name of Augustin le Blanc, in 1700, at Louvain, a work with this title: Historia Congregationum de auxiliis Gratiæ divinæ; which was answered by another history of these debates, composed by Liv. de Meyer, a Jesuit, who assumed the name of Theod. Eleutherius, in order to remain concealed from public view, and whose book is entitled, Historia Controversarium de Gratiæ divinæ Auxiliis. The Dominicans also published the Acta Congregationum et Disputationum, quæ Coram Clemente VIII. et Paulo V. de Auxiliis divinæ Gratiæ sunt celebratæ, a work composed by Thomas de Lemos, a subtle monk of their order, who, in this very congregation, had defended with great applause the glory of St. Thomas against the Jesuits. Amidst these jarring accounts, a man must be endowed with a supernatural sagacity to come to the truth; for acts are opposed to acts, testimony to testimony, and narration to narration. It is therefore a matter of doubt, which the court of Rome favoured most on this occasion, the Jesuits or the Dominicans, and which of these two parties defended their cause with the greatest dexterity and success. There is also a history of these debates written in French, which was published at Louvain in 1702, under the following title: Histoire des Congregations *de Auxiliis*, par un Docteur de la Faculte de Theologie de Paris. This historian, though he be neither destitute of learning nor of elegance, being nevertheless a flaming Jansenist, discovers throughout his enmity against the Jesuits and relates all things in a manner that favours the cause of the Dominicans

by the clergy, and were either entirely absurd or grossly superstitious, called loudly for redress; and, indeed, the council of Trent seemed disposed to correct these abuses, and prevent their further growth. But this good design was never carried into execution; it was abandoned, either through the corrupt prudence of the pope and clergy, who looked upon every check given to superstition as an attempt to diminish their authority, or through their criminal negligence about every thing that tended to promote the true interests of religion. Hence it happens, that in those countries where there are few protestants, and consequently where the church of Rome is in no danger of losing its credit and influence from the proximity and attempts of these pretended heretics, superstition reigns with unlimited extravagance and absurdity. Such is the case in Italy, Spain, and Portugal, where the feeble glimmerings of Christianity, that yet remain, are overwhelmed and obscured by an enormous multitude of ridiculous ceremonies, and absurd, fantastic, and unaccountable rites; so that a person who arrives in any one of these countries, after having passed among other nations even of the Romish communion, is immediately struck with the change, and thinks himself transported into the thickest darkness, into the most gloomy retreats of superstition.* Nor, indeed, are even those nations whom the neighbourhood of the protestants, and a more free and liberal turn of mind, have rendered somewhat less absurd, entirely exempt from the dominion of superstition, and the solemn fooleries that always attend it; for the religion of Rome, in its best form, and in those places where its external worship is the least shocking, is certainly loaded with rites and observances that are highly offensive to sound reason. If, from this general view of things, we descend to a more circumstantial consideration of the innumerable abuses that are established in the discipline of that church; if we attend to the pious, or rather impious, frauds which, in many places, are imposed with impunity upon the deluded multitude; if we pass in review the corruption of the clergy, the ignorance of the people, the devout farces that are acted in the ceremonies of public worship, and the insipid jargon and trifling rhetoric that prevails in the discourses of the Romish preachers; if we weigh all these things maturely, we shall find, that they have little regard to impartiality and truth, who pretend that, since the council of Trent, the religion and worship of the Roman church have been every where corrected and amended.

* It is well known that the French, who travel into Italy, employ the whole force of their wit and raillery in rendering ridiculous the monstrous superstition of the Italians. The Italians, in their turn, look upon the French that visit their country as totally destitute of all principles of religion. This is evidently the case, as we learn from the testimony of many writers, and particularly from that of Father Labat, in his Voyages en Italie et en Espagne. This agreeable Dominican lets no opportunity escape of censuring and exposing the superstition of the Spaniards and Italians; nor does he pretend to deny that his countrymen, and even he himself, passed for impious libertines in the opinion of those bigots

CHAPTER II.

The History of the Greek and Eastern Churches.

I. THE Christian society that goes under the general denomination of the eastern church, is dispersed throughout Europe, Asia, and Africa, and may be divided into three distinct communities. The first is that of the Greek Christians, who agree, in all points of doctrine and worship, with the patriarch residing at Constantinople, and reject the pretended supremacy of the Roman pontiff. The second comprehends those Christians who differ equally from the Roman pontiff and the Grecian patriach, in their religious opinions and institutions, and who live under the government of their own bishops and rulers. The third is composed of those who are subject to the see of Rome.

II. That society which holds religious communion with the patriarch of Constantinople, is, properly speaking, the Greek (though it assumes likewise the title of the eastern) church. This society is subdivided into two branches, of which one acknowledges the supreme authority and jurisdiction of the bishop of Constantinople, while the other, though joined in communion of doctrine and worship with that prelate, obstinately refuses to receive his legates, or to obey his edicts, and is governed by its own laws and institutions, under the jurisdiction of spiritual rulers, who are not dependent on any foreign authority.

III. That part of the Greek church which acknowledges the jurisdiction of the bishop of Constantinople, is divided, as in the early ages of Christianity, into four large districts or provinces, Constantinople, Alexandria, Antioch, and Jerusalem; and over each of these a bishop presides with the title of Patriarch, whom the inferior bishops and monastic orders unanimously respect as their common Father. But the supreme chief of all these patriarchs, bishops and abbots, and indeed of the whole church, is the patriarch of Constantinople. This prelate has the privilege of nominating the other patriarchs, (though that dignity still continues apparently elective,) and of approving the election that is made; nor is any thing of moment undertaken or transacted in the church without his express permission, or his especial order. It is true, that, in the present decayed state of the Greek churches, whose former opulence is reduced almost to nothing, their spiritual rulers enjoy little more than the splendid title of patriarchs, without being in a condition to extend their fame, or promote their cause, by any undertaking of signal importance.

IV. The spiritual jurisdiction and dominion of the first of these patriarchs are very extensive, comprehending a considerable part of Greece, the Grecian Isles, Wallachia, Moldavia, and several of the European and Asiatic provinces subject to the Turks. The patriarch of Alexandria resides generally at Cairo, and exercises his spiritual authority in Egypt, Nubia, Libya, and part of Arabia.* Damascus is

* For an account of the patriarchate of Alexandria, and the various prelates who have filled that

the principal residence of the patriarch of Antioch, whose jurisdiction extends to Mesopotamia, Syria, Cilicia, and other provinces,* while the patriarch of Jerusalem comprehends, within the bounds of his pontificate, Palestine, Syria,† Arabia, the country beyond Jordan, Cana in Galillee, and mount Sion.‡ The episcopal dominions of these three patriarchs are indeed extremely poor and inconsiderable; for the Monophysites have long since assumed the patriarchal seats of Alexandria and Antioch, and have deprived the Greek churches of the greatest part of their members in all those places where they have gained an ascendancy; and, as Jerusalem is the resort of Christians of every sect, who have their respective bishops and rulers, the jurisdiction of the Grecian patriarch is consequently confined there within narrow limits.

V. The right of electing the patriarch of Constantinople is, at this day, vested in the twelve bishops who reside nearest to that famous capital; but the Turkish emperor alone enjoys the right of confirming this election, and of enabling the new patriarch to exercise his spiritual functions. This institution, however, if it is not entirely overturned, is nevertheless, on many occasions, prostituted in a shameful manner by the corruption and avarice of the reigning ministers. Thus it happens, that many bishops, inflamed with the ambitious lust of power and pre-eminence, purchase by money what they cannot obtain by merit, and, seeing themselves excluded from the patriarchal dignity by the suffrages of their brethren, find an open and ready way to it by the mercenary services of men in power. What is yet more deplorable has frequently happened: prelates, who have been chosen in the lawful way to this eminent office, have even been deposed, in order to make way for others, whose only pretensions were ambition and bribery. And indeed, generally speaking, he is looked upon by the Turkish viziers as the most qualified for the office of patriarch, who surpasses his competitors in the number and value of the presents he employs on that occasion. It is true, that some accounts worthy of credit represent the present state of the Greek church as advantageously changed in this respect; and it is reported, that, as the Turkish manners have gradually assumed a milder and more humane cast, the patriarchs live under their dominion with more security and repose than they did some ages ago.*

The power of the patriarch among a people dispirited by oppression, and sunk, through their extreme ignorance, into the greatest superstition, may be supposed to be very considerable and extensive; and such, indeed, it is Its extent, however, is not entirely derived from the causes now mentioned, but from others that give no small weight and lustre to the patriarchal dignity. For this prelate not only calls councils by his own authority, in order to decide, by their assistance, the controversies that arise, and to make use of their prudent advice and wise deliberations in directing the affairs of the church; his prerogatives go yet farther, and, by the especial permission of the sultan, he administers justice and takes cognizance of civil causes among the members of his communion. His influence is maintained, on the one hand, by the authority of the Turkish monarch, and, on the other, by his right of excommunicating the disobedient members of the Greek church. This right gives the patriarchs a singular degree of influence and authority, as nothing has a more terrifying aspect to that people than a sentence of excommunication, which they reckon among the greatest and most tremendous evils. The revenue of this prelate is drawn particularly from the churches that are subject to his jurisdiction; and its produce varies according to the state and circumstances of the Greek Christians, whose condition is exposed to many vicissitudes.†

VI. The Scriptures and the decrees of the first seven general councils are acknowledged by the Greeks as the rule of their faith. It is received, however, as a maxim established by long custom, that no private person has a right

see, it will be proper to consult Sollerii Commentar. de Patriarchis Alexandrinis, prefixed to the fifth volume of the Acta Sanctorum Mensis Junii; as also the Oriens Christianus of Mich. Le Quien, tom. ii. p. 329. The nature of their office, the extent of their authority, and the manner of their creation, are accurately described by Eus. Renaudot, in his Dissertatio de Patriarcha Alexandrino, published in Liturg. Orient. The Grecian patriarch has, at this day, no bishops under his jurisdiction; the chorepiscopi or rural bishops alone are subject to his authority. All the bishops acknowledge as their chief the patriarch of the Monophysites, who is, in effect, the patriarch of Alexandria.

* The Jesuits have prefixed a particular and learned account of the patriarchs of Antioch to the fifth volume of the Acta SS. Mensis Julii, in which, however, there are some omissions and defects. Add to this the account that is given of the district or diocese of the patriarch of Antioch, by Le Quien, in his Oriens Christianus, tom. ii. and by Blasius Tertius, in his "Siria Sacra, o Descrittione Historico-Geographica delle due Chiese Patriarchali, Antiochia, e Gierusalemme," published at Rome, in 1695. There are three bishops in Syria who claim the title and dignity of patriarch of Antioch. The first is the bishop of the Melchites,—a name given to the Christians in Syria, who follow the doctrines, institutions, and worship of the Greek church; the second is the spiritual guide of the Syrian Monophysites; and the third is the chief of the Maronites, who hold communion with the church of Rome. This last bishop pretends to be the true and lawful patriarch of Antioch, and is acknowledged as such, or at least receives this denomination from the Roman pontiff; yet it is certain, that the pope creates at Rome a patriarch of Antioch of his own choice. Thus the see of Antioch has, at this day, four patriarchs, one from the Greeks, two from the Syrians, and one created at Rome, who is patriarch *in partibus*, i. e. titular patriarch, according to the usual signification of that phrase.

☞ † Syria is here erroneously placed in the patriarchate of Jerusalem: it evidently belongs to that of Antioch, in which also Dr. Mosheim places it in the preceding part of the sentence.

‡ Blas. Tertii Siria Sacra, lib. ii. D. Papebrochii Comment. de Patriarch. Hierosolym. tom. iii. Act. Sanct. Mens. Maii.—Le Quien, tom. iii.

* Le Quien, tom. i. p. 145.—Elsner, Beschreibung der Griechischen in der Turckey.

† Cuper, a Jesuit, has given a History of the Patriarchs of Constantinople, in the Acta Sanctorum Mensis Augusti, tom. i. p. 1—257. There is also a very ample account both of the see of Constantinople and its patriarchs, in the Oriens Christianus of Le Quien, who likewise treats of the Latin patriarchs of that city. See also a brief account of the power and revenues of the present patriarch, and of the names of the several sees under his spiritual jurisdiction, in Smith, de Eccles. Græciæ Hodierno Statu

to explain, for himself or others, either the declarations of Scripture, or the decisions of these councils; and that the patriarch and his brethren are alone authorized to consult these oracles, and to declare their meaning; and, accordingly, the declarations of this prelate are looked upon as sacred and infallible directions, whose authority is supreme, and which can neither be transgressed nor disregarded without the utmost impiety. The substance of the doctrine of the Greek church is contained in a treatise entitled, The orthodox Confession of the Catholic and Apostolic Eastern Church, which was drawn up by Peter Mogislaus, bishop of Kiow, in a provincial council assembled in that city. This confession was translated into Greek,* and publicly approved and adopted, in 1643, by Parthenius of Constantinople, and the other Grecian patriarchs. It was afterwards published in Greek and Latin, at the expense of Panagiota, the grand-signor's interpreter, a man of great opulence and liberality, who ordered it to be distributed *gratis* among the Greek Christians; and it was also enriched with a recommendatory letter composed by Nectarius, patriarch of Jerusalem.† It appears evidently from this confession, that the Greeks differ widely from the votaries of the Roman pontiff, whose doctrines they reject and treat with indignation in several places; but it appears, at the same time, that their religious tenets are equally remote from those of other Christian societies; so that whoever peruses this treatise with attention, will be fully convinced, how much certain writers mistake the case, who imagine that the obstacles which prevent the union of the Greeks with this or the other Christian community, are small and inconsiderable.‡

VII. The votaries of Rome have found this to be true on many occasions. And the Lutherans made an experiment of the same kind, when they presented a fruitless invitation to the Greek churches to embrace their doctrine and discipline, and live with them in religious communion. The first steps in this laudable attempt were taken by Melancthon, who sent to the patriarch of Constantinople a copy of the confession of Augsburg, translated into Greek by Paul Dolscius. This present was accompanied with a letter, in which the learned and humane professor represented the protestant doctrine with the utmost simplicity and faithfulness, hoping that the artless charms of truth might touch the heart of the Grecian prelate. But his hopes were disappointed; for the patriarch did not even deign to send him an answer.* After this the divines of Tubingen renewed, with his successor Jeremiah,† the correspondence which had been begun by Melancthon. They wrote frequently, during the course of several years,‡ to the new patriarch, and sent him another copy of the Confession of Augsburg, with a Compendium of Theology, composed by Heerbrand, and translated into Greek by Martin Crusius; nor did they leave unemployed any means, which a pious and well-conducted zeal could suggest as proper to gain over this prelate to their communion. The fruits, however, of this correspondence were very inconsiderable, and wholly consisted in a few letters from the Greek patriarch, written, indeed, with an amiable spirit of benevolence and cordiality, but at the same time in terms which showed the impossibility of the union so much desired by the protestants. The whole strain of these letters manifested in the Greeks an inviolable attachment to the opinions and institutions of their ancestors, and tended to demonstrate the vanity of attempting to dissolve it in the present situation and circumstances of that people.§

VIII. Nothing, indeed, more deplorable can be conceived than the state of the greatest part of the Greeks, since their subjection to the oppressive yoke of the Turkish emperors. Since that fatal period, almost all learning and science, human and divine, have been extinguished among them. They have neither schools, colleges, nor any of those literary establishments that ennoble human nature, by sowing in the mind the immortal seeds of knowledge and virtue. Those few who surpass the vulgar herd in intellectual acquirements have derived this advantage from the schools of learning in Sicily or Italy, where the studious Greeks usually repair in quest of knowledge, or from a perusal of the writings of the ancient doctors, and more especially of

* It was originally composed in the Russian language.

† This confession was published at Leipsic, with a Latin translation, by Laur. Normannus, in 1695. In the preface we are informed, that it had been composed by Nectarius: but this assertion is refuted by that prelate himself, in a letter which immediately follows the preface. It is also affirmed, both in the preface and title-page, that this is the first public edition which has been given of the Greek confession. But this assertion is also false, since it is well known that it was published in Holland in 1662, at the expense of Panagiota. The German translation of this confession was published at Frankfort and Leipsic, in 1727. The learned Jo. Christ. Kocher has given, with his usual accuracy and erudition, an ample account both of this and the other confessions received among the Greeks, in his Bibliotheca Theologiæ Symbol., and the laborious Dr. Hoffman, principal professor of divinity at Wittenberg, published, in 1751, a new edition of the Orthodox confession, with an historical account of it. Those who are desirous of a circumstantial account of the famous Panagiota, to whom this confession was indebted for a considerable part of its credit, and who rendered to the Greek church in general the most eminent services, will find it in Cantemir's Histoire de l'Empire Ottoman, tom. iii. p. 149.

‡ The learned Fabricius has given, in the tenth volume of his Bibliotheca Græca, an exact and ample list of the writers, whom it is proper to consult, in order to form a just notion of the state, circumstances, and doctrines of the Greek church.

* Leo Allatius, de perpetua Consensione Eccles. Orient. et Occident. lib. iii. cap. viii. sect. ii. p. 1005

☞ † The name of the former patriarch was Joseph. In 1559, he had sent his deacon Demetrius to Wittenberg, to inform himself upon the spot of the genius and doctrines of the protestant religion.

‡ This correspondence commenced in 1576, and ended in 1581.

§ All the acts and papers relating to this correspondence were published in 1584. See Christ. Matth. Pfaffii Liber de Actis et Scriptis publicis Ecclesiæ Wirtembergicæ, p. 50.—Jo. Alb. Fabricii Biblioth. Græca, vol. x.—Emman. a Schelstrate, Acta Ecclesiæ Orientalis contra Lutheri Hæresin.—Lami Deliciæ Eruditorum, tom. viii.

the theology of St. Thomas Aquinas, which they have translated into their native language.*

Such, at least, is the notion of the learning of the modern Greeks, that is entertained by all the European Christians, as well Roman Catholics as protestants; and it is built upon the clearest evidence, and supported by testimonies of every kind. Many of the Greeks deny with obstinacy this inglorious charge, and not only defend their countrymen against the imputation of such gross ignorance, but even go so far as to maintain, that all the liberal arts and sciences are in as flourishing a state in modern Greece, as they were in any period of the history of that nation. Among the writers that exalt the learning of the modern Greeks in such an extraordinary manner, the first place is due to an eminent historian,† who has taken much pains to demonstrate the error of those who are of a different opinion. For this purpose he has not only composed a list of the learned men who adorned that country in the last century, but also makes mention of an academy founded at Constantinople by a certain Greek, whose name was Manolax, in which all the branches of philosophy, all the liberal and useful arts and sciences, are taught with the utmost success and applause, after the manner of the ancient sages of Greece. But all this, though matter of fact, does not amount to a satisfactory proof of the point in question. It only proves, what was never doubted by any thinking person, that the populous Greek nation, in which are many ancient, noble, and opulent families, is not entirely destitute of men of learning and genius. But it does not at all demonstrate, that this nation, considered in general, is at present enriched with science either sacred or profane, or makes any shining figure in the republic of letters. In a nation which, generally speaking, is sunk in the most barbarous ignorance, some men of genius and learning may arise, and shine like meteors in a gloomy firmament. With respect to the academy founded at Constantinople, it may be observed, that a literary establishment, so necessary and yet so recent, confirms the judgment that has been almost universally formed concerning the state of erudition among the Greeks.

This ignorance, which reigns among the Greeks, has the most pernicious influence upon their morals. Licentiousness and impiety not only abound among the people, but also dishonour their leaders; and the calamities that arise from this corruption of manners, are deplorably augmented by their endless contentions and divisions. Their religion is a motley collection of ceremonies, the greatest part of which are either ridiculously trifling, or shockingly absurd. Yet they are much more zealous in retaining and observing these senseless rites, than in maintaining the doctrine, or obeying the precepts, of the religion they profess. Their misery would be extreme, were it not for the support they derive from those Greeks who perform the functions of physicians and interpreters at the emperor's court; and who, by their opulence and credit, frequently interpose to reconcile the differences, or to ward off the dangers, that so often menace their church with destruction.

IX. The Russians, Georgians, and Mingrelians, adopt the doctrines and ceremonies of the Greek church, though they are entirely free from the jurisdiction and authority of the patriarch of Constantinople. It is true, indeed, that this prelate had formerly enjoyed the privilege of a spiritual supremacy over the Russians, to whom he sent a bishop whenever a vacancy happened. But, toward the conclusion of this century, this privilege ceased in consequence of the following incident. Jeremiah II., patriarch of Constantinople, undertook a journey into Moscovy, to levy pecuniary succours against his rival Metrophanes, and to drive him, by the force of money, from the patriarchal throne. On this occasion, the Moscovite monks, in compliance, no doubt, with the secret orders of the grand duke Theodore, the son of John Basilowitz, employed all the influence both of threatenings and supplications to engage Jeremiah to place at the head of the Moscovite nation an independent patriarch. The patriarch of Constantinople, unable to resist such powerful solicitations, was forced to yield; and accordingly, in a council assembled at Moscow in 1589, he nominated and proclaimed Job, archbishop of Rostow, the first patriarch of the Moscovites. This extraordinary step was, however, taken on condition that every new patriarch of the Russians should demand the consent and suffrage of the patriarch of Constantinople, and pay, at fixed periods, five hundred gold ducats. The transactions of this Moscovite council were afterwards ratified in one assembled by Jeremiah at Constantinople in 1593, to which ratification the Turkish emperor gave his solemn consent.* But the privileges and immunities of the patriarch of Moscow were extended about the middle of the following century, when Dionysius II., the Constantinopolitan primate, and his three patriarchal colleagues, exempted him, at the renewed solicitation of the grand duke of Moscovy, from the double obligation of paying tribute, and of depending, for the confirmation of his election and installation, on a foreign jurisdiction.†

X. The Georgians and Mingrelians, or, as they were anciently called, the Iberians and Colchians, have declined so remarkably since the Mohammedan dominion has been established in these countries, that they can scarcely be ranked in the number of Christians. Such, in a more especial manner, is the depraved state of the latter, who wander about the woods and mountains, and lead a savage and undisciplined life; but, among the Geor-

☞ * The translator has inserted the note [k] of the original into that paragraph of the English text, which begins thus: *Such, at least,* &c.

† See Demetrius Cantemir's Histoire de l'Empire Ottoman, tom. ii.

* See Anton. Possevini Moscovia.—Le Quien, tom. i.—The Catalogus Codicum Manuscriptorum Biblioth. Taurinens. (p. 433—469.) contains Jeremiah's account of this transaction.

† Le Quien, tom. i.—Nic. Bergius, de Ecclesia Muscovitica, part i. sect. i. c. xviii.

gians or Iberians, there are yet some remains of religion, morals, and humanity. These nations have a pontiff at their head, whom they call the Catholic; they have also their bishops and priests; but these spiritual rulers are a dishonour to Christianity, by their ignorance, avarice, and profligacy; they surpass almost the populace in the corruption of their manners, and, grossly ignorant themselves of the truths and principles of religion, they never entertain the least thought of instructing the people. If therefore it be affirmed, that the Georgians and Mingrelians, at this day, are neither attached to the opinions of the Monophysites, nor to those of the Nestorians, but embrace the doctrine of the Greek church, this must be confirmed rather in consequence of probable conjecture, than of certain knowledge, since it is almost impossible to know, with precision, what are the sentiments of a people who seem to be involved in the thickest darkness. Any remains of religion, observable among them, are entirely comprehended in certain sacred festivals and external ceremonies, of which the former are celebrated, and the latter are performed, without the least appearance of decency; for the priests administer the sacraments of baptism and of the Lord's supper with as little respect and devotion, as if they were partaking of an ordinary repast.*

XI. The eastern Christians, who renounce the communion of the Greek church, and differ from it both in doctrine and worship, may be comprehended under two distinct classes. To the former belong the Monophysites, or Jacobites, so called from Jacob Albardai,† who declare it as their opinion, that in the Saviour of the world there is only one nature, while the latter comprehends the followers of Nestorius, frequently called *Chaldæans*, from the country where they principally reside, and who suppose that there are two distinct persons or natures in the Son of God. The Monophysites are subdivided into two sects or parties, one African, the other Asiatic. At the head of the Asiatics is the patriarch of Antioch, who resides, for the most part, in the monastery of St. Ananias, and sometimes at Merdin, his episcopal seat, or at Amida, Aleppo, and other Syrian cities.* The government of this prelate is too extensive, and the churches over which he presides are too numerous, to allow his performing, himself, all the duties of his high office; and therefore a part of the administration of the pontificate is given to a kind of colleague, who is called the *maphrian*, or primate of the East, and whose doctrine and discipline are said to be adopted by the eastern churches beyond the Tigris. This primate used formerly to reside at Tauris, a city on the frontiers of Armenia; but his present habitation is the monastery of St. Matthew, near Mosul, in Mesopotamia. It is farther observable, that all the patriarchs of the Jacobites assume the denomination of Ignatius.†

XII. The African Monophysites are under the jurisdiction of the patriarch of Alexandria, who generally resides at Grand Cairo; and they are subdivided into Copts and Abyssinians. The former denomination comprehends all those Christians who dwell in Egypt, Nubia, and the countries adjacent, and whose condition is truly deplorable. Oppressed by the insatiable avarice and tyranny of the Turks, they draw out their wretched days in misery and want, and are unable to support either their patriarch or their bishops. These are not, however, left entirely destitute; since they are, in a manner, maintained by the liberality of those Copts, who, on account of their capacity in domestic affairs, and their dexterity in the exercise of several manual arts, highly useful, though entirely unknown to the Turks, have gained admittance into the principal Moslem families.‡ As to the Abyssinians, they surpass considerably the Copts, in number, power, and opulence; nor will this appear surprising, when it is considered, that they live under the dominion of a Christian emperor; they, nevertheless, consider the Alexandrian pontiff as their spiritual parent and chief; and, consequently, instead of choosing their own bishop, receive from that prelate a primate, whom they call *abuna*, and whom they acknowledge as their spiritual ruler.§

XIII. These Monophysites differ from other

* Clementis Galini Conciliatio Ecclesiæ Armenicæ cum Romana, tom. i. p. 156.—Chardin's Voyage en Perse, &c. tom. i. p. 67, where the reader will find Jos. Mar. Zampi's Relation de la Colchide et Mingrelie.—Lamberti's Relation de la Colchide ou Mingrelie, in the Recueil des Voyages au Nord, tom. vii. p. 160. Le Quien, tom. i. p. 1333.—See also Rich. Simon's Histoire Critique des Dogmes et Ceremonies des Chretiens Orientaux, ch. v. and vi. in which the learned author endeavours to remove, at least, a part of the reproach under which the Georgians and Mingrelians labour on account of their supposed ignorance and corruption. The catholics or pontiffs of Georgia and Mingrelia are, at this day, exempt from foreign jurisdiction; they are, however, obliged to pay a certain tribute to the patriarch of Constantinople.

† This Jacob Albardai, or Baradæus, as he is called by others, restored, in the sixth century, the sect of the Monophysites, then almost expiring, to its former vigour, and modelled it anew; hence they were called Jacobites. This denomination is commonly used in an extensive sense, as comprehending all the Monophysites, except those of Armenia; it, however, more strictly and properly belongs only to those Asiatic Monophysites, of whom Jacob Albardai was the restorer and the chief. See Simon's Histoire des Chretiens Orientaux—a work, nevertheless, that often wants correction

* Assemani Dissert. de Monophysitis, tom. ii.—Biblioth. Orient. Clem. Vatican. sect. viii.—Faust. Nairon's Euoplia Fidei Catholicæ ex Syrorum Monument. par. i. p. 40.—Le Quien's Oriens Christ. tom. ii. p. 1343.

† Assemani Dissertat. de Monophysitis, sect. viii.

‡ Renaudot published, in 1713, a very learned work, relative to the history of the Eastern patriarchs, under the title of "Historia Alexandrinorum Patriarcharum Jacobitarum," &c. He also gave to the world the office used in the ordination of the Jacobite patriarch, with remarks, in the first volume of his Liturg. Orient.—The internal state of the Alexandrian or Coptic church, both with respect to doctrine and worship, is described by Wansleb, in his "Histoire de l'Eglise d'Alexandrie, que nous appelons celle des Jacobites Coptes," published in 1667. Add to this another work of the same author, entitled, "Relation d'un Voyage en Egypte," in which there is a particular account of the Coptic monasteries and religious orders. See also "Nouveaux Memoires des Missions de la Compagnie de Jesus dans le Levant;" and Maillet's Description de l'Egypte, tom. ii.

§ Job. Ludolf. Comment. in Histor. Æthiop. p. 451, 461.—Lobo, Voyage d'Abissinie, tom. ii. p. 36.—Nouveaux Memoires des Missions dans le Levant, tom. iv.—Le Quien, tom. ii.

Christian societies, whether of the Greek or Latin communion, in many points, both of doctrine and worship, though the principal reason of their separation lies in the opinion they entertain concerning the nature and person of Jesus Christ. Following the doctrine of Dioscorus, Barsuma, Xenaias, Fullo, and others, whom they consider as the heads or chief ornaments of their sect, they maintain that in Christ the divine and human natures were reduced into one, and consequently reject both the decrees of the council of Chalcedon, and the famous letter of Leo the Great. That, however, they may not seem to have the least inclination toward the doctrine of Eutyches, which they profess to reject with the most ardent zeal, they propose their own system with the utmost caution and circumspection, and hold the following obscure principles: That the two natures are united in Christ without either confusion or mixture; so that though the nature of our Saviour be really one, yet it is at the same time twofold and compound.* By this declaration it appears, that those learned men, who look upon the difference between the Monophysites, and the Greek and Latin churches, rather as a dispute about *words* than *things*, are not so far in an error as some have imagined.† Be that as it may, both the Asiatic and African Monophysites of the present times are, generally speaking, so deeply sunk in ignorance, that their attachment to the doctrine by which they are distinguished from other Christian societies, is rather founded on their own obstinacy, and on the authority of their ancestors, than on any other circumstance; nor do they even pretend to appeal, in its behalf, to reason and argument.‡

XIV. The Armenians,§ though they agree with the other Monophysites in the main doctrine of that sect relating to the unity of the divine and human nature in Christ, differ from them, nevertheless, in many points of faith discipline, and worship; and hence it comes to pass, that they hold no communion with that branch of the Monophysites who are Jacobites in the more limited sense of that term. The Armenian church is governed by three patriarchs.* The chief, whose diocese comprehends the Greater Armenia, beholds forty-two archbishops subjected to his jurisdiction, and resides in a monastery at Echmiazin. The revenues of this spiritual ruler are such as would enable him to live in the most splendid and magnificent manner;† but there are no marks of pomp or opulence in his external appearance, or in his regular economy. His table is frugal, his habit plain; nor is he distinguished from the monks, with whom he lives, by any other circumstance than his superior power and authority. He is, for the most part, elected to his patriarchal dignity by the suffrages of the bishops assembled at Echmiazin, and his election is confirmed by the solemn approbation of the Persian monarch. The second patriarch of the Armenians, who is called the Catholic, resides at Cis in Cilicia, rules over the churches established in Cappadocia, Cilicia, Cyprus, and Syria, and has twelve archbishops under his jurisdiction. He at present acknowledges his subordination to the patriarch of Echmiazin. The third patriarch, who has no more than eight or nine bishops under his dominion, resides in the island of Aghtamar (which is in the midst of the great lake of Varaspuracan,) and is looked upon by the other Armenians as the enemy of their church.

Beside these prelates, who are patriarchs in the true sense of that term, the Armenians have other spiritual leaders, who are honoured with the same appellation; but this, indeed, is no more than an empty title, unattended with the authority and prerogatives of the patriarchal dignity. Thus the archbishop of the Armenians, who lives at Constantinople, and whose authority is respected by the churches established in those provinces which form the connexion between Europe and Asia, enjoys the title of patriarch. The same denomination is given to the Armenian bishop who resides at Jerusalem, and also to the prelate of the same nation, who has his episcopal seat at Caminiec in Poland, and governs the Armenian churches that are established in Russia, Poland, and the adjacent countries. These

* Assemani Biblioth. Orien. Clement. Vatican. tom. ii. p. 25, 34, 117, 133, 277, 297, &c.—See, in the same work, Abulpharajius' subtle vindication of the doctrine of his sect, vol. ii. p. 288. There is a complete and circumstantial account of the religion of the Abyssinians, in the Theologia Æthiopica of Gregory the Abyssinian, published by Fabricius, in his Lux Evangelii toti orbi exoriens, p. 716, where may also be found a list of all the writers who have given accounts of the Abyssinians.

† See La Croze, Hist. du Christianism des Indes, p. 23. Asseman. tom. ii. p. 291, 297.—Rich. Simon, Histoire des Chretiens Orientaux, p. 119.—Jo. Joach. Schroderi Thesaurus Linguæ Armenicæ, p. 276. ☞ The truth of the matter is, that the terms used by the Monophysites are something more than equivocal; they are contradictory. It may also be farther observed, that those who pretend to hold a middle path between the doctrines of Nestorius and Eutyches, were greatly embarrassed, as it was almost impossible to oppose the one, without adopting, or at least appearing to adopt the other.

‡ The liturgies of the Copts, the Syrian Jacobites, and the Abyssinians, have been published, with learned observations, by Renaudot, in the first and second volumes of his Liturgiæ Orientales.

§ The first writer, who gave a circumstantial account of the religion and history of the Armenians, was Clement Galani, an Italian of the order of the Theatins, whose Conciliatio Ecclesiæ Armenicæ cum Romana was published in 1650. The other authors, who have treated of this branch of ecclesiastical history, are enumerated by Fabricius, in his Lux Evangelii toti Orbi exoriens, ch. xxxviii.; to which must be added, Le Quien, Oriens Christianus, tom. i.—The History of Christianity in Armenia, which the learned La Croze has subjoined to his account of the progress of the Christian religion in Abyssinia, is by no means answerable to the importance and copiousness of the subject; which must be attributed to the age and infirmities of that author. For an account of the particular institutions and rites of the Armenians, see Gemelli Carreri, Voyage autour du Monde, tom. ii.

☞ * Sir Paul Ricaut mentions four; but his authority, were it more respectable than it really is, cannot be compared with that of the excellent sources from which Dr. Mosheim draws his materials.

† R. Simon has subjoined to his Histoire des Chretiens Orient. an account of all the Armenian churches which are subject to the jurisdiction of this grand patriarch; but this account, though taken from Uscanus, an Armenian bishop, is defective in many respects. For an account of the residence and manner of life of the patriarch of Echmiazin, see Paul Lucas, Voyage au Levant, tom. ii., and Gemelli Carreri, Voyage autour du Monde, tom. ii.

bishops assume the title of patriarchs, on account of some peculiar privileges conferred on them by the great patriarch of Echmaizin; for, by an authority derived from this supreme head of the Armenian church, they are allowed to consecrate bishops, and to make, every third year, and distribute among their congregations, the holy *chrism*, or ointment; which, according to a constant custom among the eastern Christians, is the privilege of the patriarchs alone.*

XV. The Nestorians, who are also known by the denomination of Chaldeans, have fixed their habitation chiefly in Mesopotamia and the neighbouring countries. They have several doctrines, as well as some religious ceremonies and institutions, that are peculiar to themselves. But the main points that distinguish them from all other Christian societies, are, their persuasion that Nestorius was unjustly condemned by the council of Ephesus, and their firm attachment to the doctrine of that prelate, who maintained that there were not only two natures, but also two distinct persons in the Son of God. In the earlier ages of the church, this error was looked upon as of the most momentous and pernicious kind; but in our times it is deemed of less consequence, by persons of the greatest weight and authority in theological matters, even among the Roman Catholic doctors. They consider this whole controversy as a dispute about words, and the opinion of Nestorius as a nominal, rather than a real heresy; that is, as an error arising rather from the words he employed, than from his intention in the use of them. It is true, indeed, that the Chaldeans attribute to Christ two natures, and even two persons; but they correct what may seem rash in this expression, by adding, that these natures and persons are so closely and intimately united, that they have only one aspect. Now the word *barsopa*, by which they express this aspect, is precisely of the same signification with the Greek word προσωπον, which signifies a *person*;† and hence it is evident, that they attached to the word *aspect* the same idea that we attach to the word *person*, and that they understood by the word *person*, precisely what we understand by the term *nature*. However that may be, we must observe here, to the lasting honour of the Nestorians, that, of all the Christian societies established in the East, they have been the most careful and successful in avoiding a multitude of superstitious opinions and practices that have infected the Greek and Latin churches.‡

XVI. In the earlier ages of Nestorianism, the various branches of that numerous and powerful sect were under the spiritual jurisdiction of the same pontiff, or *catholic*, who resided first at Bagdad, and afterwards at Mosul; but in this century the Nestorians were divided into two sects. They had chosen, in 1552, as has been already observed, two bishops at the same time, Simeon Barmama, and John Sulaka, otherwise named Siud. The latter, to strengthen his interest, and to triumph over his competitor, hastened to Rome, and acknowledged the jurisdiction, that he might be supported by the credit, of the Roman pontiff. In 1555, Simeon Denha, archbishop of Gelu, adopted the party of the fugitive patriarch, who had embraced the communion of the Latin church; and, being afterwards chosen patriarch himself, fixed his residence in the city of Ormia, in the mountainous parts of Persia. So far down as the last century, these patriarchs persevered in their communion with the church of Rome; but they seem at present to have withdrawn themselves from it.* The great Nestorian pontiffs, who form the opposite party, and look with a hostile eye on this little patriarch, have, since the year 1559, been distinguished by the general denomination of Elias, and reside constantly in the city of Mosul.† Their spiritual dominion is very extensive, takes in a considerable part of Asia, and comprehends also within its circuit the Arabian Nestorians; as also the Christians of St. Thomas, who dwell along the coast of Malabar.‡

XVII. Beside the Christian societies now mentioned, who still retain some faint shadow at least of the system of religion delivered by Christ and his apostles, there are other sects dispersed through a great part of Asia, whose principles and doctrines are highly pernicious. These sects derive their origin from the Ebionites, Valentinians, Manicheans, Basilidians, and other separatists, who, in the early ages of Christianity, excited schisms and factions in the church. Equally abhorred by Turks and Christians, and thus suffering oppression from all quarters, they gradually declined in successive centuries, and fell at length into such barbarous superstition and ignorance, as extinguished among them every spark of true religion. Thus were they reduced to the wretched and ignominious figure they at present make, having fallen from the privileges, and almost forfeited the very name of Christians. The sectaries, who pass in the East under the denomination of Sabians, who call themselves *Mendai Ijahi*, or the disciples of John, and whom the Europeans style the Christians of St.

* See the Nouveaux Memoires des Missions de la Compagnie de Jesus, tom. iii. where there is an ample and circumstantial account, both of the civil and religious state of the Armenians. This account has been highly applauded by M. de la Croze, for the fidelity, accuracy, and industry with which it is drawn up; and no man was more conversant in subjects of this nature than that learned author.

† It is in this manner that the sentiments of the Nestorians are explained in the inscriptions which adorn the tombs of their patriarchs at Mosul.—See Assemani Biblioth. Oriental. Vatican. tom. iii. par. ii.--R. Simon, Histoire de la Creance des Chretiens Orientaux, ch. vii.—P. Strozzi, de Dogmatibus Chaldæorum, published in 1617.

‡ See the learned dissertation of Assemanus de Syris Nestorianis, which occupies entirely the fourth volume of his Biblioth. Oriental. Vatican. and which seems to have been much consulted and partly copied by Mich. Le Quien.

* See Jos. Sim. Assemani Biblioth. Orient. Vatican. tom. i. p. 538, and tom. ii. p. 456.

† A list of the Nestorian pontiffs is given by Assemanus, in his Biblioth. Orient. Vatican. tom. iii. part i. p. 711; which is corrected, however, in the same volume, part ii.—See also Le Quien, tom. iii. p. 1078.

‡ The reader will find an ample account of the Christians of St. Thomas in La Croze, Histoire du Christianisme des Indes. See also Assemani Biblioth. tom. iii. part ii. cap. ix. p. ccccxiii.

John, because they yet retain some knowledge of the gospel, are probably of Jewish origin, and the remains of the ancient Hemerobaptists, of whom the writers of ecclesiastical history make frequent mention.* This, at least, is certain, that John, whom they consider as the founder of their sect, bears no sort of similitude to John the Baptist, but rather resembles the person of that name whom the ancient writers represent as the chief of the Jewish Hemerobaptists. These ambiguous Christians, whatever their origin may be, dwell in Persia and Arabia, and principally at Basra, and their religion consists in bodily washings, performed frequently, and with great solemnity,† and attended with certain ceremonies which the priests mingle with this superstitious service.‡

☞ * The sect of Hemerobaptists among the Jews were so called from their washing themselves every day, and their performing this custom with the greatest solemnity, as a religious rite, necessary to salvation. The account of this sect given by Epiphanius, in the introduction to his book of heresies, has been treated as a fiction, in consequence of the suspicions of inaccuracy and want of veracity, under which that author too justly labours. Even the existence of the Hemerobaptists has been denied, but without reason, since they are mentioned by Justin Martyr, Eusebius, and many other ancient writers, every way worthy of credit. That the Christians of St. John descended from this sect, is rendered probable by many reasons, of which the principal and the most satisfactory may be seen in a very learned and ingenious work of Dr. Mosheim, entitled, de Rebus Christianorum ante Constantinum Magnum Commentarii.

☞ † The Mendæans at present perform these ablutions only once in a year.

‡ See the work of a learned Carmelite, named Ignatius a Jesu, published in 1652, under the following title: "Narratio Originis Rituum et Errorum Christianorum S. Johannis, cui adjungitur Discursus, per modum Dialogi, in quo confutantur xxxiv. Errores ejusdem Nationis." Engelb. Kæmpferi Amœnitates Exoticæ, Fascic. II. Relat. XI. p. 35.—Sale's Preface to his English Translation of the Koran, p. 15.—Assemani Biblioth. Oriental. tom. iii. par. ii. p. 609.—Thevenot, Voyages, tom. iv. p. 584.—Herbelot, Biblioth. Orient. p. 725.—The very learned Bayer had composed an historical account of these Mendæans, which contained a variety of curious and interesting facts, and of which he intended that I should be the editor; but a sudden death prevented his executing his intention. He was of opinion (as appears from the Thesaurus Epistolicus Crozianus) that these Mendæans, or disciples of St. John, were a branch of the ancient Manicheans; which opinion La Croze himself seems to have adopted, as may be seen in the work now cited, tom. iii. But there is really nothing, either in the doctrines or manners of this sect, that resembles the opinions and practice of the Manicheans. Hence several learned men conjecture, that they derive their origin from the ancient idolators who worshipped a plurality of gods, and more especially from those who payed religious adoration to the stars of heaven, and who were called, by the Arabians, Sabians or Sabeans. This opinion has been maintained with much erudition by the famous Fourmont, in a dissertation inserted in the eighteenth volume of the Memoires de l'Academie des Inscriptions et des Belles Lettres. But it is absolutely groundless, and has not even a shadow of probability, if we except the name which the Mohammedans usually give to this sect. The Mendæans, themselves, acknowledge that they are of Jewish origin, and that they were transferred from Palestine into the country which they at present inhabit. They have sacred books of a very remote antiquity; among others, one which they attribute to Adam, and another composed by John, whom they revere as the founder of their sect. As these books were some years ago added to the library of the king of France, it is to be hoped that they may contribute to give us a more authentic account of this people than we have hitherto received.

XVIII. The Jasidians, or Jezdæans, of whose religion and manners many reports of a very doubtful nature are given by voyage-writers, are an unsettled wandering tribe, who frequent the Gordian mountains, and the deserts of Curdistan, a province of Persia; the character of whose inhabitants has something in it peculiarly fierce and intractable. The Jezdæans are divided into black and white members. The former are the priests and rulers of the sect, who go arrayed in sable garments; while the latter, who compose the multitude, are clothed in white. Their system of religion is certainly very singular, and is not hitherto sufficiently known, though it is evidently composed of some Christian doctrines, and a motley mixture of fictions drawn from a different source. They are distinguished from the other corrupt sects, that have dishonoured Christianity, by the peculiar impiety of their opinion concerning the evil genius. This malignant principle they call *Karubin*, or Cherub, i. e. one of the great ministers of the Supreme Being; and, if they do not directly address religious worship to this evil minister, they treat him at least with the utmost respect, and not only abstain, themselves, from offering him any marks of hatred or contempt, but will not suffer any contumelious treatment to be given him by others. They carry, it is said, this reverence and circumspection to such an excessive height, that no efforts of persecution, no torments, not even death itself, can engage them to conceive or express an abhorrence of this evil genius; and it is even added, that they will make no scruple to put to death such persons as express, in their presence, an aversion to him.*

XIX. The Duruzians, or Dursians, a fierce and warlike people that inhabit the craggy rocks and inhospitable wilds of mount Libanus, give themselves out for descendants of the Franks, who, from the eleventh century, carried on the holy war with the Mohamme-

* See Hyde, Historia Relig. Veter. Persarum in Append. p. 549.—Otter, Voyage en Turquie et en Perse, tom. i. p. 121, tom. ii. p. 249. In the seventeenth century, Mich. Nau, a learned Jesuit, undertook to instruct this profane sect, and to give them juster notions of religion, (see D'Arvieux, Memoires ou Voyages, tom. vi. p. 362, 377,) and after him another Jesuit, whose name was Monier, embarked in the same dangerous enterprise, (see Memoires des Missions des Jesuites, tom. iii. p. 291;) but how they were received, and what success attended their ministry, is hitherto unknown. Rhenferdius (as appears from the letters of the learned Gisbert Cuper, published by Bayer) considers the Jezdæans as the descendants of the ancient Scythians. But this opinion is no less improbable than that which makes them a branch of the Manicheans; and this is sufficiently refuted by their sentiments concerning the Evil Genius. Beausobre, in his Histoire du Manicheisme, conjectures that the denomination of this sect is derived from the name of Jesus; but it seems rather to be borrowed from the word *Jazid*, or *Jezdan*, which, in the Persian language, signifies the *good God*, and is opposed to *Ahrimen*, or *Arimanius*, the Evil Principle, (see Herbelot, Biblioth. Orient. p. 484.—Cherefeddin Ali, Hist. de Timur-bec, tom. iii. p. 81.) so that the appellative term derived from the former points out that sect as the worshippers of the good or true God. Notwithstanding the plausibility of this account of the matter, it is not impossible that the city *Jezd*, of which Otter speaks in his Voyage en Turquie et en Perse, may have given rise to the title of *Jasidians*, or *Jezdæans*.

dans in Palestine; though this pretended origin is a matter of the greatest uncertainty. What the doctrine and discipline of this nation are at present, it is extremely difficult to know, as they are at the greatest pains imaginable to conceal their religious sentiments and principles. We find, however, both in their opinions and practice, the plainest proofs of their acquaintance with Christianity. Several learned men have imagined, that both they and the Curdi of Persia had formerly embraced the sentiments of the Manicheans, and perhaps still persist in their pernicious errors.*

The Chamsi, or Solares, who reside in a certain district of Mesopotamia, are supposed, by curious inquirers into these matters, to be a branch of the Samsæans, mentioned by Epiphanius.†

There are many other Semi-Christian sects of these kinds in the east,‡ whose principles, tenets, and institutions, are far from being unworthy of the curiosity of the learned. And those who would be at the pains to turn their researches this way, and more especially to have the religious books of these sects conveyed into Europe, would undoubtedly render eminent service to the cause of sacred literature, and obtain applause from all who have a taste for the study of Christian antiquities; for the accounts which have hitherto been given of these nations and sects are full of uncertainty and contradiction.

XX. The missionaries of Rome have never ceased to display, in these parts of the world, their dexterity in making proselytes, and accordingly have founded, though with great difficulty and expense, among the greatest part of the sects now mentioned, congregations that adopt the doctrine, and acknowledge the jurisdiction, of the Roman pontiff. It is abundantly known, that among the Greeks, who live under the empire of the Turks, and also among those who are subject to the dominion of the Venetians, the emperor of Germany, and other Christian princes, there are many who have adopted the faith and discipline of the Latin church, and are governed by their own clergy and bishops, who receive their confirmation and authority from Rome. In the latter city is a college, expressly founded with a view to multiply these apostatising societies, and to increase and strengthen the credit and authority of the Roman pontiff among the Greeks. In these colleges a certain number of Grecian students, who have given early marks of genius and capacity, are instructed in the arts and sciences, and are more especially prepossessed with the deepest sentiments of veneration and zeal for the authority of the pope. Such an institution, accompanied with the efforts and labours of the missionaries, could not fail, one would think, to gain an immense number of proselytes to Rome, considering the unhappy state of the Grecian churches. But the case is quite otherwise; for the most respectable writers, even of the Roman catholic persuasion, acknowledge fairly, that the proselytes they have drawn from the Greek churches make a wretched and despicable figure, in point of number, opulence, and dignity, when compared with those, to whom the religion, government, and the very name of Rome, are disgusting and odious. They observe farther, that the sincerity of a great part of these proselytes is of the Grecian stamp; so that, when a favourable occasion is offered them of renouncing, with advantage, their pretended conversion, they seldom fail, not only to return to the bosom of their own church, but even to recompense the good offices they received from the Romans with the most injurious treatment. The same writers mention another circumstance, much less surprising, indeed, than those now mentioned, but much more dishonourable to the church of Rome; and that circumstance is, that even those of the Greek students who are educated at Rome with such care, as might naturally attach them to its religion and government, are, nevertheless, so disgusted and shocked at the corruptions of its church, clergy, and people, that they forget, more notoriously than others, the obligations with which they have been loaded, and exert themselves with peculiar obstinacy and bitterness in opposing the credit and authority of the Latin church.*

XXI. In their efforts to extend the papal empire over the Greek churches, the designing pontiffs did not forget the church of Russia, the chief bulwark and ornament of the Grecian faith. On the contrary, frequent deliberations were holden at Rome, about the proper methods of uniting, or rather subjecting this church to the papal hierarchy. In this century John Basilides, or Basilowitz, grand duke of the Russians, seemed to discover a propensity toward this union, by sending, in 1580, a solemn embassy to Gregory XIII. to exhort that pontiff to resume the negotiations relative to this important matter, that they might be brought to a happy and speedy conclusion. Accordingly, in the year following, Antony Possevin, a learned and artful Jesuit, was charged by the pope with the commission, and sent into Moscovy, to carry it into execution. But this dexterous missionary, though he spared no pains to obtain the purposes of his ambitious court, found by experience that all his efforts were unequal to the task he had un-

* See Lucas' Voyage en Grece et Asie Mineure, tom. ii. p. 36.—Hyde's Hist. Relig. Veter. Persar. p. 491, 554.—Sir Paul Ricaut's History of the Ottoman Empire, vol. i. p. 313.

† Hyde, Histor. Relig. Veter. Persar. p. 555.

‡ The Jesuit Diusse (in the Lettres Edifiantes et Curieuses des Missions Etrangeres, tom. i. p. 63,) informs us of the existence of a sect of Christians, in the mountains which separate Persia from India, who imprint the sign of the cross on their bodies with a red-hot iron.

* See, among other authors who have treated this point of history, Urb. Cerri, Etat present de l'Eglise Romaine, in which, speaking of the Greeks, he expresses himself in the following manner: "Ils deviennent les plus violens ennemis des catholiques lorsqu'ils ont apris nos sciences, et qu'ils ont connoissance de nos imperfections:" i. e. in plain English, they (the Greeks) become the bitterest enemies of us Roman catholics, when they have been instructed in our sciences, and have acquired the knowledge of our imperfections.—Other testimonies of a like nature shall be given hereafter.—Mich. Le Quien has given us an enumeration, although a defective one, of the Greek bishops who follow the rites of the Roman church, in his Oriens Christ. tom. iii. p. 360.

dertaken; nor did the Russian ambassadors, who arrived at Rome soon after, bring any thing to the ardent wishes of the pontiff, but empty promises, conceived in dubious and general terms, on which little dependence could be placed.* And, indeed, the event abundantly showed, that Basilowitz had no other view, in all these negotiations, than to flatter the pope, and obtain his assistance, in order to bring to an advantageous conclusion the unsuccessful war which he had carried on against Poland.

The advice and exhortations of Possevin and his associates were attended with more fruit among the Russian residents in the Polish dominions, many of whom embraced the doctrine and rites of the Roman church, in consequence of an association agreed on in 1596, in a meeting at Bresty, the capital of the Palatinate of Cujavia. Those who thus submitted to the communion of Rome were called the United, while the adverse party, who adhered to the doctrine and jurisdiction of the patriarch of Constantinople, were distinguished by the title of the Non-United.† It is likewise worthy of observation here, that there has been established at Kiow, since the fourteenth century, a Russian congregation, subject to the jurisdiction of the Roman pontiff, and ruled by its own metropolitans, who are entirely distinct from the Russian bishops resident in that city.‡

XXII. The Roman missionaries made scarcely any spiritual conquests worthy of mention among either the Asiatic or African Monophysites. About the middle of the preceding century, a little insignificant church, that acknowledged the jurisdiction of the pope, was erected among the Nestorians, whose patriarchs, successively named Joseph,§ resided in the city of Diarbek. Some of the Armenian provinces embraced the doctrines and discipline of Rome so early as the fourteenth century, under the pontificate of John XXIII., who, in 1318, sent them a Dominican monk to govern their church, with the title and authority of an archbishop. The episcopal seat of this spiritual ruler was first fixed at Soldania, a city in the province of Aderbijan:‖ but was afterwards transferred to Naxivan, where it still remains in the hands of the Dominicans, who alone are admitted to that spiritual dignity.¶ The Armenian churches in Poland, which have embraced the faith of Rome, have also their bishop, who resides at Lemberg.** The Georgians and Mingrelians, who were visited by some monks of the Theatin and Capuchin orders, disgusted these missionaries by their ferocity and ignorance, remained inattentive to their counsels, and unmoved by their admonitions; so that their ministry and labours were scarcely attended with any visible fruit.*

XXIII. The pompous accounts which the papal missionaries have given of the vast success of their labours among all these Grecian sects, are equally destitute of candour and truth. It is evident, from testimonies of the best and most respectable authority, that, in some of those countries, they do nothing more than administer clandestine baptism to sick infants who are committed to their care, as they appear in the fictitious character of physicians;† and that, in other places, the whole success of their ministry is confined to the assembling of some wretched tribes of indigent converts, whose poverty is the only bond of their attachment to the Romish church, and who, when the papal largesses are suspended or withdrawn, fall from their pretended allegiance to Rome, and return to the religion of their ancestors.‡ It happens also, from time to time, that a person of distinction, among the Greeks or Orientals, embraces the doctrine of the Latin church, promises obedience to its pontiff, and carries matters so far as to repair to Rome to testify his respectful submission to the apostolic see. But in these obsequious steps the noble converts are almost always moved by avarice or ambition; and, accordingly, upon a change of affairs, when they have obtained their purposes, and have nothing more to expect, they, in general, either suddenly abandon the church of Rome, or express their attachment to it in such ambiguous terms as are only calculated to deceive. Those who, like the Nestorian bishop of Diarbek,§ continue in the profession of the Roman faith, and even transmit it with an appearance of zeal to their posterity, are excited to this perseverance by no other motive than the uninterrupted liberality of the Roman pontiff.

On the other hand, the bishops of Rome are extremely attentive and assiduous in employing all the methods in their power to maintain and extend their dominion among the Christians of the East. For this purpose, they treat, with the greatest lenity and indulgence, the proselytes they have made in those parts of the world, that their yoke may not appear intolerable. They even carry this indulgence so far, as to show evidently, that they are actuated more by a love of power, than by an attachment to their own doctrines and institutions; for they not only allow the Greek and

* See the conferences between Possevin and the duke of Moscovy, together with the other writings of this Jesuit, (relative to the negotiation in question,) subjoined to his work, called Moscovia.—See also La Vie du Pere Possevin, par Jean Dorigny, liv. v. p. 351.

† Adr. Regenvolscii Histor. Eccl. Slavonicar. lib. iv. cap. ii. p. 465.

‡ See Le Quien, tom. i. p. 1274, and tom. iii. p. 1126.—Acta Sanctorum, tom. ii. Februar. p. 693.

§ See Assemani Biblioth. Orient. Vatican. tom. iii. par. i. p. 615.—Le Quien, tom. ii. p. 1084.

‖ Odor. Raynald. Annal. tom. xv. ad An. 1318. sect. iv.

¶ Le Quien, tom. iii. p. 1362, and 1403.—Clemens Galanus, Conciliatio Ecclesiæ Armenicæ cum Romana, tom. i. p. 527.

** Memoires des Missions de la Compagnie de Jesus,

* Urb. Cerri. Etat present de l'Eglise Romaine.

† Urb. Cerri, p. 164.—Gabr. de Chinon, Relations nouvelles du Levant, par. i. c. vi. This Capuchin monk delivers his opinions on many subjects with frankness and candour.

‡ See Chardin's Voyages en Perse, tom. i. ii. iii. of the last edition published in Holland, in 4to.; for, in the former editions, all the scandalous transactions of the Roman missionaries among the Armenians, Colchians, Iberians, and Persians, are entirely wanting.—See also Chinon's Relations du Levant, part ii. for the affairs of the Armenians; and Maillet's Description d'Egypte, tom. iii., for an account of the Copts.

§ Otherwise named Amida and Caramit.

other eastern proselytes the liberty of retaining the ceremonies of their ancestors (though in direct opposition to the religious service of the church of Rome,) and of living in a manner repugnant to the customs and practice of the Latin world; but, what is much more surprising, they suffer the peculiar doctrines, that distinguish the Greeks and Orientals from all other Christian societies, to remain in the public religious books of the proselytes already mentioned, and even to be reprinted at Rome in those which are sent abroad for their use.* The truth of the matter seems to be briefly this: at Rome, a Greek, an Armenian, or a Copt, is looked upon as an obedient child, and a worthy member of the church, if he acknowledges the supreme and unlimited power of the Roman pontiff over all the Christian world.

XXIV. The Maronites who inhabit the mounts Libanus and Anti-Libanus, date their subjection to the spiritual jurisdiction of the Roman pontiff from the time that the Latins carried their hostile arms into Palestine, with a view to make themselves masters of the Holy Land.† This subjection however was agreed to, with an express condition, that neither the popes nor their emissaries should pretend to change or abolish any thing which related to the ancient rites, moral precepts, or religious opinions, of this people; so that in reality, among the Maronites, there is nothing to be found that savours of popery, if we except their attachment to the Roman pontiff,* who is obliged to pay dearly for their friendship; for, as they live in the utmost distress of poverty, under the tyrannical yoke of infidels, the bishop of Rome is under a necessity of furnishing them with such subsidies as may gratify the rapacity of their oppressors, procure a subsistence for their bishop and clergy, provide all things requisite for the support of their churches and the uninterrupted exercise of public worship, and contribute in general to lessen their misery. Besides, the college erected at Rome by Gregory XIII. with a view of instructing the young men, frequently sent from Syria, in the various branches of useful science and sacred erudition, and prepossessing them with an early veneration and attachment for the Roman pontiff, is attended with a very considerable expense. The Maronite patriarch performs his spiritual functions at Canobin, a convent of the monks of St. Antony, on mount Libanus, which is his constant residence. He claims the title of Patriarch of Antioch, and always assumes the name of Peter, as if he seemed desirous of being considered as the successor of that apostle.†

* Assemanus complains (in several passages of his Biblioth. Orient. Vatican.) that even the very books printed at Rome for the use of the Nestorians, Jacobites, and Armenians, were not corrected or purged from the errors peculiar to these sects; and he looks upon this negligence as the reason of the defection of many Roman converts, and of their return to the bosom of the eastern and Greek churches, to which they originally belonged.—See, on the other hand, the Lettres Choisies de R. Simon, tom. ii. let. xxiii., in which the author pretends to defend this conduct of the Romanists, which some attribute to indolence and neglect, others to artifice and prudence.

† The Maronite doctors, and more especially those who reside at Rome, maintain, with the greatest efforts of zeal and argument, that the religion of Rome has always been preserved among them in its purity, and exempt from any mixture of heresy or error. The proof of this assertion has been attempted, with great labour and industry, by Faust. Nairon, in his Dissertatio de Origine, Nomine, ac Religione, Maronitarum, published at Rome in 1679 It was from this treatise, and some other Maronite writers, that De la Roque drew the materials of his discourses concerning the origin of the Maronites, together with the abridgment of their history, which he inserted in the second volume of his Voyage de Syrie et du Mont Liban. But neither this hypothesis, nor the authorities by which it is supported, have any weight with the most learned men of the Roman church, who maintain, that the Maronites derived their origin from the Monophysites, and adhered to the doctrine of the Monothelites,* until the twelfth century, when they embraced the communion of Rome. See R. Simon, Histoire Critique des Chretiens Orientaux, ch. xiii.—Euseb. Renaudot, Histor. Patriarch. Alexand. in Præfat. iii. 2. in Histor. p. 49. The very learned Assemanus, who was himself a Maronite, steers a middle way between these opposite accounts, in his Biblioth. Orient. Vatic. tom. i., while the matter in debate is left undecided by Mich. le Quien, in his Oriens Christianus, tom. iii., where he gives an account of the Maronite church and its spiritual rulers.—For my own part I am persuaded, that those who consider that all the Maronites have not as yet embraced the faith, or acknowledged the jurisdiction of Rome, will be little disposed to receive with credulity the assertions of certain Maronite priests, who are, after the manner of the Syrians, much addicted to boasting and exaggeration. Certain it is, that there are Maronites in Syria, who still behold the church of Rome with the greatest aversion and abhorrence; and, what is still more remarkable, great numbers of that nation residing in Italy, even under the eye of the pontiff, opposed his authority during the last century, and threw the court of Rome into great perplexity. One body of these non-conforming Maronites retired into the valleys of Piedmont, where they joined the Waldenses; another, above six hundred in number, with a bishop and several ecclesiastics at their head, fled into Corsica, and implored the protection of the republic of Genoa against the violence of the inquisitors. See Urb. Cerri's Etat present de l'Eglise Romaine, p. 121. Now may it not be asked here, What could have excited the Maronites in Italy to this public and vigorous opposition to the Roman pontiff, if it be true that their opinions were in all respects conformable to the doctrines and decrees of the church of Rome? This opposition could not have arisen from any thing but a difference in point of doctrine and belief, since the church of Rome allowed, and still allows the Maronites, under its jurisdiction, to retain and perform the religious rites and institutions that have been handed down to them from their ancestors, and to follow the precepts and rules of life to which they have always been accustomed. Compare, with the authors above cited, Thesaur. Epistol. Crozian. t. i.

* Those who maintained, that, notwithstanding the two natures in Christ, viz. the human and divine, there was, nevertheless, but one will, which was the divine.

* The reader will do well to consult principally, on this subject, the observations subjoined by Rich. Simon to his French translation of the Italian Jesuit Dandini's Voyage to Mount Libanus, published in 1685. See also Euseb. Renaudot's Historia Patriarch. Alexandr. p. 548.

† See Petitqueux, Voyage a Canobin dans le Mont Liban, in the Nouveaux Memoires des Missions de la Compagnie de Jesus, tom. iv. p. 252, and tom. viii. p. 355.—La Roque, Voyage de Syrie, tom. ii. p. 10.—Laur. D'Arvieux, Memoires ou Voyages tom. ii. p. 418.

PART II.

THE HISTORY OF THE MODERN CHURCHES.

CHAPTER I.

The History of the Lutheran Church.

I. The rise and progress of the Evangelical or Lutheran church, have been already related, so far as they belong to the history of the Reformation. The former title was assumed by that church in consequence of the original design of its founder, which was to restore to its native lustre the Gospel of Christ, that had so long been covered with the darkness of superstition, or, in other words, to place in its proper and true light that important doctrine, which represents salvation as attainable by the merits of Christ alone. Nor did the church, now under consideration, discover any reluctance to an adoption of the name of the great man, whom Providence employed as the honoured instrument of its foundation and establishment. A natural sentiment of gratitude to him, by whose ministry the clouds of superstition had been chiefly dispelled, who had destroyed the claims of pride and self-sufficiency, exposed the vanity of confidence in the intercession of saints and martyrs, and pointed out the Son of God as the only proper object of trust to miserable mortals, excited his followers to assume his name, and to call their community the *Lutheran* Church.

The rise of this church must be dated from that remarkable period, when pope Leo X. drove Martin Luther, with his friends and followers, from the bosom of the Roman hierarchy, by a solemn and violent sentence of excommunication. It began to acquire a regular form, and a considerable degree of stability and consistence, from the year 1530, when the system of doctrine and morality which it had adopted was drawn up and presented to the diet of Augsburg; and it was raised to the dignity of a lawful and complete hierarchy, totally independent of the laws and jurisdiction of the Roman pontiff, in consequence of the treaty concluded at Passau, in 1552, between Charles V., and Maurice, elector of Saxony, relating to the religious affairs of the empire.

II. The great and leading principle of the Lutheran church, is, that the Scriptures are the only source from which we are to draw our religious sentiments, whether they relate to faith or practice; and that these inspired writings are, in all matters that are essential to salvation, so plain, and so easy to be thoroughly understood, that their signification may be learned, without the aid of an expositor, by every person of common sense, who has a competent knowledge of the language in which they are composed. There are, indeed, certain formularies adopted by this church, which contain the principal points of its doctrine, ranged, for the sake of method and perspicuity, in their natural order. But these books have no authority but what they derive from the scriptures of truth, whose sense and meaning they are designed to convey; nor are the Lutheran doctors permitted to interpret or explain these books so as to draw from them any propositions inconsistent with the express declarations of the word of God. The Confession of Augsburg, and the annexed Defence of it against the objections of the Roman catholic doctors, may be deemed the chief and the most respectable of these human productions.* In the next rank may be placed the *Articles of Smalcald*,† as they are commonly called, together with the shorter and larger Catechisms of Luther, calculated for the instruction of youth, and the improvement of persons of riper years. To these standard-books most churches add the *Form of Concord;* which, though not universally received, has not, on that account, occasioned any animosity or disunion, as the few points that prevent its being adopted by some

☞ * When the confession of Augsburg had been presented to the diet of that city, the Roman catholic doctors were employed to refute the doctrines it contained; and this pretended refutation was also read to that august assembly. A reply was immediately drawn up by Melancthon, and presented to the emperor, who, under the pretext of a pacific spirit, refused to receive it. This reply was afterwards published, under the title of Apologia Confessionis Augustanæ; and is the defence of that confession, mentioned by Dr. Mosheim as annexed to it. To speak plainly, Melancthon's love of peace and concord seems to have carried him beyond what he owed to the truth, in composing this defence of the confession of Augsburg. In that edition of the Defence which some Lutherans (and Chytræus among others) look upon as the most genuine and authentic, Melancthon makes several strange concessions to the church of Rome; whether through servile fear, excessive charity, or hesitation of mind, I will not pretend to determine. He speaks of the presence of Christ's body in the eucharist in the very strongest terms that the catholics use to express the monstrous doctrine of transubstantiation, and adopts these remarkable words of Theophylact, that 'the bread was not a figure only, but was truly changed into flesh.' He approves that canon of the mass, in which the priest prays that 'the bread may be changed into the body of Christ.' It is true, that, in some subsequent editions of the defence or apology now under consideration, these obnoxious passages were omitted and the phraseology, which had given such just offence, was considerably mitigated. There is an ample account of this whole affair, together with a history of the dissensions of the Lutheran church, in the valuable and learned work of Hospinian, entitled, 'Historiæ Sacramentariæ Pars posterior,' p. 199, et seq. These expressions, in Melancthon's Apologia, will appear still more surprising, when we recollect that, in the course of the debates concerning the manner of Christ's presence in the eucharist, he, at length, seemed to lean visibly toward the opinions of Bucer and Calvin, and that, after his death, his followers were censured and persecuted in Saxony on this account, under the denomination of Philippists. This shows either that the great man now under consideration changed his opinions, or that he had formerly been seeking union and concord at the expense of truth.

☞ † The articles here mentioned were drawn up at Smalcald by Luther, on occasion of a meeting of the protestant electors, princes, and states, at that place. They were principally designed to show how far the Lutherans were disposed to go, in order to avoid a final rupture, and in what sense they were willing to adopt the doctrine of Christ's presence in the eucharist. And though the terms in which these articles are expressed, be somewhat dubious, yet they are much less harsh and disgusting than those used in the Confession, the Apology, and the Form of Concord.

churches are of an indifferent nature,* and do not, in any degree, affect the grand and fundamental principles of true religion.†

III. The form of public worship, and the rites and ceremonies that were proper to be admitted as a part of it, gave rise to disputes in several places, during the infancy of the Lutheran church. Some were inclined to retain a greater number of the ceremonies and customs that had been so excessively multiplied in the church of Rome, than seemed either lawful or expedient to others. The latter, after the example of the Helvetic reformers, had their views entirely turned toward that simplicity and gravity which characterized the Christian worship in the primitive times; while the former were of opinion, that some indulgence was to be shown to the weakness of the multitude, and some regard paid to institutions that had acquired a certain degree of weight through long established custom. But, as these contending parties were both persuaded that the ceremonial part of religion was, generally speaking, a matter of human institution, and that consequently a diversity of external rites might be admitted among different churches professing the same religion, without any prejudice to the bonds of charity and fraternal union, these disputes could not be of any long duration. In the mean time, all those ceremonies and observances of the church of Rome, whether of a public or private nature, that carried palpable marks of error and superstition, were every where rejected without hesitation; and wise precautions were used to regulate the forms of public worship in such a manner, that the genuine fruits of piety should not be choked by a multitude of insignificant rites. Besides, every church was allowed to retain so much of the ancient form of worship as might be still observed without giving offence, and as seemed suited to the character of the people, the genius of the government, and the nature and circumstances of the place where it was founded. Hence it has happened, that, even so far down as the present times, the Lutheran churches differ considerably one from another, with respect both to the number and nature of their religious ceremonies; a circumstance so far from tending to their dishonour, that it is, on the contrary, a very striking proof of their wisdom and moderation.*

IV. The supreme civil rulers of every Lutheran state are clothed also with the dignity, and perform the functions of supremacy in the church. The very essence of civil government seems manifestly to point out the necessity of investing the sovereign with this spiritual supremacy,† and the tacit consent of the Lutheran churches has confirmed the dictates of wise policy in this respect. It must not, however, be imagined, that the ancient rights and privileges of the people in ecclesiastical affairs have been totally abolished by this constitution of things, since it is certain, that the vestiges of the authority exercised by them in the primitive times, though more striking in one place than in another, are yet more or less visible every where. Besides, it must be carefully remembered, that all civil rulers of the Lutheran persuasion are effectually restrained, by the fundamental principles of the doctrine they profess, from any attempts to change or destroy the established rule of faith and manners, to make any alteration in the essential doctrines of their religion, or in any thing that is intimately connected with them, or to impose their particular opinions upon their subjects in a despotic and arbitrary manner.

The councils, or societies, appointed by the sovereign to watch over the interests of the church, and to govern and direct its affairs, are composed of persons conversant both in civil and ecclesiastical law, and, according to a very ancient denomination, are called *Consistories*. The internal government of the Lutheran church seems equally removed from episcopacy on the one hand, and from presbyterianism on the other, if we except the kingdoms of Sweden and Denmark, which retain the form of ecclesiastical government that preceded the reformation, purged, indeed, from the superstitions and abuses that rendered it so odious.‡ This constitution of the hierarchy

☞ * Dr. Mosheim, like an artful painter, shades those objects in the history of Lutheranism which it is impossible to expose with advantage to a full view. Of this nature was the conduct of the Lutheran doctors in the deliberations relating to the famous Form of Concord here mentioned; a conduct that discovers such an imperious and uncharitable spirit, as would have been more consistent with the genius of the court of Rome than with the principles of a protestant church. The reader who is desirous of an ample demonstration of the truth and justice of this censure, has only to consult the learned work of Rod. Hospinian, entitled, 'Concordia Discors, seu de Origine et Progressu Formulæ Concordiæ Bergensis.' The history of this remarkable production is more amply related in the thirty-ninth and following paragraphs of this first chapter, and in the notes, which the translator has taken the liberty to add there, in order to cast a proper light upon some things that are too interesting to be viewed superficially. In the mean time I shall only observe that the points in the Form of Concord, that prevented its being universally received, are not of such an indifferent nature as Dr. Mosheim seems to imagine. To maintain the ubiquity or omnipresence of Christ's body, together with its real and peculiar presence in the eucharist, and to exclude from their communion the protestants, who denied these palpable absurdities, was the plan of the Lutheran doctors in composing and recommending the Form of Concord; and this plan can neither be looked upon as a matter of pure indifference, nor as a mark of Christian charity.

† See, for an account of the Lutheran confessions of faith, Christ. Locheri Biblioth. Theologiæ Symbolicæ, p. 114.

* See Balth. Meisneirus, Lib. de Legibus, lib. iv. art. iv. quæst. iv.—Jo. Adam Scherzerus, Breviar. Hulsemann. Enulc. p. 1313—1321.

☞ † Since nothing is more inconsistent with that subordination and concord, which are among the great ends of civil government, than *imperium in imperio*, i. e. two independent sovereignties in the same body politic, the genius of government, equally with the spirit of genuine Christianity, proclaims the equity of that constitution, which makes the head of the state the supreme visible ruler of the church.

☞ ‡ In these two kingdoms the church is ruled by bishops and superintendants, under the inspection and authority of the sovereign. The archbishop of Upsal is primate of Sweden, and the only archbishop among the Lutherans. The luxury and licentiousness that too commonly flow from the opulence of the Roman catholic clergy are unknown in these two northern states, since the revenues of the prelate now mentioned do not amount to more than 400 pounds yearly, while those of the bishops are proportionally small

of the Lutherans will not seem surprising, when their sentiments with respect to ecclesiastical polity are duly considered. On the one hand, they are persuaded that there is no law, of divine authority, which points out a distinction between the ministers of the Gospel, in rank, dignity, or prerogatives; and therefore they recede from episcopacy. But, on the other hand, they are of opinion, that a certain subordination, a diversity in point of rank and privileges among the clergy, are not only highly useful, but also necessary to the perfection of church communion, by connecting more closely, in consequence of a mutual dependence, the members of the same body; and thus they avoid the uniformity of the presbyterian government. They do not, however, agree with respect to the extent of this subordination, and the degrees of superiority and precedence that ought to distinguish their doctors; for, in some places, this is regulated with much more regard to the ancient rules of church-government, than is discovered in others. As the divine law is silent on this head, different opinions may be entertained, and different forms of ecclesiastical polity adopted, without a breach of Christian charity and fraternal union.

V. Every country has its own liturgies, which are the rules of proceeding in every thing that relates to external worship and the public exercise of religion. These rules, however, are not of an immutable nature, like those institutions which bear the stamp of a divine authority, but may be augmented, corrected, or illustrated, by the order of the sovereign, when such changes evidently appear to be necessary or expedient. The liturgies used in the different countries that have embraced the system of Luther, agree perfectly in all the essential branches of religion, in all matters that can be looked upon as of real moment and importance; but they differ widely in many things of an indifferent nature, concerning which the Scriptures are silent, and which compose that part of the public religion that derives its authority from the wisdom and appointment of men. Assemblies for the celebration of divine worship meet every where at stated times. Here the Scriptures are read publicly, prayers and hymns are addressed to the Deity, the sacraments are administered, and the people are instructed in the knowledge of religion, and excited to the practice of virtue by the discourses of their ministers. The wisest methods are used for the religious education of youth, who are not only carefully instructed in the elements of Christianity in the public schools, but are also examined by the pastors of the churches to which they belong, in a public manner, in order to the progressive extension of their knowledge, and the more vigorous exertion of their faculties in the study of divine truth. Hence, in almost every province, catechisms, containing the essential truths of religion and the main precepts of morality, are published and recommended by the authority of the sovereign, as rules to be followed by the masters of schools, and by the ministers of the church, both in their private and public instructions. But, as Luther left behind him an accurate and judicious production of this kind, in which the fundamental principles of religion and morality are explained and confirmed with the greatest perspicuity and force, both of evidence and expression, this compendious catechism of that eminent reformer is universally adopted as the first introduction to religious knowledge, and is one of the standard-books of that church which bears his name; and, indeed, all the provincial catechisms are no more than illustrations and enlargements of this excellent abridgment of faith and practice.

VI. Among the days deemed sacred in the Lutheran church, (beside that which is celebrated every week in memory of Christ's resurrection from the dead,) we may reckon all such as were signalised by those glorious and important events that proclaimed the celestial mission of the Saviour, and the divine authority of his holy religion.* For these sacred festivals, the grateful and well-grounded piety of ancient times had always professed the highest veneration. But the Lutheran church has gone yet farther; and, to avoid giving offence to weak brethren, has retained several which seemed to have derived the respect that is paid to them, rather from the suggestions of superstition than from the dictates of true religion. There are some churches that carry the desire of multiplying festivals so far, as to observe religiously the days formerly set apart for celebrating the memory of the twelve apostles.

It is well known, that the power of *excommunication*, i. e. of banishing from its bosom obstinate and scandalous transgressors, was a privilege enjoyed and exercised by the church from the remotest antiquity; and it is no less certain, that this privilege was often perverted to the most iniquitous and odious purposes. The founders of the Lutheran church, therefore, undertook to remove the abuses and corruptions under which this branch of ecclesiastical discipline laboured, and to restore it to it primitive purity and vigour. At first their attempts seemed to be crowned with success, since it is plain, that, during the sixteenth century, no opposition of any moment was made to the wise and moderate exercise of this spiritual authority. But, in process of time, this privilege fell imperceptibly into contempt; the terror of excommunication lost its force; and ecclesiastical discipline was reduced to such a shadow, that, in most places, there are scarcely any remains or traces of it at this day. This change may be partly attributed to the corrupt propensities of mankind, who are naturally desirous of destroying the influence of every institution that is designed to curb their licentious passions. It must, however, be acknowledged, that the relaxation of ecclesiastical discipline was not owing to this cause alone; other circumstances concurred to diminish the respect and submission that had been paid to the spiritual tribunal. On one hand, the clergy abused this important privi-

* Such (for example) are the nativity, death, resurrection, and ascension of the Son of God; the descent of the Holy Spirit upon the apostles on the day of Pentecost. &c.

'ege in various ways; some misapplying the severity of excommunication through ignorance or imprudence, while others impiously perverted an institution, in itself exceedingly useful, to satisfy their private resentments, and to avenge themselves upon those who had dared to offend them. On the other hand, the counsels of certain persons in power, who considered the privilege of excommunicating in the hands of the clergy as derogatory from the majesty of the sovereign, and detrimental to the interests of civil society, had no small influence in bringing this branch of spiritual jurisdiction into disrepute. It is however certain, that whatever causes may have contributed to produce this effect, the effect itself was much to be lamented, as it removed one of the most powerful restraints upon iniquity. Nor will it appear surprising, when this is duly considered, that the manners of the Lutherans are so remarkably depraved, and that, in a church which is almost deprived of all authority and discipline, multitudes affront the public by their audacious irregularities, and transgress, with a shameless impudence, through the prospect of impunity.

VII. The prosperous and unfavourable events which belong to the history of the Lutheran church, since the happy establishment of its liberty and independence, are neither numerous nor remarkable, and may consequently be mentioned in a few words. The rise and progress of this church, before its final and permanent establishment, have been already related; but that very religious peace, which was the instrument of its stability and independence, set bounds, at the same time, to its progress in the empire, and prevented it effectually from extending its limits.* Near the close of this century, Gebhard, archbishop of Cologne, evinced a wish to enter into its communion, and, having contracted the bonds of matrimony, formed the design of introducing the reformation into his dominions. But this arduous attempt, which was in direct contradiction to the famous ecclesiastical reservation† stipulated in the articles of the peace of religion concluded at Augsburg, proved abortive; and the prelate was obliged to resign his dignity, and to abandon his country.‡ On the other hand, it is certain, that the adversaries of the Lutheran church were not permitted to disturb its tranquillity, or to hurt, in any essential point, its liberty, prosperity, and independence. Their intentions, indeed, were malignant enough; and it appeared evident, from many striking circumstances, that they were secretly projecting a new attack upon the protestants with a view to annul the treaty of Passau, and to have them declared public enemies to the empire. Such was undoubtedly the unjust and seditious design of Francis Burckhard, in composing the famous book *de Autonomiâ*, which was published in 1586; and also of Pistorius, in drawing up the reasons, which the margrave of Baden alleged in vindication of his returning from Lutheranism into the bosom of popery.* These writers, and others of the same stamp, treated the Religious Peace, negotiated at Passau, and ratified at Augsburg, as unjust, because it was obtained by force of arms, and as null, because concluded without the knowledge and consent of the Roman pontiff. They pretended also to prove, that by the changes and interpolations, which they affirmed to have been made by Melancthon, in the confession of Augsburg, after it had been presented to the diet, the protestants forfeited all the privileges and advantages derived from the treaty now mentioned. The latter accusation gave rise to long and warm debates during this and the following century. Many learned and ingenious productions were published on that occasion, in which the Lutheran divines proved, with the utmost perspicuity and force of argument, that the Confession was preserved in their church in its original state, uncorrupted by any mixture, and that none of their brethren had ever departed in any instance from the doctrines contained in it.† They who felt most sensibly the bitter and implacable hatred of the papists against the doctrine and worship of the Lutheran Church (which they disdainfully called the *new religion*,) were such members of that church as lived in the territories of Roman Catholic princes. This is more especially true of the protestant subjects of the house of Austria,‡ who experienced, in the most affecting manner, the dire effect of bigotry and superstition seated on a throne, and who lost the greatest part of their liberty before the conclusion of this century.

VIII. While the votaries of Rome were thus meditating the ruin of the Lutheran church, and exerting, for this purpose, all the powers of secret artifice and open violence, the followers of Luther were assiduously bent on defeating their efforts, and left no means unemployed, that seemed proper to maintain their own

☞* The reason of this will be seen in the following note.

☞† In the diet of Augsburg, which was assembled in 1555, in order to execute the treaty of Passau, those states which had already embraced the Lutheran religion, were confirmed in the full enjoyment of their religious liberty. To prevent, however, as far as was possible, the progress of the reformation, Charles V. stipulated for the catholics the famous ecclesiastical reservation, by which it was decreed, that if any archbishop, prelate, bishop, or other ecclesiastic, should, in time to come, renounce the faith of Rome, his dignity and benefice should be forfeited, and his place be filled by that chapter or college which possessed the power of election.

‡ See Jo. Dav. Koleri Dissertatio de Gebhardo Truchsessio.—Jo. Pet. a Ludewig Reliquiæ Manuscriptorum omnis Ævi, tom. v. p. 383.—See also a German work entitled Unschuldige Nachritchten, An 1748 p. 484.

* See Chr. Aug. Salig. Histor. August. Confessionis, tom. i. lib. iv. cap. iii. p. 767.

† See Salig. Hist. August. Confessionis, tom. i.—It cannot indeed be denied, that Melancthon corrected and altered some passages of the Confession of Augsburg. It is certain, that, in 1555, he made use of the extraordinary credit and influence he then had, to introduce among the Saxon churches an edition of that confession, which was so far corrected as to be, upon the whole, very different from the original one. But his conduct in this step, which was extremely audacious, or at least highly imprudent, never received the approbation of the Lutheran church, nor was the Augsburg Confession, in this new shape ever admitted as one of the standard-books of its faith and doctrine.

‡ See the Austria Evangelica of the learned Raupachius, tom. i. p. 152. tom. ii p. 287.

doctrine, and to strengthen their cause. The calamities which they had suffered were fresh in their remembrance; and hence they were admonished to use all possible precautions to prevent their falling again into the like unhappy circumstances. Add to this, the zeal of princes and men in power for the advancement of true religion, which, it must be acknowledged, was much greater in this century, than it is in the times in which we live. Hence the original confederacy that had been formed among the German princes for the maintenance of Lutheranism, and of which the elector of Saxony was the chief, gradually acquired new strength; and foreign sovereigns, particularly those of Sweden and Denmark, were invited to enter into this grand alliance; and, as it was universally agreed, that the stability and lustre of the rising church depended much on the learning of its ministers, and the progress of the sciences, among those in general who professed its doctrines, so the greatest part of the confederate princes promoted, with the utmost zeal, the culture of letters, and banished, wherever their salutary influence could extend, that baneful ignorance which is the parent of superstition. The academical institutions founded by the Lutherans, at Jena, Helmstadt, and Altorf, and by the Calvinists at Franeker, Leyden, and other places; the ancient universities reformed and accommodated to the constitution and exigencies of a purer church than that under whose influence they had been at first established; the great number of schools that were opened in almost every city; the ample rewards, together with the distinguished honours and privileges that were bestowed on men of learning and genius; all these circumstances bear honourable testimony to the generous zeal of the German princes for the advancement of useful knowledge. These noble establishments were undoubtedly expensive, and required large funds for their support. These were principally drawn from the revenues and possessions, which the piety or superstition of ancient times had consecrated to the multiplication of convents, the erection or embellishment of churches, and other religious uses.

IX. These generous and zealous efforts in the cause of learning were attended with remarkable success. Almost all the liberal arts and sciences were cultivated with emulation, and brought to greater degrees of perfection. All those, whose views were turned to the service of the church, were obliged to apply themselves, with diligence and assiduity, to the study of Greek, Hebrew, and Latin literature, in order to qualify them for performing, with dignity and success, the duties of the sacred function; and it is well known that in these branches of erudition several Lutheran doctors excelled in such a manner, as to require a deathless name in the republic of letters. Melancthon, Cario, Chytræus, Reineccius, and others, were eminent for their knowledge of history. More particularly Matthias Flacius, one of the authors of the Centuriæ Magdeburgenses,* (an immortal work that restored to the light of evidence and truth the facts relating to the rise and progress of the Christian church, which had been covered with great darkness, and corrupted by innumerable fables,) may be deservedly considered as the parent of ecclesiastical history. Nor should we omit mentioning the learned Martin Chumnitz, to whose Examination of the Decrees of the Council of Trent, the history of religion is more indebted, than many, at this day, are apt to imagine. While so many branches of learning were cultivated with zeal, some, it must be confessed, were too little pursued. Among these we may place the history of literature and philosophy, the important science of criticism, the study of antiquities, and other objects of erudition connected with them. It is, however, to be observed, that, notwithstanding the neglect with which these branches of science seemed too generally to be treated, the foundations of their culture and improvement in future ages were really laid in this century. On the other hand, it is remarkable that Latin eloquence and poetry were carried to a very high degree of improvement, and exhibited orators and poets of the first order; from which circumstance alone it may be fairly concluded, that, if all the branches of literature and philosophy were not brought to that pitch of perfection, of which they were susceptible, this was not owing to the want of industry or genius, but rather to the restraints imposed upon genius by the infelicity of the times. All the votaries of science, whom a noble emulation excited to the pursuit of literary fame, were greatly animated by the example, the influence, and the instructions of Melancthon, who was deservedly considered as the great and leading doctor of the Lutheran church, and whose sentiments relating both to sacred and profane erudition, were so generally respected, that scarcely any had the courage to oppose them. In the next rank to this eminent reformer may be mentioned Joachim Camerarius of Leipsic, a shining ornament to the republic of letters in this century, who, by his zeal and application, contributed much to promote the cause of universal learning, and more especially the study of elegant literature.

X. The revolutions of philosophy among the Lutheran doctors were many and various. Luther and Melancthon seemed to set out with a resolution to banish every species of philosophy* from the church; and, though it is impossible to justify entirely this part of their conduct, they are less to be blamed than those scholastic doctors whose barbarous method of teaching philosophy was extremely disgusting, and who, by a miserable abuse of the subtle precepts of Aristotle, had perverted the dictates of common sense, and introduced the

* The joint authors of this famous work (beside Flacius Illyricus) were Nicolaus Gallus, Johannes Wigandus, and Matthias Judex, all ministers of Magdeburg; and they were assisted by Casper Nidpruckius, an Imperial counsellor, Johannes Baptista Heincelius, an Augustinian, Basil Faber, and others.

* See Christ. Aug. Heumanni Acta Philosophor. art. ii. part x. p. 579.—Jo. Herm. ab Elswich, Dissertat. de Varia Aristotelis Fortuna in Scholis Protestantium, which Launoy has prefixed to his book de Fortuna Aristotelis in Academia Parisiensi, sect viii. xiii.

greatest obscurity and confusion both into philosophy and religion. But, though these abuses led the two great men now mentioned too far, and were carrying them into the opposite extreme, their own recollection suspended their precipitation, and they both perceived, before it was too late, that true philosophy was necessary to restrain the licentious flights of mere genius and fancy, and to guard the sanctuary of religion against the inroads of superstition and enthusiasm.* It was in consequence of this persuasion that Melancthon composed, in a plain and familiar style, abridgments of almost all the branches of philosophy, which, during many years, were explained publicly to the studious youth in all the Lutheran academies and schools of learning. This celebrated reformer may not improperly be considered as an *eclectic;* for, though in many points he followed Aristotle, and retained some degree of propensity to the ancient philosophy of the schools, yet he drew many things from the fecundity of his own genius, and often had recourse also to the doctrines of the Platonists and Stoics.

XI. This method of teaching philosophy, however recommendable on account of its simplicity and perspicuity, did not long enjoy, alone and unrivalled, the great credit and authority which it had obtained. Certain acute and subtle doctors, having perceived that Melancthon, in composing his Abridgments, had discovered a peculiar and predominant attachment to the philosophy of Aristotle, thought it was better to go to the source, than to drink at the stream, and therefore read and explained to their disciples the words of the Stagirite. On the other hand, it was observed, that the Jesuits, and other votaries of Rome, artfully made use of the ambiguous terms and the intricate sophistry of the ancient schoolmen, in order to puzzle the protestants, and to reduce them to silence, when they particularly wished for such arguments as were calculated to produce conviction; and, therefore, many protestant doctors thought it might be advantageous to their cause to have the studious youth instructed in the mysteries of the Aristotelian philosophy, as it was taught in the schools, that thus they might be qualified to defend themselves with the same weapons with which they were attacked. Hence there arose, in the latter part of this century, three philosophical sects, the Melancthonian, the Aristotelian, and the Scholastic. The first declined gradually, and soon disappeared: but the other two imperceptibly grew into one, acquired new vigour by this coalition, increased daily in reputation and influence, and were adopted in all the schools of learning. It is true, that the followers of Ramus made violent inroads, in several places, upon the territories of these combined sects, and sometimes with a certain appearance of success; but their hopes were transitory; for after various struggles they were obliged to yield, and were at length entirely banished from the schools.*

XII. Such also was the fate of the disciples of Paracelsus, who, from the grand principle of their physical system, were called *Fire-Philosophers*,† and who aimed at nothing less than the total subversion of the peripatetic philosophy, and the introduction of their own reveries into the public schools. Toward the close of this century, the Paracelsists really made a figure in almost all the countries of Europe, as their sect was patronised and supported by the genius and eloquence of several great men, who exerted themselves, with the utmost zeal and assiduity, in its cause, and endeavoured, both by their writings and their transactions, to augment its credit. In England it found an eminent defender in Robert Flood, or Fludd, a man of a very singular genius,‡ who illustrated, or at least attempted to illustrate, the philosophy of Paracelsus, in a great number of treatises, which, even in our times, are not entirely destitute of readers and admirers. The same philosophy found some votaries in France, and was propagated with zeal at Paris by River, in opposition to the sentiments and efforts of the university of that city.§ Its cause was industriously promoted in Denmark, by Severinus;‖ in Germany, by Kunrath, an eminent physician at Dresden, who died in 1605;¶ and in other countries by a considerable number of warm votaries, who were by no means unsuccessful in augmenting its reputation, and multiplying its followers. As all these heralds of the new philosophy accompanied their instructions with a striking air of piety and devotion, and seemed, in propagating their strange system, to propose to themselves no other end than the advancement of the divine glory, and the restoration of peace and concord to a divided church, a motive which, in appearance, was so generous

☞ * Some writers, either through malignity, or for want of better information, have pretended that Luther rejected the scholastic philosophy through a total ignorance of its nature and precepts. Those who have ventured upon such an assertion must have been as ignorant of the history of literature in general, as of the industry and erudition of Luther in particular. For a demonstrative proof of this, see Brucker's Historia Critica Philosophiæ, tom. iv part i.

* Jo. Herm. ab. Elswich, de Fatis Aristot. in Scholis Protest. sect. xxi.—Jo. Georg. Walchius, Historia Logices, lib. ii. cap. i.—Otto Fred. Schutzius, de Vita Chytræi, lib. iv. sect iv.

☞ † This fanatical sect of philosophers had several denominations. They were called Theo-Sophists, from their declaiming against human reason as a dangerous and deceitful guide, and their representing a divine and supernatural illumination as the only means of arriving at truth. They were called *Philosophi per ignem*, i. e. Fire-Philosophers, from their maintaining that the intimate essences of natural things were only to be known by the trying efforts of fire, directed in a chemical process. They were, lastly, denominated Paracelsists, from the eminent physician and chemist of that name who was the chief ornament and leader of that extraordinary sect.

☞ ‡ The person here mentioned by Dr. Mosheim is not the famous Dominican monk of that name, who, from his ardent pursuit of mathematical knowledge, was called the Seeker, and who, from his passion for chemistry, was suspected of magic, but a famous physician born in Kent, in 1574, who was very remarkable for his attachment to the alchemists. See Wood's Athen. Oxoniens. vol. i. p. 610, and his Hist. et Antiq. Acad. Oxoniens. lib. ii. p. 390: also P. Gassendi, Examen Philosoph. Fluddanæ, tom. iii. op.

§ Boulay, Histor. Acad. Paris. tom. vi.

‖ Jo. Molleri Cimbria Literata, tom. i. p. 623

¶ Cimb. Lit. tom. ii. p. 440.

and noble, could not fail to procure friends and protectors. Accordingly, we find, that, near the close of this century, several persons, eminent for their piety, and distinguished by their zeal for the advancement of true religion, joined themselves to this sect. Of this number were the Lutheran doctors Weigelius, Arndius, and others, who were led into the snare by their ill-grounded notions of human reason, and who apprehended that controversy and argumentation might lead men to substitute anew the pompous and intricate jargon of the schools in the place of solid and sincere piety.

XIII. Among those who manifested a propensity toward the system of the Paracelsists, or Theosophists, was the celebrated Daniel Hoffman, professor of divinity in the university of Helmstadt, who, from the year 1598, had declared open war against philosophy, and who continued to oppose it with the greatest obstinacy and violence. Alleging the weight and authority of some opinions of Luther, and of various passages in the writings of that great man, he extravagantly maintained, that philosophy was the mortal enemy of religion; that truth was divisible into two branches, one philosophical and the other theological; and that what was true in philosophy, was false in theology. These absurd and pernicious tenets naturally alarmed the judicious doctors of the university, and excited a warm controversy between Hoffman and his colleagues Owen Guntherus, Cornelius Martin, John Caselius, and Duncan Liddle; a controversy also of too much consequence, to be confined within such narrow bounds, and which accordingly was carried on in other countries with the same fervour. The tumults which it excited in Germany were appeased by the interposition of Henry, duke of Brunswick, who, having made a careful inquiry into the nature of this debate, and consulted the professors of the academy of Rostoch on that subject, commanded Hoffman to retract publicly the invectives he had thrown out against philosophy in his writings and in his academical lectures, and to acknowledge, in the most open manner, the harmony and union of sound philosophy with true and genuine theology.*

XIV. The theological system that now prevails in the Lutheran academies, is not of the same tenor or spirit with that which was adopted in the infancy of the reformation. As time and experience are necessary to bring all things to perfection, so the doctrine of the Lutheran church changed, imperceptibly and by degrees, its original form, and was improved and perfected in many respects. This will appear both evident and striking to those who are acquainted with the history of the doctrines relating to free-will, predestination, and other points, and who compare the Lutheran systems of divinity of an earlier date, with those which have been composed in modern times. The case could not well be otherwise. The glorious defenders of religious liberty, to whom we owe the various blessings of the Reformation, as they were conducted only by the suggestions of their natural sagacity, whose advances in the pursuit of knowledge are gradual and progressive, could not at once behold the truth in all its lustre, and in all its extent; but, as usually happens to persons who have been long accustomed to the darkness of ignorance, their approaches toward knowledge were slow, and their views of things very imperfect. The Lutherans were greatly assisted both in correcting and illustrating the articles of their faith, partly by the controversies which they were obliged to carry on with the Roman Catholic doctors and the disciples of Zuingle and Calvin, and partly by the intestine divisions that prevailed among themselves, of which an account shall be given in this chapter. They have been absurdly reproached, on account of this variation in their doctrine, by Bossuet and other papal writers, who did not consider that the founders of the Lutheran church never pretended to divine inspiration, and that it is by discovering first the errors of others, that the wise generally prepare themselves for the investigation of truth.

XV. The first and principal object that drew the attention and employed the industry of the reformers, was the exposition and illustration of the sacred writings, which, according to the doctrine of the Lutheran church, contain all the treasures of celestial wisdom, all things that relate to faith and practice. Hence it happened, that the number of commentators and expositors among the Lutherans equalled that of the eminent and learned doctors who adorned that communion. At the head of all, Luther and Melancthon are undoubtedly to be placed; the former, on account of the sagacity and learning, discovered in his explications of several portions of Scripture, and particularly of the books of Moses, and the latter, in consequence of his commentaries on the Epistles of St. Paul, and other learned labours of that kind, which are abundantly known. A second class of expositors, of the same communion, obtained also great applause in the learned world, by their successful application to the study of the Scriptures. In this class we may rank Matthias Flacius, who composed a Glossary and Key to the sacred Writings,* very useful in unfolding the meaning of the inspired penmen; John Bugenhagius, Justus Jonas, Andrew Osiander, and Martin Chemnitz, whose Harmonies of the Evangelists are not destitute of merit; and to these we may add Victor Strigelius and Joachim Camerarius; of whom the latter, in his Commentary on the New Testament, expounds the Scriptures in a grammatical and critical manner only, and, laying aside all debated points of doctrine and religious controversy, unfolds the sense of each term, and the spirit of each phrase, by the rules of criticism and the genius of the ancient languages, in which he was a very uncommon proficient.

* There is an accurate account of this controversy, with an enumeration of the writings published on both sides of the question, in the life of Owen Guntherus, inserted by Mollerus in his Cimbria Literata, tom. i. p. 225.—See also Jo. Herm. ab Elswich, de Fatis Aristotelis in Scholis Protestant. sect. xxvii., and a German work, by Gottfried Arnold, upon the affairs of the church and the progress of heresy, entitled, Kirchen und Ketzer Historie, p. 947

* The Latin titles are *Glossa Scripturæ Sacræ* and *Clavis Scripturæ Sacræ*.

XVI. All these expositors and commentators abandoned the method of the ancient interpreters, who, neglecting the plain and evident purport of the words of Scripture, were perpetually torturing their imaginations, in order to find out a mysterious sense in each word or sentence, or were hunting after insipid allusions and chimerical applications of particular passages to objects which never entered into the views of the inspired writers. On the contrary, their principal zeal and industry were employed in investigating the natural force and signification of each expression, in consequence of that golden rule of interpretation which Luther inculcated, '*that there is only one sense annexed to the words of Scripture throughout all the books of the Old and New Testament.*'* It must, however, be acknowledged, that the examples exhibited by these judicious expositors were far from being universally followed. Many, labouring under the inveterate disease of an irregular fancy and a scanty judgment, were still seeking hidden significations and double meanings in the expressions of holy writ. They were perpetually busied in twisting all the prophecies of the Old Testament into an intimate connexion with the life, sufferings, and transactions of Jesus Christ; and were over-sagacious in pretending to find out, in the history of the patriarchal and Jewish churches, the types and figures of the events that have happened in modern, and which may yet happen in future times. In all this they discovered more imagination than judgment, more wit than wisdom. Be that as it may, all the expositors of this age may, I think, be properly divided into two classes, with Luther at the head of the one, and Melancthon presiding in the other. Some commentators followed the example of the former, who, after a familiar explication of the sense of Scripture, applied its decisions to the settlement of controverted points, and to the illustration of the doctrines and duties of religion. Others discovered a greater propensity to the method of the latter, who first divided the discourses of the sacred writers into several parts, explained them according to the rules of rhetoric, and afterwards proceeded to a more strict and almost a literal exposition of each part, taken separately, applying the result, as rarely as was possible, to points of doctrine or matters of controversy.

XVII. Complete systems of theology were far from being numerous in this century. Melancthon, the most eminent of all the Lutheran doctors, collected and digested the doctrines of the church, which he so eminently adorned, into a body of divinity, under the vague title of *Loci Communes*, i. e. a Common-Place-Book of Theology. This compilation, which was at different times reviewed, corrected, and enlarged by its author, was in such high repute during this century, and even in succeeding times, that it was considered as a model of doctrine for all those, who either instructed the people by their public discourses, or promoted the knowledge of religion by their writings.* The title prefixed to this performance, indicates sufficiently the method, or rather the irregularity that reigns in the arrangement of its material; and shows, that it was not the design of Melancthon to place the various truths of religion in that systematic concatenation, and that scientific order and connexion, which are observed by the philosophers in their demonstrations and discourses, but to propose them with freedom and simplicity, as they presented themselves to his view. Accordingly, in the earlier editions of the book under consideration, the method observed, both in delineating and illustrating these important truths, is exceedingly plain, and not loaded with the terms, the definitions, or the distinctions that abound in the writings of the philosophers. Thus did the Lutheran doctors, in the first period of the rising church, renounce and avoid, in imitation of the great reformer whose name they bore, all the abstruse reasoning, and subtle discussions, of the scholastic disputants and writers. But the sophistry of their adversaries, and their perpetual debates with the artful champions of the church of Rome, engaged them by degrees, as has been already observed, to change their language and their methods of reasoning; so that, in process of time, the simplicity that had reigned in their theological systems, and in their manner of explaining the truths of religion, almost totally disappeared. Even Melancthon himself fell imperceptibly into the new method, or rather into the old method revived, and enlarged the subsequent editions of his *Loci Communes*, by the edition of several philosophical illustrations, calculated to expose the fallacious reasonings of the Romish doctors. As yet, however, the discussions of philosophy were sparingly used, and the unintelligible jargon of the schoolmen was kept at a certain distance, and seldom borrowed. But when the founders of the Lutheran church were removed by death, and the Jesuits attacked the principles of the Reformation with redoubled animosity, armed with the intricate and perplexing dialect of the schools, the scene was changed, and theology assumed another aspect. The stratagem employed by the Jesuits corrupted our doctors, induced them to revive that intricate and abstruse manner of defending and illustrating religious truth, which Luther and his associates had rejected, and to introduce, into the plain and artless paths of theology, all the thorns and thistles, all the dark and devious labyrinths of the scholastic philosophy. This unhappy change was deeply lamented by several divines of eminent piety and learning about the commencement of the seventeenth century, who regretted the loss of that amiable simplicity which is the attendant on divine truth; but they could not prevail upon the professors, in the different universities, to sacrifice the jargon of the schools to the dictates of common sense, or to return to the plain, serious, and unaffected method of teaching theology, that had been introduced by Luther. These obstinate doctors pleaded necessity in behalf of

☞ * This golden rule will be found often defective and false, unless several prophetical, parabolical, and figurative expressions be excepted in its application.

* See Jo Franc. Buddeus, Isagoge ad Theolo lib ii. c. i. § xiii. t. i. p. 381.

their scholastic divinity, and looked upon this pretended necessity as superior to all authorities, and all examples, however respectable.

XVIII. Those who are sensible of the intimate connexion between faith and practice, between the truths and duties of religion, will easily perceive the necessity that existed for a reformation of the corrupt morality, as well as of the superstitious doctrines, of the church of Rome. It is therefore natural, that the same persons, who had spirit enough to do the one. should think themselves obliged to attempt the other. This they accordingly attempted, and not without a certain degree of success; for it may be affirmed with truth, that more genuine piety and more excellent rules of conduct are observable in the few practical productions of Luther, Melancthon, Weller, and Rivius, than are to be found in the innumerable volumes of all the ancient Casuists and Moralisers,* as they are called in the barbarous language of those remote periods. It is not, however, meant even to insinuate, that the notions of these great men concerning the important science of morality were either sufficiently accurate or extensive. It appears, on the contrary, from various debates which were carried on during this century, concerning the duties and obligations of Christians, and from the answers that were given by famous casuists to persons perplexed with religious scruples, that the true *principles* of morality were not yet fixed with perspicuity and precision, the agreement or difference between the laws of nature and the precepts of Christianity not sufficiently examined and determined, nor the proper distinctions made between those parts of the gospel dispensation, which are agreeable to right reason, and such as are beyond its reach and comprehension. Had not the number of adversaries, with whom the Lutheran doctors were obliged to contend, given them perpetual employment in the field of controversy, and robbed them of that precious leisure which they might have consecrated to the advancement of real piety and virtue, they would certainly have been free from the defects now mentioned, and would, perhaps, have equalled the best moral writers of modern times. This consideration will also diminish our wonder at a circumstance, which otherwise might seem surprising, that none of the famous Lutheran doctors attempted to give a regular system of morality. Melancthon himself, whose exquisite judgment rendered him peculiarly capable of reducing into a compendious system the elements of every science, never seems to have thought of treating morals in this manner; but has inserted, on the contrary, all his practical rules and instructions under the theological articles that relate to the law, sin, free-will, faith, hope, and charity.

XIX. All the divines of this century were educated in the school of controversy, and so trained up to spiritual war, that an eminent theologian, and a bold and vehement disputant, were considered as synonymous terms. It could scarcely, indeed, be otherwise, in an age when foreign quarrels and intestine divisions of a religious nature threw all the countries of Europe into a state of agitation, and obliged the doctors of the contending churches to be perpetually in action, or at least in a posture of defence. These champions of the Reformation were not, however, all animated with the same spirit, nor did they attack and defend with the same arms. Such of them as were contemporary with Luther, or lived near his time, were remarkable for the simplicity of their reasoning, and attacked their adversaries with no other arguments than those which they drew from the declarations of the inspired writers, and the decisions of the ancient fathers. In the latter part of the century this method was considerably changed; and we see those doctors, who were its chief ornaments, reinforcing their cause with the succours of the Aristotelian philosophy, and thus losing, in point of perspicuity and evidence, what they gained in point of subtilty and imagined science. It is true, as has been already observed more than once, that they were too naturally, though inconsiderately, led to adopt this method of disputing by the example of their adversaries the Roman catholics. The latter, having learned, by a disagreeable and discouraging experience, that their cause was unable to support that plain and perspicuous method of reasoning, which is the proper test of religious and moral truth, had recourse to stratagem, when evidence failed, and involved both their arguments and their opinions in the dark and intricate mazes of the scholastic philosophy; and it was this that engaged the protestant doctors to change their weapons, and to employ methods of defence unworthy of the glorious cause in which they had embarked.

The spirit of zeal, that animated the Lutheran divines, was, in general, very far from being tempered by a spirit of charity. If we except Melancthon, in whom a predominant mildness and sweetness of natural temper triumphed over the contagious ferocity of the times, all the disputants of this century discovered too much bitterness and animosity in their transactions and in their writings. Luther himself appears at the head of this sanguine tribe, whom he far surpassed in invectives and abuse, treating his adversaries with the most brutal asperity, and sparing neither rank nor condition, however elevated or respectable they might be. It must indeed be confessed, that the criminal nature of this vehemence will be much alleviated, when it is considered in one point of view with the genius of those barbarous times, and the odious cruelty and injustice of the virulent enemies, whom the oppressed reformers were called to encounter. When the impartial inquirer considers the abominable calumnies that were lavished on the authors and instruments of the Reformation; when he reflects upon the horrors of fire and sword employed, by bigoted and blood-thirsty tyrants, to extirpate those good men whom they wanted arguments to convince; will not his heart burn with a generous indignation? and will he not think it in some measure just, that such horrid proceedings

☞ * The moral writers of this century were called *Moralisantes*. a barbarous term, to which the English word *Moralisers* bears some resemblance.

should be represented in their proper colours, and be stigmatised by such expressions as are suited to their demerit?

XX. In order to form a just idea of the internal state of the Lutheran Church, and of the revolutions and changes which have happened in it, with their true springs and real causes, it is necessary to consider the history of that church under three periods. The first extends from the commencement of the Reformation to the death of Luther, which happened in 1546: the second takes in the time which elapsed between the death of Luther and that of Melancthon, and consequently terminates in 1560; and the remainder of the century is comprehended in the third period.

THE FIRST PERIOD.

DURING this period, all things were transacted in the Lutheran church in a manner conformable to the sentiments, counsels, and orders of Luther. This eminent reformer, whose undaunted resolution, and amazing credit and authority, rendered him equal to the most arduous attempts, easily suppressed the commotions and dissensions which arose from time to time in the church, and did not suffer the sects, that several had attempted to form in its bosom, to gather strength, or to arrive at any considerable degree of consistence and maturity. The natural consequence of this was, that, during the life of that great man, the internal state of the Lutheran church was a state of tolerable tranquillity and repose; and all such as attempted to foment divisions, or to introduce any essential changes, were either speedily reduced to silence, or obliged to retire from the new community.

XXI. The infancy of this church was troubled by an impetuous rabble of wrong-headed fanatics, who introduced the utmost confusion wherever they endeavoured to diffuse their pestilential errors, and who pretended that they had received a divine inspiration, authorizing them to erect a new kingdom of Christ, in which sin and corruption were to have no place. The leaders of this turbulent and riotous sect were Munzer, Storck, Stubner, and others, either Swiss or Germans, who kindled the flame of discord and rebellion in several parts of Europe, but chiefly in Germany, and excited among the ignorant multitude tumults and commotions, which, though less violent in some places than in others, were, nevertheless, formidable wherever they appeared.* The history of this seditious band is full of obscurity and confusion. A regular, full, and accurate account of it, neither has been, nor could well be, committed to writing; since, on one hand, the opinions and actions of these fanatics were a motley chaos of inconsistencies and contradictions, and, on the other, the age, in which they lived, produced few writers who had either the leisure or the capacity to observe with diligence, or to relate with accuracy, commotions and tumults of this extraordinary kind. It is however certain, that, from the most profligate and abandoned part of this enthusiastical multitude, those seditious armies were formed, which kindled in Germany the war of the peasants, and afterwards seized the city of Munster, involving the whole province of Westphalia in the most dreadful calamities. It is also well known, that the better part of this motley tribe, terrified by the unhappy and deserved fate of their unworthy associates, whom they saw massacred with the most unrelenting severity, saved themselves from the ruin of their sect, and, at length, embraced the communion of those who are called Mennonites.* The zeal, vigilance, and resolution of Luther, happily prevented the divisions, which the odious disciples of Munzer attempted to excite in the church he had founded, and preserved the guilty and credulous multitude from their seductions; and it may be safely affirmed, that, had it not been for the vigour and fortitude of this active and undaunted reformer, the Lutheran church would, in its infancy, have fallen a miserable prey to the enthusiastic fury of these detestable fanatics.†

XXII. Fanatics and enthusiasts of the kind now described, while they met with the warmest opposition from Luther, found, on the contrary, in his colleague Carlostadt, such a credulous attention to their seductions, as naturally flattered them with the hopes of his patronage and favour. This divine, who was a native of Franconia, was not destitute of learning or of merit; but imprudence and precipitation were the distinguished lines of his warm and violent character. Of these he gave the most evident marks, in 1523, when, during the absence of Luther, he excited no small tumult at Wittenberg, by ordering the images to be taken out of the churches, and by other enterprises of a rash and dangerous nature.‡ This tumult was

* John Baptist Ottius, in his Annales Anabaptist, has collected a considerable number of facts relating to these fanatical commotions, which are likewise mentioned by all the writers of the history of the Reformation.

☞ * The tumults of the anabaptists in Germany have already been mentioned in a cursory manner, sect. i. chap. ii. sect. xxii. For an ample account of the origin, doctrine, and progress of the Mennonites, see the third chapter of the second part of this third section, cent. xvi.

☞ † The danger that threatened the Lutheran church in these tumults of the German anabaptists, was so much the greater on account of the inclination which Munzer and Storck discovered at first for the sentiments of Luther, and the favourable disposition which Carlostadt seemed for some time to entertain with respect to these fanatics.

☞ ‡ The reader may perhaps imagine, from Dr. Mosheim's account of this matter, that Carlostadt introduced these changes merely by his own authority; but this was far from being the case; the suppression of private masses, the removal of images out of the churches, the abolition of the law which imposed celibacy upon the clergy, which are the changes hinted at by our historian as rash and perilous, were effected by Carlostadt, in conjunction with Bugenhagius, Melancthon, Jonas Amsdorff, and others, and were confirmed by the authority of the elector of Saxony; so that, there is some reason to apprehend that one of the principal causes of Luther's displeasure at these changes, was their being introduced in his absence; unless we suppose that he had not so far shaken off the fetters of superstition, as to be sensible of the absurdity and the pernicious consequences of the use of images, &c. As to the abolition of the law that imposed celibacy on the clergy, it is well known that it was the object of his warmest approbation. This appears from the following expressions in his letter to Amsdorff: "Carlostadii nuptiæ mire placent: novi puellam: comfortet eum Dominus in bonum exemplum inhibendæ et minu-

appeased by the sudden return of Luther, whose presence and exhortations calmed the troubled spirits of the people; and here we must look for the origin of the rupture between him and Carlostadt; for the latter immediately retired from Wittenberg to Orlamund, where he not only opposed the sentiments of Luther concerning the eucharist,* but also betrayed, in several instances, a fanatical turn of mind.† He was therefore commanded to leave the territories of the elector of Saxony, which he did accordingly, and repaired to Switzerland, where he propagated his doctrines, and taught with success, first at Zurich, and afterwards at Basil, retaining however, as long as he lived, a favourable disposition toward the sects of the Anabaptists, and, in general, to all enthusiastic teachers, who pretended to a divine inspiration.‡ Thus then did Luther, in a short time, allay this new storm which the precipitation of Carlostadt had raised in the church.

XXIII. The reforming spirit of Carlostadt, with respect to the doctrine of Christ's presence in the eucharist, was not extinguished, by his exile, in the Lutheran church. It was revived, on the contrary, by a man nearly of the same turn of mind, a Silesian knight, and counsellor to the duke of Lignitz, whose name was Caspar Schwenckfeld. This nobleman, seconded by Valentine Crautwald, a man of eminent learning, who lived at the court of the prince now mentioned, took notice of many things, which he deemed erroneous and defective, in the opinions and rites established by Luther; and, had not the latter been extremely vigilant, as well as vigorously supported by his friends and adherents, would have undoubtedly brought about a considerable schism in the church. Every circumstance, in Schwenckfeld's conduct and appearance, was adapted to give him credit and influence. His morals were pure, and his life, in all respects, exemplary. His exhortations in favour of true and solid piety were warm and persuasive, and his principal zeal was employed in promoting it among the people. He thus acquired the esteem and friendship of many learned and pious men, both in the Lutheran and Helvetic churches, who favoured his sentiments, and undertook to defend him against all his adversaries.* Notwithstanding all this, he was banished by his sovereign both from the court and from his country, in 1528, only because Zuingle had approved his opinions concerning the eucharist, and declared that they did not differ essentially from his own. From that time the persecuted knight wandered from place to place, under various turns of fortune, until death, in 1561, put an end to his trials.† He had founded, in Silesia, a small congregation, the members of which were persecuted and ejected by the popish possessors of that country; but they were restored to their former habitations and privileges, civil and religious, by that prince who began, in 1740, to reign over Prussia.‡

XXIV. The upright intentions of Schwenckfeld, and his zeal for the advancement of true piety, deserve, no doubt, the highest commendation; but the same thing cannot be said of

---

endæ papisticæ libidinis." He soon afterwards confirmed this approbation by his own example.

☞ * This difference of opinion between Carlostadt and Luther concerning the eucharist, was the true cause of the violent rupture between those two eminent men, and it tended very little to the honour of the latter; for, however the explication, which the former gave of the words of the institution of the Lord's Supper, may appear forced, yet the sentiments he entertained of that ordinance as a commemoration of Christ's death, and not as a celebration of his bodily presence, in consequence of a consubstantiation with the bread and wine, are infinitely more rational than the doctrine of Luther, which is loaded with some of the most palpable absurdities of transubstantiation; and if it be supposed that Carlostadt strained the rule of interpretation too far, when he alleged, that Christ pronounced the pronoun *this*, (in the words *This is my body*) pointing to his body, and not to the bread, what shall we think of Luther's explaining the nonsensical doctrine of consubstantiation by the similitude of a red-hot iron, in which two elements are united, as the body of Christ is with the bread in the eucharist?

☞ † This censure is with too much truth applicable to Carlostadt. Though he did not adopt the impious and abominable doctrines of Munzer and his band, (as Dr. Mosheim permits the uninstructed reader to imagine by mentioning him, as being a friend to these fanatics *in general*,) yet he certainly was chargeable with some extravagances that were observable in the tenets of that wrong-headed tribe. He was for abolishing the civil law, with the municipal laws and constitutions of the German empire, and proposed substituting the law of Moses in their place. He distinguished himself by railing at the universities, declaiming against human learning, and other follies.

"Great wits to madness nearly are allied."

See Val. Ern. Loscheri Historia Motuum inter Lutheranos et Reformat par. i. cap. i.—Dan. Gerdes, Vita Carolostadii, in Miscell. Groningens. novis.

☞ ‡ This affirmation of Dr. Mosheim wants much to be modified. In the original it stands thus: "Dum vixit vero anabaptistarum hominumque divina visa jactantium partibus amicum sese ostendit,"—i. e. as long as he lived, he showed himself a friend to the anabaptists and other enthusiasts who pretended to divine inspiration. But how could our historian assert this without restriction, since it is well known that Carlostadt, after his banishment from Saxony, composed a treatise against enthusiasm in general, and against the extravagant tenets and the violent proceedings of the anabaptists in particular? This treatise was even addressed to Luther, who was so affected by it, that, repenting of his unworthy treatment of Carlostadt, he pleaded his cause and obtained from the elector a permission for him to return into Saxony. See Gerdes, Vita Carolostadii. After this reconciliation with Luther, he composed a treatise on the eucharist, which breathes the most amiable spirit of moderation and humility; and, having perused the writings of Zuingle, where he saw his own sentiments on that subject maintained with the greatest perspicuity and force of evidence, he repaired a second time to Zurich, and thence to Basil, where he was admitted to the offices of pastor and professor of divinity, and where, after having lived in the exemplary and constant practice of every Christian virtue, he died, amidst the warmest effusions of piety and resignation, on the 25th of December, 1541. All this is testified solemnly in a letter of the learned and pious Grynæus of Basil, to Pitiscus, chaplain to the Elector Palatine, and shows how little credit ought to be given to the assertions of the ignorant Morreri, or to the insinuations of the insidious Bossuet.

* See Jo. Conr. Fueslini Centuria I. Epistolar. a Reformatoribus Helveticis scriptar. p. 169, 175, 225 Museum Helvetic. tom. iv. p. 445.

† Jo. Wigandi Schwenckfeldianismus.—Conr Schlusselburgi Catalog. Hæreticor lib. x.—The most accurate accounts of this nobleman have been given by Chr. Aug. Salig, in his Histor. August. Confessionis, tom. iii. lib. xi. and by Gottfried Arnold, in his Kirchen und Ketzer Historie, p. 720, both of which authors have pleaded the cause of Schwenckfeld.

‡ See an account of Schwenckfeld's Confession of Faith, in Kocher's Bibliotheca Theologiæ Symbolicæ, p. 457

his prudence and judgment. The good man had a natural propensity toward fanaticism, and fondly imagined that he had received a divine commission to propagate his opinions. He differed from Luther, and the other friends of the reformation, in three points, which it is proper to select from others of less consequence. The first of these points related to the doctrine concerning the eucharist. Schwenckfeld inverted the words of Chrsit, 'This is my body,' and insisted on their being thus understood: "*My body is this*, i. e. such as this bread which is broken and consumed; a true and real food, which nourishes, satisfies, and delights the soul. *My blood is this*, that is, such in its effects as the wine, which strengthens and refreshes the heart." The poor man imagined that this *wonderful* doctrine had been revealed to him from heaven; which circumstance alone is a sufficient demonstration of his folly.

The second point in which he differed from Luther, was in his hypothesis relating to the efficacy of the divine word. He denied, for example, that the external word, which is committed to writing in the Scriptures, was endowed with the power of healing, illuminating, and renewing the mind; and he ascribed this power to the internal word, which, according to his notion, was Christ himself. His discourses, however, concerning this internal word, were, as usually happens to persons of his turn, so full of confusion, obscurity, and contradiction, that it was difficult to find out what his doctrine really was, and whether it resembled that of the Mystics and Quakers, or was borrowed from a different source.

His doctrine concerning the human nature of Christ, formed the third subject of debate between him and the Lutherans. He would not allow Christ's human nature, in its exalted state, to be called a *creature*, or a created substance, as such denomination appeared to him infinitely below its majestic dignity, united as it is, in that glorious state, with the divine essence. This notion of Schwenckfeld bears a remarkable affinity to the doctrine of Eutyches, which, however, he professed to reject; and, in his turn, he accused those of Nestorianism, who gave the denomination of a creature to the human nature of Christ.

XXV. An intemperate zeal, by straining certain truths too far, turns them into falsehood, or, at least, often renders them the occasion of the most pernicious abuses. A striking instance of this happened during the ministry of Luther. While he was insisting upon the necessity of imprinting deeply in the minds of the people that doctrine of the Gospel, which represents Christ's merits as the source of man's salvation, and while he was eagerly employed in censuring and refuting the popish doctors, who mixed the law and the Gospel together, and represented eternal happiness as the fruit of legal obedience, a fanatic arose, who abused his doctrine, by over-straining it, and thus opened a field for the most dangerous errors. This new teacher was John Agricola, a native of Eisleben, and an eminent doctor of the Lutheran Church, though chargeable with vanity, presumption, and artifice. He first began to make a noise in 1538 when from the doctrine of Luther now mentioned, he took occasion to declaim against the law, maintaining, that it was neither fit to be proposed to the people as a rule of manners, nor to be used in the church as a mean of instruction; and that the Gospel alone was to be inculcated and explained, both in the churches and in the schools of learning. The followers of Agricola were called *Antinomians*, i. e. enemies of the law. But the fortitude, vigilance, and credit of Luther, suppressed this sect in its very infancy; and Agricola, intimidated by the opposition of such a respectable adversary, acknowledged and renounced his pernicious system. But this recantation does not seem to have been sincere, since it is said, that when his fears were dispelled by the death of Luther, he returned to his errors, and gained proselytes to his extravagant doctrine.*

XXVI. The tenets of the Antinomians, if their adversaries are to be believed, were of the most noxious nature and tendency; for they are supposed to have taught the most dissolute doctrine in point of morals, and to have maintained that it was allowable to follow the impulse of every passion, and to transgress without reluctance the divine law, provided that the transgressor took hold of Christ, and embraced his merits by a lively faith. Such, at least, is the representation that is generally given of their doctrine; but it ought not to be received with implicit credulity; for whoever looks into this matter with attention and impartiality, will soon be persuaded, that such an absurd and impious doctrine is unjustly laid to the charge of Agricola, and that the principal fault of this presumptuous man lay in some harsh and inaccurate expressions, which were susceptible of dangerous and pernicious interpretations. By the term *law*, he understood the ten Commandments, promulgated under the Mosaic dispensation; and he considered this law as enacted for the Jews, and not for Christians. He, at the same time, explained the term *Gospel* (which he considered as substituted for the law) in its true and extensive sense, as comprehending not only the doctrine of the merits of Christ rendered salutary by faith, but also the sublime precepts of holiness and virtue, delivered by the divine Saviour, as rules of obedience. If, therefore, we follow the intention of Agricola, without interpreting, in a rigorous manner, the uncouth phrases and improper expressions which he so frequently and so injudiciously employed, his doctrine will plainly amount to this: "That the ten Commandments, published during the ministry of Moses, were chiefly designed for the Jews, and on that account might be lawfully neglected and laid aside by Christians: and that it was sufficient to explain with perspicuity, and to enforce with zeal, what Christ and his apostles had taught in the New Testament, both with respect to the means of grace and salvation, and the obligations of repentance and virtue." The great

* See Caspar Sagittarius, Introd. ad Histor. Ecclesiast. tom. i. p. 838.—Bayle's Dictionaire, tom. ii. at the article Islebius.—Conr. Schlusselburg, Catalog. Hær. lib. iv.—G. Arnold, Kirchen und Ketzer Hist p. 813.

est part of the doctors of this century are chargeable with a want of precision and consistency in expressing their ideas: hence their real sentiments have been misunderstood, and opinions have been imputed to them which they never entertained.

THE SECOND PERIOD

XXVII. AFTER the death of Luther, which happened in the year 1546, Philip Melancthon was placed at the head of the Lutheran doctors. The merit, genius, and talents of this new chief were, undoubtedly, great and illustrious, though it must, at the same time, be confessed, that he was inferior to Luther in many respects,* and more especially in courage, firmness, and personal authority. His natural temper was soft and flexible; his love of peace almost excessive, and his apprehensions of the displeasure and resentment of men in power were such as betrayed a pusillanimous spirit. He was ambitious of the esteem and friendship of all with whom he had any intercourse, and was absolutely incapable of employing the force of threatenings, or the restraints of fear, to suppress the efforts of religious faction, to keep within due bounds the irregular love of novelty and change, and to secure to the church the obedience of its members. It is also to be observed, that his sentiments, on some points of moment, differed considerably from those of Luther; and it may not be improper to point out the principal subjects on which they adopted different ways of thinking.

In the first place, Melancthon was of opinion, that, for the sake of peace and concord, many things might be connived at and tolerated in the church of Rome, which Luther considered as absolutely insupportable. The former carried so far the spirit of toleration and indulgence, as to discover no reluctance against retaining the ancient form of ecclesiastical government, and submitting to the dominion of the Roman pontiff, on certain conditions, and in such a manner, as might be without prejudice to the obligation and authority of all those truths which are clearly revealed in the holy scriptures.

A second occasion of a diversity of sentiment, between these great men, was furnished by the tenets which Luther maintained in opposition to the doctrines of the church of Rome. Such were his ideas concerning faith, as the *only* cause of salvation, concerning the necessity of good works to our final happiness, and man's natural incapacity of promoting his own conversion. In avoiding the corrupt notions which were embraced by the Roman catholic doctors on these important points of theology, Luther seemed, in the judgment of Melancthon, to lean too much toward the opposite extreme.* Hence the latter was inclined to think, that the sentiments and expressions of his colleague required to be in some degree mitigated, lest they should give a handle to dangerous abuses, and be perverted to the propagation of pernicious errors.

It may be observed, thirdly, that though Melancthon adopted the sentiments of Luther in relation to the eucharist,† yet he did not consider the controversy with the divines of Switzerland on that subject, as a matter of sufficient moment to occasion a breach of church communion and fraternal concord between the contending parties. He thought that this happy concord might be easily preserved by expressing the doctrine of the eucharist, and Christ's presence in that ordinance, in general and ambiguous terms, which the two churches might explain according to their respective systems.

Such were the sentiments of Melancthon, which, though they were not entirely concealed during the life of Luther, he delivered, nevertheless, with great circumspection and modesty, yielding always to the authority of his colleague, for whom he had a sincere friendship, and of whom also he stood in awe. But no sooner were the eyes of Luther closed, than he inculcated, with the greatest plainness and freedom, what he had before only hinted with timidity and caution. The eminent rank which he held among the Luthrean doctors rendered this bold manner of proceeding extremely disagreeable to many. His doctrine accordingly was censured and opposed; and thus the church was deprived of the tranquillity which it had enjoyed under Luther, and exhibited an unhappy scene of animosity, contention, and discord.

XXVIII. The rise of these unhappy divisions must be dated from the year 1548, when Charles V. attempted to impose upon the Germans the famous edict, called the *Interim*. Maurice,

☞ * It would certainly be very difficult to point out the *many respects* in which Dr. Mosheim affirms that Luther was superior to Melancthon; for, if the single article of courage and firmness of mind be excepted, I know no other respect in which Melancthon is not superior, or at least equal, to Luther. He was certainly his equal in piety and virtue, and much his superior in learning, judgment, meekness, and humanity.

☞ * It is certain, that Luther carried [illegible] doctrine of Justification by Faith to such an excessive length, as seemed, though perhaps contrary to his intention, to derogate not only from the necessity of good works, but even from their obligation and importance. He would not allow them to be considered either as the *conditions* or *means* of salvation, or even as a preparation for receiving it.

☞ † It is somewhat surprising to hear Dr. Mosheim affirming that Melancthon adopted the sentiments of his friend with regard to the eucharist, when the contrary is well known. It is true, that in his writings, published before the year 1529 or 1530, there are passages, which show that he had not yet thoroughly examined the controversy relating to the nature of Christ's presence in the eucharist. It is also true, that during the disputes carried on between Wesphal and Calvin, after the death of Luther, concerning the *real presence*, he did not declare himself in an open manner for either side, (which however is a presumptive argument of his leaning to that of Calvin,) but expressed his sorrow at these divisions, and at the spirit of animosity by which they were inflamed. But whoever will be at the pains to read his letters to Calvin upon this subject, or those extracts of them which are collected by Hospinian, in the second volume of his Historia Sacramentaria, will be persuaded that he looked upon the doctrine of Consubstantiation not only as erroneous, but even idolatrous; and that nothing but the fear of inflaming the present divisions, and of not being seconded, prevented him from declaring his sentiments openly. See Bayle's Life of Melancthon in his Dictionary

the new elector of Saxony, desirous of knowing how far such an edict ought to be respected in his dominions, assembled the doctors of Wittenberg and Leipsic in the last-mentioned city, and proposed this nice and critical subject to their serious examination. Upon this occasion Melancthon, complying with the suggestions of that lenity and moderation which were the great and leading principles in the whole course of his conduct and actions, declared it as his opinion, that, in matters of an indifferent nature, compliance was due to the imperial edicts.* But, in the class of matters indifferent, this great man and his associates placed many things which had appeared of the highest importance to Luther, and consequently could not be considered as indifferent by his true disciples;† for he regarded, as such, the doctrine of justification by faith alone, the necessity of good works to eternal salvation, the number of the sacraments, the jurisdiction claimed by the pope and the bishops, extreme unction, the observance of certain religious festivals, and several superstitous rites and ceremonies. Hence arose that warm contest‡ which divided the church during many years, and proved highly detrimental to the progress of the Reformation. The defenders of the primitive doctrines of Lutheranism, with Flacius at their head, attacked with incredible bitterness and fury the doctors of Wittenberg and Leipsic, (particularly Melancthon, by whose council and influence every thing relating to the *Interim* had been conducted,) and accused them of apostasy from the true religion. Melancthon, on the other hand, seconded by the zeal of his friends and disciples, justified his conduct with the utmost spirit and vigour.§ In this unfortunate debate the two following questions were principally discussed: first, whether the points that seemed indifferent to Melancthon were so in reality?—this his adversaries obstinately denied:||—secondly, whether in things of an indifferent nature, and in which the interests of religion are not essentially concerned, it be lawful to yield to the enemies of the truth?

XXIX. This debate became, as might have been expected, a fruitful source of other controversies, which were equally detrimental to the tranquillity of the church, and to the cause of the Reformation. The first to which it gave rise was the warm dispute concerning the necessity of good works, that was carried on with such spirit against the rigid Lutherans, by George Major, an eminent teacher of theology at Wittenberg. Melancthon had long been of opinion, that the necessity of good works, in order to the attainment of everlasting salvation, might be asserted and taught, as conformable to the truths revealed in the Gospel; and both he and his colleagues declared this to be their opinion, when they were assembled at Leipsic, in 1548, to examine the famous edict already mentioned.* This declaration was severely censured by the rigid disciples of Luther, as contrary to the doctrine and sentiments of their chief, and as conformable both to the tenets and interests of the church of Rome; but it found an able defender in Major, who, in 1552, maintained the necessity of good works, against the extravagant assertions of Amsdorf. Hence arose a new controversy between the rigid and moderate Lutherans, which was carried on with the keenness and animosity that were peculiar to all debates of a religious nature during this century. In the course of this warm debate, Amsdorf was so far transported and infatuated by his excessive zeal for the doctrine of Luther, as to maintain that good works were an impediment to salvation; from which imprudent and odious expression, the flame of controversy received new fuel, and broke forth with redoubled fury. On the other hand, Major complained of the malice or ignorance of his adversaries, who explained his doctrine in a manner quite different from that in which he intended it should be understood; and, at length, he renounced it entirely, that he might not appear fond of wrangling, or be looked upon as a disturber of the peace of the church. This step did not, however, put an end to the debate, which was still carried on, until it was terminated at last by the *Form of Concord*.†

XXX. From the same source that produced the dispute concerning the necessity of good works, arose the *synergistical* controversy. The Synergists,‡ whose doctrine was almost the same with that of the Semi-Pelagians, denied that God was the *only* agent in the conversion of sinful man; and affirmed, that man *co-operated* with divine grace in the accomplishment of this salutary purpose. Here also Melancthon renounced the doctrine of Luther; at least, the terms he employs in expressing his sentiments concerning this intricate subject, are such as Luther would have rejected with horror; for, in the conference at Leipsic,

* The piece in which Melancthon and his associates delivered their sentiments relating to things indifferent, is commonly called in the German language *Das Leipziger Interim*, and was republished at Leipsic in 1721, by Bieckius, in a work entitled, Das Dreyfache Interim.

☞ † If they only are the true disciples of Luther, who submit to his judgment, and adopt his sentiments in theological matters, many doctors of that communion, and our historian among the rest, must certainly be supposed to have forfeited that title, as will abundantly appear hereafter. Be that as it may, Melancthon can scarcely, if at all, be justified in placing in the class of things indifferent the doctrines relating to faith and good works, which are the fundamental points of the Christian religion, and, if I may use such an expression, the very *hinges* on which the Gospel turns.

☞ ‡ This controversy was called *Adiaphoristic*, and Melancthon and his followers *Adiaphorists*, from the Greek word ἀδιάφορος, which signifies *indifferent*.

§ Schlusselburg's Catalog. Hæreticor. lib. xiii.—Arnold's Kirchen und Ketzer Histoire, lib. xvi. cap. xxvi. p. 816.—Salig's Histor. Aug. Confess. vol. i. p. 611.—The German work, entitled, Unschuldige Nachrichten, An. 1702.—Luc. Osiandri Epitome Histor. Eccles. Centur. XVI. p. 502.

☞ || See above, note (d)

* The *Interim* of Charles V.

† Schlusselburg, lib. vii. Catal. Hæreticor.—G. Arnold's Kirchen Hist. lib. xvi. cap. xxvii. p. 822.—Jo. Musæi Prælect. in Form. Concord. p. 181.—Arn. Grevii Memoria Jo. Westphali, p. 169.

☞ ‡ As this controversy turned upon the *co-operation* of the human will with the divine grace, the persons who maintained this joint agency, were called *Synergists*, from a Greek word (συνεργεια) which signifies *co-operation*

the former of these great men did not scruple o affirm, that "God drew to himself and converted adult persons in such a manner, that the powerful impression of his grace was accompanied with a certain correspondent action of their will." The friends and disciples of Melancthon adopted this manner of speaking, and used the expressions of their master to describe the nature of the divine agency in man's conversion. But this representation of the matter was far from being agreeable to the rigid Lutherans. They looked upon it as subversive of the true and genuine doctrine of Luther, relating to the absolute servitude of the human will,* and the total inability of man to do any good action, or to bear any part in his own conversion; and hence they oppose the Synergists with the utmost animosity and bitterness. The principal champions in this theological conflict were Strigelius, who defended the sentiments of Melancthon with singular dexterity and perspicuity, and Flacius, who maintained the ancient doctrine of Luther: of these doctors, as also the subject of their debate, a farther account will soon be given.†

XXXI. During these dissensions, a new university was founded at Jena by the dukes of Saxe-Weimar, the sons of the famous John Frederic, whose unsuccessful wars with the emperor Charles V. had involved him in so many calamities, and deprived him of his electoral dominions. The noble founders of this university, having designed it for the bulwark of the protestant religion, as it was taught and inculcated by Luther, were particularly careful in choosing such professors and divines as were remarkable for their attachment to the genuine doctrine of that great reformer, and their aversion to the sentiments of those moderate Lutherans, who had attempted by certain modifications and corrections, to render it less harsh and disgusting; and, as none of the Lutheran doctors were so much distinguished by their uncharitable and intemperate zeal for this ancient doctrine, as Matthias Flacius, the virulent enemy of Melancthon and all the Philippists, he was appointed, in 1557, professor of divinity at Jena. The consequences of this nomination were, indeed, deplorable. This turbulent and impetuous man, whom nature had formed with an uncommon propensity to foment divisions and propagate discord, not only revived all the ancient controversies that had distracted the church, but also excited new debates; and sowed, with such avidity and success, the seeds of contention between the divines of Weimar and those of the electorate of Saxony, that a fatal schism in the Lutheran church was apprehended by many of its wisest members.* And indeed this schism would have been inevitable, if the machinations and intrigues of Flacius had produced the desired effect; for, in 1559, he persuaded the dukes of Saxe-Weimar to order a refutation of the errors that had crept into the Lutheran church, and particularly of those which were imputed to the followers of Melancthon, to be drawn up with care, promulgated by authority, and placed among the other religious edicts and articles of faith that were in force in their dominions. But this pernicious design of dividing the church proved abortive; for the other Lutheran princes, who acted from the true and genuine principles of the Reformation, disapproved this seditious book, from a just apprehension of its tendency to increase the present troubles, and to augment, instead of diminishing, the calamities of the church.†

XXXII. This theological incendiary kindled the flame of discord and persecution even in the church of Saxe-Weimar, and in the university of Jena, to which he belonged, by venting his fury against Strigelius,‡ the friend and disciple of Melancthon. This moderate divine adopted, in many things, the sentiments of his master, and maintained, particularly, in his public lectures, that the human will, when under the influence of the divine grace leading it to repentance, was not totally inactive, but bore a certain part in the salutary work of its conversion. In consequence of this doctrine, he was accused by Flacius of Synergism at the court of Saxe-Weimar; and, by the duke's order, was cast into prison, where he was treated with severity and rigour. He was at length delivered from this confinement in 1562, and allowed to resume his former vocation, after he had made a declaration of his real sentiments, which, as he alleged, had been greatly misrepresented. This declaration, however, did not either decide or terminate the controversy, since Strigelius seemed rather to conceal his erroneous sentiments§ under ambiguous expressions, than to renounce them entirely; and indeed he was so conscious of this himself, that, to avoid being involved in new calamities and persecutions, he retired from Jena to Leipsic, and thence to Heidelberg, where he spent the remainder of his days; and appeared so unsettled in his religious opinions, that it is doubtful whether he ought to be placed among the followers of Luther or Calvin.

XXXIII. The issue of this warm controversy, which Flacius had kindled with such an intemperate zeal, proved highly detrimental to his own reputation and influence in particular, as well as to the interests of the Lutheran

☞ * The doctrines of absolute predestination, irresistible grace, and human impotence, were never carried to a more excessive length, or maintained with a more virulent obstinacy, by any divine, than they were by Luther. But in these times he has very few followers in this respect even among those who bear his name.

† See Schlusselburg's Catal. Hæreticor. lib. v.—G. Arnold, Histor. Eccles. lib. xvi. cap. xxviii. p. 826.—Bayle's Dict.—Salig's Histor. August Confess. vol. iii.—Musæi Prælect

* See the remarkable letter of Augustus, elector of Saxony, concerning Flacius and his malignant attempts; published by Arn. Grævius in his Memoria Joh. Westphalia.

† Salig's Hist. Aug. Confess. vol. iii. p. 476.

‡ See Bayle's Dict.

☞ § The sentiments of Strigelius were not, I have reason to believe, very *erroneous* in the judgment of Dr. Mosheim, nor are they such in the estimation of the greatest part of the Lutheran doctors at this day.

church in general; for, while this vehement disputant was assailing his adversary with an inconsiderate ardour, he exaggerated so excessively the sentiments, which he looked upon as orthodox, as to maintain an opinion of the most monstrous and detestable kind; an opinion which made him appear, even in the judgment of his warmest friends, an odious heretic, and a corruptor of the true religion. In 1560, a public dispute was holden at Weimar, between him and Strigelius, concerning the natural powers and faculties of the human mind, and their influence in the conversion and conduct of the true Christian. In this conference the latter seemed to attribute to unassisted nature too much, and the former too little. The one looked upon the fall of man as an event that extinguished, in the human mind, every virtuous tendency, every noble faculty, and left nothing behind it but universal darkness and corruption. The other maintained, that this degradation of the powers of nature was by no means universal or entire; that the will still retained some propensity to worthy pursuits, and a certain degree of activity that rendered it capable of attainments in virtue. Strigelius, who was well acquainted with the wiles of a captious philosophy, proposed to defeat his adversary by puzzling him, and, with that view, addressed to him the following question: "Whether original sin, or the corrupt habit which the human soul contracted by the fall, ought to be placed in the class of substances or accidents?" Flacius answered, with unparalleled imprudence and temerity, that it belonged to the former; and maintained, to his dying hour, this most extravagant and dangerous proposition, that original sin is the very substance of human nature. So invincible was the obstinacy with which he persevered in this strange doctrine, that he chose to renounce all worldly honours and advantages rather than depart from it. It was condemned by the greatest and soundest part of the Lutheran church, as a doctrine that bore no small affinity to that of the Manichæans. But, on the other hand, the merit, erudition, and credit of Flacius, procured him many respectable patrons as well as able defenders among the most learned doctors of the church, who embraced his sentiments and maintained his cause with the greatest spirit and zeal; of whom the most eminent were Cyriac Spangenberg, Christopher Irenæus, and Cælestine.*

XXXIV. It is scarcely possible to imagine how much the Lutheran church suffered from this new dispute in all those places where its contagion had reached, and how detrimental it was to the progress of Lutheranism, among those who still adhered to the religion of Rome; for the flame of discord spread to a great extent; it was communicated even to those churches which were erected in popish countries, and particularly in the Austrian territories, under the gloomy shade of a dubious toleration; and it so animated the Lutheran pastors, though surrounded by their cruel adversaries, that they could neither be restrained by the dictates of prudence, nor by the sense of danger.* Many are of opinion, that an ignorance of philosophical distinctions and definitions threw Flacius inconsiderately into the extravagant hypothesis which he maintained with such obstinacy, and that his greatest heresy was no more than a foolish attachment to an unusual term. But Flacius seems to have fully refuted this plea in his behalf, by declaring boldly, in several parts of his writings, that he knew perfectly well the philosophical signification and the whole energy of the word *substance*, and was by no means ignorant of the consequences that might be drawn from the doctrine he had embraced.† Be that as it may, we cannot but wonder at the senseless and excessive obstinacy of this turbulent man, who chose rather to sacrifice his fortune, and disturb the tranquillity of the church, than to abandon a word, which was entirely foreign to the subject in debate, and renounce an hypothesis, that was composed of the most palpable contradictions.

XXXV. The last controversy that we shall mention, of those which were occasioned by the excessive lenity of Melancthon, was set on foot by Osiander, in 1549, and produced much animosity in the church. Had its founder been yet alive, his influence and authority would have suppressed in their birth these wretched disputes; nor would Osiander, who despised the moderation of Melancthon, have dared either to publish or defend his crude and chimerical opinions within the reach of Luther. Arrogance and singularity were the principal lines in Osiander's character; he loved to strike out new notions; but his views seemed always involved in an intricate obscurity. The disputes that arose concerning the *Interim*, induced him to retire from Nuremberg, where he had exercised the pastoral charge, to Konigsberg, where he was chosen professor of divinity. In this new station he began his academical functions by propagating notions concerning the divine Image, and the nature of repentance, very different from the doctrine that Luther had taught on these interesting subjects; and, not content with this deviation from the common course, he thought proper, in the year 1550, to introduce considerable alterations and corrections into the doctrine that had been generally received in the Lutheran church, with respect to the means of our *justification* before God. When we examine his discussion of this important point, we shall

* Schlusselburg, Catalog. Hæret. lib. ii.—The Life of Flacius, written in German by Ritter.—Salig. Histor. Aug. Confessionis, vol. iii. p. 593.—Arnold's Kirchen Hist. lib. xvi. cap. xxix. p. 829.—Musæi Prælect. in Formul. Concordiæ, p. 29.—Jo. Georgii Leuckfeldii Hist. Spangenbergensis.—For a particular account of the dispute, that was holden publicly at Weimar, see the work entitled Unschuldige Nachichten, p. 383.

* See Bern. Raupach's Zwiefache Zugabe zu dem Evangelisch. Oesterrich. The same author speaks of the friends of Flacius in Austria, and particularly of Irenæus, in his Presbyterol. Austriac.—For an account of Cælestine, see the Unschuldige Nachrichten.

† This will appear evident to such as will be at the pains to consult the letters which Westphal wrote to his friend Flacius, in order to persuade him to abstain from the use of the word *substance*, with the answer of the latter. These letters and answers were published by Arnold Grevius, in his Mem. J. Westphali

find it much more easy to perceive the opinions he rejected, than to understand the system he had invented or adopted; for, as was too usual in this age, he not only expressed his notions in an obscure manner, but seemed very frequently to speak and write in contradiction to himself. His doctrine, when carefully examined, will appear to amount to the following propositions; "Christ, considered in his *human nature only*, could not, by his obedience to the divine law, obtain justification and pardon for sinners; nor can we be justified before God by embracing and applying to ourselves, through faith, the righteousness and obedience of the *man* Christ. It is only through that eternal and essential righteousness, which dwells in Christ *considered as God*, and which resides in his divine nature, that is united to the human, that mankind can obtain complete justification. Man becomes a partaker of this divine righteousness by faith, since it is in consequence of this uniting principle that Christ dwells in the heart of man, with his divine righteousness; now, wherever this divine righteousness dwells, *there* God can behold no sin, and therefore, when it is present with Christ in the hearts of the regenerate, they are, on its account, considered by the Deity as righteous, although they may be sinners. Moreover, this divine and justifying righteousness of Christ, excites the faithful to the pursuit of holiness and to the practice of virtue." This doctrine was zealously opposed by the most eminent doctors of the Lutheran church, and, in a more especial manner, by Melancthon and his colleagues. On the other hand, Osiander and his sentiments were supported by persons of considerable weight. But, upon the death of this rigid and fanciful divine, the flame of controversy was cooled, and dwindled by degrees into nothing.*

XXXVI. The doctrine of Osiander, concerning the method of being justified before God, appeared so absurd to Stancarus, professor of Hebrew at Konigsberg, that he undertook to refute it. But while this turbulent and impetuous doctor was exerting all the vehemence of his zeal against the opinion of his colleague, he was hurried by his violence into the opposite extreme, and fell into an hypothesis, that appeared equally groundless, and not less dangerous in its tendency and consequences. Osiander had maintained that the man Christ, in his character of moral agent, was obliged to obey, for *himself*, the divine law, and therefore could not, by the imputation of this obedience, obtain righteousness or justification for *others*. Hence he concluded, that the Saviour of the world had been empowered, not by his character as *man*, but by his nature as *God*, to make expiation for our sins, and reconcile us to the favour of an offended Deity. Stancarus, on the other hand, excluded entirely Christ's divine nature from all concern in the satisfaction he made, and in the redemption he procured for offending mortals, and maintained, that the sacred office of a mediator between God and man belonged to Jesus, considered in his human nature alone. Having perceived, however, that this doctrine exposed him to the enmity of many divines, and even rendered him the object of popular resentment and indignation, he retired from Konigsberg into Germany, and at length into Poland, where, after having excited no small commotions,* he concluded his days in 1574.†

XXXVII. All those who had the cause of virtue, and the advancement of the Reformation really at heart, looked with an impatient ardour for an end to these bitter and uncharitable contentions; and these desires of peace and concord in the church were still increased, by their perceiving the great assiduity with which Rome turned these unhappy divisions to the advancement of her interests. But during the life of Melancthon, who was principally concerned in these warm debates, no effectual method could be found to bring them to a conclusion. The death of this great man, which happened in 1560, changed, indeed, the face of affairs, and enabled those who were disposed to terminate the present contests, to act with more resolution, and a surer prospect of success than had accompanied their former efforts. Hence it was, that after several vain attempts, Augustus, elector of Saxony, and John William, duke of Saxe-Weimar, summoned the most eminent doctors of both the contending parties to meet at Altenburg, in 1568, and there to propose, in an amicable manner, and with a charitable spirit, their respective opinions, that thus it might be seen how far a reconciliation was possible, and what was the most probable method of bringing it about. But the intemperate zeal and warmth of the disputants, with other inauspicious circumstances, blasted the fruits that were expected from this conference.‡ Another method of restoring tranquillity and union among the members of the Lutheran church was therefore proposed; and this was, that a certain number

* See Schlusselburgii Catalogus Hæreticor. lib. vi.—Arnoldi Kirchen Hist. lib. xvi. cap. xxiv. p. 804.—Christ. Hartknoch's Preussische Kirchen Historie, p. 309.—Salig's Historia August. Confessionis, tom. ii. p. 922. The judgment that was formed of this controversy by the divines of Wittenberg, may be seen in the Unschuldige Nachrichten, and that of the doctors of Copenhagen, in the Danischen Bibliothec. part vii. p. 150, where may be found an ample list of the writings published on this subject.—To form a just idea of the insolence and arrogance of Osiander, those who understand the German language will do well to consult Hirschius, Nuremburg Interims-Historie.

* See Hartknoch's Preussische Kirch. Hist.—Schlusselburg, liv. ix.—Bayle's dict.—Before the arrival of Stancarus at Konigsberg, in 1548, he had lived for some time in Switzerland, where also he had occasioned religious disputes; for he adopted several doctrines of Luther, particularly that concerning the virtue and efficacy of the sacraments, which were rejected by the Swiss and Grisons. See the Museum Helveticum, tom. v. page 484, 490. For an account of the disturbances he occasioned in Poland in 1556, see Bullinger, in Jo. Conr. Fueslini Cent. I Epistolarum a Reformatoribus Helveticis scriptarum

☞ † The main argument alleged by Stancarus in favour of his hypothesis, was this,—that, if Christ was mediator by his divine nature only, it followed evidently, that even considered as God he was inferior to the Father; and thus, according to him, the doctrine of his adversary Osiander led directly to the Unitarian system. This difficulty, which was presented with great subtlety, engaged many to strike into a middle road, and to maintain, that both the divine and human natures of Christ were immediately concerned in the work of redemption.

‡ Casp. Sagittarii Introductio ad Histor. Ecclesiasticam, p. ii. p. 1542.

of wise and moderate divines should be employed in composing a form of doctrine, in which all the controversies that divided the church should be terminated and decided; and that this new compilation, as soon as it should be approved by the Lutheran princes and consistories, should be invested with ecclesiastical authority, and added to the symbclical* or standard books of the Lutheran church. James Andreas, professor at Tubingen, whose theological abilities had procured him the most eminent and shining reputation, had been employed, so early as in the year 1569, in this critical and difficult undertaking, by the special command of the dukes of Wirtemberg and Brunswick. The elector of Saxony,† with several persons of distinction, embarked with these two princes in the project they had formed; so that Andreas, under the shade of such a powerful protection and patronage, exerted all his zeal, travelled through different parts of Germany, negotiating alternately with courts and synods, and took all the measures which prudence could suggest, to render the form, that he was composing, universally acceptable.

XXXVIII. The persons embarked in this conciliatory design, were persuaded that no time ought to be lost in carrying it into execution, when they perceived the imprudence and temerity of the disciples of Melancthon, and the changes they were attempting to introduce into the doctrine of the church; for his son-in-law, Peucer,‡ who was a physician and professor of natural philosophy at Wittenberg, together with the divines of that city and of Leipsic, encouraged by the approbation, and relying on the credit, of Cracovius, chancellor of Dresden, and of several ecclesiastics and persons of distinction at the Saxon court, aimed at nothing less than abolishing the doctrines of Luther, concerning the eucharist and the person of Christ, with a view of substituting the sentiments of Calvin in its place. This new reformation was attempted in Saxony in 1570; and a great variety of clandestine arts and stratagems were employed, in order to bring it to a happy and successful issue. What the sentiments of Melancthon concerning the eucharist were toward the conclusion of his days, appears to be extremely doubtful. It is however certain, that he had a strong inclination to form a coalition between the Saxons and Calvinists, though he was prevented, by the irresolution and timidity of his natural character, from attempting openly this much desired union. Peucer, and the other disciples of Melancthon already mentioned, made a public profession of the doctrine of Calvin; and though they had much more spirit and courage than their soft and yielding master, yet they wanted his circumspection and prudence, which were not less necessary to the accomplishment of their designs. Accordingly in 1571, they published, in the German language, a work entitled *Stereoma,** and other writings, in which they openly declared their dissent from the doctrine of Luther concerning the eucharist and the *person of Christ;*† and, that they might execute their purposes with greater facility, they introduced into the schools a Catechism, compiled by Pezelius, which was favourable to the sentiments of Calvin. As this bold step excited great commotions and debates in the church, Augustus held at Dresden, in the same year, a solemn convocation of the Saxon divines, and of other persons concerned in the administration of ecclesiastical affairs, and commanded them to adopt *his* opinion in relation to the eucharist.‡

☞ * The Lutherans call *symbolical* (from a Greek word that signifies *collection* or *compilation*) the books which contain their articles of faith and rules of discipline.

† Augustus.

☞ ‡ This Peucer, whom Dr. Mosheim mentions without any mark of distinction, was one of the wisest, most amiable, and most learned men that adorned the annals of German literature during this century, as the well known history of his life, and the considerable number of his medical, mathematical, moral, and theological writings, abundantly testify. Nor was he more remarkable for his merit than for his sufferings. After his genius and virtues had rendered him the favourite of the elector of Saxony, and placed him at the head of the university of Wittenberg, he felt, in a terrible manner, the effects of the bigotry and barbarity of the rigid Lutherans, who, on account of his denying the corporal presence of Christ in the eucharist, united, with success, their efforts to deprive him of the favour of his sovereign, and procured his imprisonment. His confinement, which lasted ten years, was accompanied with inhuman severity. See Melchior Ad·m's Vit. Medicor. Germanor.

☞ * A term which signifies *foundation*.

☞ † The learned historian seems to deviate here from his usual accuracy. The authors of the Stereoma did not declare their dissent from the doctrine of Luther, but from the extravagant inventions of some of his successors. This great man, in his controversy with Zuingle, had indeed thrown out some unguarded expresssions, that seemed to imply a belief of the omnipresence of the body of Christ; but he became sensible afterwards that this opinion was attended with great difficulties, and particularly, that it ought not to be brought forward as a proof of Christ's corporal presence in the eucharist.* Yet this absurd hypothesis was renewed after the death of Luther, by Tinman and Westphal, and was dressed up in a still more specious and plausible form, by Brentius, Chemnitz, and Andreas, who maintained the communication of the properties of Christ's divinity to his human nature, as it was afterwards adopted by the Lutheran church. This strange system gave occasion to the Stereoma, in which the doctrine of Luther was respected, and the inventions alone of his successors were renounced, and in which the authors declared plainly, that they did not adopt the sentiments of Zuingle or Calvin, but that they admitted the real and substantial presence of Christ's body and blood in the eucharist.

☞ ‡ In this passage, compared with what follows, Dr. Mosheim seems to maintain, that the opinion of Augustus, which he imposed upon the assembled divines, was in favour of the adversaries of Melancthon, and in direct opposition to the authors of the Stereoma. But here he has committed a palpable oversight. The convocation of Dresden, in 1571, instead of approving or maintaining the doctrine of the rigid Lutherans, drew up, on the contrary, a form of agreement (*formula consensus*) in which the omnipresence or *ubiquity* of Christ's body was denied; and which was, indeed, an abridgment of the Stereoma; so that the transactions at Dresden were entirely favourable to the moderate Lutherans, who embraced openly and sincerely (and not by a feigned consent (*subdole*) as our historian remarks) the sentiment of the elector Augustus, who at that time patronised the disciples of Melancthon. This prince, it is true, seduced by the crafty and artful insinuations of the Ubiquitarians, or rigid Lutherans, who made him believe that the ancient doctrines of the church were in danger, changed sides soon after, and was pushed on to the most violent and persecuting

* See Lutheri op. tom. viii p. 375, Edit. Janiens

The assembled doctors complied with this order in appearance; but their compliance was feigned;* for, on their return to the places of their abode, they resumed their original design, pursued it with assiduity and zeal, and by their writings, as also by their public and private instructions, endeavoured to abolish the ancient doctrine of the Saxons, relating to the presence of Christ's body in that holy sacrament. The elector, informed of these proceedings, convened anew the Saxon doctors, and held, in 1574, the famous convocation of Torgaw,† where, after a strict inquiry into the doctrines of those who, from their *secret* attachment to the sentiments of the Swiss divines, were called *Crypto*-Calvinists,‡ he committed some of them to prison, sent others into banishment, and engaged a certain number by the force of the secular arm to change their sentiments. Peucer, who had been principally concerned in moderating the rigour of some of Luther's doctrines, felt, in a more especial manner, the severe effects of the elector's displeasure; for he was confined to a comfortless prison, where he lay in the most affecting circumstances of distress until the year 1585, when, having obtained his liberty through the intercession of the prince of Anhalt, who had given his daughter in marriage to Augustus, he retired to Zerbst, where he ended his days in peace.§

XXXIX. The schemes of the Crypto-Calvinists being thus disconcerted, the elector of Saxony, and those princes who had entered into his views, redoubled their zeal and diligence in promoting the Form of Concord, already mentioned. Accordingly, various conferences were holden, preparatory to this important undertaking; and, in 1576, while the Saxon divines were convened at Torgaw by the order of Augustus, a treatise was composed by James Andreas with a view of healing the divisions of the Lutheran church, and as a preservative against the opinions of the *reformed* doctors.‖ When this production, which was styled the Book of Torgaw, had been carefully examined, reviewed, and corrected by the greatest part of the Lutheran doctors in Germany, the affair was again proposed to the deliberation of a select number of divines, who met at Berg, a Benedictine monastery in the neighbourhood of Magdeburg.* Here all points relating to the intended project were accurately weighed, the opinions of the assembled doctors carefully discussed, and the result of all was the famous *Form of Concord.* The persons who assisted Andreas in the composition of this celebrated work, or at least in the revision of it at Berg, were Martin Chemnitz, Nicholas Selneccer, Andrew Musculus, Christopher Cornerus, and David Chytræus.† This new confession of the Lutheran faith was adopted first by the Saxons, in consequence of the strict order of Augustus; and their example was followed by the greatest part of the Lutheran churches, by some sooner, by others later.‡ The authority of this confession, as is sufficiently known, was employed for the following purposes: first, to terminate the controversies which divided the Lutheran church, more especially after the death of its founder; and, secondly, to preserve that church against the opinions of the Reformed in relation to the eucharist.

XL. This very form, however, which was designed to restore peace and concord in the church, and had actually produced this effect

---

measures of which the convocation of Torgaw was the first step, and the *Form of Concord* the unhappy issue.

☞ * The compliance was sincere; but the order was very different from that mentioned by our author, as appears from the preceding note.

☞ † It is to be observed, that not more than fifteen of the Saxon doctors were convened at Torgaw by the elector—a small number this to give law to the Lutheran church. For an account of the declaration drawn up by this assembly on the points relating to the presence of Christ's body in the eucharist, the omnipresence of that body, and the oral manducation of the flesh and blood of the divine Saviour, see Hospiniani Concordia Discors.

☞ ‡ i. e. Hidden, or disguised Calvinists.

☞ § See Schlusselburgii Theologia Calvinistica, lib. ii. iii. iv.—Hutteri Concordia Concors, cap. i. viii.—Arnoldi Histor. Ecclesiast. lib. xvi cap. xxxii.—Loscheri Historia Motuum inter Lutheranos et Reformat. par. ii. iii.—All these are writers favourable to the rigid Lutherans; see therefore, on the other side, Casp. Peuceri Hist. Carcerum et Liberationis divinæ, published at Zurich, in 1605, by Pezelius.

☞ ‖ The term *Reformed* was used to distinguish the other protestants of various denominations from the Lutherans: and it was equally applied to the friends of episcopacy and presbyterianism. See the following chapter.

☞ * The book that was composed by Andreas and his associates at Torgaw, was sent by the elector to almost all the Lutheran princes, with a view of its being examined, approved, and received by them. It was, however, rejected by several princes, and censured and refuted by various doctors. These censures engaged the compilers to review and correct it; and it was from this book, thus changed and new-modelled, that the *form* published at Berg was entirely drawn.

☞ † The Form of Concord, composed at Torgaw, and reviewed at Berg, consists of two parts. In the first is contained a system of doctrine, drawn up according to the fancy of the six doctors here mentioned. In the second is exhibited one of the strongest instances of that persecuting and tyrannical spirit, of which the protestants complained in the church of Rome, even a formal condemnation of all those who differed from these six doctors, particularly in their strange opinions concerning the majesty and omnipresence of Christ's body, and the real manducation of his flesh and blood in the eucharist. This condemnation branded with the denomination of heretics, and excluded from the communion of the church, all Christians, of all nations, who refused to subscribe these doctrines. More particularly in Germany, the terrors of the sword were solicited against these pretended heretics, as may be seen in the famous testament of Brentius. For a full account of the Confession of Torgaw and Berg, see Hospinian's Concordia Discors, where the reader will find large extracts from this confession, with an ample account of the censures it underwent, the opposition that was made to it, and the arguments which were used by its learned adversaries.

‡ A list of the writers who have treated of this *form*, may be found in Jo. Georgii Walchii Introduct. in Libros Symbolicos, lib. i. cap. vii. p. 707, and Kocheri Biblioth. Theol. Symbolicæ, p. 188 There are also several unpublished documents relative to this famous confession, of which there is an account in the German work entitled, Unsch. Nachricht.—The principal writers who have given the history of the *form* and the transactions relating to it, are Hospinian and Hutter, already mentioned. These two historians have written on opposite sides; and whoever will be at the pains of comparing their accounts with attention and impartiality, will easily perceive where the truth lies, and receive satisfactory information with respect to the true state of these controversies, and the motives that animated the contending parties.

in several places, became a source of new tumults, and furnished matter for the most violent dissensions and contests. It immediately met with a warm opposition from the Reformed, and also from all those who were either secretly attached to their doctrine, or who, at least, were desirous of living in concord and communion with them, from a laudable zeal for the common interest of the Protestant cause. Nor was their opposition at all unaccountable, since they plainly perceived that this form removed all the flattering hopes they had entertained, of seeing the divisions that reigned among the friends of religious liberty happily healed, and entirely excluded the Reformed from the communion of the Lutheran church. Hence they were filled with indignation against the authors of this new confession of faith, and exposed their uncharitable proceedings in writings full of spirit and vehemence. The Swiss doctors, with Hospinian at their head, the Belgic divines,* those of the palatinate,† together with the principalities of Anhalt and Baden, declared war against the form; and accordingly from this period the Lutheran, and more especially the Saxon doctors, were charged with the disagreeable task of defending this new creed and its compilers, in many laborious productions.‡

XLI. Nor were the followers of Zuingle and Calvin the only opposers of this form: it found adversaries, even in the very bosom of Lutheranism, and several of the most eminent churches of that communion rejected it with such firmness and resolution, that no arguments or entreaties could engage them to admit it as a rule of faith, or even as a mean of instruction. It was rejected by the church of Nuremberg, by those of Hesse, Pomerania, Holstein, Silesia, Denmark, Brunswick, and others.§ But though they all united in opposing it, their opposition was founded on different reasons, nor did they all act in this affair from the same motives or the same principles. A warm and affectionate veneration for the memory of Melancthon was, with some, the only, or at least the predominant, motive, that induced them to declare against the form in question; they could not behold, without the utmost abhorrence, a production in which the sentiments of this great and excellent man were so rudely treated. In this class we may rank the Lutherans of Holstein. Others were not only animated in their opposition by a regard for Melancthon, but also by a persuasion that the opinions, condemned in the new creed, were more conformable to truth, than to those which were substituted in their place. A secret attachment to the sentiments of the Helvetic doctors prevented some from approving the form under consideration; the hopes of uniting the Reformed and Lutheran churches engaged many to declare against it; and a considerable number refused their assent to it from an apprehension, whether real or pretended, that the addition of a new creed to the ancient confessions of faith would be really a source of disturbance and discord in the Lutheran church. It woud be endless to enumerae the different reasons alleged by the different individuals or communities, who declared their dissent from the Form of Concord.

XLII. This form was patronized in a more especial manner by Julius, duke of Brunswick, to whom, in a great measure, it owed its existence, who had employed both his authority and munificence in order to encourage those who had undertaken to compose it, and had commanded all the ecclesiastics, within his dominions, to receive and subscribe it as a rule of faith. But scarcely was it published, when the zealous prince, changing his mind, suffered the form to be publicly opposed by Heshusius, and other divines of his university of Helmstadt, and to be excluded from the number of the creeds and confessions received by his subjects. The reasons alleged by the Lutherans of Brunswick, in behalf of this step, were, 1st, That the Form of Concord, when printed, differed in several places from the manuscript copy to which they had given their approbation; 2dly, That the doctrine relating to the freedom of the human will was expressed in it without a sufficient degree of accuracy and precision, and was also inculcated in the harsh and improper terms that Luther had employed in treating that subject: 3dly, That the ubiquity, or universal and indefinite presence of Christ's human nature, was therein positively maintained, although the Lutheran church had never adopted any such doctrine. Besides these reasons, which were publicly avowed, some perhaps of a secret nature, contributed to the remarkable change, which was visible in the sentiments and proceedings of the duke of Brunswick. Various methods and negotiations were employed to remove the dislike which this prince, and the divines who lived in his territories, had conceived against the Creed of Berg. Particularly, in 1533, a convocation of divines from Saxony, Brandenberg, Brunswick, and the Palatinate, was holden at Quedlinburg for this purpose. But Julius persisted

* See Betri Villerii Epistola Apologetica Reformatarum in Belgio Ecclesiarum ad et contra Auctores Libri Bergensis, dicti "Concordiæ."—This work was published a second time, with the annotations of Lud. Gerard a Renesse, by the learned Dr. Gerdes of Groningen, in his Scrinium Antiquarium, seu Miscellan. Groningens. Nov. tom. i. Add to these the Unschuldige Nachricht.

† John Casimir, prince Palatine, convoked an assembly of the reformed divines at Francfort, in 1577, in order to reject and annul this form. See Hen. Altingii Histor. Eccles. Palatin. sect. clxxix.

‡ See Jo. Georg. Walchii Introd. in Libros Symbolicos Lutheranor. lib. i. cap. vii.

§ For an account of the ill success of this form in the dutchy of Holstein, see the Danische Bibliothec. vol. iv. p. 212, vol. v. p. 355, vol. viii. p. 333—461, vol. ix. p. 1.—Muhlii Dissert. Histor. Theol. Diss. i. de Reformat. Holsat. p. 108.—Arn. Grevii Memoria Pauli ab Eitzen. The transactions in Denmark, in relation to this form, and the particular reasons for which it was rejected there, may be seen in the Danish Library above quoted, vol. iv. p. 222—282, and also in Pontoppidan's Annal. Eccles Danicæ Diplomatici, tom. iii. p. 456. The last author evidently proves (p. 476,) a fact which Herman ab Elswich, and other authors, have endeavoured to represent as dubious,—that Frederic II. king of Denmark, as soon as he received a copy of the form, threw it into the fire, and saw it consumed before his eyes. The opposition that was made to it by the Hessians, may be seen in Tielemanni Vitæ Theologor. Marpugens. p. 99.—Danischen Bibliothec. vol. vii. p. 273—364. t. ix. p. 1—87.—The ill fate of this famous Confession, in the principalities of Lignitz and Brieg, is amply related in the Unsch. Nachricht.

steadfastly in his opposition, and proposed that the form should be examined, and its authority discussed in a general assembly or synod of the Lutheran church.*

XLIII. This form was not only opposed from abroad, but had likewise adversaries in the very country which gave it birth; for even in Saxony many, who had been obliged to subscribe it, beheld it with aversion, in consequence of their attachment to the doctrine of Melancthon. During the life of Augustus, they were forced to suppress their sentiments; but, as soon as he had paid the last tribute to nature, and was succeeded by Christian I., the moderate Lutherans and the secret Calvinists resumed their courage. The new elector had been accustomed, from his tender years, to the moderate sentiments of Melancthon, and is also said to have evinced a propensity to the doctrine of the Helvetic church. Under his government, therefore, an opportunity was offered to the persons above mentioned of declaring their sentiments and executing their designs; and the attempts to abolish the form now seemed to be renewed, with a view of opening a door for the entrance of Calvanism into Saxony. The persons who had embarked in this design, were greatly encouraged by the protection which they received from several noblemen of the first rank at the Saxon court, and, particularly, from Crellius, the first minister of Christian. Under the auspicious influence of such patrons it was natural to expect success; yet they conducted their affairs with circumspection and prudence. Certain laws were previously enacted, in order to prepare the minds of the people for the intended revolution in the doctrine of the church; and, some time after,† the form of exorcism was omitted in the administration of baptism.‡ These measures were followed by others still more alarming to the rigid Lutherans; for not only a new German catechism, favourable to the purpose of the secret Calvinists, was industriously distributed among the people, but also a new edition of the Bible, in the same language, enriched with the observations of Henry Salmouth, which were artfully accommodated to this purpose, was, in 1591, published at Dresden. The consequences of these vigorous measures were violent tumults and seditions among the people, which the magistrates endeavoured to suppress, by punishing with severity such of the clergy as distinguished themselves by their opposition to the views of the court. But the whole plan of this religious revolution was overturned by the unexpected death of Christian, which happened in the year 1591. Affairs then assumed their former aspect. The doctors, who had been principally concerned in the execution of this unsuccessful project, were committed to prison, or sent into banishment, after the death of the elector; and its chief encourager and patron, Crellius, suffered death in 1601, as the fruit of his temerity.*

XLIV. Towards the conclusion of this century, a new controversy was imprudently set on foot at Wittenberg, by a Swiss named Samuel Huber, professor of divinity in that university. The Calvinistical tenets of absolute predestination and unconditional decrees were extremely offensive to this adventurous theologian, and even excited his warmest indignation. Accordingly he affirmed, and taught publicly, that all mankind were elected from eternity by the Supreme being to everlasting salvation, and accused his colleagues in particular, and the Lutheran divines in general, of a propensity to the doctrine of Calvin, on account of their asserting, that the divine election was confined to those, whose *faith, foreseen* by an omniscient God, rendered them the proper objects of his redeeming mercy. The opinion of Huber, as is now acknowledged by many learned men, differed more in words than in reality, from the doctrine of the Lutheran church; for he did no more than explain in a new method, and with a different turn of phrase, what that church had always taught concerning the unlimited extent of the love of God, as embracing the whole human race, and excluding none by an *absolute* decree from everlasting salvation. However, as a disagreeable experience and repeated examples had abundantly shown, that new method of explaining or proving even received doctrines were as much adapted to excite divisions and contests, as the introduction of new errors, Huber was exhorted to adhere to the ancient method of proposing the doctrine of *election*, and, instead of his own pecular forms of expression, to make use of those which were received and authorized by the church. To this compliance he refused to submit, alleging that it was contrary to the dictates of his conscience, while his patrons and disciples, in many places, gave several indications of a turbulent and seditious zeal for his cause. These considerations engaged the magistrates of Wittenberg to depose him from his office, and to send him into banishment.†

XLV. The controversies, of which a succinct account has now been given, and others of inferior moment, which it is needless to mention, were highly detrimental to the true interests of the Lutheran church, as is abun-

* See Leon. Hutteri Concordia Concors, cap. xlv.—Phil. Jul. Richtmeyeri Braunschweig Kirchen Hist. part iii. cap. viii.—See also the authors mentioned by Christ. Matth. Pfaffius, in his Acta et Scripta Ecclesiæ Wirtembergensis, p. 62, et Histor. Literar. Theologiæ, part ii. p. 423.—For an account of the convocation of Quedlinburg, and the acts that passed in that assembly, see the Danische Bibliothec. part viii.

† In the year 1591.

☞ ‡ The custom of *exorcising*, or casting out evil spirits, was used in the fourth century at the admission of catechumens, and was afterwards absurdly applied in the baptism of infants. This application of it was retained by the greatest part of the Lutheran churches. It was indeed abolished by the elector, Christian I., but was restored after his death; and the opposition that had been made to it by Crellius was the chief reason of his unhappy end. See Justi H. Bohmeri Jus ecclesiast. Protestant. tom. iii.; as also a German work of Melchior Kraft, entitled Geschichte des Exorcismi.

* See Arnold's Kirchen und Ketzer Historie, part ii. book xvi. cap. xxxii.; as also the authors mentioned by Herm. Ascan. Engelcken, in his Dissertat de Nic. Crellio, ejusque Supplicio.

† For an account of the writers that appeared in this controversy, see Christ. Matth. Pfaffii Introductio in Histor. Liter. Theologiæ, par. ii. lib. iii. p. 431

dantly known by all who are acquainted with the history of this century. It must also be acknowledged, that the manner of conducting and deciding these debates, the spirit of the disputants, and the proceedings of the judges, if we form our estimate of them by the sentiments that prevail among the wiser sort of men in modern times, must be considered as inconsistent with equity, moderation, and charity. It betrays, nevertheless, a want, both of candour and justice, to inveigh indiscriminately against the authors of these misfortunes, and to represent them as totally destitute of rational sentiments and virtuous principles; and it is still more unjust to throw the whole blame upon the triumphant party, while the suffering side are all fondly represented as men of unblemished virtue, and worthy of a better fate. It ought not certainly to be a matter of surprise, that persons long accustomed to a state of darkness, and suddenly transported from it into the blaze of day, did not, at first, behold the objects that were presented to their view with that distinctness and precision which are natural to those who have long enjoyed the light; and such really was the case of the first protestant doctors, who were delivered from the gloom of papal superstition and tyranny. Besides, there was something gross and indelicate in the reigning spirit of this age, which made the people not only tolerate, but even applaud, many things relating both to the conduct of life and the management of controversy, which the more polished manners of modern times cannot relish, and which, indeed, are by no means worthy of imitation. As to the particular motives or intentions that guided each individual in this troubled scene of controversy, whether they acted from the suggestions of malice and resentment, or from an upright and sincere attachment to what they considered as truth, or how far these two springs of action were jointly concerned in their conduct, all this must be left to the decision of Him alone, whose privilege it is to search the heart, and to discern its most hidden intentions and its most secret motives.

XLVI. The Lutheran church furnished, during this century, a long list of distinguished men, who illustrated, in their writings, the various branches of theological science. After Luther and Melancthon, who stand foremost in this list, on account of their superior genius and erudition, we may select the following writers as the most eminent, and as persons whose names are worthy of being preserved in the annals of literature; viz. Weller, Chemnitz, Brentius, Flacius, Regius, Major, Amsdorf, Sarcerius, Matthesius, Wigandus, Lambertus, Andreas, Chytræus, Selneccer, Bucer, Fagius, Cruciger, Strigelius, Spangenberg, Judex, Heshusius, Westphal, Æpinus, Osiander, and others.*

* For an ample account of these Lutheran doctors, see Melchior Adam's Vitæ Theologorum, and Du-Pin's Bibliotheque des Auteurs separes de la Communion de l'Eglise Romaine au XVII. Siecle. The lives of several of these divines have been also composed by different authors of the present times; for example, that of Weller by Læmelius, that of Flacius by Ritter those of Heshusius and Spangenberg by Leuckfeldt, that of Fagius by Fervelin, that of Chytræus by Schutz, that of Bucer by Verpoortenius, those of Westphal and Æpinus by Arn. Grevius, &c.

CHAPTER II.

History of the Reformed Church.*

I. The reformed church, founded by Zuingle and Calvin, differs considerably, in its nature and constitution, from all other ecclesiastical communities. Every other Christian church hath some common centre of union, and its members are connected by some common bond of doctrine and discipline. But this is far from being the case of the *Reformed* church,† whose several branches are neither united by the same system of doctrine, nor by the same mode of worship, nor yet by the same form of government. It is farther to be observed, that this church does not require, from its ministers, either uniformity in their

* It has already been observed, that the denomination of *Reformed* was given to those protestant churches which did not embrace the doctrine and discipline of Luther. The title was first assumed by the French protestants, and afterwards became the common denomination of all the Calvinistical churches on the continent;—I say, on the continent; since in England the term *Reformed* is generally used as standing in opposition to popery alone Be that as it may, this part of Dr. Mosheim's work would have been, perhaps, with greater propriety entitled, 'The History of the Reformed *Churches*,' than that of the 'Reformed *Church*.' This will appear still more evident from the following note.

☞ † This, and the following observations, are designed to give the Lutheran church an air of unity, which is not to be found in the reformed. But there is a real fallacy in this specious representation of things. The *reformed* church, when considered in the true extent of the term, comprehends all those religious communities which separated themselves from the church of Rome; and, in this sense, it includes the Lutheran church, as well as the others. And even when this epithet is used in opposition to the community founded by Luther, it represents not a single church, as the episcopal, presbyterian, or independent, but rather a collection of churches; which, though they may be invisibly united by a belief and profession of the fundamental doctrines of Christianity, maintain separate places of worship, and have each a visible centre of external union peculiar to themselves, which is formed by certain peculiarities in their respective rules of public worship and ecclesiastical government.* An attentive examination of the discipline, polity, and worship of the churches of England, Scotland, Holland, and Switzerland, will set this matter in the clearest light. The first of these churches, being governed by bishops, and not admitting the validity of presbyterian ordination, differs from the other three more than any of these differ from each other. There are, however, peculiarities of government and worship that distinguish the church of Holland from that of Scotland. The institution of deacons, the use of forms for the celebration of the sacraments, an ordinary form of prayer, the observance of the festivals of Christmas, Easter, Ascension-day, and Whitsuntide, are established in the Dutch church; and it is well known that the church of Scotland greatly differs from it in these respects.—But, after all, to what does the pretended uniformity among the Lutherans amount? Are not some of the Lutheran churches governed by bishops, while others are ruled by elders? It shall moreover be shown in its proper place, that even in point of doctrine, the Lutheran churches are not so very remarkable for their uniformity.

* See the general sketch of the state of the church in the eighteenth century, paragraph xxi. and the notes annexed

private sentiments, or in their public doctrine, but permits them to explain, in different ways, several doctrines of no small moment, provided that the great and fundamental principles of Christianity, and the practical precepts of that divine religion, be maintained in their original purity. This great community, therefore, may be properly considered as an ecclesiastical body composed of many churches, that vary from each other in their form and constitution, but which are preserved from anarchy and schism, by a general spirit of equity and toleration, that runs through the whole system, and renders variety of opinion consistent with fraternal union.

II. This indeed was not the original state and constitution of the reformed church, but was the result of a certain combination of events and circumstances, that threw it, by a sort of necessity, into this ambiguous form. The divines of Switzerland, from whom it derived its origin, and Calvin, who was one of its principal founders, employed all their credit, and exerted their most vigorous efforts, in order to reduce all the churches, which embraced their sentiments, under one rule of faith, and the same form of ecclesiastical government. And although they considered the Lutherans as their brethren, yet they showed no marks of indulgence to those who openly favoured the opinions of Luther, concerning the eucharist, the person of Christ, or predestination; nor would they permit the other protestant churches that embraced their communion, to deviate from their example in this respect. A new scene, however, which was exhibited in Britain, contributed much to enlarge this narrow and contracted system of church communion; for, when the violent contest concerning the form of ecclesiastical government, and the nature and number of those ceremonies which were proper to be admitted into the public worship, arose between the abettors of episcopacy and the puritans,* it was judged necessary to extend the borders of the reformed church, and rank, in the class of its true members, even those who departed, in some respects, from the ecclesiastical polity and doctrines established at Geneva. This spirit of toleration and indulgence became still more forbearing and comprehensive after the famous synod of Dordrecht; for, though the sentiments and doctrines of the Arminians were rejected and condemned in that numerous assembly, yet they gained ground privately, and insinuated themselves into the minds of many. The church of England, in the reign of Charles I., publicly renounced the opinions of Calvin relating to the divine decrees, and made several attempts to model its doctrine and institutions after the laws, tenets, and customs, that were observed by the primitive Christians.† On the other hand, several Lutheran congregations in Germany entertained a strong propensity to the doctrines and discipline of the church of Geneva, though they were restrained from declaring themselves fully and openly on this head, by their apprehensions of forfeiting the privileges which they derived from their adherence to the confession of Augsburg. The French refugees also, who had long been accustomed to a moderate way of thinking in religious matters, and whose national turn led them to a certain freedom of inquiry, being dispersed abroad in all parts of the protestant world, rendered themselves so agreeable, by their wit and eloquence, that their example excited a kind of emulation in favour of religious liberty. All these circumstances, accompanied with others, whose influence was less palpable, though equally real, gradually instilled such a spirit of lenity and forbearance into the minds of protestants, that at this day, all Christians, if we except Roman Catholics, Socinians, Quakers, and Anabaptists, may claim a place among the members of the reformed church. It is true, that great reluctance was discovered by many against this comprehensive scheme of church communion; and, even in the times in which we live, the ancient and less charitable manner of proceeding hath several patrons, who would be glad to see the doctrines and institutions of Calvin universally adopted and rigorously observed. These zealots, however, are not very numerous, nor is their influence considerable; and it may be affirmed with truth, that, both in point of number and authority, they are much inferior to the friends of moderation, who reduce within a narrow compass the fundamental doctrines of Christianity, on the belief of which salvation depends, exercise forbearance and fraternal charity toward those who explain certain doctrines in a manner peculiar to themselves, and desire to see the enclosure (if I may use that expression) of the reformed church rendered as large and comprehensive as is possible.*

III. The founder of the reformed church was Ulric Zuingle, a native of Switzerland, and a man of uncommon penetration and acuteness, accompanied with an ardent zeal for truth. This great man was for removing out of the churches, and abolishing, in the ceremonies and appendages of public worship, many things which Luther was disposed to

☞ * The *Puritans*, who inclined to the presbyterian form of church government, of which Knox was one of the earliest abettors in Britain, derived this denomination from their pretending to a *purer* method of worship than that which had been established by Edward VI. and queen Elizabeth.

☞ † This assertion is equivocal. Many members of the church of England, with Archbishop Laud at their head, did, indeed, propagate the doctrines of Arminius, both in their pulpits and in their writings. But it is not accurate to say that the church of England renounced publicly, in that reign, the opinions of Calvin. See this matter farther discussed in the note , cent. xvii. sect. ii. p. ii. ch. ii. paragraph xx.

* The annals of theology have not yet been enriched with a full and accurate history of the Reformed Church. This task was indeed undertaken by Scultet, and even carried down so far as his own time, in his Annales Evangelii Renovatii; but the greatest part of this work is lost. Theod. Hasæus, who proposed to give the annals of that church, was prevented by death from fulfilling his purpose. The famous work of James Basnage, published in 1725 under the title of Histoire de la Religione des Eglises Reformees, instead of giving a regular history of the reformed church, is only designed to show that its peculiar and distinguishing doctrines are not new inventions, but were taught and embraced in the earliest ages of the church. Malmbourg's Histoire du Calvinisme is remarkable for nothing but the partiality of its author, and the wilful errors with which it abounds.

treat with toleration and indulgence, such as images, altars, wax-tapers, the form of exorcism, and private confession. He aimed at nothing so much as establishing, in his country, a form of divine worship remarkable for its simplicity, and as far remote as could be from every thing that might have the smallest tendency to nourish a spirit of superstition.* Nor were these the only circumstances in which he differed from the Saxon reformer; for his sentiments concerning several points of theology, and more especially his opinions relating to the sacrament of the Lord's supper, varied widely from those of Luther. The greatest part of these sentiments and opinions were adopted in Switzerland, by those who had joined themselves to Zuingle in promoting the cause of the Reformation, and were by them transmitted to all the Helvetic churches that threw off the yoke of Rome. From Switzerland these opinions were propagated among the neighbouring nations, by the ministerial labours and the theological writings of the friends and disciples of Zuingle: and thus the primitive reformed church, that was founded by this eminent ecclesiastic, and whose extent at first was not very considerable, gathered strength by degrees, and daily made new acquisitions.

IV. The separation, between the Lutheran and Swiss churches, was chiefly occasioned by the doctrine of Zuingle, concerning the sacrament of the Lord's supper. Luther maintained that the body and blood of Christ were really, though in a manner far beyond human comprehension, present in the eucharist, and were exhibited together with the bread and wine. On the contrary, the Swiss reformer looked upon the bread and wine in no other light than as the signs and symbols of the absent body and blood of Christ; and, from the year 1524, he propagated this doctrine in a public manner by his writings, having entertained and taught it privately before that period.† In a little time after this,‡ his example was followed by Œcolampadius, a divine of Basil, and one of the most learned men of that century.§ But they were both opposed with obstinacy and spirit by Luther and his associates, particularly those of the circle of Suabia. In the mean time, Philip, landgrave of Hesse, apprehending the pernicious effects that these debates might have upon the affairs of the protestants, which were, as yet, in the fluctuating and unsettled state that marks the infancy of all great revolutions, was desirous of putting an end to these differences, and, for that purpose, appointed a conference at Marpurg, between Zuingle, Luther, and other doctors of both parties.* This meeting, however, only covered the flame instead of extinguishing it; and the pacific prince, seeing it impossible to bring about a definite treaty of peace and concord between these jarring divines, was obliged to rest satisfied with having engaged them to consent to a truce. Luther and Zuingle came to an engreement about several points; but the principal matter in debate,—that which regarded Christ's presence in the eucharist,—was left undecided; each party appealing to the Fountain of wisdom to terminate this contorversy, and expressing a hope that time and impartial reflection might discover and confirm the truth.†

V. The reformed Church had scarcely been founded in Switzerland by Zuingle, when the Christian hero fell in a battle that was fought, in 1530, between the protestants of Zurich, and their Roman catholic compatriots, who drew the sword in defence of popery. It was not indeed to perform the sanguinary office of a soldier that Zuingle was present at this engagement, but with a view to encourage and animate, by his counsel and exhortations, the valiant defenders of the protestant cause.‡

☞ * The design of Zuingle was certainly excellent; but in the execution of it perhaps he went too far, and consulted rather the dictates of reason than the real exigencies of human nature in its present state. The existing union between soul and body, which operate together in the actions of moral agents, even in those who appear the most abstracted and refined, renders it necessary to consult the external senses, as well as the intellectual powers, in the institution of public worship. Besides, between a worship purely and philosophically rational, and a service grossly and palpably superstitious, there are many intermediate steps and circumstances, by which a rational service may be rendered more affecting and awakening, without becoming superstitious. A noble edifice, solemn music, a well-ordered set of external gestures, though they do not, in themselves, render our prayers more acceptable to the Deity, than if they were offered up without any of these circumstances, produce, nevertheless, a good effect. They elevate the mind, they give it a composed and solemn frame, and thus contribute to the fervour of its devotion.

Zuingle certainly taught this doctrine in private before the year 1524, as appears from Gerdes' Historia Renovati Evangelii, tom. i.

‡ In the year 1525.

§ Jo. Conr. Fueslini Centuria i. Epistol. Theolog. Reformat.—☞ Œcolampadius was not less remarkable for his extraordinary modesty, his charitable, forbearing, and pacific spirit, and his zeal for the progress of vital and practical religion, than for his profound erudition, which he seemed rather studious to conceal, than to display.

☞ * Zuingle was accompanied by Œcolampadius, Bucer, and Hideon. Luther had with him Melancthon and Justus Jonas from Saxony, and also Osiander, Brentius, and Agricola.

† Ruchat, Histoire de la Reformation de la Suisse vol. i. ii.—Hottinger, Helvetische Kirchen-Geschichte, part iii.—Loscher, Historia Motuum, par. i. cap. ii. iii. vi.—Fueslini Beytrage zur Schweizer Reformation, tom. iv.

‡ The Lutherans, who consider this unhappy fate of Zuingle as a reproach upon that great man in particular, and upon the reformed church in genera , discover a gross ignorance of the genius and manners of the Swiss nation in this century; for, as all the inhabitants of that country are at present trained to arms, and obliged to take the field when the defence of their country requires it so in the time of Zuingle this obligation was so general, that neither the ministers of the Gospel, nor the professors of theology, was exempted from this military service. Accordingly, in the same battle in which Zuingle fell, Jerome Pontanus, one of the theological doctors of Basil, also lost his iife, See Fueslini Centuria i. Epistolar. Theol. Reformator. ☞ Erasmus also spoke in a very unfriendly manner of the death of Zuingle and his friend Œcolampadius. See Jortin's Life of Erasmus, vol. i. It is not therefore surprising to find the bigoted Sir Thomas More insulting (with the barbarity that superstition seldom fails to produce in a narrow and peevish mind) the memory of these two eminent reformers, in a letter to the furious and turbulent Cochlæus; of which the following words show the spirit of the writer: "Postrema ea fuit, quam de Zuinglio et Œcolempadio, scriptam misisti, quorum nunciata mors mihi lætitiam attulit. —Sublatos e medio esse tam immanes fidei Christianæ hostes, tam intentos ubique in omnem perimendæ

After his death, several Lutheran doctors of the more moderate sort, and particularly Martin Bucer, used their utmost endeavours to bring about some kind of reconciliation between the contending parties. For this purpose they exhorted the jarring theologians to concord, interpreted the points in dispute with a prudent regard to the prejudices of both sides, admonished them of the pernicious consequences that must attend the prolongation of these unhappy contests, and even went so far as to express the respective sentiments of the contending doctors in terms of considerable ambiguity and latitude, that thus the desired union might be the more easily effected. There is no doubt, that the intentions and designs of these zealous intercessors were pious and upright;* but it will be difficult to decide, whether the means they employed were adapted to promote the end they had in view. Be that as it may, these specific counsels of Bucer excited divisions in Switzerland: for some persevered obstinately in the doctrine of Zuingle, while others adopted the explications and modifications of his doctrine, offered by Bucer.† But these divisions and commotions had not the least effect on that reconciliation with Luther, which was earnestly desired by the pious and moderate doctors of both parties. The efforts of Bucer were more successful out of Switzerland, and particularly among those divines in the upper parts of Germany, who inclined to the sentiments of the Helvetic church; for they retired from the communion of that church, and joined themselves to Luther by a public act, which was sent to Wittenberg, in 1536, by a solemn deputation appointed for that purpose.‡ The Swiss divines could not be brought to so great a length. There was, however, still some prospect of a reconciliation even between them and the Lutherans. But this fair prospect entirely disappeared in 1544, when Luther published his confession of faith in relation to the sacrament of the Lord's supper, which was directly opposite to the doctrine of Zuingle and his followers on that head. The doctors of Zurich pleaded their cause publicly against the Saxon reformer in the following year; and thus the purposes of the advocates of peace were totally defeated.§

VI. The death of Luther, which happened in the year 1546, was an event that seemed adapted to calm these commotions, and to revive, in the breast of the moderate and pacific, the hopes of a reconciliation between the contending parties. For this union, between the Lutherans and Zuinglians, was so ardently desired by Melancthon and his followers, that this great man left no means unemployed to effect it, and seemed resolved, rather to submit to a dubious and forced peace, than to see those flaming discords perpetuated, which reflected such dishonour on the protestant cause. At the same time, this salutary work seemed to be facilitated by the theological system that was adopted by John Calvin, a native of Noyn in France, who as pastor and professor of divinity at Geneva, and whose genius, learning, eloquence, and talents, rendered him respectable, even in the eyes of his enemies. This great man, whose particular friendship for Melancthon was an incidental circumstance highly favourable to the intended reconciliation, proposed an explication of the point in debate, that modified the crude hypothesis of Zuingle, and made use of all his credit and authority among the Swiss, and more particularly at Zurich, where he was held in the highest veneration, in order to obtain their assent to it.* The explication he proposed was not, indeed, favourable to the doctrine of Christ's bodily presence in the eucharist, which he persisted in denying; he supposed, however, that a certain *divine* virtue, or efficacy, was communicated by Christ, with the bread and wine, to those who approached this holy sacrament with a lively faith, and with upright hearts; and to render this notion still more satisfactory, he expressed it in almost the same terms which the Lutherans employed in inculcating their doctrine of Christ's real presence in the eucharist.† Indeed the great and common errror of all those, who, from a desire of peace, assumed the character of arbitrators in this controversy, lay in this, that they aimed rather at an uniformity of terms than of sentiments, and seemed satisfied when they had engaged the contending parties to use the same words and phrases, though their real difference in opinion remained the same, and each explained these ambiguous or figurative terms in a manner agreeable to their respective systems.

The concord, so much desired, did not, however, seem to advance much. Melancthon, although he stood foremost in the rank of those who longed impatiently for it, had not courage enough to embark openly in the execution of such a perilous project. Besides, after the death of Luther, his enemies attacked him with redoubled fury, and gave him so much disagreeable occupation, that he had neither that leisure, nor that tranquillity of mind, which were necessary to prepare his measures properly for such an arduous undertaking. A new obstacle to the execution of this pacific project was also presented, by the intemperate zeal of Joachim Westphal, pastor at Hamburg, who, in 1552, renewed, with greater vehemence than ever, this deplorable controversy, which had been for some time suspended; and who, after Flacius, was the most obstinate defender of the opinions of Luther. This violent theologian, with a spirit of acrimonious vehemence, like that which too remarkably ap-

pietatis occasionem, jure gaudere possum." Jortin, vol. ii.

* See Alb. Menon. Verpoorten, Comment. de Mart. Bucero, et ejus Sententia de Cœna Domini, sect. ix. p. 23, published in 8vo. at Coburg, in the year 1709.—Loscheri Hist. Motuum, par. i. lib. ii. and par. i. lib. iii.

† Fueslini Centur. i. Epistolar. Theolog.

‡ Loscheri Hist. cap. ii. p. 205.—Ruchat, Histoire de la Reformat. de Suisse, tom. v. p. 535.—Hottingeri Histor. Eccles. Helvet. tom. iii. lib. vi. p. 702.

§ Loscheri Hist. par. i. lib. ii. cap. iv. p. 341.

* Salig. Hist. Aug. Confessionis, tom. ii. lib. vii.

☞ † Calvin went certainly too far in this matter; and, in his explication of the benefits that arise from a worthy commemoration of Christ's death in the eucharist, he dwelt too grossly upon the allegorical expressions of Scripture, which the papists had so egregiously abused, and talked of really eating by faith the body, and drinking the blood of Christ.

heard in the polemic writings of Luther, attacked the act of uniformity, by which the churches of Geneva and Zurich declared their agreement concerning the doctrine of the eucharist. In the book which he published with this view,* he censured, with the utmost severity, the variety of sentiments concerning the sacrament of the Lord's supper, observable in the reformed church, and maintained, with his usual warmth and obstinacy, the opinion of Luther on that subject. This engaged Calvin to enter the lists with Westphal, whom he treated with as little lenity and forbearance, as the rigid Lutherans had shown toward the Helvetic churches. The consequences of this debate were, that Calvin and Westphal had, respectively, their zealous defenders and patrons: thus the breach was widened, the spirits were heated, and the flame of controversy was kindled anew with such violence and fury, that to extinguish it entirely seemed to be a task beyond the reach of human wisdom or power.†

VII. These disputes were unhappily augmented by that famous controversy concerning the decrees of God, with respect to the eternal condition of men, which was set on foot by Calvin, and became an inexhaustible source of intricate researches, and abstruse, subtle, and inexplicable questions. The most ancient Helvetic doctors were far from adopting the doctrine of those, who represent the Deity as assigning from all eternity, by an absolute, arbitrary, and unconditional decree, to some everlasting happiness, and to others endless misery, without any previous regard to the moral characters and circumstances of either. Their sentiments seemed to differ very little from those of the Pelagians; nor did they hesitate in declaring, after the example of Zuingle, that the kingdom of heaven was open to all who lived according to the dictates of right reason.‡ Calvin had adopted a quite different system with respect to the divine decrees. He maintained, that the everlasting condition of mankind in a future world was determined from all eternity, by the unchangeable order of the Deity, and that this absolute determination of his will and good pleasure, was the only source of happiness or misery to every individual. This opinion was in a very short time propagated through all the reformed churches, by the writings of Calvin, and by the ministry of his disciples; and, in some places, it was inserted in the national creeds and confessions, and thus made a public article of faith. The unhappy controversy, which took its rise from this doctrine, was opened at Strasburg, in 1560, by Jerome Zanchius, an Italian ecclesiastic, who was particularly attached to the sentiments of Calvin; and it was afterwards carried on by others with such zeal and assiduity, that it drew, in an extraordinary manner, the attention of the public, and tended as much to exasperate the passions, and foment the discord of the contending parties, as the dispute about the eucharist had already done.*

VIII. The Helvetic doctors had no prospect left of calming the troubled spirits, and tempering, at least, the vehemence of these deplorable feuds, but the moderation of the Saxon divines, who were the disciples of Melancthon, and who, breathing the pacific spirit of their master, seemed, after his death, to have nothing so much at heart as the restoration of concord and union to the protestant church. Their designs, however, were not carried on with that caution and circumspection, with that prudent foresight, or that wise attention to the nature of the times, which always distinguished the transactions of Melancthon, and which the critical nature of the cause they were engaged in, indispensably required. And hence they had already taken a step, which threatened to render ineffectual all the remedies they could apply to the healing of the present disorders; for, by dispersing artful and insidious writings, with a design to seduce the ministers of the church, and the studious youth, into the sentiments of the Swiss divines, or, at least, to engage them to treat these sentiments with toleration and forbearance, they drew upon themselves the indignation of their adversaries, and ruined the pacific cause in which they had embarked. It was this conduct that gave occasion to the composition of that famous *Form of Concord*, which condemned the sentiments of the reformed churches in relation to the person of Christ, and the sacrament of the Lord's supper; and, as this form is received by the greatest part of the Lutherans, as one of the articles of their religion, hence arises an insuperable obstacle to all schemes of reconciliation and concord.

IX. So much did it seem necessary to premise concerning the causes, rise, and progress of the controversy, which formed the separation that still subsists between the Lutheran and reformed churches. Thence it will be proper to proceed to an account of the internal state of the latter, and to the history of its progress and revolutions. The history of the reformed church, during this century, comprehends two distinct periods. The first commences with the year 1519, when Zuingle withdrew from the communion of Rome, and began to form a christian church beyond the bounds of the pope's jurisdiction; and it ex-

☞ * This book, which abounds with senseless and extravagant tenets that Luther never so much as thought of, and breathes the most virulent spirit of persecution, is entitled, "Farrago Confusanearum et inter se dissidentium de S. Cœna Opinionum ex Sacramentariorum Libris congesta."

† Loscheri Historia Motuum, par. ii. lib. iii. cap. viii. p. 83.—Molleri Cimbria Literata, tom. iii. p. 642.—Arn. Grevii Memoria Joac. Westphali.

‡ For the proof of this assertion, see Dallæi Apologia pro duabus Ecclesiarum Gallicar. Synodis adversus Fred. Spanheim, part iv. p. 946.—Jo. Alphons. Turretini Epistol. ad Antistitem Cantuariensem, inserted in the Bibliotheque Germanique, tom. xiii.—Simon, Bibliotheque Critique, published under the fictitious name of Sanior, tom. iii. ch. xxviii., and also a book, entitled, Observationes Gallicæ in Formul. Consensus Helveticam. The very learned Dr. Gerdes, instead of being persuaded by these testimonies, maintains, on the contrary, (in his Miscellan. Groningens.) that the sentiments of Calvin were the same with those of the ancient Swiss doctors; but this excellent author may be refuted, even from his own account of the tumults which were occasioned in Switzerland, by the opinion that Calvin had propagated in relation to the divine decrees.

* Loscheri Historia Motuum, part iii. lib. v. cap. ii —Salig Hist. August. Confessionis, tom. i. lib ii cap. xiii

ends to the time of Calvin's settlement at Geneva, where he acquired the greatest reputation and authority. The second period takes in the rest of this century.

During the first of these periods, the Helvetic church, which assumed the title of *Reformed* after the example of the French protestants in its neighbourhood, who had chosen this denomination, in order to distinguish themselves from the catholics, as very considerable in its extent, and was confined to the cantons of Switzerland. It was indeed augmented by the accession of some small states in Suabia and Alsace, but, in 1526, these states changed sides, through the suggestions and influence of Bucer, returned to the communion of the Saxon church, and thus made their peace with Luther. The other religious communities, which had abandoned the church of Rome, either openly embraced the doctrine of Luther, or consisted of persons who did not agree in their theological opinions, and who really seemed to stand in a kind of neutrality between the contending parties. All things being duly considered, it appears probable enough that the church founded by Zuingle, would have remained still confined to its original limits, had not Calvin arisen, to augment its extent, authority, and lustre; for the natural and political character of the Swiss, neither bent toward the lust of conquest, nor the grasping views of ambition, discovered itself in their religious transactions; and, as a spirit of contentment with what they had, prevented their aiming at an augmentation of their territory, so did a similar spirit hinder them from being extremely solicitous about enlarging the borders of their church.

X. In this infant state of the reformed church, the only point that prevented its union with the followers of Luther, was the doctrine they taught with respect to the sacrament of the Lord's supper. This first controversy, indeed, soon produced a second, relating to the *person* of Jesus Christ; which, nevertheless, concerned only a part of the Lutheran Church.* The Lutheran divines of Suabia, in the course of their debates with those of Switzerland, drew an argument in favour of the *real* presence of Christ's body and blood in the eucharist, from the following proposition: that "all the *properties* of the divine nature, and consequently its *omnipresence* were communicated to the human nature of Christ by the hypostatic union." The Swiss doctors, in order to destroy the force of this argument, denied this communication of the divine attributes to Christ's human nature; and denied, more especially, the 'ubiquity or omnipresence of the man Jesus;' and hence arose that most intricate and abstruse controversy concerning ubiquity, and the communication of properties, which produced so many learned and unintelligible treatises, so many subtle disputes, and occasioned such a multitude of accusations and invectives.

It is proper to observe, that, at this time, the Helvetic church universally embraced the doctrine of Zuingle concerning the eucharist. This doctrine, which differed considerably from that of Calvin, amounted to the following propositions: That the bread and wine were no more than a representation of the body and blood of Christ; or, in other words, the signs appointed to denote the benefits that were conferred upon mankind, in consequence of the death of Christ; that, therefore, Christians derived no other fruit from the participation of the Lord's supper, than a mere commemoration and remembrance of the merits of Christ, which, according to an expression common in the mouths of the advocates of this doctrine, was the 'only thing that was properly meant by the Lord's supper.'* Bucer, whose leading principles was the desire of peace and concord, endeavoured to correct and modify this doctrine in such a manner, as to give it a certain degree of conformity to the hypothesis of Luther; but the memory of Zuingle was too fresh in the minds of the Swiss, to permit their acceptance of these corrections and modifications, or to suffer them to depart, in any respect, from the doctrine of that eminent man, who had founded their church, and had been the instrument of their deliverance from the tyranny and superstition of Rome.

XI. In the year 1541, John Calvin, who surpassed almost all the doctors of this age in laborious application, constancy of mind, force of eloquence, and extent of genius, returned to Geneva, whence the opposition of his enemies had obliged him to retire. On his settlement in that city, the affairs of the new church were committed to his direction;† and he acquired also a high degree of influence in the political administration of that republic. This event changed entirely the face of affairs, and gave a new aspect to the reformed church. The views and projects of this great man were grand and extensive; for he not only undertook to give strength and vigour to the rising church, by framing the wisest laws and the most salutary institutions for the maintenance of order, and the advancement of true piety, but even proposed to render Geneva the mother, the seminary of all the reformed churches, as Wittenberg was of all the Lutheran communities. He formed the scheme of sending

☞ * It was only a certain number of those Lutherans, who were much more rigid in their doctrine than Luther himself, that believed the ubiquity or omnipresence of Christ's person, considered as a man. By this we may see that the Lutherans have their divisions as well as the reformed, of which several instances may be yet given in the course of this History.

* Nihil esse in Cœna quam memoriam Christi. That this was the real opinion of Zuingle, appears evidently from various testimonies, which may be seen in the Museum Helveticum, tom. i. p. 485, 490. tom. iii. p. 631. This is also confirmed by the following sentence in his book concerning baptism; (tom. ii. op. p. 85.) "Cœna Dominica non aliud quam Commemorationis nomen meretur." Compare, with all this, Fueslini Cent. I. Epist. Theol. Reform.

† Calvin, in reality, enjoyed the power and authority of a bishop at Geneva; for, as long as he lived, he presided in the assembly of the clergy, and in the consistory, or ecclesiastical judicatory. But, when he was at the point of death, he advised the clergy not to appoint a successor, and proved to them evidently the dangerous consequences of entrusting with any one man, during life, a place of such high authority. After him, therefore, the place of president ceased to be perpetual. See Spon's Histoire de Geneva, tom. ii.

forth from this little republic the succours and ministers that were to promote and propagate the protestant cause through the most distant nations, and aimed at nothing less than rendering the government, discipline, and doctrine of Geneva, the model and rule of strict imitation to all the reformed churches in the world. The undertaking was certainly great, and worthy of the extensive genius and capacity of this eminent man; and, great and arduous as it was, it was executed in part, and even carried on to a very considerable length, by his indefatigable assiduity and inextinguishable zeal. It was with this view, that, by the fame of his learning, as well as by his epistolary solicitations and encouragements of various kinds, he engaged many persons of rank and fortune, in France, Italy, and other countries, to leave the places of their nativity, and to settle at Geneva; while others repaired thither merely out of curiosity to see a man, whose talents and exploits had rendered him so famous, and to hear the discourses which he delivered in public. Another circumstance, that contributed much to the success of his designs, was the establishment of an university at Geneva, which the senate of that city founded at his request; and in which he himself, with his colleague, Theodore Beza, and other divines of eminent learning and abilities, taught the sciences with the greatest reputation. In effect, the lustre which these great men reflected upon this infant seminary of learning, spread its fame through the distant nations with such amazing rapidity, that all who were ambitious of a distinguished progress either in sacred or profane erudition, repaired to Geneva, and that England, Scotland, France, Italy, and Germany, seemed to vie with each other in the numbers of their studious youth, that were incessantly repairing to the new university. By these means, and by the ministry of these his disciples, Calvin enlarged considerably the borders of the reformed church, propagated his doctrine, and gained proselytes and patrons to his theological system, in several countries of Europe. In the midst of this glorious career, he ended his days, in the year 1564; but the salutary institutions and wise regulations, of which he had been the author, were both respected and maintained after his death. In a more especial manner, the university of Geneva flourished as much under Beza, as it had done during the life of its founder.*

XII. The plan of doctrine and discipline that had been formed by Zuingle, was altered and corrected by Calvin, more especially in three points, of which it will not be improper to give a particular account.

1st, Zuingle, in his form of ecclesiastical government, had given an absolute and unbounded power, in religious matters, to the civil magistrate, to whom he had placed the clergy in a degree of subjection that was displeasing to many. At the same time he allowed a certain subordination and difference of rank among the ministers of the church, and even thought it expedient to place at their head a perpetual president, or superintendent, with a certain degree of inspection and authority over the whole body. Calvin, on the contrary, reduced the power of the magistrate, in religious matters, within narrow bounds. He declared the church a separate and independent body, endowed with the power of legislation for itself. He maintained, that it was to be governed, like the primitive church, only by presbyteries and synods, that is, by assemblies of elders, composed both of the clergy and laity; and he left to the civil magistrate little more than the privilege of protecting and defending the church, and providing for what related to its external exigencies and concerns. Thus this eminent reformer introduced into the republic of Geneva, and endeavoured to introduce into all the reformed churches throughout Europe, that form of ecclesiastical government, which is called *Presbyterian*, from its neither admitting the institution of bishops, nor any subordination among the clergy; and which is founded on this principle, that all ministers of the Gospel are, by the law of God, declared to be equal in rank and authority. In consequence of this principle, he established at Geneva a consistory composed of ruling elders, partly pastors, and partly laymen, and invested this ecclesiastical body with a high degree of power and authority. He also convened synods, composed of the ruling elders of different churches, and, in these consistories and synods, procured laws to be enacted for the regulation of all matters of a religious nature; and, among other things, restored to its former vigour the ancient practice of excommunication. All these things were done with the consent of the greatest part of the senate of Geneva.

2dly, The system that Zuingle had adopted with respect to the eucharist, was by no means agreeable to Calvin, who, in order to facilitate the desired union with the Lutheran church, substituted in its place another, which appeared more conformable to the doctrine of that church, and, in reality, differed little from it. For while the doctrine of Zuingle supposed only a *symbolical* or figurative *presence* of the body and blood of Christ in the eucharist, and represented a pious remembrance of Christ's death, and of the benefits it procured to mankind, as the only fruits that arose from the celebration of the Lord's supper, Calvin explained this critical point in a quite different manner. He acknowledged a *real* though *spiritual presence* of Christ in this sacrament or, in other words, he maintained, that true Christians, who approached this holy ordinance with a lively faith, were, in a certain manner, united to the man Christ; and that from this union the spiritual life derived new vigour in the soul, and was still carried on, in a progressive motion, to greater degrees of purity and perfection. This kind of language

* The various projects and plans that were formed, conducted, and executed with equal prudence and resolution by Calvin, in behalf, both of the republic and church of Geneva, are related by the learned person, who, in 1730, gave a new edition (enriched with interesting historical notes, and authentic documents) of Spon's Histoire de Geneve. The particular accounts of Calvin's transactions, given by this anonymous editor, in his notes, are drawn from several curious manuscripts of undoubted credit.

had been used in the forms of doctrine drawn up by Luther; and as Calvin observed, among other things, that the divine grace was conferred upon sinners. and sealed to them by the celebtation of the Lord's supper, this induced many to suppose that he adopted the sentiment implied in the barbarous term *impanation*,* and did not essentially alter the doctrine of the Lutheran church on this important subject.† Be that as it may, his sentiments differed considerably from those of Zuingle; for, while the latter asserted, that all Christians, whether regenerate or unregenerate, might be partakers of the body and blood of Christ, Calvin confined this privilege to the pious and regenerate believer alone.

3dly, The absolute decree of God, with respect to the future and everlasting condition of the human race, which made no part of the theology of Zuingle, was an essential tenet in the creed of Calvin, who inculcated with zeal the following doctrine: that God, in predestinating, from all eternity, one part of mankind to everlasting happiness, and another to end less misery, was led to make this distinction by no other motive than his own good pleasure and free will.

XIII. The first point was of such a nature, that, great as the credit and influence of Calvin were, he could not procure an universal reception for it in the reformed churches. The English and Germans rejected it, and even the Swiss refused to adopt it. It was, however, received by the reformed churches in France, Holland, and Scotland. The Swiss remained firm in their opposition; they would not suffer the form of ecclesiastical government, that had once been established under the inspection of Zuingle, to be changed in any respect, nor the power of the civil magistrate, in religious matters, to receive the smallest prejudice. The other two points were long debated, even in Switzerland, with the greatest warmth. Several churches, more especially those of Zurich and Bern, maintained obstinately the doctrine of Zuingle concerning the eucharist;* and they could not be easily persuaded to admit, as an article of faith, the doctrine of predestination, as it had been taught by Calvin.† The prudence, however, of this great man, seconded by his resolute perseverance and his extraordinary credit, triumphed at length so far, as to bring about an union between the Swiss churches and that of Geneva, first in relation to the doctrine of the eucharist,‡ and afterwards also on the snbject of predestination.§ The followers of Calvin extended still farther the triumphs of their chief, and improved with such success the footing he had gained, that, in process of time, almost all the reformed churches adopted his theological system; a result to which, no doubt, his learned writings greatly contributed.||

XIV. It will not be improper to pass in review the different countries in which the doctrine and discipline of the reformed church, as modelled by Calvin, were established in a fixed and permanent manner. Among its chief patrons in Germany we may reckon Frederic III. elector Palatine, who, in 1560, removed from their pastoral functions the Lutheran doctors, and filled their places with Calvinists; and, at the same time, obliged his subjects to embrace the tenets, rites, and institutions of the church of Geneva.¶ This order was indeed abro-

☞ * The term *Impanation* (which signifies here the *presence* of Christ's body in the eucharist, *in* or *with* the *bread* that is there exhibited) amounts to what is called Consubstantiation. It was a modification of the monstrous doctrine of Transubstantiation, first invented by some of the disciples of Berenger, who had not a mind to break all measures with the church of Rome, and was afterwards adopted by Luther and his followers, who, in reality, made sad work of it. For, in order to give it some faint air of possibility, and to maintain it as well as they could, they fell into a wretched scholastic jargon about the nature of substances, subsistences, attributes, properties, and accidents, that did infinite mischief to the true and sublime science of gospel theology, whose beautiful simplicity it was adapted to destroy. The very same perplexity and darkness, the same quibbling, sophistical, and unintelligible logic, that reigned in the attempts of the Roman catholics to defend the doctrine of Transubstantiation, were visible in the controversial writings of the Lutherans in behalf of Consubstantiation, or Impanation. The latter had, indeed, one absurdity less to maintain; but being obliged to assert, in opposition to intuitive evidence and unchangeable truth, that the same body can be in many places at the same time, they were consequently obliged to have recourse to the darkest and most intricate jargon of the schools, to hide the nonsense of this unaccountable doctrine. The modern Lutherans are grown somewhat wiser in this respect; at least, they seem less zealous than their ancestors about the tenet in question.

† See Fueslini Centur. I. Epistol. Theol. Reform. tom. i. p. 255, 262.—Lettres de Calvin a Mons. de Falaise, p. 84.—We learn from Fueslin that Calvin wrote to Bucer a letter, intimating that he approved his sentiments. It is possible, that he may have derived from Bucer the opinion he entertained with respect to the eucharist.—See Bossuet's Histoire, des Variations des Eglises Protestantes, tom. ii.; and Courayer's Examens des Defauts de Theologiens, tom. ii. These two writers pretend that the sentiments of Calvin, with respect to the eucharist, were almost the same with those of the catholics.* The truth of the matter is, that the obscurity and inconsistency with which this great man expressed himself upon that subject, rendered it extremely difficult to give a clear and accurate acount of his doctrine.

☞ * How it could come into the heads of such men as Bossuet and Dr. Courayer to say, that "the sentiments of Calvin concerning the eucharist were almost the same with those of the catholics," is, indeed, strange enough. The doctrine of transubstantiation was to Calvin an invincible obstacle to any sort of conformity between him and Rome on that subject; for, however obscure and figurative his expressions with respect to Christ's spiritual presence in the eucharist may have been, he never once dreamed of any thing like a corporal presence in that holy sacrament.

* See Fueslini Centur. Epistolar. p. 264.—Museum Helvet. tom. i. p. 490. tom. v. p. 479, 483. tom. ii. p. 79.

† Besides Ruchat and Hottinger, see Museum Helveticum, tom. ii.—Gerdes, Miscellan. Groningens. Nova, tom. ii.

‡ This agreement was concluded in 1549, for one point; and in 1554 for the other.

§ See the Consensus Genev. et Tigurinor. in Calvini Opusculis.

|| The learned Dan. Ern. Jablonsky, in his Letters to Leibnitz, published by Kappius, maintians (p. 24, 41,) that the opinion of Zuingle has no longer any patrons among the reformed. But this is a palpable mistake: for its patrons and defenders are, on the contrary, extremely numerous; and at this very time the doctrine of Zuingle is received in England, Switzerland, and other countries, and seems to acquire new degrees of credit from day to day.

¶ Hen. Altingii Hist. Eccl. Palat. in Lud. Chr Miegii Monum. Palat. tom. i. p. 223. Loscheri Historia Motuum, par. ii. lib. iv. cap. iv. p. 125.—Salig, Hist. Confession. Aug. tom. iii lib. ix. cap. v. p. 453.

gated, in 1576, by his son and successor Louis, who restored Lutheranism to its former credit and authority. The effects of this revolution were, however, transitory; for, in 1583, under the government of the elector John Casimir, who had followed the example of his brother Frederic in embracing the discipline of the reformed church, Calvinism resumed what it had lost, and became triumphant.* From this period the church of the Palatinate obtained the second place among the reformed churches; and its influence and reputation were so considerable, that the form of instruction, which was composed for its use by Ursinus, and which is known under the title of the *Catechism of Heidelberg*, was almost universally adopted by the Calvinists.† The republic of Bremen embraced, also, the same doctrine and institutions. Albert Hardenberg, the intimate friend of Melancthon, was the first who attempted to introduce there the doctrine of Calvin concerning the eucharist. This attempt he made so early as the year 1556; and, though a powerful opposition rendered it at that time unsuccessful, and procured the expulsion of its author from the city of Bremen, yet the latent seeds of Calvinism took root, and, toward the conclusion of this century, acquired such strength, that no measures either of prudence or force were sufficient to prevent the church of Bremen from regulating its faith, worship, and government, by that of Geneva.‡ The various motives that engaged other German states to adopt by degrees the same sentiments, and the incidents and circumstances that favoured the progress of Calvinism in the empire, must be sought in those writers, who have undertaken to give an ample and complete history of the Christian church.

XV. Those among the French, who first renounced the jurisdiction and doctrine of the church of Rome, are commonly called Lutherans by the writers of these early times. This denomination, joined to other circumstances, induced some to imagine, that these French converts to the protestant cause were attached to the tenets of the Lutheran church, and averse to those of the Swiss divines.§ But this is by no means a just representation of the matter. It appears much more probable, that the first French protestants were uniform in nothing but their antipathy to the church of Rome, and that, this point being excepted, there was a great variety in their religious sentiments. It is, however, to be observed, that the vicinity of Geneva, Lausanne, and other cities which had adopted the doctrine of Calvin, together with the incredible zeal of this eminent man, and his two colleagues Farel and Beza, in nourishing the opposition to the church of Rome, and augmenting both the indignation and number of its enemies, produced a very remarkable effect upon the French churches; for, before the middle of this century, they all entered into the bonds of fraternal communion with the church of Geneva. The French protestants were called by their enemies Huguenots, by way of derision and contempt; the origin, however, of this denomination is extremely uncertain.* Their fate was severe; the storms of persecution assailed them with unparalleled fury; and, though many princes of the royal blood, and the flower of the nobility, adopted their sentiments, and stood forth in their cause,† no other part of the reformed church suffered so grievously as they did for the sake of religion. Even the peace, which they obtained from Henry III. in 1576, was the source of that civil war, in which the powerful and ambitious house of Guise, instigated by the sanguinary suggestions of the Roman pontiffs, aimed at nothing less than the extirpation of the royal family, and the utter ruin of the protestant religion; while the Huguenots, on the other hand, headed by leaders of the most heroic valour and the most illustrious rank, combated for their religion and for their sovereigns with various success. These dreadful commotions, in which both the contending parties committed such deeds as are yet (and always will be) remembered with horror, were at length calmed by the fortitude and prudence of Henry IV. This monarch, indeed, sacrificed the dictates of conscience to the suggestions of policy; and imagining, that his government could have no stable or solid foundation, as long as he persisted in disowning the authority and jurisdiction of Rome, he renounced the reformed religion, and made a solemn and public profession of popery. Perceiving, however, on the other hand, that it was not possible to extirpate or suppress entirely the protestant religion, he granted to its professors, by the famous edict promulgated at

* Alting. loc. cit.—Loscheri Hist. par. iii. lib. vi. p. 324.—See also a German work, by Gotth. Struvius, entitled Pfaelzische Kirchen Historie, p. 110.

† For an account of the catechism of Heidelberg, see Kocheri Bibliotheca Theologiæ Symbolicæ, p. 593 and 308.

‡ Salig, loc. cit. par. iii. lib. x. cap. v. p. 715. cap. vi. p. 776.—Loscherus, loc. cit. par. ii. lib. iv. cap. v. p. 134. par. iii. lib. vi. cap. vii. p. 276.—Gerdes, Historia, Renovati Evangeliii, tom. iii. p. 157.

§ Losch. par ii. cap. vi.—Salig, tom. ii. lib. v. cap. vi

☞ * Some etymologists suppose this term derived from *Huguon*, a word used in Touraine, to signify "persons who walk at night in the streets;" and as the first Protestants, like the first Christians, may have chosen that season for their religious assemblies, through the fear of persecution, the nickname of *hugiienot* may, naturally enough, have been applied to them by their enemies. Others are of opinion, that it was derived from a French and faulty pronunciation of the German word *eidgenossen*, which signifies *confederates*, and had been originally the name of that valiant part of the city of Geneva which entered into an alliance with the Swiss cantons, in order to maintain their liberties against the tyrannical attempts of Charles III. duke of Savoy. These confederates were called *egnotes;* and thence, very probably, was derived the word *huguenot*, now under consideration. The count de Villars, in a letter written to the king of France from the province of Languedoc, where he was lieutenant-general, and dated the 11th of November, 1560, calls the riotous Calvinists of the Cevennes, *Huguenots;* and this is the first time that the term is found in the registers of that province, applied to the protestants.

† See the Histoire Eccles. des Eglises Reformees au Royaume de France. published at Antwerp in 1580, and supposed by many to have been written by Beza. The writers that have given the best accounts of the French reformed churches, their confession of faith, and their forms of worship and discipline. are enumerated by Kocher, in his Biblioth. Theolog. Symbolicæ, p. 299.

Nantes in 1598, the liberty of serving God according to their consciences,* and a full security for the enjoyment of their civil rights and privileges, without persecution or molestation from any quarter.†

XVI. The church of Scotland acknowledges as its founder John Knox, the disciple of Calvin; and, accordingly, from its first reformation, it adopted the doctrine, rites, and form of ecclesiastical government established at Geneva. To these it has always adhered with the utmost uniformity, and has maintained them with the greatest jealousy and zeal; so that even in the last century the designs of those who attempted to introduce certain changes into its discipline and worship, were publicly opposed by the force of arms.‡

A quite different constitution is observable in the church of England, which could never be brought to an entire compliance with the ecclesiastical laws of Geneva, and which retained, but for a short time, even those which it adopted. It is well known, that the greatest part of those English, who first threw off the yoke of Rome, seemed much more inclined to the sentiments of Luther concerning the eucharist, the form of public worship, and ecclesiastical government, than to those of the Swiss churches. But the scene changed after the death of Henry VIII. when, by the industrious zeal of Calvin, and his disciples, more especially Peter Martyr, the cause of Lutheranism lost ground considerably; and the universities, schools, and churches, became the oracles of Calvinism, which also acquired new votaries among the people from day to day.§ Hence it happened, that, when it was proposed, in the reign of Edward VI., to give a fixed and stable form to the doctrine and discipline of the Church, Geneva was acknowledged as a sister church; and the theological system, there established by Calvin, was adopted, and rendered the public rule of faith in England. This, however, was done without any change of the form of episcopal government, which had already taken place, and was entirely different from that of Geneva; nor was this step attended with any alteration of several religious ceremonies, which were looked upon as superstitious by the greatest part of the reformed. This difference, however, between the churches, though it appeared at first of little consequence, and, in the judgment even of Calvin, was deemed an object of toleration and indulgence, was nevertheless, in succeeding times, a source of dissensions and calamities, which were highly detrimental both to the civil and ecclesiastical constitution of Great Britain.

XVII. The origin of these unhappy dissensions, which it has not yet been possible entirely to heal, must be sought in the conduct of those persecuted fugitives, who, to save their lives, their families, and their fortunes, from the sanguinarg rage and inhuman tyranny of Queen Mary, left their native country in 1554, and took refuge in Germany.* Of these fugitive congregations some performed divine worship with the rites that had been authorized by Edward VI., while others preferred the Swiss method of worship as more recommendable on account of its purity and simplicity. The former were called *Conformists*, on account of their compliance with the ecclesiastical laws enacted by that prince; and the denominations of *Nonconformists* and *Puritans* were given to the latter, from their insisting upon a form of worship, more exempt from superstition, and of a more pure kind, than the liturgy of Edward seemed to them to be. The controversy concerning the ceremonial part of divine worship that had divided these protestants when they were in exile, changed scenes, and was removed with them to England, when the auspicious accession of Elizabeth to the throne permitted them to return to their native country. The hopes of enjoying liberty, and of promoting their respective systems, increased their contests instead of diminishing them; and the breach was widened to such a degree, that the most sagacious and provident observers of things seemed to despair of seeing it healed.

☞ * This edict restored and confirmed, in the fullest terms, all the favours that had ever been granted to the protestants by other princes, and particularly by Henry III. To these privileges some were added, which had never been granted or even demanded before; such as a free admission to all employments of trust, honour, and profit; the establishment of courts and chambers, in which the professors of the two religions were equal in number; and the permitting of the children of protestants to be educated, without any molestation or constraint, in the public universities.

† Benoit, Histoire de l'Edit de Nantes, tom. i. lib. v. p. 200.—Daniel, Hist. de France, tom. ix. page 409. Boulay, Hist. Academ. Paris. tom. vi.

‡ Salig, Hist. Aug. Confessionis, part ii. lib. vi. cap. i. p. 403.—☞ Dr. Mosheim alludes in this passage, to the attempts made in the reign of Charles II. to introduce episcopacy into Scotland.

§ Luscher, par. ii. lib. iii. cap. vii.—Salig, tom. ii lib. vi. cap iii.

☞ * I cannot help mentioning the uncharitableness of the Lutherans, upon this occasion, who hated these unhappy exiles because they were *Sacramentarians*, (for so the Lutherans called those who denied Christ's bodily presence in the eucharist,) and expelled from their cities such of the English protestants as repaired to them, as a refuge from popish superstition and persecution. Such as sought an asylum in France, Geneva, and and those parts of Switzerland and Germany where the Reformation had taken place, and where Lutheranism was not professed, were received with great humanity, and allowed to have places of public worship. But it was at Frankfort that the exiles were most numerous; and there began the contest and division which gave rise to that separation from the church of England, which continues to this day. It is, however a piece of justice due to the memory of the excellent Melancthon, to observe, that he warmly condemned this uncharitable treatment, and more especially the indecent reproaches which the Lutherans cast upon the English martyrs who had sealed the Reformation, whom they called the *Devil's martyrs*. "Vociferantur quidam, (says this amiable reformer,) Martyres Angelicos esse Martyres Diaboli. Nolim hac contumelia afficere sanctum spiritum in Latimero, qui annum octogesimum egressus fuit, et in aliis sanctis viris quos novi." These are the words of this truly Christian reformer, in one of his letters to Camerarius, Epist. lib. iv. p. 959; and in another of his letters, speaking of the burning of Burgius at Paris, he thus severely censures Westphal's intolerant principles: "Tales viros ait Westphalus esse Diaboli Martyres. Hanc judicii perversitatem quis non detestetur?" Ep. lib. ii. p. 387. Such were the humane and liberal sentiments of Melancthon, which have rendered his name so precious to the lovers of piety, probity, and moderation, while the zealots of his own church have traduced his memory with obloquy, and composed dissertations *de indifferentismo Melancthonis*.

The wise queen, in her design to accomplish the reformation of the church, was fully resolved not to confine herself to the model exhibited by the protestants of Geneva, and by their adherents the Puritans; and, therefore, she recommended to the attention and imitation of the doctors, who were employed in this weighty and important matter, the practice and institutions of the primitive ages.* When her plan was put in execution, and the face of the church was changed and reformed by new rules of discipline, and purer forms of public worship, the famous *Act of Uniformity* was issued forth, by which all her subjects were commanded to observe these rules, and to submit to the reformation of the church on the footing on which it was now placed by the queen, as its supreme visible head upon earth. The Puritans refused their assent to these proceedings; pleaded the dictates of their consciences in behalf of this refusal; and complained heavily, that the gross superstitions of popery, which they had looked upon as abrogated and abolished, were now revived, and even imposed by authority. They were not indeed all equally exasperated against the new constitution of the church; nor did they in effect carry their opposition to equal degrees of excess. The more violent demanded the total abrogation of all that had been done toward the establishment of a national religion, and required nothing less than that the church of England should be exactly modelled after that of Geneva. The milder and more moderate Puritans were much more equitable in their demands, and only desired liberty of conscience, with the privilege of celebrating divine worship in their own way. The queen did not judge it proper to grant to either the object of their requests; but, rather intent upon the suppression of this troublesome sect, (as she called it,) permitted its enemies to employ for that purpose all the resources of artifice, and all the severity of the laws. Thus was that form of religion established in Britain, which separated the English equally from the church of Rome, on the one hand, and from the other churches that had renounced popery on the other; but which, t the same time, laid a perpetual foundation for dissensions and feuds, in that otherwise happy and prosperous nation.*

XVIII. The incident that gave rise to these unhappy divisions, which were productive of so many and such dreadful calamities, was a matter of very small moment, that did not seem to affect, in any way, the interests of true religion and virtue. The chief leaders among the Puritans entertained a strong aversion to the vestments worn by the English clergy in the celebration of divine worship. As these habits had been used in the times of popery, and seemed to renew the impressions that had been made upon the people by the Romish priests, they appeared to the Puritans in no other light than as the ensigns of Anti-Christ. The spirit of opposition, being once set on foot, proceeded, in its remonstrances, to matters of superior moment. The form of ecclesiastical government, established in England, was one of the first and main grievances of which the Puritans complained. They looked upon this form as quite different from that which had been instituted by Christ, the great lawgiver of the church; and, in conformity with the sentiments of Calvin, maintained, that, by the divine law, all the ministers of the Gospel were absolutely equal in point of rank and authority. They did not indeed think it unlawful, that a person distinguished by the title of bishop, or superintendant, should preside in the assembly of the clergy, for the sake of maintaining order and decency in their method of proceeding; but they deemed it incongruous and absurd, that the persons invested with this character should be ranked, as the bishops had hitherto been, among the nobility of the kingdom, employed in civil and political affairs, and distinguished so eminently by their worldly opulence and power. This controversy was not carried on, however, with excessive animosity and zeal, as long as the English bishops pretended to derive their dignity and authority from no other source than the laws of their country, and pleaded a right, purely human, to the rank they held in church and state. But the flame broke out with redoubled fury in 1588, when Bancroft, afterwards archbishop of Canterbury, ventured to assert, that the episcopal order was superior to the body of presbyters, not in consequence of any human institution, but by the express appointment of God himself.† This

☞* Dr. Mosheim seems disposed, by this ambiguous expression of the primitive ages, to insinuate that queen Elizabeth had formed a pure, rational, and evangelical plan of religious discipline and worship. It is however certain, that, instead of being willing to strip religion of the ceremonies which remained in it, she was rather inclined to bring the public worship still nearer to the Romish ritual,* and had a great propensity to several usages in the church of Rome, which were justly looked upon as superstitious. She thanked publicly one of her chaplains, who had preached in defence of the "real presence;" she was fond of images, and retained some in her private chapel; and would undoubtedly have forbidden the marriage of the clergy, if Cecil, her secretary, had not interposed.† Having appointed a committee of divines to review king Edward's liturgy, she gave them an order to strike out all offensive passages against the pope, and to make people easy about the corporal presence of Christ in the sacrament.‡

* Heylin, p. 124.
† Strype's Life of Parker, p. 107.
‡ Neal's Hist. of the Puritans, vol. i. p. 138.

* No writer has treated this part of the ecclesiastical history of Britain in a more ample and elegant manner than Daniel Neal, in his History of the Puritans, or Protestant Non-conformists. The first part of this laborious work was published at London, in 1732, and the latter part in 1738. The author, who was himself a non-conformist, has not indeed been able to impose silence so far on the warm and impetuous spirit of party, as not to discover a certain degree of partiality in favour of his brethren: for, while he relates, in the most circumstantial manner, all the injuries the Puritans received from the bishops, and those of the established religion, he in many places diminishes, excuses, or suppresses, the faults and failings of these separatists. See also, for an account of the religious history of these times, Strype's Lives of the Archbishops Parker, Grindal, and Whitgift.

† See Strype's Life and Acts of John Whitgift, archbishop of Canterbury, p. 121. ☞ The first English reformers admitted but two orders of church officers to be of divine appointment, viz. bishops and deacons;

doctrine was readily adopted by many, and the consequences that seemed naturally to flow from it in favour of episcopal ordination, happened in effect, and gave new fuel to the flame of controversy; for they who embraced the sentiments of Bancroft, considered all ministers of the Gospel, who had not received ordination from a bishop, as not properly invested with the sacred character, and also maintained that the clergy, in those countries where there were no bishops, were destitute of the gifts and qualifications that were necessary to the exercise of the pastoral office, and were to be deemed inferior to the Roman catholic priests.

XIX. All these things exasperated the puritans whose complaints, however, were not confined to the objects already mentioned. There were many circumstances that entered into their plan of reformation. They had a singular antipathy against cathedral churches, and demanded the abolition of the archdeacons, deans, canons, and other officials, that are supported by their lands and revenues. They disapproved the pompous manner of worship that is generally observed in these churches, and looked, particularly, upon instrumental music, as improperly employed in the service of God. The severity of their zeal was also very great; for they were of opinion, that not only open profligates, but even persons whose piety was dubious, deserved to be excluded from the communion of the church;* and they endeavoured to justify the rigour of this decision, by observing, that, as the church was the congregation of the faithful, nothing was more incumbent on its ministers and rulers, than to guard against its being defiled by the presence of persons destitute of true faith and piety. They found, moreover, much subject of affliction and complaint in the ceremonies that were imposed by the queen's order, and by the authority of her council.† Among these were the festivals or holydays that were celebrated in honour of the saints, the use of the sign of the cross, more especially in the sacrament of baptism, the nomination of godfathers and godmothers as sureties for the education of children, whose parents were still living,* and the doctrine relating to the validity of lay baptism.† They disliked the reading of the apocryphal books in the church; and, with respect to set forms of prayer, although they did not go so far as to insist upon their being entirely abolished, yet they pleaded for a right to all ministers, of modifying, correcting, and using them in such a manner, as might tend most to the advancement of true piety, and of addressing the Deity in such terms as were suggested by their inward feelings, instead of those which were dictated by others. In a word, they were of

a presbyter and a bishop, according to them, being merely two names for the same office; but Dr. Bancroft, in a sermon preached at Paul's cross, (January 12, 1588,) maintained, that the bishops of England were a distinct order from priests, and had superiority over them *jure divino*.

☞ * The puritans justified themselves in relation to this point, in a letter addressed from their prison to queen Elizabeth, in 1592, by observing, that their sentiments concerning the persons subject to excommunication, and also with regard to the effects and extent of that act of church discipline, were conformable to those of all the reformed churches, and to the doctrine and practice of the church of England in particular. They declared more especially, that, according to their sense of things, the censure of excommunication deprived only of spiritual privileges and comforts, without taking away either liberty, goods, lands, government private or public, or any other civil or earthly commodity of this life; and thus they distinguished themselves from those furious and fanatical anabaptists, who had committed such disorders in Germany, and some of whom were now making a noise in England.

☞ † By this council our author means, the High-Commission court, of which it is proper to give some account, as its proceedings essentially belong to the ecclesiastical history of England. This court took its rise from a remarkable clause in the act of supremacy, by which the queen and her successors were empowered to choose persons "to exercise, under her, all manner of jurisdiction, privileges, and pre-eminences, touching any spiritual or ecclesiastical jurisdiction within the realms of England and Ireland, as also to visit, reform, redress, order, correct, and amend, all errors, heresies, schisms, abuses, contempts, offences and enormities whatsoever; provided that they have no power to determine any thing to be heresy. but what has been adjudged to be so by the authority of the canonical scripture, or by the first four general councils, or any of them; or by any other great council, wherein the same was declared heresy by the express and plain words of canonical scripture, or such as shall hereafter be declared to be heresy by the high court of parliament, with the assent of the clergy in convocation." Upon the authority of this clause, the queen appointed a certain number of commissioners for ecclesiastical causes, who, in many instances, abused their power. The court they composed, was called *the Court of High-Commission*, because it claimed a more extensive jurisdiction, and higher powers, than the ordinary courts of the bishops. Its jurisdiction reached over the whole kingdom, and was much the same with that which had been lodged in the single person of lord Cromwell, vicar-general of Henry VIII These commissioners were empowered to make inquiry, not only by the legal methods of juries, and witnesses, but by all other ways and means which they could devise, that is, by rack, torture, inquisition, and imprisonment. They were invested with a right to examine such persons as they suspected, by administering to them an oath, (not allowed in their commission, and therefore called *ex officio*,) by which they were required to answer all questions, and thereby might be obliged to accuse themselves or their most intimate friends. The fines they imposed were merely discretionary; the imprisonment to which they condemned was limited by no rule but their own pleasure; they imposed, when they thought proper, new articles of faith on the clergy, and practised all the inquities and cruelties of a real inquisition. See Rapin's and Hume's History of England and Neal's History of the Puritans.

☞ * Other rites and customs displeasing to the puritans, and omitted by our author, were, kneeling at the sacrament of the Lord's supper, bowing at the name of Jesus, giving the ring in marriage, the prohibition of marriage during certain times of the year, and the licensing of it for money, as also the confirmation of children by episcopal imposition of hands.

☞ † The words of the original are "nec sacris Christianis pueros recens natos ab aliis, quam sacerdotibus, initiari patiebantur." The Roman catholics, who look upon the external rite of baptism as absolutely necessary to salvation, consequently allow it to be performed by a layman, or a midwife, where a clergyman is not at hand, or (if such a ridiculous thing may be mentioned) by a surgeon, where a still birth is apprehended. The church of England, though it teacheth in general, that none ought to baptize but men dedicated to the service of God, yet doth not deem null baptism performed by laics or women, because it makes a difference between what is essential to a sacrament, and what is requisite to the regular way of using it. The puritans, that they might neither prescribe, nor even connive at a practice that seemed to be founded on the absolute necessity of infant baptism, would allow that sacred rite to be performed by the clergy alone.

opinion, that the government and discipline of the church of England ought to have been moddled after the ecclesiastical laws and institutions of Geneva, and that no indulgence was to be shown to those ceremonies or practices, which bore the smallest resemblance to the discipline or worship of the church of Rome.

XX. These sentiments, considered in themselves, seemed neither susceptible of a satisfactory defence, nor of a complete refutation. Their solidity or falsehood depended upon the principles from which they were derived; and no regular controversy could be carried on upon these matters, until the contending parties adopted some common and evident principles, by which they might corroborate their respective systems. It is only by an examination of these, that it can be known on which side the truth lies, and what degree of utility or importance can be attributed to a contest of this nature. The principles laid down by the queen's commissioners on the one hand, and the Puritans on the other, were indeed very different.

For, in the first place, the former maintained, that the right of reformation, that is, the privilege of removing the corruptions, and of correcting the errors that might have been introduced into the doctrine, discipline, or worship of the church, was lodged in the sovereign, or civil magistrate alone; while the latter denied, that the power of the magistrate extended so far, and maintained, that it was rather the business of the clergy to restore religion to its native dignity and lustre. This was the opinion of Calvin, as has been already observed.

Secondly, the queen's commissioners maintained, that the rules of proceeding, in reforming the doctrine or discipline of the church, were not to be derived from the sacred writings alone, but also from the writings and decisions of the fathers in the primitive ages. The Puritans, on the contrary, affirmed, that the inspired word of God being the pure and only fountain of wisdom and truth, it was thence alone that the rules and directions were to be drawn, which were to guide the measures of those who undertook to purify the faith, or to rectify the discipline and worship, of the church; and that the ecclesiastical institutions of the early ages, as also the writings of the ancient doctors, were absolutely destitute of all authority.

Thirdly, the commissioners ventured to assert, that the church of Rome was a true church, though corrupt and erroneous in many points of doctrine and government; that the pontiff, though chargeable with temerity and arrogance in assuming to himself the title and jurisdiction of head of the whole church, was, nevertheless, to be esteemed a true and lawful bishop; and, consequently, that the ministers ordained by him were qualified for performing the pastoral duties. This was a point which the English bishops thought it absolutely necessary to maintain, since they could not otherwise claim the honour of deriving their dignities, in an uninterrupted line of succession, from the apostles. But the Puritans entertained very different notions of this matter; they considered the Romish hierarchy as a system of political and spiritual tyranny, that had justly forfeited the title and privileges of a true church; they looked upon its pontiff as Anti-Christ, and its discipline as vain, superstitious, idolatrous, and diametrically opposite to the injunctions of the Gospel; and, in consequence of these sentiments, they renounced its communion, and regarded all approaches to its discipline and worship as highly dangerous to the cause of true religion.

Fourthly, the commissioners considered, as the best and most perfect form of ecclesiastical government, that which took place during the first four or five centuries; they even preferred it to that which had been instituted by the apostles, because, as they alleged, our Saviour and his apostles had accommodated the form, mentioned in Scripture, to the feeble and infant state of the church, and left it to the wisdom and discretion of future ages to modify it in such a manner as might be suitable to the triumphant progress of Christianity, the grandeur of a national establishment, and also to the ends of civil policy. The Puritans asserted, in opposition to this, that the rules of church government were clearly laid down in the Scriptures, the only standard of spiritual discipline;* and that the apostles, in establishing the first Christian church on the aristocratic plan that was then observed in the Jewish Sanhedrim, designed it as an unchangeable model, to be followed in all times, and in all places.

Lastly, the court reformers were of opinion, that things *indifferent*, which are neither commanded nor forbidden by the authority of Scripture, such as the external rites of public worship, the kind of vestments that are to be used by the clergy, religious festivals, and the like, might be ordered, determined, and rendered a matter of obligation by the authority of the civil magistrate; and that, in such a case, the violation of his commands would be no less criminal than an act of rebellion against the laws of the state. The Puritans alleged, in answer to this assertion, that it was an indecent prostitution of power to impose, as necessary and indispensable, those things which Christ had left in the class of matters indifferent, since this was a manifest encroachment upon that liberty with which the divine Saviour had indulged us. To this they added, that such ceremonies as had been abused to idolatrous purposes, and had a manifest tendency to revive the impressions of superstition and popery in the minds of men, could by no means be considered as indifferent, but deserved to be rejected without hesitation as impious and profane. Such, in their estimation, were the

☞ * By this they meant, at least, that nothing should be imposed as necessary, but what was expressly contained in the Scriptures, or deduced from them by necessary consequence. They maintained still farther, that supposing it proved, that all things necessary to the good government of the church could not be deduced from those writings, yet the discretionary power of supplying this defect was not vested in the civil magistrate, but in the spiritual officers of the church.

religious ceremonies of ancient times, whose abrogation was refused by the queen and her council.*

XXI. This contest between the commissioners of the court, and those religionists who desired a more complete reformation than had yet taken place, would have been much more dangerous in its consequences, had the party, distinguished by the general denomination of *Puritans*, been united in their sentiments, views, and measures. But the case was quite otherwise; for this large body, composed of persons of different ranks, characters, opinions, and intentions, and unanimous in nothing but their antipathy to the forms of doctrine and discipline that were established by law, was suddenly divided into a variety of sects; of which some spread abroad the delusions of enthusiasm, which had turned their own brains; while others displayed their folly in inventing new and whimsical plans of church government. Of all these sects the most famous was that which was formed, about the year 1581, by Robert Brown, an insinuating man, but very unsettled and inconsistent in his views and notions of things. This innovator did not greatly differ, in point of doctrine, either from the church of England, or from the rest of the Puritans; but he had formed singular notions concerning the nature of the church, and the rules of ecclesiastical government. He was for dividing the whole body of the faithful into separate societies or congregations, not larger than those which were formed by the apostles in the infancy of Christianity; and maintained, that such a number of persons, as could be contained in an ordinary place of worship, ought to be considered as a church, and enjoy all the rights and privileges that are competent to an ecclesiastical community. These small societies he pronounced independent, *jure divino*, and entirely exempt from the jurisdiction of the bishops, in whose hands the court placed the reins of spiritual government; and also from that of synods, which the Puritans in general regarded as the supreme visible sources of ecclesiastical authority. He also maintained, that the power of governing each congregation, and providing for its welfare, resided in the people; and that each member had an equal share in this direction, and an equal right to regulate affairs for the good of the whole society.† Hence all points both of doctrine and discipline were submitted to the discussion of the whole congregation, and whatever was supported by a majority of votes passed into a law. It was the congregation also that elected some of the brethren to the office of pastors, to perform the duty of public instruction, and the several branches of divine worship; reserving, however, the power of dismissing these ministers, and reducing them to the condition of private members, whenever such a change should appear to be conducive to the spiritual advantage of the community. For these pastors were not esteemed superior, either in sanctity or rank, to the rest of their brethren, nor distinguished from them by any other circumstance than the liberty of preaching and praying, which they derived from the free will and consent of the congregation. It is, besides, to be observed, that their right of preaching was by no means of an exclusive nature, or peculiar to them alone, since any member that thought proper to exhort or instruct the brethren, was abundantly indulged in the liberty of *prophesying* to the whole assembly. Accordingly, when the ordinary teacher or pastor had finished his discourse, all the other brethren were permitted to communicate in public their sentiments and illustrations upon any useful or edifying subject, on which they supposed they could throw new light. In a word, Brown endeavoured to model the form of the church after the infant community that was founded by the apostles, without once considering the important changes which had taken place since that time, both in the religious and civil state of the world, the influence that these changes must necessarily have upon all ecclesiastical establishments, or the particular circumstances of the Christian church, in consequence of its former corruptions and its late reformation. And, if his notions were crude and chimerical, the zeal, with which he and his associates maintained and propagated them, was intemperate and extravagant in the highest degree; for he affirmed, that all communion was to be broken off with those religious societies which were founded upon a different plan from his, and treated more especially the church of England as a spurious church, whose ministers were unlawfully ordained, whose discipline was popish and antichristian, and whose sacraments and institutions were destitute of all efficacy and virtue. The sect of this hot-headed innovator, not being able to endure the severe treatment which their opposition to the established forms of religious government and worship had drawn upon them, from an administration that was not distinguished by its mildness and indulgence, retired into the Netherlands, and founded churches at Middleburg, Amsterdam, and Leyden; but their establishments were neither solid nor durable.* Their founder returned into

☞ * Dr. Mosheim, in these five articles, has followed the account of this controversy given by Mr. Neal. This writer adds a sixth article, not of debate, but of union. "Both parties (says he) agreed too well in asserting the necessity of an uniformity of public worship, and of calling in the sword of the magistrate for the support and defence of their several principles, which they made an ill use of in their turns, as they could grasp the power into their hands. The standard of uniformity, according to the bishops, was the queen's supremacy, and the laws of the land; according to the puritans, the decrees of provincial and national synods, allowed and enforced by the civil magistrate: but neither party were for admitting that liberty of conscience, and freedom of profession, which is every man's right, as far as is consistent with the peace of the government under which he lives."

☞ † It is further to be observed, that, according to this system, one church was not entitled to exercise jurisdiction over another; but each might give the other counsel or admonition, if its members walked in a disorderly manner, or abandoned the capital truths of religion; and, if the offending church did not receive the admonition, the others were allowed to disown it publicy as a church of Christ. On the other hand, the powers of the church-officers were confined within the narrow limits of their own society. The pastor of the church might not administer the sacrament of baptism, or the Lord's supper, to any but those of his own communion.

☞ * The British churches at Amsterdam and

England, and, having renounced his principles of separation, took orders in the established church, and obtained a benefice.* The Puritan exiles, whom he thus abandoned, disagreed among themselves, and split into parties; and their affairs declined from day to day.† This engaged the wiser part of them to mitigate the severity of their founder's plan, and to soften the rigour of his uncharitable decisions; and hence arose the community of the *Independents*, or *Congregational Brethren;* a sect which still subsists, and of which an account shall be given in the history of the following century.

XXII. In the Belgic provinces, the friends of the Reformation seemed for a long time uncertain, whether they should embrace the communion of the Swiss or that of the Lutheran church. Each of these had zealous friends and powerful patrons.‡ The matter was, nevertheless, decided in 1571, and the religious system of Calvin was publicly adopted; for the Belgic confession of faith, which then appeared,§ was drawn up in the spirit, and almost in the terms, of that which was received in the reformed churches of France, and differed considerably, in several respects, from the confession of Augsburg, but more especially in the article relating to Christ's presence in the eucharist.|| This will not appear surprising to those who consider the vicinity of the French to the Low-Countries, the number of French protestants constantly passing or sojourning there, the extraordinary reputation of Calvin and of the college of Geneva, and the indefatigable zeal of his disciples in extending the limits of their church, and propagating throughout Europe their system of doctrine, discipline, and government. Be that as it may, from this period, the Dutch, who had before been denominated *Lutherans*, assumed universally the title of *Reformed*, in which also they imitated the French, by whom this title had been first invented and adopted. It is true, that, as long as they were subject to the Spanish yoke, the fear of exposing themselves to the displeasure of their sovereign induced them to avoid the title of *Reformed*, and to call themselves *Associates of the Brethren of the Confession of Augsburg;* for the Lutherans were esteemed, by the Spanish court, much better subjects than the disciples of Calvin, who, on account of the tumults which had lately prevailed in France, were supposed to have a greater propensity to mutiny and sedition.*

XXIII. The light of the Reformation was first transmitted from Saxony into Poland by the disciples of Luther. Some time after this happy period, the Bohemian Brethren, whom the Romish clergy had expelled from their country, as also several Helvetic doctors, propagated their sentiments among the Polanders. Some congregations were also founded in that republic by the Anabaptists, Anti-Trinitarians, and other sectaries.† Hence it was, that three distinct communities, each of which adopted the main principles of the Reformation, were to be found in Poland,—the Bohemian Brethren, the Lutherans, and Swiss. These communities, in order to defend themselves with the greater vigour against their common enemies, formed among themselves a kind of confederacy, in a synod held at Sendomir in 1570, on certain conditions, which were comprehended in the Confession of Faith that derives its title from the city now mentioned.‡ But, as this association seemed rather adapted to accelerate the conclusion of peace, than to promote the cause of truth, the points in debate between the Lutherans and the Reformed being expressed in this reconciling confession in vague and ambiguous terms, it was soon after this warmly opposed by many of the former, and was entirely annulled in the following century. Many attempts have, indeed, been made to revive it; but they have not answered the expectations of those who have employed their dexterity and zeal in this matter. In Prussia the Reformed gained ground after the death of Luther and Melancthon, and founded the flourishing churches which still subsist in that country.§

XXIV. The Bohemian, or (as they are otherwise called) Moravian Brethren, who descended from the better sort of Hussites, and were distinguished by several religious institutions of a singular nature, which were well adapted to guard their community against the reigning vices and corruptions of the times, had no sooner heard of Luther's design of reforming the church, than they sent deputies, in 1522, to recommend themselves to his friendship and good offices. In succeeding times, they continued to discover the same zealous attachment to the Lutheran churches in Saxony, and also to those which were founded in other countries. These offers could not be well accepted without a previous examination of their religious sentiments and

Middleburg are incorporated into the national Dutch church, and their pastors are members of the Dutch synod, which is sufficient to show that there are at this time no traces of Brownism or Independency in these churches. The church at Leyden, where Robinson had fixed the standard of independency, about the year 1595, was dispersed; and it is very remarkable, that some members of this church, transplanting themselves into America, laid the foundation of the colony of New-England.

☞* Brown, in his new preferment, forgot not only the rigour of his principles, but also the gravity of his former morals; for he led a very idle and dissolute life. See Neal's History of the Puritans, vol. i.

† Neal, vol. i. chap. vi.—Hoornbeckii Summa Controvers. lib. x. p. 738.—Fuller's Ecclesiastical History of Britain, book x.

‡ Loscher, par. iii. lib. v. cap. iv.

§ Kocheri Biblioth. Theolog. Symbolicæ, p. 216.

|| See Brandt's His. of the Netherlands (written in Dutch,) vol. i. book v.

☞* Dr. Mosheim advances this on the authority of a passage in Brandt's History of the Reformation which is a most curious and valuable work, notwithstanding the author's partiality to the cause of Arminianism, of which he was one of the most respectable patrons.

† Loscher, par. iii. lib. v. cap. iii.—Salig, tom. ii. lib. vi. cap. iii. iv. v.—Regenvolscii Hist. Eccles. Slavonicar. lib. i. cap. xvi.—Solignac, Hist. de Pologne, tom. v.—Kautz, Præcipua Relig. Evangel. in Polonia Fata, published at Hamburg, in 1738.

‡ See Dan. Ernest Jablonsky's Historia Consensus Sendomiriensis, published at Berlin, in 1731; as also the Epistola Apologetica of the same author, in defence of the work now mentioned, against the objections of an anonymous author.

§ Loscher, par. iii. lib. vi cap. i.

principles: and, indeed, this examination turned to their advantage; for neither Luther nor his disciples found any thing, either in their doctrine or discipline, that was, in any great measure, liable to censure; and though he could not approve every part of their Confession of Faith, which they submitted to his judgment, yet he looked upon it as an object of toleration and indulgence.* Nevertheless, the death of Luther, and the expulsion of these Brethren from their country in 1547, gave a new turn to their religious connexions; and great numbers of them, more especially of those who retired into Poland, embraced the religious sentiments and discipline of the Reformed. The attachment of the Bohemians to the Lutherans seemed, indeed, to be revived by the Convention of Sendomir; but, as the articles of Union, drawn up in that assembly, soon lost all their force and authority, all the Bohemians gradually entered into the communion of the Swiss church.† This union was at first formed on the express condition, that the two churches should continue to be governed by their respective laws and institutions, and should have separate places of public worship; but, in the following century, all remains of dissension were removed in the synods holden at Ostrog in 1620 and 1627, and the two congregations were formed into one, under the title of The Church of the United Brethren. In this coalition the reconciled parties showed to each other reciprocal marks of toleration and indulgence; for the external form of the church was regulated by the discipline of the Bohemian Brethren, and the articles of faith were taken from the creed of the Calvinists.‡

XXV. The descendants of the Waldenses, who lived shut up in the valleys of Piedmont, were naturally led, by their situation in the neighbourhood of the French, and of the republic of Geneva, to embrace the doctrines and rites of the reformed church. So far down, however, as the year 1630, they retained a considerable part of their ancient discipline and tenets; but the plague that broke out in that year having destroyed the greatest part of this unhappy people, and among the rest a considerable number of their pastors and clergy, they addressed themselves to the French churches for spiritual succour; and the new doctors, who were sent in consequence of that invitation, made several changes in the discipline and doctrine of the Waldenses, and rendered them conformable, in every respect, with those of the protestant churches in France.§

The Hungarians and Transylvanians were engaged to renounce the errors and superstitions of the church of Rome by the writings

* See a German work of Carpzovius, entitled, Nachricht von den Bohmischen Brudern, p. 46; as also Jo Chr. Kocheri Biblioth. p. 76.

† Beside Comenius, Camerarius, and Lasitius, who have written professedly the history of the Bohemian Brethren, see Loscher, par. iii. lib. v. cap. vi.—Salig, tom. ii. lib. vi. cap. iii.—Regenvolsc. lib. i. cap. xiii. xiv. xv.

‡ Regenvolscii Hist. lib. i. cap. xiv. p. 120.

§ Leger, Histoire Generale des Eglises Vaudoises, livr. i. chap. xxxiii. p. 205, 206.—Abr. Sculeti Annales Renovati Evangelii, p. 294.—Dan. Gerdes, Hist Renovati Evangelii. tom. ii. p. 401.

of Luther, and the ministry of his disciples. But, some time after, Matthias Devay, and other doctors, began to introduce, in a secret manner, among these nations, the doctrine of the Swiss churches in relation to the eucharist, as also their principles of ecclesiastical government. This doctrine and these principles were propagated in a more open and public manner about the year 1550, by Szegedin and other Calvinist teachers, whose ministry was attended with remarkable success. This change was followed by the same dissensions that had broken out in other countries on similar occasions; and these dissensions grew into an open schism among the friends of the Reformation in these provinces, which the lapse of time has rather confirmed than diminished.*

XXVI. After the solemn publication of the famous Form of Concord, many German churches, of the Lutheran communion, dissolved their original bonds, and embraced the doctrine and discipline of Calvin. Among these we may place the churches of Nassau, Hanau, and Isenburg, with several others of less note. In 1595, the princes of Anhalt, influenced by the counsels of Wolfgang Amling, renounced also the profession of Lutheranism, and introduced into their dominions the religious tenets and rites of Geneva; this revolution, however, produced a long and warm controversy between the Lutherans and the inhabitants of the principality.† The doctrines of the Calvinist or reformed church, particularly those which relate to the eucharist, were also introduced into Denmark, toward the conclusion of this century; for, in this kingdom, the disciples and votaries of Melancthon, who had always discovered a strong propensity to a union between the protestant churches, were extremely numerous, and they had at their head Nicholas Hemmingius, a man eminent for his piety and learning. But the views of this divine, and the schemes of his party, being discovered much sooner than they expected, by the vigilant defenders of the Lutheran cause, their plans were disconcerted,‡ and the progress of Calvinism was successfully opposed by the Lutheran ministers, seconded by the countenance and authority of the sovereign.§

* Pauli Debrezeni Historia Eccles. Reform. in Hungar. et Transylvan. lib. ii. p. 64, 72, 98.—Unschuld. Nachricht, An. 1738, p. 1076.—Georg. Haneri Historia Eccles. Transylv.

† See for an account of this matter, the German work of Bechman, which is entitled Historie des Hauses Anhalt, vol. ii. p. 133, and that of Kraft, which bears the title of Ausfuhrliche Historie von dem. Exorcismo, p. 428, 497. ☞ Though the princes professed Calvinism, and introduced Calvinist ministers into all the churches, where they had the right of patronage, yet the people were left free in their choice; and the noblemen and their vassals, who were attached to Lutheranism, had secured to them the unrestrained exercise of their religion. By virtue of a convention made in 1679, the Lutherans were permitted to erect new churches. The Zerbst line, and the greatest part of its subjects, profess Lutheranism; but the three other lines, with their respective people, are Calvinists.

‡ Erici Pontoppidani Annal. Ecclesiæ Danicæ Diplomatici, t. iii. p. 57.

☞§ That is, (for our author consistently with truth can mean no more) the designs, that were formed to render Calvinism the national and established religion, proved abortive. It is certain, however that Calvinism made a very considerable ro

XXVII. It must not, however, be imagined, that the different nations which embraced the communion of the Calvinist church, adopted, at the same time, without exception, all its tenets, rites, and institutions. This universal conformity was, indeed, ardently desired by the Helvetic doctors; but their desires, in this respect, were far from being accomplished. The English, as is sufficiently known, rejected the forms of ecclesiastical government and religious worship that were adopted by the other reformed churches, and could not be persuaded to receive, as public and national articles of faith, the doctrines that were propagated in Switzerland, in relation to the sacrament of the Lord's supper and the divine decrees.* The protestants in Holland, Bremen, Poland, Hungary, and the Palatinate, followed, indeed, the French and Helvetic churches in their sentiments concerning the eucharist, in the simplicity of their worship, and in their principles of ecclesiastical polity; but not in their notions of *predestination*, which intricate doctrine they left undefined, and submitted to the free examination and private judgment of every individual.† It may farther be affirmed, that, before the synod of Dordrecht,‡ no reformed church had obliged its members, by any special law or article of faith, to adhere to the doctrine of the church of Geneva relating to the primary causes of the salvation of the elect, or the ruin of the reprobate. It is true, that, in the countries now mentioned, the greatest part of the reformed doctors fell by degrees, of their own accord, into the Calvinistical opinion concerning these intricate points; and this was principally owing, no doubt, to the great reputation of the college of Geneva, which was generally frequented, in this century, by those among the reformed who were candidates for the ministry.

XXVIII. The books of the Old and New Testament are regarded by the reformed churches as the only sources of Divine Truth; it must however be observed, that, to their authority, the church of England adds that of the writings of the Fathers during the first five centuries.* The reformed and the Lutherans agree in maintaining that the Scriptures are infallible in all things; that, in matters of which the knowledge is necessary to salvation, they are clear, and complete; and also that they are to be explained by themselves, and not by the dictates of human reason, or the decisions of the ancient Fathers. Several of the doctors among the former have indeed employed too freely the sagacity of their natural understanding, in explaining the divine mysteries that are contained in the Gospel; and this circumstance has induced many to imagine, that the reformed adopted two sources of religion, two criterions of divine truth, viz. the Scripture and human reason. But perhaps it will be found, that, in this respect, doctors of both communions have sometimes gone too far, being led on by the spirit of controversy, and animated with the desire of victory; for, if we except the singular tenets of some individuals, it may be affirmed with truth, that the Lutherans and the reformed are unanimous in the matter now under consideration. They both maintain, that contradictory propositions cannot be the objects of faith; and consequently that all doctrines which contain such ideas and notions as are repugnant to and destroy each other, must be false and incredible. It is true, indeed, that the reformed sometimes use this principle in a contentious manner, to overturn certain points of the Lutheran system, which they have thought proper to reject.†

XXIX. The reformed, if by this denomination we understand those who embrace the sentiments of Calvin, differ entirely from the Lutherans in the following points:

1st, In their notions of the sacrament of the Lord's Supper. The Lutherans affirm that the body and blood of Christ are materially present in this sacrament, though in an incom

gress in Denmark, and has still a great number of votaries in that kingdom.

☞ * It is true, that the doctrine of Zuingle, who represented the bread and wine as nothing more than the external signs of the death of Christ, was not adopted by the church of England; but the doctrine of Calvin was embraced by that church, and is plainly taught in the xxviiith article of its faith. As to what relates to the doctrine of the divine decrees, Dr. Mosheim is equally in an error. The xviith article of the church of England, is, as bishop Burnet candidly acknowledges, framed according to St. Augustin's doctrine, which scarcely differs at all from that of Calvin; and though it be expressed with a certain latitude that renders it susceptible of a mitigated interpretation, yet it is very probable, that those who penned it were patrons of the doctrine of absolute decrees. The very cautions, that are subjoined to this article, intimate, that Calvinism was what it was meant to establish. It is certain, that the Calvinistical doctrine of predestination prevailed among the first English reformers, the greatest part of whom were, at least, *Sublapsarians;* in the reign of queen Elizabeth this doctrine was predominant, but after that period it lost ground imperceptibly, and was renounced by the church of England in the reign of king Charles I. Some members of that church still adhered, nevertheless, to the tenets of Calvin, and maintained, not only that the thirty-nine articles were Calvinistical, but also affirmed that they were not susceptible of that latitude of interpretation for which the Arminians contended. These episcopal votaries of Calvinism were called *Doctrinal Puritans.* See Burnet's Exposition of the Seventeenth Article, &c., and Neal's History of the Puritans, vol. i. p. 579.

† See Grotii Apologet. eorum, qui Hollandiæ ante mutationem, An. 1618, præfuerunt, cap. iii

☞ ‡ It was in this famous synod, that was assembled in the year 1618, and of which we shall have occasion to give a more ample account in the history of the following century, that the doctrine of Calvin was fixed as the national and established religion of the Seven United Provinces.

☞ * There is nothing in the thirty-nine articles of the church of England, which implies its considering the writings of the Fathers of the first five centuries, as an authoritative criterion of religious truth. There is, indeed, a clause in the Act of Uniformity, passed in the reign of queen Elizabeth, declaring that her delegates, in ecclesiastical matters, should not determine any thing to be heresy but what was adjudged so by the authority of Scripture, or by the first four general councils; and this has perhaps misled Dr. Mosheim in the passage to which this note refers. Much respect, indeed, (perhaps too much,) has been paid to the Fathers; but that has been always a matter of choice, and not of obligation.

☞ † Our author has here undoubtedly in view the Lutheran doctrine of Consubstantiation, which supposes the same extended body to be totally present in different places at one and the same time. To call this a gross and glaring contradiction, seems rather the dictate of common sense, than the suggestion of a contentious spirit.

prehensible manner; and that they are really exhibited, both to the righteous and the wicked, to the worthy and to the unworthy receiver. The reformed hold, on the contrary, that the man Christ is only present in this ordinance by the external signs of bread and wine, though it must, at the same time, be observed, that this matter is differently explained and represented in the writings of their theologians.

2dly, In their doctrine of the eternal decrees of God, respecting man's salvation. The Lutherans maintain, that the divine decrees respecting the salvation or misery of men are founded upon a previous knowledge of their sentiments and characters; or, in other words, that God, foreseeing from all eternity the faith or incredulity of different persons, had reserved eternal happiness for the faithful, and eternal misery for the unbelieving and disobedient. The reformed entertained different sentiments concerning this intricate point. They consider the divine decrees as free and unconditional, and as founded on the will of God, which is limited by no superior order, and which is above all laws.

3dly, Concerning some religious rites and institutions, which the Reformed consider as bordering upon superstition, or tending, at least, to promote it, while the Lutherans view them in another light, and represent all of them as tolerable, and some of them as useful. Such are, the use of images in the churches, the distinguishing vestments of the clergy, the private confession of sins, the use of wafers in the administration of the Lord's supper, the form of exorcism in the celebration of baptism, and other ceremonies of like moment. The reformed doctors insist on the abolition of all these rites and institutions, upon this general principle, that the discipline and worship of the Christian church ought to be restored to their primitive simplicity, and freed from the human inventions and additions that were employed by superstition in the times of ignorance, to render them more striking to the deluded multitude.

XXX. The few heads of difference, between the two communions, which have been now briefly pointed out, have furnished an inexhaustible fund of controversy to the contending parties, and been drawn out into a multitude of intricate questions, and subjects of debate, that, by consequences, fairly or injudiciously deduced, have widened the scene of contention, and extended to almost all the important truths of religion. Thus the debate concerning the manner in which the body and blood of Christ are present in the eucharist, opened to the disputants a large field of inquiry; in which the nature and fruits of the institutions called sacraments, the majesty and glory of Christ's human nature, together with the communication of the divine perfections to it, and the inward frame of spirit that is required in the worship addressed to the Saviour, were carefully examined. In like manner, the controversy, which had for its object the divine decrees, led the doctors, by whom it was carried on, into the most subtile and profound researches concerning the nature of the divine attributes, particularly those of justice and goodness, the doctrines of fate and necessity, the connexion between human liberty and divine prescience; the extent of God's love to mankind, and of the benefits that arise from the merits of Christ as mediator; the operations of that divine spirit, or power, which rectifies the wills and sanctifies the affections of men; the perseverance of the elect in their covenant with God, and in a state of salvation; and other points of great moment. The subject of debate, that was drawn from the use of external ceremonies in religious worship, was also productive of several questions and inquiries; for, besides the researches into the origin and antiquity of certain institutions to which it gave occasion, it naturally led to a discussion of the following important questions: viz. "What are the special marks that characterize things *indifferent?*—How far is it lawful to comply with the demands of an adversary, whose opposition is only directed against things esteemed indifferent in their own nature?—What is the extent of Christian liberty? —Is it lawful to retain, in condescension to the prejudices of the people, or with a view to their benefit, certain ancient rites and institutions, which, although they carry a superstitious aspect, may nevertheless be susceptible of a favourable and rational interpretation?"

XXXI. It has always been a question much debated among protestants, and more especially in England and Holland, where it has excited great commotions and tumults,—to whom the right of governing the church, and the power of deciding in religious matters, properly belong? This controversy has been determined in favour of those who maintain, that the power of deciding, in matters of religious doctrine, discipline, and government, is, by the appointment of Christ himself, vested in the church, and therefore ought by no means to be intrusted with the civil magistrate; while, at the same time, they grant, that it is the business of the latter to assist the church with his protection and advice, to convoke and preside in its synods and councils, to take care that the clergy do not attempt to carry on any thing that may be prejudicial to the interests of the state, and, by his authority, to confirm the validity, and secure the execution of the different laws enacted by the church under his inspection. It is true, that from the time of Henry VIII. the sovereigns of England consider themselves as supreme heads of the church, in relation to its spiritual, as well as its temporal concerns; and it is plain enough, that, on the strength of this important title, both Henry and his son Edward assumed an extensive authority and jurisdiction in the church, and looked upon their spiritual power, as equal to that which had been unworthily enjoyed by the Roman pontiff.* But queen Elizabeth receded considerably from these high pretensions, and diminished the spiritual power of her successors, by declaring that the royal jurisdiction extended only to the ministers of religion, and not to religion itself; to the rulers of the church, and not to the church itself; or, in other words, that the persons of the clergy

* See Neal's History of the Puritans, vol. i. p. 11

were alone subject to their civil authority.* Accordingly, we see that the constitution of the church of England perfectly resembles that of the state, and that a striking analogy exists between the civil and ecclesiastical government established in that country. The clergy, consisting of the upper and lower houses of convocation, are immediately assembled by the archbishop of Canterbury, in consequence of an order from the sovereign, and propose in these meetings, by common consent, such measures as seem necessary to the well-being of the church. These measures are laid before the king and parliament, and derive from their approbation and authority the force of laws.† But it must be acknowledged, that this matter has given occasion to much altercation and debate; nor has it been found easy to fix the extent of the jurisdiction and prerogatives of these great bodies in a manner conformable to their respective pretensions, since the king and his council explain them in one way, and the clergy, more especially those who are zealous for the spiritual supremacy and independency of the church, understand them in another. The truth of the matter is plainly this, that the ecclesiastical polity in England has never acquired a stable and consistent form; nor has it been reduced to clear and certain principles. It has rather been carried on and administered by ancient custom and precedent, than defined and fixed by any regular system of laws and institutions.

XXXII. If it was not an easy matter to determine in what hands the power of deciding affairs of a religious nature was to be lodged, it was no less difficult to fix the form of ecclesiastical government in which this power was to be administered. Many vehement disputes were kindled on this subject, which neither the lapse of time, nor the efforts of human wisdom, have been able to bring to an amicable issue. The republic of Geneva, in consequence of the counsels of Calvin, judged it proper that the particular affairs of each church should be directed by a body of presbyters, all invested with an equal degree of power and authority; that matters of a more public and important nature were to be submitted to the judgment of an assembly, or synod, composed of elders chosen as deputies by the churches of a whole province or district; and that all affairs of such extensive influence and high moment, as concerned the welfare of the sacred community in general, should be examined and decided, as in early times, by an assembly of the whole church. This form of ecclesiastical government the church of Geneva adopted for itself,‡ and left no entreaties or methods of persuasion unemployed, that might recommend it to those reformed churches with which they lived in fraternal communion. But it was obstinately rejected by the English clergy, who regarded as sacred and immutable that ancient form of spiritual government, according to which a certain district or diocese is committed to the care and inspection of one ruler or bishop, to whom the presbyters of each church are subject, as also the deacons are to the presbyters; while the general interests of the church are treated and discussed in an assembly of bishops, and of such ecclesiastics as are next to them in rank and dignity. This form of episcopal polity was, with some small exceptions, adopted by the Bohemian and Moravian brethren,* who had become one of the reformed churches; but it was highly displeasing to those among the protestants, who had embraced the sentiments and discipline of Calvin. The dissensions, occasioned by these different schemes of ecclesiastical polity, were every way adapted to produce a violent schism in the church; so much the more, as the leaders of the contending parties pretended to derive their respective plans from the injunctions of Christ, and the practice of his disciples. And, in effect, it divided the English nation into two parties, who during a long time treated each other with great animosity and bitterness, and whose feuds, on many occasions, proved detrimental to the civil interests and prosperity of the nation. This schism, however, which did such mischief in England, was, by the prudence and piety of a few great and excellent divines, confined to that country, and prevented from either becoming universal, or interrupting the fraternal union that prevailed between the church of England and the reformed churches abroad. The worthy men, who

* See Courayer's Supplement aux deux Ouvrages pour la Defense de la Validite des Ordinations Anglicanes, chap. xv.

☞ This must be understood with many restrictions, if it can at all be admitted. The whole tenor of queen Elizabeth's reign showed plainly that she did not pretend to less power in religious matters than any of her predecessors.

☞ † Jo. Cosinus, de Ecclesiæ Anglicanæ Religione et Disciplina, in the learned Thomas Smith's Vitæ Erudítiss. Virorum, published in 1707.—See also Dav. Wilkins, de Veteri et Moderna Synodi Anglic. Constitutione, tom. i. Concil. Magn. Britann. p. 7.—Neal, vol. i.

☞ ‡ The account which Dr. Mosheim gives here and above (sect. xii. of this chapter) of the form of ecclesiastical government established by Calvin at Geneva, is far from being accurate. There are but two ecclesiastical bodies in that republic, viz. the venerable company of the pastors and professors, and the consistory: for a just description of which, see the judicious Mr. Keate's "Short Account of the Ancient History, present Government, and Laws of the Republic of Geneva," published in 1761.—I would only remark that what this sensible author observes, with respect to the consistory, in p. 124 of his interesting performance, belongs principally, if not wholly, to the venerable company. Dr. Mosheim seems to have been led into this mistake, by imagining that the ecclesiastical form of government established in Scotland, where indeed all church affairs are managed by consistorial, provincial, and national assemblies, or, in other words, by presbyteries, synods, and general synods, was a direct transcript of the hierarchy of Geneva. It is also probable, that he may have been deceived by reading, in Neal's History of the Puritans, that the Scottish reformers approved the discipline of the removed churches of Geneva and Switzerland, and followed their plan of ecclesiastical government. But he ought to have observed, that this approbation and imitation related only to the democratic form of the church of Geneva, and the parity of its ministers. Be that as it may, the plan of government which our historian here supposes to have place at Geneva, is in reality that which is observed in Scotland, and of which no more than the first and fundamental principles were taken from the discipline of Calvin. The small territory of Geneva would not admit such a form of ecclesiastical polity as Dr. Mosheim here describes.

* See Epist. de Ordinat. et Successione Episcopal in Unitate Fratrum Bohem, conservata, in Christ Matth. Pfaffii Institutionibus Juris Eccles. p. 410

thus set bounds to the influence of these unhappy divisions, found great opposition made, by the suggestions of bigotry, to their charitable purpose. To maintain, however, the bonds of union between the episcopal church of England and the presbyterian churches in foreign countries, they laid down the following maxim, which, though it be not universally adopted, tends nevertheless to the preservation of external concord among the reformed, viz. "That Jesus Christ has left upon record no express injunctions with respect to the external form of government that is to be observed in his church; and, consequently, that every nation hath a right to establish such a form, as seemeth conducive to the interests, and suitable to the peculiar state, circumstances, and exigencies of the community, provided that such an establishment be in no respect prejudicial to truth, or favourable to the revival of superstition."*

XXXIII. It was the opinion of Calvin, not only that flagitious and profligate members were to be cut off from the sacred society, and excluded from the communion of the church, but also that men of dissolute and licentious lives were punishable by the laws of the state, and the arm of the civil magistrate. In this he differed from Zuingle, who, supposing that all authority, of every kind, was lodged in the hands of the magistrate alone, would not allow to the ministers of the church the power of excluding flagitious offenders from its communion, or withholding from them the participation of its sacraments.† But the credit and influence of Calvin were so great at Geneva, that he accomplished his purpose, even in the face of a formidable opposition from various quarters. He established the severest rules of discipline to correct the licentious manners of the times, by which he exposed himself to innumerable perils from the malignity and resentment of the dissolute, and to perpetual contests with the patrons of voluptuousness and immorality. He executed, moreover, these rules of discipline with the utmost rigour, had them strengthened and supported by the authority of the state, excluded obstinate offenders from the communion of the church, by the judicial sentence of the consistory, and even went so far as to procure their banishment from the city; not to mention other kinds of punishment, of no mild nature, which, at his desire, were inflicted upon men of loose principles and irregular lives.‡ The clergy in Switzerland were highly pleased with the form of church government that had been established at Geneva, and ardently desirous of a greater degree of power to restrain the insolence of obstinate sinners, and a larger share of authority in the church, than they were intrusted with by the moderate ecclesiastical constitution of Zuingle. They devoutly wished that the discipline of Calvin might be followed in their cantons, and even made some attempts for that purpose. But their desires and their endeavours were equally vain; for the cantons of Bern, Zurich, and Basil, distinguished themselves among the others in opposing this change, and would by no means permit the bounds, that Zuingle had set to the jurisdiction of the church, to be removed, nor its power and authority to be augmented in any respect.*

XXXIV. All the various branches of learning, whether sacred or profane, flourished among the reformed during this century, as appears evidently by the great number of excellent productions which have been transmitted to our times. Zuingle, indeed, seemed disposed to exclude philosophy from the pale of the church;† but in this inconsiderate purpose he had few followers, and the succeeding doctors of the Helvetic church were soon persuaded of the necessity of philosophical knowledge, more especially in controversies, and researches of a theological kind. Hence it was, that, in 1588, an academical body was founded at Geneva by Calvin, whose first care was to place in this new seminary a professor of philosophy for the instruction of youth in the principles of reasoning. It is true, indeed, that this professor had a very limited province assigned to him, being obliged to confine his instructions to a mere interpretation of the precepts of Aristotle, who at this same time was the oracle of all the public schools,‡ and whose philosophical principles and method were exclusively adopted by all the other reformed

* See Spanhemii Opera, tom. ii. lib. viii. ix. p. 1055. This was the general opinion of the British divines who lived in the earliest period of the Reformation, and was first abandoned by Archbishop Whitgift. See Neal's History of the Puritans, vol. iii.

† See a remarkable letter of Rodolph Gualter, in Fueslin's Centuria I. Epistolarum a Reformatoribus Helveticis scriptarum, p. 478, where he expresses himself thus: "Excommunicationem neque Zuinglius . . . neque Bullingerus, unquam probarunt, et . . . obstiterunt iis qui eam aliquando voluerunt introducere . . . Basileæ quidem Œcolampadius, multum dissuadente Zuinglio, instituerat . . . sed adeo non durabilis fuit illa constitutio, ut Œcolampadius illam abrogarit. &c. See also p. 90.

‡ Of all the undertakings of Calvin, there was not one that involved him in so much trouble, or exposed him to such imminent danger, as the plan he had formed, with such resolution and fortitude, of purging the church, by the exclusion of obstinate and scandalous offenders, and inflicting severe punishments on all such as violated the laws, enacted by the church, or by the consistory, which was its representative. See the Life of Calvin, composed by Beza, and prefixed to his Letters.—Spon's Histoire de Geneve, and particularly the notes, tom. ii. p. 45, 65.—Calvin's Letters, and more especially those addressed to Jaques de Bourgogne. The party at Geneva, which Calvin called the sect of Libertines, (because they defended the licentious customs of ancient times, the erection of stews, and other vicious practices, not only by their discourse and their actions, but even by force of arms,) was both numerous and powerful. But the courage and resolution of this great reformer gained the ascendency, and triumphed over the opposition of his enemies.

* See the account of the tumults and commotions of Lausanne, in the Museum Helveticum, tom. ii The disputes that were carried on upon this occasion, in the Palatinate, which adopted the ecclesiastical discipline of Geneva, are recorded by Altingius, in his Hist. Eccles. Palat. and by Struvius, in his Hist. Eccles. Palat. German.

† Zuingle, in the dedication of his book, *de Vera et Falsa Religione*, to Francis I. king of France, expresses himself in the following terms: "Philosophiæ interdictum est a Christi scholis; at isti (Sorbonistæ) fecerunt eam cœlestis verbi magistram."

‡ Beza, in his Epist. Theol. (ep. xxxvi. p. 156,) speaks thus: "Certum nobis ac constitutum est, et in ipsis tradendis logicis et in ceteris explicandis disciplinis ab Aristotelis sententia ne tantillum quidem deflectere"

colleges; though it is certain, that the philosophy of Ramus was, for some time, preferred, by many of the doctors of Basil, to that of the Stagirite.*

XXXV. The reformed church, from its very infancy, produced a great number of expositors of Scripture, whose learned and excellent commentaries deserve a memorable place† in the history of theological science. The exposition that Zuingle has given of the greatest part of the books of the New Testament, is far from being destitute of merit.‡ He was succeeded by Bullinger, Œcolampadius, and Musculus, and also by others, who, though inferior to those great men in erudition and genius, deserve a certain degree of approbation and esteem. But the two divines who shone with a superior and unrivalled lustre in this learned list of sacred expositors, were John Calvin and Theodore Beza. The former composed an excellent commentary on almost all the books of Holy Writ; and the latter published a Latin version of the New Testament, enriched with theological and critical observations, which has passed through many editions, and enjoys, at this day, a considerable part of the reputation and applause with which it was crowned at its first appearance. It must be acknowledged, to the honour of the greatest part of these commentators, that, wisely neglecting those allegorical significations and mystical meanings which the irregular fancies of former expositors had attributed to the terms of Scripture, they employed their whole diligence and industry in investigating the literal sense and the full energy of the words, in order to find out the true intention of the sacred writer. It must, however, be observed, on the other hand, that some of these interpreters, and more especially Calvin, have been sharply censured for applying, to the temporal state and circumstances of the Jews, several prophecies that point to the Messiah and to the Christian dispensation in the most evident and palpable manner, and thus removing some of the most striking arguments in favour of the divinity of the Gospel.§

XXXVI. The state of theology, and the revolutions it underwent among the Helvetic and the other reformed churches, were nearly the same as among the Lutherans. Zuingle was one of the first reformed doctors who reduced that sacred science into a certain sort of order, in his book concerning true and false Religion, which contained a brief exposition of the principal doctrines of Christianity. This production was followed by one much more comprehensive in its contents, and perfect in its kind, composed by Calvin, and entitled Institutes of the Christian Religion, which held in the reformed churches the same rank, authority, and credit, that the Loci Communes of Melancthon obtained among us.* The example of Calvin animated the doctors of his communion, and produced a great number of writers of Common-Place Divinity, some more, others less voluminous, among whom Musculus, Peter Martyr, and Piscator, particularly excelled. The most ancient of these writers are, generally speaking, the best, on account of their simplicity and clearness, being untainted with that affectation of subtlety, and that scholastic spirit, which have eclipsed the merit of many a good genius. Calvin was a model in this respect, more especially in his Institutes; a work remarkable for the finest elegance of style, and the greatest ease and perspicuity of expression, together with the most perfect simplicity of method, and clearness of argument. But this simplicity was soon effaced by the intricate science of the schools. The philosophy of Aristotle, which was taught in almost all the seminaries of learning, and suffered much from falling into bad hands, insinuated itself into the regions of theology, and rendered them barren, thorny, intricate, and gloomy, by the enormous multitude of barbarous terms, captious questions, minute distinctions, and useless subtleties, that followed in its train.†

* See Casp. Brandtii Vita Jacobi Arminii, p. 12, 22.

☞ † Dr. Mosheim pays a tribute to these great men of the reformed church, that seems to be extorted by justice, with a kind of effort from the spirit of party. He says, that Zuingle's labours are not contemptible; that Calvin attempted an illustration of the sacred writings; that the New Testament of Beza has not, even at this day, entirely lost the reputation it formerly enjoyed. This is faint praise; and therefore the translator has, without departing from the tenor of the author's phraseology, animated a little the coldness of his panegyric.

☞ ‡ It was not only on the books of the New Testament that Zuingle employed his very learned and excellent labours. He expounded the book of Genesis, together with the twenty-four first chapters of Exodus, and gave new versions of the Psalms, of the Prophesies of Isaiah and Jeremiah.

§ See Ægidii Hunnii Calvinus Judaizans, published in 1595, which was refuted by David Pareus, in a book published the same year, under the title of Calvinus Orthodoxus.

* The reader must not forget that the learned author of this History was a Lutheran.

† It must however be acknowledged, that the scholastic method of teaching theology seems to have first infected our (the Lutheran) church, though the contagion spread itself, soon after, among the reformed doctors. It was certainly very recent in Holland at the time of the famous synod of Dordrecht. In this assembly Maccovius, professor at Franeker, a man deeply versed in all the mysteries of the scholastic philosophy, was accused of heresy by his colleague Sibrand Lubbert. When the matter was examined, the synod declard that Maccovius was unjustly accused of heresy; but that, in his divinity lectures, he had not followed that simplicity of method, and clearness of expression, which are commendable in a public teacher of Christianity; and that he rather followed the subtle manner of the scholastic doctors, than the plain and unaffected phraseology of the inspired writers. The decision of the synod is expressed by Walter Balcanqual (in the acts of that ecclesiastical assembly, subjoined to his letters to Sir Dudley Carleton) in the following words: "Maccovium . . . nullius hæreseos reum teneri . . . peccasse eum, quod quibusdam ambiguis et obscuris scholasticis phrasibus usus sit; quod scholasticum docendi modum conetur in Belgicis academiis introducere . . . Monendum esse eum, ut cum spiritu sancto loquatur, non cum Bellarmino aut Suarezio."* These admonitions produced little effect on Maccovius, as appears by his theological writings, which are richly seasoned with scholastic wit and intricate speculations. He therefore appears to have been the first who introduced the subtleties of philosophy into the theological system of the reformed churches in Holland. He was not, however, alone in this attempt, but was seconded by the acute Dr. William Ames, minister of the English church at the

* See the Acta Synodi Dord. in Hale's Golden Remains, p. 161—and Philippi Limborchii Epistolar. Ecclesiasticar Collect. p. 574.

XXXVII. The reformed doctors of this century generally concluded their treatises of didactic theology with a delineation of the moral duties that are incumbent upon Christians, and the rules of practice that are prescribed in the Gospel. This method was observed by Calvin, and was followed, out of respect for his example, by almost all the divines of his communion, who looked upon him as their model and their guide. This eminent man, toward the conclusion of his Institutes, speaks of the power of the magistrate, and the ends of civil government; and, in the last chapter, gives the portraiture of the life and manners of a true Christian, but in a much more concise manner than the copiousness, dignity, and importance of the subject seemed to require. The progress of morality among the reformed, was obstructed by the very same means that retarded its improvement among the Lutherans. It was neglected amidst the tumult of controversy; and, while every pen was drawn to maintain certain systems of doctrine, few were employed in cultivating or promoting that noblest of all sciences, which has virtue, life, and manners, for its objects.

This master-science, which Calvin and his associates had left in a rude and imperfect state, was first reduced into some kind of form, and explained with a certain degree of accuracy and precision, by William Perkins,* an English divine, as the reformed doctors universally allow. He was seconded in this laudable undertaking by Telingius, a native of Holland; and it was by a worthy and pious spirit of emulation, excited by the example of these two doctors, that William Ames, a native of Scotland, and professor of divinity at Franeker,† was engaged to compose a complete body of Christian morality.* These writers were succeeded by others, who threw farther light on this important science.

XXXVIII. The reformed church was less disturbed, during this century, by sects, divisions, and theological disputes, than the Lutheran, which was often a prey to the most unhappy dissensions. This circumstance is looked upon by the former as a matter of triumph, though it may be very easily accounted for by all such as are acquainted with the history of that church.† We have however, in the writings of Calvin, an account, and also a refutation, of a most pernicious sect that sprang up in that establishment, and produced troubles of a more deplorable kind than any that happened in our community.‡ This odious sect, which assumed the denominations of *Libertines* and *Spiritual Brethren and Sisters*, arose in Flanders, under the auspices of Pockesius, Ruffus, and Quintin; gained a certain footing in France through the favour and protection of Margaret, queen of Navarre, and sister to Francis I.; and found patrons in several of the reformed churches.§ Their doctrine, as far as it can be known by the writings of Calvin and its other antagonists, (for I do not find that these fanatics published any account of their tenets,) amounted to the following propositions: "That the Deity was the sole operating cause in the mind of man, and the immediate author of all human actions; that, consequently, the distinctions of good and evil, which had been established with re-

---

Hague, and several others of the same scholastic turn. This method of teaching theology must have been in use among almost all the reformed doctors before the synod of Dordrecht, if we give credit to Episcopius, who, in the last discourse which he addressed to his disciples at Leyden, tells them that he had carefully avoided this scholastic divinity; and that this was the principal cause that had drawn on him the vehement hatred and opposition of all the other professors and teachers of theology. His words are as follows: "Videbam veritatem multarum et maximarum rerum in ipsa scriptura sacra, elaboratis humana industria phrasibus, ingeniosis vocularum fictionibus, locorum communium artificiosis texturis, exquisitis terminorum ac formularum inventionibus, adeo involutam, perplexam et intricatam redditam esse, ut Œdipo sæpe opus esset ad Sphingem illam theologicam enodandam. Ita est, et hinc primæ lacrymæ—Reducendam itaque terminorum apostolicorum et cuivis obviorum simplicitatem semper sequendam putavi, et sequestrandas, quas academiæ et scholæ tanquam proprias sibi vendicant, logicas philosophicasque speculationes et dictiones." See Philippi Limborchii vita Episcopii, p. 123.

☞ * Mr. William Perkins was born at Marston in Warwickshire, in the first year of queen Elizabeth, and educated in Christ's College, Cambridge, of which he became fellow. He was one of the most famous practical writers and preachers of his age. His puritanical and non-conforming principles exposed him to the cognizance of the High-Commission Court; but his peaceable behaviour, and eminent reputation in the learned world, procured him an exemption from the persecutions that fell upon his brethren. His works, which were printed in three volumes folio, afford abundant proofs of his piety and industry, especially when it is considered that he died in the 44th year of his age.

☞ † Dr. William Ames, educated at Cambridge under Mr. Perkins, fled from the persecution of archbishop Bancroft, and was invited by the states of Friesland to the divinity chair in the university of Franeker, which he filled with great reputation for twelve years. He then removed to Rotterdam, at the invitation of an English church there, and became their pastor. He was at the synod of Dordrecht, and informed the ambassador of king James at the Hague, from time to time, of the debates of that assembly. Besides his controversial writings against the Arminians, he published the following: Medulla Theologiæ (the work here referred to by Dr. Mosheim;)—Manuductio Logica;—Cases of Conscience;—Analysis of the Book of Psalms;—Notes on the First and Second Epistles of St. Peter, &c. These productions are not void of merit, considering the times in which they were written.

☞ * In the preface to his famous book de Conscientia et ejus Jure, Dr. Ames observes, that an excessive zeal for doctrine had produced an unhappy neglect of morality: "Quod hæc pars prophetiæ (i. e. morality,) hactenus minus fuerit exculta, hoc inde fuit, quod primipilares nostri perpetuo in acie adversus hostes pugnare, fidem propugnare, et aream ecclesiæ purgare, necessitate quadam cogebantur, ita ut agros et vineas plantare et rigare non potuerint ex voto, sicut bello fervente usu venire solet." The address to the students of Franeker, which is subjoined to this book, under the title of Parænesis ad Studiosos, &c. deserves to be perused, as it tends to confirm what has been already observed with respect to the neglect of the science of morality. "Theologi (says he) præclare se instructos putant ad omnes officii sui partes, si dogmata tantum intelligant. Neque tamen omnia dogmata scrutantur, sed illa sola, quæ præcipue solent agitari et in controversiam vocari."

☞ † Dr. Mosheim ought to have given us a hint of his manner of accounting for this, to avoid the suspicion of having been somewhat at a loss for a favourable solution.

☞ ‡ Why all these comparisons? Our author seems, on some occasions, to tinge his historical relation with the spirit of party.

§ See "Calvini Instructio adversus fanaticam et furiosam sectam Libertinorum, qui se Spirituales vocant," among his theological tracts

spect to these actions, were false and groundless, and that men could not, properly speaking, commit sin; that religion consisted in the union of the spirit, or rational soul, with the Supreme Being; that all those who had attained this happy union, by sublime contemplation and elevation of mind, were allowed to indulge, without exception or restraint, their appetites and passions; that all their actions and pursuits were then perfectly innocent; and that, after the death of the body, they were to be united to the Deity." These extravagant tenets resemble, in such a striking manner, the opinions of the Beghards, or Brethren of the Free Spirit, that it appears to me, beyond all doubt, that the Libertines, or Spirituals, now under consideration, were no more than a remnant of that ancient sect. The place of their origin tends to confirm this hypothesis, since it is well known, that, in the fourteenth and fifteenth centuries, Flanders swarmed with licentious fanatics of this kind.

XXXIX. We must not confound (as is frequently done) with these fanatics, another kind of Libertines, whom Calvin had to combat, and who gave him much trouble and perplexity during the whole course of his life and ministry; I mean the Libertines of Geneva. These were rather a cabal of rakes than a sect of fanatics; for they made no pretences to any religious system, but pleaded only for the liberty of leading voluptuous and immoral lives. This cabal was composed of such licentious citizens as could not bear the severe discipline of Calvin, who punished with rigour, not only dissolute manners, but also whatever carried the aspect of irreligion and impiety. This irregular troop stood forth in defence of the licentiousness and dissipation that had reigned in their city before the Reformation, pleaded for the continuance of those brothels, banquetings, and other entertainments of a sensual kind, which the regulations of Calvin were designed to abolish, and employed all the bitterness of reproach and invective, all the resources of fraud and violence, all the powers of faction, to accomplish their purpose.* In this turbulent cabal there were several persons, who were not only notorious for their dissolute and scandalous manner of living, but also for their contempt of all religion. Of this odious class was Gruet, who attacked Calvin with the utmost animosity and fury, calling him bishop of Asculum, the new pope, and branding him with other contumelious denominations. This Gruet denied the divinity of the Christian religion, the immortality of the soul, the difference between moral good and evil, and rejected, with disdain, the doctrines that are deemed most sacred among Christians; for which impieties he was at last brought before the civil tribunals, in 1550, and was punished with death.†

XL. The opposition that was made to Calvin did not end here. He had contests of another kind to sustain against those who disapproved his theological system, and, more especially, his melancholy and discouraging doctrine, in relation to eternal and absolute decrees. These adversaries felt, by a disagreeable experience, the warmth and violence of his haughty temper, and that impatience of contradiction which arose from an over-jealous concern for his honour, or rather for his unrivalled supremacy. He would not suffer them to remain at Geneva; and, in the heat of controversy, being carried away by the impetuosity of his passions, he accused them of crimes from which they have been fully absolved by the impartial judgment of unprejudiced posterity.* Among these victims of Calvin's unlimited power and excessive zeal, we may reckon Sebastian Castalio, master of the public school at Geneva, who, though not exempt from failings,† was nevertheless a man of probity, and was also remarkable for the extent of his learning and the elegance of his taste. As this learned man could neither approve all the measures that were followed, nor all the opinions that were entertained by Calvin and his colleagues, and particularly that of absolute and unconditional predestination, he was deposed from his office in 1544, and banished from the city. The magistrates of Basil, however, received this ingenious exile, and gave him the Greek professorship of their university.‡

XLI. A like fate happened to Jerome Bolsec, a French monk of the Carmelite order, who, though much inferior to Castalio in genius and learning, was judged worthy of esteem, on account of the motive that brought him to Geneva; for it was a conviction of the excellence of the protestant religion that engaged him to abandon the monastic retreats of superstition, and to repair to this city, where he followed the profession of physic. His imprudence, however, was great, and was the principal cause of the misfortunes that befell him. It led him, in 1551, to lift up his voice in the full congregation, after the conclusion of divine worship, and to declaim, in the most indecorous manner, against the doctrine of absolute decrees; for which offence he was thrown into prison, and soon after, sent into banishment. He then returned to the place of his nativity, and to the communion of Rome, and published the most bitter and slanderous libels, in which the reputation, conduct, and morals of Calvin and Beza, were cruelly attacked.§ From this treatment of Bolsec arose the misunderstanding between Calvin and his intimate friend and patron Jaques de Bourgogne, a man illustrious

* Spon's Histoire de Geneve, tom. ii. p. 44, in the edition of 1730.

† Spon's Hist. tom. ii.

* At this day we may venture to speak thus freely of the rash decisions of Calvin, since even the doctors of Geneva, as well as those of the other reformed churches, ingenuously acknowledge that his eminent talents and excellent qualities were accompanied with great defects, for which, however, they plead indulgence, in consideration of his services and virtues. See the notes to Spon's Histoire de Geneve, tom. ii. p. 110, as also the preface to Calvin's Letters to Jaques de Bourgogne.

☞ † See Bayle's Dictionary, at the article Castalio, in which the merit and demerit of that learned man seem to be impartially and accurately examined.

‡ See Uytenbogard's Ecclesiastical History, part ii. where that author endeavours to defend the innocence of Castalio.—See also Colomesii Italia Orientalis, p. 99.—Bayle's Dict. tom. i.

§ See Bayle's Dict. at the article Bolsec.—Spon's Hist. de Geneve, tom. ii. p. 55, in the Notes.—Biblioth. Raisonnee, tom. xxxii. p. 446, tom. xxxiv. p. 409

by his descent from the dukes of Burgundy, who had settled at Geneva with no other view than to enjoy the pleasure of conversing with him. Jaques de Bourgogne had employed Bolsec as his physician, and was so well satisfied with his services, that he endeavoured to support him, and to prevent his being ruined by the enmity and authority of Calvin. This incensed the latter to such a degree, that he turned the force of his resentment against this illustrious nobleman, who, to avoid his vengeance, removed from Geneva, and passed the remainder of his days in a rural retreat.*

XLII. Bernardino Ochino, a native of Sienna, (and, before his conversion, general of the Capuchin order,) was, in 1543, banished from Switzerland, in consequence of a sentence passed upon him by the Helvetic church. This proselyte, who was a man of a fertile imagination, and a lively and subtle turn of mind, had been invited to Zurich as pastor of the Italian church established in that city. But the freedom, or rather the licentiousness of his sentiments, justly exposed him to the displeasure of those who had been his patrons and protectors; for, among many other opinions very different from such as were commonly received, he maintained that the law, which confined a husband to one wife, was susceptible of exceptions in certain cases. In his writings also he propagated several notions which were repugnant to the theological system of the Helvetic doctors, and pushed his inquiries into many subjects of importance, with a boldness and freedom by no means suited to the genius and spirit of the age in which he lived. Some have, however, undertaken his defence, and have alleged in his behalf, that the errors he maintained at the time of his banishment, (when, worn out with age, and oppressed with poverty, he was rather an object of compassion, than of resentment,) were not of such a heinous nature as to justify so severe a punishment. However that may have been, this unfortunate exile retired into Poland, where he embraced the communion of the Anti-Trinitarians and Anabaptists,† and ended his days in 1564.‡

XLIII. It is remarkable that those very doctors, who animadverted with such severity upon all that dared to dissent from any part of their theological system, thought proper, nevertheless, to behave with the greatest circumspection, and the most pacific spirit of mildness, in the long controversy which was carried on with such animosity between the Puritans, and the advocates of episcopacy, in England; for if, on the one hand, they could not but stand well affected to the Puritans, who were steadfast defenders of the discipline and sentiments of the Helvetic church; so, on the other, they were connected with their episcopal doctors by the bonds of Christian communion and fraternal love. In this critical situation, their whole thoughts were turned to reconciliation and peace; and they exhorted their brethren, the Puritans, to put on a spirit of meekness and forbearance toward the episcopal church, and not to break the bonds of charity and communion with its rulers or its members. Such was the gentle spirit of the doctors in Switzerland toward the church of England, notwithstanding the severe treatment the greatest part of the reformed had received from that church, which constantly insisted on the divine origin of its government and discipline, and scarcely allowed, to the other reformed communities, the privileges, or even the denomination of a true church. This moderation of the Helvetic doctors was the dictate of prudence. They did not think it expedient to contend with a generous and flourishing people, or to incur the displeasure of a mighty queen, whose authority seemed to extend not only over her own dominions, but even to the United Provinces, which were placed in her neighbourhood, and, in some measure, under her protection. Nor did the apprehensions of a general schism in the reformed church contribute a little to render them meek, moderate, and pacific. It is one thing to punish and excommunicate a handful of weak and unsupported individuals, who attempt to disturb the tranquillity of the state by the introduction of opinions, which, though neither highly absurd, nor of dangerous consequence, have yet the demerit of novelty; and another to irritate, or promote divisions in a flourishing church, which, though weakened by intestine feuds, is yet both powerful and respectable in a high degree. Besides, the dispute between the church of England and the other reformed churches, did not, as yet, turn upon points of doctrine, but only on the rites of external worship and the form of ecclesiastical government. It is, however, to be observed that, soon after the period now under consideration, certain religious doctrines were introduced into the debate between the churches, that contributed much to widen the breach, and to obscure the prospect of reconciliation.*

* See the preface to Lettres de Calvin a Jaques de Bourgogne, and La Bibliotheque Raisonee, tom. xxxii. xxxiv.

† See Boverii Annales Capucinorum; and a book entitled, La Guerre Seraphique, ou Histoire des Perils qu'a couru la Barbe des Capucins, livr. ii. p. 147. livr. iii. p. 190, 230.—Observationes Halenses Latinæ, tom. iv. Observ. xx. p. 406. tom. v. Observ. i. p. 3.—Bayle's Diction. at the article Ochin.—Christ. Sandii Biblioth. Anti-Trinitar. p. 4. Niceron's Memoires pour servir a l'Hist. des Hommes illustres, t. xix. p. 166.

☞ ‡ Ochino did not leave the accusations of his adversaries without a reply; he published, in Italian, an apology for his character and conduct, printed, with a Latin translation by Seb. Castalio, without the date of the year. The Geneva edition of this apology bears the date of 1554, and a German edition appeared in 1556. Beza, in his letter to Dudithius, insults the memory of Ochino, and pretends to justify the severity with which he was treated, in such a taunting and uncharitable manner as does him little credit. See his Epist. Theolog. Genevæ, 1575. What the writers of the Romish church have laid to the charge of Ochino, may be seen in the life of cardinal Commendoni, written by Gratiani, bishop of Amelia, (and published in a French translation by the eloquent Flechier, bishop of Nismes,) B. 2. C. 9. p. 138—149. N.

☞ * All the protestant divines of the reformed church, whether puritans or others, seemed, indeed, hitherto of one mind about the doctrines of faith. But, toward the latter end of queen Elizabeth's reign, there arose a party, that first wished to soften, and then to overthrow, the received opinions concerning predestination, perseverance, free-will, effectual grace, and the extent of Christ's redemption. These are the doctrines to which Dr Mosheim al-

XLIV. That the reformed church abounded, during this century, with great and eminent men, justly celebrated for their talents and learning, is too well known to require proof. Beside Calvin, Zuingle, and Beza, who exhibited to the republic of letters very striking instances of genius and erudition, we may place, in the list of those who have gained an immortal name by their writings, Œcolampadius, Bullinger, Farel, Viret, Martyr, Bibliander, Musculus, Pelican, Lavater, Hospinian, Ursinus, Cranmer, archbishop of Canterbury, Szegedinus, and many others, whose names and merits are recorded by the writers of literary history, particularly by Melchior Adam, Antony Wood, Gerard Brandt, and Daniel Neal, the learned and industrious author of the History of the Puritans.

CHAPTER III.

The History of the Anabaptists or Mennonites.

I. The true origin of that sect which acquired the denomination of Anabaptists* by their administering anew the rite of baptism to those who came over to their communion, and derived that of *Mennonites* from the famous man to whom they owe the greatest part of their present felicity, is hidden in the depths of antiquity, and is, of consequence, extremely difficult to be ascertained.* This uncer

ludes in this passage. The clergy of the episcopal church began to lean toward the notions concerning these intricate points, which Arminius propagated some time after this; while, on the other hand, the puritans adhered rigorously to the system of Calvin. Several episcopal doctors remained attached to the same system; and all these abettors of Calvinism, whether episcopal or presbyterian, were called *doctrinal puritans.*

* The modern Mennonites reject the denomination of Anabaptists, and also disavow the custom of repeating the ceremony of baptism, whence this denomination is derived. They acknowledge that the ancient Anabaptists practised the repetition of baptism to those who joined them from other Christian churches; but they maintain, at the same time, that this custom is at present abolished by the far greater part of their community. See Herm. Schyn's Historiæ Mennonitarum plenior deductio, cap. ii. But here, if I do not mistake, these good men forget that ingenuous candour and simplicity, of which, on other occasions, they make such ostentation, and have recourse to artifice, in order to disguise the true cause and origin of the denomination in question. They pretend, for instance, that the Anabaptists, their ancestors, were so called from their baptizing *a second time* all the adult persons who left other churches to enter into their communion. But it is certain, that the denomination in question was given to them, not only on this account, but also, and indeed principally, from the following consideration; that they did not look upon those who had been baptized in a state of infancy, or at a tender age, as rendered, by the administration of this sacrament, true members of the Christian church; and therefore insisted upon their being re-baptized, in order to their being received into the communion of the Anabaptists. It is likewise certain that all the churches of that communion, however they may vary, in other respects, and differ from each other in their tenets and practices, agree nevertheless in this opinion, and persevere obstinately in it. In a more especial manner are the ancient Flemish Anabaptists entitled to this denomination; for they not only re-baptized the children that had been already baptized in other churches, but even observed the same method with respect to persons who had reached the years of reason and discretion; and, what is still more remarkable, the different sects of Anabaptists deal in the same manner one with another; each sect re-baptizes the persons that enter into its communion, although they have already received that sacrament in another sect of the same denomination; and the reason of this conduct is, that each sect considers its baptism alone as pure and valid. It is indeed to be observed, that there is another class of Anabaptists, called Waterlandians, who are more moderate in their principles, and wiser in all respects than those now mentioned, and who do not pretend to re-baptize adult persons already baptized in other Christian churches, or in other sects of their own denomination. These moderate sectaries are, however, with propriety termed Anabaptists, on account of their re-baptizing such as had received the baptismal rite in a state of infancy or childhood. The patrons of this sect seem, indeed, very studious to conceal a practice which they cannot deny to take place among them; and their eagerness to conceal it, arises from a fear of reviving the hatred and severities which formerly pursued them. They are apprehensive that, by acknowledging the truth, the modern Mennonites may be considered as the descendants of those flagitious and fanatical Anabaptists of Munster, whose enormities rendered their very name odious to all true Christians. All this appears evident from the following passage in Schyn's Historiæ Mennonitarum plenior Deductio, tom. ii. where that author pretends to prove that his brethren are unjustly stigmatized with the odious denomination of Anabaptists. His words are: "Anabaptismus ille plane obsolevit; et a multis retro annis neminem cujuscunque sectæ Christianæ fidei, *juxta mandatum Christi* baptizatum, dum ad nostras Ecclesias transire cupit, re-baptizaverunt," i. e. That species of Anabaptism with which we are charged exists no longer, nor has it happened during the space of many years past, that any person professing Christianity, of whatever church or sect he may have been, and who had been previously baptized *according to the commandment of Christ*, has been re-baptized upon his entering into our communion. This passage would, at first sight, induce an inattentive reader to imagine that there is no such thing among the modern Mennonites, as the custom of re-baptizing those who enter into their community. But the words, *juxta mandatum Christi*, discover sufficiently the artifice and fraud that lie hidden in this apology; for the Anabaptists maintain that there is no *commandment of Christ* in favour of infant baptism. Moreover, we see the whole fallacy exposed, by what the author adds to the sentence already quoted: "Sed illam etiam *adultorum* baptismum ut sufficientem agnoscunt." Nevertheless, this author, as if he had perfectly proved his point, concludes, with an air of triumph, that the odious name of Anabaptists cannot be given, with any propriety, to the Mennonites at this day; "Quare (says he,) verissimum est, illud odiosum nomen Anabaptistarum illis non convenire." In this, however, he is certainly in an error; and the name in question is as applicable to the modern Mennonites, as it was to the sect from which they descend, since the best and wisest of the Mennonites maintain, in conformity with the principles of the ancient Anabaptists, that the baptism of infants is destitute of validity, and consequently are very careful in re-baptizing their proselytes, notwithstanding their having been baptized in their tender years, in other Christian churches. Many circumstances persuade me that the declarations and representations of things given by the modern Mennonites, are not always worthy of credit. Unhappily instructed by the miseries and calamities in which their ancestors were involved, they are anxiously careful to conceal entirely those tenets and laws which are the distinguishing characteristics of their sect; while they embellish what they cannot totally conceal, and disguise with the greatest art such of their institutions as otherwise might appear of a pernicious tendency, and might expose them to censure.

* The writers for and against the Anabaptists are amply enumerated by Caspar Sagittarius, in his Introductio ad Histor. Eccles. tom. i. p. 826. and by Christ. M. Pfaffius, in his Introduct. in Histor. Liter Theologiæ, part ii. p. 349.—Add to these a modern writer and a Mennonite preacher, Herman Schyn who published at Amsterdam, in 1723, his Historia Mennonitarum, and, in 1729, his Plenior Deductio

tainty will not appear surprising, when it is considered, that this sect started up suddenly in several countries, at the same point of time, under leaders of different talents and different intentions, and at the very period when the first contests of the reformers with the Roman pontiffs drew the attention of the world, and employed the pens of the learned, in such a manner, as to render all other objects and incidents almost matters of indifference. The modern Mennonites not only consider themselves as the descendants of the Waldenses, who were so grievously oppressed and persecuted by the despotic heads of the Romish church, but pretend, moreover, to be the purest offspring of these respectable sufferers, being equally averse to all principles of rebellion, on the one hand, and all suggestions of fanaticism on the other.* Their adversaries, on the contrary, represent them as the descendants of those turbulent and furious Anabaptists, who, in the sixteenth century, involved Holland, Switzerland, Germany, and more especially the province of Westphalia, in such scenes of blood, perplexity, and distress; and allege, that, terrified by the dreadful fate of their associates, and also influenced by the moderate counsels and wise injunctions of Mennon, they abandoned the ferocity of their primitive enthusiasm, and were gradually brought to a better mind. After having examined these different accounts of the origin of the Anabaptists with the utmost attention and impartiality, I have found that neither of them can justly be pronounced conformable to strict truth.

II. It may be observed, in the first place, that the Mennonites are not entirely in an error when they boast of their descent from the Waldenses, Petrobrusians, and other ancient sects, who are usually considered as witnesses of the truth, in the times of general darkness and superstition. Before the rise of Luther and Calvin, there lay concealed, in almost all the countries of Europe, particularly in Bohemia, Moravia, Switzerland, and Germany, many persons, who adhered tenaciously to the following doctrine, which the Waldenses, Wickliffites, and Hussites, had maintained, some in a more disguised, and others in a more open and public manner; viz. "That the kingdom of Christ, or the visible church which he established upon earth, was an assembly of true and real saints, and ought therefore to be inaccessible to the wicked and unrighteous, and also exempt from all those institutions which human prudence suggests, to oppose the progress of iniquity, or to correct and reform transgressors." This maxim is the true source of all the peculiarities that are to be found in the religious doctrine and discipline of the Mennonites; and it is most certain, that the greatest part of these peculiarities were approved by many of those, who, before the dawn of the reformation, entertained the notion already mentioned, relating to the visible church of Christ.* There were, however, different ways of thinking among the different members of this sect, with respect to the methods of attaining such a perfect church-establishment as they had in view. Some, who were of a fanatical complexion on the one hand, and were persuaded on the other, that such a visible church as they had modelled out in fancy, could not be realized by the power of man, entertained the pleasing hope, that God, in his own good time, would erect to himself a holy church, exempt from every degree of blemish and impurity, and would set apart, for the execution of this grand design, a certain number of chosen instruments, divinely assisted and prepared for this work, by the extraordinary succours of his Holy Spirit. Others, of a more prudent and rational turn of mind, entertained different views of this matter. They neither expected stupendous miracles, nor extraordinary revelations, since they were persuaded, that it was possible, by human wisdom, industry, and vigilance, to purify the church from the contagion of the wicked, and restore it to the simplicity of its original constitution, provided that the manners and spirit of the primitive Christians could recover their lost dignity and lustre.

III. The drooping spirits of these people, who had been dispersed through many countries, and persecuted every where with the greatest severity, were revived when they were informed that Luther, seconded by several persons of eminent piety, had attempted with success the reformation of the church. Then they spoke with openness and freedom; and the enthusiasm of the fanatical, as well as the prudence of the wise, discovered themselves in their natural colours. Some of them imagined, that the time was now come in which God himself was to dwell with his servants in an extraordinary manner, by celestial succours, and to establish upon earth a kingdom truly spiritual and divine. Others, less sanguine and chimerical in their expectations, flattered themselves, nevertheless, with the fond hope of the approach of that happy period, in which the restoration of the church, which had been so long expected in vain, was to be accomplished, under the divine protection, by the labours and counsels of pious and eminent men.

Histor. Mennonit. These two books, though they do not deserve the title of a History of the Mennonites, are nevertheless useful, in order to come at a thorough knowledge of the affairs of this sect; for this author is much more intent upon defending his brethren against the accusations and reproaches with which they have been loaded, than careful in tracing out the origin, progress, and revolutions of their sect. Indeed the Mennonites have not much reason to boast either of the extraordinary learning or dexterity of this their patron; and it is to be imagined, that they may easily find a more able defender. For an accurate account of the Mennonite Historians, and their confessions of faith, see Jo. Christ. Kocheri Bibliotheca Theol. Symbolicæ, p. 461.

* See Herm. Schyn's Plenior Deductio Histor. Mennon. cap. i. as also a Dutch work by Galen Abrahamzon, entitled, Verdediging der Christenen, die Doopsgesinde genand worden

* See, for an account of the religious sentiments of the Waldenses, Limborch's excellent History of the Inquisition, translated into English by the learned Dr. Samuel Chandler, book i. chap. viii.—It appears from undoubted testimonies, that the Wickliffites and Hussites did not greatly differ from the Waldenses, with regard to the point under consideration.

☞ See also Lydii Waldensia, and Allix's Ancient Churches of Piedmont, ch. xxii.—xxvi. p. 211—280. N

This sect was soon joined by great numbers, and (as usually happens in sudden revolutions of this nature) by many persons, whose characters and capacities were very different, though their views seemed to turn upon the same object. Their progress was rapid; for, in a very short time, their discourses, visions, and predictions, excited commotions in a great part of Europe, and drew into their communion a prodigious multitude, whose ignorance rendered them easy victims to the illusions of enthusiasm. It is, however, to be observed, that, as the leaders of this sect had fallen into that erroneous and chimerical notion, that the new kingdom of Christ, which they expected, was to be exempted from every kind of vice, and from the smallest degree of imperfection and corruption, they were not satisfied with the plan of reformation proposed by Luther. They looked upon it as much beneath the sublimity of their views, and, consequently, undertook a more perfect reformation, or, to express more properly their visionary enterprise, they proposed to found a true church, entirely spiritual, and truly divine.

IV. It is difficult to determine, with certainty, the particular spot that gave birth to that seditious and pestilential sect of Anabaptists, whose tumultuous and desperate attempts were equally pernicious to the cause of religion, and the civil interests of mankind. Whether this sect arose in Switzerland, Germany, or Holland, is still a point of debate, whose decision is of no great importance.* It is most probable, that several persons of this odious class made their appearance at the same time, in different countries; and we may fix this period soon after the dawn of the Reformation in Germany, when Luther arose to set bounds to the ambition of Rome. This appears from a variety of circumstances, and especially from this striking one, that the first Anabaptist doctors of any eminence were, almost all, heads and leaders of particular and separate sects; for it must be carefully observed, that though all these projectors of a new, unspotted, and perfect church, were comprehended under the general denomination of Anabaptists, on account of their opposing the baptism of infants, and their re-baptizing such as had received that sacrament in a state of childhood in other churches, yet they were, from their very origin, subdivided into various sects, which differed from each other in points of no small moment. The most pernicious faction of all those that composed this motley multitude, was the sect which pretended that the founders of the new and perfect church, already mentioned, were under the direction of a divine impulse, and were armed against all opposition by the power of working miracles. It was this detestable faction that, in 1521, began their fanatical work, under the guidance of Munzer, Stubner, Storck, and other leaders of the same furious complexion, and excited the most unhappy tumults and commotions in Saxony and the adjacent countries. They employed at first the various arts of persuasion, in order to propagate their doctrine. They preached, exhorted, admonished, and reasoned, in a manner that seemed proper to gain the multitude, and related a great number of visions and revelations, with which they pretended to have been favoured from above. But when they saw that these methods of making proselytes were not attended with such rapid success as they fondly expected, and that the ministry of Luther, and other eminent reformers, proved detrimental to their cause, they had recourse to more expeditious measures, and madly attempted to propagate their fanatical doctrine by force of arms. Munzer and his associates assembled, in 1525, a numerous army, chiefly composed of the peasants of Suabia, Thuringia, Franconia, and Saxony, and, at the head of this credulous and deluded rabble, declared war against all laws, governments, and magistrates of every kind, under the chimerical pretext, that Christ was now to take the reins of civil and ecclesiastical government into his own hands, and to rule alone over the nations. But this seditious crowd was routed and dispersed, without much difficulty, by the elector of Saxony and other princes; Munzer was ignominiously put to death, and his factious counsellors were scattered abroad in different places.*

V. This bloody defeat of one part of these seditious and turbulent fanatics, did not produce that effect upon the rest which might naturally have been expected; it rendered them, indeed, more timorous, but it did not open their eyes upon their delusion. It is certain, that, even after this period, numbers of them, who were infected with the same odious principles that occasioned the destruction of Munzer, wandered about in Germany, Switzerland, and Holland, and excited the people to rebellion by their seditious discourses. They collected congregations in several places; affected to foretel, in consequence of a divine commission, the approaching abolition of magistracy, and the downfall of civil rulers and governors; and, while they pretended to be ambassadors of the Most High, insulted on many occasions the majesty of Heaven by the most flagitious crimes. Those who distinguished themselves by the enormity of their conduct in this infamous sect, were Louis Hetzer, Balthazar Hubmeyer, Felix Mentz, Conrad Grebel, Melchior Hoffman, and George Jacob, who, if their power had seconded their designs, would have involved all Switzerland, Holland, and Germany, in tumult and bloodshed.† A great part of this rabble seemed really delirious; and nothing more extravagant or more incredible can be imagined than the dreams and visions that were constantly arising

* Fueslin has attempted to examine, whether the Anabaptists first arose in Germany or Switzerland, in a German work, entitled, *Beytrage zur Schwezerisch Reformat. Geschichte*, tom. i. p. 190; tom. ii. p 64 265, 327; tom. iii. p. 323; but without success

* See Seckendorf, Histor. Lutheranismi, lib. i. p. 192, 304. lib. ii. p. 13.—Sleidan, Commentar. lib. v. p. 47.—Joach. Camerarii Vita Melancthonis, p. 44.

† See Jo. Bapt. Ottii Annales Anabaptist. p. 21.—Jo. Hornbeckii Summa Controvers. lib. v. p. 332.—Anton. Matthæi Analect. veteris Ævi, tom. iv. p. 629, 677. 679.—Bernard. Raupachii Aust. Evangel. t. ii. p. 41.—Jo. Georg. Schelhorn, Act. ad Hist. Ec. pertin. t. i. p. 100.—See also Arnold's Kirchen Hist. lib. xvi. c. xxi. and Fueslin's Beytrage

in their disordered brains. Such of them as had some sparks of reason left, and had reflexion enough to reduce their notions into a certain form, maintained, among others, the following points of doctrine: "That the church of Christ ought to be exempt from all sin; that all things ought to be in common among the faithful; that all usury, tithes, and tribute, ought to be entirely abolished; that the baptism of infants was an invention of the devil; that every Christian was invested with a power of preaching the Gospel, and, consequently, that the church stood in no need of ministers or pastors; that in the kingdom of Christ civil magistrates were absolutely useless; and that God still continued to reveal his will to chosen persons by dreams and visions."*

It would betray, however, a strange ignorance, or an unjustifiable partiality, to maintain, that all those who professed this eccentric and absurd doctrine were chargeable with that furious and brutal extravagance which has been mentioned as the character of too great a part of their sect. This was by no means the case; several of these enthusiasts discovered a milder and more pacific spirit, and were free from any other reproach, than that which resulted from the errors they maintained, and their too ardent desire of spreading them among the multitude. It may still farther be affirmed with truth, that many of those who followed the wiser class of Anabaptists, and even some who adhered to the most extravagant factions of that sect, were men of upright intentions and sincere piety, who were seduced into this mystery of fanaticism and iniquity, on the one hand, by their ignorance and simplicity, and, on the other, by a laudable desire of reforming the corrupt state of religion.

VI. The progress of this turbulent sect, in almost all the countries of Europe, alarmed all who had any concern for the public good. Princes, and sovereign states, exerted themselves to check these rebellious enthusiasts in their career, by issuing out, first, severe edicts to restrain their violence, and employing, at length, capital punishments to conquer their obstinacy.† But here a maxim, already verified by repeated experience, received a new degree of confirmation; for the conduct of the Anabaptists, under the pressure of persecution, plainly showed the extreme difficulty of correcting or influencing, by the prospect of suffering, or even by the terrors of death, minds that are either deeply tainted with the poison of fanaticism, or firmly bound by the ties of religion. In almost all the countries of Europe, an unspeakable number of these unhappy wretches preferred death, in its worst forms, to a retraction of their errors. Neither the view of the flames that were kindled to consume them, nor the ignominy of the gibbet, nor the terrors of the sword, could shake their invincible, but ill-placed constancy, or make them abandon tenets, that appeared dearer to them than life and all its enjoyments. The Mennonites have preserved voluminous records of the lives, actions, and unhappy fate of those of their sect, who suffered death for the crimes of rebellion or heresy, which were imputed to them.* Certain it is, that they were treated with severity; and it is much to be lamented that so little distinction was made between the members of this sect, when the sword of justice was unsheathed against them. Why were the innocent and the guilty involved in the same fate? Why were doctrines purely theological, or, at worst, fanatical, punished with the same rigour that was shown to crimes inconsistent with the peace and welfare of civil society? Those who had no other marks of peculiarity than their administering baptism to adult persons only, and their excluding the unrighteous from the external communion of the church, ought undoubtedly to have met with milder treatment than that which was given to those seditious incendiaries, who were for unhinging all government and destroying all civil authority. Many suffered for errors which they had embraced with the most upright intentions, seduced by the eloquence and fervour of their doctors, and persuading themselves that they were contributing to the advancement of true religion. But, as the greatest part of these enthusiasts had communicated to the multitude their visionary notions, concerning the new spiritual kingdom that was soon to be erected, and the abolition of magistracy and civil government that was to be the immediate effect of this great revolution, this rendered the very name of an Anabaptist unspeakably odious, and made it always excite the idea of a seditious incendiary, a pest to human society. It is true, that many Anabaptists suffered death, not on account of their being considered as rebellious subjects, but merely because they were judged to be incorrigible heretics; for in this century the error of limiting the administration of baptism to adult persons only, and the practice of re-baptizing such as had received that sacrament in a state of infancy, were looked upon as most flagitious and intolerable heresies. It is, nevertheless, certain, that the greatest part of these wretched sufferers owed their unhappy fate to their rebellious principles and tumultuous proceedings, and that many also were punished for their temerity and imprudence, which had led them to the commission of various crimes.

VII. There stands upon record a most shocking instance of this, in the dreadful commotions that were excited at Munster, in 1533.

* This account of the doctrine of the Anabaptists is principally taken from the learned Fueslin already quoted.

† It was in Saxony, if I mistake not, and also in the year 1525, that penal laws were first enacted against this fanatical tribe. These laws were renewed in 1527, 1528, 1534. See a German work of the learned Kappius, entitled, Nachlese von Reformations Urkunden, part i. p. 176. Charles V. incensed at the increasing impudence and iniquity of these enthusiasts, issued out against them severe edicts, in the years 1527 and 1529. (See Ottii Annales Anabapt. p. 45.) The magistrates of Switzerland treated, at first, with remarkable lenity and indulgence, the Anabaptists who lived under their government; but when it was found that this lenity rendered them still more enterprising and insolent, it was judged proper to have recourse to a different manner of proceeding. Accordingly the magistrates of Zurich, in 1525, denounced capital punishment against this riotous sect

* See Joach. Christ. Jehring, Præfat. ad Historiam Mennonitarum

by some Dutch Anabaptists, who chose that city as the scene of their horrid operations, and committed in it such deeds as would surpass all credibility, were they not attested in a manner that excludes every degree of doubt and uncertainty. A handful of madmen, who had gotten into their heads the visionary notion of a new and spiritual kingdom, soon to be established in an extraordinary manner, formed themselves into a society, under the guidance of a few illiterate leaders chosen out of the populace; and they persuaded, not only the ignorant multitude, but even several among the learned, that Munster was to be the seat of this new and heavenly Jerusalem, whose spiritual dominion was thence to be propagated to all parts of the earth. The bold ringleaders of this furious tribe were John Matthison, John Bockhold, a tailor of Leyden, one Gerard, with some others, whom the blind rage of enthusiasm, or the still more culpable principles of sedition, had embarked in this extravagant and desperate cause. They made themselves masters of the city of Munster, deposed the magistrates, and committed all the enormous crimes, and ridiculous follies, which the most perverse and infernal imagination could suggest.* John Bockhold was proclaimed king and legislator of this new hierarchy; but his reign was transitory, and his end deplorable; for Munster was, in 1536, retaken after a long siege by its bishop and sovereign, count Waldeck, the New Jerusalem of the Anabaptists destroyed, and its mock monarch punished with a most painful and ignominious death.† The disorders occasioned by the Anabaptists at this period, not only in Westphalia, but also in other parts of Germany,‡ showed too plainly to what horrid extremities the pernicious doctrines of this wrong-headed sect were calculated to lead the inconsiderate and unwary; and therefore it is not at all to be wondered, that the secular arm employed rigorous measures to extirpate a faction, which was the occasion, and the source, of unspeakable calamities in so many countries.*

VIII. While the terrors of death, in the most dreadful forms, were presented to the view of this miserable sect, and numbers of them were executed every day, without a proper distinction being made between the innocent and the guilty, those who escaped the severity of justice were in the most discouraging situation that can well be imagined. On the one hand, they beheld, with sorrow, all their hopes blasted by the total defeat of their brethren at Munster; and, on the other, they were filled with the most anxious apprehensions of the perils that threatened them on all sides. In this critical situation they derived much comfort and assistance from the counsels and zeal of Menno Simonis, a native of Friseland, who had formerly been a popish priest, and, as he himself confesses, a notorious profligate. This man went over to the Anabaptists at first, in a clandestine manner, and frequented their assemblies with the utmost secrecy; but, in 1436, he threw off the mask, resigned his rank and office in the Romish Church, and publicly embraced their communion. About a year after this, he was earnestly solicited by many of the sect to assume among them the rank and functions of a public teacher; and as he looked upon the persons, from whom this proposal came, to be exempt from the fanatical phrenzy of their brethren at Munster, (though, according to other accounts, they were originally of the same stamp, only rendered somewhat wiser by their sufferings,) he yielded to their entreaties. From this period to the end of his days, that is, during the space of twenty-five years, he travelled from one country to another with his wife and children,

* Bockhold, or Bockelson, aliis John of Leyden, who headed them at Munster, ran naked in the streets, married eleven wives, at the same time, to show his approbation of polygamy; and entitled himself king of Sion; all which formed but a very small part of the pernicious follies of this mock monarch.

† See Anton. Corvini Narratio de miserabili Monaster. Anabapt. Excidio.—Casp. Sagittar. Introduct. in Histor. Ecclesiast. tom. i. p. 537 and 835.—Herm. Hamelmann, Historia Renati Evangelii in urbe Monaster. in Operib. Genealogico-Historicis, p. 1203.—The elegant Latin poem of Bolandus in elegiac verse, entitled, J. Fabricii Bolandi Motus Monasteriens. Libri decem,—Herm. Kerssenbrock, Histor. Belli Monaster. edited by Dan. Gerdes in Miscellan. Groningens. Nov. tom. ii. The last-mentioned author speaks also of Bernard Rothman, an ecclesiastic of Munster, who had introduced the reformation into that city, but afterwards was infected with the enthusiasm of the Anabaptists; and who, though, in other respects he had shown himself to be neither destitute of learning nor of virtue, yet enlisted himself in this fanatical tribe, and had a share in their most turbulent and furious proceedings.

☞ ‡ The scenes of violence, tumult, and sedition, that were exhibited in Holland by this odious tribe, were likewise terrible. They formed the design of reducing the city of Leyden to ashes, but were happily prevented, and severely punished. John of Leyden, the Anabaptist king of Munster, had taken it into his head that God had made him a present of the cities of Amsterdam, Deventer, and Wesel; in consequence of which, he sent bishops to these three places, to preach *his* gospel of sedition and carnage. About the beginning of the year 1535, twelve Anabaptists, of whom five were women, assembled at midnight in a private house at Amsterdam. One of them, who was a tailor by profession, fell into a trance, and, after having preached and prayed during the space of four hours, stripped himself naked, threw his clothes into the fire, and commanded all the assembly to do the same, in which he was obeyed without the least reluctance. He then ordered them to follow him through the streets in this state of nature, which they accordingly did, howling and bawling out, "Wo! wo! the wrath of God! wo to Babylon!" When, after being seized and brought before the magistrates, clothes were offered them to cover their indecency, they refused them obstinately, and cried aloud, "We are the naked truth." When they were brought to the scaffold, they sang, danced, and discovered all the marks of enthusiastic phrenzy. These tumults were followed by a regular and deep laid conspiracy, formed by Van Geelen (an envoy of the mock king of Munster, who had made a very considerable number of proselytes) against the magistrates of Amsterdam, with a design to wrest the government of that city out of their hands. This incendiary marched with his fanatical troops to the town-house on the day appointed, drums beating, and colours flying, and fixed there his head-quarters. He was attacked by the burghers, who were assisted by some regular troops, and headed by several of the burgomasters of the city. After an obstinate resistance, he was surrounded with his whole troop, who were put to death in the severest and most dreadful manner, to serve as examples to the other branches of the sect, who were exciting commotions of a like nature in Friseland, Groningen, and other provinces and cities in the Netherlands.

* Ger. Brandt. Histor. Reform. Belgicæ tom i. lib. ii.

exercising his ministry under a series of pressures and calamities of various kinds, and constantly exposed to the danger of falling a victim to the severity of the laws. East and West Friseland, together with the province of Groningen, were first visited by the zealous apostle of the Anabaptists: thence he directed his course into Holland, Guelderland, Brabant, and Westphalia, continued it through the German provinces on the coast of the Baltic sea, and penetrated as far as Livonia. In all these places his ministerial labours were attended with remarkable success, and added to his sect a prodigious number of proselytes. Hence he is deservedly looked upon as the common chief of almost all the Anabaptists, and the parent of the sect that still subsists under that denomination. The success of this missionary will not appear very surprising to those who are acquainted with his character, spirit, and talents, and who have a just notion of the state of the Anabaptists at the period now under consideration. Menno was a man of genius; though, as his writings show, his genius was not under the direction of a very sound judgment. He had the inestimable advantage of a natural and persuasive eloquence, and his learning was sufficient to make him pass for an oracle in the eyes of the multitude. He appears, moreover, to have been a man of probity, of a meek and tractable spirit, gentle in his manners, pliant and obsequious in his commerce with persons of all ranks and characters, and extremely zealous in promoting practical religion and virtue, which he recommended by his example, as well as by his precepts. A man of such talents and dispositions could not fail to attract the admiration of the people, and to gain a great number of adherents wherever he exercised his ministry. But no where could he expect a more plentiful harvest than among the Anabaptists, whose ignorance and simplicity rendered them peculiarly susceptible of new impressions, and who, having been long accustomed to leaders that resembled phrenetic Bacchanals more than Christian ministers, and often deluded by odious impostors, who involved them in endless perils and calamities, were rejoiced to find at length a teacher, whose doctrine and manners flattered them with the hopes of more prosperous days.*

IX. Menno drew up a plan of doctrine and discipline of a much more mild and moderate nature than that of the furious and fanatical Anabaptists already mentioned, but somewhat more severe, though more clear and consistent, than the doctrine of some of the wiser branches of that sect, who aimed at nothing more than the restoration of the Christian church to its primitive purity. Accordingly he condemned the plan of ecclesiastical discipline, that was founded on the prospect of a new kingdom, to be miraculously established by Jesus Christ on the ruins of civil government, and the destruction of human rulers, and which had been the pestilential source of such dreadful commotions, such execrable rebellions, and such enormous crimes. He declared, publicly, his dislike to that doctrine which pointed out the approach of a marvellous reformation in the church by the means of a new and *extraordinary* effusion of the Holy Spirit. He expressed his abhorrence of the licentious tenets which several of the Anabaptists had maintained, with respect to the lawfulness of polygamy and divorce; and finally considered, as unworthy of toleration, those fanatics who were of opinion that the Holy Ghost continued to descend into the minds of many chosen believers, in as extraordinary a manner as it did at the first establishment of the Christian church, and that it testified its peculiar presence to several of the faithful, by miracles, predictions, dreams, and visions of various kinds. He retained, indeed, the doctrines commonly received among the Anabaptists in relation to the baptism of infants, the *Millenium*, or thousand-years' reign of Christ upon earth, the exclusion of magistrates from the Christian church, the abolition of war, and the prohibition of oaths enjoined by our Saviour, and the vanity, as well as the pernicious effects, of human science. But, while Menno retained these doctrines in a general sense, he explained and modified them in such a manner, as made them resemble the religious tenets which were universally received in the protestant churches; and this rendered them agreeable to many, and made them appear inoffensive even to numbers who had no inclination to embrace them. Indeed, it so happened, that the nature of the doctrines, considered in themselves, the eloquence of Menno, which set them off to such advantage, and the circumstances of the times, gave a high degree of credit to the religious system of this famous teacher among the Anabaptists, so that it made a rapid progress in that sect. And thus it was in consequence of the ministry of Menno that the different sorts of Anabaptists agreed together in excluding from their communion the fanatics who dishonoured it, and in renouncing all tenets that were detrimental to the authority of civil government, and, by an unexpected coalition, formed themselves into one community.*

* Menno was born in the neighbourhood of Bolswert in Friseland, in 1505, and not in 1496, as most writers affirm. After a life of toil, peril, and agitation, he died in peace in 1561, at the country seat of a certain nobleman, (not far from the city of Oldesloe in Holstein,) who, moved with compassion at a view of the perils to which Menno was exposed, and the snares that were daily laid for his ruin, took him, with some of his associates, into his protection, and gave him an asylum. We have a particular account of this famous Anabaptist in the Cimbria Literata of Mollerus, tom. ii. p. 835. See also Schyn's Plenior Deduct. Histor. Mennon. cap. vi. p. 116.—The writings of Menno, which are almost all composed in the Dutch language, were published at Amsterdam, in 1651. An excessively diffused and rambling style, frequent and unnecessary repetitions, an irregular and confused method, with other defects of equal moment, render the perusal of these productions highly disagreeable.

* These facts show us plainly how the famous question concerning the origin of the modern Anabaptists may be resolved. The Mennonites oppose, with all their might, the account of their descent from the ancient Anabaptists, which we find in so many writers, and would willingly give the modern Anabaptists a more honourable origin. (See Schyn's Histor. Mennonitar. cap. viii. ix. xxi. p. 223.) The reason of their zeal in this matter is evident. Their situation has rendered them timorous. They live as

X. To preserve a spirit of union and concord in a body composed of such a motley multitude of dissonant members, required more than human power; and Menno neither had, nor pretended to have, supernatural succours. Accordingly, the seeds of dissension were, in a little time, sown among this people. About the middle of this century, a warm contest, concerning excommunication, was excited by several Anabaptists, headed by Leonard Bowenson and Theodore Philip; and its fruits are yet visible in that divided sect. These men carried the discipline of excommunication to an enormous degree of severity. They not only maintained, that open transgressors, even those who sincerely deplored and lamented their faults, should, without any previous warning or admonition, be expelled from the communion of the church, but were also audacious enough to pretend to exclude the persons, thus excommunicated, from all intercourse with their wives, husbands, brothers, sisters, children, and other relatives. The same persons, as might naturally be expected from this instance of their severity, were harsh and rigid in their manners, and were for imposing upon their brethren a course of moral discipline, which was difficult and austere in the highest degree. Many of the Anabaptists protested against this, as unreasonable and unnecessary; and thus the community was suddenly divided into two sects, one of which treated transgressors with lenity and moderation, while the other proceeded against them with the utmost rigour. Nor was this the only difference that was observable in the conduct and manners of these two parties, since the members of the latter sect were remarkable for the sordid austerity that reigned in their rules of life and practice, while the former, considering more wisely the present state of human nature, were less severe in their injunctions, and were not altogether regardless of what is called decent, agreeable, and ornamental in life and manners. Menno employed his most vigorous

---

it were, in the midst of their enemies, and are constantly filled with an uneasy apprehension, that, at some time or other, malevolent zealots may take occasion, from their supposed origin, to renew against them the penal laws, by which the seditious Anabaptists of ancient times suffered in such a dreadful manner. At least, they imagine that the odium under which they lie, will be greatly diminished, if they can prove, to the satisfaction of the public, the falsehood of the general opinion, that "the Mennonites are the descendants of the Anabaptists;" or, to speak more properly, "the same individual sect, purged indeed from the fanaticism that formerly disgraced it, and rendered wiser than their ancestors, by reflection and suffering."

After comparing diligently and impartially what has been alleged by the Mennonites and their adversaries in relation to this matter, I cannot see what it is properly, that forms the subject of their controversy; and if the merits of the case be stated with accuracy and perspicuity, I do not see how there can be any dispute at all about the matter now under consideration. For, in the first place, if the Mennonites mean nothing more than this, that Menno, whom they considered as their parent and their chief, was not infected with those odious opinions which drew the just severity of the laws upon the Anabaptists of Munster; that he neither looked for a new and spotless kingdom that was to be miraculously erected on earth, nor excited the multitude to depose magistrates, and abolish civil government; that he neither deceived himself, nor imposed upon others, by fanatical pretensions to dreams and visions of the supernatural kind; if (I say) this be all that the Mennonites mean, when they speak of their chief, no person, acquainted with the history of their sect, will pretend to contradict them. Even those who maintain that there was an immediate and intimate connexion between the ancient and modern Anabaptists, will readily allow to be true, all that has been here said of Menno.—2dly, If the Anabaptists maintain, that such of their churches as received their doctrine and discipline from Menno, have not only discovered, without interruption, a pacific spirit and an unlimited submission to civil government. (abstaining from every thing that bears the remotest aspect of sedition, and showing the utmost abhorrence of wars and bloodshed,) but have even banished from their confessions of faith, and their religious instructions, all those tenets and principles which led the ancient Anabaptists to disobedience, violence, and rebellion; this also will be readily granted.—And if they allege, in the third place, that even the Anabaptists who lived before Menno, were not *all* so delirious as Munzer, or so outrageous as the fanatical members of the sect, who rendered their memory eternally odious by the enormities they committed at Munster; that, on the contrary, many of these ancient Anabaptists abstained religiously from all acts of violence and sedition, followed the pious examples of the ancient Waldenses, Henricians, Petrobrusians, Hussites, and Wickliffites, and adopted the doctrine and discipline of Menno, as soon as that new parent arose to reform and patronise the sect; all this will be allowed without hesitation.

But, on the other hand, the Mennonites may assert many things in defence of the purity of their origin, which cannot be admitted by any person who is free from prejudice, and well acquainted with their history. If they maintain, 1st, that none of their sect descended, by birth, from those Anabaptists, who involved Germany and other countries in the most dreadful calamities, or that none of these furious fanatics adopted the doctrine and discipline of Menno, they may be easily refuted by a great number of facts and testimonies, and particularly by the declarations of Menno himself, who glories in his having conquered the ferocity, and reformed the lives and errors of many members of this pestilential sect. Nothing can be more certain than this fact, viz. that the first Mennonite congregations were composed of the different sorts of Anabaptists already mentioned, of those who had been always inoffensive and upright, and of those who, before their conversion by the ministry of Menno, had been seditious fanatics. Nor can the acknowledgment of this incontestable fact be a just matter of reproach to the Mennonites, or be more dishonourable to them, than it is to us, that our ancestors were warmly attached to the idolatrous and extravagant worship of paganism or popery.—Again, it will not be possible for us to agree with the Mennonites, if they maintain, 2dly, that their sect does not retain, at this day, any of those tenets, or even any remains of those opinions and doctrines which led the seditious and turbulent Anabaptists of old to the commission of so many, and of such enormous crimes. For, not to mention Menno's calling the Anabaptists of Munster his *Brethren*, (a denomination indeed somewhat softened by the epithet of *erring*, which he joined to it,) it is undoubtedly true, that the doctrine concerning the nature of Christ's kingdom, or the church of the New-Testament, which led by degrees the ancient Anabaptists to those furious acts of rebellion that rendered them so odious, is by no means effaced in the minds of the modern Mennonites. It is, indeed, weakened and modified in such a manner as to have lost its noxious qualities, and to be no longer pernicious in its influence; but it is not totally renounced or abolished.—I shall not now inquire how far even the reformed and milder sect of Menno has been, in time past, exempt from tumults and commotions of a grievous kind, nor shall I examine what passes at this day among the Anabaptists in general, or in particular branches of that sect, since it is certain, that the more eminent communities of that denomination, particularly those that flourish in North Holland, and the places adjacent, behold fanatics with the utmost aversion, as appears evidently from this circumstance, among others, that they will not suffer the people called Quakers to enter into their communion.

efforts to heal these divisions, and to restore peace and concord in the community; but, when he perceived that his attempts were vain, he conducted himself in such a manner as he thought the most proper to maintain his credit and influence among both parties. For this purpose he declared himself for neither side, but was constantly trimming between the two, as long as he lived; at one time, discovering an inclination toward the austere Anabaptists; and, at another, seeming to prefer the milder discipline and manners of the moderate brethren. But in this he acted in opposition to the plainest dictates of prudence; and accordingly the high degree of authority he enjoyed, rendered his inconstancy and irresolution not only disagreeable to both parties, but also the means of inflaming, instead of healing, their divisions.*

XI. These two sects are, to this very day, distinguished by the denomination of *fine* and *gross*,† or, to express the distinction in more intelligible terms, into *rigid* and *moderate* Anabaptists. The former observe, with the most religious accuracy, veneration, and precision, the ancient doctrine, discipline, and precepts of the purer sort of Anabaptists; the latter depart much more from the primitive sentiments, manners, and institutions of their sect, and more nearly approach those of the protestant churches. The gross or moderate Anabaptists consisted, at first, of the inhabitants of a district in North-Holland, called Waterland; and hence their whole sect received the denomination of Waterlandians.‡ The fine or rigid part of that community were, for the most part, natives of Flanders; and hence their sect acquired the denomination of Flemings or Flandrians. But new dissensions and contests arose among these rigid Anabaptists, not, indeed, concerning any point of doctrine, but about the manner of treating persons that were to be excommunicated, and other matters of inferior moment. Hence a new schism arose, and they were subdivided into two sects, distinguished by the appellations of Flandrians and Friselanders, who differed from each other in their manners and discipline. The members of a third division took the name of their country, like the two former sects, and were called Germans; for the Anabaptists of Germany passed in shoals into Holland and the Netherlands. But, in process of time, the greatest part of these three sects came over, by degrees, to the moderate community of the Waterlandians, with whom they lived in the strictest bonds of peace and union. Those among the rigid Anabaptists, who refused to follow this example of moderation, are still known by the denomination of the Old Flemings or Flandrians, but are few in number, when compared with the united congregations of the milder sects now mentioned.

XII. No sooner had the ferment of enthusiasm subsided among the Mennonites, than all the different sects, into which they had been divided, unanimously agreed to draw the whole system of their religious doctrine from the Holy Scriptures alone. To give a satisfactory proof of the sincerity of their resolution in this respect, they took care to have *Confessions* drawn up, in which their sentiments concerning the Deity, and the manner of serving him, were expressed in the terms and phrases of Holy Writ. The most ancient, and also the most respectable of these Confessions, is that which we find among the Waterlandians. Several others of later date, were also composed, some for the use of large communities, for the people of a whole district, and which were consequently submitted to the inspection of the magistrate; others designed only for the benefit of private societies.* It might not, perhaps, be amiss to inquire, whether all the tenets received among the Mennonites are faithfully exhibited and plainly expressed in these Confessions, or whether several points be not there omitted which relate to the internal constitution of this sect, and would give us a complete idea of its nature and tendency. One thing is certain, that whoever peruses these Confessions with an ordinary degree of attention, will easily perceive, that those tenets which appear detrimental to the interests of civil society, particularly such as relate to the prerogatives of magistracy, and the administration of oaths, are expressed with the utmost caution, and embellished with the greatest art, to prevent

* See the Historia Bellorum et Certaminum quæ, ab An. 1615, inter Mennonitas contigerunt, published by an anonymous Mennonite.—See also a German work by Simon Frederic Rues, entitled Nachrichten von dem Zustande der Mennoniten, published at Jena in 1743.

☞ † The terms *fine* and *gross* are a literal translation of *feinen* and *groben*, which are the German denominations used to distinguish these two sects. The same terms have been introduced among the protestants in Holland; the *fine* denoting a set of people, whose extraordinary and sometimes fanatical devotion resembles that of the English methodists; while the epithet *gross* is applied to the generality of Christians, who make no extraordinary pretensions to sanctity and devotion.

‡ See Fred. Spanhemii Elenchus Controvers. Theol. op. tom. iii. p. 772. The Waterlandians were also called Johannites, from John de Ries, who was of great use to them in many respects, and who, assisted by Lubert Gerard, composed their confession of faith in 1580. This confession (which far surpasses both in point of simplicity and wisdom all the other confessions of the Mennonites) has passed through several editions, and has been lately republished by Herman Schyn, in his Histor. Mennon. It was also illustrated in an ample Commentary, in 1686, by Peter Joannis, a native of Holland, and pastor among the Waterlandians. It has, however, been alleged, that this famous production is by no means the general confession of the Waterlandians, but the private one only of that particular congregation of which its author was the pastor. See Rues, Nachrichten, p. 93.

* See Schyn's Plenior Deduct. Hist. Mennon. cap iv. where he maintains, that "these Confessions prove as great an uniformity among the Mennonites, in relation to the great and fundamental doctrines of religion, as can be pretended to by any other Christian community." But should the good man even succeed in persuading us of this boasted uniformity, he will yet never be able to make his assertion go down with many of his own brethren, who are, to this day, quarrelling about several points of religion, and who look upon matters, which appear to him of little consequence, as of high moment and importance to the cause of true piety. And, indeed, how could any of the Mennonites, before the present (*eighteenth*) century, believe what Schyn here affirms, since it is well known, that they disputed about matters which he treats with contempt, as if they had been immediately connected with their eternal interests?

their bearing an alarming aspect. At the same time, the more discerning observer will see, that these embellishments are intended to disguise the truth, and that the doctrines of the Anabaptists, concerning the critical points above-mentioned, are not represented, in their public confessions, in their real colours.

XIII. The ancient Anabaptists, who trusted in an extraordinary direction of the Holy Spirit, were (under the pretended influence of so infallible a guide) little solicitous about composing a system of religion, and never once thought of instilling into the minds of the people just sentiments of the Deity. Hence warm dissensions arose among them, concerning matters of the highest consequence, such as the divinity of Christ, polygamy, and divorce. Menno and his disciples made some attempts to supply this defect. Yet we find, after his time, that the Mennonites, more especially those of the rigid class, carried the freedom of their religious speculations to such an excessive height, as bordered upon extravagance. This circumstance alone, were there no other, proves that the heads of this sect employed the smallest part of their zeal to prevent the introduction and propagation of error, and that they looked upon sanctity of life and manners alone as the essence of true religion. The Waterlandians, indeed, and after them the other Anabaptists, were obliged, at length, to draw up a summary of their doctrine, and to lay it before the public, in order to remove the odium that was cast upon them, on account of their bold tenets and their extravagant disputes, which were likely to involve them in the greatest calamities. But these confessions of the Mennonites were, in reality, little more than a method of defence, to which they were reduced by the opposition they met with, and must therefore be rather considered as an expedient to avert the indignation of their enemies, than as articles of doctrine, which all of them without exception were obliged to believe. For we do not find among the Mennonites (a part of the modern Waterlandians excepted) any injunction, which expressly prohibits individuals from entertaining or propagating religious opinions different from the public creed of the community; and, indeed, when we look attentively into the nature and constitution of this sect, it will appear to have been, in some measure, founded upon this principle, that practical piety is the essence of religion, and that the surest and most infallible mark of the true church is the sanctity of its members; it is at least certain, that this principle was always universally adopted by the Anabaptists.

XIV. If we are to form our judgment of the religion of the Mennonites from their public creeds and confessions, we shall find, that, though it differs widely from the doctrine of the Lutherans, it varies little in most points from that of the reformed church. They consider the sacraments in no other light, than as *signs* or symbols of the spiritual blessings administered in the Gospel; and their ecclesiastical discipline seems to be almost entirely the same with that of the Presbyterians. There are, however, peculiar tenets, by which they are distinguished from all other religious communities; and these may be reduced under three heads; for it is observable, that there are certain doctrines, which are holden in common by all the various sects of the Mennonites; others, which are only received in some of the more eminent and numerous sects of that community; (such were the sentiments of Menno, which hindered him from being universally acceptable to the Anabaptists;) and some, which are only to be found among the more obscure and inconsiderable societies of that denomination. These last, indeed, appear and vanish, alternately, with the transitory sects that adopt them, and therefore do not deserve to engage our attention.

XV. The opinions, entertained by the Mennonites in general, seem to be derived from this leading and fundamental principle, that 'the kingdom which Christ established upon earth is a visible church, or community, into which the holy and the just are alone to be admitted, and which is consequently exempt from all those institutions and rules of discipline that have been invented by human wisdom for the correction and reformation of the wicked.'

This fanatical principle was frankly avowed by the ancient Mennonites: their more immediate descendants, however, began to be less ingenuous; and, in their public confessions of faith, they either disguised it under ambiguous phrases, or expressed themselves as if they meant to renounce it. To renounce it entirely was, indeed, impossible, without falling into the greatest inconsistency, and undermining the very foundation of those doctrines which distinguished them from all other Christian societies.* And yet it is certain that the present Mennonites, as they have, in many other respects, departed from the principles and maxims of their ancestors, have also given a striking instance of defection in the case now before us, and have almost wholly relinquished this fundamental doctrine of their sect, relating to the nature of the Christian church. A dismal experience has convinced them of the absurdity

* That they did not entirely relinquish it, is evident from their own creeds and confessions, even from those in which the greatest caution has been employed to conceal the principles that rendered their ancestors odious, and to disguise whatever might render themselves liable to suspicion. For example, they speak in the most pompous terms concerning the dignity, excellence, utility, and divine origin, of civil magistrates; and I am willing to suppose that they speak their real sentiments in this matter. But, when they proceed to give reasons that prevent their admitting magistrates into their communion, they discover unwarily the very principles which they are otherwise so studious to conceal. Thus, in the thirtieth article of the Waterlandian Confession, they declare, that "Jesus Christ has not comprehended the institution of civil magistracy in his spiritual kingdom, in the church of the New Testament, nor has he added it to the offices of his church." The Latin words are: "Potestatem hanc politicam Dominus Jesus in regno suo spirituali, ecclesia Novi Testamenti, non instituit, neque hanc officiis ecclesiæ suæ adjunxit." Hence it appears, that the Mennonites look upon the church of the New Testament as a holy republic, inaccessible to the wicked, and, consequently, exempt from those institutions and laws which are necessary to oppose the progress of iniquity. Why then do they not speak plainly, when they deliver their doctrine concerning the nature of the church, instead of affecting ambiguity and evasions?

of this chimerical principle, which the dictates of reason, and the declarations of Scripture, had demonstrated sufficiently, but without effect. Now, that the Mennonites have opened their eyes, they seem to be pretty generally agreed about the following tenets: first, That there is an invisible church, which is universal in its extent, and is composed of members from all the sects and communities that bear the Christian name: secondly, That the mark of the true church is not, as their former doctrine supposed, to be sought in the unspotted sanctity of all its members, (since they acknowledge that the visible church is promiscuously composed of the righteous and the wicked,) but in the knowledge of the truth, as it was delivered by Christ, and in the agreement of all the members of the church in professing and defending it.

XVI. Notwithstanding all this, it is manifest, beyond all possibility of contradiction, that the religious opinions which still distinguish the Mennonites from all other Christian communities, flow directly from the ancient doctrine of the Anabaptists concerning the nature of the church. It is in consequence of this doctrine, that they admit none to the sacrament of baptism, but persons who are come to the full use of their reason; because infants are incapable of binding themselves by a solemn vow to a holy life, and it is altogether uncertain whether, in mature years, they will be saints or sinners. Influenced by the same doctrine, they neither admit civil rulers into their communion, nor allow any of their members to perform the functions of magistracy; for, where there are no malefactors, magistrates are useless. Hence they pretend also to deny the lawfulness of repelling force by force, and consider war, in all its shapes, as unchristian and unjust; for, as those who are *perfectly holy*, can neither be provoked by injuries, nor commit them, they do not stand in need of the force of arms, either for the purposes of resentment or defence. It is still the same principle that excites in them the utmost aversion to the execution of justice, and more especially to capital punishments; since according to this principle, there are no transgressions or crimes in the kingdom of Christ, and consequently no occasion for the arm of the judge. Nor can it be imagined, that they should refuse to confirm their testimony by an oath upon any other foundation than this, that the perfect members of a holy church can neither dissemble nor deceive. It was certainly then the ancient doctrine of the Anabaptists, concerning the sanctity of the church, that gave rise to the tenets now mentioned, and was the source of that rigid and severe discipline, which excited such tumults and divisions among the members of that community.

XVII. The rules of moral discipline, formerly observed by the Mennonites, were rigorous and austere in the highest degree, and thus every way conformable to the fundamental principle, which has been already mentioned as the source of all their peculiar tenets. It is somewhat doubtful whether these rules still subsist and are respected among them; but it is certain, that in former times their moral precepts were very severe. And indeed it could not well be otherwise: for, when these people had once imbibed a notion that sanctity of manners was the *only* genuine mark of the true church, it may well be imagined, that they would spare no pains to obtain this honourable character for their sect; and that, for this purpose, they would use the strictest precautions to guard their brethren against disgracing their profession by immoral practices. Hence it was, that they unanimously, and no doubt justly, exalted the rules of the Gospel, on account of their transcendant purity. They alleged, that Christ had promulgated a new law of life, far more perfect than that which had been delivered by Moses and the prophets; and they excluded from their communion all such as deviated, in the least, from the most rigorous rules of simplicity and gravity in their looks, their gestures, their clothing, and their tables; all whose desires surpassed the dictates of mere necessity; and even all who observed a certain decorum in their manners, and paid a decent regard to the innocent customs of the world. But this primitive austerity is greatly diminished in the more considerable sects of the Mennonites, and more especially among the Waterlandians and Germans. The opulence they have acquired, by their industry and commerce, has relaxed their severity, softened their manners, and rendered them less insensible of the sweets of life; so that at this day the Mennonite congregations furnish their pastors with as much matter of censure and admonition as any other Christian communion.* There are, however, still some remains of the abstinence and severity of manners that prevailed formerly among the Anabaptists; but these are only to be found among some of the smaller sects of that persuasion, and more particularly among those who live remote from great and populous cities.

XVIII. The particular sentiments and opinions that divided the more considerable societies of the Mennonites, were those which follow: 1. Menno denied that Christ derived from his mother the body he assumed; and thought, on the contrary, that it was produced out of nothing, in the womb of that blessed virgin, by the creative power of the Holy Ghost.† This opinion is yet firmly maintained by the ancient Flemings or rigid Anabaptists,

☞ * It is certain, that the Mennonites in Holland, at this day, are, in their tables, their equipages, and their country seats, the most luxurious part of the Dutch nation. This is more especially true of the Mennonites of Amsterdam, who are very numerous and opulent.

† This is the account that is given of the opinion of Menno by Herman Schyn, in his Plenior Deduct. Hist. Mennonit. which other writers represent in a different manner. After an attentive perusal of several passages in the writings of Menno, where he professedly handles this very subject, it appears to me more than probable, that he inclined to the opinion attributed to him in the text, and that it was in this sense only, that he supposed Christ to be clothed with a divine and celestial body; for that may, without impropriety, be called celestial and divine, which is produced immediately, in consequence of a creating act, by the Holy Ghost. It must, however, be acknowledged, that Menno does not seem to have been unchangeably wedded to this opinion: for, in several places, he expresses himself ambiguously on this head, and even sometimes falls into incon

but has, long since, been renounced by all other sects of that denomination.* 2. The more austere Mennonites, like their forefathers, not only animadvert, with the most unrelenting severity, upon actions manifestly criminal, and evidently repugnant to the divine laws, but also treat, in the same manner, the smallest marks of an internal propensity to the pleasures of sense, or of a disposition to comply with the customs of the world. They condemn, for example, elegant dress, rich furniture, every thing, in a word, that looks like ornament, or surpasses the bounds of absolute necessity. Their conduct also to offenders is truly merciless; for they expel them from the church without previous admonition, and never temper the rigour of their judgments by an equitable consideration of the infirmities of nature in this imperfect state. The other Mennonites are by no means chargeable with this severity toward their offending brethren; they exclude none from their communion but the obstinate contemners of the divine laws; nor do they proceed to this extremity even with regard to such, until repeated admonitions have proved ineffectual to reform them. 3. The more rigid Mennonites look upon excommunicated persons as the pests of society, who are to be avoided on all occasions, and to be banished from all the comforts of social intercourse. Neither the voice of nature, nor the ties of blood, are allowed to plead in their behalf, or to procure them the smallest degree of indulgence. In such a case the exchange of good offices, the sweets of friendly conversation, and the mutual effusions of tenderness and love, are cruelly suspended, even between parents and children, husbands and wives, and also in all the other endearing relations of human life. But the more moderate branches of this community have wisely rejected this unnatural discipline, and consider the honour and sanctity of the church as sufficiently vindicated, when its members avoid a close and particular intimacy with those who have been expelled from its communion. 4. The rigid Anabaptists enjoin it as an obligation upon their disciples, and the members of their community, to wash the feet of their guests as a token of brotherly love and affection, and in obedience to the example of Christ; which they suppose, in this case, to have the force of a positive command; and hence they are sometimes called *Podoniptæ*. But the other Mennonites deny that Christ meant, in this instance of his goodness and condescension, to recommend this custom to the imitation of his followers, or to give to his example, in this case, the authority of a positive precept.

XIX. The Anabaptists, however divided on other subjects, agreed in their notions of learning and philosophy, which, in former times, they unanimously considered as the pest of the Christian church, and as highly detrimental to the progress of true religion and virtue. Hence it happened, that among a considerable number of writers who, in this century, employed their pens in the defence of that sect, there is not one whose labours bear any inviting mark of learning and genius. The rigid Mennonites persevere still in the barbarous system of their ancestors, and, neglecting the improvement of the mind and the culture of the sciences, devote themselves entirely to trade, manual industry, and the mechanic arts. The Waterlandians, indeed, are honourably distinguished from all the other Anabaptists, in this, as well as in many other respects; for they permit several members of their community to frequent the public universities, and there to apply themselves to the study of languages, history, antiquities, and more especially of physic, whose utility and importance they do not pretend to deny; and hence it happens, that, in our times, so many pastors among the Mennonites assume the title and profession of physicians. It is not unusual to see Anabaptists of this more humane and moderate class engaged even in philosophical researches, to the excellence and advantages of which their eyes are, at length, so far opened, as to make them acknowledge their importance to the well-being of society. It was, no doubt, in consequence of this change of sentiment, that they erected, not long ago, a public seminary of learning at Amsterdam, in which there is always a person of eminent abilities chosen as professor of philosophy. But, though these moderate Anabaptists acknowledge the benefit that may be derived to civil society from the culture of philosophy and the sciences, they still persist so far in their ancient prejudices, as to deem theology a system that has no connexion with them; and, consequently, they are of opinion, that in order to preserve it pure and untainted, the utmost caution must be used not to blend the dictates of philosophy with the doctrines of religion It is farther to be observed, that, in the present times, even the Flemish or rigid Anabaptists begin gradually to divest themselves of their antipathy to learning, and allow their brethren

sistencies. Hence, perhaps, it may not be unreasonable to conclude, that he renounced indeed the common opinion concerning the origin of Christ's human nature, but was undetermined with respect to the hypothesis, which; among many that were proposed, it was proper to substitute in its place. ☞ See Fueslini Centuria I. Epistolar. a Reformator. Helveticis scriptar. p. 383.—Be that as it may, Menno is generally considered as the author of this opinion concerning the origin of Christ's body, which is still entertained by the more rigid part of his followers. It appears probable, nevertheless, that this opinion was much older than his time, and was only adopted by him with the other tenets of the Anabaptists. As a proof of this, it may be observed, that Bolandus, in his Poem, entitled, Motus Monasteriensis, lib. x. v. 49, plainly declares, that many of the Anabaptists of Munster (who certainly had not been instructed by Menno) held this very doctrine in relation to Christ's incarnation:

> Esse* Deum statuunt alii, sed corpore carnem
> Humanam sumto sustinuisse negant:
> At Diam mentem, tenuis quasi fauce canalis,
> Per Mariæ corpus virginis isse ferunt.

* Many writers are of opinion, that the Waterlandians, of all the Anabaptists, evinced the strongest propensity to adopt the doctrine of Menno, relating to the origin of Christ's body. See Histoire des Anabaptists, p. 223, and the Ceremonies et Coutumes de tous les Peuples du Monde, tom. iv. p. 200. But that these writers are in error, is abundantly manifest from the public Confession of Faith of the Waterlandians, composed by John de Ries. See also, for a farther refutation of this mistake, Herm. Schyn's Deduct. Plen. p. 165.

* Christum.

to apply themselves to the study of languages, history, and the sciences.

XX. That simplicity and ignorance, of which the ancient Anabaptists boasted, as the guardians of their piety and the sources of their felicity, contributed principally to the divisions that prevailed among them, even from their rise, in a degree unknown and unprecedented in any other Christian community. This will appear evident to such as inquire, with the smallest attention, into the more immediate causes of their dissensions; for it is observable, that their most vehement contests had not for their object any difference in opinion concerning the doctrines or mysteries of religion, but generally turned upon matters relating to the conduct of life, on what was lawful, decent, just, and pious, in actions and manners, and what, on the contrary, was to be deemed criminal, indecorous, unjust, or impious. These disputes were a natural consequence of their favourite principle, that holiness of life, and purity of manners, were the authentic marks of the true church. But the misfortune lay here, that, being ignorant themselves, and under the guidance of persons whose knowledge was little superior to theirs, they were unacquainted with the true method of determining, in a multitude of cases, what was pious, laudable and lawful, and what was impious, unbecoming, and criminal. The criterion they employed for this purpose was neither the decision of right reason, nor the authority of the divine laws, accurately interpreted, since their ignorance rendered them incapable of using these means of arriving at the truth. They judged, therefore, of these matters by the suggestions of fancy, and the opinions of others. But, as this method of discerning between right and wrong, decent and indecent, was extremely uncertain and precarious, and necessarily tended to produce a variety of decisions, according to the different feelings, fancies, tempers, and capacities of different persons, hence naturally arose diversity of sentiments, debates and contests of various kinds. These debates, produced schisms, which are never more easily excited, or more obstinately fomented and perpetuated, than where ignorance, the true source of bigotry, prevails.

XXI. The Mennonites, after having been long in an uncertain and precarious situation, obtained a fixed and unmolested settlement in the United Provinces, under the shade of a legal toleration procured for them by William, prince of Orange, the glorious founder of Belgic liberty. This illustrious chief, who acted from principle in allowing liberty of conscience and worship to Christians of different denominations, was moreover engaged, by gratitude, to favour the Mennonites, who had assisted him, in 1572, with a considerable sum of money, when his coffers were almost exhausted.* The fruits, however, of this toleration, were not immediately enjoyed by all the Anabaptists that were dispersed through the different provinces of the rising republic; for, in several places, both the civil magistrates and the clergy made a long and obstinate opposition to the will of the prince in this matter; particularly in the province of Zealand and the city of Amsterdam, where the plots formed by the Anabaptists, and the tumults they had excited, were still remembered by the people with horror.* This opposition, indeed, was in a great measure conquered before the conclusion of this century, partly by the resolution and influence of William the First, and his son Maurice, and partly by the exemplary conduct of the Mennonites, who manifested their zealous attachment to the republic on several occasions, and redoubled, instead of diminishing, the precautions which were calculated to remove all grounds of suspicion, and take from their adversaries every pretext which could render their opposition justifiable. But it was not before the following century, that their liberty and tranquillity were fixed upon solid foundations, when, by a Confession of Faith, published in 1626, they cleared themselves from the imputation of those pernicious and detestable errors which had been laid to their charge.†

XXII. The sectaries in England, who reject the custom of baptising infants, are not distinguished by the title of Anabaptists, but by that of Baptists. It is, however, probable, that they derive their origin from the German and Dutch Mennonites, and that, in former times, they adopted their doctrine in all its points. That, indeed, is by no means the case at present; for the English Baptists differ, in many things, both from the ancient and modern Mennonites. They are divided into two sects. The members of one sect are distinguished by the denomination of General or Arminian Baptists, on account of their rejection of the doctrine of absolute and unconditional decrees; and the others are called Particular or Calvinistical Baptists, from the striking resemblance of their religious system to that of the presbyterians, who have Calvin for their chief.‡ The Baptists of the latter sect settled chiefly in London, and in the adjacent towns and villages; and they have departed so far from the tenets of their ancestors, that, at this day, they retain no more of the peculiar doctrines and institutions of the Mennonites, than the administration of baptism by immersion, and the refusal of that sacrament to infants, and those of tender years; and consequently they have none of those scruples relating to oaths, wars, and the functions of magistracy, which still remain among even the most rational part of the Mennonites. They observe in their congregations the same rules of government, and the same forms of worship, that are followed by the presbyterians; and their community is under the direction of men eminent for their piety and learning.§ From their Confession of Faith, published in 1643, it appears plainly,

* See Brandt, Histoire de Reformatie in de Nederlande, vol. i. p. 525.—Ceremonies et Coutumes de tous les Peuples du Monde, tom. iv. p. 201.

* Brandt's Hist. book xi. p. 555, 586, 609; book xiv. p. 780; book xvi. p. 811.

† See Herm. Schyn's Deduct. Plen. cap. iv. p. 79.

‡ See Whiston's Memoirs of his Life and Writings, vol. ii. p. 461.

§ See a German work composed by Ant. William Bohm, under the title of the History of the Reformation in England, p. 151, 473, 536, 1152.

that their religious sentiments were then the same as they are at this day.*

XXIII. The General Baptists, or, as they are called by some, the Antipædobaptists, are dispersed in great numbers through several counties of England, and are, for the most part, persons of mean condition, and almost totally destitute of learning and knowledge. This latter circumstance will appear less surprising, when it is considered, that, like the ancient Mennonites, they profess a contempt of erudition and science. There is much latitude in their system of religious doctrine, which consists in such vague and general principles, as render their communion accessible to Christians of almost all denominations; and, accordingly, they tolerate, in fact, and receive among them, persons of every sect, even Socinians and Arians; nor do they reject, from their communion, any who profess themselves Christians, and receive the Scriptures as the source of truth, and the rule of faith.† They agree with the Particular Baptists in this circumstance, that they admit to baptism adult persons only, and administer that sacrament by dipping or total immersion; but they differ from them in another respect, that is, in their repeating the administration of baptism to those who had received it, either in a state of infancy, or by aspersion, instead of dipping; for, if the common accounts may be believed, the Particular Baptists do not carry matters so far. The following sentiments, rites, and tenets, are also peculiar to the former: 1. After the manner of the ancient Mennonites, they look upon their sect as the only true Christian church, and consequently shun, with the most scrupulous caution, the communion of all other religious societies. 2. They dip only once (and not three times, as is practised elsewhere) the candidates for baptism, and consider it as a matter of indifference, whether that sacrament be administered in the name of the Father, Son, and Holy Ghost, or in that of Christ alone. 3. They adopt the doctrine of Menno with respect to the Millenium, or the reign of the saints with Christ upon earth for a thousand years. 4. Many of them embrace his particular opinion concerning the origin of Christ's body.‡ 5. They look upon the precept of the apostles, prohibiting the use of blood and things strangled,* as a law that was designed to be in force in all ages and periods of the church. 6. They believe that the soul, from the moment that the body dies until its resurrection at the last day, remains in a state of perfect insensibility. 7. They use the ceremony of extreme unction. And, to omit matters of a more trifling nature, 8. Several of them observe the Jewish, as well as the Christian Sabbath.† These Baptists have three different classes of ecclesiastical governors, bishops, elders, and deacons; the first of these, among whom there have been several learned men,‡ they modestly call messengers,§ as St. John is known to have styled that order in the book of the Revelations.

XXIV. Before we conclude the history of the Anabaptists, it may not be improper to mention a very singular and ridiculous sect that was founded by David George, a native of Delft, and a member of that community. This enthusiast, after having laid the foundation of the sect of the Davidists, or David-Georgians, deserted the Anabaptists, and removed to Basil, in 1544, where he changed his name, and by the liberality and splendour that attended his opulence, joined to his probity and purity of manners, acquired a very high degree of esteem, which he preserved till his death. The lustre of his reputation was, however, transitory; for, soon after his decease, which happened in 1556, his son-in-law, Nicholas Blesdyck, charged him with having maintained the most blasphemous and pestilential errors. The senate of Basil, before whom this accusation was brought, being satisfied with the evidence by which it was supported, pronounced sentence against the deceased heretic, and ordered his body to be dug up and publicly burned. And indeed, nothing more horridly impious and extravagant can be conceived, than the sentiments and tenets of this fanatic, if they were really such as they have been represented, either by his accusers or his historians; for he is said to have given himself out for the Son of God, the fountain of divine wisdom, to have denied the existence of angels, good and evil, of heaven and hell, and to have rejected the doctrine of a future judgment; and he is also charged with having trampled upon all the rules of decency and modesty with the utmost contempt.|| In all

* Bibliotheque Britannique, tom. vi.

† This appears evidently from their Confession of Faith, which appeared first in 1660, was re-published by Mr. Whiston, in the Memoirs of his Life, vol. ii. p. 561, and is drawn up with such latitude, that, with the removal and alteration of a few points,* it may be adopted by Christians of all denominations.† Mr. Whiston, though an Arian, became a member of this Baptist community, which, as he thought, came nearest to the simplicity of the primitive and apostolic age. The famous Mr. Emlyn, who was persecuted on account of his Socinian principles, joined himself also to this society, and died in their communion.

☞ ‡ Namely, that the body of Jesus was not derived from the substance of the blessed Virgin, but was *created* in her womb by an omnipotent act of the Holy Spirit.

☞ * Namely, those relating to universal redemption, the perseverance of the saints, election and reprobation, which are illustrated entirely on Arminian principles, and consequently cannot be embraced by rigid Calvinists; not to mention the points relating to baptism, which are the distinctive marks of this sect.

☞ † Our author certainly does not mean to include Roman catholics, in this large class; for then his assertion would not be true.

* Acts xv. 29.

† These accounts of the doctrine of the Baptists are taken from Wall's History of Infant Baptism, vol. ii. and also from the second volume of Whiston's Memoirs.

‡ See Whiston's Memoirs, vol. ii. p. 466, as also Crosby's History of the English Baptists.

§ St. John calls them the "angels of the churches;' the word angel (in Greek αγγελος) signifies properly an envoy or messenger.

|| See Nic. Blesdyckii Historia Davidis Georgii a Jacobo Revio edita; as also the life of the same fanatic, written in the German language, by Stolterforth. Among the modern writers see Arnold's Kirchen und Ketzer Historie, tom. i. p. 750; tom. ii. p. 534 and 1183, in which there are several things that tend to clear the character of David. See also Henr. Mori Enthusiasmus Triumphatus, sect. xxiii.—and the documents I have published in relation to this matter, in the History of Servetus, p. 425.

this, however, there may be much exaggeration. The enthusiast in question, though a man of some natural genius, was, nevertheless, totally destitute of learning of every kind, and had something obscure, harsh, and illiberal in his manner of expression, that gave too much occasion to an unfavourable interpretation of his religious tenets. That he had both more sense and more virtue than he is generally supposed to have possessed, appears manifestly, not only from his numerous writings, but also from the simplicity and candour that were visible in the temper and spirit of the disciples he left behind him, some of whom are yet to be found in Holstein, Friseland, and other countries.* He deplored the decline of vital and practical religion, and endeavoured to restore it among his followers; and in this he seemed to imitate the example of the more moderate Anabaptists. But the excessive warmth of an irregular imagination threw him into illusions of the most dangerous and pernicious kind, and seduced him into a persuasion that he was honoured with the gift of divine inspiration, and had celestial visions constantly presented to his mind. Thus was he led to such a high degree of fanaticism, that, rejecting as mean and useless the external services of piety, he reduced religion to contemplation, silence, and a certain frame or habit of soul, which it is equally difficult to define and to understand. The soaring Mystics, and the visionary Quakers, may therefore, if they please, give David George a distinguished rank in their enthusiastical community.

XXV. Henry Nicolas, a Westphalian, one of the intimate companions of this fanatic, though somewhat different from him in the nature of his enthusiasm, and also in point of genius and character, founded a sect in Holland, in 1555, which he called the *Family of Love.* The principles of this sect were afterwards propagated in England, and produced no small confusion in both countries. The judgment that has been formed with respect to David George may be applied with truth, at least in a great measure, to his associate Nicolas, who, perhaps, would have prevented a considerable part of the heavy reproaches with which he has been loaded, had he been endowed with a degree of genius, discernment and knowledge, sufficient to enable him to express his sentiments with perspicuity and elegance. Be that as it may, the character, temper, and views of this man, may be learned from the spirit that reigned in his flock.† As to his pretensions, they were, indeed, visionary and chimerical; for he maintained, that he had a commission from heaven, to teach men that the essence of religion consisted in the feelings of divine love; that all other theological tenets, whether they related to objects of faith, or modes of worship, were of no moment; and consequently, that it was a matter of perfect indifference, what opinions Christians entertained concerning the divine nature, provided their hearts burned with the pure and sacred flame of piety and love. To this, his main doctrine, Nicolas may have probably added other odd fancies, as always is the case with those innovators who are endued with a warm and fruitful imagination; to obtain, however, a true notion of the opinions of this enthusiast, it will be much more advisable to consult his own writings, than to depend entirely upon the accounts and refutations of his adversaries.*

* See Jo. Melleri Introduct. in Histor. Chersones. Cimbricæ, par. ii. p. 116, and his Cimbria Literata, tom. i. p. 422.

† See Jo. Hornbeck, Summa Controvers. lib. vi. p. 393.—Arnold, p. 746.—Bohm. book iv. ch. v. p. 541.

* The most learned of all the authors who wrote against the Family of Love, was Dr. Henry More, in his Grand Explanation of the Mystery of Godliness, &c. book vi. George Fox, the founder of the sect of Quakers, inveighed also severely against this seraphic family, and called them a motley tribe of fanatics, because they took oaths, danced, sang, and made merry. See Sewell's History of the Quakers, book iii. p. 88, 89, 344.

CHAPTER IV.

The History of the Socinians.

I. The Socinians are said to have derived this denomination from the illustrious family of the Sozzini, which flourished a long time at Sienna in Tuscany, and produced several great and eminent men, and among others Lælius and Faustus Socinus, who are commonly supposed to have been the founders of this sect. The former was the son of Marianus, a famous lawyer, and was himself a man of uncommon genius and learning; to which he added, as his very enemies were obliged to acknowledge, the lustre of a virtuous life and of unblemished manners. Being obliged to leave his country, in 1547, on account of the disgust he had conceived against popery, he travelled through France, England, Holland, Germany, and Poland, in order to examine the religious sentiments of those who had thrown off the yoke of Rome, and thus at length to come at the truth. After this he settled at Zurich, where he died in 1562, before he had arrived at the fortieth year of his age.† His mild and gentle disposition rendered him averse from whatever had the air of contention and discord. He adopted the Helvetic confession of faith, and professed himself a member of the church of Switzerland; and this did not induce him to conceal entirely the doubts he had formed in relation to certain points of religion, and which he communicated, in effect, by letter, to some learned men, whose judgment he respected, and in whose friendship he could confide.‡ His sentiments were indeed propagated, in a more public manner, after his death, since Faustus, his nephew and his heir, is supposed to have drawn, from the papers he left behind him, that religious system upon which the Socinian sect was founded.

II. It is, however, to be observed, that this denomination does not always convey the same ideas, since it is susceptible of different

† Cloppenburg, Dissertatio de Origine et Progressu Socinianismi.—Jo. Hornbeck, Summa Controversiarum, p. 563.—Jo. Henr. Hottinger, Hist. Eccles. tom ix. p. 417.

‡ Zanchius, Præf. ad Libr. de tribus Elohim. Beza, Epist. lxxxi. p. 167. Certain writings are attributed to him by Sandius, in his Bibliotheca Anti-Trinitar. but it is very doubtful whether he was the real author of them.

significations, and is, in effect, used sometimes in a more strict and proper, and at others in a more improper and extensive sense. For, according to the usual manner of speaking, all are termed Socinians, whose sentiments bear a certain affinity to the system of Socinus; and those are more especially ranked in that class, who either boldly deny, or artfully explain away, the doctrines that assert the divine nature of Christ, and a trinity of persons in the Godhead. But, in a strict and proper sense, they only are deemed the members of this sect, who embrace wholly, or with a few exceptions, the form of theological doctrine, which Faustus Socinus either drew up himself or received from his uncle, and delivered to the Unitarian brethren, or Socinians, in Poland and Transylvania.*

III. The origin of Socinianism may be traced to the earliest period of the Reformation. Scarcely had the happy revolution in the state of religion taken place, when a set of men, fond of extremes, and consequently disposed to look upon as erroneous whatever had hitherto been taught and professed in the church of Rome, began to undermine the doctrine of Christ's divinity, and the other truths that are connected with it, and proposed reducing the whole of religion to practical piety and virtue. The efforts of these men were opposed with united zeal and vigilance by the Romish, Reformed, and Lutheran churches; and their designs were so far disconcerted, as to prevent their forming themselves and their followers into a regular and permanent sect. So early as the year 1524, the divinity of Christ was openly denied by Louis Hetzer, one of the wandering and fanatical Anabaptists, who, about three years afterwards, suffered death at Constance.† There were not wanting, among the first Anabaptists, several persons who entertained the opinions of Hetzer, though it would be manifestly unfair to lay these opinions to the charge of the whole community. But it was not only from that quarter that erroneous opinions were propagated in relation to the points already mentioned; others seemed to have been seized with the contagion, and it manifested itself from day to day in several countries. John Campanus, a native of Juliers, disseminated at Wittenberg and other places, various tenets of an heretical aspect; and taught, among other things, that the Son was inferior to the Father, and that the Holy Ghost was not the title of a divine person, but a denomination used to denote the *nature* of the Father and of the Son: and thus did this innovator revive, in a grea measure, the errors of the ancient Arians.* A doctrine of a similar kind was propagated, in 1530, at Augsburg and in Switzerland, by a person, whose name was Claudius, who, by his opposition to the doctrine of Christ's divinity, excited no small commotions.† But none of these new teachers were so far encouraged by the number of their followers, or the indulgence of their adversaries, as to be in a condition to form a regular sect.

IV. The attempts of Michael Servede,‡ or Servetus, a Spanish physician, were much more alarming to those who had the cause of true religion at heart, than the feeble and impotent efforts of the innovators now mentioned This man, who made so great a noise in the world, was born at Villa-Nueva, in the kingdom of Arragon, distinguished himself by the superiority of his genius, and had made a considerable progress in various branches of science. In the years 1531 and 1532, he published, in Latin, his seven books concerning the errors that are contained in the doctrine of the Trinity, and two Dialogues on the same subject, in which he attacked, in the most audacious manner, the sentiments adopted by the greatest part of the Christian church, in relation to the divine nature, and a trinity of persons in the Godhead. Some years after this he travelled into France, and, after a variety of adventures, settled at Vienne in Dauphine, where he applied himself, with success, to the practice of physic. It was here, that, letting loose the reins of his warm and irregular imagination, he invented that strange system of theology, which was printed, in a clandestine manner, in 1553, under the title of Christianity restored. He seemed to be seized with a passion for reforming (in his way;) and many things concurred to favour his designs, such as the fire of his genius, the extent of his learning, the power of his eloquence, the strength of his resolution, the obstinacy of his temper, and an external appearance, at least, of piety, that rendered all the rest doubly engaging. Add, to all this, the protection and friendship

* We have, hitherto, no complete or accurate history either of the sect called Socinians, or of Lælius and Faustus Socinus, its founders; nor any satisfactory account of those who laboured principally with them, and, after them, in giving a permanent and stable form to this community; for the accounts we have of the Socinians, and their principal doctors, from Hornbeck,* Calovius,† Cloppenburg,‡ Sandius,§ Lubieniecius,‖ and Lauterbach,¶ are far from being proper to satisfy the curiosity of those, who desire something more than a vague and superficial knowledge of this matter. The history of Socinianism, published at Paris by Lamy in 1723, is a wretched compilation from the most common-place writers on that subject; it is also full of errors, and is loaded with a variety of matters that have no sort of relation to the history of Socinus, or to the doctrine he taught. The very learned and laborious La Croze promised a complete history of Socinianism, but did not fulfil this interesting engagement.

† Sandii Bibliotheca Anti-Trinitar.—Jo. Bapt. Ottii Annal. Anabaptist.—Breitingeri Museum Helveticum, tom. v. vi.

* In his Socinianism. Confutat. vol. i.—† In his Opera Anti-Sociniana.—‡ In his Dissertat. de origine et progressu Socinianismi, tom. ii. op.—§ In his Bibliotheca Anti-Trinitariorum.—‖ In his Historia Reformationis Polonicæ.—¶ In his Ariano-Socinismus

* See the Dissertation de Joh. Campano, Anti Trinitario, in the Amœnitates Literariæ of the learned Schelhornius, tom. xi.

† See Schelhornii Dissert. Epistol. de Mino Celso Senensi, Claudio item Allobroge, homine Fanatico et SS. Trinitatis hoste.—Jac. Breitingeri Museum Helvetic. tom. vii.—Jo. Hallerus, Epistol. in Fueslin's Centuria Epistolar. Viror Eruditor.

‡ By taking away the last syllable of this name (I mean the Spanish termination *de*) there remains *Serve*, which, by placing differently the letters that compose it, makes *Reves*. Servetus assumed the latter name in the title-pages of all his books. He also called himself sometimes *Michael Villanovanus*, or *Villanovanus* alone, after the place of his nativity omitting the name of his family.

of many persons of weight, in France, Germany, and Italy, which he had obtained by his talents and abilities both natural and acquired; and it will appear, that few innovators have set out with a better prospect of success. But, notwithstanding these signal advantages, all his views were totally disappointed by the vigilance and severity of Calvin, who, when Servetus had escaped from his prison, and was passing through Switzerland, in order to seek refuge in Italy, caused him to be apprehended at Geneva, in 1553, and had an accusation of blasphemy brought against him before the council.* The issue of this accusation was fatal to Servetus, who, adhering resolutely to the opinions he had embraced, was, by a public sentence of the court, declared an obstinate heretic, and condemned to the flames. For it is observable, that, at this time, the ancient laws which had been enacted against heretics by the emperor Frederic II. and had been so frequently renewed after his reign, were still in vigour at Geneva. It must, however, be acknowledged, that this learned and ingenious sufferer was worthy of a better fate; though it is certain, on the other hand, that his faults were neither few nor trivial, since it is well known, that his excessive arrogance was accompanied with a malignant and contentious spirit, an invincible obstinacy of temper, and a considerable portion of fanaticism.†

V. The religious system that Servetus struck out of a wild and irregular fancy, was, indeed, singular in the highest degree. The greatest part of it was a necessary consequence of his peculiar notions concerning the universe, the nature of God, and the nature of things, which were equally strange and chimerical. Thus it is difficult to unfold, in a few words, the doctrine of this unhappy man; nor, indeed, would any detail render it intelligible in all its branches. He took it into his head that the true and genuine doctrine of Christ had been entirely lost, even before the council of Nice; and he was, moreover, of opinion, that it had never been delivered with a sufficient degree of precision and perspicuity in any period of the church. To these extravagant assertions he added another still more so, even that he himself had received a commission from above to reveal anew this divine doctrine, and to explain it to mankind. His notions with respect to the Supreme Being, and a trinity of persons in the Godhead, were obscure and chimerical beyond all measure, and amounted in general to the following propositions: That "the Deity, before the creation of the world, had produced within himself two *personal representations* or *manners of existence*,* which were to be the *medium* of intercourse between him and mortals, and by which, consequently, he was to reveal his will, and to display his mercy and beneficence to the children of men; that these two representatives were the Word and the Holy Ghost; that the former was united to the man Christ, who was born of the Virgin Mary by an omnipotent act of the divine will and that, on this account, Christ might be properly called God; that the Holy Spirit directed the course, and animated the whole system of nature; and more especially produced in the minds of men wise counsels, virtuous propensities, and divine feelings; and, finally, that these two representations were to cease after the destruction of this terrestial globe, and to be absorbed into the substance of the Deity, from which they had been formed." This is, at least, a general sketch of the doctrine of Servetus, who, however, did not always explain his system in the same manner, nor take any pains to avoid inconsistencies and contradictions; and who frequently expressed himself in such ambiguous terms, that it is extremely difficult to learn from them his true sentiments. His system of morality agreed in many circumstances with that of the Anabaptists, whom he also imitated in censuring, with the utmost severity, the custom of Infant Baptism.

VI. The pompous plans of reformation, that had been formed by Servetus, were not only disconcerted, but even fell into oblivion, after the death of their author. He was, indeed, according to vulgar report, supposed to have left behind him a considerable number of disciples; and we find, in the writings of the doctors of this century, many complaints and apprehensions that seem to confirm this supposition, and would persuade us that Servetus had really founded a sect; yet, when this matter is attentively examined, there will appear just reason to doubt, whether this man left behind him any one person that might properly be called his true disciple. For those who were denominated Servetians by the theological writers of this century, not only differed from Servetus in many points of doctrine, but also varied widely from him in his opinion of the Trinity, which was the peculiar and distinguishing point of his theological system. Valentine Gentili, a Neapolitan, who suffered

☞ * This accusation was brought against Servetus by a person, who lived in Calvin's family as a servant; and this circumstance displeased many.

☞ † Dr. Mosheim refers the reader here, in a note, to an ample and curious history of Servetus, composed by him in his native tongue. Those who are not acquainted with that language, will find a full account of this singular man, and of his extraordinary history, in a Latin dissertation, composed under the inspection of Dr. Mosheim, and entitled, Historia Michaelis Serveti, quam, Præside Jo. Laur. Moshemio, Doctorum examini publice exponit Henricus ab Allwaerden.' There is an accurate history of this unhappy man, written by M. de la Roche, in the first volume of the work, entitled, Memoirs of Literature, containing a Weekly Account of the State of Learning, both at home and abroad. There is also an account of him given by Mackenzie, in his Lives and Characters of the most eminent Writers of the Scottish nation. To these we may add an Impartial History of Servetus, &c. written by an anonymous author, and published at London in 1724.

It is impossible to justify the conduct of Calvin in the case of Servetus, whose death will be an indelible reproach upon the character of that great and eminent reformer. The only thing that can be alleged, not to efface, but to diminish his crime, is, that it was no easy matter for him to divest himself at once of that persecuting spirit, which had been so long nourished and strengthened by the popish religion in which he was educated. It was a remaining portion of the spirit of popery in the breast of Calvin that kindled his unchristian zeal against he wretched Servetus.

☞ * These representations, or manners of existence, Servetus also called œconomies, dispensations, dispositions, &c. for he often changed his terms in unfolding his visionary system.

death at Bern in 1566, adopted the Arian hypothesis, and not that of Servetus, as many writers have imagined; for his only error consisted in this, that he considered the Son and the Holy Ghost as subordinate to the Father.* Nearly allied to this, was the doctrine of Matthew Gribaldi, a lawyer, whom a timely death saved from the severity of an ecclesiastical tribunal, that was ready to pronounce sentence against him on account of his errors; for he supposed the divine nature to be divided into three eternal spirits, which were distinguished from each other, not only by number, but also by subordination † It is not so easy to determine the particular charge that was brought against Alciat, a native of Piedmont, and Sylvester Tellius, who were banished from the city and territory of Geneva, in 1559; nor do we know, with certainty, the errors that were embraced by Paruta, Leonardo, and others,‡ who ranked among the followers of Servetus. It is, however, more than probable, that none of the persons now mentioned were the disciples of Servetus, or adopted the hypothesis of that visionary innovator. The same thing may be affirmed with respect to Gonesius, who is said to have embraced the doctrine of that unhappy man, and to have introduced it into Poland;§ for, though he maintained some opinions that really resembled it in some of its points, his manner of explaining the mystery of the Trinity was totally different from that of Servetus.

VII. It is evident that none of the persons, now mentioned, professed the form or system of theological doctrine, that is properly called *Socinianism*, the origin of which is, by the writers of that sect, dated from the year 1546, and placed in Italy. These writers tell us, that, in this year, above forty persons eminently distinguished by their learning and genius, and still more by their generous zeal for truth, held secret assemblies, at different times, in the territory of Venice, and particularly at Vicenza, in which they deliberated upon a general reformation of the received systems of religion, and, in a more especial manner, undertook to refute the peculiar doctrines that were afterwards publicly rejected by the Socinians. They tell us farther, that the principal members of this clandestine society, were Lælius Socinus, Alciat, Ochino, Paruta, and Gentili; that their design was divulged, and their meetings were discovered, by the temerity and imprudence of some of their associates; that two of them were apprehended and put to death; while the rest, being dispersed, sought a refuge in Switzerland, Germany, Moravia, and other countries; and that Socinus, after having wandered up and down in several parts of Europe, went into Poland, first in 1551, and afterwards in 1558, and there sowed the seeds of his doctrine, which grew apace, and produced a rich and abundant harvest.* Such is the account of the origin of Socinianism that is generally given by the writers of that sect. To assert that it is, in every circumstance, fictitious and false, would perhaps be going too far; but, on the other hand, it is easy to demonstrate that the system, commonly called Socinianism, was neither invented nor drawn up in the meetings at Venice and Vicenza.†

* See Bayle's Dictionary.—Spon's Hist. de Geneve, tom. ii. p. 80.—Sandii Biblioth. Anti-Trinit. p. 26—Lamy's Histoire du Socinianisme, part ii. ch. vi. p. 251.—Fueslin's Reformations Beytrage, tom. v.

† Sandius, p. 17.—Lamy, part ii. ch. vii.—Spon, tom. ii. p. 85. not.—Haller, in Museo Tigurino, tom. ii. p. 114.

‡ For an account of these, and other persons of the same class, see Sandius, Lamy, and also Lubieniecius' Historia Reformat. Polonicæ, lib. ii. cap. v.—There is a particular and ample account of Alciat given by Bayle, in his Dictionary; see also Spon, tom. ii.

§ This is affirmed upon the authority of Wissowatius and Lubieniecius; but the very words of the latter will be sufficient to show us upon what grounds. He says, "Is Serveti sententiam de præeminentia patris in patriam attulit, eamque non dissimulavit," i. e. Gonesius introduced into Poland the opinion embraced by Servetus in relation to the pre-eminence of the Father, and was by no means studious to conceal it. Who now does not see, that, if it was the *pre-eminence of the Father* that Gonesius maintained, he must have differed considerably from Servetus, whose doctrine removed all *real* distinction in the divine nature? The reader will do well to consult Sandius with regard to the sentiments of Gonesius, since it is from this writer, that Lamy has borrowed the greatest part of what he has advanced in his Histoire du Socinianisme, tom. ii. chap. x.

* See the Bibliotheca Anti-Trinit. of Sandius, who mentions some writings that are supposed to have been published by the clandestine society of pretended reformers at Venice and Vicenza, though the truth of this supposition is extremely dubious;—Andr. Wissowatii Narratio quomodo in Polonia Reformati ab Unitariis separati sunt, which is subjoined to the Biblioth. of Sandius.—The reader may likewise consult Lubieniecius, (Histor. Reformat. Polon. lib. ii. cap. i.) who intimates, that he took this account of the origin of Socinianism from the manuscript Commentaries of Budzinus, and his Life of Lælius Socinus. See also Sam. Przipcovius, in Vita Socini.

† See Gustav. Georg. Zeltneri Historia Crypto-Socinianismi Altorfini, cap. ii. sect. xli. p. 321, note. This writer seems to think that the inquiries hitherto made into this affair are by no means satisfactory; and he therefore wishes that some men of learning, equal to the task, would examine the subject anew. This, indeed, is much to be wished. In the mean time, I shall venture to offer a few observations, which may, perhaps, contribute to cast some light upon this matter. That there was in reality such a society as is mentioned in the text, is far from being improbable. Many circumstances and relations prove sufficiently, that, immediately after the Reformation had taken place in Germany, secret assemblies were holden, and measures proposed, in several provinces that were still under the jurisdiction of Rome, with a view to combat the errors and superstition of the times. It is also, in a more especial manner, probable that the territory of Venice was the scene of these deliberations, since it is well known that a great number of the Venetians at this time, though they had no personal attachment to Luther, approved his design of reforming the corrupt state of religion, and wished well to every attempt that was made to restore Christianity to its native and primitive simplicity. It is farther highly credible, that these assemblies were interrupted and dispersed by the vigilance of the papal emissaries, and that some of their members were apprehended and put to death, while the rest saved themselves by flight. All this is probable enough; but it is extremely improbable, and utterly incredible, that all the persons who are said to have been present at these assemblies, were really so. And I therefore willingly adopt the opinion of those who affirm, that many persons, who, in after-times, distinguished themselves from the multitude by opposing the doctrine of the Trinity in Unity, were considered as members of the Venetian society, by ignorant writers, who looked upon that society as the source and nursery of the whole Unitarian sect. It is certain, for i.

VIII. While, therefore, we reject this inaccurate account of the matter under consideration, it is incumbent upon us to substitute a better in its place; and, indeed, the origin and progress of the Socinian doctrine may, I think, easily be traced out by such as are acquainted with the history of the church during this century. There were certain sects and doctors, against whom the zeal, vigilance and severity of Catholics, Lutherans, and Calvinists, were united, and, in opposing whose settlement and progress, these three communions, forgetting their dissensions, joined their most vigorous counsels and endeavours. The objects of their common aversion were the Anabaptists, and those who denied the divinity of Christ, and a trinity of persons in the Godhead. To avoid the unhappy consequences of such a formidable opposition, great numbers of both classes retired into Poland, from this persuasion, that, in a country whose inhabitants were passionately fond of freedom, religious liberty could not fail to find a refuge. However, on their first arrival, they proceeded with circumspection and prudence, and explained their sentiments with much caution, and a certain mixture of disguise, not knowing surely what might happen, nor how far their opinions would be treated with indulgence. Thus they lived in peace and in quiet during several years, mixed with the Lutherans and Calvinists, who had already obtained a solid settlement in Poland, and who admitted them into their communion, and even into the assemblies where their public deliberations were holden. They were not, however, long satisfied with this state of constraint, notwithstanding the privileges with which it was attended; but, having insinuated themselves into the friendship of several noble and opulent families, they began to act with greater spirit, and even to declare, in an open manner, their opposition to certain doctrines that were generally received among Christians. Hence arose violent contests between them and the Swiss or reformed churches, with which they had been principally connected. These dissensions drew the attention of the government, and occasioned, in 1565, a resolution of the diet of Petrikow, ordering the innovators to separate themselves from the churches already mentioned, and to form a distinct congregation or sect.* These founders of the Socinian church were commonly called Pinczovians, from the town in which the heads of their sect resided. Hitherto, indeed, they had not carried matters so far as they did afterwards; for they professed chiefly the Arian doctrine concerning the divine nature, maintaining that the Son and the Holy Ghost were two distinct natures, begotten by God the Father, and subordinate to him.†

stance, that Ochino is erroneously placed among the members of the famous society now mentioned; for, not to insist upon the circumstance, that it is not sufficiently clear whether he was really a Socinian or not, it undeniably appears, from the Annales Capucinorum of Boverius, as well as from other unquestionable testimonies, that he left Italy so early as the year 1543, and went to Geneva. See a singular book, entitled, La Guerre Seraphique, ou l'Histoire des Perils qu'a courus la Barbe des Capucins, livr. iii. p 191, 216.—What I have said of Ochino may be confidently affirmed with respect to Lælius Socinus, who, though reported to have been at the head of the society now under consideration, was certainly never present at any of its meetings. For how can we suppose that a young man only one-and-twenty years old, would leave the place of his nativity, and repair to Venice or Vicenza without any other view than the pleasure of disputing freely on certain points of religion?* Or how could it happen, that a youth of such inexperienced years should acquire such a high degree of influence and authority, as to obtain the first rank, and the principal direction, in an assembly composed of so many eminently learned and ingenious men? Besides, from the life of Lælius, which is still extant, and from other testimonies of good authority, it is easy to show, that it was the desire of improvement and the hope of being aided in his inquiries after truth, by the conversation of learned men in foreign nations, that induced him to leave Italy, and not the apprehension of persecution and death, as some have imagined. It is also certain, that he returned into his native country afterwards, and, in 1551, remained some time at Sienna, while his father lived at Bologna. See his letter to Bullinger, in the Museum Helveticum, tom. v. p. 489. Now surely it cannot easily be imagined, that a man in his senses would return to a country from which, a few years before, he had been obliged to fly, in order to avoid the terrors of a barbarous inquisition and a violent death.

But, waving this question for a moment, let us suppose all the accounts we have from the Socinians, concerning this famous assembly of Venice and Vicenza, and the members of which it was composed, to be true and exact: yet it remains to be proved, that the Socinian system of doctrine was invented and drawn up in that assembly. This the Socinian writers maintain; and this, as the case appears to me, may be safely denied; for the Socinian doctrine is undoubtedly of much later date than this assembly; it also passed through different hands, and was, during many years, reviewed and corrected by men of learning and genius, and thus underwent various changes and improvements before it was formed into a regular, permanent, and connected system. To be convinced of this, it will be sufficient to cast an eye upon the opinions, doctrines, and reasonings of several of the members of the famous society, so often mentioned; which vary in such a striking manner, as to show manifestly that this society had no fixed views, nor had ever agreed upon any consistent form of doctrine. We learn, moreover, from many circumstances in the life and transactions of Lælius Socinus, that this man had not, when he left Italy, formed the plan of a regular system of religion; and it is well known, that, for many years afterwards, his time was spent in doubting, inquiring, and disputing; and that his ideas of religious matters were extremely fluctuating and unsettled; so that it seems probable to me, that the man died in this state of hesitation and uncertainty, before he had reduced his notions to any consistent form. As to Gribaldi and Alciat, who have been already mentioned, it is manifest that they inclined toward the Arian system, and did not entertain such low ideas of the person and dignity of Jesus Christ, as those which are adopted among the Socinians. From all this it appears abundantly evident, that these Italian reformers, if their famous society ever existed in reality, (which I admit as a probable supposition, rather than as a fact sufficiently attested,) were dispersed and obliged to seek their safety in a voluntary exile, before they had agreed about any regular system of religious doctrine; so that this account of the origin of Socinianism is rather imaginary than real, though it has been adopted by many writers. Fueslin has alleged several arguments against it in his German work entitled, *Reformations Beytragen*, tom. iii. page 327

☞ * Is such a supposition really so absurd? Is not a spirit of enthusiasm, or even an uncommon degree of zeal, adequate to the production of such an effect?

* Lamy's Histoire du Socinianisme, part i. chap. vi. &c. page 16—Stoinii Epitome Originis Unitariorum in Polonia, apud Sandium, p. 183.—Georg. Schomanni Testamentum, apud eundem, p. 194.—Andr. Wissowatius de Separatione Unitar. a Reformatis, p. 211.—Lubieniecius, Histor. Reformat. Polonicæ, lib. ii. cap. vi. viii. lib. iii. cap. i.

† This will appear abundantly evident to all such as consult, with a proper degree of attention, the

IX. The Unitarians, being thus separated from the other religious societies in Poland, had many difficulties to encounter, both of an internal and external kind. From without, they were threatened with a very unfavourable prospect, arising from the united efforts of Catholics, Lutherans, and Calvinists, to crush their infant sect. From within, they dreaded the effects of intestine discord, which portended the ruin of their community before it could arrive at any measure of stability or consistence. The latter apprehension had some foundation; for, as yet, they had agreed upon no regular system of principles, which might serve as a centre and bond of union. Some of them chose to persevere in the doctrine of the Arians, and to proceed no farther; and these were called *Farnovians*.* Others, more adventurous, went much greater lengths, and attributed to Jesus Christ scarcely any other rank and dignity than those of a divine messenger and a true prophet. A third class, distinguished by the denomination of *Budneians*,† went still farther; declaring that Christ was born in an ordinary way, according to the general law of nature, and that, consequently, he was no proper object of divine worship or adoration.‡ There were also among these people many fanatics, who were desirous of introducing into the society the discipline of the enthusiastic Anabaptists; such as a community of goods, an equality of rank, and other absurdities of the same nature.§ Such were the disagreeable and perilous circumstances in which the Unitarians were placed, during the infancy of that sect, and which, no doubt, rendered their situation extremely critical and perplexing. But they were happily extricated out of these difficulties by the dexterity and resolution of some of their doctors, whose efforts were crowned with singular success, on account of the credit and influence which they had obtained in Poland. These divines suppressed, in a little time, the factions that threatened the ruin of their community, erected flourishing congregations at Cracow, Lublin, Pinczow, Luck, Smila,|| (a town belonging to the famous Dudith,)¶ and in several other parts of Poland and Lithuania, and obtained the privilege of printing their productions, and those of their brethren, without molestation or restraint.* All these advantages were crowned by a signal mark of liberality and munificence, which they received from Jo. Sienienius, palatine of Podolia, who gave them a settlement in the city of Racow, which he had himself built, in 1569, in the district of Sendomir.† This extraordinary favour was peculiarly adapted to better the state of the Unitarians, who were, at that time, scattered about in the midst of their enemies; and accordingly they now looked upon their religious establishment as permanent and stable, and presumed so far upon their good fortune, as to declare Racow the centre of their community, where their distant and dispersed members might unite their counsels, and hold their deliberations.

X. When they saw their affairs in this promising situation, the first thing that employed the attention and zeal of their doctors and spiritual rulers, was a translation of the Bible into the Polish language, which was accordingly published in 1572. They had, indeed, before this, a Polish version of the sacred writings, which they had composed jointly with the Helvetic doctors, in 1565, while they lived in communion with that church: but, after the breach of that communion, and the order they had received to separate themselves from the reformed church, this version lost its credit among them, as it did not seem proper to answer their views.‡ After they had finished their new version, they drew up a summary of their religious doctrine, which was published at Cracow, in 1574, under the title of *Catechism* or *Confession* of the *Unitarians*.§ The

writers mentioned in the preceding note. It is unquestionably certain, that all those, who then called themselves Unitarian Brethren, did not entertain the same sentiments concerning the Divine Nature. Some of the most eminent doctors of that sect adopted the notions relating to the person and dignity of Christ, that were in after-times peculiar to the Socinians; the greatest part of them, however, embraced the Arian system, and affirmed, that our blessed Saviour was created before the formation of the world, by God the Father, to whom he was much inferior, nevertheless, in dignity and perfection.

☞ * For a more particular account of the Farnovians, see sect. xxiv. of this chapter.

† See the part of this chapter referred to in the preceding note.

‡ Vita Andr. Wissowatii in Sandii Biblioth. p. 226; also Sandius in Simone Budnæo, p. 54.

§ Lubieniecius, lib. iii. cap. xii.

|| Mart. Adelt, Historia Arianismi Smiglensis.

☞ ¶ This Dudith, who was certainly one of the most learned and eminent men of the sixteenth century, was born at Buda, in 1533; and, after having studied in the most famous universities, and visited almost all the countries of Europe, was named to the bishopric of Tinia by the emperor Ferdinand, and made privy counsellor to that prince. He had, by the force of his genius, and the study of the ancient orators, acquired such a masterly and irresistible eloquence, that in all public deliberations he carried every thing before him. In the council to which he was sent in the name of the emperor and of the Hungarian clergy, he spoke with such energy against several abuses of the church of Rome, and particularly against the celibacy of the clergy, that the pope, being informed thereof by his legates, solicited the emperor to recall him. Ferdinand complied; but, having heard Dudith's report of what passed in that famous council, he approved his conduct, and rewarded him with the bishopric of Chonat. He afterwards married a maid of honour of the queen of Hungary, and resigned his bishopric; the emperor, however, still continued to be his friend and protector. The papal excommunication was levelled at his head; but he treated it with contempt. Tired of the fopperies and superstitions of the church of Rome, he retired to Cracow, where he publicly embraced the protestant religion, after having been for a considerable time its secret friend. It is said that he showed some inclination toward the Socinian system. Some of his friends deny this; others confess it, but maintain, that he afterwards changed his sentiments in that respect. He was well acquainted with several branches of philosophy and the mathematics, with physic, history, theology, and the civil law. He was such an enthusiastic admirer of Cicero, that he copied over three times, with his own hand, all the works of that immortal author. He had something majestic in his figure, and in the air of his countenance. His life was regular and virtuous, his manners were elegant and easy, and his benevolence warm and extensive.

* Sandii Biblioth. p. 201.

† Sandius, p. 201. Lubieniecius, p. 239.

‡ See a German work of Ringeltaube, entitled Von den Pohlnischen Bibeln, p. 90, 113, 142, in which there is a farther account of the Polish interpretations of the Bible composed by Socinian authors.

§ From this little performance, and indeed from it alone we may learn with certainty the true state

system of religion that is contained in this catechism, is remarkable for its simplicity, and is neither loaded with scholastic terms nor with subtle discussions; but it breathes, in several places, the spirit of Socinianism, even in those parts of it which its authors look upon as most important and fundamental. Nor will this appear surprising to those who consider,

of the Unitarian religion before Faustus Socinus; yet I do not find that it has been so much as once quoted, or even mentioned by any of the Socinian writers, by any historians who have given an account of their sect, or by any of the divines that have drawn the pen of controversy against their religious system. I am almost inclined to believe, that the Socinians (when in process of time they had gained ground, acquired more dexterity in the management of their affairs, and drawn up a new, specious, and artful summary of their doctrine) were prudent enough to desire that this primitive catechism should disappear, that it might not furnish their adversaries with an occasion of accusing them of inconstancy in abandoning the tenets of their ancestors, nor excite factions and divisions among themselves, by inducing any of their people to complain that they had deviated from the ancient simplicity of the founders of their sect. These reasons, very probably, engaged the Socinian doctors to buy up all the copies they could find of this Confession, with a view to bury it in oblivion. It will not, therefore, be improper to give here some account of the form and matter of this first Socinian creed, which contained the doctrine of that sect before the Racovian Catechism was composed. This account will throw new light upon a period and branch of ecclesiastical history that are highly interesting. The original catechism now under consideration, which is extremely rare, has the following title prefixed to it: "Catechism, or Confession of Faith of the Congregation assembled in Poland, in the name of Jesus Christ our Lord, who was crucified, and raised from the dead—Deuter. vi. Hear, O Israel, the Lord our God is one God—John viii. 54. It is my Father—of whom ye say that he is your God. Printed by Alexander Turobinus, born in the year of Christ, the Son of God, 1574."* We find, by a passage at the end of the preface, that this curious catechism was printed at Cracow; for it is said to have been published in that city, in the year 1574 from the birth of Christ. Now it is known that the Unitarians had, at that time, a printing-house at Cracow, which was, soon after, removed to Racow. Turobinus, who is said to have been the printer of this little production, is mentioned by Sandius, under the denomination of Turobinczyck, which he undoubtedly derived from Turobin, a town in the Palatinate of Chelm, in Little or Red Russia, which was the place of his nativity. The author of this catechism was the famous George Schoman, as has been evidently proved from a piece entitled Schomanni Testamentum,† and other circumstances, by Jo. Adam Mollerus, in his dissert. de Unitariorum Catechesi et Confessione omnium prima.‡ The preface, composed in the name of the whole congregation, begins with the following salutation: "To all those who thirst after eternal salvation, the little and afflicted flock in Poland, which is baptized in the name of Jesus of Nazareth, sendeth greeting, praying most earnestly that grace and peace may be shed upon them by the one supreme God and Father, through his only begotten Son, our Lord Jesus Christ, who was crucified."§ After this general salutation, the prefacers give an account of the reasons that engaged them to compose and publish this confession. The principal motives arose from the reproaches and aspersions that were cast upon the Anabaptists in several places; from which we learn that, at this time, the denomination of Anabaptists was given to those, who, in after-times, were called Socinians. The rest of this preface is employed in beseeching the reader to be firmly persuaded, that the designs of the congregation are pious and upright, to read with attention, that he may judge with discernment, and, "abandoning the doctrine of Babylon, and the conduct and conversation of Sodom, to take refuge in the ark of Noah," i. e. among the Unitarian Brethren.

In the beginning of the catechism itself, the whole doctrine of Christianity is reduced to six points. The first relates to the nature of God and his Son Jesus Christ; the second to justification; the third to discipline; the fourth to prayer; the fifth to baptism; and the sixth to the Lord's supper. These six points are explained at length, in the following manner. Each point is defined and unfolded, in general terms, in one question and answer, and is afterwards subdivided into its several branches in various questions and answers, in which its different parts are illustrated and confirmed by texts of Scripture. From this it appears, at first sight, that the primitive state of Socinianism was a state of real infancy and weakness; that its doctors were by no means distinguished by the depth or accuracy of their theological knowledge; and that they instructed their flock in a superficial manner, by giving them only some vague notions of certain leading doctrines and precepts of religion. In their definition of the nature of God, with which this catechism begins, the authors discover immediately their sentiments concerning Jesus Christ, by declaring that he is subject, with 'all other things,' to the Supreme Creator of the universe. It may also be observed, as a proof of the ignorance or negligence of these authors, that, in illustrating the nature and perfections of the Deity, they make not the least mention of his infinity, his omniscience, immensity, eternity, omnipotence, omnipresence, spirituality, or of those other perfections of the divine nature that surpass the comprehension of finite minds. Instead of this, they characterize the Supreme Being only by his wisdom, his immortality, his goodness, and unbounded dominion and empire over the creatures. By this it would seem, that, even at this early period of Socinianism, the rulers of that sect had adopted it as a maxim, that nothing incomprehensible or mysterious was to be admitted into their religious system.—Their erroneous notion concerning Christ is expressed in the following terms: "Our mediator before the throne of God is a man who was formerly promised to our fathers by the prophets, and was born in these latter days of the seed of David, and whom God the Father has made Lord and Christ; that is, the most perfect prophet, the most holy priest, and the most triumphant king, by whom he created the *new* world,* by whom he sent peace upon earth, restored all things, and reconciled them to himself; and by whom also he has bestowed eternal life upon his elect, to the end that, after the Supreme God, we should believe in him, adore and invoke him, hear his voice, imitate his example, and find in him rest to our souls."† It is here worthy of notice, that, al-

* The original title runs thus: "Cathechesis et Confessio fidei cœtus per Poloniam congregati in nomine Jesu Christi, Domini nostri crucifixi et resuscitati. Deut. vi. Audi, Israel, Dominus Deus noster Deus unus est. Johan. viii. dicit Jesus, Quem vos dicitis vestrum esse Deum, est pater meus. Typis Alexandri Turobini, anno nati Jesu Christi, filii Dei, 1574."

† This testament is published by Sandius, in his Bibliotheca Anti-Trin.

‡ The dissertation of Mollerus is to be found in a collection of pieces published by Bartholomæus under the following title: "Fortgesezten nutzlichen Anmerckungen von allerhand Materien," part xxi. p.758.

§ Omnibus salutem æternam sitientibus, gratiam ac pacem ab uno illo altissimo Deo patre, per unigenitum ejus filium, Dominum nostrum, Jesum Christum crucifixum, ex animo precatur cœtus exiguus et afflictus per Poloniam, in nomine ejusdem Christi Nazareni Baptizatus.

* This expression is remarkable; for these doctors maintained, that these declarations of Scripture, which represent the world as formed by Christ, do not relate to the visible world, but to the restoration of mankind to virtue and happiness by the Son of God. They invented this interpretation to prevent their being obliged to acknowledge the divine glory and creative power of Christ.

† Est homo, mediator noster apud Deum, patribus olim per prophetas promissus, et ultimis tandem temporibus ex Davidis semine natus, quem Deus pater fecit Dominum et Christum, hoc est, perfectissimum prophetam, sanctissimum sacerdotem, invictissimum regem, per quem mundum creavit omnia restaura-

that the papers of Lælius Socinus, which he undoubtedly left behind him in Poland, were in the hands of many; and that, by the perusal of them, the Arians, who had formerly the upper hand in the community of the Unitarians, were engaged to change their sentiments concerning the nature and mediation of Christ.* It is true, indeed, that the denomination of *Socinian* was not as yet known. Those who were afterwards distinguished by this title, passed in Poland, at the time of which we now speak, under the name of Anabaptists, because they admitted to baptism adult persons only, and also rebaptized those who joined them from other Christian churches.†

though they call Christ *a most holy priest*, and justify this title by citations from Scripture, they no where explain the nature of that priesthood which they attribute to him.—With respect to the Holy Ghost, they plainly deny his being a divine *person*, and represent him as nothing more than a divine *quality*, or virtue, as appears from the following passage: "The Holy Ghost is the energy or perfection of God, whose fulness God the Father bestowed upon his only begotten Son, our Lord, that we becoming his adopted children, might receive of his fulness."*—They express their sentiments of justification in the ensuing terms: "Justification consists in the remission of all our past sins, through the mere grace and mercy of God, in, and by our Lord Jesus Christ, without our merits and works, and in consequence of a lively faith; as also in the certain hope of life eternal, and the true and unfeigned amendment of our lives and conversation, through the assistance of the divine Spirit, to the glory of God the Father, and the edification of our neighbours."† As by this inaccurate definition justification comprehends in it amendment and obedience, so, in the explication of this point, our authors break in upon the following one, which relates to discipline, and lay down a short summary of moral doctrine, which is contained in a few precepts, and expressed for the most part in the language of Scripture. There is this peculiarity in their moral injunctions, that they prohibit the taking of oaths and the repelling of injuries. As to what regards ecclesiastical discipline, they define it thus: "Ecclesiastical discipline consists in calling frequently to the remembrance of every individual, the duties that are incumbent upon him; in admonishing, first privately, and afterwards, if that be ineffectual, in a public manner, before the whole congregation, such as have sinned openly against God, or offended their neighbour; and, lastly, in excluding from the communion of the church the obstinate and impenitent, that, being thus covered with shame, they may be led to repentance, or, if they remain unconverted, may be damned eternally."‡ By their farther explication of the point relating to ecclesiastical discipline, we see how imperfect and incomplete their notions of that matter were. For they treat, in the first place, concerning the government of the church and its ministers, whom they divide into bishops, deacons, elders, and widows. After this they enumerate, at length, the duties of husbands and wives, old and young, parents and children, masters and servants, citizens and magistrates, poor and rich; and conclude with what relates to the admonition of offenders, and their exclusion from the communion of the church, in case of obstinate impenitence. Their sentiments concerning prayer, are, generally speaking, sound and rational. But, in their notion of baptism, they differ from other Christian churches in this, that they make it to consist in immersion or dipping, and emersion or rising again out of the water, and maintain that it ought not to be administered to any but adult persons. "Baptism," say they, "is the immersion into water, and the emersion of one who believes in the Gospel, and is truly penitent, performed in the name of Father, Son, and Holy Ghost, or in the name of Jesus Christ alone; by which solemn act the person baptized publicly acknowledgeth, that he is cleansed from all his sins, through the mercy of God the Father, by the blood of Christ, and the operation of the Holy Spirit, to the end that, being engrafted into the body of Christ, he may mortify the old Adam, and be transformed into the image of the new and heavenly Adam, in the firm assurance of eternal life after the resurrection."* The last point handled in this performance is the sacrament of the Lord's Supper, of which the authors give an explication that will be readily adopted by those who embrace the doctrine of Zuingle on that head. At the end of this curious catechism there is a piece entitled, "Œconomia Christiana, seu Pastoratus Domesticus," which contains a short instruction to heads of families, showing them how they ought to proceed in order to maintain and increase in their houses a spirit of piety; in which also their devotion is assisted by forms of prayer, composed for morning, evening, and other occasions.

The copy of this catechism, which is now before me, was given in 1680, by Martin Chelmius, one of the most eminent and zealous Socinian doctors, to Mr. Christopher Heiligmier, as appears by a long inscription, written by the donor, at the end of the book. In this inscription Chelmius promises his friend other productions of the same kind, provided he receives the present one kindly, and concludes with these words of St. Paul: 'God hath chosen the weak things of the world to confound the strong.'

vit, secum reconciliavit, pacificavit, et vitam æternam electis suis donavit; ut in illum, post Deum altissimum, credamus, illum adoremus, invocemus, audiamus, pro modulo nostro imitemur, et, in illo, requiem animabus nostris inveniamus.

* Spiritus sanctus est virtus Dei, cujus plenitudinem dedit Deus pater filio suo unigenito, Domino nostro, ut ex ejus plenitudine nos adoptivi accipe-remus.

† Justificatio est ex mera gratia, per Dominum nostrum Jesum Christum, sine operibus et meritis nostris, omnium præteritorum peccatorum nostrorum in viva fide remissio, vitæque æternæ indubitata expectatio, et auxilio spiritus Dei vitæ nostræ non simulata sed vera correctio, ad gloriam Dei patris nostri et ædificationem proximorum nostrorum.

‡ Disciplina ecclesiastica est officii singulorum frequens commemoratio, et peccantium contra Deum vel proximum primum privata, deinde etiam publica, coram toto cœtu, commonefactio, denique pertinacium a communione sanctorum alienatio, ut pudore suffusi convertantur, aut, si id nolint, æternum damnentur.

* Baptismus est hominis Evangelio credentis et pœnitentiam agentis, in nomine Patris, et Filii et Spiritus Sancti, vel in nomine Jesu Christi, in aquam immersio et emersio, qua publice profitetur, se gratia Dei Patris, in sanguine Christi, opera Spiritus Sancti, ab omnibus peccatis ablutum esse, ut, in corpus Christi insertus, mortificet veterem Adamum, et transformetur in Adamum illum cælestem, certus, se post resurrectionem consequuturum esse vitam æternam.

* This appears evidently from the following passage in Schoman's Testamentum, p. 194, 195. "Sub id fere tempus (A. 1566,) ex rhapsodiis Lælii Socini quidam fratres didicerunt, Dei filium non esse secundam Trinitatis personam, patri coessentialem et coæqualem, sed hominem Jesum Christum, ex Spiritu Sancto conceptum, ex Virgine Maria natum, crucifixum, et resuscitatum: a quibus nos commoniti, sacras literas perscrutari persuasi sumus." These words show plainly, that the Unitarians, or Pinczovians, had, before their separation from the reformed church in 1565, believed in a Trinity of some kind or other, and had not gone so far as totally to divest Jesus Christ of his divinity. Schoman, now cited, was a doctor of great authority in this sect; and he tells us that, at the diet of Petricow, in 1565, he defended the unity of God the Father against the reformed, who maintained the existence of a threefold Deity. We learn nevertheless, from himself, that it was not till the year 1566, that a perusal of the papers of Lælius Socinus had engaged him to change his sentiments, and to deny the divine personality of Christ. Hence we may conclude, that, before the year last-mentioned, he and his Pinczovian flock were not Socinians, but Arians only.

† This the Unitarians acknowledge, and it is confirmed by the writer of the Epistola de Vita Andr.

XI. The dexterity and perseverance of Faustus Socinus gave a new face to the Unitarian sect, of which he became a zealous and industrious patron. He was a man of true genius, but of little learning; firm in his purposes, and steady in his measures; much inferior in knowledge to his uncle Lælius, while he surpassed him greatly in courage and resolution. This eminent sectary, after having wandered through several countries of Europe, settled, in 1579, among the Unitarians in Poland, and, at his arrival there, suffered many vexations and much opposition from a considerable number of persons, who looked upon some of his tenets as highly erroneous. And, indeed, it is evident, that his religious system, which he is said to have drawn from the papers of Lælius, was much less remarkable for its simplicity than that of the Unitarians. He triumphed, however, at last, over all the difficulties that had been laid in his way, by the power of his eloquence, the spirit and address that reigned in his compositions, the elegance and gentleness of his manner, the favour and protection of the nobility, which he had acquired by his happy talents and accomplishments, and also by some lucky hits of fortune. By seizing the occasions when it was prudent to yield, and improving the moments that demanded bold resistance and firm resolution, he stemmed dexterously and courageously the torrent of opposition, and beheld the Unitarians submitting to his doctrine, which they had before treated with indignation and contempt. They, in effect, laid aside all feuds and controversies, and formed themselves into one community under his superintendency and direction.*

XII. Thus did Socinus introduce a considerable change into the ancient Unitarian system, which, before his time, was ill digested, ill expressed, and chargeable in many places with ambiguity and incoherence. He disguised its inconsistencies, gave it an air of connexion, method, and elegance, and defended it with much more dexterity and art, than had ever been discovered by its former patrons.† And, accordingly, the affairs of the Unitarians put on a new face. Under the auspicious protection of such a spirited and insinuating chief, the little flock, that had been hitherto destitute of strength, resolution, and courage, grew apace, and suddenly arose to a high degree of credit and influence. Its number was augmented by proselytes of all ranks and orders. Of these some were distinguished by their nobility, others by their opulence, some by their address, and many by their learning and eloquence. All these contributed, in one way or another, to increase the lustre, and to advance the interests of this rising community, and to support it against the multitude of adversaries, which its remarkable prosperity and success had raised up against it from all quarters; the rich maintained it by their liberality, the powerful by their patronage and protection, and the learned by their writings. But now the system of the Unitarians, being thus changed and new-modelled, required a new confession of faith to make known its principles, and give a clear and full account of its present state. The ancient catechism, which was no more than a rude and incoherent sketch, was therefore laid aside, and a new form of doctrine was drawn up by Socinus himself. This form was corrected by some, augmented by others, and revised by all the Socinian doctors of any eminence; and, having thus acquired a competent degree of accuracy and perfection, was published under the title of the Catechism of Racow, and is still considered as the Confession of Faith of the whole sect. An unexpected circumstance crowned all the fortunate events that had happened to this sect, and seemed to leave them nothing farther to desire; and this was the zealous protection of Jacobus à Sienno, to whom Racow belonged. This new patron, separating himself from the reformed church, in 1600, embraced the doctrine and communion of the Socinians, and, about two years after, erected in his own city, which he declared their metropolis, a public school, designed as a seminary for their church, to form its ministers and pastors.*

XIII. From Poland, the doctrine of Socinus made its way into Transylvania, in 1563, principally by the credit and influence of George Blandrata, a celebrated physician, whom Sigismund, at that time sovereign of the country, had invited to his court, in order to

Wissowatii, who tells us, that his sect were distinguished by the denomination of Anabaptists and Arians, but that all other Christian communities and individuals in Poland were promiscuously called Chrzesciani, from the word Chrzest, which signifies Baptism.

* See Bayle's Dictionary.—Sandii Biblioth. Anti-Trin. p. 64.—Sam. Przypcopii Vita Socini, prefixed to the works of Socinus.—Lamy's Histoire du Socinianisme, part i. ii.

† Hence it appears, that the modern Unitarians are very properly called Socinians; for certainly the formation and establishment of that sect were entirely owing to the labours of Lælius and Faustus Socinus. The former, indeed, who was naturally timorous and irresolute, died at Zurich, in 1562, in the communion of the reformed church, and seemed unwilling to expose himself to danger, or to sacrifice his repose, by founding a new sect, that is, by appearing professedly and openly in this enterprise. Besides, many circumstances concur to render it highly probable, that he did not finish the religious system of which he had formed the plan, but died, on the contrary, in a state of uncertainty and doubt with respect to several points of no small importance. But, notwithstanding all this, he contributed much to the institution of the sect now under consideration. He collected the materials that Faustus afterwards digested and employed with such dexterity and success: he secretly and imperceptibly excited doubts and scruples in the minds of many, concerning several doctrines generally received among Christians; and, by several arguments against the divinity of Christ, which he left in writing, he so far seduced, even after his death, the Arians in Poland, that they embraced the communion and sentiments of those who looked upon Christ as a mere man, created immediately, like Adam, by God himself. What Lælius had thus begun, Faustus carried on with vigour and finished with success. It is indeed difficult, and scarcely possible, to determine precisely, what materials he received from his uncle, and what tenets he added himself; that he added several is plain enough. The difficulty arises from this circumstance, that there are few writings of Lælius extant; and of those that bear his name, some undoubtedly belong to other authors. We learn, however, from Faustus himself, that the doctrine he propagated, with respect to the person of Christ, was (at least, the greatest part of it) broached by Lælius.

* See Wissowatii Narratio de Separatione Unitariorum a Reformatis, p. 214.—Lubieniecius, lib. iii cap. xii.

the restoration of his health. Blandrata was a man of uncommon address, had a deep knowledge of men and things, and was particularly acquainted with the manners, transactions, and intrigues of courts. He was accompanied by a Socinian minister, whose name was Francis Davides, who seconded his efforts with such zeal, that, by their united solicitations and labours, they engaged the prince, and the greatest part of the nobility, in their cause, infected almost the whole province with their errors, and obtained for the ministers and members of their communion, the privilege of professing and propagating their doctrines in a public manner. The Bathori, indeed, who were afterwards chosen dukes of Transylvania, were by no means prejudiced in favour of the Socinians; but that sect had become so powerful by its numbers and its influence, that they could not, in prudence, attempt to suppress it.* Such also was the case with the successors of the Bathori; they ardently wished to extirpate this society, but never could accomplish that object; so that to this day the Socinians profess their religion publicly in this province, and, indeed, in it alone; and, relying on the protection of the laws, and the faith of certain treaties that have been adjusted with them, have their churches and seminaries of learning, and hold their ecclesiastical and religious assemblies, though exposed to perpetual dangers and snares from the vigilance of their adversaries.† About the same time the Socinians endeavoured to form settlements in Hungary‡ and Austria;§ but these attempts were defeated by the united and zealous opposition both of the Roman catholic and reformed churches.

XIV. No sooner had the Socinians obtained a solid and happy settlement at Racow, than the dictates of zeal and ambition suggested to them views of a still more extensive nature. Encouraged by the protection of men in power, and the suffrages of men of learning and genius, they began to form several plans for the enlargement of their community, and meditated nothing less than the propagation of their doctrine through all the states of Europe. The first step they took toward the execution of this purpose, was the publication of a considerable number of books, of which some were designed to illustrate and defend their theological system, and others to explain, or rather to pervert, the sacred writings into a conformity with their peculiar tenets. These books, which were composed by the most subtile and artful doctors of the sect, were printed at Racow, and dispersed with the utmost industry and zeal through different countries.‖ They also sent some of their brethren into various parts of Europe, toward the conclusion of this century, as we learn from authentic records, in order to make proselytes and erect new congregations. These missionaries seemed every way qualified to gain credit to the cause in which they had embarked, as some of them were distinguished by the lustre of their birth, and others by the extent of their learning, and the powers of their eloquence; and yet, notwithstanding these uncommon advantages, they failed, almost every where, in their attempts. A small congregation was founded at Dantzic, which subsisted for some time in a clandestine manner, and then gradually dwindled to nothing.* The first attempts to promote the cause of Socinianism in Holland, were made by a person whose name was Erasmus Johannis.† After him Christopher Ostorod, and Andrew Voidovius, who were the main pillars of the sect, used their utmost endeavours to gain disciples and followers in that country; nor were their labours wholly unsuccessful, though the zeal of the clergy, and the vigilance of the magistrates, prevented their forming any regular assemblies,‡ and thus hindered their party from acquiring any considerable degree of strength and stability.§ Socinianism did not meet with a better reception in Britain than in Holland. It was introduced into Germany by Adam Neuser, and other emissaries, who infected the Palatinate with its errors, having entered into a league with the Transylvanians, at the critical period when the affairs of the Unitarians, in Poland, carried a dubious and unpromising aspect. But this pernicious league was soon detected, and the schemes of its authors were entirely disconcerted; upon which Neuser went into Turkey, and enlisted among the Janisaries.‖

XV. Although the Socinians professed to believe that our divine knowledge is derived solely from the Holy Scriptures, they maintain in reality, that the sense of Scripture is to be investigated and explained by the dictates of right reason, to which, in consequence, they attribute a great influence in determining the nature, and unfolding the various doctrines of religion. When their writings are perused with attention, they will be found to attribute

* See Sandius, p. 28, 55.—Salig, vol. ii. lib. vi.—Debrezeni Hist. Ecclesiæ Reformatæ in Hungaria, p. 147.—Mart. Schmeizelii de Statu Ec. Lutheranæ in Transylvania, p. 55.—Lamy, His. du Socinianisme, part i. ch. xiii.

† Zeltneri Historia Crypto-Socinismi Altorfini, cap. ii. p. 357.

‡ Debrezeni Hist. p. 169.

§ Henr. Spondani Continuat. Annal. Baronii, ad An. 1568.

‖ A considerable number of these books were republished, in 1656, in one great collection, consisting of six volumes in folio, under the title of Bibliotheca Fratrum Polonorum. In this collection, indeed, many pieces are not inserted, which were composed by the most eminent leaders of the sect; but what is there published, is sufficient to give the attentive reader a clear idea of the doctrine of the Socinians, and of the nature of their institution as a religious community.

* Zelterni Hist. p. 199.

† Sandius, p. 87.

☞ ‡ Brandt, in his History of the Reformation of the Netherlands, tells us, that Ostorod and Voidovius were banished, and that their books were condemned to be publicly burned by the hands of the common hangman. Accordingly the pile was raised the executioner approached, and the multitude was assembled; but the books did not appear. The magistrates, who were curious to peruse their contents, had quietly divided them among themselves and their friends.

§ Zeltnerus, p. 31, 178.

‖ Burch. Struvii Hist. Eccles. Palat. cap. viii. sect. liii.—Alting, Hist. Eccles. Palat. in Miegii Monum. Palat. p. 266—337.—La Croze, Dissertations Historiques, tom. i. p. 101, 127, compared with Bern. Raupachius' Presbyterologia Austriaca, p. 113, where there is an account of John Matthæus, who was concerned in these troubles.

more to reason, in this matter, than most other Christian societies; for they frequently insinuate artfully, and sometimes declare plainly, that the sacred penmen were guilty of many errors, from a defect of memory, as well as a want of capacity; that they expressed their sentiments without perspicuity or precision, and rendered the plainest things obscure by their pompous and diffuse Asiatic style; and that it was therefore absolutely necessary to employ the lamp of human reason to cast a light upon their doctrine, and to explain it in a manner conformable to truth. It is easy to see what they had in view by maintaining propositions of this kind. They aimed at nothing less than the establishment of the following general rule, viz. That the history of the Jews, and also that of Jesus Christ, were indeed to be derived from the books of the Old and New Testament, and that it was not lawful to entertain the least doubt concerning the truth of this history, or the authenticity of these books in general; but that the particular doctrines which they contain, were, nevertheless, to be understood and explained in such a manner as to render them consonant with the dictates of reason. According to this representation of things, it is not the scripture that declares clearly and expressly what we are to believe concerning the nature, counsels, and perfections of the Deity; but it is human reason, which shows us the system of religion that we ought to seek in, and deduce from, the divine oracles.

XVI. This fundamental principle of Socinianism will appear more dangerous and pernicious, when we consider the sense in which the word *Reason* was understood by this sect. The pompous title of *Right Reason* was given, by the Socinians, to that measure of intelligence and discernment, or, in other words, to that faculty of comprehending and judging, which we derive from nature. According to this definition, the fundamental rule of Socinianism necessarily supposes, that no doctrine ought to be acknowledged as true in its nature, or divine in its origin, all whose parts are not level to the comprehension of the human understanding; and that, whatever the Scriptures teach concerning the perfections of God, his counsels, and decrees, and the way of salvation, must be modified, curtailed, and filed down, in such a manner, by the transforming power of art and argument, as to answer the extent of our limited faculties. Those who adopt this singular rule, must at the same time grant that the number of religions must be nearly equal to that of individuals; for, as there is a great variety in the talents and capacities of different persons, so what will appear difficult and abstruse to one, will seem evident and clear to another; and thus the more discerning and penetrating will adopt, as divine truth, what the slow and superficial will look upon as unintelligible jargon. This consequence does not at all alarm the Socinians, who suffer their members to explain, in very different ways, many doctrines of the highest importance, and permit every one to follow his particular fancy in composing his theological system, provided that they acknowledge, in general, the truth and authenticity of the history of Christ, and adhere to the precepts which the gospel lays down for the regulation of our lives and actions.

XVII. In consequence of this leading maxim, the Socinians either reject without exception, or change and accommodate to their limited capacities, all those doctrines relating to the nature of God and of Jesus Christ, the plan of redemption, and the eternal rewards and punishments unfolded in the Gospel, which they either cannot comprehend, or consider as attended with considerable difficulties. The sum of their theology is as follows: "God, who is infinitely more perfect than man, though of a similar nature in some respects, exerted an act of that power by which he governs all things; in consequence of which an extraordinary person was born of the Virgin Mary. That person was Jesus Christ, whom God first translated to heaven by that portion of his divine power, which is called the Holy Ghost; and, having there instructed him fully in the knowledge of his will, counsels, and designs, he sent him again into this sublunary world, to promulgate to mankind a new rule of life, more excellent than that under which they had formerly lived, to propagate divine truth by his ministry, and to confirm it by his death.

"Those who obey the voice of this Divine Teacher, (and this obedience is in the power of every one whose will and inclination lead that way,) shall one day be clothed with new bodies, and inhabit eternally those blessed regions, where God himself immediately resides. Such, on the contrary, as are disobedient and rebellious, shall undergo most terrible and exquisite torments, which shall be succeeded by annihilation, or the total extinction of their being."

The whole system of Socinianism, when stripped of the embellishments and commentaries with which it has been loaded and disguised by its doctors, is really reducible to the few propositions now mentioned.

XVIII. The nature and genius of the Socinian theology have an immediate influence upon the moral system of that sect, and naturally led its doctors to confine their rules of morality and virtue to the *external* actions and duties of life. On one hand, they deny the influence of a divine spirit and power upon the minds of men; and, on the other, they acknowledge, that no mortal has such an empire over himself as to be able to suppress or extinguish his sinful propensities and corrupt desires. Hence they have no conclusion left but one, and that is, to declare all such true and worthy Christians, whose words and external actions are conformable to the precepts of the divine law. It is, at the same time, remarkable, that another branch of their doctrine leads directly to the utmost severity in what relates to life and manners, since they maintain, that the great end of Christ's mission upon earth was to exhibit to mortals a new law, distinguished from all others by its unblemished sanctity and perfection. Hence it is, that a great number of Socinians have fallen into the fanatical rigour of the ancient Anabaptists, and judge it absolutely unlawful to repel injuries, to take oaths, to inflict capital punishments on malefactors, to oppose the despotic proceedings of tyrannical magistrates, or even to acquire wealth by honest industry. But, in this, there is something extremely singular, and they are here, indeed, inconsistent with themselves; for while, in matters of doctrine, they take the greatest liberty with the expressions of Scripture, and pervert them, in a violent manner, to the defence of their peculiar tenets, they proceed quite otherwise, when they come to prescribe rules of conduct from the precepts of the Gospel; for then they understand these precepts literally, and apply them without the least distinction of times, persons, and circumstances.

XIX. It must carefully be observed, that the Catechism of Racow, which most people look upon as the great standard of Socinianism, and as an accurate summary of the doctrine of that sect, is, in reality, no more than a collection of the popular tenets of the Socinians, and by no means a just representation of the secret opinions and sentiments of their doctors.* The writings, therefore, of these learned men must be perused with attention, in order to our knowing the hidden reasons and true principles from which the doctrines of the Catechism are derived. It is observable, besides, that, in this Catechism, many Socinian tenets and institutions, which might have contributed to render the sect still more odious, and to expose its internal constitution too much to public view, are entirely omitted; so that it seems to have been less composed for the use of the Socinians themselves, than to impose upon strangers, and to mitigate the indignation which the tenets of this community had excited in the minds of many.† Hence it never obtained, among the Socinians, the authority of a public confession or rule of faith; and hence the divines of that sect were authorized to correct and contradict it, or to substitute another form of doctrine in its place. It is also observable, that the most eminent writers and patrons of the Socinians, give no clear or consistent account of the sentiments of that sect in relation to ecclesiastical discipline and government, and the form of public worship. All that we know is, that they follow in these matters, generally speaking, the customs received in the protestant churches.‡

XX. The founders and first patrons of this sect were eminently distinguished by their learning and genius. Their successors, however, did not follow their steps in this respect, nor retain the reputation they had universally obtained. The Unitarians in Poland seem to have had little ambition of science. They gave no encouragement to learning or talents; and appeared little solicitous of having in their community subtle doctors and learned disputants. But, when they perceived on the one hand, that the success of their community required as able defenders, as they had learned and ingenious adversaries, and were so fortunate, on the other, as to obtain the privilege of erecting seminaries of learning at Racow and Lublin, they changed their sentiments with respect to this matter, and became sensible of the necessity under which they lay, to encourage in their community a zeal for the sciences. This zeal increased greatly from the time that Faustus Socinus undertook the restoration of their declining credit, and put himself at the head of their tottering sect. At that time many persons, distinguished by their birth, education, and talents, embraced its doctrine, and contributed to promote the love of science among its members. Then the youth were instructed in the rules of eloquence and rhetoric, and the important branches of Oriental, Greek, and Latin literature. Even the secret paths of philosophy were opened, though their treasures were disclosed only to a few, who were selected, for that purpose, from the multitude. The Racovian doctors, in compliance with the spirit and taste of the age, chose Aristotle as their guide in philosophy, as appears evidently from the Ethics of Crellius, and other literary records of these times.

XXI. Notwithstanding this progress of philosophy among the Socinians, their doctors seemed to reject its aid in theology with obstinacy and disdain. They declare, in numberless places of their writings, that both in the interpretation of Scripture, and in explaining and demonstrating the truth of religion in general, clearness and simplicity are alone to be consulted, and no regard paid to the subtleties of philosophy and logic. And, indeed, had their doctors and interpreters followed, in practice, that rule which they have laid down with so much ostentation in theory, they would have saved their adversaries, and perhaps themselves, much trouble. But this is by no means the case. For, in the greatest part of their theological productions, their pretended simplicity is frequently accompanied with much subtlety, and with the most refined intricacies of scientific art. And, what is still more inexcusable, they reason with the greatest dexterity and acuteness upon those subjects, which (as they surpass the reach of the human understanding,) are generally received, among other Christians, as facts confirmed by the most respectable testimony, and consequently as matters of pure faith, while they discover little sagacity, or strength of judgment, in those discussions which are within the sphere of reason, and are properly amenable to its tribunal. They are acute where they ought to be silent, and they reason awkwardly where sa

* We have an account of the authors of this famous catechism, and of the various success it met with, in the Commentatio de Catechesi Recoviensi, published by Schmidius in 1707. See also Kocheri Biblioth.—A new edition of the catechism itself, with a solid refutation of the doctrine it contains, was published in 1739, by the learned George Louis Oeder.

† This appears evident enough from their presenting a Latin translation of this catechism to James I. king of Great Britain, and a German one to the university of Wittenberg.

‡ This is manifest from a work which bears the following title: "Politia Ecclesiastica, quam vulgo Agenda vocant, sive forma Regiminis exterioris Ecclesiarum Christianarum in Polonia, quæ unum Deum Patrem, per filium ejus Unigenitum in Spiritu Sancto, confitentur." This work was composed in 1642, by Peter Morscovius or Morscowsky, and published at Nuremburg by Oeder. It is mentioned by Sandius, who says that it was drawn up for the use of the Belgic churches.

gacity and argument are required. These are certainly great inconsistencies; yet they proceed from one and the same principle, even the maxim universally received in this community, that all things which surpass the limits of human comprehension, are to be entirely banished from the Christian religion.

XXII. It has been already observed, that the Unitarians had no sooner separated themselves from the Reformed churches in Poland, than they became a prey to intestine divisions, and were split into several factions. The points of doctrine that gave rise to these divisions, related to the dignity of Christ's nature and character, the unlawfulness of infant baptism, and the personality of the Holy Ghost, to which were added several alterations, concerning the duties of life, and the rules of conduct that were obligatory on Christians. The sects, produced by these divisions, were not all equally obstinate. Some of them entertained pacific dispositions, and seemed inclined toward a reconciliation. But two, particularly, tenaciously maintained their sentiments, and persisted in their separation; these were the Budnæans and the Farnovians. The former were so called from their leader Simon Budnæus, a man of considerable acuteness and sagacity, who, more dexterous than the rest of his brethren in deducing consequences from their principles, and perceiving plainly the conclusions to which the peculiar principles of Lælius Socinus naturally led, peremptorily denied the propriety of offering any kind of religious worship to Jesus Christ. Nor did Budnæus stop here: in order to give a more specious colour to this capital error, and to maintain it upon consistent grounds, he asserted that Christ was not begotten by an extraordinary act of divine power, but that he was born like other men, in a natural way. This hypothesis, however conformable to the fundamental principles of Socinianism, appeared intolerable and impious to the major part even of that community. Hence Budnæus, who had gained over to his doctrine a great number of proselytes in Lithuania and Russian Poland, was deposed from his ministerial functions, in 1584, and publicly excommunicated with all his disciples. It is said, however, that he afterwards abandoned his peculiar and offensive sentiments, and was re-admitted to the communion of that sect.*

XXIII. This heretical doctrine, which had created so much trouble to Budnæus, was soon after adopted by Francis Davides, a native of Hungary, who was the superintendent of the Socinian churches in Transylvania, and who opposed, with the greatest ardour and obstinacy, the custom of offering up prayers and divine worship to Jesus Christ. Several methods were used to reclaim him from this offensive error. Blandrata employed all the power of his eloquence for this purpose, and, to render his remonstrances still more effectual, sent for Faustus Socinus, who went accordingly into Transylvania, in 1578, and seconded his arguments and exhortations with the utmost zeal and perseverance. But Davides remained unmoved, and was, in consequence of this obstinate adherence to his error, apprehended by order of Christopher Bathori, prince of Transylvania, and thrown into prison, where he died in 1579, at an advanced age.* His unhappy fate did not, however, extinguish the controversy to which his doctrine had given rise; for he left behind him disciples and friends, who strenuously maintained his sentiments, stood firm against the opposition that was made to them, and created much uneasiness to Socinus and his followers in Lithuania and Poland. The most eminent of these were Jacob Palæologus, of the isle of Chio, who was burned at Rome in 1585; Christian Francken, who had disputed in person with Socinus; and John Somer,† who was master of the academy of Clausenburg.‡ This little sect is branded, by the Socinian writers, with the ignominious appellation of Semi-Judaizers.§

* See Sandii Biblioth. Anti-Trinit. p. 54, 55.—Epistola de Vita, Wissowatii, p. 226.—Ringeltaube's German Dissertation on the Polish Bibles, p. 144, 152.—Samuel Crellius, the most learned Socinian of our times, is of opinion that Adam Neuser,* who was banished on account of his erroneous sentiments, was the author of this doctrine, which is so derogatory from the dignity of Jesus Christ. See Crellii Thesaur. Epistol. Crozian.

* See sect. xiv. of this chapter.

* Sandius, Biblioth. Anti-Trinit. p. 55.—Faust. Socin. oper. tom. i. p. 353, 395; tom. ii. p. 713, 771, where there is an account of his conference and dispute with Francis Davides.—Stan. Lubieniecii Hist. Reform. Polonicæ, lib. iii. c. xi.

† See Sandius, Biblioth. p. 57. The dispute between Socinus and Francken is related at large in the works of the former, tom. ii. p. 767.

☞ ‡ Clausenburg, otherwise Coloswar, is a town in Transylvania, extremely populous and well fortified. The Socinians have here a public school and a printing-house; and their community in this place is very numerous. Till the year 1603, they were in possession of the cathedral, which was then taken from them and given to the Jesuits, whose college and church they had pulled down.

§ Faustus Socinus wrote a particular treatise against the Semi-Judaizers. It is, however, worthy of observation, that the motive which engaged him and his friends to employ so much pains and labour in the suppression of this faction, was not a persuasion of the pernicious tendency of its doctrines or peculiar notions. On the contrary, he expressly acknowledges, that this controversy turns upon matters of very little importance, by declaring it, as his opinion, that praying or offering up divine worship to Christ, is not necessary to salvation. Thus, in his answer to Wujeck, he expresses himself in the following manner: "The Christian, whose faith is so great, as to encourage him to offer his addresses habitually and directly to the Supreme Being, and who standeth not in need of the comfort that flows from the invocation of Christ, his brother, who was tempted in all things like as he is, is not obliged to call upon the name of Jesus, by prayer or supplication."* According therefore to the opinion of Socinus, those who lay aside all regard to Christ as an intercessor, and address themselves directly to God alone, have a greater measure of faith than others. But, if this be so, why did he oppose with such vehemence and animosity the sentiment of Davides, who, in effect, did no more than exhort all Christians to address themselves directly and immediately to the Father? Here there appears to be a striking inconsistency. We find also Lubieniecius, in his Reformat. Histor. Polonicæ, lib. iii. cap. xi. speaking lightly enough of this controversy, and representing it as a matter of very little moment; for he says that in Transylvania there was 'much ado about no-

* Si quis tanta est fide præditus, ut ad Deum ipsum perpetuo recta accedere audeat, nec consolatione, quæ ex Christi fratris sui per omnia tentati invocatione proficiscitur, indigeat, hic non opus habet ut Christum invocet.

XXIV. The Farnovians were treated by the Socinians with much greater indulgence. They were neither excluded from the communion of the sect, nor obliged to renounce their peculiar tenets; they were only exhorted to conceal them prudently, and not publish or propagate them in their discourses from the pulpit.* This particular branch of the Socinian community was so named from Stantislaus Farnovius, or Farnesius, who was engaged by Gonesius to prefer the Arian system to that of the Socinians, and consequently asserted, that Christ had been engendered or produced out of nothing, by the Supreme Being, before the creation of this terrestrial globe. It is not so easy to say, what his sentiments were concerning the Holy Ghost; all we know upon that head is, that he warned his disciples against paying the tribute of religious worship to that divine Spirit.* Farnovius separated from the other Unitarians, in 1568, and was followed in this schism by several persons eminent on account of the extent of their learning, and the influence of their rank, such as Martin Czechovicius, Neimoiovius, Stanislaus Wisnowius, John Falcon, George Schoman, and others. They did not, however, form themselves into a stable or permanent sect. The lenity and indulgence of the Socinians, together with the dexterity of their disputants, brought many of them back into the bosom of the community they had deserted, and considerable numbers were dispersed or regained by the prudence and address of Faustus Socinus; so that at length the whole faction, being deprived of its chief, who died in 1615, was scattered abroad, and reduced to nothing.†

thing.'* We may therefore conclude, that Socinus and his followers were more artful than ingenuous in their proceedings with respect to Davides. They persecuted him and his followers, lest, by tolerating his doctrine, they should increase the odium under which they already lay, and draw upon themselves anew the resentment of other Christian churches, while, in their private judgment, they looked upon this very doctrine, and its professors, as worthy of toleration and indulgence.

* Epist. ad de Vita Wissowatii, p. 226.—Sandius says, that a professor of divinity at Clausenburg was prohibited from saying any thing, in his public discourses, of Christ's having existed before the Virgin Mary.

* Fluctus in simpulo excitatos esse.

* Sandius, Biblioth. p. 52, &c.

† We omit here an enumeration of the more famous Socinian writers who flourished in this century, because the greater part of them have already been mentioned in the course of this History. The rest may be easily collected from Sandius.

THE SEVENTEENTH CENTURY.

SECTION I.

THE GENERAL HISTORY OF THE CHRISTIAN CHURCH.

I. THE arduous attempts of the pontiffs, in the preceding century, to advance the glory and majesty of the see of Rome, by extending the limits of the Christian church, and spreading the Gospel among distant nations, met with great opposition; and, as they were neither well conducted nor properly supported, their fruits were neither abundant nor permanent. But in this century the same attempts were renewed with vigour, and crowned with such success, as contributed not a little to give a new degree of stability to the tottering grandeur of the papacy. They were begun by Gregory XV., who, by the advice of his confessor Narni, founded at Rome, in 1622, the famous congregation for the Propagation of the Faith, and enriched it with ample revenues. This congregation, which consists of thirteen cardinals, two priests, one monk, and a secretary,* is designed to propagate and maintain the religion of Rome in all parts of the world. Its riches and possessions were so prodigiously augmented by the munificence of Urban VIII. and the liberality of an incredible number of donors, that its funds are, at this day, adequate to the most sumptuous undertakings.* And, indeed, the enterprises of this congregation are great and extensive: by it a vast number of missionaries are sent to the remotest parts of the world; books of various kinds published, to facilitate the study of foreign and barbarous languages; the sacred writings, and other pious productions, sent abroad to the most distant corners of the globe, and exhibited to each nation and country in their own language and characters; seminaries founded for the sustenance and education of a great number of young men, set apart for the foreign missions; houses erected for the instruction and support of the pagan youths who are yearly sent from abroad to Rome, that they may return thence into their respective countries, and become the instructors of their blinded brethren: not to mention the charitable establishments that are intended for the relief and support of those who have suffered banish-

* Such is the number appropriated to this Congregation by Gregory's original *Bull*. See Bullarium Roman. tom. iii.—Cerri mentions the same number, in his Etat Present de l'Eglise Romaine. But a different account is given by Aymon, in his Tableau de la Cour de Rome, p. iii. ch. iii. p. 279, for he makes this Congregation to consist of eighteen cardinals, one of the pope's secretaries, one apostolical protonotary, one referendary, and one of the assessors or secretaries of the inquisition.

* This assertion was not strictly true at the time when it was hazarded and to our own time it is very inapplicable.—*Edit.*

ment, or been involved in other calamities, on account of their steadfast attachment to the religion of Rome, and their zeal for promoting the glory of its pontiff. Such are the arduous and complicated schemes, with the execution of which this congregation is charged; but these, though the principal, are not the only objects of its attention; its views, in a word, are vast, and its exploits almost incredible. Its members hold their assemblies in a spacious and magnificent palace, whose delightful situation adds a singular lustre to its beauty and grandeur.*

II. To this famous establishment, another, less splendid indeed, but highly useful, was added, in 1627, by Urban VIII. under the denomination of a College or Seminary for the Propagation of the Faith. This seminary is appropriated to the education of those who are designed for the foreign missions; and they are here instructed, with the greatest care, in the knowledge of all the languages and sciences that are necessary to prepare them for propagating the Gospel among the distant nations. This excellent foundation was due to the zeal and munificence of John Baptist Viles, a Spanish nobleman, who resided at the court of Rome, and who began by presenting to the pontiff all his ample possessions, together with his house, which was a noble and beautiful structure, for this pious and generous purpose. His liberality excited a spirit of pious emulation, and is followed with zeal even to this day. The seminary was at first committed by Urban to the care and direction of three canons of the patriarchal churches; but this appointment was afterwards changed, and, ever since the year 1641, it has been governed by the *congregation* founded by Gregory XV.†

III. The same zealous spirit reached France, and produced in that country several pious foundations of a like nature. In 1663, the king instituted *the Congregation of Priests of the foreign Missions;* while an association of bishops and other ecclesiastics founded the Parisian Seminary for the Missions abroad, designed for the education of those who were set apart for the propagation of Christianity among the pagan nations. Hence apostolical vicars are still sent to Siam, Tonquin, Cochin-China, and Persia, bishops to Bagdad, and missionaries to other Asiatic nations; and all these spiritual envoys are supported by the ample revenues and possessions of the *congregation* and *seminary*.‡ These priests of the foreign missions,§ and the apostles whom they send into foreign countries, are almost perpetually involved in altercations and debates with the Jesuits and their missionaries. The former are shocked at the methods which are ordinarily employed by the latter in converting the Chinese and other Asiatics to the Christian religion; and the Jesuits, in their turn, absolutely refuse obedience to the orders of the apostolical vicars and bishops, who receive their commission from the congregation above-mentioned, though this commission be issued out with the consent of the pope, or of the College *de propagandâ fide* residing at Rome. There was also another religious establishment formed in France, during this century, under the title of the Congregation of the Holy Sacrament, whose founder was Autherius, Bishop of Bethlehem, and which, in 1644, received an order from Urban VIII. to have always a number of ecclesiastics ready to exercise their ministry among the pagan nations, whenever they should be called upon by the pope, or the Congregation *de propagandâ fide*, for that purpose. It would be endless to mention other associations of less note, that were formed in several countries for promoting the cause of Christianity among the darkened nations; as also the care taken by the Jesuits, and other religious communities, to have a number of missionaries always ready for that service.

IV. These congregations and colleges sent forth those legions of missionaries, who, in this century, covered a great part of the globe, and converted to the profession of Christianity at least, if not to its temper and spirit, multitudes of persons among the fiercest and most barbarous nations. The religious orders, that made the greatest figure in these missions, were the Jesuits, Dominicans, Franciscans, and Capuchins, who, though concerned in one common cause, agreed very ill among themselves, publicly accusing each other, with the most bitter reproaches and invectives, of want of zeal in the service of Christ, and even of corrupting the purity of the Christian doctrine to promote their ambitious purposes. But none of these teachers of religion were so generally accused of sinister views and unworthy practices, in this respect, as the Jesuits, who were singularly odious in the eyes of all the other missionaries, and were looked upon as a very dangerous and pernicious set of apostles by a considerable part of the Romish church. Nor, indeed, could they be viewed in any other light, if the general report be true, that, instead of instructing their proselytes in the genuine doctrines of Christianity, they then taught, and still teach, a corrupt system of religion and morality, that is not burthensome to the conscience, and is reconcilable with the indulgence of gross appetites and passions;—that they not only tolerate, but even countenance, in new converts, several profane opinions and superstitious rites and customs;—that, by commerce, carried on with the most rapacious avidity, and various other methods, little consistent with probity and candour, they have already acquired an overgrown opulence, which they augment from day to day;—that they burn with the thirst of ambition, and are constantly gaping after worldly honours and prerogatives;—that they are perpetually employing the arts of adulation, and

* The authors who have given an account of this Congregation, are mentioned by Fabricius, in his Lux Evangelii toti Orbi exoriens, cap. xxxiii. p. 566. Add to these, Dorotheus Ascanius, de Montibus Pietatis Ecclesiæ Roman. p. 522, where may be seen a complete list of the books that have been published by this congregation, from its first institution to the year 1667.

† Helyot, Histoire des Ordres, tom. viii. cap. xii.—Urb. Cerri, Etat. Present de l'Eglise Romaine, p. 293, where, however, the founder of this college is called, by mistake, Vives.

‡ See the Gallia Christiana Benedictinorum, tom. iv. p. 1024.—Helyot, Histoire des Ordres, tom. viii. chap. xii.

§ These Ecclesiastics are commonly called, in France, *Messieurs des Missions Etrangeres.*

the seductions of bribery, to insinuate themselves into the friendship and protection of men in power;—that they are deeply involved in civil affairs, in the cabals of courts, and the intrigues of politicians;—and finally, that they frequently excite intestine commotions and civil wars, in those states and kingdoms, where their views are obstructed or disappointed, and refuse obedience to the Roman pontiff, and to the vicars and bishops that bear his commission. These accusations are indeed grievous, but they are perfectly well attested, being confirmed by the most striking circumstantial evidence, as well as by a prodigious number of unexceptionable witnesses. Among these we may reckon many of the most illustrious and respectable members of the church of Rome, whose testimony cannot be imputed to the suggestions of envy, on one hand, or be considered as the effect of temerity or ignorance on the other; such are the cardinals, the members of the Congregation *de propagandâ fide*, and even some of the popes themselves. These testimonies are supported and confirmed by glaring facts, even by the proceedings of the Jesuits in China, Abyssinia, Japan, and India, where they have dishonoured the cause of Christianity, and, by their corrupt practices, have injured, in the most sensible manner, the interest of Rome.*

V. The Jesuits exhausted all the resources of their peculiar artifice and dexterity to impose silence upon their accusers, confound their adversaries, and give a specious colour to their own proceedings. But all their stratagems were ineffectual. The court of Rome was informed of their odious frauds; and this information was, by no means, looked upon as groundless. Many circumstances concur to prove this, and among others the conduct of that congregation by which the foreign missions are carried on and directed; for it is remarkable, that, for many years past, the Jesuits have been much less employed by this congregation, than in former times, and are also treated, on almost every occasion, with a degree of circumspection that manifestly implies suspicion and diffidence. Other religious orders have evidently gained the ascendency which the Jesuits formerly held; and, in the nice and critical affairs of the church, especially in what relates to the propagation of the Gospel in foreign parts, much greater confidence is placed in the austere sobriety, poverty, industry, and patience of the Capuchins and Carmelites, than in the opulence, artifice, genius, and fortitude, of the disciples of Loyola. On the other hand it is certain, that, if the Jesuits are not much trusted, they are more or less feared, since neither the powerful congregation, now mentioned, nor even the pontiffs themselves, venture to reform all the abuses, which they silently disapprove, or openly blame, in the conduct of this insidious order. This connivance, however involuntary, is now a matter of necessity. The opulence of the Jesuits is so excessive, and their credit and influence are so extensive and formidable, in all those parts of the world which have embraced the Romish religion, that they carry their insolence so far as to menace often the pontiff himself, who cannot, without the utmost peril, oblige them to submit to his orders, when they are disposed to be refractory. Even the decisions of the pope are frequently suggested by this powerful society; and it is only in such a case that the society treats them with unlimited respect. When they come from any other quarter, they are received in a very different manner by the Jesuits, who trample upon some of them with impunity, and interpret others with their usual dexterity, in such a manner, as to answer the views and promote the interests of their ambitious order. Such, at least, are the accounts that are generally given of their proceedings, accounts which, though contradicted by them, are supported by striking and palpable evidence.

VI. The rise of these dissensions between the Jesuits and the other Romish missionaries, may be ascribed to the methods of conversion used by the former, which are entirely different from those that are employed by the latter. The crafty disciples of Loyola judge it proper to attack the superstition of the Indian nations by artifice and stratagem, and to bring them gradually, with the utmost caution and prudence, to the knowledge of Christianity. In consequence of this principle, they interpret and explain the ancient doctrines of Paganism, and also those which Confucius taught in China, in such a manner as to soften and diminish, at least in appearance, their opposition to the truths of the Gospel; and whenever they find, in any of the religious systems of the Indians, tenets or precepts that bear even the faintest resemblance to certain doctrines or precepts of Christianity, they employ all their dexterity and zeal to render this resemblance more plausible and striking, and to persuade the Indians, that there is a great conformity between their ancient theology and the new religion they are exhorted to embrace. They go still farther; for they indulge their proselytes in the observance of all their national customs and rites, except such as are glaringly inconsistent with the genius and spirit of the Christian worship. These rites are modified a little by the Jesuits, and are directed toward a different set of objects, so as to form a sort of coalition between Paganism and Christianity. To secure themselves an ascendancy over the untutored minds of these simple Indians, they study their natural inclinations and propensities, comply with them on all occasions, and carefully avoid whatever may shock them; and, as in all countries the clergy, and men of eminent learning, are supposed to have a considerable influence on the multitude, so the Jesuists are particularly assiduous in courting the friendship of the Indian priests, which they obtain by various methods, in the choice of which they are far from being scrupulous. But the protection of men in power is the great object at which they principally aim, as the surest method of establishing their authority, and extending their influence. With this view, they study all the arts that can render them agreeable or useful to great men; apply them selves to the mathematics, physic, poetry, the

* The reader will find an ample relation of these facts, in the preface to the Hist. de la Compagnie de Jesus, published at Utrecht in 1741

theory of painting, sculpture, architecture, and other elegant arts; and persevere in studying men and manners, the interests of princes, and the affairs of the world, in order to prepare them for giving counsel in critical situations, and suggesting expedients in perplexing and complicated cases. It would be endless to enumerate all the circumstances that have been complained of in the proceedings of the Jesuits. These, now mentioned, have ruined their credit in the esteem of the other missionaries, who consider their artful and insiduous dealings as every way unsuitable to the character and dignity of the ambassadors of Christ, whom it becomes to plead the cause of God with an honest simplicity, and an ingenuous openness and candour, without any mixture of dissimulation or fraud. And, accordingly, we find the other religious orders, that are employed in the foreign missions, proceeding in a very different method in the exercise of their ministry. They attack openly the superstitions of the Indians, in all their connexions and in all their consequences, and are studious to remove whatever might tend to nourish them. They show little regard to the ancient rites and customs in use among the blinded nations, and little respect for the authority of those by whom they were established. They treat, with an indifference bordering upon contempt, the pagan priests, grandees, and princes; and preach, without disguise, the peculiar doctrines of Christianity, while they attack, without hesitation or fear, the superstitions of those nations they are called to convert.

VII. These missionaries diffused the fame of the Christian religion through a great part of Asia during this century. The ministerial labours of the Jesuits, Theatins, and Augustinians, contributed to introduce some rays of divine truth, mixed, indeed, with much darkness and superstition, into those parts of India which had been possessed by the Portuguese, before their expulsion by the Dutch. But, of all the missions that were established in those distant parts of the globe, no one has been more constantly and generally applauded than that of Madura, or is said to have produced more abundant and permanent fruit. It was undertaken and executed by Robert de Nobili,* an Italian Jesuit, who took a very singular method of rendering his ministry successful. Considering, on one hand, that the Indians beheld all Europeans with an eye of prejudice and aversion, and, on the other, that they held in the highest veneration the order of Brachmans or Bramins, as descended from the Gods; and that, impatient of other rulers, they paid an implicit and unlimited obedience to them alone; he assumed the appearance and title of a Bramin who had come from a distant country, and, by smearing his countenance, and imitating that most austere and painful method of living which the Sanianes or penitents observe, he at length persuaded the credulous people that he was, in reality, a member of that venerable order.† By this stratagem he gained over to Christianity twelve eminent Bramins, whose example and influence engaged a prodigious number of the people to hear the instructions, and to receive the doctrine of this famous missionary. On the death of Robert, this singular mission was for some time at a stand, and seemed even to be neglected;* but it was renewed by the zeal and industry of the Portuguese Jesuits, and is still carried on by several missionaries of that order, from France and Portugal, who have inured themselves to the terrible austerities that were practised by Robert, and which have thus become, as it were, the appendages of that mission. These fictitious Bramins, who boldly deny their being Europeans or Franks,† and only give themselves out for inhabitants of the northern regions, are said to have converted a prodigious number of Indians to Christianity; and, if common report may be credited, the congregations which they have already founded in those countries grow more numerous from year to year. Nor, indeed, do these accounts appear, in the main, unworthy of belief,‡ though we must not be too ready to re-

* Others call this famous missionary Robert de Nobilibus.

† Urban Cerri, Etat present de l'Eglise Romaine, p. 173.

☞ Nobili, who was looked upon by the Jesuists as the chief apostle of the Indians after Francis Xavier, took incredible pains to acquire knowledge of the religion, customs, and language of Madura, sufficient for the purposes of his ministry. But this was not all; for, to stop the mouths of his opposers, and particularly of those who treated his character of Bramin as an impostor, he produced an old, dirty parchment, in which he had forged, in the ancient Indian characters, a deed, showing that the Bramins of Rome were of much older date than those of India, and that the Jesuits of Rome descended, in a direct line, from the god Brama. Father Jouvenci, a learned Jesuit, tells us, in the History of his Order, something yet more remarkable; even that Robert de Nobili, when the authenticity of his smoky parchment was called in question by some Indian unbelievers, declared *upon oath*, before the assembly of the Bramins of Madura, that he really derived his origin from the god Brama. Is it not astonishing that this reverend father should acknowledge, is it not monstrous that he should applaud, as a piece of pious ingenuity, this detestable instance of perjury and fraud? See Jouvenci, Histoire des Jesuites; and Norbet, Memoires Historiques sur les Missions de Malab. tom. ii. p. 145.

* Urban Cerri, Etat present de l'Eglise Romaine p. 173.

† The Indians distinguish all the Europeans by the general denomination of *Franks*, or, (as they pronounce the word) *Franghis*.

‡ The Jesuits seem to want words to express the glory that has accrued to their order from the remarkable success and the abundant fruits of this famous mission, as also the dreadful sufferings and hardships which their missionaries sustained in the course of their ministry. See the Lettres Curieuses et Edifiantes, ecrites des Missions Etrangeres, tom. i. where Father Martin observes, that this mission surpasses all others; that each missionary baptises, at least, a thousand converts every year; that, nevertheless, baptism is not indiscriminately administered, or granted with facility and precipitation to every one who demands it; that those who present themselves to be baptized, are accurately examined until they exhibit sufficient proofs of their sincerity, and are carefully instructed during a period of four months in order to their reception; that, after their reception, they live like angels rather than like men and that the smallest appearance of a mortal sin is scarcely, if ever, to be found among them. If any one is curious enough to inquire into the causes that produced such an uncommon degree of sanctity among these new converts, the Jesuits allege the two following: The first is modestly drawn from the holy lives and examples of the missionaries, who pass their days in the greatest austerity, and in acts of mortification that are terrible to nature; (see tom.

ceive, as authentic and well attested, the relations which have been given of the intolerable hardships and sufferings sustained by these Jesuit-Bramins in the cause of Christ. Many imagine, and not without good foundation, that their austerities are (generally speaking) more dreadful in appearance than in reality; and that, while they outwardly affect an extraordinary degree of self-denial, they indulge themselves privately in a free, and even luxurious mode of living, have their tables delicately served, and their cellars exquisitely furnished, in order to refresh themselves after their labours.

VIII. The knowledge of Christianity was first conveyed to the kingdoms of Siam, Tongking or Tonquin, and Cochin-China, by a mission of Jesuits, under the direction of Alexander of Rhodes, a native of Avignon,* whose instructions were received with uncommon docility by a prodigious number of the inhabitants of those countries. When an account of the success of this spiritual expedition was brought to pope Alexander VII. in 1658, he resolved to commit this new church to the inspection and government of a certain number of bishops, and chose for this purpose some French priests out of the Congregation of foreign Missions to carry his orders to the rising community, and to rule over it as his representatives and vicegerents. But the Jesuits, who can bear no superiors, and scarcely an equal, treated these pious men with the greatest indignity, loaded them with injuries and reproaches, and would not permit them to share their labours or partake of their glory.* Hence arose, in the court of Rome, a long and tedious contest, which served to show, in the plainest manner, that the Jesuits were ready enough to make use of the authority of the pope, when it was necessary to promote their interests, or to extend their influence and dominion; but that they did not hesitate, on the other hand, to treat the same authority with indifference and contempt in all cases, where it seemed to oppose their private views and personal interests. After this, Louis XIV. sent a solemn embassy,† in

xii. p. 206; tom. xv. p. 211;) who are not allowed, for instance, to take bread, wine, fish, or flesh, but are obliged to be satisfied with water and vegetables, dressed in the most insipid and disgusting manner, and whose clothing and other circumstances of life are answerable to their miserable diet. The second cause of this unusual appearance, alleged by the Jesuits, is the situation of these new Christians, by which they are cut off from all communication and intercourse with the Europeans, who are said to have corrupted, by their licentious manners, almost all the other Indian proselytes. Add, to all this, other considerations, which are scattered up and down, in the letters above cited, tom. i. p. 16, 17; tom. ii. p. 1; tom. iii. p. 217; tom. v. p. 2; tom. vi. p. 119; tom. ix. p. 126. Madura is a separate kingdom situated in the midst of the Indian peninsula beyond the Ganges.* There is an accurate map of the territory comprehended in the mission of Madura, published by the Jesuits in the xvth tome of the Lettres Curieuses, p. 60. The French Jesuits set on foot, in the kingdom of Carnate and in the adjacent provinces, a mission like that of Madura; and, toward the conclusion of this century, other missionaries of the same order formed an enterprise of the same nature in the dominions of the king of Marava. The Jesuits themselves acknowledge that the latter establishment succeeded much better than the former. The reason of this may perhaps be, that the French Jesuits, who founded the mission of Carnate, could not endure, with such constancy and patience, the austere and mortified manner of living which an institution of this nature required, nor imitate the rigid self-denial of the Bramins, so well as the missionaries of Spain and Portugal. Be that as it may, all these missions, which formerly made such a noise in the world, were suspended and abandoned, in consequence of a mandate issued in 1754, by Benedict XIV., who declared his disapprobation of the mean and perfidious methods of converting the Indians that were practised by the Jesuists, and pronounced it unlawful to make use of frauds or insidious artifices in extending the limits of the Christian church. See Norbert's Memoires Historiques pour les Missions Orientales, tom. i. and iv. Mammachius has given an account of this matter, and also published the mandate of Benedict, in his Orig. et Antiq. Christian. tom. ii. p. 245. See also Lockman's Travels of the Jesuits.

* See the writings of Alexander de Rhodes, who was undoubtedly a man of sense and spirit, and more especially his Travels, which were published at Paris in 1666.

☞ * This is a mistake. Madura is in the Indian peninsula on this side of the Ganges, and not beyond it. Its chief produce is rice, which is one of the principal instruments used by the rich Jesuits in the conversion of the poor Indians

* There were several pamphlets and memorials published at Paris, in the years 1666, 1674, and 1682, in which these French missionaries, whom the Jesuits refused to admit as fellow-labourers in the conversion of the Indians, relate, in an eloquent and affecting strain, the injuries they had received from that jealous and ambitious order. The most ample and accurate narration of that kind was published in 1688 by Francis Pallu, whom the pope had created bishop of Heliopolis. The same subject is largely treated in the Gallia Christiana of the learned Benedictines, tom. vii. p. 1027; and a concise account of it is also given by Urban Cerri, in his Etat present de l'Eglise Romaine, p. 199. The latter author, though a secretary of the Congregation de propaganda fide, yet inveighs with a just severity and a generous warmth against the perfidy, cruelty, and ambition of the Jesuits, and laments it as a most unhappy thing, that the congregation now mentioned, had not sufficient power to set limits to the rapacity and tyranny of that arrogant society. He farther observes, toward the end of his narrative, which is addressed to the pope, that he was not at liberty to reveal all the abominations which the Jesuits had committed, during the course of this contest, but, by the order of his holiness, was obliged to pass them over in silence. His words are, *Votre Saintete a ordonne qu'elles demeurassent sous le secret.*—See also, on this topic, Helyot's Histoire des Ordres, tom. viii.

☞ † The French bishops of Heliopolis, Berytus, and Metellopolis, who had been sent into India about the year 1663, had prepared the way for this embassy, and, by an account of the favourable dispositions of the monarch then reigning at Siam, had encouraged the French king to make a new attempt for the establishment of Christianity in those distant regions. A fixed residence had been formed at Siam for the French missionaries, together with a seminary for instructing the youth in the languages of the circumjacent nations, who had all settlements (or *camps*, as they were called) at the capital. A church was also erected there, by the king's permission, in 1667; and that prince proposed several questions to the missionaries, which seemed to discover a propensity to inform himself concerning their religion. The bishop of Heliopolis, who had gone back to Europe on the affairs of the mission, returned to Siam in 1673, with letters from Louis and pope Clement IX., accompanied with rich presents, to thank his Siamese majesty for the favours bestowed on the French bishops. In a private audience to which he was admitted, he explained, in an answer to a question proposed to him by the king of Siam, the motive that had engaged the French bishops to cross so many seas, and the French king to send his subjects to countries so far from home; observing, that a strong desire, in his prince, to extend the kingdom of the true God, was the sole reason of their voyage. Upon this we are told, that the king of Siam offered a port in any part of his dominions, where a city might be

1684, to the king of Siam, whose prime minister, at that time, was a Greek Christian, named Constantine Falcon, a man of an artful, ambitious, and enterprising spirit. The design of this embassy was to engage the pagan prince to embrace Christianity, and to permit the propagation of the Gospel in his dominions. The ambassadors were attended by a great retinue of priests and Jesuits, some of whom were well acquainted with such branches of science as were agreeable to the taste of the king of Siam. It was only, however, among a small part of the people, that the labours of these missionaries were crowned with any degree of success; for the monarch himself, and the great men of his kingdom, remained unmoved by their exhortations, and deaf to their instructions.* The king, indeed, though he chose to persevere in the religion of his ancestors, yet discovered a spirit of condescension and toleration towards the conductors of this mission; and his favourite Constantine had secretly invited the French to Siam to support him in his authority, which was beheld with an envious eye by several of the grandees. As long as this prince and his minister lived, the French retained some hopes of accomplishing their purpose, and of converting the nation to the faith; but these hopes entirely vanished in 1688, when, in a popular sedition, excited and fomented by some prince of the blood, both the king and his minister were put to death;* and then the missionaries returned home.

IX. China, the most extensive and opulent of all the Asiatic kingdoms, could not but appear, to the missionaries and their constituents, an object worthy of their pious zeal and spiritual ambition. And accordingly a numerous tribe of Jesuits, Dominicans, Franciscans, and Capuchins, set out about the commencement of this century, with a view to enlighten that immense region with a knowledge of the Gospel. All these, however they differed in other matters, agreed in proclaiming the astonishing success of their ministerial labours. It is nevertheless certain, that the principal honour of these religious exploits belonged to the Jesuits, who, with peculiar dexterity and address, removed the chief obstacles to the progress of Christianity, among a people whose natural acuteness and pride were accompanied with a superstitious attachment to the religion and manners of their ancestors. These artful missionaries studied the temper, character, taste, inclinations, and prejudices of the Chinese, with incredible attention; and perceiving that their natural sagacity was attended with an ardent desire of improvement, and that they took the highest pleasure in the study of the arts and sciences, and more especially in the mathematics, they lost no occasion of sending for such members of their order as, beside their knowledge of mankind, and prudence in transacting business, were also masters of the different branches of learning and philosophy. Some of these learned Jesuits acquired such a high degree of credit and influence by their sagacity and eloquence, the insinuating sweetness and facility of their manners, and their surprising dexterity and skill in all kinds of transactions, that they were at length gratified by the emperor with the most honourable marks of distinction, and were employed in the most secret and important deliberations and affairs of the cabinet. Under the auspicious protection of such powerful patrons, the other missionaries, though of a lower rank and of inferior talents, were delivered from all apprehension of danger in the exercise of their ministry, and were thus encouraged to exert themselves with spirit, vigour, and perseverance, in the propagation of the Gospel, in all the provinces of that mighty empire.

X. This promising scene was clouded for some time, when Xun-chi, the first Chinese

---

built to the honour of Louis the Great, and where, if he thought fit, he might send a viceroy to reside; and declared afterwards, in a public assembly of the grandees of his court, that he would leave all his subjects at liberty to embrace the Romish faith. All this raised the hopes of the missionaries to a very high pitch; but the expectations which they thence derived of converting the king himself were entirely groundless, as may be seen from a very remarkable declaration of that monarch in the following note. See the Relation des Missions et des Voyages des Eveques Francois.

☞ * When Monsieur de Chaumont, who was charged with this famous embassy, arrived at Siam, he presented a long memorial to the monarch of that country, intimating how solicitous the king of France was to have his Siamese majesty of the same religion with himself. Chaw Naraya, (for so was the latter named,) who seems to have always deceived the French by encouraging words, which administered hopes that he never intended to accomplish, answered this memorial in a very acute and artful manner. After asking who had made the king of France believe that he entertained any such sentiments, he desired his minister Falcon to tell the French ambassador, "That he left it to his most Christian majesty to judge, whether the change of a religion that had been followed in his dominions without interruption for 2229 years could be a matter of small importance to him, or a demand with which it was easy to comply;—that, besides, he was much surprised to find the king of France concern himself so zealously and so warmly in a matter which related to *God* and not to *him;* and in which, though it related to God, the Deity did not seem to interfere at all, but left it entirely to human discretion." The king asked, at the same time, "Whether the true God, who created heaven and earth, and had bestowed on mankind such different natures and inclinations, could not, when he gave to men the same bodies and souls, have also, if he had pleased, inspired them with the same religious sentiments, and have made all nations live and die in the same laws." He added that, "since order among men, and unity in religion, depend absolutely on the divine will, which could as easily introduce them into the world as a diversity of sects, it is natural thence to conclude, that the true God takes as much pleasure to be honoured by different modes of religion and worship, as to be glorified by a prodigious number of different creatures, who praise him every one in his own way." He moreover asked, "Whether that beauty and variety, which we admire in the order of nature, be less admirable in the order of supernatural things, or less becoming in the wisdom of God?—However that may be (continued the king of Siam,) since we know that God is the absolute master of the world, and we are persuaded that nothing comes to pass contrary to his will, I resign my person and dominions into the arms of his providence, and beseech his eternal wisdom to dispose thereof according to his good will and pleasure." See Tachard's Prem. Voyage de Siam, p. 218; as also the Journal of the Abbe Choisi.

* An account of this embassy, and of the transactions both of ambassadors and missionaries, is given by Tachard, Chaumont, and La Loubere. The relations, however, of the author last-mentioned, who was a man of learning and candour, deserve undoubtedly the preference

emperor of the Mogul race, died, and left, as his only heir, a son, who was a minor. The grandees of the empire, to whose tuition and care this young prince was committed, had long entertained an aversion to Christianity, and only sought for a convenient occasion of venting their rage against it. This occasion was now offered and greedily embraced. The guardians of the young prince abused his power to execute their vindictive purposes, and, after using their utmost efforts to extirpate Christianity wherever it was professed, they persecuted its patrons, more especially the Jesuits, with great bitterness, deprived them of all the honours and advantages they had enjoyed, and treated them with the utmost barbarity and injustice. John Adam Schaal, their chief, whose advanced age and extensive knowledge, together with the honourable place which he held at court, seemed to demand some marks of exemption from the calamities that pursued his brethren, was thrown into prison, and condemned to death, while the other missionaries were sent into exile. These dismal scenes of persecution were exhibited in 1664; but, about five years after this gloomy period, when Kanghi assumed the reigns of government, a new face of things appeared. The Christian cause, and the labours of its ministers, not only resumed their former credit and vigour, but even gained ground, and received such distinguished marks of protection from the throne, that the Jesuits usually date from this period the commencement of the golden age of Christianity in China. The new emperor, whose noble and generous spirit* was equal to the uncommon extent of his genius, and to his ardent curiosity in the investigation of truth, began his reign by recalling the Jesuits to his court, and restoring them to the credit and influence which they had formerly enjoyed. But his generosity and munificence did not stop here; for he sent to Europe for a still greater number of the members of that order, such of them particularly as were eminent for their skill in the arts and sciences. Some of these he placed in the highest offices of the state, and employed in civil negotiations and transactions of the greatest importance. Others he chose for his private friends and counsellors, who were to assist him with their advice in various points, and to direct his philosophical and mathematical studies. These private friends and counsellors were principally chosen from among the French Jesuits. Thus the order was raised, in a short time, to the very summit of favour, and invested with a degree of authority and lustre which it had not before attained. In such a state of things, it is natural to conclude, that the Christian religion would not want powerful patrons, and that its preachers would not be left destitute and unsupported.

* See Joach. Bouveti Icon Monarchæ Sinarum, translated into Latin by the famous Leibnitz, and published in 1699, in the second part of his Novissima Sinica. See also Du Halde's Description de la Chine, and the Lettres Edifiantes, in which the Jesuits give an account of the success of their missions. In these productions, the virtues and talents of this emperor, which seem, indeed, to be universally acknowledged, are described and celebrated with peculiar encomiums.

Accordingly a multitude of spiritual labourers from all parts of Europe repaired to China, allured by the prospect of a rich, abundant, and glorious harvest; and, indeed, the success of their ministry seemed to answer fully the extent of their expectations, since it is well known that, with very little pains, and still less opposition, they made a prodigious number of converts to the profession of the Gospel. At length Christianity seemed to triumph in 1692, when the emperor, from an excessive attachment to the Jesuits, issued that remarkable edict, by which he declared, that the Christian religion was in no wise detrimental to the safety or interests of the monarchy, as its enemies pretended; and by which also he granted to all his subjects an entire freedom of conscience, and a full permission to embrace the Gospel. This triumph was farther confirmed, when the same prince, in 1700, ordered a magnificent church to be built for the Jesuits within the precincts of the imperial palace.*

XI. This surprising success of the Christian cause may undoubtedly be attributed to the dexterity and perseverance of the Jesuits, as even the greatest enemies of that artful order are obliged to acknowledge. But it is quite another question, whether this success was obtained by methods agreeable to the dictates of reason and conscience, and consistent with the dignity and genius of the Christian religion. The latter point has been long debated, with great animosity and vehemence, on both sides. The adversaries of the Jesuits, whose opposition is as keen as their numbers are formidable, and more especially the Jansenites and Dominicans, assert boldly, that the success above mentioned was obtained by the most odious frauds, and even, in many cases, by detestable crimes. They charge the Jesuits with having given a false exposition and a spurious account of the ancient religion of the Chinese, and with having endeavoured to persuade the emperor and the nobility, that the primitive theology of their nation, and the doctrine of their great instructor and philosopher Confucius, scarcely differed in any respect from the doctrine of the Gospel. The missionaries are farther charged with having invented a variety of historical fictions, in order to persuade the Chinese, (who are warmly attached to whatever carries the air of remote antiquity,) that Jesus Christ had been known and worshipped in their nation many ages ago; and these fictions are supposed to have prejudiced the emperor in favour of Christianity, and to have engaged certain grandees not only to grant their

* There is a concise but interesting account of these revolutions, given by Du Halde, in his description de la Chine, tom. iii., and by the Jesuit Fontaney, in the Lettres Edifiantes et Curieuses, tom. viii.—They are related in a more diffuse and ample manner by other writers. See Suarez, de Libertate Religionem Christianam apud Sinas propagandi Narratio, published in 1698 by Leibnitz, in the first part of his Novissima Sinica. The other authors who have treated this branch of history are mentioned by Fabricius, in his Lux Evangelii, cap. xxxix. See also an Eccles. His. of China, which I published in German in 1748. ☞This history was translated into English, and published in 1750, with this titl Authentic Memoirs of the Christian church in China.

protection to the Jesuits, but even to become members of their society. The disciples of Loyola are also said to have lost sight of all the duties and obligations that are incumbent on the ministers of Christ, and the heralds of a spiritual kingdom, by not only accepting worldly honours and places of civil authority and power, but even aspiring to them with all the ardour of an insatiable ambition, by boasting, with an arrogant vanity, of the protection and munificence of the emperor, by deserting the simplicity of a frugal and humble appearance, and indulging themselves in all the circumstances of external pomp and splendour, such as costly garments, numerous retinues, luxurious tables, and magnificent houses. To all this is added, that they employed much more zeal and industry in the advancement of human science, especially the mathematics, than in promoting Christian knowledge and virtue; and that they even went so far as to interfere in military matters, and to concern themselves, both personally and by their counsels, in the bloody scenes of war. While these heavy crimes are laid to the charge of those Jesuits, who, by their capacity and talents, had been raised to a high degree of credit in the empire, the more obscure members of that same order, who were appointed more immediately to instruct the Chinese in the truths of the Gospel, are far from being considered as blameless. They are accused of having employed, in the practice of usury, and various kinds of traffic, the precious moments which ought to have been consecrated to the functions of their ministry, and of having used low and dishonourable methods of advancing their fortunes, and insinuating themselves into the favour of the multitude. The Jesuits acknowledge, that some of these accusations are founded upon facts; but they give a specious colour to these facts, and use all their artifice and eloquence to justify what they cannot deny. Other articles of these complaints they treat as groundless, and as the fictions of calumny, invented with no other design than to cast a reproach upon their order. An impartial inquirer into these matters will perhaps find, that if, in several points, the Jesuits defend themselves in a very weak and unsatisfactory manner, there are others, in which their misconduct seems to have been exaggerated by envy and prejudice in the complaints of their adversaries.

XII. The grand accusation that is brought against the Jesuits in China, is this: That they make an impious mixture of light and darkness, of Chinese superstition and Christian truth, in order to triumph with the greater speed and facility over the prejudices of that people against the doctrine of the Gospel; and that they allow their converts to retain the profane customs and the absurd rites of their pagan ancestors. Ricci, who was the founder of the Christian Church in that famous monarchy, declared it as his opinion, that the greatest part of those rites, which the Chinese are obliged by the laws of their country to perform, might be innocently observed by the new converts. To render this opinion less shocking, he supported and explained it upon the following principle: that these rites were of a civil and not of a sacred nature; that they were invented from views of policy; and not for any purposes of religion; and that none but the very dregs of the populace in China, considered them in any other light.* This opinion was not only rejected by the Dominicans and Franciscans, who were associated with the Jesuits in this important mission, but also by some even of the most learned Jesuits both in China and Japan, and particularly by Nicolas Lombard, who published a memorial, containing the reasons† upon which his dissent was founded. This contest, which was long carried on in a private manner, was brought, by the Dominicans, before the tribunal of the pontiff, in the year 1645; and from that period it continued to produce great divisions, cabals, and commotions, in the church of Rome. Innocent X., in the year now mentioned, pronounced in favour of the Dominicans, and highly condemned the indulgence which the Jesuits had shown to the Chinese superstitions. But, about eleven years after, this sentence, though not formally reversed, was virtually annulled by Alexander VII., at the instigation of the Jesuits, who persuaded that pontiff to allow the Chinese converts the liberty of performing several of the rites to which they had been accustomed, and for which they discovered a peculiar fondness. This, however, did not prevent the Dominicans from renewing their complaints in 1661, and also in 1674, under the pontificate of Innocent XI., though the power and credit of the Jesuits seemed to triumph over all their remonstrances. This fatal dispute, which had been suspended for many years in China, broke out there again, in 1684, with greater violence than ever; and then the victory seemed to incline to the side of the Dominicans, in consequence of a decision pronounced, in 1693, by Charles Maigrot, a doctor of the Sorbonne, who acted as the delegate or vicar of the Roman pontiff, in the province of Fokien, and who was afterwards consecrated titular bishop of Conon. This ecclesiastic, by a public edict, declared the opinions and practices of the Jesuits, in relation to the affairs of the Chinese mission, absolutely inconsistent with the purity and simplicity of the Christian religion. But the pope, to whose supreme cognisance and decision Maigrot had submitted this important edict, refused to come to a determination before the matter in debate had been carefully examined, and the reasons of each party weighed with the utmost attention; and therefore, in 1699, he appointed a congregation of chosen doctors to examine and decide this tedious controversy. This resolution of the pontiff was no sooner made public, than all the enemies of the Jesuits, in all quarters of the church of Rome, and more especially those who wished ill to the

* See Mammachii Origines et Antiquitates Christiana, tom. ii. p. 373.

† See Chr. Kortholti Præfatio ad Volumen II. Epistolar. Leibnitiar. sect. vi. To this work are subjoined the pieces composed against the Jesuits by Lombard and Antony de S. Maria, with the remarks of Leibnitz; and there is also inserted in this collection, p. 413, an ample dissertation on the Chinese philosophy, drawn up by Leibnitz, who pleads there in the cause of the Jesuits.

order in France, came forth with their complaints, their accusations, and invectives, and loaded the transactions and reputation of the whole society with the most bitter reproaches.* The Jesuits, on the other hand, were not silent or inactive. They attacked their adversaries with vigour, and defended themselves with dexterity and spirit.†—But the conclusion of this critical and momentous contest belongs to the history of the following century.

XIII. If, in considering this controversy, which employed the ablest pens of the Romish church, we confine our attention to the merits of the cause, (passing over what personally concerns the Jesuits, with some other questions of a minute and incidental kind,) it will appear, that the whole dispute turns essentially upon two great points; the one relating to the Chinese notion of the Supreme Being; and the other to the nature of those honours which that people offer to certain persons deceased.

As to the former of these points, it is to be observed, that the Chinese call the supreme object of their religious worship Tien and Shang-ti, which, in their language, signify the *Heavens*, and that the Jesuits employ the same terms when they speak of the true God, who is adored by the Christians. Hence it is inferred, that they make no distinction between the supreme God of the Chinese, and the infinitely perfect Deity of the Christians; or (to express the same thing in other words) that they imagine the Chinese entertain the same notions concerning the Tien, or Heaven, that the Christians do concerning the God whom they adore. The question then relative to this point is properly as follows: "Do the Chinese understand, by the denominations above-mentioned, the visible and material heavens? or are these terms, on the contrary, employed by them to represent the Lord of these heavens, i. e. an eternal and all perfect Being, who presides over universal nature, and, from heaven, the immediate residence of his glory, governs all things with unerring wisdom?" or, to express the object in fewer words, "Do the Chinese mean, by their Tien, such a Deity as the Christians adore?" This question the Jesuits answer in the affirmative. They maintain, that the ancient Chinese philosophers, who had an accurate knowledge of the great principles of natural religion, represented the Supreme Being almost under the very same characters that are attributed to him by Christians; and hence they not only allow their Chinese disciples to employ the terms already mentioned in their prayers to the Deity, and in their religious discourses, but even use these terms themselves, when they pronounce the name of God in their public instructions, or in private conversation. The adversaries of the Jesuits maintain the negative of this question, regard the ancient philosophy of the Chinese as an impure source of blasphemy and impiety, and affirm, that it confounded the Divine Nature with that of the universe. They assert farther, that the famous Confucius, whose name and writings are held in such veneration by the people of China, was totally ignorant of divine truth, destitute of religious principle, and referred the origin of all things that exist to an internal and inevitable necessity. This contest, concerning the first point that divided the missionaries, produced a multitude of learned dissertations on the manners, laws, and opinions of the ancient inhabitants of China, and gave rise to several curious discoveries. But all these were insufficient to serve the chief purpose they were designed to accomplish, since they were far from giving a clear and satisfactory decision of the matter in debate. It still remained a question, which were most to be believed,—the Jesuits or their adversaries? and the impartial inquirer, after long examination, thought it prudent to trust entirely to neither; since, if it appeared on the one hand, that the Tien, or supreme God of the Chinese, was much inferior, in perfection and excellence, to the God of the Christians, it was equally evident, on the other, that this Chinese Deity was looked upon by his adorers as entirely distinct from the material æther and the visible heavens.

XIV. As to the other point in dispute, it must be previously observed, that the ancient laws of China oblige the natives of that vast region to perform, annually, at a stated time, in honour of their ancestors, certain rites, which seem to be of a religious nature. It may also be observed, that it is a custom among the learned to pay, at stated times, to the memory of Confucius, whom the Chinese consider as the oracle of all wisdom and knowledge, certain marks of veneration that have undoubtedly a religious aspect, and which are, moreover, performed in a kind of temple erected to that great and illustrious philosopher. Hence arises a second question, which is thus proposed: "Are those honours that the Chinese, in general, pay to the memory of their ancestors, and which the learned, in particular, offer at the shrine of Confucius, of a *civil* or *sacred* nature? Are they to be considered as religious offerings, or are they no more than political institutions designed to promote some public good?" The Jesuits affirm, that the ancient Chinese lawgivers established these rites with no other view than to keep the people in order, and to maintain the tranquillity of the state; and that the Chinese did not pay any religious worship, either to the memory of Confucius, or to the departed souls of their ancestors, but only declared, by the performance of certain rites, their gratitude and respect to both, and their solemn resolution to imitate their virtues, and follow their

☞ * See the Lettres des Messieurs des Missions Etrangeres au Pape, sur les Idolatries et les Superstitions Chinoises—Revocation de l'Approbation donnee par M. Brisacier, Superieur des Missions Etrangeres, au Livre de la Defense des nouveaux Chretiens et des Missionaires de la Chine.—Deux Lettres d'un Docteur de l'Ordre de St. Dominique au R. P. Dez, Provincial des Jesuites, sur les Ceremonies de la Chine.

† Du Halde, Description de la Chine, tom. iii. p. 142.—See the enumeration of other writers on the same subject, given by Fabricius, in his Lux Evangelii, cap. xxxix. p. 665.—See also Voltaire's Siecle de Louis XIV. tom. ii. p. 318.—But the most ingenious patron of the Jesuits, on this occasion, was Father Daniel, himself a member of that famous order. See his Histoire Apologetique de la Conduite des Jesuites de la Chine, in the third volume of his Opuscules.

illustrious examples. Hence these missionaries conclude, that the Chinese converts to Christianity might be permitted to perform these ceremonies according to the ancient custom of their country, provided they understood their true nature, and kept always in remembrance, the political views with which they were instituted, and the civil purposes they were designed to serve. By this specious account of things, the conduct of the Jesuits is, in some measure, justified. But, whether this representation be true or false, it will still remain evident, that, in order to render the Christian cause triumphant in China, some such concessions and accommodations as those of the Jesuits seem almost absolutely necessary; and they who desire the *end* must submit to the use of the *means*.* The necessity of concession arises from this remarkable circumstance, that, by a solemn law of ancient date, it is positively declared, that no man shall be esteemed a good citizen, or be looked upon as qualified to hold any public office in the state, who neglects the observance of the ceremonies now under consideration. On the other hand, the Dominicans, and the other adversaries of the Jesuits, maintain, that the rites in question form an important branch of the Chinese religion; that the honours paid by the Chinese to Confucius and to the souls of their ancestors, are not of a civil, but of a religious nature;† and consequently, that all who perform these rites are chargeable with insulting the majesty of God, to whom alone all divine worship is due, and cannot be considered as true Christians. This account of the affair is so specious and probable, and the consequences deducible from it are so natural and just, that the more equitable and impartial among the Jesuits have acknowledged the difficulties that attend the cause they maintain; and taking, at length, refuge in the plea of necessity, allege, that certain evils and inconveniences may be lawfully submitted to when they are requisite in order to the attainment of extensive, important, and salutary purposes.

XV. The ministerial labours of the Romish missionaries, and more especially of the Jesuits, were crowned in Japan with surprising success, about the commencement of this century, and made an incredible number of converts to the Christian religion.* But this prosperous and

☞ * True; if the *means* be not either criminal in themselves, pernicious in their consequences, or of such a nature as to defeat, in a great measure, the benefits and advantages proposed by the *end*. And it is a very nice and momentous question, whether the concessions pleaded for in behalf of the Chinese converts, by the Jesuits, are not to be ranked among the means here characterized. See the following note.

☞ † The public honours paid to Confucius twice a year, used to be performed before his statue, erected in the great hall or temple that is dedicated to his memory. At present they are performed before a kind of table, placed in the most conspicuous part of the edifice, with the following inscription: "The Throne of the Soul of the most holy and the most excellent chief Teacher Confucius." The literati, or learned, celebrate this famous festival in the following manner:—The chief mandarin of the place exercises the office of priest, and the others discharge the functions of deacons, sub-deacons, &c. A certain sacrifice, which consists of wine, blood, fruits, &c. is offered, after the worshippers have prepared themselves for this ceremony by fasting and other acts of abstinence and mortification. They kneel before the inscription, prostrate the body nine times before it, until the head touches the ground, and repeat many prayers; after which the priest, taking in one hand a cup full of wine, and in the other a like cup filled with blood, makes a solemn libation to the deceased, and dismisses the assembly with a blessing. The rites performed by families, in honour of their deceased parents, are nearly of the same nature.

Now, in order to know, with certainty, whether this festival and these rites be of a civil or religious nature, we have only to inquire, whether they be the same with those ceremonies that are performed by the Chinese, in the worship they pay to certain celestial and terrestrial spirits, or *genii*, which worship is undoubtedly of a religious kind. The learned Leibnitz* undertook to affirm, that the services now mentioned were not of the same kind, and, consequently, that the Jesuits were accused unjustly. But that great man does not appear to have examined this matter with his usual sagacity and attention; for it is evident, from a multitude of relations every way worthy of credit, and particularly from the observations made on the Chinese missions by that learned and candid Franciscan, Antonio de S. Maria,* not only that Confucius was worshipped among the *idols*, and the celestial and terrestrial spirits of the Chinese, but that the oblations and ceremonies observed in honour of him, were perfectly the same with those that were performed as acts of worship to these idols and spirits. Those who desire a more ample account of this matter may consult the following authors: Budæi Annal. Histor. Philos. p. 287, where he treats *de superstitioso Demortuorum apud Sinenses Cultu*.—Wolfii Not. ad Casaubon. p. 342.—Nic. Charmos, Annot. ad Maigrotti Historiam Cultus Sinensis; and more especially Arnaud, Morale Pratique des Jesuites, tom. iii. vi. vii.; and a collection of historical relations, published in 1700, under the following title: Historia Cultus Sinensium, seu varia Scripta de Cultibus Sinarum inter Vicarios Apostolicos et P. P. S. I. controversis.

* See Præf. Novissim. Sinicorum.

* See vol. ii. Epist. Leibnitz.

☞ * Two peculiar circumstances contributed to facilitate the progress of the Romish religion in Japan. The first was the uncharitable severity and cruelty of the Japanese *bonzas* or priests toward the sick and indigent, compared with the humanity, zeal, and beneficence of the missionaries. These *bonzas* represented the poor and infirm not as objects of pity, but as wretches loaded with the displeasure of the gods, and abandoned to present and future misery by the judgments of Heaven; and inspired the rich with a contempt and abhorrence of them. The Christian religion, therefore, which declares that poverty and afflictions are often surer marks of the divine favour than grandeur and prosperity, and that the transitory evils which the righteous endure here, shall be crowned with everlasting glory and felicity hereafter, was every way proper to comfort this unhappy class of persons, and could not but meet with a most favourable reception among them. Add to this, that the missionaries were constantly employed in providing them with food, medicine, and habitations. A second circumstance that was advantageous to Christianity (that is, to such a form of Christianity as the popish missionaries preached in Japan,) was a certain resemblance or analogy between it and some practices and sentiments which prevailed among the Japanese. The latter look for present and future felicity only through the merits of Xaca Amida, and other of their deities, who, after a long course of severe mortifications freely undertaken had voluntarily, also, put an end to their lives. They sainted many melancholy persons who had been guilty of suicide, celebrated their memories, and implored their intercession and good offices. They used processions, statues, candles, and perfumes in their worship; as also prayers for the dead, and auricular confession; and had monasteries founded for devout persons of both sexes, who lived in celibacy, solitude, and abstinence; so that the Japanese religion was not an inapplicable preparation for popery. Beside these two circumstances, another may be mentioned, which we take from the letters of the Jesuits themselves, who inform us, that the princes of

flourishing state of the church was somewhat interrupted by the prejudices that the priests and grandees of the kingdom had conceived against the new religion, prejudices which proved fatal in many places, both to those who embraced it, and to those who taught it. The cause of Christianity did not, however, suffer only from the virulence and malignity of its enemies; it was wounded in the house of its friends, and received some detriment from the intestine quarrels and contentions of those to whom the care of the rising church was committed. For the same scenes of fraternal discord, that had given such offence in the other heathen countries, were renewed in Japan, where the Dominicans, Franciscans, and Augustinians, were at perpetual variance with the Jesuits. This variance produced, on both sides, the heaviest accusations, and the most bitter reproaches. The Jesuits were charged, by the missionaries of the three orders now mentioned, with insatiable avarice, with showing an excessive indulgence, both to the vices and superstitions of the Japanese, with crafty and low practices unworthy of the ministers of Christ, with an ambitious thirst after authority and dominion, and other misdemeanors of a like nature. These accusations were not only exhibited at the court of Rome, but were spread abroad in every part of Christendom. The disciples of Loyola were by no means silent under these reproaches; but, in their turn, charged their accusers with imprudence, ignorance of the world, obstinacy, asperity of manners, and a disgusting rusticity in their way of living; adding, that these circumstances rendered their ministry rather detrimental than advantageous to the cause of Christianity, among a people remarkable for their penetration, generosity, and magnificence. Such then were the contests that arose among the missionaries in Japan; and nothing but the amazing progress that Christianity had already made, and the immense multitude of those who had embraced it, could have prevented these contests from being fatal to its interests. As the case stood, neither the cause of the Gospel, nor its numerous professors, received any essential damage from these divisions; and, if no other circumstance had intervened to stop its progress, an expedient might have probably been found out, either to heal these divisions, or at least to appease them so far as to prevent them from being attended with mischievous and calamitous consequences.*

XVI. But a new and dreadful scene of opposition arose, in 1615, to blast the hopes of those who wished well to the cause of Christianity in Japan; for, in that year, the emperor issued, against the professors and ministers of that divine religion, a persecuting edict, which was executed with a degree of barbarity unparalleled in the annals of the Christian history. This cruel persecution raged for many years with unrelenting fury, and only ended with the extinction of Christianity throughout that mighty empire. That religion, which had been suffered to make such a rapid and triumphant progress in Japan, was at length considered as detrimental to the interests of the monarchy, inconsistent with the good of the people, and derogatory from the majesty of their high priest, whom they revered as a person descended from the gods; and, on these accounts, it was judged unworthy not only of protection, but even of toleration. This judgment was followed by the fatal order, by which all foreigners that were Christians, and more especially the Spaniards and Portuguese, were commanded to quit the kingdom; and the natives, who had embraced the Gospel, were required to renounce the name and doctrine of Christ, on pain of death presented to them in the most dreadful forms. This tremendous order was the signal for the perpetration of such horrors as the most sanguine and atrocious imagination will scarcely be able to conceive. Innumerable multitudes of the Japanese Christians of each sex, and of all ages, ranks, and stations, expired with magnanimous constancy, amidst the most dreadful torments, rather than apostatize from the faith they had embraced. And here it may not be amiss to observe, that both the Jesuits and their adversaries in the missions expiated, in some measure, if I may so express myself, by the agonies they endured, and the fortitude with which they suffered, the faults they had committed in the exercise of their ministry. For it is well known, that the greatest part of them died magnanimously for the cause of Christ by the hands of the executioner, and that some of them even expired with triumphant feelings of satisfaction and joy.

Historians are not entirely agreed with respect to the real causes of this merciless persecution. The Jesuits consider it as having been occasioned, in part, by the imprudence of the Dominicans and Franciscans; while the latter impute it, in a great measure, to the covetous, arrogant, and factious spirit of the Jesuits.* Both parties accuse the English and Dutch of having excited in the emperor of Japan a strong prejudice against the Spaniards, Portuguese, and the Roman pontiff, to the end

the maritime parts of Japan were so fond of this new commerce with the Portuguese, that they strove who should oblige them most, and encouraged the missionaries, less perhaps from a principle of zeal, than from views of interest. See Varenius' Descrip. Japon. lib. iii. cap. vi. x. and the Modern Univ. History.

* See the writers on this subject enumerated by Fabricius, in his Lux Evangelii, p. 678, as also Charlevoix, Histoire Generale de Japon, tom. ii. liv. xi

* There is a concise and sensible account of this tedious dispute in the sixth discourse that is subjoined to the English edition of Kæmpfer's History of Japan, sect. iv. But it will also be proper to see what is said on the other side, by an author, who, in his long and circumstantial narration, has not omitted any incident, however minute, that tends, in the least, to exculpate the Jesuits, or to procure them indulgence; that author is Charlevoix; see his Histoire Generale de Japon, tom. ii. liv. xii. The other historians that may be consulted with utility on this subject, are enumerated by Fabricius, in his Lux Evangelii, cap. x. p. 678. Add to these the Acta Sanctorum, tom. i. Mens. Februar. p. 723, where we find not only a history of the commencement and progress of Christianity in Japan, but also an account of the lives and martyrdom of those who first suffered for the cause of the Gospel in that kingdom. See likewise Mammachii Origines et Antiquitat. Christian. tom. ii. p. 376.

that they alone might engross the commerce of that vast monarchy, and be unrivalled in their credit among that powerful people. The English and Dutch allege, on the other hand, that they never attempted to undermine, by any false accusations, the credit of the Roman Catholics in that kingdom, but only detected the perfidious plots the Spaniards had laid against it. Almost all the historians, who have given accounts of this country, concur in affirming, that certain letters, intercepted by the Dutch, and other circumstances of a very striking and alarming kind, had persuaded the emperor, that the Jesuits, as also the other missionaries, had formed seditious designs against his government, and aimed at nothing less than exciting their numerous disciples to rebellion, with a view to reduce the kingdom of Japan under the dominion of Spain.* A discovery of this nature could not but make the most dreadful impressions upon a prince naturally suspicious and cruel, such as the emperor then reigning was; and, indeed, as soon as he had received this information, he concluded, with equal precipitation and violence, that he could not sit secure on his throne, while the smallest spark of Christianity remained unextinguished in his dominions, or any of its professors breathed under his government. It is from this remarkable period, that we must date the severe edict by which all Europeans are forbidden to approach the Japanese dominions, and in consequence of which all the terrors of fire and sword are employed to destroy whatever carries the remotest aspect or shadow of the Christian doctrine. The only exception from this general law is made in favour of some Dutch merchants, who are allowed to import annually a certain quantity of European commodities, and have a factory, or rather a kind of prison, allowed them, in one of the extremities of the kingdom, where they are strictly watched, and rigourously precluded from all communication with the natives, but what is essentially necessary to the commerce they are permitted to carry on.

XVII. The example of the Roman Catholic states could not but excite a spirit of pious emulation in Protestant countries, and induce them to propagate a still purer form of Christianity among those unhappy nations that lay grovelling in the darkness of Paganism and idolatry. Accordingly the Lutherans were, on several occasions, solicited by persons of eminent merit and rank in their communion, to embark in this pious and generous undertaking. Justinian Ernest, baron of Wells, distinguished himself by his zealous appearance in this good cause, having formed the plan of a society that was to be intrusted with the propagation of the Gospel in foreign parts, and to bear the name of Jesus, the divine founder of that religion which its members were anxious to promote.† But several circumstances concurred to prevent the execution of this pious design, among which we may reckon, principally, the peculiar situation of the Lutheran princes, of whom very few had any territories, forts, or settlements, beyond the limits of Europe.

This was by no means the case with the princes and states who professed the reformed religion. The English and Dutch, more especially, whose ships covered the ocean, and sailed to the most distant corners of the globe, and who, moreover, in this century, had sent colonies to Asia, Africa, and America, had abundant opportunities of spreading abroad the knowledge of Christianity among the unenlightened nations. Nor were these opportunities entirely neglected, notwithstanding the reports that have generally prevailed, of their being much more zealous in engrossing the riches of the Indians than in effecting their conversion, though it may, perhaps, be granted, that neither of these nations exerted themselves, to the extent of their power, in this salutary undertaking. In 1647, the propagation of the Gospel in foreign parts was committed, by an act of the English parliament, to the care and inspection of a society composed of persons of eminent rank and merit. The civil wars that ensued suspended the execution of the plans that were laid for carrying on this salutary work. In 1661, under the sway of Charles II., the work was resumed, and the society re-established. In 1701, this respectable society received singular marks of protection and favour from king William III. who enriched it with new donations and privileges.* Since that period, even to the present time, it has been distinguished by ample marks of the munificence of the kings of England, and of the liberality of persons of all ranks and orders, and has been, and continues to be, eminently useful in facilitating the means of instruction to the nations immersed in pagan darkness, and more especially to the Americans. Nor are the laudable efforts of the United Provinces, in the advancement and propagation of Christian knowledge, to be passed over in silence, since they also are said to have converted to the Gospel a prodigious number of Indians, in the islands of Ceylon and Formosa, on the coast of Malabar, and in other Asiatic settlements, which they either had acquired by their own industry, or obtained by conquest from the Portuguese.† Some historians, perhaps, may have exaggerated, in their relations, the number of proselytes made by the Dutch; it is nevertheless most certain, that, as soon as that nation had gained a firm footing in the East Indies, they planned with wisdom, and executed, at a great expense, various schemes for instructing the natives of those distant regions in the doctrines of the Gospel.‡

☞ * The discoveries made by the Dutch were against the Portuguese, with whom they were then at war; so that, instead of Spain, our author should have said Portugal. See Kæmpfer's Japan, and the Modern Universal History.

† See Molleri Cimbria Literata, tom. iii. as also a German work of the learned Arnold, entitled, Kirchen und Ketzer Historie, part ii. book xvii. c. xv. sect. 23. part iii. cap. xv. sect. 18.

* See Humphrey's Account of the Propagation of the Gospel in Foreign Parts.

† See Epist. de Successu Evangelii apud indos Orientales. ad Johan. Leusdenium script.

‡ See Braun's Veritable Religion des Hollandois, p. 71, 267, &c. This treatise, which was published at Amsterdam, in 1677, was intended as an answer to a malignant libel of one Stoup, entitled la Religion des Hollandois, in which that writer proposed to persuade the world that the Dutch had scarcely any religion at all.

XVIII. The inward parts of Africa remain still in the darkness of Paganism, as they have been hitherto inaccessible to the most adventurous of the Europeans. But in the maritime provinces of that great peninsula, and more especially in those where the Portuguese have their settlements, there are several districts in which the religion of Rome has prevailed over the savage superstitions of that barbarous region. It is nevertheless acknowledged, by the more ingenuous historians, even among the Roman Catholics, who have given accounts of the African colonies, that, of the proselytes made there to the Gospel, a very small number deserve the denomination of Christians, since the greatest part of them retain the abominable superstitions of their ancestors, and the very best among them dishonour their profession by various practices of a most vicious and corrupt nature. Any progress that Christianity made in these parts must be chiefly attributed to the zealous labours of the Capuchin missionaries, who, in this century suffered the most dreadful hardships and discouragements in their attempts to bring the fierce and savage Africans under the Christian yoke. These attempts succeeded so far, as to gain over to the profession of the Gospel the kings of Benin and Awerri,* and also to engage the cruel and intrepid Anna Zingha, queen of Metamba, and all her subjects, to embrace, in 1652, the Christian faith.† The African missions were allotted to this austere order by the court of Rome, and by the society *de propagandâ fide*, for wise reasons, since none could be so fitted for an enterprise attended with dreadful hardships, difficulties, and perils, as a set of men whose monastic institute had familiarized them to the severest acts of mortification, abstinence, and penance, and thus prepared them for the bitterest scenes of trial and adversity. Although the Capuchins seem to have been alone honoured with this sacred, but arduous commission, it does not appear that the other orders beheld, with the smallest sentiment of envy, their dear-bought glory.

XIX. The extensive continent of America swarms with colonies from Spain, Portugal, and France,‡ all which profess the Christian religion as it has been disfigured by the church of Rome. But it is abundantly known, that these colonists, more especially the Spaniards and Portuguese, are the most worthless and profligate set of men that bear the Christian name; and this fact is confirmed by the testimonies of Roman catholic writers of great merit and authority, who cannot be suspected of partiality in this matter. Even the clergy are not excepted from this general condemnation; but, as we learn from the same credible testimonies, surpass even the idolatrous natives in the ridiculous rites which they perform in the worship of God, as well as in the licentiousness of their manners, and the enormity of the crimes they commit without reluctance. Those of the ancient inhabitants of America, who either have submitted to the European yoke, or live near the colonies, have imbibed some faint knowledge of the Romish religion. from the Jesuits, Franciscans, and other ecclesiastics; but these feeble rays of instruction are totally clouded by the gloomy suggestions of their native superstition, and the corrupt influence of their barbarous customs and manners. As to those Indians who live more remote from the European settlements, and wander about in the woods without any fixed habitation, they are absolutely incapable either of receiving or retaining any adequate notions of the Christian doctrine, unless they be previously reclaimed from that irregular and desultory manner of life, and civilized by an intercourse with persons, whose humane and insinuating manners are adapted to attract their love, and excite their imitation. This the Jesuits, and other ecclesiastics who have been sent in later times to convert these wandering savages, have found by a constant and uniform experience.* Hence the former have erected cities, and founded civil societies, cemented by government and laws, like the European states, in several Indian provinces both in South and North America; and it is on this account that they discharge the double functions of magistrates and doctors among these their new subjects and disciples, whose morals and sentiments, it is said, they endeavour to preserve pure and uncorrupted, by permitting few or no Europeans to approach them.† These arduous and difficult attempts have furnished to the disciples of Loyola ample matter of boasting, and a lucky occasion of extolling the zeal, the dexterity, and industry of their order. But it has appeared, from relations worthy of credit, that these exploits of the Jesuits, in the internal and more inaccessible provinces of America, are not so much carried on with a view to the propagation of Christianity, as with an intention of gratifying their own insatiable avarice and boundless ambition; and, accordingly, they are reported to send yearly to the members of their order, in Eu-

* Called by some *Ouverne*.

☞ † For a more ample account of this queen, and her conversion, Dr. Mosheim refers the reader (in his note [r]) to Urban Cerri's Etat present de l'Eglise Romaine, p. 222, and to the third and fourth volumes of Father Labat's Relation Historique de l'Afrique Occidentale, in the former of which, he tells us, there is a French translation of Ant. Cavazzi's account of Africa. All these citations are inaccurate. Cerri makes no mention of Zingha, or of Metamba; nor are they mentioned by Labat, in any of the five volumes of his Historical Relation; nor is Cavazzi's account translated in that work. In general it may be observed, that the missions in Africa were greatly neglected by the Portuguese, and that the few missionaries sent thither were men absolutely void of learning, and destitute of almost every qualification that was necessary to the prosecution of such an important undertaking. See Labat's Preface, as also the Modern Univeral History.

‡ See the authors mentioned by Fabricius, in his Lux Evangelii Orbem Terrarum collustrans, cap. xlviii. xlix. p. 769.—There is a cursory account of the state of the Romish religion, in that part of America which is possessed by the European catholics in Cerri's work above-mentioned.

* A great variety of facts are alleged as a proof of this, in the Letters in which the French Jesuits gave their friends in Europe an account of the success and fruits of their mission, and which were regularly published at Paris.

☞ † That this was by no means the only, nor even the principal reason of cutting off all communication between the Indians and Europeans, will appear evident from the contents of the following note.

rope, immense quantities of gold, drawn from several American provinces where they have power and property, but chiefly from Paraguay, which belongs to them alone.*

XX. The cause of Christianity was promoted with greater wisdom, and consequently with better success, in those parts of America where the English formed settlements during this century; and, though it had the greatest ignorance, stupidity, and indolence to conquer, it quickly made a considerable progress. The English Independents who retired to America because they dissented from the established religion of their country, claimed the honour of carrying thither the first rays of divine truth, and of beginning a work that has been since continued with such pious zeal and such abundant fruit; and indeed this claim is founded in justice. Several families of this sect that had been settled in Holland, removed thence into America* in 1620, in order, as they alleged, to transmit their doctrine pure and undefiled to future ages; and there they laid the foundations of a new state.† The success that attended this first emigration engaged great numbers of the Puritans, who groaned under the oppression of the bishops, and the severity of a court by which this oppression was authorized, to follow the fortunes of these religious adventurers;‡ and this produced a second emigration in 1629. But, notwithstanding the

* While Father Labat was at Rome, Tamburini, at that time general of the Jesuits, asked him several questions relating to the progress of Christianity in America; to which, with equal courage and candour, he gave immediately this general answer: "that the Gospel had made little or no real progress in that country; that he had never met with one adult person among the Americans who could be regarded as a true proselyte to Christianity; and that the missionaries could scarcely pretend to any other exploits (*of a spiritual kind*) than their having baptized some children at the point of death." [Labat's Voyage en Espagne et en Italie, tom. viii.] He added, that, "in order to make the Americans *Christians*, it was previously necessary to make them *men*." This bold Dominican, who had been himself a missionary in the American islands, was inclined to give Tamburini some seasonable advice concerning the immense wealth and authority that the Jesuits had acquired in those parts of the world; but the cunning old man eluded artfully this part of the conversation, and turned it upon another subject. Labat gave, on another occasion, a still greater proof of his undaunted spirit and presence of mind; for when, in an audience granted him by Clement XI. that pontiff praised, in pompous terms, the industry and zeal of the Portuguese and Spanish missionaries in promoting the salvation of the Americans, and reproached the French with inactivity and indifference in a matter of such high importance, our resolute Dominican told him plainly, "that the Spaniards and Portuguese boasted of the success of their labours without any sort of foundation; since it was well known, that, instead of *converts*, they had only made *hypocrites*, all their disciples among the Indians having been forced, by the dread of punishment and the terrors of death, to embrace Christianity;" adding, "that such as had received baptism continued as open and egregious idolaters as they had been before their profession of Christianity." To this account we might add the relations of a whole cloud of witnesses, whose testimonies are every way worthy of credit, and who declare unanimously the same thing. See, among others, a remarkable piece, entitled, Memoire touchant l'Etablissement considerable des Peres Jesuites dans les Indes d'Espagne, which is subjoined to Frezier's Relation du Voyage de la Mer du Sud. See also Voyage aux Indes Occidentales, par F. Coreal, tom. ii. p. 67, and Mammachius, Orig. et Antiquit. Christian. tom. ii. p. 337. There is a particular account of the Jesuits of Paraguay, given by Don Ulloa, in his Voyage d'Amerique, tom. i. p. 540; but this account is partial in their favour. They are also zealously and artfully defended in an account of the mission of Paraguay, published by Muratori.

☞ When Dr. Mosheim wrote this note, the important discovery that placed the ambitious, despotic, and rebellious proceedings of the Jesuits in Paraguay in the plainest and most striking light, had not been yet made. The book of Muratori deceived, for some time, the over-credulous, and induced even the enemies of the Jesuits to suspect that their conduct at Paraguay was not so criminal as it had been represented; so that, notwithstanding the accusations that had been brought against these missionaries by the writers mentioned by our historian: notwithstanding a memorial sent to the court of Spain in 1730, by Don Martin de Barua, at that time Spanish governor of Paraguay, in which the Jesuits are charged with the most ambitious projects and the most rebellious designs, represented as setting up an independent government, accused of carrying on a prodigious trade, and other things of that nature; and notwithstanding the circumstantial evidence of various known facts that supported these accusations in the strongest manner; a great proportion of the public had not just ideas upon the subject. The illusion, however, did not last long. In 1750, the courts of Madrid and Lisbon entered into a treaty for fixing the limits of their respective dominions in South-America. The Jesuits, who had formed an independent republic in the heart of those dominions, composed of the Indians, whom they had gained by the insinuating softness and affected mildness, humility, and generosity of their proceedings, were much alarmed at this treaty. It was one of the fundamental laws of this new state, (which was founded under the mask of a Christian mission,) that no bishop or governor, nor any officer, civil, military, or ecclesiastical, nor even any individual, Spaniard or Portuguese, should be admitted into its territories, to the end that the proceedings and projects of the Jesuits might still remain an impenetrable secret. The members of their order were alone to be instructed in this profound and important mystery. The use of the Spanish language was prohibited in this new territory, in order to prevent more effectually all communication between the Indians and that nation. The Indians were trained to the use of arms, furnished with artillery, instructed in the art of war, taught to behold the Jesuits as their sovereigns and their gods, and to look upon all white people, except the Jesuits, as demoniacs, atheists, and moreover, as their barbarous and mortal enemies. Such was the state of affairs when, in 1752, the united troops of Spain and Portugal marched toward the eastern borders of the river Uragai, to make the exchanges of certain villages that had been agreed upon in the treaty above-mentioned. Upon this, the Jesuits, not being sufficiently prepared for their defence, demanded a delay of the execution of the treaty under various pretexts. This delay was granted: but, as the Spanish general, Gomez Frere Andrada, perceived that the *holy fathers* employed this delay in arming the Indians, and confirming them in their rebellion, he wrote to his court, and thence received new orders to proceed to the execution of the treaty. A war ensued between the Spanish and Portuguese on one side, and the Indians, animated by the Jesuits, on the other, in which the Spanish general lost his life, and of which the other circumstances are well known. This was the real and original cause of the disgrace of the Jesuits at the court of Portugal. Those who desire a more particular account of this matter, will find it in a famous pamphlet, drawn from an authentic memorial, published by the court of Lisbon, and printed in 1758, under the following title: *La Republique des Jesuites au Paraguay Renversee, ou Relation Authentique de la Guerre que ces Religieux ont ose soutenir contre les Monarques d'Espagne et de Portugal en Amerique, pour y defendre les domaines dont ils avoient usurpe la Souveraine au Paraguay sous pretexte de Religion.*

* This colony settled in that part of America which was afterwards called New Plymouth.

† See Neal's Hist. of the Puritans, vol. ii. p. 128 and also a German work entitled, Englische Refor Hist. by Ant. W. Bohm, b. vi. c. v.

‡ See Mather's History of New-England, p. 126 — Neal, vol. ii.

success which at length crowned this enterprise, its commencement was unpromising, and the colonists, immediately after their arrival, laboured under such hardships and difficulties in the dreary and uncultivated wilds of this new region, that, for several years, they could make very little progress in instructing the Indians, their whole zeal and industry being scarcely sufficient to preserve the infant settlement from the horrors of famine. But, about the year 1633,* affairs assumed a better aspect: the colony began to flourish, and the new-comers, among whom the Puritans Mayhew, Shepherd, and Elliot, made an eminent figure, had the leisure, courage, and tranquillity of mind, that were necessary for the execution of such an important and arduous design. All these devout exiles were remarkably zealous, laborious, and successful in the conversion of the Indians; but none acquired such a shining reputation, in this pious career, as John Elliot, who learned their language, (into which he translated the Bible, and other instructive and edifying books,) collected the wandering savages, and formed them into regular congregations, instructed them in a manner suited to the dulness of their comprehension, and the measure of their respective capacities; and, by such eminent displays of his zeal, dexterity, and indefatigable industry, merited, after his death, the honourable title of the Apostle of the Indians.†

The unexpected success that attended these pious attempts toward the propagation of Christian knowledge, drew the attention of the parliament and people of England; and the advancement of this good cause appeared an object of sufficient importance to employ the deliberations, and to claim the protection, of the great council of the nation. Thus was formed that illustrious society, which derives its title from the great purpose of its institution, namely, the propagation of the Gospel in foreign parts, and which, in proportion to the increase of its number, influence, revenues, and prerogatives, has still renewed and augmented its efforts for the instruction of the Pagans in all parts of the world, particularly those of the American continent. It is true, that, after all its efforts, much is yet to be done; but it is also true, and must be acknowledged by all who have examined these matters with attention and impartiality, that much has been done, and that the pious undertakings of this respectable society have been followed by unexpected fruit.—With respect to the province of Pennsylvania, which receives in its bosom, without distinction, persons of all sects and all opinions, we shall have occasion to speak of its religious state in another place. The American provinces which were taken from the Portuguese by the Dutch, under the command of count Maurice of Nassau, became immediately an object of the pious zeal of their new masters, who began, with great ardour and remarkable success, to spread the light of the Gospel among the wretched inhabitants of those benighted regions.* But this fair prospect was clouded in 1644, when the Portuguese recovered the territories they had lost. As to the Dutch settlement in Surinam, we cannot say much, having never received the smallest information of any attempts made by the colonists to instruct the neighbouring Indians in the knowledge of Christianity.†

XXI. Religion in general, and the Christian faith in particular, had many enemies to encounter in this century, though their number has been studiously diminished in the accounts of some, and greatly exaggerated in the representations of others. The English complain of the reign of Charles II as the fatal period, when corruption of manners, and vice, in the most licentious and profligate forms, overran their nation, engendered a spirit of scepticism and infidelity, and formed a set of unhappy men, who employed all the wantonness of inconsiderate wit, all the sallies of imagination, and even all the force of real talent and genius, to extinguish a sense of religion in the minds of mankind. That this complaint is far from being groundless, appears, on one hand, from the number of those writers among the English, who either directed their attacks against all religion, or endeavoured to confine the belief of men to natural religion alone; and, on the other from the still superior number of learned and ingenious treatises in which the divinity, dignity, and intrinsic excellence of the Gospel, were demonstrated and displayed in the most striking and conspicuous manner. But nothing is more adapted to confirm the accounts that have been given of the progress of infidelity and licentiousness at the period now under consideration, than the famous Lectures founded by that illustrious ornament of religion and humanity, Mr. Robert Boyle, who, in 1691, consecrated a considerable part of his large fortune to the service of Christianity, by leaving, in his last will, a sum to be distributed successively to a number of learned divines, who were to preach, in their turns, eight sermons every year, in defence of natural and revealed religion.‡ This pious and honourable task has been generally committed to men of the most eminent genius and abilities, and is still undertaken with zeal, and

☞ * Dr. Mosheim says in the year 1623; but this is probably an error of the press; for it is well known, that the emigration of Shepherd and Elliot happened between 1631 and 1634.

† Hornbeckius, de Conversione Indorum et Gentil. lib. ii. cap. xv. p. 260.—Crescentii Matheri Epistola de Successu Evangelii apud Indos Occidentales ad Joh. Leusdenium. ☞ The Letter to Leusden, by Increase Mather, is translated into English, and inserted in Cotton Mather's Life of Elliot, and in his History of New-England, book iii. N.

* Jo. Henr. Hottingeri Topographia Ecclesiastica, p. 47.—Janicon, Etat Present des Provinces Unies, tom. i. p. 396. The same author gives an account of Surinam, and of the state of religion in that colony, chap. xiv. p. 407.

☞ † There are three churches in that settlement for the use of the colonists; but no attempt has been made to spread the knowledge of the Gospel among the natives.

‡ See Ricotier's preface to his French translation of Dr. Clarke's Discourses on the Being and Attributes of God. For an account of the pious, learned, and illustrious Mr. Boyle, see Budgell's Memoirs of the Lives and Characters of the illustrious Family of the Boyles: see also the Bibliotheque Brittanique, tom. xii. ☞ But, above all, see the late learned Dr. Birch's Life of Boyle, and that very valuable collection of lives, the Biographia Britannica, Article *Boyle (Robert)* note z. See also the article *Hobbes* in the same collection. N.

performed with remarkable dignity and success. The discourses that have been delivered in consequence of this admirable institution have always been published; and they form at this day a large and important collection, which is known throughout all Europe, and has done eminent service to the cause of religion and virtue.*

XXII. The leader of the impious band in England, which, so early as the reign of Charles II., attempted to obscure the truth, and to dissolve the solemn obligations of religion, was Thomas Hobbes of Malmesbury, a man whose audacious pride was accompanied with an uncommon degree of artifice and address, whose sagacity was superior to his learning, and whose reputation was more owing to the subtilty and extent of his genius, than to any progress he had made either in sacred or profane erudition.† This man, notwithstanding the pernicious nature and tendency of his principles, had several adherents in England; and found also, in foreign countries, more than one apologist, who, though they acknowledge that his sentiments were erroneous, yet deny that he went such an impious length as to introduce the disbelief, or to overturn the worship of a Supreme Being.‡ But if it should be granted, on one hand, that Hobbes was not totally destitute of all sense of a Deity, or of all impressions of religion, it must be allowed, on the other, by all who peruse his writings with a proper degree of attention, that his tenets lead, by natural consequences, to a contempt of religion and of divine worship; and that, in some of his productions, there are visible marks of an extreme aversion to Christianity. It has, indeed, been said of him, that, at an advanced age, he returned to a better mind, and condemned publicly the opinions and tenets he had formerly entertained;§ but how far this recantation was sincere, we shall not pretend to determine, since the reality of his repentance has been strongly questioned.

The same thing cannot be said of John, earl of Rochester, who had insulted the majesty of God, and trampled upon the truths of religion and the obligations of morality with a profane sort of phrensy, that far exceeded the impiety of Hobbes, but whose repentance and conversion were also as palpable as had been his folly, and much more unquestionable than the dubious recantation of the philosopher of Malmesbury. The earl was a man of uncommon sagacity and penetration, of a fine genius and an elegant taste; but these natural talents were accompanied with the greatest levity and licentiousness, and the most impetuous propensity to unlawful pleasure. As long as health enabled him to answer the demands of passion, his life was an uninterrupted scene of debauchery.* He was, however, so happy in the last years of a very short life, as to see the extreme folly and guilt of his past conduct, in which salutary view he was greatly assisted by the wise and pathetic reasonings and exhortations of Doctor Burnet, afterwards bishop of Sarum. This conviction of his guilt produced a deep contrition and repentance, an ardent recourse to the mercy of God, as it is manifested in the Gospel of Jesus Christ, and a sincere abhorrence of the offences he had committed against the Best of Beings. In these pious sentiments he died in 1680.†

In this list we may also place Anthony, earl of Shaftesbury, who died of a consumption at Naples, in the year 1713; not that this illustrious writer attacked openly and professedly

* There is a complete list of these learned discourses in the Bibliotheque Angloise, tom. xv. part ii. p. 416.—The late Reverend Mr. Gilbert Burnet published a judicious, comprehensive, and well-digested abridgment of such of the Lectures as had been preached before the year 1737. This abridgment comprehends the discourses of Bentley, Kidder, Williams, Gastrell, Harris, Bradford, Blackhall, Stanhope, Clarke, Hancock, Whiston, Turner, Butler, Woodward, Derham, Ibbot, Long, J. Clarke, Gurdon, Burnet, Berriman.

† See Bayle's Dictionary, and Wood's Athenæ Oxonienses.

‡ Among the patrons and defenders of Hobbes, we may reckon Nic. Hier. Gundlingius, in his Observationes Selectæ, and in his Gundlingiana, and also Arnold, in the second part of his German history of the church and of heresy. These writers are refuted by the learned Buddeus, in his Theses de Atheismo et Superstitione.

§ This recantation depends upon the testimony of Wood, who informs us, that Hobbes composed an apology for himself and his writings, in which he declared, that the opinions he had published in his Leviathan were by no means conformable to his real sentiments; that he had only proposed them as a matter of debate, to exercise his mind in the art of reasoning; that, after the publication of that book, he had never maintained them either in public or in private, but had left them entirely to the judgment and decision of the church; more especially that the tenets, in this and his other writings, which seemed inconsistent with the received doctrines concerning God and religion, were never delivered by him as *truths*, but proposed as *questions* to be decided by divines and ecclesiastical judges endued with a proper authority.—Such is the account that Wood gives of the apology now under consideration; but he does not tell us the year in which it was published, which is a proof that he himself had never seen it; nor does he inform us whether it appeared during the life of Hobbes, or after his death. As indeed it is placed in the catalogue of his writings, with a date posterior to the year 1682, it is natural to suppose that it was not published during his life, since he died in 1679. It is, therefore, no easy matter to determine what stress is to be laid upon this recantation of Hobbes, or what opinion we are to form of his supposed repentance. That the apology exists, we do not pretend to deny; but it may have been composed by some of his friends, to diminish the odium which it was natural to think, his licentious principles would cast on his memory. But should it be granted, that it was drawn up and published by Hobbes himself, even this concession would contribute little to save, or rather to recover, his reputation, since it is well known, that nothing is more common among those who, by spreading corrupt principles and pernicious opinions, have drawn upon themselves the just indignation of the public, than, like Hobbes, to deceive the world by insidious and insincere declarations of the soundness of their belief, and the uprightness of their intentions. It is thus that they secure themselves against the execution of the laws that are designed to fence religion, while they persevere in their licentious sentiments, and propagate them, wherever they can do it with security.

* See an account of his life and writings in Wood's Athenæ Oxonienses, vol. ii. His poetical genius is justly celebrated by Voltaire, in his Melanges de Literature et de Philosophie.

† Bishop Burnet has given a particular account of this last and very affecting scene of the life of this nobleman, in a pamphlet written expressly on that subject, and entitled, Some Passages of the Life and Death of John, Earl of Rochester, written, at his desire, on his death-bed, by Gilbert Burnet, D. D. containing more amply their Conversations on the great principles of Natural and Revealed Religion

the Christian religion, but that the most seducing strokes of wit and raillery, the most enchanting eloquence, and the charms of a genius, in which amenity, elegance, copiousness, and elevation, were happily blended, rendered him one of its most dangerous, though secret enemies; and so much the more dangerous, because his opposition was carried on under a mask. His works have been published in various forms, and have passed through many editions. They are remarkable for beauty of diction, and contain very noble and sublime sentiments; but they ought to be read with the utmost caution, as being extremely dangerous to inexperienced, youthful and unwary minds.* The brutal rusticity and uncouth turn of John Toland, a native of Ireland, who, toward the conclusion of this century, was rendered famous by several injurious libels against Christianity, must naturally appear doubly disgusting, when compared with the amiable elegance and specious refinement of the author now mentioned. However, as those writers, who flatter the passions by endeavouring to remove all the restraints that religion imposes upon their excessive indulgence, will never want patrons among the licentious part of mankind; so this man, who was not destitute of learning, imposed upon the ignorant and unwary; and, notwithstanding the excess of his arrogance and vanity, and the shocking rudeness and ferocity of his manners, acquired a certain measure of fame.*

* His works were first collected and published under the title of Characteristics, in 1711, and, since that time, have passed through many editions. See Le Clerc's account of them in his Bibliotheque Choise, tom. xxiii. The critical reflections of the learned and ingenious Leibnitz on the philosophy of Lord Shaftesbury were published by Dez-Maizeaux, in the second volume of his Receuil de diverses Pieces sur la Philosophie, p. 245.—There are some writers who maintain, that this noble philosopher has been unjustly charged, by the greatest part of the clergy, with a contempt for revealed religion; and it is to be wished, that the arguments they employ to vindicate him from this charge were more satisfactory and solid than they really are. But, if I do not greatly mistake, whoever peruses his writings, and more especially his famous letter concerning enthusiasm, will be inclined to adopt the judgment that was formed of him by the ingenious Dr. Berkeley, bishop of Cloyne, in his Alciphron, or the Minute Philosopher, vol. i. p. 200.—Nothing is more easy than to observe, in the writings of Lord Shaftesbury, a spirit of raillery, mingling itself even with those of his reflections upon religious subjects that seem to be delivered with the greatest seriousness and gravity. But, at the same time, this unseemly mixture of the solemn and the ludicrous, renders it difficult for those who are not well acquainted with his manner, to know whether he is in jest or in earnest. It may also be added, that this author has perniciously endeavoured to destroy the influence and efficacy of some of the great motives that are proposed in the Scriptures to render men virtuous, by representing these motives as mercenary, and even turning them into ridicule. He substitutes, in their place, the intrinsic excellence and beauty of virtue, as the great source of moral obligation, and the true incentive to virtuous deeds. But, however alluring this sublime scheme of morals may appear to certain minds of a refined, elegant, and ingenious turn, it is certainly little adapted to the taste, the comprehension, and the character of the multitude. Take away from the lower orders of mankind the prospects of reward and punishment, that lead them to virtue and obedience, by the powerful suggestions of hope and fear; and the great supports of virtue, and the most effectual motives to the pursuit of it will, with respect to them, be removed.

☞ Since Dr. Mosheim wrote this note, the very learned and judicious Dr. Leland published his View of the Principal Deistical Writers that have appeared in England during the last and present Century, &c. in which there is a full account of the free-thinkers and deists mentioned by our historian, with a review of the writings of the earl of Shaftesbury. This review merits a particular attention, as it contains an impartial account, an accurate examination, and a satisfactory refutation, of the erroneous principles of that great man. Like all other eminent innovators, the earl has been misrepresented both by his friends and his enemies. Dr. Leland has steered a middle course between the blind enthusiasm of the former, and the partial malignity of the latter. He points out, with singular penetration and judgment, the errors, inconsistencies, and contradictions, of that illustrious author; does justice to what is good in his ingenious writings; separates carefully the wheat from the chaff; and neither approves nor condemns in the lump, as too many have done. In a more particular manner he has shewn, with his usual perspicuity and good sense, that the being influenced by the hope of the reward promised in the Gospel, has nothing in it disingenuous and slavish, and is so far from being inconsistent with loving virtue for its own sake, that it tends, on the contrary, to heighten our esteem of its amiableness and worth. The triumphant manner in which the learned Dr. Warburton has refuted Shaftesbury's representation of raillery and ridicule as a test of truth, is too well known to be mentioned here. See also Dr. Brown's Three Essays on the Characteristics, in which that sensible author treats of ridicule considered as a test of truth; of the obligations of men to virtue, and of the necessity of religious principle, and of revealed religion and Christianity.

☞ * Dr. Mosheim, in a short note, refers to an account he had given of the Life and Writings of Toland, prefixed to his confutation of the Nazarenus of that contemptible author. He also quotes a life of Toland, prefixed to his posthumous works by Des-Maizeaux. Dr. Mosheim says, that this man *was not destitute of learning*. Should that be granted, it must, nevertheless, be acknowledged that this learning lay quite undigested in his head, and that the use he made of it, in his works, was equally injudicious and impudent. His conference with M. Beausobre, concerning the authenticity of the Holy Scriptures, which was holden at Berlin in presence of the queen of Prussia, and in which he made such a despicable figure, is a proof of the former; and his writings, to all but half-scholars and half-thinkers, will be a proof (as long as they endure,) of the latter.—It is remarkable that (according to the maxim of Juvenal. *Nemo repente fuit turpissimus*,) Toland arrived only gradually, and by a progressive motion, at the summit of infidelity. His first step was Socinianism, which appeared in his book, entitled, Christianity not Mysterious. This book procured him hard treatment from the Irish parliament, and was answered by Mr. Brown, afterwards bishop of Cork who, unhappily, did not think good arguments sufficient to maintain a good cause, unless they were seconded by the secular arm, whose ill-placed succours he solicited with ardour. The second step that Toland made in the devious fields of religion, was in the publication of his Amyntor, which, in appearance, was designed to vindicate what he advanced in his Life of Milton, to prove that king Charles I. was not the real author of the *Eikon Basilike*, but, in reality, was intended to invalidate the Canon of the New Testament, and to render it uncertain and precarious. This piece, as far as it attacked the authenticity of Scripture, was answered in a triumphant manner by Dr. Clarke, in his Reflections on that part of the Book called Amyntor, which relates to the Writings of the Primitive Fathers, and the Canon of the New Testament; by Mr. Richardson, in his learned and judicious Vindication of the Canon of the New Testament; and by Mr. Jones, in his new and full Method of settling the Canonical Authority of the New Testament. These learned writers have exposed, in the most striking manner, the disingenuity, the blunders, the false quotations, the insidious fictions, and ridiculous mistakes of Toland, who, on various accounts, may pass for one of the most harmless writers against the Christian religion. For an account of the Adeisidæmon, the Nazarenus, the Letters to Serena, the Pantheisticon, and the

It is not necessary to mention other authors of this class, who appeared in England, during this century, but are long since consigned to oblivion. The reader may, however, add, to those who have been already named, lord Herbert of Cherbury, a philosopher of some note, who, if he did not absolutely deny the divine origin of the Gospel,* maintained, at least, that it was not essentially necessary to the salvation of mankind; and Charles Blount, who composed a book, entitled the Oracles of Reason, and, in 1693, died by his own hand.†

XXIII. Infidelity, and even atheism, showed themselves also on the continent during this century. In France, Julius Cæsar Vanini, the author of two books, one entitled, the Amphitheatre of Providence,* and the other, Dialogues concerning Nature,† was publicly burned at Toulouse, in 1629, as an impious and obstinate atheist. It is nevertheless to be observed, that several learned and respectable writers consider this unhappy man rather as a victim to bigotry and envy, than as a martyr to impiety and atheism; and maintain, that neither his life nor his writings were so absurd or blasphemous as to entitle him to the character of a despiser of God and religion.‡ But, if Vanini had his apologists, this was by no means the case of Cosmo Ruggieri, a native of Florence, whose atheism was as impudent as it was impious, and who died in the most desperate sentiments of irreligion at Paris, in 1615, declaring that he looked upon all the accounts that had been given of the existence of a Supreme Being, and of evil spirits, as idle

other irreligious works of this author, and also of the excellent answers that have been made to them, see his Life in the General Dictionary, or rather in Chauffepied's Supplement to Bayle's Dictionary, entitled, Nouveau Dictionnaire Historique et Critique, as this author has not only translated the articles added to Bayle's Dictionary by the English editors of that work, but has augmented and improved them by several interesting anecdotes drawn from the literary history of the continent.

☞ * Lord Herbert did not presume to deny the divinity of the Gospel; he even declared that he had no intention to attack Christianity. He expressly calls it the "best religion," and admits that it tends to establish the five great articles of that universal, sufficient, and absolutely perfect religion, which he pretends to deduce from reason and nature. But, notwithstanding these fair professions, his lordship loses no occasion of throwing out insinuations against al. revealed religion, as absolutely uncertain, and of little or no use. But this same deist, who was the first, and, indeed, the least contemptible of that tribe in England, has left upon record one of the strongest instances of fanaticism and absurdity, that perhaps ever were heard of, and of which he himself was guilty. This instance is preserved in a manuscript life of lord Herbert, drawn up from memorials penned by himself, which is now in the possession of a gentleman of distinction,* and is as follows: that lord, having finished his book *de Veritate*, apprehended that he should meet with much opposition, and was, consequently, dubious for some time, whether it would not be prudent to suppress it. "Being thus doubtful (says his lordship,) in my chamber (*at Paris, where he was ambassador, in* 1624,) one fair day in the summer, my casement being open towards the south, the sun shining clear, and, no wind stirring, I took my book *de Veritate* in my hands, and, kneeling on my knees, devoutly said these words: O thou Eternal God, author of this light that now shines upon me, and giver of all inward illuminations, I do beseech thee, of thine infinite goodness, to pardon a greater request than a sinner ought to make; I am not satisfied enough whether I shall publish this book; if it be for thy glory, I beseech thee, give me some sign from heaven; if not, I shall suppress it." What does the reader now think of this corner-stone of deism, who demands a supernatural revelation from heaven in favour of a book that was designed to prove all revelation uncertain and useless? But the absurdity does not end here; for our deist not only sought for this revelation, but also obtained it, if we are to believe him. "I had no sooner (says he,) spoken these words, but a loud though yet gentle noise came forth from the heavens, (for it was like nothing on earth,) which did so cheer and comfort me, that I took my petition as granted." Rare credulity this in an unbeliever! but these gentlemen can believe even against reason, when it answers their purpose. His lordship continues, "This, however strange it may seem, I protest before the Eternal God, is true: neither am I superstitiously deceived herein," &c. See Leland's View of the Deistical Writers, vol. i.

† This is sufficiently known to those who have perused lord Herbert's book de Causis Errorum, as also his celebrated work de Religione Gentilium. This author is generally considered as the chief and founder of the sect or society that are called Naturalists, from their attachment to natural religion alone. See Arnoldi Historia Eccles. at Hæret. part ii. p. 1083.—The peculiar tenets of this famous deist have been refuted by Musæus and Kortholt, two German divines of eminent learning and abilities. ☞ Gassendi also composed an answer to lord Herbert's book de Veritate. In England it was refuted by Mr. Richard Baxter, in a treatise entitled, More Reasons for the Christian Religion, and no Reason against it. Mr. Locke, in his Essay on the Human Understanding, shows, with great perspicuity and force of evidence, that the five articles of natural religion, proposed by this noble author, are not, as he represents them, common notices, clearly inscribed by the hand of God in the minds of all men, and that a divine revelation is necessary to indicate, develope, and enforce them. Dr. Whitby has also treated the same matter amply in his learned work, entitled, The Necessity and Usefulness of the Christian Revelation, by reason of the Corruptions of the Principles of Natural Religion among the Jews and Heathens.

* The translator probably alludes to Horace Walpole, earl of Orford, who afterwards published it. —EDIT.

* See the Nouveau Dictionnaire Historique et Critique of Chauffepied, who, however, has omitted the mention of this gentleman's unhappy fate, out of a regard, no doubt, to his illustrious family. ☞ Mr. Chauffepied only translated the article *Charles Blount*, from that of the English continuators of Bayle.

☞ This book was published at Lyons in 1615, was approved by the clergy and magistrates of that city, and contains many things absolutely irreconcilable with atheistical principles: its title is as follows: Amphitheatrum Æternæ Providentiæ, Divino-Magicum Christiano-Physicum Astrologico-Catholicum, adversus Veteres Philosophos, Atheos, Epicureos, Peripateticos, Stoicos, &c. This book has been deemed innocent by several writers, impious by others; but, in our judgment, it would have escaped reproach, had Vanini published none of his other productions, since the impieties it may contain, according to the intention of its author, are carefully concealed. This is by no means the case of the book mentioned in the following note.

☞ † This book, concerning the Secrets of Queen Nature, the Goddess of Mortals, was published with this suspicious title at Paris, in 1616, and contains glaring marks of impiety and atheism; and yet it was published with the king's permission, and the approbation of the Faculty of Theology. This scandalous negligence or ignorance is unaccountable in such a reverend body. The Jesuit Garasse pretends that the Faculty was deceived by Vanini, who substituted another treatise in the place of that which had been approved. See a wretched book of Garasse, entitled, Doctrine Curieuse; as also Durand's Vie de Vanini.

‡ See Buddeus's Theses de Atheismo et Superstitione. The author of the Apologia pro Vanino, which appeared in Holland in 1712, was Peter Frederic Arp, a learned lawyer; and we may also place, among the defenders of Vanini, Elias Frederic Heister, author of the Apologia pro Medicis.

dreams.* Casimir Leszynski, a Polish knight, was capitally punished at Warsaw, in 1689, for denying the Being and Providence of God; but whether this accusation was well founded, can only be known by reading his trial, and examining the nature and circumstances of the evidence adduced against him.† In Germany, a senseless and frantic man, called Matthew Knutzen, a native of Holstein, attempted to found a new sect, whose members, laying aside all considerations of God and religion, were to follow the dictates of reason and conscience alone, and thence were to assume the title of Conscientiarians. But this wrong-headed sectary was easily obliged to abandon his extravagant undertakings; and thus his idle attempt proved abortive.‡

XXIV. The most acute and eminent of the atheists of this century, whose system represented the Supreme Author of all things as a Being bound by the eternal and immutable laws of necessity or fate, was Benedict de Spinosa, a Portuguese Jew. This man, who died at the Hague in 1677, observed in his conduct the rules of wisdom and probity, much better than many who profess themselves Christians; nor did he ever endeavour to pervert the sentiments or corrupt the morals of those with whom he lived, or to inspire, in his discourse, a contempt of religion or virtue.§ It is true, indeed, that in his writings, more especially in those which were published after his death, he maintains openly, that God and the universe are one and the same Being, and that all things happen by the eternal and immutable law of *nature*, i. e. of an all-comprehending and infinite Being, that exists and acts by an invincible necessity. This doctrine leads directly to consequences equally impious and absurd; for, if the principle now mentioned be true, each individual is his own God, or, at least, a *part* of the universal Deity, and is, therefore, impeccable and perfect.|| Be that as it may, it is evident that Spinosa was seduced into this monstrous system by the Cartesian philosophy, of which he was a passionate admirer, and which was the perpetual subject of his meditation and study. When he had adopted the general principle (about which philosophers of all sects are agreed) that all realities are possessed by the Deity in the most eminent degree, and had annexed to this principle, as equally evident, the opinion of Des-Cartes, that there are only two realities in nature, thought and extension, one essential to spirit, and the other to matter,* the natural consequence was, that he should attribute to the Deity both these realities, even thought and extension, in an eminent degree, or, in other words, should represent them as infinite and immense in God. Hence the transition seemed easy to that enormous system, which confounds God with the universe, represents them as one and the same Being, and supposes only one substance whence all things proceed, and into which they all return. It is natural to observe here, that even the friends of Spinosa are obliged to acknowledge, that this system is neither attended with that luminous perspicuity, nor with that force of evidence, which are proper to make proselytes. It is too dark, too intricate, to allure men from the belief of those truths relating to the Deity, which the works of nature, and the plainest dictates of reason, are perpetually enforcing upon the human mind. Accordingly, the followers of Spinosa tell us, without hesitation, that it is rather by the suggestions of a certain sense, than by the investigations of reason, that his doctrine is to be comprehended; and that it is of such a nature, as to be easily misunderstood even by persons of the greatest sagacity

* See Bayle's Dictionary.

† See Arnold's History of the Church.—The famous library of Offenbach formerly contained a complete collection of all the papers relating to the trial of Leszynski, and a full account of the proceedings against him.

‡ See Molleri Cimbria Literata, tom. i. p. 304; and Isagoge ad Historiam Chersonesi Cimbr. part ii. cap. vi. sect. viii.—La Croze, Entretiens sur divers sujets d'Histoire, p. 400.

§ The life of Spinosa was accurately written by Colerus, whose performance was published at the Hague in 1706. But a more ample and circumstantial account of this singular man was given by Lenglet du Fresnoy, and prefixed to Boulainvilliers' Exposition of the Doctrine of Spinosa. See Bayle's Dictionary. ☞ Lenglet du Fresnoy republished the work of Colerus, and added to it several anecdotes and circumstances, borrowed from a Life of Spinosa, written by an infamous profligate, whose name was Lucas, and who practised physic at the Hague. See the notes † & ‡, p. 172.

|| The learned Fabricius, in his Bibliotheca Græca, and Jenichen, in his Historia Spinosismi Lenhofiani, have given us an ample list of the writers who have refuted the system of Spinosa. The real opinion which this subtle sophist entertained concerning the Deity, is to be learned in his Ethics, that were published after his death, and not in his Tractatus Theologico-Politicus, which was printed during his life. In the latter treatise, he reasons like one who was persuaded that there exists an eternal Deity, distinct from matter and the universe, who has sent upon earth a religion designed to form men to the practice of benevolence and justice, and has confirmed that religion by events of a wonderful and astonishing, though not of a supernatural kind; but in his Ethics he throws off the mask, explains clearly his sentiments, and endeavours to demonstrate, that the Deity is nothing more than the universe, producing a series of necessary movements or acts, in consequence of its own intrinsic, immutable, and irresistible energy. This diversity of sentiment, that appears in the different productions of Spinosa, is a sufficient refutation of those who, forming the estimate of his system from his Tractatus Theologico Politicus alone, pronounce it less pernicious, and its author less impious, than they are generally supposed to be. But, on the other hand, how shall this diversity be accounted for? Are we to suppose that Spinosa proceeded to atheism by gradual steps, or is it more probable, that, during his life, he prudently concealed his real sentiments? Whether the former, or the latter, be the real case, it is not easy to determine. It appears, however, from testimonies, every way worthy of credit, that he never, during his whole life, either made, or attempted to make, converts to irreligion, and never said any thing in public that tended to encourage disrespectful sentiments of the Supreme Being, or of the worship that is due to him. It is well known, on the contrary, that, when subjects of a religious nature were incidentally treated in the course of conversation where he was present, he always expressed himself with the utmost decency on the occasion, and often with an air of piety and seriousness more adapted to edify than to give offence.

☞* The hypothesis of Des-Cartes is not, perhaps, represented with sufficient accuracy and precision, by saying that he looked upon thought as essential to spirit, and extension as essential to matter, since it is well known that this philosopher considered thought as the very essence or substance of the soul, and extension as the very essence and substance of matter.

and penetration.* His disciples assumed the denomination of Pantheists, choosing rather to derive their distinctive title from the nature of their doctrine, than from the name of their master.† The most noted members of this strange sect were a physician, whose name was Louis Meyer,* a person called Lucas,† count Boulainvilliers,‡ and some others, equally contemptible on account of their sentiments and morals.

* There is certainly no man so little acquainted with the character of Bayle as to think him void of discernment and sagacity; and yet this most subtle metaphysician has been accused by the followers of Spinosa, of misunderstanding and misrepresenting the doctrine of that Pantheist, and consequently of answering it with very little solidity. This charge is brought against Bayle, with peculiar severity, by L. Meyer, in his preface to the posthumous works of Spinosa, in which, after complaining of the misrepresentations that have been given of the opinions of that writer, he pretends to maintain, that his system was, in every point, conformable to the doctrines of Christianity. Boulainvilliers also, another of Spinosa's commentators and advocates, declares, in his preface to a book, whose perfidious title is mentioned below in note ‡, that all the antagonists of that famous Jew either ignorantly misunderstood, or maliciously perverted, his true doctrine; his words are: Les refutations de Spinosa m'ont induit a juger, ou que leurs auteurs n'avoient pas voulu mettre la doctrine, qu'ils combattent, dans une evidence suffisante, ou qu'ils l'avoient mal entendue. If this be true, if the doctrine of Spinosa be not only far beyond the comprehension of the vulgar, but also difficult to be understood, and liable to be mistaken and misrepresented by men of the most acute parts and the most eminent abilities, what is the most obvious conclusion deducible from this fact? It is plainly this, that the greatest part of the Spinosists, whose sect is supposed by some to be very numerous in Europe, have adopted the doctrine of that famous atheist, not so much from a conviction of its truth, founded on an examination of its intricate contents, as from the pleasure they take in a system that promises impunity to all transgressions that do not come within the cognisance of the law, and thus lets loose the reins to every irregular appetite and passion; for it would be senseless, in the highest degree, to imagine, that the pretended multitude of the Spinosists, many of whom never once dreamed of exercising their minds in the pursuit of truth, or accustoming them to philosophical discussion, should all accurately comprehend a system, which, according to their own account, has escaped the penetration and sagacity of the greatest geniuses.

† Toland, unable to purchase a dinner, composed and published, in order to supply the sharp demands of hunger, an infamous and impious book under the following title: Pantheisticon, sive Formulæ celebrandæ Societatis Socraticæ, in tres Particulas divisæ, quæ Pantheistarum sive Sodalium continent, I. Mores et Axiomata; II. Numen et Philosophiam; III. Libertatem et non fallentem Legem neque fallendam, &c. The design of this book, which was published at London in 1720, appears by the title. It was intended to draw a picture of the licentious morals and principles of his brethren the *Pantheists* under the fictitious description of a Socratical Society, which they are represented as holding in all the places where they are dispersed. In the Socratical, or rather Bacchanalian Society, described in this pernicious work, the president and members are said to converse freely on several subjects. There is also a Form or Liturgy read by the president, who officiates as priest, and is answered by the assembly in suitable responses. He recommends earnestly to the members of the Society the care of truth, liberty, and health; exhorts them to guard against superstition, that is, religion; and reads aloud to them, by way of lesson, certain select passages out of Cicero and Seneca, which seem to favour irreligion. His colleagues promise solemnly to conform themselves to his injunctions and exhortations. Sometimes all the members, animated with enthusiasm and joy, raise their voices together, and sing, out of the ancient Latin poets, certain verses which are suitable to the laws and principles of their sect. See Des-Maizeaux, Life of John Toland, p. 77.—Bibliotheque Angloise tom. viii. If the pantheistical community be really such as it is here represented, it is not so much the duty of wise and good men to dispute with or refute its members, as it is the business of the civil magistrate to prevent such licentious and turbulent spirits from troubling the order of society, and seducing honest citizens from their religious principles, and the duties of their respective stations.

* This Meyer was the person who translated into Latin the pieces that Spinosa had composed in the Dutch language; who assisted him in his last moments, after having attempted in vain to remove his disorder; and who published his Posthumous Works, with a preface, in which, with great impudence and little success, he endeavours to prove, that the doctrine of Spinosa differs in nothing from that of the Gospel. Meyer is also the author of a well-known treatise, entitled, Philosophia Scripturæ Interpres, in which the merit and authority of the sacred writings are examined by the dictates of philosophy, that is to say, of the philosophy of Mr. Meyer.

† Lucas was a physician at the Hague, and was as famous for what he called his Quintessences, as he was infamous on account of the profligacy of his morals. He left behind him a Life of Spinosa, from which Lenglet du Fresnoy took all the additions that he made to the life of that atheist written by Colerus. He also composed a work which is still handed about, and bought at an extravagant price, by those in whose judgment rarity and impiety are equivalent to merit. This work is entitled, l'Esprit de Spinosa, and surpasses infinitely, in atheistical profaneness, even those productions of Spinosa that are generally looked upon as the most pernicious; so far has this miserable writer lost sight of every dictate of prudence, and triumphed even over the restraints of shame.

‡ This fertile and copious, but paradoxical and inconsiderate writer, is abundantly known by his various productions relating to the history and political state of the French nation, by a certain prolix Fable, entitled, the Life of Mohammed, and by the adverse turns of fortune that pursued him. His character was so made up of inconsistencies and contradictions, that he is almost equally chargeable with superstition and atheism; for, though he acknowledged no other Deity than the universe, or nature, yet he looked upon Mohammed as authorized, by a divine commission, to instruct mankind; and he was of opinion, that the fate of nations, and the destiny of individuals, could be foreknown, by an attentive observation of the stars. Thus the man was, at the same time, an atheist and an astrologer. Now this medley of a man was greatly concerned (in consequence, forsooth, of his ardent zeal for the *public good*) to see the *admirable* doctrine of Spinosa so generally misunderstood, and therefore he formed the laudable design of expounding, illustrating, and accommodating it, as is done with respect to the doctrines of the Gospel in books of piety, to ordinary capacities. This design, indeed, he executed, but not so fortunately for his master as he might fondly imagine, since it appeared most evidently from his own account of the system of Spinosa, that Bayle and the other writers who had represented his doctrine as repugnant to the plainest dictates of reason, and destructive of all religion, had judged rightly, and were not misled by ignorance or by temerity. In short, the book of Boulainvilliers set the atheism and impiety of Spinosa in a much more clear and striking light than ever they had appeared before This infamous book, which was worthy of eternal oblivion, was published by Lenglet du Fresnoy, who, that it might be bought with avidity, and read without reluctance, prefixed to it the attractive but perfidious title of a Refutation of the Errors of Spinosa, adding to it, indeed, some separate pieces, to which this title may, in some measure, be thought applicable. The whole title runs thus: Refutation des Erreurs de Benoit de Spinosa, par M. de Fenelon, Archeveque de Cambray, par le Pere Lami Benedictin, et par M. le Comte de Boulainvilliers, avec la Vie de Spinosa, ecrite par Jean Colerus, Ministre de l'Eglise Lutherienne de la Haye, augmentée de beaucoup de Particularites tirees d'une Vie Manuscrite de ce Philosophe, faite par un de ses Amis (this friend was Lucas, the atheistical physician mentioned in the

XXV. The progressive and flourishing state of the arts and sciences, in the seventeenth century, is abundantly known; and we see the effects, and enjoy the fruits, of the efforts then made for the advancement of learning. No branch of literature seemed to be neglected. Logic, philosophy, history, poetry, and rhetoric; in a word, all the sciences that belong to the respective provinces of reason, experience, observation, genius, memory, and imagination, were cultivated and improved with remarkable success throughout the Christian world. While the learned men of this happy period discovered such zeal for the improvement of science, their zeal was both inflamed and directed by one of the greatest and rarest geniuses that ever arose for the instruction of mankind. This was Francis Bacon, lord Verulam, who, toward the commencement of this century, opened the paths that lead to true philosophy in his admirable works.* It must be acknowledged, indeed, that the rules he prescribes, to direct the researches of the studious, are not all practicable amidst the numerous prejudices and impediments to which the most zealous inquirers are exposed in the pursuit of truth; and it appears plainly that this great man, to whose elevated and comprehensive genius all things seemed easy, was at certain times so far carried away by the vastness of his conceptions, as to require, from the application and abilities of men, more than they were capable of performing, and to desire the *end*, without always examining whether the *means* of attaining it were possible. At the same time it must be confessed that a great part of the improvements in learning and science, which distinguished Europe during this century, arose from the counsels and directions of this extraordinary man. This is more particularly true of the progress then made in natural philosophy, to which noble science Bacon did such important service, as is alone sufficient to render his name immortal. He opened the eyes of those who had been led blindfold by the dubious authority of traditionary systems, and the uncertain directory of hypothesis and conjecture. He led them to Nature, that they might consult that oracle directly and near at hand, and receive her answers; and, by the introduction of experimental inquiry, he placed philosophy upon a new and solid basis. It was thus undoubtedly that he removed the prejudices of former times, which led men to consider all human knowledge as circumscribed within the bounds of Greek and Latin erudition, and an acquaintance with the more elegant and liberal arts; and thus, in the vast regions of nature, he opened scenes of instruction and science, which, although hitherto unknown or disregarded, were infinitely more noble and sublime, and much more productive of solid nourishment to the minds of the wise, than the learning that was cultivated before his time.

XXVI. It is remarkable, in general, that the sciences of natural philosophy, mathematics, and astronomy, were carried in this century, in all the nations of Europe, to such a high degree of perfection, that they seemed suddenly to rise from the puny weakness of infancy to a state of full maturity. There is certainly no sort of comparison between the philosophers, mathematicians, and astronomers, of the sixteenth and seventeeth centuries. The former look like pygmies, when compared with the gigantic stature of the latter. At the head of the latter appears Galileo, the ornament of natural science in Italy, who was encouraged, in his astronomical researches and discoveries, by the munificence and protection of the grand dukes of Tuscany.* In France appeared Des-Cartes and Gassendi, who left behind them a great number of eminent disciples; in Denmark Tycho Brahe; in England Boyle and Newton; in Germany Kepler, Hevelius, and Leibnitz; and in Switzerland the brothers, James and John Bernoulli. These philosophers of the first magnitude, if I may use that expression, excited such a spirit of emulation in Europe, and were followed by such a multitude of admirers and rivals, that, if we except those countries which had not yet emerged from a state of ignorance and barbarism, there was scarcely any nation that could not boast of possessing a profound mathematician, a famous astronomer, or an eminent philosopher. Nor were the dukes of Tuscany, however distinguished by their hereditary zeal for the sciences, and their liberality to the learned, the only patrons of philosophy at this time, since it is well known that the monarchs of Great-Britain and France, Charles II. and Louis XIV., honoured the sciences, and those who cultivated them, with their protection and encouragement. It is to the munificence of those two princes that the Royal Society of London, and the Academy of Sciences at Paris, owe their origin and establishment, their privileges, honours and endowments, and that we, in consequence, are indebted for the interesting discoveries that have been made by these two learned bodies, the end of whose institution is the study and investigation of nature, and the culture of all those arts and sciences which lead

preceding note,) a Bruxelles, chez Francois Foppens, 1731. Here we see the poison and the antidote joined, but the latter perfidiously distributed in a manner and measure every way insufficient to remove the noxious effects of the former: in a word, the wolf is shut up with the sheep. The account and defence of the philosophy of Spinosa, given by Boulainvilliers under the insidious title of a Refutation, take up the greatest part of this book, and are placed first, and not the last in order, as the title would insinuate. Besides, the whole contents of this motley collection are not enumerated in the title: for at the end of it we find a Latin treatise, entitled Certamen Philosophicum propugnatæ Veritatis divinæ et naturalis, adversus Jo. Bredenburgii Principia, in fine annexa. This *philosophical controversy* contains a Defence of the Doctrine of Spinosa, by Bredenburg, and a Refutation of that Defence by Isaac Orobio, a learned Jewish physician at Amsterdam, and was first published in 1703.

* More especially in his treatise de Dignitate et Augmentis Scientiarum, and in his Novum Organum. See the life of that great man, prefixed to his works published in four volumes, in folio, 1740.—Bibliotheque Britannique, tom. xv.—In Mallet's Life of Bacon there is a particular and interesting account of his noble attempt to reform the miserable philosophy that prevailed before his time. See also Voltaire's Melanges de Literature et de Philosophie.

* See Heuman's Acta Philosophorum, the xivth, xvth, and xviith parts.

to truth, and are useful to mankind.* These establishments, and the inquiries they were so naturally adapted to encourage and promote, proved not only beneficial, in the highest degree, to the civil interests of mankind, but were also productive of inestimable advantages to the cause of true religion. By these inquiries, the empire of superstition, which is always the bane of genuine piety, and often a source of rebellion and calamity in sovereign states, was greatly shaken; by them the fictitious prodigies, that had so long kept miserable mortals in a painful state of servitude and terror, were deprived of their influence; by them natural religion was built upon solid foundations, and illustrated with admirable perspicuity and evidence; as by them the infinite perfections of the Supreme Being were demonstrated with the utmost clearness and force from the frame of the universe in general, and also from the structure of its various parts.

XXVII. The improvements made in history, and more especially the new degrees of light that were thrown upon the ancient history of the church, were of eminent service to the cause of genuine Christianity; for thus the original sources and reasons of many absurd opinions and institutions, which antiquity and custom had rendered sacred, were discovered and exposed in their proper colours; and innumerable errors that had possessed and perplexed the anxious spirits of the credulous and superstitious multitude, were happily deprived of their authority and influence. Thus, in consequence, the cheerful light of truth, and the calm repose and tranquillity that attend it, arose upon the minds of many; and human life was delivered from the crimes that have been sanctified by superstition, and from the tumults and agitations in which it has so often involved unhappy mortals. The advantages that flowed from the improvement of historical knowledge were both innumerable and inestimable. By this many pious and excellent persons, whom ignorance or malice had stigmatised as heretics, were delivered from reproach, recovered their good fame, and thus were secured against the malignity of superstition. By this it appeared, that many of those religious controversies, which had divided nations, friends, and families, and involved so often sovereign states in bloodshed, rebellion, and crimes of the most horrid kind, were owing to the most trifling and contemptible causes, to the ambiguity and obscurity of certain theological phrases and terms, to superstition, ignorance and envy, to spiritual pride and ambition. By this it was demonstrated with the fullest evidence, that many of those religious ceremonies, which had been long considered as of divine institution, were derived from the most inglorious sources, being either borrowed from the manners and customs of barbarous nations, or invented with a design to deceive the ignorant and credulous, or dictated by the idle visions of senseless enthusiasm. By this the ambitious intrigues of the bishops and other ministers of religion, who, by perfidious arts, had encroached upon the prerogatives of the throne, usurped a considerable part of its authority and revenues, and held princes in subjection to their yoke by the terrors of the church, were brought to light. And to mention no more instances, it was by the lamp of history that those councils, whose decrees had so long been regarded as infallible and sacred, and revered as the dictates of celestial wisdom, were exhibited to the attentive observer as assemblies, where an odious mixture of ignorance and knavery very frequently presided. Our happy experience, in these later times, furnishes daily instances of the salutary effects of these important discoveries on the state of the Christian church, and on the condition of all its members. Hence flow that lenity and moderation which are mutually exercised by those who differ in their religious sentiments; the prudence and caution that are used in estimating opinions and deciding controversies; the protection and support that are granted to men of worth, when attacked by the malice of bigotry; and the visible diminution of the errors, frauds, crimes, and cruelties, with which superstition formerly embittered the pleasures of human life, and the enjoyments of social intercourse

XXVIII. Many of the doctors of this century applied themselves, with eminent success, to the study of Hebrew and Greek literature, and of the oriental languages and antiquities; and, as their progress in this kind of erudition was rapid, so, in many instances, was the use they made of it truly excellent and laudable, for they were thus enabled to throw light on many difficult passages of the sacred writings that had been ill understood and injudiciously applied, and which some had even employed in supporting erroneous opinions, and giving a plausible colour to pernicious doctrines. Hence it happened, that many patrons and promoters of popular notions, and of visionary and groundless fancies, were deprived of the fallacious arguments by which they maintained their errors. It cannot also be denied, that the cause of religion received considerable benefit from the labours of those, who either endeavoured to preserve the purity and elegance of the Latin language, or who, beholding with emulation the example of the French, employed their industry in improving and polishing the languages of their respective countries; for it must be evidently both honourable and advantageous to the Christian church, to have always in its bosom men of learning qualified to write and discourse upon theological subjects with precision, elegance, ease, and perspicuity, that so the ignorant and perverse may be allured to receive instruction, and also be able to comprehend with facility the instructions they receive.

XXIX. The rules of morality and practice, which were laid down in the sacred writings by Christ and his apostles, assumed an advantageous form, received new illustrations, and were supported upon new and solid principles

* The history of the Royal Society of London, was published by Dr. Sprat, in the year 1722.* Fontenelle composed the History of the Academy of Sciences at Paris. The reader will find a comparison between these learned bodies in Voltaire's Melanges de Literature et de Philosophie.

☞ * A much more interesting and ample history of this respectable society was afterwards composed, and published by Dr. Birch, its learned secretary.

when that great system of law, which results from the constitution of nature, and the dictates of right reason, began to be studied with more diligence, and investigated with more accuracy and perspicuity than had been the case in preceding ages. In this sublime study of the law of nature, the immortal Grotius led the way in his excellent book concerning the Rights of War and Peace: and, from the dignity and importance of the subject, his labours excited the zeal and emulation of men of the most eminent genius and abilities,* who turned their principal attention to this noble science. How much the labours of these great men contributed to assist the ministers of the Gospel, both in their discourses and writings concerning the duties and obligations of Christians, may be easily seen by comparing the books of a practical kind, published since the period now under consideration, with those which were in vogue before that time.—[☞ There is scarcely a discourse upon any subject of Christian morality, how inconsiderable soever it may be, that does not bear some marks of the improvement which was introduced into the science of morals by those great men, who studied that science in the paths of nature, in the frame and constitution of rational and moral beings, and in the relations by which they are rendered members of one great family, under the inspection and government of one common and universal† Parent.] It is unquestionably certain, that since this period the dictates of natural law, and the duties of Christian morality, have been more accurately defined; certain evangelical precepts, whose nature and foundations were imperfectly comprehended in the times of old, have been more clearly illustrated; the superiority which distinguishes the morality of the Gospel from the course of duty that is deducible from the mere light of nature, has been more fully demonstrated; and those common notions and general principles, which are the foundations of moral obligation, and are every way adapted to dispel all doubts that may arise, and all controversies that may be started, concerning the nature of evangelical righteousness and virtue, have been established with greater evidence and certainty. It may also be added, that the impiety of those infidels who have had the effrontery to maintain that the precepts of the Gospel are contrary to the dictates of sound reason, repugnant to the constitution of our nature, inconsistent with the interests of civil society, adapted to enervate the mind, and to draw men off from the business, the duties, and enjoyments of life,‡ has been much more triumphantly refuted in the seventeenth and eighteenth centuries, than in any other period of the Christian church.

XXX. To these reflections upon the state of learning and science in general, it may not be improper to add a particular and separate account of the progress and revolutions of philosophy in the Christian schools. At the beginning of this century, almost all the European philosophers were divided into two classes, one of which comprehended the *Peripatetics*, and the other the *Chemists*, or *Fire-Philosophers*, as they were often styled. These two classes, during many years, contended warmly for the pre-eminence; and a great number of laboured and subtile productions were published amidst this philosophical contest. The Peripatetics were in possession of the professorships in almost all the schools of learning, and looked upon all such as presumed, either to reject, or even amend the doctrines of Aristotle, as objects of indignation, little less criminal than traitors and rebels. It is, however, observable, that the greatest part of these supercilious and persecuting doctors, if we except those of the universities of Tubingen, Altorf, Juliers, and Leipsic, were less attached to Aristotle himself than to his modern interpreters and commentators. The Chemists spread themselves through almost all Europe, and assumed the obscure and ambiguous title of *Rosecrucian Brethren*,* which drew at first some degree of respect, as it seemed to be borrowed from the arms of Luther, which were a *cross* placed upon a *rose*. They inveighed against the Peripatetics with a singular degree of bitterness and animosity, represented them as corruptors both of religion and philosophy, and published a multitude of treatises against them, which discovered little else than their folly and their malice. At the head of these fanatics were Robert Fludd,† a native of Eng-

* See Adam. Fred. Glafey's Historia Juris Naturæ; to which is subjoined his Bibliotheca Juris Naturæ et Gentium.

† This sentence, beginning with "*There is scarcely a discourse*," and ending with "*common and universal Parent*," is added by the translator.

‡ Le Contra Social, par Rousseau.

* The title of *Rosecrucians* evidently denotes the chymical philosophers, and those who blended the doctrines of religion with the secrets of chymistry. The denomination itself is drawn from the science of chymistry; and they only who are acquainted with the peculiar language of the chymists can understand its true signification and energy. It is not compounded, as many imagine, of the two words *rosa* and *crux*, which signify *rose* and *cross*, but of the latter of these words, and the Latin word *ros*, which signifies *dew*. Of all natural bodies, *dew* is the most powerful dissolvent of gold. The *cross*, in the chymical style, is equivalent to *light;* because the figure of the cross (†) exhibits, at the same time, the three letters of which the word *lux*, i. e. *light*, is compounded. Now *lux* is called by this sect the seed or menstruum of the red dragon; or, in other words, that gross and corporeal light, which, when properly digested and modified, produces gold. From all this it follows, that a Rosecrucian philosopher is one who, by the intervention and assistance of the dew, seeks for light, or, in other words, the substance called the Philosopher's Stone. All other explications of this term are false and chimerical. The interpretations that are given of it by the chymists, who love, on all occasions, to involve themselves in intricacy and darkness, are invented merely to deceive those who are strangers to their mysteries. The true energy and meaning of this denomination of Rosecrucians, did not escape the penetration and sagacity of Gassendi, as appears by his Examen Philosophiæ Fluddanæ, sect. xv. It was, however, still more fully explained by Renaudot, a famous French physician, in his Conferences Publiques, t. iv. A great number of materials and anecdotes relating to the fraternity, rules, observances, and writings, of the Rosecrucians, (who made such a noise in this century,) may be found in Arnold's Kirchen-und-Ketzer, Historie, part ii. p. 1114.

† See, for an account of this singular man, from whose writings Jacob Behmen derived all his mystical and rapturous doctrine, Wood's Athenæ Oxonienses, vol. i. p. 610. and Histor. et Antiq. Acade-

land, and a man of surprising genius; Jacob Behmen, a shoemaker, who lived at Gorlitz, and Michael Mayer.* These leaders of the sect were followed by John Baptist Helmont, and his son Francis, Christian Knorrius de Rosenroth, Khulman, Nollius, Sperber, and many others of various fame. A uniformity of opinion, and a spirit of concord, seem scarcely possible in such a society as this; for, as a great part of its doctrine is derived from certain internal feelings and flights of imagination, which can neither be comprehended nor defined, and is supported by testimonies of the external senses, whose reports are illusory and changeable, so it is remarkable, that, among the more eminent writers of this sect, there are scarcely any two who adopt the same tenets and sentiments. There are, nevertheless, some common principles that are generally embraced, and which serve as a centre of union to the society. They all maintain, that the dissolution of bodies, by the power of fire, is the only way through which men can arrive at true wisdom, and come to discern the first principles of things. They all acknowledge a certain analogy and harmony between the powers of nature and the doctrines of religion, and believe that the Deity governs the kingdom of grace by the same laws with which he rules the kingdom of nature; and hence it is that they employ chemical denominations to express the truths of religion. They all hold, that there is a sort of divine energy, or soul, diffused through the frame of the universe, which some call Archæus, others the Universal Spirit, and which others mention under different appellations. They all talk in the most obscure and superstitious manner of what they call the signatures of things, of the power of the stars over all corporeal beings, and their particular influence upon the human race, of the efficacy of magic, and the various species and classes of demons. In fine, they all agree in throwing out the most crude and incomprehensible notions and ideas, in the most obscure, quaint, and unusual expressions.

XXXI. This controversy, between the Chemists and Peripatetics, was buried in silence and oblivion, as soon as a new and more seemly form of philosophy was presented to the world by two great men, who reflected a lustre upon the French nation,—Gassendi and Des-Cartes. The former, whose profound knowledge of geometry and astronomy was accompanied with the most engaging eloquence, and an acquaintance with the various branches of solid erudition and polite literature, was canon of Digne, and professor of mathematics at Paris. The latter, who was a man of quality and bred a soldier, surpassed the greatest part of his contemporaries in acuteness, subtlety, and extent of genius, though he was much inferior to Gassendi in point of learning.

;niæ Oxoniensis, lib. ii. p. 308.—For an account of Helmont, the father, see Hen. Witte, Memor. Philosoph.—Consult also Joach. Fred. Feller, in Miscelan. Leibnitian.—Several writers beside Arnold have given an account of Jacob Behmen.*

* See Molleri Cimbria Literata, tom. i. p. 376.

* See, also sect. ii. part 1 chap. i. sect. xl. of this century

In 1624, Gassendi attacked Aristotle, and the whole body of his commentators and followers, with great resolution and ingenuity;* but the resentment and indignation which he drew upon himself from all quarters by this bold attempt, and the sweetness of his natural temper, which made him an enemy to dissention and contest, engaged him to desist, and to suspend an enterprise, that, by opposing the prejudices, was so adapted to inflame the passions of the learned. Hence no more than two books of the work he had composed against the Aristotelians were made public; the other five were suppressed.† He also wrote against Fludd, and, by refuting him, refuted at the same time the Rosecrucian Brethren; and here the Aristotelians seemed to behold his labours with a favourable eye. After having overturned several false and visionary systems of philosophy, he began to think of substituting something more solid and satisfactory in their place, and in pursuance of this design he proceeded with the utmost circumspection and caution. He recommended to others, and followed himself, that wise method of philosophical investigation, which, with a slow and timorous pace, rises from the objects of sense to the discussions of reason, and arrives at truth by assiduity, experiment, and an attentive observation of the laws of nature; or, to express the same thing in other words, he struck out that judicious method, which, by an attention to facts, to the changes and motions of the natural world, leads by degrees to general principles, and lays a solid foundation for rational inquiry. In the application of this method, he had recourse chiefly to mathematical succours, from a persuasion that demonstration and certainty were the peculiar fruits of that accurate and luminous science. He drew no assistance from metaphysics, which he overlooked from an opinion that the greatest part of its rules and decisions were too precarious to satisfy a sincere inquirer, animated with the love of truth.‡

XXXII. Des-Cartes followed a very different method in his philosophical researches He abandoned mathematics, which he had at first looked upon as the tree of knowledge, and employed the science of abstract ideas, or metaphysics, in the investigation of truth Having accordingly laid down a few plain and general principles, which seemed to be deduced immediately from the nature of man his next business was to form distinct notions of the Deity, of matter, soul, body, space, the universe, and the various parts of which it is composed. From these notions, examined with attention, compared and combined ac-

* The title of his book against the Aristotelians is as follows: Exercitationum paradoxicarum adversus Aristoteleos Libri VII. in his quibus præcipua totius Peripateticæ Doctrinæ Fundamenta excutiuntur, Opiniones vero, ut ex vetustioribus obsoletæ, stabiliuntur.

† See Bougerelle's Vie de Gassendi.

‡ See Gassendi's Institutiones Philosophiæ; a diffuse production, which takes up the two first volumes of his works, and in which his principal design is to show, that those opinions, both of the ancient and modern philosophers, which are deduced from metaphysical principles, have little solidity, and are generally defective in point of evidence and perspicuity.

cording to their mutual relations, connexions, and resemblances, and reduced into a kind of system, he proceeded still farther, and made admirable use of them in reforming the other branches of philosophy, and giving them a new degree of stability and consistence. This he effected by connecting all his branches of philosophical reasoning in such a manner, that principles and consequences were placed in the most accurate order, and the latter seemed to flow from the former in the most natural manner. This method of pursuing truth could not fail to attract the admiration of many; and so indeed it happened; for no sooner had Des-Cartes published his discoveries in philosophy, than a considerable number of eminent men, in different parts of Europe, who had long entertained a high disgust to the inelegant and ambiguous jargon of the schools, adopted these discoveries with zeal, declared their approbation of the new system, and expressed their desire that its author should be substituted in the place of the Peripatetics, as a philosophical guide to the youth in the public seminaries of learning. On the other hand, the Peripatetics, or Aristotelians, seconded by the influence of the clergy, who apprehended that the cause of religion was aimed at, and endangered, by these philosophical innovations, made a prodigious noise, and left no means unemployed to prevent the downfall of their old system, and diminish the growing reputation of the new philosophy. To execute this invidious purpose with the greater facility, they not only accused Des-Cartes of the most dangerous and pernicious errors, but went so far, in the extravagance of their malignity, as to bring a charge of atheism against him. This furious zeal of the Aristotelians will not appear so extraordinary, when it is considered, that they contended, not so much for their philosophical system, as for the honours, advantages, and profits they derived from it. The Theosophists, Rosecrucians, and Chymists, entered into this contest against Des-Cartes, but conducted themselves with greater moderation than the Aristotelians, notwithstanding their persuasion that the Peripatetic philosophy, though chimerical and impious, was much less intolerable than the Cartesian system.* The consequences of this dispute were favourable to the progress of science; for the wiser part of the European philosophers, although they did not adopt the sentiments of Des-Cartes, were encouraged and animated by his example to carry on their inquiries with more freedom from the restraints of traditional and personal authority than they had formerly done, and to throw resolutely from their necks that yoke of servitude, under which Aristotle and his followers had so long kept them in subjection.

XXXIII. The most eminent contemporaries of Des-Cartes applauded, in general, the efforts he made toward the reformation of philosophy, and that noble resolution with which he broke the shackles of magisterial authority, and struck out new paths, in which he proceeded without a guide, in the search after truth. They also approved his method of rising, with caution and accuracy, from the most simple, and, as it were, the primary dictates of reason and nature, to truths and propositions of a more complex and intricate kind, and of admitting nothing as truth, that was not clearly and distinctly apprehended as such. They went still farther, and unanimously acknowledged, that he had made most valuable and important discoveries in philosophy, and had demonstrated several truths, which, before his time, were received upon no other evidence than that of tradition and conjecture. But these acknowledgments did not prevent some of those who made them with the greatest sincerity, from finding several essential defects in the philosophy of this great man. They considered his account of the causes and principles of natural things, as for the most part hypothetical, and founded on fancy, rather than experience. They even attacked the fundamental principles upon which the whole system of his philosophy was built, such as his ideas of the Deity, of the universe, of matter and spirit, of the laws of motion, and other points that were connected with these. Some of these principles they pronounced uncertain; others, they said, were of a pernicious tendency, and likely to engender the most dangerous errors; and they affirmed, that some were directly contrary to the language of experience. At the head of these objectors appeared his fellow-citizen, Gassendi, who had made war before him upon the Aristotelians and Chymists; who, in genius, was his equal; in learning, greatly his superior; and whose mathematical knowledge was most uncommon and extensive. This formidable adversary directed his first attacks against the metaphysical principles which supported the whole structure of the Cartesian philosophy. He then proceeded still farther; and, for the physical system of Des-Cartes, substituted one that resembled not a little the natural philosophy of Epicurus, though far superior to it in solidity, much more rational, consistent, and perfect, being founded, not on the illusory visions of fancy, but on the testimony of sense and the dictates of experience.* This new and sagacious observer of nature had not many followers, and his disciples were much less numerous than those of Des-Cartes. But what he wanted in number, was sufficiently compensated by the merit and reputation of those who adopted his philosophical system; for he was followed by some of the most eminent men in Europe, by persons who were distinguished in the highest degree by their indefatigable application, and

* See Baillet's Vie de Rene Des-Cartes, and also the General Dictionary.

* See his Disquisitio Metaphysica, seu Dubitationes et Instantiæ adversus Cartesii Metaphysicam, et Responsa, in the third volume of his works.—Bernier, a celebrated French physician, has given an accurate view of the philosophy of Gassendi in his abridgment of it, published at Lyons, in 1684. This abridgment will give the reader a better account of this philosophy than even the works of Gassendi himself, in which his meaning is often expressed in an ambiguous manner, and which are, besides, loaded with superfluous erudition. The Life of Gassendi, accurately written by Bougerelle, a priest of the oratory, was published in 1737.—See Biblioth. Francoise, tom. xxvii. p 353.

their extensive knowledge both of natural philosophy and mathematics. He had certainly few disciples in his own country; but, among the English, who in his time were remarkable for their application to studies of a physical and mathematical kind, a considerable number adopted his philosophical system. It may here be observed, that even those eminent philosophers and divines, such as Whichcot, Gale, Cudworth, and More, who entered the lists with Hobbes, (whose doctrine came nearer to the principles of Gassendi than to the system of Des-Cartes,) and revived ancient Platonism, in order to crush under its weight the philosopher of Malmesbury, placed Gassendi and Plato in the same class, and explained the sentiments of the latter in such a manner as to make them appear quite agreeable to the principles of the former.*

XXXIV. From this period must be dated the famous schism that divided the philosophical world into two great sects, which, though they almost agree upon those points that are of the greatest utility and importance in human life, differ widely about the principles of human knowledge, and the fundamental points whence the philosopher must proceed in his search of truth. Of these sects, one may properly be called *Metaphysical*, and the other *Mathematical*. The metaphysical sect follows the system of Des-Cartes; the mathematical one directs its researches by the principles of Gassendi. Philosophers of the former class look upon truth as attainable by abstract reasoning; those of the latter seek it by observation and experience. The follower of Des-Cartes attributes little to the external senses, and much to meditation and discussion. The disciple of Gassendi, on the contrary, places little confidence in metaphysical discussion, and principally has recourse to the reports of sense and the contemplation of nature. The Cartesian, from a small number of abstract truths, deduces a long series of propositions, in order to arrive at a precise and accurate knowledge of God and nature, of body and spirit; the Gassendian admits these metaphysical truths, but at the same time denies the possibility of erecting, upon their basis, a regular and solid system of philosophy, without the aid of assiduous observation and repeated experiments, which are the most natural and effectual means of philosophical progress and improvement. The one, eagle-like, soars with an intrepid flight to the first fountain of truth, and to the general relations and final causes of things; and thence descending, explains, by them, the various changes and appearances of nature, the attributes and counsels of the Deity, the moral constitution and duties of man, the frame and structure of the universe. The other, more difficult and cautious, observes with attention, and examines with assiduity, the objects that are before his eyes; and rises gradually from them to the first cause, and the primordial principle of things. The Cartesians suppose, that many things are known by man with the utmost certainty; and hence arises their propensity to form their opinions and doctrines into a regular system. The followers of Gassendi consider man as in a state of ignorance with respect to an immense number of points, and, consequently, think it incumbent upon them to suspend their judgment in a multitude of cases, until time and experience dispel their darkness; and hence it is also, that they consider a *system* as an attempt of too adventurous a nature, and by no means proportioned to the narrow extent of human knowledge; or, at least, they think, that the business of system-making ought to be left to the philosophers of future times, who, by joining the observations and experience of many ages, may acquire a more satisfactory and accurate knowledge of nature than has been yet attained.

These dissensions and contests concerning the first principles of human knowledge, produced various debates upon other subjects of the utmost moment and importance; such as, the nature of God, the essence of matter, the elements or constituent principles of bodies, the laws of motion, the manner in which the Divine Providence exerts itself in the government of the world, the frame and structure of the universe, the nature, union, and joint operations of soul and body. If we consider attentively the profound and intricate nature of these subjects, together with the limits, debility, and imperfections of the human understanding, we shall see too much reason to fear, that these contests will last as long as the present state of man.* The wise and the good, sensible of this, will carry on such debates with a spirit of mildness and mutual forbearance; and, knowing that differences in opinions are inevitable where truth is so difficult of access, will guard against that temerity with which too many disputants accuse their antagonists of irreligion and impiety.†

* See the preface to the Latin translation of Cudworth's Intellectual System; and also the *remarks* added to that translation. ☞ Dr. Mosheim is the author of that *translation* and of those *remarks*.

* Voltaire published, in 1740, at Amsterdam, a pamphlet, entitled, La Metaphysique de Newton, ou Parallele des Sentimens de Newton et de Leibnitz, which, though superficial and inaccurate, may be useful to those readers who have not application enough to draw from better sources, and are desirous of knowing how much these two philosophical sects differ in their principles and tenets.

† It is abundantly known that Des-Cartes and his metaphysical followers were accused by many of striking at the foundations of all religion; nor is this accusation entirely withdrawn even in our times. See, in the miscellaneous works of Father Hardouin, his Atheists Unmasked. Among these pretended atheists, Des-Cartes, and his two famous disciples, (Antoine Le Grand and Sylvain Regis,) hold the first rank; nor is Father Malebranche, though he seems rather chargeable with fanaticism than atheism, exempted from a place in this odious list. It is true that Hardouin, who gives so liberally a place in the atheistical class to these great men, was himself a visionary dreamer, whose judgment, in many cases, is little to be respected; but it is also true, that, in the work now under consideration, he does not reason from his own whimsical notions, but draws all his arguments from those followers of Aristotle and Gassendi, who have opposed, with the greatest success and acuteness, the Cartesian system. Even Voltaire, notwithstanding the moderation with which he expresses himself, seems plainly enough to give his assent to the accusers of Des-Cartes. On the other hand, it must be observed that these accusers are censured in their turns by several modern metaphysicians. Gassendi, for example, is charged by Arnauld with overturning the doctrine

XXXV. Those who had either adopted, without exception, the principles of Des-Cartes, or who, without going so far, approved the method and rules laid down by him for the investigation of truth, employed all their zeal and industry in correcting, amending, confirming, and illustrating, the metaphysical species of philosophy; and its votaries were exceedingly numerous, particularly in France and in the United Provinces. But among the members of this philosophical sect there were some who aimed at the destruction of all religion, more especially Spinosa, and others, who, like Balthasar Becker,* made use of the principles of Des-Cartes, to overturn some doctrines of Christianity, and to pervert others. This circumstance proved disadvantageous to the whole sect, and brought it into disrepute in many places. The metaphysical philosophy fell, however, afterwards into better hands, and was treated with great wisdom and acuteness by Malebranche, a man of uncommon eloquence and subtlety; and by Leibnitz, whose name is consigned to immortality as one of the greatest geniuses that ever appeared in the world.† Neither of these great men, indeed, adopted all the principles and doctrines of Des-Cartes; but both of them approved, upon the whole, his philosophical method, which they enlarged, amended, and improved, by several additions and corrections, that rendered its procedure more luminous and sure. This is more especially true of Leibnitz, who, rejecting the suggestions of fancy, seemed to follow no other guides than reason and judgment; for Malebranche, having received from nature a warm and exuberant imagination, was too much ruled by its dictates, and was thus often imperceptibly led into the visionary regions of enthusiasm.

XXXVI. The mathematical philosophy already mentioned, was much less studied and adopted than the metaphysical system, and its followers in France were very few in number. But it met with a favourable reception in Great Britain, whose philosophers perceiving, in its infant and unfinished features, the immortal lines of Verulam's wisdom, snatched it from its cradle, in a soil where it was ready to perish, cherished it with parental tenderness, and have still continued their zealous efforts to bring it to maturity and perfection. The Royal Society of London, which may be considered as the philosophical seminary of the nation, took it under their protection, and have neither spared expense nor pains to cultivate and improve it, and to render it subservient to the purposes of life. It owed, more especially, a great part of its progress and improvement to the countenance, industry, and genius of that immortal protector of science, the pious and venerable Robert Boyle, whose memory will be ever precious to the worthy and the wise, the friends of religion, learning, and mankind. The illustrious names of Barrow, Wallis, and Locke, may also be added to the list of those who contributed to the progress of natural knowledge. Nor were the learned divines of the British nation (though that order has often excited the complaints of philosophers, and been supposed to behold, with a jealous and suspicious eye, the efforts of philosophy as dangerous to the cause of religion) less zealous than the other patrons of science in this noble cause. On the contrary, they looked upon the improvement of natural knowledge not only as innocent, but as of the highest utility and importance; as admirably adapted to excite and maintain in the minds of men a profound veneration for the Supreme Creator and Governor of the world, and to furnish new supports to the cause of religion; and also as agreeable both to the laws and the spirit of the Gospel, and to the sentiments of the primitive church. And hence it was that those doctors, who, in the lectures founded by Mr. Boyle, attacked the enemies of religion, employed in this noble and pious attempt the succours of philosophy with the most happy and triumphant success. But the immortal man, to whose immense genius and indefatigable industry philosophy owed its greatest improvements, and who carried the lamp of knowledge into paths of nature that had been unexplored before his time, was Sir Isaac Newton,* whose name was revered, and whose genius was admired, even by his warmest adversaries. This

of the soul's immortality in his controversy with Des-Cartes, and by Leibnitz with corrupting and destroying the whole system of natural religion: see Des-Maizeaux, Recueil de diverses pieces sur la Philosophie, tom. ii.* Leibnitz has also ventured to affirm, that Sir Isaac Newton and his followers rob the Deity of some of his most excellent attributes, and sap the foundations of natural religion. In short, the controversial writings on both sides are filled with rash and indecorous reproaches of this kind.

☞ * See, for a farther account of the particular tenets and opinions of Becker, sect. ii. part ii. chap. ii. sect. xxxv. of this century.

† For an ample and interesting account of Malebranche and his philosophy, see Fontenelle's Eloges des Academiciens, tom. i. p. 317, and, for a view of the errors and defects of his metaphysical system, see Hardouin's Atheists Unmasked, in his Œuvres Melees, p. 43. Fontenelle has also given an account of the life and philosophical sentiments of Leibnitz, in the work already quoted, vol. ii.; but a much more ample one has been published in German by Charles Gunther Ludewig, in his history of the Leibnitian Philosophy. However, the genius and philosophy of this great man are best to be learned from his letters, published by Kortholt.

☞ * It appears, on reference, that the censure is not conveyed in such strong terms as those employed by our historian; Leibnitz merely says, that Gassendi appeared to hesitate and waver too much concerning the nature of the soul and the principles of natural religion.

☞ * Mr. Hume's account of this great man is extremely just, and contains some peculiar strokes that do honour to this elegant painter of minds. "In Newton, (*says he*,) this island may boast of having produced the greatest and rarest genius that ever arose for the ornament and instruction of the species. Cautious in admitting no principles but such as were founded in experiment; but resolute to adopt every such principle, however new and unusual; from modesty, ignorant of his superiority above the rest of mankind, and thence less careful to accommodate his reasonings to common apprehensions; more anxious to merit than to acquire fame; he was, from these causes, long unknown to the world; but his reputation, at last, broke out with a lustre, which scarcely any writer, during his own life-time, had ever before attained. While Newton seemed to draw off the veil from some of the mysteries of nature, he showed, at the same time, the imperfections of the mechanical philosophy; and thereby restored her ultimate secrets to that obscurity, in which they ever did and ever will remain.'

great man spent, with uninterrupted assiduity, the whole of a long life in correcting, digesting, and enlarging, the new philosophy, and in throwing upon it the light of demonstration and evidence, both by observing the laws of nature, and by subjecting them to the rules of calculation; and thus he introduced a great change into natural science, and brought it to a very high degree of perfection.* The English look upon it as an unquestionable proof of the solidity and excellence of the Newtonian philosophy, that its most eminent votaries were friends to religion, and have transmitted to posterity shining examples of piety and virtue; while, on the contrary, the Cartesian or metaphysical system has exhibited, in its followers, many flagrant instances of irreligion, and some demonstrations of the most horrid impiety.

XXXVII. The two famous philosophical sects now mentioned, deprived, indeed, all the ancient systems of natural science, both of their credit and their disciples; and hence it might have been expected that they would have totally engrossed and divided between them the suffrages of the learned. But this was not the case; the liberty of thinking being restored by Des-Cartes and Newton, who broke the fetters of prejudice, in which philosophical superstition had confined, in former times, the human understanding, a variety of sects sprang up. Some trusting to their superior genius and sagacity, and others, more remarkable for the exuberance of their fancy than for the solidity of their judgment, pretended to strike out new paths in the unknown regions of nature, and new methods of investigating truth; but of their disciples the number was small, and the duration of their inventions transitory; and therefore it is sufficient to have barely mentioned them. There appeared also another sort of men, whom mediocrity of genius, or an indolent turn of mind, indisposed for investigating truth by the exertion of their own talents and powers, and who, terrified at the view of such an arduous task, contented themselves with borrowing from the different sects such of their respective tenets as seemed to them most remarkable for their perspicuity and solidity, more especially those concerning which all the different sects were agreed. These they compiled and digested into a system, and pushed their inquiries no farther. The philosophers of this class are generally termed *Eclectics*. From these remarkable differences of sentiment and system that reigned among the jarring sects, some persons, otherwise distinguished by their acuteness and sagacity, took occasion to represent truth as unattainable by such a short-sighted being as man, and to revive the desperate and uncomfortable *doctrine* (shall I call it, or *jargon*) of the Sceptics, that had long been buried in the silence and oblivion which it deserved. The most eminent of these cloudy philosophers were Sanchez, a physician of Toulouse,* de la Mothe le Vayer,† Huet, bishop of Avranches,‡ to whom we may justly add Peter Bayle,§ who, by the erudition and wit that abound in his voluminous works, acquired a distinguished reputation in the republic of letters.

* The Mathematical Principles of Natural Philosophy, as also the other writings, whether philosophical, mathematical, or theological, of this great man, are abundantly known. There is an elegant account of his life, and literary and philosophical merit, given by Fontenelle, in his Eloge des Academiciens, tom. ii. p. 293.—See also the Biblioth. Angloise, tom. xv. par. ii. p. 545, and Biblioth. Raisonee, tom. vi. par. ii. p. 478. ☞ See more especially the late learned and ingenious **Mr. Maclaurin's Account of Sir Isaac Newton's Discoveries.**

* There is still extant a famous book of this writer, entitled, *de eo quod nihil scitur*, which, with the rest of his works, and an account of his life, appeared at Toulouse, in 1636. See Bayle's Dictionary, and Villemandi Scepticismus debellatus, cap. iv.

† See Bayle's Dictionary for an account of this author.

‡ Huet's book concerning the Weakness of Human Reason was published after his death, in French, at Amsterdam, in 1723, and lately in Latin. It appears, however, that this eminent writer had, long before the composition of this book, recommended the sceptical method of conducting philosophical researches, and looked upon it as the best adapted to establish the truth of Christianity upon solid foundations. See the Commentarius de Rebus ad eum pertinentibus, lib. iv. p. 230; and Demonstrat Evangelicæ Præfat. sect. iv. p. 9, where he commends *their* manner of proceeding, *who*, by sceptical arguments, invalidate all philosophical principles, before they begin to prove the truth of Christianity to those who doubt of its evidence. It is well known that the Jesuits, who were particularly favoured by Huet have, on many occasions, employed this method to throw dust in the eyes of the Protestants, and thus lead them blindfold into the Romish communion, and that they still continue to practise the same insidious instrument of seduction.

§ Every thing relating to the life and sentiments of Bayle is abundantly and universally known. His life, composed by M. Des-Maizeaux, was published at the Hague in 1732.—The scepticism of this insidious and seducing writer was unmasked and refuted, with great learning and force of argument, by J. P. de Crousaz, in a voluminous French work, entitled, Traite du Pyrrhonisme, of which M. Formey gave an elegant and judicious abridgment under the title of Triomphe de l'Evidence.

SECTION II.

PART I.

THE HISTORY OF THE MORE ANCIENT CHURCHES

CHAPTER I.

Containing the History of the Romish Church.

I. HIPPOLITO ALDOBRANDINI, under the papal name of Clement VIII. continued to rule the church of Rome at the commencement of this century, having been elected to that high dignity toward the conclusion of the preceding one. The eminent abilities and insidious dexterity of this pontiff, as also his ardent desire of extinguishing the Protestant religion, and extending the limits of the Romish church, are universally acknowledged; but it is much questioned, whether his prudence was equal to the arduous nature of his pontifical station, and the critical circumstances of an incidental kind that arose during his administration.* He was succeeded in 1605 by Leo XI. of the house of Medici, who died a few weeks after his election, and thus left the papal chair open to Camillo Borghese, by whom it was filled under the denomination of Paul V. This pontiff was of a haughty and violent spirit, jealous to excess of his authority, and insatiably furious in the execution of his revenge upon such as encroached on his pretended prerogative, as appears in a striking manner by his rash and unsuccessful contest with the Venetians.†—Gregory XV.,‡ who was raised to the pontificate in 1621, seemed to be of a milder disposition, though he was not less defective than his predecessor in equity and clemency toward those who had separated themselves from the church of Rome. An unjust severity against the friends of the Reformation is, indeed, the general and inevitable character of the Roman pontiffs; for, without this, they would be destitute of the predominant and distinctive mark of the papacy. A pope inspired with sentiments of toleration and charity toward those who refuse a blind submission to his opinions and decisions, is a contradiction in terms. Urban VIII., who previously bore the name of Meffei Barberini, and who, by his interest in the conclave, ascended the papal throne in 1623, was a man of letters, an elegant writer, an elegant poet, and a generous and munificent patron of learning and genius;* but nothing could equal the rigour and barbarity with which he treated all who bore the name of Protestants. He may be indeed considered as a good and equitable ruler of the church, when compared with Innocent X. of the family of Pamphili, who succeeded him in 1644. This unworthy pontiff, to a profound ignorance of all those things which it was necessary for a Christian bishop to know, joined the most shameful indolence and the most notorious profligacy; for he abandoned his person, his dignity, the administration of his temporal affairs, and the government of the church, to the disposal of Donna Olympia,† a woman of corrupt morals, insatiable avarice, and boundless ambition.‡ His zealous endeavours to prevent the peace of Westphalia, however odious they may appear when considered in themselves, ought not to be reckoned among his personal crimes, since it is to be sup-

---

* This pontiff had an edition of the Vulgate published, which was very different from that of pope Sixtus; and this is one of the many instances of that *contrariety* of opinion which has prevailed amongst the *infallible* heads of the church of Rome.

☞ † This contest arose, partly from two edicts of the republic of Venice for preventing the unnecessary increase of religious buildings, and the augmentation of the enormous wealth of the clergy; and partly from the prosecution of two ecclesiastics for capital crimes, who had not been delivered up to the pope at his requisition. It is not surprising that these proceedings of the Venetians, however just and equitable, should inflame the ambitious fury of a pontiff, who called himself Vice-God, the Monarch of Christendom, and the Supporter of Papal Omnipotence. Accordingly, Paul subjected all the dominions of the republic to an interdict, while the Venetians, on the other hand, declared that unjust and tyrannical mandate null and void, and banished from their territory the Jesuits and Capuchins, who had openly disobeyed the laws of the state. Preparations for war were proceeding on both sides, when an accommodation, not very honourable to the pope, was brought about by the mediation of Henry IV. of France. This controversy between the pope and the Venetians produced several important pieces, composed by Sarpi on the side of the republic, and by Baronius and Bellarmine in behalf of the pontiff. The controversy concerning the nature and limits of the pope's pretended supremacy is judiciously stated, and the papal pretensions are accurately examined, by Sarpi, in his history of this tyrannical interdict, which, in Italian, occupies the fourth volume of his works, and was translated into Latin by William Bedell, of Cambridge.—It was Paul V. that dishonoured his title of *Holiness*, and cast an eternal stain upon his *infallibility*, by an express approbation of the doctrine of Suarez, the Jesuit, in defence of the murder of kings.

☞ ‡ His family name was Alexander Ludovisio.

* See Leonis Allatii Apes Urbanæ. This little work is a sort of index, or list, of all the learned and eminent men who adorned Rome, under the pontificate of Urban VIII. and experienced the munificence and liberality of that pontiff; and their number is far from being small. The Latin poems of Urban, which are not without a considerable portion of wit and elegance, have passed through several editions. ☞ These poems were composed while he was yet a cardinal. After his elevation to the pontificate, he published a remarkable edition of the Romish Breviary and several bulls; among which, that which abolishes the order of Female Jesuits and certain festivals, those relating to image-worship, and to the condemnation of Jansenius' Augustinus, and that which confers the title of Eminence upon the cardinal-legates, the three ecclesiastical electors, and the grand master of Malta, are the most worthy of notice.

☞ † This Donna Olympia Maldachini was his brother's widow, with whom he had lived, before his elevation to the pontificate, in an illicit commerce, in which his *holiness* continued afterwards.

‡ See the Memoires du Cardinal de Retz, tom. iii. and iv. of the last edition published at Geneva.—For an account of the disputes between this pontiff and the French, see Bougeant's Histoire de la Paix de Westphalia, tom. iv.

posed, that any other pontiff, in his place, would have made the same attempts without hesitation or remorse. He was succeeded in the papal chair, in 1655, by Fabio Chigi, who assumed the title of Alexander VII. and who, though less odious than his predecessor, nevertheless possessed all the pernicious qualities that are necessary to constitute a true pope, and without which the papal jurisdiction and majesty cannot be maintained. The other parts of his character are drawn much to his disadvantage, by several ingenious and eminent writers of the Romish church, who represent him as a man of a mean genius, unequal to great or difficult undertakings, full of craft and dissimulation, and chargeable with the most shameful levity and the greatest inconsistency of sentiment and conduct.* The two Clements IX. and X. who were elected successively to the papacy in 1668 and 1669, were concerned in few transactions that deserve to be transmitted to posterity.† This was not the case of Benedict Odeschalchi, who is known in the list of pontiffs by the denomination of Innocent XI. and was raised to that high dignity in 1677.‡ This respectable pontiff acquired a very high and permanent reputation by the austerity of his morals, his uncommon courage and resolution, his dislike of the grosser superstitions that reigned in the Romish church, his attempts to reform the manners of the clergy, and to abolish a considerable number of those fictions and frauds that dishonour their ministry, and also by other solid and eminent virtues. But it appeared manifestly by his example that those pontiffs, who respect truth, and act from virtuous and Christian principles, may, indeed, form noble plans, but will never be able to carry them into execution, or at least to give them that measure of stability and perfection, which is the object of their wishes. By his example and administration it appeared, that the wisest institutions, and the most judicious establishments, will be unable to stand firm, for any considerable time, against the insidious stratagems, or declared opposition of a deluded multitude, who are corrupted by the prevalence of licentious morals, whose imaginations are impregnated with superstitious fictions and fables, whose credulity is abused by pious frauds, and whose minds are nourished, or rather amused, with vain rites and senseless ceremonies.* Be that as it may, all the wise and salutary regulations of Innocent XI. were suffered to go almost to ruin by the criminal indolence of Peter Ottoboni, who was raised to the head of the Romish church, in 1689, and assumed the name of Alexander VIII. A laudable attempt was made to revive them by Innocent XII., a man of uncommon merit and eminent talents, whose name was Pignatelli, and who, in 1691, succeeded Alexander in the papal chair; nor were his zealous endeavours absolutely destitute of success. But it was also his fate to learn, by experience, that the most prudent and resolute pontiffs are unequal to such an arduous task, such an Herculean labour, as the reformation of the church and court of Rome; nor were the fruits of this good pope's wise administration enjoyed long after his decease.† The pontiff, whose reign concluded this century, was John Francis Albani, who was raised to the head of the Romish church in 1699, and assumed the name of Clement XI. He surpassed in learning the whole college of cardinals, and was inferior to none of the preceding pontiffs in sagacity, lenity, and a desire, at least, to govern well; but he was very far from opposing, with a proper degree of vigour and resolution, the inveterate corruptions and superstitious observances of the church over which he presided; on the contrary, he inconsiderately aimed at, what he thought, the honour and advantage of the church (that is, the glory and interests of its pontiff) by measures that proved detrimental to both; and thus showed, by a striking example, that popes, even of the best disposition, may fall imperceptibly into the greatest mistakes, and commit the most pernicious blunders, through an imprudent zeal for extending their jurisdiction, and augmenting the influence and lustre of their station.‡

* See the Memoires du Cardinal de Retz, tom. iv. p. 16, 77.—Memoires de M. Joly, tom. ii. p. 186, 210, 237.—Archenholtz, Memoires de la Reine Christine, tom. ii. p. 125. ☞ The craft and dissimulation attributed to this pontiff really constituted an essential part of his character; but it is not strictly true that he was a man of a mean genius, or unequal to great and difficult undertakings. He was a man of learning, and discovered very eminent abilities at the treaty of Munster, where he appeared in the character of nuncio. Some writers relate, that, while he was in Germany, he had formed the design of abjuring popery, and embracing the Protestant religion, but was deterred from the execution of this purpose by the example of his cousin count Pompey, who was poisoned at Lyons, on his way to Germany, after he had abjured the Romish faith. These writers add, that Chigi was confirmed in his religion by his elevation to the cardinalship. See Bayle, Nouvelles de la Repub. des Lettres, Oct. 1688.

☞ † Clement IX. was of the family of Rospigliosi, and the family name of Clement X. was Altieri. See Memoires de la Reine Christine, tom. ii. There are upon record several transactions of Clement IX. that do him honour, and prove his dislike of nepotism, and his love of peace and justice.

☞ ‡ Some maintain, and with the strongest appearance of truth, that this pontiff had formerly been a soldier, though this report is treated as groundless by count Turrezonico, in his dissertation 'de suppositiis militaribus Stipendiis Bened. Odeschalchi.' See an interesting account of this pontiff in Bayle's Dictionary.

* See Journal Universel, tom. i. p. 441; tom. vi. p. 306. The present pope, Benedict XIV.,* attempted, in the year 1743, the *canonization* of Innocent XI.; but the king of France, instigated by the Jesuits, opposed this design, chiefly on account of the misunderstandings that always subsisted between Louis XIV. and Innocent, of which more will be said hereafter.

† For an account of the character, morals, and election of Innocent XII., see the Letters of cardinal Norris, published in the fifth volume of his Works, p 362.

‡ In the year 1752, there appeared, at Padua, a Life of Clement XI., composed in French by the learned and eloquent M. Lafitau, bishop of Sisteron. In the same year M. Reboulet, chancellor of Avignon, published his Histoire de Clement XI. These two productions, and more especially the latter, are written with uncommon elegance; but they abound with historical errors, which the French writers, in general, are at too little pains to avoid. Besides, they are both composed rather in the strain of pane-

* This note was written during the life of Benedict XIV

II. The incredible pains that were taken by the pontiffs and clergy of the Romish church, to spread their doctrine and to erect their dominion among the nations that lay in the darkness of Paganism, have been already mentioned. We are, therefore, at present, to confine our narration to the schemes they laid, the cabals they formed, and the commotions they excited, with an uninterrupted and mischievous industry, in order to recover the possessions and prerogatives they had lost in Europe, to oppress the Protestants, and to extinguish the light of the glorious Reformation. Various were the stratagems and projects they formed for these purposes. The resources of genius, the force of arms, the seduction of the most alluring promises, the terrors of the most formidable threatenings, the subtle wiles of controversy, the influence of pious, and often of impious frauds, the arts of dissimulation, in short, all possible means, fair or disingenuous, were employed for the destruction of the reformed churches, but in most cases without success. The plan of a dreadful attack upon the friends of the Reformation had been, for some time, formed in secret; and the bigoted and persecuting house of Austria, at the pope's persuasion, undertook to put it in execution. However, as injustice, however arrogant, usually seeks some pretext to mask, or at least to diminish its deformity, so the church of Rome endeavoured before-hand to justify the persecution, of which the flame was ready to break out. For this purpose, the pens of the perfidious and learned Scioppius,* of the Jesuits Tanner, Possevin, Hager, Hederic, and Forer, jurists of Dillingen, were employed to represent the treaty of peace, concluded between Charles V. and the protestants of Germany, as unjust, null, and even rendered void by the Protestants themselves, by their departing from, or at least perverting, by various changes and modifications, the confession of Augsburg.† This injurious charge was proved groundless by several Lutheran doctors who, of their own accord, defended their communion against this instance of popish calumny; and it was also refuted by public authority, by the express order of John George, elector of Saxony. The task was committed to Matthew Hoe, who, in the years 1628 and 1631, published an accurate and laborious defence of the Protestants, entitled, Defensio Pupillæ Evangelicæ. The mouth of calumny was not stopped by these performances. The accusers continued their clamours, multiplied their libels, and had recourse to the succours of indecent raillery and sarcastic wit, to cover as well as they were able, the striking defects of a bad cause. On the other hand, the Lutheran writers exerted themselves in exposing the sophistry, and refuting the arguments and invectives of their adversaries.

III. The first flames of that religious war, which the Roman pontiffs proposed to carry on by the arms of the Austrians and Spaniards, their servile and bigoted instruments, broke out in Austria, where, about the commencement of this century, the friends of the Reformation were cruelly persecuted and oppressed by their Roman catholic adversaries.* The solemn treaties and conventions, by which the religious liberty and civil rights of these Protestants had been secured, were trampled upon, and violated in the most shocking manner; nor had these unhappy sufferers resolution, vigour, or strength, sufficient to maintain their privileges. The Bohemians, who were involved in the same vexations, proceeded in a different manner. Perceiving plainly that the votaries of Rome earnestly wished to deprive them of that religious liberty which had been purchased by the blood of their ancestors, and so lately confirmed to them by an imperial edict, they came to a resolution of taking up arms to defend themselves against a set of men, whom, in consequence of the violence they offered to conscience, they could look upon in no other light than as the enemies of their souls. Accordingly a league was formed by the Bohemian Protestants; and they began to avenge, with great spirit and resolution, the injuries that had been committed against their persons, their families, their religion, and their civil rights and privileges. But it must be acknowledged, that, in this just attempt to defend what was dear to them as men and Christians, they lost sight of the dictates of equity and moderation, and carried their resentment beyond the bounds, both of reason and religion. Their adversaries were alarmed at a view of their intrepidity, but were not dismayed. The Bohemians, therefore, apprehending still farther opposition and vexations from bigotry, animated by a spirit of vengeance, renewed their efforts to provide for their security. The death of the emperor Matthias, which happened in 1619, furnished them, as they thought, with an opportunity of striking at the root of the evil, and removing the source of their calamities, by choosing a sovereign of the reformed religion; for they considered themselves as authorized by the ancient laws and customs of the kingdom, to reject any one who pretended to the throne by virtue of an hereditary right, and to demand a prince whose title to the crown should be derived from the free suffra-

gyric than of history. An attentive reader will, however, easily perceive, even in these panegyrics, that Clement XI., notwithstanding his acknowledged sagacity and prudence, took several rash and inconsiderate steps, in order to augment the power, and multiply the prerogatives of the Roman pontiffs; and thus, through his own temerity, involved himself in various perplexities.

☞ * Scioppius seems rather to merit the titles of *malevolent* and *furious*, than that of *perfidious*, unless his turning papist be considered by Dr. Mosheim as an instance of perfidy. This is the intemperate and odious satirist who was caned by the servants of the English ambassador at Madrid, for the invectives he had thrown out against king James I. in a book which was burned by the hands of the common hangman at Paris.

† See Salig, Hist. August. Confessionis, t. i. lib. iv. cap. iii. p. 768.

* Raupachius, in his Austria Evangelica, (a German work with a Latin title,) has given an accurate account of this persecution and these commotions. The same learned and worthy author had formed the design of publishing an authentic and circumstantial relation of the sufferings of the Protestants in Styria, Moravia, and Carinthia, with an account of the perfidious snares that were laid for them, the whole drawn from unexceptionable records; but death prevented the execution of this scheme.

ges of the states. Accordingly, Frederic V., elector Palatine, who professed the reformed religion, was, in the same year, chosen king of Bohemia, and solemnly crowned at Prague.*

IV. This bold step, from which the Bohemians expected such signal advantages, proved to them a source of complicated misfortunes. Its consequences were highly detrimental to their new sovereign, and fatal to their own liberties and privileges; for by it they were involved in the most dreadful calamities, and deprived of the free exercise of the Protestant religion, the security of which was the ultimate end of all the measures they had pursued. Frederic was defeated, before Prague, by the imperial army, in 1620, and by this unfortunate battle was not only deprived of his new crown, but also of his hereditary dominions. Reduced thus to the wretched condition of an exile, he was obliged to leave his fruitful territories, and his ample treasures, to the merciless discretion of the Austrians and Bavarians, who plundered and ravaged them with the most rapacious barbarity. The defeat of this unfortunate prince was attended with dreadful consequences to the Bohemians, and more especially to those who, from a zeal for religious liberty and the interests of the Reformation, had embarked in his cause. Some of them were committed to a perpetual prison, others banished for life; several had their estates and possessions confiscated; many were put to death; and the whole nation was obliged, from that fatal period, to embrace the religion of the victor, and bend an unwilling neck under the yoke of Rome. The triumph of the Austrians would neither have been so sudden nor so complete, nor would they have been in a condition to impose such rigorous and despotic terms on the Bohemians, had they not been powerfully assisted by John George I., elector of Saxony, who, partly from a principle of hatred toward the Reformed,† and partly from considerations of a political kind, reinforced with his troops the imperial army.‡ This invasion of the Palatinate was the occasion of that long and bloody war, that was so injurious to Germany, and in which the greatest part of the princes of Europe were, in one way or another, unhappily engaged. It began by a confederacy formed between some German powers and the king of Denmark, in order to assert the rights of the elector Palatine, unjustly excluded from his dominions, against the despotic proceedings of the emperor. The confederates maintained, that the invasion of Bohemia, by this unhappy prince, was no just subject of offence to the emperor; and that the house of Austria, whose quarrel the emperor was not obliged by any means to adopt, was alone the sufferer in this case. However that may have been, the progress and issue of the war were unfavourable to the allies.

V. The success of the imperial arms filled the votaries of popery and Rome with the warmest transports of joy and exultation, and presented to their imaginations the most flattering prospects. They thought that the happy period was now approaching, when the whole tribe of heretics, that had withdrawn their necks from the papal yoke, should either perish by the sword, or be reduced under the dominion of the church. The emperor himself seemed to have imbibed no small portion of this odious spirit, which was doubly prepared, to convert or destroy. The flame of ambition that burned within him was nourished by the suggestions of bigotry. Hence he audaciously carried his arms through a great part of Germany, suffered his generals to harass, with impunity, such princes and states as refused a blind obedience to the court of Rome, and showed plainly, by all his proceedings, that a scheme had been laid for the extinction of the Germanic liberty, civil and sacred. The Saxon elector's zealous attachment to the emperor, which he had abundantly discovered by his warm and ungenerous opposition to the unfortunate Frederic, together with the lamentable discord that reigned among the German princes, persuaded the papal faction, that the difficulties which seemed to oppose the execution of their project, were far from being invincible. Accordingly, the persons concerned in this grand enterprise began to act their respective parts. In 1629, Ferdinand II., to give some colour of justice to this religious war, issued out the terrible *restitution-edict*, by which the Protestants were ordered to restore to the church of Rome all the possessions of which they had become masters in consequence of the religious peace, concluded in the preceding century.* This edict principally arose from the suggestions of the Jesuits. That greedy and ambitious order claimed a great part of these goods and possessions as a recompense due to their labours in the cause of religion; and hence arose a warm contest between them and the ancient and real proprietors.†

* Beside Caroli and Jagerus, who have composed the ecclesiastical history of this century, see Burch. Gotth. Struvii Syntagma Historiæ Germanicæ, p. 1487, 1510, 1523, 1538; as also the writers whom he recommends. See also the Histoire de Louis XIII., composed by the learned and accurate Le Vassor, tom. iii. p. 223.

☞ † By the Reformed, as has been already observed, we are to understand the Calvinists, and also, in general, those Protestants who are not of the Lutheran persuasion. And here we see a Lutheran elector drawing his sword to support the cause of popery and persecution against a people generously struggling for the Protestant religion, and the rights of conscience.

‡ See the Commentarii de Bello Bohemico-Germanico, ab A. C. 1617 ad An. 1630.—Abraham Scultet, Narratio Apologetica de Curriculo Vitæ suæ, p. 86. –It is well known, that the Roman catholics, and more especially Martin Becan, a Jesuit, persuaded Matthew Hoe, who was an Austrian by birth, and the elector's chaplain, to represent to his prince the cause of the elector Palatine (which was the cause of the reformed religion) as not only unjust, but also as detrimental to the interest of Lutheranism, and to recommend to him the cause and interests of the house of Austria. See Unschuldige Nachricht, An. 1747, p. 858. ☞ What Dr. Mosheim observes here may be true; but then it is as true that Matthew Hoe must have been a great fool, or a great knave, to listen to such insinuations, not only on account of their glaring absurdity, but also considering the persons from whom they came. This is the same Hoe that is mentioned above, as a learned defender of the Lutheran faith.

* See, for an illustration of this matter, the authors mentioned by Struvius, in his Syntagma Histor. Germaniæ, p. 1553.

† See Salig, His. August. Confessionis, t. i. lib iv c. iii. § xxv. p. 810.

This contest, indeed, was decided by the law of force. It was the depopulating soldier, who, sword in hand, gave weight and authority to the imperial edict, wresting out of the hands of the lawful possessor, without form of process, whatever the Romish priests and monks thought proper to claim, and treating the innocent and plundered sufferers with all the severity that the most barbarous spirit of oppression and injustice could suggest.*

VI. Germany groaned under these dismal scenes of tumult and oppression, and looked about for succour in vain. The enemy assailed her on all sides; and not one of her princes seemed qualified to stand forth as the avenger of her injuries, or the assertor of her rights. Some were restrained from appearing in her cause by the suggestions of bigotry, others by a principle of fear, and others again by an ungenerous attention to their own private interest, which choked in their breasts all concern for the public good. An illustrious hero, whose deeds even envy was obliged to revere, and whose name will descend with glory to the latest ages, came forth, nevertheless, at this critical season; Gustavus Adolphus took the field, and maintained the cause of the Germanic liberties against the oppression and tyranny of the house of Austria. At the earnest request of the French court, which beheld, with uneasiness, the overgrown power of that aspiring house, he set sail for Germany, in 1629, with a small army; and, by his repeated victories, blasted, in a short time, the sanguine hopes which the pope and emperor had entertained of suppressing the Protestant religion in the empire. These hopes, indeed, seemed to revive in 1632, when this glorious assertor of Germanic liberty fell in the battle of Lutzen;† but this very serious loss was, in some measure, made up in process of time, by the conduct of those who succeeded Gustavus at the head of the Swedish army. And, accordingly, the war was obstinately carried on in bleeding Germany, during many years, with various success, until the exhausted treasures of the contending parties, and the pacific inclinations of Christina, the daughter and successor of Gustavus, put an end to these desolations, and brought on a treaty of peace.

VII. Thus, after a war of thirty years, carried on with the most unrelenting animosity and ardour, the wounds of Germany were closed, and the drooping states of Europe revived, in 1648, by the peace of Westphalia, so called from the cities of Munster and Osnabrug, where the negotiations were prosecuted and concluded. The Protestants, indeed, did not derive from this treaty all the privileges they claimed, or all the advantages they had in view; for the emperor, among less important instances of obstinacy, absolutely refused to reinstate the Bohemian and Austrian protestants in their religious privileges, or to restore the Upper Palatinate to its ancient and lawful proprietor. Yet they obtained, by this peace, privileges and advantages which the votaries of Rome beheld with great displeasure and uneasiness; and it is unquestionably evident, that the treaty of Westphalia gave a new and remarkable degree of stability to the Lutheran and reformed churches in Germany. By this treaty the peace of Augsburg, which the Lutherans had obtained from Charles V. in the preceding century, was firmly secured against all the machinations and stratagems of the court of Rome; it abrogated the edict that commanded the protestants to restore to the Romish church the ecclesiastical revenues and lands of which they had taken possession after that peace; and it confirmed both the contending parties in the perpetual possession of whatever they had occupied in the beginning of the year 1624. It would be entering into a very long detail, were we to enumerate the advantages that accrued to the protestant princes from this treaty.* All this was a source of vexation to the court of Rome, and made its pontiff feel the severest pangs of disappointed ambition. He, accordingly, used various stratagems, without being very scrupulous in his choice, in order to annul this treaty, or elude its effects; but his attempts were unsuccessful, since neither the emperor, nor the princes that had embarked in this cause, thought it advisable to involve themselves anew in the tumults of war, whose issue is so uncertain, and whose most fatal effects they had lately escaped with so much difficulty. The treaty, therefore, was executed in all its parts; and all the articles that had been agreed upon at Munster and Osnabrug

☞ * When the consequences of these iniquitous and barbarous proceedings were represented to this emperor, and he was assured that the country must be utterly ruined, if the Bohemians, rendered desperate by his enormous cruelty and oppression, should exert themselves in defence of their liberties, and endeavour to repel force by force, he is reported to have answered, with great zeal and calmness, *Malumus regnum vastatum, quam damnatum.* See the Historia Persecutionum Ecclesiæ Bohemicæ, published in 1648. This little book contains an ample recital of the deplorable effects of lawless power, inhuman bigotry, and blood-thirsty zeal, and proves, by numberless facts, that Dr. Mosheim had the strongest evidence for the account he gives of Ferdinand and his missionaries. It is impossible to reflect upon the sanguinary spirit of such converters, without expressing, at the same time, a generous detestation and abhorrence of their unjust and violent proceedings.

† See Archenholtz, Memoires de la Reine Christine, tom. i. in which are many very interesting anecdotes, relating to the life, exploits, and death of Gustavus. The learned compiler of these *Memoires* has also thrown much light upon this period, and particularly upon the peace that terminated this long and dreadful war.

* An account of this whole matter, sufficient to satisfy the curiosity of the most inquisitive reader, may be found in that most elaborate and excellent work, compiled by the very learned and judicious John Godfrey de Meyern, under the following title: Acta Pacis Westphalicæ et Executionis ejus Norimbergensis. See also the more compendious, though valuable work of Adam Adami, bishop of Hierapolis, entitled, Relatio Historica de Pacificatione Osnabrugo-Monasteriensi, of which the illustrious author published a new edition in 1737, more accurate and ample than the preceding one. We must not omit here the ingenious Father Bougeant's elegant history of this treaty, which though chiefly drawn from the papers of the French ambassadors, is nevertheless (generally speaking) composed with accuracy, impartiality, and candour; it was published in 1746, under the title of Histoire de la Paix de Westphalie

were confirmed and ratified, in 1650, at Nuremberg.*

VIII. After this period, the court of Rome and its creatures were laid under a considerable degree of restraint. They no longer dared to make war, in an open and public manner, upon the protestants, since the present state of affairs blasted all the hopes they had fondly entertained of extinguishing the light of the reformation, by destroying, or reducing under their spiritual yoke, the princes and states that had encouraged and protected it in their territories. But, wherever they could exert the spirit of persecution with impunity, they oppressed the protestants in the most grievous manner, and, in defiance of the most solemn conventions and the most sacred obligations, encroached upon their rights, privileges, and possessions. Thus, in Hungary, during the space of ten years,† both Lutherans and Calvinists were involved in an uninterrupted series of the most cruel calamities and vexations.‡ The injuries and insults they suffered from various orders of men, and more especially from the Jesuits, both before and after the period now under consideration, are not to be numbered. In Poland, all those who ventured to differ from the pope, found, by a bitter experience, during the whole course of this century, that no treaty or convention that tended to set bounds to the authority or rapacity of the church, was deemed sacred, or even regarded at Rome; for many of these were ejected out of their schools, deprived of their churches, robbed of their goods and possessions, under a variety of perfidious pretexts, and frequently condemned to the most severe and cruel punishments, without having been even chargeable with the appearance of a crime.§ The remains of the Waldenses, that lived in the valleys of Piedmont, were persecuted often with the most inhuman cruelty, (and more especially in the years 1632, 1655, and 1685,) on account of their magnanimous and steady attachment to the religion of their ancestors; and this persecution was carried on, with all the horrors of fire and sword, by the dukes of Savoy.‖ In Germany, the same spirit of bigotry and persecution produced, almost every where, flagrant acts of injustice. The infractions of the famous treaty above mentioned, and of the Germanic liberty that was founded upon it, would furnish matter for many volumes;* and all these infractions were occasioned by a preposterous and extravagant zeal for augmenting the authority, and extending the jurisdiction of the church of Rome. And, indeed, as long as that church and its assuming pontiff shall persist in maintaining that they have a right to extend their lordly sceptre over all the churches of the Christian world, so long must those who have renounced their authority, but are more or less within their reach, despair of enjoying the inestimable blessings of security and peace. They will always be considered as rebellious subjects, against whom the greatest acts of severity and violence are lawful.

IX. The over-zealous instruments of the court of Rome at length accomplished, in this century, (what had often been attempted without success,) the deliverance of Spain from the infidelity of the Moors, and of France from the heresy of the protestants. The posterity of the Moors or Saracens, who had formerly been masters of the greatest part of Spain, and hitherto lived in that kingdom, mixed with the other inhabitants of the country, and their number was still considerable. They were Christians, at least in their external profession and manners; industrious also, and inoffensive; and, upon the whole, good and useful subjects: but they were strongly suspected of a secret propensity to the doctrine of Mohammed, which was the religion of their ancestors. Hence the clergy beset the monarch with their importunate solicitations, and never ceased their clamorous remonstrances before a royal edict was obtained to drive the Saracens out of the Spanish territories. This imprudent step was highly detrimental to the kingdom, and its pernicious effects are more or less visible even at the present time; but the church, whose interest and dominion are, in popish countries, considered as distinct from the interests and authority of the state, and of a much more sublime and excellent nature, acquired new accessions of wealth and power by the expulsion of the Moors.† In proportion as the community lost, the church gained; and thus the public good was sacrificed to the demands of bigotry and superstition.

In France, the persecuting spirit of the Romish church exhibited scenes still more shocking. The Huguenots, after having long groaned under various forms of cruelty and oppression, and seen multitudes of their brethren put to death, by secret conspiracies or open tyranny and violence, were, at length, obliged either to save themselves by a clandestine flight, or to profess, against their consciences, the Romish religion. This barbarous and iniquitous scene of French persecution, than which the annals of modern history present nothing more unnatural and odious, will find its place below, in the history of the Reformed Church.‡

* Pope Innocent X. opposed, to this treaty of peace, in 1651, a flaming bull, on which Hornbeck published an ample and learned commentary, entitled, Examen Bulli Papalis, qua Innocentius X. abrogare nititur Pacem Germaniæ. This *bull* might, perhaps, have produced some effect upon the emperor and his allies, had it been properly *gilded*.

† From 1671 to 1681.

‡ See Historia Diplomatica de Statu Religionis Evangelicæ in Hungaria, p. 69.—Pauli Debrezeni Historia Ecclesiæ Reformatæ in Hungaria, lib. ii. p. 447.—Schelhornius, in Museo Helvetico, tom. vii. page 46—90.

§ See Ad. Regenvolscii Historia Ecclesiæ Sclavonicæ, lib. ii. cap. xv. p. 216, 235, 253. The grievances which the dissenters from the church of Rome suffered in Poland, after the death of Regenvolscius, may be learned from various memorials that have been published in our times.

‖ See Gilles' Histoire Ecclesiastique des Eglises Vaudoises, ch. xlviii. p. 339.

* The histories of the grievances suffered by the protestants of Germany on account of their religion that have been composed by Struvius and Hoffman, contain ample details of this matter.

† See the history of this impolitic expulsion by Michael Geddes, in his Miscellaneous Tracts, vol. i.

‡ In the second chapter of the second part of this section.

X. All the resources of inventive genius and refined policy, all the efforts of insinuating craft and audacious rebellion, were employed to bring back Great Britain and Ireland under the yoke of Rome. But all these attempts were without effect. About the beginning of this century, a set of desperate and execrable wretches, in whose breasts the suggestions of bigotry and the hatred of the protestant religion had suppressed all the feelings of justice and humanity, were instigated by three Jesuits, of whom Garnet, the superior of the society in England, was the chief, to form the most horrid plot that is known in the annals of history. The design of this conspiracy was nothing less than to destroy, at one blow, James I., the prince of Wales, and both houses of parliament, by the explosion of an immense quantity of gunpowder, which was concealed for that purpose, in the vaults situated under the house of lords. The sanguinary bigots concerned in it imagined, that, as soon as this horrible deed was performed, they would be at full liberty to restore popery to its former credit, and substitute it in the place of the protestant religion.* This odious conspiracy, whose infernal purpose was providentially discovered, when it was ripe for execution, is commonly known in Britain under the denomination of the *gunpowder plot*.†

This discovery did not suspend the efforts and stratagems of the court of Rome, which carried on its schemes in the succeeding reign, but with less violence, and more caution. Charles I. was a prince of a soft and gentle temper, and was entirely directed by the counsels of Laud, archbishop of Canterbury, a man who was neither destitute of learning nor of good qualities,‡ though he carried things to excessive and intolerable lengths through his warm and violent attachment to the ancient forms and ceremonies of the church. The queen also, Henrietta Maria, who was a princess of France, was warmly devoted to the interests of popery; and from all this it seemed probable, that, though treason and violence had failed, yet artifice and mild measures might succeed, and that a reconciliation might be brought about between England and Rome.§ This prospect, which had smiled in the imaginations of the friends of popery, vanished entirely when the civil war broke out between the king and parliament. In consequence of these commotions, both the unfortunate Charles, and his imprudent and bigoted counsellor Laud, were brought to the scaffold; and Oliver Cromwell, a man of unparalleled resolution, dexterity, and foresight, and a declared enemy to every thing that bore even the most distant resemblance to popery, was placed at the helm of government, under the title of Protector of the Commonwealth.

The hopes of Rome and its votaries were nevertheless revived by the restoration of Charles II., and from that period grew more lively and sanguine from day to day. For that monarch, as appears from unquestionable authorities,* had been initiated, during his exile, into the mysteries of popery, and had secretly embraced that religion, while his only brother, the presumptive heir to the crown, professed it openly, and had publicly apostatized from the protestant faith. Charles, indeed, was not a proper instrument for the propagation of any theological system. Indolent and voluptuous on one hand, and inclined to infidelity and irreligion on the other, it was not from him that the Roman pontiff could expect the zeal and industry which were necessary to force upon the English nation, a religion so contrary as popery was to the tenor of the laws and the spirit of the people.† This zeal was found in his bigoted successor James II.; but it was accompanied with such excessive vehemence and imprudence as entirely defeated its own purposes; for that inconsiderate monarch, by his passionate attachment to the court of Rome, and his blind obsequious-

☞ * There is a letter extant written by Sir Everard Digby, one of the conspirators, to his wife, after his condemnation, which deserves an eminent place in the history of superstition and bigotry, and shows abundantly their infernal spirit and tendency. The following passage will confirm this judgment: "Now for my intention," says Digby, "let me tell you, that if I had thought there had been the least sin in the plot, I would not have been of it for all the world; and no other cause drew me to hazard my fortune and life, but zeal to God's religion." See the Papers relating to the popish plot, published by the orders of secretary Coventry.

† See Rapin's Hist. d'Angleterre, t. vii. livre xviii. and Heidegger's Historia Papatus.

☞ ‡ Mr. Hume, speaking of Laud's learning and morals, expresses himself in the following manner: "This man was virtuous, if severity of manners alone, and abstinence from pleasure, could deserve that name. He was learned, if polemical knowledge could entitle him to that praise."

§ See Cerri's Etat Present de l'Eglise Romaine, p. 315.—Neal's History of the Puritans, vol. iii. p. 194

* Burnet's History of his Own Time, vol. i. book iii.—Neal, vol. iv.—Rapin, livre. xxiii.

☞ † Such is the representation given of Charles II. by almost every historian; so that Dr. Mosheim is excusable in mistaking a part of this monarch's character, which was known to very few before him. Mr. Hume, whose history of the reign of that prince is a master-piece in every respect, gave a like account of Charles, as fluctuating between deism and popery. But this eminent historian having had occasion, during his residence at Paris, to peruse the manuscript memoirs of king James II. which were written by himself, and are kept in the Scottish college there, received from them new information with respect to the religious character of Charles, and was convinced that his zeal for popery went much farther than has been generally imagined. For it appears, with the utmost evidence, from these memoirs, that the king had laid with his ministry a formal plan for subverting the constitution in favour of popery; and that the introduction of popery, as the established religion, was the great and principal object which Charles had in view when he entered into the French alliance, which was concluded at Versailles in June 1670, by lord Arundel of Wardour. By this treaty, Louis was to give Charles 200,000 pounds a-year, in quarterly payments, in order to enable him to establish the Roman catholic religion in England; and he also engaged to supply him with 6000 men in case of any insurrection. The division of the United Provinces between England and France was another article of this treaty. But we are told that the subversion of the protestant religion in England was the point that Charles had chiefly at heart, and that he insisted warmly on beginning with the execution of this part of the treaty; but the duchess of Orleans, in the interview at Dover, persuaded him to begin with the Dutch war. The king (says Mr. Hume) was so *zealous a papist*, that he *wept for joy* when he entertained the project of re-uniting his kingdom to the catholic church. See the Corrections and Additions to Mr. Hume's History of Charles II., and also Macpherson's Appendix to his History of Great Britain.

ness to the unreasonable and precipitate counsels of the Jesuits, who were the oracles of his cabinet, gave a mortal blow to that religion which he meant to promote, and lost that royalty which he was attempting to fix on the basis of despotism. He openly attempted to restore to its former vigour, both in England and Ireland, the authority of the pontiff, which had been renounced and annulled by the laws of both realms; and that he might accomplish with the more facility this most imprudent purpose, he trampled upon those rights and privileges of his people, that had ever been deemed most respectable and sacred, and which he had bound himself, by the most solemn engagements, to support and maintain. Justly exasperated and provoked by repeated insults from the throne upon their religion and liberties, and alarmed with natural apprehensions of the approaching ruin of both, the English looked about for a deliverer, and fixed their views, in 1688, on William prince of Orange, (son-in-law to their despotic monarch,) by whose wisdom and valour, affairs were so conducted that James was obliged to retire from his dominions, and to abdicate the crown; and the pope and his adherents were disappointed in the fond expectations they had formed of restoring popery in England.*

XI. When the more prudent defenders and patrons of the Romish faith perceived the ill success that attended all their violent and sanguinary attempts to establish its authority, they thought it expedient to have recourse to softer methods; and, instead of conquering the protestants by open force, proposed deluding them back into the church of Rome by the insinuating influence of secret artifice. This way of proceeding was approved by many of the votaries of Rome; but they did not all agree about the particular manner of employing it, and therefore followed different methods. Some had recourse to the appointment of public disputations or conferences between the principal doctors of the contending parties; and this from a notion, which past experience had rendered so vain and chimerical, that the adversaries of popery would either be vanquished in the debate, or at least be persuaded to look upon the Roman catholics with less aversion and disgust. Others declared it as their opinion, that all contest was to be suspended; that the great point was to find out the proper method of reconciling the two churches; and that, in order to promote this salutary purpose, as little stress as possible was to be laid upon those matters of controversy which had been hitherto looked upon as of the highest moment and importance. A different manner of proceeding was thought more advisable by a third set of men, who, from a persuasion that their doctors had more zeal than argument, and were much more eminent for their attachment to the church of Rome, than for their skill in defending its cause, prepared their combatants with greater care for the field of controversy, taught them a new art of theological war, and furnished them with a new and artful method of vanquishing, or at least of perplexing, their heretical adversaries.

XII. A public conference took place at Ratisbon, in 1601, at the joint desire of Maximilian, duke of Bavaria, and Philip Louis, elector Palatine, between some eminent Lutheran doctors on one side, and three celebrated Jesuits on the other. The dispute turned upon the two great points, to which almost all the contests between the Protestants and Roman Catholics are reducible, namely, the rule of faith and the judge of controversies. In 1615, James Heilbronner, a learned Lutheran, held a conference at Neuburg with James Keller, a celebrated Jesuit, by the appointment of Wolfgang William, prince Palatine, who had recently embraced the Romish faith. But the most famous conference of this kind, was that which was holden in 1645, at Thorn, by the express order of Uladislaus IV. king of Poland, between several eminent doctors of the Romish, Lutheran, and Reformed churches. This meeting, which was designed to heal the division that reigned among these churches, and to find out some method of reconciling their differences, and bringing about their re-union, was thence called the *Charitable Conference*.

Some time after this, Ernest, landgrave of Hesse, in order to give a plausible colour to his apostasy from the Protestant religion, and make it appear to be the result of examination and conviction, obliged Valerianus Magnus, a learned Capuchin, to enter the lists with Peter Habercorn, a reformed minister, in the castle of Rheinfeld. Beside these public conferences, there were some of a private nature during this century, between the doctors of the contending churches. Of these the most remarkable was the famous dispute between John Claude, the most learned of the reformed divines in France, and Jaques Benigne de Bossuet, whose genius and erudition placed him at the head of the Romish doctors in that country. This dispute, which occurred in 1683, ended like all the rest. They all widened the breach instead of healing it. Neither of the contending parties could be persuaded to yield:* on the contrary, they both returned from the field of controversy more riveted in their own opinions, and more unfriendly to the tenets of their adversaries.

XIII. Those Roman catholics, whose views were turned toward union and concord, did not omit the use of *pious* artifice, in order to accomplish this salutary purpose. They endeavoured to persuade the zealous protestants and the rigid catholics, that their differences in opinion were less considerable, and less important, than they themselves imagined; and that the true way to put an end to their dissensions,

* The circumstances of this famous and ever-memorable revolution are accurately recorded by Burnet, in the second volume of his History of his Own Times; and also by Rapin, in the tenth volume of his History of England. Add to these, Neal's History of the Puritans, vol. iv. ch. xi. p. 536.

* The reader who desires a more particular account of what passed in these conferences, may satisfy his curiosity by consulting the writers mentioned by Sagittarius, in his Introduct. in Historiam Ecclesiast. tom. ii. p. 1569, 1581, 1592, 1598. An account of the conference between Claude and Bossuet, was composed and published by each of these famous combatants.

and to promote union, was not to nourish the flames of discord by disputes and conferences, but to see whether their systems might not be reconciled, and apparent inconsistencies removed, by proper and candid explications. They imagined that a plausible and artful exposition of those doctrines of the church of Rome, which appeared the most shocking to the Protestants, would tend much to conquer their aversion to popery. Such was the general principle in which the Romish peacemakers agreed, and such the basis on which they proposed to carry on their pacific operations; but they differed so widely in their manner of applying this general principle, and pursued such different methods in the execution of this nice and hazardous stratagem, that the event did not answer their expectations. In the way they proceeded, instead of promoting the desired union by their representations of things, by their exhortations and counsels, this union seemed to be previously necessary, in order to render their explications and exhortations acceptable, or even supportable; so little were the means proportioned to the end!

The first, as well as the most eminent, of those who tried the force of their genius in this arduous enterprise, was cardinal Richelieu, that great minister, who employed all the influence of promises and threats, all the powers of sophistry and eloquence, all the arts of persuasion, in order to bring back the French protestants into the bosom of the Romish church.* The example of this illustrious prelate was followed, with less dignity and less influence, by Masenius, a German Jesuit,† Volusius, a theologian of Mentz,‡ Prætorius, a Prussian,§ Gibbon de Burg, an Irish doctor, who was professor at Erfort,‖ Marcellus, a Jesuit,¶ and other divines of inferior note. But, of all modern adepts in controversy, none pursued this method with such dexterity and art as Bossuet, bishop of Meaux, a man of true genius, directed by the most consummate circumspection and prudence. The famous Exposition of the Roman Catholic Faith, that was drawn up by this subtle and insinuating author, was designed to show the protestants, that their reasons against returning to the bosom of the Romish church would be easily removed, if they would view the doctrines of that church in their true light, and not as they had been erroneously represented by protestant writers.** This notion was propagated, though with less dexterity and success, by Dezius, a Jesuit of Strasbourg, who wrote a book expressly to prove, that there was little if any difference between the doctrine of the council of Trent, and that of the confession of Augsburg, than which no two systems can be more irreconcilably opposite.* It is, however, remarkable, that all these pacific attempts to reunite the two churches, were made by the persons now mentioned on their own private authority; they were not avowed by the higher powers, who alone were qualified to remove, modify, or explain away those doctrines and rites of the Romish church, that shocked the protestants and justified their separation. It is true, that, in 1686, this plan of reconciliation was warmly recommended by a person properly commissioned, or, at least, who gave himself out for such. This pacificator was Christopher de Roxas, bishop of Tinia, in the district of Bosnia; who, during several years, frequented, with these reconciling views, the courts of the protestant princes in Germany; intimated the assembling of a new council, that was to be more impartial in its decisions, and less restrained in its proceedings, than the council of Trent; and even assured the protestants, that they might obtain, without difficulty, whatever rights, privileges, and immunities, they should think proper to demand from the Roman pontiff, provided they would

* Rich. Simon, Lettres Choisies, tom. i.—Bayle's Dictionary, at the articles Amyraut, Beaulieu, Ferry, and Milletiere.

† See F. Spanhemii Stricturæ ad Bossueti Expositionem Fidei Catholicæ, tom. iii. op. Theolog. pars ii. p. 1042.

‡ There is extant a book composed by this writer under the following title: Aurora Pacis religiosæ divinæ Veritate amica.

§ In his Tuba Pacis, of which the reader may see a curious account in Bayle's Nouvelles de la Republique des Lettres for the year 1685.

‖ In a treatise, entitled, Luthero Calvinismus schismaticus quidem sed reconciliabilis.

¶ The book of Marcellus, entitled, Sapientia Pacifica, was refuted by Seldius, at the express desire of the duke of Saxe-Gotha.

** This book might furnish topics for a multitude of reflections. See a particular account of its history and its effects in Pfaff's Historia Literaria Theologiæ, tom. ii., and Le Clerc's Bibliotheque Universelle et Historique, tom. xi. ☞ It is remarkable, that nine years passed before this work could obtain the pope's approbation. Clement X. refused it positively; and several Catholic priests were rigorously treated, and severely persecuted, for preaching the doctrine contained in the Exposition, which was, moreover, formally condemned by the university of Louvain, in 1685, and declared to be scandalous and pernicious. The Sorbonne also disavowed the doctrine contained in that book, though by a late edict we learn, that the fathers of that theological seminary have changed their opinion on that head, and thus given a new instance of the variations that reign in the Romish church, which boasts so much of its uniformity in doctrinal matters. The artifice that was employed in the composition of this book, and the tricks that were used in the suppression and alteration of the first edition that was given of it, have been detected with great sagacity and evidence by the learned and excellent archbishop Wake, in the Introduction to his Exposition of the Doctrine of the Church of England. See also his two Defences of that Exposition, in which the perfidious sophistry of Bossuet is unmasked and refuted in the most satisfactory manner. There was an excellent answer to Bossuet's book published by M. de la Bastide, one of the most eminent protestant ministers in France. Of this answer the French prelate took no notice during eight years; at the end of which, he published an advertisement, in a new edition of his Exposition, which was designed to remove the objections of Bastide. The latter replied in such a demonstrative and victorious manner, that the learned bishop, notwithstanding all his eloquence and art, was obliged to quit the field of controversy. See a very interesting account of this insidious work of Bossuet, and the controversies it occasioned, in the Bibliotheque des Sciences, published at the Hague, vol. xviii. This account, which is curious, accurate, ample, and learned, was given partly on occasion of a new edition of the Exposition, printed in 1761, and accompanied with a Latin translation by Fleury, and partly on occasion of Burigny's Life of Bossuet.

* This book is entitled, La Re-union des Protestans de Strasbourg a l'Eglise Romaine, and was published in 1689.—See Phil. Jac. Speneri Consilia Theol. German. in parte iii. p. 650, 662

acknowledge his paternal authority, and no longer refuse submission to his mild and gentle empire. But the artifice and designs of this specious missionary were easily detected; the protestant doctors, and also their sovereigns, soon perceived that a fair and candid plan of reconciliation and union was not what the court of Rome had in view; but that a scheme was in agitation for restoring its pontiffs to their former despotic dominion over the Christian world.*

XIV. The Romish peace-makers found among the protestants, and more especially among those of the reformed church, certain doctors, who, by a natural propensity to union and concord, seconded perhaps, in some, by views of interest, or by the suggestions of ambition, were disposed to enter into their plan, and to assist them in the execution of it. These theologians maintained, that the points in debate between the churches were not of sufficient importance to justify their separation. Among the French protestants, Louis Le Blanc, and his disciples, were suspected of a strong inclination to go too far in this matter.† The same accusation was brought, with fuller evidence, against Huisseaux, professor of divinity at Saumur, Milletiere, Le Fevre, and others of less note.‡ Among the British divines, this excessive propensity to diminish the shocking absurdities of popery was less remarkable; William Forbes was the principal person who discovered an extreme facility to compose a considerable number of the differences that contributed to perpetuate the separation between the churches.§ With respect to the Dutch, it is abundantly known, how ardently the great and learned Grotius desired the re-union of all Christian churches in one general bond of charity and concord, and with what peculiar zeal he endeavoured to reform some enormities of the church of Rome, and to excuse others. But these, and all the other arbitrators, whose names and whose efforts in this pacific cause it would be tedious to mention, derived no other fruit from their (perhaps, well-intended) labours, than the displeasure of both the contending parties, and the bitter reproaches of their respective churches.

In the number of the protestant doctors who betrayed an inconsiderate zeal for the re-union of these churches, many writers place George Calixtus, a man of eminent learning, and professor of divinity in the university of Helmstadt. It is nevertheless certain, that this great man discovered and exposed the errors and corruptions of popery with a degree of learning and perspicuity scarcely surpassed by any writer in this century, and persisted in maintaining that the decrees and anathemas of the council of Trent had banished all hopes of a reconciliation between the protestant churches and the see of Rome. He looked, indeed, upon some of the controversies that divided the two communions with much greater indulgence than was usually shown, and decided them in a manner that did not seem suited to the taste and spirit of the times; he was also of opinion that the church of Rome had not destroyed the genuine principles of Christianity, but had only deformed them with its senseless fictions, and buried them under a heap of rubbish, under a motley multitude of the most extravagant and intolerable doctrines and ceremonies. It was undoubtedly on this account that he has been ranked by some in the class of the imprudent peace-makers already mentioned.

XV. It was no difficult matter to defeat the purposes, and ruin the credit of these pacific arbitrators, who, upon the whole, made up but a motley and ill composed society, weakened by intestine discords. It required more dexterity, and greater efforts of genius, to oppose the progress, and disconcert the sophistry of a set of men who had invented new methods of defending popery, and attacking its adversaries. This new species of polemic doctors were called Methodists, and the most eminent of them arose in France, where a perpetual scene of controversy, carried on with the most learned among the Huguenots, had augmented the dexterity, and improved the theological talents of the catholic disputants. The Methodists, from their different manner of treating the controversy in question, may be divided into two classes. In one we may place those doctors whose method of disputing was disingenuous and unreasonable, and who followed the examples of those military chiefs, who shut up their troops in entrenchments and strong-holds, in order to cover them from the attacks of the enemy. Such was the manner of proceeding of the Jesuit Veron, who was of opinion that the protestants should be obliged to prove the tenets of their church* by plain passages of

* See Jo. Wolf. Jaegeri Historia Ecclesiast. Sæculi XVII.—Christ. Eberhardi Weismanni. Hist. Ecclesiast. Sæc. XVII. p. 735. The reader will find, in the Commercium Epistolico-Leibnitianum of Grubarus, vol. i. an account of the particular conditions of reconciliation that were proposed to the German courts in 1660, by the elector of Mentz, authorised, as it is alleged, by the Roman pontiff.

† See a particular and interesting account of Le Blanc, in Bayle's Dictionary, at the article Beaulieu.

‡ See the above-mentioned Dictionary, at the article Milletiere. For an account of Huisseaux, and his pacific counsels, see Rich. Simon's Lettres Choisies, tom. iii., and Aymon's Synodes Nationaux des Eglises Reformees en France, tom. ii. The labours of Le Fevre, father to the famous Madame Dacier, in the same cause, are mentioned by Morhoff, in his Polyhistor, tom. i.

§ See Forbes' "Considerationes modestæ et pacificæ Controversiarum de Justificatione, Purgatorio," &c., which were published at London in 1658, and afterwards more correctly in Germany, under the inspection of John Fabricius, professor of divinity at Helmstadt. Forbes is mentioned by Grabe with the highest encomiums, in his Notæ ad Bulli Harmoniam Apostolicam; and, if we consider his probity, and the exemplary regularity of his life and conversation, he must be allowed to deserve the praise that is due to piety and good morals. Nevertheless, he had his infirmities, and the wiser part of the English doctors acknowledge, that his propensity toward a reconciliation with the church of Rome, was carried too far. See Burnet's History of his own Time, vol. i. On this account he has been lavishly praised by the catholic writers; see R. Simon's Lettres Choisies, tom. iii. lettre xvii.—He was undoubtedly one of those who contributed most to spread among the English a notion, (the truth or falsehood of which we shall not here examine,) that king Charles I. and archbishop Laud had formed the design of restoring popery in England.

☞ * More especially the doctrines that peculiarly oppose the decrees and tenets of the council of Trent

Scripture, without being allowed to have the liberty of illustrating these passages, reasoning upon them, or drawing any conclusions from them.* In the same class may be ranked Nihusius, an apostate from the protestant religion,† the two Walenburgs, and other polemics, who, looking upon it as an easier matter to maintain their pretensions, than to show upon what principles they were originally founded,‡ obliged their adversaries to prove all their assertions and objections, whether of an affirmative or negative kind, and confined themselves to the mere business of answering objections, and repelling attacks. We may also place among this kind of Methodists cardinal Richelieu, who judged it the shortest and best way to attend little to the multitude of accusations, objections, and reproaches, with which the protestants loaded the various branches of the Romish government, discipline, doctrine, and worship, and to confine the whole controversy to the single article of the divine institution and authority of the church, which he thought it essential to establish by the strongest arguments, as the grand principle that would render popery impregnable.§

The *Methodists* of the second class were of opinion, that the most expedient manner of reducing the protestants to silence, was not to attack them partially, but to overwhelm them at once, by the weight of some general principle or presumption, some universal argument, which comprehended, or might be applied to, all the points contested between the churches. They imitated the conduct of those military leaders, who, instead of spending their time and strength in sieges and skirmishes, endeavour to put an end to a war by a general and decisive action. This method, if not invented,‖ was at least improved and seconded, with all the aids of eloquence and genius, by Nicole, a celebrated doctor among the Jansenists;¶ and it was followed by many of the disputants of the church of Rome, who were so fully persuaded of its irresistible influence, that they looked upon any one of the general points already mentioned as sufficient, when properly handled, to overturn the whole protestant cause. Hence it was, that some of these polemics rested the defence of popery upon the single principle of prescription; others upon the vicious lives of several of those princes who had withdrawn their dominions from the yoke of Rome; and some upon the criminal nature of religious schism, with which they reproached the promoters of the Reformation; and they were all convinced, that, by urging their respective arguments, and making good their respective charges, the mouths of their adversaries must be stopped, and the cause of Rome and its pontiff triumph.* The famous Bossuet stood foremost in this class, which he peculiarly adorned, by the superiority of his genius and the insinuating charms of his eloquence. His arguments, indeed, were more specious than solid, and the circumstances from which they were drawn were imprudently chosen. From the variety of opinions which had taken place among the protestant doctors, and the changes which had happened in their discipline and doctrine, he endeavoured to demonstrate, that the church founded by Luther was not the true church; and, on the other hand, from the perpetual sameness and uniformity that prevailed in the tenets and worship of the church of Rome, he pretended to prove its divine original.† Such an argument must indeed sur-

* Musæus de Usu Principiorum Rationis in Controversiis Theologicis, lib. i. c. iv.—G. Calixti Digressio de Arte nova, p. 125. Simon's Lettres Choisies, tom. i.

† See a particular account of this vain and superficial doctor in Bayle's Dictionary. His work, entitled Ars nova dicto Sacræ Scripturæ unico lucrandi a Pontificiis plurimas in partes Lutheranorum detecta, &c., was refuted in the most satisfactory manner by Calixtus, in his digressio de Arte Nova contra Nihusium, a curious and learned work, published at Helmstadt in 1634.

☞ ‡ That is to say, in other words, that they pleaded *prescription* in favour of popery, and acted like one who, having been for a long time in possession of an estate, refused to produce his title, and requires that those who question it should prove its insufficiency or falsehood.

§ For a more ample account of these methods of controversy, and of others used by the church of Rome, the curious reader may consult Fred. Spanheim's Strictur. ad Expositionem Fidei Bossueti, tom. iii. op. par. ii. p. 1037.—Heidegger's Histor. Papatus, Period. vii. sect. ccxviii. p. 316.—Walchii Introduct. ad Controvers. Theolog. tom. ii.—Weismanni Histor. Ecclesiastica, sæc. xvii. p. 726.

☞ ‖ This method certainly was not the invention of Nicole, for it seems to differ little, if at all, from the method of cardinal Richelieu. We may observe farther, that Richelieu seems rather to belong to the second class of Methodists than to the first, where Dr. Mosheim has placed him.

¶ Nicole is supposed to be the author of a book entitled, "Prejugez legitimes contre les Calvinistes," which was answered in a satisfactory manner by several learned men. ☞ It is very remarkable, that some of the principal arguments employed in this book against the protestants, are precisely the same that the deists make use of to show that it is impossible for the general body of Christians to believe upon a rational foundation. The learned Claude, in his Defence of the Reformation, showed in a demonstrative manner, that the difficulties arising from the incapacity of the multitude to examine the grounds and principles of the protestant religion, are much less than those which occur to a papist, whose faith is founded, not on the plain word of God alone, but on the dictates of tradition, on the decrees of councils, and a variety of antiquated records that are beyond his reach. The protestant divine goes still farther, and proves that there are arguments in favour of Christianity and the protestant faith, that are intelligible by the lowest capacity, and, at the same time, sufficient to satisfy an upright and unprejudiced mind.

* Fred. Spanhemii Diss. de Præscriptione, in Rebus Fidei, adversus novos Methodistas, tom. iii. par. ii. op. p. 1079.

† This is the purpose of Bossuet's Historie des Variations des Eglises Protestantes, which was published in 1688, and is still considered by the catholics as one of the strongest bulwarks of popery. Let them go on in their delusions, and boast of this famous champion and defender; but, if they have any true zeal for the cause he defends, or any regard for the authority of the supreme head of *their* church, they will bury in oblivion that maxim of this *their* champion, that "the church, which frequently modifies, varies, and changes its doctrines, is destitute of the direction of the Holy Spirit." ☞ This observation might be verified by numberless instances of variations in the doctrine and worship of Rome, that must strike every one who has any tolerable acquaintance with the history of that church.—But, without going any farther than one instance, we may observe, that Bossuet had a striking proof of the variations of his own church, in the different reception that his Exposition of the Roman Catholic Faith met with from different persons, and at different times. It was disapproved by one pope, and approved by another; it was applauded by the archbishop

prise, coming from a man of learning, who could not be ignorant of the temporising spirit of the Roman pontiffs, or of the changes they had permitted in their discipline and doctrine, according to the genius of time and place, and the different characters of those whom they were desirous to gain over to their interest. It was still more surprising in a French prelate, since the doctors of that nation generally maintain, that the leaden age does not differ more from the age of gold, than the modern church of Rome differs from the ancient and primitive church of that famous city.

XVI. These various attempts of the votaries of Rome, though they gave abundant exercise to the activity and vigilance of the protestant doctors, were not, however, attended with any important revolutions, or any considerable fruits. Some princes, indeed, and a few learned men, were thereby seduced into the communion of that church, from whose superstition and tyranny their ancestors had delivered themselves and others; but these defections were only personal, nor could any people or province be persuaded to follow these examples. Among the more illustrious deserters of the Protestant religion, we may place Christina, queen of Sweden,* who was a princess of great spirit and genius, but was precipitate and vehement in almost all her proceedings, and preferred her ease, pleasure, and liberty, to all other considerations;† Wolfgang William, count Palatine of the Rhine; Christian William, marquis of Brandenburg; Ernest, prince of Hesse;‡ John Frederic, duke of Brunswick; and Frederic Augustus, king of Poland. The learned men that embraced the communion of the church of Rome were, baron Boineburg, secretary to the elector of Mentz, and a zealous patron of erudition and genius,* Christopher Ranzow, a knight of Holstein,† Caspar Scioppius, Peter Bertius, Christopher Besold, Ulric Hunnius, Nicolas Stenon, a Danish physician, of great reputation in his profession, John Philip Pfeiffer, professor at Konigsberg, Luke Holstenius, Peter Lambecius, Henry Blumius, professor at Helmstadt, a man of learning, and of excessive vanity,‡ Daniel Nesselius, Andrew Fromius, Barthold Nihusius, Christopher Hellwigius, Matthew Prætorius, and a few others of inferior rank in the learned world. But these conversions, when considered with the motives that produced them, will be found, in *reality*, less honourable to the church of Rome than they are *in appearance;* for if, from this list of princes and learned men, we efface those whom the temptations of adversity, the impulse of avarice and ambition, the suggestions of levity, the effects of personal attachments, the power of superstition upon a feeble and irresolute mind, and other motives of like merit, engaged to embrace the Romish religion, these proselytes will be reduced to a number too small to excite the envy of the protestant churches.§

XVII. The Christian churches in the East, which were not dependent on the yoke of Rome, did not stand less firm against the attempts of the papal missionaries than those of Europe. The pompous accounts which several Roman catholic writers have given of the wonderful success of the missionaries among the Nestorians and Monophysites, are little else than splendid fables, designed to amuse and dazzle the multitude; and many of the wisest and best of the Romish doctors acknowledge, that they ought to be considered in no other light. As little credit is to be given to those who mention the strong propensity discovered by several of the heads and superin-

of Rheims, and condemned by the university of Louvain; it was censured by the Sorbonne in 1671, and declared by the same society a true exposition of the catholic faith in the following century. For a full proof of the truth of these and other variations, see Wake's Exposition, &c.—the Biblioth. Univ. of Le Clerc, tom. xi. p. 438.—the General Dictionary, at the article Wake, in the note, and the Biblioth. des Sciences, tom. xviii.

* See Archenholtz, Memoires de la Reine Christine, which contain a variety of agreeable and interesting anecdotes.

☞ † The candid and impartial writer, mentioned in the preceding note, has given an ample account of the circumstances that attended this queen's change of religion, and of the causes that might have contributed to determine her to a step so unexpected and inexcusable. It was neither the subtlety of Des-Cartes, nor the dexterity of Canut, that brought about this event, as Baillet would persuade us. The true state of the case seems to have been this: Christina, having had her sentiments of religion in general considerably perverted by the licentious insinuations of her favourite Bourdelot, was prepared for embracing any particular religion, that pleasure, interest, or ambition, should recommend to her. Upon this foundation, the Jesuits Macedo, Malines, and Cassati, under the immediate protection of Pimentel, and encouraged by the courts of Rome, Spain, and Portugal, employed their labours and dexterity in the conversion of this princess, whose passion for Italy, together with that taste for the fine arts and the precious remains of antiquity, which rendered her desirous of sojourning there, may have contributed not a little to make her embrace the religion of that country.

‡ This learned and well-meaning prince was engaged, by the conversation and importunities of Valerius Magnus, a celebrated monk of the Capuchin order, to embrace popery, in 1651. See Gruberi Commercium Epistol. Leibnitianum, t. i. p. 27, 35. Memoires de la Reine Christine, t. i. p. 216.—It is, however, to be observed, that this prince, with Anthony Ulric, duke of Brunswick, and several others, who went over to the church of Rome, did not go over to *that* church of Rome which is now exhibited to us in the odious forms of superstition and tyranny, but to another kind of church, which, perhaps, never existed but in their idea, and which at least has long ceased to exist. That this was the case appears evidently from the theological writings of prince Ernest.

* This eminent man, who had more learning than philosophy, and who was more remarkable for the extent of his memory than for the rectitude of his judgment, followed the example of the prince of Hesse, in 1653. See Gruberi Commercium Epistol. Leibnitianum, in which his letters, and those of Conringius, are published, tom. i.

† See Molleri Cimbria Literata, tom. i. p. 520.

‡ Blumius deserted the protestant church in 1654. —See Burckhardi Historia Biblioth. Augustæ, pars iii. p. 223.—Gruberi Comm. Epist. tom. i. p. 41, 95, &c. In some of these letters he is called Florus, probably in allusion to his German name Blum, which signifies a *flower*.

§ See, for a particular account of these proselytes to popery, Weisman's Historia Eccles. sæc. XVII. p. 738.—Walchius' Introductio in Controversias, tom. ii. p. 728.—Arnold's Kirchen und Ketzer Historie, pars ii. p. 912, and other writers of civil and literary history.

pendents of the Christian sects in those remote regions, to submit to the jurisdiction of the Roman pontiff.* It is evident, on the contrary, that Rome, in two remarkable instances, suffered a considerable diminution of its influence and authority in the eastern world during this century. One instance was the dreadful revolution in Japan, which has been already related, and which was unhappily followed by the total extinction of Christianity in that great monarchy. The other was the downfall of popery by the extirpation of its missionaries in the empire of Abyssinia, of which it will not be improper, or foreign from our purpose, to give here a brief account.

About the commencement of the seventeenth century, the Portuguese Jesuits renewed, under the most auspicious encouragement, the mission to Abyssinia that had been for some time interrupted and suspended; for the emperor Susneius or Socinios, who assumed the denomination of Sultan Segued, after the defeat of his enemies and his accession to the throne, covered the missionaries with his peculiar protection. Gained over to their cause, partly by the eloquence of the Jesuits, and partly by the hopes of maintaining himself upon the throne by the succours of the Portuguese, he committed the whole government of the church to Alphonso Mendez, a missionary from that nation; created him patriarch of the Abyssinians; and, in 1626, not only swore, in a public manner, allegiance to the Roman pontiff, but also obliged his subjects to abandon the religious rites and tenets of their ancestors, and to embrace the doctrine and worship of the Romish church. But the new patriarch, by his intemperate zeal, imprudence, and arrogance, ruined the cause in which he had embarked, and occasioned the total subversion of the Roman pontiff's authority and jurisdiction, which seemed to have been established upon solid foundations. He began his ministry with the most inconsiderate acts of violence and despotism. Following the spirit of the Spanish inquisition, he employed formidable threatenings and cruel tortures to convert the Abyssinians; the greatest part of whom, together with their priests and ministers, held the religion of their ancestors in the highest veneration, and were willing to part with their lives and fortunes rather than forsake it. He also ordered those to be re-baptized, who, in compliance with the orders of the emperor, had embraced the faith of Rome, as if their former religion had been nothing more than a system of Paganism.† This the Abyssinian clergy looked upon as a shocking insult to the religious discipline of their ancestors, as even more provoking than the violence and barbarities practised against those who refused to submit to the papal yoke. Nor did the insolent patriarch rest satisfied with these arbitrary and despotic proceedings in the church; he excited tumults and factions in the state, and, with an unparalleled spirit of rebellion and arrogance, encroached upon the prerogatives of the throne, and attempted to give law to the emperor himself. Hence arose civil commotions, conspiracies, and seditions, which excited in a little time the indignation of the emperor, and the hatred of the people against the Jesuits, and produced, at length, in 1631, a public declaration from the throne, by which the Abyssinian monarch annulled the orders he had formerly given in favour of popery, and left his subjects at liberty, either to persevere in the doctrine of their ancestors, or to embrace the faith of Rome. This rational declaration was mild and indulgent toward the Jesuits, considering the treatment which their insolence and presumption had so justly deserved; but, in the following reign, much severer measures were employed against them. Basilides or Facilidas, the son of Segued, who succeeded his father in 1632, thought it expedient to free his dominions from these troublesome and despotic guests; and accordingly, in 1634, he banished from his territories the patriarch Mendez, with all the Jesuits and Europeans who belonged to his retinue, and treated the Roman Catholic missionaries with excessive severity.* From this period the very name of Rome, its religion, and its pontiff, were objects of the highest aversion among the Abyssinians, who guarded their frontiers

* See the remarks made by Chardin in several places of the last edition of his travels. See also what Cerri, in his Etat Present de l'Eglise Romaine, says of the Armenians and Copts. It is true, that, among these sects, the papal missionaries sometimes form congregations that are obedient to the see of Rome; but these congregations are poor, and composed only of a very small number of individuals. Thus the Capuchins, about the middle of the century now under consideration, founded a small congregation among the Monophysites of Asia, whose bishop resided at Aleppo. See Lequien, Oriens Christianus, t. ii. p. 1408.

☞ † The reader will recollect, that the Abyssinians differ very little from the Copts, and acknowledge the patriarch of Alexandria as their spiritual chief. They receive the old and new Testament, the three first Councils, the Nicene Creed, and the Apostolical Constitutions. Their first conversion to Christianity is attributed by some to the famous prime minister of their queen Candace, mentioned in the acts of the Apostles: it is, however, probable, that the general conversion of that great empire was not perfected before the fourth century, when Frumentius, ordained bishop of Axuma by Athanasius, exercised his ministry among the people with the most astonishing success. They were esteemed a pure church before they fell into the errors of Eutyches and Dioscorus; and even since that period they still form a purer church than that of Rome.

* See Ludolfi Histor. Æthiopica, lib. iii. cap. xii.—Geddes' Church History of Ethiopia, p. 233.—La Croze, Histoire du Christianisme d'Ethiopie, p. 79.—Lobo. Voyage d'Abyssinie, p. 116, 130, 144, with the additions of Le Grand, p. 173, and the fourth Dissertation that is subjoined to the second volume. In this dissertation, Le Grand, himself a Roman Catholic, makes the following remark upon the conduct of the patriarch Mendez: "It is to be wished that the patriarch had never intermeddled in such a variety of affairs," (*by which mitigated expression the author means his ambitious attempts to govern in the cabinet as well as in the church*,) "or carried his authority to such a height, as to behave in Ethiopia as if he had been in a country where the inquisition was established: for, by this conduct, he set all the people against him, and excited in them such an aversion to the Roman Catholics in general, and to the Jesuits in particular, as nothing has been hitherto able to diminish, and which subsists in its full force to this day." ☞ The third book of La Croze's History, which relates to the progress and ruin of this mission, is translated by Mr. Lockman into English, and inserted in the Travels of the Jesuits, vol. i. p. 308, &c. as also in Poncet's Voyage mentioned in the following note.

with the greatest vigilance and the strictest attention, lest any Jesuit or Romish missionary should steal into their territories in disguise, and excite new tumults and commotions in the kingdom. The Roman pontiffs indeed made more than one attempt to recover the authority they had lost by the ill success and misconduct of the Jesuits. They began by sending two Capuchin monks to repair their loss; but these unfortunate wretches were no sooner discovered than they were stoned to death. They afterwards employed more artful and clandestine methods of reviving the missions, and had recourse to the influence and intercession of Louis XIV. to procure admission for their emissaries into the Abyssinian empire;* but, as far we have learned, neither the pontiffs nor their votaries have yet been able to calm the resentment of that exasperated nation, or to conquer its reluctance against the worship and jurisdiction of the church of Rome.†

XVIII. Hitherto we have confined our views to the external state and condition of this church, and to the good or ill success that attended its endeavours to extend its dominion in the different parts of the world. It will be now proper to change the scene, to consider this establishment in its internal constitution, and to review its polity, discipline, institutions, and doctrine. Its ancient form of government still remained; but its pontiffs and bishops lost, in many places, no small part of that extensive authority which they had so long enjoyed. The halcyon days were now over, in which the papal clergy excited with impunity seditious tumults in the state, interfered openly in the transactions of government, struck terror into the hearts of sovereigns and subjects by the thunder of their anathemas, and, imposing burthensome contributions on the credulous multitude, filled their coffers by notorious acts of tyranny and oppression. The pope himself, though still honoured with the same pompous titles and denominations, frequently found, by a mortifying and painful experience, that these titles had lost a considerable part of their former signification, and that the energy of these denominations daily diminished. For now almost all the princes and states of Europe had adopted the important maxim, formerly peculiar to the French nation; that the power of the Roman pontiff is confined to matters of a religious and spiritual nature, and cannot, under any pretext whatever, extend to civil transactions or worldly affairs. In the schools, indeed, and colleges of Roman catholic countries, and in the writings of the Romish priests and doctors, the majesty of the pope was still exalted in the most emphatic terms, and his prerogatives were displayed with all imaginable pomp. The Jesuits also, who have been always ambitious of a distinguished place among the assertors of the power and pre-eminence of the Roman see, and who give themselves out for the pope's most obsequious creatures, raised their voices, in this ignoble cause, even above those of the schools and colleges. Even in the courts of sovereign princes, very flattering terms and high-sounding phrases were sometimes used, to express the dignity and authority of the head of the church. But as it happens in other cases, that men's actions are frequently very different from their language, so was this observation particularly verified in the case of *Rome's holy father.* He was extolled in words, by those who despised him most in reality; and, when any dispute arose between him and the princes of his communion, the latter respected his authority no farther than they found expedient for their own purposes, and measured the extent of his prerogatives and jurisdiction, not by the slavish adulation of the colleges and the Jesuits, but by a regard to their own interests and independence.

XIX. This the pontiffs learned by disagreeable experience, as often as they endeavoured, in this century, to resume their former pretensions, to interpose their authority in civil affairs, and encroach upon the jurisdiction of

* These projects are mentioned by Cerri, and by Le Grand in his Supplement to Lobo's Itinerarium Æthiopicum.* The reader who would know what credit is to be given to what the Jesuits say of the attachment and veneration which the Asiatic and African Christians express for the church of Rome, will do well to compare the relations of Le Grand, who was a Roman Catholic, and no enemy to the Jesuits, and who drew his relations from the most authentic records, with those of Poncet, a French physician, who went into Ethiopia in 1698, accompanied by Father Brevedent, a Jesuit, who died during the voyage. This comparison will convince every ingenuous and impartial inquirer, that the accounts of the Jesuits are not to be trusted, and that they surpass the ancient Carthaginians themselves in the art of deceiving. Poncet's Voyage is published in the fourth volume of the Jesuitical work, entitled, Lettres Curieuses et Edifiantes des Missions Etrangeres.

† Lafitau and Reboulet, who have composed each a Life of pope Clement XI., tell us, that the emperor of Abyssinia desired that pontiff, in 1703, to send to his court missionaries and legates to instruct him and his people, and to receive their submission to the see of Rome. These biographers go still farther, and assert that this monarch actually embraced the communion of Rome, in 1712. But these assertions are idle fictions, forged by the Jesuits and their creatures. It is well known, on the contrary, that, not many years ago, the edict prohibiting the entrance of Europeans within the Abyssinian frontier, was still in force, and was executed with the greatest severity. Even the Turks are included in this prohibition; and what is still more remarkable, the Egyptian Monophysites, who have once entered within the Abyssinian territories, are not allowed to return into their own country. All these facts are confirmed by a modern writer of the most unquestionable authority, the learned and worthy M. Maillet, the French consul-general in Egypt, and ambassador from Louis XIV. to the emperor of Abyssinia, in his Description de l'Egypte, par. i. p. 325. See also Le Grand's Supplement. The last-mentioned author, after relating all the attempts that have been made in our times, by the French nation and the pope, to introduce Romish priests into Abyssinia, adds, that all such attempts must appear vain and chimerical to all those who have any knowledge of the empire of Abyssinia, and of the spirit and character of its inhabitants; his words are: "Toutes ces entreprises paroitront chimeriques a ceux qui connoitron l'Abissinie et les Abissins."

☞ * Father Lobo, who resided nine years in Ethiopia, has given an elegant and lively, though simple and succinct description, of that vast empire, in his Itinerarium Æthiopicum. This itinerary was translated into French by M. Le Grand, and enriched by him with curious anecdotes and dissertations. Hence Dr. Mosheim sometimes quotes the Itinerarium, under the title of Voyage d'Abyssinie, referring to Le Grand's French translation of it.

sovereign states. The conduct of Paul V. and its consequences, furnish a striking example that abundantly verifies this observation. This haughty and arrogant pontiff, in 1606, laid the republic of Venice under an interdict. The reasons alleged for this insolent proceeding, were the prosecution of two ecclesiastics for capital crimes, and the promulgation of two edicts, one of which prohibited the erection of any more religious edifices in the Venetian territories, without the knowledge and consent of the senate, while the other forbade the alienation of any lay possessions or estates in favour of the clergy, without the express approbation of the republic. The assembled senators received this papal insult with dignity, and conducted themselves under it with becoming resolution and fortitude. Their first step was to prevent their clergy from executing the interdict, by an act prohibiting that cessation of public worship, and that suspension of the sacraments, which the pope had so imperiously commanded. Their next step was equally vigorous; for they banished from their territories the Jesuits and Capuchins, who intended to obey the orders of the pope, in opposition to their express commands. In the process of this controversy they employed their ablest pens, and particularly that of the learned and ingenious Paul Sarpi, of the order of Servites, to demonstrate, on one hand, the justice of their cause, and to determine, on the other, after an accurate and impartial inquiry, the true limits of the pontiff's jurisdiction and authority. The arguments of these writers were so strong and cogent, that Baronius, and the other learned advocates whom the pope had employed in supporting his pretensions and defending his measures, struggled in vain against irresistible evidence. In the mean time all things tended toward a rupture; and Paul was assembling his forces in order to make war upon the Venetians, when Henry IV., king of France, interposed as mediator,* and adjusted a peace between the contending parties, on conditions not very honourable to the ambitious pontiff;† for the Venetians could not be persuaded, either to repeal the edicts and resolutions they had issued against the court of Rome on this occasion, or to recall the Jesuits from their exile.* It is remarkable, that, at the time of this rupture, the senate entertained serious thoughts of a total separation from the church of Rome, in which the ambassadors of England and Holland did all that was in their power to confirm that assembly. But many considerations of a momentous nature intervened to prevent the execution of this design, which, as it would seem, had had not the approbation of the sagacious and prudent Father Paul, notwithstanding his aversion to the tyranny and maxims of the court of Rome.†

XX. Had the Portuguese acted with the same wisdom and resolution that distinguished the Venetians, their contest with the court of Rome, which began under the pontificate of Urban VIII. in 1641, and was carried on until the year 1666, would have been terminated in a manner equally disadvantageous to the haughty pretensions of the pontiffs. The Portuguese, unable to bear any longer the tyranny and oppression of the Spanish government, threw off the yoke, and chose Don John, duke of Braganza, for their king. Urban and his

☞ * It must be observed here, that it was at the request of the pope, and not of the Venetians, that Henry acted as mediator. The Venetians had nothing to fear. Their cause was considered as the common cause of all the sovereign states of Italy: and the dukes of Urbino, Modena, and Savoy, had already offered their troops and services to the republic. The rash pontiff, perceiving the storm that was gathering against him, took refuge in the French monarch's intercession.

† Beside De Thou and other historians, see Daniel's Histoire de la France, tom. x.—Heidegger's Historia Papatus, period. vii. sect. ccxx.—Jaeger's Historia Eccles. sæc. XVII. decenn. i.—More especially the writings of the famous Paul Sarpi, commonly called Fra-Paolo, and of the other divines and canonists that defended the cause of the republic, deserve a careful and attentive perusal; for these writings were composed with such solidity, learning, and eloquence, that they produced remarkable effects, and contributed much to open the eyes of several princes and magistrates, and to prevent their submitting blindly and implicitly, as their ancestors had done, to the imperious dictates of the pontiffs. Among the most masterly pieces written in this cause, we must place Fra-Paolo's Istoria delle Cose passate entre Paolo V. e la Republ. di Venetia, published at Mirandola in 1624, and his Historia Interdicti Veneti, which was published at Cambridge in 1626, by bishop Bedell, who, during these troubles, had been chaplain to the English ambassador at Venice. Paul V., by forcing the Venetians to expose, in these admirable productions, his arrogance and temerity, on one hand, and many truths unfavourable to the pretensions of the popes on the other, was the occasion of the greatest perplexities and oppositions that the court of Rome had to encounter in after-times.

* When peace was concluded between the Venetians and the pope, in 1607, the Capuchins and the other ecclesiastics, who had been banished on account of their partiality to the cause of Rome, were all re-instated in their respective functions, except the Jesuits; and even the latter were recalled in 1657, under the pontificate of Alexander VII. in consequence of the earnest and importunate requests of Louis XIV. king of France, and several other princes, who gave the Venetians no rest until they re-admitted these dangerous guests into their territories. It is, nevertheless, to be observed, that the Jesuits never recovered the credit and influence they had formerly enjoyed in that republic, nor, at this present time, are there any people of the Romish communion, among whom their society has less power than among the Venetians, who have never yet forgotten their rebellious behaviour during the quarrel now mentioned. See the Voyage Historique en Italie, Allemagne, Suisse, (published at Amsterdam in 1736,) tom. i. p. 291. It is farther worthy of observation, that, since this famous quarrel, the bulls and rescripts of the popes have just as much authority at Venice, as the senate judges consistent with the rules of wise policy, and the true interests and welfare of the community. For proof of this, we need go no farther than the respectable testimony of cardinal Henry Norris, who, in 1676, wrote to Magliabecchi in the following terms: *Poche Bulle passevane quelle acque verso la parte del Adriatico, per le massime lasciate nel Testamento di* Fra-Paolo; i. e. Few papal Bulls pass the Po, or approach the coasts of the Adriatic sea: the maxims bequeathed to the Venetians by Fra-Paolo, render this passage extremely difficult.

† This intention is particularly mentioned by Burnet, in his life of Bishop Bedell, and by M. Courayer in his Defense de la Nouvelle Traduction de l'Histoire du Concile de Trente. The latter writer shows plainly, that Father Paul, though his sentiments differed in many points from the doctrine of the church of Rome, did not approve all the tenets received by the protestants, or suggest to the Venetians the idea of renouncing the Romish faith.

successors obstinately refused, notwithstanding the most earnest and pressing solicitations, both of the French and Portuguese, either to acknowledge Don John's title to the crown, or to confirm the bishops whom that prince had named to fill the vacant sees in Portugal. Hence it happened, that the greatest part of the kingdom remained for a long time without bishops. The pretended vicar of Christ upon earth, whose character ought to set him above the fear of man, was so slavishly apprehensive of the resentment of the king of Spain, that, rather than offend that monarch, he violated the most solemn obligations of his station, by leaving such a number of churches without pastors and spiritual guides. The French and other European courts, advised and exhorted the new king of Portugal to follow the noble example of the Venetians, and to assemble a national council, by which the new-created bishops might be confirmed, in spite of the pope, in their respective sees. Don John seemed disposed to listen to their counsels, and to act with resolution and vigour at this important crisis; but his enterprising spirit was checked by the formidable power of the court of inquisition, the incredible superstition of the people, and the blind zeal and attachment that the nation in general discovered for the person and authority of the pontiff. Hence the popes continued their insults with impunity; and it was not before peace was concluded between Portugal and Spain, five-and-twenty years after this revolution, that the bishops nominated by the king were confirmed by the pope. It was under the pontificate of Clement IX. that an accommodation was brought about between the courts of Portugal and Rome. It must, indeed, be observed, to the honour of the Portuguese, that, notwithstanding their superstitious attachment to the court of Rome, they vigorously opposed its ambitious pontiff in all his attempts to draw from this contest an augmentation of his power and authority in their kingdom; nor did the bishops permit, in their respective sees, any encroachment to be made, at this time, upon the privileges and rights enjoyed by their monarchs in former ages.*

XXI. There had subsisted, during many preceding ages, an almost uninterrupted variance between the French monarchs and the pontiffs, which had often occasioned an open rupture, and which produced more than once that violent effect during this century. The greatest exertions of industry, artifice, and assiduous labour, were employed by the popes, during the whole of this period, to conquer the aversion that the French had conceived against the pretensions and authority of the court of Rome, and to undermine imperceptibly, and enervate and destroy by degrees, the liberties of the Gallican church. In this arduous and important enterprise the Jesuits acted a principal part, and seconded, with all their dexterity and craft, the designs of the aspiring pontiffs. But these attempts and stratagems were effectually defeated and disconcerted by the parliament of Paris, while many able pens exposed the tyranny and injustice of the papal claims. Richer, Launoy, Peter de Marca, Natalis Alexander, Elias du-Pin, and others, displayed their learning and talents in this contest, though with different degrees of merit. They appealed to the ancient decrees of the Gallican church, which they confirmed by recent authorities, and enforced by new and victorious arguments. It will naturally be thought, that these bold and respectable defenders of the rights and liberties, both of the church and state, were amply rewarded, for their generous labours, by peculiar marks of the approbation and protection of the court of France. But this was so far from being always the case, that they received, on the contrary, from time to time, several marks of its resentment and displeasure, designed to appease the rage and indignation of the threatening pontiff, whom it was thought expedient to treat sometimes with artifice and caution. Rome, however, gained little by this mild policy of the French court; for it has been always a prevailing maxim with the monarchs of that nation, that their prerogatives and pretensions are to be defended against the encroachments of the pontiffs with as little noise and contention as possible, and that pompous memorials, and warm and vehement remonstrances, are to be carefully avoided, except in cases of urgent necessity.* Nor do these princes think it beneath their dignity to yield, more or less, to time and occasion, and even to pretend a great veneration for the orders and authority of the pontiffs, in order to obtain from them, by fair means, the immunities and privileges which they look upon as their due. But they are, nevertheless, constantly on their guard; and, as soon as they perceive the court of Rome taking advantage of their lenity to extend its dominion, and the lordly popes growing insolent in consequence of their mildness and submission, they then alter their tone, change their measures, and resume the language that becomes the monarchs of a nation, that could never bear the tyranny and oppression of the papal yoke. This appears evidently in the contests that arose between the courts of France and Rome, under the reign of Louis XIV., of which it will not be improper to give here some remarkable instances.†

XXII. The first of these contests happened in the pontificate of Alexander VII., and arose from the temerity and insolence of his Corsican guards, who, in 1662, insulted the French

* See Geddes' History of the Pope's Behaviour toward Portugal, from 1641 to 1666, in his Miscellaneous Tracts, vol. ii. p. 73—186.—The cause of the Portuguese, in this quarrel, is defended with great learning and sagacity by a French writer, whose name was Bulliald, in a book entitled, Pro Ecclesiis Lusitanis ad Clerum Gallicanum Libelli Duo.

☞ * It is with a view to this that Voltaire, speaking of the manner in which the court of France maintains its prerogatives against the Roman pontiff, says, pleasantly, that "the king of France kisses the pope's feet, and ties up his hands."

☞ † The long note l of the original, in which Dr Mosheim has examined that interesting question, "Whether the papal authority gained or lost ground in France during the seventeenth century?" is transposed by the translator into the text, and placed at the end of our author's account of the quarrels of Louis XIV. with the pope, where it comes in with the utmost propriety. See sect. xxiii.

ambassador and his lady, the duke and duchess of Crequi, at the instigation, as it is supposed, of the pope's nephews. Louis demanded satisfaction for the insult offered to his representative; and, on the pope's delaying to answer this demand, actually ordered his troops to file off for Italy, and to besiege the arrogant pontiff in his capital. Alexander, terrified by these warlike preparations, implored the clemency of the incensed monarch, who granted pardon and absolution to the humble pontiff, and concluded a peace with him at Pisa, in 1664, upon the most inglorious and mortifying conditions. These conditions were, that the pope should send his nephew to Paris, in the character of a suppliant for pardon; that he should brand the Corsican guards with perpetual infamy, and break them by a public edict; and should erect a pyramid at Rome, with an inscription destined to preserve the memory of this audacious instance of papal insolence, and of the exemplary manner in which it was chastised and humbled by the French monarch. It is however to be observed, that, in this contest, Louis did not chastise Alexander, considered as head of the church, but as a temporal prince violating the law of nations.* Yet he showed, on other occasions, that, when seriously provoked, he was as much disposed to humble papal as princely ambition, and that he feared the head of the church as little as the temporal ruler of the ecclesiastical state. This appeared evidently by the important and warm debate he had with Innocent XI. considered in his spiritual character, which began about the year 1678, and was carried on for several years with great animosity and contention. The subject of this controversy was a right called in France the *regale*, by which the French king, upon the death of a bishop, claimed the revenues and fruits of his see, and also discharged several parts† of the episcopal function, until a new bishop was elected. Louis was desirous that all the churches in his dominions should be subject to the *regale*. Innocent pretended, on the contrary, that this claim could not be granted with such universality; nor would he consent to any augmentation of the prerogatives of this nature, that had formerly been enjoyed by the kings of France. Thus the claims of the prince and the remonstrances of the pontiff, both urged with warmth and perseverance, formed a sharp and violent contest, which was carried on by both parties with spirit and resolution. The pontiff sent forth his bulls and mandates. The monarch opposed their execution by the terror of penal laws, and the authority of severe edicts against all who dared to treat them with the smallest regard. When the pope refused to confirm the bishops who were nominated by the king, the latter took care to have them consecrated and inducted into their respective sees; and thus, in some measure, declared to the world, that the Gallican church could govern itself without the intervention of the Roman pontiff. Innocent, who was a man of a high spirit, and inflexibly obstinate in his purposes, did not lose courage at a view of these resolute and vigorous proceedings, but threatened the monarch with the divine vengeance, issued out bull after bull, and did every thing in his power to convince his adversaries, that the vigour and intrepidity, which formerly distinguished the lordly rulers of the Romish church, were not yet totally extinguished.* This obstinacy, however, only served to add fuel to the indignation and resentment of Louis; and accordingly that monarch summoned the famous assembly of bishops,† which met at Paris in 1682. In this convocation, the ancient doctrine of the Gallican church, that declares the power of the pope to be merely spiritual, and also inferior to that of a general council, was drawn up anew in four propositions,‡ which were solemnly adopted by the whole assembly, and were proposed to the whole body of the clergy and to all the universities throughout the kingdom, as a sacred and inviolable rule of faith. But even this respectable decision of the affair, which gave such a severe wound to the authority of Rome, did not shake the constancy of its resolute pontiff, or reduce him to silence.§

* See Jaegeri Histor. Eccles. sæc. XVII. decenn. vii. lib. ii. cap. ii. p. 180.—Voltaire, Siecle de Louis XIV. tom. i. p. 134. *Edit. de Dresde*, 1753.—Archenholtz, Memoires de la Reine Christine, tom. ii. p. 72.

☞ † The author means here undoubtedly the collation of all benefices, which became vacant in the diocese of a deceased bishop, before the nomination of his successor. The right of collation, in such cases, was comprehended in the *regale*. See note †.

* See Jo. Hen. Heideggeri Historia Papatus, period. vii. sect. cccxli. p. 555. ☞ Voltaire's Siecle de Louis XIV. tom. i. p. 221. A great number of writers have either incidentally or professedly treated the subject of the *regale*, and have given ample accounts of the controversies it has occasioned. But no author has traced out more circumstantially the rise and progress of this famous right than cardinal Henry Norris, in his Istoria delle Investiture Ecclesiast. p. 547.

☞ † This assembly, which consisted of thirty-five bishops, and as many deputies of the second order, extended the *regale* to all the churches in France without exception. The bishops, at the same time, thought proper to represent it to the king, as their humble opinion, that those ecclesiastics whom he should be pleased to nominate, during the vacancy of the see, to benefices attended with cure of souls, were bound to apply for induction and confirmation to the grand vicars appointed by the chapters.

☞ ‡ These four propositions were to the following purport:

1. That neither St. Peter nor his successors have received from God any power to interfere, directly, or indirectly, in what concerns the temporal interests of princes and sovereign states; that kings and princes cannot be deposed by ecclesiastical authority, nor their subjects freed from the sacred obligation of fidelity and allegiance, by the power of the church, or the bulls of the Roman pontiff.

2. That the decrees of the council of Constance, which represent the authority of general councils as superior to that of the pope, in spiritual matters, are approved and adopted by the Gallican church.

3. That the rules, customs, institutions, and observances, which have been received in the Gallican church, are to be preserved inviolable.

4. That the decisions of the pope, in points of faith, are not infallible, unless they be attended with the consent of the church.

§ This pope was far from keeping silence with respect to the famous propositions mentioned in the preceding note. As they were highly unfavourable to his authority, so he took care to have them refuted and opposed, both in private and in public. The principal champion for the papal cause, on this occasion, was the cardinal Celestin Sfondrati, who, in 1684, published, under the feigned name of Eugenius Lombardus, a treatise, entitled, Regale Sacerdotium Romano Pontifici assertium, et quatuor Propositionibus explicatum. This treatise was printed

Another contest arose, some time after the one now mentioned, between these princes, whose mutually jealousy and dislike inflamed their divisions. This new dispute broke out in 1687, when Innocent wisely resolved to suppress the franchises, and the right of asylum, which had formerly been enjoyed by the ambassadors residing at Rome,* and had, on many occasions, proved a sanctuary for rapine, violence, and injustice, by procuring impunity for the most heinous malefactors. The marquis de Lavardin refused, in the name of the French king, to submit to this new regulation; and Louis took all the violent methods that pride and resentment could invent to oblige the pontiff to restore to his ambassador the immunities above mentioned.† Innocent, on the other hand, persisted in his purpose, opposed the king's demands in the most open and intrepid manner, and could not be induced by any consideration to yield, even in appearance, to his ambitious adversary.‡ His death, however, put an end to this long debate, which had proved really detrimental to both parties. His successors, being men of a softer and more complaisant disposition, were less averse to the concessions that were necessary to bring about a reconciliation, and to the measures that were adapted to remove the chief causes of these unseemly contests. They were not, indeed, so far unmindful of the papal dignity, and of the interests of Rome, as to patch up an agreement on inglorious terms. On the one hand, the right of *asylum* was suppressed with the king's consent; on the other the right of the *regale* was settled, with modifications.§ The four famous propositions, relating to the pope's authority and jurisdiction, were softened, by the king's permission, in private letters addressed to the pontiff by certain bishops; but they were neither abrogated by the prince, nor renounced by the clergy: on the contrary, they still remain in force, and occupy an eminent place among the laws of the kingdom.

XXIII. * Several protestant writers of great merit and learning, lament the accessions of power and authority which the Roman pontiffs are supposed to have gained in France during the course of this century. They tell us, with sorrow, that the Italian notions of the papal majesty and jurisdiction, which the French nation had, in former ages, looked upon with abhorrence, gained ground now, and had infected not only the nobility and clergy, but almost all ranks and orders of men; and hence they conclude, that the famous rights and liberties of the Gallican church have suffered greatly by the perfidious stratagems of the Jesuits. They are led into this opinion by certain measures that were taken by the French court, and which seemed to favour the pretensions of the Roman pontiff. They are confirmed in it by the declamations of the Jansenists, and other modern writers among the French, who complain of the high veneration that was paid to the papal bulls during this century; of the success of the Jesuits in instilling into the mind of the king and his counsellors, the maxims of Rome, and an excessive attachment to its bishop; of the violence and ill-treatment that were offered to all those who firmly adhered to the doctrine and maxims of their forefathers; and of the gradual attempts that were made to introduce the formidable tribunal of the inquisition into France. But it will perhaps appear, on mature consideration, that too much stress is laid, by many, on these complaints, and that the rights and privileges of the Gallican church were in this century, and are actually at this day, in the same state and condition in which we find them during those earlier ages, of which the writers and declaimers above mentioned, incessantly boast. It might be asked, where are the victories that are said to have been obtained over the French by the popes, and which some protestant doctors, lending a credulous ear to the complaints of the Jansenists and Appellants, think they perceive with the utmost clearness? I am persuaded that it would be difficult, if not impossible, to give a satisfactory answer in the affirmative to this question.

It is true, indeed, that, as the transactions of government, in general, are now carried on in France, with more subtlety, secrecy, and art, than in former times, so, in particular, the stratagems and machinations of the pontiffs have been opposed and defeated with more artifice and less noise, than in those more rude and unpolished ages, when almost every contest was terminated by brutal force and open violence. The opposition between the court of France and the bishop of Rome, still subsists; but the manner of conducting it is changed; and the contests are carried on with less clamour, though not with less animosity and vigour, than in former times. This new and prudent manner of disputing is not agreeable to the restless, fiery, and impatient temper of

in Switzerland, as appears evidently by the character or form of the letters. Several German, Flemish, Italian, and Spanish doctors, stood forth to support the tottering majesty of the pontiff against the court of France; and more especially the learned Nicolas du Bois, professor at Louvain, whose writings in defence of the pope are mentioned by Bossuet. But all these papal champions were defeated by the famous prelate last mentioned, the learned and eloquent bishop of Meaux, who, by the king's special order, composed that celebrated work, which appeared in 1730, under the following title: Defensio Declarationis celeberrimæ, quam de Potestate Ecclesiastica sanxit Clerus Gallicanus, xix Martii, MDCLXXXII, Luxemburgi. The late publication of this defence was owing to the prospect of a reconciliation between the courts of France and Rome, after the death of Innocent; which reconcilation actually took place, and engaged Louis to prohibit the publication of this work.

☞ * This right of asylum extended much farther than the ambassador's palace, whose immunity the pope did not mean to violate; it comprehended a considerable extent of ground which was called a *quarter*, and undoubtedly gave occasion to great and flagrant abuses.

☞ † The marquis de Lavardin began his embassy by entering Rome, surrounded with a thousand men in arms.

‡ See Jaegeri Historia Ecclesiastic. sæc. XVII. decenn. ix. p. 19, and Legatio Lavardini; but, above all, the Memoires de la Reine Christine, tom. ii. p. 248, for Christina took part in this contest, and adopted the cause of the French monarch.

§ See Fleury's Institutions du Droit Ecclesiastique Francois, which excellent work is translated into Latin. Dr. Mosheim refers to p. 454 of the Latin version.

* See Note †, p. 196.

the French, who have an irresistible propensity to noisy, clamorous, and expeditious proceedings; and hence undoubtedly arise all the complaints we have heard, and still hear, of the decline of the liberties of the Gallican church, in consequence of the growing influence and perfidious counsels of the Jesuits. If those, however, who are accustomed to make these complaints, would for a moment suspend their prejudices, and examine with attention the history, and also the present state of their country, they would soon perceive that their ecclesiastical *liberties*,* instead of declining, or of being neglected by their monarchs, are maintained and preserved with greater care, resolution, and foresight, than ever. It must indeed be acknowledged, that, in France, there are multitudes of cringing slaves, who basely fawn upon the pontiffs, exalt their prerogatives, revere their majesty, and, through the dictates of superstition, interest, or ambition, are ever ready to hug the papal chain, and submit their necks blindly to the yoke of those spiritual tyrants; but it may be proved, by the most undoubted facts, and by innumerable examples, that these servile creatures of the pope abounded as much in France in former ages as they do at this day; and it must be also considered, that it is not by the counsels of this slavish tribe, that the springs of government are moved, or the affairs of state and church transacted. It must be farther acknowledged, that the Jesuits have attained a very high degree of influence and authority,† and sometimes have credit enough to promote measures that are by no means consistent with the rights of the Gallican church, and must consequently be considered as heavy grievances by the patrons of the ancient ecclesiastical liberty. But here it may be observed, on one hand, that many such measures were proposed and followed before the rise of the Jesuits; and, on the other, that many affairs of great consequence are daily transacted in a manner highly displeasing and detrimental to that society, and extremely disagreeable to the Roman pontiffs. If it be alleged, that those who defend, with learning and judgment, the ancient doctrines and maxims of the Gallican church, scarcely escape public censure and punishment, and that those who maintain them with vehemence and intemperate zeal are frequently rewarded with exile or a prison; and that even the most humble and modest patrons of these doctrines are left in obscurity without encouragement or recompense; all this must be granted. But it must be considered, that the cause they maintain, and the ancient doctrines and maxims they defend, are not condemned, nor even deserted; the matter is only this, that the prince and his ministry have fallen upon a new method of maintaining and supporting them. It appears to them much more conducive to public peace and order, that the stratagems and attempts of the pontiffs should be opposed and defeated by secret exertions of resolution and vigour, without noise or ostentation, than by learned productions and clamorous disputes; which, for the most part, excite factions in the kingdom, inflame the spirits of the people, throw the state into tumult and confusion, exasperate the pontiffs, and alienate them still more and more from the French nation. In the mean time the doctors and professors, who are placed in the various seminaries of learning, are left at liberty to instruct the youth in the ancient doctrine and discipline of the church, and to explain and inculcate those maxims and laws by which, in former times, the papal authority was restrained and confined within certain limits. If these laws and maxims are infringed, and if even violent methods are employed against those who firmly adhere to them, this happens very rarely, and never but when their suspension is required by some case of extreme necessity, or by the prospect of some great advantage to the community. Besides, those who sit at the political helm, always take care to prevent the pope's reaping much benefit from this suspension or neglect of the ancient laws and maxims of the church. This circumstance, which is of so much importance in the present question, must appear evident to such as will be at the pains to look into the history of the debates that attended, and the consequences that followed the reception of the *Bull Unigenitus* in France, than which no papal edict could seem more repugnant to the rights and liberties of the Gallican church. In the business of this bull, as in other transactions of a like nature, the court proceeded upon this political maxim, that a smaller evil is to be submitted to, when a greater may be thereby prevented.

In a word, the kings of France have almost always treated the Roman pontiffs as the heroes, who are said in pagan story to have descended into Tartarus, behaved toward the triple-jawed guardian of that lower region: sometimes they offered a soporiferous cake to suppress his grumbling and menacing tone; at others they terrified him with their naked swords, and the din of arms; and this with a view to stop his barking, and to obtain the liberty of directing their course in the manner they thought proper. There is nothing invidious designed by this comparison, which certainly represents, in a lively manner, the caresses and threatenings that were employed by the French monarchs, according to the nature of the times, the state of affairs, the characters of the pontiffs, and other incidental circumstances, in order to render the court of Rome favourable to their designs. We have dwelt, perhaps, too much upon this subject; but we thought it not improper to undeceive many protestant writers, who, too much in

☞ * It is scarcely necessary to inform the reader, that by these *liberties* we do not mean that rational and Christian liberty which entitles every individual to follow the light of his own conscience and the dictates of his own judgment in religious matters; for no such liberty is allowed in France. The liberties of the Gallican church consist in the opposition which that church has made, at different times, to the overgrown power of the Roman pontiff, and to his pretended *personal* infallibility.

☞ † Dr. Mosheim wrote this in 1753, before the suppression of the order of Jesuits in France. The downfall of that society, and the circumstances that attended it, seem both to illustrate and confirm his judicious notion with respect to the degree of credit and influence which the popes have had in that kingdom for some time past.

fluenced by the bitter complaints and declamations of certain Jansenists, and not sufficiently instructed in the history of these ecclesiastical contentions, have formed erroneous notions concerning that point which we have here endeavoured to examine and discuss.

XXIV. The corruptions that had been complained of in preceding ages, both in the higher and inferior orders of the Romish clergy, were rather increased than diminished during this century, as the most impartial writers of that communion candidly confess. The bishops were rarely indebted for their elevation to eminent learning, or superior merit. The intercession of potent patrons, services rendered to men in power, connexions of blood, and simoniacal practices, were, generally speaking, the steps to preferment; and, what was still more deplorable, their promotion was sometimes obtained by their vices. Their lives were such, as might be expected from persons who had risen in the church by such unseemly means; for, had they been obliged by their profession, to give public examples of those vices which the holy laws of the Gospel so solemnly and expressly condemn, instead of exhibiting patterns of sanctity and virtue to their flock, they could not have conducted themselves otherwise than they did.* Some indeed there were, who, sensible of the obligations of their profession, displayed a true Christian zeal, in administering useful instruction, and exhibiting pious examples to their flock, and exerted their utmost vigour and activity, in opposing the vices of the sacred order in particular, and the licentiousness of the times in general. But these rare cultivators of virtue and piety were either ruined by the resentment and stratagems of their envious and exasperated brethren, or were left in obscurity, without that encouragement and support which were requisite to enable them to execute effectually their pious and laudable purposes. The same treatment fell to the lot of those among the lower order of the clergy, who endeavoured to maintain the cause of truth and virtue. But the number of sufferers in this noble cause was small, compared with the multitude of corrupt ecclesiastics, who were carried away with the torrent, instead of opposing it, and whose lives were spent in scenes of pleasure, or in the anxiety and toils of avarice and ambition. While we acknowledge, that, among the bishops and inferior clergy, there were several exceptions from that general prevalence of immorality and licentiousness with which the sacred order was chargeable, it is also incumbent upon us to do justice to the merit of some of the Roman pontiffs, in this century, who used their most zealous endeavours to reform the manners of the clergy, or, at least, to oblige them to observe the rules of external decency in their conduct and conversation. It is however matter of surprise, that these pontiffs did not perceive the insurmountable obstacles to the success of their counsels, and the fruits of their wise and salutary edicts, that arose from the internal constitution of the Romish church, and the very nature of the papal government; for, if the pontiffs were even divinely inspired, and really infallible, yet, unless this inspiration and infallibility were attended with a miraculous power, and with the supernatural privilege of being present in many places at the same time, it is not conceivable how they should ever entertain a notion of the possibility of restoring or maintaining order, or good morals, among the prodigious multitude of persons of all classes and characters that are subject to their jurisdiction.

XXV. Though the monks, in several places, behaved with much more circumspection and decency than in former times, yet they had every where departed, in a great measure, from the spirit of their founders, and the primitive laws of their respective institutions About the commencement of this age, their convents and colleges made a most wretched and deplorable figure, as we learn from the accounts of the wisest and most learned, even of their own writers. But, in the progress of the century, several attempts were made to remove this disorder. Some wise and pious Benedictines, in France and other countries, reformed several monasteries of their order, and endeavoured to bring them back, as near as was possible, to the laws and discipline of their founders.* Their example was followed by the monks of Clugni, the Cistercians, the regular canons, the Dominicans, and Franciscans.† It is from this period that we are to date the division of the monastic orders into two general classes. One comprehends the reformed monks, who, reclaimed from that licentiousness and corruption of manners which had formerly dishonoured their societies, lead more strict and regular lives, and discover in their conduct a greater regard to the primitive laws of their order. The other is composed of the un-reformed orders, who, forgetting the spirit of their founders, and the rules of their institutes, spend their days in ease and pleasure, and have no taste for the austerities and hardships of the monastic life. The latter class is evidently the most numerous; and the majority, even of the reformed monks, not only fall short of that purity of manners which

* The reader may see these disagreeable accounts of the corruptions of the clergy confirmed by a great number of unexceptionable testimonies, drawn from the writings of the most eminent doctors of the Romish church, in the Memoires de Port Royal, tom. ii. p. 308.

* Le Bœuf, Memoires sur l'Histoire d'Auxerre, tom. ii p. 513, where an account is given of the first *reforms* made in the convents during this century.—See Martenne's Voyage Literaire de deux Benedictins, par. ii. p. 97.

† There is an account of all the convents reformed in this century, in Helyot's Histoire des Ordres, tom. v. vi. vii. to which, however, several interesting circumstances may be added, by consulting other writers. The reform of the monks of Clugni is amply described by the Benedictines, in the Gallia Christiana, tom. vii. p. 544. The same authors speak of the reform of the Regular Canons of St. Augustin, tom. vii. p. 778, 787, 790.—For an account of that of the Cistercians, see Mabillon's Annal. Benedict. tom. vi. p. 121; and the Voyage Literaire de deux Benedictins, tom. i. p. 7; tom. ii. p. 133, 229, 269, 303. The Cistercians were no sooner reformed, than they used their most zealous endeavours for the reformation of the whole society, (i. e. of the Benedictine order,) but in vain See Meaupou's Vie de l'Abbe de la Trappe. tom. i.

their rules enjoin, but are moreover gradually and imperceptibly relapsing into their former indolence and disorder.

XXVI. Among the reformed monks, a particular degree of attention is due to certain Benedictine societies, or congregations, who surpass all the other monastic orders, both in the excellence and utility of their rules and constitution, and in the zeal and perseverance with which they adhere to them. Of these societies the most distinguished is the congregation of St. Maur,* which was founded in 1620 by the express order of Gregory XV., and was enriched by Urban VIII. in 1627, with various donations and privileges. It does not indeed appear, that even this society adheres strictly to the spirit and maxims of Benedict, whose name it bears, nor is it beyond the reach of censure in other respects; but these imperfections are compensated by the great number of excellent rules and institutions that are observed in it, and by the regular lives and learned labours of its members. For, in this congregation, a select number of men of genius and talent are set apart for the study of sacred and profane literature, and more especially of history and antiquities; and these learned members are furnished with all the means and materials of knowledge in a rich abundance, and with every thing that can tend to facilitate their labours and render them successful.† It must be abundantly known, to those who have any acquaintance with the history and progress of learning in Europe, what signal advantages the republic of letters has derived from the establishment of this famous Congregation, whose numerous and admirable productions have cast a great light upon the various branches of philology and the *belles lettres*, and whose researches have embraced the whole circle of science, philosophy excepted.*

XXVII. Though these pious attempts to reform the monasteries were not entirely unsuccessful, yet the effects they produced, even in those places where they had succeeded most, came far short of that perfection of austerity that had seized the imaginations of a set of persons, whose number is considerable in the Romish church, though their credit be small, and their severity be generally looked upon as excessive and disgusting. These rigid censors, having always in their eyes the ancient discipline of the monastic orders, and being bent on reducing the modern convents to that austere discipline, looked upon the changes abovementioned as imperfect and trifling. They considered a monk as a person obliged, by the sanctity of his profession, to spend his whole time in prayer, tears, contemplation, and si-

* See the Gallia Christiana Nova, an admirable work, composed by the Congregation of St. Maur, tom. vii. p. 474.—Helyot, tom. vi. cap. xxxvii. p. 256. The letters patent of Gregory XV., by which the establishment of this famous congregation was approved and confirmed, were criticised with great severity and rigour by Launoy, that formidable scourge of all the monastic orders, in his Examen. Privil. S. Germani, tom. iii. p. i. op. p. 303. The same author, (in his Assert. Inquisit. in priv. S. Medardi, tom. iii. op.) gives an account of the dissentions that arose in this congregation, immediately after its establishment; but this account savours too much of that partiality with which he is chargeable, whenever he treats of monastic affairs.

† The Benedictines celebrate, in pompous terms, the exploits of this congregation in general, and more especially its zealous and successful labours in restoring order, discipline, and virtue, in a great number of monasteries, which were falling into ruin through the indolence and corruption of their licentious members; see the "Voyage de deux Religieux Benedictins de la Congregation de S. Maur," tom. i. p. 16; tom. ii. p. 47. This eulogy, though perhaps exaggerated, is not entirely unmerited; and there is no doubt that the Benedictines have contributed much to restore the credit of the monastic orders. There are, nevertheless, several classes of ecclesiastics in the Romish church, who are no well-wishers to this learned congregation, though their dislike be founded on different reasons. In the first class, we may place a certain number of ambitious prelates, whose artful purposes have been disappointed by this ingenious fraternity; for the monks of St. Maur, having turned their principal study toward ancient history and antiquities of every kind, and being perfectly acquainted with ancient records, diplomas, and charters, are thus peculiarly qualified to maintain their possessions, their jurisdictions, and privileges, against the litigious pretensions of the bishops, and have, in fact, maintained them with more success than their order could do in former times, when destitute of learning, or ill furnished with the knowledge of ancient history. The Jesuits form the second class of adversaries, with whom this learned congregation has been obliged to struggle; for, their lustre and reputation being considerably eclipsed by the numerous and admirable productions of these Benedictines, they have used their utmost endeavours to sink, or at least to diminish, the credit of such formidable rivals. See Simon's Lettres Choisies, tom. iv. p. 36, 45. These Benedictines have a third set of enemies, who are instigated by superstition; and it is not improbable that this superstition may be accompanied with a certain mixture of envy. To understand this fully, it must be observed, that the learned monks, of whom we are now speaking, have substituted an assiduous application to the culture of philology and literature in the place of that bodily and manual labour, which the rule of St. Benedict prescribes to his followers. The more robust, healthy, and vigorous monks, indeed, are obliged to employ a certain portion of the day in working with their hands; but those of a weaker constitution and superior genius, are allowed to exchange bodily for mental labour, and, instead of cultivating the lands or gardens of the convent, to spend their days in the pursuit of knowledge, both human and divine. The lazy monks envy this bodily repose; and the superstitious and fanatical ones, who are vehemently prejudiced in favour of the ancient monastic discipline, behold with contempt these learned researches as unbecoming the monastic character, since they tend to divert the mind from divine contemplation. This superstitious and absurd opinion was maintained with peculiar warmth and vehemence, by Armand John Bouthillier de Rance, Abbot of La Trappe, in his book des Devoirs Monastiques; upon which the Benedictines employed Mabillon, the most learned of their fraternity, to defend their cause, and to expose the reveries of the abbot in their proper colours. This he did with remarkable success, in his famous book, de Studiis Monasticis, which was published in 1691, passed through many editions, and was translated into different languages. Hence arose that celebrated question, which was long debated with great warmth and animosity in France;—"How far a monk may, consistently with his character, apply himself to the study of literature?" There is an elegant and interesting history of this controversy given by Vincent Thuillier, a most learned monk of the congregation of St. Maur; see the Opera Posthuma of Mabillon and Ruinart, tom. i. p. 365—425.

* The curious reader will find an account of the authors and learned productions with which the congregation of St. Maur has enriched the republic of letters, in Ph. le Cerf's Bibliotheque Historique et Critique des Auteurs de la Congregation de St. Maur and also in Bernard Pez's Bibliotheca Benedictino Maurina.—These Benedictines still maintain their literary fame by the frequent publications of laborious and learned works both in sacred and profane literature.

lence; in the perusal of holy books, and the hardships of bodily labour: they even went so far as to maintain, that all other designs and occupations, however laudable and excellent in themselves, were entirely foreign from the monastic vocation, and, on that account, vain and sinful in persons of that order. This severe plan of monastic discipline was recommended by several persons, whose obscurity put it out of their power to influence many in its behalf; but it was also adopted by the Jansenists, who reduced it to practice in some parts of France,* and in none with more success and reputation than in the female convent of Port Royal, where it has subsisted from the year 1618 to our time.† These steps of the Jansenists excited a spirit of emulation, and several monasteries exerted themselves in the imitation of this austere model; but they were all surpassed by the famous Bouthillier de Rance, abbot de la Trappe,‡ who, with the most ardent zeal, and indefatigable labour, attended with uncommon success, introduced into his monastery this discipline, in all its austere and shocking perfection. This abbot, so illustrious by his birth, and so remarkable for his extraordinary devotion, was so happy as to vindicate his fraternity from the charge of excessive superstition, which the Jansenists had drawn upon themselves by the austerity of their monastic discipline; and yet his society observed the severe and laborious rule of the ancient Cistercians, whom they even surpassed in abstinence, mortifications, and self-denial. This order still subsists, under the denomination of the Reformed Bernardins of La Trappe, and has several monasteries both in Spain and Italy; but, if credit may be given to the accounts of writers who seem to be well informed, it is degenerating gradually from the austere and painful discipline of its famous founder.*

* See the Memoires de Port Royal, tom. ii. p. 601. Martin Barcos, the most celebrated Jansenist of this century, introduced this austere rule of discipline into the monastery of St. Cyran, of which he was abbot. See the Gallia Christiana, tom. ii. p. 132, and Moleon's Voyages Liturgiques, p. 135; but, after the death of this famous abbot, the monks of his cloister relapsed into their former disorder, and resumed their former manners. See the Voyage de deux Benedictins, tom. i.

† Helyot, tom. v. chap. xliv. p. 455.

‡ This illustrious abbot showed very early an extraordinary genius for the *belles lettres*. At the age of ten, he was master of several of the Greek and Roman poets, and understood Homer perfectly. At the age of twelve or thirteen, he gave an edition of Anacreon, with learned annotations. Some writers alleged, that he had imbibed the voluptuous spirit of that poet, and that his subsequent application to the study of theology in the Sorbonne did not entirely extinguish it. They also attribute his conversion to a singular incident. They tell us, that returning from the country, after six weeks' absence from a lady whom he loved passionately, (and not in vain,) he went directly to her chamber by a back-stair, without having the patience to make any previous inquiry about her health and situation. On opening the door, he found the chamber illuminated, and hung with black; and, on approaching the bed, saw the most hideous spectacle that could be presented to his eyes, and the most adapted to mortify passion, inspire horror, and engender the gloom of melancholy devotion, in a mind too lively and too much agitated to improve this shocking change to the purposes of rational piety; he saw his fair mistress in her shroud—dead of the small pox—all her charms fled—and succeeded by the ghastly lines of death, and the frightful marks of that terrible disorder. From that moment, it is said, our abbot retired from the world, repaired to La Trappe, the most gloomy, barren, and desolate spot in the whole kingdom of France, and there spent the forty last years of his life in perpetual acts of the most austere piety

XXVIII. The Romish church, from whose prolific womb all the various forms of superstition issued forth in an amazing abundance, saw several new monastic establishments arise within its borders during this century. The greatest part of them we shall pass over in silence, and confine ourselves to the mention of those which have obtained some degree of fame.

We begin with the Fathers of the Oratory of the Holy Jesus, a famous order, instituted by cardinal Berulle, a man of genius and talents, who displayed his abilities with such success, in the service both of state and church, that he was generally looked upon as equally qualified for shining in these very different spheres. This order, which, both in the nature of its rules, and in the design of its establishment, seems to be in direct opposition to that of the Jesuits, was founded in 1613, has produced a considerable number of persons eminent for their piety, learning, and eloquence, and still maintains its reputation in this respect. Its members however have, on account of certain theological productions, been suspected of introducing new opinions; and this suspicion has not only been raised but is also industriously fomented and propagated by the Jesuits. The priests who enter into this society are not obliged to renounce their property or possessions, but only to refuse all ecclesiastical cures or offices to which any fixed revenues or honours are annexed, as long as they continue members of this fraternity, from which they are, however, at liberty to retire whenever they think proper.† While they continue in the order, they are bound to perform, with the greatest fidelity and accuracy, all the priestly functions, and to turn the whole bent of their zeal and industry to one point, namely, the task of preparing and qualifying themselves and others for discharging them daily with greater perfection and more abundant fruits. If, therefore, we consider this order in the original end of its institution, its convents may, not improperly, be called the schools of *sacerdotal divinity*.‡ It is nevertheless to be observed, that, in later times, the Fathers of the Oratory have not confined themselves to this object, but have imperceptibly extended their original plan, and applied themselves to the

* Marsolier's Vie de l'Abbe de la Trappe.—Meaupou's Vie de M. l'Abbe de la Trappe.—Felibien's Descrip. de l'Ab. de la Trappe.—Helyot, t. vi.

☞ † The Fathers, or Priests (as they also are called) of the Oratory, are not, properly speaking religious, or monks, being bound by no vows, and their institute being purely ecclesiastical or sacerdotal.

‡ See Hubert de Cerisi, Vie du Cardinal Berulle, Fondateur de l'Oratoire de Jesus.—Morini Vita Antiq. prefixed to his Orientalia, p. 3, 110.—R. Simon, Lettres Choisies, tom. ii. p. 60, and his Bibliotheque Critique, (published under the fictitious name of Saint Jorre,) tom. iii. p. 303, 324, 330. For an account of the genius and capacity of Berulle, see Baillet's Vie de Richer, p. 220, 342.—Le Vassor's Histoire de Louis XIII. tom. iii. p. 397.—Helyot, tom. viii. chap. x.—Gallia Christiana Benedictinorum, tom. vii. p. 976.

study of polite literature and theology, which they teach with reputation in their colleges.*

After these Fathers, the next place is due to the Priests of the Missions; an order founded by Vincent de Paul, (who obtained, not long ago, the honours of saintship,) and formed into a regular congregation, in 1632, by pope Urban VIII. The rule prescribed to this society, by its founder, lays its members under the three following obligations: first, to purify themselves, and to aspire daily to higher degrees of sanctity and perfection, by prayer, meditation, the perusal of pious books, and other devout exercises; secondly, to employ eight months in the year in the villages, and, in general, among the country people, in order to instruct them in the principles of religion, form them to the practice of piety and virtue, accommodate their differences, and administer consolation and relief to the sick and indigent; thirdly, to inspect and govern the seminaries in which persons designed for holy orders receive their education, and to instruct the candidates for the ministry, in the sciences that relate to their respective vocations.†

The Priests of the Missions were also intrusted with the direction and government of a female order called Virgins of Love, or Daughters of Charity, whose office it was to administer assistance and relief to indigent persons, who were confined to their beds by sickness and infirmity. This order was founded by a noble virgin, whose name was Louisa le Gras, and received, in 1660, the approbation of Clement IX.‡ The Brethren and Sisters of the pious and Christian schools, who are now commonly called Pietists, were formed into a society in 1678, by Nicolas Barre, and obliged by their engagements to devote themselves to the education of poor children of both sexes.§ It would be endless to mention all the religious societies which rose and fell, were formed by fits of zeal, and dissolved by external incidents, or by their own internal principles of instability and decay.

XXXI. If the Company of Jesus, which may be considered as the soul of the papal hierarchy, and the main-spring that directs its motions, had not been invincible, it must have sunk under the attacks of those formidable enemies, who, during the course of this century assailed it on all sides and from every quarter. When we consider the multitude of the adversaries the Jesuits had to encounter, the heinous crimes with which they were charged, the innumerable affronts they received, and the various calamities in which they were involved, it must appear astonishing that they yet subsist; and still more so, that they enjoy any degree of public esteem, and are not, on the contrary, sunk in oblivion, or covered with infamy. In France, Holland, Poland, and Italy, they experienced, from time to time, the bitter effects of a warm and vehement opposition, and were, both in public and private, accused of the greatest enormities, and charged with maintaining pestilential errors and maxims, that were equally destructive of the temporal and eternal interests of mankind, by their tendency to extinguish the spirit of true religion, and to trouble the order and peace of civil society. The Jansenists, and all who espoused their cause, distinguished themselves more especially in this opposition. They composed an innumerable multitude of books, in order to cover the sons of Loyola with eternal reproach, and to expose them to the hatred and scorn of the universe. Nor were these productions mere defamatory libels dictated by malice alone, or pompous declamations, destitute of argument and evidence. On the contrary, they were attended with the strongest demonstration, being drawn from undeniable facts, and confirmed by unexceptionable testimonies.* Yet all this was

☞ * *The Fathers of the Oratory* will now be obliged, in a more particular manner, to extend their plan, since, by the suppression of the Jesuits in France, the education of youth is committed to them.

† Abely's Vie de Vincent de Paul.—Helyot, tom. viii. chap. xi.—Gallia Christiana, tom. vii. p. 998.

‡ Gobillon's Vie de Madame le Gras, Fondatrice des Filles de la Charite, published at *Paris*, in 1676.

§ Helyot's Histoire des Ordres, tom. viii. chap. xxx.

* An account of this opposition to, and of these contests with the Jesuits, would furnish matter for many volumes, since there is scarcely any Roman catholic country which has not been the theatre of violent divisions between the sons of Loyola, and the magistrates, monks, or doctors, of the Romish church. In these contests, the Jesuits seemed almost always to be vanquished; and, nevertheless, in the issue, they always came victorious from the field of controversy. A Jansenist writer proposed, some years ago, to collect into one relation the dispersed accounts of these contests, and to give a complete history of this famous order. The first volume of his work accordingly appeared at Utrecht, in 1741, was accompanied with a curious preface, and entitled, Histoire des Religieux de la Compagnie de Jesus. If we may give credit to what this writer tells us of the journeys he undertook, the dangers and difficulties he encountered, and the number of years he spent in investigating the proceedings, and in detecting the frauds and artifices of the Jesuits, we must certainly be persuaded, that no man could be better qualified for composing the history of this insidious order. But this good man, returning imprudently into France, was discovered by his exasperated enemies the Jesuits, and is said to have perished miserably by their hands. Hence not above a third part of his intended work was either published, or finished for the press. ☞ Some things may be added, both by way of correction and illustration, to what Dr. Mosheim has here said concerning the history of the Jesuits and its author. In the first place, its author or compiler is still alive, resides at the Hague, passes by the name of Benard, is supposed to be a Jansenist, and a relative of the famous Father Quesnel whom the Jesuits persecuted with such violence in France. He is a native of France, and belonged to the oratory. It is also true that he went thither from Holland several years ago; and it was believed, that he had fallen a victim to the resentment of the Jesuits, until his return to the Hague proved that report false. Secondly, this history is carried no farther down than the year 1572, notwithstanding the express promises and engagements, by which our author bound himself, four and twenty years ago,* (in the preface to his first volume,) to publish the whole in a very short time, declaring that it was ready for the press. This suspension is far from being honourable to M. Benard, as he is at full liberty to accomplish his promise. This has made some suspect, that, though he is too much out of the Jesuits' reach to be influenced by their threatenings, he is not too far from them to be moved by the eloquence of their promises, or sufficiently firm and resolute to stand out against the weighty remonstrances they may have employed to prevent the farther publication of his history. It may be observed, thirdly, that the character of a traveller, who has studied the manners and conduct of the Jesuits in the most remarkable scenes of their transactions in Europe, and

* The translator wrote this note in 1765

far from overturning that fabric of profound and insidious policy which the Jesuits had raised, under the protection of the Roman pontiffs, and the connivance of deluded princes and nations. It seemed, on the contrary, as if the opposition of such a multitude of enemies and accusers had strengthened their interest instead of diminishing it, and added to their affluence and prosperity, instead of bringing on their destruction. Amidst the storm that threatened them with a fatal shipwreck, they directed their course with the utmost dexterity, tranquillity and prudence. Thus they safely reached the desired harbour, and rose to the very summit of spiritual authority in the church of Rome. Avoiding, rather than repelling the assault of their enemies, opposing, for the most part, patience and silence to their redoubled insults, they proceeded uniformly and steadily to their great purpose, and they seemed to have attained it. For those very nations who formerly looked upon a Jesuit as a kind of monster, and as a public pest, commit, at this day, some through necessity, some through choice, and others through both, a great part of their interests and transactions to the direction of this most artful and powerful society.*

XXX. All the different branches of literature received, during this century, in the more polished Roman Catholic countries, a new degree of lustre and improvement. France, Spain, Italy, and the Netherlands, produced several men eminent for their genius, erudition, and acquaintance with the learned languages. This happy circumstance must not, however, be attributed to the labour of the schools, or to the methods and procedure of public education; for the old, dry, perplexing, inelegant, scholastic method of instruction prevailed then, and indeed still takes place in both the higher and lower seminaries of learning; and it is the peculiar tendency of this method to damp genius, to depress (instead of exciting and encouraging) the generous efforts of the mind toward the pursuit of truth, and to load the memory with a multitude of insignificant words and useless distinctions. It was beyond the borders of these pedantic seminaries, that genius was encouraged, and directed by great and eminent patrons of science, who opened new paths to the attainment of solid learning, and presented the sciences under a new and engaging aspect to the studious youth. It must be observed here, in justice to the French, that they bore a distinguished part in this literary reformation. Excited by their native force of genius, and animated by the encouragement which learning and learned men received from the munificence of Louis XIV., they cultivated with success almost every branch of literature, and, rejecting the barbarous jargon of the schools, exhibited learning under an elegant and alluring form, and thereby multiplied the number of its votaries and patrons.* It is well known how much the example and labours of this polite nation contributed to deliver other countries from the yoke of scholastic bondage.

XXXI. The Aristotelians of this century were a set of intricate dialecticians, who had the name of the Stagirite always in their mouths, without the least portion of his genius, or any tolerable knowledge of his system; and they maintained their empire in the schools, notwithstanding the attempts that had been made to diminish their credit. It was long before the court of Rome, which beheld with terror whatever bore the smallest aspect of novelty, could think of consenting to the introduction of a more rational philosophy, or permit the modern discoveries in that noble science to be explained with freedom in the public seminaries of learning. This appears sufficiently from the fate of Galileo, the famous mathematician of Florence, who was cast into prison by the court of Inquisition, for adopting the sentiments of Copernicus, with regard to the constitution of the solar system. It is true, that Des-Cartes and Gassendi,† one by his new philosophy, and the other by his admirable writings, gave a mortal wound to the Peripatetics, and excited a spirit of liberty and emulation that changed the face of science in France. It was under the auspicious influence of these adventurous guides, that several ingenious men of that nation abandoned the perplexed and intricate wilds of the philosophy that was taught by the modern Aristotelians; and, throwing off the shackles of mere authority, dared to consult the dictates of reason and experience, in the study of nature, and in the investigation of truth. Among these converts to

the other parts of the globe, is here assumed by M. Benard as the most pleasing manner of conveying the accounts which he compiled in his closet. These accounts do not appear to be false, though the character of a traveller, assumed by the compiler, be fictitious. It must be allowed, on the contrary, that M. Benard has drawn his relations from good sources, though his style and manner cannot well be justified from the charge of acrimony and malignity.

* It may perhaps be affirmed with truth, that none of the Roman catholic nations attacked the Jesuits with more vehemence and animosity than the French did upon several occasions; and it is certain, that the Jesuits in that kingdom have been, more than once, involved in great difficulties and distress. To be convinced of this, the reader has only to consult Du-Boulay's Hist. Academiæ Parisiensis, tom. vi. page 559, 648, 676, 738, 742, 763, 874, 890, 909, in which he will find an ample and accurate account of the resolutions and transactions of the parliament and university of Paris, and also of the proceedings of the people in general, to the detriment of this artful and dangerous society. But what was the final issue of all these resolutions and transactions, and in what did all this opposition end? I answer, in the exaltation and grandeur of the Jesuits. They had been banished with ignominy out of the kingdom, and were recalled from their exile, and honourably restored to their former credit in 1604, in the reign of Henry IV., notwithstanding the remonstrances of many persons of the highest rank and dignity, who were shocked beyond expression at this unaccountably mean and ignoble step, (see the Memoires de Sully, modern edition, published at Geneva, tom. v. p. 83, 314.) After that period, they moved the mainsprings of government both in church and state, and still continue to sit, though invisibly, at the helm of both. ☞ The reader must be reminded, that this note was written by Dr. Mosheim some years before the suppression of the society of Jesuits in France.

* For an ample account of this matter, see Voltaire's Siecle de Louis XIV. and more especially the chapter in the second volume relative to the arts and sciences.

† See Gassendi Exercitationes Paradoxæ adversus Aristoteleos, tom. iii. op. This subtle and judicious work contributed, perhaps more than any thing else to hurt the cause and ruin the credit, of the Peripatetic*

true philosophy, several Jesuits, and a still greater number of Jansenists and priests of the Oratory, distinguished themselves; and, accordingly, we find in this list the respectable names of Malebranche, Arnauld, Lami, Nicole, Pascal, who acquired immortal fame by illustrating and improving the doctrine of Des-Cartes, and accommodating it to the purposes of human life.* The modesty, circumspection, and self-diffidence of Gassendi, who confessed the scanty measure of his knowledge, and pretended to no other merit than that of pointing out a rational method of arriving at truth, while others boasted that they had already found it out, rendered him disagreeable in France. The ardent curiosity, the fervour, precipitation, and impatience of that lively people, could not bear the slow and cautious method of proceeding that was recommended by the cool wisdom of this prudent inquirer. They wanted to get at the summit of philosophy, without climbing the steps that lead to it.

Toward the conclusion of this century, many eminent men, in Italy and in other countries, followed the example of the French, in throwing off the yoke of the Peripatetics, and venturing into the paths that were newly opened for the investigation of truth. This desertion of the old philosophy was at first attended with that timidity and secrecy which arose from apprehensions of the displeasure and resentment of the court of Rome; but, as soon as it was known that the pontiffs beheld, with less indignation and jealousy, the new discoveries in metaphysics, mathematics, and natural philosophy, the deserters broke their chains with greater confidence, and proceeded with greater freedom and boldness in the pursuit of truth.

XXXII. After this general account of the state of learning in the catholic countries, it will not be improper to point out, in a more particular manner, those Romish writers, who contributed most to the propagation and improvement both of sacred and profane erudition during this century. The Jesuits, for a long time, not only possessed an undisputed pre-eminence in this respect, but were, moreover, considered as almost the sole fountains of universal knowledge, and the only religious order that made any great figure in the literary world. And it must be allowed by all, who are not misled by want of candour or of proper information, that this famous society was adorned by many persons of uncommon genius and learning. The names of Petau, Sirmond, Poussin, Labbe, and Abram, will live as long as literature shall be honoured and valued; and even that of Hardouin, notwithstanding the singularity of his disordered fancy, and the extravagance of many of his opinions, will escape oblivion.

It is at the same time to be observed, that the literary glory of the Jesuits suffered a remarkable eclipse in this century, from the growing lustre of the Benedictine order, and more especially of the Congregation of St. Maur. The Jesuits were perpetually boasting of the eminent merit and lustre of their society on the one hand, and exposing, on the other, to public contempt, the ignorance and stupidity of the Benedictines, who, indeed, formerly made a very different figure from what they do at present. Their view in this was to form a plausible pretext for invading the rights of the latter, and engrossing their ample revenues and possessions; but the Benedictines resolved to disconcert this insidious project, to wipe off the reproach of ignorance that had heretofore been cast upon them with too much justice, and to disappoint the rapacious avidity of their enemies, and rob them of their pretexts. For this purpose they not only erected schools in their monasteries, for the instruction of youth in the various branches of learning and science, but also employed such of their select members, as were distinguished by their erudition and genius, in composing a variety of learned productions that were likely to survive the waste of time, adapted to vindicate the honour of the fraternity, and to reduce its enemies to silence. This important task was executed with incredible ability and success by Mabillon, D'Achery, Massuet, Ruinart, Beaugendre, Garnier, De la Rue, Martenne, Montfaucon, and other eminent men of that learned order It is to these Benedictines that we are indebted for the best editions of the Greek and Latin fathers; for the discovery of many curious records, and ancient documents, that throw a new light upon the history of remote ages, and upon the antiquities of various countries; for the best accounts of ancient transactions, whether ecclesiastical or political, and of the manners and customs of the earliest times; for the improvement of chronology, and the other branches of literature. In all these parts of philology and the belles lettres, the religious order, now under consideration, has shone with a distinguished lustre, and given specimens of knowledge, discernment, and industry, that are worthy of being transmitted to the latest posterity. It would be perhaps difficult to assign a reason for that visible decline of learning among the Jesuits, which commenced precisely at the very period when the Benedictines began to make this eminent figure in the republic of letters. The fact, however is undeniable; and the Jesuits have long been at a loss to produce any one or more of their members who are qualified to dispute the pre eminence, or even to claim an equality, with the Benedictines. The latter still continue to shine in the various branches of philology, and, almost every year, enrich the literary world with productions that furnish abundant proofs of their learning and industry; whereas, if we except a single work published by the Jesuits of Antwerp, (the Acts of the Saints,) many

* These great men were, indeed, very ill treated by the Peripatetics, on account of their learned and excellent labours. They were accused, by these exasperated scholastics, of irreligion, and were even charged with atheism by father Hardouin, who was really intoxicated with the large draughts he had taken from the muddy fountains of Peripatetic and scholastic science. See his Athei Detecti, in his Op. Posthum.—It is easy to perceive the reasons of all this resentment, since the Cartesian system, which aimed at restoring the authority of reason, and the light of true philosophy, was by no means so proper to defend the pretensions of Rome and the cause of popery, as the dark and intricate jargon of the Peripatetics.

years have passed since the sons of Loyola have given any satisfactory proofs of their boasted learning, or added to the mass of literature any work worthy to be compared with the labours of the followers of Benedict.

These learned monks excited the emulation of the Priests of the Oratory, whose efforts to resemble them were far from being destitute of success. Several members of the latter order distinguished themselves by their remarkable proficiency in various branches both of sacred and profane literature. This, to mention no more examples, appears sufficiently from the writings of Morin, Thomassin, and Simon, and from that admirable work of Charles le Cointe, entitled, The Ecclesiastical Annals of France. The Jansenists also deserve a place in the list of those who cultivated letters with industry and success. Many of their productions abound with erudition, and several of them excel both in elegance of style and precision of method; and it may be said, in general, that their writings were eminently serviceable in the instruction of youth, and also proper to contribute to the progress of learning among persons of riper years. The writings of those who composed the community of Port-Royal,* the works of Tillemont, Arnauld, Nicole, Pascal, and Lancelot, with many other elegant and useful productions of persons of this class, were undoubtedly an ornament to French literature during this century. The other religious societies, the higher and lower orders of the clergy, had also among them men of learning and genius, who reflected a lustre upon the respective classes to which they belonged. Nor ought this to be a matter of astonishment, since nothing is more natural than that, in an immense multitude of monks and clergy, all possessing abundant leisure for study, and the best opportunities of improvement, there should be some who, unwilling to hide or throw away such a precious talent, would employ with success this leisure, and these opportunities, in the cultivation of the sciences. It is nevertheless certain, that the eminent men who were to be found beyond the limits of the four classes already mentioned,† were few in number, comparatively speaking, and scarcely exceeded the list that any one of these classes could furnish.

XXXIII. Hence it comes, that the church of Rome can produce a long list of writers who have arisen in its bosom, and acquired a shining and permanent reputation by their learned productions. At the head of the eminent authors, found among the monastic orders and the regular clergy, must be placed the cardinals Baronius and Bellermine, who have obtained an immortal name in their church, one by his laborious Annals, and the other by his books of controversy. The other writers who belong to this class, are, Serrarius, Fevardentius, Possevin, Gretser, Combefis, Natalis Alexander, Becan, Sirmond, Petau, Poussin, Cellot, Caussin, Morin, Renaud, Fra-Paolo, Pallavicini, Labbe, Maimbourg, Thomassin, Sfondrati, Aguirre, Henry Norris, D'Achery, Mabillon, Hardouin, Simon, Ruinart, Montfaucon, Galloni, Scacchi, Cornelius à Lapide, Bonfrere, Menard, Seguenot, Bernard, Lamy, Bolland, Henschen, Papebroch, and others.

The principal among the secular clergy, who are neither bound by vows, nor attached to any peculiar community and rules of discipline, were, Perron, Estius, Launoy, Albaspinæus, Peter de Marca, Richelieu, Holstenius, Baluze, Bona, Huet, Bossuet, Fenelon, Godeau, Tillemont, Thiers, Du-Pin, Leo Allatius, Zaccagnia, Cotelier, Filesac, Visconti, &c.* This list might be considerably augmented by adding to it those writers among the laity who distinguished themselves by their theological or literary productions.

XXXIV. If we take an accurate view of the religious system of the Romish church during this century, both with respect to articles of faith and rules of practice, we shall find that, instead of being improved by being brought nearer to the perfect model of doctrine and morals, exhibited to us in the Holy Scriptures, it had contracted new degrees of corruption and degeneracy, partly by the negligence of the pontiffs, and partly by the dangerous maxims and influence of the Jesuits. This is not only the observation of those who have renounced the Romish communion, and in the despotic style of that church are called heretics; it is the complaint of the wisest and worthiest part of that communion, of all its members who have a zeal for the advancement of true Christian knowledge and genuine piety.

As to the doctrinal part of the Romish religion, it is said, and not without foundation, to have suffered extremely in the hands of the Jesuits, who, under the connivance, and sometimes even by the immediate assistance of the pontiffs, have perverted and corrupted such of the fundamental doctrines of Christianity as were left entire by the council of Trent. There are proofs sufficient to support this charge; inasmuch as the subtle and insidious fathers have manifestly endeavoured to diminish the authority and importance of the Scriptures, have extolled the power of human nature, changed the sentiments of many with respect to the necessity and efficacy of divine grace, represented the mediation and sufferings of Christ as less powerful and meritorious than they are said to be in the sacred writings, turned the Roman pontiff into a terrestrial Deity, and put him almost upon an equal footing with the Divine Saviour; and, finally, have rendered, as far as they can, the truth of the Christian religion dubious, by their fallacious reasonings, and their artful and pernicious sophistry. The testimonies adduced to support these accusations by men of weight and merit, particularly among the Jansenists, are of very great autho-

* The denomination of Messieurs de Port-Royal comprehended all the Jansenist writers; but it was applied, in a more confined and particular sense, to those Jansenists who passed their days in pious exercises and literary pursuits in the retreat of Port-Royal, a mansion situated near Paris. It is well known, that several writers of superior genius, extensive learning, and uncommon eloquence, resided in this sanctuary of letters.

† The Jesuits, Benedictines Priests of the Oratory, and Jansenists.

* For a particular account of the respective merit of the writers here mentioned, see Du-Pin's His. des Ecrevains Eccles. t. xvii. xviii. xix.

rity; and it is extremely difficult to refuse our assent to them, when they are impartially examined: but, on the other hand, it may be easily proved, that the Jesuits, instead of inventing these pernicious doctrines, did no more, in reality, than propagate them as they found them in that ancient system of religion which preceded the Reformation, and was directly calculated to raise the authority of the pope, and the power and prerogatives of the church, to the highest pitch of despotic grandeur. To inculcate this form of doctrine was the direct vocation of the Jesuits, who were to derive all their credit, opulence, and influence, from their being considered as the main support of the papacy, and the peculiar favourites of the pontiffs. If the ultimate end and purpose of these pontiffs were to render the church more pure and holy, and to bring it as near as possible to the resemblance of its Divine Founder, and if this were the commission they gave to their favourite emissaries the doctors, then the Jesuits would be at liberty to preach a very different doctrine from what they now inculcate. But that liberty cannot be granted to them as long as their principal orders from the papal throne are, to use all their diligence and industry, to the end that the pontiffs may hold what they have acquired, and recover what they have lost, and that the bishops and other ministers of the church may daily see their opulence increase, and the limits of their authority extended and enlarged. The chief crime then of the Jesuits is really this, that they have explained, with more openness and perspicuity, those points which the leading managers in the council of Trent had either entirely omitted, or slightly mentioned, that they might not shock the friends of true religion, who composed a part of that famous assembly. And here we see the true reason why the pontiffs, notwithstanding the ardent solicitations and remonstrances that have been employed to arm their just severity against the Jesuits, have always maintained that artful order, and have been so deaf to the accusations of their adversaries, that no entreaties have been able to persuade them to condemn their religious principles and tenets, however erroneous in their nature, and pernicious in their effects. On the contrary, the court of Rome has always opposed, either in a public or clandestine manner, all the vigourous measures that have been used to procure the condemnation and suppression of the doctrine of the Jesuits; and it has constantly treated all such attempts as the projects of rash and imprudent men, who, through involuntary ignorance or obstinate prejudice, were blind to the true interest of the church.

XXXV. In the sphere of morals, the Jesuits made still more dreadful and atrocious inroads than in that of religion. In affirming that they have perverted and corrupted almost every branch and precept of morality, we should not express sufficiently the pernicious tendency of their maxims. Were we to go still farther, and maintain, that they have sapped and destroyed its very foundations, we should maintain no more than what innumerable writers of the Romish church abundantly testify, and what many of the most illustrious communities of that church publicly lament. Those who bring this dreadful charge against the sons of Loyola, have taken abundant precautions to vindicate themselves from the reproach of calumny They have published several maxims, inconsistent with all regard for virtue and even decency, which they have drawn from the moral writings of that order, and more especially from the numerous productions of its casuists. They observe, more particularly, that the whole society adopts and inculcates the following maxims:

"That persons truly wicked, and void of the love of God, may expect to obtain eternal life in heaven, provided that they be impressed with a fear of the divine anger, and avoid all heinous and enormous crimes through the dread of future punishment.

"That those persons may transgress with safety, who have a probable reason for transgressing, i. e. any plausible argument or authority in favour of the sin they are inclined to commit.*

"That actions intrinsically evil, and directly contrary to the divine laws, may be innocently performed, by those who have so much power over their own minds, as to join, even ideally, a good end to this wicked action, or (to speak in the style of the Jesuits) who are capable of rightly directing their intention.†

"That philosophical sin is of a very light

☞ * This is one of the most corrupt and most dangerous maxims of the Jesuits. On one hand, they have among them doctors of different characters and different principles, that thus they may render their society recommendable in the eyes of all sorts of persons, the licentious as well as the austere. On the other, they maintain, that an opinion or practice, recommended by any one doctor, becomes thereby probable, as it is not to be supposed, that a learned divine would adopt an opinion, or recommend a practice, in favour of which no considerable reason could be alleged.—But here lies the poison: this probable opinion or practice *may* be followed, say the Jesuits, when the contrary is still more probable, and even when it is *sure*, because, though the man may err, he errs under the authority of an eminent doctor. Thus Escobar affirms, that a judge may decide in favour of that side of a question which is the least probable, and even against his own opinion, if he be supported by any tolerable authority. See the viiith of the Lettres Provinciales.

☞ † For example, an ecclesiastic who buys a benefice, in order to direct his intention rightly, must, by a powerful act of abstraction, turn away his thoughts from the crime of simony, which he is committing, to some lawful purpose, such as that of acquiring an ample subsistence, or that of doing good by instructing the ignorant. Thus again, a man who runs his neighbour through the body in a duel, on account of a trivial affront, to render his action lawful, has only to turn his thoughts from the principal of vengeance, to the more decent principal of honour, and the murder he commits will, by the magic power of Jesuitical morality, be converted into an innocent action. There is no crime or enormity to which this abominable maxim may not be extended. "A famous Jesuit has declared, that a son may wish for the death of his father, and even rejoice at it when it arrives, provided that his wish does not arise from any personal hatred, but only from a desire of the patrimony which this death will procure him." See Gaspard Hurtado, de sub. peccat. definit. 9, quoted by Diana, p. 5. tr. 14. R. 99. and another has had the effrontery to maintain, that a monk or ecclesiastic may lawfully assassinate a calumniator, who threatens to impute scandalous crimes to their community, when there is no other way of preventing the execution of his purpose. See the works of Father L'Amy, tom. v. disp. 36 n. 118.

and trivial nature, and does not deserve the pains of hell:—By philosophical sin the Jesuists mean an action contrary to the dictates of nature and right reason, done by a person who is ignorant of the written law of God, or doubtful* of its true meaning.

"That the transgressions committed by a person blinded by the seduction of lust, agitated by the impulse of tumultuous passions, and destitute of all sense and impression of religion, however detestable and heinous they may be in themselves, are not imputable to the transgressor before the tribunal of God; and that such transgressions may often be as involuntary as the actions of a madman:

"That the person who takes an oath, or enters into a contract, may, to elude the force of the one, and the obligation of the other, add, to the form of words by which they are expressed, certain mental additions and tacit reservations."

These, and other enormities of a like nature,† are said to make an essential part of the system of morality inculcated by the Jesuits. And they were complained of, in the strongest remonstrances, not only by the Dominicans and Jansenists, but also by the most eminent theologians of Paris, Poictiers, Louvain, and other academical cities, who expressed their abhorrence of them in such a public and solemn manner, that the pontiff neither thought it safe nor honourable to keep silence on that head. Accordingly some of these maxims were condemned, in 1659, by Pope Alexander VII. in a public edict; and, in 1690, the article relating to philosophical sin met with the same fate, under the pontificate of Alexander VIII.* It was natural to think, that, if the order of Jesuits did not expire under the terrible blows it received from such a formidable list of adversaries, yet their system of morals must at least have been suppressed, and their pestilential maxims banished from the schools This is the least that could have been expected from the complaints and remonstrances of the clerical and monastic orders, and the damnatory bulls of the pontiffs. And yet, if we may credit the testimonies of many learned and pious men in the communion of Rome, even this effect was not produced; and the remonstrances of the monks, the complaints of the clergy, and the bulls of the popes, rather served to restrain, in a certain measure, the enormous licentiousness that had reigned

☞ * It would perhaps be more accurate to define the philosophical sin of the Jesuits to be "an action contrary to right reason, which is done by a person who is either absolutely ignorant of God, or does not think of him during the time this action is committed."

† The books that have been written to expose and refute the corrupt and enormous maxims of the Jesuits, would make an ample library, were they collected. But nothing of this kind is equal to the learned, ingenious, and humourous work of the famous Pascal, entitled, Les Provinciales, ou Lettres ecrites par Louis de Montalte a un Provincial de ses amis, et aux Jesuites, sur la Morale et la Politique de ces Peres. This exquisite production is accompanied, in some editions of it, with the learned and judicious observations of Nicole, who, under the fictitious name of Guillaume Wenderock, fully demonstrated the truth of those facts which Pascal had advanced without quoting his authorities, and placed, in a full and striking light, several interesting circumstances which that great man had treated with, perhaps, too much brevity. These letters, which did the Jesuits more real mischief than either the indignation of sovereign princes, or any other calamity that had heretofore fallen upon their order, were translated into Latin by Rachelius. On the other hand, the sons of Loyola, sensibly affected and alarmed by this formidable attack upon their reputation, left no means unemployed to defend themselves against such a respectable adversary. They sent forth their ablest champions to defend their cause, or, at least, to cover them from shame: among which champions the subtle and eloquent Father Daniel, the celebrated author of the History of France, shone forth with a superior lustre; and, as if they thought it unsafe to trust to the powers of argument, and the force of evidence alone, they applied themselves for help to the secular arm, and had credit enough to obtain a sentence, condemning the Provinciales to be burned publicly at Paris. See Daniel's Opuscules, vol. i. p. 363. This author, however, acknowledges that the greatest part of the answers which the Jesuits opposed to the performance of Pascal were weak and unsatisfactory. Certain it is, that (whether it was owing to the strength of argument, or to the elegant wit and humour that reigned in them,) the Provincial Letters lost not the smallest portion of their credit and reputation by all the answers that were made to them, but continued to pass through a great number of editions, which could scarcely be printed off with rapidity sufficient to satisfy the desires of the public.

Another severe attack was made upon the Jesuits, in a book inferior to Pascal's work in point of wit and genteel pleasantry, but superior to it in point of evidence, since it abounds with passages and testimonies, which are drawn from the most applauded writings of the Jesuits, and demonstrate fully the corruption and enormity of the moral rules and maxims inculcated by that famous order. This book, which was published at Mons in 1702, bears the following title: La Morale des Jesuites, extraite fidelement de leurs Livres imprimez avec la permission et l'approbation des Superieurs de leur Compagnie, par un Docteur de Sorbonne. The author was Perrault (son of Charles Perrault, who began the famous controversy in France concerning the respective merits of the ancients and moderns,) and his book met with the some fate with the Provinciales of Pascal: for it was burned at Paris in 1670, at the request of the Jesuits. See the Opuscules du Pere Daniel, t. i. p. 356. Nor indeed is it at all surprising, that the Jesuits exerted all their zeal against this compilation, which exhibited, in one shocking point of view, all that had been complained of and censured in their maxims and institutions, and unfolded the whole mystery of their iniquity.

It has also been laid to the charge of the Jesuits, that they reduced their pernicious maxims to practice, especially in the remoter parts of the world. Arnauld, and some of his Jansenist brethren, ably endeavoured to support this charge in that laborious and celebrated work, entitled La Morale Pratique des Jesuites. In this important work, a multitude of authentic relations, documents, facts, and testimonies, are employed to demonstrate the criminal conduct and practices of the Jesuits. For an ample account of the Jesuitical doctrine concerning philosophical sin, and the dissensions and controversies it occasioned, see Jacobi Hyacinthi Serry.* Addenda ad Histor. Congregationum de Auxiliis, p. 82; as also his Auctarium, p. 289.

* There is a concise and accurate account of the contests and divisions, to which the morality of the Jesuits gave rise in France and in other countries, in a work, entitled, Catechisme Historique et Dogmatique sur les Contestations qui divisent maintenant l'Eglise, published in 1730. See tom. ii. p. 26.—It is very remarkable, that the two bulls of Alexander VII. and VIII. against the Jesuits are not to be found in the Bullarium Pontificum; but the Jansenists and Dominicans, who are careful in perpetuating whatever may tend to the dishonour of the Jesuits, have preserved them industriously from oblivion.

☞ * This is a fictitious name; the true **name of the author of the Addenda was Augustin Le Blanc.**

among the writers of this corrupt order, than to purify the seminaries of instruction from the contagion of their dissolute maxims.—After what has been observed in relation to the moral system of the Jesuits, it will not be difficult to assign a reason for the remarkable propensity that is discovered by kings, princes, the nobility and gentry of both sexes, and an innumerable multitude of persons of all ranks and conditions, to commit their consciences to the direction, and their souls to the care, of the brethren of this society. It is, no doubt, highly convenient for persons, who do not pretend to a rigid observance of the duties of religion and morality, to have spiritual guides, who diminish the guilt of transgression, disguise the deformity of vice, let loose the reins to all the passions, and even nourish them by their dissolute precepts, and render the way to heaven as easy, agreeable, and smooth as is possible.*

What has here been said concerning the erroneous maxims and corrupt practices of the Jesuits, must, however, be understood with modifications and restrictions. It must not be imagined, that these maxims are adopted, or these practices justified, by all the sons of Loyola, without exception, or that they are publicly taught and inculcated in all their schools and seminaries: for this, in reality, is not the case. As this order has produced men of learning and genius, so neither has it been destitute of men of probity and candour; nor would it be a difficult task to compile from the writings of the Jesuits a much more just and proper representation of the duties of religion and the obligations of morality, than that hideous and unseemly exhibition of both, which Pascal and his followers have drawn from the Jesuitical casuists, summists, and moralists. Those who censure the Jesuits in general, must, if their censures be well founded, have the following circumstances in view; first, that the rulers of that society not only suffer many of their members to propagate publicly impious opinions and corrupt maxims, but even go so far as to set the seal of their approbation to the books in which these opinions and maxims are contained;† secondly, that the system of religion and morality, taught in the greatest part of their seminaries, is so loose, vague, and ill-digested, that it not only may be easily perverted to bad purposes and erroneous conclusions, but even seems peculiarly susceptible of such abuse; and lastly, that the select few, who are initiated into the grand mysteries of the society, and set apart to transact its affairs, to carry on its projects, to exert their political talents in the closet of the minister, or in the cabinet of the prince, commonly make use of the dangerous and pernicious maxims that are complained of to augment the authority and opulence of their order. The candour and impartiality that become an historian, oblige us to acknowledge, at the same time, that, in demonstrating the turpitude and enormity of certain maxims and opinions of the Jesuits, their adversaries have gone too far, and permitted their eloquence and zeal to run into exaggeration. This we might show, with the fullest evidence, by examples deduced from the doctrines of probability and mental reservation, and the imputations that have been made to the Jesuits on these heads; but this would lead us too far from the thread of our history. We shall only observe, that what happens frequently in every kind of controversy, happened here in a singular manner; I mean, that the Jesuits were charged with tenets, which had been drawn *consequentially* from their doctrine, by their accusers, without their consent; that their phrases and terms were not always interpreted according to the precise meaning which they annexed to them; and that the tendency of their system was represented in too partial and unequitable a light.

XXXVI. The Scriptures did not acquire any new degrees of public respect and authority under the pontiffs of this century. It can be proved, on the contrary, by the most authentic records, that the votaries of Rome, and more especially the Jesuits, employed all their dexterity and art, either to prevent the word of God from falling into the hands of the people, or at least to have it explained in a manner consistent with the interest, grandeur, and pretensions of their church. In France and the Netherlands there arose, indeed, several commentators and critics, who were very far from being destitute of knowledge and erudition; but it may nevertheless be said of them, that, instead of illustrating and explaining the divine oracles, they rendered them more obscure, by blending their own crude inventions with the dictates of celestial wisdom. This is chargeable even upon the Jansenists, who, though superior to the other Roman catholic expositors, in most respects, yet fell into that absurd method of disfiguring the pure word of God, by far-fetched allusions, mystic interpretations, and frigid allegories, compiled from the reveries of the ancient fathers.* Here, nevertheless, an exception is to be made in favour of Pasquier Quesnel, a priest of the oratory, whose edition of the New Testament, accompanied with pious meditations and remarks, made such a prodigious noise in the theological world,† and even in our time has continued to furnish matter of warm and violent contest, and to split the Roman catholic doctors into parties and factions.‡

* The translator has here inserted in the text the note q of the original.

☞ † This is, no doubt, true. The Jesuits have doctors of all sorts and sizes; and this, indeed, is necessary, in order to the establishment of that universal empire at which they aim. See Lettres Provinciales, let. v. p. 62 of the tenth Cologne edition.

* The reader will find a striking example of this in the well-known Bible of Isaac le Maitre, commonly called Sacy, which contains all the crude and extravagant fancies and allegories, with which the ancient doctors obscured the beautiful simplicity of the Scriptures, and rendered their clearest expressions intricate and mysterious.

☞ † That is, in the Roman Catholic part of the theological world. Never perhaps did any thing show, in a more striking manner, the blind zeal of faction than the hard treatment this book met with. See Cent. xviii. sect. x. note.

‡ The first part of this work, which contains observations on the four Gospels, was published in 1671; and, as it was received with general applause this encouraged the author not only to revise and augment it, but also to enlarge his plan, and com-

XXXVII. The majority of the public schools retained that dry, intricate, and captious method of teaching theology, which had prevailed in the ages of barbarism and darkness, and which could only excite disgust in all such as were endowed with a liberal turn of mind. There was no possibility of ordering matters so, that didactic or biblical theology, which is supposed to arrange and illustrate the truths of religion by the dictates of Scripture, should be placed upon the same footing, and holden in the same honour with scholastic divinity, which had its source in the metaphysical visions of the Peripatetic philosophy. Even the edicts of the pontiffs were insufficient to accomplish this object. In the greatest part of the universities, the scholastic doctors domineered, and were constantly molesting and insulting the biblical divines, who, generally speaking, were little skilled in the captious arts of sophistry and dialectical chicane. It is nevertheless to be observed, that many of the French doctors, and more especially the Jansenists, explained the principal doctrines and duties of Christianity in a style and manner that were at least recommendable on account of their elegance and perspicuity; and indeed it may be affirmed, that almost all the theological or moral treatises of this age, that were composed with any tolerable degree of simplicity and good sense, had the doctors of Port-Royal, or the French priests of the oratory, for their authors. We have already taken notice of the changes that were introduced, during this century, into the method of carrying on theological controversy. The German, Belgic, and French divines, being at length convinced, by disagreeable experience, that their captious, incoherent, and uncharitable manner of disputing, exasperated those who differed from them in their religious sentiments, and confirmed them in their respective systems, instead of converting them;—and perceiving, moreover, that the arguments in which they had formerly placed their principal confidence, proved feeble and insufficient to make the least impression,—found it necessary to look out for new and more specious methods of attack and defence.

XXXVIII. The Romish church has, notwithstanding its boasted uniformity of doctrine, been always divided by a multitude of controversies. It would be endless to enumerate the disputes that have arisen between the seminaries of learning, and the contests that have divided the monastic orders. The greatest part of these, as being of little moment, we shall pass over in silence; for they have been treated with indifference and neglect by the popes, who never took notice of them but when they grew violent and noisy, and then suppressed them with an imperious nod, that imposed silence upon the contending parties. Besides, these less momentous controversies, which it will never be possible entirely to extinguish, are not of such a nature as to affect the church in its fundamental principles, to endanger its constitution, or to hurt its interests. It will, therefore, be sufficient to give a brief account of those debates which by their superior importance and their various connexions and dependencies, may be said to have affected the church in general, and to have threatened it with alarming changes and revolutions.

And here the first place is naturally due to the famous debates, carried on between the Jesuits and Dominicans concerning the nature and necessity of divine grace; the decision of which important point had, toward the conclusion of the preceding century, been committed by Clement VIII. to a select assembly of learned divines. These arbiters, after having employed several years in deliberating upon this nice and critical subject, and in examining the arguments of the contending parties, intimated, plainly enough, to the pontiff, that the sentiments of the Dominicans, concerning grace, predestination, human liberty, and original sin, were more conformable to the doctrine of Scripture and the decisions of the ancient fathers than the opinions of Molina, which were patronised by the Jesuits. They observed, more especially, that the former leaned toward the tenets of Augustine, while the latter bore a striking resemblance to the Pelagian heresy. In consequence of this declaration, Clement seemed resolved to pass condemnation on the Jesuits, and to determine the controversy in favour of the Dominicans. Affairs were in this state in 1601, when the Jesuits, alarmed at the dangers that threatened them, beset the old pontiff night and day, and so importuned him with entreaties, menaces, arguments, and complaints, that, in 1602, he consented to re-examine this intricate controversy, and undertook himself the critical task of principal arbitrator. For this purpose, he chose a council* (composed of fifteen cardinals, nine professors of divinity, and five bishops,) which, in the course of three years,† assembled seventy-eight times, or, to speak in the style of Rome, held so many *congregations*. At these meetings, the pontiff heard, at one time, the Jesuits and Dominicans disputing in favour of their respective systems; and, at another, ordered the assembled doctors to weigh their reasons, and examine the proofs that were adduced on both sides of this difficult question. The result of this examination is not known with certainty; as the death of Clement, which happened on the fourth day of March, 1605, prevented his pronouncing a decisive sentence. The Dominicans assure us, that the pope, had he lived, would have condemned Molina. The Jesuits, on the contrary, maintain, that he would have acquitted him publicly from all charge of heresy and error. They alone who have seen the records of this council and the journals of its proceedings, are qualified to determine which of the two we are to believe; but these records are kept with the utmost secrecy at Rome.

XXXIX. The proceedings of the congregation that had been assembled by Clement were

pose observations on the other books of the N. Test. See the Catech. Hist. sur les Contest. de l'Eglise. t. ii. p. 150.—Ch. Eberh. Weismanni Hist. Eccles. sæc. XVII. p 588

☞ * This council was called the congregation *de Auxiliis*.

† From the 20th of March 1602, to the 22d of January, 1605.

suspended for some time, by the death of that pontiff; but they were resumed, in the same year, by the order of Paul V. his successor. Their deliberations, which were continued from September to the following March, did not turn so much upon the merits of the cause, which were already sufficiently examined, as upon the prudent and proper method of finishing the contest. The great question now was, whether the well-being of the church would admit the decision of this controversy by a papal bull; and, if such a decision should seem advisable, it still remained to be considered, in what terms the bull should be drawn up. All these long and solemn deliberations resembled the delivery of the mountain in the fable, and ended in this resolution, that the whole controversy, instead of being *decided*, should be *suppressed*, and that each of the contending parties should have the liberty of following their respective opinions. The Dominicans assert, that the two pontiffs, together with the congregation of divines employed by them in the review of this important controversy, were fully persuaded of the justice of *their* cause, and of the truth of *their* system; they moreover observe, that Paul had expressly ordered a solemn condemnation of the doctrine of the Jesuits to be drawn up, but was prevented from finishing and publishing it, by the unhappy war that was kindled about that time between him and the Venetians. The Jesuits, on the other hand, represent these accounts of the Dominicans as entirely fictitious, and affirm that neither the pontiff, nor the more judicious and respectable members of the congregation, found any thing in the sentiments of Molina that was worthy of censure, or stood in much need of correction. In a point which is rendered thus uncertain by contradictory testimonies and assertions, it is difficult to determine what we are to believe; it however appears exceedingly probable, that, whatever the private opinion of Paul may have been, he was prevented from pronouncing a public determination of this famous controversy, by his apprehensions of offending either the king of France, who protected the Jesuits, or the king of Spain, who warmly maintained the cause of the Dominicans. It is farther probable, and almost certain, that, had the pontiff been independent of all foreign influence, and at full liberty to decide this knotty point, he would have pronounced one of those *ambiguous* sentences, for which the oracle of Rome is so famous, and would have so conducted matters as to shock neither of the contending parties.*

XL. The flame of controversy, which seemed thus extinguished, or at least covered, broke out again with new violence, in 1640, and formed a kind of schism in the church of Rome, which involved it in great perplexity, and proved highly detrimental to it in various respects. The occasion of these new troubles was the publication of a book, entitled Augustinus, composed by Cornelius Jansenius, bishop of Ypres, and published after the death of the author.* In this book, which even the

* Beside the authors we have above recommended as proper to be consulted in relation to these contests, see Le Clerc, Memoires pour servir a l'Histoire des Controverses dans l'Eglise Romaine sur la Predestination et sur la Grace, in his Bibliotheque Universelle et Historique, tom. xiv. p. 235. The conduct, both of the Jesuits and Dominicans, after their controversy was hushed, affords much reason to presume that they had been both secretly exhorted by the pontiff to mitigate their respective systems, and so to modify their doctrines or expressions, as to avoid the reproach of heresy that had been cast upon them; for the Jesuits had been accused of Pelagianism, and the Dominicans of a propensity to the tenets of the protestant churches. This appears, in a more particular manner, from a letter written by Claudius Aquaviva, general of the Jesuits, in 1613, and addressed to all the members of his order. In this letter the prudent general modifies with great dexterity and caution the sentiments of Molina, and enjoins it upon the brethren of the society to teach every where the doctrine which represents the Supreme Being as electing, freely, to eternal life, without any regard had to their merits, those whom he has been pleased to render partakers of that inestimable blessing; but, at the same time, he exhorts them to inculcate this doctrine in such a manner, as not to give up the tenets relating to divine grace, which they had maintained in their controversy with the Dominicans. Never, surely, was such a contradictory exhortation or order heard of; the good general thought, nevertheless, that he could reconcile abundantly these contradictions, by that branch of the divine knowledge which is called, by the schoolmen, *scientia media*. See the Catechisme Historique sur les Dissensions de l'Eglise, tom. i. p. 207.

On the other hand, the Dominicans, although their sentiments remain the same as they were before the commencement of this controversy, have learned to cast a kind of ambiguity and obscurity over their theological system, by using certain terms and expressions, which are manifestly borrowed from the schools of the Jesuits; and this they do to prevent the latter from reproaching them with a propensity to the doctrine of Calvin. They are, moreover, much less remarkable than formerly, for their zealous opposition to the Jesuits, which may be owing perhaps to prudent reflections on the dangers they may have been involved in by this opposition, and the fruitless pains and labour it has cost them. The Jansenists reproach them severely with this change of conduct, and consider it as a manifest and notorious apostacy from divine truth. See the Lettres Provinciales of Pascal, lettre ii. We are not, however, to conclude, from this change of style and external conduct among the Dominicans, that they are reconciled to the Jesuits, and that there remain no traces of their ancient opposition to that perfidious order. By no means; for, besides that many of them are shocked at the excessive timidity or prudence of a great part of their brethren, the whole body retain some hidden sparks of the indignation with which they formerly beheld the Jesuits; and, when a convenient occasion of discovering this indignation is offered, they do not let it pass unimproved. The Jansenists are here embarked in the same cause with the Dominicans since the sentiments of St. Thomas, concerning divine grace, differ very little from those of St. Augustine. Cardinal Henry Noris, the most eminently learned among the followers of the latter, expresses his concern, that he is not at liberty to publish what passed in favour of Augustine, and to the disadvantage of Molina and the Jesuits, in the famous congregation *de Auxiliis*, so often assembled by the popes Clement VIII. and Paul V. See his Vindiciæ Augustinianæ, cap. vi. p. 1175, tom. i. op.—"Quando," says he, "recentiori Romano decreto id vetitum est, cum dispendio causæ, quam defendo, necessariam defensionem omitto."

* For an account of this famous man, see Bayle's *Dictionaire*.—Leydecker, de Vita et Morte Jansenii lib. iii. which makes the first part of his History of Jansenism. *Dictionaire des Livres Jansenistes*, tom. i This celebrated work of Jansenius, which gave such a wound to the Romish church, as neither the power nor wisdom of its pontiffs will ever be able to heal, is divided into three parts. The first is historical, and contains a relation of the Pelagian controversy, which arose in the fifth century. In the second we find an accurate account and illustration of the doctrine of Augustine, relating to the Constitution and Powers of Human Nature, in its original, fallen and renewed state. The third contains the doctrine

Jesuits acknowledge to be the production of a man of learning and piety, the doctrine of Augustine, concerning man's natural corruption, and the nature and efficacy of that divine grace, which alone can efface this unhappy stain, is unfolded at large, and illustrated, for the most part, in Augustine's own words: for the end, which Jansenius proposed to himself in this work, was not to give his own private sentiments concerning these important points, but to show in what manner they had been understood and explained by that celebrated father of the church, now mentioned, whose name and authority were highly revered in all parts of the Roman catholic world.* No incident could be more unfavourable to the cause of the Jesuits, and the progress of their religious system, than the publication of this book; for, as the doctrine of Augustine scarcely differed from that of the Dominicans;† as it was held sacred, and almost respected as divine, in the church of Rome, on account of the extraordinary merit and authority of that illustrious bishop, and, at the same time, was almost diametrically opposite to the sentiments generally received among the Jesuits, the latter could scarcely consider the book of Jansenius in any other light than as a tacit, but formidable refutation of their opinions concerning human liberty and divine grace; and accordingly, they not only drew their pens against this famous book, but also used their most zealous endeavours to obtain a public condemnation of it from Rome. Their endeavours were not unsuccessful. The Roman inquisitors began the opposition by prohibiting the perusal of it, in 1741; and, in the following year, Urban VIII. condemned it by a solemn bull, as infected with various errors that had been long banished from the catholic church.

XLI. There were nevertheless places, even within the bounds of the Romish church, where neither the decisions of the inquisitors, nor the bull of the pontiff, were in the least respected. The doctors of Louvain in particular, and the followers of Augustine in general, who were very numerous in the Netherlands, opposed, with the utmost vigour, the proceedings of the Jesuits and the condemnation of Jansenius; and hence arose a warm contest, which proved a source of much trouble to the Belgic provinces. But it was not confined within such narrow limits; it reached the neighbouring countries, and broke out with peculiar vehemence in France, where the abbot of St. Cyran,‡ a man of an elegant genius, and equally distinguished by the extent of his learning, the lustre of his piety, and the sanctity of his manners, had procured to Augustine many zealous followers, and to the Jesuits as many bitter and implacable adversaries.* This respectable abbot was the intimate friend and relative of Jansenius, and one of the most strenuous defenders of his doctrine. On the other hand, the far greater part of the French theologists appeared on the side of the Jesuits, whose religious tenets seemed more honourable to human nature, or, at least, more agreeable to its propensities, more suitable to the genius of the Romish religion, and more adapted to promote and advance the interests of the Romish church, than the doctrine of Augustine. The party of Jansenius had also its patrons; and they were such as reflected honour on the cause. In this respectable list we may reckon several bishops eminent for their piety, and some of the first and most elegant geniuses of the French nation, such as Arnauld, Nicole, Pascal, and Quesnel, and the other famous and learned men, who are known under the denomination of the Authors of Port-Royal. This party was also considerably augmented by a multitude of persons, who looked upon the usual practice of piety in the Romish church (which consists in the frequent use of the eucharist, the confession of sins, and the performance of certain external acts of religion,) as much inferior to what the Gospel requires, and who considered Christian piety as the vital and internal principle of a soul, in which true faith and divine love have gained a happy ascendency. Thus one of the contending parties excelled in the number and power of its votaries, the other in the learning, genius, and piety of its adherents; and, things being thus balanced, it is not difficult to comprehend, how a controversy, which began about a century ago, should be still carried on with vehement contention and ardour.†

---

of the same great man relating to the Aids of sanctifying Grace procured by Christ, and to the eternal Predestination of Men and Angels. The style of Jansenius is clear, but not sufficiently correct.

* Thus Jansenius expresses himself in his Augustinus, tom. ii. lib. proœmial. cap. xxix. p. 65.—Non ego hic de aliqua nova sententia reperienda disputo . . . sed de antiqua Augustini. Quæritur, non quid de naturæ humanæ statibus et viribus, vel de Dei gratia et prædestinatione sentiendum est, sed quid Augustinus olim, ecclesiæ nomine et applausu, tradiderit, prædicaverit, scriptoque multipliciter consignaverit.

† The Dominicans followed the sentiments of Thomas Aquinas, concerning the nature and efficacy of Divine Grace.

‡ The name of this abbot was Jean du Verger de Haurane.

* This illustrious abbot is considered by the Jansenists as equal in merit and authority to Jansenius himself, whom he is supposed to have assisted in composing his Augustinus. The French, more especially, (I mean such of them as adopt the doctrine of Augustine,) revere him as an oracle, and even extol him beyond Jansenius. For an account of the life and transactions of this pious abbot, see Lancelot's Memoires touchant la Vie de M. de S. Cyran.—Recueil de plusieurs Pieces pour servir a l'Histoire de Port-Royal.—Arnaud D'Andilly, Memoires au sujet de l'Abbe de S. Cyran, published in the first volume of his Vies des Religieuses de Port-Royal.—Bayle's Dictionary, at the article Jansenius. Dictionaire des Livres Jansenistes, tom. i. For an account of the earlier studies of the abbot in question, see Gabriel Liron's Singularites Historiques et Literaires, tom. iv. p. 507.

† The history of this contest is to be found in many authors, who have either given a relation of the whole, or treated apart some of its most interesting branches. The writers that ought to be principally consulted on this subject are the following: Gerberon, Histoire Generale du Jansenisme, published at Amsterdam in 1700; and Du-Mas, Histoire des Cinq Propositions de Jansenius. The former maintains the cause of the Jansenists, while the latter favours that of the Jesuits.—Add, to these, Melch. Leydecker's Historia Jansenismi, and Voltaire's Siecle de Louis XIV. Several books, written on both sides, are enumerated in the Bibliotheque Janseniste, ou Catalogue Alphabetique des Principaux Livres Jansenistes, the author of which is said to be Domin. Colonia, a learned Jesuit.

XLII. Those who have taken an attentive view of this long, and indeed endless controversy, cannot but think it a matter both of curiosity and amusement to observe the contrivances, stratagems, arguments, and arts employed by both Jesuits and Jansenists; by the former in their methods of attack, and by the latter in their plans of defence. The Jesuits came forth into the field of controversy, armed with sophistical arguments, odious comparisons, papal bulls, royal edicts, and the protection of a great part of the nobility and bishops; and, as if all this had appeared to them insufficient, they had recourse to still more formidable auxiliaries, even the secular arm, and a competent number of dragoons. The Jansenists, far from being dismayed at the view of this warlike host, stood their ground with steadiness and intrepidity. They evaded the seemingly mortal blows that were levelled at them in the royal and papal mandates, by the help of nice interpretations and subtle distinctions, and by the very same sophistical refinements which they blamed in the Jesuits. To the threats and frowns of the nobles and bishops, who protected their adversaries, they opposed the favour and applause of the people; to sophisms they opposed sophisms, and invectives to invectives; and to human power they opposed the Divine Omnipotence, and boasted of the miracles by which Heaven had declared itself in their favour. When they perceived that the strongest arguments, and the most respectable authorities, were insufficient to conquer the obstinacy of their adversaries, they endeavoured, by their religious exploits, and their application to the advancement of piety and learning, to obtain the favour of the pontiffs, and strengthen their interest with the people. Hence they declared war against the enemies of the Romish church; formed new stratagems to ensnare and ruin the protestants; took extraordinary pains in instructing the youth in all the liberal arts and sciences; drew up a variety of useful, accurate, and elegant abridgments, containing the elements of philosophy and the learned languages; published a multitude of treatises on practical religion and morality, whose persuasive eloquence charmed all ranks and orders of men; introduced and cultivated an easy, correct, and agreeable manner of writing; and gave accurate and learned interpretations of several ancient authors. To all these various kinds of merit, the greatest part of which were real and solid, they added others that were at least visionary and chimerical; for they endeavoured to persuade, and did in effect persuade many, that the Supreme Being interposed particularly in support of their cause, and, by prodigies and miracles of a stupendous kind, confirmed the truth of the doctrine of Augustine, in a manner adapted to remove all doubt, and triumph over all opposition.* All this rendered the Jansenists extremely popular, and held the victory of the Jesuits for some time dubious, and it is more than probable, that the former would have triumphed, had not the cause of the latter been the cause of the papacy, and had not the stability and grandeur of the Romish church depended, in a great measure, upon the success of their religious maxims.

XLIII. It appears from several circumstances, that Urban VIII., and after him Innocent X., were really bent on appeasing these dangerous tumults, in the same manner as the

* It is well known that the Jansenists, or Augustinians, have long pretended to confirm their doctrine by miracles; and they even acknowledge, that these miracles have sometimes saved them, when their affairs have been reduced to a desperate situation. See the Memoires de Port-Royal, tom. i. p. 256, tom. ii. p. 107.—The first time we hear mention made of these miracles, is in 1656, and the following years, when a thorn of the derisive crown that was put upon our Saviour's head by the Roman soldiers, is reported to have performed several marvellous cures in the convent of Port-Royal. See the Recueil de plusieurs Pieces pour servir a l'Histoire de Port-Royal, p. 228, 448; and Fontaine's collections upon the same subject, tom. ii.—Other prodigies followed in 1661 and 1664; and the fame of these miracles rose to a great height during the last century, and proved singularly advantageous to the cause of the Jansenites; but they are now fallen, even in France, into oblivion and discredit. The Jansenists, therefore, of the present age, being pressed by their adversaries, were obliged to have recourse to new prodigies, as the old ones had entirely lost their credit; and they seemed, indeed, to have had miracles at command, by the considerable number they pretended to perform. Thus, (if we are credulous enough to believe their reports,) in 1725, a woman, whose name was La Fosse, was *suddenly* cured of a bloody flux, by imploring the aid of the host, when it was, one day, carried by a *Jansenist* priest. About two years after this, we are told, that the tomb of Gerard Rouse, a canon of Avignon, was honoured with miracles of a stupendous kind; and, finally, we are informed, that the same honour was conferred, in 1731, on the bones of the abbe de Paris, which were interred at St. Medard, where innumerable miracles are said to have been wrought. This last story has given rise to the warmest contests, between the superstitious or crafty Jansenists and their adversaries in all communions. Beside all this, Quesnel Levier, Desangins, and Tournus, the great ornaments of Jansenism, are said to have furnished extraordinary succours, on several occasions, to sick and infirm persons, who testified a lively confidence in their prayers and *merits*. See a famous Jansenist book composed in answer to the *Bull Unigenitus*, and entitled, Jesus Christ sous l'Anatheme et sous l'Excommunication, art. xvii. xviii.—There is no doubt that a great part of the Jansenists defend these miracles from principle, and in consequence of a persuasion of their truth and reality; for that party abounds with persons, whose piety is blended with a most superstitious credulity, who look upon their religious system as celestial truth, and their cause as the immediate cause of Heaven, and who are consequently disposed to think that it cannot be neglected by the Deity, or left without extraordinary marks of his approbation and supporting presence. It is however amazing, and almost incredible, on the other hand, that the more judicious defenders of this cause, those eminent Jansenists, whose sagacity, learning, and good sense, discover themselves so abundantly in other matters, do not consider that the powers of nature, the efficacy of proper remedies, or the effects of imagination, produce many important changes and effects, which, from imposture, or a blind attachment to some particular cause, many are led to attribute to the miraculous interposition of the Deity. We can easily account for the delusions of weak enthusiasts, or the tricks of egregious impostors; but when we see men of piety and judgment appearing in defence of such miracles as those now under consideration, we must conclude, that they look upon fraud as lawful in the support of a good cause, and make no scruple of deceiving the people, when they propose, by this delusion, to confirm and propagate what they take to be the truth.

popes in former times had prudently suppressed the controversies excited by Baius and the Dominicans. But the vivacity, inconstancy, and restless spirit of the French doctors, threw all into confusion, and disconcerted the measures of the pontiffs. The opposers of the doctrine of Augustine selected five propositions out of the work of Jansenius already mentioned, which appeared to them the most erroneous in their nature, and the most pernicious in their tendency; and, being set on by the instigation, and seconded by the influence of the Jesuits, employed their most zealous endeavours and their most importunate entreaties at the court of Rome, to have these propositions condemned. On the other hand, a great part of the Gallican clergy used their utmost efforts to prevent this condemnation; and, for that purpose they sent deputies to Rome, to entreat Innocent to suspend his final decision until the true sense of these propositions should be deliberately examined, since the ambiguity of style, in which they were expressed, rendered them susceptible of a false interpretation. But these entreaties were ineffectual: the interest and importunities of the Jesuits prevailed; and the pontiff, without examining the merits of the cause with a suitable degree of impartiality and attention, condemned, by a public bull, on the 31st of May, 1653, the propositions of Jansenius. These propositions contained the following doctrines: 1. "That there are divine precepts which good men, notwithstanding their desire to observe them, are, nevertheless, absolutely unable to obey; nor has God given them that measure of grace, which is essentially necessary to render them capable of such obedience: 2. That no person, in this corrupt state of nature, can resist the influence of divine grace, when it operates upon the mind: 3. That, in order to render human actions meritorious, it is not requisite that they be exempt from necessity, but only that they be free from constraint:* 4. That the Semi-Pelagians err grievously in maintaining, that the human will is endowed with the power of either receiving or resisting the aids and influences of preventing grace: 5. That whosoever affirms, that Jesus Christ made expiation, by his sufferings and death, for the sins of all mankind, is a Semi-Pelagian."—Of these propositions the pontiff declared the first four only heretical; but he pronounced the fifth rash, impious, and injurious to the Supreme Being.†

XLIV. This sentence of the supreme ecclesiastical judge was indeed painful to the Jansenists, and in consequence highly agreeable to their adversaries. It did not however either drive the former to despair, or satisfy the latter to the extent of their desires; for while the *doctrine* was condemned, the *man* escaped. Jansenius was not named in the bull, nor did the pontiff even declare that the five propositions were maintained, in the book entitled Augustinus, in the sense in which he had condemned them. Hence the disciples of Augustine and Jansenius defended themselves by a distinction invented by the ingenious and subtle Arnaud, in consequence of which they considered separately in this controversy the matter of doctrine and the matter of fact; that is to say, they acknowledged themselves bound to believe, that the five propositions were justly condemned by the pontiff;* but they maintained, that the pope had not declared, and consequently that they were bound not to believe, that these propositions were to be found in Jansenius' book, in the sense in which they had been condemned.† They did not however enjoy long the benefit of this artful distinction. The restless and invincible hatred of their enemies pursued them in every quarter where they looked for protection or repose, and at length engaged Alexander VII., the successor of Innocent, to declare, by a solemn bull, issued in 1656, that the five condemned propositions were the tenets of Jansenius, and were contained in his book. The pontiff did not stop here; but to this flagrant instance of imprudence added another still more shocking; for, in 1665, he sent into France the form of a declaration, that was to be subscribed by all those who aspired to any preferment in the church, and in which it was affirmed, that the five propositions were to be found in the book of Jansenius, in the same sense in which they had been condemned by the church.‡ This declaration, whose temerity and contentious tendency appeared in the most odious colours, not only to the Jansenists, but also to the wiser part of the French nation, produced deplorable divisions and tumults. It was immediately opposed with vigour by the Jansenists, who maintained, that in matters of fact the pope was fallible, especially when his decisions were merely personal, and not confirmed by a general council; and, in consequence, that it was neither obligatory nor necessary to subscribe this papal declaration, which had only a matter of fact for its object The Jesuits, on the contrary, audaciously asserted, even openly, in the city of Paris, and in the face of the Gallican church, that faith and confidence in the papal decisions relating to matter of fact, had no less the characters of a well-grounded and divine faith, than when these decisions related merely to matters of doctrine and opinion. It is to be remarked, on the other hand, that all the Jansenists were by no means so resolute and intrepid as those above-mentioned. Some of them declared. that they would neither subscribe nor reject the Form in question, but would show their

* Augustine, Leibnitz, and a considerable number of modern philosophers, who maintain the doctrine of necessity, consider this necessity, in moral actions, as consistent with true liberty, because it is consistent with spontaneity and choice. According to them, constraint alone and external force destroy merit and imputation.

† This bull is still extant in the Bullarium Romanum, tom. vi. p. 456. It has also been published, together with several other pieces relating to this controversy, by Du-Plessis D'Argentre, in his Collectio Judiciorum de novis Erroribus tom. iii. p. ii.

☞ * This was what our author calls the *quæstio de jure*.

☞ † This is the *quæstio de facto*.

‡ This bull, and several other pieces, are also to be found in D'Argentre's Collectio Judiciorum, tom. iii.—See the form of Alexander's declaration, with the Mandate of Louis XIV. *ibid.*

veneration for the authority of the pope, by observing a profound silence on that subject. Others professed themselves ready to subscribe it, not indeed without exception and reserve, but on condition of being allowed to explain, either verbally or in writing, the sense in which they understood it, or the distinctions and limitations with which they were willing to adopt it. Others employed a variety of methods and stratagems to elude the force of this tyrannical declaration.* But nothing of this kind was sufficient to satisfy the violent demands of the Jesuits; nothing less than the entire ruin of the Jansenists could appease their fury. Such, therefore, among the latter, as made the least opposition to the declaration in question, were thrown into prison, or sent into exile, or involved in some other species of persecution; and it is well known, that this severity was a consequence of the suggestions of the Jesuits, and of their influence in cabinet-councils.

XLV. The lenity or prudence of Clement IX. suspended, for a while, the calamities of those who had sacrificed their liberty and their fortunes to their zeal for the doctrine of Augustine, and gave them both time to breathe, and reason to hope for better days. This change, which happened in 1669, was occasioned by the fortitude and resolution of the bishops of Angers, Beauvais, Pamiers, and Alet, who obstinately and gloriously refused to subscribe, without the proper explications and distinctions, the oath or declaration that had produced such troubles and divisions in the church. They did not indeed stand alone in the breach; for, when the court of Rome began to menace and level its thunder at their heads, nineteen bishops more arose with a noble intrepidity, and adopted their cause, in solemn remonstrances, addressed both to the king of France and the pontiff. These resolute protesters were joined by Ann Genevieve de Bourbon, duchess of Longueville, a heroine of the first rank both in birth and magnanimity, who, having renounced the pleasures and vanities of the world, which had long employed her most serious thoughts, espoused, with a devout ardour, the doctrines and cause of the Jansenists, and most earnestly implored the pope's clemency in their behalf. Moved by these entreaties, and also by other arguments and considerations of like moment, Clement became so indulgent as to accept a conditional subscription to the famous declaration, and to permit doctors of scrupulous consciences to sign it according to the mental interpretation they thought proper to give it. This instance of condescension and lenity was no sooner made public, than the Jansenists began to come forth from their lurking-places, to return from their voluntary exile, and to enjoy their former tranquillity and freedom, being exempt from all uneasy apprehensions of any farther persecution.

This remarkable event is commonly called the Peace of Clement IX.; its duration, nevertheless, was but transitory.* It was violated in 1676, at the instigation of the Jesuits, by Louis XIV., who declared, in a public edict, that it had only been granted for a time, out of condescending indulgence to the tender and scrupulous consciences of a certain number of persons; and it was totally abolished after the death of the duchess of Longueville, which happened in 1679, and deprived the Jansenists of their principal support. From that time their calamities were renewed, and they were pursued with the same malignity and rage that they had before experienced. Some of them avoided the rising storm by a voluntary exile; others sustained it with invincible fortitude and constancy of mind; others turned aside its fury, and escaped its violence, as well as they could, by dexterity and prudence. Antoine Arnaud, who was the head and leader of the party, fled into the Netherlands in 1679;† and in this retreat he not only escaped the fury of his enemies, but had it in his power to hurt them considerably, and actually made the Jesuits feel the weight of his talents and the extent of his influence. For the admirable eloquence and sagacity of this great man gave him such an ascendency in the Netherlands, that the greatest part of the churches there embraced his opinions, and adopted his cause; the Romish congregations in Holland also were, by his influence, and the ministry of his intimate friends and adherents, John Neercassel and Peter Coddeus, bishops of Castorie and Sebasto,‡ entirely gained over to the Jansenist party. The latter churches still persevere with the utmost

* See Du-Mas, Histoire des Cinq Propositions, p. 158.—Gerberon, Histoire Generale du Jansenisme, p. ii. p. 516.

* The transactions relating to this event, which were carried on under the pontificate of Clement IX., are circumstantially related by cardinal Rospigliosi, in his Commentaries, which Du-Plessis D'Argentre has subjoined to his Elementa Theologica published at Paris, in 1716. See also the last-mentioned author's Collectio Judiciorum, tom. iii. p. ii. p. 336, in which the letters of Clement are inserted. Two Jansenists have written the History of the Clementine Peace.—Varet, vicar to the archbishop of Sens, in an anonymous work, entitled, Relation de ce qui s'est pass dans l'Affaire de la Paix de l'Eglise sous le Pape Clement IX.; and Quesnel, in an anonymous production also, entitled, La Paix de Clement IX. ou Demonstration des deux Faussetes capitales avancees dans l'Histoire des Cinq Propositions contre la Foi des Disciples de St. Augustin. That Varet was the author of the former work is asserted in the Catechisme Historique sur les Contestations de l'Eglise, tom. i. p. 352; and that the latter came from the pen of Quesnel, we learn from the writer of the Bibliotheque Janseniste, p. 314. There was another accurate and interesting account of this transaction published in 1706, under the following title: Relation de ce qui s'est passe dans l'Affaire de la Paix de l'Eglise sous le Pape Clement IX. avec les Lettres, Actes, Memoires, et autres Pieces qui y ont rapport. The important services that the duchess of Longueville rendered to the Jansenists in this affair are related with elegance and spirit by Villefort, in his Vie d'Anne Genevieve de Bourbon, Duchesse de Longueville tom. ii. livr. p. 89, of the edition of Amsterdam (1739,) which is more ample and complete than the edition of Paris.

† For an account of this great man, see Bayle's Dictionary, and the Histoire abregee de la Vie et des Ouvrages de M. Arnaud, published at Cologne. The change introduced into the Romish churches in Holland is mentioned by Lafiteau, Vie de Clement XI. tom. i. p. 123. For an account of Coddeus, Neercassel, and Varet, and the other patrons of Jansenism among the Dutch, see the Dictionaire des Livres Jansenistes, tom. i. ii. iv.

‡ Bishops *in partibus infidelium*.

steadiness in the principles of Jansenism; and, secured under the protection of the Dutch government, defy the threats, and hold in derision the resentment, of the Romish pontiffs.*

XLVI. It is not only on account of their embracing the doctrine of Augustine concerning divine grace (a doctrine which bears a striking resemblance to that of the Calvinists,) that the Jansenists have incurred the displeasure and resentment of the Jesuits. They are charged with many other circumstances, which appear intolerable to the warm votaries of the church of Rome. And, indeed, it is certain, that the various controversies, which have been mentioned above, were excited in that church principally by the Jansenists, and have been propagated and handed down by them, even to our times, in a prodigious multitude of their books published both in France and in the Netherlands.† But that which offends most the Jesuits, and the other creatures of the pontiff, is the austere severity that reigns in the system of moral discipline and practical religion adopted by the Jansenists. For the members of this sect cry out against the corruptions of the church of Rome, and complain that neither its doctrines nor morals retain any traces of their former purity. They reproach the clergy with an universal depravation of sentiments and manners, and an entire forgetfulness of the dignity of their character, and the duties of their vocation. They censure the licentiousness of the monastic orders, and insist upon the necessity of reforming their discipline according to the rules of sanctity, abstinence, and self-denial, that were originally prescribed by their respective founders. They maintain, also, that the people ought to be carefully instructed in all the doctrines and precepts of Christianity, and that, for this purpose, the Scriptures and public liturgies should be offered to their perusal in their mother tongue; and, finally, they look upon it as a matter of the highest moment to persuade all Christians that true piety does not consist in the observance of pompous rites, or in the performance of external acts of devotion, but in inward holiness and divine love.

These sentiments of the Jansenists, on a general view, seem just and rational, and suitable to the spirit and genius of Christianity; but, when we examine the particular branches into which they extend these general principles, the consequences they deduce from them, and the manner in which they apply them, in their rules of discipline and practice, we shall find, that the piety of this famous party is deeply tinged both with superstition and fanaticism; that it more especially favours the harsh and enthusiastical opinion of the Mystics; and, in consequence, that the Jansenists are not undeservedly branded by their adversaries with the appellation of Rigorists.‡ This denomination they merited in a peculiar manner, by their doctrine concerning repentance and penance, whose tendency, considered both in a civil and religious point of view, is singularly pernicious;

☞ * It must, however, be observed, that, notwithstanding the ascendency which the Jansenists have in Holland, the Jesuits, for some time past, have by artifice and disguise gained a considerable footing among the Romish churches that are tolerated by the republic.

† See Hist. Eccles. Rom. sæc. XVI. sect. xxxi.

‡ They who desire to form a just notion of the dismal piety of the Jansenists, (which carries the unseemly features of the gloomy devotion that was formerly practised by fanatical hermits in the deserts of Syria, Libya, and Egypt, but is entirely foreign from the dictates of reason and the amiable spirit of Christianity,) have only to peruse the epistles and other writings of the abbot of St. Cyran, who is the great oracle of the party. This abbot was a well-meaning man; and his piety, such as it was, carried in it the marks of sincerity and fervour; he was also superior, perhaps, as a pastor, to the greatest part of the Roman catholic doctors; and his learning, more especially his knowledge of religious antiquity, was very considerable; but to propose this man as a complete and perfect model of *genuine* piety, and as a most accurate and accomplished teacher of *Christian* virtue, is an absurdity peculiar to the Jansenists, and can be adopted by no person who knows what genuine piety and Christian virtue are. That we may not seem to detract rashly, and without reason, from the merit of this eminent man, it will not be improper to confirm what we have said by some instances. This good abbot, having undertaken to vanquish the *heretics*, (*i. e.* the protestants,) in a prolix and extensive work, was obliged to read, or at least to look into the various writings published by that *impious tribe;* and this he did in company with his nephew Martin de Barcos, who resembled him entirely in his sentiments and manners. But before he would venture to open a book composed by a protestant, he constantly marked it with the sign of the cross, to expel the evil spirit. What weakness and superstition did this ridiculous proceeding discover! for the good man was persuaded that Satan had fixed his residence in the books of the protestants; but it is not so easy to determine where he imagined the wicked spirit lay, whether in the paper, in the letters, between the leaves, or in the doctrines of these *infernal* productions. Let us see the account that is given of this matter by Lancelot, in his Memoires touchant la Vie de M. l'Abbe de S. Cyran, tom. i. p. 226. His words are as follow: "Il lisoit ces livres avec tant de piete, qu'en les prenant il les exorcisoit toujours en faisant la signe de la croix dessus, ne doutant point que le demon n'y residoit actuellement." His attachment to Augustine was so excessive, that he looked upon as sacred and divine even those opinions of that great man, which the wiser part of the Romish doctors had rejected as erroneous and highly dangerous. Such, (among others,) was the extravagant and pernicious tenet, that the saints are the only lawful proprietors of the world, and that the wicked have no right, by the divine law, to those things which they possess justly, in consequence of the decisions of human law. To this purpose is the following assertion of our abbot, as we find it in Fontaine's Memoires pour servir a l' Histoire de Port-Royal, tom. i. p. 201. "Jesus Christ n'est encore entre dans la possession de son royaume temporel, et des biens du monde qui lui appartiennent, que par cette *petite portion* qu'en tient l'eglise par les benefices de ses clercs, qui ne sont que les fermiers et les depositaires de Jesus Christ." If, therefore, we are to give credit to this visionary man, the golden age is approaching, when Jesus Christ, having pulled down the mighty from their seats, and dethroned the kings and princes of the earth, shall reduce the whole world under his sole dominion, and give it over to the government of priests and monks, who are the princes of his church.—After we have seen such sentiments as these maintained by their oracle and chief, it is natural to be surprised when we hear the Jansenists boasting of their zeal in defending sovereign states, and, in general, the civil rights of mankind, against the stratagems and usurpations of the pontiffs.

The notions of the abbot of St. Cyran concerning prayer, which breathe the fanatical spirit of mysticism, will farther confirm what we have said of his propensity to enthusiasm. It was, for example, a favourite maxim with him, that the Christian who prays, ought never to recollect the good things he stands in need of in order to ask them of God, since true prayer does not consist in distinct motions and clear ideas of what we are doing in that solemn act,

for they make repentance consist chiefly in those voluntary sufferings, which the transgressor inflicts upon himself, in proportion to the nature of his crimes and the degree of his guilt. As their notions of the extent of man's original corruption are greatly exaggerated, they prescribe remedies to it that are of the same nature. They look upon Christians as bound to expiate this original guilt by acts of mortification performed in solitude and silence, by torturing and macerating their bodies, by painful labour, excessive abstinence, continual prayer and contemplation; and they hold every person obliged to increase these voluntary pains and sufferings, in proportion to the degree of corruption derived by each from nature, or contracted by a vicious and licentious course of life. They even carry these austerities to so high a pitch, that they do not scruple to call those *holy* self-tormentors, who have gradually put an end to their days by excessive abstinence or labour, the 'sacred victims of repentance, that have been *consumed* by the fire of divine love.' Not satisfied with this fanatical language, they go still farther, and superstitiously maintain, that the conduct of these self-murderers is peculiarly meritorious in the eye of Heaven; and that their sufferings, macerations, and labours, appease the anger of the Deity, and not only contribute to their own felicity, but draw down abundant blessings upon their friends and upon the church. We might confirm this account by various examples, and more especially by that of the famous abbe de Paris, the great wonder-worker of the Jansenists, who put himself to a most painful death, in order to satisfy the justice of an incensed God:* such was the picture he had formed of the best of beings in his disordered fancy.

XLVII. A striking example of this austere, forbidding, and extravagant species of devotion, was exhibited in that celebrated female convent called Port-Royal in the Fields, which was situated in a retired, deep, and gloomy vale, not far from Paris. Henry IV. committed the inspection and government of this austere society, about the commencement of this century, to Jaqueline, daughter of Antoine Arnaud,† who, after her conversion, assumed the name of Marie Angelique de la Sainte-Madelaine. This lady had at first led a very dissolute life,‡ which was the general case of the cloistered fair in France about this period; but a remarkable change happened in her sentiments and manners, in 1609, when she resolved no more to live like a nun, but to consecrate her future days to deep devotion and penitential exercises. This holy resolution was strengthened by her acquaintance with the famous Francois de Sales, and the abbot of St. Cyran. The last of these pious connexions she formed in 1623, and regulated both her own conduct and the manners of her convent by the doctrine and example of these devout men. Hence it happened, that, during the whole course of this century, the convent of Port-Royal excited the indignation of the Jesuits, the admiration of the Jansenists, and the attention of Europe. The holy virgins observed, with the utmost rigour and exactness, that ancient rule of the Cistercians, which had been almost every where abrogated on account of its excessive and intolerable austerity: they even went beyond its most cruel demands.§ Such was the fame of this devout

but in a certain blind impulse of divine love. Such is the account given of the abbot's sentiments on this head by Lancelot, tom. ii. p. 44.—"Il ne croyoit pas, (says that author,) que l'on put faire quelque effort pour s'appliquer a quelque point, ou a quelque pensee particuliere—parce que la veritable priere est plutot un attrait de son amour, qui emporte notre cœur vers lui, et nous enleve comme hors de nous-memes, qu'une occupation de notre esprit, qui se remplisse de l'idee de quelque objeti quoi que divin." According to this hypothesis, the man prays best who neither *thinks* nor *asks*, in that act of devotion. This is, indeed, a very extraordinary account of the matter, and contains an idea of prayer which seems to have been quite unknown to Christ, and his apostles; for the former has commanded us to address our prayers to God in a set form of words; and the latter frequently tell us the subjects of their petitions and supplications.

But, of all the errors of this Arch-Jansenist, not one was so pernicious as the fanatical notion he entertained of his being the *residence* of the Deity, the *instrument* of the Godhead, by which the divine nature itself essentially operated. It was in consequence of this dangerous principle, that he recommended it as a duty incumbent on all pious men to follow, without consulting their judgment or any other guide, the first motions and impulses of their minds, as the dictates of Heaven. And, indeed, the Jansenists, in general, are intimately persuaded, that God operates immediately upon the minds of those who have composed, or rather suppressed, all the motions of the understanding and of the will, and that to such he declares, from above, his intentions and commands; since whatever thoughts, inclinations, or designs, arise within them, in this calm state of tranquillity and silence, are to be considered as the direct suggestions and oracles of the divine wisdom. See, for a farther account of this pestilential doctrine, the Memoires de Port Royal, tom iii. p. 246.

* See Morin's Com. de Pœnitentia, præf. p. 3, in which there is a tacit censure of the penance of the Jansenists.—See, on the other hand, the Memoires de Port-Royal.—The Jansenists, among all the meritorious actions of the abbot of St. Cyran, find none more worthy of admiration and applause than his restoring from oblivion the true system of penitential discipline; and they consider him as the second author or parent of the doctrine of penance. This very doctrine, however, was one of the principal reasons of his being committed to prison by the order of cardinal Richelieu.

† An eminent lawyer, and father to the famous Arnaud, doctor of the Sorbonne.

☞ ‡ The dissolute life imputed to this abbess by Dr. Mosheim is an egregious mistake, which seems to have proceeded from his misunderstanding a passage in Bayle's Dictionary, vol. i. p. 338, note f, the fourth French edition.

§ There is a prodigious multitude of books still extant, in which the rise, progress, laws, and sanctity, of this famous convent, are described and extolled by eminent Jansenists, who, at the same time, deplore its fate in the most doleful strains. Of this multitude we shall mention those only which may easily be procured, and which contain the most modern and circumstantial accounts of that celebrated establishment.—The Benedictines of St. Maur have given an exact, though dry history of this convent in their Gallia Christiana, tom. vii. A more elegant and agreeable account of it, charged, however, with imperfection and partiality, was composed by the famous poet Racine, under the title of Abrege de l'Histoire de Port-Royal, and was published, after having passed through many editions, in the year 1750, at Amsterdam, among the works of his son Louis Racine, tom. ii. The external state and form of this convent are professedly described by Moleon, in his Voyages Liturgiques, p. 234.—Add to these, Nic. Fontaine's Memoires pour servir a l'Histoire de

sisterhood, that multitudes of pious persons were ambitious to dwell in the neighbourhood of Port-Royal, and that a great part of the Jansenist Penitents, or self-tormentors, of both sexes, built huts without its precincts, where they imitated the manners of those austere and gloomy fanatics, who, in the fourth and fifth centuries, retired into the wild and uncultivated places of Syria and Egypt, and were commonly called the Fathers of the Desert. The end which these penitents had in view was, by silence, hunger, thirst, prayer, bodily labour, watchings, sorrow, and other voluntary acts of self-denial, to efface the guilt, and remove the pollution which the soul had derived from natural corruptions or evil habits.* They did not, however, all observe the same discipline, or follow the same kind of application and labour. The more learned consumed their strength in composing laborious productions filled with sacred and profane erudition, and some of these have, no doubt, deserved well of the republic of letters: others were employed in teaching youth the rudiments of language and the principles of science; but the far greatest part exhausted both the health of their bodies and the vigour of their minds in servile industry and rural labour, and thus pined away by a slow kind of death. What is singularly surprising is, that many of these voluntary victims of an inhuman piety were persons illustrious both by their birth and stations, who, after having distinguished themselves in civil or military employments, debased themselves so far in this penitential retreat, as to assume the character, offices, and labours, of the lowest servants.

This celebrated retreat of the devout and austere Jansenists was subject to many vicissitudes during the whole course of this century: at one time it flourished in unrivalled glory; at another, it seemed eclipsed, and on the brink of ruin. At length, however, the period of its extinction approached. The nuns obstinately refused to subscribe the declaration of pope Alexander VII., that has been so often mentioned; on the other hand, their convent and rule of discipline were considered as detrimental to the interests of the kingdom, and a dishonour to some of the first families in France; hence Louis XIV., in 1709, instigated by the violent counsels of the Jesuits, ordered the convent to be suppressed, the whole building to be levelled with the ground, and the nuns to be removed to Paris. And, lest there should still remain some secret fuel to nourish the flame of superstition in that place, he ordered the very carcases of the nuns and devout Jansenists to be dug up and buried elsewhere.

XLVIII. The other controversies that disturbed the tranquillity of the church of Rome, were but light blasts when compared with this violent hurricane. The old debate, however, between the Franciscans and Dominicans, concerning the immaculate conception of the Virgin Mary, which was maintained by the former, and denied by the latter, gave much trouble and perplexity to the pontiffs, and more especially to Paul V., Gregory XV., and Alexander VII. The kingdom of Spain was so agitated and divided into factions by this controversy, in the former part of this century, tha solemn embassies were sent to Rome, both by Philip III., and his successor, with a view to engage the Roman pontiff to determine the question, or, at any rate, to put an end to the contest by a public edict. But, notwithstanding the weighty solicitations of these monarchs, the oracle of Rome pronounced nothing but ambiguous words; and its high priests prudently avoided coming to a plain and positive decision of the affair. If they were awed, on one hand, by the warm remonstrances of the Spanish court, which favoured the sentiment of the Franciscans, they were restrained, on the other, by the credit and influence of the Dominicans: so that, after the most earnest entreaties and importunities, all that could be obtained from the pontiff, by the court of Spain, was a declaration, intimating that the opinion of the Franciscans had a high degree of probability on its side, and forbidding the Dominicans to oppose it in a public manner; but this declaration was accompanied with

Port-Royal, published in 1738.—The Memoires (by Du-Fosse) pour servir a l'Histoire de Port-Royal; and the Recueil de plusiers Pieces pour servir a l'Histoire de Port-Royal.—The editor of this last compilation promises, in his preface, farther collections of pieces relative to the same subject, and seems to insinuate, that a complete history of Port-Royal, drawn from these and other valuable and authentic records, will sooner or later see the light. See, beside the authors above-mentioned, Lancelot's Memoires touchant la Vie de l'Abbe de St. Cyran. All these authors confine their relations to the external form and various revolutions of this nunnery. Its internal state, its rules of discipline, the manners of its virgins, and the incidents and transactions that happened between them and the holy neighbourhood of Jansenists, are described and related by another set of writers. See the Memoires pour servir a l'Histoire de Port-Royal, et a la Vie de Marie Angelique D'Arnaud, published at Utrecht in 1742; also the Vies interessantes et edifiantes des Religieuses de Port-Royal, et de plusieurs Personnes qui leur etoient attachees; and, for an account of the suppression and abolition of this convent, see the Memoires sur la Destruction de l'Abbaye de Port-Royal des Champs. If we do not mistake, all these histories and relations have been much less serviceable to the reputation of this famous convent than the Jansenist party are willing to think. When we view Arnaud, Tillemont, Nicole, Le Maitre, and the other authors of Port-Royal, in their learned productions, they then appear truly great; but, when we lay aside their works, and, taking up these histories of Port-Royal, see these great men in private life, in the constant practice of that austere discipline of which the Jansenists boast so foolishly, they shrink almost to nothing, appear in the contemptible light of fanatics, and seem totally unworthy of the fame they have acquired. When we read the Discourses that Isaac le Maitre, commonly called Sacy, pronounced at the bar, together with his other ingenious productions, we cannot refuse him the applause that is due to such an elegant and accomplished writer; but when we meet with this polite author at Port-Royal, mixed with labourers and reapers, and with the spade or the sickle in his hand, he certainly makes a ludicrous or comical figure, and can scarcely be looked upon as perfectly right in his head.

* Among the most eminent of these penitents was Isaac le Maitre, a celebrated advocate at Paris, whose eloquence had procured him a shining reputation, and who, in 1637, retired to Port-Royal, to make expiation for his sins. The retreat of this eminent man raised new enemies to the abbot of St. Cyran. See the Memoires pour l'Histoire de Port-Royal, tom. i. p. 223. The example of Le Maitre was followed by some persons of the highest distinction, and by a great number of persons of all ranks. See the Vies des Religieuses de Port Royal, t. i. p. 141

another,* by which the Franciscans were prohibited, in their turn, from treating as erroneous the doctrine of the Dominicans. This accommodation of the dispute would have been highly laudable in a prince or civil magistrate, who, unacquainted with theological questions of such an abstruse nature, preferred the tranquillity of his people to the discussion of such an intricate and unimportant point; but whether it was honourable to a supreme pontiff, who boasts of a divine right to decide all religious controversies, and pretends to a degree of inspiration that places him beyond the possibility of erring, we leave to the consideration of those who have his glory at heart.

XLIX. The controversies with the Mystics were now renewed; and that sect, which in former times enjoyed such a high degree of reputation and authority, was treated with the greatest severity, and involved in the deepest distress, toward the conclusion of this century. This unhappy change in its affairs was principally occasioned by the fanaticism and imprudence of Michael de Molinos, a Spanish priest, who resided at Rome, and the fame of whose ardent piety and devotion procured him a considerable number of disciples of both sexes. A book published at Rome in 1681, by this ecclesiastic, under the title of the Spiritual Guide, alarmed the doctors of the church.† This book contained, beside the usual precepts and institutions of mystic theology, several notions relating to a spiritual and contemplative life, that seemed to revive the pernicious and infernal errors of the Beghards, and open a door to all sorts of licentiousness and profligacy. The principles of Molinos, which have been very differently interpreted by his friends and enemies, amount to this: "that the whole of religion consists in the perfect tranquillity of a mind removed from all external and finite things, and centred in God, and in such a pure love of the Supreme Being, as is independent of all prospect of interest or reward;" or, to express the doctrine of this Mystic, in other words, "The soul, in the pursuit of the supreme good, must retire from the reports and gratifications of sense, and, in general, from all corporeal objects, and, imposing silence upon all the motions of the understanding and will, must be absorbed in the Deity." Hence the denomination of Quietist was given to the followers of Molinos; though that of Mystic, which was their vulgar title, was more applicable, and expressed with greater propriety their fanatical system; for the doctrine of Molinos had no other circumstance of novelty attending it, than the singular terms he employed in unfolding his notions, and the ingenuity he discovered in digesting what the ancient Mystics had thrown out in the most confused and incoherent jargon, into something that looked like a system. The Jesuits, and other zealous votaries of Rome, soon perceived that his system was a tacit censure of the Romish church, as having departed from the spirit of true religion, by placing the essence of piety in external works, and in the performance of a certain round of ceremonies. But the warmest opposition that he met with was from the French ambassador* at Rome, who raised a most violent persecution against him. This made many imagine, that it was not his theological system alone that had inflamed the resentment of that minister, but that some considerations of a political nature had been blended with this famous controversy, and that the Spanish Mystic had opposed the designs and negotiations of the French monarch at the court of Rome. However that may have been, Molinos, unable to resist the storm, and abandoned by those from whom he chiefly expected succour, yielded to it in 1685, when, notwithstanding the number, rank, and credit of his friends at Rome, and the particular marks of favour he had received from the pontiff,† he was thrown into prison. Two years after this, he was obliged to renounce, in a public manner, the errors of which he was accused; and this solemn recantation was followed by a sentence of perpetual imprisonment, from which he was, in an advanced age, delivered by death, in 1696.‡ The candid and impartial will be obliged to acknowledge, that the opinions and expressions of this enthusiast were perfidiously misrepresented and perverted by the Jesuits and others, whose interest it was that he should be put out of the way, and excluded from every

* See Fred. Ulr. Calixti Historia Immaculatæ Conceptionis B. Virginis Mariæ, published in 1696.—Hornbeckii Comm. ad Bullam Urbani VIII. de diebus Festis, p. 250.—Launoii Præscriptiones de Conceptu Virginis Mariæ, tom. i. p. i. oper.—Long after this period, Clement XI. went a step farther, and appointed, in 1708, a festival to be celebrated, in honour of the immaculate conception, throughout the Romish church. See the Memoires de Trevoux for the year 1709, art. xxxviii. p. 514. But the Dominicans obstinately deny that the obligation of this law extends to them, and persist in maintaining their ancient doctrine, though with more modesty and circumspection than they formerly discovered in this debate; and when we consider that their opinion in this respect has never been expressly condemned by any pope, and that they are not in the least molested, or even censured, for refusing to celebrate the festival above-mentioned, it appears evidently, from all this, that the terms of the papal edict are to be understood with certain restrictions, and interpreted in a mild and indulgent manner; and that the spirit of this edict is not contrary to the tenor of the former declarations of the pontiffs on this head. See Lamindus Pritanius (a fictitious name assumed by the author Muratori) de Ingeniorum Moderatione in Religionis Negotio, p. 254.

† This work, which was published in 1675, was honoured with the approbation and encomiums of many eminent and respectable personages. It was translated into Latin, Italian, French, and Dutch, and passed through many editions. There is another work of Molinos composed in the same spirit, concerning the daily celebration of the communion, which was also condemned. See the "Recueil de diverses Pieces concernant le Quietisme et les Quietistes, ou Molinos, ses Sentimens et ses Disciples," published at Amsterdam, in 1688, in which the reader will find a French translation of the Spiritual Guide, together with a collection of letters on various subjects, written by Molinos.

* Cardinal d'Estrees.

† Innocent XI.

‡ He was born in the diocese of Saragossa, in 1627; see the Biblioth. Janseniste, p. 469.—For an account of this controversy, see the Narrative of the Proceedings of the Controversy concerning Quietism, subjoined to the German translation of Burnet's Travels as also Arnoldi Histor. Eccles. et Hæretic. tom. iii c. xvii.—Jaegeri Histor. Eccles. et Polit. Sæculi XVII. decen. ix.—Plessis D'Argentre, Collectio Judiciorum de novis Erroribus. t. iii. p. 357, where may be seen the papal edicts relating to this controversy.

thing but contemplation and repose; and it is most certain, that his doctrine was charged with consequences which he neither approved nor even apprehended. But, on the other hand, it must also be confessed, that his system was chargeable with the greatest part of the reproaches that are justly thrown upon the Mystics, and favoured much the illusions and follies of those fanatics, who would make the crude visions of their disordered fancies pass for divine revelations.*

L. It would have been truly surprising had a system of piety, that was so adapted to seduce the indolent mind, to captivate the warm imagination, and melt the tender heart, been destitute of votaries and followers. This was by no means the case. In Italy, Spain, France, and the Netherlands, Molinos had a considerable number of disciples; and, beside the reasons we have now hinted, another circumstance must have contributed much to multiply his votaries; for, in all parts of the Romish dominion, there were numbers of persons, who had sense and knowledge enough to perceive, that the whole of religion could not consist in external rites and bodily mortifications, but too little to direct themselves in religious matters, or to substitute what was right in the place of what they knew to be wrong; and hence it was natural for them to follow the first plausible guide that was offered to them. But the church of Rome, apprehensive of the consequences of this mystic theology, left no method unemployed that could contribute to stop its progress; and, by the force of promises and threats, of severity and mildness properly applied, stifled in the birth the commotions and changes it seemed adapted to excite. The death of Molinos contributed also to dispel the anxiety of the Romish doctors, since his disciples and followers seemed too inconsiderable to deserve any notice. Among these are generally reckoned cardinal Petrucci, Francis de la Combe, a Barnabite friar, (the spiritual director of Madame Guyon,) Francis Malavalle, Bernier de Louvigni, and others of less note. These enthusiasts, as is common among the Mystics, differ from Molinos in several points, and are also divided among themselves. This diversity is, however, rather nominal than real; and, if we consider the true signification of the terms by which they express their respective notions, we shall find that they all set out from the same principles, and tend to the same conclusions.†

LI. One of the principal patrons and propagators of Quietism in France was Marie Bouvieres de la Mothe Guyon, a woman of fashion, remarkable for the goodness of her heart and the regularity of her manners, but of an inconstant and unsettled temper, and subject to be drawn away by the seduction of a warm and unbridled fancy. This female apostle of mysticism derived all her ideas of religion from the feelings of her own heart,* and described its nature to others as she felt it herself; a manner of proceeding which is extremely uncertain and delusive. And, accordingly, her religious sentiments made a great noise in 1687, and gave offence to many. Hence, after they had been attentively and accurately examined by several men of eminent piety and learning, they were pronounced erroneous and unsound, and, in 1697, were professedly confuted by the celebrated Bossuet. This gave rise to a controversy of still greater moment, between the prelate last mentioned, and Francis Salignac de Fenelon, archbishop of Cambray, whose sublime virtue and superior genius were beheld with veneration in all the countries of Europe. Of these two disputants, who, in point of eloquence, were avowedly without either superiors or equals in France, the latter seemed disposed to favour the religious system of Madame Guyon; for, when Bossuet desired his approbation of the book he had composed in answer to the sentiments of that female mystic, Fenelon not only refused it, but openly declared that this pious woman had been treated with great partiality and injustice, and that the censures of her adversary were unmerited and groundless. Nor did the warm imagination of this amiable prelate permit him to stop here, where the dictates of prudence ought to have set bounds to his zeal; for, in the same year, he published a book,† in which he adopted several of the tenets of Madame Guyon, and more expecially that favourite doctrine of the Mystics, which teaches that the love of the Supreme Being must be pure and disinterested; that is, exempt from all views of interest and all hope of reward.‡ This doctrine Fenelon explained with pathetic eloquence, and confirmed it by the authority of many of the most eminent and pious among

* All that can be alleged in defence of Molinos has been collected by Weisman, in his Histor. Ecclesiast. sæc. XVII.

† The writings of these fanatics are enumerated and sharply criticised by Colonia, in the Bibliotheque Quietiste (which he has subjoined to his Biblioth. Janseniste,) p. 455, 488.—See also God. Arnoldi Hist. et Descriptio Theologiæ Mysticæ, p. 364, and Poiret's Biblio. Mysticorum.

* The writings of this lady abound with childish allegories and mystic ejaculations. She wrote an account of her own life and spiritual adventures; but her principal production was La Bible de Mad. Guyon, avec des Explications et Reflexions qui regardent la Vie interieure. This Bible, with Annotations relating to the hidden or internal Life, was published in 1715, in twenty volumes in 8vo. and the notes abundantly discover the fertile imagination and shallow judgment of this female mystic.—See a farther account of her in the Letters of Mad. de Maintenon, tom. i. ii.

† This book was entitled, Explication des Maximes des Saints sur la Vie interieure. It has been translated into Latin.

☞ ‡ This doctrine has thus far a foundation in reason and philosophy, that the moral perfections of the Deity are, in themselves, *intrinsically amiable;* and that their excellence is as much adapted to excite our esteem and love, as the experience of their beneficent effects in promoting our well-being, is to inflame our gratitude. The error, therefore, of the mystics lay in their drawing extravagant conclusions from a right principle, and in their requiring in their followers a perpetual abstraction and separation of ideas which are intimately connected, and, as it were, blended together, such as felicity and perfection; for, though these two are inseparable in fact, yet the mystics, from a fantastic pretension to disinterestedness, would separate them right or wrong, and turned their whole attention to the latter. In their views also of the Supreme Being, they overlooked the important relations he bears to us as *benefactor* and *rewarder;* relations which certainly give rise to noble sentiments and important duties, and confined their views to his supreme beauty, excellence, and perfection.

the Romish doctors. Bossuet, whose leading passion was ambition, and who beheld with anxiety the rising fame and eminent talents of Fenelon as an obstacle to his glory, was highly exasperated by this opposition, and left no method unemployed which artifice and jealousy could suggest to mortify a rival whose illustrious merit had rendered him so formidable. For this purpose, he threw himself at the feet of Louis XIV., implored the pope's aid, and, by his importunities and stratagems, obtained the condemnation of Fenelon's book. This censure was pronounced, in 1699, by Innocent XII., who, in a public brief, declared that book unsound in general, and branded with peculiar marks of disapprobation twenty-three propositions, specified by that Congregation which had been appointed to examine it. The book, however, was condemned alone, without any mention of the author; and the conduct of Fenelon on this occasion was very remarkable. He declared publicly his entire acquiescence in the sentence by which his book had been condemned, and not only read that sentence to his people in the pulpit at Cambray, but exhorted them to respect and obey the papal decree.* This step was differently interpreted by different persons, according to their notions of this great man, or their respective ways of thinking. Some considered it as an instance of true magnanimity, as the mark of a meek and gentle spirit, that preferred the peace of the church to every private view of interest or glory. Others, less charitable, looked upon this submissive conduct as ignoble and pusillanimous, as denoting manifestly a want of integrity, inasmuch as it implied, that the prelate condemned with his lips what in his heart he believed to be true. One thing indeed seems generally agreed on; and that is, that Fenelon persisted, to the end of his days, in the sentiments which, in obedience to the order of the pope, he retracted and condemned in a public manner.

LII. Beside these controversies, which derived their importance chiefly from the influence and reputation of the disputants, and thus became productive of great tumults and divisions in the church, there were others excited by several innovators, whose new and singular opinions were followed by troubles, though of a less momentous and permanent nature. Such was the strange doctrine of Isaac la Peyrere, who, in two small treatises, published in 1655, maintained that it is the origin of the Jewish nation, and not of the human race, that we find recorded in the books of Moses, and that our globe was inhabited by many nations before Adam, whom he considered as merely the father of the Jews. Though Peyrere was a protestant when he published this opinion, yet the doctors of the Romish church thought themselves bound to punish an error that seemed to strike at the foundation of all revealed religion; and, therefore, in 1656, had him seized at Brussels, and thrown into prison, where, to escape the flames, he publicly renounced his erroneous system, and, to make a full expiation for it, embraced the popish religion.*

Thomas White, known at different times, and in different countries, by the names of Albius, Anglus, Candidus, Bianchi,† which he assumed successively, made a considerable figure, about the middle of this century, in England, Portugal, France, and the Netherlands, by the number and subtlety of his philosophical productions; but he also incurred the displeasure of many of the doctors of his communion, on account of the novelty and singularity of his opinions. He was undoubtedly a man of genius and penetration; but, being a passionate admirer of the Peripatetic philosophy, he ventured to employ it in the explication of some of the peculiar doctrines of the Romish church. This bold attempt led him imperceptibly out of the beaten road of popery, opened to him new views of things, and made him adopt notions that had never been heard of in the church of Rome; and hence his books were prohibited and condemned in several places, and particularly at Rome by the Congregation of the Index. This innovator is said to have died in England, his native country, and to have left a sect behind him that embraced his doctrine, but which, in process of time, fell into oblivion.‡

His peculiarities, however, were nothing, in comparison with the romantic notions of Joseph Francis Borri, a Milanese knight, eminent for his knowledge of chemistry and physic; but who, at the same time, appears to have been rather a madman than a heretic. The fancies broached by this man, concerning the Virgin Mary, the Holy Ghost, the erection of a new celestial kingdom, of which he himself was to be the founder, and the downfall of the Roman pontiff, are so extravagant, childish, and absurd, that no sober person can view them in any other light than as the crude reveries of a disordered brain. Besides, the conduct of this fanatic, in many instances, discovered the greatest vanity and levity, attended with that spirit of imposture which is usually visible in quacks and mountebanks; and, indeed, in the whole of his behaviour, he seemed destitute of sense, integrity, and prudence. The inquisitors had spread their snares for Borri; but he fortunately escaped them, and wandered up and down through a great part of Europe, giving himself out for another Æsculapius, and pretending to be initiated into the most profound mysteries of chemical science. But, in 1672, he imprudently fell

* An ample and impartial account of this controversy has been given by Toussaint du Plessis, a Benedictine, in his Histoire de l'Eglise de Meaux, livre v. tom. i. p. 485—523.—Ramsay, in his life of Fenelon, is less impartial, but is nevertheless worthy of being consulted on this subject. See Voltaire's Siecle de Louis XIV. tom. ii. p. 301.—The public acts and edicts relating to this controversy have been collected by M. du Plessis Argentre, in his Collectio Judiciorum, tom. iii.

* Bayle's Dictionary.—Arnold's Histor. Eccles. et Hæret. tom. iii.—Menagiana, published by M. de la Monnoye, tom. ii.

☞ † All these denominations bear reference to his true name, which was White. This man was a peculiar favourite of Sir Kenelm Digby, and mentions him with singular veneration in his philosophical writings. See more of this White in Wood's Athenæ Oxon. second edit. vol. ii. p. 665, and in the Biograph. Brit. article Glanville, vol. iv. p. 2296.

‡ See Bayle's Dictionary, at the article *Anglus*.—Baillet, Vie de M. Des Cartes, tom. ii.

into the power of the pontiff, who pronounced against him a sentence of perpetual imprisonment.*

The last innovator we shall here mention is Celestine Sfondrati, who, having formed the design of terminating the disputes concerning predestination, by new explications of that doctrine, wrote a book upon that knotty subject, which threw into combustion, in 1696, a considerable part of the Romish church, since it was, in some things, agreeable to none of the contending parties, and neither satisfied entirely the Jesuits nor their adversaries.† Five French bishops, of great credit at the court of Rome, accused the author, notwithstanding the high rank of cardinal to which he had been raised on account of his extensive learning, of various errors, and more especially of having departed from the sentiments and doctrine of Augustine. This accusation was brought before Innocent XII. in 1696; but the contest which it seemed calculated to excite was nipped in the bud. The pontiff appeased, or rather put off, the French prelates, with a fair promise that he would appoint a congregation to examine the cardinal's doctrine, and then pronounce sentence accordingly; but he forgot his promise, imitated the prudent conduct of his predecessors on like occasions, and did not venture to decide this intricate controversy.

LIII. There was scarcely any change introduced into the Romish ritual during this century, if we except an edict of Urban VIII., issued in 1643,‡ for diminishing the number of holidays: we shall therefore conclude this account with a list of the saints added to the calendar by the Roman pontiffs during the period now before us.

In the year 1601, Clement VIII. raised to that spiritual dignity Raymond of Pennafort, the famous compiler of the Decretals; in 1608, Frances Pontiani, a Benedictine nun; and, in 1610, the eminent and illustrious Charles Borromeo, bishop of Milan, so justly celebrated for his exemplary piety, and almost unparalleled liberality and beneficence.

Gregory XV. conferred, in 1622, the honour of saintship on Theresa, a native of Avila in Spain, and a nun of the Carmelite order.

Urban VIII. in 1623, conferred the same spiritual honours on Philip Neri, the founder of the order entitled Fathers of the Oratory, in Italy; on Ignatius Loyola, the parent of the Jesuits; and on his chief disciple Francis Xavier, the Apostle of the Indians.

Alexander VII. canonized, in 1658, Thomas de Villanueva, a Spanish monk, of the order of St. Augustin; and, in 1665, Francis de Sales, bishop of Geneva.

Clement X. added to this honourable list, in 1670, Pedro de Alcantara, a Franciscan monk, and Maria Magdalena Pactii, a Florentine nun of the Carmelite order; and, in 1671, Rose, an American virgin, of the third order of Dominick, and Louis Bertrand, a Dominican monk.

Under the pontificate of Innocent XII. saintship was conferred upon Caietan of Vicenza, a regular clerk of the order of Theatins, for whom that honour had been designed twenty years before by Clement X. who died at the time when the canonization was to have been performed. John of Leon, also, a hermit of St. Augustine; Pascal Baylonio, a Franciscan monk of the kingdom of Arragon; and John de Dieu, a Portuguese, and one of the order of the Brethren of Hospitality, all of whom had been marked for a place in the calendar by Alexander VIII., were solemnly canonized, in 1691, by Innocent XII.*

CHAPTER II.

The History of the Greek and Oriental Churches.

I. THE history of the Greek and Eastern Christians, faithfully and accurately composed, would, no doubt, furnish us with a variety of entertaining and useful records; but the events that happen, and the transactions that are carried on in those distant regions, are very rarely transmitted to us genuine and uncorrupted. The spirit of religious party, and the pious frauds which it often engenders, want of proper information, and undistinguishing credulity, have introduced a fabulous mixture into the accounts we have of the state of the Christian religion in the East; and this consideration has engaged us to treat in a more concise manner than would otherwise have been expedient, this particular branch of ecclesiastical history.

The Greek church, whose wretched situation was mentioned in the history of the preceding century, continued, during the present one, in the same deplorable state of ignorance and decay, destitute of the means of acquiring or promoting solid and useful knowledge. This

* There is a very interesting article in Bayle's Dictionary relating to Borri, in which all the extravagances of that wrong-headed man are curiously related. See also Arnold's History, p. iii. c. xviii. p. 193.

† This book, which was published at Rome in 1696, is entitled, Nodus Prædestinationis dissolutus. The letters of the French bishops, with the answer of the pontiff, are to be found in Du-Plessis D'Argentre's Collectio Judiciorum, tom. iii. and in Natalis Alexander's Theologia Dogmatica et Moralis, p. 877. The letters of the bishops are remarkable in this respect, that they contain sharp animadversions upon the Jesuits and their discipline. The prelates express, in the strongest terms, their abhorrence of the doctrine of philosophical sin, which rendered the Jesuits so deservedly infamous, and their detestation of the methods of propagating Christianity employed by the missionaries of that order in China; and, to express their aversion to the doctrine of Sfondrati, they say, that his opinions are still more erroneous and pernicious than even those of the Molinists. The doctrine of this cardinal has been accurately represented and compared with that of Augustin by the learned Basnage, in his Histoire de l'Eglise, livre xii. c. iii. sect. xi.

‡ This bull may be seen in the Nouvelle Bibliotheque, tom. xv. p. 88.

* The diplomas of the pontiffs, relative to all these canonizations, may be seen in Fontanini's Codex Constitutionum, quas summi Pontifices ediderunt in solemni Canonizatione sanctorum, p. 260, published at Rome, in 1729. As they contain the particular reasons which occasioned the elevation of these persons to a place in the calendar, and the peculiar kind of merit on which each promotion was founded, they offer abundant matter for reflection and censure to a judicious reader. Nor would it be labour ill employed to inquire, without prejudice or partiality, into the justice, piety, and truth of what the popes allege in these diplomas, as the reasons for conferring saintship on the persons therein mentioned.

account is, however, to be considered as taken from a general view of that church; for several of its members may be alleged as exceptions from the prevailing character of ignorance, superstition, and corruption. Among the multitude of Greeks who travel into Sicily, Italy, England, Holland, and Germany, or carry on trade in their own country, or fill honourable and important posts in the courts of the Turkish emperors, there are undoubtedly some who are exempt from this reproach of ignorance and stupidity, of superstition and profligacy, and who make a figure by their opulence and credit.* But nothing can be more rooted and invincible than the aversion the Greeks in general discover to the Latin or Romish church; an aversion which neither promises nor threats, artifice nor violence, have been able to conquer, or even to temper or diminish, and which has continued inflexible and unrelenting amidst the most zealous efforts of the Roman pontiffs, and the various means employed by their numerous missionaries, to gain over this people to their communion and jurisdiction.† It is true, indeed, that the Latin Christians have founded churches in some of the islands of the Archipelago; but these congregations are poor and inconsiderable; nor will either the Greeks or their masters, the Turks, permit the Romish missionaries to extend farther their spiritual jurisdiction.

II. Under the pontificate of Urban VIII great hopes were entertained of softening the antipathy of the Greeks against the Latin church,* and of engaging them and the other Christians of the East, to embrace the communion of Rome, and acknowledge the supremacy and jurisdiction of its pontiff. This was the chief object that excited the ambitious zeal and employed the assiduous labour and activity of Urban, who called to his assistance such ecclesiastics as were most eminent for their acquaintance with Greek and Oriental learning, and with the tempers, manners, and characters of the Christians in those distant regions, that they might suggest the shortest and most effectual method of bringing them and their churches under the Roman yoke. The wisest of these counsellors advised the pontiff to lay it down for a preliminary in this difficult negotiation, that the Greek and Eastern Christians were to be indulged in almost every point that had hitherto been refused them by the Romish missionaries, and that no alteration was to be introduced either into their ritual or doctrine; that their ceremonies were to be tolerated, since they did not concern the essence of religion; and that their doctrine was to be explained and understood in such a manner as might give it a near and striking resemblance to the doctrine and institutions of the church of Rome. In defence of this method of proceeding, it was judiciously observed, that the Greeks would be much more tractable and obsequious, were they told by the missionaries, that it was not meant to convert them; that they had always been Roman catholics in reality, though not in profession; and that the popes had no intention of persuading them to abandon the doctrine of their ancestors, but only desired that they would understand it in its true and genuine sense. This plan gave rise to a variety of laborious productions, in which there was more learning than probity, and more dexterity than candour and good faith. Such were the treatises published by Leo Allatius, Morinus, Clement Galanus, Lucas Holstenius, Abraham Ecchellensis,† and

* I have been led to these remarks by the complaints of Alexander Helladius, and of others who see things in the light in which he has placed them. There is still extant a book published in Latin by this author, in 1714, entitled, The present State of the Greek Church, in which he throws out the bitterest reproaches upon several authors of eminent merit and learning, who have given accounts of that church, and maintains that his brethren of the Greek communion are much more pious, learned, wise, and opulent, than they are commonly supposed to be. Instead of envying the Greeks the merit and felicity which this panegyrist supposes them to possess, we sincerely wish them much greater degrees of both. But we observe at the same time, that from the very accounts given by Helladius it would be easy to prove, that the state of the Greeks is not a whit better than it is generally supposed to be; though it may be granted, that the same ignorance, superstition, and immorality, do not abound alike in all places, or among all persons. See what we have remarked on this subject in the accounts we have given of the Eastern church, during the sixteenth century.

† The Jesuit Tarillon has given an ample relation of the numerous missions in Greece and the other provinces of the Ottoman empire, and of the present state of these missions, in his letter to Pontchartrain, sur l'Etat present des Missions des Peres Jesuites dans la Grece, published in the Nouveaux Memoires des Missions de la Compagnie de Jesus, tom. i. p. 1125. For an account of the state of the Romish religion in the islands of the Archipelago, see the letter of the Jesuit Xavier Portier, in the Lettres edifiantes et curieuses, ecrites des Missions etrangeres, t. x. p. 328. These accounts are, it is true, somewhat embellished, in order to advance the glory of the Jesuits; but the exaggerations of these missionaries may be easily corrected by the accounts of other writers, who, in our times, have treated this branch of ecclesiastical history. See, above all others, R. Simon's (under the fictitious name of Saint-Jore) Bibliotheque Critique, tom. i. c. xxiii. p. 340, and especially p. 346, where the author confirms a remarkable fact, which we have mentioned above upon the authority of Cerri, namely, that, amidst the general dislike which the Greeks have to the Romish church, no persons carry this dislike to such a high degree of antipathy and aversion, as those very Greeks who have been educated at Rome, or in the other schools and seminaries belonging to its spiritual jurisdiction. "Ils sont (says Father Simon) les premiers a crier contre et a medire du pape et des Latins. Ces pelerins Orientaux qui viennent chez nous, fourbent et abusent de notre credulite, pour acheter un benefice, et tourmenter les missionaries Latins, &c." We have still more recent and ample testimonies of the invincible hatred of the Greeks toward the Latins, in the preface to Cowell's Account of the present Greek church.

* See the Life of Morinus, prefixed to his Antiquitates Eccles. Orient. p. 37.

† The book of Leo Allatius, *de Concordia Ecclesiæ Orientalis et Occidentalis*, is well known, and deservedly looked upon, by the most learned protestants, as the work of a disingenuous and insidious writer. The Græcia Orthodoxa of the same author, which was published at Rome in 1652, and contains a compilation from all the books of the Grecian doctors who were well affected to the Latin church, is still extant.—We have nothing of Lucas Holstenius (who was superior to Allatius in learning and sagacity) upon this subject, except two posthumous dissertations, *de Ministro et Forma Sacramenti Confirmationis apud Græcos*, which were published at Rome in 1666.—The treatises of Morinus, de Pœnitentia et Ordinationibus, are known to all the learned, and seem expressly composed to make the world believe, that there is a striking conformity of sentiment between the Greek and Latin churches on these two

others who pretended to demonstrate, that there was little or no difference between the religion of the Greeks, Armenians and Nestorians, and that of the church of Rome, a few ceremonies excepted, together with some unusual phrases and terms that are peculiar to the Christians of the East.

The design of bringing, by artful compliances, the Greek and Eastern churches under the jurisdiction of Rome, was opposed by many, but by none with more resolution and zeal than by Cyril Lucar, patriarch of Constantinople, a man of extensive learning and knowledge of the world, who had visited a great part of Europe, and was well acquainted with the doctrine and discipline, both of the protestant and papal churches. This prelate declared openly, and indeed with more courage than prudence, that he had a strong propensity to the religious sentiments of the English and Dutch churches, and had conceived the design of reforming the doctrine and ritual of the Greeks, and bringing them nearer to the purity and simplicity of the Gospel. This was sufficient to render the venerable patriarch odious to the friends of Rome; and accordingly the Jesuits, seconded by the credit and influence of the French ambassador, and assisted by the treacherous stratagems of some perfidious Greeks, continued to perplex and persecute the good man in various ways, and at length accomplished his ruin; for, by the help of false witnesses, they obtained an accusation of treason against him; in consequence of which he was put to death, in 1638, by the mandate of the Turkish emperor.* He was succeeded by Cyril, bishop of Berea, a man of a dark, malignant, and violent spirit, and the infamous instrument the Jesuits had chiefly employed in bringing him to an untimely end. As this new patriarch declared himself openly in favour of the Latins, the reconciliation of the Greeks with the church of Rome seemed more probable than ever, and almost certain;* but the dismal fate of this unworthy prelate suddenly dispelled the pleasing hopes and the anxious fears with which Rome and its adversaries beheld the approach of this important event. The same violent death that had concluded the days of Cyril Lucar pursued his successor, in whose place Parthenius, a zealous opposer of the doctrine and ambitious pretensions of Rome, was raised to the patriarchal dignity. After this period the Roman pontiffs desisted from their attempts upon the Greek church, no opportunity being offered either of deposing its patriarchs, or gaining them over to the Romish communion.

III. Notwithstanding these unsuccessful attempts of the pontiffs to reduce the Greek church under their dominion, many allege, and more especially the reformed clergy complain, that the doctrine of that church has been manifestly corrupted by the emissaries of Rome. It is supposed, that, in later times, the munificence of the French ambassadors at the Porte, and the persuasive sophistry of the Jesuits, have made such irresistible impressions on the avarice and ignorance of the Greek bishops, whose poverty is great, that they have departed, in several points, from the religious system of their ancestors, and have adopted, among other errors of the Romish church, the monstrous and unnatural doctrine of transubstantiation. This change is said to have been more especially brought about in the famous council, which was assembled, in 1672, at Jerusalem, by Dositheus, the patriarch of that city.† Without entering into an examination of the truth and equity of this charge brought against the Greek bishops, we shall only observe, that it was the controversy between the catholics and protestants in France that first gave rise to it. The latter, and more especially John Claude, so justly celebrated for his extensive learning and masterly eloquence, maintained, that many of the doctrines of the Romish church, and more particularly that of transubstantiation, were of a modern date, and had never been heard of before the ninth century. The catholics on the contrary, with Arnaud at their head, affirmed, that the doctrine of Rome concerning the eucharist, and the real conversion of the bread and wine

important points, when laying aside the difference that scholastic terms and peculiar modes of expression may appear to occasion, we attend to the meaning that is annexed to these terms by the members of the two communions. Galanus, in a long and laborious work, has endeavoured to prove, that the Armenians differ very little from the Latins in their religious opinions; and Abraham Ecchellensis has attempted to convince us in several treatises, (and more especially in his Animadversiones ad Hebed. Jesu Catalogum librorum Chaldaicorum) that all Christians throughout Africa and Asia have the same system of doctrine that is received among the Latins.

* The Confession of Faith, drawn up by Cyril Lucar, was published in Holland, in 1645; and is also inserted by Aymon in his Monumens authentiques de la Religion des Grecs, p. 237. By this confession, it appears evidently, that this prelate had a stronger inclination toward the doctrine of the reformed churches, than to that which was commonly received among the Greeks. Nor was he, by any means, ill-affected toward the Lutherans, since he addressed several letters to the Swedish clergy about this time, and solicited their friendship, as appears from the learned Archenholtz' Memoires de la Reine Christine. —Aymon has published, in the work already mentioned, twenty-seven letters of this patriarch to the clergy of Geneva, and to the doctors of the reformed church, in which his religious sentiments are still more plainly discovered. His life, transactions, and deplorable fate, have been recorded by Thomas Smith, a learned divine of the English church, in his Narratio de Vita, Studiis, Gestis et Martyrio Cyrilli Lucaris, which is the third article of his Miscellanea; as also by Hottinger, and by other authors mentioned by Fabricius in his Bibliotheca Græca.

* See Eliæ Vegellii Defensio Exerc. de Ecclesia Græca, p. 300, where we find the letters of pope Urban VIII. to Cyril of Berea, in which he loads with applause this new patriarch, for having been so instrumental in banishing from among the Greeks the pernicious errors of Cyril Lucar, and warmly exhorts him to depose all the Greek patriarchs and bishops who are not favourable to the Latin church. These exhortations are seconded by flattering promises, and, particularly, by an assurance of protection and succour from the king of Spain. Cyril of Berea died in the communion of the Romish church. See Hen. Hilarii Not. ad Phil. Cyprii Chron. Ecclesiæ Græcæ, p. 470.

† See, for an account of this council, Aymon's Memoires Authentiques de la Religion des Grecs, tom. i. p. 263; and Gisberti Cuperi Epistolæ, p. 404, 407.—See, more especially, the judicious and learned observations of Basnage on the transactions of this council, in his Histoire de la Religion des Eglises Reformees, period iv. p. i. c. xxxii. p. 452, and Cowell's Account of the Present State of the Greek Church, book i. ch. v.

into the body and blood of Christ in that holy ordinance, had been received by Christians in all ages of the church.* To strengthen their cause by authorities, which they imagined would have no small influence upon their adversaries, they ventured to assert that this doctrine was adopted by all the Eastern Christians, and particularly by the Greek churches.† This bold assertion required striking and authentic testimonies to give it any degree of credit. Accordingly the ambassador of France, residing at Constantinople, received orders from his court to concur with the Jesuits, and to leave no methods unemployed in procuring certificates from the Greek clergy to confirm this assertion. On the other hand, the English and Dutch ambassadors, persuaded that no such doctrine was really professed in the Greek church, procured also the testimonies of several ecclesiastics, in order to take from the catholic disputants this pretext; which, after all, was of no great consequence, as it did not affect the merits of the cause. The result, however, of this scrutiny was favourable to the Romish doctors, whose agents in foreign parts procured a more numerous list of testimonies than their adversaries could produce. The protestants invalidated these testimonies, by proving fully, that many of them were obtained by bribery from the indigent Greeks, whose deplorable poverty made them sacrifice truth to lucre; and that a great number of them were drawn by artifice from ignorant priests, whom the Jesuits deceived, by disguising the doctrines of Rome in such a manner as to give them a Grecian air, and make them resemble the religious system of the Eastern churches.‡ If we grant this to be true, we may nevertheless justly question, whether the admission of certain doctrines in the Greek church, that resemble the errors of popery, ought to be dated from the period now before us; and whoever examines this controversy with a spirit of impartiality, accompanied with a competent knowledge of the history of the religious doctrine of the Greek churches, will perhaps find that a certain vague and obscure notion, similar to the Romish doctrine of transubstantiation, was received during many ages by several of these churches; though, in these later times, they may have learned, from the Romish missionaries, the popish manner of expressing this very absurd and unaccountable tenet.§

IV. Of those independent Greek churches, which are governed by their own laws, and are not subject to the jurisdiction of the patriarch of Constantinople, there is not one that can furnish any matter for an ecclesiastical historian, except the church established in Russia; the rest are sunk in the most deplorable ignorance and barbarity that can be imagined. About the year 1666, a certain sect, which assumed the name of *Isbraniki*, i. e. the multitude of the Elect, but were called by their adversaries *Roscolskika*, or the seditious Faction, arose in Russia, and excited considerable tumults and commotions in that kingdom.* The reasons alleged by this sect in defence of its separation from the Russian church, are not yet known with certainty; nor have we any satisfactory or accurate account of its doctrines and institutions;† we only know in general, that its members affect an extraordinary air of piety and devotion, and complain of the corruptions introduced into the ancient religion of the Russians, partly by the negligence, and partly by the ambition, of the episcopal order.‡ On the other hand, great pains were taken to conquer the obstinacy of this factious sect; arguments, promises, threatenings, dragoonings, the authority of synods and councils, seconded by racks and gibbets; in a word, all the methods that artifice or barbarity could suggest, were practised to bring back these se-

☞ * It was to prove this most groundless assertion, that the famous Nicole published his artful book, de la Perpetuite de la Foi, in 1664, which was answered, with a victorious force of evidence, by the learned Claude.

† The names and productions of the principal writers that appeared in this controversy may be found in the Bibliotheca Græca of Fabricius, vol. x. p. 444, and in the learned Pfaff's Dissertatio contra Ludov. Rogerii Opus Eucharisticum.

‡ Here, above all other histories, the reader will do well to consult Cowell's Account of the Present State of the Greek Church, as this author was actually at Constantinople when the scene of fraud and bribery was carried on, and was an eye-witness of the insidious arts and perfidious practices employed by the Jesuits to obtain, from the Greek priests and monks, testimonies in favour of the doctrine of the Latin or Romish church.

§ The learned La Croze, who cannot be suspected of any propensity to favour the cause of Rome in general, or that of the Jesuits in particular, was of opinion that the Greeks had been long in possession of the foolish doctrine of transubstantiation. See Gisberti Cuperi Epistolæ.

* These, perhaps, are the same persons of whom the learned Gmelin speaks, under the denomination of Sterowerzi, in the account of his Voyage into Siberia, tom. iv. p. 404.

☞ † This sect is called, by other authors, the sect of the Roskolniki. According to the account of Voltaire, who pretends to have drawn the materials of his History of the Russian Empire under Peter I from authentic records furnished by the court of Petersburg, this sect made its first appearance in the twelfth century. The members of it alleged, in defence of their separation, the corruptions, both in doctrine and discipline, which had been introduced into the Russian church. They profess a rigorous zeal for the *letter* of Scripture, which they do not understand; and the transposition of a single word in a new edition of the Russian Bible, though it tended only to correct an uncouth phrase in the translation commonly received, threw them into the greatest combustion and tumult. They will not allow a priest to administer baptism after having tasted spirituous liquor; and in this, perhaps, they do not amiss, since it is well known, that the Russian priests seldom touch the flask without drinking deeply. They hold that there is no subordination of rank, no superior or inferior, among the faithful; that a Christian may kill himself for the love of Christ; that it is a great sin to say *Hallelujah* thrice, and that a priest must never give a blessing but with three fingers. They are regular, even to austerity, in their manners; but, as they have always refused to admit Christians of other denominations into their religious assemblies, they have been suspected of committing, at those meetings, various abominations, which ought not to be believed without the strongest demonstrative proof. They are accused, for example, of killing a child in these assemblies, and of drinking its blood, and of lascivious commerce in its most irregular forms.

‡ See Bergius, de Statu Ecclesiæ et Religionis Moscoviticæ, sect. xi. cap. vii. sect. ii. cap. xvi.—Append. 270.—Heineccius' Account of the Greek Church, written in German; and Haven's Iter Russicum.—Some writers conjecture, that the Roskolniki are a branch descended from the ancient Bogomilians, of whom we have already given some accoun cent. xii. p. ii. chap. v. sect. ii

ditious heretics into the bosom of the church. But the effect of these violent measures by no means answered the expectations of the Russian government; they exasperated, instead of reclaiming, these schismatics, who retired into the woods and deserts, and, as it often happens, were rendered more fierce and desperate by the calamities and sufferings in which they were involved. From the time that Peter the Great ascended the throne of Russia, and made such remarkable changes both in its civil and ecclesiastical government, this faction has been treated with greater humanity and mildness; but it is alleged, that these mild proceedings have by no means healed the schism, and that, on the contrary, the Roskolniki have gained strength, and have become still more obstinate since the period now mentioned.

V. It will not be improper here to give some account of this reformation of the church of Russia, which resulted from the active zeal and wisdom of Peter; for, though this interesting event belongs to the history of the following century, yet the scheme, by which it was brought about, was formed toward the conclusion of the seventeenth. This great prince made no change in the articles of faith received among the Russians, and which contain the doctrine of the Greek church. But he took the utmost pains to have this doctrine explained in a manner conformable to the dictates of right reason and the spirit of the Gospel; and he used the most effectual methods to destroy, on one hand, the influence of the hideous superstition that sat brooding over the whole nation, and, on the other, to dispel the ignorance of the clergy, which was incredible, and that of the people, which would have exceeded it, had that been possible. These were great and arduous undertakings; and the reformation to which they pointed, was such as seemed to require whole ages to accomplish and bring to any tolerable degree of perfection. To accelerate the execution of this glorious plan, Peter became a zealous protector and patron of arts and sciences. He encouraged, by various instances of munificence, men of learning and genius to settle in his dominions. He reformed the schools that were sunk in ignorance and barbarism, and erected new seminaries of learning. He endeavoured to excite in his subjects a desire of emerging from their ignorance and brutality, and a taste for knowledge and the useful arts. And, to crown all these noble attempts, he extinguished the infernal spirit of persecution; abolished the penal laws against those who differed merely in religious opinion from the established church; and granted to Christians of all denominations liberty of conscience, and the privilege of performing divine worship in the manner prescribed by their respective liturgies and institutions. This liberty, however, was modified in such a prudent manner, as to restrain and defeat any attempts that might be made by the Latins to promote the interests of popery in Russia, or to extend the jurisdiction of the Roman pontiff beyond the tolerated chapels of that communion; for, though Roman Catholics were allowed to have places for the celebration of divine worship, the Jesuits were not permitted to exercise the functions of missionaries or public teachers in Russia; and a particular charge was given to the council, to which belonged the cognizance of ecclesiastical affairs, to use the utmost care and vigilance to prevent the propagation of Romish tenets among the people.

Beside all this, a remarkable change was now introduced into the manner of governing the church. The splendid dignity of patriarch, which approached too near the lustre and prerogatives of majesty, not to be offensive to the emperor, and burthensome to the people, was suppressed, or rather assumed by this spirited prince, who declared himself the supreme pontiff and head of the Russian church.* The functions of this high and important office were committed to a council assembled at Petersburg, which was called the Holy Synod, and in which one of the archbishops, the most distinguished by his integrity and prudence, acted as president. This honourable office was filled by the famous Stephen Javorski, who composed a laborious work, in the Russian language, against heresy.† The other orders of the clergy continued in their respective ranks and offices; but both their revenues and their authority were considerably diminished. It was resolved at first, in this general reformation, to abolish all monasteries and convents, as prejudicial to the community, and unfriendly to population; but this resolution was not executed; on the contrary, the emperor himself erected a magnificent monastery in honour of Alexander Newsky, whom the Russians place in the list of their heroes.‡

VI. A small body of the Monophysites in Asia abandoned, for some time, the doctrine and institutions of their ancestors, and embraced the communion of Rome. This step was entirely occasioned by the suggestions and intrigues of a person named Andrew Achigian, who had been educated at Rome, where he imbibed the principles of popery, and, having obtained the title and dignity of patriarch from the Roman pontiff, assumed the denomination of Ignatius XXIV.§ After the death of this

☞ * This account is not perhaps entirely accurate. Dr. Mosheim seems to insinuate that Peter assumed not only the authority, but also the office and title of patriarch or supreme pontiff and head of the church. This, however, was not the case; he retained the power without the title, as may be seen by the oath that every member of the synod he had established was obliged to take when he was appointed to that office. It was in consequence of his authority, as emperor, that he claimed an absolute authority in the church, and not from any spiritual character or denomination. The oath now mentioned ran thus: "I swear and promise to be a faithful and obedient subject and servant to my true and natural sovereign, and to the august successors whom it shall please him to appoint, in consequence of the indisputable power he has to regulate the succession to the crown.—I acknowledge him as the supreme judge of this spiritual college," &c. See Voltaire's Histoire de l'Empire de Russie sous Pierre le Grand tom. i. p. 174.

† Le Quien, Oriens Christianus, tom. i. p. 1295.

‡ Those who are acquainted with either the Danish or German language, will find several interesting anecdotes relating to these changes in Haven's Iter Russicum.

§ From the fifteenth century downwards, all the patriarchs of the Monophysites have taken the name of Ignatius, for no other reason than to show that they are the lineal successors of Ignatius, (who was

pretended patriarch, another usurper, whose name was Peter, aspired to the same dignity, and, taking the title of Ignatius XXV., placed himself in the patriarchal chair; but the lawful patriarch of the sect had credit enough with the Turks to procure the deposition and banishment of this pretender; and thus the small congregation which acknowledged his jurisdiction was entirely dispersed.* The African Monophysites, and more especially the Copts, notwithstanding that poverty and ignorance which exposed them to the seductions of sophistry and gain, stood firm in their principles, and made an obstinate resistance to the promises, presents, and attempts, employed by the papal missionaries to bring them under the Roman yoke. With respect to the Abyssinians, we have mentioned already, in its proper place, a revolution by which they delivered themselves from that tyrannical yoke, and resumed the liberty they had so imprudently renounced. It is proper, however, to take notice here of the zeal discovered by the Lutherans, in their attempts to dispel the ignorance and superstition of this people, and to bring them to the knowledge of a purer religion and a more rational worship. It was with this pious design that the learned Heyling, of Lubec, undertook a voyage into Ethiopia in 1634, where he resided many years, and acquired such a distinguished place in the favour and esteem of the emperor, that he was honoured with the important office of prime minister of that mighty empire. In this eminent station he gave many instances of his zeal both for the interests of religion and the public good; after which he set out for Europe, but never arrived there; nor is it known in what manner, or by what accident, he ended his days.†

Several years after this, Ernest, duke of Saxe-Gotha, surnamed the Pious, on account of his sanctity and virtue, formed the resolution of making a new attempt to diffuse the knowledge of the Gospel, in its purity and simplicity, among the ignorant and superstitious Abyssinians. This design was formed by the counsels and suggestions of the famous Ludolph, and was to have been executed by the ministry of the abbot Gregory, an Abyssinian, who had resided for some time in Europe.‡ The unhappy fate of this missionary, who perished in a shipwreck in 1657, did not totally discourage the prince from pursuing his purpose; for, in 1663, he entrusted the same pious and important commission to John Michael Wansleb, a native of Erfort, to whom he gave the wisest orders, and whom he charged particularly to leave no means unemployed that might contribute to give the Abyssinian nation a favourable opinion of the Germans, as it was upon this basis alone that the success of the present enterprise could be built. Wansleb, however, whose virtue was by no means equal to his abilities, instead of continuing his journey to Abyssinia, remained several years in Egypt. On his return thence into Europe, he began to entertain uneasy apprehensions of the account that would naturally be demanded both of his conduct, and of the manner in which he had employed the sums of money he had received for his Abyssinian expedition. These apprehensions rendered him desperate, because they were attended with a consciousness of guilt. Hence, instead of returning into Germany, he went to Rome, where, in 1667, he embraced, at least in outward profession, the doctrine of that church, and entered into the Dominican order.* Thus the pious design of the best of princes failed in the execution. To his formation of that scheme, however, we are indebted for the great light that has been thrown by the learned and laborious Ludolph on the history, doctrine, literature, and manners of the Abyssinians, which before this period were very superficially known in Europe.

VII. The state of the Christians in Armenia underwent a considerable change soon after the commencement of this century, in consequence of the incursions of Abbas the Great, king of Persia, into that province. This prince ravaged that part of Armenia which lay contiguous to his dominions, and ordered the inhabitants to retire into Persia. These devastations were intended to prevent the Turks from approaching his frontier; for the Eastern monarchs, instead of erecting fortified towns on the borders of their respective kingdoms, as is done by the European princes, laid waste their borders upon the approach of the invaders, that, by thus cutting off the means of their subsistence, their progress might be either entirely stopped, or considerably retarded. In this general emigration, the more opulent and the better sort of the Armenians removed to Ispahan, the capital of Persia, where the generous monarch granted them a beautiful suburb for their residence, with the free exercise of their religion under the jurisdiction of a bishop or patriarch Under the sway of this magnanimous prince, who cherished his people with a paternal tenderness, these happy exiles enjoyed the sweets of liberty and abundance; but after his death the scene changed, and they were involved in calamities of various kinds.† The storm of persecution that arose upon them shook their constancy; many of them apostatised to the Mohammedan religion, so that it was justly to be feared that this branch of the Armenian church would gradually be lost. On the other hand, the state of religion in that church derived considerable advantages from the settle-

bishop of Antioch in the first century,) and of consequence the lawful patriarchs of Antioch. A like reason induces the religious chief of the Maronites, who also claims the same dignity, to assume the name of Peter; for St. Peter is said to have governed the church of Antioch before Ignatius.

* Jo. Simon. Assemani Biblioth. Oriental. Clementino-Vatican. tom. ii. p. 482, and his Dissert. de Monophysitis, sect. iii.

† A very curious life of Heyling was published in German by Dr. Michaelis at Halle, in 1724.—See also Moller's Cimb. Litera. t. i. p. 253.

‡ See Ludolphi Proemium ad Comm. in Hist. Ethiop. p. 31.—Junckeri Vita Jobi Ludolphi, p. 63.

* For an account of this inconstant and worthless, but learned man, see Lobo's Voyage d'Abyss. tom. i. p. 198, 227, 233, 248.—Cyprian's Catalog. MSS. Biblioth. Gothanæ, p. 64.—Eus. Renaudot's Præf. ad Histor. Patriarch. Alexand. and his Historia Ecclesiæ Alexandrinæ: see also Scriptor. Ordin. Prædicatorum, edited by Echard and Quetif. t. ii. p. 693.

† See Chardin's Voyages en Perse, tom. ii. p. 106; and the Nouvelles Relations au Levant, by Gabriel de Chinon. p. 206.

ment of a great number of Armenians in different parts of Europe for the purposes of commerce. These merchants, who had fixed their residence, during this century, at London, Amsterdam, Marseilles, and Venice,* were not unmindful of the interests of religion in their native country; and their situation furnished them with opportunities of exerting their zeal in this good cause, and particularly of supplying their Asiatic brethren with Armenian translations of the Scriptures, and of other theological books, from the European presses, especially from those of England and Holland. These pious and instructive productions, being dispersed among the Armenians, who lived under the Persian and Turkish governments, contributed, no doubt, to preserve that illiterate and superstitious people from falling into the most consummate and deplorable ignorance.

VIII. The divisions that reigned among the Nestorians in the preceding century still subsisted, as all the methods employed to heal them had hitherto proved ineffectual. Some of the Nestorian bishops discovered a propensity to accommodate matters with the church of Rome. Elias II., bishop of Mosul, sent two private embassies to the pope, in 1607 and 1610, to solicit his friendship; and, in the letter he addressed upon that occasion to Paul V., he declared his desire of effecting a reconciliation between the Nestorians and the Latin church.† Elias III., though at first extremely averse to the doctrine and institution of that church, changed his sentiments in this respect; and, in 1657, addressed a letter to the congregation *de propagandâ Fide*, in which he intimated his readiness to join with the church of Rome, on condition that the pope would allow the Nestorians a place of public worship in that city, and would abstain from all attempts to alter the discipline of the sect.‡ The Romish doctors could not but perceive that a reconciliation, founded on such conditions as these, would be attended with no advantage to their church, and promised nothing that could flatter the ambition of their pontiff; and accordingly we do not find that the proposal above-mentioned was accepted. It does not appear that the Nestorians were received, at this time, into the communion of the Romish church, or that the bishops of Mosul were, after this period, at all solicitous about the friendship or good-will of the pope. The Nestorian bishops of Ormus, who successively assume the name of Simeon, proposed also, more than once,* plans of reconciliation with the church of Rome; and, with that view, sent to the pontiff a confession of their faith, which gave a clear idea of their religious tenets and institutions. But these proposals were little attended to by the court of Rome, either in consequence of its disapprobation of the doctrine of these Nestorians,† or of that contempt which their poverty and want of influence excited in the pontiffs, whose ambition and avidity aimed at acquisitions of greater consequence; for it is well known, that, since the year 1617, the bishops of Ormus have been in a low and declining state, both in point of opulence and credit, and are no longer in a condition to excite the envy of their brethren at Mosul.‡ The Romish missionaries gained over, nevertheless, to their communion, a small number of Nestorians, whom they formed into a congregation or church, about the middle of this century. The bishops or patriarchs of this little flock reside in the city of Amida, or Diarbek, and all assume the denomination of Joseph.§ The Nestorians, resident on the coast of Malabar, called also the Christians of St. Thomas, suffered innumerable vexations, and the most grievous persecution, from the Romish priests, and more especially from the Jesuits, while those settlements were in the hands of the Portuguese; but neither artifice nor violence could engage them to embrace the communion of Rome.‖ When Cochin was taken by the Dutch, in 1663, and the Portuguese were driven out of these quarters, the persecuted Nestorians resumed their primitive liberty, and were reinstated in the privilege of serving God without molestation, according to their consciences. These blessings they still continued to enjoy; nor are such of them as entered into the communion of Rome disturbed by the Dutch, who are accustomed to treat with toleration and indulgence all sects that live peaceably with those who differ from them in religious opinions and ceremonies.¶

* For an account of the Armenians who settled at Marseilles, and of the books which they ordered to be printed in that city for the use of their brethren in foreign parts, see Richard Simon's Lettres Choisies, tom. ii. p. 137.—The same author (tom. iv. p. 160,) and the learned Joachim Schroder, in a dissertation prefixed to his Thesaurus Linguæ Armenicæ, give an account of the Armenian Bible that was printed in Holland. The latter also takes notice of the other Armenian books that were published at Venice, Lyons, and Amsterdam.

† Jos. Sim. Assemani Biblioth. Orient. Clement, Vatican. tom. i. ii. iii.

‡ Idem Opus, tom. iii

* In the years 1619 and 1658.

† Assemani Biblioth. tom. i. ii. iii.

‡ Pet. Strozza, Præf. ad Librum de Chaldæorum Dogmatibus.

§ See Le Quien, Oriens Christianus, tom. ii. p 1078.

‖ La Croze, Histoire du Christianisme des Indes liv. v. p. 334.

¶ Schouten, Voyage aux Indes Orient. tom. i p 319, 446.

SECTION II.

PART II.

THE HISTORY OF THE MODERN CHURCHES.

CHAPTER I.

The History of the Lutheran Church.

I. We have already seen* the calamities and vexations that were entailed on the Lutheran church, by the persecuting spirit of the Roman pontiffs, and the intemperate zeal of the house of Austria, which, on many occasions, showed too great a propensity to second their ambitious and despotic measures; we shall, therefore, at present confine our view to the losses it sustained from other quarters. The cause of Lutheranism suffered considerably by the desertion of Maurice, landgrave of Hesse, a prince of uncommon genius and learning, who not only embraced the doctrine and discipline of the *reformed* church,† but also, in 1604, removed the Lutheran professors from their places in the university of Marpurg, and the doctors of that communion from the churches they had in his dominions. After taking this vigorous step, on account of the obstinacy with which the Lutheran clergy opposed his design, he took particular care to have his subjects instructed in the doctrine of the Helvetic church, and introduced into the Hessian churches the form of public worship that was observed at Geneva. This plan was not executed without some difficulty; but it acquired a complete degree of stability and consistence in 1619, when deputies were sent by this prince to the synod of Dordrecht, with express orders to consent, in the name of the Hessian churches, to all the acts that should be passed in that assembly. The doctors of the reformed church, who lived at this period, strenuously defended the measures followed by Maurice, and maintained, that in all these transactions he observed the strictest principles of equity, and discovered an uncommon spirit of moderation. Perhaps the doctors of modern days may view this matter in a different light. They will acknowledge, perhaps without hesitation, that if this illustrious prince had been more influenced by the sentiments of the wisest of the reformed doctors, concerning the conduct we ought to observe toward those who differ from us in religious matters, and less by his own will and humour, he would have ordered many things otherwise than he actually did.‡

II. The example of the landgrave of Hesse was followed, in 1614, by John Sigismund, elector of Brandenburg, who also renounced Lutheranism, and embraced the communion of the reformed churches, though with certain restrictions, and without employing any acts of mere authority to engage his subjects in the same measure; for it is observable, that this prince did not adopt all the peculiar doctrines of Calvinism. He introduced, indeed, into his dominions the Genevan form of public worship, and embraced the sentiments of the reformed churches concerning the person of Christ, and the manner in which he is present in the eucharist, as they appeared to him much more conformable to reason and Scripture than the doctrine of the Lutherans relating to these points. But, on the other hand, he refused to admit the Calvinistical doctrines of divine grace and absolute decrees; and, on this account, he neither sent deputies to the synod of Dordrecht, nor adopted the decisions of that famous assembly on these intricate subjects. This way of thinking was so exactly followed by the successors of Sigismund, that they never would allow the opinion of Calvin, concerning the divine decrees, to be considered as the public and received doctrine of the reformed churches in their dominions. It must be particularly mentioned, to the honour of this wise prince, that he granted to his subjects an entire liberty in religious matters, and left it to their unrestrained and free choice, whether they would remain in the profession of Lutheranism, or follow the example of their sovereign; nor did he exclude from civil honours and employments, or from the usual marks of his protection and favour, those who continued in the faith of their ancestors. This lenity and moderation, which seemed so adapted to prevent jealousy and envy, and to satisfy both parties, did not however produce this natural and salutary effect; nor were they sufficient to restrain within the bounds of decency and charity several warm and inconsiderate votaries of Lutheranism. These over-zealous persons, who breathed the violent spirit of an age in which matters of consequence were usually carried on with vehemence and rigour, deemed it intolerable and highly provoking, that the Lutherans and Calvinists should enjoy the same honours and prerogatives; that all injurious terms and odious comparisons should be banished from religious debates; that the controverted points in theology should either be entirely omitted in the public discourses of the clergy, or explained with a spirit of mo-

* In the History of the Romish Church.—See above.

☞ † The reader must always remember, that the writers of the continent generally use the denomination of *reformed* in a limited sense, to distinguish the church of England and the Calvinistical churches from those of the Lutheran persuasion.

‡ The reader will find a more ample account of this matter in the controversial writings of the divines of Cassal and Darmstadt, of which Salig speaks largely in his Hist. Aug. Confess. tom. i. lib. iv. cap. ii. p. 756. Those who understand the German language, may also consult Garth's Historischer Bericht von dem Religions-Wesen in Furstenthum Hessen—Cyprian's Unterricht von Kirchlicher Vereinigung der Protestanten, and the Acts published in the Un schuld. Nachrich. An. 1749.

---d Christian charity; that certain rites which displeased the Calvinists should be totally abolished; and that they who differed in opinion should be obliged to live in peace, concord, and the mutual exchange of good offices. If it was unreasonable in them to be offended at injunctions of this nature, it was still more so to discover their indignation in a manner, that excited not only sharp and uncharitable debates, but also civil commotions and violent tumults, that disturbed considerably the tranquillity of the state, and nourished a spirit of sedition and revolt, which the labour of years was in vain employed to extinguish. In this troubled state of things, the divines of Saxony, and more especially those of Wittenberg, undertook to defend the Lutheran cause; but if it be acknowledged, on one hand, that their views were good, and their intentions upright, it must be owned, on the other, that their style was keen even to a degree of licentiousness, and their zeal warm beyond all measure. And, indeed, as it generally happens, their want of moderation injured, instead of promoting, the cause in which they had embarked; for it was in consequence of their violent proceedings, that the Form of Concord was suppressed in the territories of Brandenburg, and the subjects of that electorate were prohibited, by a solemn edict, from studying divinity in the university of Wittenberg.*

III. It was deplorable to see two churches, which had discovered an equal degree of pious zeal and fortitude in throwing off the despotic yoke of Rome, divided among themselves, and living in discords that were highly detrimental to the interests of religion and the welfare of society. Hence several eminent divines and leading men, both among the Lutherans and Calvinists, anxiously sought some method of uniting the two churches, though divided in their opinions, in the bonds of Christian charity and ecclesiastical communion. A competent knowledge of human nature and human passions served to persuade these wise and pacific mediators, that a perfect uniformity of religious opinion was not practicable, and that it would be entirely extravagant to imagine that either of these communities could ever be brought to embrace universally, and without limitation, the doctrines of the other. They made it, therefore, their principal business to persuade those, whose spirits were inflamed with the heat of controversy, that the points in debate between the churches were not essential to true religion;—that the fundamental doctrines of Christianity were received and professed in both communions;—and that the difference of opinion between the contending parties, turned either upon points of an abstruse and incomprehensible nature, or upon matters of indifference, which did not tend to render mankind wiser or better, and in which the interests of genuine piety were in no respects concerned. Those who viewed things in this point of light, were obliged to acknowledge, that the diversity of opinion was by no means a sufficient reason for the separation of the churches, and that in consequence they were called, by the dictates of that Gospel which they both professed, to live not only in the mutual exercise of Christian charity, but also to enter into the fraternal bonds of church communion. The greatest part of the reformed doctors seemed disposed to acknowledge, that the errors of the Lutherans were not of a momentous nature, or of a pernicious tendency, and that the fundamental doctrines of Christianity had not undergone any remarkable alteration in that communion; and thus on their side an important step was made toward peace and union between the churches. But the majority of the Lutheran doctors declared, that they could not form a like judgment with respect to the doctrine of the reformed churches; they maintained tenaciously the importance of the points which divided the two communions, and affirmed, that a considerable part of the controversy turned upon the fundamental principles of all religion and virtue. It is not at all surprising, that the opposite party branded this steadiness and constancy with the epithets of morose obstinacy, supercilious arrogance, and the like odious denominations. The Lutherans were not behind-hand with their adversaries in acrimony of style; they recriminated with vehemence, and charged their accusers with instances of misconduct, different in kind, but equally condemnable. They reproached them with having dealt disingenuously, by disguising, under ambiguous expressions, the real doctrine of the reformed churches; they observed farther, that their adversaries, notwithstanding their consummate prudence and circumspection, gave plain proofs, on many occasions, that their propensity to a reconciliation between the churches arose from views of private interest, rather than from a zeal for the public good.

IV. Among the public transactions relative to the project of an union between the reformed and Lutheran churches, we must not omit mentioning the attempt made in 1615 by James I., king of Great Britain, to accomplish this salutary purpose. The person employed for this end by the British monarch, was Peter du Moulin, the most eminent among the Pro

* The edicts of Sigismund and his successors, relating to this change in the state of religion in Brandenburg, have been several times republished in one collection. Beside these, there are many books, treatises, and pamphlets, which give an account of this remarkable transaction, and of which the reader will find a complete list in the German work, entitled, Unschuldigen Nachrichten, An. 1745, p. 34; An. 1746, p. 326, compared with Jo. Carol. Kocheri. Biblioth. Theolog. Symbol. p. 312.—The reader who desires to attain a perfect acquaintance with this controversy, and to be able to weigh the merits of the cause, by having a true state of the case before him, will do well to consult Arnold's Histor. Eccles. et Hæret. p. ii. lib. xvii. c. vii. p. 965.—Cyprian's Unterricht von der Vereinigung der Protestant. p. 75, and Append. Monum. p. 225. Unschuldigen Nachrichten, An. 1727, p. 1069, et An. 1732, p. 715. They who affirm that the elector's ultimate end, in changing the face of religion in his dominions, was not the prospect of augmenting and extending his authority, found their opinion rather on conjecture than on demonstration; nor do they confirm this assertion by testimonies that are sufficient to produce full conviction. It must, however, be acknowledged, on the other hand, that their conjectures have neither an absurd nor an improbable aspect.

testant doctors in France;* but this design was neither carried on with spirit, nor attended with success.† Another attempt of the same pacific nature was made in 1631, in the synod of Charenton, in which an act was passed by the reformed doctors of that respectable assembly, declaring the Lutheran system of religion conformable with the spirit of true piety, and free from pernicious and fundamental errors. By this act, an opportunity was offered to the Lutherans of joining with the reformed church upon honourable terms, and of entering into the bonds both of civil and religious communion with their Calvinistical brethren.‡ But this candid and charitable proceeding was attended with very little fruit, since few of the Lutherans were disposed to embrace the occasion that was here so freely offered to them, of terminating the dissensions that separated the two churches. In the same year, a conference took place at Leipsic between the Saxon doctors, Koe, Lyser, and Hopfner, on one side, and some of the most eminent divines of Hesse-Cassel and Brandenburg, on the other; to the end that, by exposing with fidelity and precision their respective doctrines, it might be more easily seen, what were the real obstacles to the union projected between the churches. This conference was conducted with decency and moderation, and the deliberations were neither disturbed by intemperate zeal nor by a proud spirit of contention and dispute; but that openness of heart, that mutual trust and confidence, which are so essential to the success of all kinds of pacification, were not manifested on this occasion; for, though the doctors of the reformed party exposed, with great precision and fairness, the tenets of their church, and even made several concessions, which the Lutherans themselves could scarcely expect; yet the latter, suspicious and fearful, and always apprehensive of schemes, formed by artifice under the mask of candour, to betray and ensnare them, did not dare to acknowledge, that they were satisfied with these explications and offers; and thus the conference broke up without having contributed in any respect to promote the salutary work of peace.§ To form a true idea of these pacific deliberations, of the reasons that gave rise to them, and of the principles by which they were conducted, it will be necessary to study the civil history of this interesting period with attention and care.

V. Uladislaus IV., king of Poland, formed a still more extensive plan of religious union than those which have been mentioned; he proposed a reconciliation, not only between the Reformed and Lutheran churches, but also between these communions and that of Rome. For this purpose, he ordered a conference to be holden at Thorn, in 1645, the issue of which, as might naturally have been expected, was far from being favourable to the projected union; for the persons employed by the three churches to heal their divisions, or at least to calm their animosities, returned from this conference with a greater measure of party zeal, and a smaller portion of Christian charity, than they had brought to it.

The conference which took place at Cassel in 1661, by the order of William VI., landgrave of Hesse, between Musæus and Henichius, professors at Rintelen, on the side of the Lutherans, and Curtius and Heine, of the university of Marpurg, on that of the reformed, was attended with better success; and, if it did not bring about a perfect uniformity of opinion, it produced what was more desirable, a spirit of Christian charity and forbearance. For these candid doctors, after having diligently examined the nature, and weighed the importance, of the controversies that divided the two churches, embraced each other with reciprocal marks of affection and esteem, and mutually declared that their respective doctrines were less different than was generally imagined, and that this difference was not of sufficient moment to prevent their fraternal union and concord. But it unfortunately happened, that these moderate theologians could not infuse the same spirit of peace and charity that animated *them*, into their Lutheran brethren, nor persuade them to view the diversities of opinion that divided the Protestant churches, in the same indulgent point of view in which they had considered them in the conference at Cassel. On the contrary, this their moderation drew upon them the hatred of almost all the Lutherans; and they were loaded with bitter reproaches in a multitude of pamphlets,* that were composed expressly to refute their sentiments, and to censure their conduct. The pains that were taken after this period by the princes of the house of Brandenberg, and more especially by Frederic William and his son Frederic, in order to compose the dissensions and animosity that divided the Protestants, and particularly to promote a fraternal union between the reformed and Lutheran churches in the Prussian territories, and in the rest of their dominions, are well known; and it is also equally notorious, that innumerable difficulties opposed the execution of this salutary design.

* See Le Vassor, Hist. de Louis XIII. tom. ii. part ii.

☞ † King James, who would have abandoned the most important and noble design, at any time, to discuss a point of grammar or theology, or to gain a point of interest for himself or his minions, neglected this union of the Lutheran and reformed churches, which he had begun to promote with such an appearance of piety and zeal.

‡ Benoit, Histoira de l'Edit de Nantes, tom. ii. p. 544.—Aymon, Actes des Synodes Nationaux des Eglises Reformees de France, tom. ii. p. 500.—Ittigii Dissert. de Synodi Carentoniensis Indulgentia erga Lutheranos. Lips. 1705. 4to.

§ Timanni Gesselii Historia Sacra et Ecclesiastica, p. ii. in addendis, p. 597—613, in which the acts of this conference are published.—Jo. Wolfg. Jaegeri Historia Sæculi XVII. decenn. iv. p. 497. ☞ This testimony of Dr. Mosheim, who was himself a Lutheran, is singularly honourable to the reformed doctors.

* The writers who have given accounts of the conferences of Thorn and Cassel, are enumerated by Sagittarius, in his Introd. ad Hist. Ecclesiast. tom. ii. p 1604. See also Jaegeri Historia Sæculi XVII. decenn. v. p. 68), and decenn. vii. p. 160, where the acts of the two conferences are extant.—Add to these Jo. Alphons. Turretini Nubes Testium pro moderato in Rebus theologicis Judicio, p. 178.—There is an ample account of the conference of Cassel in the life of Musæus, given by Moller, in his Cimbria Literata, tom. ii. p. 566. The reader will find, in the same work, an accurate index of the accounts of this conference, published on both sides.

VI. Beside these public conferences, holden by the authority of princes, in order to promote union and concord among Protestants, a multitude of individuals, animated by a spirit of true Christian charity, embarked in this pious cause on their own private authority, and offered their mediation and good offices to reconcile the two churches. It is true, indeed, that these peace-makers were, generally speaking, of the reformed church, and that those among the Lutherans, who appeared in this amiable character, were but few, in comparison with the great number of Calvinists that favoured this benevolent but arduous design. The most eminent Calvinistical advocate of peace was John Dureus, a native of Scotland, justly celebrated on account of his universal benevolence, solid piety, and extensive learning, but, at the same time, more remarkable for genius and memory, than for nicety of discernment and accuracy of judgment, as might be evinced by several proofs and testimonies, were this the proper place for discussions of that nature. Be that as it will, never, perhaps, were greater zeal and perseverance manifested than by Dureus, who, during a period of forty-three years,* suffered vexations and underwent labours which required the firmest resolution and the most inexhaustible patience; wrote, exhorted, admonished, entreated, and disputed; in a word, tried every method that human wisdom could suggest, to put an end to the dissensions and animosities that reigned among the Protestant churches. It was not merely by the persuasive eloquence of his pen, or by forming plans in the silence of the closet, that this worthy divine performed the task which his benevolence and zeal engaged him to undertake; his activity and industry were equal to his zeal; he travelled through all the countries in Europe, where the Protestant religion had obtained any footing; he formed connexions with the doctors of both parties; he addressed himself to kings, princes, magistrates, and ministers; and by representing, in lively and striking colours, the utility and importance of the plan he had formed, hoped to engage them more or less in this good cause, or at least to derive some succour from their influence and protection. But here his views were considerably disappointed; for, though his undertaking was generally applauded, and though he met with a favourable and civil reception from the greatest part of those to whom he addressed himself, he found very few who were seriously disposed to alleviate his labours, by lending him their assistance, and seconding his attempts by their influence and counsels. Some, suspecting that his fervent and extraordinary zeal arose from mysterious and sinister motives, and apprehending that he had secretly formed a design of drawing the Lutherans into a snare, even attacked him in their writings with animosity and bitterness, and loaded him with the sharpest invectives and reproaches: so that this well-meaning man, neglected at length by those of his own communion, opposed and rejected by the followers of Luther, involved in various perplexities and distress, exhausted by unsuccessful labour, and oppressed and dejected by injurious treatment, perceived, by a painful experience, that he had undertaken a task which was beyond the power of a private person, and spent the remainder of his days in repose and obscurity at Cassel.*

It may not be improper to observe here, that Dureus, who, notwithstanding the general uprightness of his intentions, was sometimes deficient in ingenuous frankness, had annexed to his plan of reconciliation certain doctrines which, were they susceptible of proof, would serve as a foundation for the union, not only of the Lutherans and Calvinists, but also of all the different sects that bear the Christian name, for, among other things, he maintained, that the Apostles' Creed was a complete body of divinity; that the Ten Commandments formed a perfect system of morals, and the Lord's Prayer a comprehensive series of petitions for all the blessings contained in the divine promises. Now if this notion, that these sacred compositions contain all that is essential to faith, obedience, and devotion, had been universally entertained, or evidently demonstrated, it would not have been a chimerical project to aim at a reconciliation of all Christian churches upon this basis, and to render these compositions the foundation of their coalition and the bond of their union. But it would have been highly chimerical to expect, that the Christian sects would universally adopt this notion, or be pleased to see the doctrines of Christianity reduced to such general principles. It is farther to be observed, with respect to Dureus, that he showed a peculiar propensity toward the sentiments of the Mystics and Quakers, on account of their tendency to favour his conciliatory and pacific project. Like them, he placed the essence of religion in the ascent of the soul to God, in calling forth the hidden word, in fanning the divine spark that resides in the recesses of the human mind; and, in consequence of this system, he was intimately persuaded, that differences merely in theological opinions did not at all concern the essence of true piety.

VII. Among the Lutherans, those who ap-

* From the year 1631 to 1674.

* See Coleri Historia Joh. Duræi, to which many important additions might be made from public records, and also from documents that have not yet seen the light. Some records and documents of the kind here referred to, have been published by Hasæus, in his Bibliotheca Bremens. Theologico-Philologica, tom. i. p. 911, and tom. iv. p. 683 A still greater number are given by Gesselius, in the addenda to his Historia Ecclesiastica, tom. ii. p. 614. The transactions of Duræus at Marpurg, are mentioned by Schenck, in his Vitæ Professorum Theologiæ Marpurg. p. 207.—His attempts in Holstein may be learned from the letters of Lackman and Lossius, which are joined together in the same volume. His exploits in Prussia and Poland are recorded by Jablonsky, in his Historia Consensus Sendomiriensis, p. 127; and his labours in Switzerland, Denmark, and the Palatinate, are mentioned respectively in the Museum Helveticum, tom. iii. iv. v. by Elswich, in his Fasciculus Epistol. Theolog. p. 147, and by Seelen, in the Deliciæ Epistol. p. 353. See also Jaegeri Historia Sæculi XVII. decenn. vii. p. 171; the Englische Reformations Historie, by Bohm, and more especially an account of Duræus, published under my direction at Helmstadt, in 1744, by Benzelius, and entitled, Dissertatio de Johan. Duræo, maxime de Actis ejus Suecanis.

peared the most zealous in this pacific cause, were John Matthias,* bishop of Strengnes in Sweden, and George Calixtus, professor of divinity at Helmstadt, whom Dureus had animated with a portion of his charitable and indulgent spirit. The former was a man of capacity and merit; the latter was eminently distinguished among the divines of this century, by his learning, genius, probity, and candour; but both failed in the arduous undertaking in which they had engaged, and suffered considerably in their attempts to promote the cause of unity and concord. The *Olive-branches*† of Matthias, who entitled thus his pacific productions, were, by a royal edict, publicly condemned and suppressed in Sweden; and their author, in order to appease the fury of his enemies, was obliged to resign his bishopric, and pass the rest of his days in retirement.‡ The zeal of Calixtus, in calming the tumultuous and violent spirit of the contending parties, drew upon him the bitterest reproaches, and the warmest animosity and resentment from those who were more bent on maintaining their peculiar opinions, than in promoting that charity which is the end of the commandment; and, while he was labouring to remove all sects and divisions, he appeared to many of his brethren in the light of a new sectary, who was founding the most pernicious of all sects, even that of the Syncretists, who were supposed to promote peace and concord at the expense of truth. We shall, before we finish this chapter, endeavour to give a more particular and circumstantial account of the sentiments and trials of this great man, to whose charge many other things were laid, beside the *crime* of endeavouring to unite the disciples of the same master in the amiable bonds of charity, concord, and mutual forbearance, and whose opinions and designs excited warm contests in the Lutheran church.

VIII The external state of the Lutheran church at this period was attended with various circumstances of prosperity, among which we may reckon its standing firm against the assaults of Rome, whose artifice and violence were in vain employed to effect its destruction. It is well known, that a very considerable number of Lutherans resided in those provinces where the public exercise of their religion was prohibited. It has more especially been shown by the late memorable emigration of the Saltzburgers,§ that a still greater number of them lay concealed in that land of despotism and bigotry, where the smallest dissent from popery, with whatever secrecy and circumspection it may be disguised, is considered as an enormous and capital crime; and that they preserved their religious sentiments and doctrines pure and uncorrupted amidst the contagion of Romish superstition, which they always beheld with aversion and horror. In those countries which are inhabited by persons of different communions, and whose sovereigns are members of the Romish church, we have numberless instances of the cruelty and injustice practised by the papists against those who dissent from them; and these cruelties are exercised under a pretext suggested by the most malevolent bigotry, which represents these dissenters as seditious subjects, and consequently as worthy of the most rigorous treatment. And yet it is certain that, amidst all these vexations, the Lutheran church stood its ground; nor could either the craft or fury of its enemies, in any country, deprive it entirely of its rights and privileges. It may also be observed, that the doctrine of Luther was carried into Asia, Africa, and America, by several persons who fixed their habitations in those distant regions, and was also introduced into some parts of Europe, where it had hitherto been unknown.

IX. When we turn our view to the internal state of the Lutheran church during this century, we shall find it improved in various respects. Though several blemishes yet remained that clouded its lustre, it must be acknowledged, to the honour of the Lutherans, that they cultivated all the branches of literature, both sacred and profane, with uncommon industry and success, and made several improvements in the sciences, which are too well known to stand in need of a particular mention, and of which a circumstantial enumeration would be inconsistent with the brevity required in an historical compendium. But if it cannot be denied, on one hand, that the cause of religion gained by these improvements in learning, it must be owned, on the other, that some branches of science were perverted by injudicious or ill-designing men, to corrupt the pure simplicity of genuine Christianity, and to render its doctrines abstruse and intricate. Thus it too often happens in life, that the best things are the most egregiously abused. About the commencement of this century, the sciences chiefly cultivated in the schools were logic and metaphysics, though the manner in which they were treated was almost entirely destitute of elegance, simplicity, and precision. But, in process of time, the scene changed in the seminaries of learning; and the more entertaining and agreeable branches of literature, that polish wit, excite taste, exercise judgment, and enrich memory, such as civil and natural history, philology, antiquities, criticism, and eloquence, gained the ascendency. Both these kinds of knowledge acquired also a more graceful, consistent, and regular form than that under which they had hitherto appeared. But it unfortunately happened, that, while the boundaries of science were extended from day to day, and new discoveries and improvements were constantly enriching the republic of letters, the credit of learning began sensibly to decrease, and learned men seemed gradually to lose

☞ * Matthias had been chaplain to Gustavus Adolphus, and was afterwards appointed, by that prince, preceptor to his daughter Christina, so famous in history, on account of the whimsical peculiarities of her character, her taste for learning, and her desertion of the Swedish throne and the Protestant religion.

† Rami Olivæ Septentrionalis.

‡ See Schefferi Suecia Literata, p. 123, and Joh. Molleri ad eam Hypomnemata, p. 317.—Archenholtz. Memoires de la Reine Christine, tom. i. p. 320, 505; tom. ii. p. 63.

☞ § For an account of the persecuted Lutherans in the archbishopric of Saltzburg, see Burnet's Travels. See more especially a famous Latin discourse, entitled, Commentariolus Theologicus de non tolerandis in Religione Dissentientibus pub. at Tubingen, in 1732, by W. L. Letching.

those peculiar marks of veneration and distinction that the novelty of their character, as well as the excellence and importance of their labours, had hitherto drawn from the public. Among the various circumstances that contributed to this decline of literary glory, we may particularly reckon the multitude of those who, without natural capacity, taste, or inclination, were led, by authority or a desire of applause, to literary pursuits, and, by their ignorance or their pedantry, cast a reproach upon the republic of letters.

X. The only kind of philosophy that was taught in the Lutheran schools, during the greatest part of this century, was that of Aristotle, dressed up in that scholastic form which increased its native intricacy and subtlety; and such was the devout and excessive veneration entertained by many for this abstruse system, that any attempt to reject the Grecian oracle, or to correct its decisions, was looked upon as of the most dangerous consequence to the interests of the church, and as equally criminal with a like attempt upon the sacred writings. Those who distinguished themselves in the most extraordinary manner by their zealous and invincible attachment to the Peripatetic philosophy, were the divines of Leipsic, Tubingen, Helmstadt, and Altorf. The enchantment, however, was not universal; and there were many who, withdrawing their private judgment from the yoke of authority, were bold enough to see with their own eyes, and thus discerned the blemishes that were indeed sufficiently visible in the pretended wisdom of the Grecian sage. The first attempt to reduce his authority within narrow bounds was made by certain pious and prudent divines,* who, though they did not pretend to discourage all philosophical inquiries, yet were desirous of confining them to a few select subjects, and complained, that the pompous denomination of philosophy was too frequently prostituted by being applied to unintelligible distinctions, and words (or rather sounds) destitute of sense. These were succeeded in their repugnance to the Peripatetic philosophy by the disciples of Ramus, who had credit enough to banish it from several seminaries of learning, and to substitute in its place the system of their master, which was of a more practical kind, and better adapted to the purposes of life.† But, if the philosophy of Aristotle met with adversaries, who opposed it upon solid and rational principles, it had also enemies of a very different character, who imprudently declaimed against philosophy in general, as highly detrimental to the cause of religion and the interests of society. Such was the fanatical extravagance of Daniel Hoffman, professor at Helmstadt, who betrayed, in this controversy, an equal degree of ignorance and animosity; and such also were the followers of Robert Fludd, Jacob Behmen, and the Rosecrucians, who boasted of having stricken out, by the assistance of *fire* and *divine illumination*, a new, wonderful, and celestial system of philosophy, of which mention has been already made.* These adversaries of the Stagirite were divided among themselves; and this diminished the strength and vigour of their opposition to the common enemy. But, even if they had been very closely united in their sentiments and measures, they would not have been able to overturn the empire of Aristotle, which was deeply rooted in the schools through long possession, and had a powerful support in the multitude of its votaries and defenders.

XI. The Peripatetic system had still more formidable adversaries to encounter in Des-Cartes and Gassendi, whose writings were composed with such perspicuity and precision as rendered them highly agreeable to many of the Lutheran doctors of this century, who were hence induced to look with contempt on that obsolete and barren philosophy of the schools, which was expressed in uncouth terms and barbarous phrases, without taste, elegance, or accuracy. The votaries of Aristotle beheld with envy these new philosophers, used their most zealous endeavours to bring them into discredit, and, for this purpose, represented their researches and principles as highly injurious to the interests of religion and the growth of true piety. But when they found, by experience, that these methods of attack proved unsuccessful, they changed their method of proceeding, and, (like a prudent general, who, besieged by a superior force, abandons his outworks and retires into the citadel) they relinquished much of their jargon, and defended only the main and essential principles of their system. To render these principles more palatable, they began to adorn them with the graces of elocution, and to mingle with their philosophical tenets the charms of polite literature. They even went so far as to confess, that Aristotle, though the prince of philosophers, was chargeable with errors and defects, which it was both lawful and expedient to correct. But these concessions only served to render their adversaries more confident and enterprising, since they were interpreted as resulting from a consciousness of their weakness, and were looked upon as a manifest acknowledgment of their defeat. In consequence of this, the enemies of the Stagirite renewed their attacks with redoubled impetuosity, and with a full assurance of victory; nor did they confine them to those branches of the Peripatetic philosophy which were allowed by its votaries to stand in need of correction, but levelled them, without distinction, at the whole system, and aimed at nothing less than its total dissolution. Grotius, indeed, who marched at the head of these philosophical reformers, proceeded with a certain degree of prudence and moderation. Puffendorf, in treating of the law of nature and of the duties of morality, threw off, with more boldness and freedom, the Peripatetic yoke, and pursued a method entirely different from that which had been hitherto observed in the schools. This freedom drew upon him a multitude of enemies, who loaded him with the bitterest reproaches; his example, however,

* Among these we find Wenceslaus Schellingius, of whom a particular account is given by Arnold, in his Histor. Eccles. et Hæret. p. ii. lib. xvii. cap. vi.

† See Jo. Herman ab Elswich, de varia Aristotelis fortuna, § xxi. p. 54, and Walchius, His. Logices, lib. ii. c. ii. § iii. v. in Parergis ejus Academicis, p. 613.

* See above, in the Gen. His. of the Church, § 31.

was imitated by Thomasius, professor of law in the academy of Leipsic, and afterwards at Hall, who attacked the Peripatetics with new degrees of vehemence and zeal. This eminent man, though honourably distinguished by the excellence of his genius and the strength of his resolution, was not, perhaps, the most proper person that could be fixed upon to manage the interests of philosophy. His views, nevertheless, were vast; he aimed at the reformation of philosophy in general, and of the Peripatetic system in particular; and he assiduously employed both the power of exhortation and the influence of example, in order to persuade the Saxons to reject the Aristotelian system, which he had never read, and which most certainly he did not understand. The scheme of philosophy, that he substituted in its place, was received with little applause, and soon fell into oblivion; but his attempt to overturn the system of the Peripatetics, and to restore the freedom of philosophical inquiry, was attended with remarkable success, made, in a little time, the most rapid progress, and produced such admirable effects, that Thomasius is justly looked upon, to this day, as the chief of those bold spirits who pulled down philosophical tyranny from its throne in Germany, and gave a mortal blow to what was called the Sectarian Philosophy* in that country. The first seminary of learning that adopted the measures of Thomasius was that of Hall in Saxony, where he was professor; this example was followed by the rest of the German schools, by some sooner, and by others later; and thence a spirit of philosophical liberty began to spread itself into other countries where the Lutheran religion was established; so that, toward the conclusion of this century, the Lutherans enjoyed a perfect liberty of conducting their philosophical researches in that manner which they judged the most conformable with truth and reason, of departing from the mere dictates of authority in matters of science, and of proposing publicly every one his respective opinions. This liberty was not the consequence of any positive decree of the state, nor was it inculcated by any law of the church; it seemed to result from that invisible disposal of things, which we call accident, and certainly proceeded from the efforts of a few great men, seconding and exciting the natural propensity toward free inquiry, that can never be totally extinguished in the human mind. Many employed this liberty in extracting, after the manner of the ancient Eclectics, what they thought most conformable to reason, and most susceptible of demonstration, from the productions of the different schools, and connecting these extracts in such a manner as to constitute a complete body of philosophy. But some made a yet more noble use of this inestimable privilege, by employing, with indefatigable zeal and industry, their *own faculties* in the investigation of truth, and building upon solid and unchangeable principles a new and sublime system of philosophy.* At the head of these we may place Leibnitz, whose genius and labours have deservedly rendered his name immortal.

In this conflict between the reformers of philosophy and the votaries of Aristotle, the latter lost ground from day to day; and his system, in consequence of the extremes into which reformers often fall, became so odious, that condemnation was passed on every part of it. Hence the science of Metaphysics, which the Grecian sage had considered as the master science, as the original fountain of all true philosophy, was despoiled of its honours and fell into contempt; nor could the authority and influence even of Des-Cartes (who also set out, in his inquiries, on metaphysical principles) support it effectually against the prejudices of the times. However, when the first heat of opposition began to cool, and the rage of party to subside, this degraded science was not only recalled from its exile, by the interposition and credit of Leibnitz, but was also reinstated in its former dignity and lustre.

XII. The defects and vices of the Lutheran clergy have been circumstantially exposed and even exaggerated by many writers, who seem to require in the ministers of the Gospel a degree of perfection, which ought indeed always to be aimed at, but which no wise observer of human nature can ever hope to see generally reduced to practice. These censors represent the leading men of the Lutheran church as arrogant, contentious, despotic, and uncharitable; as destitute of Christian simplicity and candour; fond of quibbling and dispute; judging of all things by the narrow spirit of party; and treating with the utmost antipathy and aversion those who differ from them very slightly in religious matters. The less considerable among the Lutheran doctors are charged with ignorance, with a neglect of the sacred duties of their station, and with a want of talent in their characters as public teachers; and avarice, indolence, want of piety, and corruption of manners, are boldly imputed to the whole body.

It will be acknowledged, without difficulty, by those who have studied with attention and impartiality the genius, manners, and history of this century, that the Lutheran clergy were not wholly irreproachable with respect to the matters that are here laid to their charge, and that many Lutheran churches were under the direction of pastors who were highly deficient, some in zeal, others in abilities, many in both, and consequently ill qualified for propagating the truths of Christianity with wisdom and success. But this reproach is not peculiarly applicable to the seventeeth century; it is a general charge, that, with too much truth, may be brought against all the ages of the church. On the other hand, it must be acknowledged, by all such as are not blinded by ignorance or partiality, that the whole of the Lutheran clergy did not consist of these un-

☞ * By the Sectarian Philosophers were meant those who followed implicitly some one of the ancient philosophical sects, without daring to use the dictates of their private judgment, to correct or modify the doctrines or expressions of these hoary guides.

* The curious reader will find an accurate and ample account of this revolution in philosophy, in the learned Brucker's Historia Critica Philosophiæ.

worthy pastors, and that many of the Lutheran doctors of this century were distinguished by their learning, piety, gravity, and wisdom; and perhaps it might be difficult to decide, whether in our times, in which some pretend that the sanctity of the primitive doctors is revived in several places, there be not as many that do little honour to the pastoral character as in the times of our ancestors It must farther be observed, that many of the defects which are invidiously charged upon the doctors of this age, were in a great measure occasioned by the infelicity of the times. They were the unhappy effects of those public calamities which a dreadful war of thirty years produced in Germany; they derived strength from the influence of a corrupt education, and were sometimes encouraged by the protection and countenance of vicious and profligate magistrates.

XIII. That the vices of the Lutheran clergy were partly owing to the infelicity of the times, will appear evident from some particular instances. It must be acknowledged that, during the greatest part of this century, neither the discourses of the pulpit, nor the instructions of the schools, were adapted to promote, among the people, just ideas of religion, or to give them a competent knowledge of the doctrines and precepts of the Gospel. The eloquence of the pulpit, as some ludicrously and too justly represent it, was reduced, in many places, to the noisy art of bawling (during a certain space of time measured by a sand-glass) upon various points of theology, which the orators understood very imperfectly, and which the people did not understand at all; and, when the important doctrines and precepts of Christianity were introduced in these public discourses, they were frequently disfigured by tawdry and puerile ornaments, wholly inconsistent with the spirit and genius of the divine wisdom that shines forth in the Gospel, and were thus, in a great measure, deprived of their native beauty, efficacy, and power. All this must be confessed; but perhaps it may not appear an object of wonder, when all things are duly considered. The ministers of the Gospel had their heads full of sonorous and empty words, of trivial distinctions and metaphysical subtleties, and very ill furnished with that kind of knowledge which is adapted to touch the heart and to reform the life; they had also few models of true eloquence before their eyes; and therefore it is not very surprising, that they dressed out their discourses with foreign and tasteless ornaments.

The charge brought against the universities, that they spent more time in subtle and contentious controversy, than in explaining the Scriptures, teaching the duties of morality, and promoting a spirit of piety and virtue, though too just, yet may also be alleviated by considering the nature and circumstances of the times. The Lutherans were surrounded with a multitude of adversaries, who obliged them to be perpetually in a posture of defence; and the Roman catholics, by threatening their destruction, contributed, in a more particular manner, to excite in their doctors that polemic spirit which unfortunately became a habit, and had an unhappy influence on the exercise both of their academical and pastoral functions. In time of war, the military art not only becomes singularly respectable, but is preferred, without hesitation, to all others, on account of its tendency to maintain the inestimable blessings of liberty and independence; and thus, in the midst of theological commotions, the spirit of controversy, by becoming necessary, gains an ascendency, which, even when the danger is over, it is unwilling to lose. It is indeed ardently to be wished, that the Lutherans had treated with more mildness and charity those who differed from them in religious opinions, and had discovered more indulgence and forbearance toward such, more especially, as by ignorance, fanaticism, or excessive curiosity, were led into error, yet without pretending to disturb the public tranquillity by propagating their particular systems. But they had unhappily imbibed a spirit of persecution in their early education; this was too much the spirit of the times, and it was even a leading maxim with our ancestors, that it was both lawful and expedient to use severity and force against those whom they looked upon as heretics. This maxim was derived from Rome; and even those who separated from that church did not find it easy to throw off, suddenly, that despotic and uncharitable spirit which had so long been the main-spring of its government, and the general characteristic of its members. In their narrow views of things, their very piety seemed to suppress the generous movements of fraternal love and forbearance; and the more they felt themselves animated with a zeal for the divine glory, the more difficult did they find it to renounce that ancient and favourite maxim, which had so often been ill interpreted and ill applied, that 'whoever is found to be an enemy to God, ought also to be declared an enemy to his country.'*

XIV. There were few or no changes introduced, during this century, into the form of government, the method of worship, and the external rites and ceremonies of the Lutheran church. Many alterations would indeed have been made in all these, had the princes and states of that communion judged it expedient to put in execution the plans that had been laid by Thomasius, and other eminent men, for reforming its ecclesiastical polity. These plans were built upon a new principle, which supposed, that the majesty and supreme authority of the sovereign formed the only source of church-power. On this fundamental principle, which these great men took all imaginable pains to prove, by solid and striking arguments, they raised a voluminous system of laws, which, in the judgment of many, evidently tended to these conclusions;—that the

☞ * It is to be wished that the Lutherans had not, in many places, persevered in these severe and despotic principles longer than other Protestant churches. Until this very day, the Lutherans of Frankfort on the Maine have always refused to permit the Reformed to celebrate public worship within the bounds, or even in the suburbs of that city Many attempts have been made to conquer their obstinacy in this respect, but hitherto without success

same sovereign who presides in the state ought to rule in the church; that prince and pontiff are inseparable characters; and that the ministers of the Gospel are not the ambassadors of the Deity, but the deputies or vicegerents of the civil magistrate. These reformers of Lutheranism did not stop here; they reduced within narrower bounds the few privileges and advantages that the clergy yet retained; and treated many of the rites, institutions, and customs of our church, as the remains of popish superstition. Hence an abundant source of contention was opened, and a long and tedious controversy was carried on with warmth and animosity between the clergy and civilians. We leave it to others to determine with what views these debates were commenced and fomented, and with what success they were respectively carried on. We shall only observe, that their effects and consequences were unhappy, as, in many places, they proved seriously detrimental to the reputation of the clergy, to the dignity and authority of religion, and to the peace and prosperity of the Lutheran church.* The present state of that church verifies too plainly this observation. It is now its fate to see few entering into its public service, who are adapted to restore the reputation it has lost, or to maintain that which it yet retains. Those who are distinguished by illustrious birth, uncommon genius, and a liberal and ingenuous turn of mind, look upon the study of theology, which has so few external honours and advantages to recommend it, as below their ambition; and hence the number of wise, learned, and eminent ministers may be said gradually to decrease. This circumstance is deeply lamented by those among us who consider with attention the dangerous and declining state of the Lutheran church; and it is to be feared, that our descendants will have reason to lament it still more bitterly.

XV. The eminent writers that adorned the Lutheran church through the course of this century, were many in number. We shall only mention those whom it is most necessary for a student of ecclesiastical history to be more particularly acquainted with; such are Giles and Nicolas Hunnius—Leonard Hutter—Joseph and John Ernest Gerard—George and Frederic Ulric Calixtus—the Mentzers—Godfrey and John Olearius—Frederic Baldwin—Albert Grawer—Matthias Hoe—two of the name of Carpzovius—John and Paul Tarnovius—John Affelman—Eilhart Luber—the Lysers—Michael Walther—Joachim Hildebrand—John Valentine Andreas—Solomon Glassius—Abraham Calovius—Theodore Hackspan—John Hulseman—Jacob Weller—Peter and John Musæus, brothers—John Conrad Danhaver—John George Dorschæus—John Arndt—Martin Geyer—John Adam Schartzer—Balthazar and John Meisner—Augustus Pfeiffer—Henry and John Muller—Justus Christopher Schomer—Sebastian Schmidt—Christopher Kortholt—the Osianders—Philip Jacob Spener—Geb. Theodore Meyer—Fridem. Bechman—and others.*

XVI. The doctrine of the Lutheran church remained entire during this century; its fundamental principles received no alteration, nor could any doctor of that church, who should have presumed to renounce or invalidate any of those theological points which are contained in the symbolical books of the Lutherans, have met with toleration and indulgence. It is, however, to be observed, that, in later times, various circumstances contributed to diminish, in many places, the authority of these oracles, which had so long been considered as almost infallible rules of faith and practice. Hence arose that unbounded liberty, which is at this day enjoyed by all who are not invested with the character of public teachers, of dissenting from the decisions of these symbols or creeds, and of declaring this dissent in the manner they judge the most expedient. The case was very different in former times: whoever ventured to oppose any of the received doctrines of the church, or to spread new religious opinions, among the people, was called before the higher powers to give an account of his conduct, and very rarely escaped without suffering in his fortune or reputation, unless he renounced his innovations. But the teachers of novel doctrines had nothing to apprehend, when toward the conclusion of this century, the Lutheran churches adopted the leading maxim of the Armenians, that "Christians were accountable to God alone for their religious sentiments, and that no individual could be justly punished by the magistrate for his erroneous opinions, while he conducted himself like a virtuous and obedient subject, and made no attempts to disturb the peace and order of civil society." It is to be wished, that this religious liberty, which the advocates of equity must approve, but of which the virtuous mind alone can make a wise and proper use, had never degenerated into the unbridled licentiousness that holds nothing sacred, but with an audacious insolence tramples under foot the solemn truths of religion, and is constantly endeavouring to throw contempt upon the respectable profession of its ministers.

XVII. The various branches of sacred erudition were cultivated with uninterrupted zeal and assiduity among the Lutherans, who, in no period, were without able commentators, and learned and faithful guides for the interpretation of the Holy Scriptures. It is proper to mention here Tarnovius, Gerard, Hackspan, Calixtus, Erasmus Schmidt, to whom might be added a numerous list of learned and judicious expositors of the sacred oracles. But what appears more peculiarly worthy of observation is, that the very period which some look upon as the most barren of learned productions, and

☞ * It has been the misfortune even of well-meaning persons to fall into pernicious extremes, in the controversies relating to the foundation, power, and privileges of the church. Too few have steered the middle way, and laid their plans with such equity and wisdom as to maintain the sovereignty and authority of the *state*, without reducing the *church* to a mere creature of civil policy. The reader will find a most interesting view of this nice and important subject in the learned and ingenious bishop Warburton's Alliance between Church and State, and in his dedication of the second volume of his Divine Legation of Moses, to the earl of Mansfield.

* For an account of the lives and writings of these authors, see Witte's Memoriæ Theologorum and his Diarium Biographicum; as also Pippingius Goesius and other writers of literary history.

the most remarkable for a general inattention to the branch of erudition now under consideration, produced that inestimable and immortal work of Solomon Glassius, which he published under the title of Sacred Philology, and than which none can be more useful for the interpretation of Scripture, as it throws an uncommon degree of light upon the language and phraseology of the inspired writers. It must, at the same time, be candidly acknowledged, that a considerable part of this century was more employed, by the professors of the different universities, in defending, with subtlety and art, the peculiar doctrines of the Lutheran church, than in illustrating and explaining the Scripture, the only genuine source of divine truth. Whatever was worthy of censure in this manner of proceeding, was abundantly repaired by the more modern divines of the Lutheran communion: for no sooner did the rage of controversy begin to subside, than the greatest part of them turned their principal studies toward the exposition and illustration of the sacred writings; and they were particularly animated in the execution of this laborious task, by observing the indefatigable industry of those among the Dutch divines, who, in their interpretations of Scripture, followed the sentiments and method of Cocceius. At the head of these modern commentators we may place, with justice, Sebastian Schmidt, who was at least the most laborious and voluminous expositor of this age. After this learned writer, may be ranked Calovius, Geyer, Schomer, and others of inferior note.* The contests excited by the persons called Pietists, though unhappy in several respects, were nevertheless attended with this good effect, that they engaged many to apply themselves to the study of the Scriptures, which they had too much neglected before that period, and to the perusal of the commentators and interpreters of the sacred oracles. These commentators pursued various methods, and were unequal both in their merit and success. Some confined themselves to the mere signification of the words, and the literal sense that belonged to the phrases of the inspired writers; others applied their expositions to the decision of controverted points, and attacked their adversaries, either by refuting their false interpretations, or by making use of their own commentaries to overturn their doctrines; a third sort, after unfolding the sense of Scripture, applied it carefully to the purposes of life and the direction of practice. We might mention another class of interpreters, who, by an assiduous perusal of the writings of the Cocceians, are said to have injudiciously acquired their defects, as appears by their turning the sacred history into allegory, and seeking rather the more remote and mysterious sense of Scripture, than its obvious and literal signification.

XVIII. The principal doctors of this century, followed, at first, the loose method of deducing their theological doctrines from Scripture under a few general heads. This method had been observed in ancient times by Melancthon, and was vulgarly called *common-place* divinity. They, however, made use of the principles, terms, and subtle distinctions of the Peripatetic philosophy, which was yet in high reputation, in explaining and illustrating each particular doctrine. The first person that reduced theology into a regular system, and gave it a truly scientific and philosophical form, was George Calixtus, a man of great genius and erudition, who had imbibed the spirit of the Aristotelian school. His general design was not so much censured, as the particular method he followed, and the form he gave to his system; for he divided the whole science of divinity into three parts, viz. the *end*, the *subject* the *means;* and this division, which was borrowed from Aristotle, appeared to many extremely improper. This philosophical method of arranging the truths of Christianity was followed, with remarkable zeal and emulation, by the most eminent doctors in the different schools of learning; and even in our times it has its votaries. Some indeed had the courage to depart from it, and to exhibit the doctrines of religion under a different, though still under a scientific form; but they had few followers, and struggled in vain against the empire of Aristotle, who reigned with a despotic authority in the schools.

There were, however, many pious and good men, who beheld, with great displeasure, this irruption of metaphysics into the sphere of theology, and never could be brought to approve this philosophical method of teaching the doctrines of Christianity. They earnestly desired to see divine truth freed from captious questions and subtleties, delivered from the shackles of an imperious system, and exhibited with that beautiful simplicity, perspicuity, and evidence, in which it appears in the sacred writings. Persons of this turn had their wishes and expectations in some measure answered, when, toward the conclusion of this century, the learned Spener, and others who were animated by his exhortations and example, began to inculcate the truths and precepts of religion in a more plain and popular manner, and when the eclectics had succeeded so far as to dethrone Aristotle, and to banish his philosophy from the greatest part of the Lutheran schools. Spener was not so far successful as to render universal his popular method of teaching theology; it was nevertheless adopted by a considerable number of doctors: and it cannot be denied, that, since this period, the science of divinity, delivered from the jargon of the schools, has assumed a more liberal and graceful aspect. The same observation may be applied to controversial productions; it is certain that polemics were totally destitute of elegance and perspicuity so long as Aristotle reigned in the seminaries of learning, and that they were more or less embellished and improved after the suppression and disgrace of the Peripatetic philosophy. It is, however, to be lamented, that controversy did not lose, at this period, all the circumstances which had so justly rendered it displeasing; and that the defects, that had given such offence in the theological disputants of all parties, were far from being entirely removed. These defects still subsist. though perhaps in a less shocking de

* See J. Franc. Buddei Isagoge in Theologiam, lib. ii. cap. viii. p. 1686.

gree; and, whether we peruse the polemic writers of ancient or modern times, we shall find too few among them who may be said to be animated by the pure love of truth, without any mixture of pride, passion, or partiality, and whom we may pronounce free from the illusions of prejudice and self-love.

XIX. The science of morals, which must ever be esteemed the master-science, from its immediate influence upon life and manners, was, for a long time, neglected among the Lutherans. If we except a few eminent men, such as Arndt and Gerard, who composed some popular treatises concerning the internal worship of the Deity, and the duties of Christians, there did not appear, in the former part of this century, any moral writer of distinguished merit. Hence it happened, that those who applied themselves to the business of resolving what are called Cases of Conscience, were holden in high esteem, and their tribunals were much frequented. But, as the true principles and foundations of morality were not yet established with a sufficient degree of precision and evidence, their decisions were often erroneous, and they were liable to fall into daily mistakes. Calixtus was the first who separated the objects of faith from the duties of morality, and exhibited the latter under the form of an independent science. He did not, indeed, live to finish this work, the beginning of which met with general applause; his disciples, however, employed, with some degree of success, the instructions they had received from their master, in executing his plan, and composing a system of Moral Theology. This system, in process of time, fell into discredit on account of the Peripatetic form under which it appeared; for, notwithstanding the striking dissimilarity that exists, in the very nature of things, between the beautiful science of morals, and the perplexing intricacies of metaphysics, Calixtus could not abstain from the latter in building his moral system. The moderns, however, stripped morality of the Peripatetic garment. Calling to their assistance the law of nature, which had been explained and illustrated by Puffendorf and other authors, and comparing this law with the sacred writings, they not only discovered the true springs of Christian virtue, and entered into the true spirit and sense of the divine laws, but also digested the whole science of morals into a better order, and demonstrated its principles with a new and superior degree of evidence.

XX. These improvements in theology and morality did not diffuse such a spirit of concord in the Lutheran church, as was sufficient to heal ancient divisions, or to prevent new ones. That church, on the contrary, was involved in the most lamentable commotions and tumults, during the whole course of this century, partly by the controversies that arose among its most eminent doctors, and partly by the intemperate zeal of violent reformers, the fanatical predictions of pretended prophets, and the rash measures of innovators, who studiously spread among the people singular notions and (for the most part) extravagant opinions. The controversies that divided the Lutheran doctors may be ranged under two classes, according to their different importance and extent, as some of them involved the whole church in tumult and discord, while others were less general in their pernicious effects. Of the former class there were two controversies, that gave abundant exercise to the polemic talents of the Lutheran divines during the greatest part of this century; and these turned upon the religious systems that are generally known under the denominations of *Syncretism* and *Pietism*. Nothing could be more amiable than the principles that gave rise to the former, and nothing more respectable and praiseworthy than the design that was proposed by the latter. The Syncretists,* animated with that fraternal love and that pacific spirit, which Jesus Christ had so often recommended as the peculiar characteristics of his true disciples, used their warmest endeavours to promote union and concord among Christians; and the Pietists had undoubtedly in view the restoration and advancement of that holiness and virtue, which had suffered so much by the influence of licentious manners on the one hand, and by the turbulent spirit of controversy on the other. These two great and amiable virtues, that gave rise to the projects and efforts of the two orders of persons now mentioned, were combated by a third, even a zeal for maintaining the truth, and preserving it from all mixture of error. Thus the love of truth was unhappily found to stand in opposition to the love of union, piety, and concord; and thus, in the present critical and corrupt state of human nature, the unruly and turbulent passions of men can, by an egregious abuse, draw the worst consequences from the best things, and render the most excellent principles and views productive of discord, confusion, and calamity.

XXI. The origin of Syncretism was owing to George Calixtus, of Sleswick, a man of eminent and distinguished abilities and merit, and who had few equals in this century, either in point of learning or genius. This great man being placed in an university,† which, from the very time of its foundation, had been remarkable for encouraging freedom of inquiry, improved this happy privilege, examined the respective doctrines of the various Christian sects, and found, in the notions commonly received among divines, some things defective and erroneous. He accordingly gave early intimations of his dissatisfaction at the state of theology, and lamented, in a more particular manner, the divisions and factions that reigned among the servants and disciples of the same great master. He therefore turned his views to the salutary work of softening the animosities produced by these divisions, and showed the warmest desire, not so much of establishing a perfect harmony and concord between the jarring sects, which no human power seemed capable of effecting, as of extinguishing the hatred, and appeasing the resentment, which the contending parties discovered too much in their conduct toward each other. His col-

* The Syncretists were also called Calixtines, from their chief, George Calixtus; and Helmstadians, from the university where their plan of doctrine and union took its rise.

† The university of Helmstadt, in the duchy of Brunswick, founded in 1576.

leagues did not seem at all averse to this pacific project; and the surprise that this their silence or acquiescence must naturally excite, in such as are acquainted with the theological spirit of the seventeenth century, will be diminished, when it is considered, that the professors of divinity at Helmstadt bind themselves, at their admission, by an oath, to use their best and most zealous endeavours to heal the divisions, and terminate the contests that prevail among Christians. Neither Calixtus, however, nor his friends, escaped the opposition which it was natural to expect in the execution of such an unpopular and comprehensive project. They were warmly attacked, in 1639, by Statius Buscher, a Hanoverian ecclesiastic, a bigoted votary of Ramus, a declared enemy to all philosophy, and a man of great temerity and imprudence. This man, exasperated at the preference given by Calixtus and his companions to the Peripatetic philosophy over the principles of the Ramists, composed a very malignant book, entitled, Crypto-Papismus novæ Theologiæ Helmstadiensis,* in which Calixtus was charged with a long list of errors. Though this production made some small impression on the minds of certain persons, it is nevertheless probable that Buscher would have almost universally passed for a partial, malicious, and rash accuser, had his invectives and complaints rendered Calixtus more cautious and prudent. But the upright and generous heart of this eminent man, which disdained dissimulation to a degree that bordered upon the extreme of imprudence, excited him to speak with the utmost frankness his private sentiments, and thus to give a certain measure of plausibility to the accusations of his adversary. Both he and his colleague Conrad Horneius maintained, with boldness and perseverance, several propositions, which appeared, to many others beside Buscher, new, singular, and of a dangerous tendency; and Calixtus more especially, by the freedom and plainness with which he declared and defended his sentiments, drew upon himself the resentment and indignation of the Saxon doctors, who, in 1645, were present at the conference of Thorn. He had been chosen by Frederic William, elector of Brandenburg, as colleague and assistant to the divines sent from Konigsberg to these conferences; and the Saxon deputies were greatly incensed to see a Lutheran ecclesiastic in the character of an assistant to a deputation of reformed doctors. The first cause of offence was followed by other incidents, in the course of these conferences, which increased the resentment of the Saxons against Calixtus, and made them accuse him of leaning to the side of the reformed churches. We cannot enter here into a circumstantial account of this matter, which would lead us from our main design. We shall only observe, that, when these conferences broke up, the Saxon doctors, and more especially Hulseman, Weller, Scharfius, and Calovius, turned the whole force of their polemic weapons against Calixtus, and, in their public writings, reproached him with apostacy from the principles of Lutheranism, and with a propensity toward the sentiments both of the reformed and Romish churches. This great man did not receive tamely the insults of his adversaries. His consummate knowledge of the philosophy that reigned in the schools, and his perfect acquaintance with the history of the church, rendered him an able disputant; and accordingly he repelled, with the greatest vigour, the attacks of his enemies, and carried on, with uncommon spirit and erudition, this important controversy, until the year 1656, when death put an end to his labours, and transported him from these scenes of dissension and tumult into the regions of peace and concord.*

XXII. Neither the death of Calixtus, nor the decease of his principal adversaries, could extinguish the flame they had kindled: on the contrary, the contest was carried on, after that period, with greater animosity and violence than ever. The Saxon doctors, and more especially Calovius, insulted the ashes and attacked the memory of this great man with unexampled bitterness and malignity; and in the judgment of many eminent and worthy divines, who were by no means the partisans of Calixtus, conducted themselves with such imprudence and temerity, as tended to produce an open schism in the Lutheran church. They drew up a new creed, or confession of faith,† which they proposed to place in the class of what the members of our communion call their Symbolical Books, and which, consequently, all professors of divinity and all candidates for the ministry would be obliged to subscribe, as containing the true and genuine doctrine of the church. By this new production of intemperate zeal, the friends and followers of Calixtus were declared unworthy of the communion of that church, and were accordingly supposed to have forfeited all right to the privileges and tranquillity that were granted to the Lutherans by the laws of the empire. The reputation of Calixtus found, nevertheless, some able defenders, who pleaded his cause with modesty and candour; such were Titius, Hildebrand, and other ecclesiastics,

* i. e. Popery disguised under the mask of the new theological system of Helmstadt.

* Those who desire to be more minutely acquainted with the particular circumstances of this famous controversy, the titles and characters of the books published on that occasion, and the doctrines that produced such warm contests and such deplorable divisions, will do well to consult Walchius, Carolus, Weisman, Arnold, and other writers; and, above all, the third volume of the Cimbria Literata of Moller, in which there is an ample account of the life, transactions, and writings of Calixtus. But, if any reader should push his curiosity still farther, and be solicitous to know the more secret springs that acted in this whole affair, the remote causes of the events and transactions relating to it, the spirit, views, and characters of the disputants, the arguments used on both sides,—in a word, those things which are principally interesting and worthy of attention in controversies of this kind,—he will find no history that will satisfy him fully in these respects. A history that would throw a proper light upon these important matters, must be composed by a man of great candour and abilities; by one who knows the world, has studied human nature, is furnished with materials and documents that lie yet concealed in the cabinets of the curious, and is not unacquainted with the spirit that reigns, and the cabals that are carried on in the courts of princes.—But were such an historian to be found, I question very much, whether, even in our times, he could publish without danger all the circumstances of this memorable contest.

† The title of this new creed was, Consensus repetitus Fidei veræ Lutheranæ.

who were distinguished from the multitude by their charity, moderation, and prudence. These good men showed with the utmost evidence, that the new creed would be a perpetual source of contention and discord, and would thus have a fatal effect upon the true interests of the church: but their counsels were overruled, and their admonitions neglected. Among the writers who opposed this creed, was Frederic Ulric Calixtus, who was not destitute of abilities, though much inferior to his father in learning, genius, and moderation. Of those who stood forth in its vindication and defence, the most considerable were Calovius and Strauchius. The polemic productions of these contending parties were multiplied from day to day, and yet remain as deplorable monuments of the intemperate zeal of the champions. The invectives, reproaches, and calumnies, with which these productions were filled, showed too plainly that many of these writers, instead of being animated with a love of truth and a zeal for religion, were rather actuated by a keen spirit of party, and by the suggestions of vindictive pride and vanity. These contests were of long duration; they were, however, at length suspended toward the close of this century, by the death of those who had been the principal actors in this scene of theological discord, by the abolition of the creed that had produced it, by the rise of debates of a different nature, and by various circumstances of inferior moment, which do not require particular notice.

XXIII. It will be proper to give here some account of the accusations adduced against Calixtus by his adversaries. The principal charge was, his having formed a project, not of uniting into one ecclesiastical body, as some have understood it, the Romish, Lutheran, and Reformed churches, but of extinguishing the hatred and animosity that reigned among the members of these different communions, and joining them in the bonds of charity, mutual benevolence, and forbearance. This is the project, which was at first condemned, and is still known under the denomination of *Syncretism*.* Several singular opinions were also laid to the charge of this great man, and were exaggerated and blackened, as the most innocent things generally are, when they pass through the medium of malignity and party-spirit. Such were his notions concerning the obscure manner in which the doctrine of the Trinity was revealed under the Old Testament dispensation, the appearances of the Son of God during that period, the necessity of good works to the attainment of everlasting salvation, and God's being occasionally* the author of sin. These notions have been considered, by many of the best judges of theology, as of an indifferent nature, as opinions which, even were they false, would not affect the great and fundamental doctrines of Christianity. But the two great principles that Calixtus laid down as the foundation of all his reconciling and pacific plans, gave much greater offence than the plans themselves, and drew upon him the indignation and resentment of many. Those principles were; first, that the fundamental doctrines of Christianity (by which he meant those elementary principles from which all its truths flow) were preserved pure and entire in all the three communions, and were contained in the ancient form of doctrine, vulgarly known by the name of the Apostles' Creed; and secondly, that the tenets and opinions,

* It is neither my design nor my inclination to adopt the cause of Calixtus; nor do I pretend to maintain that his writings or his doctrines are exempt from error. But the love of truth obliges me to observe, that it has been the ill fortune of this eminent man to fall into the hands of bad interpreters; and that even those who imagine they have been more successful than others in investigating his true sentiments, have most grievously misunderstood them. Calixtus is commonly supposed to have formed the plan of a formal reconciliation of the Protestants with the church of Rome and its pontiffs; but this notion is entirely groundless, since he publicly and expressly declared, that the Protestants could by no means enter into the bonds of concord and communion with the Romish church, as it was constituted at this time; and that, if there had ever existed any prospect of healing the divisions that reigned between it and the Protestant churches, this prospect had entirely vanished since the council of Trent, whose violent proceedings and tyrannical decrees had rendered the union now under consideration absolutely impossible. He is further charged with having either approved or excused the greatest part of those errors and superstitions, that are looked upon as a dishonour to the church of Rome; but this charge is abundantly refuted, not only by the various treatises in which he exposed the falsehood and absurdity of the doctrines and opinions of that church, but also by the declarations of the Roman Catholics themselves, who acknowledge that Calixtus attacked them with much more learning and ingenuity than had been discovered by any other protestant writer.* It is true, he maintained that the Lutherans and Roman Catholics did not differ about the fundamental doctrines of the Christian faith; and it is to be wished, that he had never asserted any such thing, or, at least, that he had expressed his meaning in more proper and inoffensive terms. It must however be considered, that he always looked upon the popes and their votaries, as having adulterated these fundamental doctrines with an impure mixture or addition of many opinions and tenets, which no wise and good Christian could adopt; and this consideration diminishes a good deal the extravagance of an assertion, which, otherwise, would deserve the severest censure. We shall not enter farther into a review of the imputations that were cast upon Calixtus, by persons more disposed to listen to his accusers, than to those who endeavour, with candour and impartiality, to represent his sentiments and his measures in their true point of view. But if it should be asked here, what this man's real design was, we answer, that he laid down the following maxims: first, "that if it were possible to bring back the church of Rome to the state in which it was during the first five centuries, the Protestants would be no longer justified in rejecting its communion: secondly, that the modern members of the Romish church, though polluted with many intolerable errors, were not all equally criminal; and, that such of them, more especially, as sincerely believed the doctrines they had learned from their parents or masters, and by ignorance, education, or the power of habit, were hindered from perceiving the truth, were not to be excluded from salvation, or deemed heretics, provided they gave their assent to the doctrines contained in the Apostles' Creed, and endeavoured seriously to govern their lives by the precepts of the Gospel." I do not pretend to defend these maxims, which seem, however, to have many patrons in our times; I would only observe, that the doctrine they contain is much less intolerable than that which was commonly imputed to Calixtus.

* *Per accidens.*

* Bossuet, in his Traite de la Communion sous les deux Especes, speaks thus of the eminent man now under consideration; "Le fameux George Calixte, le plus habile des Lutheriens de notre tems, qui a ecrit le plus doctement contre nous" &c.

which had been constantly received by the ancient doctors during the first five centuries, were to be considered as of equal truth and authority with the express declarations and doctrines of Scripture. The general plan of Calixtus was founded upon the first of these propositions; and he made use of the second to give some degree of plausibility to certain Romish doctrines and institutions, which have been always rejected by the protestant church, and to establish a happy concord between the various Christian communions that had hitherto lived in a state of dissension and separation from each other.

XXIV. The divines of Rintelen, Konigsberg, and Jena, were more or less involved in these warm contests. Those of Rintelen, more especially Henichius and Peter Musæus, had, on several occasions, and particularly at the conference of Cassel, shown plainly that they approved the plan of Calixtus for removing the discords and animosities that reigned among Christians, and that they beheld with peculiar satisfaction that part of it which had, for its objects, union and concord among the protestant churches. Hence they were opposed with great animosity by the Saxon doctors and their adherents, in various polemic productions.*

The pacific spirit of Calixtus discovered itself also at Konigsberg. John Laterman, Michael Behmius, and the learned Christopher Dryer, who had been the disciples of that great man, were at little pains to conceal their attachment to the sentiments of their master. By this discovery, they drew upon them the resentment of their colleagues John Behmius and Celestine Mislenta, who were seconded by almost the whole body of the clergy of Konigsberg; and thus a warm controversy arose, which was carried on, during many years, in such a manner as did very little honour to either of the contending parties. The interposition of the civil magistrate, together with the decease of Behmius and Mislenta, put an end to this intestine war, which was succeeded, however, by a new contest of long duration between Dryer and his associates on one side, and several foreign divines on the other, who considered the system of Calixtus as highly pernicious, and looked upon its defenders as the enemies of the church. This new controversy was managed, on both sides, with as little equity and moderation as those which preceded it.†

XXV. It must, at the same time, be acknowledged, to the immortal honour of the divines of Jena, that they discovered the most consummate prudence and the most amiable moderation in the midst of these theological debates; for, though they ingenuously confessed, that all the sentiments of Calixtus were not of such a nature, as to be reasonably adopted without exception, yet they maintained, that the greatest part of his tenets were much less pernicious than the Saxon divines had represented them, and that several of them were innocent, and might be freely admitted without any danger to the cause of truth. Solomon Glassius, an ecclesiastic renowned for the mildness of his temper and the equity of his proceedings, examined with the utmost candour and impartiality the opposite sentiments of the doctors who were engaged in this important controversy, and published the result of this examination, by the express order of Ernest, prince of Saxe-Gotha, surnamed the Pious.* John Musæus, a man of superior learning and exquisite penetration and judgment, so far adopted the sentiments of Calixtus and Horneius, as to maintain that good works might, in a certain sense, be considered as necessary to salvation; and that, of the erroneous doctrines imputed to the former of these divines, several were of little importance. It is very probable, that the followers of Calixtus would have willingly submitted this whole controversy to the arbitration of such candid and impartial judges. But this laudable moderation so highly offended the Saxon doctors, that they began to suspect the university of Jena of several erroneous opinions, and marked out Musæus, in a particular manner, as a person who had in various respects apostatized from the true and orthodox faith.†

XXVI These debates were suppressed and succeeded by new disputes, which are commonly known under the denomination of the *Pietistical Controversy*. This dispute arose from the zeal of a certain set of persons, who, no doubt, with pious and upright intentions, endeavoured to stem the torrent of vice and corruption, and to reform the licentious manners both of the clergy and the people. But, as the best things may be abused, so this reforming spirit inflamed persons who were ill qualified to exert it with wisdom and success. Many, deluded by the suggestions of an irregular imagination and an ill-informed understanding, or guided by principles and views of a criminal nature, spread abroad new and singular opinions, false visions, unintelligible maxims, austere precepts, and imprudent clamours against the discipline of the church; all which excited dreadful tumults, and kindled the flames of contention and discord. The commencement of Pietism was indeed laudable and decent. It was set on foot by the pious and learned Philip James Spener, who, by the private societies which he formed at Francfort, with a view of promoting vital religion, roused the lukewarm from their indifference, and excited a spirit of vigour and resolution in those who had been satisfied to lament, in silence, the progress of impiety. The remarka-

* See Abrah. Calovii Historia Syncretistica, p. 618.—Jo. Georgii Walchii Introductio in Controversias Lutheran. vol. i. p. 286.

† See Christopher Hartknoch's Church History of Prussia, book ii. chap. x. p. 602.—Moller's Cimbria Literata, tom. iii. p. 150.—See also the Acts and Documents contained in the famous collection, entitled, Unschuldige Nachrichten, A. 1740. p. 144. A. 742. p 29. A. 1745. p. 91.

* This piece, which did not appear in public till after the death of Glassius, in 1662, exhibits a rare and shining instance of theological moderation, and is worthy of a serious and attentive perusal.

† For an account of the imputations cast upon the divines of Jena, and more especially on Musæus, see a judicious and solid work of the latter, entitled, Der Jenischen Theologen Ausführliche Erklarung, &c. See also Jo. Georgii Walchii Introductio in Controversias Ecclesiæ Lutheranæ, vol i. p. 405

ble effect of these pious meetings was increased by a book published by this well-meaning man, under the title of Pious Desires, in which he exhibited a striking view of the disorders of the church, and proposed the remedies that were proper to heal them. Many persons of good intentions were highly pleased both with the proceedings and writings of Spener; and indeed the majority of those who had the cause of virtue and practical religion at heart, applauded the designs of this good man, though an apprehension of abuses restrained numbers from encouraging them openly. These abuses actually happened. The remedies proposed by Spener to heal the disorders of the church fell into unskilful hands, were administered without sagacity or prudence, and thus, in many cases, proved to be worse than the disease itself. The religious meetings above-mentioned (or the *Colleges of Piety*, as they were usually called by a phrase borrowed from the Dutch,) tended in many places to kindle in the breasts of the multitude the flames of a blind and intemperate zeal, whose effects were impetuous and violent, instead of that pure and rational love of God, whose fruits are benign and peaceful. Hence complaints arose against these institutions of Pietism, as if, under a striking appearance of sanctity, they led the people into false notions of religion, and fomented in those who were of a turbulent and violent character, the seeds and principles of mutiny and sedition.

XXVII. These first complaints would have been undoubtedly hushed, and the tumults which they occasioned would have subsided by degrees, had not the contests that arose at Leipsic, in 1689, added fuel to the flame. Some pious and learned professors of philosophy, and particularly Franckius, Schadius, and Paulus Antonius, the disciples of Spener, who at that time was ecclesiastical superintendant of the court of Saxony, began to consider with attention the defects that prevailed in the ordinary method of instructing the candidates for the ministry; and this review persuaded them of the necessity of using their best endeavours to supply what was deficient, and to correct what was amiss. For this purpose, they undertook to explain in their colleges certain books of Scripture, in order to render these genuine sources of religious knowledge better understood, and to promote a spirit of practical piety and vital religion in the minds of their hearers. The novelty of this method drew attention, and rendered it singularly pleasing to many; accordingly, these lectures were much frequented, and their effects were visible in the lives and conversations of several persons, whom they seemed to inspire with a deep sense of the importance of religion and virtue. Whether these first effusions of religious fervour, which were, in themselves, most certainly laudable, were always kept within the strict bounds of reason and discretion, is a question not easily decided. If we are to believe the report of common fame, and the testimonies of several persons of great weight, this was by no means the case; and many things were both said and done in these *Biblical Colleges* (as they were called) which, though they might be looked upon, by equitable and candid judges, as worthy of toleration and indulgence, were contrary to custom, and far from being consistent with prudence.—Hence rumours were spread, tumults excited, animosities kindled, and the matter at length brought to a public trial, in which the pious and learned men above-mentioned were, indeed, declared free from the errors and heresies that had been laid to their charge, but were, at the same time, prohibited from carrying on that plan of religious instruction which they had undertaken with such zeal. It was during these troubles and divisions that the invidious denomination of Pietist was first invented; it may, at least, be affirmed, that it was not commonly known before this period. It was at first applied by some giddy and inconsiderate persons to those who frequented the Biblical Colleges, and lived in a manner suitable to the instructions and exhortations that were addressed to them in those seminaries of piety. It was afterwards used to characterise all who were either distinguished by the excessive austerity of their manners, or who, regardless of truth and opinion, were only intent upon practice, and turned the whole vigour of their efforts toward the attainment of religious feelings and habits. But, as it is the fate of all those denominations by which peculiar sects are distinguished, to be variously and often very improperly applied, so the title of Pietist was frequently given, in common conversation, to persons of eminent wisdom and sanctity, who were equally remarkable for their adherence to truth and their love of piety; and, not seldom, to persons whose motley characters exhibited an enormous mixture of profligacy and enthusiasm, and who deserved the title of delirious fanatics rather than any other denomination.

XXVIII. This contest was by no means confined to Leipsic, but diffused its contagion, with incredible celerity, through all the Lutheran churches, in the different states and kingdoms of Europe; for, from this time, in all the cities, towns, and villages, where Lutheranism was professed, there suddenly started up persons of various ranks and professions, of both sexes, learned and illiterate, who declared that they were called, by a divine impulse, to pull up iniquity by the root, to restore to its primitive lustre, and propagate through the world, the declining cause of piety and virtue, to govern the Church of Christ by wiser rules than those by which it was at present directed; and who, partly in their writings, and partly in their private and public discourses, pointed out the means and measures that were necessary to bring about this important revolution. All those who were stricken with this imaginary impulse, unanimously agreed, that nothing could have a more powerful tendency to propagate among the multitude solid knowledge, pious feelings, and holy habits, than the private meetings which had been first contrived by Spener, and were afterwards introduced into Leipsic. Several religious assemblies were accordingly formed in various places, which, though they differed in some circumstances, and were not

assemblies; and experience and observation all composed and conducted with equal wisdom, piety, and prudence, were intended to promote the same general purpose. In the mean time, these unusual, irregular and tumultuous proceedings, filled, with uneasy and alarming apprehensions, both those who were intrusted with the government of the church, and those who sat at the helm of the state. These apprehensions were justified by this important consideration, that the pious and well-meaning persons who composed these assemblies, had indiscreetly admitted into their community a number of extravagant and hot-headed fanatics, who foretold the approaching destruction of Babel, (by which they meant the Lutheran church,) terrified the populace with fictitious visions, assumed the authority of prophets honoured with a divine commission, obscured the sublime truths of religion by a gloomy kind of jargon of their own invention, and revived doctrines that had long before been condemned by the church. These enthusiasts also asserted, that the *millennium*, (or thousand-years' reign of the saints on earth,) mentioned by St. John, was near at hand. They endeavoured to overturn the wisest establishments, and to destroy the best institutions, and desired that the power of preaching and administering public instruction might be given promiscuously to all sorts of persons. Thus was the Lutheran church torn asunder in the most deplorable manner, while the votaries of Rome stood by and beheld, with a secret satisfaction, these unhappy divisions. The most violent debates arose in all the churches; and persons, whose differences were occasioned rather by mere words and questions of little consequence, than by any doctrines or institutions of considerable importance, attacked one another with the bitterest animosity; and, in many countries, severe laws were at length enacted against the Pietists.*

XXIX. These revivers of piety were of two kinds, who, by their different manner of proceeding, deserve to be placed in two distinct classes. One sect of these practical reformers proposed to carry on their plan without introducing any change into the doctrine, discipline, or form of government, established in the Lutheran church. The other maintained, on the contrary, that it was impossible to promote the progress of real piety among the Lutherans, without making considerable alterations in their doctrine, and changing the whole form of their ecclesiastical discipline and polity. The former had at their head the learned and pious Spener, who, in 1691, removed from Dresden to Berlin, and whose sentiments were adopted by the professors of the new university at Halle, and particularly by Franckius and Paulus Antonius, who had been invited thither from Leipsic; where they began to be suspected of Pietism. Though few pretended to treat either with indignation or contempt the intentions and purpose of these good men (which, indeed, no one could despise without affecting to appear the enemy of practical religion and virtue,) yet many eminent divines, and more especially the professors and pastors of Wittenburg, were of opinion, that, in the execution of this laudable purpose, several maxims were adopted, and certain measures employed, that were prejudicial to the truth, and also detrimental to the interests of the church. Hence they thought themselves obliged to proceed publicly, first against Spener, in 1695, and afterwards against his disciples and adherents, as the inventors and promoters of erroneous and dangerous opinions. These debates are of a recent date; so that those who are desirous of knowing more particularly how far the principles of equity, moderation, and candour, influenced the conduct and directed the proceedings of the contending parties, may easily receive satisfactory information.

XXX. These debates turned upon a variety of points; and therefore the matter of them cannot be comprehended under any one general head. If we consider them indeed in relation to their origin, and the circumstances that gave rise to them, we shall be able to reduce them to some fixed principles. It is well known that those who had the advancement of piety most zealously at heart, entertained a notion that no order of men contributed more to retard its progress than the clergy, whose peculiar vocation it was to inculcate and promote it. While they considered this as the root of the evil, it was natural that their plans of reformation should begin here; and, accordingly, they laid it down as an essential principle, that none should be admitted into the ministry, but such as had received a proper education, were distinguished by their wisdom and sanctity of manners, and had hearts filled with divine love. Hence they proposed, in the first place, a thorough reformation of the schools of divinity; and they explained clearly enough what they meant by this reformation, which consisted in the following points: That the systematical theology, which reigned in the colleges, and was composed of intricate and disputable doctrines, and obscure and unusual forms of expression, should be totally abolished; that polemical divinity, which comprehended the controversies subsisting between Christians of different communions, should be less eagerly studied, and less frequently treated, though not entirely neglected; that all mixture of philosophy and human learning

* This whole matter is amply illustrated by the learned John George Walchius, in his Introductio ad Controversias, vol. ii. and iii. who exhibits successively the various scenes of this deplorable contest, with a view of the principal points that were controverted, and his judgment concerning each, and a particular account of the writers who displayed their talents on this occasion. It would, indeed, be difficult for any one man to give an ample and exact history of this contest, which was accompanied with so many incidental circumstances, and was, upon the whole, of such a tedious and complicated nature. It is therefore to be wished, that a society of prudent and impartial persons. furnished with a competent knowledge of human nature and political transactions, and also with proper materials, would undertake to compose the history of Pietism. If several persons were employed in collecting from public records, and also from papers that are yet concealed in the cabinets of the curious, the events which happened in each country where this controversy reigned; and if these materials, thus carefully gathered on the spot, were put into the hands of a man capable of digesting the whole; this would produce a most interesting and useful history

with divine wisdom was to be most carefully avoided; that, on the contrary, all those who were intended for the ministry, should be accustomed from their early youth to the perusal and study of the Scriptures; that they should be instructed in a plain system of theology, drawn from these unerring sources of truth; and that the whole course of their education was to be so directed, as to render them useful in life, by the practical power of their doctrine and the commanding influence of their example. As these maxims were propagated with the greatest industry and zeal, and were explained inadvertently by some, without those restrictions which prudence seemed to require, these professed patrons and revivers of piety were suspected of designs that could not but render them obnoxious to censure. They were supposed to despise philosophy and learning, to treat with indifference, and even to renounce, all inquiries into the nature and foundations of religious truth, to disapprove the zeal and labours of those who defended it against such as either corrupted or opposed it, and to place the whole of their theology in certain vague and incoherent declamations concerning the duties of morality. Hence arose those famous disputes concerning the use of philosophy and the value of human learning, considered in connexion with the interests of religion—the dignity and usefulness of systematic theology—the necessity of polemic divinity—the excellence of the mystic system—and also concerning the true method of instructing the people.

The second great object, that employed the zeal and attention of the persons now under consideration, was, that the candidates for the ministry should not only, for the future, receive such an academical education as would tend rather to solid utility than to mere speculation, but also that they should dedicate themselves to God in a peculiar manner, and exhibit the most striking examples of piety and virtue. This maxim, which, when considered in itself, must be acknowledged to be highly laudable, not only gave occasion to several new regulations, calculated to restrain the passions of the studious youth, to inspire them with pious sentiments, and to excite in them holy resolutions; but also produced another maxim, which was a lasting source of controversy and debate, namely, "that no person, who was not himself a model of piety and divine love, was qualified to be a public teacher of piety, or a guide to others in the way of salvation." This opinion was considered by many as derogatory from the power and efficacy of the word of God, which cannot be deprived of its divine influence by the vices of its ministers, and a sort of revival of the long-exploded errors of the Donatists; and what rendered it peculiarly liable to an interpretation of this nature was, the imprudence of some Pietists, who inculcated it without those restrictions that were necessary to render it unexceptionable. Hence arose endless and intricate debates concerning the following questions; "whether the religious knowledge acquired by a wicked man can be termed theology?"—"whether a vicious person can, in effect, obtain a true knowledge of religion?"—"how far the office and ministry of an impious ecclesiastic can be pronounced salutary and efficacious?"—"whether a licentious and ungodly man can be susceptible of illumination?"—and other questions of a like nature.

XXXI. These revivers of declining piety went yet farther. In order to render the ministry of their pastors as successful as possible, in rousing men from their indolence, and in stemming the torrent of corruption and immorality, they judged two things indispensably necessary. The first was, to suppress entirely, in the course of public instruction, and more especially in that delivered from the pulpit, certain maxims and phrases which the corruption of men leads them frequently to interpret in a manner favourable to the indulgence of their passions. Such, in the judgment of the Pietists, were the following propositions:—"No man is able to attain that perfection which the divine law requires: good works are not necessary to salvation: in the act of justification, on the part of man, faith alone is concerned, without good works." Many, however, were apprehensive, that, by the suppression of these propositions, truth itself must suffer deeply, and that the Christian religion, deprived thus of its peculiar doctrines, would be exposed naked and defenceless, to the attacks of its adversaries. The second step they took, in order to give efficacy to their plans of reformation, was to form new rules of life and manners, much more rigorous and austere than those which had been formerly practised, and to place in the class of sinful and unlawful gratifications several kinds of pleasure and amusement, which had hitherto been looked upon as innocent in themselves, and which could only become good or evil, in consequence of the respective characters of those who used them with prudence, or abused them with intemperance. Thus, dancing, public sports, pantomimes, theatrical diversions, the reading of humorous and comical books, with several other kinds of pleasure and entertainment, were prohibited by the Pietists, as unlawful and unseemly, and, therefore, by no means of an indifferent nature. Many, however, thought this rule of moral discipline far too rigid and severe; and thus was revived the ancient contest of the schoolmen, concerning the famous question, whether any human actions are truly indifferent? i. e. equally removed from moral good on the one hand, and from moral evil on the other; and whether, on the contrary, it be not true, that all actions, whatever, must be either considered as good or as evil? The discussion of this question was attended with a variety of debates upon the several points of the prohibition now mentioned; and these debates were often carried on with animosity and bitterness, and very rarely with that precision, temper, and judgment, which the nicety of the matters in dispute required. The third point, on which the Pietists insisted, was, that beside the stated meetings for public worship, private assemblies should be holden for prayer and other religious exercises. But many were of opinion, that the cause of true piety and virtue was rather endangered than promoted by these

seemed to confirm this opinion. It would be both endless and unnecessary to enumerate all the little disputes that arose from the appointment of these private assemblies, and, in general, from the notions entertained, and the measures pursued by the Pietists.* It is nevertheless proper to observe, that the lenity and indulgence shown by these people to persons whose opinions were erroneous, and whose errors were by no means of an indifferent nature, irritated their adversaries to a very high degree, and made many suspect, that the Pietists laid a much greater stress upon practice than upon belief, and that, separating what ought ever to be inseparably joined, they held virtuous manners in higher esteem than religious truth. Amidst the prodigious numbers that appeared in these controversies it was not at all surprising, if the variety of their characters, capacities, and views, be duly considered, that some were chargeable with imprudence, others with intemperate zeal, and that many, to avoid what they looked upon as unlawful, fell injudiciously into the opposite extreme.

XXXII. The other class of Pietists already mentioned, whose reforming views extended so far, as to change the system of doctrine, and the form of ecclesiastical government, established in the Lutheran church, comprehended persons of various characters and different ways of thinking. Some of them were totally destitute of reason and judgment; their errors were the reveries of a disordered brain; and they were rather to be considered as lunatics than as heretics. Others were less extravagant, and tempered the singular notions, which thev had derived from reading or meditation, with a certain mixture of the important truths and doctrines of religion. Of this class we shall mention those only who were distinguished from the rest by superior merit and reputation. Among these we find Godfrey Arnold, a native of Saxony, a man of extensive reading, tolerable parts, and richly endowed with that natural and unaffected eloquence, which is so wonderfully adapted to touch and to persuade. This man disturbed the tranquillity of the church, toward the conclusion of this century, by a variety of theological productions, that were full of new and singular opinions, and more especially by his ecclesiastical history, which he had the assurance to impose upon the public, as a work composed with candour and impartiality. His natural complexion was dark, melancholy and austere; and these seeds of fanaticism were so expanded and nourished by the perusal of the mystic writers, that the flame of enthusiasm was kindled in his breast, and broke forth in his conduct and writings with peculiar vehemence. He looked upon the Mystics as superior to all other writers, and even as the only depositories of true wisdom; reduced the whole of religion to certain internal feelings and motions, of which it is difficult to form a just idea; neglected entirely the study of truth; and employed the whole power of his genius and eloquence in enumerating, deploring, and exaggerating, the vices and corruptions of human nature. If it is universally allowed to be the first and most essential obligation of an historian to avoid all appearance of partiality, and neither to be influenced by personal attachments nor by private resentment in the recital of facts, it may fairly be acknowledged, that no man could be less fit for writing history than Arnold. His whole history, as every one must see who looks into it with the smallest degree of attention, is the production of a violent spirit, and is dictated by a vehement antipathy to the doctrines and institutions of the Lutheran church. A fundamental principle that influences the judgment, and directs the opinions and decisions of this historian, through the whole course of his work, is, that all the abuses and corruptions that have found admittance into the church since the time of the apostles, have been introduced by its ministers and rulers, men of vicious and abandoned characters. From this principle he draws the following goodly consequence: that all those who opposed the measures of the clergy, or felt their resentment, were persons of distinguished sanctity and virtue; and that, on the contrary, such as either favoured the ministers of the church or were favoured by them, were strangers to the spirit of true and genuine piety. Hence proceeded Arnold's unaccountable partiality to almost all that bore the denomination of heretics;* whom he defended with the utmost zeal, without having always understood their doctrine, and, in some cases, without having even examined their arguments. This partiality was highly detrimental to his reputation, and rendered his history peculiarly obnoxious to censure. He did not, however, continue in this way of thinking; but, as he advanced in years and experience, perceived the errors into which he had been led by the impetuosity of his passion and the contagious influence of pernicious examples. This sense of his mistakes corrected the vehemence of his natural temper and the turbulence of his party spirit, so that, as we learn from witnesses worthy of credit, he became at last a lover of truth and a pattern of moderation.†

XXXIII. Arnold was far exceeded in fanatical malignity and insolence by John Conrad Dippelius, a Hessian divine, who assumed the denomination of the Christian Democritus, inflamed the minds of the simple by a variety of productions, and excited considerable tumults and commotions near the close of this century. This vain, supercilious, and arrogant doctor, who seemed formed by nature for a satirist and

* These debates were first collected, and also needlessly multiplied, by Schelvigius, in his Synopsis Controversiarum sub Pietatis Prætextu motarum, published in 1701. The reader will also find the arguments, used by the contending parties in this dispute, judiciously summed up in two different works of Langius, one entitled Anti-Barbarus, and the other the Middle Way, (*die Mittel-strasse;*) the former composed in Latin, the latter in German.*

* See also the Timotheus Verinus of Val. Ern. Loscher

☞* Arnold's history is entitled Historia Ecclesiastica et Hæretica. Dr. Mosheim's account of this learned man is drawn up with much severity, and perhaps is not entirely destitute of partiality. See the Life of Arnold in the General Dictionary.

† See Coleri Vita Arnoldi, and also the Nouveau Diction. Histor. et Critique tom. i. p. 485.

a buffoon, instead of proposing any new system of religious doctrine and discipline, was solely employed in overturning those which were received in the protestant church. His days were principally spent in throwing out sarcasms and invectives against all denominations of Christians; and the Lutherans, to whose communion he belonged, were more especially the objects of his raillery and derision, which, on many occasions, spared not those things which had formerly been looked upon as the most respectable and sacred. It is much to be doubted, whether he had formed any clear and distinct notions of the doctrines he taught, since, in his views of things, the power of imagination domineered evidently over the dictates of reason and common sense. But, if he really understood the religious maxims he was propagating, he certainly had not the talent of rendering them clear and perspicuous to others; for nothing can be more ambiguous and obscure than the expressions under which they are conveyed, and the arguments by which they are supported. A man must have the gift of divination, to be able to deduce a regular and consistent system of doctrine from the various productions of this incoherent and unintelligible writer, who was a chemist into the bargain, and whose brain seems to have been heated into a high degree of fermentation by the fire of the laboratory. If the rude, motley, and sarcastic writings of this wrong-headed reformer should reach posterity, it will be certainly a just matter of surprise to our descendants, that a considerable number of their ancestors should have been so blind as to choose, for a model of genuine piety and a teacher of religion, a man who had audaciously violated the first and most essential principles of solid piety and sound sense.*

XXXIV. The mild and gentle temper of John William Petersen, minister and first member of the ecclesiastical consistory of Lunenburg, distinguished him remarkably from the fiery enthusiast now mentioned. But the mildness of this good-natured ecclesiastic was accompanied with a want of resolution, that might be called weakness, and a certain floridness and warmth of imagination, which rendered him peculiarly susceptible of illusion himself, and a fit instrument to lead others innocently into error. Of this he gave a very remarkable specimen in 1691, by maintaining publicly that Rosamond Juliana, countess of Asseburg (whose disordered brain suggested to her the most romantic and chimerical notions) was honoured with a vision of the Deity, and commissioned to make a new declaration of his will to mankind. He also revived and propagated openly the absolute doctrine of the Millennium, which Rosamond had confirmed by her pretended authority from above. This first error produced many; for error is fertile, especially in those minds where imagination has spurned the yoke of reason, and considers all its airy visions as solid and important discoveries. Accordingly, Petersen went about prophesying with his wife,* who also gave herself out for a kind of oracle, and boasted of her extensive knowledge of the secrets of heaven. They talked of a general restitution of all things; at which grand and solemn period all intelligent beings were to be restored to happiness, the gates of hell opened, and wicked men, together with evil spirits, delivered from the guilt, power and punishment of sin. They supposed that two distinct natures, and both of them human, were united in Christ; one assumed in heaven before the formation of this globe, the other derived, upon earth, from the Virgin Mary. These opinions were swallowed down by many among the multitude, and were even embraced by some of superior rank; they met, however, with great opposition, and were refuted by a considerable number of authors, to whom Petersen, who was amply furnished with leisure and eloquence, wrote voluminous replies. In the year 1692, he was deposed; and, from that period, passed his days in the tranquillity of a rural retreat in the territory of Magdeburg, where he cheered his solitude by epistolary commerce, and spent the remainder of his life in composition and study.†

* His works were all published in 1747; and his memory is still highly honoured and respected by many, who consider him as having been, in his day, an eminent teacher of true piety and wisdom. No kind of authors find such zealous readers and patrons as those who deal largely in invective, and swell themselves, by a vain self-sufficiency, into an imagined superiority over the rest of mankind. Besides, Dippelius was an excellent chemist, and a good physician; and this procured him many friends and admirers, as all men are fond of riches and long life, and these two sciences were supposed to lead to the one and the other.

XXXV. It is not easy to determine whether John Caspar Schade and George Bosius may be associated properly with the persons now mentioned. They were both good men, full of zeal for the happiness and salvation of their brethren; but their zeal was neither directed by prudence, nor tempered with moderation. The former, who was minister at Berlin, propagated several notions that seemed crude and uncouth, and, in 1697, inveighed with the greatest bitterness against the custom that prevails in the Lutheran church of confessing privately to the clergy. These violent remonstrances excited great commotions, and were even attended with popular tumults. Bosius performed the pastoral functions at Soraw; and, to awaken sinners from their security, and prevent their treating, with negligence and indifference, interests that are most important by being eternal, denied that God would continue always propitious and placable with respect to those offenders, whose incorrigible obstinacy he had foreseen from all eternity; or that he would offer to them beyond a certain period, marked in his decrees, those succours of grace which are necessary to salvation. This tenet, in the judgment of many grave divines, seemed highly injurious to the bound-

* Her name was Johanna Eleonora a Merlau.

† Petersen wrote an account of his own life in German; his wife added her life to it, by way of supplement; and these pieces of biography will satisfy such as are desirous of a particular account of the character, manners, and talents, of this extraordinary pair. For an account of the troubles they excited at Lunenburg, see Moller's Cimbria Literata, tom. ii. p. 639; the Unschuldigen Nachrichten, An. 1748. p. 974; An. 1749. p. 30—200.

less mercy of God, and was accordingly refuted and condemned in several treatises: it found, nevertheless, an eminent patron and defender in the learned Rechenberg, professor of divinity at Leipsic, not to mention others of less note, who appeared in its behalf.*

XXXVI. Among the controversies of inferior moment that divided the Lutheran church, we shall first mention those that broke out between the doctors of Tubingen and Giessen so early as the year 1616. The principal part of this debate related to the abasement and humiliation, or to what divines call the *exinanition* of Jesus Christ; and the great point was, to know in what this exinanition properly consisted, and what was the precise characteristic of this singular situation. That the man Christ possessed, even in the most dreadful periods of his abasement, the divine properties and attributes he had received in consequence of the hypostatic union, was unanimously agreed on by both parties; but they differed in their sentiments relating to this subtle and intricate question, whether Christ during his mediatorial sufferings and sacerdotal state, really suspended the exertion of these attributes, or only concealed this exertion from the view of mortals? The latter was maintained by the doctors of Tubingen, while those of Giessen were inclined to think, that the exertion of the divine attributes was really suspended in Christ during his humiliation and sufferings. This main question was followed by others which were much more subtle than important, concerning the manner in which God is present with all his works, the reasons and foundation of this universal presence, the true cause of the omnipresence of Christ's body, and others of a like intricate and unintelligible nature. The champions who distinguished themselves on the side of the doctors of Tubingen were, Lucas Osiander, Melchior Nicolas, and Theodore Thummius. The most eminent of those who adopted the cause of the divines of Giessen were Balthasar Menzer and Justus Feverborn. The contest was carried on with zeal, learning, and sagacity: it is to be wished that one could add, that it was managed with wisdom, dignity, and moderation. This, indeed, was far from being the case; for such was the complexion of the age, that many things were now treated with indulgence, or beheld with approbation, which the wisdom and decency of succeeding times have justly endeavoured to discountenance and correct. In order to terminate these disagreeable contests, the Saxon divines were commanded by their sovereign, to offer themselves as arbitrators between the contending parties in 1624: their arbitration was accepted; but it did not at all contribute to decide the matters in debate. Their decisions were vague and ambiguous, and were therefore not adapted to give satisfaction. They declared, that they could not fully or entirely approve the doctrine of either; but insinuated, at the same time, that a certain degree of preference was due to the opinions maintained by the doctors of Giessen.† Those of Tubingen rejected the decision of the Saxon arbitrators; and it is very probable, that the divines of Giessen would have appealed from it also, had not the public calamities, in which Germany began to be involved at this time, suspended this miserable contest, by imposing silence upon the disputants, and leaving them in the quiet possession of their respective opinions.

XXXVII. Before the cessation of the controversy now mentioned, a new one was occasioned, in 1621, by the writings of Herman Rathman, minister at Dantzic, a man of eminent piety, some learning, and a zealous patron and admirer of Arndt's famous book concerning true Christianity. This good man was suspected by his colleague Corvinus, and several others, of entertaining sentiments derogatory from the dignity and power of the sacred writings. These suspicions they derived from a book published by him in 1621, concerning Christ's Kingdom of Grace, which, according to the representations of his adversaries, contained the following doctrine: "That the word of God, as it stands in the sacred writings, has no innate power to illuminate the mind, to excite in it a principle of regeneration, and thus to turn it to God: that the external word shows, indeed, the way to salvation, but cannot effectually lead men to it; but that God himself, by the ministry of another, and an internal word, works such a change in the minds of men, as is necessary to render them agreeable in his sight, and enables them to please him by their words and actions." This doctrine was represented by Corvinus and his associates as the same which had been formerly maintained by Schwenckfeld, and was professed by the Mystics in general. But whoever will be at the pains to examine with attention the various writings of Rathman on this subject, must soon be convinced, that his adversaries either misunderstood his true sentiments, or wilfully misrepresented them. His real doctrine may be comprised in the four following points: "first, that the divine word, contained in Scripture, is endowed with the power of healing the minds of men, and bringing them to God; but that, secondly, it cannot exert this power in the minds of corrupt men, who resist its divine operation and influence; and that, in consequence, thirdly, it is absolutely necessary, that the word be preceded or accompanied by some divine energy, which may prepare the minds of sinners to receive it, and remove those impediments that oppose its efficacy; and, fourthly, that it is by the power of the holy spirit, or internal word, that the external word is rendered capable of exerting its efficacy in enlightening and sanctifying the minds of men."* There is, indeed, some difference between these opinions and the doctrine commonly received in the Lutheran church, relat-

* See the first part of Walchius' Introductio ad Controversias, cap. iv.

† Jo. Wolf. Jager, Histor. Eccles. et. Polit. sæc. XVII. decenn. iii. p. 329.—Christ. Eberh. Weisman, Histor. Ecclesiast. sæc. XVII. p. 1178.—Walchius, p. 203.—See also Carolus, Arnold, and the other writers, who have written the ecclesiastical history of these times.

* See Moller's Cimbria Literata, tom. iii. p. 559.—Hartknoch's German work, entitled, Preussische Kirchen-Geschichte, book iii. ch. viii. p. 812. Arnold's Kirchen Historie, part iii. chap. xii

ing to the efficacy of the divine word; but a careful perusal of the writings of Rathman on this subject, and a candid examination of his inaccurate expressions, will persuade the impartial reader, that this difference is neither great nor important; and he will only perceive, that this pious man had not the talent of expressing his notions with order, perspicuity, and precision. However that may have been, this contest grew more general from day to day, and, at length, extended its polemic influence through the whole Lutheran church, the greatest part of whose members followed the example of the Saxon doctors in condemning Rathman, while a considerable number, dazzled by the lustre of his piety, and persuaded of the innocence of his doctrine, espoused his cause. He died in 1628, when this controversy was at the greatest height, and the warmth and animosity of the contending parties gradually subsided.

XXXVIII. It would be repugnant to the true end of history, as well as to all principles of candour and equity, to swell this enumeration of the controversies that divided the Lutheran church, with the private disputes of individuals concerning particular points of doctrine and worship. Some writers have, indeed, followed this method, not so much with a design to enrich their histories with a multitude of facts, and to show men and opinions in all their various aspects, as with a view to render the Lutherans ridiculous or odious. In the happiest times, and in the best-modelled communities, there will always remain sufficient marks of human imperfection, and abundant sources of private contention, at least, in the imprudence, inadvertency, and misconceptions of some, and the impatience and severity of others; but it must betray a great want of sound judgment, as well as of candour and impartiality, to form a general estimate of the state and character of a whole church upon such particular instances of imperfection and error. Certain singular opinions and modes of expression were censured by many in the writings of Tarnovius and Affelman, two divines of Rostoch, who were otherwise men of distinguished merit. This, however, will surprise us less if we consider, that these doctors often expressed themselves improperly, when their sentiments were just; and that, when their expressions were accurate and proper, they were frequently misunderstood by those who pretended to censure them. Joachim Lutkeman, whose reputation was considerable, and, in many respects, well deserved, conceived the idea of denying that Christ remained *a true man* during the three days that intervened from his death to his resurrection. This sentiment appeared highly erroneous to many; and hence arose a contest, which was merely a dispute about words, resembling many other debates, which, like bubbles, are incessantly swelling and vanishing on the surface of human life. Of this kind, more especially, was the controversy which, for some time, exercised the talents of Boetius and Balduin, professors of divinity (the former at Helmstadt, and the latter at Wittenberg,) and had for its subject the following question, whether the wicked shall one day be restored to life by the merits of Christ? In the duchy of Holstein, Reinboth distinguished himself by the singularity of his opinions. After the example of Calixtus, he reduced the fundamental doctrines of religion within narrower bounds than were usually prescribed to them; he also considered the opinion of those Greeks, who denied that the Holy Ghost proceeds from the Son, as an error of very little consequence. In both these respects, his sentiments were adopted by many; they, however, met with opposition from several quarters, and were censured with peculiar warmth by the learned John Conrad Danhaver, professor of divinity at Strasbourg: in consequence of this, a kind of controversy was kindled between these eminent men, and was carried on with more vehemence than the nature and importance of the debated points could justify.* But these and other contests of this nature, must not be admitted into that list of controversies, from which we are to form a judgment of the internal state of the Lutheran church during this century.

XXXIX. We cannot make the same observation with regard to certain controversies, which were of a personal rather than a real nature, and related to the orthodoxy or unsoundness of certain men, rather than to the truth or falsehood of particular opinions: for these are more particularly connected with the internal state and history of the church, than the contests last mentioned. It is not unusual for those who professedly embark in the cause of declining piety, and aim, in a solemn, zealous, and public manner, at its revival and restoration, to be elated with high and towering views, and warmed with a certain enthusiastic, though noble fervour. This ardent elevation of mind is by no means a source of accuracy and precision; on the contrary, it produces many unguarded expressions, and prevents men of warm piety from framing their language by those rules which are necessary to render it clear, accurate, and proper; it frequently dictates expressions and phrases that are pompous and emphatic, but, at the same time, allegorical and ambiguous; and leads pious and even sensible men to adopt uncouth and vulgar forms of speech, employed by writers whose style is as low and barbarous as their intentions are upright and pious, and whose practical treatises on religion and morality have nothing to recommend them but the zeal and fervour with which they are penned. Persons of this warm and enthusiastic turn fall with more facility than any other set of men into the suspicion of heresy, on account of the inaccuracy of their expressions. This many doctors found to be true, by a disagreeable experience, during the course of this century; but it was, in a more particular manner, the fate of Stephen Prætorius, minister of Saltzwedel, and of John Arndt, whose piety and virtue have rendered his memory precious

* For a general account of these controversies, see Arnold's Kirchen Hist. p. ii. lib. xvii. cap. vi. p. 957. That which was occasioned by Reinboth is amply and circumstantially related by Moller, in part ii. of his Introd. ad Hist. Chersonesi Cimbricæ and in his Cimbria Literata, t. ii

to the friends of true religion. Prætorius had, so early as the preceding century, composed certain treatises, designed to revive a spirit of vital religion, and awaken in the minds of men a zeal for their future and eternal interests. These productions, which were frequently republished during this century, were highly applauded by many, while, in the judgment of others, they abounded with expressions and sentiments, that were partly false, and partly adapted by their ambiguity to lead men into error. It cannot be denied, that there are in the writings of Prætorius some improper and unguarded expressions, which may too easily deceive the ignorant and unwary, as also several marks of a credulity that borders upon weakness; but those who peruse his works with impartiality will be fully persuaded of the uprightness of his intentions.

The unfeigned piety and integrity of Arndt could not secure him from censure. His famous book concerning true Christianity, which is still perused with the utmost pleasure and edification by many persons eminent for the sanctity of their lives and manners, met with a warm and obstinate opposition. Osiander, Rostius, and other doctors, inveighed against it with great asperity, pretended to find in it various defects, and alleged, among other things, that its style was infected with the jargon of the Paracelsists, Weigelians, and other Mystico-chemical philosophers. It must, indeed, be acknowledged, that this eminent man was highly disgusted at the philosophy that, in his time, reigned in the schools; nor can it be denied, that he had a high, perhaps an excessive degree of respect for the chemists, and an ill-placed confidence in their obscure decisions and pompous undertakings. This led him sometimes into conversation with those fantastic philosophers, who, by the power and ministry of fire, pretended to unfold both the secrets of nature and the mysteries of religion. But, notwithstanding this, he was declared exempt from any errors of moment by a multitude of grave and pious divines, among whom were Egard, Dilger, Breler, Gerard, and Dorschæus; and in the issue the censures and opposition of his adversaries seemed rather to give a new lustre to his reputation than to cover him with reproach.*

We may place, in the class now under consideration, Valentine Weigel, a minister of the church of Zscopavia in Misnia; for, though he died in the preceding century, yet it was in this that the greatest part of his writings were published, and also censured as erroneous and of a dangerous tendency. The science of chemistry, which at this time was making such a rapid progress in Germany, proved also detrimental to this ecclesiastic; who, though in the main a man of probity and merit, neglected the paths of right reason, and chose rather to wander in the devious wilds of a chimerical philosophy.†

* See Arnoldi Hist. Eccles. p. ii. lib. xvii. cap. vi p. 940.—Weismanni Histor. Eccles. sæc. XVII. p 1174, 1189.—Godof. Balth, Scharfii. Supplementum Historiæ Litisque Arndtianæ.

† There is an account of Weigel, more ample than impartial, given by Arnold, lib. xvii. cap. xvii. p. 1088.

XL. There were a set of fanatics among the Lutherans, who in the flights of their enthusiasm far surpassed those now mentioned, and who had such a high notion of their own abilities as to attempt melting down the present form of religion, and casting a new system of piety after a model drawn from their wanton and irregular fancies; it is with some account of the principal of these spiritual projectors that we shall conclude the history of the Lutheran church during this century.

At the head of this visionary tribe we may place Jacob Behmen, a tailor at Gorlitz, who was remarkable for the multitude of his patrons and adversaries, and whom his admirers commonly called the German Theosophist. This man had a natural propensity toward the investigation of mysteries, and was fond of abstruse and intricate inquiries of every kind, and having, partly by books, and partly by conversation with certain physicians,* acquired some knowledge of the doctrine of Robert Fludd and the Rosecrusians, which was propagated in Germany with great ostentation during this century, he struck out of the element of fire, by the succours of imagination, a species of theology much more obscure than the numbers of Pythagoras, or the intricacies of Heraclitus. Some have bestowed high praises on this enthusiast, on account of his piety, integrity, and sincere love of truth and virtue; and we shall not presume to contradict these encomiums. But such as carry their admiration of his doctrine so far as to honour him with the character of an inspired messenger of Heaven, or even of a judicious and wise philosopher, must be themselves deceived and blinded in a very high degree; for never did there reign such obscurity and confusion in the writings of any mortal, as in the miserable productions of Jacob Behmen, which exhibit a motley mixture of chemical terms, crude visions, and mystic jargon. Among other dreams of a disturbed and eccentric fancy, he entertained the following chimerical notion: "That the divine grace operates by the same rules, and follows the same methods, which the divine providence observes in the natural world, and that the minds of men are purged from their vices and corruptions in the same way that metals are purified from their dross;" and this maxim was the principle of his fire-theology. Behmen had a considerable number of followers in this century, the most eminent of whom were John Louis Giftheil, John Angelus Werdenhagen, Abraham Frankenberg, Theodore Tzetsch, Paul Felgenhauer, Quirinus Kuhlman, John Jacob Zimmermann; and he has still many votaries and admirers even in our times. Some of his followers retained, notwithstanding their attachment to his extravagant system, a certain degree of moderation and good sense, while others seemed entirely out of their wits, and by their phrensy excited the compassion of those who were the spectators of their conduct; such were Kuhlman and Gichtel, of whom the former was burned at Moscow in 1684; but, indeed, it may be affirmed in general, that none of his disciples propa

* Tobias Kober and Balthaser Walther.

gated his doctrine, or conducted themselves, in such a manner as to do honour either to their master or to his cause in the judgment of the wise.*

XLI. Another class of persons, who deserve to be placed immediately after Behmen, were they, whom a disordered brain persuaded that they were prophets sent from above, and that they were divinely inspired with the power of prediction. A considerable number of these delirious fanatics arose in this century, more especially at that juncture when the house of Austria was employed in maintaining its power in the empire, against the united armies of Sweden, France, and Germany. It is remarkable, that pretended prophets and diviners are never more numerous than at those critical and striking periods when great revolutions are expected, or sudden and heavy calamities have happened, as such periods, and the scenes they exhibit, inflame the imagination of the fanatic, and may be turned to the profit of the impostor. The most eminent of the fanatical prophets now under consideration, were Nicholas Drabicius, Christopher Kotter, Christina Poniatovia (all of whom found an eloquent defender and patron in John Amos Comenius,) Joachim Greulich, Anne Vetter, Mary Frolich, and George Reichard; beside several others, who audaciously assumed the same character. It is not necessary to enter into a circumstantial detail of the history of this visionary tribe, since none of them arose to such a degree of reputation and consequence, as to occasion any considerable tumults by their pretended predictions. It is sufficient to have observed in general, that, even in this century, there were among the Lutherans some crazy fanatics, who, under the impulse of a disordered imagination, assumed the character and authority of prophets sent from above to enlighten the world.†

XLII. It will not, however, be improper to mention, somewhat more circumstantially, the case of those, who, though they did not arrive at that enormous height of folly which leads men to pretend to divine inspiration, yet deceived themselves and deluded others, by entertaining and propagating the strangest fancies, and the most monstrous and impious absurdities. Some time after the commencement of this century, Isaiah Stiefel and Ezekiel Meth, natives of Thuringia, were observed to throw out the most extraordinary and shocking expressions, while they spoke of themselves and their religious attainments. These expressions, in the judgment of many, amounted to nothing less, than attributing to themselves the divine glory and majesty, and thus implied a blasphemous, or rather a phrenetic, insult on the Supreme Being and his eternal Son. It is nevertheless scarcely credible, however irrational we may suppose them to have been, that these fanatics should have carried their perverse and absurd fancies to such an amazing height; and it would perhaps be more agreeable both to truth and charity to suppose, that they only imitated the pompous and turgid language of the mystic writers in such an extravagant manner, as to give occasion to the heavy accusation above stated. Considering the matter even in this candid and charitable light, we may see by their examples what an effect the constant perusal of the writings of the Mystics may have in shedding darkness, delusion, and folly, into the imaginations of weak and ignorant men.* The reveries of Paul Nagel, professor of divinity at Leipsic, were highly absurd, but of a less pernicious tendency than those already mentioned. This prophetic dreamer, who had received a superficial tincture of mathematical knowledge, pretended to see, in the position of the stars, the events that were to happen in church and state; and, from a view of these celestial bodies, affected to foretell, in a more particular manner, the erection of a new and most holy kingdom in which Christ should reign here upon earth.†

XLIII. Christian Hoburg, a native of Lunenburg, a man of a turbulent and inconstant spirit, and not more remarkable for his violence, than for his duplicity, threw out the most bitter reproaches and invectives against the whole Lutheran church without exception,‡ and thereby involved himself in various perplexities. He long deceived the multitude by his dissimulation and hypocrisy; and, by a series of frauds, which he undoubtedly looked upon as lawful, he so far disguised his true character that he appeared to many, and especially to persons of a candid and charitable turn, much less contemptible than he was in reality; and though the acrimony and violence of his proceedings were condemned, yet they were supposed to be directed, not against re-

* It is needless to mention the writers who employed their pens in stemming the torrent of Behmen's enthusiasm. The works of this fanatic are in every body's hands, and the books that were composed to refute them are well known, and to be found every where. All that has been alleged, in his favour and defence, has been carefully collected by Arnold, who is, generally speaking, peculiarly eloquent in the praises of those whom others treat with contempt. For an account of Kuhlman, and his unhappy fate, see the German work, entitled, Unschuld. Nachrichten, An. 1748.

☞ Behmen, however, had the good fortune to meet with, in our days, a warm advocate and an industrious disciple, in the late well meaning but gloomy and visionary Mr. William Law, who employed himself, for many years, in preparing a new edition and translation of Behmen's works, which, after his death, a friend gave to the world.

† Arnold is to be commended for giving us an accurate collection of the transactions and visions of these enthusiasts, in the third and fourth parts of his History of Heretics, since those who are desirous of full information in this matter may easily see, by consulting this historian, that the pretended revelations of these prophets were no more than the phantoms of a disordered imagination. A pious but ignorant man, named Benedict Bahnsen, who was a native of Holstein, and lived at Amsterdam about the middle of the seventeenth century, was so delighted with the effusions and writings of these fanatics, that he collected them carefully, and published them. In 1670, a catalogue of his library was printed at Amsterdam, which was full of chemical, fanatical, and pretendedly-prophetic books.

* See Arnold's Historia Eccles. p. iii. cap. iv. p. 32.—Thomasius' German work, entitled, Histoire der Weisheit und Narrheit, vol. i.

† Arnold, p. iii. cap. v. p. 53.—Andr. Caroli Memorabilia Ecclesiæ, sæc. XVII. in parte i. lib. iii. cap. iv. p. 513.

‡ Hoburg, in some of his petulant and satirical writings, assumed the names of Elias Prætorius and Bernard Baumann.

ligion itself, but against the licentiousness and vices of its professors, and particularly of its ministers. At length, however, the mask fell from the face of this hypocrite, who became an object of general indignation and contempt, and, deserting the communion of the Lutheran church, went over to the Mennonites.* There was a striking resemblance between this petulant railer and Frederic Breckling; the latter, however, surpassed even the former in impetuosity and malignity. Breckling had been pastor, first in the duchy of Holstein, and afterwards at Zwoll, a city in the United Provinces, where he was deposed from his ministry, and lived many years afterward without being attached to any religious sect or community. There are several of his writings extant, which, indeed, recommend warmly the practice of piety and virtue, and seem to express the most implacable abhorrence of vicious persons and licentious manners; and yet, at the same time, they demonstrate plainly that their author was destitute of that charity, prudence, meekness, patience, and love of truth, which are essential and fundamental virtues of a real Christian.† It is undoubtedly a just matter of surprise, that these vehement declaimers against the established religion and its ministers, who pretend to be so much more sagacious and sharp-sighted than their brethren, do not perceive a truth, which the most simple may learn from daily observation; even that nothing is more odious and disgusting than an angry, petulant, and violent reformer, who comes to heal the disorders of a community, armed as it were with fire and sword, with menaces and terrors. We may also wonder, that these men are not aware of another consideration equally obvious, namely, that it is scarcely credible, that a *spiritual* physician will cure another, with entire success, of the disorders under which he himself is known to labour.

George Laurence Seidenbecher, pastor at Eisfeld in Saxony, adopted himself, and propagated among the multitude, the doctrine of the Millennium, which scarcely ever gains admittance but in disordered brains, and rarely produces any other fruits than incoherent dreams and idle visions. Seidenbecher was censured on account of this doctrine, and deposed from his pastoral charge.‡

XLIV. It would be superfluous to name the other fanatics, that seem to demand a place in the class now before us, since they almost all laboured under the same disorder, and such uniformity prevailed in their sentiments and conduct, that the history of one may, in a great measure, be considered as the history of all. We shall therefore conclude this crazy list with a short account of the very worst of the whole tribe, namely, Martin Seidel, a native of Silesia, who endeavoured to form a sect in Poland toward the conclusion of the preceding century and the commencement of this, but could not find followers, even among the Socinians; so wild were his views, and so extravagant his notions. This audacious adventurer in religious novelty was of opinion, that God had, indeed, promised a Saviour or Messiah to the Jews; but that this Messiah had never appeared, and never would appear, on account of the sins of the Jewish people, which rendered them unworthy of this great deliverer. Hence he concluded, that it was erroneous to look upon Christ as the Messiah; that the only office of Jesus was, to interpret and republish the law of nature, which had been perverted and obscured by the vices, corruptions, and ignorance of men; and that the whole duty of men, and all the obligations of religion, were fulfilled by an obedience to this law, republished and explained by Jesus Christ. To render this doctrine more defensible and specious, or, at least, to get rid of a multitude of arguments and express declarations that might be drawn from the Scriptures to prove its absurdity, he boldly rejected all the books of the New Testament. The small number of disciples, that adopted the fancies of this intrepid innovator, were denominated *semi-judaizers*.* Had he appeared in our times, he would have given less offence than at the period in which he lived; for, if we except his singular notion concerning the Messiah, his doctrine was such as would at present be highly agreeable to many persons in Great Britain, Holland, and other countries.†

CHAPTER II.

The History of the Reformed Church.

I. It has been already observed, that the Reformed Church, considered in the most comprehensive sense of that term, as forming a *whole*, composed of a great variety of parts, is rather united by the principles of moderation and fraternal charity than by a perfect uniformity in doctrine, discipline, and worship. It will, therefore, be proper first to take a view of those events which related to this great body collectively considered, and afterwards to enter into a detail of the most memorable occurrences that happened in the particular communities of which it is composed. The principal accessions it received during this century have already been mentioned, when, in the history of the Lutheran church, we related the changes and commotions that happened in the princi-

* Arnold, p. iii. cap. xiii. p. 130.—Andr. Caroli Mem. Eccles. vol. i. p. 1065. Jo. Hornbeck's Summa Controvers. p. 535.—Moller's Cimbria Literata, tom. ii. p. 337.

† Arnold has given an account of Breckling, in the third and fourth parts of his History; he has also published some of his writings, which sufficiently demonstrate the irregularity and exuberance of his fancy. There is a particular account of this degraded pastor given in the Cimbria Literata, tom. iii. p. 72.

‡ There is a circumstantial account of this man given by Alb. Meno. Verpoorten, in his Commentat. de Vita et Institutis G. L. Seidenbecheri.

* See Gustavi Georgii Zeltneri Historia Crypto-Socinismi Altorffini, vol. i. p. 268, 335.

☞ † We are much at a loss to know what Dr Mosheim means by this insinuation, as also the persons he has in view; for, on one hand, it is sufficiently evident he cannot mean the deists; and, on the other, we know of no denomination of Christians, who "boldly reject all the books of the New Testament." Our author probably meant that the part of Seidel's doctrine which represents Christ's mission as only designed to republish and interpret the law of nature, and the whole religious and moral duty of man, as consisting in an obedience to this law, would have been well received by many persons in Great Britain and Holland; but he should have said so: nothing requires such precision as accusations.

palities of Hesse-Cassel and Brandenburg.* These, however, were not the only changes that took place in favour of the reformed church. Its doctrine was embraced, early in this century, by Adolphus, duke of Holstein; and it was naturally expected, that the subjects would follow the example of their prince: but this expectation was disappointed by the death of Adolphus, in 1616.† Henry, duke of Saxony, withdrew also from the communion of the Lutherans, in whose religious principles he had been educated, and, in 1688, embraced the doctrine of the reformed church at Dessau, in consequence, as some allege, of the solicitations of his duchess.‡ In Denmark, about the beginning of this century, there were still a considerable number of persons who secretly espoused the sentiments of that church, and more especially could never reconcile themselves to the Lutheran doctrine of Christ's bodily presence with the sacrament of the eucharist. They were confirmed in their attachment to the tenets of the reformed by Hemming, and the other followers of Melancthon, whose secret ministry and public writings were attended with considerable success. The face of things, however, changed; and the reformed in Denmark saw their expectations vanish, and their credit sink, in 1614, when Canute, bishop of Gothenburg, who had given too plain intimations of his propensity to the doctrines of Calvin, was deprived of his episcopal dignity.§ The progress of the reformed religion in Africa, Asia, and America, is abundantly known; it was carried into those distant regions by the English and Dutch emigrants, who formed settlements there for the purposes of commerce, and founded flourishing churches in the various provinces where they fixed their habitations. It is also known, that, in several places where Lutheranism was established, the French, German, and British members of the reformed church were allowed to enjoy the free exercise of their religion.

II. Of all the calamities that tended to diminish the influence, and eclipse the lustre, of the reformed church, none proved more dismal in its circumstances, and more unhappy in its effects, than the deplorable fate of that church in France. From the time of the accession of Henry IV. to the throne of that kingdom, this church had acquired the form of a body politic.* Its members were endowed with considerable privileges; they were also secured against insults of every kind by a solemn edict, and possessed several fortified places, particularly the strong city of Rochelle; in which, to render their security still more complete, they were permitted to have their own garrisons. This body politic was not, indeed, always under the influence and direction of leaders eminent for their prudence, or distinguished by their permanent attachment to the interests of the crown, and the person of the sovereign. Truth and candour oblige us to acknowledge, that the Reformed conducted themselves, on some occasions, in a manner inconsistent with the demands of regular subordination. Sometimes, amidst the broils and tumults of faction, they joined the parties that opposed the government; at others, they took important steps without the king's approbation or consent; they even went so far as to solicit, more than once, without so much as disguising their measures, the alliance and friendship of England and Holland, and formed views which, at least in appearance, were scarcely consistent with the tranquillity of the kingdom, or with a proper respect for the authority of its monarch. Hence contests arose in 1621, and subsisted long, between Louis XIII. and his protestant subjects; and these civil broils furnished a pretence for the severe and despotic maxim of Richelieu, the first minister of that monarch, that the kingdom could never enjoy the sweets of peace, or the satisfaction that was founded upon the assurance of public safety, before the protestants were deprived of their towns and strong-holds, and before their rights and privileges, together with their ecclesiastical polity, were crushed to pieces, and totally suppressed. This haughty minister, after many violent efforts and hard struggles, at length obtained his purpose; for, in 1628, Rochelle, the chief bulwark of the reformed interest in France, was taken, after a long and difficult siege, and annexed to the crown. From this fatal event the party, defenceless and naked, dated its decline; since, after the reduction of their chief city, these protestants had no other resource than the pure clemency and generosity of their sovereign.† Those who judge of the reduction of this place by the maxims of civil policy, consider the conduct of the French court as entirely consistent with the principles both of wisdom and justice; since nothing can be more detrimental to the tranquillity and safety of any nation, than a body politic erected in its bosom, independent of the supreme authority of the state, and secured against its influence or inspection by an external force; and if the French monarch, satisfied with depriving the protestants of their strong-holds, had continued to maintain them in the possession of that liberty of conscience, and that free exercise of

* See sect. ii. part ii. chap. i. sect. i. ii. where the History of the Lutheran church commences with an account of the loss which that church sustained by the secession of Maurice, landgrave of Hesse-Cassel, and John Sigismund, elector of Brandenburg, who embraced solemnly the doctrine of the reformed church, the former in 1604, and the latter in 1614.

† Jo. Molleri Introd. ad Histor. Chersonesi Cimbricæ, v. ii. p. 101.—Erici Pontoppidani Annales Ecclesiæ Danicæ Diplomatici, tom. iii. p. 691.

‡ See Moebii Selectæ Disp. Theolog. p. 1137. The duke of Saxony published a Confession of his Faith, containing the reasons of his change. This piece, which the divines of Leipsic were obliged by a public order to refute, was defended against their attacks by the learned Isaac de Beausobre, at that time pastor at Magdeburg, in a book entitled, "Defense de la Doctrine des Reformes, et en particulier de la Confession de S. A. S. Mon-Seigneur le Duc Henri de Saxe, contre un Livre compose par la Faculte de Theologie a Leipsic."

§ Pontoppidani Annal. Eccles. Danicæ, tom. iii. p. 695.

* *Imperium in imperio*, i. e. an empire within an empire.

† See Le Clerc, Vie du Cardinal Richelieu, tom. i. p. 69, 77, 177, 199, 259.—Le Vassor, Histoire de Louis XIII. tom. iii. p. 676, tom. iv. p. 1, and the following volumes. See also the third, fourth, and fifth volumes of the Memoirs of Sully (the friend and confidant of Henry IV.) who, though a protestant, acknowledges frankly the errors of his party.

their religion, for which they had shed so much blood, and to the enjoyment of which their eminent services to the house of Bourbon had given them such a fair and illustrious claim, it is highly probable that they would have borne with patience this infraction of their privileges, and the loss of that liberty which had been confirmed to them by the most solemn edicts.

III. But the court and the despotic minister were not satisfied with this success. Having destroyed that form of civil polity which had been annexed to the reformed church as a security for the maintenance of its religious privileges, and was afterwards considered as detrimental to the supreme authority of the state, they proceeded still farther, and regardless of the royal faith, confirmed by the most solemn declarations, perfidiously invaded those privileges of the church which were merely of a spiritual and religious nature. At first, the court, and the ministers of its tyranny, put in practice all the arts of insinuation and persuasion, in order to gain over the heads of the reformed church, and the more learned and celebrated ministers of that communion. Pathetic exhortations and alluring promises were tried; artful interpretations of those doctrines of popery which were most disagreeable to the protestants were brought forward; in a word, every insidious method was employed to conquer their aversion to the church of Rome. Richelieu exhausted all the resources of his dexterity and artifice, and eagerly practised, with the most industrious assiduity, all the means that he thought the most adapted to seduce the protestants into the Romish communion. When all these stratagems were observed to produce little or no effect, barbarity and violence were employed to extirpate and destroy a set of men, whom mean perfidy could not seduce, and whom weak arguments were insufficient to convince. The most inhuman laws that the blind rage of bigotry could dictate, the most oppressive measures that the ingenious efforts of malice could invent, were put in execution to damp the courage of a party become odious by their resolute adherence to the dictates of their consciences, and to bring them by force under the yoke of Rome. The French bishops distinguished themselves by their intemperate and unchristian zeal in this horrid scene of persecution and cruelty: many of the protestants sunk under the weight of despotic oppression, and yielded up their faith to armed legions, that were sent to convert them; a considerable number fled from the storm, and deserted their families, their friends, and their country; and the greatest part persevered, with a noble and heroic constancy, in the purity of that religion, which their ancestors had delivered, and happily separated, from the manifold superstitions of a corrupt and idolatrous church.

IV. When at length every method which artifice or perfidy could invent had been practised in vain against the protestants under the reign of Louis XIV., the bishops and Jesuits, whose counsels had a peculiar influence in the cabinet of that prince, judged it necessary to extirpate, by fire and sword, this resolute people, and thus to ruin, as it were by one mortal blow, the cause of the Reformation in France. Their insidious arguments and importunate solicitations had such an effect upon the weak and credulous mind of Louis, that, in 1685, trampling on the most solemn obligations, and regardless of all laws, human and divine, he revoked the edict of Nantes, and thereby deprived the protestants of the liberty of serving God according to their consciences. This revocation was accompanied with the applause of Rome; but it excited the indignation even of many Roman Catholics, whose bigotry had not effaced or suspended, on this occasion, their natural sentiments of generosity and justice. It was, moreover, followed by a measure still more tyrannical and shocking, even an express order, addressed to all the reformed churches, to embrace the Romish faith. The consequences of this cruel and unrighteous proceeding were highly detrimental to the true interests and the real prosperity of the French nation,* by the prodigious emigrations it occasioned among the protestants, who sought, in various parts of Europe, that religious liberty, and that humane treatment, which their mother-country had so cruelly refused them. Those among them, whom the vigilance of their enemies guarded so closely as to prevent their flight, were exposed to the brutal rage of an unrelenting soldiery, and were assailed by every barbarous form of persecution that might tend to subdue their courage, exhaust their patience, and thus engage them to a feigned and external profession of popery, which in their consciences they beheld with the utmost aversion and disgust. This crying act of perfidy and injustice in a prince, who, on other occasions, gave evident proofs of his generosity and equity, is sufficient to show, in their true and genuine colours, the spirit of the Romish church and pontiffs, and the manner in which they stand affected to those whom they consider as *heretics*. It is peculiarly adapted to convince the impartial and attentive observer, that the most solemn oaths, and the most sacred treaties, are never looked upon by this church and its pontiffs as respectable and obligatory, when the

* See the Life of Isaac de Beausobre, written by the ingenious Armand de la Chapelle, and subjoined to Beausobre's Remarques Historiques, Critiques, et Philologiques sur le Nouveau Testament.

☞ Some late hireling writers, employed by the Jesuits, have been audacious enough to plead the cause of the revocation of the edict of Nantes. But it must be observed, to the honour of the French nation, that these impotent attempts, to justify the measures of a persecuting and unrelenting priesthood, have been treated almost universally at Paris with indignation and contempt. They who are desirous of seeing a true statement of the losses the French nation sustained, by the revocation of that famous edict, have only to consult the curious and authentic account of the state of that nation, taken from memorials drawn up by the intendants of the several provinces, for the use of the duke of Burgundy, and published in 1727 with the following title: "Etat de la France, extrait, par M. le Comte de Boulainvilliers, des Memoires dresses par les Intendans du Royaume, par l'Ordre du Roi Louis XIV. a la Solicitation du Duc de Bourgogne." See also Voltaire, Sur la Tolerance, p. 41 and 201; and, for an account of the conduct of the French court toward the protestants at that dismal period, see the incomparable memorial of the learned and pious Claude, entitled, Plaintes des Protestans de France.

violation of them may contribute to advance their interest, or to accomplish their views.

V. The Waldenses, who lived in the vallies of Piedmont, and had embraced the doctrine, discipline, and worship of the church of Geneva, were oppressed and persecuted, in the most inhuman manner, during the greatest part of this century, by the ministers of Rome. This persecution was carried on with peculiar marks of rage and enormity in the years 1655, 1686, and 1696, and seemed to portend nothing less than the total extinction of that unhappy nation.* The most horrid scenes of violence and bloodshed were exhibited on this theatre of papal tyranny; and the small numbers of the Waldenses that yet survive, are indebted for their existence and support, precarious and uncertain as it is, to the continual intercession made for them by the English and Dutch governments, and also by the Swiss cantons, who never cease to solicit the clemency of the duke of Savoy in their behalf.

The church of the Palatinate, which had been long at the head of the Reformed churches in Germany, declined apace from the year 1685, when a catholic prince was raised to that electorate. This decline became at length so visible, that, instead of being the first, it was the least considerable of all the Protestant assemblies in that country.

VI. The eminent and illustrious figure that the principal members of the reformed church made in the learned world is too well known, and the reputation they acquired, by a successful application to the various branches of literature and science, is too well established, to require our entering into a circumstantial detail upon that head. We shall also pass in silence the names of those celebrated men who have acquired immortal fame by their writings, and transmitted their eminent usefulness to succeeding times in their learned and pious productions. Out of the copious list of famous authors that adorned this church, it would be difficult to select the most eminent; and this is a sufficient reason for our silence.† The supreme guide and legislator of such as applied themselves to the study of philosophy had been Aristotle, who, for a long time, reigned unrivalled in the reformed, as well as in the Lutheran schools, and was exhibited, in both, not in his natural and genuine aspect, but in the motley and uncouth form in which he had been dressed up by the scholastic doctors. But, when Gassendi and Des-Cartes appeared, the Stagirite began to decline, and his fame and authority diminished gradually. Among the French and Dutch, many adopted the Cartesian philosophy on its first promulgation; and a considerable number of the English embraced the principles of Gassendi, and were singularly pleased with his prudent and candid manner of investigating truth. The Aristotelians every where, and more especially in Holland, were greatly alarmed at this revolution in the philosophical world, and set themselves, with all their vigour, to oppose its progress. They endeavoured to persuade the people, that the cause of truth and religion must suffer considerably by the efforts that were made to dethrone Aristotle, and bring into disrepute the doctrine of his interpreters; but the principal cause of their anxiety and zeal, was the apprehension of losing their places in the public schools; a thought which they could not bear with any degree of patience.* However, the powerful lustre of truth, which unfolded daily more and more its engaging charms, and the love of liberty, which had been kept in chains by Peripatetic tyranny, obliged this obstinate sect to yield, and reduced them to silence; and hence it is, that the doctors of the reformed church carry on, at this day, their philosophical inquiries with the same freedom that is observable among the Lutherans. It may, indeed, be a question with some, whether Aristotle be not, even yet, secretly revered in some of the English universities. It is at least certain, that, although, under the government of Charles II. and in the two succeeding reigns, the mathematical philosophy had made a most extensive progress in Great Britain, there were, both at Oxford and Cambridge, some doctors who preferred the ancient system of the schools to the new discoveries now under consideration.

VII. All the interpreters and expositors of Scripture that made a figure in the reformed church about the commencement of this century, followed scrupulously the method of Calvin in their illustrations of the sacred writings, and unfolded the true and natural signification of the words of Scripture, without perplexing their brains to find out deep mysteries in plain expressions, or to force, by the inventive efforts of fancy, a variety of singular notions from the metaphorical language that is frequently used by the inspired writers. This attachment to the method of Calvin, was indeed considerably

* Leger, Histoire Generale des Eglises Vaudoises, p. ii. c. vi. p. 72.—Gilles, Histoire Ecclesiast. des Eglises Vaudoises, ch. xlix. p. 353.—A particular history of the persecution suffered by these victims of papal cruelty in 1686, appeared at Rotterdam in 1688.

☞ See also a pamphlet, entitled, An Account of the late Persecutions of the Waldenses by the duke of Savoy and the French king in 1686; and likewise a detail of the miseries endured by these unfortunate objects of papal persecution in the years 1655, 1662, 1663, and 1686, related by Peter Boyer, in his history of the Vaudois.

☞ † The list of the eminent divines and men of learning who were ornaments to the Reformed church in the seventeenth century, is indeed extremely ample. Among those who adorned Great Britain, we shall always remember, with peculiar veneration, the immortal names of Newton, Barrow, Cudworth, Boyle, Chillingworth, Usher, Bedell, Hall, Pocock, Fell, Lightfoot, Hammond, Calamy, Walton, Baxter, Pearson, Stillingfleet, Mede, Parker, Oughtred, Burnet, Tillotson, and many others well known in the literary world. In Germany we find Pareus, Scultet, Fabricius, the two Altings, Pelargus, and Bergius; in Switzerland and Geneva, Hospinian, the two Buxtorfs, Hottinger, Heidegger, and Turretin. In the churches and universities of Holland, we meet with the following learned divines: Drusus, Amama, Gomar, Rivet, Cloppenburg, Vossius, Cocceius, Voet, Des-Marets, Heidan, Momma, Burman, Wittichius Hornbeck, the Spanheims, Le Moine, De Maestricht, and others. Among the French doctors, we may reckon Cameron, Chamier, Du-Moulin, Mestrezat, Blondel, Drelincourt, Daille, Amyrault, the two Capels, De la Place, Gamstole, Croy, Morus, Le Blanc, Pajon, Bochart, Claude, Allix, Jurieu, Basnage, Abbadie, Beausobre, L'Enfant, Martin, Des-Vignoles &c.

* See Baillet's Vie de Rene Des-Cartes.

diminished, in the sequel, by the credit and influence of two celebrated commentators, who struck out new paths in the sphere of sacred criticism. These were Hugo Grotius, and John Cocceius. The former departed less from the manner of interpretation generally received than the latter. Like Calvin, he followed in his commentaries, both in the Old and New Testament, the literal and obvious signification of the words employed by the sacred writers; but he differed considerably from that great man in his manner of explaining the predictions of the prophets. The hypothesis of Grotius, upon that important subject, amounts to this: "That the predictions of the ancient prophets were all accomplished in the events to which they directly pointed before the coming of Christ; and that therefore the natural and obvious sense and import of the words and phrases, in which they were delivered, do not terminate in our blessed Lord; but that in some of these predictions, and more especially in those which the writers of the New Testament apply to Christ, there is, beside the literal and obvious signification, a hidden and mysterious sense, that lies concealed under the external mask of certain persons, events, and actions, which are *representative* of the person, ministry, sufferings, and merits of the Son of God."

The method of Cocceius was entirely different from this. He looked upon the whole history of the Old Testament as a perpetual and uninterrupted representation or mirror of the history of the divine Saviour, and of the Christian church; he maintained, moreover, that all the prophecies have a literal and direct relation to Christ; and he finished his romantic system by laying it down as a certain maxim, that all the events and revolutions which shall happen in the church, until the end of time, are prefigured and pointed out, though not all with the same degree of evidence and perspicuity, in different places of the Old Testament.* Each of these eminent commentators had his zealous disciples and followers. The Arminians in general, many of the English and French divines, together with those warm votaries of ancient Calvinism who are called Voetians (from their chief Gisbert Voet, the great adversary of Cocceius,) adopted the method of interpreting Scripture introduced by Grotius. On the other hand, many of the Dutch, Swiss, and Germans, were singularly delighted with the learned fancies of Cocceius. There are, however, still great numbers of prudent and impartial divines, who, considering the extremes into which these two eminent critics ran, and disposed to profit by what is really solid in both their systems, neither reject nor embrace their opinions in the aggregate, but agree with them both in some things, and differ from them both in others. It may also be observed, that neither the followers of Grotius nor those of Cocceius are agreed among themselves, and that these two general classes of expositors may be divided into many subordinate ones. A considerable number of English divines of the episcopal church refused to adopt the opinions, or to respect the authority, of these modern expositors; they appealed to the decisions of the primitive fathers, and maintained, that the sacred writings ought always to be understood in that sense *only*, which has been attributed to them by these ancient doctors of the rising church.*

VIII. The doctrines of Christianity, which had been so sadly disfigured among the Lutherans by the obscure jargon and the intricate tenets of the scholastic philosophy, met with the same fate in the Reformed churches. The first successful effort, that prevented these churches from falling entirely under the Aristotelian yoke, was made by the Arminians, who were remarkable for expounding, with simplicity and perspicuity, the truths and precepts of religion, and who censured, with great plainness and severity, those ostentatious doctors, who affected to render them obscure and unintelligible, by expressing them in the *terms*, and reducing them under the *classes* and divisions, used in the schools. The Cartesians and Cocceians contributed also to deliver theology from the chains of the Peripatetics; though it must be allowed, that it had not, in some respects, a much better fate in the hands of these its deliverers. The Cartesians applied the principles and tenets of their philosophy, in illustrating the doctrines of the Gospel; the Cocceians imagined, that they could not give a more sublime and engaging aspect to the Christian religion, than by representing it under the notion of a *covenant* concluded between God and man;† and both these modes of proceeding

* It is become almost a proverbial saying, that in the Books of the Old Testament Cocceius finds Christ every where, while Grotius meets him no where. The first part of this saying is certainly true; the latter much less so: for it appears, with sufficient evidence, from the Commentaries of Grotius, that he finds Christ prefigured in many places of the Old Testament, not, indeed, *directly* in the *letter* of the prophecies, where Cocceius discovers him, but *mysteriously*, under the appearance of certain persons, and in the *secret* sense of certain transactions.

☞ * These have been confuted by the learned Dr. Whitby, in his important work, concerning the Interpretation of Scripture after the Manner of the Fathers, which was published in 1714, under the following title: "Dissertatio de Scripturarum Interpretatione secundum Patrum Commentarios," &c.—In this dissertation, which was the forerunner of the many remarkable attempts that were afterwards made to deliver the right of private judgment in matters of religion, from the restraints of human authority, the judicious author has shown, first, that the Scripture is the only rule of faith, and that by it alone we are to judge of the doctrines that are necessary to salvation; secondly, that the fathers, both of the primitive times and also of succeeding ages, are extremely deficient and unsuccessful in their explications of the sacred writings; and, thirdly, that it is impossible to terminate the debates concerning the Trinity, by the opinions of the fathers, the decisions of councils, or by any tradition which is really universal. The contradictions, absurdities, the romantic conceits and extravagant fancies, that are to be found in the commentaries of the fathers, were never represented in such a ridiculous point of view as they are in this performance. The worst part of the matter is, that such a production as Dr. Whitby's, in which all the mistakes of these ancient expositors are culled out and compiled with such care, may tend to prejudice young students even against what may be good in their writings, and thus give them a disgust to a kind of study, which, when conducted with impartiality and prudence, has its uses. It is the infirmity of our nature to be fond of extremes.

☞ † It is somewhat surprising, that Dr. Mosheim should mention this circumstance as an invention of Cocceius, or as a manner of speaking peculiar to him. The representation of the Gospel dispensa-

were disliked by the wisest and most learned divines of the reformed church. They complained with reason, that the tenets and distinctions of the Cartesian philosophy had as evident a tendency to render the doctrines of Christianity obscure and intricate as the abstruse terms, and the endless divisions and subdivisions of the Peripatetics. They observed also, that the metaphor of a covenant, applied to the Christian religion, must be attended with many inconveniences, by leading uninstructed minds to form a variety of ill-grounded notions, which is the ordinary consequence of straining metaphors; and that it must contribute to introduce into the colleges of divinity the captious terms, distinctions, and quibbles, that are employed in the ordinary courts of justice, and thus give rise to the most trifling and ill-judged discussions and debates about religious matters. Accordingly, the greatest part, both of the British and French doctors, refused to admit the intricacies of Cartesianism or the imagery of Cocceius into their theological system, and followed the free, easy, and unaffected method of the Arminian divines in illustrating the truths, and enforcing the duties of Christianity.

IX. We have had occasion to observe, that Dr. William Ames, a Scottish divine, was one of the first among the Reformed who attempted to treat morality as a separate science, to consider it abstractedly from its connexion with any particular system of doctrine, and to introduce new light, and a new degree of accuracy and precision, into this master-science of life and manners. The attempt was laudable, had it been well executed; but the system of this learned writer was dry, theoretical, and subtle, and was thus much more adapted to the instruction of the studious than to the practical direction of the Christian. The Arminians, who are known to be much more zealous in enforcing the duties of Christianity than in illustrating its truths, and who generally employ more pains in directing the will than in enlightening the understanding, engaged several authors of note to exhibit the precepts and obligations of morality in a more useful, practical, and popular manner; but the English and French surpassed all the moral writers of the Reformed church in penetration and solidity, and in the ease, freedom, and perspicuity, of their method and compositions. Moses Amyrault, a man of a sound understanding and subtle genius, was the first French divine who distinguished himself in this kind of writing. He composed an accurate and elaborate system of morality, in a style, indeed, that is now obsolete; and those more moderate French writers, such as La Placette and Pictet, who acquired such a high reputation on account of their moral writings, owe to the excellent work now mentioned a considerable part of their glory. While England groaned under the horrors and tumults of a civil war, it was chiefly the Presbyterians and Independents that employed their talents and their pens in promoting the cause of practical religion. During this unhappy period, indeed, these doctors were remarkable for the austere gravity of their manners, and for a melancholy complexion and turn of mind which appeared abundantly in their compositions. Some of these were penned with such rigour and severity, as discovered either a total ignorance of the present imperfect state of humanity, or an entire want of indulgence for its unavoidable infirmities. Others were composed with a spirit of enthusiasm, that betrayed an evident propensity to the doctrine of the Mystics. But, when Hobbes appeared, the scene changed. A new set of illustrious and excellent writers arose to defend the truths of religion, and the obligations of morality, against this author, who aimed at the destruction of both, since he subjected the unchangeable nature of religion to the arbitrary will of the sovereign, and endeavoured to efface the eternal distinction that exists between moral good and evil. Cudworth, Cumberland, Sharrock, and others,* alarmed at the view of a system so false in its principles, and so pernicious in its effects, rendered eminent service to the cause of religion and morals by their immortal labours, in which, rising to the first principles of things, and opening the primitive and eternal fountains of truth and good, they illustrated clearly the doctrines of the one with the fairest evidence, and established the obligations of the other on the firmest foundations.

X. About the commencement of this century, the college of Geneva was in such high repute among the reformed churches, that it was resorted to from all quarters by persons who were desirous of a learned education, and more especially by those students of theology, whose circumstances in life permitted them to frequent this famous seminary.† Hence it very naturally happened, that the opinions of Calvin, concerning the decrees of God and divine grace, became daily more general, and were gradually introduced every where into the schools of learning. There was not, however, any public law or confession of faith that obliged the pastors of the reformed churches, in any part of the world, to conform their sen-

tion under the idea of a *Covenant*, whether this representation be literal or metaphorical, is to be found, almost every where, in the Epistles of St. Paul, and of the other apostles, though rarely, (scarcely more than twice) in the Gospels. The same phraseology has also been adopted by Christians of almost all denominations. It is, indeed, a manner of speaking that has been grossly abused by those divines, who, urging the metaphor too closely, exhibit the sublime transactions of the divine wisdom under the narrow and imperfect forms of human tribunals, and thus lead to false notions of the springs of action, as well as of the dispensations and attributes of the Supreme Being. We have remarkable instances of this abuse, in a book lately translated into English; I mean the Œconomy of the Covenants, by Witsius, in which that learned and pious man, who has deservedly gained an eminent reputation by other valuable productions, has inconsiderately introduced the captious, formal, and trivial terms, employed in human courts, into his descriptions of the stupendous scheme of redemption.

☞ * See Leland's View of the Deistical Writers, vol. i. p. 48.

† The lustre and authority of the college of Geneva began gradually to decline, from the time that, the United Provinces being formed into a free and independent republic, universities were founded at Leyden, Franeker, and Utrecht.

timents to the theological doctrines that were adopted and taught at Geneva.* And accordingly there were many, who either rejected entirely the doctrine of that college on these intricate points, or received it with certain restrictions and modifications. Even those who were in general attached to the theological system of Geneva, did not perfectly agree about the manner of explaining the doctrines relating to the divine decrees. The majority were of opinion, that God had only *permitted* the first man to fall into transgression, without positively *predetermining* his fall. But others went much farther, and presumptuously forgetting their own ignorance on the one hand, and the wisdom and equity of the divine counsels on the other, maintained, that God, in order to exercise and display his awful justice and his free mercy, had decreed from all eternity the transgression of Adam, and so ordered the course of events, that our first parents could not possibly avoid their unhappy fall. Those who held this latter sentiment were denominated *Supralapsarians*, to distinguish them from the *Sublapsarian* doctors, who maintained the doctrine *of permission* already mentioned.

XI. It is remarkable that the Supralapsarian and Sublapsarian divines forgot their debates and differences, as matters of little consequence, and united their force against those who thought it their duty to represent the Deity, as extending his goodness and mercy to all mankind. This gave rise, soon after the commencement of this century, to a deplorable schism, which all the efforts of human wisdom have since been unable to heal. James Arminius, professor of divinity in the university of Leyden, rejected the doctrine of the church of Geneva, in relation to the deep and intricate points of predestination and grace; and maintained, with the Lutherans, that God has excluded none from salvation by an absolute and eternal decree. He was joined in these sentiments by several persons in Holland, who were eminently distinguished by the extent of their learning, and the dignity of their stations; but he met with the warmest opposition from Francis Gomar, his colleague, and from the principal professors in the Dutch universities. The magistrates exhorted the contending parties to moderation and charity; and observed, that, in a free state, their respective opinions might be treated with toleration, without any detriment to the essential interests of true religion. After long and tedious debates, which were frequently attended with popular tumults and civil broils, this intricate controversy was, by the counsels and authority† of Maurice, prince of Orange, referred to the decision of the church, assembled in a general synod at Dordrecht, in 1618. The most eminent divines of the United Provinces, and many learned deputies from the churches of England, Scotland, Switzerland, Bremen, Hesse, and the Palatinate, were present at this numerous and solemn assembly. It was by the sentence of these judges, that the Arminians lost their cause, and were declared corruptors of the true religion. It must be observed, at the same time, that the doctors of Geneva, who embraced the Sublapsarian system, triumphed over their adversaries in this synod; for, though the patrons of the Supralapsarian cause were far from being contemptible either in point of number or of abilities, yet the moderation and equity of the British divines prevented the synod from giving its sanction to the opinions of that presumptuous sect. Nor indeed would even the Sublapsarians have obtained the accomplishment of their desires, had the doctors of Bremen, who for weighty reasons were attached to the Lutherans, been able to execute their purposes.*

XII. It is greatly to be doubted, whether this victory, gained over the Arminians, was, upon the whole, advantageous or detrimental to the church of Geneva in particular, and to the reformed church in general. It is at least certain, that, after the synod of Dordrecht, the doctrine of absolute decrees, lost ground from day to day; and its patrons were put to the hard necessity of holding fraternal communion with those whose doctrine was either professedly Arminian, or at least nearly resembled it. The leaders of the vanquished Arminians were eminently distinguished by their eloquence, sagacity, and learning; and, being highly exasperated by the injurious and oppressive treatment they met with, in consequence of their condemnation, they defended themselves, and attacked their adversaries with such spirit and vigour, and also with such dexterity and eloquence, that multitudes were persuaded of the justice of their cause. It is particularly to be observed, that the authority of the synod of Dordrecht was far from being universally acknowledged among the Dutch; the provinces of Friseland, Zealand, Utrecht, Guelderland, and Groningen, could not be persuaded to adopt its decisions; and though, in 1651, they were at length gained over so far as to intimate, that they would see with pleasure the reformed religion maintained upon the footing on which it had been placed and confirmed by the synod, yet the most eminent adepts in Belgic jurisprudence deny that this intimation has the force or character of a law.†

In England, the face of religion changed considerably, in a very little time after the famous synod now mentioned; and this change, which was entirely in favour of Arminianism, was principally effected by the counsels and influence of William Laud, archbishop of Canterbury. This revolution gave new courage to the Arminians; and, from that period to the present time, they have had the pleasure of

* See, for a full demonstration of this assertion, Grotius' Apologeticus, &c.; as also several treatises, written in Dutch by Theod. Volkh. Coornhert, of whom Arnold makes particular mention in his Historia Eccles. tom. ii.

☞ † It was not by the authority of prince Maurice, but by that of the States-General, that the national synod was assembled at Dordrecht. The states were not indeed unanimous; three of the seven provinces protested against the holding of this synod, viz. Holland, Utrecht, and Over-Yssel.

* We shall give, in the History of the Arminians, a list of the writers who appeared in this controversy, and a more particular account of the transactions of the synod of Dordrecht.

† See the very learned and illustrious president Bynkershoek's Quæstiones Juris publici, lib. ii. cap xviii.

seeing the decisions and doctrines of the synod, relating to the points in debate between them and the Calvinists, treated in England, with something more than mere indifference, beheld by some with aversion, and by others with contempt.* And, indeed, if we consider the genius and spirit of the church of England during this period, we shall plainly see, that the doctrine of the Gomarists, concerning predestination and grace, could not meet there with a favourable reception, since the leading English divines were zealous in modelling its doctrine and discipline after the sentiments and institutions that were received in the primitive times, and since those early fathers of the church, whom they followed with a profound submission, had never presumed, before Augustine, to set limits to the extent of the divine grace and mercy.

The reforemd churches in France seemed, at first, disposed to give a favourable reception to the decisions of this famous synod; but, as these decisions were highly displeasing to the votaries of Rome among whom they lived, and kindled anew their rage against the protestants, the latter thought it their duty to be circumspect in this matter; and, in process of time, their real sentiments, and the doctrines they taught, began to differ extremely from those of the Gomarists. The churches of Brandenburg and Bremen, which made a considerable figure among the reformed in Germany, would never suffer their doctors to be tied down to the opinions and tenets of the Dutch divines; and thus it happened, that the liberty of private judgment, (with respect to the doctrines of predestination and grace,) which the spirit that prevailed among the divines of Dordrecht seemed so much calculated to suppress or discourage, acquired rather new vigour, in consequence of the arbitrary proceedings of that assembly; and the reformed church was immediately divided into Universalists, Semi-Universalists, Supralapsarians, and Sublapsarians, who, indeed, notwithstanding their dissensions, which sometimes become violent and tumultuous, live generally in the exercise of mutual toleration, and are reciprocally restrained by many reasons from indulging a spirit of hostility and persecution. What is still more remarkable, and therefore ought not to be passed over in silence, we see the city of Geneva, which was the parent, the nurse, and the guardian of the doctrine of absolute predestination and particular grace, not only display sentiments of charity, forbearance, and esteem for the Arminians, but become itself almost so far Arminian, as to deserve a place among the churches of that communion.

XIII. While the reformed church in France yet subsisted, its doctors departed, in several points, from the common rule of faith that was received in the other churches of their communion. This, as appears from several circumstances, in a great measure resulted from their desire of diminishing the prejudices of the catholics against them, and of repelling a part of the odious conclusions which were drawn by their adversaries from the doctrines of Dordrecht, and laid to their charge with that malignity which popish bigotry so naturally inspires. Hence we find, in the books that were composed by the doctors of Saumur and Sedan after the synod, many things which seem conformable, not only to the sentiments of the Lutherans, concerning grace, predestination, the person of Christ, and the efficacy of the sacraments, but also to certain peculiar opinions of the Romish church. This moderation may be dated from the year 1615, when the opinion of John Piscator, pastor at Herborn, concerning the obedience of Christ, was tacitly adopted, or at least pronounced free from error, by the synod of the isle of France,* though it had been condemned and rejected in several preceding assemblies of the same nature.† Piscator maintained, that it was not by his obedience to the divine law that Christ made a satisfaction to that law in our stead, since this obedience was his duty considered as a man; and, therefore, being obliged to obey this law himself, his observance of it could not merit any thing for others from the Supreme Being. This opinion, as every one may see, tended to confirm the doctrine of the Romish church, concerning the merit of good works, the natural power of man to obey the commands of God, and other points of a like nature.‡ These less

* Sev. Lintrupii Dissertatio de Contemptu Concilii Dordraceni in Anglia, in Dissert. Theologicis Hect. Godofr. Masii, tom. i. n. xix.

* Aymon, Actes de tous les Synodes Nationaux des Eglises Reformees de France, tom. ii. p. 275, 276.

† See Aymon, tom. i. p. 400, 401, 457. tom. ii. p. 13.—Bossuet, Histoire des Variations des Eglises Protestantes, livr. xii. tom. ii. p. 268, where this prelate, with his usual malignity and bitterness, reproaches the protestants with their inconstancy. The learned Basnage has endeavoured to defend the reformed churches against this charge, in the second volume of his Histoire de l'Eglise, p. 1533: but his defence is not satisfactory. ☞ To Dr. Mosheim, who speaks more than once of the reformed church and its doctors with partiality and prejudice, this defence may not appear satisfactory; it has, nevertheless, been judged so by many persons of uncommon discernment; and we invite the reader to judge for himself.

☞ ‡ It does not appear to me that any one, who looks with an unprejudiced eye, can see the least connexion between the opinion of Piscator (which I shall not here either refute or defend,) and the popish doctrine which maintains the merit of good works; for, though we are not justified (i. e. pardoned or treated as if we had not offended) in consequence of Christ's active obedience to the divine law, yet we may be so by his death and sufferings; and it is really to these, that the Scriptures, in many places, ascribe our acceptance. Now a person who ascribes his acceptance and salvation to the death and mediation of Christ, does not surely give any countenance to the doctrine of the strict and rigorous merit of works, although he should not be so *sharp-sighted* as to perceive the influence which certain doctors attribute to what is called Christ's *active obedience*. But let it be observed here, in a particular manner, that the opinion of Piscator is much more unfavourable to popery than our author imagined, since it overturns totally, by a direct and most natural consequence, the popish doctrine concerning works of supererogation, which is as monstrous an absurdity in morals, as transubstantiation is in the estimation of common sense; for, if Christ, in his universal and perfect obedience to the divine laws, did no more than he was morally obliged to do by his character as a man, is it not absurd, if not impious, to seek in the virtue of the Romish saints (all of whom were very imperfect, and some of them very worthless mortals) an exuberance of obedience, a superabundant quantity of virtue, to which they were not obliged and

important concessions were followed by others of a much more weighty and momentous kind, of which some were so erroneous that they were strongly disapproved and rejected, even by those of the French protestants themselves, who were the most remarkable for their moderation, charity, and love of peace.*

XIV. The doctors of Saumur revived a controversy, that had for some time been suspended, by their attempts to reconcile the doctrine of predestination, as it had been taught at Geneva, and confirmed at Dordrecht, with the sentiments of those who represent the Deity as offering the displays of his goodness and mercy to all mankind. The first person who made this fruitless attempt was John Cameron, whose sentiments were supported and illustrated by Moses Amyrault, a man of uncommon sagacity and erudition. The latter applied himself, from the year 1634, with unparalleled zeal, to this arduous work, and displayed in it extraordinary exertions of capacity and genius; and so ardently was he bent on bringing it into execution, that he made, for this purpose, no small changes in the doctrine commonly received among the reformed in France. The form of doctrine which he had devised, in order to accomplish this important reconciliation, may be briefly summed up in the following propositions: "That God desires the happiness of all men, and that no mortal is excluded, by any divine decree, from the benefits that are procured by the death, sufferings, and gospel of Christ:

"That, however, no one can be made a partaker of the blessings of the Gospel, and of eternal salvation, without believing in Jesus Christ:

"That such, indeed, is the immense and universal goodness of the Supreme Being, that he refuses to none the power of believing, though he does not grant unto all his assistance and succour, that they may wisely improve this power to the attainment of everlasting salvation:

"And, that, in consequence of this, multitudes perish through their own fault, and not from any want of goodness in God."*

Those who embraced this doctrine were called Universalists, because they represented God as willing to show mercy to all mankind· and Hypothetical Universalists, because the condition of faith in Christ was necessary to render them the objects of this mercy. It is the opinion of many that this doctrine differs little from that which was established by the synod of Dordrecht: but such do not seem to have attentively considered either the principles whence it is derived, or the consequences to which it leads. The more I examine this reconciling system, the more I am persuaded, that it is no more than Arminianism or Pelagianism artfully dressed up, and ingeniously covered with a half-transparent veil of specious, but ambiguous expressions; and this judgment is confirmed by the language that is used in treating this subject by the modern followers of Amyrault, who express their sentiments with greater courage, plainness, and perspicuity, than the spirit of the times permitted their master to do. A cry was raised in several French synods, against the doctrine of Amyrault; but, after it had been carefully examined by them, and defended by him at their public meetings with his usual eloquence and erudition, he was honourably acquitted.† The opposition he met with from Holland was still more formidable, as it came from the celebrated pens of Rivet, Spanheim, Des-Marets, and other learned adversaries. He nevertheless answered them with great spirit and vigour; and his cause was powerfully supported afterwards by Daille, Blondel, Mestrezat, and

which they are supposed to deposit in the hands of the popes, who are empowered to distribute it, for love or money, among such as have need of it, to make up their accounts?

* This affirmation is groundless, and I wish it were not liable to the charge of malignity. The accusation that Dr. Mosheim brings here against the reformed church in France is of too serious a nature not to require the most evident and circumstantial proofs. He has, however, alleged none; nor has he given any one instance of these weighty and momentous concessions that were made to popery. It was not, indeed, in his power either to give arguments or examples of a satisfactory kind; and it is highly probable, that the unguarded words of Elias Saurin, minister of Utrecht, in relation to the learned Louis Le Blanc, professor of Sedan (which dropped from the pen of the former, in his Examen de la Theologie de M. Jurieu,) are the only testimony Dr. Mosheim had to allege, in support of an accusation, which he has not limited to any one person, but inconsiderately thrown out upon the French churches in genera . Those who are desirous of a full illustration of this matter, and yet have not an opportunity of consulting the original sources of information, may satisfy their curiosity by perusing the articles *Beaulieu* and *Amyrault* in Bayle's Dictionary, and the articles *Pajon* and *Papin* in M. de Chauffepied's supplement to that work. Any concessions that seem to have been made by the protestant doctors in France to their adversaries, consisted in giving an Arminian turn to some of the more rigid tenets of Calvin relating to original sin, predestination, and grace; and this turn would undoubtedly have been given to these doctrines, had popery been out of the question. But these concessions are not certainly what our historian had in view; nor would he, in effect, have treated such concessions as erroneous

* See Jo. Wolfg. Jaegeri Hist. Eccles. sæc. XVII. decenn. iv. p. 522. ☞ This mitigated view of the doctrine of predestination has only one defect; but it is a capital one. It represents God as desiring a thing (*i. e.* salvation and happiness) for all, which, in order to its attainment, requires a degree of his assistance and succour, which he refuses to many. This rendered grace and redemption universal only in words, but partial in reality, and therefore did not at all mend the matter. The Supralapsarians were consistent with themselves; but their doctrine was harsh and terrible, and was founded on the most unworthy notions of the Supreme Being; and, on the other hand, the system of Amyrault was full of inconsistencies; even the sublapsarian doctrine has its difficulties, and rather palliates than removes the horrors of Supralapsarianism. What then is to be done? from what quarter shall the candid and well disposed Christian receive that solid satisfaction and wise direction, which neither system is adapted to administer? These he will receive by turning his dazzled and feeble eye from the secret decrees of God, which were neither designed to be rules of action, nor sources of comfort to mortals here below; and by fixing his view upon the mercy of God, as it is manifested through Christ, upon the pure laws and sublime promises of his gospel, and the equity of his present government and his future tribunal.

† See Aymon's Actes des Synodes Nationaux des Eglises Reformees en France, tom. ii. p. 571, 604.— Blondel's Actes Authentiques des Eglises Reformees touchant la Paix et la Charite fraternelle.

Claude.* This controversy was carried on for a long time, with great animosity, and little fruit to those who opposed the opinions of the French innovator: for the sentiments of Amyrault were not only received in all the colleges of the Huguenots in France, and adopted by divines of the highest note in that nation, but also spread themselves as far as Geneva, and were afterwards disseminated by the French protestants, who fled from the rage of persecution, through all the reformed churches of Europe; and they now are so generally received, that few have the courage to oppose or decry them.

XV. The desire of mitigating certain doctrines of the reformed church, which drew upon it the heaviest censures from both the Roman catholics and some protestant communions, was the true origin of the opinion propagated, in the year 1640, by Joshua de la Place, concerning the imputation of original sin. This divine, who was the intimate friend of Amyrault, and his colleague at Saumur, rejected the opinion generally received in the schools of the reformed, that the personal and actual transgression of the first man is imputed to his posterity. He maintained, on the contrary, that God imputes to every man his natural corruption, his personal guilt, and his propensity to sin; or, to speak in the theological style, he affirmed, that original sin is indirectly, and not directly, imputed to mankind. This opinion was condemned as erroneous, in 1642, by the synod of Charenton, and many Dutch and Helvetic doctors of great name endeavoured to refute it,† while the love of peace and union prevented its author from defending it in a public and open manner.‡ But neither the sentence of the synod, nor the silence of M. de la Place, could preclude this sentiment from making a deep impression on the minds of many, who deemed it conformable to the plainest dictates of justice and equity; nor could they prevent its being transmitted, with the French exiles, into other countries.

In the class of those who, to diminish or avoid the resentment of the papists, made concessions inconsistent with truth, and detrimental to the purity of the protestant religion, many place Louis Capel, professor at Saumur, who, in a voluminous and elaborate work,§ undertook to prove that the Hebrew points were not used by the sacred writers, and were a modern invention added to the text by the Masoretes.|| It is at least certain, that this hypothesis was highly agreeable to the votaries of Rome, and seemed manifestly adapted to diminish the authority of the Scriptures, and to put them upon a level with oral tradition, if not to render their decisions still less respectable and certain.* On these accounts, the system of this famous professor was opposed, with the most ardent efforts of erudition and zeal, by several doctors both of the reformed and Lutheran churches, who were eminent for their knowledge of the Hebrew language, and their general acquaintance with Oriental learning.†

XVI. Though these great men gave offence to many, by the freedom and novelty of their sentiments, yet they had the approbation and esteem of the greatest part of the reformed churches; and the equity of succeeding generations removed the aspersions that envy had thrown upon them during their lives, and made ample amends for the injuries they had received from several of their contemporaries. This was far from being the case of those doctors who either openly attempted to bring about a complete reconciliation and union between the reformed and Romish churches, or explained the doctrines of Christianity in such a manner as lessened the difference between the communions, and thereby rendered the passage from the former to the latter less disgusting and painful. The attempts of these advocates of peace were looked upon as odious; and in the issue they proved utterly unsuccessful. The most eminent of these reconciling doctors were Louis Le Blanc, professor at Sedan, and Claude Pajon, minister of Orleans,‡ who were both remarkable for the persuasive power of their eloquence, and discovered an uncommon degree of penetration and sagacity in their writings and negotiations. The former passed in review many of the controversies that divided the two churches, and seemed clearly to prove, that some of them were merely disputes about words, and that the others were of much less consequence than was generally imagined.§ This manner of stating the differences between the two churches drew upon Le Blanc the indignation of those who considered all attempts to soften and modify controverted doctrines as dangerous and de-

* Bayle's Dictionary, vol. i. at the articles *Amyrault* and *Blondel;* and vol. ii. at the article *Daille.*—See Christ. Pfaffius, de Formula Consensus, cap. i.

† Aymon, tom. ii. p. 680.

‡ Christ. Eberh. Weismanni Histor. Eccles. sæc. XVII. p. 817.

§ This work, which is entitled, Arcanum Punctuationis Revelatum, may be found with its Vindiciæ in the works of Capel, printed at Amsterdam in 1689, and in the Critica Sacra Veteris Testamenti, published at Paris in 1650.

☞ || It was also Capel who affirmed that the characters which compose the Hebrew text, were such as the Chaldeans used after the Babylonian captivity, the Jews having always made use of the Samaritan characters before that period.

☞ * This absurd notion of the tendency of Capel's hypothesis is now almost entirely exploded by the learned world. Be that as it may, the hypothesis in question is by no means peculiar to Capel; it was adopted by Luther, Zuingle, Calvin, the three great pillars of the Reformation; as also by Munster, Olivetan, Masius, Scaliger, Casaubon, Drusius, De Dieu, Walton, and Bochart, those eminent men, who have thrown such light on sacred philology; so that Capel had only the merit of supporting it by new arguments, and placing it in a striking and luminous point of view.

† See B. Jo. Christ. Wolfii Biblioth. Hebraica.

☞ ‡ It is difficult to conceive what could engage Dr. Mosheim to place Pajon in the class of those who explained the doctrines of Christianity in such a manner, as to diminish the difference between the doctrines of the reformed and papal churches. Pajon was, indeed, a moderate divine, and leaned toward the Arminian system; and this propensity was not uncommon among the French protestants. But few doctors of this time wrote against popery with more learning, zeal, and judgment, than Claude Pajon, as appears from his excellent treatise against Nicole, entitled, "Examen du Livre qui porte pour titre prejugez legitimes contre les Calvinistes."

§ In his Theses Theologicæ, which are highly worthy of an attentive perusal.

trimental to the cause of truth.* On the other hand, the acuteness and dexterity with which he treated this delicate affair, made a considerable impression upon many persons, and procured him disciples, who still entertain his reconciling sentiments, but either conceal them entirely, or discover them with caution, as they are known to be displeasing to the greatest part of the members of both communions.

XVII. The modifications under which Pajon exhibited some of the doctrines of the reformed church, were also extremely offensive and unpopular. This ecclesiastic applied the principles and tenets of the Cartesian philosophy, of which he was a warm and able defender, to an explication of the opinions of that church relating to the corruption of human nature, the state of its moral faculties and powers, the grace of God, and the conversion of sinners; and, in the judgment of many, he gave an erroneous interpretation of these opinions. It is, indeed, very difficult to determine what were the real sentiments of this man; nor is it easy to say, whether this difficulty be most owing to the affected obscurity and ambiguity under which he disguised them, or to the inaccuracy with which his adversaries, through negligence or malignity, have represented them. If we may give credit to the latter, his doctrine amounts to the following propositions: "That the corruption of man is less, and his natural power to amend his ways greater, than is generally imagined:—That original sin lies in the understanding alone, and consists principally in the obscurity and imperfection of our ideas of divine things:—That this imperfection of the human understanding has a pernicious influence upon the will, excites in it vicious propensities, and thus leads it to sinful actions:—That this internal disorder is healed, not by the mere efforts of our natural faculties and powers, but by the assistance and energy of the Holy Spirit, operating upon the mind by the divine word as its mean or instrument:—That, however, this word is not endowed with any divine intrinsic energy, either natural or supernatural, but only with a moral influence, i. e. it corrects and improves the understanding, in the same manner as human truth does, even by imparting clear and distinct notions of spiritual and divine things, and furnishing solid arguments for the truth and divinity of the Christian religion, and its perfect conformity with the dictates of right reason;—and that, in consequence, every man, if no internal or external impediments destroy or suspend the exertion of his natural powers and faculties, may, by the use of his own reason, and a careful and assiduous study of the revealed will of God, be enabled to correct what is amiss in his sentiments, affections, and actions, without any extraordinary assistance from the Holy Ghost."†

Such is the account of the opinions of Pajon, given by his adversaries. On the other hand, if we take our ideas of his doctrine from himself, we shall find this account disingenuous and erroneous. Pajon intimates plainly his assent to the doctrines that were confirmed by the synod of Dordrecht, and which are contained in the catechisms and confessions of faith of the reformed churches; he complains that his doctrine has been ill understood or wilfully perverted; and he observes, that he did not deny entirely an immediate operation of the Holy Spirit on the minds of those who are really converted to God, but only such an immediate operation as was not accompanied with the ministry and efficacy of the divine word; or, to express the matter in other terms, he declared that he could not adopt the sentiments of those who represent that word as no more than an instrument void of intrinsic efficacy, a mere external sign of an immediate operation of the Spirit of God.* This last declaration is, however, both obscure and captious. Be that as it may, Pajon concludes by observing, that we ought not to dispute about the manner in which the Holy Spirit operates upon the minds of men, but content ourselves with acknowledging that this spirit, is the true and original author of all that is good in the affections of our heart, and the actions that proceed from them. Notwithstanding these declarations, the doctrine of this learned and ingenious ecclesiastic was not only deemed heterodox by some of the most eminent divines of the reformed church, but was also condemned, in 1677, by several synods in France, and, in 1686, by a synod assembled at Rotterdam.

XVIII. This controversy, which seemed to be brought to a conclusion by the death of Pajon, was revived, or rather continued, by Isaac Papin, his nephew, a native of Blois, who, by his writings and travels, was highly instrumental in communicating to England, Holland, and Germany, the contagion of these unhappy debates. This ecclesiastic expressed his sentiments without ambiguity or reserve, and zealously propagated the doctrine of his uncle, which, according to his crude and harsh manner of representing it, he reduced to the two following propositions:—

"That the natural powers and faculties of man are more than sufficient to lead him to the knowledge of divine truth:

"That, in order to produce that amendment of the heart, which is called regeneration, nothing more is requisite than to put the body, if its habit is bad, into a sound state by the power of physic, and then to set truth and falsehood before the understanding, and virtue and vice before the will, in their genuine colours, clearly and distinctly, so that their nature and properties may be fully apprehended."

This and the other opinions of Papin were refuted with a considerable degree of acrimony, in 1686, by the famous Jurieu, professor of divinity, and pastor of the French church a Rotterdam; and they were condemned in the following year by the synod of Bois-le-duc

* See Bayle's Dictionary, at the article *Beaulieu*.

† Fred. Spanheim's Append. ad Elenchum Controversiar. tom. iii. op. p. 882.—Jurieu's Traite de la Nature et de la Grace, p. 35.—Val. Ern. Loscher's Exercit. de Claud. Pajonii ejusque Sectatorum Doctrina et Fatis.

* All these declarations made by Pajon may be seen in a confession of his faith, supposed to have been drawn up by himself, and published by the learned M. de Chauffepied, in his Nouveau Dictionnaire Histor. et Critique, tom. ii. p. 164.

In 1688, they were condemned, with still greater marks of severity, by the French synod at the Hague, where a sentence of excommunication was pronounced against their author. Exasperated at these proceedings, Papin returned into France in 1690, where he publicly abjured the protestant religion, and embraced the communion of the church of Rome, in which he died in 1709.* It has been affirmed by some, that this ingenious man was treated with great rigour and injustice, and that his theological opinions were unfaithfully represented by his violent and unrelenting adversary, Jurieu, whose warmth and impetuosity in religious controversy are well known. How far this affirmation may be supported by evidence, we cannot pretend to determine. A doctrine in some degree resembling that of Pajon, was maintained in several treatises, in 1684, by Charles le Cene, a French divine of uncommon learning and sagacity, who gave a new and very singular translation of the Bible.† But he entirely rejected the doctrine of original sin, and of the impotency of human nature; and asserted, that it was in every man's power to amend his ways, and arrive at a state of obedience and virtue, by the mere use of his natural faculties, and an attentive study of the divine word; more especially, if those were seconded by the advantage of a good education, and the influence of virtuous examples. Hence several divines pretend that his doctrine is, in many respects, different from that of Pajon.‡

XIX. The church of England had, for a long time, resembled a ship tossed on a boisterous and tempestuous ocean. The opposition of the Papists on the one hand, and the discontents and remonstrances of the Puritans on the other, had kept it in a perpetual ferment. When, on the death of Elizabeth, James I. ascended the throne, the latter conceived the warmest hopes of seeing more serene and prosperous days, and of being delivered from the vexations and oppressions to which they had been constantly exposed on account of their attachment to the discipline and worship of the church of Geneva. These hopes were so much the more natural, as the king had received his education in Scotland, where the Puritans prevailed, and had, on some occasions, made the strongest declarations of his attachment to their ecclesiastical constitution.§ And some of the first steps taken by this prince seemed to encourage those hopes, as he appeared desirous of assuming the character and office of an arbitrator, in order to accommodate matters between the church and the Puritans.* But these expectations soon vanished and, under his government, affairs assumed a new aspect. As the desire of unlimited power and authority was his reigning passion, so all his measures, whether of a civil or religious nature, were calculated to answer the purposes of his ambition. The presbyterian form of ecclesiastical government seemed less favourable to his views than the episcopal hierarchy, as the former exhibits a kind of republic, which is administered by various rules of equal authority, while the latter approaches much nearer to the spirit and genius of monarchy. The very name of a republic, synod, or council, was odious to James, who dreaded every thing that had a popular aspect; hence he distinguished the bishops with peculiar marks of his favour, extended their authority, increased their prerogatives, and publicly adopted and inculcated the following maxim, 'No bishop, no king.' At the same time, as the church of England had not yet abandoned the Calvinistical doctrines of predestination and grace, he also adhered to them for some time, and gave his theological representatives, in the synod of Dordrecht, an order to join in the condemnation of the sentiments of Arminius, in relation to these deep and intricate points. Abbot, archbishop of Canterbury, a man of remarkable gravity,† and of eminent

* See Jurieu de la Nature et de la Grace—Molleri Cimbria Literata, tom. ii. p. 608.

† This translation was published at Amsterdam in 1741, and was condemned by the French synod in Holland.

‡ See the learned and laborious M. Chauffepied's Nouv. Diction. tom. ii. p. 160.

☞ § In a general assembly holden at Edinburgh, in 1590, this prince is said to have made the following public declaration: "I praise God that I was born in the time of the light of the Gospel, and in such a place as to be the king of the sincerest (i. e. *purest*) kirk in the world. The kirk of Geneva keep pasche and yule (i. e. Easter and Christmas.) What have they for them? They have no institution. As for our neighbour kirk of England, their service is an evil-said mass in English; they want nothing of the mass but the liftings (i. e. *the elevation of the host*.) I charge you, my good ministers, doctors, elders, nobles, gentlemen, and barons, to stand to your purity, and to exhort your people to do the same; and I, forsooth, as long as I brook my life, shall do the same." Calderwood's History of the Church of Scotland p. 256.

* The religious disputes between the church and the puritans induced James to appoint a conference between the two parties at Hampton-Court, at which nine bishops, and as many dignitaries of the church appeared on one side, and four puritan ministers on the other. The king himself took a considerable part in the controversy against the latter; and this was an occupation well adapted to his taste; for nothing could be more pleasing to this royal pedant, than to dictate magisterially to an assembly of divines upon points of faith and discipline, and to receive the applause of these holy men for his superior zeal and learning. The conference continued three days. On the first day, it was managed between the king and the bishops and deans, to whom James proposed some objections against certain expressions in the liturgy, and a few alterations in the ritual of the church; in consequence of which, some slight alterations were made. On the two following days, the puritans were admitted, whose proposals and remonstrances may be seen in Neal's History of the Puritans, vol. ii. Dr. Warner, in his Ecclesiastical History of England, observes, that this author must be read with caution, on account of his unfairness and partiality: why therefore did he not take his account of the Hampton-Court conference from a better source? The different accounts of the opposite parties, and more particularly those published by Dr. Barlow, dean of Chester, on one hand, and Patrick Galloway, a Scottish writer, on the other. (both of whom were present at the conference,) must be carefully consulted, in order to our forming a proper idea of these theological transactions. James at least obtained, on this occasion, the applause he had in view. The archbishop of Canterbury (Whitgift) said, that "undoubtedly his majesty spoke by the special assistance of God's spirit;" and Bancroft, falling on his knees, with his eyes raised to —— James, expressed himself thus: "I protest my heart melteth for joy, that Almighty God, of his singular mercy, has given us such a king, as since Christ's time has not been."

☞ † The earl of Clarendon says, in his History

zeal both for civil and religious liberty, whose lenity toward their ancestors the Puritans still celebrate in the highest strains,* used his utmost endeavours to confirm the king in the principles of Calvinism, to which he himself was thoroughly attached. But scarcely had the British divines returned from the synod of Dordrecht, and given an account of the laws that had been enacted, and the doctrines that had been established by that famous assembly, when the king, and the greatest part of the episcopal clergy, discovered, in the strongest terms, their dislike of these proceedings, and judged the sentiments of Arminius, relating to the divine decrees, preferable to those of Gomar and of Calvin.† This sudden change in

of the Rebellion, that "Abbot was a man of very morose manners, and of a very sour aspect, which at that time was called *gravity*." If, in general, we strike a medium between what Clarendon and Neal say of this prelate, we shall probably arrive at the true knowledge of his character. See the History of the Rebellion, vol. i. p. 88; and Neal's History of the Puritans, vol. ii. p. 243. It is certain, that nothing can be more unjust and partial than Clarendon's account of this eminent prelate, particularly when he says, that "he neither understood nor regarded the constitution of the church." But it is too much the custom of this writer, and others of his stamp, to give the denomination of latitudinarian indifference to that charity, prudence, and moderation, by which alone the best interests of the church (though not the personal views of many of its ambitious members) can be established upon firm and permanent foundations. Abbot would have been reckoned a good churchman by some, if he had breathed that spirit of despotism and violence, which, being essentially incompatible with the spirit and character of a people, not only free, but jealous of their liberty, has often endangered the church, by exciting that resentment which always renders opposition excessive. Abbot was so far from being indifferent about the constitution of the church, or inclined to the presbyterian discipline, (as the noble author affirms,) that it was by his zeal and dexterity that the clergy of Scotland, who had refused to admit the bishops as moderators in their synods, were brought to a more tractable temper, and affairs put into such a situation as afterwards produced the entire establishment of the episcopal order in that nation. It is true, that Abbot's zeal in this affair was conducted with great prudence and moderation; and it was by these that his zeal was rendered successful. Nor have these his transactions in Scotland, where he went as chaplain to the lord-treasurer Dunbar, been sufficiently attended to by historians: they even seem to have been entirely unknown to some, who have pretended to depreciate the conduct and principles of this virtuous and excellent prelate. King James, who had been so zealous a presbyterian in appearance before his accession to the crown of England, had scarcely set his foot out of Scotland, when he conceived the design of restoring the ancient form of episcopal government in that kingdom; and it was Abbot's conduct there that brought him to that high favour with the king, which, in a short time, raised him from the deanery of Winchester to the see of Canterbury. For it was by Abbot's mild and prudent counsels, that Dunbar procured that famous act of the general assembly for Scotland, by which it was provided, "that the king should have the calling of all general assemblies, that the bishops (or their deputies) should be perpetual moderators of the diocesan synods, that no excommunication should be pronounced without their approbation, that all presentations of benefices should be made by them, that the deprivation or suspension of ministers should belong to them, that the visitation of the diocese should be performed by the bishop or his deputy only, and that the bishop should be moderator of all conventions for exercisings or *prophesyings* (i. e. preaching) within their bounds." See Calderwood's True History of the Church of Scotland, p. 588, 589. Heylin's History of the Presbyterians, p. 381, 382; and above all, Speed's History of Great Britain, book x. The writers who seem the least disposed to speak favourably of this wise and good prelate, bear testimony, nevertheless, to his eminent piety, his exemplary conversation, and his inflexible probity and integrity; and it may be said with truth, that, if his moderate measures had been pursued, the liberties of England would have been secured, popery discountenanced, and the church prevented from running into those excesses which afterwards proved so injurious to it. If Abbot's candour failed him on any occasion, it was in the representations, which his rigid attachment, not to the discipline, but to the doctrinal tenets of Calvinism, led him to give of the Arminian doctors. There is a remarkable instance of this in a letter of his to Sir Ralph Winwood, dated at Lambeth, the first of June, 1613, and occasioned by the arrival of Grotius in England, who had been expressly sent from Holland, by the Remonstrants, or Arminians, to mitigate the king's displeasure and antipathy against that party. In this letter, the archbishop represents Grotius (with whom he certainly was not worthy to be named, either in point of learning, sagacity, or judgment) as a pedant, and mentions, with a high degree of complacency and approbation, the absurd and impertinent judgment of some civilians and divines, who called this immortal ornament of the republic of letters, a *smatterer* and a *simple fellow*. See Winwood's Memorials, vol. iii p. 459.

* See Wood's Athenæ Oxonienses, t. i. p. 583.—Neal's History of the Puritans, vol. ii. ch. iv. p. 242.—Clarendon's History of the Rebellion, vol. i.

† See Heylin's History of the Five Articles.—Neal, vol. ii. ch. ii. p. 117. The latter author tells us, that the following verses were made in England, with a design to pour contempt on the synod, and to turn its proceedings into ridicule:

"Dordrechti Synodus, nodus: chorus integer, æger;
Conventus, ventus; sessio, stramen. Amen!"*

With respect to James, those who are desirous of forming a just idea of the character, proceedings, and theological fickleness and inconstancy of that monarch, must peruse the writers of English history, more especially Larrey and Rapin. The majority of these writers tell us, that, toward the close of his life, James, after having deserted from the Calvinists to the Arminians, began to discover a strong propensity toward popery; and they affirm positively, that he entertained the most ardent desire of bringing about an union between the churches of England and Rome. In this, however, these writers seem to have gone too far; for, though many of the proceedings of this injudicious prince justly deserve the sharpest censure, yet it is both rash and unjust to accuse him of a design to introduce popery into England. It is not to be believed, that a prince, who aspired to arbitrary power and uncontrolled dominion, could ever have entertained a thought of submitting to the yoke of the Roman pontiff.† The truth of the matter seems to be this, that, toward the end of his reign, James began to have less aversion to the doctrines and rites of the Romish church, and permitted certain religious observances, that were conformable to the spirit of that church, to be used in England. This conduct was founded upon a manner of reasoning, which he had learned from several bishops of his time, that the primitive church is the model which all Christian churches ought to imitate in doctrine and worship: that, in proportion as any church approaches to this original standard of truth and purity, it must become proportionably

☞ * It would be a difficult, and indeed an impracticable task, to justify all the proceedings of this synod; and it is much to be wished, that they had been more conformable to the spirit of Christian charity, than the representations of history, impartially weighed, show them to have been. We are not, however, to conclude, from the insipid monkish lines here quoted by Dr. Mosheim, that the transactions and decisions of that synod were universally condemned or despised in England. It had its partisans in the established church, as well as among the Puritans: and its decisions, in point of doctrine, were looked upon by many, and not without reason, as agreeable to the tenor of the book of articles established by law in the church of England.

† This remark is confuted by fact, observation, and the perpetual contradictions that are observable in the conduct of men: besides, see the note

the theological opinions of the court and clergy, was certainly owing to a variety of reasons, as will appear evident to those who have any acquaintance with the spirit and transactions of these times. The principal one, if we are not deceived, must be sought in the plans of a farther reformation of the church of England, which were proposed by several eminent ecclesiastics, whose intention was to bring it to as near a resemblance as was possible of the primitive church; and every one knows, that the peculiar doctrines to which the victory was assigned by the synod were absolutely unknown in the first ages of the Christian church.* Be that as it may, this change was very injurious to the Puritans; for, the king being indisposed to the opinions and institutions of Calvinism, those sectaries were left without defence, and exposed anew to the animosity and hatred of their adversaries, which had been, for some time, suspended, but now broke out with redoubled vehemence, and at length kindled a religious war, whose consequences were deplorable beyond expression. In 1625 this prince died, of whom it may be observed, that he was the bitterest enemy of the doctrine and discipline of the Puritans, to which he had been in his youth most warmly attached; the most inflexible and ardent patron of the Arminians, in whose ruin and condemnation in Holland he had been highly instrumental; and the most zealous defender of episcopal government, against which he had more than once expressed himself in the strongest terms. He left the constitution of England, both ecclesiastical and civil, in a very unsettled and fluctuating state, languishing under intestine disorders of various kinds.

XX. His son and successor Charles, who had imbibed his political and religious principles, had nothing so much at heart as to bring to perfection what his father had left unfinished. All the exertions of his zeal, and the whole tenor of his administration, were directed toward the three following objects: "The extending the royal prerogative, and raising the power of the crown above the authority of the law—the reduction of all the churches in Great Britain and Ireland under the jurisdiction of bishops, whose government he looked upon as of divine institution, and also as the most adapted to guard the privileges and majesty of the throne—and, lastly, the suppression of the opinions and institutions that were peculiar to Calvinism, and the modelling of the doctrine, discipline, ceremonies, and polity of the church of England, after the spirit and constitution of the primitive church." The person whom the king chiefly intrusted with the execution of this arduous plan, was William Laud, bishop of London, who was raised, in 1633, to the see of Canterbury, and exhibited in these high stations a mixed character, composed of great qualities and great defects. The voice of justice must celebrate his fortitude, his erudition, his zeal for the sciences, and his munificence and liberality to men of letters; and, at the same time, even charity must acknowledge, with regret, his inexcusable imprudence, his excessive superstition, his rigid attachment to the sentiments, rites, and institutions of the ancient church, which made him behold the Puritans and Calvinists with horror,* and that violent spirit of animosity and persecution which discovered itself in the whole course of his ecclesiastical administration.† This haughty prelate executed the plans of his royal master, and fulfilled the views of his own ambition, without using those mild and moderate methods, which prudence employs in the prosecution of unpopular schemes. He carried things with a high hand: when he found the laws opposing his views, he treated them with contempt, and violated them without hesitation; he loaded the Puritans with injuries and vexations, and aimed at nothing less than their total extinction; he publicly rejected, in 1625, the Calvinistical doctrine of predestination, and, notwithstanding the opposition and remonstrances of Abbot, substituted the Arminian system in its place;‡ he revived many religious

pure and perfect; and that the Romish church retained more of the spirit and manner of the primitive church than the Puritan or Calvinist churches.—☞ Of these three propositions, the two first are undoubtedly true, and the last is evidently and demonstrably false. Besides, this makes nothing to the argument: for, as James had a manifest aversion to the Puritans, it could, in his eyes, be no very great recommendation of the Romish church, that it surpassed that of the Puritans in doctrine and discipline.

* Dr. Mosheim has annexed the following note to this passage: "Perhaps the king entered into these ecclesiastical proceedings with the more readiness, when he reflected on the civil commotions and tumults that an attachment to the presbyterian religion had occasioned in Scotland. There are also some circumstances that intimate plainly enough, that James, before his accession to the crown of England, was very far from having an aversion to popery." Whoever, indeed, looks into the Historical View of the Negotiations between the Courts of England, France, and Brussels, from the year 1592 to 1617, extracted from the manuscript State Papers of Sir Thomas Edmondes and Anthony Bacon, Esq., and published in 1749 by the learned and judicious Dr. Birch, will be persuaded, that, about the year 1595, this fickle and unsteady prince had really formed an intention of embracing the faith of Rome. See, in the curious collection now mentioned, the postscript of a letter from Sir Thomas Edmondes to the lord high treasurer, dated the 20th of December, 1595. We learn also, from the Memoirs of Sir Ralph Winwood, that, in 1596, James sent Mr. Ogilvie, a Scottish baron, into Spain, to assure his catholic majesty, that he was then ready and resolved to embrace popery, and to propose an alliance with that king and the pope against the queen of England. See State Tracts. vol. i. p. 1. See also an extract of a letter from Tobie Matthew, D. D. dean of Durham, to the lord-treasurer Burghley, containing an information of Scotch affairs, in Strype's Annals, vol. iv. p. 201. Above all, see Harris' Hist. and Critical Account of the Life and Writings of James I., p. 29, note (N.) This last writer may be added to Larrey and Rapin, who have exposed the pliability and inconsistency of this self-sufficient monarch

* See Wood's Athenæ Oxon. t. ii. p. 55.—Heylin's Cyprianus Angelicus, or Hist. of Life and Death of Wm. Laud.—Clarendon's His. vol. i.

† "Sincere he undoubtedly was, (says Mr. Hume,) and, however misguided, actuated by religious principles in all his pursuits; and it is to be regretted that a man of such spirit, who conducted his enterprises with such warmth and industry, had not entertained more enlarged views, and embraced principles more favourable to the general happiness of human society."

‡ See Mich. le Vassor, Hist. de Louis XIII. tom. v. p. 262.

☞ This expression may lead the uninformed reader into a mistake, and make him imagine that Laud had caused the Calvinistical doctrine of the xxxix Articles to be abrogated, and the tenets of

ceremonies, which though stamped with the sanction of antiquity, were nevertheless marked with the turpitude of superstition, and had been on that account justly abrogated; he forced bishops upon the Scots, who were zealously attached to the discipline and ecclesiastical polity of Geneva, and had shown, on all occasions, the greatest reluctance against an episcopal government; and, lastly, he gave many, and very plain intimations, that he looked upon the Romish church, with all its errors, as more pure, more holy, and preferable upon the whole to those Protestant churches which were not subject to the jurisdiction of bishops. By these his unpopular sentiments and violent measures, Laud drew an odium on the king, on himself, and on the episcopal order in general. Hence, in 1644, he was brought before the public tribunals of justice, declared guilty of high treason, and condemned to lose his head on a scaffold; which sentence was accordingly executed.

After the death of Laud, the dissentions that had reigned for a long time between the king and parliament, grew still more violent, and rose at length to so great a height, that they could not be extinguished but by the blood of that excellent prince. The great council of the nation, heated by the violent suggestions of the Puritans and Independents,* abolished episcopal government; condemned and abrogated every thing in the ecclesiastical establishment that was contrary to the doctrine, worship, and discipline of the church of Geneva; turned the vehemence of their opposition against the king himself, and, having brought him into their power by the fate of arms, accused him of treason against the majesty of the nation; and, in 1649, while the eyes of Europe were fixed with astonishment on this strange spectacle, ordered him to be decapitated on a public scaffold. Such are the calamities that flow from religious zeal without knowledge, from that en-

---

Arminius to be substituted in their place. It may therefore be proper to set this matter in a clearer light. In 1625, Laud wrote a small treatise to prove the orthodoxy of the Arminian doctrines; and, by his credit with the duke of Buckingham, had Arminian and anti-puritanical chaplains placed about the king. This step increased the debates between the Calvinistical and Arminian doctors, and produced the warmest animosities and dissensions. To calm these, the king issued out a proclamation, dated the 14th of January, 1626, the literal tenor of which was, in truth, more favourable to the Calvinists than to the Arminians, though, by the manner in which it was interpreted and executed by Laud, it was turned to the advantage of the latter. In this proclamation it was said expressly, "that his majesty would admit no innovations in the *doctrine*, discipline, or government of the church;" (N. B. *The doctrine of the church, previously to this, was Calvinistical,*) "and therefore charges all his subjects, and especially the clergy, not to publish or maintain, in preaching or writing, any *new inventions* or *opinions*, contrary to the said doctrine and discipline established by law, &c." It was certainly a very singular instance of Laud's indecent partiality, that this proclamation was employed to suppress the books that were expressly written in the defence of the xxxix Articles, while the writings of the Arminians, who certainly opposed these articles, were publicly licensed. I do not here enter into the merits of the cause; I only speak of the tenor of the proclamation, and the manner of its execution.

This manner of proceeding showed how difficult and arduous a thing it is to change systems of doctrine established by law, since neither Charles, who was by no means diffident of his authority, nor Laud, who was far from being timorous in the use and abuse of it, attempted to reform articles of faith, that stood in direct opposition to the Arminian doctrines, which they were now promoting by the warmest encouragements, and which were daily gaining ground under their protection. Instead of reforming the xxxix Articles, which step would have met with great opposition from the house of commons, and from a considerable part of the clergy and laity, who were still warmly attached to Calvinism, Laud advised the king to have these articles reprinted, with an ambiguous declaration prefixed to them, which might tend to silence or discourage the reigning controversies between the Calvinists and Arminians, and thus secure to the latter an unmolested state, in which they would daily find their power growing under the countenance and protection of the court. This declaration, which, in most editions of the Common Prayer, is still to be found at the head of the articles, is a most curious piece of political theology; and, if it had not borne hard upon the right of private judgment, and been evidently designed to favour one party, though it carried the aspect of a perfect neutrality, it might have been looked upon as a wise and provident measure to secure the tranquillity of the church; for, in the tenor of this declaration, precision was sacrificed to prudence and ambiguity; and even contradictions were preferred to consistent, clear, and positive decisions, that might have fomented dissensions and discord. The declaration seemed to favour the Calvinists, since it prohibited the affixing any new sense to any article: it also in effect favoured the Arminians, as it ordered all curious search about the contested points to be laid aside, and these disputes to be shut up in God's promises, as they are set forth to us in the holy scriptures, and in the general meaning of the articles of the church of England according to them. But what was singularly preposterous in this declaration was, its being designed to favour the Arminians, and yet prohibiting expressly any person, either in sermons or writings, from giving his own sense or comment as the meaning of the article, and ordering every one, on the contrary, to take each article in its literal and grammatical sense, and to submit to it in the full and plain meaning thereof; for certainly, if the 17th article has a plain, literal, and grammatical meaning, it is a meaning unfavourable to Arminianism: and bishop Burnet was obliged afterwards to acknowledge, that, without enlarging the sense of the articles, the Arminians could not subscribe them consistently with their opinions, or without violating the demands of common candour and sincerity. See Burnet's remarks on the examination of his exposition, &c. p. 3.

This renders it probable, that the declaration now mentioned (in which we see no royal signature, no attestation of any officer of the crown, no date, in short, no mark to show where, when, or by what authority it was issued out) was not composed in the reign of king Charles. Burnet, indeed, was of opinion, that it was composed in that reign to support the Arminians, who, when they were charged with departing from the true sense of the articles, answered, "that they took the articles in their literal and grammatical sense, and therefore did not prevaricate." But this reasoning does not appear conclusive to the acute and learned author of the Confessional. He thinks it more probable that the declaration was composed, and first published, in the latter part of king James' reign; for though, says he, there be no evidence that James ever turned Arminian in principle, yet this was the party that adhered to him in his measures, and which it became necessary for him on that account to humour, and to render respectable in the eyes of the people by every expedient that might not bring any reflection on his own consistency. "And whoever (continues this author) considers the quibbling and equivocal terms in which this instrument is drawn, will, I am persuaded, observe the distress of a man divided between his principles and his interests, that is, of a man exactly in the situation of king James I. in the three last years of his reign." It is likely then, that this declaration was only republished at the head of the articles, which were reprinted by the order of Charles I.

* The origin of this sect has been already mentioned.

thusiasm and bigotry which inspire a blind and immoderate attachment to the external unessential parts of religion, and to certain doctrines ill-understood! These broils and tumults tended also unhappily to confirm the truth of an observation often made, that all religious sects, while they are kept under and oppressed, are remarkable for inculcating the duties of moderation, forbearance, and charity toward those who dissent from them; but, as soon as the scenes of persecution are removed, and they in their turn arrive at power and pre-eminence, they forget their own precepts and maxims, and leave both the recommendation and practice of charity to those who groan under their yoke. Such, in reality, was the behaviour of the Puritans during their transitory exaltation; they showed as little clemency and equity to the bishops and other patrons of episcopacy, as they had received from them when the reins of government were in their hands.*

XXI. The Independents, who have been just mentioned among the promoters of civil discord in England, are generally represented by the British writers in a much worse light than the Presbyterians or Calvinists. They are commonly accused of various enormities, and they are even charged with the crime of parricide, as having borne a principal part in the death of the king. But whoever will be at the pains of examining, with impartiality and attention, the writings of that sect, and their confession of faith, must soon perceive, that many crimes have been imputed to them without foundation, and will probably be induced to think, that the bold attempts of the civil Independents (i. e. of those warm republicans who were the declared enemies of monarchy, and wished to extend the liberty of the people beyond all bounds of wisdom and prudence,) have been unjustly laid to the charge of those Independents whose principles were merely of a religious kind.† The religious Independents derived their denomination from the following principle, which they held in common with the Brownists;—that every Christian congregation ought to be governed by its

* Beside Clarendon and the other writers of English history already mentioned, see Neal's History of the Puritans, vol. ii. and iii.

† This sect is of recent date, and still subsists in England; there is, nevertheless, not one, either of the ancient or modern sects of Christians, that is less known, or has been more loaded with groundless aspersions and reproaches. The most eminent English writers, not only among the patrons of episcopacy, but even among those very presbyterians with whom those sectaries are now united, have thrown out against them the bitterest accusations and severest invectives that the warmest indignation could invent. They have not only been represented as delirious, mad, fanatical, illiterate, factious, and ignorant both of natural and revealed religion, but also as abandoned to all kinds of wickedness and sedition, and as the only authors of the odious parricide committed on the person of Charles I.* And as the writers who have given these representations, are considered by foreigners as the best and most authentic narrators of the transactions that passed in their own country, and are therefore followed as the surest guides, the Independents appear, almost every where, under the most unfavourable aspect. It must indeed be candidly acknowledged, that, as every class and order of men consist of persons of very different characters and qualities, the independent sect has been likewise dishonoured by several turbulent, factious, profligate, and flagitious members. But if it be a constant maxim with the wise and prudent, not to judge of the spirit and principles of a sect from the actions or expressions of a handful of its members, but from the manners customs, opinions, and behaviour of the generality of those who compose it, from the writings and discourses of its learned men, and from its public and avowed forms of doctrine, and confessions of faith, I make no doubt that, by this rule of estimating matters, the Independents will appear to have been unjustly loaded with so many accusations and reproaches.

We shall take no notice of the invidious and severe animadversions that have been made upon this religious community by Clarendon, Echard, Parker, and so many other writers. To set this whole matter in the clearest and most impartial light, we shall confine ourselves to the account of the Independents given by a writer, justly celebrated by the English themselves, and who, though a foreigner, is generally supposed to have had an accurate knowledge of the British nation, its history, parties, sects and revolutions. This writer is Rapin de Thoyras, who, (in the twenty-first book of his History of England) represents the Independents under such horrid colours, that, were his portrait just, they would not deserve to enjoy the light of the sun, or to breathe the free air of Britain, much less to be treated with indulgence and esteem by those who have the cause of virtue at heart. Let us now examine the account which this illustrious historian gives of this sect. He declares, in the first place, that, notwithstanding all the pains he had taken to trace out the true origin of it, his inquiries had been entirely fruitless; his words may be thus translated: "After all my researches, I have not been able to discover, precisely, the origin of the Independent sect, or faction." It is very surprising to hear a man of learning, who had employed seventeen years in composing the History of England, and had admittance to so many rich and famous libraries, express his ignorance of a matter, about which it was so easy to acquire ample information. Had he only looked into the work of the learned Hornbeck, entituled, Summa Controversiarum, lib. x. p. 775, he would have found, in a moment, what he had been so long and so laboriously seeking in vain. Rapin proceeds to the doctrines and opinions of the Independents, and begins this part of his work by a general declaration of their tendency to throw the nation into disorder and combustion. He says, "It is at least certain, that their principles were* very proper to put the kingdom

* Durell, (whom, nevertheless, Louis de Moulin, the most zealous defender of the Independents, commends on account of his ingenuity and candour,) in his Historia Rituum Sanctæ Ecclesiæ Anglicanæ, c. i. p. 4, expresses himself thus: "Fateor, si atrocis illius tragœdiæ tot actus fuerint, quot ludicrarum esse solent, postremum fere Independentium fuisse;—adeo ut non acute magis, quam vere, dixerit L'Estrangius noster, Regem primo a Presbyterianis interemtum, Carolum deinde ab Independentibus interfectum

☞ * Dr. Mosheim's defence of the Independents is certainly specious; but he has not sufficiently distinguished the times; and he has, perhaps, in defending them, strained too far that equitable principle, that we must not impute to a sect any principles that are not contained in, or deducible from, their religious system. This maxim does not entirely answer here the purpose to which it is applied. The religious system of a sect may be in itself pacific and innocent, while incidental circumstances, or certain associations of ideas, may render that sect more turbulent and restless than others, or at least involve it in political factions and broils. Such perhaps was the case of the Independents at certain periods, and more especially at the period now under consideration. When we consider their religious form of government, we shall see evidently, that a principle of analogy (which influences the sentiments and imaginations of men much more than is generally supposed,) must naturally have led the greatest part of them to republican notions of civil government; and it is farther to be observed, that, from a republican government, they must have expected much more protection and favour, than from a kingly one. When these two points are consider

own laws, without depending on the jurisdiction of bishops, or being subject to the authority of synods, presbyteries, or any ecclesiastical assembly composed of the deputies from

in a flame; and this they did effectually." What truth may be in this assertion, will be seen by what follows. Their sentiments concerning government were, if we are to believe this writer, of the most pernicious kind, since, according to him, they wanted to overturn the monarchy, and to establish a democracy in its place: his words are, "With regard to the state, they abhorred monarchy, and approved only a republican government." I will not pretend to deny, that there were among the Independents several persons who were unfriendly to a kingly government; persons of this kind were to be found among the Presbyterians, Anabaptists, and all the other religious sects and communities that flourished in England during this tumultuous period; but I want to see it proved, in an evident and satisfactory manner, that these republican principles were embraced by all the Independents, and formed one of the distinguishing characteristics of that sect. There is, at least, no such thing to be found in their public writings. They declared, on the contrary, in a public memorial drawn up by them in 1647, that, as magistracy in general is the ordinance of God, "they do not disapprove any form of civil government, but do freely acknowledge, that a kingly government, bounden by just and wholesome laws, is both allowed by God, and also a good accommodation unto men." I omit the mention of several other circumstances which unite to prove that the Independents were far from looking with abhorrence on a monarchical government.

Their sentiments of religion, according to Rapin, were highly absurd, since he represents their principles as entirely opposite to those of all other religious communities: "As to religion, (says he,) their principles were contrary to those of all the rest of the world." With respect to this accusation, it may be proper to observe, that there are extant two Confessions of Faith, one of the English Independents in Holland, and another drawn up by the principal members of that community in England. The former was composed by John Robinson, the founder of the sect, and was published at Leyden in 1619, under the following title: "Apologia pro Exulibus Anglis, qui Brownistæ vulgo appellantur:" the latter appeared at London, for the first time, in 1658, and was thus entitled: "A declaration of the Faith and Order owned and practised in the Congregational churches in England, agreed upon, and consented unto by their elders and messengers, in their meeting at the Savoy, October 12, 1658." Hornbeck gave, in 1659, a Latin translation of this Declaration, and subjoined it to his Epistolæ ad Duræum de Independentismo. It appears evidently from these two public and authentic pieces, not to mention other writings of the Independents, that they differed from the presbyterians or calvinists in no single point of any consequence, except that of ecclesiastical government. To put this matter beyond all doubt, we have only to attend to the following passage in Robinson's Apology for the English Exiles, p. 7, 11, where that founder of the Independent sect expresses his own private sentiments, and those of his community, in the plainest manner: "Profitemur coram Deo et hominibus, adeo nobis convenire cum ecclesiis reformatis Belgicis in re religionis, ut omnibus et singulis earundem ecclesiarum fidei articulis, prout habentur in harmonia confessionum fidei, parati simus subscribere.—Ecclesias reformatas pro veris et genuinis habemus, cum iisdem in sacris Dei communionem profitemur, et, quantum in nobis est, colimus." It clearly appears from this declaration, that, instead of differing totally from all other Christian societies, it may rather be said of the Independents, that they perfectly agreed with the far greater part of the reformed churches. To show, as he imagines, by a striking example, the absurdity of their religion and worship, our eminent historian tells us, that they not only reject all kind of ecclesiastical government, but, moreover, allow all their members promiscuously, and without exception, to perform in public the pastoral functions, i. e. to preach, pray, and expound the Scriptures; his words are, "They were not only averse to episcopacy and the ecclesiastical hierarchy," (this charge is true, but it may equally be brought against the Presbyterians, Brownists, Anabaptists, and all the various sects of Nonconformists,) "but they would not so much as endure ordinary ministers in the church. They maintained, that every man might pray in public, exhort his brethren, and interpret the Scriptures, according to the talents with which God had endowed him. So with them every one preached, prayed, admonished, interpreted the Scriptures, without any other call than what he himself drew from his zeal and supposed gifts, and without any other authority than the approbation of his auditors." This whole charge is evidently false and groundless. The Independents have, and always have had, *fixed* and *regular* ministers, approved by their people; nor do they allow to teach in public every person who thinks himself qualified for that important office. The celebrated historian has here confounded the Independents with the Brownists, who, as is well known, permitted all to pray and preach in public without distinction. We shall not enlarge upon the other mistakes into which he has fallen on this subject; but only observe, that if so eminent a writer, and one so well acquainted with the English nation, has pronounced such an unjust sentence against this sect, we may the more easily excuse an inferior set of authors, who have loaded them with groundless accusations.

It will, however, be alleged, that, whatever may have been the religious sentiments and discipline of the Independents, innumerable testimonies concur in proving, that they were chargeable with the death of Charles I., and many will consider this single circumstance as a sufficient demonstration of the impiety and depravity of the whole sect. I am well aware, indeed, that many of the most eminent and respectable English writers have given the Independents the denomination of Regicides; and if, by the term Independents, they mean those licentious republicans, whose dislike of a monarchical form of government carried them to the most pernicious and extravagant lengths, I grant that this denomination is well applied. But if, by this term, we are to understand a religious sect, the ancestors of those who still bear the same title in England, it appears very questionable to me, whether the unhappy fate of the worthy prince above mentioned ought to be imputed entirely to that set of men. They who affirm that the Independents were the only authors of the death of king Charles, must mean one of these two things, either that the regicides were animated and set on by the seditious doctrines of that sect, and the violent suggestions of its members, or that all who were concerned in this atrocious deed were themselves Independents, zealously attached to the religious community now under consideration. Now it may be proved, with the clearest evidence, that neither was the case. There is nothing in the doctrines of this sect, so far as they are known to me, that seems in the least adapted to excite men to such a horrid deed; nor does it appear from the history of those times, that the Independents were a whit more exasperated against Charles, than were the Presbyterians. And as to the latter supposition, it is far from being true, that all those who were concerned in bringing this unfortunate prince to the scaffold were Independents, since we learn from the best English writers, and from the public declarations of Charles II., that this violent faction was composed of persons of different sects. That there were Independents among them may be easily conceived. After all, this matter will be best unravelled by the

ed, together with their situation under the reign of Charles I. when the government was unhinged, when affairs were in great confusion, when the minds of men were suspended upon the issue of the national troubles, and when the eager spirit of party, nourished by hope, made each faction expect that the chaos would end in some settled system, favourable to their respective views, sentiments, and passions; we may be induced to think, that the Independents, at that time, were much more tumultuous and republican than the sect which bears that denomination in our times. The reader who would form just ideas of the matter of fact, must examine the relations given by the writers of both parties. See particularly the histories of Clarendon, Neal, Burnet, and Hume.

different churches.* It is in this their notion of ecclesiastical government, that the difference between them and the Presbyterians, principally consists; for their religious doctrines, if we except some points of very little moment, are almost entirely the same with those of the church of Geneva. The founder of this sect was John Robinson, a man wh. had much of the solemn piety of the times, and was master of a congregation of Brownists that had settled at Leyden. This well-meaning man, perceiving the defects that reigned in the discipline of Brown, and in the spirit and temper of his followers, employed his zeal and diligence in correcting them, and in modelling anew the society, in such a manner as to render it less odious to its adversaries, and less liable to the just censure of those true Christians, who looked upon charity as the end of the commandment. The Independents, accordingly, were much more commendable than the Brownists in two respects. They surpassed them both in the moderation of their sentiments, and the order of their discipline. They did not, like Brown, pour forth bitter and uncharitable invectives against the churches that were governed by rules entirely different from theirs, nor pronounce them, on that account, unworthy of the Christian name. On the contrary, though they considered their own form of ecclesiastical government as of divine institution, and as originally introduced by the authority of the apostles, or by the apostles themselves, yet they had candour and charity enough to acknowledge that true religion and solid piety might flourish in those communities, which were under the jurisdiction of bishops, or the government of synods and presbyteries. They were also much more attentive than the Brownists to the establishment of a regular ministry in their communities; for, while the latter allowed promiscuously all ranks and orders of men to teach in public, and to perform the other pastoral functions, the Independents had, and still have, a certain number of ministers, chosen respectively by the congregations where they are fixed; nor is any person among them permitted to speak in public, before he has

English writers, who know best in what sense the term is used, when it is applied to those who brought Charles I. to the block.*

On inquiring, with particular attention, into the causes of the odium that has been cast upon the Independents, and of the heavy accusations and severe invectives with which they have been loaded, I was more peculiarly struck with the three following considerations, which will perhaps furnish a satisfactory account of this matter. In the first place, the denomination is ambiguous, and is not peculiar to any one distinct order of men. For, not to enumerate the other notions that have been annexed to this term, it is sufficient to observe, that it is used sometimes by the English writers to denote those who aim at the establishment of a purely democratical or popular government, in which the body of the people is clothed with the supreme dominion. Such a faction there was in England, composed, in a great measure, of persons of an enthusiastical character and complexion; and to it, no doubt, we are to ascribe those scenes of sedition and misery, whose effects are still justly lamented. The violence and folly that dishonoured the proceedings of this tumultuous faction have been, if I mistake not, too rashly imputed to the religious Independents now under consideration, who, with all their defects, were a much better set of men than the party now mentioned. It may be observed, secondly, that almost all the religious sects, which divided the English nation in the reign of Charles I. and more especially under the administration of Cromwell, assumed the denomination of Independents, in order to screen themselves from the reproaches of the public, and to share a part of that popular esteem which the true and genuine Independents had acquired, on account of the regularity of their lives, and the sanctity of their manners. This is confirmed, among other testimonies, by the following passage of a letter from Toland to Le Clerc. "Au commencement tous les sectaires se disoient Independans, parce que ces derniers etoient fort honores du peuple a cause de leur piete." See Le Clerc's Biblioth. Univers. et Histor. tom. xxiii. p. ii. p. 506. As this title was of a very extensive signification, and of great latitude, it might thus easily happen, that all the enormities of the various sects that sheltered themselves under it, and several of which were but of short duration, might unluckily be laid to the charge of the true Independents. But it must be particularly remarked, in the third place, that the usurper Cromwell preferred the Independents to all other religious communities. He looked, with an equal eye of suspicion and fear, upon the presbyterian synods and the episcopal visitations; every thing that looked like an extensive authority, whether it was of a civil or religious nature, excited uneasy apprehensions in the breast of the tyrant; but, in the limited and simple form of ecclesiastical discipline that was adopted by the Independents, he saw nothing that was calculated to alarm his fears. This circumstance was sufficient to render the Independents odious in the eyes of many, who would be naturally disposed to extend their abhorrence of Cromwell to those who were the objects of his favour and protection.

* The Independents were undoubtedly so called from their maintaining that all Christian congregations were so many independent religious societies, which had a right to be governed by their own laws, without being subject to any ulterior or foreign jurisdiction. Robinson, the founder of the sect, makes express use of this term in explaining his doctrine relating to ecclesiastical goverment; "Cœtum quemlibet particularem (says he, in his Apologia, cap. v. p. 22,) esse totam, integram, et perfectam ecclesiam ex suis partibus constantem, immediate et *independenter* (quoad alias ecclesias) sub ipso Christo." It may possibly have been from this very passage that the title of *Independent* was originally derived. The disciples of Robinson did not reject it; nor indeed is there any thing shocking in the title, when it is understood in a manner conformable to the sentiments of those to whom it is applied. It was certainly utterly unknown in England before the year 1640; at least it is not once mentioned in the ecclesiastical canons and constitutions that were drawn up, during that year, in the synods or visitations holden by the archbishops of Canterbury, York, and other prelates, in which canons all the various sects that then existed in England are particularly mentioned. See Wilkins' Concilia Magnæ Britanniæ et Hiberniæ, vol. iv. cap. v. p. 548, where are the "constitutions and canons ecclesiastical treated upon by the archbishops of Canterbury and York, and the rest of the bishops and clergy, in their several synods." An. MDCXL. It is true, that not long after this period, and more particularly from the year 1642, we find this denomination very frequently in the English annals. The English Independents were so far from being displeased with it, that they assumed it publicly in a piece they published in their own defence in 1644, under the following title; Apologetical Narration of the Independents. But when, in process of time, a great variety of sects, as has been already observed, sheltered themselves under the cover of this extensive denomination, and even seditious subjects, who aimed at nothing less than the death of their sovereign and the destruction of the government, employed it as a mask to hide their deformity, then the true and genuine Independents renounced this title, and substituted a less odious appellation for it, calling themselves *Congregational Brethren*, and their religious assemblies *Congregational Churches.*

* Tout-a-fait propres a mettre l'Angleterre en combustion.

submitted to a proper examination of his capacity and talents, and has been approved by the heads of the congregation. This community, which was originally formed in Holland in 1610, made at first but a very small progress in England;* it worked its way slowly, and in a clandestine manner; and its members concealed their principles from public view, to avoid the penal laws that had been enacted against Non-conformists. But during the reign of Charles I., when, amidst the shocks of civil and religious discord, the authority of the bishops and the cause of episcopacy began to decline, and more particularly about the year 1640, the Independents became more courageous, and came forth, with an air of resolution and confidence, to public view. After this period, their affairs took a prosperous turn; and, in a little time, they became so considerable, both by their numbers, and by the reputation they acquired, that they vied in point of pre-eminence and credit, not only with the bishops, but also with the Presbyterians, while these were in the very zenith of their power. This rapid progress of the Independents, no doubt, arose from a variety of causes; among which justice obliges us to reckon the learning of their teachers, and the regularity and sanctity of their manners.† During the administration of Cromwell, whose peculiar protection and patronage they enjoyed on more than one account, their credit rose to the greatest height, and their influence and reputation were almost universal; but, after the Restoration, their cause declined, and they fell back gradually into their primitive obscurity. The sect, indeed, still subsisted, but in such a state of dejection and weakness, as engaged them, in 1691, under the government of King William, to enter into an association with the Presbyterians residing in and about London, under certain heads of agreement, that tended to the maintenance of their respective institutions.‡

☞ * In 1616, Mr. Jacob, who had adopted the religious sentiments of Robinson, set up the first Independent or Congregational church in England.

† Neal's History, vol. ii. p. 107, 393; vol. viii. p. 141, 276, 303, 437, 549. See also Bohm's Englische Reformations-Historie, p. 794.

‡ From this time they were called *United Brethren*. The heads of agreement that formed and cemented this union are to be found in the second volume of Whiston's Memoirs of his Life and Writings; and they consist of nine articles. The first relates to "Churches and Church Members," in which the United Ministers, Presbyterians and Independents, declare, among other things, "That each particular church hath a right to choose its own officers, and, being furnished with such as are duly qualified and ordained according to the Gospel rule, hath authority from Christ for exercising government and enjoying all the ordinances of worship within itself: that, in the administration of church-power, it belongs to the pastors and other elders of every particular church (if such there be) to rule and govern, and to the brotherhood to consent, according to the rule of the Gospel." In this both the Presbyterians and Independents depart from the primitive principles of their respective institutions. Article II. relates to "the Ministry," which they grant to have been instituted by Jesus Christ, "for the gathering, guiding, edifying, and governing of his church." In this article it is farther observed, "that ministers ought to be endued with competent learning, sound judgment, and solid piety; that none are to be ordained to the work of the ministry, but such as are chosen and called thereunto by a particular church;" that, in such a weighty matter, "it is ordinarily requisite, that every such church consult and advise with the pastors of neighbouring congregations· and that, after such advice, the person thus consulted about, being chosen by the brotherhood of that particular church, be duly ordained and set apart to his office over them." Article III. relates to "Censures," and prescribes, first, the admonishing, and, if this prove ineffectual, the excommunication of offending and scandalous members, to be performed by the pastors, with the consent of the brethren. Article IV. concerning the "Communion of Churches," lays it down as a principle, that there is no subordination between particular churches; that they are all equal, and consequently independent; that the pastors, however, of these churches "ought to have frequent meetings, that, by mutual advice, support, encouragement, and brotherly intercourse, they may strengthen the hearts and hands of each other in the ways of the Lord." In Article V. which relates to "Deacons and Ruling Elders," the United Brethren acknowledge, that, "the office of a deacon is of divine appointment, and that it belongs to his office to receive, lay out, and distribute, the stock of the church to its proper uses;" and as there are different sentiments about the office of Ruling Elders, who labour not in word and doctrine, they agree that this difference makes no breach among them. In article VI. concerning "Occasional Meetings of Ministers," &c. the brethren agree, that it is needful, in weighty and difficult cases, that the ministers of several churches meet together, "in order to be consulted and advised with about such matters;" and that particular churches "ought to have a reverential regard to their judgment so given, and not dissent therefrom without apparent grounds from the word of God." Article VII. which relates to "the Demeanour of the Brethren towards the Civil Magistrate," prescribes obedience to, and prayers for God's protection and blessing upon, their rulers. In Article VIII. which relates to a "Confession of Faith," the brethren esteem it sufficient, that a church acknowledge the Scriptures to be the word of God, the perfect and only rule of faith and practice, and "own either the doctrinal part of the articles of the church of England," or the Westminster Confession and Catechisms, drawn up by the Presbyterians, or the Confession of the Congregational Brethren (i. e. the Independents) to be agreeable to the said rule. Article IX. which concerns the "duty and deportment of the Brethren towards those who are not in communion with them," inculcates charity and moderation. It appears from these articles, that the Independents were led by a kind of necessity to adopt, in many things, the sentiments of the Presbyterians, and to depart thus far from the original principles of their sect.

XXII. While Oliver Cromwell held the reigns of government in Great Britain, all sects, even those that dishonoured true religion in the most shocking manner by their fanaticism or their ignorance, enjoyed a full and unbounded liberty of professing publicly their respective doctrines. The Episcopalians alone were excepted from this toleration, and received the most severe and iniquitous treatment. The bishops were deprived of their dignities and revenues, and felt, in a particular manner, the heavy hand of oppression. But, though toleration was extended to all other sects and religious communities, yet the Presbyterians and Independents were treated with peculiar marks of distinction and favour. Cromwell, though attached to no one particular sect, gave to the latter extraordinary proofs of his good-will, and augmented their credit and authority, as this seemed the easiest and least exasperating method of setting bounds to the ambition of the Presbyterians, who aimed at a very high degree of ecclesiastical power.* It was du-

☞ * Soon after Cromwell's elevation, it was resolved by the parliament, at the conclusion of a debate concerning public worship and church-govern

ring this period of religious anarchy, that the Fifth-Monarchy-Men arose—a set of wrong-headed and turbulent enthusiasts, who expected Christ's sudden appearance upon earth to establish a new kingdom, and, acting in consequence of this illusion, aimed at the subversion of all human government, and were for turning all things into the most deplorable confusion.* It was at this time also, that the Quakers, of whom we propose to give a more particular account,† and the hot-headed Anabaptists,‡ propagated, without restraint, their visionary doctrines. It must likewise be observed, that the Deists, headed by Sidney, Neville, Martin, and Harrington, appeared with impunity, and promoted a kind of religion, which consisted in a few plain precepts, drawn from the dictates of natural reason.§

XXIII. Among the various religious factions that sprang up in England during this period of confusion and anarchy, we may reckon a certain sect of Presbyterians, who were called by their adversaries *Antinomians*, or enemies of the law, and still subsist even in our times. The Antinomians are a more rigid kind of Calvinists, who pervert Calvin's doctrine of absolute decrees to the worst purposes, by drawing from it conclusions highly detrimental to the interests of true religion and virtue. Such is the judgment that the other Presbyterian communities form of this perverse and extravagant sect.‖ Several of the Antinomians (for they are not all precisely of the same mind) look upon it as unnecessary for Christian ministers to exhort their flock to a virtuous practice, and a pious obedience to the divine law, "since they whom God has elected to salvation, by an eternal and immutable decree, will, by the irresistible impulse of divine grace, be led to the practice of piety and virtue; while those who are doomed by a divine decree to eternal punishment, will never be engaged, by any exhortations or admonitions, how affecting soever they may be, to a virtuous course: nor have they it in their power to obey the divine law, when the succours of divine grace are withholden from them." From these principles they concluded, that the ministers of the Gospel discharged sufficiently their pastoral functions, when they inculcated the necessity of faith in Christ, and proclaimed to their people the blessings of the new covenant. Another, and a still more hideous form of Antinomianism, is that which is exhibited in the opinions of other doctors of that sect,* who maintain, "That, as the elect cannot fall from grace or forfeit the divine favour, the wicked actions they commit, and the violations of the divine law with which they are chargeable, are not really sinful, nor are to be considered as instances of their departing from the law of God; and, consequently, they have no occasion either to confess their sins or to break them off by repentance. Thus adultery, for example, in one of the elect, though it may appear sinful in the sight of men, and be considered universally as an enormous violation of the divine law, yet is not a sin in the sight of God, because it is one of the essential and distinctive characters of the elect, that they cannot do any thing which is either displeasing to God, or prohibited by the law."†

XXIV. The public calamities, that flowed from these vehement and uncharitable disputes about religion, afflicted all wise and good men, and engaged several who were not less eminent for their piety than for their moderation and wisdom, to seek some method of uniting such of the contending parties as were capable of listening to the dictates of charity and reason, or at least of calming their animosities, and persuading them to mutual forbearance. These pacific doctors offered themselves as mediators between the more violent Episcopalians on the one hand, and the more rigid Presbyterians and Independents on the other; and hoped that, when their differences were accommodated, the minor factions would fall of themselves. The contests that reigned between the former turned partly on the forms of church government and public worship, and partly on cer-

ment, that the Presbyterian system should be the established government. The Independents had not yet agreed upon any standard of faith and discipline; and it was only a little before Cromwell's death that they held a synod, by his permission, in order to publish to the world an uniform account of their doctrine and principles.

* See Burnet's History of his own Time, vol. i. p. 67.

† See the History of the Quakers, in the present volume.

☞ ‡ We are not to imagine, by the term hot-headed, (*furiosi*,) that the Anabaptists resembled the furious fanatics of that name who formerly excited such dreadful tumults in Germany, and more especially at Munster. This was by no means the case; the English Anabaptists differed from their Protestant brethren about the subject and mode of baptism alone, confining the former to grown Christians, and the latter to immersion, or dipping. They were divided into Generals and Particulars, from their different sentiments upon the Arminian controversy. The latter, who were so called from their belief of the doctrines of particular election, redemption, &c. were strict Calvinists, who separated from the Independent congregation at Leyden in 1638. Their confession was composed with a remarkable spirit of modesty and charity. Their preachers were generally illiterate, and were eager in making proselytes of all that would submit to their immersion, without a due regard to their religious principles, or their moral characters. The writers of these times represent them as tinctured with a kind of enthusiastic fury against all that opposed them. There were, nevertheless, among them some learned and pious persons, who highly disapproved all violent and uncharitable proceedings.

§ Neal's History, vol. iv. p. 87.

‖ See Toland's Letters to Le Clerc, in the periodical work of the latter, entitled, Bibliotheque Universelle et Historique, tom. xxiii. p. 505; and also Hornbeck's Summa Controversiarum, p. 800, 812.

☞ * This second Antinomian hypothesis has certainly a still more odious aspect than the first; and it is therefore surprising that our author should use, in the original, these terms; *Alii tantum statuunt, Electos, &c.*

† There is an account of the other tenets of the Antinomians, and of the modern disputes that were occasioned by the publication of the posthumous works of Crisp, a flaming doctor of that extravagant and pernicious sect, given by Pierre François le Courayer, in his Examen des Defauts Theologiques, tom. ii. p. 198. Baxter and Tillotson distinguished themselves by their zeal against the Antinomians; and they were also completely refuted by Dr. Williams, in his famous book, entitled, Gospel Truth Stated and Vindicated. ☞ I have been informed, since the first edition of this history was published, that the book entitled Examen des Defauts Theologiques, which our author supposes to have been written by Dr. Courayer, is the production of another pen.

tain religious tenets, more especially those that were debated between the Arminians and Calvinists. To lessen the breach that kept these two great communities at such a distance from each other, the arbitrators, already mentioned, endeavoured to draw them out of their narrow enclosures, to render their charity more extensive, and widen the paths of salvation, which bigotry and party-rage had been labouring to render inaccessible to many good Christians. This noble and truly evangelical method of proceeding procured to its authors the denomination of Latitudinarians.* Their views, indeed, were generous and extensive. They were zealously attached to the forms of ecclesiastical government and worship that were established in the church of England, and they recommended episcopacy with all the strength and power of their eloquence; but they did not go so far as to look upon it as of divine institution, or as absolutely and indispensably necessary to the constitution of a Christian church; and hence they maintained, that those who followed other forms of government and worship, were not, on that account, to be excluded from their communion, or to forfeit the title of brethren. As to the doctrinal part of religion, they took the system of the famous Episcopius for their model; and, like him, reduced the fundamental doctrines of Christianity (or those doctrines, the belief of which is necessary to salvation,) to a few points. By this manner of proceeding, they showed, that neither the Episcopalians, who, generally speaking, embraced the sentiments of the Arminians, nor the Presbyterians and Independents, who as generally adopted the doctrine of Calvin, had any reason to oppose each other with such animosity and bitterness, since the subjects of their debates were matters of an indifferent nature, with respect to salvation, and might be variously explained and understood, without any prejudice to their eternal interests. The chief leaders of these Latitudinarians were Hales and Chillingworth, whose names are still pronounced in England with that veneration which is due to distinguished wisdom and rational piety.† The respectable names of More, Cudworth, Gale, Whichcot, and Tillotson, add a high degree of lustre to this eminent list. The undertaking of these great men, was indeed bold and perilous; and it drew upon them much opposition, and many bitter reproaches. They received, as the first fruits of their charitable zeal, the odious appellations of Atheists, Deists, and Socinians, both from the Roman Catholics and the more rigid of the contending protestant parties; but, on the restoration of Charles II., they were raised to the first dignities of the church, and were deservedly holden in general esteem. It is also well known, that, even at the present time, the church of England is chiefly governed by Latitudinarians of this kind, though there be among both bishops and clergy, from time to time, ecclesiastics who breathe the narrow and despotic spirit of Laud, and who, in the language of faction, are called High-Churchmen, or Church-Tories.*

XXV. No sooner was Charles II. re-established on the throne of his ancestors, than the ancient forms of ecclesiastical government and public worship were restored with him, and the bishops reinstated in their dignities and honours. The Non-conformists hoped, that *they* should be allowed to share some part of the honours and revenues of the church; but their expectations were totally disappointed, and the face of affairs changed very suddenly with respect to them; for Charles subjected to the government of bishops, not only the church of Ireland, but also that of Scotland, a nation which was peculiarly attached to the ecclesiastical discipline and polity of Geneva; and, in 1662, a public law was enacted, by which all who refused to observe the rites, and subscribe the doctrines of the church of England, were entirely excluded from its communion.† From this period until the reign of William III. the Non-conformists were in a precarious and changing situation, sometimes involved in calamity and trouble, at others enjoying some intervals of tranquillity and gleams of hope, according to the varying spirit of the court and ministry, but never entirely free from perplexities and fears.‡ But, in 1689, their affairs took a favourable turn, when a bill for the toleration of all protestant dissenters from the church of England, except the Socinians, passed in parliament almost without opposition, and delivered them from the penal laws to which they had been subjected by the act of uniformity, and other statutes enacted under the sway of the Stuart family.§ Nor did the

* See Burnet's History of his own Time, vol. i. book ii.

† The life of the ingenious and worthy Mr. Hales was composed in English by M. Des-Maizeaux, and published at London in 1719; it was considerably augmented in the Latin translation of it, which I prefixed to the account of the synod of Dordrecht, drawn from the letters of that great man, and published at Hamburg in 1724 A life of Mr. Hales, written in French, is to be found in the first volume of the French translation of Chillingworth's Religion of Protestants, a safe Way to Salvation. The life of Chillingworth also was drawn up by Des-Maizeaux in English: and a French translation of it appeared in 1730, at the head of the excellent book now mentioned, which was also translated into that language, and published at Amsterdam in 1730. Those who are desirous of acquiring a thorough knowledge of the doctrines, government, laws, and present state of the church of England, will do well to read the history of these two men, and more especially to peruse Chillingworth's admirable book already mentioned.

* See Rapin's Dissertation on the Whigs and Tories. ☞ See an admirable defence of the Latitudinarian divines, in a book entitled, The Principles and Practices of certain moderate Divines of the Church of England (greatly misunderstood) truly represented and defended, London, 1670. This book was written by Dr. Fowler, afterwards bishop of Gloucester. N.

☞ † This was the famous Act of Uniformity, in consequence of which the validity of presbyterian ordination was renounced, the ministration of the foreign churches were disowned, the terms of conformity rendered more difficult, and raised higher than before the civil wars; and by which (contrary to the manner of proceeding in the times of Elizabeth and Cromwell, both of whom reserved for the subsistence of each ejected clergyman a fifth part of his benefice) no provision was made for those who should be deprived of their livings. See Wilkins' Concilia Magnæ Britanniæ et Hiberniæ, tom. iv. p. 573.—Burnet's History of his own Time, vol. ii. p. 190, &c. Neal's History of the Puritans, vol. iv. p. 358.

‡ See the whole fourth volume of Neal's History.

§ This was called the Toleration Act; and it may

protestant dissenters in England enjoy, alone, the benefits of this act; for it extended also to the Scottish church, which was permitted thereby to follow the ecclesiastical discipline of Geneva, and was delivered from the jurisdiction of bishops, and from the forms of worship that were annexed to episcopacy. It is from this period that the non-conformists date the liberty and tranquillity they have long been blessed with, and which they still enjoy; but it is also observable, that it is to the transactions carried on during this period, in favour of religious liberty, that we must chiefly impute the multitude of religious sects and factions, that start up from time to time in that free and happy island, and involve its inhabitants in the perplexities of religious division and controversy.*

XXVI. In the reign of King William, and in the year 1689, the divisions among the friends of episcopacy ran high, and terminated in that famous schism in the church of England, which has never hitherto been entirely healed. Sancroft, archbishop of Canterbury, and seven of the other bishops,† all of whom were eminently distinguished both by their learning and their virtue, deemed it unlawful to take the oath of allegiance to the new king, from a mistaken notion that James II., though banished from his dominions, remained their rightful sovereign. As these scruples were deeply rooted, and no arguments or exhortations could engage these prelates to acknowledge the title of the prince of Orange to the crown of Great Britain, they were deprived of their ecclesiastical dignities, and their sees were filled by other men of eminent merit.‡ The deposed bishops and clergy formed a new episcopal church, which differed, in some points of doctrine, and certain circumstances of public worship, from the established church. The members of this new religious community were denominated *Non-jurors*, on account of their refusing to take the oath of allegiance, and were also called the *High-Church* party, on account of the high notions they entertained of the dignity and power of the church, and the extent they gave to its prerogatives and jurisdiction. Those, on the other hand, who disapproved this schism, who distinguished themselves by their charity and moderation toward dissenters, and were less ardent in extending the limits of ecclesiastical authority, were denominated *Low-Churchmen.** The bishops who were deprived of their sees, and those who embarked in their cause, maintained openly that the church was not dependent on the jurisdiction of the king or the parliament, but was subject to the authority of God alone, and empowered to govern itself by its own laws; that consequently the sentence, pronounced against these prelates by the great council of the nation, was destitute both of justice and validity; and that it was only by the decree of an ecclesiastical council that a bishop could be deposed. These high notions of the authority and prerogatives of the church were maintained and propagated, with peculiar zeal, by the famous Henry Dodwell, who led the way in this important cause, and who, by his example and abilities, formed a considerable number of champions for its defence. Hence arose a very nice and intricate controversy, concerning the nature, privileges, and authority of the church, which has not yet been brought to a satisfactory conclusion.†

XXVII. The Non-jurors or High-Church-

be seen at length in the Appendix, subjoined to the fourth volume of Neal's History of the Puritans.— ☞ It is entitled, An Act for exempting their Majesties' Protestant Subjects, dissenting from the Church of England, from the Penalties of certain Laws. In this bill the Corporation and Test acts are omitted, and consequently still remain in force. The Socinians are also excepted; but provision is made for Quakers, upon their making a solemn declaration, instead of taking the oaths to the government. This act excuses protestant dissenters from the penalties of the laws therein mentioned, provided they take the oaths to the government, and subscribe the doctrinal articles of the church of England.

* Burnet's History of his own Time, vol. ii. p. 23.

☞ † The other non-juring bishops were Lloyd, bishop of Norwich; Turner, of Ely; Kenn, of Bath and Wells; Frampton, of Gloucester; Thomas, of Worcester; Lake, of Chichester, and White, of Peterborough.

☞ ‡ Among these were Tillotson, Moore, Patrick, Kidder, Fowler, and Cumberland, names that will be ever pronounced with veneration by such as are capable of esteeming well employed learning and genuine piety, and that will always shine among the brightest ornaments of the church of England.

* The denomination of High-church is given certainly, with great propriety, to the Non-jurors, who have very proud notions of church power; but it is commonly used in a more extensive signification, and is applied to all those who, though far from being Non-jurors, or otherwise disaffected to the present happy establishment, yet form pompous and ambitious conceptions of the authority and jurisdiction of the church, and would raise it to an absolute exemption from all human control. Many such are to be found even among those who go under the general denomination of the Low-Church party.

☞ † Dodwell himself was deprived of his professorship of history, for refusing to take the oath of allegiance to King William and Queen Mary; and this circumstance, no doubt, augmented the zeal with which he interested himself in the defence of the bishops, who were suspended for the same reason. It was on this occasion that he published his "Cautionary Discourse of Schism, with a particular regard to the case of the bishops, who are suspended for refusing to take the new oath." This book was fully refuted by the learned Dr. Hody, in 1691, in a work entitled, "The Unreasonableness of a Separation from the new Bishops: or a Treatise out of Ecclesiastical History, showing, that although a bishop was unjustly deprived, neither he nor the church ever made a separation, if the successor was not a heretic;" translated out of an ancient Greek manuscript (among the Baroccian MSS.) in the public library at Oxford. The learned author translated this work afterwards into Latin, and prefixed to it some pieces out of ecclesiastical antiquity, relative to the same subject. Dodwell published, in 1692, an answer to it, which he called, "A Vindication of the deprived Bishops," &c., to which Dr. Hody replied, in a treatise entitled, "The Case of the Sees vacant by an unjust or uncanonical Deprivation stated, in reply to the Vindication," &c. The controversy did not end here; for it was extremely difficult to reduce Mr. Dodwell to silence. Accordingly he came forth a third time with his stiff and rigid polemics, and published, in 1695, his Defence of the Vindication of the deprived Bishops. The preface which he designed for this work, was at first suppressed, but appeared afterwards under the following title: "The Doctrine of the Church of England concerning the independency of the Clergy on the Lay-power, as to those rights of theirs which are purely spiritual, reconciled with our oath of supremacy and the lay-deprivation of the popish Bishops in the beginning of the Reformation." Several other pamphlets were published on the subject of this controversy.

men, who boast with peculiar ostentation of their orthodoxy, and treat the Low-Church as unsound and schismatical, differ in several things from the members of the episcopal church, in its present establishment; but they are more particularly distinguished by the following principles: 1. That it is never lawful for the people, under any provocation or pretext whatever, to resist the sovereign. This is called in England passive obedience, and is a doctrine warmly opposed by many, who think it both lawful and necessary, in certain circumstances, and in cases of an urgent and momentous nature, to resist the prince for the happiness of the people. They maintain farther, 2. That the hereditary succession to the throne is of divine institution, and therefore can never be interrupted, suspended, or annulled, on any pretext: 3. That the church is subject to the jurisdiction, not of the civil magistrate, but of God alone, particularly in matters of a religious nature: 4. That, consequently, Sancroft, and the other bishops, deposed by King William III., remained, notwithstanding their deposition, true bishops, to the day of their death; and that those who were substituted in their places were the unjust possessors of other men's property: 5. That these unjust possessors of ecclesiastical dignities were rebels against the state, as well as schismatics in the church; and that all, therefore, who held communion with them, were also chargeable with rebellion and schism: 6. That this schism, which rends the church in pieces, is a most heinous sin, and that the punishment due to it must fall heavy upon all those who do not return sincerely to the true church, from which they have departed.*

XXVIII. It will now be proper to change the scene, and to consider a little the state of the reformed church in Holland. The Dutch Calvinists thought themselves happy after the defeat of the Arminians, and were flattering themselves with the agreeable prospect of enjoying long, in tranquillity and repose, the fruits of their victory, when new scenes of tumult arose from another quarter. Scarcely had they triumphed over the enemies of absolute predestination, when, by an ill hap, they became the prey of intestine disputes, and were divided among themselves in such a deplorable manner, that, during the whole of this century, the United Provinces were a scene of contention, animosity, and strife. It is not necessary to mention all the subjects of these religious quarrels; nor indeed would this be an easy task. We shall therefore pass over in silence the debates of certain divines, who disputed about some particular, though not very momentous, points of doctrine and discipline; such as those of the famous Voet and the learned Des-Marets; as also the disputes of Salmasius, Boxhorn, Voet, and others, concerning usury, ornaments in dress, stage-plays, and other minute points of morality; and the contests of Apollonius, Trigland, and Vedelius, concerning the power of the magistrate in matters of religion and ecclesiastical discipline, which produced such a flaming division between Frederic Spanheim and John Vander-Wayen. These, and other debates of the like nature and importance rather discover the sentiments of certain learned men, concerning some particular points of religion and morality, than exhibit a clear view of the internal state of the Belgic church. The knowledge of this must be derived from those controversies alone in which the whole church, or at least the greatest part of its doctors, have been directly concerned.

XXIX. Such were the controversies occasioned in Holland by the philosophy of Des-Cartes, and the theological novelties of Cocceius. Hence arose the two powerful and numerous factions, distinguished by the denominations of Cocceians and Voetians, which still subsists, though their debates are now less violent, and their champions somewhat more moderate than they were in former times. The Cocceian theology and the Cartesian philosophy have, indeed, no common features, nor any thing, in their respective tenets and principles, that was in the least adapted to form a connexion between them; and, in consequence, the debates they excited, and the factions they produced, had no natural relation to, or dependence on, each other. It nevertheless so happened, that the respective votaries of these very different sciences formed themselves into one sect; so far at least, that those who chose Cocceius for their guide in theology, took Des-Cartes for their master in philosophy.* This will appear less surprising when we consider, that the very same persons who opposed the progress of Cartesianism in Holland were the warm adversaries of the Cocceian theology; for this opposition, equally levelled at these two great men and their respective systems, laid the Cartesians and Cocceians under a kind of necessity of uniting their force, in order to defend their cause, in a more effectual manner, against the formidable attacks of their numerous adversaries. The Voetians were so called from Gisbert Voet, a learned and eminent professor of divinity in the university of Utrecht, who first sounded the alarm of this theologico-philosophical war, and led on, with zeal, the polemic legions against those who followed the standard of Des-Cartes and Cocceius.

XXX. The Cartesian philosophy, at its first appearance, attracted the attention and esteem of many, and seemed more conformable to truth and nature, as well as more elegant and pleasing in its aspect, than the intricate labyrinths of Peripatetic wisdom. It was considered in this light in Holland; it however met there with a formidable adversary, in 1639, in the famous Voet above mentioned, who taught theology with the greatest reputation, and gave plain intimations of his looking upon Cartesianism as a system of impiety. Voet was a man of uncommon application and immense learning; he had made an extraordinary progress in the various branches of erudition and philosophy; but he was not endowed

* See Whiston's Memoirs of his Life and Writings, vol. i. p. 30.—Hickes' Memoirs of the Life of John Kettlewell.—Nouveau Diction. Histor. et Crit. at the article Collier.—Ph. Masson, Histoire Critique la Repub. des Lettres, tom. xiii. p. 298.

* See Fred. Spanhemii Epistola de novissimis in Belgio Dissidiis, tom. ii. op. p. 973.

with a large portion of that philosophical spirit, which judges with acuteness and precision of natural science and abstract truths. While Des-Cartes resided at Utrecht, Voet found fault with many things in his philosophy; but what induced him to cast upon it the aspersion of impiety, was its being introduced by the following principles: "That the person who aspires to the character of a true philosopher must begin by doubting of all things, even of the existence of a Supreme Being—that the nature or essence of spirit, and even of God himself, consists in thought—that space has no real existence, and is no more than the creature of fancy,—and that, consequently, matter is without bounds."

Des-Cartes defended his principles, with his usual acuteness, against the professor of Utrecht; his disciples and followers thought themselves obliged, on this occasion, to assist their master; and thus war was formally declared. On the other hand, Voet was not only seconded by those Belgic divines who were the most eminent, at this time, for the extent of their learning and the soundness of their theology, such as Rivet, Des-Marets, and Maestricht, but also was followed and applauded by the greatest part of the Dutch clergy.* While the flame of controversy burned with sufficient ardour, it was considerably augmented by the proceedings of certain doctors, who applied the principles and tenets of Des-Cartes to the illustration of theological truth. Hence, in 1656, an alarm was raised in the Dutch churches and schools, and a strong resolution was taken in several of their ecclesiastical assemblies (commonly called *classes*,) to make head against Cartesianism, and not to permit that imperious philosophy to make such encroachments upon the domain of theology. The states of Holland not only approved this resolution, but also gave a new force and efficacy by a public edict, issued in the same year, by which both the professors of philosophy and theology were forbidden either to explain the writings of Des-Cartes to the youth under their care, or to illustrate the doctrines of the Gospel by the principles of philosophy. It was farther resolved in an assembly of the clergy, holden at Delft in the following year, that no candidate for holy orders should be received into the ministry before he made a solemn declaration, that he would neither promote the Cartesian philosophy, nor disfigure the divine simplicity of religion, by loading it with foreign ornaments. Laws of a like tenor were afterwards passed by the States-general, and by the governments of other countries.† But as there is in human nature a strange propensity to struggle against authority, and to pursue, with a peculiar degree of ardour, things that are forbidden, so it happened, that all these edicts proved insufficient to stop the progress of Cartesianism, which at length obtained a solid and permanent footing in the seminaries of learning, and was applied, both in the universities and churches, and sometimes indeed very preposterously, to explain the truths and precepts of Christianity. Hence it was, that the United Provinces were divided into the two great factions already mentioned, and that the whole remainder of this century was spent amidst their contentions and debates.

XXXI. John Koch of Cocceius, a native of Bremen, and professor of divinity in the university of Leyden, might have certainly passed for a great man, had his vast erudition, his exuberant fancy, his ardent piety, and his uncommon application to the study of the Scriptures, been under the direction of a sound and solid judgment. This singular man introduced into theology a multitude of new tenets and strange notions, which had never before entered into the brain of any other mortal, or at least had never been heard of before his time. In the first place, as has been already hinted, his manner of explaining Scripture was totally different from that of Calvin and his followers. Departing entirely from the admirable simplicity that reigns in the commentaries of that great man, he represented the whole history of the Old Testament as a mirror, that held forth an accurate view of the transactions and events which were to happen in the church under the dispensation of the New Testament, and to the end of the world. He even went so far as to maintain, that the miracles, actions, and sufferings of Christ and of his apostles, during the course of their ministry, were types and images of future events. He affirmed, that the far greater part of the ancient prophecies foretold Christ's ministry and mediation, and the rise, progress, and revolutions of the church, not only under the figures of persons and transactions, but in a literal manner, and by the very sense of the words, used in these predictions; and he completed the extravagance of this chimerical system, by turning, with wonderful art and dexterity, into holy riddles and typical predictions, even those passages of the Old Testament which seemed intended for no other purpose than to celebrate the praises of the Deity, convey some religious truth, or inculcate some rule of practice. In order to give an air of solidity and plausibility to these eccentric notions, he first laid it down as a fundamental rule of interpretation, "That the words and phrases of Scripture are to be understood in every sense of which they are susceptible; or, in other words, that they signify, in effect, every thing that they can signify;" a rule which, when followed by a man who had more imagination than judgment, could not fail to produce very extraordinary comments on the sacred writings. After having laid down this singular rule, he divided the whole history of the church into seven periods, conformable to the seven trumpets and seals mentioned in the Revelations.

XXXII. One of the great designs formed by Cocceius, was that of separating theology from philosophy, and of confining the Christian doctors, in their explications of the former, to the words and phrases of the Scriptures. Hence it was, that, finding, in the language of the sacred writers, the Gospel dispensation

* See Baillet's Vie de M. Des-Cartes, tom. ii. chap. v. and Daniel's Voyage du Monde de M. Des-Cartes.

† Fred. Spanheim, de novissimis in Belgio Dissidiis, tom. ii. op. p. 959.—The reader may also consult the historians of this century, such as Arnold, Weismann, Jager, Carolus, and also Walchius' Histor. Controvers. Germanic. tom. iii.

represented under the image of a covenant made between God and man, he looked upon the use of this image as admirably adapted to exhibit a complete and well connected system of religious truth. But while he was labouring this point, and endeavouring to accommodate the circumstances and characters of human contracts to the dispensations of divine wisdom, which they represent in such an inaccurate and imperfect manner, he fell imprudently into some erroneous notions. Such was his opinion concerning the covenant made between God and the Jewish nation by the ministry and the mediation of Moses, which he affirmed to be "of the same nature with the new covenant obtained by the mediation of Jesus Christ." In consequence of this general principle, he maintained, "That the Ten Commandments were promulgated by Moses not as a rule of obedience, but as a representation of the covenant of grace; that when the Jews had provoked the Deity, by their various transgressions, particularly by the worship of the golden calf, the severe and servile yoke of the ceremonial law was added to the decalogue, as a punishment inflicted on them by the Supreme Being in his righteous displeasure; that this yoke, which was painful in itself, became doubly so on account of its typical signification, since it admonished the Israelites, from day to day, of the imperfection and uncertainty of their state, filled them with anxiety, and was a standing and perpetual proof that they had merited the displeasure of God, and could not expect, before the coming of the Messiah, the entire remission of their transgressions and iniquities; that, indeed, good men, even under the Mosaic dispensation, were immediately after death made partakers of everlasting happiness and glory; but that they were, nevertheless, during the whole course of their lives, far removed from that firm hope and assurance of salvation, with which the faithful are gratified under the dispensation of the Gospel, and that their anxiety flowed naturally from this consideration, that their sins, though they remained unpunished, were not pardoned, because Christ had not then offered himself up a sacrifice to the Father to make an entire atonement for them." These are the principal lines that distinguish the Cocceian from other systems of theology; it is attended, indeed, with other peculiarities; but we shall pass them over in silence, as of little moment, and unworthy of notice. These notions were warmly opposed by the persons who had declared war against the Cartesian philosophy; and the contest was carried on for many years with various success. But in the issue, the doctrines of Cocceius, like those of Des-Cartes, maintained their ground; and neither the dexterity nor the vehemence of his adversaries could exclude his disciples from the public seminaries of learning, or hinder them from propagating, with surprising success and rapidity, the tenets of their master in Germany and Switzerland.*

XXXIII. The other controversies that divided the Batavian church during this century, arose from the immoderate propensity that certain doctors discovered toward an alliance between the Cartesian philosophy and their theological system. This will appear, with the utmost evidence, from the debates excited by Roell and Becker, which surpassed all the others, both by the importance of their subjects and by the noise they made in the world. About the year 1686, certain Cartesian doctors of divinity, headed by the ingenious Herman Alexander Roell, professor of theology in the university of Franeker, seemed to attribute to the dictates of reason a more extensive authority in religious matters, than they had hitherto possessed. The controversy occasioned by this innovation was reducible to the two following questions: "1. Whether the divine origin and authority of Scripture can be demonstrated by reason alone, or whether an inward testimony of the Holy Spirit in the hearts of Christians be necessary in order to the firm belief of this fundamental point? 2. Whether the sacred writings propose to us, as an object of faith, any thing that is repugnant to the dictates of right reason?" These questions were answered, the former in the affirmative, and the latter in the negative, not only by Roell, but also by Vander-Wayen, Wessel, Duker, Ruard ab Andala, and other doctors, who were opposed on this occasion by Ulric Nuber, an eminent lawyer, Gerard de Vries, and others of inferior note.* The flame excited by this controversy spread itself far and wide through the United Provinces; and its progress seemed to be increasing from day to day, when the states of Friseland prudently interposed to restore the peace of the church, by imposing silence on the contending parties. Those whose curiosity may engage them to examine, with attention and accuracy, the points debated in this controversy, will find, that a very considerable part of it was merely a dispute about words, and that the real difference of sentiment that existed between these learned disputants might have been easily accommodated, by proper explications on both sides.

XXXIV. Not long after this controversy had been hushed, Roell alarmed the orthodoxy of his colleagues, and more particularly of the learned Vitringa, by some other new tenets, that rendered the soundness of his religious principles extremely doubtful, not only in their opinion, but likewise in the judgment of many Dutch divines;† for he maintained, "That the account we have of the generation of the Son, in the sacred writings, is not to be understood in a literal sense, or as a real generation of a natural kind;" he also affirmed, "That the afflictions and death of the righteous are as truly the penal effects of original sin, as the afflictions and death of the wicked and impenitent;" and he entertained notions concerning the divine decrees, original sin, the satisfaction of Christ, and some points of less moment, which

* See Baillet's Vie de M. Des-Cartes, tom. ii. p. 33. —Daniel's Voyage du Monde de Des-Cartes.—Val. Alberti Διπλοῦν κάππα, Cartesianismus et Cocceianismus descripti et refutati.

* See the Biblioth. Univers. et Historique of Le Clerc, tom. vi.

† For an account of Roell, see the Bibliotheca Bremens, Theologico-Philolog. tom. ii. p. vi. p. 707 and Casp. Burmanni Trajectum Eruditum. p. 306.

differed in reality, or by the manner of expressing them seemed to differ greatly, from the doctrines received and established in the Dutch church.* The magistrates of Friseland used all the precautions that prudence could suggest, to prevent these controversies from being propagated in their province; and they enacted several laws for this purpose, all tending toward peace and silence. This conduct, however, was not imitated by the other provinces, where Roell and his disciples were condemned, both in private and in public, as heretics and corruptors of divine truth.† Nor did the death of this eminent man extinguish the animosity and resentment of his adversaries; for his disciples were still treated with severity; and, notwithstanding the solemn protestations they have given of the soundness and purity of their religious sentiments, they labour under the imputation of many concealed errors.

XXXV. The controversy set on foot by the ingenious Balthasar Becker, minister at Amsterdam, must not be omitted. This learned ecclesiastic took occasion, from the Cartesian definition of spirit, of the truth and precision of which he was intimately persuaded, to deny boldly all the accounts we have in Scripture of the seduction, influence, and operations of the devil and his infernal emissaries, as also all that has been said in favour of the existence of ghosts, spectres, and magicians. The long and elaborate work which he published in 1691, upon this interesting subject, is still extant. In this singular production, which bears the title of the World Bewitched, he modifies and perverts, with the greatest ingenuity, but also with equal temerity and presumption, the accounts given by the sacred writers of the power of Satan and wicked angels, and of persons possessed by evil spirits; he affirms, moreover, that the unhappy and malignant being, who is called in Scripture Satan, or the Devil, is chained down with his infernal ministers in hell; so that he can never come forth from this eternal prison to terrify mortals, or to seduce the righteous from the paths of virtue. According to the Cartesian definition above mentioned, the essence of spirit consists in thought; and, from this definition, Becker drew his doctrine, since none of that influence, or of those operations which are attributed to evil spirits, can be effected by mere thinking.* Rather, therefore, than call in question the accuracy or authority of Des-Cartes, Becker thought proper to force the narrations and doctrines of Scripture into a conformity with the principles and definitions of this philosopher. This error excited great tumults and divisions, not only in all the United Provinces, but also in some parts of Germany, where several doctors of the Lutheran church were alarmed at its progress, and arose to oppose it.† Its inventor and promoter, though refuted victoriously by a multitude of adversaries, and publicly deposed from his pastoral charge, died in 1718, in the full persuasion of the truth of those opinions which had drawn upon him so much opposition, and professed, with his last breath, his sincere adherence to every thing he had written on that subject; nor can it be said, that this his doctrine died with him, since it is abundantly known, that it has still many votaries and patrons, who either hold it in secret, or profess it publicly.

XXXVI. The curious reader can be no stranger to the multitude of sects, some Christian, some half-Christian, some totally delirious, that have started up at different times both in England and Holland. It is difficult, indeed, for those who live in other countries, to give accurate accounts of these separatists, as the books that contain their doctrines and views are seldom dispersed among foreign nations. We have, however, been lately favoured with

* Those who are desirous of the most accurate account of the errors of Roell, will find them enumerated in a public piece composed by the faculty of theology at Leyden, in order to confirm the sentence of condemnation that had been pronounced against them by the Dutch synods. This piece is entitled, Judicium Ecclesiasticum, quo Opiniones quædam Cl. H. A. Roellii synodice damnatæ sunt, laudatum a Professoribus Theologiæ in Academia Lugduno-Batava.

☞ † This affirmation is somewhat exaggerated; at least we must not conclude from it, that Roell was either deposed or persecuted; for he exercised the functions of his professorship for several years after this at Franeker, and was afterwards called to the chair of divinity at Utrecht, upon the most honourable and advantageous terms. The states of Friseland published an edict, enjoining silence, and forbidding all professors, pastors, &c. in their province, to teach the particular opinions of Roell; and this pacific divine sacrificed the propagation of his opinions to the love of peace and concord. His notion concerning the Trinity did not essentially differ from the doctrine generally received upon that mysterious and unintelligible subject; and his design seemed to be no more than to prevent Christians from humanising the relation between the Father and Son. But this was wounding his brethren, the rigorous systematic divines, in a tender point; for, if Anthropomorphism, or the custom of attributing to the Deity the kind of procedure in acting and judging that is usual among men (who resemble him only as imperfection resembles perfection,) should be banished from theology, orthodoxy would be deprived of some of its most precious phrases, and our confessions of faith and systems of doctrine would be reduced within much narrower bounds.

☞ * Our historian relates here somewhat obscurely the reasoning which Becker founded upon the Cartesian definition of mind or spirit. The substance of his argument is as follows: "The essence of mind is thought, and the essence of matter extension. Now since there is no sort of conformity or connexion between thought and extension, mind cannot act upon matter, unless these two substances be united, as soul and body are in man: therefore no separate spirits, either good or evil, can act upon mankind. Such acting is miraculous, and miracles can be performed by God alone. It follows of consequence that the scriptural accounts of the actions and operations of good and evil spirits must be understood in an allegorical sense." This is Becker's argument; and it does, in truth, little honour to his acuteness and sagacity. By proving too much, it proves nothing at all; for, if the want of a connexion or conformity between thought and extension renders mind incapable of acting upon matter, it is hard to see how their union should remove this incapacity, since the want of conformity and of connexion remains notwithstanding this union. Besides, according to this reasoning, the Supreme Being cannot act upon material beings. In vain does Becker maintain the affirmative, by having recourse to a miracle; for this would imply, that the whole course of nature is a series of miracles, that is to say, that there are no miracles at all.

† See Lilienthalii Selectæ Historiæ Literar. p. i. observat. ii. p. 17.—Miscellan. Lipsiens, tom. i. p. 361, where may be found an explication of a satirical medal, struck to expose the sentiments of Becker. See also Nouveau Diction. Hist. et Critique, tom. i. p. 193.

some relations that give a more just idea of the Dutch sects, called Verschorists and Hattemists, than we had before entertained; and it will not therefore be improper to give here some account of these remarkable communities. The former derives its denomination from Jacob Verschoor, a native of Flushing, who in 1680, out of a perverse and heterogeneous mixture of the tenets of Cocceius and Spinosa, produced a new form of religion, equally remarkable for its extravagance and impiety. His disciples and followers were called Hebrews, on account of the zeal and assiduity with which they all, without distinction of age or sex, applied themselves to the study of the Hebrew language.

The Hattemists were so called from Pontian Van Hattem, a minister in the province of Zealand, who was also addicted to the sentiments of Spinosa, and was on that account degraded from his pastoral office. The Verschorists and Hattemists resemble each other in their religious systems, though there must also be some points in which they differ, since it is well known, that Van Hattem could never persuade the former to unite their sect with his, and thus to form one communion. Neither of the two would wish the public to conclude that they have abandoned the profession of the Reformed religion; they affect, on the contrary, an apparent attachment to it; and Hattem, in particular, published a treatise upon the Catechism of Heidelberg. If I rightly understand the imperfect relations that have been given of the sentiments and principles of these two communities, both their founders began by perverting the doctrine of the Reformed church concerning absolute decrees, so as to deduce from it the impious system of a fatal and uncontrollable necessity. Having laid down this principle to account for the origin of all events, they went a step farther into the domain of atheism, and denied "the difference between moral good and evil, and the corruption of human nature." Hence they concluded, "That mankind were under no sort of obligation to correct their manners, to improve their minds, or to endeavour after a regular obedience to the divine laws; that the whole of religion consisted, not in acting, but in suffering; and that all the precepts of Jesus Christ are reducible to this single one, that we should bear with cheerfulness and patience the events that happen to us through the divine will, and make it our constant and only study to maintain a permanent tranquillity of mind."

This, if we mistake not, was the common doctrine of the two sects under consideration. There were, however, certain opinions or fancies, which were peculiar to Hattem and his followers, who affirmed, "That Christ had not satisfied the divine justice, nor made an expiation for the sins of men by his death and sufferings, but had only signified to us, by his mediation, that there was nothing in us that could offend the Deity." Hattem maintained, "that this was Christ's manner of justifying his servants, and presenting them blameless before the tribunal of God." These opinions seem perverse and pestilential in the highest degree; and they evidently tend to extinguish all virtuous sentiments, and to dissolve all moral obligation. It does not, however, appear, that either of these innovators directly recommended immorality and vice, or thought that men might safely follow, without any restraint, the impulse of their irregular appetites and passions. It is at least certain, that the following maxim is placed among their tenets, that God does not punish men *for* their sins, but *by* their sins; and this maxim seems to signify, that, if a man does not restrain his irregular appetites, he must suffer the painful fruits of his licentiousness, both in a present and future life, not in consequence of any judicial sentence pronounced by the will, or executed by the immediate hand of God, but according to some fixed law or constitution of nature.* The two sects still subsist, though they bear no longer the names of their founders.

XXXVII. The churches of Switzerland, so early as the year 1669, were alarmed at the progress which the opinions of Amyrault, De la Place, and Capel, were making in different countries; and they were apprehensive that the doctrine they had received from Calvin, and which had been so solemnly confirmed by the Synod of Dordrecht, might be altered and corrupted by these supposed improvements in theology. This apprehension was so much the less chimerical, as at that very time there were, among the clergy of Geneva, certain doctors eminent for their learning and eloquence, who not only adopted these new opinions, but were also desirous, notwithstanding the opposition and remonstrances of their colleagues, of propagating them among the people.† To set bounds to the zeal of these innovators, and to stop the progress of the new doctrines, the learned John Henry Heidegger, professor of divinity at Zurich, was employed in 1675, by an assembly composed of the most eminent Helvetic divines, to draw up a form of doctrine, in direct opposition to the tenets and principles of the celebrated French writers mentioned above. The magistrates were engaged, without much difficulty, to give to this production the stamp of their authority, and to add to it the other confessions of faith received in the Helvetic church, under the peculiar denomination of the *Form of Concord.* This step, which seemed to be taken with pacific views, proved an abundant source of division and discord. Many declared, that they could not conscientiously subscribe this new form; and thus unhappy tumults and contests arose in several places. Hence it happened, that the canton of Basil and the republic of Geneva, perceiving the inconveniences that proceeded from this new article of church communion, and being strongly solicited, in 1686, by Frederic William, elector of Brandenburg, to ease the burthened consciences of their clergy, abrogated this form.‡ It is neverthe-

* See Theod. Hasæi Dissert. in Museo Bremensi Theol. Philolog. vol. ii. p. 144.—Bibliotheque Belgique, tom. ii. p. 203.

† See Leti Istoria Genevina, part iv. book v. p. 448, 488, 497, &c.

☞ ‡ It must not be imagined, from the expressions of our historian, that this *Consensus*, or Form of Agreement, was abrogated at Basil by a positive edict. The case stood thus: Mr Peter Werenfels

less certain, that in the other cantons it maintained its authority for some time after this period; but, in our time, the discords it has excited in many places, and more particularly in the university of Lausanne, have contributed to deprive it of all its authority, and to plunge it into utter oblivion.*

CHAPTER III.

The History of the Arminian Church.

I. THERE sprang forth from the bosom of the reformed church, during this century, two new sects, whose birth and progress were, for a long time, painful and perplexing to the parent that bore them. These sects were the Arminians and Quakers, whose origin was owing to very different principles, since the former derived its existence from an excessive propensity to improve the faculty of reason, and to follow its dictates and discoveries: while the latter sprang up, like a rank weed, from the neglect and contempt of human reason. The Arminians derive their name and their origin from James Arminius, or Harmensen, who was first pastor at Amsterdam, afterwards professor of divinity at Leyden, and who attracted the esteem and applause of his very enemies, by his acknowledged candour, penetration, and piety.† They received also the denomination of *Remonstrants*, from an humble petition, entitled their Remonstrance, which they addressed, in 1610, to the states of Holland and West-Friseland; and, as the patrons of Calvinism presented an address in opposition to this, which they called their Counter-Remonstrance, the latter received the name of *Counter-Remonstrants.*

II. Arminius, though he had imbibed in his tender years the doctrines of Geneva, and had even received his theological education in the university of that city, yet rejected, when he arrived at the age of manhood, the sentiments, concerning predestination and the divine decrees, that were adopted by the greatest part of the reformed churches, and embraced the principles and communion of those, whose religious system extended the love of the Supreme Being, and the merits of Jesus Christ, to all mankind.* As time and deep meditation had only served to confirm him in these principles, he thought himself obliged, by the dictates both of candour and conscience, to profess them publicly, when he had obtained the chair of divinity in the university of Leyden, and to oppose the doctrine and sentiments of Calvin on these heads, which had been followed by the greatest part of the Dutch clergy. Two considerations encouraged him, in a particular manner, to venture upon this open declaration of his sentiments; for he was persuaded, on one hand, that there were many persons, beside himself, and, among these, some of the first rank and dignity, who were highly disgusted at the doctrine of absolute decrees; and, on the other, he knew that the Dutch divines and doctors were neither obliged by their confession of faith, nor by any other public law, to adopt and propagate the principles of Calvin. Thus animated and encouraged, he taught his sentiments publicly, with great freedom and equal success, and persuaded many of the truth of his doctrine: but, as Calvinism was at this time in a flourishing state in Holland, this freedom procured him a multitude of enemies, and drew upon him the severest marks of disapprobation and resentment from those who adhered to the theological system of Geneva, and more especially from Francis Gomar, his colleague. Thus commenced that long, tedious, and intricate controversy, which afterwards made such a noise in Europe. Arminius died in 1609, when it was just beginning to involve his country in contention and discord.‡

who was at the head of the ecclesiastical consistory of that city, paid such regard to the letter of the elector, as to avoid requiring a subscription to this form from the candidates for the ministry: and his conduct, in this respect, was imitated by his successors. The remonstrances of the elector do not seem to have had the same effect upon those who governed the church of Geneva; for the form maintained its credit and authority there until the year 1706, when, without being abrogated by any positive act, it fell into disuse. In several other parts of Switzerland, it was still imposed as a rule of faith, as appears from the letters addressed by George I., king of Great Britain, and by the king of Prussia, in 1723, to the Swiss cantons, in order to procure the abrogation of this form, which was considered as an obstacle to the union of the Reformed and Lutheran churches. See the Memoires pour servir a l'Histoire des Troubles arrivees en Suisse a l'occasion du Consensus, published at Amsterdam in 1726.

* See the work last quoted, and also Christ. Matth. Pfaffii. Schediasma de Formula Consens. Helvet.

† The most ample account we have of this eminent man is given by Caspar Brandt, in his Historia Vitæ Jac. Arminii, published at Leyden, in 1724, and the year after by me at Brunswick, with an additional preface and some annotations. See also Nouveau Dictionaire Histor. et Critique, tom. i. p. 471. They who would form a just and accurate notion of his temper, genius, and doctrine, will do well to peruse, with particular attention, his Disputationes publicæ et privatæ. There are in his manner of reasoning, and also in his phraseology, some little remains of the scholastic jargon of that age; yet we find in his writings, upon the whole, much of that simplicity and perspicuity which his followers have always looked upon, and still consider, as among the principal qualities of a Christian minister. For an account of the Arminian confessions of faith, and the historical writers who have treated of this sect, see J Christ. Kocher's Biblioth. Theol. Symbolicæ, p. 481.

* Bertius in his Funeral Oration on Arminius, Brandt in his history of the life of that divine, and almost all the ecclesiastical historians of this period, mention the occasion of this change in his sentiments. It happened in 1591, as appears from the remarkable letter of Arminius to Grynæus, dated in that year, in which the former proposes to the latter some of his theological doubts. This letter is published in the Biblioth. Brem. Theol. Philolog. tom. iii. p. 384.

‡ The history of this controversy, and of the public discords and tumults it occasioned, is more circumstantially related by Brandt, in the second and third volumes of his History of the Reformation, than by any other writer. This excellent history is written in Dutch; but there is an abridgment of it in French, which has been translated into English. Add to this, Uytenbogard's Ecclesiastical History, written also in Dutch; Limborchi Historia Vitæ Episcopii; and the Epistolæ Clarorum Virorum, published by Limborch. Those who desire a more concise view of this contest, will find it in Limborch's Relatio Historica de Origine et Progressu Controversiarum in Fœderato Belgio de Prædestinatione et capitibus annexis, which is subjoined to the latter editions of his Theologia Christiana, or Body of Divinity. It is true, all these are Arminians; and, as impartiality requires our hearing both sides, the reader may consult Trigland's Ecclesiastical History, composed like

III. After the death of Arminius, the contest seemed to be carried on, during some years, with equal success; so that it was not easy to foresee which side would gain the ascendency. The demands of the Arminians were moderate; they required no more than a bare toleration of their religious sentiments;* and some of the first men in the republic, such as Olden-Barneveldt, Grotius, Hoogerbeets, and several others, looked upon this demand as reasonable and just. It was the opinion of those great men, that, as the points in debate had not been determined by the Belgic confession of faith, every individual had an unquestionable right to judge for himself, more especially in a free state, which had thrown off the yoke of spiritual despotism and civil tyranny. In consequence of this persuasion, they used their utmost efforts to accommodate matters, and left no methods unemployed to engage the Calvinists to treat with Christian moderation and forbearance their dissenting brethren. These efforts were at first attended with some prospect of success. Maurice, prince of Orange, and the princess dowager, his mother, countenanced these pacific measures, though the former became afterwards one of the warmest adversaries of the Arminians. Hence a conference was holden in 1611, at the Hague, between the contending parties; another took place at Delft in 1613; and with the same view, a pacific edict was issued in 1614 by the states of Holland to exhort them to charity and mutual forbearance; not to mention a number of expedients applied in vain to prevent the schism that threatened the church.† But these measures confirmed, instead of removing, the apprehensions of the Calvinists; from day to day they were still more firmly persuaded, that the Arminians aimed at nothing less than the ruin of all religion; and hence they censured their magistrates with great warmth and freedom, for interposing their authority to promote peace and union with such adversaries;‡ and those, who are well informed and impartial, must candidly acknowledge, that the Arminians were far from being sufficiently cautious in avoiding connexions with persons of loose principles, and that, by frequenting the company of those, whose sentiments were entirely different from the received doctrines of the reformed church, they furnished their enemies with a pretext for suspecting their own principles, and representing their theological system in the worst colours.

IV. It is worthy of observation, that this unhappy controversy, which assumed another form, and was rendered more comprehensive by new subjects of contention, after the synod of Dordrecht, was at this time confined to the doctrines relating to predestination and grace. The sentiments of the Arminians concerning these intricate points, were comprehended in five articles. They held,

1. "That God, from all eternity, determined to bestow salvation on those who, as he foresaw, would persevere to the end in their faith in Christ Jesus, and to inflict everlasting punishments on those who should continue in their unbelief, and resist, to the end of life, his divine succours:

2. "That Jesus Christ, by his death and sufferings, made an atonement for the sins of mankind in general, and of every individual in particular: that, however, none but those who believe in him can be partakers of that divine benefit.

3. "That true faith cannot proceed from the exercise of our natural faculties and powers, or from the force and operation of free-will, since man, in consequence of his natural corruption, is incapable either of thinking or doing any good thing; and that therefore it is necessary to his conversion and salvation, that he be *regenerated* and renewed by the operation of the Holy Ghost, which is the gift of God, through Jesus Christ.

4. "That this divine grace, or energy of the Holy Ghost, which heals the disorders of a corrupt nature, begins, advances, and brings to perfection, every thing that can be called good in man; and that, consequently, all good works, without exception, are to be attributed to God alone, and to the operation of his grace; that, nevertheless, this grace does not *force* the man to act against his inclination, but may be resisted and rendered ineffectual by the perverse will of the impenitent sinner.

5. "That they who are united to Christ by faith are thereby furnished with abundant strength, and with succours sufficient to enable them to triumph over the seductions of Satan, and the allurements of sin and temptation; but that the question, Whether such *may* fall from their faith, and forfeit finally this state of grace, has not been yet resolved with sufficient perspicuity, and must, therefore, be yet more carefully examined by an attentive study of what the Scriptures have declared in relation to this important point."

It is to be observed, that this last article was afterwards changed by the Arminians, who, in process of time, declared their sentiments with less caution, and positively affirmed, that the saints might fall from a state of grace.*

If we are to judge of men's sentiments by

wise in Dutch, and a prodigious number of polemical writings published against the Arminians.

☞ * This toleration was offered to them in the conference holden at the Hague in 1611, provided they would renounce the errors of Socinianism. See Trigland's History, and also Henry Brandt's Collatio Scriptorum habita Hagæ-Comitum.

† The writers who have given accounts of these transactions are well known: we shall only mention the first and second volumes of the Histoire de Louis XIII. by Le Vassor, who treats largely and accurately of these religious commotions, and of the civil transactions that were connected with them.

‡ The conduct of the states of Holland, who employed not only the language of persuasion, but also the voice of authority, in order to calm these commotions, and restore peace to the church, was defended, with his usual learning and eloquence, by Grotius, in two treatises. One, which contains the general principles on which this defence is founded, is entitled, "De Jure summarum Potestatum circa Sacra;" the other, in which these principles are peculiarly applied in justifying the conduct of the states, was published, in 1613, under the following title: "Ordinum Hollandiæ ac West-Frisiæ Pietas a multorum Calumniis vindicata."

* The history of these five articles, and more particularly of their reception and progress in England, has been written by Dr. Heylin, whose book was translated into Dutch by the learned and eloquent Brandt, and published at Rotterdam in 1687

their words and declarations, the tenets of the Arminians, at the period now under consideration, bear a manifest resemblance to the Lutheran system. But the Calvinists did not judge in this manner; on the contrary, they explained the words and declarations of the Arminians according to the notions they had formed of the hidden sentiments of those sectaries; and, instead of judging of their opinions by their expressions, they judged of their expressions by their opinions. They maintained, that the Arminians designed, under these specious and artful declarations, to insinuate the poison of Socinianism and Pelagianism into unwary and uninstructed minds. The secret thoughts of men are only known to Him, who is the searcher of hearts; and it is his privilege alone to pronounce judgment upon those intentions and designs which are concealed from public view. But if we were allowed to interpret the five articles now mentioned in a sense conformable to what the leading doctors among the Arminians have taught in later times concerning these points, it would be difficult to show, that the suspicions of the Calvinists were entirely groundless; for it is certain, whatever the Arminians may allege to the contrary, that the sentiments of their most eminent theological writers, after the synod of Dordrecht, concerning divine grace, and the doctrines that are connected with it, are much more accordant to the opinions of the Pelagians and Semi-Pelagians, than to those of the Lutheran church.*

V. The mild and favourable treatment which the Arminians received from the magistrates of Holland, and from several persons of merit and distinction, encouraged them to hope, that their affairs would take a prosperous turn, or at least that their cause was not desperate, when an unexpected storm arose against them, and blasted their expectations. This change was produced by causes entirely foreign to religion; and its origin must be sought in those connexions which can scarcely be admitted as possible by the philosopher, but are perpetually presented to the view of the historian. A secret misunderstanding had for some time subsisted between the stadtholder Maurice, prince of Orange, and some of the principal magistrates and ministers of the new republic, such as Olden-Barneveldt, Grotius, and Hoogerbeets; and this misunderstanding had at length broken out into an open enmity and discord. The views of this great prince are differently represented by different historians. Some allege, that he had formed the design of getting himself declared count of Holland, a dignity which William I., the glorious founder of Belgic liberty, is also said to have had in view.† Others affirm, that he only aspired to a greater degree of authority and influence than seemed consistent with the liberties of the republic; it is at least certain, that some of the principal persons in the government suspected him of aiming at supreme dominion. The leading men above mentioned opposed these designs; and these leading men were the patrons of the Arminians. The Arminians adhered to these their defenders, without whose aid they could have no prospect of security or protection. Their adversaries the Gomarists, on the contrary, seconded the views and espoused the interests of the prince, and inflamed his resentment, which had been already kindled by various suggestions, to the disadvantage of the Arminians, and of those who protected them. Thus, after mutual suspicions and discontents, the flame broke out with violence; and Maurice aimed at the ruin of those who ruled the republic without showing a proper regard to his counsels, and also of the Arminians, who espoused their cause. The men who sat at the helm of government, were cast into prison. Olden-Barneveldt, a man of gravity and wisdom, whose hairs were grown grey in the service of his country, lost his life on a public scaffold; while Grotius and Hoogerbeets were condemned to perpetual imprisonment;* under

* This is a curious remark. It would seem as if the Lutherans were not Semi-Pelagians; as if they considered man as absolutely passive in the work of his conversion and sanctification; but such an opinion surely has never been the general doctrine of their church, however rigorously Luther may have expressed himself on that head, in some unguarded moments: more especially it may be affirmed, that in later times the Lutherans are, to a man, Semi-Pelagians; and let it not be thought that this is imputed to them as a reproach.

† That Maurice aimed at the dignity of count of Holland we learn from Aubery's Memoires pour servir a l'Histoire d'Hollande et des autres Provinces Unies, sect. ii. If we are to believe Aubery (informed by his father, who was, at that time, ambassador of France at the Hague,) Olden-Barneveldt disapproved this design, prevented its execution, and lost his life by his bold opposition to the views of the prince. This account is looked upon as erroneous by Le Vassor, who takes much pains to refute it, and indeed with success, in his Histoire de Louis XIII., t. ii. p. ii. Le Clerc, in his Biblioth. Choisie, and in his History of the United Provinces, endeavours to confirm what is related by Aubery; and also affirms, that the project formed by Maurice had been entertained before by his father. The determination of this debated point is not necessary to our present purpose. It is sufficient to observe, what is acknowledged on all sides, that Olden-Barneveldt and his associates suspected prince Maurice of a design of encroaching upon the liberties of the republic, and arrogating to himself the supreme dominion. Hence arose the zeal of Barneveldt to weaken his influence, and to set bounds to his authority; hence the indignation and resentment of Maurice; and hence the downfall of the Arminian sect, which enjoyed the patronage and adhered to the interests of Olden-Barneveldt and Grotius.

* The truth of this general account of these unhappy divisions will undoubtedly be acknowledged by all parties, particularly at this period, when these tumults and commotions have subsided, and the spirit of party is less blind, partial, and violent; and the candid and ingenuous Calvinists who acknowledge this, will not thereby do the smallest prejudice to their cause. If they should even grant (what I neither pretend to affirm nor deny) that their ancestors, carried away by the impetuous spirit of the times, defended their religious opinions in a manner that was far from being consistent with the dictates of moderation and prudence, no rational conclusion can be drawn from this, either against them or the goodness of their cause; for it is well known, both by observation and experience, that unjustifiable things have often been done by men, whose characters and intentions, in general, were good and upright, and that a good cause has frequently been maintained by methods that would not bear a rigorous examination. What I have said with brevity on this subject is confirmed and amplified by Le Clerc, in his Histoire des Provinces Unies, and in the Biblioth. Choisie, tom. ii. p. 134; and also by Grotius, in his Apologeticus eorum, qui Hollandiæ et West-Frisiæ, et vicinis quibusdam Nationibus, præfuerunt ante Mutationem, quæ evenit Anno 1618. The life of Olden-Barne-

what pretext, or in consequence of what accusations or crimes, is unknown to us.* As the Arminians were not charged with any violation of the laws, but merely with departing from the established religion, their cause was not of such a nature as rendered it cognisable by a civil tribunal. That, however, this cause might be regularly decided, it was judged proper to bring it before an ecclesiastical assembly, or national synod. This method of proceeding was agreeable to the sentiments and principles of the Calvinists, who are of opinion, that all spiritual concerns and religious controversies ought to be judged and decided by an ecclesiastical assembly or council.†

VI. Accordingly a synod was convoked at Dordrecht, in 1618, by the counsels and influence of prince Maurice,‡ at which were present ecclesiastical deputies from the United Provinces, as also from the churches of England, Hesse, Bremen, Switzerland, and the Palatinate. The leading men among the Arminians appeared, before this famous assembly, to defend their cause; and they had, at their head, Simon Episcopius, who was, at that time, professor of divinity at Leyden, had formerly been the disciple of Arminius, and admired, even by his enemies, on account of the depth of his judgment, the extent of his learning, and the force of his eloquence. This eminent man addressed a discourse, full of moderation, gravity, and elocution, to the assembled divines; but this was no sooner finished, than difficulties arose, which prevented the conference the Arminians had demanded, in order to show the grounds, in reason and Scripture, on which their opinions were founded. The Arminian deputies proposed to begin the defence of their cause by refuting the opinions of the Calvinists. This proposal was rejected by the synod, which looked upon the Arminians as a set of men that lay under the charge of heresy, and therefore thought it incumbent upon them to declare and prove their own opinions, before they could be allowed to combat the sentiments of others. The design of the Arminians, in the proposal they made, was probably to get the people on their side, by such an unfavourable representation of the Calvinistical system, and of the harsh consequences that seem deducible from it, as might excite, in the minds of those who were present, a disgust to its patrons and abettors; and it is more than probable, that one of the principal reasons, that engaged the members of the synod to reject this proposal, was a consideration of the genius and talents of Episcopius, and an apprehension of the effects of his eloquence upon the multitude. When all the methods employed to persuade the Arminians to submit to the manner of proceeding, proposed by the synod, proved ineffectual, they were excluded from that assembly, and returned home, complaining bitterly of the rigour and partiality with which they had been treated. Their cause was nevertheless tried in their absence; and, in consequence of a strict examination of their writings, they were pronounced guilty of pestilential errors, and condemned as corruptors of the true religion. This sentence was followed by its natural effects, which were the excommunication of the Arminians, the suppression of their religious assemblies, and the deprivation of their ministers. In this unhappy contest, the candid and impartial observer will easily perceive that faults were committed on both sides. Which of the contending parties may justly be thought most worthy of censure, is a point, whose discussion is foreign to our present purpose.*

veldt, written in Dutch, was published in 1648. The history of his trial, and of the judgment pronounced on the famous triumvirate, mentioned above, was drawn by Gerard Brandt from authentic records, and published under the following title: Historie van de Rechts-pleginge gehouden in den jaaren 1618 en 1619, omtrent de drie gevangene Heeren Johan van Olden-Barneveldt, Rombout Hoogerbeets, en Hugo de Groot; a third edition of this book, augmented with annotations, appeared in 1723. The History of the Life and Actions of Grotius, composed in Dutch by Casper Brandt and Adrian van Cattenburg, and drawn mostly from original papers, throws a considerable degree of light on the history of these transactions. This famous work was published in 1727, under the following title: Historie van het leven des Heeren Huig de Groot, beschrewen tot den Anfang van zyn Gesand chap wegens de Koninginne en Kroone van Zweden aanit Hof van Vrankryck, door Caspard Brandt, en vervolgt tot zyn doodt door Adrian van Cattenburg. Those who desire to form a true and accurate notion of the character and conduct of Grotius, and to see him as it were near hand, must have recourse to this excellent work, since almost all the other accounts of this great man are insipid, lifeless, and exhibit little else than a poor shadow, instead of a real and animated substance. The life of Grotius, composed by Burigni in French, deserves perhaps to be included in this general censure; it is at least a very indifferent and superficial performance. ☞ There appeared in Holland a warm vindication of the memory of this great man, in a work published in 1727, and entitled, Grotii Manes ab iniquis Obtrectationibus vindicati; accedit Scriptorum ejus, tum editorum tum in editorum, Conspectus Triplex. See the following note.

☞ * Dr. Mosheim, however impartial, seems to have consulted more the authors of one side than of the other, probably because they are more numerous, and more generally known. When he published this history, the world had not been favoured with the Letters, Memoirs, and Negotiations of Sir Dudley Carleton; which lord Royston (afterwards earl of Hardwicke) drew forth from his inestimable treasure of historical manuscripts, and presented to the public, or rather at first to a select number of persons, to whom he distributed a small number of copies of these Negotiations, printed at his own expense. They were soon translated both into Dutch and French; and though it cannot be affirmed that the spirit of party is no where discoverable in them, yet they contain anecdotes with respect both to Olden-Barneveldt and Grotius, which the Arminians, and the other patrons of these two great men, have been studious to conceal. These anecdotes, though they may not be sufficient to justify the severities exercised against these eminent men, would, however, have prevented Dr. Mosheim from saying that he knew not under what pretext they were arrested.

☞ † The Calvinists are not particular in this; and indeed it is natural that debates, purely theological, should be discussed in an assembly of divines.

☞ ‡ Our author always forgets to mention the order, issued by the states-general, for the convocation of this famous synod; and, by his manner of expressing himself, and particularly by the phrase (Mauritio *auctore*,) would seem to insinuate, that it was by the prince that this assembly was called together. The legitimacy of the manner of convoking this synod was questioned by Olden-Barneveldt, who maintained that the states-general had no sort of authority in matters of religion, not even the power of assembling a synod; affirming that this was an act of sovereignty, that belonged to each province separately and respectively. See Carleton's Letters.

* The writers who have given accounts of the sy-

VII. We shall not here appreciate either the merit or demerit of the divines who were assembled in this famous synod; but we cannot help observing that their sanctity, wisdom, and virtue, have been exalted beyond all measure by the Calvinists, while their partiality, violence, and their other defects, have been exaggerated with some degree of malignity by the Arminians.* There is no doubt that, among the members of this assembly, who sat in judgment upon the Arminians, there were several persons equally distinguished by their learning, piety, and integrity, who acted with upright intentions, and had not the least notion, that the steps they were taking, or encouraging, were inconsistent with equity and wisdom. On the other hand it clearly appears, that the Arminians had reason to complain of several circumstances that strike us in the history of this remarkable period. It is evident in the first place, that the ruin of their community was a point not only premeditated, but determined even before the meeting of the national synod;† and that this synod was not so much assembled to examine their doctrine, in order to see whether it was worthy of toleration and indulgence, as to publish and execute, with a certain solemnity, with an air of justice, and with the suffrages and consent of foreign divines, whose authority was respectable, a sentence already drawn up and agreed upon by those who had the principal direction of these affairs. It is farther to be observed, that the accusers and adversaries of the Arminians were their judges, and that Bogerman, who presided in this synod, was distinguished by his peculiar hatred of that sect; that neither the Dutch nor foreign divines had the liberty of giving their suffrages according to their own private sentiments, but were obliged to deliver the opinions of the princes and magistrates, of whose orders they were the depositories;‡ that the influence of the lay deputies, who appeared in the synod with commissions from the states-general and the prince of Orange, was still superior to that of the ecclesiastical members, who sat as judges; and, lastly, that the solemn promise, made to the Arminians, when they were summoned before the synod, that they should be allowed to enjoy the liberty of explaining and defending their opinions as far as they thought proper or necessary to their justification, was manifestly violated.*

VIII. The Arminians, in consequence of the decision of the synod, were considered as enemies of their country and of its established religion; and they were accordingly treated with great severity. They were deprived of all their posts and employments, whether ecclesiastical or civil; and, which they looked upon as a yet more intolerable instance of the rigour of their adversaries, their ministers were silenced, and their congregations were suppressed. They refused obedience to the order, by which their pastors were prohibited from performing, in public, their ministerial functions; and thus they drew upon themselves anew the resentment of their superiors who punished them by fines, imprisonment, exile, and other marks of ignominy. To avoid these vexations, many of them retired to Antwerp, others fled into France; while a considerable number, accepting the invitation sent to them by Frederic, duke of Holstein, formed a colony, which settled in the dominions of that prince, and built for themselves a handsome town called Fredericstadt, in the duchy of Sleswick, where their descendants still live unmolested, in the open profession and free exercise of their religion. The heads of this colony were persons of distinction, who had been obliged to leave their native country on account of these troubles, particularly Adrian Vander-Wael, who was the first governor of the new city.† Among the persecuted ecclesiastics, who followed this colony, were, the famous Vorstius, (who, by his religious sentiments, which differed little from the Socinian system, had rendered the Arminians particularly odious,) Grevinckhovius (a man of a resolute spirit, who had been pastor at Rotterdam,) Goulart, Grevius, Walther, Narsius, and others.‡

IX. After the death of prince Maurice, which happened in 1625, the Arminian exiles

nod of Dordrecht, are mentioned by Jo. Albert Fabricius, in his Biblioth. Græc. vol. xi. p. 723. The most ample account of this famous assembly has been given by Brandt, in the second and third volumes of his History of the Reformation in the United Provinces; but, as this author is an Arminian, it will not be improper to compare his relation with a work of the learned Leydekker, in which the piety and justice of the proceedings of this synod are vindicated against the censures of Brandt. This work, which is composed in Dutch, was published in 1707 under the following title: Eere van de nationale Synode van Dordrecht, voorgestaan en bevestigd tegen de beschuldingen, van G. Brandt. After comparing diligently these two productions, I can see no enormous error in Brandt; for, in truth, these two writers do not so much differ about facts, as they do in the reasoning they deduce from them, and in their accounts of the causes whence they proceeded. The reader will do well to consult the Letters of the learned and worthy Mr. John Hale of Eton, who was an impartial spectator of the proceedings of the synod, and who relates with candour and simplicity what he saw and heard.

* All that appeared unfair to the Arminians in the proceedings of this synod has been collected in a Dutch book, entitled, Nulliteyten, Miskandelingen, ende onbyllike, Proceduren des nationalen Synodi gehouden binnen Dordrecht, &c. 1619.

† This assertion is of too weighty a nature to be advanced without sufficient proof. Our author quotes no authority for it.

☞ ‡ Here our author has fallen into a palpable mistake. The Dutch divines had no commission but from their respective consistories, or subordinate ecclesiastical assemblies; nor are they ever depositories of the orders of their magistrates, who have lay-deputies to represent them both in provincial and national synods. As to the English and other foreign doctors who appeared in the synod, the case perhaps may have been somewhat different.

* See Le Vassor, Histoire du Regne de Louis XIII. tom. iii. livr. xii. p. 365,—and Mosheim's preface to the Latin translation of the account of the synod of Dordrecht, written by the *ever-memorable* John Hale.

† The history of this colony is accurately related in the famous letters published by Philip Limborch and Christian Hartsoeker, entitled, Epistolæ præstantium et eruditorum virorum ecclesiasticæ et theologicæ, of which the last edition was published at Amsterdam in 1704. See also Molleri Introductio in Histor. Chersonesi Cimbricæ, p. ii. p. 108. and Pontoppidani Annales Ecclesiæ Danicæ Diplomatici, tom. iii. p. 714.

‡ For an ample account of Vorstius, see Molleri Cimbria Literatr. tom. ii. where we find a particular account of the other ecclesiastics above mentioned.

experienced the mildness and clemency of his brother and successor Frederic Henry, under whose administration they were recalled from banishment, and restored to their former reputation and tranquillity. Those who had taken refuge in the kingdom of France, and in the Spanish Netherlands, were the first that embraced this occasion of returning to their native country, where they erected churches in several places, and more particularly in the cities of Amsterdam and Rotterdam, under the mild shade of religious toleration. That they might also have a public seminary for the instruction of their youth, and the propagation of their theological principles, they founded a college at Amsterdam, in which two professors were appointed to instruct the candidates for the ministry, in the various branches of literature and science, sacred and profane. Simon Episcopius was the first professor of theology among the Arminians; and, since his time, the seminary now mentioned has been, in general, furnished with professors eminent for their learning and genius, such as Courcelles, Poelenburg, Limborch, Le Clerc, Cattenburg,* and Wetstein.

X. We have already seen that the original difference, between the Arminians and the Calvinists, was entirely confined to the five points mentioned above, relative to the doctrines of predestination and grace; and it was the doctrine of the former concerning these points alone that occasioned their condemnation in the synod of Dordrecht. It is farther to be observed, that these points, as explained at that time by the Arminians, seemed to differ very little from the Lutheran system. But after the dissolution of the synod, and especially after the return of the Arminian exiles into their native country, the theological system of this community underwent a remarkable change, and assumed an aspect that distinguished it entirely from that of all other Christian churches; for then they gave a new explication of these five articles, that made them almost coincide with the doctrine of those who deny the necessity of divine succours in the work of conversion, and in the paths of virtue. They even went farther; and, bringing the greatest part of the doctrines of Christianity before the tribunal of reason, they modified them considerably, and reduced them to an excessive degree of simplicity. Arminius, the parent and founder of the community, was undoubtedly the inventor of this new form of doctrine, and taught it to his disciples;† but it was first digested into a regular system, and embellished with the charms of a masculine eloquence, by Episcopius, whose learning and genius have given him a place among the Arminian doctors, next to their founder.*

XI. The great and ultimate end which the Arminians seem to have in view is, that Christians, though divided in their opinions, may be united in fraternal charity and love, and thus be formed into one family or community, notwithstanding the diversity of their theological sentiments. In order to execute their benevolent purpose, they maintain, that Christ demands from his servants more *virtue* than *faith;* that he has confined, to a few articles, that belief which is essential to salvation; that, on the other hand, the rules of practice he has prescribed are extremely large in their extent; and that charity and virtue ought to be the principal study of true Christians. Their definition of a true Christian is somewhat latitudinarian in point of belief. According to their account, every person is a genuine subject of the kingdom of Christ, "1. who receives the Scriptures, and more especially the New Testament, as the rule of his faith, however he may think proper to interpret and explain these sacred oracles; 2. who abstains from idolatry, polytheism, and all their concomitant absurdities; 3. who leads a decent, honest, and virtuous life, directed and regulated by the laws of God; and, 4. who never discovers a spirit of persecution, discord, or ill-will, toward those who differ from him in their religious sentiments, or in their manner of interpreting Scripture." Thus the wide bosom of the Arminian church is open to Christians in general, however they may differ in some of their theologi-

* There is an accurate account of these and the other Arminian writers given by Adrian van Cattenburg, in his Bibliotheca Scriptorum Remonstrantium, printed at Amsterdam in 1728.

† It is a common opinion, that the ancient Arminians, who flourished before the synod of Dordrecht, were much more sound in their opinions, and strict in their morals, than those who have lived since that period; that Arminius himself only rejected the Calvinistical doctrine of absolute decrees, and what he took to be its immediate consequences; adopting in all other points the doctrines received in the reformed churches: but that his disciples, and more especially Episcopius, had boldly transgressed the bounds which had been wisely prescribed by their master, and had gone over to the Pelagians, and even to the Socinians. Such, I say, is the opinion commonly entertained concerning this matter. But it appears, on the contrary, evident to me, that Arminius himself had laid the plan of that theological system, which was, in after-times, embraced by his followers, and that he had instilled the main principles of it into the minds of his disciples; and that these latter, and particularly Episcopius, did really no more than bring this plan to a greater degree of perfection, and propagate, with more courage and perspicuity the doctrines it contained. I have the testimony of Arminius to support this notion, beside many others that might be alleged in its behalf: for, in the last will made by this eminent man, a little before his death, he plainly and positively declares, that the great object he had in view, in all his theological and ministerial labours, was to unite in one community, cemented by the bonds of fraternal charity, all sects and denominations of Christians, the papists excepted. His words, as they are recorded in the funeral oration, which was composed on occasion of his death by Bertius, are as follow: "Ea proposui et docui . . . quæ ad propagationem amplificationemque veritatis religionis Christianæ, veri Dei cultus, communis pietatis, et sanctæ inter homines conversationis, denique ad convenientem Christiano nomini tranquillitatem et pacem juxta verbum Dei possent conferre, excludens ex iis papatum, cum quo nulla unitas fidei, nullum pietatis aut Christianæ pacis vinculum servari potest." These words, in their amount, coincide perfectly with the modern system of Arminianism, which extends the limits of the Christian church, and relaxes the bonds of fraternal communion in such a manner, that Christians of all denominations, whatever their sentiments and opinions may be (papists excepted,) may be formed into one religious body, and live together in brotherly love and concord.

* The life of this eminent man was composed in Latin by the learned and judicious Limborch, and is singularly worthy of an attentive perusal. It was published at Amsterdam in 1701

cal opinions. The papists alone are excluded from this extensive communion, because they deem it lawful* to persecute those who will not submit to the yoke of the Roman pontiff.† It is not our design here either to justify or condemn these latitudinarian terms of communion; but it may be said, that, if other Christian churches should adopt them, diversity of sentiment would be no longer an obstacle to mutual love and concord.

XII. From all this it appears, that the Arminian community was a kind of medley, composed of persons of different principles, and that, properly speaking, it could have no fixed and stable form or system of doctrine. The Arminians, however, foreseeing that this circumstance might be objected to them as a matter of reproach, and unwilling to pass for a society connected by no common principles or bond of union, have adopted, as their Confession of Faith, a kind of theological system, drawn up by Episcopius, and expressed, for the most part, in the words and phrases of Scripture.‡ But as none of their pastors are obliged, either by oath, declaration, or tacit compact, to adhere strictly to this confession, and as, on the contrary, by the fundamental constitution of this community, every one is authorized to interpret its expressions (which are in effect susceptible of various significations) in a manner conformable to their peculiar sentiments; it evidently follows, that we cannot thence deduce an accurate and consistent view of Arminianism, or know, with certainty, what doctrines are adopted or rejected by this sect. Hence it happens, that the Arminian doctors differ widely among themselves concerning some of the most important doctrines of Christianity;* and they can scarcely be said to agree universally, or to be entirely uniform, in their sentiments of any one point, if we except the doctrines of predestination and grace. They all, indeed, unanimously adhere to the doctrine that excluded their ancestors from the communion of the reformed churches, importing 'that the love of God extends itself equally to all mankind; that no mortal is rendered finally unhappy by an eternal and invincible decree; and that the misery of those who perish comes from themselves;' but they explain this doctrine in a very different manner from that in which it was formerly understood. Be that as it may, this is the fundamental doctrine of the Arminians, and whoever opposes it, becomes thereby an adversary to the whole community; whereas those whose objections are levelled at particular tenets which are found in the writings of the Arminian divines, cannot be said, with any degree of propriety, to attack or censure the Arminian church, whose theological system, a few articles excepted, is vague and uncertain,† and is not characterised by any fixed set of doctrines and principles. Such only attack certain doctors of that communion, who are divided among themselves, and do not agree, even in their explications of the doctrine relating to the extent of the divine love and mercy, though this be the fundamental point that occasioned their separation from the reformed churches.

XIII. The Armenian church makes at present but an inconsiderable figure, when compared with the reformed; and, if credit may be given to public report, it declines from day to day. The Arminians have only in the United Provinces thirty-four congregations more or less numerous, which are furnished with forty-four pastors; beside these, their church at Fredericstadt, in the duchy of Sleswick, still subsists. It cannot, however, be said, that the credit and influence of their religious principles have declined with the external lustre of their community, since it is well known that their sentiments were early adopted in several countries, and were secretly received by many who had not the courage to profess them openly. Every one is acquainted with the change that has taken place in the established church of England, whose clergy, generally speaking, since the time of archbishop Laud, have em-

☞ * It is not only on account of their persecuting spirit, but also on account of their idolatrous worship, that the Arminians exclude the Papists from their communion. See the following note.

† For a full and accurate representation of this matter, it will be sufficient for the reader to have recourse to that treatise which is published in the first volume of the works of Episcopius (p. 508.) under the following title: Verus Theologus Remonstrans, sive veræ Remonstrantium Theologiæ de errantibus dilucida Declaratio. This treatise is written with precision and perspicuity. Le Clerc, in the dedication prefixed to his Latin translation of Dr. Hammond's Paraphrase and Commentary on the New Testament, gives a brief account of the Arminian principles and terms of communion in the following words, addressed to the learned men of that sect: 'You declare," says he, "that they *only* are excluded from your communion, who are chargeable with idolatry, who do not receive the Scriptures as the rule of faith, who trample upon the precepts of Christ by their licentious manners and actions, and who persecute those who differ from them in matters of religion."* Many writers affirm, that the Arminians acknowledge, as their brethren, all those who receive that form of doctrine which is known under the denomination of the Apostles' Creed. But that these writers are in an error, appears sufficiently from what has been already said on this subject, and is confirmed by the express testimony of Le Clerc, who (in his Biblioth. Ancienne et Mod. tom. xxv. p. 110,) declares, that it is not true that the Arminians admit to their communion all those who receive the Apostles' Creed; his words are, "Ils se trompent; ils (the Arminians) offrent la communion a tous ceux qui recoivent l'ecriture sainte comme la seule regle de la foi et des mœurs, et qui ne sont ni idolatres ni persecuteurs."

‡ This Confession of Faith is extant in Latin, Dutch, and German. The Latin edition of it is to be found in the works of Episcopius, tom. ii. p. ii. p. 69; where may be found also a Defence of this Confession against the objections of the professors of divinity at Leyden.

* The original words of Le Clerc are, "Profiteri soletis.... eos duntaxat a vobis excludi, qui idololatria sunt contaminati, qui minime habent Scripturam pro fidei norma, qui impuris moribus sancta Christi præcepta conculcant, aut qui denique alios religionis causa vexant."

* They who will be at the pains of comparing the theological writings of Episcopius, Courcelles, Limborch, Le Clerc, and Cattenburg, will see clearly the diversity of sentiment that reigns among the Arminian doctors.

☞ † What renders the Arminian Confession of Faith an uncertain representation of the sentiments of the community, is, the liberty in which every pastor is indulged of departing from it, when he finds any of its doctrines contradictory to his private opinions. See the Introduction to the Arminian Confession of Faith, in the third volume of the French abridgment of Brandt's History.

braced the Arminian doctrine concerning predestination and grace, and, since the restoration of Charles II., have discovered a strong propensity to several other tenets of the Arminian church. Beside this, whoever has any acquaintance with the world, must know, that, in many of the courts of protestant princes, and, in general, among those persons who pretend to be wiser than the multitude, the following fundamental principle of Arminianism is adopted: "That those doctrines, whose belief is necessary to salvation, are very few in number; and that every one is to be left at full liberty, with respect to his private sentiments of God and religion, provided his life and actions be conformable to the rules of piety and virtue." Even the United Provinces, which saw within their bosom the defeat of Arminianism, are at this time sensible of a considerable change in that respect; for, while the patrons of Calvinism in that republic acknowledge, that the community, which makes an external profession of Arminianism, declines gradually both in its numbers and influence, they, at the same time, complain, that its doctrines and spirit gain ground from day to day; that they have even insinuated themselves more or less into the bosom of the established church, and infected the theological system of many of those very pastors who are appointed to maintain the doctrine and authority of the synod of Dordrecht. The progress of Arminianism, in other countries, is abundantly known; and its votaries in France, Geneva, and many parts of Switzerland, are certainly very numerous.*

The external forms of divine worship and ecclesiastical government, in the Arminian church, are almost the same with those which are in use among the Presbyterians. As, however, the leading men among the Arminians are peculiarly ambitious of maintaining their correspondence and fraternal intercourse with the church of England, and leave no circumstance unimproved that may tend to confirm this union; so they discover, upon all occasions, their approbation of the episcopal form of ecclesiastical government, and profess to regard it as most ancient, as truly sacred, and as superior to all other institutions of church-polity.*

CHAPTER IV.

The History of the Sect called Quakers.

I. THE sect of Quakers received this denomination, in the year 1650, from Gervas Bennet, a justice of peace in Derbyshire,† partly on account of the convulsive agitations and shakings of the body with which their discourses to the people were usually attended, and partly on account of the exhortation addressed to this magistrate by Fox and his companions, who, when they were called before him, desired him, with a loud voice and a vehement emotion of body, 'to tremble at the word of the Lord.' However sarcastical this appellation may be, when considered in its origin, the members of this sect are willing to adopt it, provided it be rightly understood; they prefer, nevertheless, to be called, in allusion to that doctrine which is the fundamental principle of their association, 'Children or Confessors of Light.' In their conversation and intercourse

☞ * It may not, however, be improper to observe here, that the progress of Arminianism has been greatly retarded, and that its cause daily declines in Germany and several parts of Switzerland, in consequence of the ascendency which the Leibnitian and Wolfian philosophy has gained in these countries, and particularly among the clergy and men of learning. Leibnitz and Wolff, by attacking that liberty of *indifference*, which is supposed to imply the power of acting, not only *without* but *against* motives, struck at the very foundation of the Arminian system. But this was not all: for, by considering the multiplicity of words that compose the universe, as one system or whole, whose greatest possible perfection is the ultimate end of creative goodness, and the sovereign purpose of governing wisdom, they removed from the doctrine of predestination those arbitrary procedures and narrow views, with which the Calvinists are supposed to have loaded it, and gave it a new, a more pleasing, and a more philosophical aspect. As the Leibnitians laid down this great end, as the supreme object of God's universal dominion, and the scope to which *all* his dispensations are directed, so they concluded, that, if this *end* was proposed, it *must* be accomplished. Hence the doctrine of necessity seemed proper to fulfil the purposes of a predestination founded in wisdom and goodness; a necessity, physical and mechanical in the motions of material and inanimate things, but moral and spiritual in the voluntary determinations of intelligent beings, in consequence of prepollent motives, which produce their effects with certainty, though these effects be contingent, and by no means the offspring of an absolute and essentially immutable fatality. These principles are evidently applicable to the main doctrines of Calvinism; by them predestination is confirmed, though modified with respect to its reasons and its ends; by them irresistible grace (irresistible in a moral sense) is maintained upon the hypothesis of prepollent motives and a moral necessity. The perseverance of the saints is also explicable upon the same system, by a series of moral causes producing a series of moral effects. In consequence of all this, several divines of the German church have applied the Leibnitian and Wolfian philosophy to the illustration of the doctrines of Christianity; and the learned Canzius has written a book expressly to show the eminent use that may be made of that philosophy in throwing light upon the chief articles of our faith. See his Philosophiæ Leibnitianæ et Wolfianæ Usus in Theologia per præcipua Fidei capita. auctore Israele Theoph. Canzio. See also Wittenbach's Tentamen Theologiæ Dogmaticæ Methodo Scientifica pertractatæ; but, above all, consult the famous work of Leibnitz, entitled, "Essais de Theodicee. sur la Bonte de Dieu, la Liberte de l'Homme, et l'Origine du Mal." It is remarkable enough, that the Leibnitian system has been embraced by very few, scarcely by any of the English Calvinists. Can this be owing to a want of inclination toward philosophical discussions? This cannot be said. The scheme of necessity, and of partial evils tending to universal good. has indeed been fostered in some parts of Great Britain, and even has turned some zealous Arminians into moderate and philosophical Calvinists. But the zealous Calvinists have, for the most part, adhered firmly to their theology, and blended no philosophical principles with their system: and it is certain, that the most eminent philosophers have been found, in general, among the Arminians. If both Calvinists and Arminians claim a King, it is certain that the latter alone can boast of a Newton, a Locke, a Clarke, and a Boyle.

* Hence, to omit many other circumstances that show unquestionably the truth of this observation, the Arminians have been at great pains to represent Grotius, their hero and their oracle, as a particular admirer of the constitution and government of the church of England, which he preferred to all other forms of ecclesiastical polity. See what Le Clerc has published on this subject at the end of the edition of Grotius' book, de Veritate Religionis Christianæ which he gave at the Hague in 1724, p. 376.

† See George Sewell's History of the Quakers, p 23.—Neal's History of the Puritans, vol. iv. p. 32.

with each other, they use no other term of appellation than that of *Friend*.*

This sect had its rise in England, in those unhappy times of confusion, anarchy, and civil discord, when every political or religious fanatic, who had formed a new plan of government, or invented a new system of theology, came forth with his novelties to public view, and propagated them with impunity among a fickle and unthinking multitude. Its parent or founder was George Fox,† a shoemaker of a dark and melancholy complexion, and of a visionary and enthusiastic turn of mind. About the year 1647, which was the twenty-fourth year of his age, he began to stroll through several counties in England, giving himself out for a person divinely inspired, and exhorting the people to attend to the voice of the divine word, that lies hidden in the hearts of all men. After the decapitation of Charles I., when all laws, both civil and ecclesiastical, seemed to be entirely suspended, if not extinct, Fox exerted his fanatical powers with new vigour, and formed more ambitious and extensive views. Having acquired a considerable number of disciples of both sexes, who were strongly infected with his wild enthusiasm, he excited great tumults in several parts of England, and, in 1650, went so far as to disturb the devotion of those who were assembled in the churches for the purposes of public worship, declaring that all such assemblies were useless and unchristian. For these extravagances, both he and his companions were sometimes thrown into prison, and chastised, as disturbers of the peace, by the civil magistrate.*

II. The first association of Quakers consisted chiefly of visionary fanatics, and of persons who really seemed to be disordered in their brains; and hence they committed many enormities, which the modern Quakers endeavour to alleviate and diminish, but which they neither pretend to justify nor to approve; for the greatest part of them were riotous and tumultuous in the highest degree, and even their female disciples, forgetting the delicacy and decency peculiar to their sex, bore their part in these disorders. They ran, like Bacchanals, through the towns and villages, declaiming against episcopacy, presbyterianism, and every fixed form of religion; railed at public and stated worship; affronted and mocked the clergy, even in the very exercise of their ministerial functions;† trampled upon the laws

* Sewell, p. 624.

☞ † The anonymous writer of a letter to Dr. Formey seems much offended at that gentleman on account of his calling George Fox a man of a turbulent spirit, &c. He tells us, on the contrary, that, from all the information worthy of credit which he was able to procure, Fox was "a man of so meek, contented, easy, steady, and tender a disposition, that it was a pleasure to be in his company; that he exercised no authority but over evil, and that every where, and in all, but with love, compassion, and long-suffering." This account he takes from Penn; and it is very probable that he has looked no farther, unless it be to the curious portrait which Thomas Ellwood, another Quaker, has given of Fox,—a portrait in which there is such an affected jingle of words as shows the author to have been more attentive to the arrangement of his sentences, than to a true exhibition of the character of his original: for we are told by Ellwood that this same George Fox was deep in divine knowledge, powerful in preaching, fervent in prayer, quick in discerning, sound in judgment (*risum teneatis, amici?*)—manly in personage, grave in gesture, courteous in conversation, weighty in communication, &c. After having thus painted George after the *fancy* of his two brethren (for fancy is the Quaker's fountain of light and truth,) the letter-writer observes, that Dr. Formey has taken his account of George's turbulence and fanaticism from Mosheim's Ecclesiastical History. As Mosheim is dead, and cannot defend himself, may I be permitted to request this anonymous letter-writer, who appears to be a candid and rational man, to cast an eye upon Sewell's History of the Quakers, and to follow this *meek, courteous* and *modest* George, running like a wild man through several counties, refusing to pay due homage to his sovereign, interrupting the ministers in the public celebration of divine service at Nottingham, Mansfield, and Bosworth? It is remarkable, that the very learned and worthy Dr. Henry More, who was not himself without a strong tincture of enthusiasm, and who looked upon Penn as a pious Christian, treated nevertheless George Fox as a melancholy fanatic, and as one possessed with the Devil. See his Myst. of Godliness, B x. ch. xiii. and also Schol. in Dialogue v. sect. 5

* Beside the ordinary writers of the ecclesiastical history of this century, the curious reader will do well to consult Croesii Historia Quakeriana, tribus libris comprehensa. A physician named Kohlhansius, who was born a Lutheran, but afterwards became a Quaker, published critical remarks upon this history, under the title of Dilucidationes, and it must be acknowledged, that there are many inaccuracies in the work of Croesius: it is, however, much less faulty than another history of this sect, which was published at Cologne in 1692, under the following title: Histoire abregee de la Naissance et du Progres du Kouakerisme, avec celle de ses Dogmes; for the anonymous author of the latter history, instead of relating well-attested facts, has compiled, without either discernment or choice, such an extravagant medley of truth and falsehood, as is rather adapted to excite laughter than to administer instruction. See the second book of Croesius' Historia Quakeriana, p. 322, and 376, as also Le Clerc, Biblioth. Universelle et Historique, tom. xxii. p. 53.—The most ample and authentic account of this sect is that which was composed by George Sewell from a great variety of genuine records, and partly from the papers of Fox, its founder, and published under the following title: "The History of the Christian people called Quakers." This work is remarkable for the industry and accuracy which the author has discovered in compiling it; but, as Sewell was himself a Quaker, he is sometimes chargeable with concealing, diminishing, or representing under artful colours, many things, which, if impartially related, *must* have appeared dishonourable, and *might* have been detrimental, to his community. It must however be granted, that, notwithstanding these defects, his history is abundantly sufficient to enable an impartial and intelligent reader to form a just and satisfactory idea of this visionary sect. Voltaire has also entertained the public with four Letters, concerning the religion, manners, and history of the Quakers, in his Melanges de Literature, d'Histoire et de Philosophie, which are written with his usual wit and elegance, but are rather adapted to amuse than instruct. The conversation between him and Andrew Pitt, an eminent Quaker in London (which is related in these letters,) may be true in general; but, to render the account of it still more pleasing, the ingenious writer has embellished it with effusions of wit and fancy, and even added some particulars, that are rather drawn from imagination than memory. It is from the books already mentioned that the French Dissertation on the Religion of the Quakers (which is inserted in the third volume of the splendid work, entitled, Ceremonies et Coutumes Religieuses de tous les Peuples,) is chiefly compiled, though with less attention and accuracy than might have been expected. A Lutheran writer, named Frederic Ernest Meis, has given an account of the English Quakers in a German work, entitled, Entwurff der Kirchen Ordnung und Gebrauche der Quacker in Engeland, 1715.

† A female, contrary to the modesty of her sex, appeared in Whitehall chapel *stark naked*, in the midst of public worship, when Cromwell was there

and the authority of the magistrates, under the pretext of being actuated by a divine impulse; and made use of their pretended inspiration to excite vehement commotions both in state and church. Hence it is not at all surprising, that the secular arm was at length raised against these pernicious fanatics, and that many of them were severely chastised for their extravagance and folly.* Cromwell himself, who was, in general, an enemy to no sect, however enthusiastical it might be, entertained uneasy apprehensions from the frantic violence of the Quakers, and therefore, in his first thoughts, formed a resolution to suppress their rising community. But when he perceived that they treated with contempt both his promises and threats, and were, in effect, too powerful or too headstrong to yield to either, he prudently abstained from the use of force, and contented himself with employing wise measures and precautions to prevent their fomenting sedition among the people, or undermining the foundations of his new sovereignty.†

III. In process of time, the fumes of this excessive fanaticism began to evaporate, and the ardent impetuosity of the rising sect seemed gradually to subside; nor did the *divine light*, of which the Quakers boast, produce such tumults in church and state, as at the first declaration of their celestial pretensions. In the reign of Charles II. both their religious doctrine and discipline assumed a more regular and permanent form, by the care and industry of Fox, assisted, in this very necessary undertaking, by Robert Barclay, George Keith, and Samuel Fisher, men of learning and abilities, who became, notwithstanding, members of this strange community. Fox stood in urgent need of such able assistants; for his gross ignorance had rendered his religion, hitherto, a confused medley of incoherent tenets and visions. The new triumvirate, therefore, used their utmost endeavours to digest these under certain heads, and to reduce them to a sort of theological system.* But such was the change of times, that the wiser and more moderate Quakers of England suffered more vexations, and were involved in greater calamities, than had fallen to the lot of their frantic and turbulent ancestors. These vexations, indeed, were not so much the consequence of their religious principles, as of their singular customs and manners in civil life; for they would never give to magistrates those titles of honour and pre-eminence which are designed to mark the respect due to their authority; they also refused obstinately to take the oath of allegiance to their sovereign,† and to pay tithes to the clergy; hence they were looked upon as rebellious subjects, and, on that account, were frequently punished with great severity.‡ In the reign of James II. and more particularly about the year 1685, they began to see more prosperous days, and to enjoy the sweets of toleration and liberty, which they owed, not to the clemency of the government, but to the friendship of that monarch for the famous William Penn,§ who had been employed by him in matters of the utmost moment, and had rendered him signal and important services.‖ What James had

present. Another entered the parliament-house, with a trencher in her hand, which she broke in pieces, saying, "Thus shall he be broken in pieces." Thomas Adams, having complained to the protector of the imprisonment of some of his friends, and not finding redress, took off his cap and tore it in pieces, saying, "So shall thy government be torn from thee and thy house." Several, pretending an extraordinary message from heaven, went about the streets, denouncing the judgments of God against the protector and his council; and one approached the door of the parliament-house with a drawn sword, and wounded several persons, saying, that "he was inspired by the Holy Spirit to kill every man who sat in that house." The most extravagant Quaker who appeared at this time, was James Naylor, formerly an officer, a man of parts, and so much admired by these fanatics, that they blasphemously styled him, "the everlasting son of righteousness, the prince of peace, the only begotten son of God, the fairest among ten thousand." See Neal's History of the Puritans, and the Life and Trial of Naylor. The anonymous author of the Letter to Dr. Formey, seems to have lost sight of the state of Quakerism in the time of Fox, when he denies that the charge of turbulence and fanaticism can be proved against him or his friends, and gives the gentle denomination of *imprudence* to the extravagances exhibited by the Quakers under Charles I. and the commonwealth. The single story of Naylor, who was the convert and pupil of Fox, and the letters, full of blasphemous absurdity, written to this "Rose of Sharon," this "new Jesus," by Hannah Stranger, Richard Fairman, and others, show the horrid vein of fanaticism that ran through this visionary sect. See these letters in the Life and Trial of Naylor, who, though cruelly scourged, was, however, whipped into his senses, or at least, brought by his sufferings into a calmer state of mind. See also Satan Enthroned. If Quakerism be now in England on a more rational footing, we may congratulate its members upon the happy change, but at the same time condole with them on the approaching annihilation of their sect; for, if *reason* gets in among them, the *spirit* (I mean *their* spirit,) will soon be quenched, and fancy being no more the only criterion of truth, the fundamental principle of their existence will be destroyed. In such a catastrophe, the abettors of ancient Quakerism will find some resource among the Methodists.

* Neal's History, vol. iv.—Sewell.

† The earl of Clarendon tells us, in his History of the Rebellion, that the Quakers always persevered in their bitter enmity against Cromwell! See Sewell's History, book i.

* For an account of the life and writings of Barclay, see the General Dictionary. Sewell, in his History, gives an ample account of Keith. There is also particular mention made of Fisher, in the Unschuldige Nachrichten, An. 1750, p. 338.

☞ † This refusal to take the oath of allegiance did not proceed from any disaffection to the government, but from a persuasion that all oaths were unlawful, and that swearing, even upon the most solemn occasions, was forbidden in the New Testament. They also sincerely believed, that they were as much obliged to obedience by an affirmation, which they were willing to make, as by an oath.

‡ See a circumstantial account of their sufferings under Charles II. in Neal's fourth volume, p. 313, 353, 396, 432, 510, 552, 569.—Burnet's History of his own Time, vol. i. p. 271.—Sewell's Hist.

§ See Sewell's History.

☞ ‖ The indulgence of James toward the Quakers and other dissenters from the established church, was, in fact, founded on a zeal for popery, and designed to favour the Roman Catholics. More particularly the order which he sent to the lord-mayor of London, on the 7th of November, 1687, to dispense with an oath from the Quakers, was evidently designed to open a door to the catholics to bear offices in the state without a legal qualification. At the same time it is probable enough, that a personal attachment to the famous William Penn may have contributed to render this monarch more indulgent to this sect than he would otherwise have been. The reasons of this attachment are differently represented. Some suppose it to have been owing to the services of his father in the fleet commanded against the Dutch in 1665, by James, when duke of York

done, from motives of a personal or political nature, in favour of the Quakers, King William III. confirmed and continued, from a zeal for maintaining the rights of conscience, and advancing the cause of religious liberty. From these motives, he procured a full and ample toleration for dissenters of almost all denominations; and the Quakers, in consequence of this grant, enjoyed at length, upon a constitutional footing, tranquillity and freedom.*

IV. Fatigued with the vexations and persecutions which they suffered in their native country during the reign of Charles II., the Quakers looked about for some distant settlements, where they might shelter themselves from the storm; and with this view they began to disseminate their religious principles in various countries. Attempts of this nature were made in Germany, Prussia, France, Italy, Greece, Holland, and Holstein, but with little success. The Dutch, however, were, after much importunity, persuaded to allow a certain number of these enthusiasts to settle in Holland, where their descendants still continue to reside. Multitudes of them had already gone over to America, and formed settlements there, not long after the rise of their sect; and it afterwards happened, by a singular concourse of events, that this new world became the chief seat of their prosperity and freedom. William Penn, son of the famous vice-admiral of that name, who embraced Quakerism in 1668, received, in 1680, from Charles and from the English parliament, the grant of an ample and fertile but uncultivated province in America, as a reward for the eminent services of his father. This illustrious Quaker, who was far from being destitute of parts, and whose activity and penetration were accompanied with an uncommon degree of eloquence,† carried over with him into his new dominions a considerable colony of his *Friends* and Brethren; and he founded in those distant regions a republic, whose form, laws, and institutions, resembled no other known system of government, whose pacific principles and commercial spirit have long blessed it with tranquillity and opulence, and which still continues in a prosperous and flourishing state.‡ The Quakers predominate in this colony, both by their influence and their numbers; but all those who acknowledge the existence and providence of one Supreme Being, and show their respect to that Being, either by external worship, or at least by the regularity of their lives and actions, are admitted to the rights and privileges of citizens in this happy republic. The large province that constitutes its territory was called Pennsylvania, from the name of its proprietor; and its capital city was named Philadelphia, from the spirit of union and fraternal love that reigned at first, and is still supposed to prevail, among its inhabitants.

V. Even during the life of their founder, the Quakers, notwithstanding their extraordinary pretensions to fraternal charity and union, were frequently divided into parties, and involved in contests and debates. These debates, indeed, which were carried on in the years 1656, 1661, and 1683, with peculiar warmth, were not occasioned by any doctrines of a religious nature, but by a diversity of opinions about matters of discipline, about certain customs and manners, and other affairs of little moment; and they were generally terminated in a short time, and without much difficulty.* But, after the death of Fox, which happened in 1691, some Friends, and more especially George Keith, who was indisputably the most learned member of their community, excited, by their doctrines and innovations, discords of a more serious and momentous kind than those which had before divided the Brethren. This fountain of contention was opened in Pennsylvania, where Keith was charged with erroneous opinions respecting several points of theology, and more particularly concerning the human nature of Christ, which he supposed to be two-fold, one part being spiritual and celestial, the other corporeal and terrestrial.† This and other inventions of Keith would perhaps have passed without censure, among a people who reduce the whole of religion to fancy and a kind of spiritual instinct, had not this learned man animadverted, with a certain degree of severity, upon some of the fantastic notions of the American brethren, and opposed, in a more particular manner, their method of converting the whole history of Christ's life and sufferings into a mere allegory, or symbolical representation of the duties of Christianity. The European Quakers dare not so far presume upon the indulgence of the civil and ecclesiastical powers, as to deny openly the *reality* of the history of the life, mediation, and sufferings of Christ; but in America, where they have nothing to fear, they are said to express themselves without ambiguity, on this subject, and to maintain publicly, that Christ never existed but in the hearts of the *faithful*. This point was debated between Keith and his adversaries, in several general assemblies of the sect

Others attribute this attachment to his personal services. From the high degree of favour he enjoyed at court, they concluded that he was a concealed papist, and assisted the king in the execution of his designs. That the imputation of popery was groundless, appears from his correspondence with Dr. Tillotson, which is published in the life of Penn, prefixed to the first volume of the works of the latter. It is nevertheless certain, that he was very intimate with Father Petre, the hot-headed Jesuit, whose bigotry framed the king's projects, and whose imprudence rendered them abortive. It is also certain, that, in 1686, he went over to Holland, in order to persuade the prince of Orange to support the measures of king James.

* Œuvres de M. de Voltaire, tom. iv. p. 182.

☞ † Bishop Burnet, who knew Penn personally, says, that "he was a talking, vain man, who had such a high opinion of his own eloquence, that he thought nothing could stand before it;" and that "he had a tedious *luscious* way, that was not apt to overcome a man's reason, though it might tire his patience."

‡ The laws and charters of the colony of Pennsylvania may be seen in Rapin's History, Penn's Works, and in other collections of public records; they are also inserted in the Bibliothèque Britannique, tom. xv. p. 310; tom. xvi. p. 127.—Penn acquired a great reputation, both by his writings and the active figure he made in life. See the accounts given of him by Sewell and Burnet.

* See Sewell's History.

☞ † Ceremonies et Coutumes de tous les Peuples du Monde, tom. iv. p. 141.—Croesii Historia Quakeriana, lib iii p 446.

holden in England, and was at length brought before the parliament. The contest was terminated, in 1695, by the excommunication of Keith and his adherents. which so exasperated this famous Quaker,* that he returned, some years after this, into the bosom of the English church, and died in its communion.† His friends and followers long continued to hold their assemblies, and to exercise their religion in a state of separation from the rest of the sect; but now, if we may believe public fame, they are reconciled with their brethren.‡

VI. The religion of this sect has an air of novelty that strikes at first sight; but, when viewed closely, it will appear to be nothing more than a certain modification of that famous Mystic Theology, which arose so early as the second century, was fostered and embellished by the luxuriant fancy of Origen, and, passing through various hands, assumed different aspects until it was adopted by the Quakers, who set off the motley form with their own inventions. Fox, indeed, is not chargeable with these inventions; his ignorant and inelegant simplicity places him beyond the reach of suspicion in this matter; but it is, at the same time, undoubtedly certain, that all his notions concerning the internal word, the divine light within, and its operations and effects, were either borrowed from the writings of the Mystics, which were, at that time, in the hands of many, or at least collected from the conversation and expressions of some persons of the Mystic order. The tenets, however, which this blunt and illiterate man expressed in a rude, confused, and ambiguous manner, were dressed up and presented under a different form by the masterly hands of Barclay, Keith, Fisher, and Penn, who digested them with such sagacity and art, that they assumed the aspect of a regular system. The Quakers may therefore be deemed with reason the principal branch of the Mystics, as they not only embraced the precepts of their hidden wisdom, but even saw its whole tendency, and adopted, without hesitation, all its consequences.§

VII. The fundamental doctrine of Quakerism, from which all the other tenets of the sect are derived, is that famous and ancient opinion of the mystic school, "that there lies concealed in the minds of all men a certain portion of divine reason, a spark of the same wisdom that exists in the Supreme Being Therefore, those who are desirous of arriving at true felicity and eternal salvation, must, (according to their system) by self-converse, contemplation, and perpetual efforts to subdue their sensual affections, endeavour to draw forth, kindle, and inflame that divine, hidden

☞ * Bishop Burnet, who was certainly better acquainted with the history of Keith (with whom he had been educated) than Dr. Mosheim, attributes his return to the church of England to a much worthier motive than irritation and resentment. He tells us that Keith, after the American quakers had appeared to him as little better than deists, opposed them so warmly, that they sent him back to England. Here he opened a new meeting, and by printed summons called together the whole party to convince them of these errors. "He continued those meetings, (says the bishop,) being still, in outward appearance, a Quaker, for some years; till having prevailed as far as he saw any appearance of success, he laid aside their exterior, and was reconciled to the church."

† See Burnet's History, and also that of Sewell; but it is proper to observe, that the latter was either unacquainted with the true nature and state of this controversy, which, as he was an illiterate man, may easily be supposed to have been the case, or he has given designedly a false and ambiguous representation of the matter. See the life of Kuster, in the Europa Erudita of Rahtlef (a work written in German,) where this controversy is placed in its true light. Kuster was a man of probity, who lived at that time in America, and was an eye-witness of these divisions.

‡ See Rogers' Christian Quaker; as also the Quakers a divided People, and Unschuld. Nachricht. 1744, p. 496.

§ Most people are of opinion that we are to learn the true doctrine and sentiments of the Quakers from the Catechism of Robert Barclay, and more especially from his Apology for the true Christian Divinity, &c. which was published in 1676, and was translated into several foreign languages; nor do I deny, that the members of this sect are very desirous that we should judge of their religious sentiments by the doctrine that is exhibited in these books: but, if those who are disposed to judge by this rule, go so far as to maintain, that these books contain all the religious tenets that were formerly advanced, or are at present adopted by the people called Quakers, they may be refuted without difficulty, from a great variety of books and records of unquestionable authenticity. It is necessary to enter into the true spirit of Barclay's writings. This ingenious man appeared as a patron and defender of Quakerism, and not as a professed teacher or expositor of its various doctrines; and he interpreted and modified the opinions of this sect after the manner of a champion or advocate, who undertakes the defence of an odious cause. How then does he go to work? In the first place, he observes an entire silence in relation to those fundamental principles of Christianity, concerning which it is of great consequence to know the real opinions of the Quakers; and thus he exhibits a system of theology that is evidently lame and imperfect; for it is the peculiar business of a prudent apologist to pass over in silence points that are scarcely susceptible of a plausible defence, and to enlarge upon those only which the powers of genius and eloquence may be able to embellish and exhibit in an advantageous point of view. It is observable, in the second place, that Barclay touches, in a slight, superficial, and hasty manner, some tenets, the explanation of which had already exposed the Quakers to severe censures; and in this he discovers plainly the weakness of his cause. Lastly (to omit many other observations that might be made here,) this writer employs the greatest dexterity and art in softening and modifying those invidious doctrines which he cannot conceal, and presumes not to disavow; for which purpose he carefully avoids all those phrases and terms which are used by the Quakers, and are peculiar to their sect, and expresses their tenets in ordinary language, in terms of a vague and indefinite nature, and in a style that casts a sort of mask over their natural aspect. At this rate the most enormous errors may be maintained with impunity; for there is no doctrine, however absurd, to which a plausible air may not be given by following the insidious method of Barclay; and it is well known that even the doctrine of Spinosa was, with a like artifice, dressed out and disguised by some of his disciples. The other writers of this sect have declared their sentiments with more freedom, perspicuity, and candour, particularly the famous William Penn and George Whitehead, whose writings deserve an attentive perusal, preferably to all the other productions of that community. There is, among other writings of these eminent Quakers, one in whose composition they were both concerned, and which was published in 1674, under the following title: The Christian Quaker and his divine Testimony vindicated by Scripture, Reason, and Authority, against the injurious Attempts that have been lately made by several Adversaries. The first part of this book was written by Penn, and the second by Whitehead. There is also, in Sewell's History, a confession of faith that was published by the Quakers in 1693, during their controversy with Keith; but this confession is composed with great caution, and is full of ambiguity.

spark, which is overpowered by the darkness of the flesh, and suffocated, as it were, by that mass of matter with which it is surrounded. They who observe this rule, will feel (say the Quakers) a divine glow of warmth and light, and hear a celestial and divine voice proceeding from the inward recesses of their souls; and by this light and this voice, they will be led to all truth, and be perfectly assured of their union with the Supreme Being." This hidden treasure, which is possessed, though not improved, by all the human race, bears different denominations in the language of this fanatical sect. They frequently call it *divine light*, sometimes *a ray of the eternal wisdom*, at others, the *heavenly Sophia*, whom they suppose married to a mortal, and whose wedding garments some of their writers describe with the most gaudy and pompous eloquence. But the most usual epithets given to this spiritual treasure are those of the *internal word*, and of Christ *within;* for as, on the one hand, they adopt that doctrine of Origen, and the ancient Mystics, which represents Christ as the eternal reason or wisdom of God, and, on the other, maintain, that all men are endowed naturally with a certain portion of the divine wisdom, they are thus directly led to affirm, that Christ, or the word of God, dwells and speaks in the hearts of all men.*

VIII. All the singularities and wonderful fancies which are to be found in the religious system of the Quakers, are the immediate consequences of the fundamental principle now mentioned; for, since Christ resides in the inward frame of every mortal, it follows, "first, that the whole of religion consists in calling off the mind from external objects, in weakening the influence and ascendancy of the outward senses, and in every one's entering deeply into the inmost recesses of his heart, and listening attentively to the divine instructions and commands that the internal word, or Christ within, delivers there; secondly, that the external word, i. e. the Scripture, neither points out the way of salvation, nor leads men to it, since it only consists of letters and words, which, being void of life, have not a sufficient degree of efficacy and power to illuminate the human mind, and unite it to God. The only advantage that, in their opinion, results from a perusal of the Scripture, is, that it excites the mind to listen to the dictates of the internal word, and to go to the school of Christ, who teaches within them; or (to express the same thing in other words,) they look upon the Bible as a mute master, who, by signs and figures, points out and discovers that living master, that effective guide, who dwells in the mind. Thirdly, they who are without this written word, such as the Jews, Mohammedans, and savage nations, are not, on that account, either removed from the path, or destitute of the doctrine of salvation, though they indeed want this inferior and subordinate help to its attainment; for, if they only attend to this inward teacher, who always *speaks* when the *man is silent*, they will learn abundantly, from him, all that is necessary to be known and practised in order to their final happiness. In consequence, fourthly, the kingdom of Christ is of a vast extent, and comprehends the whole race of mankind; for all have Christ within them, and therefore, even those who are deprived of the means of knowledge, and live in the grossest ignorance of the Christian religion, are capable of obtaining, through him, wisdom here, and happiness hereafter. Hence also they conclude, that those who lead virtuous lives, and resist the impulse of their lusts and passions, whether they be Jews, Moslems, or Polytheists, shall be united to God in this life, by means of the Christ that lies hidden within them, and shall enjoy the fruits of this union in the life to come. To these tenets they add, in the fifth place, that a heavy, dark body, composed of corrupt matter, hinders men from discerning, with ease, this hidden Christ, and from hearing his divine and internal voice. Therefore they look upon it as a matter of the highest importance, to watch against the pernicious consequences of this union between the soul and body, that the latter may not blunt the powers of the former, disturb its tranquillity, or, by the ministry of the outward senses, fill it with images of vain, sensible, and external objects." The consideration now mentioned engages them, lastly, "to look upon it as utterly incredible, that God should ever again shut up, in the same material habitation, the souls that are set free by death from their bodily prison;" and therefore they affirm, that the Gospel-account of the resurrection of the body must either be interpreted in a figurative sense, or be understood as pointing out the creation of a new and celestial body.*

IX. It evidently appears from all this, that the existence of the man of Christ Jesus, and the circumstantial accounts we have in Scripture of his divine origin, his life, and actions, his satisfaction, merits and sufferings, make no essential part of the theological system of the Quakers, which is built upon a different foundation, and derives the whole plan and method of salvation from the Christ *within*. Hence several members of that sect, as we learn from writers of unquestionable authority, went such an extravagant length as to maintain, that the accounts we have of Jesus Christ, in the evangelical history, do not relate to the Son of God, who took upon him the nature of man, but to that Christ within, whose operations are recorded by the sacred historians in figurative and allegorical language. This opinion, if we may confide in the testimonies of unexceptionable witnesses, is so far from having lost its credit among them, that it is still openly professed by the American Quakers. Those of

* It is nevertheless to be observed, that the modern Quakers, as appears from the writings of Martyn and others, are, in general, ignorant of the system of their ancestors, and perpetually confound the innate divine light above-mentioned, with the operations of the Holy Ghost in the minds of the faithful.

* The Quakers adopt all these tenets; they are at least obliged to adopt them, unless they renounce the fundamental principles of their system. We have omitted the mention of those points about which they dispute among themselves, that we may not appear to take pleasure in representing them under odious colours.

Europe, whether from the force of conviction or the suggestions of prudence, differ entirely from their brethren in this respect. They hold, "That the divine wisdom, or reason, resided in the son of the Virgin Mary, and conveyed its instructions to mankind by his ministry;" and they profess to believe, "that this divine man really did and suffered what is recorded concerning him by the sacred writers." It is nevertheless certain, that they express themselves in a very ambiguous manner on many points that relate to the history of the divine Saviour; and, in a more particular manner, their notions respecting the fruits of his sufferings, and the efficacy of his death, are so vague and obscure, that it is very difficult to know what is their real opinion about the degree of this efficacy, and the nature of these fruits. It is also worthy of observation, that the European Quakers, though they acknowledge the reality of the life, actions, and sufferings of Christ, yet do not entirely reject the allegorical interpretation of our Saviour's history mentioned above; for they consider the events that happened to Christ, in the course of his ministry upon earth, as the signs and emblems of those scenes through which the mental Christ must pass, in order to render us partakers of eternal salvation. Hence they talk in high and pompous strains (like their models the Mystics) of the birth, life, sufferings, death, and resurrection of Christ 'in the hearts of the faithful.'

X. The religious discipline, worship, and practice of the Quakers, flow from the same source from which, as we have already observed, their doctrine and tenets were immediately derived. They meet for the purposes of religion on the same days which are set apart for the celebration of public worship in all other Christian churches; but they neither observe festivals, nor use external rites and ceremonies, nor suffer religion, which they place entirely in the mental worship of the hidden Christ, to be shackled and cramped by positive institutions. All the members of their community, whether male or female, have an equal right to teach and exhort in their public meetings; for who, say they, will presume to exclude, from the liberty of speaking to the Brethren, those persons in whom Christ dwells, and by whom he speaks? They reject the use of prayers, hymns, and the various outward forms of devotion by which, in other Christian churches, public worship is distinguished; and this, indeed, is an instance of their consistency with themselves, as it is the immediate consequence of their religious system; for, in their judgment, it is not the person who expresses his desires in a set form of words, that can be said to pray truly, but he, on the contrary, who, by a deep recollection, withdraws his mind from every outward object, reduces it to a state of absolute tranquillity, silences every inward motion and affection, and plunges it, as it were, into the abyss of Deity. They neither observe the institution of baptism, nor do they renew the remembrance of Christ's death, and of the benefits that result from it, by the celebration of the eucharist. They look upon these two institutions as merely Judaical, and allege, that our Saviour observed them for no other end than to show for once, in a visible manner, the mystical purification of the soul, under the figure of baptism, and the spiritual nourishment of the inward man, under that of the eucharist.

XI. The moral doctrine of this sect, which is remarkable for its excessive austerity, is chiefly comprehended in the two following precepts. One is of this import: That the faithful are either to avoid entirely every thing that tends to gratify the external senses and passions, every thing that can be ranked under the denomination of sensual or bodily pleasure; or, if such rigorous abstinence be impossible in this present state, and contrary to the evident laws of nature, such pleasure is to be so modified and restrained by reason and meditation, as to prevent it from debasing and corrupting the mind; for, as the whole attention of the mind must be given to the voice and orders of the internal guide, so, for this purpose, all possible care must be taken to remove it from the contagion of the body, and from all intimate and habitual commerce with corporeal objects." By another leading precept of morality among the Quakers, all imitation of those external manners, that go by the name of civility and politeness, as also several matters of form, usual in the conduct of life, and in the connexions of human society, are strictly prohibited as unlawful. Hence they are easily distinguished from all other Christian sects, by their outward deportment and their manner of life. They never salute any person whom they meet in their way, nor employ in their conversation the usual manner of address, or the appellations that civility and custom have rendered a matter of decency, at least, if not of duty; they never express their respect for magistrates, or persons in authority, either by bodily gestures, titles of honour, or in general by any of the marks of homage that are paid to them by persons of all other denominations. They carry their pacific sentiments to such an extravagant length as to renounce the right of self-defence, and let pass with impunity, and even without resistance, the attacks that are made on their possessions, their reputation, and even on their lives. They refuse to confirm their testimonies by an oath, to appear in behalf of their property before a civil tribunal, or to accuse those who have injured them. To these negative parts of their external conduct, they add peculiar circumstances of a positive kind, that discover the same austere, stiff, proud, and formal spirit; for they distinguish themselves, in a striking manner, from the rest of their fellow-citizens, by the gravity of their aspects, the rustic simplicity of their apparel, the affected tones of their voices, the stiffness of their conversation, and the frugality of their tables. It is, however, affirmed by persons of credit, who are eye-witnesses of what passes among the members of this sect, that the modern, and more especially the English Quakers, whom trade has furnished with the means of luxury, have departed from this rigid and austere manner of life, and gradually become more reconciled to the outward pleasures and enjoyments of the world. These more sociable Quakers are also said to modify and explain the theology of their ancestors, in such a manner as to render it more rational than it was in its primitive state. At the same time it is certain, that many of the members of this sect have either a false notion, or no notion at all, of that theology.

XII. The principles of this community seem to exclude the very idea of order, discipline, and ecclesiastical government. Its leading members, however, began to perceive in process of time, that without laws and rulers it could not subsist, but must inevitably fall into confusion and ruin. They accordingly erected a council of elders, who discuss and determine matters of a doubtful or difficult nature, and use all possible care and diligence in inspecting the conduct of the Brethren, and in preventing whatever they look upon as prejudicial to the interests of the community. The names of those who enter into the state of matrimony are given in to those leading members, who also keep an exact register of the births and deaths that happen in their society. They exercise, moreover, a certain degree of authority over those who speak in their meetings, since it is well known, that in some places these speakers show their discourses to the ruling elders before they deliver them, in order that they may judge whether they are fit to be repeated in public; for, since the abuse that was made of the unbounded liberty that every individual had to instruct and exhort the congregation, and to speak and harangue when the pretended spirit moved them, new regulations have been observed; and this liberty has been considerably modified, in several places, to avoid the mockery, contempt, and censure, to which the community was constantly exposed, by the absurd, incoherent, and insipid discourses of many of its members. There are also in some of the more considerable congregations, and more especially in those which are formed at London, certain persons whose duty it is to be always prepared to speak to the people, if none of the congregation should seem to be inwardly moved or disposed to rise and harangue. The appointment of these professed speakers was designed to remedy an inconvenience that frequently happened in the Quaker-meetings, the whole assembly being dismissed without either instruction or exhortation, because no persons found themselves *moved* to speak. It is indeed to be observed, that this public discourse is not looked upon by the Quakers as an essential part of their religion and worship; for the Brethren and Sisters do not meet that they may hear the words of an external teacher, but that they may listen with recollection to the voice of the divine instructor, which every one carries with him in his own breast, or, to use their own phrase, that they may 'commune with themselves.' Nevertheless, as these mute assemblies excite the laughter of their adversaries, and expose them to the reproach of enthusiasm and folly, they have, on that account, appointed fixed speakers to whom they give a small salary, that the whole time of their meeting may not be passed in silence.*

The Quakers have, annually, a general assembly, which meets at London in the week before Whitsuntide,* and is composed of deputies from all their particular congregations. They still complain, notwithstanding the toleration they enjoy, of certain severities and hardships; but these are entirely owing to their obstinate refusal to pay those tithes, which, by the laws of the land, are designed for the support of the established church.

VINDICATION OF THE QUAKERS.

[*The following* VINDICATION *was added to the Philadelphia edition of Mosheim's Ecclesiastical History, published in* 1799.]

AN American edition of Mosheim's Ecclesiastical History being nearly completed, in which is contained a very false account of the principles, doctrine and discipline of our religious society, a very erroneous character of George Fox, and divers other misrepresentations and untrue charges; and although full answers and refutations of these calumnies have been heretofore published, yet as this book may fall into the hands of persons unacquainted with the true state of facts, we think it a point of justice due to the cause of truth and to our religious society, and for the information of candid and unprejudiced minds, briefly to give what from authentic histories and our own knowledge we have ascertained is a just narration.

Men who consider themselves accountable for their words and actions, and think it highly criminal to deceive others by either disguising or falsification, who are well informed and acquainted with the facts and subjects they relate or write upon, are entitled to greater credit than professed and avowed opposers, who from mistaken motives publish distortions and misconstructions. From the misrepresentations and wrong accounts given by our adversaries, we have no doubt Mosheim has taken most of his narrative.

The true character of George Fox has been drawn by men of the first respectability and the fullest information; men who were conversant with him from his youth to his close: and a cloud of witnesses and authentic testimonies can be produced to prove that he was a pious, sober, solid and exemplary man, and no fanatic, eminently qualified for the work he was raised up to promote. As we wish to be brief, we shall omit recurring to other documents,

☞ * The truth of this account of fixed speakers appointed to discourse and exhort (when the spirit does not move any of the other brethren,) and rewarded for their pains, is denied by the writer of the letter to Dr. Formey. We leave the decision of the matter to those who have an opportunity of examining the supposed fact. The translator, instead of leaving this point unsettled, ought to have inquired into the circumstance; but, as he was unwilling to take that trouble, the *editor* is induced to supply the deficiency, by stating that for Dr. Mosheim's assertion there is no authority. Many persons are in the habit of preaching, exhorting, or advising, at the different meetings; but they are not selected or appointed by the congregation, and do not act as stipendiary ministers. The *Friends* know that the labourer is worthy of his hire, and follow that rule in ordinary cases; but the idea of remuneration for religious instruction is neither entertained by the preacher himself, nor by the *Brethren* and *Sisters* who listen to his extemporaneous effusions.

* It is now fixed for the third Sunday in May.

and only cite a few sentences from a preface to George Fox's Journal written by William Penn, as follows:

"He was a man that God endowed with a clear and wonderful depth, a discerner of others spirits, and very much a master of his own.

"He was of an innocent life, no busy body nor self-seeker, neither touchy nor critical. So meek, contented, modest, steady, tender, it was a pleasure to be in his company.

"As he was unwearied, so he was undaunted in his services for God. For in all things he acquitted himself like a man, a new and heavenly-minded man, a divine and a naturalist, and all of God Almighty's making. I have been surprised at his questions and answers in natural things, that whilst he was ignorant of useless and sophistical science, he had in him the foundation of useful and commendable knowledge, and cherished it every where.

"Thus he lived and sojourned among us, and as he lived so he died, feeling in his last moments the same eternal power that had raised and preserved him."

Instead of the first association of Quakers "being mostly composed of visionary fanatics, and of persons that really seemed to be disordered in their brains," William Penn, in his aforesaid preface, gives the names of a number of eminent men who became members of this society, and who were instrumental with many others in spreading and propagating the doctrines which they had espoused, and also of establishing a discipline and church government which must be allowed to be a compact and well regulated system of good order.

The charge of their "running like bacchanals through the towns and villages, declaiming against Episcopacy, Presbyterianism, and every fixed form of religion, &c. trampling upon the laws, and making use of their pretended inspirations to excite the most vehement commotions both in church and state," and divers other scandalous aspersions, we deny.

That tumults were raised by their opposers, is very true, and also that they refused complying with laws which they conceived as violating the rights of conscience; but that in any one instance they offered violence to the person of any man, or departed from their peaceable testimony, is false. That they bore beatings, imprisonment and death, with patience, meekness, and perseverance, praying for their enemies, is a fact indisputable and of great notoriety; so that in time, when the clouds of prejudice were dissipated and their innocence fully manifested, way was made in the minds of rulers for their toleration; and this may with truth be said, that such of them as keep true to their principles, are as good members of civil society as any other people, and have never been found in any plots or combinations against the governments which in the course of providence have been set over them.

The conduct of James Naylor, in his dark and bewildered state, we freely condemn; but his punishment was rigorous in the extreme. That two or three weak persons were deluded and paid a sort of divine honour to him, is confessed; but that this was in any degree countenanced by our religious society is positively denied, but on the contrary was fully reprobated by them. Although James Naylor had lamentably missed his way, yet we have reason to believe he was through divine mercy restored to a sound mind. He published a condemnation of his misconduct, and we reverently hope he died in peace with God and love to all men.

As to the absurd story of "one of these people going to the parliament house with a drawn sword and wounding several, and saying he was inspired by the Holy Spirit to kill every man that sat in that house," it is a very fiction, and we deny that any acknowledged member among us ever was guilty of such conduct.

We have also made diligent search and cannot find any account of a female going naked as mentioned in the same note, and believe it is untrue.

That George Keith was a man of learning and a member of our society, and wrote several pieces in support of our tenets, is true; but that he gave way to a contentious spirit, and endeavoured to lay waste what he himself had assisted to build up, and was, after much patient labour and forbearance, disowned by friends, we acknowledge, and that an opposition was made to the establishment of meetings for discipline, by some through ignorance, who afterwards saw their error and condemned it, and by others from mistaken motives, but that our fundamental opinions have been the same from the first promulgation of them, we confidently assert.

We believe the Scriptures of the Old and New Testament to be of divine original, and give full credit to the historical facts, as well as the doctrines therein delivered; and never had any doubt of the truth of the actual birth, life, sufferings, death, resurrection and ascension of our Lord and Saviour Jesus Christ, as related by the evangelists, without any mental or other reserve, or the least diminution by allegorical explanation: and there is not, nor ever has been, any essential difference in faith or practice between Friends in Europe and America; but a correspondence is regularly maintained, and love, harmony, and unity have been preserved down to this day; and we hope and believe, under divine favour, nothing will be able to scatter or divide us.

We do not wish to meddle with those, called mystics, or to adopt many of their expressions. We presume there were sincerely religious people among them; but we think religion is a simple thing, the work of the Spirit of God in the hearts of men: and as to our tenets and history we refer to Fox, Barclay, Penn, Sewell, Gough, &c. and declare, that we never had, nor now have, any other doctrines to publish, and that there are no religious opinions or practices among us which have not been made known to the world.

When any person by submitting to the influence and operation of the Spirit of God, becomes thereby qualified, and is called to the work of the ministry, after having made full proof thereof to the satisfaction of the congregation, he or she is accepted and recommended as such; but as to any person being appointed with a stipend, small or great, or preparing a sermon to be delivered in our meetings to be previously examined, or without such examination, there never was any such practice among us. Our ministers, elders, overseers, and other friends appointed to religious services, receive no pecuniary pay, but spend their time and their own money freely on such occasions, at home and abroad; yet proper attention is given to those in low or poor circumstances of every description, besides contributing our full proportion to the support of the general poor. Equally untrue is the insinuation that we are ashamed of our silent meetings, having experienced them to be both profitable and refreshing, as by waiting on the Lord we renew our strength in him.

Having referred to divers books for further information respecting us, and a more minute refutation of the other false charges, we shall content ourselves at present with this general answer.

Signed by direction and on behalf of a meeting representing the religious society called Quakers in Pennsylvania, New-Jersey, &c. held in Philadelphia the 22d of 11th month, 1799.

JOHN DRINKER, *Clerk.*

CHAPTER V.

Concerning the Mennonites, or Anabaptists.

I. AFTER various scenes of trial and perplexity, the Mennonites at length found, during this century, that tranquillity which they had long sought in vain. They arrived, indeed, at this state of repose by very slow steps; for though, in the preceding age, they were admitted to the rights and privileges of citizens in the United Provinces, yet it was a long time before their solicitations and pleas of innocence could engage the English, the Swiss, and Germans, to receive them in their bosom, and to abrogate the laws that had been enacted against them. The civil magistrates, in these countries, had still before their eyes the enormities committed by the ancient Anabaptists; and, besides, they could not persuade themselves, that a set of men, who looked upon all oaths as sinful, and declared that magistracy and penal laws have no place in the kingdom of Christ, had the qualities and sentiments that are necessary to constitute a good citizen. Hence we find, even in this century, several examples of great severities employed against the Anabaptists, and some instances of even capital punishments being inflicted on them.* But now, that the demonstrations of their innocence and probity are clear and unquestionable, they enjoy the sweets of security and repose, not only in the United Provinces, but also in England, Germany, and Prussia, where they procure by their honest industry, and particularly by their application to trade and commerce, an ample subsistence for themselves and their families.

II. The wiser members of this community easily perceived, that their external tranquillity would not be staple or permanent, unless their intestine discords were removed, and their ancient disputes about trifling and unimportant matters charitably terminated. They accordingly used their most zealous endeavours to diffuse the sweets of charity and concord throughout their sect; nor were their labours altogether unsuccessful. In 1630, a considerable part of the Anabaptists of Flanders, Germany, and Friseland, concluded their debates in a conference at Amsterdam, and entered into the bonds of fraternal communion; each, notwithstanding, reserving a liberty of retaining certain opinions. This association was renewed, and confirmed by new resolutions in 1649, by the Anabaptists of Flanders and Germany, among whom great divisions had reigned.* All these formed a bond of union with those branches of the sect that were most distinguished by their moderation; and they mitigated and corrected, in various respects, the rigorous laws of Menno and his successors.

III. At this day, therefore, the whole community may be divided into two large sects. One comprehends the more *refined* Anabaptists, remarkable for their austerity, who are also called Flemings or Flandrians; and those who form the other sect are styled the *Gross* Anabaptists, who are of a milder complexion, and an easier and more moderate character, and go commonly under the denomination of Waterlandians. We have already given a particular account of the origin and etymology of these denominations. Each sect is subdivided into a variety of branches, more especially the refined and austere Anabaptists; who have not only produced two separate societies, distinguished by the names of Groningenists,† and Dantzickers, or Prussians,‡ but also a considerable number of more obscure factions, which differ in doctrine, discipline, and manners, and agree in nothing but the name of Anabaptists, and in some ancient opinions that have been unanimously embraced by all the members of that sect. All the refined Anabaptists are the rigid followers of Simon Menno, and firmly maintain, though not all with the same degree of severity and rigour, the sentiments of their chief on the following points—the human nature of Christ—the obligation that binds us to

* The severities exercised in Switzerland against the Mennonites are recorded by Ottius, in his Annal. Anabapt. p. 337, and more particularly those which they suffered in the year 1693, by Hottinger, in his German work, entitled Schweizerische Kirchen-Historie. vol. i. p. 1101, nor even in the present* century have they been treated more mildly in the canton of Bern, as appears from Schyn's Historia Mennonitar. cap. x. p. 239, in which we find the letters of the states-general of the United Provinces, interceding with that canton in their behalf. A severe persecution was set on foot against them in the Palatinate in 1694, which was suspended by the intercession of William III. king of Great Britain. See Schyn's Hist. p. 265. Bishop Burnet mentions some instances of Anabaptists suffering death in England during the seventeenth century, in the first volume of his History of his own Time.

* The eighteenth.

* Herm. Schyn, Plenior Deductio Historiæ Mennonit. p. 41, 42.

† So called, because they met at certain stated times in Groningen.

‡ They derive this denomination from their adopting the manners and discipline of the Prussians

wash the feet of strangers in consequence of our Saviour's command—the necessity of excommunicating and of avoiding, as one would do the plague, not only avowed sinners, but also those who depart, even in some light instances, from the simplicity of their ancestors, and are tainted with any appearance of evil—the contempt that is due to human learning, and other matters of less moment.* It is however to be observed, that, in our times, some of the congregations of this refined sect have been gradually departing from their austere system, and are proceeding, though with a slow pace, toward the opinions and discipline of the moderate Anabaptists.

IV. All these Anabaptists adopt a form of ecclesiastical government and discipline, that is administered by three distinct orders of persons. The first order is that of the Bishops or Presbyters, who always preside in the consistory, and are alone invested with the power of administering the sacraments of baptism and the Lord's supper. The second is that of the Teachers, who are set apart for the purposes of public instruction, and the celebration of divine worship. The third comprehends the Deacons, who are chosen out of both sexes. These three orders compose the consistory, or council, by which the church is governed. All matters of importance are proposed, examined, and decided, in the meetings of the Brethren. By their suffrages the ministers are elected to their holy office, and are all, the deacons excepted, installed by public prayers, attended with imposition of hands.

V. Among the inferior sects of the rigid Anabaptists, the most considerable is that which passes under the denomination of Ukewallists, and is so called after its founder Uke Walles, a native of Friseland. This rustic, rigid, and ignorant sectary, not only exhorted his followers to maintain the primitive and austere doctrine of Menno, without suffering it to be softened or altered in the smallest degree, but also, in the year 1637, began to propagate, jointly with another innovator, named John Leus, a singular opinion concerning the salvation of Judas, and the rest of Christ's murderers. To give an air of plausibility to the favourable opinion he entertained concerning the eternal state of this arch-apostate, he invented the following odd hypothesis: "That the period which extended from the birth of Christ to the descent of the Holy Ghost, and was, as it were, the distinctive term that separated the Jewish from the Christian dispensation, was a time of deep ignorance and darkness, during which the Jews were void of light, and entirely destitute of divine succour; and that, in consequence, the sins and enormities that were committed during this interval were in a great measure excusable, and could not merit the severest displays of the divine justice." This idle fiction met with no indulgence, either from the Mennonites on the one hand, or from the magistrates of Groningen on the other; for the former excluded its inventor from their communion, and the latter banished him from their city. He fixed his residence in the adjacent province of East-Friseland, and there drew after him a considerable number of disciples, whose descendants still subsist in Friseland, and also in Lithuania and Prussia, and have their own religious assemblies, separate from those of the other Mennonites. As they have little intercourse with any but those of their own communion, it is not an easy matter to know, with certainty, whether they persevere in the singular opinion that proved so detrimental to the interest of their leader. It is at least certain, that they follow scrupulously the steps of their original founder, Menno, and exhibit a lively image of the primitive manners and constitution of the Mennonites. They re-baptize all those who leave other Christian churches to embrace their communion. Their apparel is mean beyond expression, and they avoid every thing that has the most distant appearance of elegance or ornament. They suffer their beards to grow to an enormous length; their hair, uncombed, lies in a disorderly manner on their shoulders; their countenances are marked with the strongest lines of dejection and melancholy; and their habitations and household furniture are such as are only fitted to answer the demands of mere necessity. Such moreover is the severity of their discipline, that any member of their community, who departs in the smallest instance from this austere rule, is immediately excluded from the society, and avoided by all the Brethren as a public pest. Their inspectors or bishops, whom they distinguish from the ministers, whose office is to preach and instruct, are chosen by an assembly composed of all the congregations of the sect. The ceremony of washing the feet of strangers, who come within the reach of their hospitality, is looked upon by them as a rite of divine institution. We shall not enlarge upon the other circumstances of their ritual, but only observe, that they prevent all attempts to alter or modify their religious discipline, by preserving their people from every thing that bears the remotest aspect of learning and science; from whatever, in a word, might have a tendency to enlighten their devout ignorance.

VI. The more gross or moderate and less scrupulous Anabaptists are composed of certain inhabitants of Waterland, Flanders, Friseland, and Germany, who entered into an association, as has been already observed, and commonly pass under the denomination of Waterlandians. The members of this community have abandoned the severe discipline and singular opinions of Menno, whom, nevertheless, they generally respect as their primitive parent and founder, and have advanced a step nearer than the other Anabaptists to the religious doctrines and customs of other Christian churches. They are, however, divided into two distinct sects, which bear the respective denominations of Friselanders and Waterlandians, and are both without bishops, employing no other ecclesiastical ministers than presbyters and deacons. Each congregation of this sect is independent of all foreign jurisdiction, having its own ecclesiastical council or consistory, which is composed of presbyters and deacons. The supreme

* See a German work, entitled, Nachrichten von dem gegenwartigen Zustande der Mennoniten, by Rues, 1743.

spiritual power is, nevertheless, in the hands of the people, without whose consent nothing of importance can be carried into execution. Their presbyters are, generally speaking, men of learning, and apply themselves with success to the study of physic and philosophy: and a public professor is supported, at present, by the sect at Amsterdam, for the instruction of their youth in the various branches of philosophy and sacred erudition.

VII. One of these Waterlandian sects divided itself, in 1664, into two factions, which were respectively called Galenists and Apostoolians, from the names of their two leaders. The founder of the former sect was Galen Abraham Haan, a doctor of physic, and pastor of a Mennonite congregation at Amsterdam, who received the applause even of his enemies, on account of his uncommon penetration and eloquence. This eminent Anabaptist, in imitation of the Arminians, considered the Christian religion as a system that laid much less stress upon faith than upon practice; and he was inclined to receive, into the communion of the Mennonites, all who acknowledged the divine origin of the books of the Old and New Testament, and led holy and virtuous lives. Such, in his judgment, were true Christians, and had an undoubted right to all the rights and privileges that belonged to that character. These comprehensive terms of communion were peculiarly favourable to his own theological sentiments, since his notions concerning Christ's divinity, and the salvation of mankind by his death and merits, were very different from those of the Mennonites, and coincided in a great measure with the Socinian system.

Several persons opposed the sentiments of this latitudinarian, and more especially Samuel Apostool, an eminent pastor among the Mennonites at Amsterdam, who not only defended, with the utmost zeal, the doctrines generally received among the Mennonites, in relation to the divinity of Christ and the fruits of his death, but also maintained the ancient hypothesis of a visible and glorious church of Christ upon earth, that was peculiar to this sect.* Thus a controversy was excited which produced the division now mentioned; a division which the zealous efforts of several of the wisest and most respectable members of this community have hitherto proved insufficient to heal. The Galenists are not less disposed than the Arminians to admit, as members of their community, all who call themselves Christians; and they are the only sect of the Anabaptists who reject the denomination of Mennonites. The Apostoolians, on the contrary, admit to their communion those only who profess to believe all the points of doctrine which are contained in their public confession of faith.†

CHAPTER VI.

Concerning the Socinians and Arians.

I. ABOUT the commencement of this century, the sect of the Socinians seemed to be well established, and their affairs were even in a flourishing condition. In Transylvania and Lucko, they enjoyed the liberty of holding, without molestation, their religious assemblies, and professing publicly their theological opinions. The advantages that attended their situation in Poland were still more considerable; for they had at Racow a public seminary, which was furnished with professors eminently distinguished by their erudition and genius, together with a press for the publication of their writings; they had also a considerable number of congregations in that district, and were supported by the patronage of several persons of the highest distinction. Elate with this scene of prosperity, they began to form more extensive views, and aimed at enlarging the borders of their community, and procuring it patrons and protectors in other countries. Authentic records are extant, from which it appears, that they sent emissaries with this view, about the commencement of the century, into Holland, England, Germany, and Prussia, who endeavoured to make proselytes to Socinianism in these countries, among men of learning and men in power; for it is remarkable, that the Socinians, in propagating their religious principles, have always followed a quite different method from that which has been observed by other sects. It has been the general practice of sectaries and innovators to endeavour to render themselves popular, and to begin by gaining the multitude to their side; but the disciples of Socinus, who are perpetually exalting the dignity, prerogatives, and authority of reason, have this peculiarity in their manner of proceeding, that they are at very little pains to court the favour of the people, or to make proselytes to their cause among those who are not distinguished from the multitude by their rank or their abilities; it is only among the learned and the great that they seek disciples and patrons with zealous assiduity.

II. The effect of the missions now mentioned, though they were conducted and executed by persons of whom the greatest part were eminent, both on account of their rank and abilities, was nevertheless far from answering the views and expectations of the community. In most places the success of the cause was doubtful, at best inconsiderable; in some, however, the missionaries were favourably received, and seemed to employ their labours with effect. They had no where a more flattering prospect of success than in the university of Altorf, where their sentiments and their cause were promoted with dexterity by Ernest Sohner, an acute and learned cultivator of the peripatetic system, who was also professor of physic and natural philosophy. This subtle philosopher, who had joined the Socinians during his residence in Holland, instilled their principles into the minds of his scholars with much greater facility, by his having acquired the highest reputation, both for learning and piety. The death, indeed, of this eminent man, which happened in 1612, deprived the rising society of its chief ornament and support; nor could the remaining friends of Socinianism carry on the cause of their community

* For a more particular account of these two Mennonites, see Schyn's Deductio plenior Histor. Mennonit. cap. xv. page 318, and xviii. page 237.

† Casp. Commelini Descriptio Urbis Amstelodami, tom. i. p. 500.—Stoupa's Religion des Hollandois, p. 20.—Benthem's Hollandischer Schul and Kirchen Staat, p. 1. ch. xix. p. 830

with such art and dexterity, as to escape the vigilant and severe eye of the other professors. Their secret designs were accordingly brought to light in 1616; and the contagion of Socinianism, which was gathering strength from day to day, and growing imperceptibly into a reigning system, was suddenly dissipated and extinguished by the vigilant severity of the magistrates of Nuremberg. The foreign students, who had been infected with these doctrines, saved themselves by flight; while those natives, who were chargeable with the same reproach, accepted the remedies that were presented to them by the healing hand of orthodoxy, and returned quietly to their former theological system.*

III. The establishment of the Socinians in Poland, though it seemed to rest upon solid foundations, was nevertheless of a short duration.† Its chief supports were withdrawn, in 1638, by a public decree of the diet. It happened in this year that some of the students of Racow vented, in an irregular and tumultuous manner, their religious resentment against a crucifix, at which they threw stones, till they beat it down out of its place. This act of violence excited such a high degree of indignation, in the catholics, that they vowed revenge, and severely fulfilled this vow; for it was through their importunate solicitations that the terrible law was enacted at Warsaw, by which it was resolved, that the college of Racow should be demolished, its professors banished with ignominy, the printing-house of the Socinians destroyed, and their churches shut. All this was executed without the smallest alleviation or the least delay, notwithstanding the efforts made by the powerful patrons of the Socinians to ward off the blow.‡ But a catastrophe, still more terrible, awaited them; and the persecution now mentioned was the forerunner of that dreadful revolution, which, about twenty years afterwards, brought on the entire ruin of this community in Poland: for, by a public and solemn act of the diet holden at Warsaw, in 1658, all the Socinians were banished for ever from the territory of that republic, and capital punishment was denounced against all who should either profess their opinions, or harbour their persons. The unhappy exiles were, at first, allowed the space of three years to settle their affairs, and to dispose of their possessions; but this term was afterwards abridged by the cruelty of their enemies, and reduced to two years. In 1661, the terrible edict was renewed; and all the Socinians that yet remained in Poland were barbarously driven out of that country, some with the loss of their property, others with the loss of their lives, as neither sickness, nor any domestic consideration, could suspend the execution of that rigorous sentence.*

IV. A part of these exiles, who sought refuge among their brethren in Transylvania, sunk under the burthen of their calamities, and perished amidst the hardships to which they were exposed. A considerable number of these unhappy emigrants were dispersed through the adjacent provinces of Silesia, Brandenburg, and Prussia; and their posterity still subsists in those countries. Several of the more eminent members of the sect, in consequence of the protection granted to them by the duke of Brieg, resided for some time at Crossen in Silesia.† Others went in search of a convenient settlement for themselves and their brethren, into Holland, England, Holstein, and Denmark. Of all the Socinian exiles, none discovered such zeal and industry for the interests and establishment of the sect as Stanislaus Lubieniecius, a Polish knight, distinguished by his learning, and singularly esteemed by persons of the highest rank, and even by several sovereign princes, on account of his eloquence, politeness, and prudence. This illustrious patron of Socinianism succeeded so far in his designs, as to gain the favour of Frederic III. king of Denmark, of Christian Albert duke of Holstein, and Charles Louis elector Palatine; and thus he had almost obtained a secure retreat and settlement for the Socinians, about the year 1662, at Altena, Fredericstadt, and Manheim; but his measures were disconcerted, and all his hopes entirely frustrated, by the opposition and remonstrances of the clergy established in those countries; he was opposed in Denmark by Suaning bishop of Sealand, in Holstein by Reinboth, and in the Palatinate by John Louis Fabricius.‡ Several other attempts were made, in different countries, in favour of Socinianism; but their success was still less considerable; nor could any of the European nations be persuaded to grant a public settlement to a sect, whose members denied the divinity of Christ.

V. The remains, therefore, of this unfortunate community are, at this day, dispersed through different countries, particularly in the kingdoms of England and Prussia, the electorate of Brandenburg, and the United Provinces, where they lie more or less concealed, and hold their religious assemblies in a clandestine manner. They are, indeed, said to exercise their religion publicly in England,§ not in conse-

* The learned Gustavus George Zeltner, formerly professor of divinity in the university of Altorf, composed an ample and learned account of this theological revolution, drawn principally from manuscript records; which Gebauer published at Leipsic, in 1729, under the following title, "Historia Crypto-Socinianismi Altorfinæ quondam Academiæ infesti, arcana."

† We have a circumstantial account of the flourishing state of the Racovian seminary, while it was under the direction of the learned Martin Ruarus, in the Cimbria Literata of Moller, tom. i. p. 572, where we learn that Ruarus was a native of Holstein, who became a proselyte to the Socinian system.

‡ Epistola de Wissowatii Vita in Sandii Bib. Anti-Trinitar, p. 233.—Gust. Georg. Zeltneri His. Crypto-Socinianismi Altorfini, vol. i. p. 299.

* Stanislai Lubieniecii Hist. Reformat. Polonicæ. lib. iii. c. xvii. xviii. p. 279.—Equitis Poloni Vindiciæ pro Unitariorum in Polonia Religionis Libertate, apud Sandium, p. 267.

† Lubieniecii Hist. cap. xviii. p. 285, where there is a letter written by the Socinians of Crossen.

‡ See Sandii Biblioth. p. 165.—Historia Vitæ Lubieniecii, prefixed to his History.—Molleri Introductio in Histor. Chersones. Cimbricæ, p. ii. p. 105, and his Cimbria Literata, tom. ii. p. 487.—Jo. Henr. Heideggeri Vita Joh. Lud. Fabricii, subjoined to the works of the latter.

☞ § The Socinians in England have never made any figure as a community, but have rather been dispersed among the great variety of sects that have arisen in a country where liberty displays its most glorious fruits, and at the same time exhibits its

quence of a legal toleration, but through the indulgent connivance of the civil magistrate.* Some of them have embraced the communion of the Arminians; others have joined with those Anabaptists who form a sect distinguished by the name of Galenists; and in this there is nothing at all surprising, since neither the Arminians nor Anabaptists require, from those who enter into their communion, an explicit or circumstantial declaration of their religious sentiments. It is also said, that a considerable number of this dispersed community became members of the religious society called Collegiants.† Amidst such frequent changes and vicissitudes, it was not possible that the Socinians could maintain a uniform system of doctrine, or preserve unaltered and entire the religious tenets handed down to them by their ancestors. On the contrary, their peculiar and distinctive opinions are variously explained and understood both by the learned and illiterate members of their community, though they all agree in rejecting the doctrine of the Trinity, and that also of the divinity and satisfaction of Jesus Christ.*

most striking inconveniences. Besides, few ecclesiastics, or writers of any note, have adopted the theological system now under consideration, in all its branches. The Socinian doctrine relating to the design and efficacy of the death of Christ had, indeed, many abettors in England during the seventeenth century; and it may be presumed, that its votaries are rather increased than diminished in the present; but those divines who have abandoned the Athanasian hypothesis concerning the Trinity of Persons in the Godhead, have more generally gone into the Arian and Semi Arian notions of that inexplicable subject, than into those of the Socinians, who deny that Jesus Christ existed before his appearance in the human nature. The famous John Biddle, after having maintained, both in public and in private, during the reign of Charles and the protectorship of Cromwell, the Unitarian system, erected an Independent congregation in London, the only British church we have heard of, in which all the peculiar doctrines of Socinianism were inculcated; for, if we may give credit to the account of Sir Peter Pett, this congregation held the following notions: "That the fathers under the old covenant had only temporal promises; that saving faith consisted in universal obedience performed to the commands of God and Christ; that Christ rose again only by the power of the Father, and not by his own; that justifying faith is not the pure gift of God, but may be acquired by men's natural abilities; that faith cannot believe any thing contrary to, or above reason; that there is no original sin; that Christ has not the same body now in glory, in which he suffered and rose again; that the saints shall not have the same bodies in heaven which they had on earth; that Christ was not Lord or King before his resurrection, or Priest before his ascension: that the saints shall not, before the day of judgment, enjoy the bliss of heaven; that God does not certainly know future contingencies; that there is not any authority of fathers or general councils in determining matters of faith; that Christ, before his death, had not any dominion over the angels; and that Christ, by dying, made not satisfaction for us." See the preface to Sir Peter Pett's Happy future State of England, printed in 1688.

* The Socinians, who reside at present in the district of Mark, used to meet, some years ago, at stated times, at Koningswald, a village in the neighbourhood of Frankfort, on the Oder. See the Recueil de Literature, de Philosophie et d'Historie (published at Amsterdam, in 1731,*) p. 44. They published, in 1716, at Berlin, their confession of faith, in the German language, which is to be found, with a refutation thereto annexed, in a book entitled, Den Theologischen Heb. Opfern, part x. p. 852.

☞ † This community, of which an account is given in the following chapter, called their religious meetings *Colleges*, that is, congregations or assemblies; and hence they were denominated *Collegiants*.

☞ * The author of this collection was one Jordan, who was pastor of a church in the neighbourhood of Berlin.

VI. After the Socinians, as there is a great affinity between the two sects, it is proper to mention the Arians, who had several celebrated writers in this century, such as Sandius and Biddle.† Of those who also passed under the general denomination of Anti-Trinitarians and Unitarians, there are many that may be placed in the class of the Socinians and Arians; for the term *Unitarian* is very comprehensive, and is applicable to a great variety of persons, who agree in this common principle, that there is no real distinction in the divine nature. The denomination of Arian is also given in general to those who consider Jesus Christ as inferior and subordinate to the Father. But, as this subordination may be understood and explained in various ways, it is evident that the term *Arian*, as it is used in modern language, is susceptible of different significations; and that, in consequence, the persons to whom it is applied cannot be all considered in the same point of light with the ancient Arians, or supposed to agree perfectly with each other in their religious tenets.

CHAPTER VII.

Concerning some Sects of Inferior Note.

I. It will not be improper to take notice here of a few sects of inferior consequence and note, which we could not conveniently mention in the history of the more extensive and important communities that we have been surveying, and which, nevertheless, we cannot omit, for several reasons. While the disputes and tumults, produced in Holland in 1619 by the Arminian system, were at the greatest height, a religious society arose, whose members hold at Rhinsberg, near Leyden, a solemn assembly in every half-year, and are generally known by the denomination of *Collegiants*.‡ This community was founded by three brothers, of the name of Vander-Kodde, who

* Many examples might be alleged in proof of this. It will be sufficient to mention that of the learned Crellius, who, though he was professor of theology among the Socinians, yet differed in his opinions about many points of doctrine, from the sentiments of Socinus and the Racovian Catechism, and would not be called a Socinian, but an Artemonite.* See the Journal Literaire, tom. xvii. part i. and the account I have given of this celebrated man in my Syntagm. Dissertationum ad sanctiores Disciplinas pertinentium, p. 352.—Unschuld. Nachricht. 1750, p. 942.—Nouveau Diction. Historique et Critique, tom. ii. p. 88.

☞ This last citation is erroneous; there is no account of Crellius in the place here referred to.

† For an account of Sandius, father and son, see Arnold and other writers. The life of Biddle is to be found in the Nouveau Diction. Historique et Critique, tom. i. p. ii. p. 288. ☞ Dr. Mosheim places Biddle improperly among the Arians; it is manifest that he belongs to the Socinian sect, since, in the third article of his Confession of Faith, he professes to believe that Christ has no other than a human nature. See the Socinian Tracts, entitled, the Faith of one God, &c. published at London in 1691. See also notes [* †.]

‡ See note [†,] in the preceding chapter.

☞ * After Artemon, who lived in the reign of th Emperor Severus, and denied the pre-existence an divinity of Jesus Christ.

passed their days in the obscurity of a rural life, and are said to have been men of eminent piety, well acquainted with sacred literature, and great enemies to religious controversy. They had for their associate Anthony Cornelius, a man also of a mean condition, and who had no qualities that could give any degree of weight or credit to their cause. The descendants and followers of these men acquired the name of *Collegiants*, because they called their religious assemblies *Colleges*. All are admitted to the communion of this sect who acknowledge the divinity of the Scriptures, and endeavour to live suitably to the precepts and doctrines contained in those writings, whatever their peculiar sentiments may be concerning the nature of the Deity and the truths of Christianity. Their numbers are very considerable in the provinces of Holland, Utrecht, East and West-Friseland. They meet twice in every week, namely, on Sundays and Wednesdays, for the purpose of divine worship; and, after singing a psalm or hymn, and addressing themselves to the Deity by prayer, they explain a certain portion of the New Testament. The female members of the community are not allowed to speak in public; but all others, without any exception founded on rank, condition, or incapacity, have a right to communicate the result of their meditations to the assembly, and to submit their sentiments to the judgment of the brethren. All likewise have an unquestionable right to examine and oppose what has been advanced by any of the brethren, provided that their opposition be attended with a spirit of Christian charity and moderation. There is a printed list of the passages of Scripture, that are to be examined and illustrated at each of their religious meetings; so that any one who is ambitious of appearing among the speakers, may study the subject beforehand, and thus come fully prepared to descant upon it in public. The brethren, as has been already observed, have a general assembly twice a year at Rhinsberg, where they have ample and convenient houses for the education of orphans and the reception of strangers; and there they remain together during the space of four days, which are employed in hearing discourses that tend to edification, and exhortations which are principally designed to inculcate brotherly love and sanctity of manners. The sacrament of the Lord's supper is also administered during this assembly; and those adult persons who desire to be baptized, receive the sacrament of baptism, according to the ancient and primitive manner of celebrating that institution, that is, by immersion. Those Collegiants, who reside in the province of Friseland, have at present an annual meeting at Leewarden, where they administer the sacraments, as the distance at which they live from Rhinsberg renders it inconvenient for them to repair thither twice a year. We shall conclude our account of these sectaries by observing, that their community is of a most ample and extensive kind; that it comprehends persons of all ranks, orders, and sects, who profess themselves Christians, though their sentiments concerning the person and doctrine of the divine Founder of Christianity be extremely different; that it is kept together and its union maintained, not by the authority of rulers and doctors, the force of ecclesiastical laws, the restraining power of creeds and confessions, or the influence of positive rites and institutions, but merely by a zeal for the advancement of practical religion, and a desire of drawing instruction from the study of the Scriptures.*

II. In such a community, or rather amidst such a multitude as this, in which opinion is free, and every one is permitted to judge for himself in religious matters, dissensions and controversies can scarcely have place. However, a debate attended with some warmth, arose in 1672, between the merchants John and Paul Bredenburg, on one side, and Abraham Lemmerman and Francis Cuiper on the other John Bredenburg had erected a particular society, or college, in which he gave a course of lectures upon the religion of nature and reason; but this undertaking was highly disapproved by Lemmerman and Cuiper, who were for excluding reason altogether from religious inquiries and pursuits. During the heat of this controversy, Bredenburg discovered a manifest propensity toward the sentiments of Spinosa; he even defended them publicly, and yet, at the same time, professed a firm attachment to the Christian religion.† Other debates of less

* See the Dissertation sur les Usages de Ceux qu'on appelle en Hollande Collegiens et Rhinobourgeois, in the Ceremonies Religieuses de tous les Peuples du Monde, tom. iv. p. 323; as also a Dutch book, containing an account of the Collegiants, and published by themselves in 1736, under the following title: "De Oorspronck, Natuur, Handelwyze en Oogmerk der zo genaamde Rynburgsche Vergadering."

† The names of John Bredenburg, and Francis Cuiper, are well known among the followers and adversaries of Spinosa; but the character and profession of these two disputants are less generally known. Bredenburg, or (as he is otherwise called) Breitenburg, was a Collegiant, and a merchant of Rotterdam, who propagated in a public manner the doctrine of Spinosa, and pretended to demonstrate mathematically its conformity to the dictates of reason. The same man not only professed Christianity, but moreover explained, recommended, and maintained the Christian religion in the meetings of the Collegiants, and asserted, on all occasions, its divine original. To reconcile these striking contradictions, he declared, on one hand, that reason and Christianity were in direct opposition to each other; but maintained, on the other, that we were obliged to believe, even against the evidence of the strongest mathematical demonstrations, the religious doctrines comprehended in the Scriptures; (this, indeed, was adding absurdity to absurdity.) He affirmed, that truth was two-fold, theological and philosophical; and that those propositions, which were false in theology, were true in philosophy. There is a brief but accurate account of the character and sentiments of Bredenburg, in the learned work of the Jew, Isaac Orobio, entitled, "Certamen Philosophicum propugnatæ Veritatis, divinæ et naturalis, adversus Jo. Bredenburgii Principia, ex quibus, quod Religio Rationi repugnat, demonstrare nititur." This work, which contains Bredenburg's pretended demonstrations of the philosophy of Spinosa, was first published at Amsterdam in 1703, and afterwards at Brussels, in 1731. His antagonist, Francis Cuiper, acquired a considerable reputation by his Arcana Atheismi detecta, i. e. the secrets of Atheism detected. He was a bookseller at Amsterdam; and it was he that published, among other things, the Bibliotheca Fratrum Polonorum seu Unitariorum. Those who have a tolerable acquaintance with the literary history of this century, know that Cuiper, on account of the very book which he wrote against Bredenburg, was suspected of Spinocism, though he was a Collegiant, and a

consequence arose in this community; and the effect was a division of the Collegiants into two parties, which held their assemblies separately at Rhinsberg. This division happened in 1686; but it was healed about the commencement of the following century, by the death of those who had principally occasioned it; and then the Collegiants returned to their former union and concord.*

III. The Labadists were so called from their founder John Labadie, a native of France, a man of no mean genius, and remarkable for a natural and masculine eloquence. This man was born in the Romish communion, entered into the order of the Jesuits, and, being dismissed by them,† became a member of the reformed church, and exercised with reputation the ministerial functions in France, Switzerland, and Holland. He at length erected a new community, which resided successively at Middleburg in Zealand, and at Amsterdam. In 1670, it was transplanted to Hervorden in Westphalia, at the particular desire of the princess Elizabeth, daughter of the elector Palatine, and abbess of Hervorden.‡ It was soon driven from that part of Germany, notwithstanding the protection of this illustrious princess; and, in 1672, settled at Altena, where its founder died two years after his arrival. After the death of Labadie, his followers removed the wandering community to Wiewert, in the district of North-Holland, where it found a peaceful retreat, and soon fell into oblivion; so that few, if any, traces of it are now to be found.

Among the persons that became members of this sect, there were some, whose learning and abilities gave it a certain degree of credit and reputation, particularly Anna Maria Schurman, of Utrecht, whose extensive erudition rendered her so famous in the republic of letters. The members of this community, if we may judge of them by their own account, did not differ from the reformed church so much in their tenets and doctrines, as in their manners and rules of discipline;* for their founder exhibited in his own conduct a most austere model of sanctity and obedience, which his disciples and followers were obliged to imitate; and they were taught to look for the communion of saints, not only in the invisible church, but also in a visible one, which, according to their views of things, ought to be composed of none but such persons as were distinguished by their sanctity and virtue, and by a pious progress toward perfection. There are still extant several treatises composed by Labadie, which sufficiently discover the temper and spirit of the man, and bear evident marks of a lively and glowing imagination, not tempered by the influence of a sober and accurate judgment; and, as persons of this character are sometimes carried, by the impetuosity of pas-

zealous defender of the Christian faith, as also of the perfect conformity that subsists between right reason and true religion. ☞ Dr. Mosheim said a little before, in the text, that Lemmerman and Cuiper were for excluding reason altogether from religion; how then can he consistently say here of the latter, that he was a defender of the conformity between reason and religion?

* Beside the authors who have been already mentioned, those who understand the German language may consult the curious work of Simon Frederic Rues, entitled, "Nachrichten vom Zustande der Mennoniten," p. 267.

☞ † From this expression of our author, some may be led to imagine that Labadie was expelled by the Jesuits from their society; and many have, in effect, entertained this notion. But this is a palpable mistake; and whoever will be at the pains of consulting the letter of the abbe Goujet to father Niceron (published in the Memoires des Hommes illustres, tom. xx. p. 142,) will find that Labadie had long solicited his discharge from that society, and, after many refusals, obtained it at length in an honourable manner, by a public act signed at Bordeaux, by one of the provincials, on the 17th of April, 1639. For a full account of this restless, turbulent, and visionary man, who, by his plans of reformation, conducted by a zeal destitute of prudence, produced much tumult and disorder, both in the Romish and reformed churches, see his Life, composed with learning, impartiality, and judgment, by M. Chauffepeid, and inserted in that author's Supplement to Bayle.

☞ ‡ This illustrious princess seems to have had as strong a taste for fanaticism as her grandfather king James I. of England had for scholastic theology. She carried on a correspondence with Penn, the famous Quaker, and other members of that extravagant sect. She is, nevertheless, celebrated by certain writers, on account of her application to the study of philosophy and poetry. That a poetical fancy may have rendered her susceptible of fanatical impressions, is not impossible; but how these impressions could be reconciled with a philosophical spirit, is more difficult to imagine.

☞ * Labadie always declared, that he embraced the doctrines of the reformed church. Nevertheless, when he was called to perform the ministerial functions to a French church at Middleburgh in Zealand, he refused to subscribe its confession of faith. Besides, if we examine his writings, we shall find that he entertained very odd and singular opinions on various subjects. He maintained, among other things, "that God may and does, on certain occasions, deceive men; that the Scriptures are not sufficient to lead men to salvation, without certain particular illuminations and revelations from the Holy Ghost; that, in reading them, we ought to give less attention to the literal sense of the words, than to the inward suggestions of the spirit, and that the efficacy of the word depends upon the preacher;—that the faithful ought to have all things in common; that there is no subordination or distinction of rank in the true church of Christ;—that Christ is to reign a thousand years upon earth; that the contemplative life is a state of grace and union with God, and the very height of perfection; that the Christian, whose mind is contented and calm, sees all things in God, enjoys the Deity, and is perfectly indifferent about every thing that passes in the world; and that the Christian arrives at that happy state by the exercise of a perfect self-denial, by mortifying the flesh and all sensual affections, and by mental prayer." Beside these, he had formed singular ideas of the Old and New Testaments, considered as covenants, as also concerning the Sabbath, and the true nature of a Christian church.

It is remarkable, that almost all the sectaries of an enthusiastical turn were desirous of entering into communion with Labadie. The Brownists offered him their church at Middleburg, when he was suspended by the French synod from his pastoral functions. The Quakers sent their two leading members, Robert Barclay and George Keith, to Amsterdam, while he resided there, to examine his doctrine; and, after several conferences with him, these commissioners offered to receive him into their communion, which he refused, probably from a principle of ambition, and the desire of remaining head of a sect. It is even said, that the famous William Penn made a second attempt to gain over the Labadists; and that he went for that purpose to Wiewert, where they resided after the death of their founder, but without success. We do not pretend to answer for the truth of these assertions, but shall only observe, that they are related by Moller, in his Cimbria Literata, on the authority of a manuscript journal, of which several extracts have been given by Joach. Fred. Feller, in his Trimest. ix Monumentorum ineditorum, sect. iii. A. 1717. p. 498—500.

sion and the seduction of fancy, both into erroneous notions and licentious pursuits, we are not perhaps to reject, in consequence of an excessive charity or liberality of sentiment, the testimonies of those who have found many things worthy of censure, both in the life and doctrine of this turbulent enthusiast.*

IV. Among the fanatical contemporaries of Labadie was the famous Antoinette Bourignon de la Porte, a native of Flanders, who pretended to be divinely inspired, and set apart, by a particular interposition of Heaven, to revive the true spirit of Christianity, that had been extinguished by theological animosities and debates. This female enthusiast, whose religious feelings were accompanied with an unparalleled vivacity and ardour, and whose fancy was exuberant beyond all expression, joined to these qualities a volubility of tongue, less wonderful indeed, yet much adapted to seduce the unwary. Furnished with these useful talents, she began to propagate her theological system, and her enthusiastical notions made a great noise in Flanders, Holland, and some parts of Germany, where she had resided some years. Nor was it only the ignorant multitude that swallowed down with facility her visionary doctrines, since it is well known that several learned and ingenious men were persuaded of their truth, and caught the contagion of her fanaticism. After experiencing various turns of fortune, and suffering much vexation and ridicule on account of her religious fancies, she ended her days at Franeker, in Friseland, in 1680. Her writings were voluminous; but it would be a fruitless attempt to endeavour to draw from them an accurate and consistent scheme of religion; for the pretended divine light, that guides people of this class, does not proceed in a methodical way of reasoning and argument; it discovers itself by flashes, which shed nothing but thick darkness in the minds of those who investigate truth with the understanding, and do not trust to the reports of fancy, that is so often governed by sense and passion. An attentive reader will, however, learn something by perusing the writings of this fanatical virgin: he will be persuaded, that her intellect must have been in a disordered state; that her *divine effusions* were principally borrowed from the productions of the Mystics; and that by the intemperance of her imagination, she gave an additional air of extravagance and absurdity to the tenets which she derived from those pompous enthusiasts. If we attend to the main and predominant principle that appears in the incoherent productions of Bourignon, we shall find it to be the following: "That the Christian religion neither consists in knowledge nor in practice, but in a certain internal feeling, and divine impulse, arising immediately from communion with the Deity."† Among the more considerable patrons of this fanatical doctrine, we may reckon Christian Bartholomew de Cordt, a Jansenist, and priest of the oratory at Mechlin, who died at Nordstrand, in the duchy of Sleswick;* and Peter Poiret, a man of a bold and penetrating genius, who was a great master of the Cartesian philosophy.† The latter was shown in a striking manner by his own example, that knowledge and ignorance, reason and superstition, are often divided by thin partitions; and that they sometimes not only dwell together in the same person, but also, by an unnatural and unaccountable union, afford mutual assistance, and thus engender monstrous productions.

V. The same spirit, the same views, and the same kind of religion that distinguished Bourignon, were observable in an English, and also a female fanatic, named Jane Leadley, who, toward the conclusion of this century, seduced by her visions, predictions, and doctrines, a considerable number of disciples, among whom were some persons of learning; and thus gave rise to what was called the Philadelphian Society. This woman was of opinion that all dissensions among Christians would cease, and the kingdom of the Redeemer become, even here below, a glorious scene of charity, concord, and felicity, if those who bear the name of Jesus, without regarding the forms of doctrine or discipline which distinguish particular communions, would all join in committing their souls to the internal guide, to be instructed, governed, and formed by his divine impulse and suggestions. She even went farther, and declared, in the name of the Lord, that this desirable event would happen, and that she had a divine commission to proclaim the approach of this glorious communion of saints, who were to be collected in one visible universal church, or kingdom, before the dissolution of this earthly globe. This prediction she delivered with a peculiar degree of confidence, from a notion that her Philadelphian society was the true kingdom of Christ, in which alone the divine spirit resided and reigned. We shall not mention the other dreams of this enthusiast, among which the famous doctrine of the final restoration of all intelligent beings to perfection and happiness held an eminent place. Leadley was less fortunate than Bourignon in this respect, that she had not such an eloquent and ingenious patron as Poiret to plead her cause, and to give an air of philosophy to her wild reveries; for Pordage and Bromley, who were the chief of her associates, had nothing to recommend them but their mystic piety and contemplative turn of mind. Pordage, indeed, was so far destitute

* Moller's Cimbria Literata, tom. iii. p. 35, and his Isagoge ad Histor. Chersones. Cimbricæ, p. 2, cap. v. p. 121.—Arnold's Hist. Eccles. v. i. p. ii. lib. xvii. cap. xxi. p. 1186.—Weissman's Hist. Eccles. sæc. xvii. p. 927.—For an account of the two famous companions of Labadie, namely, Du Lignon and Yvon, see Cimbria Literata, tom. ii. p. 472, 1020.

† See, for an ample account of Bourignon, Moller's Cimbria Literata, and his Isagoge.—Bayle's Dict. at the article Bourignon.—Arnold, vol. ii. ☞ See also Poiret's Epist. de Auctoribus Mysticis, sect. xiv. p. 565. This treatise is inserted at the end of his book, de Euriditione solida et superficiaria

* Molleri Cimbria Literata, tom. ii. p. 149.

† Poiret dressed out in an artful manner and reduced to a kind of system, the wild and incoherent fancies of Bourignon, in his large work, entitled, L'Œconomie Divine, ou Systeme Universel, which was published, both in French and Latin, at Amsterdam, in 1686. For an account of this mystic philosopher, whose name and voluminous writings made such a noise, see Bibliotheca Brem. Theolog. Philol. tom. iii. p. 75.

of the powers of elocution and reasoning, that he even surpassed Jacob Behmen, whom he admired, in obscurity and nonsense; and, instead of imparting instruction to his readers, did no more than excite in them a stupid kind of awe by a high-sounding jingle of pompous words.*

* Jo. Wolf. Jaegeri Historia Sacra et Civilis, sæc. xvii. decenn. x. p. 90.—Petri Poireti Bibliotheca Mysticor. p. 161, 174, 283, 286.

A SHORT VIEW;

OR,

GENERAL SKETCH OF THE ECCLESIASTICAL HISTORY

OF THE

EIGHTEENTH CENTURY.

I. The History of the Christian Church during this period, instead of a few pages, would alone require a volume; such are the number and importance of the materials that it exhibits to an attentive inquirer. It is therefore to be hoped that, in due time, some able and impartial writer will employ his labours on this interesting subject. At the same time, to render the present work as complete as possible, and to give a certain clue to direct those who teach or who study ecclesiastical history, through a multitude of facts that have not yet been collected, or digested into a regular order, we shall draw a general sketch that will exhibit the principal outlines of the state of religion since the commencement of the eighteenth century. That this sketch may not swell to too great an extent, we shall omit the mention of the authors who have furnished materials for this period of church history. Those who are acquainted with modern literature must know, that there are innumerable productions extant, whence such a variety of lines and colours might be taken, as would render this group and general draught a finished piece.

II. The doctrines of Christianity have been propagated in Asia, Africa, and America, with equal zeal, both by the Protestant and Popish missionaries. But we cannot say the same thing of the true spirit of the Gospel, or of the religious discipline and institutions which it recommends to the observance of Christians; for it is an undeniable fact, that many of those whom the Romish missionaries have persuaded to renounce their false gods, are Christians only as far as an external profession and certain religious ceremonies go; and that, instead of departing from the superstitions of their ancestors, they observe them still, though under a different form. We have, indeed, pompous accounts of the mighty success with which the Jesuistical ministry has been attended among the barbarous and unenlightened nations; and the French Jesuits, in particular, are said to have converted innumerable multitudes in the course of their missions. This perhaps cannot be altogether denied, if we are to call those converts to Christianity who have received some faint and superficial notions of the doctrines of the Gospel; for it is well known, that several congregations of *such* Christians have been formed by the Jesuits in the East-Indies, and more especially in the Carnatic, the kingdoms of Madura and Marava, some territories on the coast of Malabar, in the kingdom of Tonquin, the Chinese empire, and also in certain provinces of America. These conversions have, in outward appearance, been carried on with particular success, since Antony Veri has had the direction of the foreign missions, and has taken such especial care, that neither hands should fail for this spiritual harvest, nor any expenses be spared that might be necessary to the execution of such an arduous and important undertaking. But these pretended conversions, instead of effacing the infamy under which the Jesuits labour in consequence of the iniquitous conduct of their missionaries in former ages, have only served to augment it, and to show their designs and practices in a still more odious point of view; for they are known to be much more zealous in satisfying the demands of their avarice and ambition, than in promoting the cause of Christ, and are said to corrupt and modify, by a variety of inventions, the pure doctrine of the Gospel, in order to render it more generally palatable, and to increase the number of their ambiguous converts.

III. A famous question arose in this century, relating to the conduct of the Jesuits in China, and their manner of promoting the cause of the Gospel, by permitting the new converts to observe the religious rites and customs of their ancestors. This question was decided to the disadvantage of the missionaries, in 1704, by Clement XI., who, by a solemn edict, forbade the Chinese Christians to practise the religious rites of their ancestors, and more especially those which are celebrated by the Chinese in honour of their deceased parents, and of their great lawgiver Confucius. This severe edict was, nevertheless, considerably mitigated in 1715, in order to appease, no doubt, the resentment of the Jesuits, whom it exasperated in the highest degree; for the pontiff allowed the missionaries to make use of the word *tien*, to express the divine nature, with the addition of the word *tchu*, to remove its ambiguity, and make it evident, that it was not the *heaven*, but the *Lord of heaven*, that the Christian doctors worshipped:* he also permitted the observance of those ceremonies which had so highly offended the adversaries of the Jesuits, on condition that they should be considered merely as marks of respect to their parents, and as tokens of civil homage to their lawgivers, without being abused to the purposes of superstition, or even being viewed in a religious point of light. In consequence of this second papal edict, considerable indulgence is granted to the Chinese converts: among other things, they have in their houses tablets, on which the names of their ancestors, and particularly of Confucius, are written in golden letters; they are allowed to light candles before these tablets, to make offerings to them of rich perfumes, victuals, fruits, and other delicacies, and even to prostrate the body before them until the head touches the ground. The same ceremony of prostration is performed by the Chinese Christians at the tombs of their ancestors.

The former edict, which was designed to prevent the motley mixture of Chinese superstition with the institutions of Christianity, was conveyed into China, in 1705, by cardinal Tournon, the pope's legate; and the second, which was of a more indulgent nature, was sent, in 1721, with Mezzabarba, who went to China with the same character. Neither the emperor nor the Jesuits were satisfied with these edicts. Tournon, who executed the orders of his spiritual employer with more zeal than prudence, was, by the express command of the emperor, thrown into prison, where he died in 1710. Mezzabarba, though more cautious and prudent, yet returned home without having succeeded in his negotiation; nor could the emperor be engaged, either by arguments or entreaties, to make any alteration in the institutions and customs of his ancestors.† At present the state of Christianity in China being extremely precarious and uncertain, this famous controversy is entirely suspended; and many reasons induce us to think, that both the pontiffs and the enemies of the Jesuits will unite in permitting the latter to depart from the rigour of the papal edicts, and to follow their own artful and insinuating methods of conversion; for they will both esteem it expedient and lawful to submit to many inconveniences and abuses, rather than to risk the entire suppression of popery in China.

IV. The attempts made since the commencement of the present century, by the English and Dutch, and more especially by the former to diffuse the light of Christianity through the benighted regions of Asia, and America, have been carried on with more assiduity and zeal than in the preceding age. That the Lutherans have borne their part in this salutary work appears abundantly from the Danish mission, planned with such piety in 1706 by Frederic IV. for the conversion of the Indians who inhabit the coast of Malabar, and attended with such remarkable success. This noble establishment, which surpasses all that have been yet erected for the propagation of the Gospel, not only subsists still in a flourishing state, but progressively acquires new degrees of perfection under the auspicious and munificent patronage of that excellent monarch Christian VI. We will, indeed, readily grant, that the converts to Christianity, made by the Danish missionaries, are less numerous than those which we find in the lists of the popish legates; but it may be affirmed, that they are much better Christians, and far excel the latter in sincerity and zeal. There is a great difference between Christians in reality, and Christians in appearance; and it is very certain, that the popish missionaries are much more ready than the protestant doctors, to admit into their communion proselytes, who have nothing of Christianity but the name.

We have very imperfect accounts of the labours of the Russian clergy, the greatest part of whom are still involved in that gross ignorance which covered the most unenlightened ages of the church: but we learn, from the modern records of that nation, that some of their doctors have employed, with a certain degree of success, their zeal and industry in spreading the light of the Gospel in those provinces which border upon Siberia.

V. While the missionaries now mentioned exposed themselves to the greatest dangers and sufferings, in order to diffuse the light of divine truth among these remote and darkened nations, there arose in Europe, where the Gospel had obtained a firm footing, a multitude of adversaries who shut their eyes upon its excellence, and endeavoured to eclipse its immortal lustre. There is no country in Europe where infidelity has not exhaled its poison; and scarcely any denomination of Christians among whom we may not find several persons, who either aim at the extinction of all religion, or at least endeavour to invalidate the authority of the Christian system. Some carry on these unhappy attempts in an open manner, others under the mask of a Christian profession; but no where have these enemies of the purest religion, and consequently of mankind, whom it was designed to render wise and happy, appeared with more effrontery and insolence, than under the free governments of Great Britain and the United Provinces. In England, more especially, it is not uncommon to meet with books, in which not only the doctrines of the Gospel, but also the perfections of the Deity, and the solemn obligations of piety and virtue, are impudently called in question, and turned into derision.* Such impious produc-

* The phrase *Tien Tchu*, signifies the Lord of heaven.

☞ † Tournon had been made, by the pope, patriarch of Antioch; and Mezzabarba, to add a certain degree of weight to his mission, was created patriarch of Alexandria. After his return, the latter was promoted to the bishopric of Lodi, a preferment which, though inferior in point of station to his imaginary patriarchate, was far more valuable in point of ease and profit.

See a more ample account of this mission in Dr. Mosheim's Memoirs of the Christian Church in China

☞ * This observation, and the examples by

tions have cast a deserved reproach on the names and memories of Toland, Collins, Tindal, and Woolston, a man of an inauspicious genius, who made the most audacious though senseless attempts to invalidate the miracles of Christ. Add to these Morgan, Chubb, Mandeville, and others. And writers of the same class will be soon found in all the countries of Europe, particularly in those where the Reformation has introduced a spirit of liberty, if mercenary booksellers are still allowed to publish, without distinction or reserve, every wretched production that is addressed to the passions of men, and designed to obliterate in their minds a sense of religion and virtue.

VI. The sect of Atheists, by which, in strictness of speech, those only are to be meant who deny the existence and moral government of an infinitely wise and powerful Being, by whom all things subsist, is reduced to a very small number, and may be considered as almost totally extinct. Any who yet remain under the influence of this unaccountable delusion, adopt the system of Spinosa, and suppose the universe to be one vast substance, which excites and produces a great variety of motions, all uncontrollably necessary, by a sort of internal force, which they carefully avoid defining with perspicuity and precision.

The Deists, under which general denomination those are comprehended who deny the divine origin of the Gospel in particular, and are enemies to all revealed religion, form a motley tribe, which, on account of their jarring opinions, may be divided into different classes. The most decent, or to use a more proper expression, the least extravagant and insipid form of Deism, is that which aims at an association between Christianity and natural religion, and represents the Gospel as no more than a republication of the original laws of nature and reason, that were more or less obliterated in the minds of men. This is the hypothesis of Tindal, Chubb, Mandeville, Morgan, and several others, if we are to give credit to their own declarations, which, indeed, ought not always to be done without caution. This also appears to have been the sentiment of an ingenious writer, whose eloquence has been ill employed in a book, entitled, Essential Religion distinguished from that which is only accessory;* for the whole religious system of this author consists in the three following points:—That there is a God, that the world is governed by his wise providence, and that the soul is immortal; and he maintains, that it was to establish these three points by his ministry, that Jesus Christ came into the world.

VII. The church of Rome has been governed, since the commencement of this century, by Clement XI. Innocent XIII. Benedict XIII Clement XII. and Benedict XIV. who may be all considered as men of eminent wisdom, virtue, and learning, if we compare them with the pontiffs of the preceding ages. Clement XI. and Prosper Lambertini, who at present fills the papal chair under the title of Benedict XIV.,† stand much higher in the list of literary fame than the other pontiffs now mentioned; and Benedict XIII. surpassed them all in piety, or at least in its appearance, which, in the whole of his conduct, was extraordinary and striking. It was he that conceived the laudable design of reforming many disorders in the church, and restraining the corruption and licentiousness of the clergy; and for this purpose, in 1725, he held a council in the palace of the Lateran, whose acts and decrees have been made public. But the event did not answer his expectations; nor is it probable that Benedict XIV. who is attempting the execution of the same worthy purpose, though by different means, will meet with better success.

We must not omit observing here, that the modern bishops of Rome make but an indifferent figure in Europe, and exhibit little more than an empty shadow of the authority of the ancient pontiffs. Their prerogatives are diminished, and their power is restrained within very narrow bounds. The sovereign princes and states of Europe, who embrace their communion, no longer tremble at the thunder of the Vatican, but treat their anathemas with contempt. They, indeed, load the holy father with pompous titles, and treat him with all the external marks of veneration and respect; yet they have given a mortal blow to his authority, by the prudent and artful distinction they make between the court of Rome and the Roman pontiff; for, under the cover of this distinction, they buffet him with one hand, and stroke him with the other; and, under the most respectful profession of attachment to his person, oppose the measures, and diminish still more, from day to day, the authority of his court. A variety of modern transactions might be alleged in confirmation of this, and more especially the debates that have arisen in this century, between the court of Rome and those of France, Portugal, Naples, and Sardinia, in all of which that

which it is supported in the following sentence, stand in need of some correction. Many books have, indeed, been published in England against the divinity both of the Jewish and Christian dispensations; and it is justly to be lamented, that the inestimable blessing of religious liberty, which the wise and good have improved to the glory of Christianity, by setting its doctrines and precepts in a rational light, and bringing them back to their primitive simplicity, has been so far abused by the pride of some, and the ignorance and licentiousness of others, as to excite an opposition to the Christian system, which is both designed and adapted to lead men, through the paths of wisdom and virtue, to happiness and perfection. It is, nevertheless, carefully to be observed, that the most eminent of the English unbelievers were far from renouncing, at least in their writings and profession, the truths of what they call natural religion, or denying the unchangeable excellence and obligations of virtue and morality. Dr. Mosheim is more especially in an error, when he places Collins, Tindal, Morgan, and Chubb, in the list of those who called in question the perfections of the Deity and the obligations of virtue: it was sufficient to put Mandeville, Woolston, and Toland, in this infamous class.

☞ * The original title of this book (which is supposed to have been written by one Muralt, a Swiss, author of the Lettres sur les Anglois et sur les Francois,) is as follows: "Lettres sur la Religion essentielle a l'Homme, distinguee de ce qui n'en est que l'accessoire." There have been several excellent refutations of this book published on the continent; among which the Lettres sur les vrais Principes de la Religion, composed by the late learned and ingenious M. Bouiller, deserve particular notice.

☞ † This history was published before the death of Benedict XIV.

ghostly court has been obliged to yield, and to discover its insignificancy and weakness.

VIII. There have been no serious attempts made in recent times to bring about a reconciliation between the Protestant and Romish churches; for, notwithstanding the pacific projects formed by private persons with a view to this union, it is justly considered as an impracticable scheme. The difficulties that attended its execution were greatly augmented by the bull *Unigenitus*, which deprived the peacemakers of the principal expedient they employed for the accomplishment of this union, by putting it out of their power to soften and mitigate the doctrines of popery, that appeared the most shocking to the friends of the Reformation. This expedient had been frequently practised in former times, in order to remove the disgust that the Protestants had conceived against the church of Rome; but that edict put an end to all these modifications, and, in most of those points that had occasioned our separation from Rome, represented the doctrine of that church in the very same shocking light in which it had been viewed by the first reformers. This shows, with the utmost evidence, that all the attempts the Romish doctors have made, from time to time, to give an air of plausibility to their tenets, and render them palatable, were so many snares insidiously laid to draw the Protestants into their communion; that the specious conditions they proposed as the terms of a reconciliation, were perfidious stratagems; and that, consequently, there can be no firm dependence upon the promises and declarations of such a disingenuous set of men.

IX. The intestine discords, tumults, and divisions, that reigned in the Romish church, during the preceding century, were so far from being terminated in this, that new fuel was added to the flame. These divisions still subsist; and the animosities of the contending parties seem to grow more vehement from day to day. The Jesuits are at variance with the Dominicans, and some other religious orders, though these quarrels make little noise, and are carried on with some regard to decency and prudence; the Dominicans are on bad terms with the Franciscans; the controversy concerning the nature, lawfulness, and expediency of the Chinese ceremonies, still continues, at least in Europe; and were we to mention all the debates that divide the Romish church, which boasts so much of its unity and infallibility, the enumeration would be almost endless. The controversy relating to Jansenism, one of the principal sources of that division which reigned within the papal jurisdiction, has been carried on with great spirit and animosity in France and in the Netherlands. The Jansenists, or, as they rather choose to be called, the disciples of Augustin, are inferior to their adversaries the Jesuits, in number, power, and influence; but they equal them in resolution, prudence, and learning, and surpass them in sanctity of manners and superstition, by which they excite the respect of the people. When their affairs take an unfavourable turn, and they are oppressed and persecuted by their victorious enemies, they find an asylum in the Low-Countries; for the greatest part of the catholics in the Spanish Netherlands, and all the Romanists who live under the jurisdiction of the United Provinces, embrace the principles and doctrines of Jansenius.* The latter have almost renounced their allegiance to the pope, though they profess a warm attachment to the doctrine and communion of the church of Rome; nor are either the exhortations or threats of the holy father, sufficient to subdue the obstinacy of these wayward children, or to reduce them to a state of subjection and obedience.

X. The cause of the Jansenists acquired a peculiar degree of credit and reputation, both in this and the preceding century, by a French translation of the New Testament, made by the learned and pious Pasquier Quesnel, a priest of the Oratory, and accompanied with practical annotations, adapted to excite lively impressions of religion in the minds of men. The quintessence of Jansenism was blended, in an elegant and artful manner, with these annotations, and was thus presented to the reader under the most pleasing aspect. The Jesuits were alarmed at the success of Quesnel's book, and particularly at the change it had wrought in many, in favour of the doctrines of Jansenius; and, to remove out of the way an instrument which proved so advantageous to their adversaries, they engaged that weak prince Louis XIV. to solicit the condemnation of this production at the court of Rome. Clement XI. granted the request of the French monarch, because he considered it as the request of the Jesuits; and, in 1713, issued the famous bull Unigenitus, in which Quesnel's New Testament was condemned, and a hundred and one propositions contained in it were pronounced heretical.† This bull, which is also known by the name of *The Constitution*, gave a favourable turn to the affairs of the Je-

☞ * This assertion is too general. It is true, that the greatest part of the catholics in the United Provinces are Jansenists, and that there is no legal toleration of the Jesuits in that republic. It is, nevertheless, a known fact, and a fact that cannot be indifferent to those who have the welfare and security of these provinces at heart, that the Jesuits are daily gaining ground among the Dutch papists. They have a flourishing chapel in the city of Utrecht, and have places of worship in several other cities, and in a great number of villages. It would be worthy of the wisdom of the rulers of the republic to put a stop to this growing evil, and not to suffer, in a protestant country, a religious order which has been suppressed in a popish one, and declared hostile to the state.*

☞ † To show what a political weathercock the *infallibility* of the holy father was upon this occasion, it may not be improper to introduce an anecdote which is related by Voltaire in his Seicle de Louis XIV. vol. ii. The credit of the narrator, indeed, weighs lightly in the balance of historical fame; but the anecdote is well attested, and is as follows: "The abbe Renaudot, a learned Frenchman, happening to be at Rome in the first year of the pontificate of Clement XI., went one day to see the pope, who was fond of men of letters, and was himself a learned man, and found his holiness reading Father Quesnel's book. On seeing Renaudot enter the apartment, the pope said, in a kind of rapture, 'Here is a most excellent book: we have nobody at Rome that is capable of writing in this manner;—I wish I could engage the author to reside here!'" And yet this same book was condemned afterwards by this same pope

* This note is left for the purpose of showing the state of affairs, at the time when Dr Maclaine inserted it; but its purport is superseded by the effect of the French revolution.—Edit.

suits; but it was highly detrimental to the interests of the Romish church, as many of the wiser members of that communion candidly acknowledge; for it not only confirmed the Protestants in their separation, by convincing them that the church of Rome was resolved to adhere obstinately to its ancient superstitions and corruptions, but also offended many of the catholics who had no particular attachment to the doctrines of Jansenius, and were only bent on the pursuit of truth and the advancement of piety. It must also be observed, that the controversy relating to Jansenism was much heated and augmented, instead of being mitigated or suspended, by this despotic and ill-judged edict.

XI. The dissensions and tumults excited in France by this edict were violent in the highest degree. A considerable number of bishops, and a large body composed of persons eminently distinguished by their piety and erudition, both among the clergy and laity, appealed from the bull to a general council. It was more particularly opposed by the cardinal Louis Antoine de Noailles, archbishop of Paris, who, equally unmoved by the authority of the pontiff, and by the resentment and indignation of Louis XIV., made a noble stand against the despotic proceedings of the court of Rome. These defenders of the ancient doctrine and liberties of the Gallican church were persecuted by the popes, the French monarch, and the Jesuits, from whom they received a series of injuries and affronts. Even their total ruin was aimed at by these unrelenting adversaries; but this inhuman purpose could not be entirely effected. Some of the Jansenists, however, were obliged to fly for refuge to their brethren in Holland; others were forced, by the terrors of penal laws, and by various acts of tyranny and violence, to receive the papal edict; while a considerable number, deprived of their places, and ruined in their fortunes, looked for subsistence and tranquillity at a greater distance from their native country. The issue of this famous contest was favourable to the bull, which was at length rendered valid by the authority of the parliament, and was registered among the laws of the state. This contributed, in some measure, to restore the public tranquillity; but it was far from diminishing the number of those who complained of the despotism of the pontiff; and the kingdom of France is still full of appellants,* who reject the authority of the bull, and only wait for an opportunity of reviving a controversy which is rather suspended than terminated, and of re-kindling a flame, that is covered without being extinguished.

XII. Amidst the calamities in which the Jansenists have been involved, they have only two methods left of maintaining their cause against their powerful adversaries; and these are their *writings* and their *miracles*. The former alone have proved truly useful to them; the latter gave them only a transitory reputation, which being ill founded, contributed in the issue to sink their credit. The writings in which they have attacked both the pope and the Jesuits are innumerable; and many of them are composed with such eloquence, spirit, and solidity, that they have produced a remarkable effect. The Jansenists, however, looking upon all human means as insufficient to support their cause, turned their views toward supernatural succours, and endeavoured to make it appear, that their cause was the peculiar object of the divine protection and approbation. For this purpose they persuaded the multitude, that God had endowed the bones and ashes of certain persons, who had distinguished themselves by their zeal in the cause of Jansenius, and had, at the point of death, appealed a second time from the pope to a general council, with the power of healing the most inveterate diseases. The person whose remains were principally honoured with this efficacy, was the abbe Paris, a man of a respectable family, whose natural character was dark and melancholy; whose superstition was excessive beyond all credibility; and who, by an austere abstinence from bodily nourishment, and the exercise of other inhuman branches of penitential discipline, was the voluntary cause of his own death.* To the miracles which were said to be wrought at the tomb of this fanatic, the Jansenists added a great variety of visions and revelations to which they audaciously attributed a divine origin; for several members of the community, and more especially those who resided at Paris, pretended to be filled with the Holy Ghost; and, in consequence of this prerogative, delivered instructions, predictions, and exhortations, which, though frequently extravagant, and almost always insipid, yet moved the passions, and attracted the admiration, of the ignorant multitude. The prudence, however, of the court of France, put a stop to these fanatical tumults and false miracles; and, in the situation in which things are at present, the Jansenists have nothing left but their genius and their pens to maintain their cause.†

XIII. We can say very little of the Greek and Eastern churches. The profound ignorance in which they live, and the despotic yoke under which they groan, prevent their forming any plans to extend their limits, or making any attempts to change their state. The Russians, who, in the reign of Peter the Great, assumed a less savage and barbarous aspect than they had before that memorable period, have in this century given some grounds to hope that they may one day be reckoned among the civilized

☞ * This was the denomination assumed by those who appealed from the bull and the court of Rome to a general council.

* The imposture, that reigned in these pretended miracles, has been detected and exposed by various authors, but by none with more acuteness, perspicuity, and penetration, than by the ingenious Dr. Douglass, in his excellent treatise on miracles, entitled the Criterion, published in 1754.

☞ † Things are greatly changed since the learned author wrote this paragraph. The storm of just resentment that has arisen against the Jesuits, and has been attended with the extinction of their order in Portugal, France, and in all the Spanish dominions, has disarmed the most formidable adversaries of Jansenism, and must consequently be considered as an event highly favourable to the Jansenists.*

* In consequence of the French revolution, more important changes have taken place since the translator wrote the last note.—Edit.

nations. There are, nevertheless, immense multitudes of that rugged people, who are still attached to the brutish superstition and discipline of their ancestors; and there are many in whom the barbarous spirit of persecution still so far prevails, that, were it in their power, they would cut off the Protestants, and all other sects that differ from them, by fire and sword. This appears evident from a variety of circumstances, and more especially from the book which Stephen Javorski has composed against heretics of all denominations.

The Greek Christians are said to be treated at present by their haughty masters with more clemency and indulgence than in former times. The Nestorians and Monophysites in Asia and Africa persevere in their refusal to enter into the communion of the Romish church, notwithstanding the earnest intreaties and alluring offers that have been made from time to time by the pope's legates, to conquer their inflexible constancy.—The pontiffs have frequently attempted to renew, by another sacred expedition, their former connexions with Abyssinia; but they have not yet been able to find out a method of escaping the vigilance of that court, which still persists in its abhorrence of popery. Nor is it at all probable that the embassy which is now preparing at Rome for the Abyssinian emperor, will be attended with success.* The Monophysites propagate their doctrine in Asia with zeal and assiduity, and, not long ago, gained over to their communion a part of the Nestorians who inhabit the coasts of India.

XIV. The Lutheran church, which dates its foundation from the year 1517, and the confession of Augsburg from 1530, celebrated in peace and prosperity the secular return of those memorable periods in the years 1717 and 1730. It received, some years ago, a considerable accession to the number of its members by the emigration of those protestants, who abandoned the territory of Saltzburg, and the town of Berchtolsgaden, in order to breathe a free air, and to enjoy unmolested the exercise of their religion. One body of these emigrants settled in Prussia, another in Holland; and many of them transplanted themselves and their families to America, and other distant regions. This circumstance contributed greatly to propagate the doctrine, and extend the reputation of the Lutheran church, which thus formed several congregations of no small note in Asia and America. The state of Lutheranism at home has not been so prosperous, since we learn both from public transactions, and also from the complaints of its professors and patrons, that, in several parts of Germany, this church has been injuriously oppressed, and unjustly deprived of some of its privileges and advantages, by the votaries of Rome.

XV. It has been scarcely possible to introduce any change into the doctrine and discipline of that church, because the ancient confessions and rules that were drawn up to point out the tenets that were to be believed, and the rites and ceremonies that were to be performed, still remain in their full authority, and are considered as the sacred guardians of the Lutheran faith and worship. The method, however, of illustrating, enforcing, and defending the doctrines of Christianity, has undergone several changes. About the commencement of this century, an artless simplicity was generally observed by the Lutheran ministers, and all philosophical terms and abstract reasonings were relinquished, as more adapted to obscure than to illustrate the truths of the Gospel. But, in process of time, a very different way of thinking began to take place; and several learned men entertained a notion that the doctrines of Christianity could not maintain their ground, if they were not supported by the aids of philosophy, and exhibited and proved in geometrical order.

The adepts in jurisprudence, who undertook, in the last century, the revision and correction of the ecclesiastical code that is in force among the Lutherans, carried on their undertaking with great assiduity and spirit; and our church-government would at this day bear another aspect, if the ruling powers had judged it expedient to listen to their counsels and representations. We see, indeed, evident proofs that the directions of these great men, relating to the external form of ecclesiastical government, discipline, and worship, are highly respected; and that their ideas, even of doctrine, have been more or less adopted by many. Hence it is not surprising, that warm disputes have arisen between them and the rulers of the church concerning several points. The Lutheran doctors are apprehensive that, if the sentiments of some of these reformers should take place, religion would become entirely subservient to the purposes of civil policy, and be converted into a mere state-machine; and this apprehension is not peculiar to the clergy, but is also entertained by some persons of piety and candour, even among the civilians.

XVI. The liberty of thinking, speaking, and writing, concerning religious matters, which began to prevail in the last century, was, in this, confirmed and augmented; and it extended so far as to encourage both infidels and fanatics to pour forth among the multitude, without restraint, all the crudities of their enthusiasm and extravagance. Accordingly we have seen, and still see, numbers of fanatics and innovators start up, and, under the influence of enthusiasm or of a disordered brain, divulge their crude fancies and dreams among the people, by which they either delude many from the communion of the established church, or at least occasion contests and divisions of the most disagreeable kind. We mentioned formerly several of these disturbers of the tranquillity of the church, to whom we may now add the notorious names of Tennhart, Gichtel, Uberfeld, Rosenbach, Bredel, Seiz, Roemeling, and many others, who either imagined that they were divinely inspired, or, from a persuasion of their superior capacity and knowledge, set up for reformers of the doctrine and discipline of the church. Many writers drew their pens against this presumptuous and fanatical tribe, though the greatest part of those who composed it were really below the notice of men of character, and were rather worthy of contempt than of opposition. And, indeed

* See the *Continuation*.

it was not so much the force of reason and argument, as the experience of their ill success, that convinced these fanatics of their folly, and induced them to desist from their chimerical projects. Their attempts could not stand the trial of time and common sense; and therefore, after having made a transitory noise, they fell into oblivion. Such is the common and deserved fate of almost all the fanatic ringleaders of the deluded populace; they suddenly start up, and make a figure for a while; but, in general, they ruin their own cause by their imprudence or obstinacy, by their austerity or perverseness, by their licentious conduct or their intestine divisions.

XVII. Many place in this fanatical class the Brethren of Herrenhut, who were first formed into a religious community in the village so named, in Lusatia, by the famous count Zinzendorff, and afterwards grew so numerous that their emigrants were spread abroad in almost all the countries of Europe, formed settlements in the Indies, and even penetrated to the remotest parts of the globe. They call themselves the descendants of the Bohemian and Moravian Brethren, who, in the fifteenth century, threw off the despotic yoke of Rome, animated by the zealous exhortations and heroic example of John Huss. They may, however, be said, with more propriety, to imitate the example of that famous community, than to descend from those who composed it; for it is well known, that there are very few Bohemians and Moravians in the fraternity of the Herrnhutters; and it is extremely doubtful, whether even this small number are to be considered as the posterity of the ancient Bohemian Brethren, that distinguished themselves so early by their zeal for the Reformation.

If we are to give credit to the declarations of the Herrenhutters, they agree with the Lutherans in their doctrine and opinions, and only differ from them in their ecclesiastical discipline, and in those religious institutions and rules of life which form the resemblance between the Bohemian Brethren and the disciples of Zinzendorff. There are, indeed, many who doubt much of the truth of this declaration, and suspect that the society now under consideration, and more especially their rulers and ringleaders, speak the language of Lutheranism when they are among the Lutherans, in order to obtain their favour and indulgence; and those who have examined this matter with the greatest attention, represent this fraternity as composed of persons of different religions, as well as of various ranks and orders. Be that as it may, it is at least very difficult to guess the reason that induces them to live in such an entire state of separation from the Lutheran communion, and to be so ambitiously zealous in augmenting their sect, if there be no other difference between them and the Lutherans than that of discipline and of ceremony; for the true and genuine followers of Jesus Christ are little concerned about the outward forms of ecclesiastical government and discipline, knowing that real religion consists in faith and charity, and not in external rites and institutions.*

XVIII. It was the opinion of many, that the succours of philosophy were absolutely necessary to stem the torrent of superstition, and stop its growing progress, and that these alone were adapted to accomplish this desirable purpose. Hence the study of philosophy, which, toward the conclusion of the last century, seemed to decline, was now revived, established upon a more rational footing, and pursued with uncommon assiduity and ardour. The branch of philosophy which is commonly known under the denomination of *Metaphysics*, was generally preferred, as it leads to the first principles of things; and the improvements made in this important science were very considerable. These improvements were chiefly produced by the genius and penetration of Leibnitz, who threw a new light upon metaphysics, and gave

☞ * It is somewhat surprising to hear Dr. Mosheim speak in such vague and general terms of this sect, without taking the least notice of their pernicious doctrines and their flagitious practices, that not only disfigure the sacred truths of the Gospel, but also sap all the foundations of morality To be persuaded of this, the reader, beside the accounts which Rimius has given of this enormous sect, will do well to consult a curious Preface, prefixed to the French translation of a Pastoral Letter against Fanaticism, addressed by Mr. Stinstra, an Anabaptist minister in Friseland, to his congregation, and published at Leyden in 1752. It may not be amiss to add here a passage relating to this odious community, from the bishop of Glocester's treatise, entitled, the Doctrine of Grace. The words of that great and eminent prelate are as follow: "As purity respects practice, the Moravians give us little trouble. If we may credit the yet unconfuted relations, both in print and in MS., composed by their own members, the participants in their most sacred mysterious rites, their practices in the consummation of marriage are so horribly, so unspeakably flagitious, that this people seem to have no more pretence to be put into the number of Christian sects, than the Turlupins of the thirteenth century, a vagabond crew of miscreants, who rambled over Italy, France, and Germany, calling themselves the Brothers and Sisters of the Free Spirit, who, in speculation, professed that species of atheism called Pantheism, and, in practice, pretended to be exempted from all the obligations of morality and religion." See the Doctrine of Grace, vol. ii. As to the doctrines of this sect, they open a door to the most licentious effects of fanaticism. Such among many others are the following, drawn from the express declarations of count Zinzendorff. the head and founder of the community that the law is not a rule of life to a believer;—that the moral law belongs only to the Jews;—that a converted person cannot sin against light. But of all the singularities for which this sect is famous, the notions they entertain of the organs of generation in both sexes are the most enormously wild and extravagant. I consider (says Zinzendorff, in one of his sermons) the parts for distinguishing both sexes in Christians, as the most honourable of the whole body, my Lord and God having partly inhabited them, and partly worn them himself. This raving sectary looks upon the conjugal act as a piece of scenery, in which the male represents Christ the husband of souls, and the female the church. 'The married brother (says he) knows matrimony, respects it, but does not think upon it of his own accord; and thus the precious member of the covenant (i. e. the penis) is so much forgotten, becomes so useless, and consequently is reduced to such a natural numbness, by not being used, that afterwards, when he is to marry, and use it, the Saviour must restore him from this deadness of body. And when an Esther by grace, and sister according to her make, gets sight of this member, her senses are shut up, and she piously perceives that God the Son was a boy. *Ye holy matrons, who as wives are about your Vice-Christs, honour that precious sign with the utmost veneration.*' We beg the chaste reader's pardon for presenting him with this odious specimen of the horrors of the Moravian theology.

this interesting branch of philosophy a more regular form. This science received a still greater degree of perfection from the philosophical labours of the acute and indefatigable Wolff, who reduced it into a scientific order, and gave to its decisions the strength and evidence of a geometrical demonstration. Under this new and respectable form it captivated the attention and esteem of the greatest part of the German philosophers, and of those in general who pursue truth through the paths of strict evidence; and it was applied with great ardour and zeal to illustrate and confirm the great truths both of natural and revealed religion. This application of the First Philosophy gave much uneasiness to some pious men, who were extremely solicitous to preserve, pure and unmixed, the doctrines of Christianity; and it was accordingly opposed by them with great eagerness and obstinacy. Thus the ancient contest between philosophy and theology, faith and reason, was unhappily revived, and has been carried on with much animosity for several years past. For many are of opinion, that this metaphysical philosophy inspires youthful minds with notions that are far from being favourable either to the doctrines or to the positive institutions of religion; that, seconded by the warmth of fancy, at that age of levity and presumption, it engenders an arrogant contempt of Divine Revelation, and an excessive attachment to human reason, as the only infallible guide of man; and that, instead of throwing new light on the science of theology, and giving it an additional air of dignity, it has contributed, on the contrary, to cover it with obscurity, and to sink it into oblivion and contempt.

XIX. In order to justify this heavy charge against the metaphysical philosophy, they appeal to the writings of Laurent Schmidt, whom they commonly call the Wertheim interpreter, from the place of his residence. This man, who was by no means destitute of abilities, and had acquired a profound knowledge of the philosophy now under consideration, undertook, some years ago, a new German translation of the Holy Scriptures, to which he prefixed a new system of theology, drawn up in a geometrical order, that was to serve him as a guide in the exposition of the sacred oracles. This undertaking proved highly detrimental to its author, as it drew upon him from many quarters severe marks of opposition and resentment; for he had scarcely published the Five Books of Moses, as a specimen of his method and abilities, when he was not only attacked by several writers, but also brought before the supreme tribunal of the empire, and there accused as an enemy of the Christian religion, and a caviller at divine truth. This severe charge was founded upon this circumstance only, that he had boldly departed from the common explication of certain passages in the books of Moses, which are generally supposed to prefigure the Messiah.* On this account he was sent to prison, and his errors were looked upon as capitally criminal; but he escaped the vigilance of his keepers, and saved himself by flight.

XX. The bare indication of the controversies that have divided the Lutheran church since the commencement of this century would make up a long list. The religious contests that were set on foot by the Pietists were carried on in some places with animosity, in others with moderation, according to the characters of the champions, and the temper and spirit of the people. These contests, however, have gradually subsided, and seem at present to be all reduced to the following question, whether a wicked man be capable of acquiring a true and certain knowledge of divine things, or be susceptible of any degree or species of divine illumination. The controversy that has been excited by this question is considered by many as a mere dispute about words; its decision, at least, is rather a matter of curiosity than importance. Many other points, that had been more or less debated in the last century, occasioned keen contests in this, such as the eternity of hell torments; the reign of Christ upon earth during a thousand years; and the final restoration of all intelligent beings to order, perfection, and happiness. The mild and indulgent sentiments of John Fabricius, professor of divinity at Helmstadt, concerning the importance of the controversy between the Lutherans and Catholics, excited also a warm debate; for this doctor and his disciples went so far as to maintain, that the difference, between those churches, was of so little consequence, that a Lutheran might safely embrace popery. The warm controversies that have been carried on between certain divines, and some eminent civilians, concerning the rites and obligations of wedlock, the lawful grounds of divorce, and the nature and guilt of concubinage, are sufficiently known. Other disputes of inferior moment, which have been of a sudden growth, and of a short duration, we shall pass over in silence, as the knowledge of them is not necessary to our forming an accurate idea of the internal state of the Lutheran church.

XXI. The reformed church still carries the same external aspect under which it has been already described;* for, though there be every where extant certain books, creeds, and confessions, by which the wisdom and vigilance of ancient times thought proper to perpetuate the truths of religion, and to preserve them from the contagion of heresy, yet, in most places, no person is obliged to adhere strictly to the doctrines they contain; and those who profess the main and fundamental truths of the Christian religion, and take care to avoid too *great an intimacy*† with the tenets of Soci-

☞ * Dr. Mosheim gives here but one half of the accusation brought against Schmidt, in 1737, when he was charged with attempting to prove, that there was not the smallest trace or vestige of the doctrine of the Trinity, nor any prediction pointing out the Messiah, to be found in the Five Books of Moses. It was by the authority of an edict addressed by Charles VI. to the princes of the empire, that Schmidt was imprisoned.

☞ * This description the reader will find above, at the beginning of the preceding century.

☞ † *Nimiam consuetudinem.* The expression is remarkable and malignant; it would make the ignorant and unwary apt to believe, that the reformed church allows its members certain approaches toward popery and Socinianism, provided they do not carry these approaches too far, even to an intimate

nianism and popery, are deemed worthy members of the reformed church.* Hence, in our times, this great and extensive community comprehends, in its bosom, Arminians, Calvinists, Supralapsarians, Sublapsarians, and Universalists, who lived together in charity and friendship,† and unite their efforts in healing the breach, and diminishing the weight and importance of those controversies that separate them from each other.‡ This moderation is, indeed, severely censured by many of the reformed divines in Switzerland, Germany, and more especially in Holland, who lament, in the most sorrowful strains, the decline of the ancient purity and strictness that characterized the doctrine and discipline of the church, and sometimes attack, with the strongest marks of indignation and resentment, these modern contemners of primitive orthodoxy. But, as the moderate party have an evident superiority in point of number, power, and influence, these attacks of their adversaries are, in general, treated with the utmost indifference.

XXII. Whoever considers all these things with due attention, will be obliged to acknowledge that neither the Lutherans nor Arminians have, at this day, any farther subject of controversy or debate with the reformed church, considered in a general point of view, but only with individual members of this great community;* for the church, considered in its

union with them. This representation of the reformed church is too glaringly false to proceed from ignorance; and Dr. Mosheim's extensive knowledge places him beyond the suspicion of an involuntary mistake in this matter. It is true, this reflection bears hard upon his candour; and we are extremely sorry that we cannot, in this place, do justice to the knowledge of that great man, without arraigning his equity.

☞ * Nothing can be more unfair, or at least more inaccurate, than this representation of things. It proceeds from a supposition that is quite chimerical, even that the reformed churches in England, Scotland, Holland, Germany, Switzerland, &c. form one general body, and, beside their respective and particular systems of government and discipline, have some general laws of religious toleration, in consequence of which they admit a variety of sects into their communion. But this general hierarchy does not exist. The friends of the Reformation, whom the multiplied horrors and absurdities of popery obliged to abandon the communion of Rome, were formed, in process of time, into distinct ecclesiastical bodies, or national churches, every one of which has its peculiar form of government and discipline. The toleration that is enjoyed by the various sects and denominations of Christians, arises in part from the clemency of the ruling powers, and from the charity and forbearance which individuals think themselves bound to exercise one toward another. See the following note.

☞ † If the different denominations of Christians here mentioned live together in the mutual exercise of charity and benevolence, notwithstanding the diversity of their theological opinions, this circumstance, which Dr. Mosheim seems to mention as a reproach, is, on the contrary, a proof, that the true and genuine spirit of the Gospel (which is a spirit of forbearance, meekness, and charity,) prevails among the members of the reformed churches. But it must be carefully observed, that this charity, though it discovers the amiable *bond of peace*, does not, by any means, imply uniformity of sentiment or indifference about truth, or lead us to suppose that the reformed churches have relaxed or departed from their system of doctrine. Indeed, as there is no general reformed church, so there is no general reformed Creed or Confession of Faith. The church of England has its peculiar system of doctrine and government, which remains still unchanged, and in full force; and to which an assent is demanded from all its members, and in a more especial, solemn, and express manner from those who are its ministers. Such is the case with the national reformed churches in the United Provinces. The dissenters in these countries, who are tolerated by the state, have also their respective bonds of ecclesiastical union; and such of them, particularly in England and Ireland, as differ from the establishment only in their form of government and worship, and not in matters of doctrine, are treated with indulgence by the moderate members of the national church, who look upon them as their brethren.

☞ ‡ In the 4to edition of this work, I mistook, in a moment of inadvertency, the construction of this sentence in the original Latin, and rendered the passage as if Dr. Mosheim had represented the reformed churches as diminishing the weight and importance of those controversies that 'separate them from the church of Rome;' whereas he represents them (and, indeed, what he says is rather an encomium than a reproach) as diminishing the weight of those controversies which 'separate them from each other.' One of the circumstances that made me fall more easily into this mistake was my having read, the moment before I committed it, Dr Mosheim's insinuation with respect to the spirit of the church of England in the very next page, where he says, very inconsiderately, that we may judge of that spirit by the conduct of Dr. Wake, who formed a project of peace and union between the English and Gallican churches, founded upon this condition, that each community should retain the greatest part of its peculiar doctrines. This is supposing, though upon the foundation of a mistaken fact, that the church of England, at least, is making evident approaches to the church of Rome.—When I had made the mistake, which turned really an encomium into an accusation, I thought it incumbent on me to defend the reformed church against the charge of an approximation to popery. For this purpose, I observed (in note z of the 4to edition,) "that the reformed churches were never at such a distance from the spirit and doctrine of the church of Rome as they are at this day; and that the improvements in science, that characterize the last and the present age, seem to render a relapse into Romish superstition morally impossible in those who have been once delivered from its baneful influence." The ingenious author of the Confessional did not find this reasoning conclusive; but the objections he has started against it, do not appear to me insurmountable. I have, therefore, thrown upon paper some farther thoughts upon the present state of the reformed religion, and the influence of improvements in philosophy upon its advancement; and these thoughts the reader will find in the third part of the Appendix.

☞ * Even if we grant this to be true with respect to the Arminians, it cannot be affirmed, with equal truth, in regard to the Lutherans, whose doctrine concerning the corporal presence of Christ in the eucharist, and the communication of the properties of his divine to his human nature, is rejected by all the reformed churches, without exception. But it is not universally true, even with respect to the Arminians; for, though the latter are particularly favoured by the church of England; though Arminianism may be said to have become predominant among the members of that church, or at least to have lent its influence in mitigating some of its articles in the private sentiments of those who subscribe them; yet the thirty-nine Articles of the same church still maintain their authority; and, when we judge of the doctrine and discipline of any church, it is more natural to form this judgment from its established creeds and confessions of faith, than from the sentiments and principles of particular persons; so that, with respect to the church of England, the direct contrary of what Dr. Mosheim asserts is strictly true; for it is rather with that church, and its rule of faith, that the Lutherans are at variance, than with private persons, who, prompted by a spirit of Christian moderation, mitigate some of its doctrines, in order charitably to extend the limits of its communion. But, if we turn our view to the reformed churches in Holland, Germany, and a part of Switzerland, the mistake of our author will still appear more palpable; for some of these churches consider certain doctrines both of the Arminians and Lutherans, as a just cause of excluding them

collective and general character, allows now to all its members the full liberty of entertaining the sentiments which they think most reasonable, in relation to those points of doctrine that formerly excluded the Lutherans and Arminians from its communion, and looks upon the essence of Christianity and its fundamental truths as in no wise affected by these points, however variously they may be explained by the contending parties. But this moderation, instead of facilitating the execution of the plans that have been proposed by some for the re-union of the Lutheran and Reformed churches, contributes rather to prevent this re-union, or at least to render it much more difficult; for those among the Lutherans who are zealous for the maintenance of the truth, complain, that the reformed church has rendered too wide the way of salvation, and opened the arms of fraternal love and communion, not only to us (Lutherans,) but also to Christians of all sects and denominations. Accordingly, we find, that when, about twenty years ago, several eminent doctors of our communion, with the learned and celebrated Matthew Pfaff at their head, employed their good offices with zeal and sincerity in order to our union with the reformed church, this specific project was so warmly opposed by the majority of the Lutherans, that it was soon rendered abortive.*

XXIII. The church of England, which is now the chief branch of the great community denominated the Reformed Church, continues in the same state, and is governed by the same principles, that it assumed at the Revolution. The established form of church government is episcopacy, which is embraced by the sovereign, the nobility, and the greatest part of the people. The Presbyterians, and the numerous sects that are comprehended under the general title of Non-conformists, enjoy the sweets of religious liberty, under the influence of a legal toleration. Those, indeed, who are best acquainted with the present state of the English nation, confidently affirm that the dissenting interest is declining, and that the cause of nonconformity owes this gradual decay, in a great measure, to the lenity and moderation that are practised by the rulers of the established church. The members of this church may be divided into two classes, according to their different ideas of the origin, extent, and dignity of episcopal jurisdiction. Some look upon the government of bishops as founded on the authority of a divine institution, and are immoderately zealous in extending the power and prerogatives of the church; others, of a more mild and sedate spirit, while they consider that form of government as far superior to every other system of ecclesiastical polity, and warmly recommend all the precautions that are necessary to its preservation and the independence of the clergy, yet do not carry this attachment to such an excessive degree, as to refuse the name of a *church* to every religious community that is not governed by a bishop, or to defend, with intemperate zeal, the prerogatives and pretensions of the episcopal order.*—These two classes are sometimes involved in warm debates, and oppose each other with no small degree of animosity, of which this century has exhibited the following remarkable example. Dr. Benjamin Hoadly, bishop of Winchester, a prelate eminently distinguished by the accuracy of his judgment, and the purity of his flowing and manly eloquence, used his utmost endeavours, and not without success, to lower the authority of the church, or at least to reduce the power of its rulers within narrow bounds. On the other hand, the church and its rulers found several able defenders; and, among the rest, Dr. John Potter, archbishop of Canterbury, maintained the rights and pretensions of the clergy with great eloquence and erudition. As to the spirit of the established church of England, in relation to those who dissent from its rules of doctrine and government, we see it no where better than in the conduct of Dr. Wake, archbishop of Canterbury, who formed a project of peace and union between the English and Gallican churches, founded upon this condition, that each community should retain the greatest part of its peculiar doctrines.†

from their communion. The question here is not, whether this rigour is laudable; it is the matter of fact that we are examining at present. The church of England, indeed, if we consider its present temper and spirit, does not look upon any of the errors of the Lutherans as *fundamental*, and is therefore ready to receive them into its communion; and the same thing may, perhaps, be affirmed of several of the reformed churches upon the continent. But this is very far from being a proof, that the "Lutherans have at this day (as Dr. Mosheim asserts) no farther subject of controversy or debate with these churches;" it only proves, that these churches nourish a spirit of toleration and charity worthy of imitation.

☞ * The project of the very pious and learned Dr. Pfaff for uniting the Lutheran and Reformed churches, and the reasons on which he justified this project, are worthy of the truly Christian spirit, and do honour to the accurate and sound judgment of that most eminent and excellent divine;* and it is somewhat surprising, considering the proofs of moderation and judgment that Dr. Mosheim has given in other parts of this valuable history, that he neither mentions the project of Dr. Pfaff with applause, nor the stiffness of the Lutherans on this occasion with any mark of disapprobation.

☞ * See this learned author's Collectio Scriptorum Irenicorum ad Unionem inter Protestantes facientium, published at Hall, in 1723.

☞ * The learned and pious archbishop Wake, in a letter to Father Courayer, dated from Croydon-House, July 9, 1724, expresses himself thus: "I bless God that I was born and have been bred in an episcopal church, which, I am convinced, has been the government established in the Christian church from the very time of the apostles. But I should be unwilling to affirm, that, where the ministry is not episcopal, there is no church, nor any true administration of the sacraments; and very many there are among us who are zealous for episcopacy, yet dare not go so far as to annul the ordinances of God performed by any other ministry."

☞ † Archbishop Wake certainly corresponded with some learned and moderate Frenchmen on this subject, particularly with M. Du-Pin, the ecclesiastical historian: and no doubt the archbishop, when he assisted Courayer in his Defence of the Validity of the English Ordinations, by furnishing him with unanswerable proofs drawn from the registers at Lambeth-Palace, had it in his view to remove certain groundless prejudices, which, while they subsisted among catholics, could not but defeat all projects of peace and union between the English and Gallican churches. The interests of the protestant religion could not be in safer hands than those of archbishop Wake. He who had so ably and so successfully defended protestantism, as a controversial writer, could not surely form any project of peace and union with a Roman catholic church, the terms

XXIV. The unbounded liberty which every individual in England enjoys of publishing, without restraint, his religious opinions, and of worshipping God in the manner which he deems the most conformable to reason and Scripture, naturally produces a variety of sects, and gives rise to an uninterrupted succession of controversies about theological matters. It is scarcely possible for any historian who has not resided for some time in England, and examined with attention, upon the spot, the laws, the privileges, the factions, and opinions of that free and happy people, to give a just and accurate account of these religious sects and controversies. Even the names of the greatest part of these sects have not yet reached us; and many of those which have come to our knowledge, we know but imperfectly. We are greatly in the dark with respect to the grounds and principles of these controversies, because we are destitute of the sources from which proper information might be drawn. At present the ministerial labours of George Whitefield, who has formed a community, which he proposes to render superior in sanctity and perfection to all other Christian churches, make a considerable noise in England, and are not altogether destitute of success. If there is any consistency in this man's theological system, and if we are not to look upon him as a mere enthusiast, led by the blind impulse of an irregular fancy, his doctrine seems to amount to these two propositions:—"That true religion consists alone in holy affections, or in a certain inward *feeling*, which it is impossible to explain; and that Christians ought not to seek truth by the dictates of reason, or by the aids of learning, but by laying their minds open to the direction and influence of divine illumination."

XXV. The Dutch church is still divided by the controversies that arose from the philosophy of Des-Cartes and the theology of Cocceius; but these controversies are carried on with less bitterness and animosity at present than in former times. It is even to be hoped that these contests will soon be totally extinguished, since it is well known, that the Newtonian philosophy has expelled Cartesianism from almost all the seminaries of learning in the United Provinces. We have already mentioned the debates that were occasioned by the opinions of Roell. In 1703, Frederic Van Leenhof was suspected of a propensity toward the system of Spinosa, and drew upon himself a multitude of adversaries, by a remarkable book, entitled Heaven upon Earth, in which he maintained literally, that it was the duty of Christians to rejoice always, and to suffer no feelings of affliction and sorrow to interrupt their gaiety. The same accusations were brought against an illiterate man, named William Deurhoff, who, in some treatises composed in the Dutch language, represented the Divine Nature under the idea of a certain force, or energy, that is diffused throughout the whole universe, and acts in every part of the great fabric. The more recent controversies that have made a noise in Holland, were those that sprang from the opinions of James Saurin and Paul Maty, on two very different subjects. The former, who was minister to the French at the Hague, and acquired a shining reputation by his genius and eloquence, fell into an error, which, if it may be called such, was at least an error of a very pardonable kind; for, if we except some inaccurate and incautious expressions, his only deviation from the received opinions consisted in his maintaining, that it was sometimes lawful to swerve from truth, and to deceive men by our speech, in order to the attainment of some great and important good.* This sentiment did not please, as the most considerable part of the reformed churches adopt the doctrine of Augustin, "That a lie or a violation of the truth can never be allowable in itself, or advantageous in the issue." The conduct of Maty was much more worthy of condemnation; for, in order to explain the mystery of the Trinity, he invented the following unsatisfactory hypothesis: "That the Son and the Holy Ghost were two finite Beings, who had been created by God, and at a certain time were united to the divine nature.†

XXVI. The particular confession of faith, that we have already had occasion to mention under the denomination of the Formulary of Agreement or Concord, has, since the commencement of this century, produced warm and vehement contests in Switzerland, and more especially in the canton of Bern. In 1718, the magistrates of Bern published an order, by which all professors, and particularly

of which would have reflected on his character as a negotiator. ☞ This note has been misunderstood and censured by the acute author of the Confessional. This censure gave occasion to the fourth Appendix, which the reader will find in this volume, and in which the matter contained in this note is fully illustrated, and the conduct of archbishop Wake set in its true light.

☞ * See Saurin's Discours Historiques, Theologiques, Critiques, et Moraux, sur les Evenements les plus memorables du Vieux et du Nouveau Testament, tom. i. of the folio edition.

☞ † Dr. Mosheim, in another of his learned productions, has explained, in a more accurate and circumstantial manner, the hypothesis of Maty, which amounts to the following propositions: "That the Father is the pure Deity; and that the Son and the Holy Ghost are two other persons, in each of whom there are two natures; one divine, which is the same in all the three persons, and with respect to which they are one and the same God, having the same numerical divine essence; and the other a finite and dependent nature, which is united to the divine nature in the same manner in which the orthodox say, that Jesus Christ is God and man." See Dissertationes ad Historiam Ecclesiasticam pertinentes, (published at Altena in 1743,) vol. ii. p. 498, but principally the original work of Mr. Maty, which was published (at the Hague) in 1729, under the following title: Lettre d'un Theologien a un autre Theologien sur le Mystere de la Trinite.—The publication of this hypothesis was unnecessary, as it was destitute even of the merit of novelty, being very little more than a repetition of what Dr. Thomas Burnet, prebendary of Sarum, had said, about ten years before, upon this mysterious subject, which nothing but presumption can make any man attempt to render intelligible. See a treatise published without his name by Dr. Burnet, in 1720, with this title: The Scripture Trinity intelligibly explained; or, An Essay towards the Demonstration of a Trinity in Unity from Reason and Scripture, in a Chain of Consequences from certain Principles, &c. by a Divine of the Church of England. See also the same author's Scripture Doctrine of the Redemption of the World by Christ, intelligibly explained, &c.

those of the university and church of Lausanne, who were suspected of entertaining erroneous opinions, were obliged to declare their assent to this Formulary, and to adopt it as the rule of their faith. This injunction was so much the more grievous, as no demand of that kind had been made for some time before this period; and the custom of requiring subscription to this confession had been suspended in the case of several who were promoted in the university, or had entered into the church. Accordingly many pastors and candidates for holy orders refused the assent that was demanded by the magistrates, and some of them were punished for this refusal. Hence arose warm contests and heavy complaints, which engaged the king of Great Britain, and the states general of the United Provinces, to offer their intercession, in order to terminate these unhappy divisions; and hence the Formulary lost much of its credit and authority.

Nothing memorable happened during this period in the German churches. The Reformed church that was established in the Palatinate, and had formerly been in such a flourishing state, suffered greatly from the persecuting spirit and the malignant counsels of the votaries of Rome.

XXVII. The Socinians, dispersed through the different countries of Europe, have not hitherto been able to form a separate congregation, or to celebrate publicly divine worship, in a manner conformable to the institutions of their sect, although, in several places, they hold clandestine meetings of a religious kind. The person that made the principal figure among them in this century, was the learned Samuel Crellius, who died in an advanced age at Amsterdam: he indeed preferred the denomination of Artemonite to that of Socinian, and departed in many points from the received doctrines of that sect.

The Arians found a learned and resolute patron in William Whiston, professor of mathematics in the university of Cambridge, who defended their doctrine in various productions, and chose rather to resign his chair, than to renounce his opinions. He was followed in these opinions, as is commonly supposed, by Dr. Samuel Clarke, a man of great abilities, judgment, and learning, who, in 1724, was accused of altering and modifying the ancient and orthodox doctrine of the Trinity.* But it must argue a great want of equity and candour, to rank this eminent man in the class of Arians, taking that term in its proper and natural signification; for he only maintained what

☞ * It is too evident that few controversies have so little augmented the sum of knowledge, and so much hurt the spirit of charity, as the controversies that have been carried on in the Christian church in relation to the doctrine of the Trinity. Mr. Whiston was one of the first divines who revived this controversy in the xviiith century. About the year 1706, he began to entertain some doubts about the proper eternity and omniscience of Christ. This led him to review the popular doctrine of the Trinity; and, in order to execute this review with a degree of diligence and circumspection suitable to its importance, he read the New Testament twice over, and also all the genuine monuments of the Christian religion prior to the conclusion of the second century. By this inquiry, he was led to think, that, at the incarnation of Christ, the *Logos*, or Eternal Wisdom, supplied the place of the *rational soul*, or πνευμα; that the eternity of the Son of God was not a real *distinct* existence, as of a son properly *co-eternal* with his father by a true eternal generation, but rather a metaphysical existence *in potentia*, or in some sublimer manner, in the Father, as his wisdom or word; that Christ's real *creation* or *generation* (for both these terms are used by the earliest writers) took place some time before the creation of the world; that the council of Nice itself established no other eternity of Christ; and, finally, that the Arian doctrine, in these points, was the original doctrine of Christ himself, of his holy apostles, and of the primitive Christians. Mr. Whiston was confirmed in these sentiments by reading Novatian's treatise concerning the Trinity, but more especially by the perusal of the Apostolical Constitutions, the antiquity and authenticity of which he endeavoured, with more zeal than precision and prudence, to prove, in the third part of his Primitive Christianity Revived.

This learned visionary, and upright man, was a considerable sufferer by his opinions. He was not only removed from his theological and pastoral functions, but also from his mathematical professorship as if Arianism had extended its baneful influence even to the science of lines, angles, and surfaces This measure was undoubtedly singular, and it appeared rigid and severe to all those, of both parties who were dispassionate enough to see things in their true point of light; and, indeed, though we should grant that the good man's mathematics might, by erroneous conclusions, have corrupted his orthodoxy, it will still remain extremely difficult to comprehend, how his heterodoxy could hurt his mathematics. It was not therefore consistent, either with clemency or good sense, to turn Mr. Whiston out of his mathematical chair, because he did not believe the explication of the Trinity that is given in the Athanasian creed; and I mention this as an instance of the unfair proceedings of immoderate zeal, which often confounds the plainest distinctions, and deals its punishments without measure or proportion.

Dr. Clarke also stepped aside from the notions commonly received concerning the Trinity; but his modification of this doctrine was not so remote from the popular and orthodox hypothesis, as the sentiment of Whiston. His method of inquiring into that incomprehensible subject was modest, and, at least, promised fairly as a guide to truth. For he did not begin by abstract and metaphysical reasonings in his illustrations of this doctrine, but turned his first researches to the word and to the testimony, being persuaded that, as the doctrine of the Trinity was a matter of mere revelation, all human explications of it must be tried by the declarations of the New Testament, interpreted by the rules of grammar, and the principles of sound criticism. It was this persuasion that produced his famous book, entitled, The Scripture Doctrine of the Trinity, wherein every Text in the New Testament relating to that Doctrine is distinctly considered, and the Divinity of our blessed Saviour, according to the Scriptures, proved, and explained. The doctrine, which this learned divine drew from his researches, was comprehended in 55 propositions, which, with the proper illustrations, form the second part of the work. As the reader will find them in that work at full length, we shall only observe here, that Dr. Clarke, if he was careful in searching for the true meaning of those scriptural expressions that relate to the divinity of the Son and the Holy Ghost, was equally circumspect in avoiding the accusation of heterodoxy, as appears by the series of propositions now referred to. There are three great rocks of heresy on which many bold adventurers on this Anti-Pacific ocean have been seen to split violently. These rocks are Tritheism Sabellianism, and Arianism. Dr. Clarke got evidently clear of the first, by denying the self-existence of the Son and the Holy Ghost, and by maintaining their derivation from, and subordination to, the Father. He strenuously laboured to avoid the second, by acknowledging the personality and distinct agency of the Son and the Holy Ghost; and he flattered himself with having escaped from the dangers of the third, by his asserting the eternity (for he believed the possibility of an eternal production which Whiston could not digest,) of the two divine subordinate

is commonly called the Arminian Subordination, which has been, and is still, adopted by some of the greatest men in England, and even by some of the most learned bishops in that country. This doctrine he illustrated with greater care and perspicuity than any before him had done, and taught that the Father, Son, and Holy Ghost, are equal in nature, and different in rank, authority, and subordination.* A great number of English writers have endeavoured, in a variety of modes, to invalidate and undermine the doctrine of the holy Trinity; and it was this consideration that engaged a lady,† eminently distinguished by her orthodoxy and opulence, to bequeath a valuable legacy as a foundation for a lecture, in which eight sermons are preached annually by a learned divine, who is nominated to that office by the trustees. This foundation has subsisted since the year 1720, and promises to posterity an ample collection of learned productions in defence of this branch of the Christian faith.

---

persons. But, with all his circumspection, Dr. Clarke did not escape opposition and censure. He was answered and abused; and heresy was subdivided and modified, in order to give him an opprobrious appellation, even that of Semi-Arian. The convocation threatened; but the doctor calmed by his prudence the apprehensions and fears which his scripture-doctrine of the Trinity had excited in that learned and reverend assembly. An authentic account of the proceedings of the two houses of convocation upon this occasion, and of Dr. Clarke's conduct in consequence of the complaints that were made against his book, may be seen in a piece supposed to have been written by the Rev. Mr. John Laurence, and published at London, in 1714, under the following title: An Apology for Dr. Clarke, containing an account of the late Proceedings in Convocation upon his Writings concerning the Trinity. The true copies of all the original papers relating to this affair are published in this apology.

If Dr. Clarke was attacked by authority, he was also combatted by argument. The learned Dr. Waterland was one of his principal adversaries, and stands at the head of a polemical body, composed of eminent divines, such as Gastrell, Wells, Nelson, Mayo, Knight, and others who appeared in this controversy. Against these, Dr. Clarke, unawed by their numbers, defended himself with great spirit and perseverance, in several letters and replies. This prolonged a controversy, which may often be suspended through the fatigue of the combatants, or the change of the mode in theological researches, but which will probably never be terminated: for nothing affords such an endless subject of debate as a doctrine above the reach of human understanding, and expressed in the ambiguous and improper terms of human language, such as persons, generations, substance, &c. which, in this controversy, either convey no ideas at all, or false ones. The inconveniences, accordingly, of departing from the divine simplicity of the scripture-language on this subject, and of converting a matter of mere revelation into an object of human reasoning, were palpable in the writings of both the contending parties. For, if Dr. Clarke was accused of verging toward Arianism, by maintaining the derived and caused existence of the Son and the Holy Ghost, it seemed no less evident that Dr. Waterland was verging toward Tritheism, by maintaining the self-existence and independence of these divine persons, and by asserting that the subordination of the Son to the Father is only a subordination of office and not of nature: so that, if the former divine was deservedly called a Semi-Arian, the latter might, with equal justice, be denominated a Semi-Tritheist. The difference between these learned men lay in this, that Dr. Clarke, after making a faithful collection of the texts in Scripture that relate to the Trinity, thought proper to interpret them by those maxims and rules of right reasoning, which are used on other subjects; whereas Dr. Waterland denied that this method of reasoning was to be admitted in illustrating the doctrine of the Trinity, which was far exalted above the sphere of human reason; and therefore he took the texts of Scripture in their direct, literal, and grammatical sense. Dr. Waterland, however, employed the words persons, subsistence, &c. as useful for fixing the notion of distinction; the words uncreated, eternal, and immutable, for ascertaining the divinity of each *person;* and the words interior, generation, and procession, to indicate their *union.* This was departing from his grammatical method, which ought to have led him to this plain conclusion, that the Son and the Holy Ghost, to whom divine attributes are ascribed in Scripture, (and even the denomination of God to the former,) possess these attributes in a manner which it is impossible for us to understand in this present state, and the understanding of which is consequently unessential to our salvation and happiness. The doctor, indeed, apologises in his *queries* (p. 321.) for the use of these metaphysical terms, by observing, that "they are not designed to enlarge our views, or to add any thing to our stock of ideas, but to secure the plain fundamental truth, that Father, Son, and Holy Ghost, are all strictly divine, and uncreated; and yet are not three Gods, but one God." It is, however, difficult to comprehend how terms that neither enlarge our views, nor give us ideas, can secure any truth. It is difficult to conceive what our faith gains by being entertained with a certain number of sounds. If a Chinese should explain a term of his language which I did not understand, by another term, which he knew beforehand that I understood as little, his conduct would be justly considered as an insult against the rules of conversation and good breeding; and I think it is an equal violation of the equitable principles of candid controversy, to offer, as illustrations, propositions or terms that are as unintelligible and obscure as the thing to be illustrated. The words of the excellent and learned Stillingfleet (in the Preface to his Vindication of the Doctrine of the Trinity,) administer a plain and a wise rule which, if observed by divines, would greatly contribute to heal the wounds which both truth and charity have received in this controversy. "Since both sides yield (says he,) that the matter they dispute about is above their reach, the wisest course they can take is, to assert and defend what is revealed, and not to be peremptory and quarrelsome about that which is acknowledged to be above our comprehension; I mean as to the *manner* how the *three persons* partake of the *divine nature.*"

Those who are desirous of a more minute historical view of the manner in which the Trinitarian controversy has been carried on during the present century, may consult a pamphlet that was published in 1720, entitled, An Account of all the considerable Books and Pamphlets that have been written on either Side in the Controversy concerning the Trinity since the year 1712; in which is also contained an Account of the Pamphlets written this last year, on each side, by the Dissenters, to the end of the year 1719. The more recent treatises on the subject of the Trinity are sufficiently known.

☞ * It will appear to those who read the preceding note [*] that Dr. Mosheim has here mistaken the true hypothesis of Dr. Clarke, or, at least, expresses it imperfectly; for what he says here is rather applicable to the opinion of Dr. Waterland. Dr. Clarke maintained an equality of perfections in the three persons, but a subordination of nature in point of existence and derivation.

† Lady Moyer.

THE FIRST APPENDIX.

Mosheim's Ecclesiastical History can be justly appreciated only by considering it as a general epitome. As such, it is indeed excellent; the arrangement is luminous; the style both of the author and of his translator, is in general perspicuous; and though topics of the greatest importance are, from the nature of the work, necessarily treated with a brevity which the reader may sometimes regret, the references at the bottoms of the pages inform him where he may, on every subject, find fuller information. It must, however, be confessed, that those references, being for the most part made to the works of German authors, are of less value to us than to those for whose use the history was originally composed; and, perhaps, it cannot be wholly denied, that the author, learned and pious as he undoubtedly was, either had not studied the works of the primitive fathers of the Christian church with sufficient care, or laboured under some prejudices, from which the most powerful minds are not wholly exempt, that made him refer to learned moderns for the decision of questions, which the ancients alone can decide. This we think, appears most remarkably in the view which he exhibits of the constitution, government, and discipline, of the primitive church, of which it is obvious that we can know nothing but from the testimony of the primitive writers.

The Fathers, as they are called, may have been bad critics, as we think they generally were; they may have been extremely credulous, and ready to attribute, to the miraculous interposition of God, natural events, for which their philosophy did not enable them to account; and their speculative doctrines may have been often corrupted by that science, falsely so called, which spread from the Alexandrian school over the whole Christian world; but the *integrity* of men who laid down their lives for what they *believed to be the truth*, cannot surely be questioned. "I see no reason," said one,* who did not pay to them undue deference, "why their veracity should be questioned, when they bear witness to the state of religion in their own times, because they disgraced their judgment, in giving ear to every strange tale of monkish extraction. Controversy apart, their testimony to common facts may yet stand good;" and surely the constitution, government and discipline of the church, were common facts, about which none of them could be deceived.

The view however which Dr. Mosheim has given of the primitive church appears not to us to be countenanced by any primitive writer; and accordingly he rarely appeals directly to them in support of what he advances, but refers to modern authors, generally French or Germans, who have written on the subject, and who could write nothing on it authentic, which they did not derive from the ancients.

* Warburton in his introduction to Julian.

The qualifications indeed which he thinks essential to an historian, and the rules which he lays down for the manner of treating ecclesiastical history, though highly valuable in themselves, are by him stated in such a manner as cannot fail to excite, in the reflecting mind, suspicions of the authenticity of his account of the government and discipline of the primitive church. After observing that, in order to render the history of the church useful and interesting, it is necessary to trace effects to their causes, and to connect events with the circumstances, views, principles, and instruments that have contributed to their existence, he adds, "In order to discover the secret causes of public events, some general succours are to be derived from the history of the times in which they happened, and the testimonies of the authors by whom they are recorded. But, beside these, a considerable acquaintance with human nature, founded on long observation and experience, is extremely useful in researches of this kind. The historian who has acquired a competent knowledge of the views that occupy the generality of men, who has studied a great variety of characters, and attentively observed the force and violence of human passions, together with the infirmities and contradictions they produce in the conduct of life, will find, in this knowledge, a key to the secret reasons and motives which gave rise to many of the most important events of ancient times. A knowledge also of the manners and opinions of the persons concerned in the events that are related, will contribute much to lead us to the true origin of things.*

There is unquestionably much truth as well as good sense in this account of the qualifications requisite to render an historian instructive and interesting; for it is obvious that he who has merely studied human nature through the medium of books, not in the society of men, and who has not observed the motives which generally influence human conduct, can never trace events to their causes, or discover the springs of those actions on which perhaps the happiness or misery of millions may depend. But, if this knowledge of human nature be ever employed to counteract the testimony of ancient authors, who were under no conceivable temptation to write falsely; or if the actions of men in one stage of society be traced to the same motives from which similar actions are observed to spring in another stage altogether different, and in many respects the reverse; if, because men are prompted by avarice and ambition to solicit offices which at one period lead to honour and opulence, it be inferred that they must have been influenced by similar motives at a period when such offices led not to opulence or honour, but to certain death, in its most hideous forms; if an historian reason thus from the observations which he has made on the force and violence

* Introduction, sect. xii

of human passions, and set his conclusions in opposition to facts recorded by ancient authors, who were witnesses of what they relate; it is obvious that his confidence in the knowledge which he has acquired of human nature by mixing in society, may lead him into the greatest errors; by inducing him either to neglect entirely, or to inspect carelessly, those writings from which alone he can derive any authentic information concerning the events of which he is writing.

That Dr. Mosheim was not entirely free from some bias of this kind, seems evident, as, without appealing to any ancient authority whatever, he represents the government of the primitive church as democratical—a form of government unknown in the religious societies of that age, as well heathen as Jewish.

He had witnessed the tyranny of the Romish clergy, and had traced the steps and discovered the causes by which the bishops of Rome had gradually reached the summit of ecclesiastical usurpation; and not adverting perhaps to the fact that, before the conversion of Constantine, ecclesiastical preferment could be no object of worldly ambition or avarice, he appears to have hastily concluded that this progress had commenced from the very beginning.

Accordingly, as if the matter were self-evident, he affirms, in the introduction to his work,* "that, when we look back to the commencement of the Christian church, *we find its government administered jointly by the pastors and the people*. But, in process of time, the scene changes, and we see these pastors affecting an air of pre-eminence and superiority, trampling upon the rights and privileges of the community, and assuming to themselves a supreme authority, both in civil and religious matters."

Of this joint administration of the government of the original church by the pastors and the people, he thinks it not necessary here to offer any evidence whatever; but, when he enters on the subject as an historian, and observes that the form of government, which the primitive churches borrowed from that of Jerusalem established by the apostles themselves, must be esteemed as of divine institution, he gives the following account of that form, which he endeavours to support by the authority of Scripture.

"In those early times, every Christian church consisted of the people, their leaders, and the ministers, or deacons; and these indeed belong essentially to every religious society. The people were, undoubtedly, the first in authority; for the apostles showed by their own example, that nothing of moment was to be carried on or determined without the consent of the assembly; and such a method of proceeding was both prudent and necessary in those critical times. It was, therefore, the assembly of the people, which chose their own rulers and teachers, or received them by a free and authoritative consent, when recommended by others. The same people rejected or confirmed, by their suffrages, the laws that were proposed by their rulers to the assembly; excommunicated profligate and unworthy members of the church; restored the penitent to their forfeited privileges; passed judgment upon the different subjects of controversy and dissension, that arose in the community; examined and decided the disputes which happened between the elders and deacons; and, in a word, exercised all that authority which belongs to such as are invested with the sovereign power."*

* Sect. vii.

Such, according to our author, was the government of the Christian church during the greater part of the first century; and he infers this supreme authority of the people from the Acts of the Apostles, chap. i. v. 15. vi. 3. xv. 4. xxi. 22; but it is difficult to conceive by what mode of interpretation these texts can be made to countenance the supreme authority of the *people* in the church.

At the time of the transaction mentioned in the fifteenth and following verses of the first chapter of the Acts of the Apostles, we know, from the testimony of St. Paul,† that the number of believers in Jerusalem and its neighbourhood amounted at least to five hundred; but St. Luke assures us that the number of names met together at the appointment of Matthias to the apostleship, did not exceed one hundred and twenty. If the authority of the people was at that period supreme, and if it belonged to them to elect by their own suffrages even a successor in the apostleship to Judas, how came so very large a majority to be deprived of their right at the election of Matthias? On this question Dr. Lightfoot says,‡ Quum Matthias et Joses coram apostolis, ut par candidatorum, sisterentur, haud constat universum fidelium cœtum, sive individuum quemvis in eorum electione suo nomine suffragia tulisse, quin in presbyterio potius, sive in collegio virorum 108, inter se coacto, jus et potestatem eligendi resedisse." And though in ordinary cases it belonged to the apostles to ordain, by imposition of hands, such as were chosen to fill any office in the church by those to whom they had deputed the right of election, yet in the present case, they left the determination between the candidates wholly to the giving-forth of lots, after solemnly praying that the divine head of the church would show which of them he had chosen to take part of the ministry and apostleship from which Judas had fallen; and all this was done, as the same learned writer observes, "utpote qui gradus apostolicos immediatâ quasi Christi manuductione adierint."

The second text quoted by our author in support of the power of the people, appears to us to teach the very opposite doctrine in terms which cannot be mistaken. When the murmuring of the Grecians against the Hebrews arose on account of the neglect, real or supposed, of their widows in the daily ministration, the sovereign people did not take the treasure of the church into their own hands, and by their supreme authority appoint officers to distribute it to the poor with greater equity. They seem not indeed to have imagined that

* Cent. I. part ii. chap. ii. sect. 5, &c.
† 1 Cor. xv. 6.
‡ Oper. Omn. tom. ii. p 758, edit. Roterodam

they had a right to take any step whatever in the matter, till "the twelve called them together, and said—Look ye out among you seven men of honest report, full of the Holy Ghost and wisdom, whom *we* (not *ye*) may appoint over this business;" thus giving the people authority to elect, specifying the number and qualifications of the persons to be elected, and still reserving to themselves the authoritative appointment of those persons to the work for which they were to be chosen.

In the fifteenth chapter of the Acts of the Apostles we are told, that a deputation was sent from Antioch to Jerusalem to consult—not the people—but the apostles and elders about the necessity of circumcision; that, when the deputies had come to Jerusalem, they were received by the church and by the apostles and elders; that these distinguished persons came together to consider of the matter referred to their decision; that, after much disputing among the apostles and elders, the question was decided against the necessity of circumcision; and that then it pleased the apostles and elders, with the whole church, to send chosen men of their own company to Antioch with their synodical decree. In all this there is not the slightest countenance given to the authority of the multitude. The people were not called together on the arrival of the deputies from Antioch; and indeed their number was so great long before that period, that the tenth part of them could not have been contained in any house at the command of the apostles within the city of Jerusalem; nor would such a multitude have been allowed by the civil power to assemble quietly in the street or in the field. As many of them as could find admission were doubtless present at the deliberations of the apostles and elders on a question of such great and general importance; but the multitude is mentioned but once, and then as keeping profound silence. The synodical epistle to the Gentiles at Antioch and in Syria and Cilicia, is indeed written in the name of the apostles and elders and brethren; but this was, in those days, the common style of such epistles. Thus St. Paul's epistle to the Galatians is written, not in his own name only, but also in the names of all the brethren who were with him; and the first epistle of St. Clement his fellow-labourer (which is undoubtedly genuine) is in the name of "the church of God which dwelleth or sojourneth at Rome, to the church of God which sojourneth at Corinth;" though it is certain that all the brethren who were with St. Paul had no authority over the Galatians, nor the lay members of the church in Rome any right to expostulate with the church in Corinth. The synodical decree issued at Jerusalem may indeed, with the greatest propriety, be called the decree of the church, because it was enacted by the undoubted governors of the church; just as the acts of the British parliament are called the laws of Great Britain, though the people at large were not consulted in the framing of one of them.

The last text appealed to by Dr. Mosheim as a proof of the supreme authority of the people in the church, not only proves no such thing, but, if it be at all applicable to the question at issue, is of itself a complete proof that they had then no such authority, and indeed that they were wholly unfit to be entrusted with such authority.

The case was this. St. Paul, after an absence of some length from Jerusalem, returned to that city, and on the day after his arrival went into the house of James, who is represented as having *all* the elders about him; but, as is evident from what passed, with not so much as *one* of the multitude of laymen in the company. When St. Paul had declared particularly what things God had wrought among the Gentiles by his ministry, James and the elders glorified the Lord, and said unto him, "Thou seest, brother, how many thousands of Jews there are who believe; and they are all zealous of the law; and they are informed of thee, that thou teachest all the Jews who are among the Gentiles to forsake Moses, saying, that they ought not to circumcise their children, neither to walk after the customs. What is it (what is to be done) therefore? The multitude must needs come together, (it cannot be but they will come together,) for they will hear that thou art come. Do therefore this that we say unto thee: we have four men which have a vow on them; them take, and purify thyself with them, and be at charges with them, that they may shave their heads: and all may know (think or judge)* that those things whereof they were informed concerning thee are nothing but that thou thyself also walkest orderly and keepest the law." (Acts xxi. 19—24.)

This advice St. Paul followed, not however in *obedience* to the people as possessing in his opinion the supreme authority in the church of Jerusalem, but to humour a harmless prejudice, upon that principle which induced him, as he declares to the Corinthians,† "to become unto the Jews as a Jew, that he might gain the Jews: to them that were under the law, as under the law, that he might gain them that were under the law; to them that were without the law, as without the law, that he might gain them that were without the law;" and, even in matters indifferent, "to become all things to all men, that he might by all means save some." Had the multitude possessed the supreme power in the church of Jerusalem, St. James and the elders would undoubtedly have called them together to hear St. Paul's declaration of the things which God had wrought among the Gentiles by his ministry, and not have left them to be drawn together by their own curiosity and zeal, when they should hear of his arrival. At any rate St. James and the elders could not have proposed, nor would St. Paul have agreed, to impose on the people by even an innocent deception, had those people in the church of Jerusalem been the first in authority; for, in that case, it would have been the duty of the two apostles and elders to give a full and fair account of their own conduct to their superiors.

* In Stephens' Thesaurus, and even in Scapula's Lexicon, the reader will find a number of extracts from Xenophon, Plutarch, and other Greek writers, in which γινωσκω is of the same import with *censeo*, *existimo*, and *judico* in Latin. That it is used in that sense by St. Luke is obvious, since the multitude could not *know* that to be false which was undoubtedly true.

† 1 Cor. ix. 20—28.

It was certainly known to St. Paul and St. James, and probably to the elders, that from the moment when the veil of the temple was rent in twain, the ceremonies of the Mosaic law were no longer obligatory on the disciples of their master. This, however, it appears, was not known to the great body of Jewish Christians dwelling at Jerusalem, who still continued zealous for the law as well as for the faith, and strongly attached to the customs of their fathers. Were men labouring under prejudices so inveterate, and in truth so inconsistent with the final object of the Gospel, fit to be entrusted with sovereign power in the Christian church; with authority to excommunicate unworthy members, or even with the privilege of choosing their own teachers? What should we think of the constitution of a great school, in which the sovereign power was committed to the scholars, with authority to expel every member whom they might deem unworthy, and even to dismiss the masters, and choose teachers for themselves out of their own number? Could such a school be reasonably expected to prove a seminary of learning, science, virtue, or truth? Surely not; and yet Dr. Mosheim supposes that the Christian church, founded by the Son of God himself for the purpose of training up mankind in the faith, piety, and virtue necessary to render them "meet to be partakers of the inheritance of the saints in light," was thus constituted. That he is in an error, no man can doubt, who reflects that the doctrines to be taught in the church were, till the manifestation of Christ, unknown in the world, and such as human reason could never have discovered; that of such doctrines half-converted Jews and Heathens were incompetent to judge; that these doctrines were therefore revealed, not to every individual in the church, but to those who were "given for the perfecting of the saints, for the work of the ministry, for the edifying of the body of Christ;" and that by those inspired teachers they were "committed only to faithful men, whom *they* (not the multitude at large) judged able to teach others also." How this was done, we shall endeavour to show, when we come to give a view of the rise, progress, constitution, and object of the Christian church, from the infallible records of the New Testament, illustrated, where they seem obscure, by primitive practice; but, before we enter on that detail, it will be proper to analyse our author's account of the officers or ministers of the church, and of their different privileges, about which he seems to have fallen into mistakes as great as those which led him to attribute the supreme authority in each church to the people.

According to Dr. Mosheim, "the rulers of the church were called either *presbyters* or *bishops*, which two titles are, in the New Testament, undoubtedly applied to the same order of men, and such as had distinguished themselves by their superior sanctity and merit. Their particular functions were not always the same; for, while some of them confined their labours to the instruction of the people, others contributed in different ways to the edification of the church. Among the first professors of Christianity, there were few men of learning; few who had capacity enough to insinuate, into the minds of a gross and ignorant multitude, the knowledge of divine things. God, therefore, in his infinite wisdom, judged it necessary to raise up, in many churches, extraordinary teachers, who were to discourse, in the public assemblies, upon the various points of the Christian doctrine, and to treat with the people in the name of God, as guided by his direction, and clothed with his authority. Such were the *prophets* of the New Testament, an order of men which ceased, when the want of teachers, which gave rise to it, was abundantly supplied.

"The church was undoubtedly provided from the beginning with inferior ministers or *deacons*. No society can be without its servants, and still less such societies as those of the first Christians were; and it appears not only probable, but evident, that the young men, who carried away the dead bodies of Ananias and Sapphira, were the subordinate ministers or deacons of the church of Jerusalem, who attended the apostles to execute their orders. All the other Christian churches followed the example of that of Jerusalem, in whatever related to the choice and office of the deacons. Some, particularly the eastern churches, elected deaconesses, and chose, for that purpose, matrons or widows of eminent sanctity, who also ministered to the necessities of the poor, and performed several other offices, that tended to the maintenance of order and decency in the church.

"Such was the constitution of the Christian church in its infancy, when its assemblies were neither numerous nor splendid. Three or four presbyters, men of remarkable piety and wisdom, ruled these small congregations in perfect harmony; nor did they stand in need of any president or superior to maintain concord and order where no dissensions were known. But the number of presbyters and deacons increasing with that of the churches, and the sacred work of the ministry growing more painful and weighty, by a number of additional duties, these new circumstances required new regulations. It was then judged necessary that a man of distinguished gravity and wisdom should preside in the council of presbyters, in order to distribute among his colleagues their several tasks, and to be a centre of union to the whole society. This person was at first styled the *angel* of the church to which he belonged, but was afterwards distinguished by the name of *bishop*, or inspector; a name borrowed from the Greek language, and expressing the principal part of the episcopal function, which was to inspect and superintend the affairs of the church. It is highly probable, that the church of Jerusalem, grown considerably numerous, and deprived of the ministry of the apostles, who were gone to instruct the other nations, was the first which chose a president or bishop; and it is no less probable, that the other churches followed by degrees such a respectable example.

"A bishop, during the first and second centuries, was a person who had the care of one Christian assembly, which at that time, was, generally speaking, small enough to be contained in a private house. In this assembly he acted, not so much with the authority of a *master*, as with the zeal and diligence of a faithful *servant*. He charged, indeed, the presbyters with the performance of those duties and services, which the multiplicity of his engagements rendered it impossible for him to fulfil; but he had not the power to decide or enact any thing without the consent of the presbyters and people; and, though the episcopal office was both laborious and singularly dangerous, yet its revenues were extremely small, since the church had no certain income, but depended on the gifts or oblations of the multitude, which were, no doubt, inconsiderable, and were, moreover, to be divided between the bishop, presbyters, deacons, and poor.

"The power and jurisdiction of the bishops were not long confined to these narrow limits, but soon extended themselves, and that by the following means. The bishops, who lived in the cities, had, either by their own ministry, or that of their presbyters, erected new churches in the neighbouring towns and villages. These churches, continuing under the inspection and ministry of the bishops, by whose labours and counsels they had been engaged to embrace the Gospel, grew imperceptibly into ecclesiastical provinces, which the Greeks afterwards called *dioceses*. But, as the bishop of the city could not extend his labours and inspection to all those churches in the country and in the villages, so he appointed certain suffragans or deputies to govern and to instruct these new societies; and they were distinguished by the title of *Chorepiscopi*, i. e. country bishops. This order held the middle rank between bishops and presbyters, being inferior to the former and superior to the latter."*

Such, according to our author, was the constitution of the Christian church during the first century and part of the second: for he affirms,† that the jurisdiction of a bishop extended not over more than one Christian assembly, and that the authority of the people continued supreme, until the middle of the second century, when the ancient privileges of the people were considerably diminished, and the power and authority of the bishops greatly augmented, by *councils*, of which, he says, we find not the smallest trace before that period. It was not, he adds,‡ till some time after the reign of Adrian, that the Christian doctors had the good fortune to persuade the people, that the ministers of the Christian church succeeded to the character, rights, and privileges of the Jewish priesthood. Then, indeed, the bishops began to consider themselves as invested with a rank and character similar to those of the high-priest among the Jews, while the presbyters represented the priests, and the deacons the Levites.

In support of this detail, the author appeals not to one ancient writer; and the consequence is, that the greater part of it is in direct opposition to the unanimous testimony of all antiquity. He refers, indeed, to several texts in the Acts of the Apostles and in the Epistles of St. Paul, as proofs of what, we believe, has never been controverted—that the titles of bishop and presbyter are in the New Testament indifferently applied to the same order of men. He seems, however, to mistake when he supposes that the order, to which these titles were commonly applied, consisted of the *rulers* of the church; for, though the apostles sometimes call themselves elders, the order to which that title as well as the title of bishop more properly belonged, was evidently subordinate to the apostles, as well as to the church rulers, whom he admits to have been known by the appellation of angels.

That the bishops or elders of the New Testament were subordinate to the apostles, has never been controverted; and that they were likewise subordinate to the *angels* of the churches, appears indisputable from the charges given by "him who hath the sharp sword with two edges, who hath his eyes like unto a flame of fire, and his feet like fine brass," to the angels of the churches of Pergamos and Thyatira.* These angels are described as eminent for their "good works, charity, service, steadfastness in the faith, and patience;" and yet they are both severely blamed, and the former threatened for suffering in their respective churches false teachers, whom, if they were themselves nothing more than such presidents of congregational presbyteries as Dr. Mosheim describes, it is obvious that they could not remove from their churches. According to him, these presidents, afterwards called bishops, were chosen by the joint suffrages of the other presbyters and of the lay members of the congregation to which they respectively belonged; when thus chosen, they acted in their respective congregations, not with the authority of masters, but with the zeal and diligence of faithful servants; they had not the power to decide or enact any thing without the consent of the presbyters and the people, who were in every church the first in authority; and therefore the censure and threatening, for suffering false teachers in the churches of Pergamos and Thyatira, were on his principles due, not to the *angels* of those churches, but to the presbyters and *people!* That the principles are erroneous which infer injustice in the Son of God, Dr. Mosheim would have been as ready as any man to confess; and therefore we have not a doubt that, if, instead of paying undue deference to the opinions of some of his less candid countrymen, he had duly weighed in his own mind the import of what the Spirit said to the seven churches, he would have perceived that the *angels* must have been of an order superior to the presbyters properly so called; and that they must have derived their superiority from some other source than the mere choice of the presbyters and people.

To the truth of this inference it is no objection, that, in the New Testament, all officers in the church above the order of deacons are indiscriminately called sometimes bishops and sometimes presbyters. In the Old Testament, the individuals of every order of priesthood, with the exception of the mere Levites, are

* Cent. I. part ii. chap ii. sections 8, 9, 11, 12, 13.
† Cent. II. part ii. chap. ii. sect 1, 2, 3.
‡ Sect. 4.

* Rev. chap. ii. 12—21.

generally styled priests without any distinction; though every Jew and every Christian know, that the high-priest was of an order superior to the rest, and authorised to perform at least one ministration to which none of his inferiors were competent.

Dr. Mosheim, indeed, seems to think, that there is no resemblance, and hardly any analogy between the Jewish priesthood and the Christian ministry; but this is a mistake so palpable, that a man of learning and integrity could not have fallen into it, but through the influence of some deep-rooted prejudice. In the fifth chapter of the Epistle to the Hebrews there is an evident analogy pointed out between the Jewish and Christian churches, and, of course, between their respective ministers; and the first epistle of St. Clement of Rome furnishes incontrovertible evidence, that long before the reign of Adrian—and even in the first century,—the bishops, presbyters, and deacons, were considered as invested with rank and characters similar to those of the high-priest, priests, and Levites among the Jews. That apostolical father, whose name, we are assured by St. Paul, was in the book of life, expostulating with the Corinthians, then in a state of schism among themselves, and of sedition against the governors of their church, thus reasons with them:—

"Let us consider those who fight under our *earthly* governors; how orderly, how readily, and with what exact obedience they perform those things which are commanded them. All are not generals, nor commanders of thousands, nor centurions, nor captains of fifties, and so on; but every one doeth those things which are enjoined him by the king, and by those officers who have the command over him. They who are great, cannot yet subsist without those that are little; nor the little without the great. There is a certain mixture in all things, and in these *there is* fitness, χρησις. Let us take our own body: the head is nothing without the feet; so neither are the feet of use without the head: even the smallest members of our body are necessary and useful to the whole body: all conspire together, and are *adapted by one subordination** to the preservation of the whole. Let therefore our whole body be saved in Christ Jesus; and let every one be subject to his neighbour according to the order in which he is placed by the grace given him. Let not the powerful despise the weak, and let the weak reverence the powerful.

"Seeing then that these things are manifest unto us, even looking into the depths of the divine knowledge, we ought to do, in order, all things which the Lord hath commanded us to do; at stated times to perform our offerings and public services; for he hath commanded them to be done not rashly and disorderly, but at predetermined times and hours. He hath determined also by his own supreme will, *where* and *by whom* he would have them to be celebrated; that so all things being piously done, unto all well-pleasing, they may be acceptable to his will. They therefore who make their offerings at the appointed seasons, are accepted and happy; for, following the instituted laws (νομιμοις) of the Lord, they do not go astray. For to the chief priest his proper services (λειτουργιαι) are committed; and to the priests their proper place is ordained and on the Levites their proper minister (διακονιαι) are imposed; and the layman is con fined by the laws ordained for laymen."*

It is impossible for an unprejudiced man to read these extracts with attention, and to entertain a doubt that St. Clement considered the bishops, priests, and Levites in the Christian church, as succeeding to the high-priest, priests, and Levites in the Jewish. Indeed, if he understood, as he appears to have done, the great scheme of human redemption; if he believed, as our church believes, that, in the Old as well as in the New Testament, "everlasting life is offered to mankind by Christ, who is the only mediator between God and man;" if, with St. Paul and the inspired author of the Epistle to the Hebrews, he considered Judaism as Christianity under a veil; he must have considered the Jewish and Christian churches as essentially the same, though the ministrations of the former were more carnal than those of the latter, on account of the grossness of the people. With this view of the stupendous plan of redemption, it seems impossible that he, or indeed any other man, could have considered the bishops, presbyters, and deacons of the church, as succeeding to any thing else than the rank and character of the high-priest, priests and Levites of the temple; unless, indeed, there had been any text of Scripture *plainly declaring*, that the Jewish and Christian churches were wholly unconnected with each other, and that the former was not intended to serve as a school-master to lead the descendants of Abraham to Christ Such a text as this, however, none of the sons of latitude have yet pretended to discover.

It seems likewise very strange that Dr. Mosheim should have supposed that, in the church of Jerusalem, there was no fixed president over the presbyters or elders, till the dispersion of the apostles; and that the jurisdiction of such presidents, who were then styled angels, and afterwards bishops, extended no farther, during the first and second centuries, than over one Christian assembly, which was generally small enough to be contained in a private house.

It has been already observed that St. James is represented, with the elders about him, as bishop of Jerusalem, when St. Paul returned to that city, and declared what things God had wrought among the Gentiles by his ministry. Indeed the part which, in the New Testament, James appears to have acted from a very early period, cannot be accounted for on any other supposition, than that he really was, what the concurring testimony of all antiquity declares him to have been, the fixed bishop or angel of the church of Jerusalem. When St. Peter was miraculously delivered from prison, and had been received into the house of Mary the mother of John, whose surname was Mark, (Acts xii.) he said, "Go show these things to

* υποταγη μια χρηται.

* Chapters 37 38 and 40.

James and to the brethren." Why to James in particular? and why were the brethren with James rather than with John, who had acted a more conspicuous part than he during the life of our Lord, as well as at the first preaching of the apostles after the shedding abroad of the Holy Ghost, and who had not at the period of St. Peter's deliverance, or for four years afterwards, left Jerusalem? In the second chapter of the Epistle to the Galatians, St. Paul says, that "when Peter was come to Antioch, he withstood him to the face, because he was to be blamed. For before that certain came from James, he (Peter) did eat with the Gentiles; but, when they were come, he withdrew, and separated himself, fearing them who were of the circumcision." In the Acts of the Apostles we have no other account of persons from Judea teaching the Gentiles of Antioch, that, except they should be circumcised, they could not be saved, than that which is given in the fifteenth chapter; and it is indeed highly improbable, that, after the synodical decree at Jerusalem, St. Peter could have acted the part of which he was accused by St. Paul, or have *attempted* "to *compel* the Gentiles to live as do the Jews," contrary to the solemn decision of himself and the whole church under the immediate influence of the Holy Ghost. There is therefore no room for reasonable doubt that it was on the occasion mentioned in the fifteenth chapter of the Acts, and some time before the meeting of the council at Jerusalem, that this dissension took place between those great apostles. But by St. Luke the certain men, who wished to impose circumcision and the other rites of the Mosaic law on the Gentile Christians at Antioch, are said only to have come from *Judea;* whereas by St. Paul they are said to have come from *James.* Why are certain men, who came down from Judea, represented as having come from James, rather than from the other apostles and elders, of whom it is evident, from the short history of the council, that there must have been many then residing in Jerusalem.

If St. James was the proper bishop of Jerusalem, all these facts, which, upon any other supposition, cannot be accounted for, were perfectly natural; for, to whom was it so expedient that St. Paul should give an account of "the things which God had wrought among the Gentiles by his ministry," as to the bishop and presbyters of the mother church of the Hebrews? To what individual of the church of Jerusalem should St. Peter have sent the earliest account of his miraculous deliverance from prison, but to the bishop of that church? If St. James had not been that bishop, is it conceivable that St. Peter would have sent such welcome intelligence to him rather than to his more intimate friend and companion, St. John, who was the disciple peculiarly dear to their divine Master? And could any thing be more natural than for St. Paul to say that certain brethren, who came to Antioch from the church of Judea, came from the *governor* of that church? This accounts likewise for St. James's presiding in the council of apostles and elders, which was holden in Jerusalem, for determining the question about circumcising the Gentiles; for that he was president of that council is incontrovertible, if any credit be due to the testimony of antiquity, to the unanimous opinion of critics and commentators, (a few members of the modern church of Rome excepted,) or, indeed, to the obvious meaning of his words, Διο εγω κρινω, &c

But if James was bishop of the church of Jerusalem, and if the constitutions of all other churches were framed after that model, there is surely no reason to suppose that even in the first century, and still less in the second, the bishop or angel of any church had the care of only one Christian assembly. The episcopal care of James unquestionably extended over many assemblies. By the preaching of St. Peter on the day of Pentecost, after the miraculous effusion of the Holy Ghost, we are assured,* that to the number of the disciples "there were added about three thousand souls." It is indeed probable, that of these many were strangers, who, after the celebration of the feast, which had brought them to Jerusalem, departed from that city, and returned to their respective countries. It appears, however, that, soon afterwards, the number of believers resident in Jerusalem amounted to five thousand; and, by the time that St. Paul returned to give an account to James and the elders, of what things God had done by his ministry among the Gentiles, even that number had greatly increased.† But ten or even five thousand men could not meet for public worship, for the breaking of bread and for prayers, in any private house, or any ten private houses, belonging to the Christians in Jerusalem; and, therefore, as James appears to have had the episcopal care of them all, that care must have extended over many assemblies.

That such was the nature of episcopal jurisdiction even in that age appears still more evident, if possible, from St. John's epistle, in the Apocalypse, to the seven churches in Asia. That epistle is addressed, not επτα εκκλησιαις των εν τη 'Ασια, as it probably would have been, had it been intended for seven of a greater number of churches in Asia Minor, but ταις επτα εκκλησιαις ταις (εκκλησιαις) εν τη 'Ασια, to the seven churches, the churches in Asia. Those seven, therefore, must have been the only societies in Asia Minor so organized as to be entitled to the appellation of churches, at the time when St. John wrote the Apocalypse. But is it conceivable that, in an age when "so mightily grew the word of God, and prevailed," the number of believers, in a country so extensive, which had been visited by different apostles and apostolical men, should, in the year 96, have been so very small as to constitute only seven Christian congregations? Even if this could be conceived, the Christians in Asia Minor were too much scattered over the face of the country, to repair, every one, for the purpose of public worship, to one or other of the small oratories of Ephesus, Smyrna, Pergamos, Thyatira, Sardes, Philadelphia, and Lao-

* Acts ii. 41.

† The words of St. James in the original Greek are, Θεωρεις, αδελφε ποσαι μυριαδες εισιν 'Ιουδαιων των πεπιστευκοτων, &c. You see, brother, how many *myriads* there are of Jews who believe, &c.

dicea. From the Acts of the Apostles, and the Epistles of St. Paul, we know that, long before the writing of the Apocalypse, there were believers in various provinces and towns of Asia Minor, and even regular churches in the province of Galatia and the city of Colosse; but it seems evident, from the manner in which St. John expresses himself, that, before the year 96, "the candlesticks of Galatia and Colosse," to use the apostle's language, "had been removed out of their places." This indeed can excite no wonder, when we reflect that every where the churches were in that age beset by persecution without, and by heresies within; that the churches of the Galatians appear to have been exceedingly corrupt, even when St. Paul wrote his Epistle to them; and that the city of Colosse was destroyed by an earthquake during the reign of Nero, and, if ever rebuilt, certainly not when the Apocalypse was written. It is not however to be supposed that there were then no Christians in Galatia or the neighbourhood of Colosse, or that those Christians did not meet regularly in different congregations for "the breaking of bread and for prayers." The only inferences that can be drawn, are, that those assemblies did not constitute what St. John called *churches*, and that they, with their presbyters and deacons, were under the temporary inspection either of the apostle himself, or of some of the angels of the seven churches, of which he speaks as the only churches then in Asia.

That the jurisdiction of Timothy and Titus extended over more than one Christian assembly at Ephesus and in Crete; that by the apostle they were invested with authority over the presbyters as well as people of those assemblies; and that to them an exclusive right was given to ordain elders or presbyters in every city under their jurisdiction; are facts which no man has ventured to deny, and which no man can deny, who has read St. Paul's epistles to Timothy and Titus, and at the same time possesses common sense and honesty. Attempts have indeed been made to get rid of the inference from these facts, by representing the extensive authority with which Timothy and Titus were entrusted, as the authority, not of fixed governors of the churches over which they were to preside, but of *Evangelists!* This, however, cannot be admitted. We are not aware of a single instance in the New Testament, where an evangelist, as such, is represented as ordaining elders or even deacons; and it is certain that Timothy and Titus neither acted nor could act as evangelists at Ephesus or in Crete, except in a sense which, under that denomination, includes elders.

The word *evangelist* is unquestionably derived from the verb ευαγγελιζω, which, according to an able critic* not prejudiced in behalf of a hierarchy, "relates to the *first* intimation that is given to a person or people, that is, when the subject may be properly called *good news.* Thus, in the Acts of the Apostles, it is frequently used for the first publication of the Gospel in a city or village, or amongst a particular people." But if this be essential to the radical import of the verb, of which indeed there can be no doubt, then it follows that an evangelist, considered as a distinct character, could only be one, whether apostle, elder, deacon, or lay man, who first carried the glad tidings of the Gospel to an individual or a people. Hence it is, that of the seven deacons not one is called an evangelist but Philip, because, though Stephen preached the Gospel as well and as ably as he, Philip is the only one of the number mentioned by St. Luke as having carried the glad tidings of the Gospel beyond the limits of Judea, within which these tidings were *first told* by Christ and his apostles. Hence too it follows, that those, whom St. Paul says that Christ, after his ascension, "gave as *evangelists* for the work of the ministry," must have been men miraculously inspired with the knowledge of the Gospel, which cannot be said of Timothy or of Titus, and impelled by the same heavenly influence to communicate that knowledge to those to whom it was *new.* But in this sense Timothy and Titus could not be evangelists to the churches of Ephesus and Crete, because St. Paul himself had preached the Gospel in those churches before them, and had even ordained presbyters in the church of Ephesus.

It has indeed been said that ευαγγελιζομαι is occasionally used in the same sense with διδασκω. If we grant this for the sake of argument, though we are not aware of a single instance in which one of these verbs could be properly substituted for the other, still we must observe, that the character of an evangelist, in this sense of the word, could give to Timothy no superiority over the elders of Ephesus, who were *teachers* as well as he, and enjoined by the apostle to "feed the church of God, which he had purchased with his own blood." Timothy was indeed exhorted by St. Paul to "do the work of an evangelist" at Ephesus; but the elders were in duty bound, as well as he, to do the work of evangelists; for in Ephesus there were then many people who had not *heard* of the Gospel, which every minister of Christ is bound, as he has opportunity, to propagate among the heathens as well as to preach among Christians. Timothy was likewise exhorted, in the very same verse, to "accomplish his deaconship"—την διακονιαν σου πληροφορησον; but it would surely be absurd to infer from such an exhortation that the overseer of the presbyters and people of Ephesus was himself nothing more than a deacon.

If it be thus evident that the bishops known in the first century by the titles of apostles or angels of the churches presided each over more than one Christian assembly, we need not pursue the argument through the second and third centuries, since it is on all hands agreed, that the powers of the bishops were not diminished as the boundaries of the church were enlarged. This would have been extremely absurd; though we see no evidence that, during the second and third centuries, the bishops in general either claimed or had the smallest inducement to claim any power or pre-eminence which they possessed not in the first. What the hierarchy was in the beginning of the second century is apparent from the epistles of Igna

* Dr. Campbell of Aberdeen.

tius, and from the fragments of other primitive writers preserved by Eusebius, whilst the canons commonly called apostolical, with the writings of St. Cyprian and other fathers of the church, define the powers and privileges of each of the three orders in the third century in terms which cannot be mistaken. From these canons and writings it appears evident, that no bishop in that century, with the exception perhaps of Victor and Stephen, bishops of Rome, arrogated to himself any authority which was not committed to the angels of the Asiatic churches, and which Timothy and Titus were not enjoined to exercise in the churches of Ephesus and Crete.

The only thing else, in Dr. Mosheim's view of the constitution of the primitive church, which calls for animadversion, is the account which he gives of the origin of *chorepiscopi*, and of deacons in the church of Jerusalem, before the ordination of the seven recorded in the sixth chapter of the Acts of the Apostles.

There is no evidence of *chorepiscopi* being any where established in the first or second century, or in the beginning of the third. They are not mentioned in the apostolical canons, nor in the writings of Clement of Rome, Ignatius of Antioch, or even St. Cyprian. The first council that takes any notice of them is that of Ancyra, holden in 315, which prohibits them from ordaining priests and deacons. They are mentioned by the great council of Nice, which provides the place of a village-bishop or *chorepiscopus* for such of the Novatian bishops as should abjure their schism, and be reconciled to the catholic church. But the fullest, as well as the most accurate and at the same time concise account, that is perhaps any where extant of the *chorepiscopi*, is in the tenth canon of the Synod of Antioch, holden in the year 341, which decrees,

"That village-bishops, though they have received episcopal ordination, shall yet keep within their bounds, and administer the affairs of the churches subject to them, and be content with the management of them, and ordain readers, and sub-deacons, and exorcists, and content themselves with the power of promoting men to these offices, and not dare to ordain a priest or deacon, without the consent of the bishop of the city to which they themselves and their districts are subject; and, if any one dare to transgress, what has now been determined, he shall be deprived of the honour which he has. A village-bishop is made by the bishop of the city to which he is subject."[*]

From this canon it is evident that the *chorepiscopi* were bishops regularly ordained; that they were chosen or nominated by the city-bishop, or diocesan, to take upon them part of his labour, and were in all things to be directed by him, when their duty was not expressly pointed out by any canon. They seem to have been introduced into the church toward the end of the third century, when the extent of some dioceses, the poverty of the bishops, and the occasional severity of persecution, rendered it difficult, if not impossible, for the diocesan to perform, as often as was proper, the various duties of his function; but those village-bishops appear to have sometimes acted very irregularly, by multiplying without reason the number of the inferior clergy,[*] and therefore were soon laid aside. They were indeed retained for some time after the danger of persecution was over, and when the revenues of the city-bishop enabled him, without inconvenience, to visit every church under his jurisdiction; but, in 367, it was decreed by the council of Laodicea, that no more village-bishops or *chorepiscopi* should be ordained.

Though we see no evidence whatever that the young men, who carried away the dead bodies of Ananias and Sapphira, were such ministers of the church of Jerusalem, as Stephen and Philip and the other five, who were ordained at the same time with them by the apostles; yet we readily admit that the words νεωτεροι and νεανισκοι *may* signify the inferior ministers of the church, as well as the word πρεσβυτεροι signifies those of a higher order: we even readily adopt Dr. Mosheim's opinion, that the words μειζων and νεωτεβος (St. Luke xxii. 26) νεωτεροι and πρεσβυτεροις (1 Peter v. 5.) relate to *offices* and not to *age*, and that νεωτεροι *may*, in both these texts, mean those ministers of the church, who from the beginning have been known by the designation of deacons: but it does not therefore follow that the young men, who carried out the dead bodies of Ananias and Sapphira, were likewise deacons in the ecclesiastical sense of the word.

Among the Jews, every person who touched a dead body was hereby rendered unclean; and it is not very probable that St. Peter would wantonly give offence to that people, by ordering the ministers of the religion which it was his duty to preach, but against which he knew them to entertain the most inveterate prejudices, to render themselves unclean by doing what the door-keepers could have done as well as they. The young men who were employed to carry away the dead bodies, may indeed have been διακονοι in the sense of menial servants of the infant church; but, in the Acts of the Apostles, there is not the slightest allusion to *ordained* deacons until we come to the sixth chapter, which gives so full an account of the ordination of the seven. Accordingly an ancient commentator, whose testimony, respecting a matter of fact, is surely entitled to greater credit than the mere conjecture of the most learned modern, says expressly, when speaking of the conversion and baptism of Cornelius the centurion,—*Adhuc enim præter septem diaconos nullus fuit ordinatus.*[†]

The difficulty in ascertaining the original

* Τȣς εν ταις κωμαις, η ταις χωραις, η τȣς καλȣμενȣς χωρεπισκοπȣς, ει και χειροθεσιαν ειεν επισκοπων ειληφοτες, εδοξε τη αγια συνοδω ειδεναι τα εαυτων μετρα, και διοικειν τας υποκειμενας αυτοις εκκλησιας, και τη τȣτων αρκεισθαι φροντιδι και κηδεμονια, καθισταν δε αναγνωστας, και υποδιακονȣς, και εφορκιστας, και τη τȣτων αρκεισθαι προαγωγη, μητε δε πρεσβυτερον, μητε διακονον χειροτονειν τολμαν, διχα τȣ εν τη πολει επισκοπȣ, η υποκεινται αυτος τε και η χωρα. Ει δε τολμησειεν τις παραβηναι τα ορισθεντα, καθαιρεσθαι αυτον, ης μετεχει τιμης. Χωρεπισκοπον δε γινεσθαι υπο τȣ της πολεως, η υποκειται επισκοπȣ.

* See the Canons of St. Basil, bishop of Cæsarea in Cappadocia, canon 90.

† Hilar. in Eph. cap. iv

constitution of the church is indeed greater than he can easily conceive, who has not attended to the power of prejudice. The controversies on the subject have been so acrimonious, and the tendency to confound Christianity with a mere system of what is called natural religion, is in the present age so very prevalent, that few men have brought, to the inquiry, minds so completely divested of prepossession, as to be capable of judging impartially. The truth may be detailed in the Scriptures with sufficient clearness; but we all study those writings under a bias, more or less powerful, in favour of the party to which we belong; and that bias, especially if we have ourselves been engaged in controversy, is very apt to prevent us from seeing what is written even as with a sun-beam. We may be ambitious of making *discoveries* in theology, and of becoming the founders of new sects; and such ambition must necessarily impel us to differ as much as possible from the luminaries of antiquity, that we may display the vigour of our own minds, and our superiority to what we are pleased to call prejudice: or we may be so attached to antiquity as to consider every practice and every rite of the primitive church, as of perpetual obligation, not distinguishing between what was deemed essential, and what was even then considered as only expedient, in consequence of the circumstances in which the church was placed.

To avoid as much as possible the errors which flow from these sources, it will be proper to trace the progress of the Gospel from the first preaching of John the Baptist, to the completion of the canon of the New Testament, ascertaining, as we proceed, the import of the principal doctrines preached, as well as the offices and authority of the several preachers; and pointing out at the same time the privileges of the people. As all parties appeal to Scripture in support of their own opinions and systems, it would be fortunate if men could agree on some rule, by which Scripture, where it appears obscure, should be interpreted: and the constitution of the church being a matter of fact obvious to all mankind, it seems not difficult to find the rule, by which whatever relates to it may be interpreted with little danger of mistake. If the principles of the persons, to whom the writings which compose the New Testament were immediately addressed, can be ascertained, it will be easy, in cases of any importance, to discover how those writings should themselves be understood; and with respect to *matters of fact*, there can be no doubt, that they who conversed with the apostles, perfectly understood their meaning. Indeed, as long as the pastors of the Christian church had no worldly ambition to gratify, by bringing themselves into public notice; as long as pre-eminence among them led not to opulence and power, but to poverty, persecution and death, it would be in the highest degree unreasonable to question their veracity, when they are giving an account of the constitution of the church, as established by the apostles. Their testimony therefore may be safely employed, not as of authority in itself, but as an authentic commentary on what is taught on that subject in the sacred pages; and as such only do we mean to appeal to it.

That the church, whatever be its constitution, is something of great importance, is unquestionable, since it was deemed worthy of being alluded to, even by the *forerunner* of our Lord. The very first words on record, of the venerable Baptist's preaching, are, "repent ye, for the kingdom of Heaven is at hand;" by which was undoubtedly meant the kingdom of the Messiah, or the church of Christ, soon to be established instead of the Jewish polity and temple. He goes on to say, "that every valley should be filled, and every mountain and hill be made low; that the crooked should be made straight, and the rough ways smooth; and that all flesh should see the salvation of God;" and soon afterwards, when he saw Jesus coming unto him, he said to the multitude, "Behold the lamb of God, which taketh away the sin of the world."

Our blessed Lord began his own preaching with the very same words—"Repent, for the kingdom of Heaven is at hand;" or, as St Mark expresses it, "Jesus came into Galilee, preaching the Gospel of the kingdom of God, and saying, The time is fulfilled, and the kingdom of God is at hand: repent ye, and believe the Gospel." According to St. Luke, "When Jesus returned, in the power of the Spirit, into Galilee, from the scene of his temptation, he came to Nazareth, where he had been brought up; and, as his custom was, he went into the Synagogue on the Sabbath-day, and stood up to read. And there was delivered to him the book of the prophet Esaias; and, when he had opened the book, he found the place where it is written, the Spirit of the Lord is upon me, because he hath anointed me to preach the Gospel to the poor, he hath sent me to heal the broken-hearted, to preach deliverance to the captives, and recovering of sight to the blind, to set at liberty them that are bruised; to preach the acceptable year of the Lord;" and this passage of the prophet, he applied to himself.

No Christian can be ignorant, that, in this first preaching of our Lord and his faithful forerunner, there is at least one very important truth, which was wholly unknown to the Gentiles, and very little understood by the generality of the Jews. It is contained in these words of the Baptist—"Behold the Lamb of God which taketh away *the sin*, (την αμαρτιαν) not the *sins*, of the world." What is the sin of the world? Evidently the transgression of our first parents, which brought death and many other miseries on themselves, and all their posterity; and to take away these consequences of that sin, was the purpose for which a redeemer was first promised to the fallen pair, from which the "Word, which was in the beginning with God, and was God," condescended to take upon him human nature, and, with the patience of a lamb led to the slaughter, to die on a cross. Controversies have been agitated in the church from a very early period, concerning the nature of that *death*, which was brought upon the human race by the fall of our first parents. This is not a proper place for discussing such topics: but, whatever more may be included in the signification of the words *mōt tamoot*, it is evident from the whole scope of the Christian revelation, that the death incurred by the first transgression was absolute, without any reason to hope for a resurrection from the dead, but through the interposition of that seed of the woman, which was to bruise the head of the serpent.

Our Saviour says expressly—"*I am the resurrection and the life:* he that believeth in me, though he were dead, yet shall live; and whosoever liveth, and believeth in me, shall never die:" and, in another place, he says, "I am he that liveth and was dead: and behold, I am alive for evermore; and have the keys of hell (hades) and death." In perfect conformity with this, St. Paul taught the Corinthians, and, through them, the whole Christian world, that "Christ is risen from the dead, and become the first fruits of them that slept; for, since by man came death, by man came also the resurrection of the dead: and, as in Adam all die, even so in Christ shall all be made alive." That these salutary truths were not wholly unknown to the ancient prophets, and such other Israelites as could look through the shadows of the law to the substance of the Gospel, is indisputable: but that they were not fully comprehended by any Jew, in the days of our Saviour's sojourning on earth, is evident from a variety of passages in the New Testament, as well as from the unquestionable fact, that the Sadducees, "who said that there is no resurrection, neither angel nor spirit," were not only in communion with the other Jews, but capable even of executing the office of high-priest. The people therefore were not prepared, at our blessed Lord's first appearance, to receive these truths in all their lustre; but, as it would have been improper—and too like the common practice of impostors—to conceal entirely the great object of his mission even for a moment, he proclaimed in the words of the prophet Isaiah, that he was sent to preach the Gospel to the poor, and "deliverance to the captives," and to "set at liberty them that were bruised," which can mean nothing but deliverance from the curse of death, brought on mankind when the serpent bruised Adam's heel.

As these truths are wholly discovered by revelation, they could not be left to make their way in the world, like the dogmas of philosophy, by the discussions of human reason; for, by the philosophers of that age, a resurrection from the dead was deemed impossible. Accordingly both our Lord and his forerunner declared that a *kingdom* was at hand—even the kingdom of heaven or of God, in which all obstacles to their reception were to be taken away; which should comprehend the Gentiles here called the *blind*,* and in which "*all flesh* should see the salvation of God." That by the kingdom of Heaven was meant the church of Christ, will be seen more clearly in the sequel. At present it is sufficient to observe that, though at hand, it was not yet come.

Our Saviour, however, began to lay the foundation of it immediately after his baptism, by preaching the Gospel, by inviting all the Jews to become his disciples, and by working miracles to prove the truth of his mission. By these means he attracted many disciples, whom he baptised, not, as John had done, in the name of "one to come after him,"* but probably in general terms unto faith in the Messiah, declaring that without his baptism no man should enter into *the kingdom of God*† or the church. Of these disciples, after continuing all night in prayer to God, "he chose twelve, that they should be with him, and that he might send them forth to preach, whom he named apostles;"‡ and some time afterwards "he appointed other seventy also, and sent them two and two before his face into every city and place whither he himself would come."§ That the seventy were subordinate to the twelve, and that they were all subject to their divine Master, is evident from every passage in the Gospels, in which any mention is made of these two orders of ministers; and in this arrangement for laying the foundation of the Christian church, there is a striking resemblance to the means employed for conducting the Israelites to the land of promise.

The Israelites were delivered from Egyptian slavery by Moses the *servant* of God; the members of the Christian church, who walk worthy of the vocation wherewith they are called, are delivered from slavery infinitely more intolerable by Jesus Christ the *Son* of God. The twelve tribes of Israel were conducted under Moses through the wilderness, by twelve officers, the heads of their respective tribes; and, on the foundation of the Christian church, Christ appointed twelve apostles, who, when he should sit on the throne of his "Glory, should also sit on twelve thrones, judging the twelve tribes of Israel." And to complete the analogy, as the Lord commanded Moses to gather unto him seventy men of the elders of Israel, who, partaking of the spirit that was upon him, should bear the burthen of the people with him;‖ so Christ appointed the like number of disciples to go before his face to every place, whither he himself should come.

An analogy so striking could not escape the observation of the apostles, after their divine Master had "opened their understandings, that they might understand the Scriptures,"¶ and perceive the close connexion between the Mosaic and Christian dispensations. But, if the analogy between what may be called the civil polity of the Israelites in the wilderness, and the subordination established among our Lord's immediate followers, be thus evident, the analogy between the polity of the Jewish church and the same subordination is surely not less evident.

In what relates to religion, the disciples could not but perceive that the station of Jesus himself resembled that of the high-priest, that the twelve held a place in the little flock

* That such is the meaning of the word *blind*, in this passage of St. Luke's gospel, appears unquestionable, when it is compared with other parts of Scripture, more especially with St. John, chap. x. 16, and Rom. xi. 17, 21.

* Acts xix. 4.
† John iii. 5.
‡ St. Luke vi. 12, 13.
§ St. Luke x. 1.
‖ Numbers xi. 16.
¶ St. Luke xxiv. 45.

similar to that of the priests among the Jews; and that the seventy answered to the Levites in the temple service. The twelve were sent out to preach the Gospel to all the Jews; to baptize* the converts to the Christian faith; and, a little before the death of their Master, they were authorised to administer the rite commemorative of his sacrifice on the cross. To the seventy no other commission was given than to go before the face of Christ, and prepare the people for his reception, as "the Levites were given to Aaron and his sons, to wait upon the service of the tabernacle of the congregation."† But neither the twelve nor the seventy had yet power to admit a single labourer into the vineyard, or to cast an individual out of the flock.

The church indeed was not yet built,‡ though its foundation was laid, and a model exhibited for its future superstructure. As it is the purchase of Christ's blood, who gave himself for it,§ the building could not be completed till after his resurrection from the dead, and his ascension into heaven; and therefore the apostles were from the beginning intended to be the builders,‖ as soon as they should, for that purpose, be endowed with power from on high. It has accordingly been justly observed by an eminent prelate of the church of England,¶ that they were gradually raised to their high office in a manner strikingly analogous to that in which their blessed Master was raised to his; and that hardly any power is said to have belonged to him, which he did not delegate to them, when he commissioned them to complete the work which he had begun.

Although he was anointed, from his first appearance in this world, to be a king, priest, and prophet, he did not actually enter on any of those offices, until the Holy Ghost, descending visibly from heaven, had anointed him to them a second time. In like manner, though at an early period of his ministry he had separated the twelve from the multitude of believers, and promised even then that they "should sit on twelve thrones judging the twelve tribes of Israel," and that "whatsoever they should bind on earth should be bound in heaven, and whatsoever they should loose on earth should be loosed in heaven;" they did not actually receive this high commission, till after the resurrection of their divine Master, when he appeared to them, saying,—"Peace be unto you; as my Father hath sent me, even so send I you. And when he had said this, he breathed on them, saying—Receive ye the Holy Ghost; whose soever sins ye remit, they are remitted unto them; and whose soever sins ye retain, they are retained."**

Whilst our blessed Lord sojourned on earth, he was the king of the Jews only, and, as such, when he sent forth the twelve to preach, he said, "Go not into the way of the Gentiles, and into any city of the Samaritans enter ye not; but go rather to the lost sheep of the house of Israel."†† After his resurrection from the dead, as the limits of his kingdom were extended, he extended likewise the commission of his apostles; for he said unto them, "All power is given unto me in heaven and in earth. Go ye therefore and teach *all nations*, baptizing them in the name of the Father, and of the Son, and of the Holy Ghost; teaching them to observe all things whatsoever I have commanded you: and lo, I am with you alway, even unto the end of the world."* They were not however to enter on this great office of converting the nations, and opening to them the kingdom of heaven, until they should receive the promise of the Father, which they had heard from him; for, added he, "John truly baptized with water, but ye shall be baptized with the Holy Ghost not many days hence;"† alluding undoubtedly to his own baptism, when the Holy Ghost visibly descended on himself, as he did on them at the ensuing festival of Pentecost.

Thus striking is the analogy between the manner in which the man Christ Jesus was raised to his high office, and that in which he raised the apostles to theirs; and thus ample was the authority which he conferred on those master-builders of his church. As the promise of the keys of the kingdom was first made to St. Peter, he had the honour to make the first converts both among the Jews and the Gentiles. It was in consequence of his preaching on the day of Pentecost, that three thousand souls were added to the number of the disciples; and then we read for the first time of a *church* as actually *built*. Immediately after the effects of that preaching it is said that "the Lord added to *the church* daily such as should be saved."‡ St. Peter was likewise employed to open the door of the kingdom of Heaven, or the church, to the Gentiles,§ who, being "aliens to the commonwealth of Israel, and strangers to the covenant of promise," had hitherto been shut out from it: and this personal distinction—the reward of his heroic zeal in confessing his master—is the only foundation on which the supremacy of his successors in the see of Rome is endeavoured to be built, although it is obviously a distinction in which he could have no successor, being indeed temporary, and consisting in two single acts.‖

Of these acts one was performed in Jerusalem, and in that city was the first Christian church gradually organized; but it was not placed under the government of St. Peter, nor was it governed by the apostles in common. We have already seen that he who presided over the church of Jerusalem, even before the dispersion of the apostles, was James, called the Lord's brother; that under him was a college of elders (we know not how many,) and subordinate to them were the seven deacons. When it is said that the church of Jerusalem was not governed by the apostles in common, nothing more is meant than that James was its *immediate* governor, or stood in a relation

* St. John iv. 1, 2.
† Numbers iii. 9. viii. 24.
‡ St. Matth. xvi. 18, 19.
§ Gal. v. 25.
‖ 1 Cor. iii. 10, 11.
¶ Archbishop Potter.
** St. John xx. 21. 22, 23.
†† St. Matth. x. 5, 6.

* St. Matth. xxviii. 18, &c.
† Acts i. 4, 5.
‡ Acts ii. 14, &c.
§ Acts x.
‖ This has been proved by bishop Horsley, in one of his published sermons, with a force of reasoning that admits no reply. See his Sermons

to the elders, deacons and people of that church, in which the other apostles did not stand; and of this fact no man can doubt who has read without prejudice the Acts of the Apostles. That James was ready to be guided by the judgment of the apostles; that he consulted them, as long as he had an opportunity, in all the trials to which he must have been subjected; and that he occasionally enforced his own admonitions by the weight of their authority, is readily granted; but he never appears in the Acts, or is mentioned in the epistles of St. Paul, but as the chief governor of the church of Jerusalem, of which he is called by the unanimous voice of antiquity the first bishop.

Here then is one church, of which the constitution was unquestionably not democratical; and all the other churches that we read of in the New Testament appear to have been constituted on the same model with the church of Jerusalem. The apostles, in the discharge of the duties of their high commission, not only preached the Gospel every where, but also "ordained presbyters or elders in every church;"* and in the churches of Ephesus and Philippi,† and doubtless in all the rest, they appear to have ordained deacons as well as presbyters. It has indeed been contended that the deacons were merely trustees for the poor in matters purely secular, and therefore no order of those who have long been known in every church by the denomination of *the clergy;* but the solemnity with which the first deacons were ordained by prayer and imposition of hands, the qualifications required of those who were to be ordained deacons in the church of Ephesus, and the universal practice of the primitive church, prove this to be a palpable mistake. To distribute the public charity has indeed been one part of the deacon's office in all ages, and in every church where a legal establishment was not made for the support of the poor; and it was that part of the office which gave rise to the order at *the particular time* at which it was instituted; but that the office included something more—and that the seven were, in the language of antiquity, διακονοι λογου—ministers of the word, as well as διακονοι τραπεζων—ministers of the tables,—is evident from every thing that we read of deacons in the New Testament.

It has been already observed that in the churches of Ephesus, Crete, and Asia Minor, as well as in the church of Jerusalem, there were officers of a higher order than the presbyters; and to these officers alone belonged the right to ordain the presbyters and deacons; to exhort them to the due discharge of their respective duties; to reprove them for their faults,‡ and by consequence to degrade them from their offices when no longer worthy of them. If Timothy and Titus had not been invested with all this authority, the admonitions of St. Paul to them would surely have been different from what we find them in his three epistles. Timothy is particularly instructed in the qualifications requisite for presbyters and deacons; cautioned against laying hands suddenly on any man, lest he should be partaker of other men's sins; and directed how to receive accusations against presbyters; but, if the supreme power in the church of Ephesus had been vested in the people, or if the presbyters had shared equally with Timothy authority to ordain and reprove each other, such instructions as these to any individual would have been palpably absurd. It would likewise have been absurd to appoint Titus to ordain presbyters in *every* city of Crete, and after the first and second admonition to reject heretics; for, if it had belonged to the office of a presbyter to ordain, and finally to judge of heresies, the presbyter first ordained by him, might, *ex officio*, and with the aid of the people, have either supported or resisted him in the discharge of these duties. The governors of churches, to whom the presbyters as well as people were thus subject, appear, as Dr. Mosheim acknowledges, to have been generally called, during the first century, the *angels* or *apostles* of their respective churches. Such a governor certainly was Epaphroditus, styled by St. Paul his "brother, and companion in labour, and fellow-soldier; but the *apostle* of the church of Philippi," and therefore to "be holden by the Philippians in reputation."* Such likewise were Sosthenes and Sylvanus, whom he so frequently associates with himself as his partners, fellow helpers and brethren; and such were those brethren whom he calls αποστολοι εκκλησιων, δοξα Χριστου—"apostles of the churches, the glory of Christ."†

Doubtless there were presbyters ordained in some places, where no men were sufficiently qualified for the government of the infant church; and the care of such churches was retained by the apostle by whom they were founded, until some persons could be found to whom the immediate inspection both of the presbyters and the people might be safely entrusted. Hence it is that St. Paul, when enumerating his labours and sufferings for the promotion of the Gospel, expressly mentions, as one of those labours which came upon him daily—"the care of all the churches which he had planted." It is however evident that each church was, as soon as possible, placed under the superintendance of an apostle or angel of its own, that the twelve, with St. Paul and Barnabas, might be as little as possible interrupted in their glorious career of converting all nations; but it does not appear that in the appointment of these *angels* or secondary *apostles*, or indeed of the *presbyters*, the people were, in the first century, so much as consulted. Paul and Barnabas ordained elders or presbyters in every church which they planted; but St. Paul himself assures us that the presbyters so ordained in the church of Ephesus, "were made overseers of the flock (not by the people but) by the Holy Ghost, to feed the church of God which he hath purchased with his own blood."‡ He likewise informs us that God, and not the people, had set, in the church, governments and governors of different orders, of which the apostles were the first;§ that there were in the

* Acts xiv. 23.
† 1 Philip. i. 1; and 1 Tim. iii. 8.
‡ See the Epistles to Timothy and Titus *passim*.

* Philip. ii. 25, 29. † 2 Cor. viii. 23.
‡ Acts xx. 28.
§ Cor. xii. 28, and Eph. iv. 11, 12.

church of Thessalonica those who, as the people were exhorted to *know* them, as well as esteem them very highly for their work's sake, could not have been *appointed* by those people themselves to "labour among them, and be over them in the Lord,"* and that in all churches there are overseers, whom the people are bound to "obey as those who have the rule over them, and to submit themselves as to those who watch for their souls."†

Who those rulers were, it is not difficult to discover. We have seen that, in every completely organized church mentioned in the New Testament, there were three orders of men, who, each in his station, laboured in the word and doctrine. Of these the lowest order was that of deacons, who appear, from the conduct of Stephen and Philip, to have preached and occasionally administered the sacrament of baptism. Superior to the deacons was the order of presbyters, often called bishops, whose duty it was to feed the flock of Christ, by preaching the word, and administering both the sacraments; and over both these orders we find a president, who is generally called in the New Testament the angel or apostle of the particular church over which he presided; whose pastoral care extended over more than one congregation; to whom alone belonged the privilege of ordaining presbyters and deacons; who was himself always ordained by apostolic hands; and who alone could finally cut off unworthy Christians from the communion of the church.

It has been often said that the apostles neither had nor could have successors, and that therefore the elders, whom all admit to be often called bishops in the New Testament, are the highest order of ministers intended to continue in the church of Christ. This, however, is said, not only without authority, but in direct contradiction to the plainest testimony of Scripture, and the consequent practice of all antiquity. It was to the apostles alone, and not to the multitude of believers, or even to the seventy, that our blessed Lord said, "Go ye and teach all nations." It was to them alone that he gave the keys of the kingdom of heaven, saying, "whatsoever ye shall bind on earth, shall be bound in heaven; and whatsoever ye shall loose on earth, shall be loosed in heaven:" and the apostles alone were sent by him, as his Father had sent him, with authority to govern that kingdom which he had purchased with his own blood. As he knew all things, he was fully aware that the apostles were mortal, and that, in fact, none of them would long survive the approaching destruction of Jerusalem. It could not therefore be with themselves personally, but with their successors in office from age to age, that he was to be always even to the end of the world. The church, which he every where calls his kingdom, and which he declared to Pilate was not to be of this world, was founded by himself, and built by his apostles acting under his authority; and its privileges, whatever they may be, are derived wholly from him. No man could be admitted into the church, or cast out of it, but by the authority which he conferred on the apostles for these purposes; and therefore, if they were to have no successors, the church must have been swept from the face of the earth, almost as soon as that ritual service, which was established among the Jews, merely as preparatory to it. After the death of St. John, no man could either have been received into the church, or cast out of it; and the church itself must have perished with that generation. Yet Christ himself solemnly promised, that "against the church to be built on the faith confessed by St. Peter, the gates of hell—πυλαι αδου—the gates of *death*, or of the *receptacle* of the dead—should never prevail;" for he well knew, that the perpetuity of the church is necessary to the perpetuity of the faith.

There are indeed men of some learning, who seem to think otherwise; who profess great regard for the doctrines and morality of the Gospel; but who raise hideous outcries against every claim to any other authority in the church of Christ, than what is exercised in literary clubs, or philosophical societies. But what must have been the consequence to the faith, if, on the death of the apostles and other inspired preachers of the Gospel, all ecclesiastical authority had ceased, or devolved on the multitude at large? With the Old and New Testaments in their hands, could the rabble have maintained the purity of the faith? Could *they* have discovered, even from those writings, the consequences of the first transgression; the necessity of a redeemer to fallen man; or the nature and extent of the redemption wrought for him? Could they have discovered the necessity of divine aid to enable us to work out our own salvation with fear and trembling, or have guarded that doctrine, supposing it discovered, from the opposite and dangerous extremes, to which it is too often carried even by learned ministers of the church? Could such men have preserved in purity the doctrine of one God in three persons; or would they not rather have immediately relapsed into polytheism and idolatry, with which, as they had themselves but lately emerged from it, they were still surrounded? Would they have long maintained the resurrection of the dead, and a general judgment, against the sophisms of those philosophers, who considered the body as the prison of the soul, who thought a resurrection of the dead impossible even to omnipotence, and who taught, either that the gods could not be offended with men, or that the human soul is no subject either of reward or of punishment; being in fact a portion of το εν, or the soul of the world, in which it was finally to be re-absorbed.

Even the morality of the Gospel, so justly admired, would, if left to the guardianship of the people at large, have been as liable to corruption as its peculiar doctrines. From the epistles of St. Paul, as well as from the philosophers, satirists, and profane historians of the age, it appears that the morals of the heathen world, at the period when the Gospel was first preached to all nations, were sunk to a state of the lowest depravity; that the sensual appetites of our nature were indulged to the ut

* 1 Thess. v. 12. 13. † Heb. xii. 17.

most excess; that some of those, who were converted to the faith, had themselves, in their unregenerated state, given way to every inordinate affection; and that vices, not even to be named among Christians, were countenanced by the teaching, if not the practice, even of some of the philosophers. Had the multitude been left, each to interpret the scriptures for himself; had they been left without control, to choose their own teachers and governors; had the power of the *keys*, or the supreme authority in the church, been committed to them, is it not probable—is it not, indeed, morally certain, that they would soon have relapsed into their former courses, "as the dog turns to his vomit again, and the sow that is washed to her wallowing in the mire?"

Although all the doctrines and precepts of Christianity, which are essential to salvation, are easily understood by candour, combined with attention, yet some of them, such as St. Paul's doctrine of justification by faith for instance, are very liable to be misapprehended, where either candour or attention is wanting. But candour and attention are not to be looked for in ignorant and illiterate men, when they are under the dominion of corrupt habits, or are impelled by the strongest propensities of our animal nature; and therefore such men, and the teachers chosen by such men, may be expected to interpret that doctrine so as to make it encourage their "continuance in sin that grace may abound," and enable them to reconcile their impure practices with their profession of Christianity. This is not a mere hypothesis formed for the sake of argument. It is a fact well known to ecclesiastical historians, and occasionally pointed out by our author, that some of the ancient sects, who renounced the communion of the regular church, taught that Christ hath set men free, not only from the ritual law of Moses, but even from the obligations of morality; and there is reason to suspect that some of the mob-commissioned teachers of the present age, acquire their popularity by the same execrable doctrine.

All this was well known to Christ, who therefore established a society or church in the world, to be "the pillar and ground of his truth,"* and the guardian of the morals of his disciples. To that society are confined all the privileges of the Gospel;† men are to be admitted into it only by baptism;‡ he who, when the Gospel has been fully preached to him, refuses to be baptised, has no claim, by the Christian covenant, to salvation;§ and he who submits not to the discipline of the church, is in the state of a heathen man or a publican.‖ But we have seen that the apostles alone had received authority to admit into the church, or cast out of it; and that therefore the apostolical order must be continued by succession from those, who were originally raised to that order by the divine head of the church, even to the end of the world. Accordingly St. Paul speaks of apostles ordained by men¶ in his time, of whom Epaphroditus appears to have been one,

* 1 Tim. iii. 15. † Acts ii. 47. Luke xviii. 18.
‡ St. Matth. xxviii. 19.
§ St. Mark xvi 16. ‖ St. Matth. xviii. 17, 18.
¶ Gal. i. 1.

as Barnabas certainly was another, and warn the Corinthians against false apostles,* whilst our blessed Lord, by the pen of St. John, makes express mention of some, who "said they were apostles, and were not, but were found liars."† Nothing of all this could have happened, if it had been understood, that the primary apostles were to have no successors; for the twelve with St. Paul were all, except St. John, dead some time before the false apostles were detected by the angel of the church of Ephesus; and, had they been alive, they must have been too well known for the most impudent liars then existing, to personate them in a church which had been founded by St. Paul, and so lately governed by his son Timothy.

The case appears to have been as Theodoret and others expressly represent it—"That those now called bishops were anciently called apostles; but in process of time the name of apostle was left to them, who were truly apostles (viz the twelve and St. Paul;) and the name of bishop was restrained to those who were anciently called apostles. Thus Epaphroditus was the apostle of the Philippians, Titus of the Cretans, and Timothy of the Asiatics."‡ This change of the denomination of the highest order of ecclesiastics, from apostle to bishop, seems to have been made about the beginning of the second century, soon after the death of St. John, and probably gave occasion to Ignatius to insist so much on the obedience due to the bishops, lest the churches, to which his epistles were addressed, should imagine that the authority of their chief pastors had been diminished by the change of their designation That change, however, appears not to have been strictly attended to, for several centuries, by those who had occasion to write of the immediate successors of the apostles in particular churches; for Clement, bishop of Rome, is by Clement of Alexandria, called§ Αποστολος Κλημης, and Ignatius, one of the first bishops of Antioch, is by Chrysostom‖ styled αποστολος και επισκοπος.

Thus, then, it appears that the constitution of the church, in the first century, was episcopal in the diocesan sense of that word; that the bishop was the chief pastor of a greater or less number of congregations, according to the extent of his diocese; that though both presbyters and deacons preached and administered the sacrament of baptism, and the former the Lord's supper, they could perform no ecclesiastical office, but by authority derived from the bishop;¶ that the people had

* 2 Cor. xi. 13. † Rev. ii. 2.

‡ Τους δε νυν καλουμενους επισκοπους αποστολους ωνομαζον, του δε χρονου προιοντος το μεν της αποστολης ονομα τοις αληθως αποστολοις κατελιπον την δε της επισκοπης προσηγοριαν τοις παλαι καλουμενοις αποστολοις επεθεσαν, &c. Theod. in Tim. cap. 3. He repeats the same thing, Com. in Phil. i. 1, and ii. 25. The author under the name of Ambrose, generally believed to be Hilary the deacon, asserts that all bishops were at first called apostles, and that it was to distinguish himself from such apostles, that St. Paul called himself an "apostle, not of men, neither by men, but by Jesus Christ and God the Father." Ambros. Com. in Eph. iv. and in Gal. i. 1.

§ Strom. lib. 4. ‖ Encom. Ign.

¶ Μηδεις χωρις του επισκοπου τι πρασσετω των ανηκοντων εις την εκκλησιαν......ουκ εξον εστιν χωρις του

no such authority in the church, as Dr. Mosheim supposes; and that neither the presbyters, nor people, nor both united, could excommunicate any person, or cast him entirely out of the church, but by the sentence of the bishop. It does not however appear that for several centuries a bishop's diocese, or the tract of country over which his pastoral care extended, was every where divided into what we now call *parishes*, each with its resident pastor. On the contrary, this division became not general before the fifth century, and seems not to have been made in England previous to the seventh. It is indeed hardly supposable that in the first century the Christians had any buildings wholly set apart for the service of the church. During that period, the probability is that the bishop, with one or two inferior clergymen to assist him, convened part of his flock in his own or some other house; that the presbyters were sent by him to other private houses, where, in different divisions, the remainder of the flock assembled themselves together, for the breaking of bread and for prayer; and it is certain, that, when the presbyters returned to their bishops, they delivered, each into the common stock of the church, the oblations which had been made by their respective congregations. When the number of Christians every where increased, presbyters appear, indeed, even during the æra of persecution, to have been stationed in a suburb, or in the country-region of the bishop's diocese; but even then the oblations of the people were all delivered into the common stock of the mother-church, and there distributed into shares, for the maintenance of the bishop, for the support of the clergy under him, for assisting the poor and strangers, and for purchasing whatever was necessary for the public service of the church. After the empire became Christian, what we now call parish churches were built, and endowed, sometimes by the public, and more frequently by opulent individuals; and hence the origin of patronage, or the right granted to individuals, to present their own clerks to the churches which they had endowed. This practice seems to have become general about the year 500, as there are two laws by Justinian of that date, authorising and confirming it; but even then no clerk could be presented without the concurrence of the bishop under whom he was to minister, nor be supported by any patron against the censures of his diocesan, when so unhappy as to have incurred them.

In the first and second centuries there seems to have been a perfect equality of rank among the several bishops of the church, he presiding in provincial synods, in whose diocese the synod was holden. Thus, though St. Peter certainly took the place of St. James in the college of the Apostles, St. James appears to have presided in the first council, because it took place in Jerusalem, of which he was acknowledged to be the bishop. This perfect equality, however, was gradually done away; for, by the middle of the third century, it is evident that, without acknowledging any superiority of order, the bishops of every province paid a particular respect to the bishop of the chief city and hence the origin of metropolitans and patriarchs. To this deviation from primitive practice several things contributed. In the chief city, it must have been the practice of the church, from the beginning, to place as bishop a man of approved talents, and piety, and virtue; and even when the clergy subsisted on the voluntary oblations of the faithful, the bishops of the larger cities must have been more opulent than those of the smaller; and in every age of the church—the purest as well as the most corrupt—opulence has always commanded a degree of respect, especially when in the possession of talents and virtue.

There was, however, another and a better motive than this for giving precedency to the bishops of the chief cities. The whole Christian church is, or ought to be, one society or kingdom, united under its divine head, by the profession of the same faith, by the administration of the same sacraments, and by the same government and discipline. In the apostolic age, whoever had the misfortune to be expelled from one particular church, found himself expelled from all particular churches, or, in other words, excommunicated by the church universal; and, by the authority of Christ himself, was reduced to the state of a heathen man or a publican. Hence St. Cyprian says*—"Episcopatus unus est, cujus a singulis in solidum pars tenetur:"—and elsewhere, "Idcirco copiosum est sacerdotium concordiæ mutuæ glutino atque unitatis vinculo copulatum, ut siquis ex collegio nostro hæresin facere, et gregem Christi lacerare et vastare tentaverit, subveniant cæteri, et, quasi pastores utiles et misericordes, oves Dominicas in gregem colligant."† This is indeed the doctrine of a much greater man than Cyprian. It is the doctrine of the illustrious apostle of the Gentiles, who compares the unity of the church, and the due subordination of its several members, to the unity of the human body, and the adaptation of its members to their respective uses;‡ beseeching Christians "to keep the unity of the spirit in the bond of peace, because, among them, there is but one body and one spirit, even as they are called in one hope of their calling, one Lord, one faith, one baptism, one God and Father of all, who is above all, and through all, and in them all."§ It is the doctrine of a still greater—an infinitely greater personage than St. Paul—even of our Lord himself, who declared, that the whole Christian world was to be "one fold under him the one shepherd," and who, when praying for his immediate followers, added—"Neither pray I for these alone, but for them also who shall believe in me through their word, that they all may be one, as thou, Father, art in me, and I in thee, that they also may be one in us; that the world may believe that thou hast sent me."‖

επισκοπου, ουτε βαπτιζειν, ουτε αγαπην ποιειν· αλλ, ο αν εκεινος δοκιμαση, τουτο και τω Θεω ευαρεστον. Ignatii Epist. ad Smyrn. cap. 8.

* De Unitate Ecclesiæ.
† Epist. 67. ed. Pamel. 68. ed. Fell.
‡ Rom. xii. 4, 5. 1 Cor. xii. 12. 31.
§ Ephesians iv. 3, 17.
‖ St. John x. 16. xvii. 20, 21.

That this catholic unity might be preserved entire, every bishop elect was obliged, before his ordination, to make a declaration of his faith to the bishops who ordained him, and, immediately after his ordination, to send, by the hands of some confidential clergymen, circular or *encyclical* letters, as they were called, to foreign churches, declaratory of his faith, announcing his promotion to such a see, and professing his communion with the churches to which the letters were sent. If his faith was deemed catholic, and nothing irregular appeared to have taken place in the various steps of his promotion, answers were immediately returned to his letters, approving what had been done, and acknowledging him as a bishop of the catholic church; but, if doubts were excited in the minds of those to whom the encyclical letters were addressed, no answer was returned until proper inquiries were made, and all doubts respecting the faith of the lately consecrated bishop, or the regularity of his promotion, were completely removed. It was thus that Christian communion was maintained between the remotest churches. But had the bishops been, in the modern sense of the word, *parochial*, and therefore as numerous as the various congregations of Christians, which assembled under separate roofs for the celebration of the mysteries of their religion, it is obvious that this salutary process could not have been carried on; the doctrines taught in distant churches must have been unknown to each other; and catholic unity could have been nothing but a name. Even among diocesan bishops, when all of equal rank, such a correspondence must have become so difficult and tedious, after churches were planted in every corner of the empire, that the authors of heresies might, as Cyprian expresses it, have divided and laid waste the flock of Christ, before the bishops at a distance could have stepped in to its assistance; but, by the institution of metropolitans and patriarchs, it became easy and expeditious, as the bishops corresponded with their own metropolitans, the metropolitans with their respective patriarchs, and the patriarchs with each other.

After the conversion of Constantine, the distinctions of rank which had thus been introduced among the bishops of the church, were confirmed by the council of Nice, and modelled according to the precedency that was allowed among the civil provinces into which the empire was divided; but, if such an arrangement was attended by some advantages, it was productive likewise of many evils. It was the parent of those fierce contentions between the bishops of Rome and Constantinople for precedency, which disgrace the character of both as the ministers of the meek and lowly Jesus; and, at last, it furnished the former of those prelates with the means of erecting that tyranny, which he so long exercised over the whole western church.

About the æra of the council of Nice, if not at an earlier period, distinctions, unknown in the apostolic age, were introduced likewise among the inferior clergy of the same order. When parochial churches were endowed and provided each with a resident pastor, it was judged expedient to give to the bishop a permanent council, which might supply the place of those presbyters who had hitherto lived with him, but were now removed to their respective cures; and from this appointment may be dated the origin of deans and chapters.

At a very early period there seems to have been, in every church where there were many deacons, one who by the bishop's authority had precedence of the rest; but there is no good evidence that visiting presbyters were any where appointed to offices similar to those of our archdeacons, until the abolition of the order of *chorepiscopi*. That the appointment took place then, is rendered unquestionable by the 57th canon of the council of Laodicea, which substitutes visiting presbyters for those village-bishops, of whom it decreed that no more were to be ordained.

Whether the church acted prudently in all these apparent deviations from primitive simplicity, is a question which we are not called upon to answer; but it is certain that in none of them did she exceed that authority, with which, as an independent society to be spread over the whole world, she must have been invested by her divine lawgiver, to adapt her constitution, as much as possible, to the circumstances in which she might be placed. To this authority St. Paul repeatedly alludes; and if her metropolitans and patriarchs, her deans and chapters, her visiting presbyters and archdeacons, &c., contributed in any degree to the maintenance of order and decency, she had an unquestionable right to appoint them. Her patriarchs and metropolitans, however dignified with titles and outward splendour, derived from Christ, by apostolical succession, no authority which was not equally possessed by every other bishop; the visiting presbyters, though the bishop devolved on them such parts of his authority as presbyters were capable of exercising, were still nothing more than mere presbyters; and an archdeacon, although he had precedence among his brethren, could not administer the Lord's supper, and was therefore inferior to the lowest presbyter in the church.

The authority of the church to decree rites or ceremonies and to make such regulations in the mode of administering her discipline, as are best adapted to produce the effects for which her discipline itself was instituted, are facts which cannot indeed be questioned. When incorporated with the state, her governors may certainly be armed by the civil magistrate with civil rank and civil power; but she has no authority to depart in a single article from the faith which was once delivered to the saints, or to surrender to any man that authority which her bishops derive by succession from the apostles. The church is a kingdom not of this world; and therefore, as she derives not her inherent authority from the potentates of this world, to the potentates of this world she cannot resign that authority. Wherever the faith is maintained in purity, and the episcopal succession preserved, there is a true church, or the elements of a true church:

"quando," to use the words of Cyprian, "Ecclesia in episcopo, et clero, et in omnibus stantibus, sit constituta;"* and to the efficacious administration of the word and sacraments, it is of no consequence whether the bishop of such a church be a prince, a peer, or an obscure pastor; for, as another ancient writer* observes, "potestas peccatorum remittendorum apostolis data est, et ecclesiis quas illi a Christo missi constituerunt, et episcopis qui eis ordinatione vicariâ successerunt."

* Epist. 27, edit. Pamel.—33, edit. Fell.

* Firmilian. inter Cyp. Epistolas, Ep. 75. edit. Pamelii et Fell.

THE SECOND APPENDIX,

BY DR. MACLAINE;

CONCERNING THE SPIRIT AND CONDUCT OF THE FIRST REFORMERS, AND THE CHARGE OF ENTHUSIASM (*i. e.* FANATICISM) THAT HAS BEEN BROUGHT AGAINST THEM BY A CELEBRATED AUTHOR.

THE candour and impartiality, with which Dr. Mosheim represents the transactions of those who were agents and instruments in bringing about the reformation, are highly laudable. He acknowledges that imprudence, passion, and even a low self-interest, mingled sometimes their rash proceedings and ignoble motives in this excellent cause; and, in the very nature of things, it could not be otherwise. It is one of the inevitable consequences of the subordination and connexions of civil society, that many improper instruments and agents are set to work in all great and important revolutions, whether of a religious or political nature. When great men appear in these revolutions, they draw after them their dependents; and the unhappy effects of a party spirit are unavoidably displayed in the best cause. The subjects follow their prince; the multitude adopt the system of their leaders, without entering into its true spirit, or being judiciously attentive to the proper methods of promoting it; and thus irregular proceedings are employed in the maintenance of the truth. Thus it happened in the important revolution that delivered a great part of Europe from the ignominious yoke of the Roman pontiff. The sovereigns, the ecclesiastics, the men of weight, piety, and learning, who arose to assert the rights of human nature, the cause of genuine Christianity, and the exercise of religious liberty, came forth into the field of controversy with a multitude of dependents, admirers, and friends, whose motives and conduct cannot be entirely justified. Besides, when the eyes of whole nations were opened upon the iniquitous absurdities of popery, and upon the tyranny and insolence of the Roman pontiffs, it was scarcely possible to set bounds to the indignation of an incensed and tumultuous multitude, who are naturally prone to extremes, generally pass from blind submission to lawless ferocity, and too rarely distinguish between the use and abuse of their undoubted rights. In a word, many things, which appear to us extremely irregular in the conduct and measures of some of the instruments of our happy reformation, will be entitled to a certain degree of indulgence, if the spirit of the times, the situation of the contending parties, the barbarous provocations of popery, and the infirmities of human nature, be duly and attentively considered.

The question here is, what was the spirit which animated the first and principal reformers, who arose in times of darkness and despair to deliver oppressed kingdoms from the dominion of Rome, and upon what principles a Luther, a Zuingle, a Calvin, a Melancthon, a Bucer, &c. embarked in the ardous cause of the Reformation? This question, indeed, is not at all necessary to the defence of the Reformation, which rests upon the strong foundations of Scripture and reason, and whose excellence is absolutely independent of the virtues of those who took the lead in promoting it. Bad men may be, and often are, embarked in the best causes, as such causes afford the most specious mask to cover mercenary views, or to disguise ambitious purposes. But until the more than Jesuitical and disingenuous Philips resumed the trumpet of calumny,* even the voice of popery had ceased to attack the moral characters of the leading reformers.

These eminent men were indeed attacked from another quarter, and by a much more respectable writer. The truly ingenious Mr. Hume, so justly celebrated as one of the first favourites of the historic muse, has, in his history of England, and more especially in the history of the houses of Tudor and Stuart, represented the character and temper of the first reformers in a point of view, which undoubtedly shows, that he had not considered them with the close and impartial attention that ought always to precede personal reflections. He has laid it down as a principle, that *superstition* and *enthusiasm* are two species of religion that stand in diametrical opposition to each other; and seems to establish it as a fact, that the former is the genius of popery, and the latter the characteristic of the Reformation. Both the principle and its application must appear extremely singular; and three sorts of persons must be more especially surprised at it.

In the first place, persons of a philosophical

* See the various answers that were made to this biographer by the ingenious Mr. Pye, the learned Dr. Neve, and other commendable writers who have appeared in this controversy.

turn, who are accustomed to study human nature, and to describe with precision both its regular and eccentric movements, must be surprised to see superstition and fanaticism* represented as opposite and jarring qualities. They have been often seen together, holding with each other a most friendly correspondence; and indeed if we consider their nature, and their essential characters, their union will appear, not only possible, but in some cases natural, if not necessary. *Superstition*, which consists in false and abject notions of the Deity, in the gloomy and groundless fears of invisible beings, and in the absurd rites, that these notions and these fears naturally produce, is certainly the root of various branches of fanaticism. For what is *fanaticism*, but the visions, illuminations, impulses, and dreams of an overheated fancy, converted into rules of faith, hope, worship, and practice? This fanaticism, as it springs up in a melancholy or a cheerful complexion, assumes a variety of aspects, and its morose and gloomy forms are certainly most congenial with superstition, in its proper sense. It was probably this consideration that led the author of the article *Fanaticism*, in the famous Dictionnaire Encyclopedique, to define it† as "a blind and passionate zeal, which arises from superstitious opinions, and leads its votaries to commit ridiculous, unjust, and cruel actions, not only without shame, but even with certain internal feelings of joy and comfort;" from which the author concludes, that "fanaticism is really nothing more than superstition set in motion." This definition unites perhaps too closely these two kinds of false religion, whose enormities have furnished very ill-grounded pretexts for discrediting and misrepresenting the true. It is, however, a testimony from one of the pretended oracles of modern philosophy, in favour of the compatibility of fanaticism with superstition. These two principles are evidently distinct; because superstition is, generally speaking, the effect of ignorance, or of a judgment perverted by a sour and splenetic temper; whereas fanaticism is the offspring of an inflamed imagination, and may exist where there is no superstition, *i. e.* where no false or gloomy notions of the divinity are entertained. But, though distinct, they are not opposite principles; on the contrary, they lend on many occasions, some strength and assistance to each other.

If persons accustomed to philosophical precision will not relish the maxim of the celebrated writer which I have been now considering, so neither, in the second place, can those who are versed in ecclesiastical history look upon superstition as a more predominant characteristic of popery than fanaticism; and yet this is a leading idea, which is not only visible in many parts of this author's excellent History, but appears to be the basis of all the reflections he employs, and of all the epithets he uses, in his speculations upon the Romish religion.

And nevertheless it is manifest, that the multitudes of fanatics, which arose in the church of Rome before the Reformation, are truly innumerable; and the operations of fanaticism in that church were, at least, as visible and frequent, as the restless workings of superstition; they went, in short, hand in hand, and united their visions and their terrors in the support of the papacy. It is, more especially, well known, that the greatest part of the monastic establishments (that alternately insulted the benignity of Providence by their austerities, and abused it by their licentious luxury,) were originally founded in consequence of pretended illuminations, miraculous dreams, and other wild delusions, of an over-heated fancy. Whenever a new doctrine was to be established, that could augment the authority of the pope, or fill the coffers of the clergy; whenever a new convent was to be erected, there was always a vision or a miracle ready to facilitate the business; nor must it be imagined, that forgery and imposture were the only agents in this matter;—by no means;—imposture there was; and it was frequently employed; but impostors made use of fanatics; and in return fanatics found impostors, who spread abroad their fame, and turned their visions to profit. Were I to recount with the utmost simplicity, without the smallest addition of ludicrous embellishment, the ecstacies, visions, seraphic amours, celestial apparitions, that are said to have shed such an odour of sanctity upon the male and female saints of the Romish church; were I to pass in review the famous conformities of St. Francis, the illuminations of St. Ignatius, and the enormous cloud of fanatical witnesses that have dishonoured humanity in bearing testimony to popery, this dissertation would become a voluminous history. Let the reader cast an eye upon Dr. Mosheim's account of those ages which more immediately preceded the Reformation, and he will see what a number of sects, *purely fanatical*, arose in the bosom of the Romish church.

But this is not all—for it must be carefully observed, that even those extravagant fanatics, who produced such disorders in Germany about the commencement of the Reformation, were nursed in the bosom of popery, were professed papists before they adopted the cause of Luther; and that many of them even passed directly from popery to fanaticism, without even entering into the outward profession of Lutheranism. It is also to be observed, that beside the fanatics, who exposed themselves to the contempt of the wise upon the public theatre of popery, Seckendorf speaks of a sect that merits this denomination, which had spread in the Netherlands, before Luther raised his voice against popery, and whose members were engaged, by the terror of penal laws, to dissemble their sentiments, and even affected a de

* I use the word *fanaticism* here, instead of *enthusiasm*, to prevent all ambiguity; because, as shall be shown presently, Mr. Hume takes *enthusiasm* in its worse sense when he applies it to the reformers; and in that sense it is not only equivalent to, but is perfectly synonymous with, fanaticism. Besides, the latter term is used indiscriminately with enthusiasm, by this celebrated historian, in characterising the Reformation.

† The words of the original are, "Le fanatisme est un zele aveugle et passione, qui nait des opinions superstitieuses, et fait commettre des actions ridicules, injustes et cruelles, non seulement sans honte, mais avec une sorta de joye et de consolation. Le fanatisme donc n'est que la superstition mise en mouvement."

vout compliance with the ceremonies of the established worship, until religious liberty, introduced by the reformation, encouraged them to pull off the mask, and propagate their opinions, several of which were licentious and profane.

But, in the third place, the friends of the Reformation must naturally be both surprised and displeased to find enthusiasm, or fanaticism, laid down by Mr. Hume, as the character and spirit of its founders and abettors, without any exception or distinction in favour of any one of the reformers. That fanaticism was visible in the conduct and spirit of many who embraced the Reformation, is a fact which I do not pretend to deny; and it may be worthy of the reader's curiosity to consider, for a moment, how this came to pass. That religious liberty, which the Reformation introduced and granted (in consequence of its essential principles) indiscriminately to all, to the learned and unlearned, rendered this eruption of enthusiasm inevitable. It is one of the imperfections annexed to all human things, that our best blessings have their inconveniences, or, at least, are susceptible of abuse. As liberty is a natural right, but not a discerning principle, it could not open the door to truth without letting error and delusion come with it. If reason came forth with dignity, when delivered from the despotism of authority, and the blind servitude of implicit faith; imagination, also set free and less able to bear the prosperous change, came forth likewise, but with a different aspect, and exposed to view the reveries which it had been long obliged to conceal.

Thus many fanatical phantoms were exhibited, which neither arose from the spirit of the Reformation, nor from the principles of the reformers, but which had been engendered in the bosom of popery, and which the fostering rays of liberty had disclosed; similar in this, to the enlivening beams of the sun, which fructify indiscriminately the salutary plant in the well cultivated ground, and the noxious weed in a rank and neglected soil. And as the Reformation had no such miraculous influence (not to speak of the imperfection that attended its infancy, and that has not entirely been removed from its more advanced stages) as to cure human nature of its infirmities and follies, to convert irregular passions into regular principles, or to turn men into angels before the time, it has still left the field open, both for fanaticism and superstition to sow their tares among the good seed; and this will probably be the case until the end of the world. It is here, that we must seek for the true cause of all that condemnable enthusiasm which has dishonoured the Christian name, and often troubled the order of civil society, at different periods since the Reformation; and for which the reformation is no more responsible, than a free government is for the weakness or corruption of those who abuse its lenity and indulgence. The Reformation established the sacred and inalienable right of private judgment; but it could not hinder the private judgment of many from being wild and extravagant.

The Reformation, then, which the multiplied enormities of popery rendered so necessary, must be always distinguished from the abuses that might be, and were often made, of the liberty it introduced. If you ask, indeed, what was the temper or spirit of the first heralds of this happy Reformation, Mr. Hume will tell you, that they were universally inflamed with the highest enthusiasm. This assertion, if taken singly, and not compared with other passages relating to the reformers, might be understood in a sense consistent with truth, and even honourable to the character of these eminent men. For, if by enthusiasm we understand that spirit of ardour, intrepidity, and generous zeal, which leads men to brave the most formidable obstacles and dangers in defence of a cause, whose excellence and importance have made a deep impression upon their minds, the first reformers will be allowed by their warmest friends to have been enthusiasts. This species of enthusiasm is a noble affection, when fitly placed and wisely exerted. It is this generous sensibility, this ardent feeling of the great and excellent, that forms heroes and patriots; and, without it, nothing difficult and arduous, that is attended with danger, or prejudice to our temporal interests, can either be attempted with vigour, or executed with success. If this ingenious writer had even observed, that the ardour of the first reformers was more or less violent, that it was more or less blended with the warmth and vivacity of human passions, candour would be obliged to avow the charge.

But it is not in any of these points of view, that our eminent historian considers the spirit, temper, and enthusiasm of the first reformers. The enthusiasm he attributes to them is fanaticism in its worst sense. He speaks indeed of the 'inflexible intrepidity, with which they braved dangers, torments, and even death itself;' but he calls them 'the fanatical and enraged reformers;' he represents fanaticism, through the whole course of his history, as the characteristic of the protestant religion and its glorious founders: the terms, 'protestant fanaticism—fanatical churches'—are interspersed in various parts of his work; and we never meet with the least appearance of a distinction between the rational and enthusiastic, the wise and indiscreet friends of the Reformation. In short, we find a phraseology constantly employed upon this subject, which discovers an intention to confound protestantism with enthusiasm, and to make *reformers* and *fanatics* synonymous terms. We are told, that, while absurd rites and burthensome superstitions reigned in the Romish church, the reformers were 'thrown, by a spirit of opposition, into an enthusiastic strain of devotion;' and, in another place, that the latter 'placed all merit in a mysterious species of faith, in inward vision, rapture, and ecstasy.' It would be endless to quote the passages in which this representation of things is repeated in a great variety of phrases, and artfully insinuated into the mind of the reader, by dexterous strokes of a seducing pencil; which, though scattered here and there, yet gradually unite their influence on the imagination of an uninstructed and unwary reader, and form, imperceptibly, an unfavourable impression of that great event, to which we owe at this day our civil and religious liberty, and our deliverance from a yoke of superstitious and barbarous despotism. Protestants, in all ages and places, are stigmatised by Mr. Hume with very dishonourable titles; and it struck me particularly to see even the generous opposers of the Spanish inquisition in Holland, whose proceedings were so moderate, and whose complaints were so humble, until the barbarous yoke of superstition and tyranny became intolerable; it struck me, I say, to see these generous patriots branded with the general character of *bigots*. This is certainly a severe appellation; and were it applied with much more equity than it is, I think it would still come with an ill grace from a lover of freedom, from a man who lives and writes with security under the auspicious shade of that very liberty which the Reformation introduced, and for which the Belgic heroes (or *bigots*—if we must call them so) shed their blood. I observe with pain, that the phraseology and mode of expression, employed perpetually by Mr. Hume, on similar occasions, seem to discover a keen dislike of every opposition made to power in favour of the Reformation. Upon the too general principle which this eminent writer has diffused through his history, we shall even be obliged to brand, with the opprobrious mark of fanaticism, those generous friends of civil and religious liberty, who, in the revolution of 1688, opposed the measures of a popish prince and an arbitrary government, and to rank the Burnets, Tillotsons, Stillingfleets, and other immortal ornaments of the protestant name, among the enthusiastic tribe; it is a question, whether even a Boyle, a Newton, or a Locke, will escape a censure which is lavished without mercy and without distinction.—But my present business is with the first reformers, and to them I return.

Those who more especially merit that title, were Luther, Zuingle, Calvin, Melancthon, Bucer, Martyr, Bullinger, Beza, Œcolampadius, and others. Now these were *all* men of learning, who came forth into the field of controversy (in which the fate of future ages, with respect to liberty, was to be decided) with a kind of arms that did not at all give them the aspect of persons agitated by the impulse, or seduced by the delusions of fanaticism. They pretended not to be called to the work they undertook by visions, or internal illuminations and impulses;—they never attempted to work miracles, or pleaded a divine commission;—they taught no new religion, nor laid claim to any extraordinary vocation;—they respected government, practised and taught submission to civil rulers, and desired only the liberty of that conscience which God has made free, and which ceases to be conscience if it be not free. They maintained, that the faith of a Christian was to be determined by the word of God alone; they had recourse to reason and argument, to the rules of sound criticism, and to the authority and light of history. They translated the Scriptures into the popular languages of different countries, and appealed to them as the only test of religious truth. They exhorted Christians to judge for themselves, to search the Scriptures, break asunder the bonds of ignorant prejudice and lawless authority, and assert that liberty of conscience to which they had an inalienable right as reasonable beings. Mr. Hume himself acknowledges, that they offered to submit 'all religious doctrines to private judgment, and exhorted every one to examine the principles formerly imposed upon him.' In short, it was their great and avowed purpose to oppose the gross corruptions and the spiritual tyranny of Rome,* of which Mr. Hume himself complains with a just indignation, and which he censures in as keen and vehement terms as those which were used by Luther and Calvin in their warmest moments.

I have already insinuated, and I acknowledge it here again, that the zeal of the reformers was sometimes intemperate; but I cannot think this circumstance sufficient to justify the aspersion of *fanaticism*, which is cast both on the spirit of the Reformation, and the principal agents concerned in it. A man may be overzealous in the advancement of what he supposes to be the true religion, without being entitled to the denomination of a fanatic, unless we depart from the usual sense of this word, which is often enough employed to have acquired, before this time, a determinate signification. The intemperate zeal of the reformers was the result of that ardour, which takes place in all divisions and parties that are founded upon objects of real or supposed importance; and it may be affirmed, that, in such circumstances, the most generous minds, filled with a persuasion of the goodness of their end, and of the uprightness of their intentions, are the most liable to transgress the exact bounds of moderation, and to adopt measures, which, in the calm hour of deliberate reflection, they themselves would not approve. In all great divisions, the warmth of natural temper,—the provocation of unjust and violent opposition,—a spirit of sympathy, which connects, in some cases, the most dissimilar characters, renders the mild violent, and the phlegmatic warm;—and frequently the pride of conquest, which mingles itself, imperceptibly, with the best principles and the most generous views,—produce or nourish an intemperate zeal; and this zeal is, in some cases, almost inevitable. On the other hand, it may be suspected, that some writers, and Mr. Hume among others, may have given too high colours to their descriptions of this intemperate zeal. There is a passage of Sir Robert Cotton, that has much meaning. "Most men *(says he)* grew to be frozen in zeal and benumbed, so that whoso ever pretended a little *spark of earnestness*, seemed no less than red fire hot, in comparison of the other."

Nothing can be more foreign from my temper and sentiments, than to plead the cause of an excessive zeal; more especially, every kind of zeal that approaches to a spirit of intole-

* See the sensible and judicious Letters on Mr. Hume's History of Great Britain, that were publish-ed at Edinburgh in 1756, and in which some points, which I have barely mentioned here, are enlarged upon and illustrated, in an ample and satisfactory manner

ance and persecution ought to be regarded with aversion and horror by all who have at heart the interest of genuine Christianity, and the happiness of civil society. There may be, nevertheless, cases, in which a zeal (not that breathes a spirit of persecution, but) that mounts to a certain degree of intemperance, may be not only inevitable, but useful; and not only useful but necessary. This assertion I advance almost against my will, because it is susceptible of great and dangerous abuse; the assertion, however, is true, though the cases must be singularly important and desperate to which such zeal may be applied. It has been observed, that the reformation was one of these cases, and, all things attentively considered, the observation appears to be entirely just; and the violence of expression and vehement measures employed by some of the reformers *might have been* (I do not say that they *really were*) as much the effect of provident reflection, as of natural fervour and resentment. To a calculating head, which considered closely, in those times of corruption and darkness, the strength of the court of Rome, the luxury and despotism of the pontiffs, the ignorance and licentiousness of the clergy, the superstition and stupidity of the people; in a word, the deep root which the papacy had gained through all these circumstances combined,—what was the first thought that must naturally have occurred? No doubt, it was this—the improbability that cool philosophy, dispassionate reason, and affectionate remonstrances, would ever triumph over these multiplied and various supports of popery. And, if a calculating head must have judged in this manner, a generous heart, which considered the blessings that must arise upon mankind from religious liberty and a reformation of the church, would naturally be excited to apply even a violent remedy, if that were *necessary*, to remove such a desperate and horrible disease. It would really seem that Luther acted on such a view of things. He began mildly, and did not employ the fire of his zeal, before he saw that it was essential to the success of his cause. Whoever looks into Dr. Mosheim's history, or any other impartial account of the sixteenth century, will find, that Luther's opposition to the infamous traffic of indulgences, was carried on at first in the most submissive strain, by humble remonstrances addressed to the pope, and the most eminent prelates of the church. These remonstrances were answered not only by the despotic voice of authority, but also by opprobrious invectives, perfidious plots against his person, and the terror of penal laws. Even under these he maintained his tranquillity; and his conduct at the famous diet of Worms, though resolute and steady, was nevertheless both respectful and modest. But, when all moderate measures proved ineffectual, then, indeed, he acted with redoubled vigour, and added a new degree of warmth and impetuosity to his zeal; and (I repeat it) reflection might have dictated those animated proceedings, which were owing, perhaps, merely to his resentment, and the natural warmth of his temper inflamed by opposition. Certain it is at least, that neither the elegant satires of Erasmus (had he even been a friend to the cause of liberty,) nor the timid remonstrances of the gentle Melancthon, (who was really such,) would ever have been sufficient to bring about a reformation of the church. The former made many *laugh*, the latter made some *reason;* but neither of the two could make them *act*, or set them in motion. At such a crisis, bold speech and ardent resolution were necessary to produce that happy change in the face of religion, which has crowned with inestimable blessings one part of Europe, and has been productive of many advantages even to the other, which censures it.

As to Calvin, every one, who has any acquaintance with history, knows how he set out in promoting the Reformation. It was by a work composed with a classic elegance of style, and which, though tinctured with the scholastic theology of the times, breathes an uncommon spirit of good sense and moderation. This work was the Institutes of the Christian religion, in which the learned writer shows, that the doctrines of the reformers were founded in Scripture and reason; and one of the designs of this book was to show that the reformers ought not to be confounded with certain fanatics, who, about the time of the Reformation, sprang from the bosom of the church of Rome, and excited tumults and commotions in several places. The French monarch (Francis I.) to cover, with a specious pretext, his barbarous persecution of the friends of the Reformation, and to prevent the resentment of the protestants in Germany, with whom it was his interest to be on good terms, alleged that his severity fell *only* upon a sect of enthusiasts, who, under the title of Anabaptists, substituted their visions in the place of the doctrines and declarations of the Scriptures. To vindicate the reformers from this reproach, Calvin wrote the book now under consideration: and though the theology that reigns in it be chargeable with some defects, yet it is as remote from the spirit and complexion of fanaticism, as any thing can be. Nor indeed is this spirit visible in any of the writings of Calvin that I have perused. His commentary upon the Old and New Testament is a production that will always be esteemed, on account of its elegant simplicity, and the evident marks it bears of an unprejudiced and impartial inquiry into the plain sense of the sacred writings, and of sagacity and penetration in the investigation of it.

If we were to pass in review the writings of the other eminent reformers, whose names have been already mentioned, we should find abundant matter to justify them in the same respect. They were men of letters, and some of them were even men of taste for the age in which they lived; they cultivated the study of languages, history, and criticism, and applied themselves with indefatigable industry to these studies, which, of all others, are the least adapted to excite or nourish a spirit of fanaticism. They had, indeed, their errors and prejudices; nor perhaps were they few in number; but who is free from the same charge? We have ours too, though they may turn on a different set of objects. Their theology savoured somewhat of the pedantry and jargon of the schools;—how could it be otherwise, considering the dismal state of philosophy at that period? The advantages we enjoy above them, give them, at least, a title to our candour and indulgence; perhaps to our gratitude, as the instruments who prepared the way through which these advantages have been conveyed to us. To conclude, let us regret their infirmities; let us reject their errors; let us even condemn any instances of ill-judged severity and violence with which they may have been chargeable; but let us never forget, that, through perils and obstacles almost insurmountable, they opened the path to that religious liberty, which we cannot too highly esteem, nor be too careful to improve to rational and worthy purposes.

THE THIRD APPENDIX.

SOME OBSERVATIONS RELATIVE TO THE PRESENT STATE OF THE REFORMED RELIGION, AND THE INFLUENCE OF IMPROVEMENTS IN PHILOSOPHY AND SCIENCE ON ITS PROPAGATION AND ADVANCEMENT; OCCASIONED BY SOME PASSAGES IN THE PREFACE TO A BOOK, ENTITLED, *THE CONFESSIONAL.*

In one of the notes,* which I added to those of Dr. Mosheim, in my translation of his Ecclesiastical History, I observed, that 'the reformed churches were never at such a distance from the spirit and doctrine of the church of Rome as they are at this day;—that the improvements in science, that characterise the last and the present age, seem to render a relapse into Romish superstition morally impossible in those who have been once delivered from its baneful influence: and that, if the dawn of science and philosophy toward the end of the sixteenth, and the commencement of the seventeenth centuries, was favourable to the cause of the Reformation, their progress, which has a kind of influence even upon the multitude, must confirm us in the principles that occasioned our separation from the church of Rome.'

This reasoning did not appear conclusive to the ingenious author of the *Confessional*, who has accordingly made some critical reflections upon it in the preface to that work. However, upon an impartial view of these reflections, I find that this author's excessive apprehensions of the progress of popery have had an undue influence on his method of reasoning on this subject. He supposes that the improvements in science and philosophy, in some popish countries, have been as considerable as in any reformed country; and afterwards asks, 'What intelligence have we from these popish countries of a proportionable progress of religious reformation? Have we no reason to suspect (adds he) that, if an accurate account were to be taken, the balance, in point of conversions, in the *most improved* of these countries, would be greatly against the reformed religion?'

I cannot see how these observations, or rather conjectures, even were they founded in truth and fact, tend to prove my reasoning inconclusive. I observed that the progress of science was adapted to confirm *us* (namely, *Protestants*) in the belief and profession of the reformed religion; and I had here in view, as every one may see, those countries in which the Protestant religion is established; and this author answers me by observing, that the progress of reformation in some popish countries, is not proportionable to the progress of science and philosophy in these countries. This, surely, is no answer at all, since there are in popish countries accidental circumstances, that counteract, in favour of popery, the influence of those improvements in science, which are in direct opposition to its propagation and advancement; circumstances that I shall consider presently, and which do not exist in protestant states. This subject is interesting; and I therefore presume, that some farther thoughts upon it will not be disagreeable to the candid reader.

The sagacious author of the Confessional cannot, I think, seriously call in question the *natural* tendency of improvements in learning and science to strengthen and confirm the cause of the Reformation; for, as the foundations of popery are a blind submission to an usurped authority over the understandings and consciences of men, and an implicit credulity that adopts, without examination, the miracles and visions that derive their existence from the crazy brains of fanatics, or the lucrative artifice of impostors, so it is unquestionably evident, that the progress of sound philosophy, and the spirit of free inquiry it produces, strike directly at these foundations. I say the progress of sound philosophy, that the most inattentive reader may not be tempted to imagine (as the author of the Confessional has been informed,) that 'improvements in philosophy have made many sceptics in all churches reformed and unreformed.' For I am persuaded, that, as true Christianity can never lead to superstition, so true philosophy will never be a guide to infidelity and scepticism. We must not be deceived by the name of philosophers, which some poets and wits have assumed in our days, particularly upon the continent, and which many lavish upon certain subtle refiners in dialectics who bear a much greater resemblance to overweening sophists, than to real sages. We must not be so far lost to all power of distinguishing as to confound, in one common mass, the philosophy of a Bacon, a Newton, a Boyle, and a Nieuwentyt, with the incoherent views and rhetorical rants of a Bolingbroke, or the flimsy sophistry of a Voltaire; and though candour must acknowledge, that some men of true

* This note was occasioned by my inadvertently mistaking the true sense of the passage to which it relates. It has since been corrected.

learning have been so unhappy as to fall into infidelity, and charity must weep to see a Hume and a D'Alembert joining a set of men who are unworthy of their society, and covering a dark and uncomfortable system with the lustre of their superior talents, yet equity itself may safely affirm, that neither their science nor their genius are the causes of their scepticism.

But if the progress of science and free inquiry have a natural tendency to destroy the foundations of popery, how comes it to pass, that, in popish countries, the progress of religious reform bears no proportion to the progress of science? and how can we account for the ground which popery (if the apprehensions of the author of the Confessional are well founded) gains even in England?

Before I answer the first of these questions, it may be proper to consider the matter of fact, and to examine, for a moment, the state of science and philosophy in popish countries: this examination, if I mistake not, will confirm the theory I have laid down with respect to the influence of philosophical improvement upon true religion. Let us then turn our view first to one of the most considerable countries in Europe, I mean Germany; and here we shall be struck with this undoubted fact, that it is in the Protestant part of this vast region only, that the improvements of science and philosophy appear, while the barbarism of the fifteenth century reigns, as yet, in those districts of the empire which profess the Romish religion. The celebrated M. D'Alembert, in his treatise, entitled, 'de l'Abus de la Critique en Matiere de Religion,' makes the following remarkable observation on this head: "We must acknowledge, though with sorrow, the present superiority of the Protestant universities in Germany over those of the Romish persuasion. This superiority is so striking, that foreigners who travel through the empire, and pass from a Romish college to a Protestant university, even in the same neighbourhood, are induced to think that they have ridden, in an hour, four hundred leagues, or lived, in that short space of time, four hundred years; that they have passed from Salamanca to Cambridge, or from the times of Scotus to those of Newton." Will it be believed (says the same author,) "in succeeding ages, that, in the year 1750. a book was published in one of the principal cities of Europe (Vienna) with the following title: 'Systema Aristotelicum de Formis substantialibus et Accidentibus absolutis, *i. e.* 'The Aristotelian System concerning substantial Forms and absolute Accidents?' Will it not rather be supposed, that this date is an error of the press, and that 1550 is the true reading?' See D'Alembert's Melanges de Literature, d'Histoire, et de Philosophie, vol. iv. p. 376.—This fact seems evidently to show the connexion that subsists between improvements in science, and the free spirit of the reformed religion. The state of letters and philosophy in Italy and Spain, where canon law, monkish literature, and scholastic metaphysics, have reigned during such a long course of ages, exhibits the same gloomy spectacle. Some rays of philosophical light are now breaking through the cloud in Italy; Boscovich, and some geniuses of the same stamp. have dared to hold up the lamp of science, without feeling the rigour of the Inquisition, or meeting with the fate of Galileo. If this dawning revolution be brought to any degree of perfection, it may, in due time produce effects that at present we have little hope of.

France, indeed, seems to be the country which the author of the Confessional has principally in view, when he speaks of a considerable progress in philosophy in popish states, that has not been attended with a proportionable influence on the reformation of religion. He even imagines that, 'if an account were to be taken, the balance, in point of conversions, in this most improved of the popish countries, would be greatly against the reformed religion.' The reader will perceive, that I might grant this, without giving up any thing that I maintained in the note which this judicious author censures. I shall, however, examine this notion, that we may see whether it is to be adopted without restriction; and perhaps it may appear, that the improvements in philosophy have had more influence on the spirit of religion in France than this author is willing to allow.

And here I observe, in the first place, that it is no easy matter, either for him or for me, to calculate the number of conversions that are made, on both sides, by priests armed with the secular power, and Protestant ministers, discouraged by the frowns of government, and the terrors of persecution. If we judge of this matter by the external face of things, the calculation may, indeed, be favourable to his hypothesis, since the *apostate Protestant* comes forth to view, and is publicly enrolled in the registers of the church, while the *converted Papist* is obliged to conceal his profession, and to approach the truth, like Nicodemus, secretly and by night. This evident diversity of circumstances, in the respective proselytes, shows that we are not to form our judgment by external appearances, and renders it but equitable to presume, that the progress of knowledge may have produced many examples of the progress of reformation, which do not strike the eye of the public. Is it not, in effect, to be presumed, that if either a toleration, or even an indulgent connivance, were granted to French Protestants, many would appear friends of the Reformation, who, at present, have not sufficient strength of mind to become martyrs, or confessors, in its cause? History informs us of the rapid progress which the Reformation made in France in former times, when a legal toleration was granted to its friends. When this toleration was withdrawn, an immense number of Protestants abandoned their country, their relations, and their fortunes, for the sake of their religion. But when that abominable system of tyranny was set up, which would neither permit the Protestants to profess their religion at home, nor to seek for the enjoyment of religious liberty abroad, and when they were thus reduced to the sad alternative of dissimulation or martyrdom, the courage of many failed, though their persuasion remained the same. In the South of France many continued, and still continue, their profession, even in the face of those booted apostles, who are sent, from time to time, to dragoon them into popery. In other places (particularly in the metropolis, where the empire of the mode, the allurements of court favour, the dread of persecution, unite their influence in favour of popery,) the public profession of protestantism lies under heavy discouragements, and would require a zeal that rises to heroism,—a thing too rare in modern times! In a word, a religion like popery, which forms the main spring in the political machine, which is doubly armed with allurements and terrors, must damp the fortitude of the feeble friend to truth, and attract the *external* respect even of libertines, free-thinkers, and sceptics.

In the second place, if it should be alleged, that men eminent for learning and genius have adhered *seriously* to the profession of popery, the fact cannot be denied. But what does it prove? It proves only that, in such persons, there are circumstances that counteract the natural influence of learning and science. It cannot be expected that the influence of learning and philosophy will always obtain a complete victory over the attachment to a superstitious church, that is riveted by the early prejudices of education, by impressions formed by the examples of respectable persons who have professed and defended the doctrine of that church, by a habit of veneration for authority, and by numberless associations of ideas, whose combined influence gives a wonderful bias to the mind, and renders the impartial pursuit of truth extremely difficult. Thus knowledge is acquired with an express design to strengthen previous impressions and prejudices. Thus many make considerable improvements in science, who have never once ventured to review their *religious* principles, or to examine the authority on which they have been taken up.

Others observe egregious abuses in the Romish church, and are satisfied with rejecting them in secret, without thinking them sufficient to justify a separation. This class is extremely numerous; and it cannot be said that the improvements in science have had no effect upon their religious sentiments. They are neither thorough Papists nor entire Protestants; but they are manifestly verging toward the Reformation.

Nearly allied to this class is another set of men, whose case is singular and worthy of attention. Even in the bosom of the Romish church, they have tolerably just notions of the sublime simplicity and genuine beauty of the Christian religion; but, either from false reasonings upon human nature, or an observation of the powerful impressions that authority makes upon the credulity, and a pompous ritual upon the senses of the multitude, imagine that Christianity, in its native form, is too pure and elevated for vulgar souls, and therefore countenance and maintain the absurdities of popery, from a notion of their utility. Those who conversed intimately with the sublime Fenelon, archbishop of Cambray, have declared, that such was the nature of his sentiments with respect to the public religion of his country.

To all this I may add, that a notion of the necessity of a visible universal church, and of a visible centre or bond of union, has led many to adhere to the papacy (considered in this light,) who look upon some of the principal and fundamental doctrines of the Romish church as erroneous and extravagant. Such is the case of the learned and worthy Dr. Courayer, whose unshaken fortitude in declaring his sentiments obliged him to seek an asylum in England; and who, notwithstanding his persuasion of the absurdities which abound in the church of Rome, has never totally separated himself from its communion; and such is known to be the case with many men of learning and piety in that church. Thus it happens, that particular and accidental circumstances counteract, in favour of popery, the natural effects of improvements in learning and philosophy, which have their full and proper influence in Protestant countries, where any thing that resembles these circumstances is directly in favour of the reformed religion.

But I beg that it may be attentively observed, in the third place, that, notwithstanding all these particular and accidental obstacles to the progress of the Reformation among men of knowledge and letters, its spirit has in fact, gained more ground than the ingenious author of the Confessional seems to imagine. I think it must be allowed, that every branch of superstition that is retrenched from popery, as well as every portion of authority that is taken from its pontiff, is a real gain to the cause of the Reformation; and, though it does not render that cause absolutely triumphant, yet prepares the way for its progress and advancement. Now (in this point of view,) I am persuaded it will appear that, for twenty or thirty years past, the Reformation, or at least its spirit, has rather gained than lost ground in Roman catholic states. In several countries, and more particularly in France, many of the gross abuses of popery have been corrected. We have seen the saintly legend, in many places, deprived of its fairest honours. We have seen a mortal blow given in France to the absolute power of the pope. What is still more surprising, we have seen, even in Spain and Portugal, the display of a spirit of opposition to the pretended infallible ruler of the church. We have seen the very order, that has been always considered as the chief support of the papacy, the order of the Jesuits, the fundamental characteristic of whose institute is an inviolable obligation to extend, beyond all limits, the despotic authority of the pontiffs; we have seen, I say, that order suppressed, banished, covered with deserved infamy, in three powerful kingdoms;* and we see, at this moment, their credit declining in other Roman catholic states. We see, in several popish countries, and more especially in France, the Scriptures more generally in the hands of the people than in former times. We have seen the senate of Venice, not many months ago, suppressing, by an express edict,† the officers of the inquisition in all the small towns, reducing their power to a shadow in the larger cities, extending the liberty of the press; and all this in a steady op

* France, Spain, and Portugal.

† This edict was issued in the month of February 1767.

position to the repeated remonstrances of the court of Rome. These, and many other facts that might be collected here, facts of a recent date, show that the essential spirit of popery, which is a spirit of unlimited despotism in the pretended head of the church, and a spirit of blind submission and superstition in its members, is rather losing than gaining ground, even in those countries that still profess the religion of Rome.

If this be the case, it would seem, indeed, very strange, that popery, which is losing ground at home, should be gaining it abroad, and acquiring new strength, as some imagine, even in Protestant countries. This, at first sight, must appear a paradox of the most enormous size; and it is to be hoped that it will continue to appear such, upon the closest examination.—While the spirit and vigour of popery are actually declining on the continent, I would fondly hope, that the apprehensions of some worthy persons, with respect to its progress in England, are without foundation. To account for the growth of popery in an age of light would be incumbent upon me, if the *fact* were true. Until this fact be *proved*, I may be excused from undertaking such a task. The famous story of the golden tooth, that employed the laborious researches of physicians, chemists, and philosophers, stands upon record, as a warning to those who are overhasty tc account for a thing which has no existence My distance from England, during many years past, renders me, indeed, less capable of judging of the state of popery, than those who are upon the spot: I shall therefore confine myself to a few reflections upon this interesting subject.

When it is said that popery gains ground in England, one of the two following things must be meant by this expression: either that the spirit of the established, and other reformed churches, is leaning that way; or that a number of individuals are made proselytes, by the seduction of popish emissaries, to the Romish communion. With respect to the established church, I think that a candid and accurate observer must vindicate it from the charge of a spirit of approximation to Rome. We do not live in the days of a Laud; nor do his successors seem to have imbibed his spirit. I do not hear that the claims of church-power are carried high in the present times, or that a spirit of intolerance characterises the episcopal hierarchy; and though it may be wished, that the case of subscription might be made easier to good and learned men, whose scruples deserve indulgence, and be better accommodated to what is known to be the reigning theology among the episcopal clergy, yet it is straining matters too far to allege the demand of subscription as a proof that the established church is verging toward popery. As to the Protestant dissenting churches in England and Ireland, they stand so avowedly clear of all imputations of this nature, that it is utterly unnecessary to vindicate them on this head. If any thing of this kind is to be apprehended from any quarter within the pale of the Reformation, it is from the quarter of fanaticism, which, by discrediting free inquiry, crying down human learning, and encouraging those pretended illuminations and impulses which give imagination and undue ascendency in religion, lays weak minds open to the seductions of a church, which has always made its conquests by wild visions and false miracles, addressed to the passions and fancies of men. Cry down reason, preach up implicit faith, extinguish the lamp of free inquiry, make inward experience the test of truth; and then the main barriers against popery will be removed. Persons who follow this method possibly *may* continue Protestants; but there is no security against their becoming Papists, if the occasion is presented. Were they placed in a scene where artful priests and enthusiastic monks could play their engines of conversion, their Protestant faith would be very likely to fail.

If by the supposed growth of popery be meant, the success of the Romish emissaries in making proselytes to their communion, here again the question turns upon a matter of fact, upon which I cannot venture to pronounce. There is no doubt that the Romish hierarchy carries on its operations under the shade of an indulgent connivance; and it is to be feared that its members are '*wiser* (i. e. more artful and zealous) in their generation than the children of light.' The establishment of the Protestant religion inspires, it is to be feared, an indolent security into the hearts of its friends. Ease and negligence are the fruits of prosperity; and this maxim even extends to religion. It is not unusual to see a victorious general sleep upon his laurels, and thus give advantage to an enemy, whom adversity renders vigilant. All good and true Protestants will heartily wish that this were otherwise. They will be sincerely afflicted at any decline that may happen in the zeal and vigilance that ought ever to be employed against popery and its emissaries, since they can never cease to consider it as a system of wretched superstition and political despotism, and must particularly look upon popery in the British isles as pregnant with the principles of disaffection and rebellion, and as at invariable enmity with our religious liberty and our happy civil constitution. But still there is reason to hope, that it makes very little progress, notwithstanding the apprehensions that have been entertained on this subject The insidious publications of a Taafe and a Philips, who abuse the terms of charity, philanthropy, and humanity, in their flimsy apologies for a church whose *tender mercies* are known to be *cruel*, have alarmed many well-meaning persons. But it is much more wise, as well as noble, to be vigilant and steady against the enemy, than to take the alarm at the smallest of his motions, and to fall into a panic, as if we were conscious of our weakness. Be that as it will, I return to my first principle, and am still persuaded, that the Protestant church, and its prevailing spirit, are, at this present time, as averse to popery, as they were at any period since the Reformation, and that the thriving state of learning and philosophy, is adapted to confirm them in this well-founded aversion. Should it even be granted that proselytes to popery have been made, among the ignorant and unwary, by the emissaries of

Rome, this would by no means invalidate what I here maintain, though it may justly be considered as a powerful incentive to the zeal and vigilance of rulers temporal and spiritual, of the pastors and people of the reformed churches, against the encroachments of Rome.

The author of the Confessional complains, and perhaps justly, of the bold and public appearance which popery has of late made in England. "The papists (*says he*) strengthened and animated by an influx of Jesuits, expelled even from popish countries for crimes and practices of the worst complexion, open public mass-houses, and affront the laws of this Protestant kingdom in other respects, not without insulting some of those who endeavour to check their insolence. And we are told, with the utmost coolness and composure, that popish bishops go about here, and exercise every part of their function, without offence, and without observation." This is, indeed, a circumstance that the friends of reformation and religious liberty cannot behold without offence: I say, the friends of religious liberty; because the maintenance of all liberty, both civil and religious, depends on circumscribing popery within proper bounds, since it is not a system of *innocent* speculative opinions, but a yoke of despotism, an enormous mixture of princely and priestly tyranny, designed to enslave the consciences of mankind, and to destroy their most sacred and invaluable rights. But, at the same time, I do not think we can, from this public appearance of popery, rationally conclude that it gains ground, much less (as the author of the Confessional suggests,) 'that the two hierarchies (i. e. the episcopal and the popish) are growing daily more and more into a resemblance of each other.' The natural reason of this bold appearance of popery is the spirit of toleration, that has been carried to a great height, and has rendered the execution of the laws against papists, in recent times, less rigorous and severe.

How it may be proper to act with regard to the growing insolence of popery, is a matter that must be left to the wisdom and clemency of government. Rigour against any thing that bears the name of *religion*, gives pain to a candid and generous mind; and it is certainly more eligible to extend too far, than to circumscribe too narrowly, the bounds of forbearance and indulgent charity.

If the dangerous tendency of popery, considered as a pernicious system of policy, should be pleaded as a sufficient reason to except it from the indulgence due to *merely speculative* systems of theology;—if the voice of history should be appealed to, as declaring the assassinations, rebellions, conspiracies, the horrid scenes of carnage and desolation, that popery has produced;—if standing principles and maxims of the Romish church should be quoted, which authorize these enormities;—if it should be alleged, finally, that popery is much more malignant and dangerous in Great Britain than in any other Protestant country;—I acknowledge that all these pleas against it are well-founded, and plead for modifications to the connivance which the clemency of government may think proper to grant to that unfriendly system of religion. All I wish is, that mercy and humanity may ever accompany the execution of justice, and that nothing like *merely religious* persecution may stain the British annals; and all I maintain with respect to the chief point under consideration is, that the public appearance of popery, which is justly complained of, is no *certain* proof of its growth, but rather shows its indiscretion than its strength, and the declining vigour of *our* zeal than the growing influence of *its* maxims.

THE FOURTH APPENDIX.

A CIRCUMSTANTIAL AND EXACT ACCOUNT OF THE CORRESPONDENCE THAT WAS CARRIED ON, IN THE YEARS 1717 AND 1718, BETWEEN DR. WILLIAM WAKE, ARCHBISHOP OF CANTERBURY, AND CERTAIN DOCTORS OF THE SORBONNE AT PARIS, RELATIVE TO A PROJECT OF UNION BETWEEN THE ENGLISH AND GALLICAN CHURCHES.

——Magis amica veritas.

When the famous Bossuet, bishop of Meaux, laid an insidious snare for unthinking Protestants, in his artful Exposition of the Doctrine of the Church of Rome, the pious and learned Dr. Wake unmasked this deceiver; and the writings he published on this occasion gave him a distinguished rank among the victorious champions of the Protestant cause. Should any person, who had perused these writings, be informed, that this 'pretended champion of the Protestant religion had set on foot a project of union with a popish church, with concessions in favour of the grossest superstition and idolatry,'* he would be apt to stare; at least he would require the strongest possible evidence for a fact, in all appearance so contradictory and unaccountable. This accusation has, nevertheless, been brought against the eminent prelate, by the ingenious and intrepid author of the Confessional; and it is founded upon an extraordinary passage in Dr Mosheim's Ecclesiastical History; where we are told, that Dr. Wake 'formed a project of peace and union between the English and Gallican churches, founded upon this condition, that each of the two communities should retain the greatest part of their respective and peculiar doctrines.'* This passage, though it

* See the Confessional, 2d edition, *Pref.* p. lxxvi.

* Dr. Mosheim had certainly a very imperfect idea of this correspondence; and he seems to have been misled by the account of it, which Kiorning has gi

is, perhaps, too uncharitably interpreted by the author already mentioned, would furnish, without doubt, just matter of censure, were it founded in truth. I was both surprised and perplexed while I was translating it. I could not immediately procure proper information with respect to the fact, nor could I examine Mosheim's proofs of this strange assertion, because he alleged none. Destitute of materials, either to invalidate or confirm the fact, I made a slight mention, in a short note, of a correspondence which had been carried on between archbishop Wake and Dr. Du-Pin, with the particulars of which I was not acquainted; and, in this my ignorance, only made a general observation, drawn from Dr. Wake's known zeal for the Protestant religion, which was designed, not to confirm that assertion, but rather to insinuate my disbelief of it. It never could come into my head, that the interests of the Protestant religion would have been safe in archbishop Wake's hands, had I given the smallest degree of credit to Dr. Mosheim's assertion, or even suspected that this eminent prelate was inclined to form a union between the English and Gallican churches, 'founded on this condition, that each of the two communities should retain the greatest part of their respective and peculiar doctrines.'

If the author of the Confessional had given a little more attention to this, he could not have represented me, as confirming the fact alleged by Mosheim, much less as giving it what he is pleased to call the *sanction* of my approbation. I did not confirm the fact; for I only said there was a correspondence on the subject, without speaking a syllable of the unpleasing *condition* that forms the charge against Dr. Wake. I shall not enter here into a debate about the grammatical import of my expressions, as I have something more interesting to present to the reader, who is curious of information about archbishop Wake's *real* conduct in relation to the correspondence already mentioned. I have been favoured with authentic copies of the letters which passed in this correspondence, which are now in the hands of Mr. Beavoir of Canterbury, the worthy son of the clergyman who was chaplain to lord Stair in the year 1717, and also with others, from the valuable collection of manuscripts left by Dr. Wake to the library of Christ-Church College in Oxford. It is from these letters that I have drawn the following account, at the end of which copies of them are printed, to serve as proofs of the truth of this relation, which I publish with a disinterested regard to truth. This impartiality may be, in some measure, expected from my situation in life, which has placed me at a distance from the scenes of religious and ecclesiastical contention in England, and cut me off from those personal connexions, that nourish the prejudices of a party spirit, more than many are aware of; but it would be still more expected from my principles, were they known.

From this narrative, confirmed by authentic papers, it will appear with the utmost evidence,

1st, That archbishop Wake was not the *first mover* in this correspondence, nor the person who formed the project of union between the English and Gallican churches.

2dly, That he never made any concessions, nor offered to give up, for the sake of peace, any one point of the established doctrine and discipline of the church of England, in order to promote this union.

3dly, That any desires of union with the church of Rome, expressed in the archbishop's letters, proceeded from the hopes (well founded, or illusory, is not my business to examine here) that he at first entertained of a considerable reformation in that church, and from an expectation that its most absurd doctrines would fall to the ground, if they could once be deprived of their great support, the papal authority;—the destruction of which authority was the very basis of this correspondence.

ven in his dissertation De Consecrationibus Episcoporum Anglorum, published at Helmstadt in 1739; which account, notwithstanding the means of information its author seemed to have by his journey to England, and his conversations with Dr. Courayer, is full of mistakes. Thus Kiorning tells us, that Dr. Wake submitted to the judgment of the Romish doctors, his correspondents, the conditions of peace between the two churches, which *he* had drawn up;—that he sent a learned man (Dr. Wilkins, his chaplain) to Paris, to forward and complete, if possible, the projected union;—that, in a certain assembly holden at Paris, the difficulties of promoting this union without the pope's concurrence were insisted upon by some men of high rank, who seemed inclined to the union, and that these difficulties put an end to the conferences:—that, however, two French divines (whom he supposes to be Du-Pin and Girardin) were sent to England to propose new terms. It now happens unluckily for Mr. Kiorning's reputation as an historian, that not one syllable of all this is true, as will appear sufficiently to the reader, who peruses with attention the account and the pieces which I here lay before the public. But one of the most egregious errors in the account given by Kiorning, is at page 61 of his Dissertation, where he says, that archbishop Wake was so much elated with the prospect of success in the scheme of an accommodation, that he acquainted the divines of Geneva with it in 1719, and plainly intimated to them, that he thought it an easier thing than reconciling the Protestants with each other.—Let us now see where Kiorning received this information.—Why, truly, it was from a letter of Dr. Wake to Professor Turretin of Geneva, in which there is not one syllable relative to a scheme of union between the English and Gallican churches; and yet Kiorning quotes a passage in this letter as the only authority he has for this affirmation. The case was this: Dr. Wake, in the former part of his letter to Turretin, speaks of the sufferings of the Hungarian and Piedmontese churches, which he had successfully endeavoured to alleviate, by engaging George I. to intercede in their behalf; and then proceeds to express his desire of healing the differences that disturbed the union of the Protestant churches abroad. 'Interim (says he) dum hæc (i. e. the endeavours to relieve the Hungarian and Piedmontese churches) feliciter peraguntur, ignoscite, Fratres Dilectissimi, si majoris quidem laboris atque difficultatis, sed longe maximi omnibus commodi inceptum vobis proponam; unionem nimirum, &c.' Professor Turretin, in his work entitled, Nubes Testium, printed only the latter part of Dr. Wake's letter, beginning with the words 'Interim, &c.' and Kiorning, not having seen the preceding part of this letter, which relates to the Hungarian and Piedmontese churches, and with which these words are connected, took it into his head that these words were relative to the scheme of union between the English and Gallican churches. Nor did he only take this into his head by way of conjecture, but he affirms, very sturdily and positively, that the words have this signification: 'Hæc verba (says he) tangunt pacis cum Gallis instaurandæ negotium, quod ex temporum rationibus manifestum est.' To show him, however, that he grossly errs, I have published among the annexed pieces (No. XX.) the *whole* letter of archbishop Wake to Turretin.

It will farther appear, that Dr. Wake considered union in external worship, as one of the best methods of healing the uncharitable dissensions that are often occasioned by a variety of sentiments in point of doctrine, in which a perfect uniformity is not to be expected. This is undoubtedly a wise principle, when it is not carried too far; and whether or no it was carried too far by this eminent prelate, the candid reader is left to judge from the following relation:

In the month of November, 1717, archbishop Wake wrote a letter to Mr. Beauvoir, chaplain to the earl of Stair, then ambassador at Paris, in which his grace acknowledges the receipt of several obliging letters from Mr. Beauvoir. This is manifestly the first letter which the prelate wrote to that gentleman, and the whole contents of it are matters of a literary nature.* In answer to this letter, Mr. Beauvoir, in one dated the eleventh of December, 1717, O. S. gives the archbishop the information he desired, about the method of subscribing to a new edition of St. Chrysostom, which was at that time in the press at Paris, and then mentions his having dined with Du-Pin, and three other doctors of the Sorbonne, who talked as if the whole kingdom of France was to appeal (in the affair of the Bull *Unigenitus*) to a future general council, and who 'wished for a union with the church of England, as the most effectual means to unite all the western churches.' Mr. Beauvoir adds, that Dr. Du-Pin had desired him to give his duty to the archbishop.† Here we see a first hint, the very first overture that was made relative to a project of union between the English and Gallican churches; and this hint comes *originally* from the doctors of the *Sorbonne*, and is not occasioned by any thing contained in preceding letters from archbishop Wake to Mr. Beauvoir, since the one only letter, which Mr. Beauvoir had hitherto received from that eminent prelate, was entirely taken up in inquiries about some new editions of books that were then publishing at Paris.

Upon this the archbishop wrote a letter to Mr. Beauvoir, in which he makes honourable mention of Du-Pin as an author of merit, and expresses his desire of serving him, with that benevolent politeness which reigns in our learned prelate's letters, and seems to have been a striking line in his amiable character.* Dr

---

* The perusal of this letter (which the reader will find among the pieces here subjoined, No. I.) is sufficient to remove the suspicions of the author of the Confessional, who seems inclined to believe, that archbishop Wake was the first mover in the project of uniting the English and Gallican churches. This author, having mentioned Mr. Beauvoir's letter, in which Du-Pin's desire of this union is communicated to the archbishop, asks the following question: 'Can any man be certain that Beauvoir mentioned this merely out of his own head, and without some previous occasion given, in the archbishop's letter to him, for such a conversation with the Sorbonne doctors?' I answer to this question, that every one who reads the archbishop's letter of the 28th of November, to which this letter of Mr. Beauvoir is an answer, may be *very certain* that Dr. Wake's letter did not give him the least occasion for such a conversation, but relates entirely to the Benedictine edition of St. Chrysostom, Martenne's Thesaurus Anecdotorum, and Moreri's Dictionary. 'But, says our author, *there is an &c.* in this copy of Mr. Beauvoir's letter, very suspiciously placed, as if to cover something improper to be disclosed.'* But really if any thing was covered here, it was covered from the archbishop as well as from the public, since the very name, *&c.* that we see in the printed copy of Mr. Beauvoir's letter, stands in the original. Besides, I would be glad to know, what there is in the placing of this, *&c.* that can give rise to suspicion? The passage of Beauvoir's letter runs thus: 'They (the Sorbonne doctors) talked as if the whole kingdom was to appeal to the future general council, &c. They wished for a union with the church of England, as the most effectual means to unite all the Western churches.' It is palpably evident, that the *&c.* here has not the least relation to the union in question, and gives no sort of reason to *suspect* any thing but the spirit of discontent, which the insolent proceedings of the court of Rome had excited among the French divines.

† See the Letters subjoined, No. II.

* The other reflections that the author has there made upon the correspondence between archbishop Wake and the doctors of the Sorbonne, are examined in the following note.

* This 'handsome mention' of Dr. Du-Pin, made by the archbishop, gives new subject of suspicion to the author of the *Confessional*. He had learned the fact from the article Wake, in the Biographia Britannica; 'but, says he, we are left to guess what this handsome mention was;—had the biographer given us this letter, together with that of November 27, they might probably (it would have been more accurate to have said *possibly*,) have discovered what the biographer did not want we should know, namely, the share Dr. Wake had in forming the project of a union between the two churches.' This is guessing with a witness:—and it is hard to imagine how the boldest calculator of probabilities could conclude from Dr. Wake's *handsome mention* of Dr. Du-Pin, that the former had a *share*, of any kind, *in forming* the project of union now under consideration. For the ingenious guesser happens to be quite mistaken in his conjecture; and I hope to convince him of this, by satisfying his desire. He desires the letter of the 27th (or rather the 28th) of November; I have referred to it in the preceding note, and he may read it at the end of this account. He desires the letter in which handsome mention is made of Du-Pin; and I can assure him, that in that letter there is not a single syllable relative to a union. The passage that regards Dr. Du-Pin is as follows: I am much obliged to you (says Dr. Wake, in his letter to Mr. Beauvoir, dated January 2, 1717–18) for making my name known to Dr. Du-Pin. He is a gentleman by whose labours I have profited these many years; and I do really admire how it is possible for one man to publish so much, and yet so correctly, as he has generally done. I desire my respects to him; and that, if there be any thing here whereby I may be serviceable to him, he will freely command me.' Such was the archbishop's handsome mention of Du-Pin; and it evidently shows that, till then, there never had been any communication between them. Yet these are all the proofs which the author of the Confessional gives of the probability that the archbishop was the first mover in this affair.

But 'his grace accepted the party, a formal treaty commences, and is carried on in a correspondence of some length,' says the author of the Confessional. And I would candidly ask that author, upon what principles of Christianity, reason, or charity, Dr. Wake could have refused to hear the proposals, terms, and sentiments of the Sorbonne doctors, who discovered an inclination to unite with his church? The author of the Confessional says elsewhere, 'that it was, at the best, officious and presumptuous in Dr. Wake to enter into a negotiation of this nature, without authority from the church or the government.' But the truth is, that he entered into no negotiation or treaty on this head; he considered the letters that were written on both sides as a personal correspondence between individuals, who could not commence a negotiation, until they had received the proper powers from their respective sovereigns; and I do think he was greatly in the right to enter into this correspondence, as it seemed very likely, in the *then* circumstances of the Gallican church, to serve the Protestant interest and the cause of reformation. If, indeed, in the course of this correspondence, he had discovered any thing like what Mosheim [illegible] to him, even a disposition toward a union [illegible]

Du-Pin improved this favourable occasion of writing to the archbishop a letter of thanks, dated January 31, (February 11, N. S.) 1717–18; in which, toward the conclusion, he intimates his desire of a union between the English and Gallican churches, and observes, that the difference between them, in most points, was not so great as to render a reconciliation impracticable; and that it was his earnest wish, that all Christians should be united in one sheepfold. His words are: 'Unum addam cum bonâ veniâ tuâ, me vehementer optare, ut unionis inter Ecclesias Anglicanam et Gallicanam ineundæ via aliqua inveniri posset: non ita sumus ab invicem in plerisque dissiti, ut non possimus mutuo reconciliari. Atque utinam Christiani omnes essent unum ovile.' The archbishop wrote an answer to this letter, dated February 13–24, 1717–18, in which he asserts, at large, the purity of the church of England, in faith, worship, government, and discipline, and tells his correspondent, that he is persuaded that there are few things in the doctrine and constitution of that church, which even he himself (Du-Pin) would desire to see changed; the original words are: 'Aut ego vehementer fallor, aut in eâ pauca admodum sunt, quæ vel tu—immutanda velles;' and again, 'Sincere judica, quid in hac nostrâ ecclesiâ invenias, quod jure damnari debeat, aut nos atrâ hæreticorum, vel etiam schismaticorum, notâ inurere.' The zeal of the venerable prelate goes still farther; and the moderate sentiments which he observed in Dr. Du-Pin's letter induced him to exhort the French to maintain, if not to enlarge, the rights and privileges of the Gallican church, for which the existing diputes, about the constitution *Unigenitus*, furnished the most favourable occasion. He also expresses his readiness to concur in improving any opportunity, that might be offered by these debates, to form a union that might be productive of a farther reformation, in which, not only the most rational Protestants, but also a considerable number of the Roman catholic churches, should join with the church of England; 'si exhinc (says the archbishop, speaking of the recent commotions excited by the Constitution) aliquid amplius elici possit ad unionem nobiscum ecclesiasticum ineundam; unde forte nova quædam reformatio exoriatur, in quam non solum ex Protestantibus optimi quique, verum etiam pars magna ecclesiarum Communionis Romano-Catholicæ, unâ nobiscum conveniant.'

Hitherto we see, that the expressions of the two learned doctors of the English and Gallican churches, relating to the union under consideration, are of a vague and general nature. When they were thus far advanced in their correspondence, an event happened, which rendered it more close, serious, and interesting, and even brought on some particular mention of preliminary terms, and certain preparatives for a future negotiation. The event I mean, was a discourse delivered, in an extraordinary meeting of the Sorbonne, March 17–28, 1717–18, by Dr. Patrick Piers de Girardin, in which he exhorts the doctors of that society to proceed in their design of revising the doctrines and rules of the church, to separate things necessary from those which are not so, by which they will show the church of England that they do not hold every decision of the pope for an article of faith. The learned orator observes farther (upon what foundation it is difficult to guess,) that the English church may be more easily reconciled than the Greek was; and that the disputes between the Gallican church and the court of Rome, removing the apprehensions of papal tyranny, which terrified the English from the Catholic communion, will lead them back into the bosom of the

upon the condition that each of the two churches should retain the greatest part of their respective and peculiar doctrines, I should think his conduct liable to censure. But no such thing appears in his letters, which I have subjoined to this account, that the candid examiner may receive full satisfaction in this affair. Mosheim's mistake is palpable, and the author of the Confessional seems certainly to have been too hasty in adopting it. He alleges, that Dr. Wake might have maintained the justice and orthodoxy of every individual article of the church of England, and yet 'give up some of them for the sake of peace.' But the archbishop expressly declares, in his letters, that he would give up none of them, and that, though he was a friend to peace, he was still a greater friend to truth. The author's reflection, that, without some concessions on the part of the archbishop, the treaty could not have gone a step farther, may be questioned in theory; for treaties are often carried on for a long time without concessions on both sides, or perhaps on either; and the archbishop might hope that Du-Pin, who had yielded several things, would still yield more; but this remark is overturned by the plain fact. Besides, I repeat what I have already insinuated, that this *correspondence* does not deserve the name of a *treaty*.* Proposals were made only on Du-Pin's side; and these proposals were positively rejected by the archbishop, in his letters to Mr. Beauvoir. Nor did he propose any thing in return to either of the Sorbonne doctors, but that they should entirely renounce the authority of the pope, hoping, though perhaps too fancifully, that, when this was done, the two churches might come to an agreement about other matters, as far as was necessary. But the author of the Confessional supposes, that the archbishop must have made some concessions, because the letters on both sides were sent to Rome, and received there as 'so many trophies gained from the enemies of the church.' This supposition, however, is somewhat hasty. Could nothing but concessions from the archbishop make the court of Rome consider those letters in that light? Would they not think it a great triumph, that they had obliged Du-Pin's party to give up the letters as a token of their submission, and defeated the archbishop's design of engaging the Gallican church to assert its liberty, by throwing off the papal yoke? If Dr. Wake made concessions, where are they? And if these were the trophies, why did not the partisans of Rome publish authentic copies of them to the world? Did the author of the Confessional ever hear of a victorious general, who carefully hid under ground the standards he had taken from the enemy? This, indeed, is a new method of dealing with trophies. Our author, however, does not, as yet, quit his hold; he alleges, that the French divines could not have acknowledged the *catholic benevolence* of the archbishop, if he made no concessions to them. This reasoning would be plausible, if charity toward those who err consisted in embracing their errors; but this is a definition of charity, that, I fancy, the ingenious author will give up, upon second thoughts. Dr. Wake's catholic benevolence consisted in his esteem for the merit and learning of his correspondents, in his compassion for their servitude and their errors, in his desire of the reformation and liberty of their church, and his inclination to live in friendship and concord, as far as was possible, with all that bear the Christian name; and this disposition, so suitable to the benevolent genius of Christianity, will always reflect a true and solid glory upon his character as a Christian bishop.

* See post, note * and the letters subjoined, No. XI.

church, with greater celerity than they formerly fled from it: 'Facient (says he) profecto offensiones, quæ vos inter et senatum Capitolinum videntur intervenisse, ut Angli deposito servitutis metu, in ecclesiæ gremium revolent alacrius quam olim inde, quorundam exosi tyrannidem, avolârunt. Meministis ortas inter Paulum et Barnabam dissensiones animorum tandem eo recidisse, ut singuli propagandæ in diversis regionibus fidei felicius insudaverint sigillatim, quam junctis viribus fortasse insudâssent.' This last sentence (in which Dr. Girardin observes, that Paul and Barnabas probably made more converts in consequence of their separation, than they would have done had they travelled together, and acted in concert,) is not a little remarkable; and, indeed, the whole passage discovers rather a desire of making proselytes, than an inclination to form a coalition founded upon concessions and some reformation on the side of popery. It may, perhaps, be alleged, in opposition to this remark, that prudence required a language of this kind, in the infancy of a project of union, whatever concessions might be offered afterwards to bring about its execution; and this may be true.

After the delivery of this discourse in the Sorbonne, Dr. Du-Pin showed to Girardin archbishop Wake's letter, which was also communicated to cardinal de Noailles, who admired it greatly, as appears from a letter of Dr. Piers de Girardin to Dr. Wake, written, I believe, April 18–29, 1718. Before the arrival of this letter the archbishop had received a second from Dr. Du-Pin, and also a copy of Girardin's discourse. But he does not seem to have entertained any notion, in consequence of all this, that the projected union would go on smoothly. On the contrary, he no sooner received these letters, than he wrote to Mr. Beauvoir (April 15, 1718,) that it was his opinion, that neither the regent nor the cardinal would ever come to a rupture with the court of Rome; and that nothing could be done, in point of doctrine, until this rupture was brought about. He added, that fundamentals should be distinguished from matters of less moment, in which differences or errors might be tolerated. He expresses a curiosity to know the reception which his former letter to Du-Pin had met with; and he wrote again to that ecclesiastic, and also to Girardin (May 1, 1718,) and sent both his letters toward the end of that month.

The doctors of the Sorbonne, whether they were set in motion by the real desire of a union with the English church, or only intended to make use of this union as the means of intimidating the court of Rome, began to form a plan of reconciliation, and to specify the terms upon which they were willing to bring it into execution. Mr. Beauvoir acquaints the archbishop, in July, 1718, that Dr. Du-Pin had made a rough draught of an essay toward a union, which cardinal de Noailles desired to peruse before it was sent to his grace; and that both Du-Pin and Girardin were highly pleased with his grace's letters to them. These letters, however, were written with a truly Protestant spirit; the archbishop insisted, in them, upon the truth and orthodoxy of the articles of the church of England, and did not make any concession, which supposed the least approximation to the peculiar doctrines, or the smallest approbation of the ambitious pretensions of the church of Rome; he observed, on the contrary, that it was now the time for Dr Du-Pin, and his brethren of the Sorbonne, to declare openly their true sentiments with respect to the superstition and tyranny of that church; that it was the interest of all Christians to unmask that court, and to reduce its authority to its primitive limits; and that, according to the fundamental principle of the Reformation in general, and of the church of England in particular, Jesus Christ is the only founder, source, and head of the church. Accordingly, when Mr. Beauvoir had acquainted the archbishop with Du-Pin's having formed a plan of union, his grace answered in a manner which showed that he looked upon the removal of the Gallican church from the jurisdiction of Rome as an essential preliminary article, without which no negotiation could even be commenced. "To speak freely (says the prelate, in his letter of the 11th of August, to Mr. Beauvoir,) I do not think the regent (the duke of Orleans) yet strong enough in his interest, to adventure at a separation from the court of Rome. Could the regent openly appear in this, the divines would follow, and a scheme might fairly be offered for such a union, as alone is requisite, between the English and Gallican churches. But, till the time comes that the state will enter into such a work, all the rest is mere speculation. It may amuse a few contemplative men of learning and probity, who see the errors of the church, and groan under the tyranny of the court of Rome. It may dispose them secretly to wish well to us, and think charitably of us; but still they must call themselves Cathòlics, and us heretics; and, to all outward appearance, say mass, and act so as they have been wont to do. If, under the shelter of Gallican privileges, they can now and then serve the state by speaking big in the Sorbonne, they will do it heartily: but that is all, if I am not greatly mistaken."

Soon after this the archbishop received Du Pin's Commonitorium, or advice relating to the method of re-uniting the English and Gallican churches; of the contents of which it will not be improper to give here a compendious account, as it was read in the Sorbonne, and was approved there, and as the concessions it contains, though not sufficient to satisfy a true Protestant, are yet such as one would not expect from a very zealous papist. Dr. Du-Pin, after some reflections, in the tedious preface, on the Reformation, and the present state of the church of England, reduces the controversy between the churces to three heads, v.z. articles of faith,—rules and ceremonies of ecclesiastical discipline,—and moral doctrine, or rules of practice; and these he treats, by entering into an examination of the XXXIX articles of the church of England. The first five of these articles he approves. With regard to the VIth, which affirms that the Scripture contains all things necessary to salvation, he expresses himself thus: "This we will readily grant, provided that you do not entirely exclude tradition, which does not exhibit new articles of faith, but confirms and illustrates those which are contained in the sacred writings, and places about them new guards to defend them against gainsayers,"* &c. He thinks that the apocryphal books will not occasion much difficulty. He is, indeed, of opinion, that "they ought to be deemed *canonical*, as those books concerning which there were doubts for some time;" yet, since they are not in the first or Jewish canon, he will allow them to be called *Deutero-Canonical*. He consents to the Xth article, which relates to free-will, provided that by the word *power* be understood what school-divines call *potentia proxima*, or a direct and immediate power, since, without a *remote* power of doing good works, sin could not be imputed.

With respect to the XIth article, which contains the doctrine of justification, he thus expresses the sentiments of his brethren: "We do not deny that it is by faith alone that we are justified, but we maintain that faith, charity, and good works, are necessary to salvation; and this is acknowledged in the following article.†

Concerning the XIIIth article, he observes, "that there will be no dispute, since many divines of both communions embrace the doctrine contained in that article," (viz. that works done before the grace of Christ are not pleasing to God, and have the nature of sin.) He indeed thinks "it very harsh to say, that all those actions are sinful which have not the grace of Christ for their source;" but he considers this rather as a matter of theological discussion than as a term of fraternal communion.‡

On the XIVth article, relating to works of supererogation (undoubtedly one of the most absurd and pernicious doctrines of the Romish church,) he observes, "that works of supererogation mean only works conducive to salvation, which are not matters of strict precept, but of counsel only; that the word, being new, may be rejected, provided it be owned that the faithful do some such works."

He makes no objections to the XV, XVI, XVII, and XVIIIth articles.

His observation on the XIXth is, that to the definition of the church, the words, *under lawful pastors*, ought to be added; and that though all particular churches, even that of Rome, may err, it is needless to say this in a confession of faith.

He consents to the decision of the XXth article, which refuses to the church the power of ordaining any thing that is contrary to the word of God; but he says, it must be taken for granted, that the church will never do this in matters which overturn essential points of faith, or, to use his own words, 'quæ fidei substantiam evertant.'

It is in consequence of this notion that he remarks on the XXIst article, that general councils, received by the universal church, cannot err; and that, though particular councils may, yet every private man has not a right to reject what he thinks contrary to Scripture.

As to the important points of controversy contained in the XXIId article, he endeavours to mince matters as nicely as he can, to see if he can make the cable pass through the eye of the needle; and for this purpose observes, that souls must be *purged*, *i. e.* purified from all defilement of sin, before they are admitted to celestial bliss; that the church of Rome does not affirm this to be done by fire; that indulgences are only relaxations or remissions of temporal penalties in this life; that the Roman catholics do not worship the cross, or relics, or images, or even saints before their images, but only pay them an external respect, which is not of a religious nature; and that even the external demonstration of respect is a matter of indifference, which may be laid aside or retained without harm.

He approves the XXIIId article; and does not pretend to dispute about the XXIVth, which ordains the celebration of divine worship in the vulgar tongue. He, indeed, excuses the Latin and Greek churches for preserving their ancient languages; but, as great care has been taken that every thing be understood by translations, he allows, that divine service may be performed in the vulgar tongue, where that is customary.

Under the XXVth article he insists that the five Romish sacraments be acknowledged as such, whether instituted immediately by Christ or not.

He approves the XXVIth and XXVIIth articles; and he proposes expressing the part of the XXVIIIth that relates to Transubstantiation (which term he is willing to omit entirely,) in the following manner: "That the bread and wine are really changed into the body and blood of Christ, which last are truly and really received by all, though none but the faithful partake of any benefit from them." This extends also to the XXIXth article.

With regard to the XXXth, he is for mutual toleration, and would have the receiving of the communion in both kinds held indifferent, and liberty left to each church to preserve, or change, or dispense with its customs on certain occasions.

He is less inclined to concessions on the XXXIst article, and maintains that the sacrifice of Christ is not only commemorated, but continued, in the eucharist, and that every communicant offers him along with the priest.

He is not a warm stickler for the celibacy of the clergy, but consents so far to the XXXIId article, as to allow that priests may marry, where the laws of the church do not prohibit it.

* The original words are: 'Hoc lubenter admittemus, modo non excludatur traditio, quæ articulos fidei novos non exhibet, sed confirmat et explicat ea, quæ in sacris literis habentur, ac adversus aliter sapientes munit eos novis cautionibus, ita ut non nova dicantur, sed antiqua nove.'

† The original words are: 'Fide sola in Christum nos justificari, quod articulo XImo exponitur, non inficiamur; sed fide, charitate, et adjunctis bonis operibus, quæ omnino necessaria sunt ad salutem, ut articulo sequenti agnoscitur.'

‡ 'De articulo XIIImo nulla lis erit, cum multi theologi in eadem versentur sententia. Durius videtur id dici, cas omnes actiones quæ ex gratia Christi non fiunt, esse peccata. Nolim tamen de hac re disceptari nisi inter theologos.'

In the XXXIIId and XXXIVth articles, he acquiesces without exception.

He suspends his judgment with respect to the XXXVth, as he never perused the homilies mentioned therein.

As to the XXXVIth, he would not have the English ordinations pronounced null, though some of them, perhaps, are so; but thinks that, if a union be made, the English clergy ought to be continued in their offices and benefices, either by right or indulgence, 'sive ex jure, sive ex indulgentiâ ecclesiæ.'

He admits the XXXVIIth, so far as relates to the authority of the civil power; denies all temporal and all immediate spiritual jurisdiction of the pope; but alleges, that, by virtue of his primacy, which moderate, (he ought to have said *immoderate*) Church-of-England-men do not deny, he is bound to see that the true faith be maintained; that the canons be observed every where; and, when any thing is done in violation of either, to provide the remedies prescribed for such disorders by the canon laws, 'secundum leges canonicas, ut malum resarciatur, procurare.' As to the rest, he is of opinion, that every church ought to enjoy its own liberties and privileges, which the pope has no right to infringe. He declares against going *too far* (the expression is vague, but the man probably meant well) in the punishment of heretics, against admitting the inquisition into France, and against war without a just cause.

The XXXVIIIth and XXXIXth articles he approves. Moreover, in the discipline and worship of the church of England, he sees nothing amiss, and thinks no attempts should be made to discover or prove by whose fault the schism was begun. He farther observes, "that a union between the English and French bishops and clergy may be completed, or at least advanced, without consulting the Roman pontiff, who may be informed of the union as soon as it is accomplished, and may be desired to consent to it; that, if he consents to it, the affair will then be finished; and that, even without his consent, the union shall be valid; that, in case he attempts to terrify by his threats, it will then be expedient to appeal to a general council."* He concludes by observing, "that this arduous matter must first be discussed between a few; and, if there be reason to hope that the bishops, on both sides, will agree about the terms of the designed union, that then application must be made to the civil power, to advance and confirm the work," to which he wishes all success.

It is from the effect which these proposals and terms made upon archbishop Wake, that it will be most natural to form a notion of his sentiments with respect to the church of Rome. It appears evident, from several passages in the writings and letters of this eminent prelate, that he was persuaded that a reformation in the church of Rome could only be made gradually; that it was not probable that they would renounce all their follies at once; but that, if they should once begin to make concessions, this would set in motion the work of reformation, which, in all likelihood, would receive new accessions of vigour, and go on until a happy change should be effected. This way of thinking might have led the archbishop to give an indulgent reception to these proposals of Du-Pin, which contained some concessions, and might be an introduction to more. And yet we find that he rejected this piece, as insufficient to serve as a basis, or ground-work, to the desired union. On receiving the piece, he immediately perceived that he had not sufficient ground for carrying on this negotiation, without previously consulting his brethren, and obtaining a permission from the king for this purpose. Besides this, he was resolved not to submit either to the direction of Dr. Du-Pin, or to that of the Sorbonne, in relation to what was to be retained, or what was to be given up, in the doctrine and discipline of the two churches; nor to treat with the church of Rome upon any other footing, than that of a perfect equality in point of authority and power. He declared, more especially, that he would never comply with the proposals made in Du-Pin's Commonitorium, of which I have now given the contents; observing that, though he was a friend to peace, he was still more a friend to truth: and that, "unless the Roman catholics gave up some of their doctrines and rites," a union with them could never be effected. All this is contained in a letter written by the archbishop to Mr. Beauvoir, on receiving the Commonitorium. This letter is dated August 30, 1718; and the reader will find a copy of it subjoined to this appendix.* About a month after, his grace wrote a letter to Dr. Du-Pin, dated October 1, 1718, in which he complains of the tyranny of the pope, exhorts the Gallican doctors to throw off the papal yoke in a national council, since a *general* one is not to be expected; and declares, that this must be the great preliminary and fundamental principle of the projected union, which being settled, a uniformity might be brought about in other matters, or a diversity of sentiments mutually allowed, without any violation of peace or concord. The archbishop commends, in the same letter, the candour and openness that reign in the Commonitorium; entreats Dr. Du-Pin to write to him always upon the same footing, freely, and without disguise or reserve; and tells him he is pleased with several things in that piece, and with nothing more than with the doctor's declaring it as his opinion, that there is not a great difference between their respective sentiments; but adds, that he cannot at present give his sentiments at large concerning that piece.†

Dr. Wake seems to have aimed principally, in this correspondence, at bringing about a separation between the Gallican church and the court of Rome. The terms in which the French divines often spoke about the liberties of their

* 'Unio fieri potest aut saltem promoveri, inconsulto pontifice, qui, facta unione, de ea admonebitur, ac suppliciter rogabitur, ut velit ei consentire. Si consentiat, jam peracta res erit: sin abnuat, nihilominus valebit hæc unio. Et si minas intentet, ad concilium generale appellabitur.'

* See this Letter, No. III.

† See this Letter to Du-Pin, No. V. as also the archbishop's letters to Dr. P Piers de Girardin, No. VI.

church, might give him some hope that this separation would take place, if ever these divines should be countenanced by the civil power of France. But a man of the archbishop's sagacity could not expect that they would enter into a union with any other national church *all at once*. He acted, therefore, with dignity, as well as with prudence, when he declined to explain himself on the proposals contained in Du-Pin's Commonitorium. To have answered ambiguously, would have been mean; and to have answered explicitly, would have blasted his hopes of separating them from Rome, which separation he desired upon the principles of civil and ecclesiastical liberty, independent of the discussion of theological tenets. The archbishop's sentiments in this matter will still appear farther from the letters he wrote to Mr. Beauvoir, in October, November, and December, 1718, and the January following, of which the proper extracts are here subjoined.* It appears from these letters, that Dr. Wake insisted still upon the abolition of the pope's jurisdiction over the Gallican church, and leaving him no more than a primacy of rank and honour, and that merely by ecclesiastical authority, as he was once bishop of the imperial city; to which empty title our prelate seems willing to have consented, provided that it should be attended with no infringement of the independence and privileges of each particular country and church. "Si quam prærogativam," (says the archbishop in his letter to Girardin,† after having defied the court of Rome to produce any precept of Christ in favour of the primacy of its bishop) "ecclesiæ concilia sedis imperialis episcopo concesserint (etsi cadente imperio etiam eâ prærogativâ excidisse merito possit censeri) tamen, quod ad me attinet, servatis semper regnorum juribus, ecclesiarum libertatibus, episcoporum dignitate, modo in cæteris conveniatur, per me licet, suo fruatur qualicumque primatu: non ego illi locum primum, non inanem honoris titulum invideo. At in alias ecclesias dominari, &c. hæc nec nos unquam ferre potuimus, nec vos debetis."

It appears farther, from these letters, that any proposals or terms conceived by the archbishop, in relation to this project of union, were of a vague and general nature, and that his views terminated rather in a plan of mutual toleration, than in a scheme for effecting an entire uniformity. The scheme that seemed to his grace the most likely to succeed was, that "the independence of every national church, or any other, and its right to determine all matters that arise within itself, should be acknowledged on both sides; that, for points of doctrine, they should agree as far as possible, in all articles of any moment (as in effect the two churches either already did, or easily might;) and, in other matters, that a difference should be allowed until God should bring them to a union in them also."‡ It must be allowed, however, though the expression is still general, that the archbishop was for "purging out of the public offices of the church all such things as hinder a perfect communion in divineservice, so that persons coming from one church to the other might join in prayers, and the holy sacrament, and the public service."* He was persuaded, that, in the liturgy of the church of England, there was nothing but what the Roman catholics would adopt, except the single rubric relating to the eucharist; and that in the Romish liturgy there was nothing to which Protestants object, but what the more rational Romanists agree might be laid aside, and yet the public offices be not the worse, or more imperfect, for the want of it. He therefore thought it proper to make the demands already mentioned the ground-work of the project of union, at the beginning of the negotiation; not that he meant to stop here, but that, being thus far agreed, they might the more easily go farther, descend to particulars, and render their scheme more perfect by degrees.†

The violent measures of the court of Rome against that part of the Gallican church which refused to admit the constitution *Unigenitus* as an ecclesiastical law, made the archbishop imagine that it would be no difficult matter to bring this opposition to an open rupture, and to engage the persons concerned in it to throw off the papal yoke, which seemed to be borne with impatience in France. The despotic bull of Clement XI. dated August 28, 1718, and which begins with the words, *Pastoralis officii*, was a formal act of excommunication, thundered out against all the anti-constitutionists, as the opposers of the bull *Unigenitus* were called; and it exasperated the doctors of the Sorbonne in the highest degree. It is to this that the archbishop alludes, when he says, in his letter to Mr. Beauvoir, dated the 23d of January, 1718,‡ "At present he (the pope) has put them out of his communion. We have withdrawn ourselves from his; both are out of communion with him, and I think it is not material on which side the breach lies." But the wished-for separation from the court of Rome, notwithstanding all the provocations of its pontiff, was still far off. Though, on numberless occasions, the French divines showed very little respect for the papal authority, yet the renouncing it altogether was a step which required deep deliberation, and which, however inclined they might be to it, they could not make, if they were not seconded by the state. But from the state they were not likely to have any countenance. The regent of France was governed by the abbe Du Bois; and Du Bois was aspiring eagerly after a cardinal's cap. This circumstance (not more unimportant that many secret connexions and trivial views that daily influence the course of public events, the transactions of government, and the fate of nations) was sufficient to stop the Sorbonne and its doctors in the midst of their career; and, in effect, it contributed greatly to stop the correspondence of which I have been now giving an account, and to nip the project of union in the bud. The correspondence between the archbishop and the two doctors of the Sorbonne had been carried on with a high

* See No. IV, VII, VIII, IX, X. † No. VI.
‡ See the pieces subjoined to this appendix, No. VIII

* See the pieces subjoined to this appendix, No. VIII. † See No. VIII. ‡ See No. X

degree of secrecy. This secrecy was prudent, as neither of the corresponding parties had been authorised by the civil power to negotiate a union between the two churches;* and, on Dr. Wake's part, it was partly owing to his having nobody that he could trust with what he did. He was satisfied (as he says in a letter to Mr. Beauvoir) "that most of the high-church bishops and clergy would readily come into such a design; but these (adds his grace) are not men either to be confided in, or made use of, by me."†

The correspondence, however, was divulged; and the project of union engrossed the whole conversation of the city of Paris. Lord Stanhope and the earl of Stair were congratulated thereupon by some great personages in the royal palace. The duke regent himself and the abbe Du Bois, minister of foreign affairs, and Mr. Joli de Fleury, the attorney-general, gave the line at first, appeared to favour the correspondence and the project, and let things run on to certain lengths. But the Jesuits and Constitutionists sounded the alarm, and overturned the whole scheme, by spreading a report, that the cardinal de Noailles, and his friends the Jansenists, were upon the point of making a coalition with the heretics. Hereupon the regent was intimidated; and Du Bois had an opportunity of appearing a meritorious candidate for a place in the sacred college. Dr. Piers Girardin was sent for to court, was severely reprimanded by Du Bois, and strictly charged, upon pain of being sent to the Bastile, to give up all the letters he had received from the archbishop of Canterbury, as also a copy of all his own. He was forced to obey; and all the letters were immediately sent to Rome, "as so many trophies (says a certain author) gained from the enemies of the church."‡ The archbishop's letters were greatly admired, as striking proofs both of his catholic benevolence and extensive abilities.

Mr. Beauvoir informed the archbishop, by a letter dated February 8, 1719, N. S. that Dr. Du-Pin had been summoned by the abbe Du Bois, to give an account of what had passed between him and Dr. Wake. This step naturally suspended the correspondence, though the archbishop was at a loss, at first, whether he should look upon it as favourable, or detrimental, to the projected union.§ The letters which he wrote to Mr. Beauvoir and Dr. Du Pin after this, express the same sentiments which he discovered through the whole of this transaction.* The letter to Du-Pin, more especially, is full of a pacific and reconciling spirit, and expresses the archbishop's desire of cultivating fraternal charity with the doctors, and his regret at the ill success of their endeavours toward the projected union. Du-Pin died before this letter, which was retarded by some accident, arrived at Paris.† Before the archbishop had heard of his death, he wrote to Mr. Beauvoir, to express his concern, that an account was going to be published of what had passed between the two doctors and himself, and his hope, "that they would keep in generals, as the only way to renew the good design, if occasion should serve, and to prevent themselves trouble from the reflections of their enemies," on account (as the archbishop undoubtedly means) of the concessions they had made, which, though insufficient to satisfy true Protestants, were adapted to exasperate bigoted papists. The prelate adds, in the conclusion of this letter, "I shall be glad to know that your doctors still continue their good opinion of us; for, though we need not the approbation of men on our own account, yet I cannot but wish it as a mean to bring them, if not to a perfect agreement in all things with us, (which is not presently to be expected,) yet to such a union as may put an end to the odious charges against, and consequential aversion of us, as heretics and schismatics, and in truth, make them cease to be so."

Dr. Du-Pin (whom the archbishop very sincerely lamented, as the only man, after Mr Ravechet, on whom the hopes of a reformation in France seemed to depend) left behind him an account of this famous correspondence. Some time before he died, he showed it to Mr. Beauvoir, and told him, that he intended to communicate it to a very great man (probably the regent.) Mr. Beauvoir observed to the doctor, that one would be led to imagine, from the manner in which this account was drawn up, that the archbishop made the first overtures with respect to the correspondence, and was the first who intimated his desire of the union· whereas it was palpably evident that he (Dr Du-Pin) had first solicited the one and the other. Du-Pin acknowledged this freely and candidly, and promised to rectify it, but was prevented by death. It does not, however, appear, that his death put a final stop to the correspondence; for we learn by a letter from the archbishop to Mr. Beauvoir, dated August 27, 1719, that Dr. Piers Girardin frequently wrote to his grace. But the opportunity was past; the appellants from the bull *Unigenitus*, or the anti-constitutionists, were divided; the court did not smile at all upon the project, because the regent was afraid of the Spanish party and the Jesuits; and therefore the continuation of this correspondence after Du-Pin's death was without effect.

Let the reader now, after having perused this historical account, judge of the appearance which Dr. Wake makes in this transaction

* Dr. Wake seems to have been sensible of the impropriety of carrying on a negotiation of this nature without the approbation and countenance of government. "I always (says he, in his letter to Mr. Beauvoir, which the reader will find at the end of this Appendix, No. XI.) took it for granted, that no step should be taken toward a union, but with the knowledge, approbation, and even by the authority of civil powers. All, therefore, that has passed hitherto stands clear of any exception as to the civil magistrate. It is only a consultation, in order to find out a way how a union might be made, if a fit occasion should hereafter be offered."

† See the letters subjoined, No. IX.

‡ These *trophies* were the defeat of the moderate part of the Gallican church, and the ruin of their project to break the papal yoke, and unite with the church of England. See above, note *, p. 170, where the conclusion which the author of the Confessional has drawn from this expression is shown to be groundless.

§ See his letter to Mr. Beauvoir, in the pieces subjoined, No. XI dated February 5 (16,) 1718-19.

* See No. XI.—XVIII.

† See his letter to Mr. Beauvoir, No. XV.

An impartial reader will certainly draw from this whole correspondence the following conclusions: that archbishop Wake was invited to this correspondence by Dr. Du-Pin, the most moderate of all the Roman catholic divines; that he entered into it with a view to improve one of the most favourable opportunities that could be offered, of withdrawing the church of France from the jurisdiction of the pope; a circumstance which must have immediately weakened the power of the court of Rome, and, in its consequences, offered a fair prospect of a farther reformation in doctrine and worship, as the case happened in the church of England, when it happily threw off the papal yoke;—that he did not give Du-Pin, or any of the doctors of the Sorbonne, the smallest reason to hope that the church of England would give up any one point of belief or practice to the church of France; but insisted, on the contrary, that the latter should make alterations and concessions, in order to be reconciled to the former;—that he never specified the particular alterations, which would be requisite to satisfy the rulers and doctors of the church of England, but only expressed a general desire of a union between the churches, if that were possible, or at least of a mutual toleration; that he never flattered himself that this union could be perfectly accomplished, or that the doctors of the Gallican church would be entirely brought over to the church of England; but thought that every advance made by them, and every concession, must have proved really advantageous to the Protestant cause.

The pacific spirit of Dr. Wake did not only discover itself in his correspondence with the Romish doctors, but in several other transactions in which he was engaged by his constant desire of promoting union and concord among Christians; for it is well known, that he kept up a constant friendly correspondence with the most eminent ministers of the foreign Protestant churches, and showed a fraternal regard to them, notwithstanding the difference of their discipline and government from that of the church of England. In a letter written to the learned le Clerc in 1716, he expresses, in the most cordial terms, his affection for them, and declares positively, that nothing can be farther from his thoughts, than the notions adopted by certain bigoted and furious writers who refuse to embrace the foreign Protestants as their brethren, will not allow to their religious assemblies the denomination of *churches*, and deny the validity of their sacraments. He declares, on the contrary, these churches to be true Christian churches, and expresses a warm desire of their union with the church of England. It will be, perhaps, difficult to find, in any epistolary composition, ancient, or modern, a more elegant simplicity, a more amiable spirit of meekness, moderation, and charity, and a happier strain of that easy and unaffected politeness which draws its expressions from a natural habit of goodness and humanity, than we meet with in this letter.* We see this active and benevolent prelate still continuing to interest himself in the welfare of the Protestant churches abroad. In several letters written in the years 1718 and 1719, to the pastors and professors of Geneva and Switzerland, who were then at variance about the doctrines of predestination and grace, and some other abstruse points of metaphysical theology, he recommends earnestly to them a spirit of mutual toleration and forbearance, entreats them particularly to be moderate in their *demands* of subscription to articles of faith, and proposes to them the example of the church of England as worthy of imitation in this respect. In one of these letters, he exhorts the doctors of Geneva not to go too far in explaining the nature, determining the sense, and imposing the belief of doctrines, which the divine wisdom has not thought proper to reveal clearly in the Scriptures, and the ignorance of which is very consistent with a state of salvation; and he recommends the prudence of the church of England, which has expressed these doctrines in such general terms, in its articles, that persons who think very differently about the doctrines may subscribe the articles, without wounding their integrity.* His letters to professor Schurer of Bern, and to the excellent and learned John Alphonso Turretin of Geneva, are in the same strain of moderation and charity, and are here subjoined,† as every way worthy of attentive perusal. But what is more peculiarly worthy of attention here, is a letter written May 22, 1719,‡ to Mr. Jablonski of Poland, who, from a persuasion of Dr. Wake's great wisdom, discernment, and moderation, had proposed to him the following question, viz. "Whether it was lawful and expedient for the Lutherans to treat of a union with the church of Rome; or whether all negotiations of this kind ought not to be looked upon as dangerous and delusive?" The archbishop's answer to this question contains a happy mixture of Protestant zeal and Christian charity. He gives the strongest cautions to the Polish Lutherans against entering into any treaty of union with the Roman catholics, except on a footing of perfect equality, and in consequence of a previous renunciation, on the part of the latter, of the tyranny, and even of the superiority and jurisdiction of the church of Rome and its pontiff; and as to what concerns points of doctrine, he exhorts them not to sacrifice truth to temporal advantages, or even *to a desire of peace*. It would carry us too far, were we to give a minute account of Dr. Wake's correspondence with the Protestants of Nismes, or of Lithuania and other countries: it may however be affirmed, that no prelate, since the Reformation, had so extensive a correspondence with the Protestants abroad, and none could have a more friendly one.

It does not appear, that the dissenters in England made to the archbishop any proposals relative to a union with the established church, or that he made any proposals to them on that head. The spirit of the times, and the situation of the contending parties, offered lit

* See an extract of it among the pieces subjoined, No. XIX.

* See the pieces here subjoined, No. XX.
† See these letters, No. XXI, XXII, XXIII.
‡ No. XXV.

tle prospect of success to any scheme of that nature. In queen Anne's time, he was only bishop of Lincoln; and the disposition of the house of commons, and of all the Tory part of the nation, was then so unfavourable to the dissenters, that it is not at all likely that any attempt toward re-uniting them to the established church would have passed into a law. And, in the next reign, the face of things was so greatly changed in favour of the dissenters, and their hopes of recovering the rights and privileges, of which they had been deprived, were so sanguine, that it may be well questioned whether they would have accepted the offer of a union, had it been made to them. Be that as it will, one thing is certain, and it is a proof of archbishop Wake's moderate and pacific spirit, that, in 1714, when the spirit of the court and of the triumphant part of the ministry was, with respect to the Whigs in general, and to dissenters in particular, a spirit of enmity and oppression, this worthy prelate had the courage to stand up in opposition to the schism-bill, and to protest against it as a hardship upon the dissenters. This step, which must have blasted his credit at court, and proved detrimental to his private interest, as matters then stood, showed that he had a friendly and sincere regard for the dissenters. It is true, four years after this, when it was proposed to repeal the schism-bill and the act against occasional conformity, both at once, he disapproved this proposal; and this circumstance has been alleged as an objection to the encomiums that have been given to his tender regard for the dissenters, or at least as a proof that he changed his mind; and that Wake, bishop of Lincoln, was more their friend than Wake, archbishop of Canterbury. I do not pretend to justify this change of conduct. It seems to have been, indeed, occasioned by a change of circumstances. The dissenters, in their state of oppression during the ministry of Bolingbroke and his party, were objects of compassion; and those who had sagacity enough to perceive the ultimate object which that ministry had in view in oppressing them, must have interested themselves in their sufferings, and opposed their oppressors, from a regard to the united causes of Protestantism and liberty. In the following reign, their credit rose; and, while this encouraged the wise and moderate men among them to plead with prudence and with justice their right to be delivered from several real grievances, it elated the violent (and violent men there are in all parties even in the cause of moderation) to a high degree. This rendered them formidable to all those who were jealous of [*zealous for*] the power, privileges, and authority, of the established church; and archbishop Wake was probably of this number. He had protested against the shackles that were imposed upon them when they lay under the frowns of government; but apprehending, perhaps, that the removal of these shackles in the day of prosperity would render their motions toward power too rapid, he opposed the abrogation of the very acts which he had before endeavoured to stifle in their birth. In this, however, it must be acknowledged, that the spirit of party mingled too much of its influence with the dictates of prudence; and that prudence, thus accompanied, was not very consistent with Dr. Wake's known principles of equity and moderation. As I was at a loss how to account for this part of the archbishop's conduct, I addressed myself to a learned and worthy clergyman of the church of England, who gave me the following answer: "Archbishop Wake's objection to the repeal of the schism-act was founded on this consideration only, that such a repeal was needless, as no use had been made, or was likely to be made, of that act. It is also highly probable, that he would have consented without hesitation to rescind it, had nothing farther been endeavoured at the same time. But, considering what sort of spirit was then shown by the dissenters and others, it ought not to be a matter of great wonder, if he was afraid that, from the repeal of the other act (viz. that against occasional conformity,) considerable damage might follow to the church over which he presided; and, even supposing his fears to be excessive, or quite groundless, yet certainly they were pardonable in a man who had never done, or designed to do, any thing disagreeable to the dissenters in any other affair, and who, in this, had the concurrence of some of the greatest and wisest of the English lords, and of the earl of Ilay, among the Scotch, though a professed Presbyterian."

However some may judge of this particular incident, I think it will appear from the whole tenor of archbishop Wake's correspondence and transactions with Christian churches of different denominations, that he was a man of a pacific, gentle, and benevolent spirit, and an enemy to the feuds, animosities, and party prejudices, which divide the professors of one holy religion, and by which Christianity is exposed to the assaults of its virulent enemies, and wounded in the house of its pretended friends. To this deserved eulogy, we may add what a learned and worthy divine* has said of this eminent prelate, considered as a controversial writer, even, "that his accurate and superior knowledge of the nature of the Romish hierarchy, and of the constitution of the church of England, furnished him with victorious arms, both for the subversion of error and the defence of truth."

AUTHENTIC COPIES OF THE ORIGINAL LETTERS FROM WHICH THE PRECEDING ACCOUNT IS DRAWN.

No. I.

A Letter from Archbishop Wake to Mr. Beauvoir.

Lambeth, Nov. 28, S. V. 1717.

I AM indebted to you for several kind letters, and some small tracts, which I have had

* Dr. William Richardson, master of Emanuel college in Cambridge, and canon of Lincoln. See his noble edition, and his very elegant and judicious continuation of Bishop Godwin's Commentarius de Præsulibus Angliæ, published in 1743, at Cambridge. His words, (p. 167,) are: "Nemo usbiam ecclesiæ Romanæ vel Anglicanæ statum penitius cognitum exploratum habuit; et proinde in disputandi arenam prodiit tum ad oppugnandum tum ad propugnandum instructissimus."

the favour to receive from you. The last, which contains an account of the new edition that is going on of Chrysostom, I received yesterday. It will, no doubt, be a very valuable edition; but, as they propose to go on with it, I shall hardly live to see it finished. They do not tell us, to whom here we may go for subscriptions: and it is too much trouble to make returns to Paris. They should, for their own advantage, say, where subscriptions will be taken in London, and where one may call for the several volumes as they come out, and pay for the next that are going on.

Among the account of books you were pleased to send me, there is one with a very promising title, *Thesaurus Anecdotorum*, five volumes. I wish I could know what the chief of those anecdotes are; it may be a book very well worth having. I admire they do not disperse some sheets of such works. What they can add to make Moreri's Dictionary so very voluminous, I cannot imagine. I bought it in two exorbitant volumes, and thought it big enough so. While I am writing this, company is come in, so that I am forced to break off; and I can only assure you, that, upon all occasions, you shall find me very sincerely,

Reverend Sir, Your faithful friend,

W. Cant.

N. B. This is the earliest letter in the whole collection; and, by the beginning of it, seems to be the first which the archbishop wrote to Mr. Beauvoir.

No. II.

A Letter from Mr. Beauvoir to Archbishop Wake.

Paris, Dec. 11, 1717, O. S.

My Lord,—I had the honour of your grace's letter of the 28th ultimo but Sunday last, and therefore could not answer it sooner. A person is to be appointed to receive subscriptions for the new edition of St. Crysostom, and deliver the copies. Inclosed is an account of *Thesaurus Anecdotorum.* Dr. Du-Pin, with whom I dined last Monday, and with the Syndic of the Sorbonne and two other doctors, tells me, that what swells Moreri's Dictionary are several additions, and particularly the families of Great Britain. He hath the chief hand in this new edition. They talked as if the whole kingdom was to appeal to the future general council, &c. They wished for a union with the church of England, as the most effectual means to unite all the western churches. Dr. Du-Pin desired me to give his duty to your grace, upon my telling him, that I would send you an arrêt of the parliament of Paris relating to him, and a small tract of his. I have transmitted them to Mr. Prevereau, at Mr. Secretary Addison's office.

No. III.

A Letter from Archbishop Wake to Mr. Beauvoir.

Aug. 30, 1718.

I told you in one of my last letters, how little I expected from the present pretences of a union with us. Since I received the papers you sent me, I am more convinced that I was not mistaken. My task is pretty hard, and I scarce know how to manage myself in this matter. To go any farther than I have done in it, even as a divine only of the church of England, may meet with censure: and, as archbishop of Canterbury, I cannot treat with these gentlemen. I do not think my character at all inferior to that of an archbishop of Paris: on the contrary, without lessening the authority and dignity of the church of England, I must say it is in some respects superior. If the cardinal were in earnest for such a union, it would not be below him to treat with me himself about it. I should then have a sufficient ground to consult with my brethren, and to ask his majesty's leave to correspond with him concerning it. But to go on any farther with these gentlemen, will only expose me to the censure of doing what, in my station, ought not to be done without the king's knowledge; and it would be very odd for me to have an authoritative permission to treat with those who have no manner of authority to treat with me. However, I shall venture at some answer or other to both their letters and papers; and so have done with this affair.

I cannot tell well what to say to Dr. Du-Pin. If he thinks we are to take their direction what to retain, and what to give up, he is utterly mistaken. I am a friend to peace, but more to truth. And they may depend upon it, I shall always account our church to stand upon an equal foot with theirs: and that we are no more to receive laws from them, than we desire to impose any upon them. In short, the church of England is free, is orthodox: she has a plenary authority within herself, and has no need to recur to any other church to direct her what to retain, or what to do. Nor will we, otherwise than in a brotherly way, and in a full equality of right and power, ever consent to have any treaty with that of France. And therefore, if they mean to deal with us, they must lay down this for the foundation, that we are to deal with one another upon equal terms. If, consistently with our own establishment, we can agree upon a closer union with one another, well: if not, we are as much, and upon as good grounds, a free independent church, as they are. And, for myself, as archbishop of Canterbury, I have more power, larger privileges, and a greater authority, than any of their archbishops: from which, by the grace of God, I will not depart—no, not for the sake of a union with them.

You see, Sir, what my sense of this matter is; and may perhaps think that I have a little altered my mind since this affair was first set on foot. As to my desire of peace and union with all other Christian churches, I am still the same: but with the doctor's Commonitorium I shall never comply. The matter must be put into another method; and, whatever they think, they must alter some of their doctrines, and practices too, or a union with them can never be effected. Of this, as soon as I have a little more leisure, I shall write my mind as inoffensively as I can to them, but yet freely too.

If any thing is to come of this matter, it will be the shortest method I can take of accomplishing it, to put them in the right way. If nothing (as I believe nothing will be done in it,) 'tis good to leave them under a plain knowledge of what we think of ourselves and our church, and to let them see, that we neither need nor seek the union proposed, but for their sake as well as our own; or rather neither for theirs nor ours; but in order to the promotion of a catholic communion (as far as is possible) among all the true churches of Christ.

I have now plainly opened my mind to you: you will communicate no more of it than is fitting to the two doctors, but keep it as a testimony of my sincerity in this affair; and that I have no design, but what is consistent with the honour and freedom of our English church, and with the security of that true and sound doctrine which is taught in it, and from which no consideration shall ever make me depart.

I am, Reverend Sir,

Your affectionate friend and brother,

W. CANT.

No. IV.

From Archbishop Wake to Mr. Beauvoir.

Oct. 8, 1718.

WHATEVER be the consequence of our corresponding with the Sorbonne doctors about matters of religion, the present situation of our affairs plainly seems to make it necessary for us so to do. Under this apprehension I have written, though with great difficulty, two letters to your two doctors, which I have sent to the secretary's office, to go with the next packet to my lord Stair. I beg you to inquire after them; they made up together a pretty thick packet, directed to you. In that to Dr. Du-Pin, I have, in answer to two of his MSS., described the method of making bishops in our church. I believe he will be equally both pleased and surprised with it. I wish you could show him the form of consecration, as it stands in the end of your large common prayer-books. The rest of my letters, both to him and Dr. Piers, is a venture which I know not how they will take, to convince them of the necessity of embracing the present opportunity of breaking off from the pope, and going one step farther than they have yet done in their opinion of his authority, so as to leave him only a primacy of place and honour; and that merely by ecclesiastical authority, as he was once bishop of the imperial city. I hope they both show you my letters: they are at this time very long, and upon a nice point. I shall be very glad if you can any way learn how they take the freedom I have used, and what they really think of it. I cannot so much trust to their answers, in which they have more room to conceal their thoughts, and seldom want to overwhelm me with more compliments than I desire, or am well able to bear.

Pray do all you can to search out their real sense of, and motions at the receipt of these two letters; I shall thereby be able the better to judge how far I may venture hereafter to offer any thing to them upon the other points in difference between us; though after all, I still think, if ever a reformation be made, it is the state that must govern the church in it. But this between ourselves.

No. V.

A Letter from Archbishop Wake to Dr. Du-Pin, dated October 1, 1718.

Spectatissimo Viro, eruditorum suæ gentis, si non et sui sæculi principi; Dno. L. Ell. Du-Pin, Doctori Parisiensi.

Gul. prov. div. Cant. Archs. in omnibus ευφρονειν και ευπραττειν.

DIU est, amplissime Domine, ex quo debitor tibi factus sum ob plures tractatus MSS. quos tuo beneficio a dilecto mihi in Christo D. Beauvoir accepi. Perlegi diligenter omnes, nec sine fructu: plurima quippe ab iis, cognitu dignissima, vel primùm didici, vel clariùs intellexi; beatamque his difficillimis temporibus censeo ecclesiam Gallicanam, quæ talem sibi in promptu habeat doctorem, in dubiis consiliarium, in juribus suis tuendis advocatum; qui et possit et audeat, non modo contra suos vel erroneos vel perfidos symmystas dignitatem ejus tueri, sed et ipsi summo pontifici (ut olim B. Apostolus Paulus Petro) in faciem resistere, quia reprehensibilis est. Atque utinam hæc quæ jam Romæ aguntur, tandem aliquando omnibus vobis animum darent ad jura vestra penitùs asserenda! Ut deinceps non ex pragmaticis (ut olim) sanctionibus non (ut hoc ferè tempore) ex concordatis, non ex præjudicatis hominum opinionibus, res vestras agatis; sed eâ authoritate quâ decet ecclesiam tam illustris ac præpotentis imperii; quæ nullo jure, vel divino, vel humano, alteri olim aut ecclesiæ aut homini subjicitur; sed ipsa jus habet intra se sua negotia terminandi, et in omnibus, sub rege suo Christianissimo, populum suum commissum propriis suis legibus et sanctionibus gubernandi.

Expergiscimini itaque, viri, eruditi; et quod ratio postulat, nec refragatur religio, strenuè agite. Hoc bonorum subditorum erga regem suum officium. Christianorum erga episcopos suos, heu! nimiùm extraneorum tyrannide oppressos, pietas exigit, flagitat, requirit. Excutite tandem jugum istud, quod nec patres vestri, nec vos ferre potuistis. Hic ad reformationem non prætensam, sed veram, sed justam, sed necessariam ecclesiæ nostræ, primus fuit gradus. Quæ Cæsaris erant, Cæsari reddidimus; quæ Dei, Deo. Coronæ imperiali regni nostri suum suprematum, episcopatui suam ἀξίαν, ecclesiæ suam libertatem restituit, vel eo solùm nomine semper cum honore memorandus, rex Henricus VIII. Hæc omnia sub pedibus conculcaverat idem ille tunc nobis, qui jam vobis inimicus. Sæpiùs authoritas papalis intra certos fines legibus nostris antea fuerat coërcita; et iis quidem legibus, quas siquis hodie inspiceret, impossibile ei videretur eas potuisse, aliquâ vel vi vel astutiâ, perrumpere. Sed idem nobis accidit quod illis, qui dæmoniacum vinculis ligare voluere. Omnia frustrà tentata: nihil perfacere inania legum repagula, contra nescio quos prætextus potestatis divinæ nullis humanis constitutionibus subditæ. Tandem defatigato regno dura necessitas sua jura tuendi oculos omnium aperuit. Proponitur quæstio episcopis ac clero in utriusque provinciæ synodo congregatis, an episcopus Romanus in sacris scripturis habeat aliquam majorem jurisdictionem in regno Angliæ quàm quivis alius externus episcopus? In partem sanam, justam, veram, utriusque concilii suffragia concurrêre. Quod episcopi cum suo clero statuerant, etiam regni academiæ calculo suo approbârunt, rex cum parliamento sancivit, adeoque tandem, quod unicè fieri poterat, sublata penitùs potestas, quam nullæ leges, nulla jura, vel civilia vel ecclesiastica, intra debitos fines unquam poterant continere. En nobis promptum ac paratum exemplum; quod sequi vobis gloriosum, nec minus posteris vestris utile fuerit! Quo solo pacem, absque veritatis dispendio, tueri valeatis, ac irridere bruta de Vaticano fulmina, quæ jumdudum ostenditis vobis non ultra terrori esse, uptote à sacris scripturis edoctis, quod *maledictio absque causâ prolata non superveniet.*—Prov. xxvi. 2.

State ergo in libertate quâ Christus vos donaverit. Frustra ad concilium generale nunquam convocandum res vestras refertis. Frustra decretorum vim suspendere curatis, quæ ab initio injusta, erronea, ac absurda, ac plane nulla erant. Non talibus subsidiis vobis opus est. Regiâ permissione, authoritate suâ a Christo commissâ, archiepiscopi et episcopi vestri in concilium nationale coëant: academiarum, cleri, ac præcipuè utrorumque principis theologicæ facultatis Parisiensis, concilium atque auxilium sibi assumant: sic muniti quod æquum et justum fuerit decernant: quod decreverint etiam civili authoritate firmandum curent: nec patiantur factiosos homines aliò res vestras vocare, aut ad judicem appellare qui nullam in vos authoritatem exposcere debeat, aut, si exposcat, meritò a vobis recusari et poterit et debuerit.

Ignoscas, vir πολυμαθέστατε, indignationi dicam an amori meo, si forte aliquanto ultrà modum commoveri videar ab iis quæ vobis his proximis annis acciderint. Veritatem Christi omni quâ possum animi devotione colo. Hanc vos tuemini: pro hac censuras pontificias subiistis, et porrò ferre parati estis.

Ille, qui se pro summo ac ferè unico Christi vicario venditat, veritatem ejus sub pedibus proterit, conculcat. Justitiam veneror: ac proinde vos injustè, ac planè tyrannicè, si non oppressos, at petitos, at comminatos; at ideo solum non penitùs obrutos, subversos prostratos, qui a Deus furori ejus obicem posuit, nec permiserit vos in ipsius manus incidere; non possum non vindicare, et contra violentum oppressorem, meum qualecunque suffragium ferre.

Jura ac libertates inclyti regni, celeberrimæ ecclesiæ, præstantissimi cleri cum honore intueor. Hæc papa reprobat, contemnit; et, dum sic alios tractat, merito se aliis castigandum, certè intra justos fines coërcendum, exhibet. Siquid ei potestatis supra alios episcopos Christus commiserit, proferantur tabulæ; jus evincatur; cedere non recusamus.

Siquam prærogativam ecclesiæ concilia sedis imperialis episcopo concesserint (etsi cadente imperio, etiam eâ prærogativâ excidisse merito possit censeri;) tamen quod ad me attinet, servatis semper regnorum juribus, ecclesiarum libertatibus, episcoporum dignitate, modo in cæteris conveniatur, per me licet, suo fruatur, qualicunque primatu: non ego illi locum primum, non inanem honoris titulum invideo. At in alias ecclesias dominari; episcopatum, cujus partem Christus unicuique episcopo in solidum reliquit, tantum non in solidum sibi soli vindicare; siquis ejus injustæ tyrannidi sese opposuerit, cœlum ac terram in illius perniciem commovere; hæc nec nos unquam ferre potuimus, nec vos debetis. In hoc pacis fundamento si inter nos semel conveniatur, in cæteris aut idem sentiemus omnes, aut facilè alii aliis dissentiendi libertatem absque pacis jacturâ concedemus.

Sed abripit calamum meum nescio quis Ἐνθουσιασμος, dum de vestris injuriis nimiùm sum solicitus; et forte liberiùs quàm par esset de his rebus ad te scripsisse videbor.

Ego verò uti ea omnia, quæ tu in tuo commonitorio, exaraveris, etiam illa in quibus ab invicem dissentimus, grato animo accipio: ita ut apertè, ut candidè, et absque omni fuco porrò ad me scribere pergas, eâque παρρησια quâ amicum cum amico agere deceat, imprimis a te peto; eo te mihi amiciorem fore existimans, quo simpliciùs quo planiùs, quicquid censueris, liberè dixeris.

Nec de commonitorio tuo amplius aliquid hoc tempore reponam; in quo cum plurima placeant, tum id imprimis, quod etiam tuo judicio, non adeo longe ab invicem distemus, quin si de fraternâ unione ineundâ publicâ aliquando authoritate deliberari contigerit, via facile inveniri poterit ad pacem inter nos stabiliendam, salvâ utrinque ecclesiæ catholicæ fide ac veritate.

Quod ad alteros tuos tractatus de constitutione episcoporum in ecclesiis vacantibus, siquidem papa, legitimè requisitus, facultates suas personis a rege nominatis obstinate pernegaverit; in iis sane reperio quod non tuâ eruditione et judicio sit; quare, ne prorsus ἀσυμβολος discedam, ordinem tibi breviter delineabo constituendi episcopos in hâc reformatâ nostrâ ecclesiâ.

Tu judicabis, an aliquid magis canonicè vel excogitari vel statui potuerit.

No. VI.

A Letter from Archbishop Wake to Dr. P. Piers Girardin, written in October, 1718.

Præstantissimo Viro, consummatissimo Theologo Dno Patricio Piers de Girardin, sacræ Facultatis Parisiensis Theologiæ Doctori.

Gul. prov. div. Cant. Archs. Gratiam, Pacem, ac Salutem in Domino.

Post prolixiores epistolas eruditissimo con fratri tuo Dno Dri Du-Pin hoc ipso tempore exaratas; quasque ego paulo minùs tuas quàm illius existimari, velim; faciliùs a te veniam impetrabo, vir spectatissime, si aliquanto brevius ad te rescribam; et in illis quidem animi mei vel amori vel indignationi liberè indulsi; eâque simplicitate, quâ decet Christianum, et maxime episcopum, quid vobis, meâ saltem sententiâ, factu opus sit, apertè exposui. Siquid, vel tuo vel illius judicio, asperius quàm par esset a me exciderit, cum vestri causâ adeo commotus fuerim, facile id homini tam benevolè erga vos animato, uti spero condonabitis: unaque reminiscemini, nullam unquam vobis stabilem inter vos pacem, aut catholicam cum aliis unionem, haberi posse, dum aliquid ultra merum honoris primatum ac προεδρίαν pontifici Romano tribuitis. Hoc nos per aliquot sæcula experti sumus; vos jam sentire debetis, qui, nescio quò insano ipsius beneficio, adeo commodam occasionem nacti estis, non tam ab illius decretis appellandi, quàm ab ipsius dominio ac potestate vos penitùs subducendi. Ipse vos pro schismaticis habet; qualem vos eum censere debetis. Ipse a vestrâ communione se suos-que separandos publicē denunciat. Quid vobis in hoc casu faciendum? Liceat mihi veteris illius Cæsareæ episcopi Firmilani verbis respondere; sic olim Stephanum papam acriter quidem, sed non ideo minus juste, castigavit: *Vide quâ imperitiâ reprehendere audeas eos qui contra mendacium pro veritate nituntur. Peccatum verō quām magnum tibi exaggerâsti, quando te a tot gregibus scidisti: excidisti enim te ipsum, noli te fallere; siquidem ille est vere schismaticus qui se a communione ecclesiasticâ unitatis apostatam fecerit. Dum enim putas omnes a te abstineri posse, solum te ab omnibus abstinuisti.* Cypr. Op. Epist. 75.

Agite ergo, viri eruditi, et quo vos divina providentia vocat, libenter sequimini. Clemens papa vos abdicavit; a suâ et suorum communione repulit, rejecit. Vos illius authoritati renunciate. Cathedræ Petri, quæ in omnibus catholicis ecclesiis conservatur, adhærete: etiam nostram ne refugiatis communionem; quibuscum si non in omnibus omninō doctrinæ Christianæ capitibus conveniatis, at in præcipuis, at in fundamentalibus, at in omnibus articulis fidei ad salutem necessariis, planē concentitis; etiam in cæteris, uti speramus, brevi concensuri. Nobis certē eo minus vos vel hæreticos vel schismaticos fore confidite, quod ā papâ ejecti pro hæreticis et schismaticis Romæ æstimemini. Sed contrahenda vela, nec indulgendum huic meo pro vobis zelo, etsi sit secundūm scientiam. Prudentibus loquor; vos ipsi, quod dico, judicate.

Ad literas tuas, præstantissime Domine, redeo; in quibus uti tuum de mediocritate meâ judicium, magis ex affectu erga me tuo, quām secundūm merita mea prolatum gratanter accipio, ita in eo te nunquam falli patiar, quod me pacis ecclesiasticæ amantissimum credas, omniaque illi consequendæ danda putem, præter veritatem. Quantum ad illam promovendam tu jamjam contuleris, ex sex illis propositionibus quas tuis inseruisti literis, gratus agnosco: ac nisi ambitiosē magis quām hominem privatum deceat, me fracturum existimarem, etiam eruditissimis illis confratribus tuis doctoribus Sorbonicis, quibus priores meas literas communicâsti, easdem per te gratias referrem. Sanē facultas vestra Parisiensis, uti maximum in his rebus pondus meritō habere debeat, sive numerum, sive dignitatem, sive denique eruditionem suorum membrorum spectemus; ita a vobis exordium sumere debebit unio illa inter nos tantopere desiderata, siquidem eam aliquando iniri voluerit Deus.

Interim gratulor vobis post illustrissimum card. Noaillium, alterum illum ecclesiæ Gallicanæ, fidei catholicæ, columnam et ornamentum, procuratorem regium D. D. Joly de Fleury; quem virum ego non jam primum ex tuis literis debito prosequi honore didici, verum etiam ob ea quæ vestri causâ his proximis annis publicē egerit, anteā suspicere, et penē venerari, consueveram. Sub his ducibus, quid non sperandum ir [illegible] vestrum ac catholicæ ecclesiæ commodum? Intonet de Vaticano pontifex Romanus; fremant inter vos ipsos conjurata turba, Romanæ curiæ servi magis quām suæ Galliæ fideles subditi. His præsidiis ab eorum injuriis tuti, vanas eorum iras contemnere valeatis.

Ego vero, uti omnia vobis publicē fausta ac felicia precor, ita tibi, spectatissime vir, me semper addictissimum fore promitto. De quo quicquid aliās senseris, id saltem ut de me credas jure postulo; me sincerē veritatem Christi et amare et quærere, et, nisi omninō me fallat animus, etiam assecutum esse Nulli. Christiano inimicus antehac aut fui aut deinceps sum futurus: sic de erroribus eorum, qui a me dissident, judico, ut semper errantes Deo judicandos relinquam. Homo sum, errare possum; sic verō animatus audacter dicam, hæreticus esse nolo. Te verō, siquidem id permittas, fratrem; sin id minus placeat, saltem id indulgebis, ut me verē et ex animo profitear, excellentissime Domine, tui amantissimum.

W. C.

No. VII.

Extract of a Letter from Archbishop Wake to Mr. Beauvoir.

Nov. 6, O. S. 1718.

Your last letter gives me some trouble, but more curiosity. I little thought, when I wrote to your two doctors, that my letters should have been read, much less copies of them given to any such great persons as you mention. I write in haste, as you know, and trust no amanuensis to copy for me, because I will not be liable to be betrayed. And upon a review of my foul, and only copy of them, since I had your account from Paris, I find some things might have been more accurately expressed, had I taken more time to correct my style But I wish that may be the worst exceptions against them: I fear the freedom I took in exhorting them to do somewhat in earnest, upon so fair a provocation, with regard to the papal authority, though excused as well as I could will hardly go down so effectually as I could wish with them. This raises my curiosity to know truly and expressly how that part of my letters operated on both your doctors; which by a wary observation, you may in good measure gather from their discourse. I cannot tell whether they showed my letters to you; if they did, I am sure you will think I did not mince the matter with them in that particular.

Of your two doctors, Dr. Piers seems the more polite: he writes elegantly both for style and matter, and has the free air, even as to the business of a union. Yet I do not despair of Dr. Du-Pin, whom, thirty years ago, in his collection of tracts relating to church discipline, I did not think far from the kingdom of God.

No. VIII.

Extract of a Letter from Archbishop Wake to Mr. Beauvoir.

Nov. 18, 1718.

At present, my more particular curiosity leads me to know the sentiments of the leading men in France with regard to the court of Rome; from which, if we could once divide the Gallican church, a reformation in other matters would follow of course. The scheme that seems to me most likely to prevail, is, to agree in the independence (as to all matters of authority) of every national church on any others; and in their right to determine all matters that arise within themselves; and, for points of doctrine, to agree, as far as possible, in all articles of any moment (as in effect we either already do, or easily may;) and, for other matters, to allow a difference, till God shall bring us to a union in those also. One only thing should be provided for, to purge out of the public offices of the church such things as hinder a perfect communion in the service of the church, that so, whenever any come from us to them, or from them to us, we may all join together in prayers and the holy sacraments with each other. In our liturgy there is nothing but what they allow, save the single rubric relating to the eucharist; in theirs nothing but what they agree may be laid aside, and yet the public offices be never the worse or more imperfect for want of it. Such a scheme as this, I take to be a more proper ground of peace, at the beginning, than to go to more particulars; if in such a foundation we could once agree, the rest would be more easily built upon it. If you find occasion, and that it may be of use, you may extract this object, and offer it to their consideration, as what you take to be my sense in the beginning of a treaty; not that I think we shall stop here, but that, being thus far agreed, we shall the more easily go into a greater perfection hereafter. I desire you to observe, as much as you can, when it is I may the most properly write to the doctors. I took the subject of the pope's authority in my last, as arising naturally from the present state of their affairs, and as the first thing to be settled in order to a union. How my freedom in that respect has been received, I desire you freely to communicate.

No. IX.

Extract of a Letter from Archbishop Wake to Mr. Beauvoir.

Dec. 2, O. S. 1718.

I AM glad the two doctors seem to receive my last letters so well. The truth is, that while they manage as they do with the court of Rome, nothing will be done to any purpose. And all ends in trifling at the last. We honestly deny the pope all authority over us: they pretend, in words, to allow him so much as is consistent with what they call their Gallican privileges; but let him ever so little use it contrary to their good liking, they protest against it, appeal to a general council, and then mind him as little as we can do. In earnest, I think we treat his holiness not only with more sincerity, but more respect than they: for, to own a power, and yet keep a reserve to obey that power only so far, and in such cases as we make ourselves judges of, is a greater affront, than honestly to confess that we deny the power, and, for that reason, refuse to obey it. But my design was partly to bring them to this, and partly to see how they would bear, at least the proposal, of totally breaking off from the court and bishop of Rome.

What you can observe, or discover more of their inclinations in this particular, will be of good use; especially if it could be found out what the court would do, and how far that may be likely to countenance the clergy in such a separation. In the mean time, it cannot be amiss to cultivate a friendship with the leading men of that side, who may in time be made use of to the good work of reforming in earnest the Gallican church. I am a little unhappy that I have none here I yet dare trust with what I do; though I am satisfied most of our high church bishops and clergy would readily come into such a design. But these are not men either to be confided in, or made use of, by

Your assured friend,

W. Cant

P. S. Did cardinal de Noailles know what authority the archbishop of Canterbury has gotten by the reformation, and how much a greater man he is now than when he was the pope's *legatus natus*, it might encourage him to follow so good a pattern, and be assured (in that case) he would lose nothing by sending back his cardinal's cap to Rome. I doubt your doctors know little of these matters.

No. X.

Extract of a Letter from Archbishop Wake to Mr. Beauvoir.

Jan. 23, O. S. 1718.

WHEN you see my letter (for I conclude the doctor will show it you,) you may do well to bring on the discourse of our episcopal rights and privileges in England, and particularly of the prerogatives of the archbishop of Canterbury, which, I believe, are greater than those of the archbishop of Rheims, or of all the archbishops in France. This may raise in them a curiosity to know more of this matter, which if they desire, I will take the first little leisure I have to give them a more particular account of it. We must deal with men in their own way, if we mean to do any good with them. They have been used to a pompous ministry, and, like the Jews heretofore, would despise the Messiah himself if he should come in a poor and low estate to them. And therefore, though, for myself, I account all temporal grandeur as nothing, and am afraid it has rather hurt the church of Christ, and the true spirit of piety and religion, than done any real service to either; yet it may be the means of disposing these gentlemen to a more favourable thought of, and inclination towards a reformation; to convince them that they may return to the truth of Christianity, and leave the corruptions of Rome, without losing any honour, any power, that a servant of Christ would desire to be troubled withal. Had the first reformers in France yielded to this scheme as we in England showed them an example, the whole Gallican church had come in to them, and been at this day as we are now: we must therefore hit off the blot which they made, and satisfy their ambition so far as to show them that they may reform, without giving up either their authority or revenues, and be still as great, but much better bishops, under our circumstances, than under their own

As to the pope's authority, I take the difference to be only this; that we may all agree (without troubling ourselves with the reason) to allow him a primacy of order in the episcopal college. They would have it thought necessary to hold communion with him, and allow him a little canonical authority over them, as long as he will leave them to prescribe the bounds of it. We fairly say we know of no authority he has in our realm; but for actual submission to him, they as little mind it as we do.

At present he has put them out of his communion; we have withdrawn ourselves from his; both are out of communion with him, and I think it is not material on which side the breach lies.

No. XI.

A Letter from Archbishop Wake to Mr. Beauvoir.

Feb. 5, 1718–19, O. S.

I do not doubt that mine of the 18th of January, with the two inclosed for my lord Stair and Dr. Du-Pin, are before this come safe to you. I should not be sorry if, upon this late transaction between the doctor and ministry, you have kept it in your hands, and not delivered it to him. I had just begun a letter to Dr. Piers, but have thrown aside what I writ of it, since I received your last; and must beg the favour of you to make my excuse to him, with the tenders of my hearty service, till I see a little more what the meaning of this present inquisition is. I am not so unacquainted with the finesses of courts, as not to apprehend, that what is now done may be as well in favour of the doctor's attempt, as against it. If the *procureur-general* be indeed well affected to it, he might take this method, not only to his own security, but to bring the affair under a deliberation, and give a handle to those whom it chiefly concerns, to discover their sentiments of it. But the matter may be also put to another use, and nobody can answer that it shall not be so: and till I see what is the meaning of this sudden turn, I shall write no more letters for the French ministry to examine, but content myself to have done enough already to men who cannot keep their own counsel, and live in a country where even the private correspondence of learned men with one another must be brought to a public inquiry, and be made the subject of a state inquisition. I am not aware, that in any of my letters there is one line that can give a just offence to the court. I always took it for granted, that no step should be taken toward a union, but with the knowledge and approbation, and even by the authority of civil powers; and indeed if I am in the right, that nothing can be done to any purpose in this case but by throwing off the pope's authority, as the first step to be made in order to it, it is impossible for any such attempt to be made by any power less than the king's. All therefore that has passed hitherto, stands clear of any just exception as to the civil magistrate; it is only a consultation, in order to find out a way how a union might be made, if a fit occasion should hereafter be offered for the doing of it. Yet still I do not like to have my letters exposed in such a manner, though satisfied there is nothing to be excepted against in them; and think I shall be kind to the doctors themselves to suspend, at least for a while, my farther troubling of them. I hope you will endeavour, by some or other of your friends, to find out the meaning of this motion; from whom it came; how far it has gone; what was the occasion of it; and what is like to be the consequence of it; what the abbe Du-Bois says of my letters, and how they are received by him and the other ministers. I shall soon discover whether any notice has been taken of it to our ministry; and I should think, if the abbe spoke to your lord about it, he would acquaint you with it.

No. XII.

Extract of a Letter from Archbishop Wake to Mr. Beauvoir.

Feb. 24, 1718.

I do not at all wonder that the cardinals Rohan and Bissi should do all they can to blacken the good cardinal de Noailles, and in him the party of the Anti-Constitutionists, but especially the Sorbonne, their most weighty and learned adversaries; and I am sensible that such a complaint is not only the most proper to do this, but to put the court itself under some difficulties, which way soever it acts upon it. But I am still the more curious to learn, if it were possible, not only the proceedings of the ministry above board hereupon, but their private thoughts and opinions about it. I am under no concern upon my own account, farther than that I would be unwilling to have my letters scanned by so many great men, which will scarcely bear the judgment of my very friends. You must do me the favour to get out of your doctors what will be most obliging to them, whether to continue to write to them, or to be silent for a while, till we see what will be the effect of this inquiry. In the mean time, it grows every day plainer what I said from the beginning, that no reformation can be made but by the authority, and with the concurrence of the court; and that all we divines have to do, is to use our interest to gain them to it, and to have a plan ready to offer to them, if they would be prevailed upon to come into it.

I am at present engaged in two or three other transactions of moment to the foreign protestants, which take up abundance of my time; God knows what will be the effect of it. Nevertheless, if I can in any way help to promote this, though I am at present without any help, alone, in this project, I shall do my utmost, both to keep up my poor little interest with the two doctors and their friends, and to concert proper methods with them about it. The surest way will be, to begin as well, and to go as far as we can, in settling a friendly correspondence one with another; to agree to own each other as true brethren, and members of the catholic Christian church; to agree to communicate in every thing we can with one another (which, on their side, is very easy, there being nothing in our offices, in any degree, contrary to their own principles;) and would they purge out of theirs what is contrary to ours, we might join in the public service with them, and yet leave one another in the free liberty of believing transubstantiation or not, so long as we did not require any thing to be done by either in pursuance of that opinion. The Lutherans do this very thing; many of them communicate not only in prayers, but in the communion with us; and we never inquire whether they believe consubstantiation, or even pay any worship to Christ as present with the elements, so long as their outward actions are the same with our own, and they give no offence to any with their opinions.

P. S. Since this last accident, and the public noise of a union at Paris, I have spoken something more of it to my friends here, who, I begin to hope, will fall in with it. I own a correspondence, but say not a tittle how far, or in what way, I have proceeded, more than that letters have passed, which can no longer be a secret. I have never shown one of my own or the doctors to any body.

No. XIII.

Extract of a Letter from Archbishop Wake to Mr. Beauvoir.

March 16, S. V. 1718.

I THANK you for your account of what passed between Mons. Hop and you, relating to the project of a union: I doubt that gentleman will not be pleased with it; because, indeed, the Gallican church will never unite with any church that has not an orderly episcopacy in it. I am very sorry my poor letters are made so public. The next thing will be, that either the imprudence of our friends, or the malice of our enemies, will print them; and then I shall have censures enough for them, perhaps some reflections printed upon them, or answers made to them; but this shall not engage me in any defence of them, or in taking any farther notice of them. I beg you to keep those I have written to yourself from all view; for I have no copies of them, and I wrote them as I do my other ordinary letters, without any great thought or consideration, more than what my subject (as I was writing) led me in that instant to. This is the liberty to be taken with a friend, where one is sure what he writes shall go no farther; but, for the same reason will require the strictest suppression from any other view. I cannot yet guess what this turn means, nor how it will end: I wish your doctors could give you some farther light into it.

P. S. I entreat you never to forget me to the two good doctors, whom I love and honour: keep up the little interest I have with them. As soon as ever the present turn is over, I will write to Dr. Girardin. I hope my letters will not always be carried as crimimals before the secretary of state, though I am persuaded he bears no ill-will to me.

No. XIV.

Extract of a Letter from Archbishop Wake to Mr. Beauvoir.

April 29, 1718.

I AM much concerned to hear that Dr. Du-Pin decays so fast: I feared by his last letter that he was sinking apace. Pray, is there any good print of him taken these last years? for I have one that was made when he was a young man. I am sorry Dr. Piers grows faint-hearted: I never thought any thing could be done as to a reformation in France, without the authority of the court; but I was in hopes the regent and others might have found their account in such an attempt; and then the good disposition of the bishops, clergy and Sorbonne, with the parliament of Paris, would have given a great deal of spirit and expedition to it. I have done what was proper for me in that matter: I can now go no farther, till the abbot Du-Bois is better disposed; yet I shall still be pleased to keep up a little esteem between those gentlemen, which will do *us* some good, if it does not do *them* any service. I am apt to think, the good old man (Du-Pin) does not think us far from the kingdom of heaven. I have with this sent a letter of friendship to Dr. Piers, which you will be so kind as to send him, with my kind respects.

No. XV.

Extract of a Letter from Archbishop Wake to Dr. Du-Pin, dated Lambeth, May 1, 1719.

N. B. Du-Pin was dead before it arrived at Paris.

SPERAVERAM equidem tuâ auctoritate, constantiâ, eruditione, pietate, moderatione, quæ omnia adeō in te perfecta esse noscuntur, ut vix in aliis singula, præclari aliquid ad Dei gloriam, ecclesiæque Gallicanæ utilitatem, perfici potuisse. Crediderim advenisse tempus, in quo, excusso Romanæ tyrannidis jugo, unā nobiscum in eandem communionem coalesceretis. In dogmatibus, prout ā te candidē proponuntur, non admodūm dissentimus: in regimine ecclesiastico minus: in fundamentalibus, sive doctrinam sive disciplinam spectemus, vix omninō. Quām facilis erat ab his initiis ad concordiam progressus, modō animos haberemus ad pacem compositos! Sed hoc principibus seculi non arridet, unionis inimicis etiam plurimum displicet: neque nobis fortē dabit Deus esse tam felicibus, ut ad hujusmodi unionem nostram qualemcunque operam conferamus. Relinquamus hoc illi, in cujus manu sunt rerum omnium tempora et occasiones. Sufficiat voluisse aliquid in tam insigni opere, fortē et semina in terram projecisse, quæ fructum tandem multiplicem proferant. Interim, quod nemo nobis denegare possit, nos invicem ut fratres, ut ejusdem mystici corporis membra, amplectamur.

No. XVI.

Extract of a Letter from Archbishop Wake to Mr. Beauvoir.

Feb. 9, S. V. 1719-20.

I HEARTILY wish there were either spirit or inclination enough in the Sorbonne to go on with our friend the abbe's project: but the fire decays, men's inclinations cool: the court will do nothing, and you are very sensible, that without the court nothing can be done in any such affair. Nevertheless, their good opinion of the church of England should be kept up as much as possible; we should encourage them all we can to account of us as of brethren, who have only thrown off, what they are weary of, the tyranny of the court of Rome, without any change in any fundamental article, either of the doctrine or government of the Ca holic church; and upon this ground I shall be ready to continue a brotherly correspondence with any of their great men, provided it be done with such caution, as may not expose my letters to be made prisoners to a secretary of state,—a thing which can never become my character, and may carry an ill aspect, even in our own court, till the thing be rightly understood.

No. XVII.

Extract of a Letter from the Archbishop to Mr. Beauvoir.

March 31, 1720.

I THANK you for your account of the present state of the French church. It is a very odd one indeed, but will settle into an agreement at last. When once the appellants begin to break, the court will drive all the *obstinate* (as they will call them; I should name them, the *honest* men, of courage and constancy) to a compliance.

No. XVIII.

Extract of a Letter from the Archbishop to Mr. Beauvoir.

April 19, O. S. 1720.

I PERCEIVE, by some late letters from him (Piers Girardin,) that he begins to despair of the business of the constitution. He has reason: the cardinal de Noailles is ensnared, and has gone too far to retire. The new archbishop of Cambray will be a cardinal; and this affair of the constitution must procure the *calot* for him. The regent himself is afraid of the Spanish party, and the Jesuits; and he will gain, or at least appease them. For all these reasons, the doctrine of the church, and the Gallican liberties, must be abandoned; and, on the slight pretence of a commt. of no esteem with the opposite party, an accommodation will certainly be made; and those who will not voluntarily go, shall be driven into it. If our poor friend be one of those who must hereby suffer, why may he not consider of a retreat hither, and, since he cannot yet bring on a union with the two churches, unite himself with ours, from which I am sure his principles, and I believe his inclinations, are not greatly distant? But this must be managed very tenderly, and rather by a kind of rallying, than a direct proposal of it. If he inclines to it, he will easily understand your meaning; if not, 'tis best not to go on far with him in a matter in which you will have no good success.

No. XIX.

Extract of a Letter from Archbishop Wake to Mr. le Clerc.

April, 1719.

NOVUM Testamentum Gallicum, notis tuis feliciter ornatum, totum, nec sine fructu, perlegi. Præfatione tuâ eidem præfixâ mirificè affectus sum; legi, relegi, quin et sæpiũs deinceps repetam. Ita me in ipso præsertim ejus initio commovit, ut veræ pietatis in eâ relucentem spiritum nunquam satis laudare possim, vel animo meo satis altè imprimere.

Et quamvis in annotationibus tuis quædam liberiũs dicta occurrant, quæ non æque omnibus placeant, neque mihi ipsi ubique satisfaciant; fero tamen, et vel in ipso tuo a communi sententiâ discessu aliquid mihi invenire videor, quod ignoscere magis quãm acerbiũs reprehendere debeam, multo minũs inclementiũs damnare. Libertatem prophetandi, modo pia ac sobria sit, cum charitate ac mansuetudine conjuncta, nec contra analogiam fidei semel sanctis traditæ, adeõ non vituperandam, ut etiam probandam, censeam. De rebus adiaphoris cum nemine contendendum puto. Ecclesias reformatas, etsi in aliquibus a nostrâ Anglicanâ dissentientes, libenter amplector. Optarem equidem regimen episcopale benè temperatum, et ab omni injustâ dominatione sejunctum, quale apud nos obtinet, et, siquid ego in his rebus sapiam, ab ipso apostolorum ævo in ecclesiâ receptum fuerit, et ab iis omnibus fuisset retentum; nec despero quin aliquando restitutum, si non ipse videam, at posteri videbunt. Interim absit ut ego tam ferrei pectoris sim, ut ob ejusmodi defectum (sic mihi absque omni invidiâ appellare liceat) aliquas earum a communione nostrâ abscindendas credam; aut, cum quibusdam furiosis inter nos scriptoribus, eas nulla vera ac valida sacramenta habere, adeõque vix Christianos esse pronuntiem. Unionem arctiorem inter omnes reformatos procurare quovis pretio vellem. Hæc si in regimine ecclesiastico ac publicis ecclesiarum officiis obtineri potuit; aut ego plurimum fallor, aut id solum brevi conduceret ad animorum inter eos unionem conciliandam, et viam sterneret ad plenam in omnibus majoris momenti dogmatibus concordiam stabiliendam. Quantum hoc ad religionis nostræ securitatem conduceret; quantum etiam ad pseudo-catholicorum Romanensium conversionem, cæcus sit qui non videat.—Sed abripuit me longius quãm par esset hæc semper mihi dulcis de pace ac unione ecclesiarum reformatarum cogitatio, &c.

No. XX.

Archbishop Wake's letter to the pastors and professors of Geneva.

8th April, 1719.

QUAMVIS literis vestris nihil mihi gratius potuit afferri, non tamen absque summo dolore, vix oculis siccis, eas perlegi; neque credo quenquam esse tam ferrei pectoris, qui ad ea mala quæ in illis referentur non perhorrescat, mireturque talia ab hominibus erga homines, a popularibus erga populares suos, a Christianis denique erga Christianos, idque (quod fidem omnem exuperare valeat) etiam religionis causâ, fieri et perpetrari.

Vos interim, venerandi viri, quod vestri erat officii, sedulo præstitistis. Delegatos ecclesiarum Hungaricarum amicè accepistis. Querimoniam eorum, eâ quâ par erat charitate atque sympathiâ fraternâ audivistis; nullâque morâ ad hibatâ, ad remedium malis ipsorum inveniendum omnes vestras cogitationes convertistis. Per illustres magistratus vestros, cæteros reformatæ religionis principes atque senatores, ad persecutiones horum fratrum vestrorum seriõ considerandas, excitavistis, et ut suam authoritatem interponerent ad sedandas eorum oppressiones enixissimè obsecrâstis

Denique, nequid vel minimi ponderis desideretur quo studium vestrum in hoc tam insigni charitatis opere exequendo ostendatis, etiam meâ qualicunque operâ uti voluistis, ad animum augustissimi regis nostri commovendum, ne in hâc tam gravi suâ necessitate afflictis Christi servis deesset.

O amorem vere Christianum! et qualem deceat ejusdem corporis membra erga se invicem habere! Dignum profecto et vobis, et eximio illo vestro congressu, opus; ut quo præcipuè tempore convenistis ad laudes Dei celebrandas, qui per duo jam secula religionem reformatam vobis incolumem servaverit, eodem etiam illam ipsam religionem evangelicam in aliis regionibus oppressam, concussam, ac tantum non extremum quasi spiritum trahentem, sublevetis et si fieri possit, in integrum restituatis.

Ego vero, fratres charissimi, et propriâ voluntate motus, et vestro tam illustri exemplo impulsus, adeo eodem vobiscum ardore accendor, ut nihil non tentandum putem, quo vestris tam piis, tam justis, tamque benignis conatibus optatum successum compararem.

Imprimis igitur nobilem virum comitem Sunderlandiæ primarium regis ministrum sedulò adivi: literas vestras illi communicavi; petii, oravi, ut in hâc re suam mihi operam utque auxilium concedere vellet; utque simul regiam majestatem adiremus; non quod de ipsius promptâ voluntate dubitarem, sed ut quæ in hâc causâ facienda essent, eo majori vigore atque promptitudine perficerentur. Successit, ferè ultrà spem, conatis noster. Utriusque ecclesiæ tum Hungaricæ tum vicinæ Vallensis, oppressiones regi, eo quo par erat affectu, exposuimus. Favorem ejus atque authoritatem apud Cæsarem regemque Sardiniæ obnixè imploravimus, ut ab his tam injustis vexationibus, eorum jussu et mandatis, liberentur. Et præcipuè quod ad Pedemontanas ecclesias attinet etiam adhortati sumus, ut jure suo a rege Sardiniæ postularet, ut pacta in his quæ religionis exercitium concernent, earum gratiâ inita, meliori fide in posterum observentur. Annuit votis nostris rex serenissimus; neque dubito quin legatis suis jamdudum præceperit, ut omnem quam possunt operam suo nomine impendant, quo ab istis adeo iniquis oppressionibus utriusque ecclesiæ membra liberentur. Orandus Deus ut tanti principis conatibus, in hâc tam justâ, tam piâ, tam religioni Christianæ proficuâ interpellatione, aspirare dignetur, et oppressis suis servis exoptatam requiem tandem concedere, pro immensâ suâ misericordiâ, velit.

Interim, dum hæc feliciter, uti spero, peraguntur, ignoscite, fratres dilectissimi, si majoris quidem laboris atque difficultatis, sed longè maximi omnibus commodi, inceptum, vobis proponam; in quo et sæpe alias et hoc tempore complures primariæ dignitatis viri summo studio allaborant; et quod ab omnibus, quibus puritas Evangelii reipsa cordi sit, unâ secum allaborandum sperant. Jamdudum sentitis quo mea tendit adhortatio; ad unionem nimirum inter omnes quæ ubique sunt ecclesias, quæ his ultimis seculis a communione, seu veriùs tyrannide pontificis Romani, sese subduxerunt, sedulò promovendam. Quin hoc fieri possit, si quidem animum ad concordiam promptum omnes attulerimus, nullatenus dubitandum est: quin fieri debeat, nemo prudens negaverit, &c. &c.

Vos interim, F. C. hoc agite, ut saltum inter vos ipsos pax atque concordia inviolabiliter conserventur. Summo quippe dolore, anno præterito, accepi dissensiones inter vos ortas fuisse, de capitulis aliquot circa doctrinam de gratiâ universali, aliisque quæstionibus longè difficillimis, in quibus optimi viri et doctissimi theologi idem per omnia haudquaquam sentiunt. Angit hoc sanè, idque non mediocriter, animum meum. Et quamvis nollem vobis videri ἀλλοτριοεπισκοπεῖν, aut in alienam (quod aiunt) messem falcem meam immittere; permittite tamen ut in spiritu charitatis, eoque quo erga vos feror amore fraterno, vos obsecrem, et in Domino obtester, ut in hujusmodi rebus, quatenus id fieri possit, idem sentiatis omnes; quod si id non assequi veleatis, ut saltem sic alii alios feratis, ut nullum sit inter vos schisma, nullus querimoniæ aliquorum adversus alios locus; ut non nimium curiosi sitis in iis determinandis quæ Deus non admodum clarè revelaverit, quæque absque salutis dispendio tutò nesciri poterint; quæ sapientissimi prædecessores nostri, in omnibus suis confessionibus, cautè tractanda censuerunt, eâque moderatione, ut universi in iis subscribendis consentirent; et à quorum prudenti cautelâ sicubi posteà discessum fuerit, contentiones, lites inimicitiæ, aliaque infinita incommoda, protinus subsecuta sunt.

In his disquisitionibus Lutherani à reformatis dissident; nec reformati ipsi prorsus inter se conveniunt. Ecclesia Anglicana optimo consilio, exemplo ab omnibus imitando, nullius conscientiæ, his in rebus, jugum imponit. Quæ de illis in articulis suis statuerit, talia sunt, ut ab omnibus ex æquo admittantur. His contenta, nec ipsa aliquid amplius requirit curiosiùs statuere. Hinc summa inter nos pax cum sobriâ sentiendi libertate conjuncta. Utinam et vobis, iisdem conditionibus, concordia stabiliatur, utque veteri confessione vestrâ Helveticâ contenti, neque alicui permitteretis aliter docere, neque ab aliquo quidpiam profitendum requireretis ultrâ id quod ab initio requisitum fuerit; cum tamen summi illi viri Calvinus et Beza (ut de aliis taceatur) secus de his articulis sentirent, quàm alii plures; quos tamen non solùm tolerandos, sed et pro fratribus habendos ritè ac sapienter judicârunt.

Hoc vobis non modò pacem inter vos ipsos conciliabit, verùm etiam concordiam cum aliis ecclesiis reformatis sartam tectam tuebitur. Absque hujusmodi temperamine, unio illa cum Protestantibus, tantopere desiderata, nullo modo iniri poterit; vos, igitur, seriò hæc, ut par est, considerate: nec a nobis, a plerisque aliis reformatis, etiam a vestris antecessoribus, novis ac durioribus impositionibus secedite, &c.

N. B. The former part of this letter, which relates to the intercession of archbishop Wake in behalf of the Hungarian and Piedmontese churches, has never been hitherto published. The latter part, beginning with these words, "Interim dum hæc feliciter peraguntur, ignoscite," &c. was inserted, by Professor Turretin of Geneva, in his work entitled, Nubes Testium. The words "Interim dum hæc," &c. were, from an ignorance of their connex ion with what goes before, supposed by some learned men to relate to the projected union between the English and Gallican churches; and Kiorning, who says in his Dissertation de Consecrationibus Episcoporum Anglorum, that Dr. Wake communicated this project to the divines of Geneva, fell into this mistake, and probably drew Dr. Mosheim after him.

No. XXI.

Extract from Archbishop Wake's Letter to Professor Schurer, of Bern, July, 1718.

De Angliâ nostrâ te peramanter et sentire et scribere plurimūm gaudeo. Quanquam enim non adeō cæcus sim patriæ meæ amator, ut non plurima hîc videam quæ vel penitūs sublata vel in meliūs mutata quovis pretio vellem, tamen aliqua etiam in hac temporum fæce occurrere, optimis etiam seculis digna, et quæ ipsa primæva ecclesia Christiana probare, ne dicam et laudare, potuisset, et tu æquissimè agnoscis et nos nobis gratulamur.

No. XXII.

To Professor Turretin, July, 1718.

Speaking of Bishop Davenant's opinion as agreeable to his own.

Utinam sic sentiremus omnes, et, fundamentalibus religionis articulis semper salvis, nihil ultrā ab aliquo subscribendum requireremus, quod bonorum hominum conscientiis oneri esse potest, certè ecclesiæ utilitatem parūm promovebit.—Ut enim de hâc ecclesiarum reformatarum utilitate paucis dicam; primum earum stabilimentum in hoc consistere, ut omnes sese, quantūm fieri possit, contra papalem potentiam ac tyrannidem tueantur, nemini credo dubium esse posse. Ut in hunc finem quām arctissimè inter se uniantur, et in idem corpus coalescant, adeō ut siquid alicui ex iis ecclesiæ damni aut detrimenti ā communi hoste fuerit illatum, id ab omnibus tanquām suum haberetur, concedi etiam necesse est.

Ut denique pax et concordia cujuslibet ecclesiæ reformatæ inter suos, ac cum aliis omnibus ejusmodi ecclesiis conserventur; unicuique viro bono, sed præsertim ecclesiarum illarum magistratibus atque ministris, totis viribus enitendum esse, adeō clarè apparet, ut nullâ probatione firmiori indigeat.

Afterwards:

Quid in hâc re aliud faciendum restat, nisi ut tuâ et amicorum tuorum auctoritate primō facultas vestra theologica, magistratus, ministri, cives Genevenses, deinde eorum exemplo atque hortatu reliqua etiam fœderis Helvetici membra reformata, omnem lapidem moveant, ut pacem ecclesiis Bernensibus restituant? Neque id ego sic fieri vellem, ut non simul et religionis veritati et doctrinæ puritati consulatur. Subscribant ministri, professores, theologi, confessioni vestræ veteri anno* [ ] editæ: prohibeantur, sub quâvis-libet pœnâ, ne ullam in concionibus, scriptis, thesibus, prælectionibus, sententiam publicè tueantur illi confessioni quovis modo contrariam. Id solum caveatur, ne multiplicentur hujusmodi subscriptiones absque necessitate; neque strictè nimis inquiratur in privatas hominum eruditorum sententias; modo suis opinionibus frui pacificè velint, et neque docendo, neque disputando, neque scribendo, ā publicâ confessione secedere, aut errores suos (si tamen errores reverâ fuerint) in scandalum cujus-vis, multō magis ecclesiæ aut reipublicæ divulgare.—Habes, vir spectatissime, sententiam meam.

* The date of the confession of faith is omitted in the archbishop's letter.

No. XXIII.

Extract from a Letter of Archbishop Wake to Professor Schurer, July, 1719.

Quæ de formulâ Consensûs mihi narras, abundè placent, qui, uti nolim laqueum absque causâ injici conscientiis bonorum atque eruditorum hominum, ita neque fræna laxanda censeo quibuscunque novatoribus ad pacem publicè turbandam, eaque vel scribenda vel docenda, quæ viris piis jure scandalum præbeant, quæque confessioni vestræ olim stabilitæ falsitatis notam injuriâ inurere videantur Intra hos igitur limites si steterint magistratus vestri, neque aliquid ampliùs à Lausannensibus requirant, nisi ut hoc demūm fine formulæ consensûs subscribant; sperandum est nullum schisma, eâ de causâ, inter vos exoriturum. Pacem publicam tueri, etiam in rebus ad fidem spectantibus, magistratus Christianus et potest et debet. Conscientiis hominum credenda imponere, nisi in rebus claris et perspicuis, et ad salutem omninō necessariis, nec potest, nec debet. Quod si contra faciat, subditis tamen semper licebit ad apostolorum exemplar, si quidem aliquid falsi, aut incertæ veritatis, iis subscribendum injunxerint, obedire Deo potiūs quām hominibus.

No. XXIV.

Extracts from Archbishop Wake's Letter to Professor Turretin, in answer to one from him, dated December 1, 1718.

Res Bernensium ecclesiasticas nondum penitūs tranquillas esse et doleo et miror; eōque magis, quod hisce temporibus hæ de decretis divinis altercationes ubique ferè alibi ad exitum sint perductæ. Quæ mea sit de iis sententia, nec adhuc cuiquam apertè declaravi, neque, ut deinceps patefaciam, facilè me patiar induci. Hoc apud nos, tum ex mandatis regiis, tum ex diu servatâ (utinam semper servandâ) consuetudine fixum est atque stabilitum, neque ā quoquam exquirere quid de his rebus sentiat, modo articulis religionis, publicâ auctoritate constitutis, subscribat; neque in concionibus aut etiam disputationibus theologicis, aliquid amplius de iis determinare, quam quod illi articuli expressè statuant, et ab omnibus ad ministerii munus admittendis profitendum requirant.

Then follows an historical narrative of the rise, and occasion, and censure of the Lambeth articles; as also of the rise and progress of Arminianism under the reigns of James I. and Charles I., and of the subsiding of all dis-

putes of that kind under Charles II.—He then subjoins,

Et quidem illud imprimis observatu dignum æstimo, quàm moderatè, quàm prudenter, in hâc tam difficili disquisitione, optimi illi viri, martyres ac confessores Christi constantissimi, quos Divina Providentia ad reformandam hanc nostram ecclesiam seligere dignatus est, se gesserunt. Non illi curiositati cujusvis aliquid indulgendum putârunt; non vanis et incertis hominum hypothesibus de decretis divinis alicujus fidem alligare fas esse consuerunt. Sciebant quàm inscrutabilia sint consilia Dei, et quanto intervallo omnes nostras cogitationes exuperent. Ideòque non religiosè minùs quàm sapienter inter justos terminos sese continuerunt; neque in necessariis ad fidem nostram de hisce mysteriis stabiliendam deficientes; neque in nonnecessariis determinandis officiosi; unde fortè pro verâ fide errorem, pro pace discordiam, pro fraternâ unione ac charitate divisionem, odia, inimicitias in ecclesiam Christi inducere poterant.

Hæc fuit eorum simplicitas verè evangelica; pietate non minùs quàm sapientiâ commendabilis; eòque magis suspicienda, ac ferè pro divinâ habenda, quod tot annorum experientiâ reperta sit non solùm optimam fuisse pacis ac concordiæ regulam, verùm etiam unicum contra schismata et divisiones remedium.

HISTORY

OF THE

CHRISTIAN CHURCH

DURING

THE EIGHTEENTH CENTURY;

FORMING

A CONTINUATION OF DR. MOSHEIM'S WORK.

INTRODUCTION

THE generality of readers, more intent on the consideration of modern affairs than on the contemplation of ancient occurrences, are induced to expect, from historic writers, a much more copious detail of recent than of early transactions. The expectation is natural and reasonable; and it is therefore readily gratified by historians. But, like other rules, this also may be allowed to have an exception. In modern times, the affairs of the church move in a more regular course, and are conducted with far greater tranquillity, than in earlier periods; and hence a narrative of such occurrences may prove less interesting than the ecclesiastical history of many preceding ages, and may consequently require a less minute detail and less frequent reflection.

Dr. Mosheim, in all probability, if he had lived to the close of the eighteenth century, would have given an elaborate and ample sequel to his valuable history;* but the writer who has undertaken to continue that work has neither the leisure nor the inclination to expatiate upon the subject. It would not, perhaps, be very difficult for him to fill volumes with a specification of the religious and ecclesiastical affairs of the last century: but he does not conceive hat such diffusion is necessary, and he hopes that a concise statement, with incidental remarks, will content his readers.

Those who wish for a copious history of the Christian church during that period, must wait for the exertions of some erudite and able divine, who may have time and patience for the accomplishment of the task.

April 3, 1811. C. COOTE.

* Such a conclusion may be drawn from what he says at the beginning of his sketch of that century 'Sæculi, quod vivimus, historia Christiana voluminis, non paginarum paucarum, materies est, suumque inter posteros scriptorem ingenuum et æquum expectat;'—a passage which may be thus translated· 'The history of the Christian church, during the century in which we live, is the proper subject of a considerable volume, rather than of only a few pages; and it demands from posterity a writer who will pay due attention to it,—a liberal impartial, and judicious author.

HISTORY OF THE CHRISTIAN CHURCH

DURING

THE EIGHTEENTH CENTURY.

CHAPTER I.

History of the Romish Church, during the Eighteenth Century.

The continued attacks of the Protestants upon the church of Rome had forced the outworks, and weakened the barriers of that establishment: but it still presented a bold front to its assailants, and numbered among its votaries the major part of the inhabitants of Europe. Its greatness was impaired, but not subverted; and it had an imposing, if not a very formidable aspect. The pope's power of interdiction and excommunication had ceased to fill nations with dismay. Some of the potentates of his communion addressed him in a tone which many of his predecessors would not have endured; harassed him with various pretensions, and encroached upon that authority which he deemed legitimate and even divine. Notwithstanding these assaults, he retained some degree of power and a considerable portion of influence, and was supported in the dignity of supreme pontiff by the greatest princes of the continent.

The prelate who occupied this high station at the commencement of that century of which we are now treating, was Clement XI. or John Francis Albani, who, having acquired reputation by his skill in the management of affairs, and being also of a spirited character, had been unanimously chosen by the conclave at a time when the political horizon of Europe threatened a storm. He rejected the offered tiara with a greater appearance of sincerity than that which an English divine usually displays when he says, on the offer of a bishopric, *nolo episcopari;* but his scruples and objections were removed by the arguments, representations, and importunities of the cardinals.

He made a good beginning of administration. He redressed some grievances, discountenanced vice and criminality of every kind, performed acts of beneficence, gave an example of devotional regularity, and filled vacant offices and preferments with men of merit. He then directed his attention to politics, and testified a desire of preventing a war between the king of France and the emperor, on the subject of the Spanish succession. He wrote a letter to each of those princes, exhorting them to accommodate all disputes without rushing into hostilities. They received his advice with professions of respect for his character, but did not suffer it to regulate their conduct. Ambition still inflamed the aged Louis: his thirst of dominion still urged him to send forth his legions, and *wantonly* (for a lust of power was no *sufficient motive*,) to shed the blood of his unoffending fellow creatures. Leopold professed an equal regard for religion, but was equally uninfluenced by justice or humanity.

With respect to the religious principles of these royal sons of the church, we may observe, that they were not animated by true piety, or a genuine spirit of religion. They may have believed the doctrines of Christianity; or, perhaps, they merely affected to give credit to the faith which they found established in their dominions. They attended mass with decorous regularity, witnessed ceremonial observances with a serious and devout aspect, and promoted among their subjects a religious uniformity. But they did not endeavour, like true Christians, to correct their evil propensities, amend their hearts, or reform their lives. They did not study to preserve "peace upon earth;" they did not cherish "good will towards men." Their religion (in the language applied by a respectable historian* to William the Conqueror) "prompted them to endow monasteries, but at the same time allowed them to pillage kingdoms: it threw them on their knees before a relic or a cross, but suffered them unrestrained to trample upon the liberties and the rights of mankind."

We have no concern with the war into which the rival princes entered, as it is unconnected with the history of the church. It arose from temporal motives, and referred to grand political objects. Both princes promised that, if the war should extend to Italy, the papal territories should remain uninjured and unmolested: but this promise was violated, on the part of Leopold, by the irruption of an Austrian detachment into the province of Ferrara. Clement having bitterly complained of this conduct, the troops retired: but, as they again encroached, he ordered an army to be levied. Louis, and his grandson the new king of Spain, earnestly requested his holiness to enter into an alliance with them, promising great advantages not only to the holy see, but to the pontiff himself, as the price of his condescension. He had no wish to take part with either of the contending families, and therefore refused to accede to the confederacy. A report was propagated of his assent to the offered terms; and it derived strength from the appearance of the duke of Berwick at Rome; but that nobleman was merely sent from France by the royal exile, James II., to congratulate Albani on his elevation to the papal throne.

Unable to check the rage of war, the pope soothed his anxiety, and gratified his religious zeal, by promoting the diffusion of the catholic faith. He even expressed a wish that he could visit the remotest parts of the globe for that pious and salutary purpose, and lamented his inability of accomplishing his desire. Contracting his views he contented himself with

* George Lord Lyttleton.

sending legates into various regions, particularly into Persia, India, and China, to support and extend the interests of Christianity: but the success of these heralds of the Gospel did not correspond with the wishes of the religious world. We are informed, however, that his entreaties and expostulations procured, for the catholics of Thrace, Armenia, and Syria, a respite from Mohammedan persecution, and an allowance of the free exercise of their religion.* This freedom, however, was occasionally interrupted and disturbed by the brutality of furious infidels, and the animosity of barbarian zealots.

The legate upon whom he chiefly depended, for the success of the eastern mission, was Maillard de Tournon, who was ready to encounter every danger in the cause of Christianity. This missionary visited India and China with a weak and declining frame, but with a heart full of pious zeal. He introduced himself to the Chinese emperor at Pekin; was politely received, and complimented with various presents; and was gratified with permission to preach the Gospel, and expound the doctrines of the catholic faith. The imperial potentate, however, did not mean that this permission should so far operate, as to authorise the legate and his associates to oppose the prevalence of popular institutions and ceremonies, sanctioned by long practice. Unwilling to make any concessions to the prejudices of paganism, Tournon loudly exclaimed against the idolatrous usages of the Chinese, and sharply reproved the ministers of state and of religion, for suffering the continuance of such degrading absurdities. By this freedom he gave great offence to the court; and he was even accused of treason against the emperor. Defying the odium which he considered as unmerited, he proceeded in his pious career, until he was banished from the capital, in 1707, and sent to the island of Macao, where he was imprisoned with five of his fellow missionaries. Admiring his undaunted zeal, the pope elevated him to the dignity of a cardinal; an honour which he declared he would not accept, if he should be expected to relinquish his mission; for he was prepared to suffer every inconvenience, and undergo every species of persecution, in the discharge of Christian duties. When the governor of the Philippine islands offered to facilitate his escape, he peremptorily refused to quit his prison. He died, not without suspicion of poison, after he had been confined above three years. The mission was continued after his death; but it did not promise to be successful, as the prejudices of the Chinese were too firmly fixed to be easily eradicated.†

Clement, in the mean time, continued to observe, with an anxious eye, the commotions of Europe. When the emperor had proclaimed his son (the archduke Charles) king of Spain, his holiness refused to acknowledge the young prince in that capacity. A new invasion of Ferrara followed; but the Austrians did not venture to make a conquest of that territory, as Leopold was unwilling to inflict any serious injury on the pontiff. As soon as Joseph became emperor, he manifested a stronger inclination than his father had evinced, to thwart and harass the head of the church. He restricted the papal authority in point of presentation to benefices; seized Comacchio, and claimed Parma and Placentia as imperial fiefs. His troops levied contributions in the ecclesiastical state, and alarmed the timid inhabitants. At length, however, he consented to an accommodation,* and ceased to be a refractory son of the church.

A revival of the contest between the Jansenists and the Jesuits had for some time conspired with politics and war to disturb the tranquillity of the court of Rome.† M. Du-Pin had published, in 1703, a Case of Conscience, in which (according to the pope's letter to the king of France) various errors already condemned were revived, and the heretical tenets of Jansenius defended; and for this offence he was banished from Paris into the province of Bretagne. Forty doctors of the Sorbonne, whose names appeared among the signatures of approbation that accompanied the *Case*, were desired to submit to the will of the pontiff; and many of them recanted, while others denied that they had given assent to the book. For the more effectual repression of Jansenism, a new apostolical constitution was issued in 1705, condemning such errors with menaces of papal indignation. The archbishop of Sebaste, vicar of the holy see in Holland, was removed from his employment for a supposed collusion with the Jansenists; and these sectaries were again subjected to ecclesiastical censure in 1708, when the pope condemned the Moral Reflections of their celebrated associate, Quesnel, upon the New Testament. This theologian answered the damnatory bull with a spirit which inflamed the contest. The partisans of Rome called for a new and more explicit condemnation of the Reflections; and the king of France, prejudiced against a sect which the Jesuits represented as even more dangerous to the church than that of the Huguenots, earnestly solicited the promulgation of a rigorous edict. Hence arose that decree which was addressed to the whole catholic world, but which more particularly demanded the attention and observance of the Gallican church.‡

The Anti-Jansenist ordinance, as it commenced with the terms *Unigenitus Dei Filius*, was quickly known throughout Christendom by the appellation of the bull *Unigenitus*. Alleging and lamenting the inefficacy of the former condemnation of Quesnel's book, the pontiff was determined, he said, to apply a stronger remedy to the growing disease. Some catholic truths, he allowed, were mingled with the mass of corrupt doctrine: but, as the insidious

* Guarnacci, Vit. et Res Gest. Pontificum Romanorum et Cardinalium, usque ad Clementem XII. tom. ii p. 7.

† Guarnacci, Vit. Pontif. et Cardin. tom. ii. p. 143, 144.

* In the year 1708.

† For an account of the rise of this controversy, and of the doctrines propagated by Jansenius, see Dr. Mosheim's fifth volume. cent. xvii. sect. ii. part i. chap. i.

‡ Guarnacci, Vit. Pontif. et Cardin. tom. ii. p. 11, 18, 19.—Histoire de France, sous le Regne de Louis XIV. par M. de Larrey, tom. iii.– This bull made its appearance on the 8th of September, 1713. N. S.

and seductive manner in which the errors were brought forward, had occasioned a neglect of the sound portion of the work, it was necessary to separate the tares from the wheat. He and his counsellors, therefore, had extracted a hundred and one propositions from the book; and these he now condemned as false, captious, scandalous, pernicious, rash, seditious, impious, blasphemous, schismatic, and heretical. Not content with censuring these passages, he subjoined a prohibition of the whole performance, and cautioned the people, on pain of excommunication, against the perusal of any vindication or defence of it, which had been, or might be, offered to the public.

This bull, perhaps, the good sense of Clement would have forborne to promulgate, if the zeal of the bigoted and domineering Louis had not overawed or perverted the pontiff; though it may with equal plausibility be supposed, that the pope's zeal was sufficient for the object, without any solicitation whatever. The Jansenists, persecuted by that intolerant prince for disregarding the new papal *constitution*, expected less rigorous treatment when Philip duke of Orleans became regent of France. The cardinal de Noailles, who had warmly supported their cause, was introduced into the cabinet: those who had been banished were recalled: the resolutions which the Sorbonne had adopted in favour of the bull, were annulled, as the effect of constraint; and the conduct of the court of Rome was publicly and acrimoniously condemned. The pope remonstrated against these proceedings, and urged the propriety of submitting to the holy see: but the Jansenists called for a general council, calculated to heal the disorders of the church. The Jesuits denied the necessity of such a convocation, and complained of the arrogance of the demand. The regent at length began to listen to the persuasions of the bigoted party, and menaced the opposers of the bull with his resentment. He banished M. Ravechet, syndic of the Sorbonne, into Roussillon; but he would not consent to the disposition of that resolute academic, who died in the midst of these disputes. An assembly of prelates, convoked by Philip, in vain endeavoured to reconcile the parties; and twenty commissioners, nominated for the same purpose, were not more successful in their exertions. The parliament of Paris took cognizance of the affair, in consequence of an appeal from some priests whom the archbishop of Rheims had excommunicated for their opposition to the will of his holiness. The spiritual sentence was declared null and void, and the prelate who had pronounced it was condemned in costs and damages. The Jansenists now became more bold in their attacks, until the regent, alleging the inutility of these disputes, imposed silence by a royal declaration.*

An edict which confounded the advocates of truth and of sound doctrine with misguided zealots, displeased both parties. The pope accused the regent of insincerity and injustice, and of enmity to that church which he was bound to protect. To the cardinal de Noailles he sent a letter, mingling expostulations with entreaty, which did not subdue the firmness of that prelate. The cardinal's appeal from the bull or "constitution of the holy father to the pope better advised, and to a future general council," was condemned by the court of inquisition at Rome as a scandalous libel; and its circulation and perusal were strictly prohibited. A papal brief afterwards appeared,* commanding all Christians throughout the world to withhold their favour and regard from the opposers of the constitution, and threatening these unworthy sons of the church, in case of prolonged contumacy, with a forfeiture of all ecclesiastical privileges. This brief, exciting the indignation of the Parisian parliament, was suppressed by an *arret*.

In the progress of the contest, the pope's adherents strengthened their party; and the Jansenist leaders assumed a more conciliatory tone. The cardinal declared his readiness to accept the constitution, according to his own explanation of it; and, with this qualification, he condemned the work of Quesnel. Some of the clergy disapproved the explanations, as being almost equally objectionable with the bull itself; and, on the other hand, the chief promoters of that act or decree insisted on an absolute and unreserved submission to its obvious import. Many of the French bishops condescended to explain it, in the hope of removing the scruples of the conscientious Jansenists; but the pope, while he commended the zeal and good intentions of those prelates, denied the necessity of their exertions, as the wisdom and authority of the head of the church, who was allowed to dictate to the faithful, did not require, from any of its members, explanatory aid or argumentative enforcement.

The pope ultimately prevailed in the contest. The regent resolved to gratify the majority of the higher clergy by giving the sanction of the court to the papal edict, after it had been for seven years an object of dispute. It was ordained,† that the constitution *Unigenitus*, received by the bishops, should be observed by all orders of people in the French dominions; that no university or incorporated society, and no individual of any description whatever, should speak, write, maintain or teach, directly or indirectly, any thing repugnant to the ordinance, or to the explanations given of it by the dignitaries of the Gallican church; that all appeals and proceedings against it should be deemed void; and that the courts of parliament, and all judges, should assist the prelates in the execution of spiritual censures. The parliament of Paris at first refused to register this decree, which, said some of its members, not only derogated from the dignity of the crown, but militated against the rights of the subject, and the liberties of the Gallican church; but it was confirmed by the great council, and promulgated as an operative law. Even the cardinal de Noailles at length acquiesced in it; and a parliamentary registration was procured by menaces of removal or of exile.‡

* October 7, 1717, N. S.—Guarnacci, Vit. Pontificum et Cardin. tom. ii. p. 21. 22.

* Dated August 28, 1718.

† August 4, 1720.

‡ Memoires de la Regence

The exertions of the cardinal Du-Bois were of signal service in subduing the spirit of the principal Jansenists, and, after the registration of the edict, he made occasional use of *lettres de cachet* against refractory individuals, and revived the oath introduced by Louis XIV. which all candidates for holy orders, and for academical degrees, were obliged to take, importing that the five propositions of Jansenius, respecting grace and free will, were justly condemned.

Clement was highly pleased at this accommodation; but his joy was allayed by the consideration of his declining health. He died in the spring of the following year, at the age of seventy-one years, during twenty of which he had occupied the pontifical throne. His catholic biographer ascribes to him an acute understanding and a tenacious memory, an unwearied zeal in the pursuit of learning, a firmness of mind united with benevolence of disposition and courtesy of manners, and a freedom from anger and resentment.*

His secretary, cardinal Paulucci, would have been chosen to succeed him, if the intrigues of the Austrian faction had not baffled the views of the Italian members of the conclave, whose advantage in point of number yielded to imperial tyranny. After a vacancy of seven weeks, the pontifical chair was filled with Michael Angelo Conti, son of the duke of Poli, who assumed the designation of Innocent XIII. Being in a weak state of health at the time of his election, he did not long preside over the church, his government not being extended by Providence to the end even of the third year.

It was one of the first cares of this pontiff to accommodate the dispute respecting the investiture of the kingdom of Naples. The emperor and the king of Spain had in vain solicited that favour from the late pope: but it was now granted to the former prince, on the acknowledgement of tributary subjection to the holy see. Another object of Innocent's attention was the maintenance of the papal claim to the sovereignty of Parma and Placentia; but he did not, in that respect, succeed to his wish. In the mean time he exercised his authority at Rome with mildness, and sometimes with that severity which appeared to be necessary. To other parts of Christendom he also extended his care and vigilance: and Spain, in particular, felt his corrective hand. Observing with serious concern, and indeed with strong disgust, the dissolute manners both of the clergy and laity in that country, he issued an admonitory and threatening edict for the repression of irregular, disorderly, and vicious practices. He had no doubt of the religious zeal and decorous behaviour of his catholic majesty,† but lamented, on this occasion, the insufficient influence even of royal example.‡

Amidst the cares of spiritual and temporal government, Innocent found his health seriously declining. Hydropic symptoms alarmed him; and other disorders conspired to put an end to his life, in the spring of the year 1724, at the age of 68. Few pontiffs were ever more popular among their temporal subjects than Innocent XIII., whose death, therefore, was sincerely lamented. His successor was cardinal Vincent Orsini (eldest son of the duke of Gravina,) who, having an early sense of piety, had rejected the offer of a splendid marriage, renounced a rich inheritance in favour of a younger brother, and entered into the clerical order, in which he distinguished himself by his indefatigable zeal as a preacher, by his rigid attention to all points of duty, and his scrupulous avoidance of every species of luxury and excess.

The beginning of the pontificate of Benedict XIII,—for so the new pope was styled—was marked by an edict against luxury and fantastic extravagance in dress; and, that he might not seem to attend more to *minutiæ* than to objects of importance, he took every opportunity of recommending a strict regard to moral and social duties, and a steady practice of Christian virtues. His exhortations and injunctions had some effect: but, when one head of the *hydra* of vice was stricken off, another instantly grew in its place. If the wishes of Benedict, however, were not answered, he consoled himself by reflecting that he had done his duty. That consciousness will always impart pleasure to a pious mind. It will soothe the Christian moralist amidst the evils of life, and at the approach of death.

It was in the first year of his government that the affair of Thorn occurred, which, while it contributed to the supposed advantage of the catholic church by injuring the protestant interest in Poland, wounded the feelings of the pontiff, who lamented and reprobated the cruelty that attended the triumph of the Romanists on that occasion. Some Lutherans neglecting or refusing to kneel at a procession of the host, a student of the Jesuits' college reproached and even struck them, and some other zealots of that seminary afterwards insulted the peaceful inhabitants. The aggressor being apprehended and confined, his comrades demanded and obtained his release: but they were not suffered to rescue another who had been seized by the city-guard. Enraged at this disappointment, they committed various outrages; and, in retaliation, the college was attacked and plundered by the populace. The president of the city, on pretence of his connivance at this tumult on the part of the people, was decapitated by order of a Polish tribunal: nine other citizens were subjected to the same fate; and the privileges of the Lutheran inhabitants were arbitrarily annulled. This barbarity disgusted those catholics who had any sense of humanity, and excited the indignation of every protestant community. The Jesuits, however, maintained, that they had only inflicted due chastisement on their insolent adversaries, who had entered into a nefarious conspiracy against their catholic fellow-citizens; and the king of Poland boasted, in the same spirit of bigotry that he had vindicated, by the punishment of profane heretics, the honour and dignity of true religion That prince seemed to think that he had sufficiently blended mercy with justice, by sparing the

* Guarnacci Vit. Pontificum et Cardinalium, tom. ii. p. 36. † Philip V.
‡ Guarnacci, Vit. Pontif. tom. ii. p. 384, 385.

lives of the vice-president and some other citizens who had been condemned. The Jesuits had, at this time, too great an influence at the court of Warsaw; and they rarely exerted that influence in the cause of justice or of humanity.

The more humane and benevolent pontiff consoled himself, amidst these sanguinary deeds, by a bloodless triumph of that religion which he superintended. We allude to the jubilee of the year 1725, which he opened with great solemnity, and which gladdened the faithful with the confident hopes of a plenary remission of their sins. He afterwards held a provincial council in the Lateran church, chiefly for a reform of the conduct of the clergy; and the assembly voted for an enforcement of some decrees that had been enacted by the council of Trent, but which had fallen into disuse. On another occasion, he rose above the bigotry of his predecessors, by expressing a wish for the diffusion of scriptural knowledge; and, with that view, he permitted the people in general to peruse the sacred volume, and encouraged the multiplication of copies in the modern languages. This permission displeased the rigid catholics; but it was approved by a majority of the members of that church. Benedict, about the same time, testified his devotion to the Muses, by publicly decorating Perfetti, a Tuscan poet, with a crown of laurel.

A grand scheme of religious comprehension was formed by this respectable ruler of the church. It was of no less magnitude than the union of the four communities that divided Christendom. He proposed, that four councils should be holden at different places at the same time, each consisting of a certain number of representatives of the Romish, Greek, Lutheran, and Calvinist churches, with a president of one or other church in each assembly; that the mass should be so altered as not to be repugnant to the feelings of the three last denominations of Christians; that unpleasing or obnoxious doctrines should be mutually softened, and various concessions reciprocally made. A scheme of this kind can only be expected to be successful, when the greater part of the professors of each religion have relinquished all remains of cool animosity, overweening conceit, and contemptuous illiberality, and when they have learned to distinguish properly between essential objects and immaterial points. Such a state of mind has never yet been observed to influence the members of different sects, assembled for deliberation and discussion; and we may easily conclude, that, if the four councils had met, and the result of their separate meetings had been submitted to the consideration of a general assembly, the desired union would not have taken place. The scheme, indeed, was not prosecuted by the pontiff who entertained it; and the churches in question are still divided.

However disposed was his holiness to remain upon amicable terms with the catholic princes, he could not easily avoid all occasions of dispute. A contest had long subsisted with the court of Turin, upon three grounds,—the right of patronage, the extent of jurisdiction, and the sovereignty of different towns. The king of Sardinia asserted his pretensions with a high tone; and the prudence of Benedict suggested the propriety of compliance, not indeed in every particular, but in most of the litigated points. An allowance of the general right of royal presentation to bishoprics and other preferments, a considerable diminution of the papal fees, and a precise settlement of jurisdiction, allayed the displeasure of Victor Amadeus; and an agreement was signed in the year 1727. An accommodation was not so easily adjusted with the king of Portugal, who, not being gratified with regard to the appointment of a priest whom he recommended as a candidate for the dignity of cardinal, recalled his ambassador from Rome, ordered the papal nuncio to quit his realm, and permitted the patriarch of Lisbon to grant dispensations, and decide those points and causes which had usually been subject to the pope's determination. Benedict left the settlement of this dispute to his successor: but he found an opportunity of effecting an accommodation with the emperor, on the subject of ecclesiastical jurisdiction and discipline in the Neapolitan realm; a reconciliation which he purchased by relinquishing some of the rights of the holy see.*

In the devotional and ritual concerns of the church, this pontiff approved the *office* of Gregory VII. and ordered it to be read and observed in every church dependent on the Romish hierarchy. The laity, in France and other countries, were not very willing to comply with the order: but Benedict, in this point, insisted upon their obedience and submission. If the sovereigns of those states had interfered on this occasion, he would probably have given up the point.

Indefatigable in his apostolical duties, he continued to pray and preach, attend to all pontifical and sacerdotal functions, and direct the conduct of subordinate prelates and ministers of the church. He frequently visited the poor, and not only gave them spiritual comfort, but relieved them by his bounty; selling for that purpose the presents which he received. He habituated himself to the plainest fare, and lived in the most frugal manner, like a hermit in his cell, that he might more liberally bestow upon others the blessings of fortune. But it is to be lamented, that, from inattention to his political duty, he suffered cardinal Coscia, an unprincipled Neapolitan, to pursue a shameful course of rapine and extortion.† Yet he died‡ without losing his popularity, in the eighty-second year of his age, and the sixth of his pontificate.

Clement XII., of the Corsini family, was

* Guarnacci, Vit. Pontif. t. ii. p. 417—22.—Hist. de Portugal, t. iii.

† So we are informed by the baron de Polnitz; and the assertion is not disputed by the impartial. Guarnacci, without stating any particulars of the cardinal's misconduct and criminality, says, that he greatly increased his fortune, and governed the pope's dominions at his discretion. Clement XII. punished him with a long imprisonment, subjected him to a heavy fine, and deprived him of the archbishopric of Benevento.

‡ On the 21st of February, 1730.—He ought to be mentioned as an author; for many sermons, some accounts of the proceedings of synods, a commentary upon the book of Exodus, and sacred epigrams, have been published as his productions. His literary merit, however is not of the highest kind.

chosen, after a long contest, to succeed the mild and humble Benedict. He quickly reformed some abuses, which had crept into the administration of the Roman state, and then directed his attention to foreign affairs. In the canton of Lucerne, in Switzerland, the laic magistracy of the chief town had presumed to take cognisance of the delinquency of ecclesiastics, and had disobeyed the injunctions of the papal nuncio, who had therefore retired into the territory of Uri. The pope now adjusted the dispute, and defined the jurisdiction, without any material derogation from the dignity of the holy see. Casting an eye upon Germany, he checked in the catholic states the practice of pluralism, and only in some cases allowed the same person to hold two bishoprics, but never three. In the Saxon electorate, he strenuously promoted the return of the protestants to catholicism, which some were inclined to embrace, in imitation of their sovereign Augustus: but these converts were not very numerous. Not neglecting France, he opposed by new edicts the progress of Jansenism in that realm. Being disgusted at the conduct of the Spaniards, who had seized the duchy of Parma without acknowledging his claim of sovereignty over it, he at first refused to bestow a cardinal's hat upon a Spanish prince, who was then too young to be canonically invested with so important a dignity: but, moved by the importunities of his catholic majesty, he suffered the prince to enjoy the title, and to be administrator of the temporalities, assigning the spiritual jurisdiction to the archbishop of Larissa. A new cause of offence soon arose; for the Spaniards had the audacity to enlist the pope's subjects, and the cruelty to commit outrages upon those who resisted such unwarrantable acts. Philip, however, soothed the irritated feelings of Clement, from whom he procured, for his son don Carlos, the investiture of Naples and Sicily. With the court of Lisbon the pontiff had previously secured a reconciliation, by complying with the request of Joseph: but he was not so acquiescent toward the king of Sardinia; for he annulled the convention which that prince had obtained from Benedict, alleging that it was too favourable to the civil and temporal power.*

This pontiff was a man of respectable abilities; had a regard for justice; was cautious and prudent, yet not destitute of spirit; economical, without being meanly parsimonious; easy of access, without rendering himself indecorously familiar. He had a taste for the polite arts, and was an encourager of literary merit. Dying in his eighty-eighth year,† he was succeeded by Prosper Laurence Lambertini, archbishop of Bologna, who entered upon his high office under the designation of Benedict XIV.

Lambertini had acquired the character of religious moderation, and the fame of learning; and, during a pontificate of eighteen years, he acted in general with prudence and propriety. He did not profess himself a politician, or claim the merit of activity and address in the important concerns of temporal government: yet he was not so negligent or remiss as his patron, the thirteenth Benedict. His chief minister was cardinal Valenti, who was at once a *virtuoso* and a man of business.

* Guarnacci, tom. ii. p. 579, 580, &c

† In February 1740.

In the administration of the church, Benedict XIV. was mild and conciliatory, rather than rigid or severe. He was aware of the relaxed morality of the clergy in the catholic states: but, however he might wish to check their licentiousness, he did not take any strong or violent measures for that purpose. He was disposed to promote a union or accommodation between the Roman see, and the Greek and protestant churches; and, if he could have succeeded by concession or compromise, he would have reconciled all religious differences among Christian communities: but that was a task which exceeded his powers of exertion, and which, indeed, no man can expect to accomplish. He was censured by many of the Romanists for attempting to diminish the number of festivals, and to abolish some ceremonies which appeared to him to be useless, improper, or absurd;* and he also gave offence by the occasional levity of his conversation, which, however, was unaccompanied with immorality or profligacy.

With the catholic courts he had no violent disputes. During the war in which the French were opposed to the house of Austria, he seemed inclined to favour the former; but he endeavoured to avoid giving offence to either of the rival families. He carried on a negotiation, for some years, with Ferdinand, king of Spain, on a subject which had frequently been a cause of altercation. His catholic majesty claimed the right of presentation to all the benefices in his ample dominions; but he at length consented to the disposal of fifty-two of the number by the pontiff, on condition that they should be given to Spaniards alone, and that no pensions should be exacted from the occupants. By the compact then adjusted,† the revenues of vacant benefices were left to a clergyman named by the king, not to the rapacity of a committee of papal agents; and, in some other respects, the receipts of the apostolical chamber were considerably diminished.

At the solicitation of those princes who were displeased at the intrigues, and offended at the mal-practices of the Jesuits, Benedict promised to exert his authority for the reform of that order; and the bull which he issued for this purpose was one of the last acts of his life. He died in 1758, when he had attained the age of eighty-three years. He was an erudite and able theologian, as his numerous works evince; a liberal patron of learning and the elegant arts; a lively companion, a benevolent and friendly man. Cardinal Rezzonico, bishop of Padua, who succeeded him as Clement XIII., had a greater reputation for piety, and was

* He had prepared bulls for these purposes: but the monks excited such a clamour on the occasion, that he did not carry them into effect. *Voyages en differens Pays de l'Europe.*——Haye, 1777; lettre 15.

It has been affirmed, that he abolished *autos da fe* in Portugal, at the desire of king Joseph; and, if he had, such a suppression would have been honourable to his memory: but the assertion appears to be untrue.

† In the year 1753.

more zealous for the high claims of the church: but he was not so generally esteemed as his amiable predecessor.

The doctrines of the Romish church, at this period, remained in the same state in which they had long subsisted. The worship of the Virgin Mary, the tenet of transubstantiation, the idea of purgatory, the propriety of invoking saints, the right and power of absolution, and other parts of the catholic creed, were still retained, and still had considerable influence. The pageantry of procession, the multitude of ceremonies, and the forms of worship, were nearly the same as they had been in the preceding century; and the church-government and discipline were not materially altered. But the majority of the people entertained less exalted ideas of the pope's supremacy, and preferred the authority of general councils. The catholic sovereigns were more enlightened, and more disposed to tolerate other religions; and the ecclesiastics themselves were less bigoted, and more indulgent to the supposed errors of those who differed from them.

While the affairs of the church were in this predicament, the conduct of the Jesuits, and the proceedings against that society, drew the public attention more particularly to ecclesiastical concerns. The rise and progress of that celebrated fraternity, and the chief incidents of its history, have been well related by Dr. Mosheim; and, in our *continuation* of his work,* we have given a concise (but, we hope, a satisfactory) account of that renewal of contest, with the advocates of Jansenism, which distinguished the pontificate of Clement XI. The effect was, in appearance, favourable to the Jesuits: yet they impaired their interest by the violent proceedings of their party against the Jansenists. After a long interval of comparative tranquillity, the animosities of contest were revived by the refusal of sacramental favours to dying persons, who were supposed to be attached to the Jansenian heresy.

But, before we enter into any detail upon this subject, it may not be improper to advert to the progress of that infidel philosophy, which had no inconsiderable effect in promoting the ruin of the Jesuits. Bayle, and other writers in the reign of Louis XIV., had propagated a freedom of opinion on religious topics, which had shaken the faith of many readers; and Voltaire, following more openly a similar course, had disseminated an anti-christian spirit, which menaced the establishment with peril. Diderot and d'Alembert, who, in 1751, sent the *Encyclopedie* into the world, insinuated scepticism and impiety in the midst of scientific discussions; and free-thinking became so prevalent, as to alarm the clergy, and call forth their zeal in the defence of an endangered church. The Jesuits, nursed in priest-craft, and devoted to the holy see, were peculiarly exposed to these profane attacks. Their arts and intrigues were developed, and their selfish policy was reprobated with pointed severity Their Jansenist opponents, at the same time, were not spared, as they had too much religion to be in favour with sceptics.

The archbishop of Paris was a friend to the Jesuits; and, therefore, when he was desired by the court to allay, by his high authority, the dispute between them and the Jansenists, he replied, that it was customary to withhold the sacraments of the church from such as could not produce certificates of confession signed by an orthodox priest; a refusal which had been originally introduced with a view of stigmatizing the Huguenots. The parliament of Paris fined a priest for having repeatedly evinced this kind of bigotry, and issued an ordinance, in 1752, prohibiting all acts tending to schism, and all refusal of sacraments on pretence of non-adherence to the bull *Unigenitus*. The king wavered between the parties, and hoped to keep them so well poised, that no serious inconvenience would ensue from the ferment: but he did not steadily preserve the balance; and both the church and state were convulsed.

The archbishop of Paris took the lead, as a supporter of the cause of orthodoxy against the encroachments of Jansenism; and he exhorted the court to oppose with vigour the presumptuous magistrates who countenanced that heresy. Louis, however, by the advice of the chancellor Lamoignon, adopted the expedient of an arbitration, and appointed delegates of both parties, to accommodate the dispute; a measure which only inflamed mutual acrimony. The parliament persisted in prosecuting such priests as withheld the sacraments; and, when the king commanded a discontinuance of these processes, an animated remonstrance was voted by the magistrates. He punished their disobedience by dispersion and exile, and instituted temporary tribunals to act in their stead. But the clamours of the public soon induced him to recall them; and an ordinance was then registered, for a cessation of all religious disputes.*

The tranquillity which ensued was of short continuance. The archbishop was banished from the capital for reviving the dispute, and some inferior ecclesiastics of his party were more rigorously punished. The clergy sat in council for several months, in 1755, without terminating the schism. They addressed a letter to pope Benedict, who, in an indecisive answer, seemed to leave the settlement of the affair to his most Christian majesty. The embarrassed monarch, after various temporising measures, held a bed of justice, in which he peremptorily ordered all his subjects to pay respect and submission to the bull, without considering it, however, as a rule of faith, although the bishops, in the late council, had declared that it bore that character. By another ordinance, he regulated the meetings and altered the constitution of the magistracy; and two courts of the parliament immediately resigned their functions in disgust.

The Jesuits were highly pleased at the spirit

* This term has been used, as being, upon the whole, the most applicable: but, in some parts, it is a *supplement*, rather than a *sequel*. For instance, in addition to Dr. Mosheim's sketch of the contest between the church and the Jansenists in the reign of Louis XIV., and under the following regency, we have given a more detailed account of the proceedings on that occasion.

* Vie Privee de Louis XV.

which the king evinced on this occasion; but, while they exulted in the depression of the parliament, they did not foresee that their own ruin was approaching. The intrigues of the members of that order in Portugal had induced Joseph, sovereign of that realm, to watch them closely, and to make such reformative arrangements as disgusted the fraternity. Hence, when his life was threatened by a conspiracy, from which he had a narrow escape,* it was found that many Jesuits were concerned in the nefarious plot, particularly father Gabriel de Malagrida, whom the court, however, out of regard to the church, did not put to death as a traitor, but as a heretic. The incensed monarch now suppressed the colleges of the Jesuits; and, to restrain the future attempts of ecclesiastics against the state, he insisted upon a grant (from the pope) of perpetual jurisdiction over the whole clerical body, in cases of treason and sedition. Clement promised to accede to the demand, if a prelate nominated by him or any of his successors should preside on such occasions: but he afterwards consented that the king should name a bishop for these trials.†

No intercession in behalf of the Portuguese Jesuits could soften the inflexibility of Joseph, who, in addition to the guilt of the late conspiracy, accused them of a usurpation of sovereign power in South America, alleging that they had concurred with their Spanish brethren in tyrannising over the natives of Paraguay, whom they had tutored to take arms against him and his catholic majesty. On account of their various enormities, all the members of the fraternity were declared outlaws, in 1759, and banished from the dominions of Portugal; and other courts were invited to follow the rigorous example.

In the meanwhile, the Parisian parliament, so hostile to the Jesuits, procured from the court a full re-establishment; and, at the same time, the clerical exiles were recalled. The magistracy now resumed the proceedings against the withholders of the sacramental favours, and waited for an opportunity of wreaking signal vengeance upon the sons of Loyola. Their commercial rapacity furnished the desired opportunity. Two merchants whom they were bound to supply with articles of traffic, stopped payment on the seizure of those goods by British cruisers; and the Jesuits did not take prompt or adequate measures to avert the shock. Numerous creditors appeared against them; and the cause was referred, at their desire, to the grand chamber of the parliament. They disavowed the imputed agency of Father de la Valette, the manager of their trade, whose offence against the church, by engaging in commerce, only concerned himself: but it was maintained against them, that their superior, or general, superintended their trade, as well as other concerns, and directed the conduct of the agent. The judges insisted upon seeing the constitutions of the society; and an exposure was consequently made of the devoted submission of all the members to a foreign head, and of their dangerous maxims in politics and morality. It also appeared that they did not constitute a regular religious order, as the intended contract between them and the state had never been completed: their fraternity had been merely tolerated, not adopted. Their enemies took advantage of these circumstances, and represented in so strong a light the danger of keeping such men embodied, that the king resolved to suppress the society; not, however, before the general had refused to submit to a plan of regulation, proposed by the French court. The parliament ordained, on the 6th of August, 1762, that the Jesuits of France should no longer wear the habit of the society, live in community, or obey the orders of foreign directors. Their partisans loudly exclaimed against an edict, which they considered as extremely severe and unjust, because those whom it affected were not heard in their own defence, and were condemned upon false reports, for misrepresented doctrines and unproved delinquency. The opinion of the lawfulness of regicide in certain cases, they said, seemed to be the chief offence of the fraternity; but it ought first to be proved that this was justly imputable to the Jesuits, who, as their enemies knew, had no concern in Damien's attempt to assassinate the French king, and were also entirely innocent with regard to other crimes of the same nature, of which they had been malignantly accused.*

A regular edict of suppression was delayed for some years: but it was at length registered, on the 7th of December, 1764, and promulgated by the royal authority. The parliaments of Normandy and Bretagne followed, with little hesitation, the example of the Parisian magistracy; but other parliaments were not fully convinced of the justice or expediency of the measure. The pope was shocked at the profane audacity of a court that could act with such determined hostility against a holy society: but his bull, for the reinstatement of the fraternity, was suppressed in France by an *arret* of parliament, and was declared inoperative in Portugal by the king's express command.

The king of Spain was not more friendly to the Jesuits than Louis or Joseph. He was disgusted at their intriguing spirit, and resolved not merely to humble them, but to annihilate their power in his dominions. He seized their temporalities in 1767, and banished them, as dangerous subjects, from every part of Spain and its dependencies. His son Ferdinand also freed the kingdom of Naples and the island of Sicily from the obnoxious fraternity. A great number of these exiles were admitted into the Roman territories, and some other parts of Italy; and many found protection among Protestants. The duke of Parma, soon afterwards, commanded all members of the order to retire from his dominions; and he, at the same time, hazarded an open rupture with the see of Rome, by abolishing the papal jurisdiction in Parma and Placentia. His holiness declared the duke's ordinance to that effect null and void, and menaced its promulgator with the thunders of the church. Being supported by the majority of the catholic princes, the duke persisted in his

* In September, 1758.

† Historia de Portugal, Lisb. 1802; tom. iv. p. 22, 27.

* Vie Privée de Louis XV.

purpose; and the pontiff was equally resolute. With a view of intimidating him into a revocation of his brief, the French king dispossessed him of Avignon; and some portions of his Italian territory were seized by his Neapolitan majesty. His spiritual authority and his revenues were diminished by the duke of Modena; and the Venetians, of whose republic he was born a subject, assailed him with similar hostilities. Mortified at this treatment, yet unwilling to yield, he was observed to decline gradually in his health. Uneasiness and chagrin hastening the effect of age, he died in his seventy-sixth year,* with the character of a pious and well-meaning prelate, who was, however, more influenced by the zeal of bigotry than by common sense or wisdom. He ought to have been content with maintaining the doctrine and worship of the church, without obstinately upholding papal usurpations.

The enemies of the Jesuits had in vain solicited the dissolution of that order, while Clement XIII. filled the papal chair: but they conceived strong hopes of success, when a prelate of a more philosophical character was chosen pontiff. This was a Franciscan monk named Francis Laurence Ganganelli, who thought proper to assume the name of his immediate predecessor.

Instead of conciliating the new pope, the king of France declared that he would retain Avignon, and its dependencies: but he condescended to offer a sum of money for a dereliction of them on the part of his holiness. The king of Naples also insisted upon the cession of the district which he had seized, and concurred with Louis in urging Clement to suppress that society which was so odious to the Christian world; but the importunities of these princes, aided by the influence of Spain and Portugal, were for some years unsuccessful. Clement XIV. felt the difficulties of his situation, and demanded time for mature reflection. He conceived it to be his duty to patronise and support a religious order, if its utility to the church or to society overbalanced its demerits; and, at the same time, he wished to avoid a rupture with those courts which had evidently the power, and seemingly the inclination, to inflict serious wounds on the papacy.

In taking a survey of Europe, he found *few* of its sovereigns inclined to support him against the house of Bourbon: we may rather say, that *none* would authoritatively interpose in his behalf. Yet he would not tamely or too readily yield to dictatorial demands. He apprehended that one concession, on his part, would lead to new requisitions; and he knew that a facility of compliance would only serve to encourage domineering insolence. Amidst these reflections, delay did not seem likely to be injurious; and, if he should be obliged to submit, a protraction of the evil day would at least save appearances, even in the eyes of the zealous advocates of papal supremacy. In this, and in other affairs of moment, he resolved to think for himself, rather than follow the example of those pontiffs who had resigned their own judgments to the influence and authority of the cardinals. Many members of the sacred college were displeased at his want of confidence in men of their rank and merit; but he disregarded their murmurs, and declared that he would not be governed. It was, he thought, better for a sovereign to be in a great measure, his own minister and negotiator, than to suffer others, as is too frequently the practice, to act for him at their discretion. With a *volto sciolto*, he deemed it expedient for a prince to have *pensieri stretti;* not from a mean spirit of hypocrisy or dissimulation, but from a politic desire of concealing those views and schemes of which an unfair advantage might be taken.

The Jesuits affected to believe (and probably many of them really thought,) that Clement would not dare to suppress their order. But, in the fifth year of his pontificate, he resolved, in defiance of all the clamours and menaces of the zealots, to disembody the fraternity, and amalgamate its members with the unprivileged mass of society. He declared it to be his opinion, that the order had ceased to answer the ends of its institution, and that the members, by the impropriety of their conduct, their loose casuistry, and their mischievous arts, had forfeited all claim to farther encouragement. A bull for the annihilation of the society was therefore promulgated;* its colleges were seized, and its revenues confiscated. Lorenzo Ricci, the refractory general of the order, was sent to the castle of St. Angelo, and died in confinement.

Pleased at the ruin of the Jesuits, the French court complimented Ganganelli on the justice and expediency of his edict, and restored the Venaissin to the holy see. The other remonstrating courts also adjusted their disputes with the pontiff; who, having thus settled the great point which had long engaged his attention, might be expected to feel little anxiety after the decision which he had so deliberately adopted. But, perhaps, he seriously apprehended the effects of the secret resentment of the ex-Jesuits, who could not look with a favourable eye upon the enemy of their order. However that may be, he died in the autumn of the following year, at the age of sixty-eight. It was supposed that he had been poisoned; but this suspicion has not been verified.

Of all the priests who for some centuries had filled the papal throne, Ganganelli seems to have been, if we except Benedict XIV., the most unprejudiced, candid, and liberal. He did not devote his chief attention to the selfish interests of the see of Rome; nor did he treat other religious establishments with supercilious arrogance, studied contempt, or marked reprobation. His moderation entailed upon him the censures of the rigid and severe, who alleged that he was too lukewarm and indifferent in religious concerns to be a proper defender of the fortress of catholicism, which required for its support the most strenuous exertions of active zeal. He was even accused of being a well-wisher to Protestantism; a heavy charge against the head of that church to which the protestants were determined foes; but this charge amounted to no more, in effect, than

* In February, 1769.

* On the 21st of July, 1773

that he was not a bigot to popery. His treatment of the Jesuits exposed him to censures still more severe, and to all the rancour of malignity; but, in acting against that order, he only complied with the wishes of the most enlightened members of the grand community of Christendom, and justly dissolved a most immoral and unprincipled society. The time was opportune for such dissolution; the clamours which it excited soon spent their force; and a phalanx, once potent and formidable, had not the power of withstanding the energies of papal hostility; energies that were undoubtedly declining, but which, in the present case, were supported by the chief catholic princes and states.

The government of the church was now consigned to John Angelo Braschi, who had been created cardinal by Ganganelli, and was regarded as a moderate man, rather than a bigot or zealot. He was more indebted for his election to the clashing of parties, than to the peculiar favour or interest of any one faction. He was less popular, at the time of his elevation, than his predecessor; and his partiality and indulgence to his nephews did not tend to increase his popularity. Having a graceful person and a pleasing countenance, he was fond of show and parade, and took every opportunity of exhibiting himself to the public. In capacity and eloquence he was not deficient; but he had no extraordinary vigour of mind.

When he had superseded the vulgar name of John by the pontifical appellation of Pius *the Sixth*, some of those who were not inclined to think favourably of his disposition or his abilities, applied to him a reproachful verse, predicting the ruin of Rome under a *Sextus*.* His friends, on the other hand, ridiculed this gloomy prophecy, and boasted of his ability, and the goodness of his heart and character. He commenced his administration with acts of benevolence and charity, with the selection of deserving men for various offices, and the removal or discouragement of some individuals who had misbehaved. He also formed the resolution of undertaking a work calculated for national benefit—the draining of the Pontine marshes. A bank was instituted to receive subscriptions for this purpose; but, after much labour and expense, the work was only effected in part. For what was done, however, Pius deserved thanks and praise.

After the suppression of the order of Jesuits, many who had belonged to the fraternity found protection in the dominions of the Prussian monarch, who intimated to the new pope, that he would not pay the least regard to the edict. His holiness replied, that he was bound to enforce the bull promulgated by his predecessor; but he at the same time declared, according to Frederic's agent Ciofani, that he would not treat the body of ex-Jesuits, then residing in the territories of that prince, as an irregular establishment. At the instigation, however, of the ministers of France and Spain, he afterwards required that the habit of the dissolved order should no longer be worn in the territories of Frederic, and that none of the ex-Jesuits should either preach, or administer the eucharist or other sacraments. The monarch, adverting to the ability which the Jesuits had displayed in the task of education, wished them to remain as a society for that purpose, in those provinces* in which his catholic subjects were numerous; and, when Pius conceded this point, the king agreed to the requisitions of the pontiff.†

The Jesuits were also protected by the empress of Russia; and from the bishop of Mohiloff, who, bred a Calvinist, had become a catholic, and who domineered over the church in Poland, they experienced peculiar favour and patronage. He was so eager to re-establish their society, that he gave public permission to a body of ex-Jesuits, assembled in the province of White Russia, to take probationary candidates for the privileges of their order. He pretended that Pius had allowed him so to exercise his authority: but this assertion was disclaimed by the pontiff, and probability favours the denial. When the Spanish court remonstrated with the empress on the subject, she maintained her pretensions and those of the prelate whom she protected, and declared that she would not submit to dictation from any court whatever. She afterwards authorised her Jesuit subjects to choose a vicar-general, who should enjoy all the former privileges of the institution; and, in defiance of all the enemies of the Jesuits, she continued to favour the members of an order proscribed and stigmatised by the catholic princes. While she disapproved the conduct of many who had been enrolled among the sons of Loyola, she said that the general demerits of the society did not appear to her to be so atrocious, as to justify its dissolution, or the severities which had preceded and followed that act.‡

In France, the cause of Jesuitism was still abetted by many of the dignified clergy; but they were not so open in expressing their wishes for the restoration of the order, as they were in counteracting the claims of the Huguenots, whom the government had ceased to persecute. Some, who hated the Jesuits, joined this party in opposing the protestants, and also in reprobating the licentiousness of infidels. In an assembly holden in the year 1765, an animated remonstrance had been voted by the prelates against the new philosophy. They conjured the king to take vigorous measures for the repression of that profane boldness, that impious freedom, which villified whatever had for ages been deemed sacred among mankind, and aimed at the subversion of all holy and venerable institutions. If he should be tame or passive at so alarming a crisis, the most portentous mischief, they said, might be apprehended. They accused the protestants of being deeply concerned in these practices, and blamed his majesty for not enforcing the laws against those presumptuous sectaries. In the year 1770, the progress of infidelity gave occasion for another remonstrance, in which the

* "Semper sub Sextis perdita Roma fuit."

* Particularly Silesia.

† Memoires Hist. et Philosophiques sur Pie VI. et son Pontificat, ch. iii.

‡ Memoires Hist. et Philos. sur Pie VI chap. iv.

assembled clergy pointed out various works of the new philosophers, as objects of condemnation,* and called for the exertion of all the powers of government in the defence and support of religion, morality, and good order. An assembly of bishops, in 1772, renewed the attack upon the new philosophy; but their fulminations were ineffective; and the contagion continued to spread.

Louis XVI., who had a stronger sense of religion than his predecessor, lamented the prevalence of scepticism: yet he sometimes gave his confidence to men who were known to be infidels. Alarmed at the ministerial influence of Turgot, the clergy, in a council which they held in the year 1775, agreed to such a remonstrance as the danger of the church seemed to require. They represented to the young monarch, in strong terms, the alarming progress of infidelity and atheism, the illegal boldness of the protestants, (who had dared even to erect churches,) the flagrant licentiousness of the press, and the prevalence of a restless and inquisitive spirit, which threatened to unhinge society. Louis promised to attend to these complaints; but he did not take any measures of remedial efficacy. When he was influenced by free-thinking ministers, he was taught to believe that it was not necessary to interfere; and, when he was under other guides, he was too irresolute to act with vigour. To govern a nation so impetuous and volatile as the French, at a time when freedom of thought began to prevail, a prince of more energetic character was requisite. Sometimes, indeed, he was peremptory; but he was not consistently firm or steadily resolute. He acquiesced in measures which in his heart he disapproved; and he neglected the enforcement of those which he conceived to be just, expedient, and salutary. Under his sway, infidelity and faction alarmingly gained ground; and by assisting the American colonists, he increased the agitations of his realm.

Even in Spain and Portugal, though in a much less degree than in France, freedom of thought, in the affairs of religion, began to diffuse itself among the higher and middle classes. The vigilance of the government, however, prevented it from being dangerous. In the extensive territories of the house of Austria, a similar freedom was repressed by the spirit of Maria Theresa, whose bigotry, at the same time, prompted her to infringe the rights of her protestant subjects.† Her son, the emperor Joseph, was himself a free-thinker, while he professed an adherence to the doctrines of the Romish church. This prince might justly be called the imperial projector. Many of his *whims*, like those of the ingenious but profligate duke of Buckingham, "died in thinking:" others were matured into *schemes*. With his political plans we have no concern on this occasion: it is only requisite that we should take notice of his regulations in the affairs of the church. He would not, he said, impeach the established doctrines; but he had a strong inclination to abridge the papal power in his dominions; and, with him, an inclination was soon converted into an act. Pius, being acquainted with the freedom of Joseph's sentiments, apprehended an attack from that enterprising innovator; and his fears were not visionary; for the emperor, in 1781, began with imposing restrictions upon the operation of bulls and rescripts sent from Rome. This ordinance was followed by an exemption of monasteries from all obedience to the chiefs of the different orders at Rome; a measure which the partisans of the pope, as might be expected, reprobated in warm terms. The generals of the orders desired the subalterns to maintain with spirit the constitutions of their establishments; but they were overawed into submission by the firmness of the emperor, who also released all the colleges of missionaries from their dependance on the papal court. He farther displeased the pontiff by ordering that no money should be sent into foreign countries for masses; that no dignity should be solicited at Rome without his permission; that pilgrimages should be discontinued; and that the number of images and ornaments in churches should be diminished. The disgust felt by Pius at this conduct, was not allayed by the liberal edict of Joseph,* granting full toleration to all the protestants in his dominions, as well as to all members of the Greek church; and the dissolution of a great number of monasteries, with the conversion of the buildings into colleges, hospitals, or barracks, increased the indignation of the vicar of St. Peter.†

Thus harassed and (as he thought) insulted, Pius resolved to visit the emperor, who, among other demands, had insisted upon presenting, in future, to all vacant bishoprics and benefices in the Milanese and Mantuan territories. The pope remonstrated against this profane encroachment upon his supposed right of patronage; but he was persuaded by some of his counsellors to promise acquiescence in this point, if Joseph would engage to desist from his career of reform. This was an engagement which none who knew that potentate could expect from him; and, with regard to the intended visit, he declared that it would be wholly fruitless, although, in a private letter to Pius, he had hinted that all disputes might be better accommodated in such a way than by mere correspondence. His holiness, to the surprise of all, repaired to Vienna, in the hope of warding off a storm which blew with increasing violence. Joseph, in one of his interviews with his spiritual father, claimed the right of altering the ecclesiastical government in his own territories, while he suffered the catholic doctrines to remain unimpaired. The pontiff, finding expostulation useless, returned to Rome, and suffered the storm to

* These were, among other publications, Christianity Unveiled, God and Men, the System of Nature, Sacred Contagion, and Hell Destroyed; which the parliament ordered to be publicly committed to the flames.

† "Under the virtuous Theresa," the protestants of Hungary (says Dr. Townson) "were not less vexed than under the profligate prince, who was taught, that his deviations from virtue might be made up for by zeal to the true church."

* Promulgated on the 13th of October, 1781.

† Memoires Hist. et Philos. sur Pie VI. chap. xi.—Coxe's Hist. of the House of Austria, vol. ii chap. [illegible]

rage. He probably thought, that Joseph was little better than a heretic, however he might pretend to doctrinal purity; and, on the other hand, the emperor imputed to the pope the narrowness of bigotry, and a want of philosophic liberality of sentiment.

The continuance of Joseph's reformative measures no longer surprised the pope, who had now witnessed the inflexibility of that prince's character. The see of Rome lost the presentation to bishoprics in Lombardy and other Austrian dependencies: its nuncios were deprived of their power and jurisdiction in Germany; and, by these and other attacks, the lustre of the papacy was visibly eclipsed.

Other catholic sovereigns, even those who had acquired the reputation of piety, did not scruple to assail that fabric which was thus weakened. Unfortunately for the cause of the papacy, there seemed to be a general disposition, during the pontificate of Pius, to diminish the authority of the see over which he presided. The court of Madrid assumed a greater degree of religious freedom than it had been accustomed to exercise; claimed rights nearly equal to those which the Gallican church had long maintained; reduced the inquisition to a state of passive subserviency; and made a farther diminution of the papal demands of revenue. Even the bigoted court of Lisbon entertained ideas of reform. The queen was a devout catholic, superstitiously faithful to the doctrines and attached to the ceremonies of popery: but she suffered her son, the prince of Brazil, to lead her into anti-papal measures. Some publications which had been introduced by the emperor into the schools at Vienna, were translated into the language of Portugal, and ordered to be studied, for the promotion of free inquiry, in several new seminaries founded in that realm. Questions tending to weaken the fabric of papal supremacy, to abridge the power of the clerical body, and even to recommend toleration of various religions, were authoritatively proposed for discussion in the universities; and the press was permitted to aid the progress of such argumentation, although it was not allowed to impugn the peculiar doctrines of catholicism. No persons were suffered to devote themselves to monastic confinement, without the particular sanction of the sovereign. Even after the death of the prince, the court continued to encroach on the claims of the pope and the immunities of the church. The courts of Naples and Florence took greater liberties in this respect than that of Lisbon. A considerable number of monasteries were suppressed by the king and the grand duke: bishoprics and rich benefices were granted without consulting his holiness with regard to the individuals proper to occupy them; and contributions to the Roman treasury were abolished or restricted. The republic of Venice dissolved some conventual foundations, and applied their revenues to better purposes than the support of superstitious indolence. The duke of Modena put an end to the horrors of the inquisition in his dominions, and treated with less respect the general authority of the pontiff.*

* Memoires sur Pie VI. chap. xviii. xix. xxii.

These incidents and transactions occurred at different times: but they are here mentioned together, to preserve a continuity of subject. They tend to show the reduced state of the papacy at the period in question: but it may be observed, that, for its total extinction, Europe was not then prepared.

The pope could only resist these assaults by remonstrances, to which the reforming courts paid no regard. He was fully sensible of the decline of his influence, but concealed his chagrin under the appearance of composure. With the pomp of ceremony, and with ritual formalities, he amused himself and his people, while his authority was exposed to rude shocks. He also attended to the improvement of the museum, which had been formed at Rome by Benedict XIV., and which Ganganelli had considerably augmented.

The catholic princes, in general, not only annihilated, or materially reduced, the papal authority over their subjects, but suffered public opinion so far to operate, as to check the arbitrary use of their own authority: and the protestant governments also relaxed, in some degree, the rigours of power. Much, however, remained to be done for the purposes of popular benefit; for, even in Great Britain, the land of boasted freedom, the government was rather a combination of monarchy and aristocracy, than a proper mixture of those two kinds of polity with democracy.

While almost every nation in Europe seemed to be gradually advancing to a melioration of its government, and to a greater freedom of inquiry, the French unfortunately took the lead, and obscured the rising prospect by senseless precipitancy and by absurd innovations. They overturned former establishments before they had concerted or devised rational plans of substitution: they indulged in all the wildness of theory and all the licentiousness of caprice. The most outrageous cruelty was mingled with their political fanaticism; and the effects were calamitous and deplorable.

A revolution like that which convulsed France, could not be expected to prove favourable to the interests of religion. Men who were inclined to cherish a boundless freedom of opinion, and who boasted of their being wholly uninfluenced by the wisdom of former times, were not likely to feel any high degree of respect for that system of religion which had long prevailed. Not content with ridiculing and reprobating the Romish ritual and establishment, they spoke contemptuously of all other creeds; and a neglect of religion became the order of the day. The Constituent Assembly, however, amidst all its innovations, made provision for the continuance of public worship; and the catholic religion was still the predominant system. The papal interest, indeed, was materially affected by the change of government. The vote against the payment of fees to the pope, the order for the suppression of monasteries, the seizure of all the possessions of the church as the property of the nation, and the entire subjection of the clergy to the civil power, struck at the vitals of the court of Rome. Pius, incensed at these proceedings, seemed ready to hurl the thunderbolts of nontifical vengeance upon the audacious and profane revolutionists; but prudence checked his arm. He apprehended that his menaces and edicts would be disregarded, and might only serve to provoke embittered hostilities. In the mean time, he endeavoured to secure the friendship of those princes whose power might afford him some protection amidst the revolutionary storm.

The bishops and priests, who acted under the new constitution of France, were not regarded as true members of the *Romish* church, by the clergy of the old school, however observant they might be of the *catholic* creed. The pope sent a brief to the king, condemning the new arrangements; but Louis was constrained to acquiesce in these and other innovations. Only three of the former bishops retained their stations: all the other prelates became non-jurors, and, with the majority of parochial ministers, were deprived of their preferments. The legislative assembly, affecting to be alarmed at the intrigues of the clerical non-jurors, menaced them with imprisonment or exile. Many of their number emigrated in the sequel; and many were assassinated by the populace.

Under the sway of the democratic convention, so little attention was paid to religion, that it seemed to be in danger of being wholly absorbed by worldly politics. The assembly did not, indeed, expressly vote for its extinction in the new republic; but contented itself with encouraging the surrender of letters of priesthood, and the open renunciation of all religious sentiments. At length, however, Robespierre pretended to be shocked at the growing spirit of atheism, and moved for the promulgation of a decree, favourable to the cause of religion. By this ordinance, a periodical festival was instituted in honour of the Creator of the world, or the Supreme Being; the propriety of public worship was allowed; and the immortality of the soul was recommended to universal belief. The clergy of the old school, however, were still harassed, and in danger of exile or confinement, until the legislature, in the year 1797, released them from the oaths with which their consciences were offended, and merely required them to promise submission to the government. Two years before this concession was obtained, five bishops had ventured to address a circular letter to the clergy; in which they affirmed, that religion, in the altered government of their country, had no longer a political foundation; that the connexion was dissolved between the church and the state; that the former still expected justice and protection from the latter; but, being left to itself, was obliged to take measures for the establishment of doctrinal uniformity and general regularity of discipline. They recognized the pope as the head of the church and acknowledged the doctrines of catholicism, as interpreted and explained by Bossuet, the celebrated bishop of Meaux.*

Before the end of the same year, another letter was addressed to the friends of the church, proposing ten metropolitan churches for the whole republic, and a bishopric for each department; recommending a popular election both of prelates and parochial ministers; disowning the authority of apostolical vicars, or papal delegates, and advising the peremptory rejection of all bulls or briefs from Rome, unless it should fully appear that they were consonant with the ordinances and the spirit of the Gallican church.*

When a sufficient time had been allowed for the operation of these letters, and for the private influence of clerical exhortations, an ecclesiastical council met in the French metropolis,† consisting of thirty-eight prelates, and fifty-three representatives of the inferior clergy. The members agreed to a profession of faith, founded on the creed promulgated, in 1560, by pope Pius IV.;‡ but they were not so bigoted to this faith, as to give license or encouragement to the perpetration of any acts of violence under the pretence of defending it. However the church might be called *militant*, "it knew and authorized no other *arms* (they said) than prayer and the word of God." The country, they added, might be lawfully defended by the people, with the arm of flesh; and the clergy were desired to inculcate the propriety and justice of such patriotic hostilities: but the church ought only to defend itself by spiritual arms. Episcopacy was declared to be essential to the proper government of the church; but royalty, of which that system was the usual accompaniment among Christian nations, did not meet with so favourable a testimony; for it was enjoined that royalty should be the object of determined hatred, because a proper knowledge of national interest strongly condemned that form of government; and it was affirmed, that the exaction of an oath, against the revival of such an obnoxious system in France, was by no means repugnant to the laws of the Gospel.§

The proceedings of this assembly were closed by an order for the communication of its decrees to the pope, who was, at the same time, earnestly solicited to convoke a general council. But his holiness declined a compliance with this request, being probably of opinion that the political convulsions of the times precluded ecclesiastical accommodation and religious union.

Amidst these arrangements, the pontiff remained at Rome, in a state of suspense and anxiety. He had already surrendered three provinces to French invaders; and he had not power to defend the rest of his territories. A republic being formed at Rome, in the year 1798, he retired into Tuscany; and, when that duchy was also revolutionized, he was sent as a prisoner of war into Dauphine. Harassed, insulted, and oppressed, he died at Briancon,‖ in the eighty-second year of his age.

* See Mosheim's History, cent. xvii. sect. ii. part i. chap. i.

* Lettre Encyclique de plusieurs Eveques de France, a leurs Freres, et aux Eglises vacantes, 1795.

† On the 15th of August, 1797.

‡ See Mosheim, cent. xvi. sect. iii. part i. chap. i.

§ Canons et Decrets du Concile national de France, tenu a Paris, en l'An de l'Ere Chretienne 1797; mis en ordre par les Eveques reunis a Paris.

‖ In April, 1799.

CHAPTER II.

History of the Greek Church, and of the Christian Communities in Asia and Africa.

If we did not know that trifles (such is the weakness of man!) frequently produce serious animosities and permanent divisions, we might be surprised at the long dissension between the Greek and Romish churches. At the time of their separation, both communities agreed in the essentials of Christianity; and they ought to have contented themselves with that agreement, without expecting their fellow-Christians to concur with them in every trivial notion or fantastic opinion, in every idle ceremony, or in all circumstances of exterior worship. But, forgetting the obligations of brotherly love, they continued at variance for ages; and they are still sufficiently estranged from each other, to render the idea of a union visionary and hopeless.

The Greek church, at the beginning of the century, extended from the Red Sea to the Frozen Ocean, and from the Adriatic to the Caspian. The patriarch of Constantinople was, nominally, the head of this church; but his authority was not co-extensive with the similarity of doctrine. He held a monthly synod in that city, with the metropolitans of Antioch and Jerusalem, and twelve other prelates. In these councils he had no decisive authority: the influence of the majority, the intrigues of the more artful members, and sometimes reason or argument, decided the questions. He did not retain that effective supremacy which some of his predecessors enjoyed over the patriarchs of Egypt, Syria, and Palestine: in the extensive regions subject to the Russian despot, he had not even the shadow of power; and, between the eastern boundaries of Asia Minor and the Caspian, his jurisdiction was not honoured with regard or acquiescence. Living also under the government of an infidel prince, to whom every form of Christianity was odious, he was, in fact, a slave to an arbitrary barbarian.

In the provinces of European Turkey, the members of the Greek church were, and are still, very numerous, notwithstanding the discouragement given to population by the tyranny of the government. Almost every successive Grand Seignior thought it his duty to oppress them, that he might evince his zeal as a defender of the Moslem faith. Mustafa III. was more lenient to them than many of his predecessors; but, even under his administration, they were insulted and plundered by his Turkish subjects, and maltreated in every mode of capricious tyranny. Their hierarchy, however, was suffered to subsist; and they were allowed to transmit to their posterity their favourite doctrines.

Frequent attempts were made by the zealous catholics, in the course of the century, to draw the Greeks into the Romish communion, not by concessions on the part of the former, but by derelictions of opinion on the part of the latter. In consequence of these endeavours, a schism was maintained in various parts of Greece and Asia Minor, and the number of proselytes to the papal church became considerable. The Mainotes, in the Morea, withstood the arts of the Romish missionaries more vigorously, even to the end of the century, than the generality of the Greeks. They assured the intruders, that they were strongly attached to the system of their own church, as opposed to that of the Romanists, whose head they considered as an unchristian schismatic, for having corrupted the purity of the true faith. They particularly condemned the prohibition of the marriage of priests, and ridiculed the issuing of bulls for the pretended rescue of souls from purgatory. They then had only one bishop; and he, like the priests, had no regular allowance, but received occasional contributions for particular masses, and cultivated the soil, or performed other labours, to procure the necessaries of life. The ecclesiastics, in general, led exemplary lives, and thus deserved that respect with which the laity treated them; and such was their spirit, that they were the first to take arms in defence of their country.*

The schism of which we have spoken was very prevalent in Syria. At Aleppo, the northern capital of that province, the Christian church, about the middle of the century, was in a state of deplorable division.

The orthodox Greeks, or those who adhered to the old system, were less numerous than the followers of the Latin church; but, having greater interest at the Porte, they kept the bishopric in their hands. They were more rigid in the observance of fasts than the opposite party: yet the latter attended more to that point of supposed duty than the generality of Roman catholics. The Armenians were still more scrupulous in this respect; and some, it is said, would rather perish for want of proper sustenance during illness, than solicit a dispensation from the rigours of abstinence. Like the Greeks, they were divided into orthodox and schismatic Christians. The advantage of number was on the side of the former; but the others had the superiority in point of opulence. The Maronites continued to be attached to the Romish church, retaining, however, some doctrinal and ritual differences. They had a higher opinion of the sanctity or the convenience of a monastic life than the other Christians of Aleppo; but they had no monasteries in that city. The priests of these three communities were in general so poor, that those who had families were obliged to have recourse to some branch of temporal business for the augmentation of their income.†

The state of the Greek church, in point of doctrine and practice, may be thus briefly exhibited. Its chief sacraments are baptism and the Lord's supper. To the former, which is deemed necessary to salvation, is annexed the *chrism*, or unction; and the child is dipped under water three times, in allusion to the Trinity. In the eucharist, three liturgies are used; but the ordinary one is that of St. Chrysostom. This sacrament is administered, even

* Voyage de Dimo et Nicolo Stephanopoli en Grece, pendant les Annees 1797 et 1798; chap. xxxix.

† Natural History of Aleppo, by Alexander Russell, M. D. vol. ii. chap. ii.

to the laity, in both kinds; and children are allowed to receive it. Transubstantiation is not a decided doctrine in this church. It is apparently maintained in one of the public confessions of faith; but the words used in the service itself* seem merely to imply, that the supposed change is an act of the mind, not a physical conversion of the sacramental elements into the body and blood of Christ.

The Romish notion of purgatory is denied by the votaries of this church: but they offer up prayers for those who have been removed from the world, and therefore seem to think that the soul has some place of residence from the day of death to the final judgment. They invoke a multitude of saints, and even burn incense to them. Next to Christ, the Virgin Mary and the twelve apostles are particularly honoured. Works of supererogation are disallowed. Faith and good works united are deemed requisite to produce justification.

Confession is practised, but not considered as a sacrament. It is enjoined four times in the year: but, in general, it is performed only once in that time. The penitents, however, are not required, as in the church of Rome, to make a full disclosure of all their sins, or to give a minute detail of circumstances.

Marriage is regarded as a very important object, yet not as an indissoluble obligation. Three offices or services are used in its celebration; namely, that of betrothing, crowning the individuals, and dissolving the crowns.† All the clergy, except bishops and monks, are allowed to enter into this union. Beyond a third time, all renewals of marriage are forbidden; and even second marriages are discountenanced. No solemnizations of matrimony are permitted during the fasts, which are usually kept with great strictness.

The ecclesiastical body consists of five orders, if readers and sub-deacons be reckoned among the number: the others are, deacons, presbyters, and bishops. The ordination of the highest class is a very impressive ceremony. It terminates with a prayer from the officiating archbishop, that Christ will render the new prelate an imitator of himself, the true shepherd; that he will make him a teacher of infants, a leader of the blind, a light to those who walk in darkness; that he may shine in the world, and at last receive the great reward prepared for those who boldly contend in the cause of the Gospel, and persevere in the service of God.

Although the head of this church has lost his controlling authority over the ecclesiastical establishment of Russia, he still has the gratification of reflecting, that the *doctrinal* prevalence of the system which he superintends, includes that great empire. The Russian clergy had long enjoyed important immunities; and, although these were in some measure abridged by Peter the Great, the order still can boast of considerable privileges. Among these we may mention an exemption from taxes; and we may add, that ecclesiastics are so far favoured in a judicial process, as not to be amenable before a temporal judge, unless commissaries of their own order be assessors at the trial. Before the year 1791, the commandant or chief magistrate of a district used to send to the bishop, on every new occasion, for commissaries; but, since that time, clerical deputies have been regularly and permanently appointed for that function, by a general order of the holy synod.*

Under this synod, in the reign of Catharine II., were thirty-one *eparchies*, or spiritual governments. That council in 1789, was composed of two metropolitans, three archbishops, two bishops, a regular and a secular proto-pope, or chief priest, an archimandrite, or abbot, and some inferior officers. To each eparchy belonged a consistory, formed of an archimandrite, some priors, and secular clergy. The titles of metropolitan and archbishop were not attached to a particular see, but were distinctions merely personal.

The *roskolniki*, or schismatics, as those were called who objected to the prevailing system, which they said, involved various corruptions of the doctrine and discipline of the ancient Greek church, were not only discountenanced, but were sometimes cruelly oppressed, before the time of Catharine. Many of them were put to death by the unchristian barbarity of the clergy; and it is particularly recorded, that, in the year 1722, whole families of those unfortunate sectaries, unwilling to submit to the emperor's demand of a renunciation of their opinions, enclosed themselves in barns, and perished in the flames kindled by their own hands. At the time of this persecution the chief ecclesiastical adviser of Peter, was Theophanes, bishop of Pleskoff, afterwards archbishop of Novogorod, whose liberality of mind, however, must have rendered him averse to the murder of reputed heretics. This prelate distinguished himself by writing against the multiplication of ceremonies, the practice of idolatry, the rigours of monastic seclusion, and the various absurdities of superstition; and, while he exhorted the people to be content with praying, singing psalms, and reading the Scriptures, he advised the clergy to preach sermons of practical utility, rather than of doctrinal refinement.†

This schism has continued to our times. Catharine treated the sectaries with lenity; and we do not find that they have been persecuted since her decease. Her chief attacks, in poin of persecution, were directed against the abet tors and advocates of democracy, and her son Paul, in that respect, followed her example.

The Russian plebeians and peasants are remarkable for superstition. Many absurdities are related of them in that particular: but it

* The prayer is, that God the Father would send down his Holy Spirit to sanctify the elements, and make them the body and blood of Christ, for pardon, grace, and salvation, to all who devoutly receive them.

† The idea of dissolving the crowns may seem ominous; but it is the ceremony which indicates that the marriage is concluded.

* Tooke's View of the Russian Empire, vol. ii.

† Historico-Geographical Description of Russia, Siberia, and Great Tartary, by Philip John von Strahlenberg, chap. viii.—The Catechism prepared by this prelate was stamped with the approbation of the holy synod, and published in the year 1766. A summary of Christian Divinity, compiled by Plato, archbishop of Moscow, was about the same time recommended to general use.

will be sufficient to mention the practice of having about the person, or in the apartments of a house, representations of saints (called *gods*) painted on boards. These pictures are viewed with an air of high respect and reverence; and, on entering a room, persons bow to them, and repeatedly cross themselves. Even many of the opulent have these little idols in their possession, and court the favour of these imaginary gods.

Among the multiplicity of tribes subject to the Russian emperor, are many Mohammedan and Pagan communities. The former are indulged with a toleration of their worship; and missionaries are employed to convert the latter, without dragooning them into the adoption of Christianity.

In Armenia, the majority of the people are still Christians, of the Monophysite sect. They appear to be more addicted to fasting than the professors of any other religion whatever; for it is said, that they have one hundred and fifty-six fast-days in the year. Their festivals also amount to a surprising number: but it is not true, that all the days in the year are appropriated to one or other of those opposite observances. Many of the natives of Armenia are dispersed over the different countries of the East, being tolerated as sectaries, and encouraged as traders. The Georgians were accustomed to steer between the doctrines and practices of the Greeks and Armenians: but, as they are now subject to the sway of the Russian emperor, they lean more to the former system.

The Nestorians, whose leading opinion is contrary to that of the Monophysites,* are scattered over a great part of Asia. It has been disputed, whether the Christians who inhabit the Malabar coast are really Nestorians. Dr. Buchanan denies that they are of that sect; but Mr. Wrede maintains that they are. The probability is, that the members of many of the churches upon that coast are of the Nestorian persuasion, while others have become Jacobites or Monophysites. However that may be, these congregations are far from being respectable, the members being in a state of ignorance and misery.

That species of Christianity which had been introduced into China, was tolerated for many years by the emperor Kang-hi: but in the year 1716, he was persuaded by his pagan ministers to revive two edicts against the Christians. By one of these ordinances, they were prohibited from building churches, and making converts; and, by the other, no missionaries were suffered to preach, unless they were furnished with an imperial patent, specifying their native country, the religious order to which they belonged, the time of their arrival in China, and their engagement not to return to Europe. They remained in this state of depression until the death of Kang-hi, in 1722; and then, instead of being relieved from it, they were subjected to farther restrictions. Young-ching, the new emperor, banished or imprisoned some of the princes of his family, and many grandees, for their favourable dispositions toward Christianity, and ordered the missionaries and their associates to be driven from the provinces into the city of Canton. Ten years afterward, they were sent to the isle of Macao; and all attempts of Christians to re-enter the empire were forbidden by the jealousy of the court. The churches were demolished or secularized; and the natives who had embraced catholicism, were compelled to renounce it, or conceal their obnoxious opinions.

The religion of Jesus can boast of very few triumphs in Africa. The Christianity of Congo, or of Zanguebar is unworthy of mention: but, in our religious progress, we must take notice of Egypt and Abyssinia.

The Copts, or the descendants of the primitive Christians of Egypt, persist in their attachment to the Monophysite doctrine. Their priests are ignorant and uninformed; but the people treat them with great respect. Monastic seclusion is very common among this sect, and great austerities are practised by many of the monks and nuns. Beside a Coptic patriarch, there is a Greek patriarch in Egypt; but the church which he rules is in a declining state.

Christianity flourishes more in Abyssinia than in Egypt, because the sovereign is himself a Christian. The hopes of restoring the Romish worship in that empire were entertained by pope Innocent XII., who was encouraged in his views for that purpose by Louis XIV. The Jesuits were eager to obtain the honour of this employment; and Poncet, a French apothecary, was sent from Cairo by the consul Maillet, with Brevedent, a respectable member of the former fraternity. The latter died in Abyssinia; but M. Poncet was introduced to the king (Yasous I.,) whom, however, he did not find willing to become a convert, or to suffer his people to re-embrace catholicism. M. du Roule was afterwards deputed to the same court: but he had scarcely reached Sennaar, in 1704, when he was murdered by the natives. at the instigation of the Franciscans, who were disgusted at seeing the Abyssinian mission in the hands of the Jesuits. Ousts, who usurped the throne in 1709, was well affected to the Romish system, and secretly communed with those Franciscans who yet remained in the country: but he did not attempt to influence the consciences of his people. David, who succeeded him in 1714, ordered three of those strangers to be apprehended; and, being condemned as heretics in an assembly of the clergy, they were stoned to death.*

Another convocation followed, which led to intestine commotions. A new *abuna* or metropolitan announced to the clergy his idea of the consubstantiality of Christ; an opinion contrary to that which had been proclaimed at the gate of the palace.† The ecclesiastics of his party,

* See Mosheim's History, cent. v. part ii. chap. v. sect. ix. xxii.

* Bruce's Travels to discover the Source of the Nile, book iv.

† The abuna represented Christ as being "one God, of the Father alone, united to a body perfectly human, consubstantial with ours, and by that union becoming the Messiah." The emperor maintained, that the Redeemer was "perfect God and perfect man by the union, one Christ, whose body was composed of a precious substance called *bahery*, not consubstantial with ours, or derived from his mother." Neither of these opinions will be deemed strictly orthodox by sound divines.

elate with their supposed triumph, insulted the emperor and his court by songs and shouts; for which offence, above a hundred of them were instantly massacred by a body of pagan soldiers, and the streets of the capital were filled with slaughter. During several subsequent reigns, the affairs of the Abyssinian church were not so important as to claim our notice. With regard to the embassy prepared by pope Benedict XIV. for the purpose of effecting a reconciliation with that church, it may suffice to observe, that it was an abortive attempt.

The state of this church, during the eighteenth century, was less corrupt and degenerate than the Jesuit missionaries represented it. It was said, that a repetition of baptism was annually administered to all adults; but this assertion has been disproved, or, at least strongly denied. It was also imputed to the priests that they gave the eucharist improperly. They do not, indeed, make use of words so fully expressive of a belief in transubstantiation, as those of the Romish ecclesiastics: but that point reflects not the least discredit upon them.

When Mr. Bruce visited Abyssinia, he was surprised at the extraordinary number of churches in that empire. These were erected near running water, for the convenience of those ablutions which the people practised according to the Levitical law. The walls were almost covered with pictures of saints or other representations; but no figures embossed or in *relievo* were exhibited; for they considered the use of these as a species of idolatry. Each parish had an arch-priest, who superintended both its spiritual and secular concerns. The priests and deacons were allowed to marry; but the monks, who occupied huts near the churches, were required to live in a state of celibacy. The reading of Scripture, and recitation of homilies of the fathers, formed, beside the eucharist, the chief portions of divine service.

CHAPTER III.

History of the Ecclesiastical Communities of the Lutherans and Calvinists.

A SENSE of religion seems to be impressed on the minds of all nations, even the most rude and uncivilized: but, as it appeals less to the external senses than to the mind and the heart, its nature renders it peculiarly liable to dispute. The attributes of the Deity, the mode in which he governs the world, and interferes in the concerns of mortals, give occasion for varieties of sentiment, among those who are unwilling to suppose that God ever revealed his will to mankind; and, even where revelation is believed and fully admitted, many doubts arise, and diverse opinions are entertained and defended. Persons who agree in essential points, differ in those of less moment, and contend, as *pro aris et focis*, with all the vehemence of animosity, and all the bitterness of zeal. Hence, among the opposers of popery, who, in one sense, maintained a common cause, various sects were formed, and various controversies occurred. The followers of Luther were hostile to those of Calvin: the disciples of Arminius also disagreed with the partisans of the Genevan reformer.

The Lutherans and Calvinists continued, at the beginning of the eighteenth century, to compose the most numerous protestant establishments of the European continent. The former still flourished in the northern kingdoms, and in different parts of Germany; while the latter enjoyed their religion in many of the free towns of that empire, and under the protection of several of its princes, and also retained their influence in some of the cantons of Switzerland.

Frederic, elector of Brandenburg, who became king of Prussia in the first year of the century, was more disposed to favour the Calvinists than the Lutherans; and the *reformed* took advantage of this circumstance to establish ministers of their persuasion in places where the Lutherans had hitherto exercised the chief sway. The king, however, would not suffer the animosities of the two parties to proceed to the violence of outrage; and he was not unwilling to tolerate Catholics and Jews in his dominions.*

Reflecting on the affairs of religion, this prince was of opinion that a union of his protestant subjects would be conducive to the happiness of his people, and reflect credit on his reign; and he was encouraged in this desirable object, by the doctors Ursinus and Jablonski. The former, though a Calvinist, had accepted from his majesty the episcopal title; and the latter was the first chaplain at court, and also superintendant of the protestant church in Poland. These ecclesiastics suggested, that one of the first steps to be taken in this business, should be the publication of the liturgy of the church of England in a German dress; and, when this translation was completed, Ursinus wrote to the archbishop of Canterbury, (Dr. Tenison,) to request his advice with regard to the proceedings best calculated for the attainment of the desired uniformity. By some negligence or mistake, the letter did not reach the primate, though it was said that he had received it, and refused to answer it. When he was informed of the scheme by a friend of Dr. Ursinus, he did not give it the least encouragement; alleging that a reported declaration of the university of Helmstadt, in the case of the queen of Spain, allowing in certain circumstances a dereliction of the protestant religion, had given him too unfavourable an opinion of the protestant churches of Germany, to permit him conscientiously to correspond with any of them.†

The reason alleged by the English prelate may be pronounced inadequate and unsatisfactory. For the supposed opinion of one protestant university, he condemned the whole reformed body of Germany, and declined assisting in a measure that promised benefit to the protestant cause, as well as credit to the church over which he presided.

This discouragement did not prevent a renewal of the attempt after the lapse of a few years. Jablonski, in 1710, submitted the af-

* Memoires pour servir a l'Histoire de la Maison de Brandebourg, par le Roi de Prusse.

† Relation des Mesures qui furent prises dans les Annees 1711, 1712, et 1713, pour introduire la Liturgie Anglicane dans le Roiaume de Prusse et dans l'Electorat d'Hanovre. Londres, 4to. 1767.

fair to the consideration of Dr. Sharp, archbishop of York, who was pleased at the application, and promised his zealous aid in promoting the pious views of his Prussian majesty. Queen Anne adopted the scheme, and ordered lord Raby, her representative at Berlin, to treat upon the subject with the baron von Printzen, the chief counsellor of Frederic in ecclesiastical concerns. Several conferences ensued; and the affair seemed to be in a favourable train. Bonnet, the Prussian minister at London, was assured by secretary Saint-John, that the court and clergy in general were very well disposed to expedite religious union; and his communication to the king invigorated the zeal of the cabinet of Berlin. Jablonski was now ordered to compose a regular plan of ecclesiastical comprehension and reform. He had already entered, with some minuteness, into the considerations of public worship and church government: and, after ulterior deliberation, he presented to the baron a plan for the establishment of episcopacy in the Prussian dominions. Mr. Ayerst, chaplain to lord Raby, proposed that the court of Hanover should be requested to join in the scheme, at least in the liturgical part of it; and Leibnitz intimated to that divine, that the princess Sophia would probably permit an English chaplain to officiate at her court, if queen Anne would defray the expense of his support.*

When the general attention was called to the diplomatic deliberations at Utrecht, the concerns of religious union were neglected, being deemed by politicians comparatively insignificant. The zeal of Frederic declined; and, although he assigned a fund for the maintenance and theological education of some of his subjects at the English universities, he took no farther measures in the scheme of comprehension. He did not, indeed, live to see the conclusion of the treaty of Utrecht: the archbishop of York, and his royal mistress, also died in the following year; and the scheme was then not merely neglected, but abandoned.

Frederic William, who obtained the crown in the year 1713, contented himself with promoting peace among his subjects of different religions, without requiring uniformity of worship; and he not only maintained toleration in his own territories, but endeavoured to secure to the protestants, in other parts of Germany, that free exercise of their religion, which had been granted by the treaty of Westphalia. Considering him as one of the champions of their cause, they requested his interposition when they were ill treated by their religious adversaries.

The influence of the French court had procured the insertion of a clause in the treaty of Ryswick, importing that the catholic religion, in the places given back by France, should be continued in the same state in which it subsisted at the time of restitution. When the diet took the affair into consideration, the protestant members refused to concur in this clause; but their remonstrances did not prevail on the emperor to withhold that confirmation of the treaty which the Romanists desired. In the negotiations which followed the war for the Spanish succession, the claims of the protestants were neglected, and the clause was not repealed. They were even ill-treated by the elector Palatine, who deprived them of many of their public places of worship; and, as the courts of Berlin and Hanover made reprisals on the catholics, the latter were still farther inflamed into acts of intolerance, illiberality, and outrage. A convention, indeed, was signed between the contending parties, for an observance of the treaty of Westphalia; and an imperial edict was issued in the year 1720, for the redress of those grievances of which the protestants complained in the Palatinate; but both the agreement and the edict were disregarded.*

In Sweden and Denmark, the Lutherans continued to predominate, and the established church was under their government. In the former of those realms, clerical representatives composed a part of the states or national council: but, in the latter, the clergy had no share of political power; and the superintendants, who acted in lieu of bishops, were required by the rulers of the state to propagate the doctrine of passive obedience. Charles XI. of Sweden, and his son the adventurous warrior, kept the states so far in subjection, that neither the clergy nor the laity dared to exercise the authority which the constitution allowed them: but, when Ulrica became queen, they recovered their power, and even extended it beyond the bounds of moderation, reducing the royal authority within very narrow limits. The queen's husband, the prince of Hesse-Cassel, renounced Calvinism to please the clergy, who were almost as unwilling to coalesce with the *reformed* church, as with catholics. It was not without great difficulty that he prevailed upon the diet to grant toleration to the Calvinists. In the year 1741, an edict was issued, by which those sectaries, and also the members of the church of England, were allowed to erect churches, and enjoy a full freedom of worship, in all the maritime towns, except Carlscrone. The Danish government likewise condescended to grant a partial toleration to the Calvinistic protestants; but the people still viewed them with an unfavourable eye.

The Lutherans lived in greater harmony with the Calvinists, (or rather in less discord,) in the electorates of Brandenburg and Hanover, than in most of the German principalities, or in either of the northern kingdoms. The Hanoverian clergy, in particular, seemed to indicate a stronger desire of fraternal union, than the ecclesiastics of other states. In the bishopric of Osnaburg, the protestants were on better terms with the catholics than in many other parts of Germany, because the sovereignty was alternately enjoyed by a Lutheran and a Romanist. In Saxony, when the elector had become a catholic, the majority of the people retained their attachment to Lutheranism, and would not suffer him to obstruct their

* Relation des Mesures qui furent prises dans les Annees 1711, 1712, et 1713, pour introduire la Liturgie Anglicane dans le Roiaume de Prusse et dans l'Electorat d'Hanovre. Londres, 4to 1767.

* Coxe's History of the house of Austria, vol. ii. chap. vii. and x.

profession of that faith. In a part of that electorate, a protestant sect, neither absolutely devoted to the Lutheran nor to the Calvinistic creed, yet professing a regard for the former system, established itself in the year 1722. When the Hussite sect seemed only to be remembered in history, and the catholics supposed it to be extinct, a party of religionists who honoured the memory of the Bohemian reformer, and entertained similar sentiments, appeared in Moravia; but could not obtain, from the Austrian government, the favour of toleration. Count Zinzendorff, admiring their zeal, and expecting, in some degree, to influence their opinions, invited them into Upper Lusatia: and the village of *Herrenhut*,* erected under his auspices, soon rose into a considerable Moravian settlement. As he had been educated in the Lutheran persuasion, he exhorted them to join that church: but they preferred a retention of their own principles to an entire association with any other church. He was allowed to style himself guardian of the fraternity, and at length became its bishop. Disputes which arose among the members were repressed by his authority, and rules of discipline and conduct were framed under his eye. Their ministers did not deny the doctrine of the Trinity, but directed their immediate adoration to Jesus Christ. They affirmed that a Christian might ensure salvation by grace arising from a lively faith, without the absolute necessity of good works: yet the Brethren, in their conduct, by no means neglected morality. Although they professed to consider their church as an episcopal establishment, they did not suffer the bishops to exercise any jurisdiction in the first instance; for all authority originated in their grand synod, which consisted not only of bishops, but also of elders, and of deputies from every congregation. Subordinate to that assembly, were the meetings of elders, both general and particular. When questions had been fully discussed by the assembled brethren, they were frequently decided by lot, which was regarded as an appeal to the Deity.

The zeal of the United Brethren gradually diffused their system over various parts of Germany, and also introduced it into Great Britain and the United Provinces. It likewise made some progress in the northern states. In Livonia, the success of its promoters at first excited the jealousy of the Russian government; and two of the brethren were committed to prison: but the court afterwards consented to tolerate the sect.

The missionary enterprises of this fraternity were prosecuted with indefatigable ardour. In the icy regions of Greenland and Labrador, and in the glowing climate of the West Indies, the labours of conversion were cheerfully sustained. The inveterate prejudices of the Hindoos were softened by the earnest appeals of the Brethren; and the brutish barbarism of the Hottentots yielded to the force of pious persuasion.†

With regard to the religion of the United Provinces. we may observe, that Calvinism still enjoyed the honour of being the established church, and the canons of the council of Dordrecht remained in force: but the tenets of Arminius were preferred to those of Calvin by a great number of people, in every class of society. Anabaptists, Lutherans, and other protestant sects, were freely tolerated; and the government connived at the practice of the catholic worship, long before it was regularly permitted. With respect to the form of the establishment, we may add, that each Calvinist congregation, beside one or more ministers, had deacons and elders: each deputed a minister and an elder to the classes; and each class sent deputies to the synod of the province.

In the progress of the century, religious zeal declined among the Dutch: public worship was less frequently attended; and education was less impregnated with a Christian spirit. If the theological faculty at any of the universities, the members of a class or a synod, condemned particular publications as repugnant to the established creed, or hostile to religion in general, many exclaimed against the bigotry and intolerance of these censors: but the rulers of the republic thought proper to support the decisions of the church, and ministers were sometimes deposed, for betraying, in the pulpit or with their pens, the interests of Calvinism or of Christianity. For the defence and support of that religion, the Teylerian society was formed at the Hague in 1786; and some judicious publications have arisen from the rewards offered out of the endowment.

Among the subjects of France, notwithstanding the revocation of the edict of Nantes, and the consequent exile or destruction of many thousand families of conscientious protestants, Calvinism was not extinct. There was great danger in professing it under a bigoted government: yet a considerable number retained a strong attachment to its doctrines. The inhabitants of the Cevennes mountains, and of the Vivarais, in particular, were zealous in the cause; and their zeal was invigorated by the eloquence of several bold Huguenots, who had returned from exile to preach their favourite doctrines. The inhuman violence of a Romish priest added fuel to the flame. The people rose against this oppressor, put him to death, and sacrificed other catholics to their revenge. Troops were sent to restore order by summary process: the insurgents retired before them, but were not over-awed into submission. The cruel punishments to which the soldiery subjected the captive malcontents, produced severe retaliation; and the increasing numbers of the latter so alarmed the court, that three marechals were successively sent to subdue them. Villars at length prevailed upon Cavalier, a young baker, who had assumed the command over them, to enter into a treaty in their name; and it was agreed, in the year 1704, that a general amnesty should

* Signifying the guard or watch of the Lord.

† The Moravians do not appear to deserve the severe censures thrown out against them by Dr. Maclaine. in a note that is justly stigmatised by Dr. Haweis as *impure* and *malignant*, and which, indeed, must excite the disgust of every chaste and candid reader.—See the note on page 309 of the present volume for this specimen of vulgar calumny, which could not reasonably have been expected from the translator of Mosheim.

be granted to the party; and that this leader, and four regiments of the protestants, should serve in the French army as foreign subsidiaries, enjoying the free exercise of their religion.* Cavalier was afterwards introduced at court; but, thinking himself in danger amidst the catholics, and finding that he could not procure so many followers in his new plan as he expected, he retired from France. Roland, a Calvinist who disdained submission, now acted at the head of a body of insurgents; but he soon lost his life, and many of the Huguenots of Languedoc quitted France, while the generality of those who remained, ceased to profess openly the tenets which had embroiled them with the Romanists. Some commotions occasionally ensued, from the violent proceedings of the catholics, against those who were known to be (or suspected of being) still attached to Calvinism; and, for a long course of years, the flame was rather smothered than extinguished.†

The dissolute successor of the fourteenth Louis had not sufficient liberality of mind to restore to the protestants the plenitude of toleration. To their religion he preferred that in which he had been educated; and, though he probably would not, like his predecessor, have spontaneously annulled the edict of Nantes, he did not think that it was either consonant with the dignity or conducive to the advantage of the church to favour those who were hostile to the establishment. He therefore, by an edict of the year 1724, menaced protestant preachers with death, and their abettors with imprisonment, or the labours of galley-slaves. He also renewed the prohibition of return to all emigrants, unless they should abjure the protestant tenets, and ordered that no molestation should be given to the present possessors of the estates of refugees, while the latter retained their anti-catholic opinions. At length, however, he so far yielded to the advice of the less bigoted members of his cabinet, as to allow the votaries of the reformation to become legal husbands and wives, by having the clergy to witness their marriages as civil contracts; and it was also intimated to them, that no notice should be taken of their religious assemblies. Upon these terms, the marechal Richelieu, in 1754, re-established the tranquillity of Languedoc, where compulsory attendance upon the Romish worship, and constrained abjurations of supposed heresy, had not effected that conversion which the court so earnestly wished to produce.‡

In the disputes between Louis XV. and the provincial and Parisian parliaments, the protestants were prompted, by their zeal for liberty, to side with the opposers of the court; but they were obliged to be cautious in their proceedings, that they might not entail upon themselves the indignation and vengeance of royalty. They witnessed with secret joy the ruin of the Jesuits, the zealous supporters of catholicism, and looked forward with renovated hope to the grant of a full toleration.

The French protestants maintained an amicable correspondence with the Genevans, to whose sacramental celebrations a multitude of the inhabitants of Languedoc and Dauphine resorted at the four great festivals of the year They also encouraged the anti-papal perseverance of the Vaudois, who, though molested by the catholic zeal of the king of Sardinia, would not suffer his priests to pervert their principles.

The inhabitants of Bern, and other protestant cantons of Switzerland, refused to grant to the Lutherans that toleration to which they were entitled. The liberal example of the Genevans, who held out a friendly hand to that sect, did not excite imitation among the followers of the Helvetic confession.

While Christian VII. and Gustavus III. reigned in Denmark and Sweden, the spirit of toleration became more prevalent in those kingdoms. By the former prince, the Calvinists were gratified with a greater degree of freedom in point of religion; but, in some places, they were not suffered to preach against other creeds and modes of worship, or to make proselytes. The Mennonites, though protestants, were placed on the same footing with Romanists; were not allowed to contract marriage with Lutherans without a license, and were obliged to acquiesce in the Lutheran education of their children of both sexes. In Sweden, the diet (in 1779) granted, to foreigners settling in that country, the freedom of worship, with an exception of public ceremonies and processions; at the same time excluding them from offices in the state, and forbidding them to propagate their opinions in seminaries.*

The Danish church, at that time, consisted of twelve superintendants or bishops, many provosts or directors of districts, parochial priests, and chaplains. The annual revenue of the metropolitan did not exceed one thousand pounds; and the income of some pastors in Iceland scarcely amounted to five pounds. In Sweden, there were fourteen bishoprics, the occupants of which had not, in general, a greater income than the superintendants of Denmark. Associated with deputies from each archdeaconry, they formed the second component body of the states or national council. The clergy of that kingdom, by order of the states, had the care of the general education of the people, all of whom, females as well as males, were required to learn the easy arts of reading and writing.

In Germany, the frequent controversies between the Lutherans and Calvinists, and also between them and the catholics, had cherished

* Many of these sectaries pretended to the gift of divination; and, in the year 1705, some of them came over to Great Britain, where they met with little encouragement. Those who ventured to appear in Holland were confined as fanatics, that, amidst hard labour, they might have time to recover their senses.

† Histoire de France sous le Regne de Louis XIV. par M. de Larrey.—Essai sur l'Hist. Generale, par M. de Voltaire; *art.* de Calvinisme.

‡ Vie Privee de Louis XV.

* Dr. Erskine's Sketches and Hints of Church History and Theological Controversy.—Yet a writer in the Encyclopædia Britannica, (edit. 1791,) after speaking of the Lutheran establishment, says, "There is not another sect in these kingdoms," [*Denmark Sweden*, and *Norway*.] He probably borrowed the remark from some *old* geographical work.

and kept up that spirit of free inquiry which originally produced the reformation. In the discussion of doctrinal points, and in bringing them to the test of Scripture, writers of different capacities and dispositions gave such varied interpretations, that many readers were perplexed and confounded, and began to doubt whether any doctrines had ever been revealed to mankind. Some protestant authors, having seduced themselves into scepticism in the solitude of their closets, propagated their doubts among the people; still pretending, however, to be well-wishers to the cause of religion. Others openly ventured to recommend reason as a substitute for religion.

The Pietists, on the other hand, continued to promote the diffusion of religious zeal and vital Christianity. They not only withstood the efforts of infidel philosophy, but also reprobated latitudinarian indifference, censured the predication of mere morality, and raised their voices against the worldly spirit and increasing dissipation of the age. They were "exposed to much obloquy" (says an English Pietist)* "for their rigid maxims, and resolute rejection of all unhallowed conformity to the manners and amusements of a wicked world." "As the century advanced" (he adds) "the fervour of Pietism abated; and, inquity abounding, the love of many waxed cold." The same zealous censor represents the generality of the Lutheran clergy, as sinking at that time into a *Laodicean state*, and "maintaining the forms and formulæ of Lutheranism, instead of the spirit of Christianity." Undoubtedly, this was the case with many of the ministers of that church: but it does not follow, because they were not continually speaking of faith and grace, that they were destitute of a Christian spirit, or regardless of the purity of religion. They might have less cant, less ostentation of piety, than those who considered themselves as the only sincere votaries of evangelical truth; but it is uncandid to insinuate that they were Christians only in name and in form, not in principle or in substance.

In Saxony and the Prussian territories, the metaphysical philosophy of Wolff, privy counsellor to Frederic William, king of Prussia, had a considerable effect in the diffusion of a sceptical spirit; and, although he was publicly censured for his pernicious writings, and deprived of a professorship at Halle, he continued to propagate his sentiments after his retreat into the principality of Hesse Cassel. He was subsequently protected by the Swedish court, but was more particularly favoured by that philosophic prince who became king of Prussia in the year 1740. Professor Kant, the celebrated metaphysician, was patronised by the same monarch; and his system likewise tended to generate scepticism.

This prince, the well-known Frederic, was fond of free inquiry, and eager to evince his superiority to what he considered as idle prejudice. He therefore easily suffered himself to be persuaded by infidel philosophers, that religion was the invention of interested hypocrites and artful statesmen. He was not more favourable in this respect to Christianity than to the Moslem creed. Priests of all persuasions were, in his eye, either wilful deluders of the multitude, or the credulous instruments of delusion. These opinions he gloried in propagating among his friends; and his court thus became the seat of irreligion, and a school of impiety. It was a matter of indifference to such a monarch, what religion his subjects professed, or whether they followed any religion at all, provided that they were subservient to his military and political despotism. He considered the morality of different sects as nearly the same;* and, while he tolerated all, his active vigilance kept his dominions in tranquillity, undisturbed by open animosities or serious dissensions. His people were free in a religious sense, but in no other respect.

Societies of *illuminati*, or enlightened reasoners, were at length formed in some of the protestant towns and principalities of Germany, and even in several of the catholic states. At Munich, professor Weishaupt, who had received his education among the Jesuits, became the founder of a club of reformists; and, when he had been banished from Bavaria for his dangerous principles, he was protected and encouraged by the duke of Saxe-Gotha. Baron Knigge strenuously laboured in the same cause; and, although greater effects have been attributed to these societies than their real importance may induce us to believe, it must be allowed that they paved the way for revolutionary mischief, and aided the pernicious influence of Gallic impiety and sedition.

While Louis XVI. filled the French throne, the clergy of the establishment repeatedly complained of his connivance at the encroachments of the protestants, who insulted or derided the institutions of the holy church, presumed to draw within their pale the children of catholics, taxed the people for the payment of salaries to unlicensed ministers, obtained the direction of public schools, and procured admission into the seats of magistracy. They did not, however, dare to recommend an infliction of the rigours of vengeance upon these "deluding and deluded men," but merely advised that the protestants should be *bribed* into an adoption of the Romish faith. Louis did not wish that considerations of interest should have any influence upon religious conversions; but he was willing, by occasional grants out of the royal temporalities, to assist those converts who required relief. The proselytes thus made by the church were not very numerous. The number of protestants, on the contrary, continued to increase, until the court thought it expedient to accede to their wishes. Under the administration of M. de Brienne, archbishop of Toulouse, the king issued an edict, by which they were admitted (in January, 1788) to the free practice of their religion, and to all the rights of citizens. The revolution soon followed; and all religions were then confounded in the vortex of politics.

Before that revolution commenced its attack upon all former institutions, religious as well

* Dr. Haweis.

* "Il n'y a aucune religion (he said) qui, sur le sujet de la morale, s'ecarte beaucoup des autres."

as political, Frederic William, the successor of the infidel king of Prussia, endeavoured to stem the torrent of latitudinarianism and of irreligion by a spirited and not injudicious proclamation.* We take notice of this edict, not only because it is remarkable in itself, and tends to show the state of religion in the Prussian dominions at that time, but also because it produced a warm controversy. His majesty ordained, in the first place, that the three principal Christian creeds and systems (the Reformed, Lutheran, and Romish) should be preserved genuine. The second article provided for a continued toleration of Moravians, Mennonites, and the Bohemian brethren, beside Jews; but prohibited sects, pernicious to the state, from holding public assemblies. Thirdly, all endeavours to make proselytes, in any confession, were forbidden: yet all persons were at liberty to change their religion. Popish emissaries, monks, and ex-Jesuits, were particularly prohibited from attempting to convert those whom they called heretics. After commending the general harmony in which the clergy and laity of the three confessions seemed to live, the king ordered, that the two first churches should preserve their liturgies and directories: they might, he said, abolish immaterial ceremonies; but he would not suffer them to change any essential part of their old systems; an injunction which appeared to him to be the more necessary, as he had observed that many of the preachers of those communities denied important articles of Protestantism and Christianity, depreciated the authority of the Scriptures, and "served up again the often-refuted errors of Socinians, Naturalists,† and Deists," under the pretence of enlightening the people. Such ministers as disapproved the creed which they had originally adopted, were required to resign their pastoral charges, rather than teach any thing contrary to the received doctrines of their church.

Several free-thinkers and latitudinarians fiercely attacked the edict, as if it had been an unwarrantable invasion of liberty of conscience; but it was ably defended by Doctor Semler of Halle, and other divines. Its assailants reprobated the arbitrary spirit that fettered the freedom of inquiry, and which commanded individuals to believe without conviction; affirmed that Christ's kingdom was not of this world, and that the penal laws of temporal governments were inapplicable to religion, and wholly unjustifiable when employed for the coercion of the conscience; and animadverted on the inconsistency manifested by a protestant ruler, in condemning and counteracting a freedom of opinion analogous to that which had produced the Reformation. The supporters of the decree denied, that it enforced belief, as people might still believe only what suited their ideas, and might even freely publish their thoughts: but when a minister, in the exercise of his pastoral charge, taught doctrines repugnant to those which he had formerly undertaken to maintain, or inconsistent with the fundamental truths of religion, there was no injustice, they said, in preventing such a preacher from continuing to be unfaithful to his trust.

Infidelity was less observable in Poland than in Prussia or Brandenburg: but that country was a frequent scene of religious dissension. The Polish protestants had long enjoyed, not merely toleration, but an equality of privilege with the catholics. After the expulsion of the Socinians, the Romanists obtained the ascendency, and gradually encroached on the rights of the protestants, for whose exclusion from the diet they procured, in the year 1733, a decree of the majority of that assembly. After the election of Stanislaus Poniatowski to the sovereignty, in 1764, the *dissidents* (under which term the members of the Greek church were included with the Lutherans and Calvinists) had recourse to the kings of Great Britain, Prussia, and Denmark, and to the empress of Russia, who readily promised to assist them by intercession for the recovery of those privileges which had been stipulated for them in the treaty of Oliva. The diet, however, for some years, would only allow them the freedom of worship; but, in 1768, being overawed by a Russian army, the assembly acceded to the requisitions of the four courts. Many of the catholic nobles, resenting this compliance, and disgusted at the domineering influence of Russia, took up arms for religion and liberty; and a desultory warfare commenced, which did not entirely cease before the first partition of Poland. The dissidents were then less favoured than they had been by the preceding diet; but, beside toleration, they obtained seats in some of the courts of justice. When the czarina, and her allies in spoliation (the empress of Germany and king of Prussia,) had seized three considerable portions of the country, her influence was paramount over that part which still retained the name of a kingdom; and she preserved peace among the votaries of the different religions. In the provinces which were ceded to Austria, the catholics gave little molestation to the dissidents, as it was apprehended that, if oppressed, they would offer themselves as subjects to the tolerant Catharine, or take refuge under the wings of the Prussian eagle.*

By that constitution which Poland obtained in 1791 from the spirit of her nobles, but which her potent adversaries would not suffer long to subsist, toleration was more fully allowed; and, when the kingdom was finally dismembered, however unjust was the spoliation, the new rulers of the country established the security of religious opinion and worship.

In Hungary, the protestants did not enjoy, during the reign of Joseph, the full effect of his liberal declarations and fair promises. They complained that his edict was not properly enforced; but, after his death, their solicitations procured a favourable decree from his successor Leopold. It was ordained by the diet, in 1791, that persons of all ranks should enjoy a perfect freedom of public worship, and the liberty of erecting churches, even with steeples and bells; but that, when the protestants should

* Dated at Potsdam, July 9, 1788.

† Not the cultivators of natural history or philosophy, but the teachers of natural religion, as opposed to Christianity. The count de Buffon, indeed, was a naturalist in both senses.

* Coxe's Travels in Poland.

wish to build a church, parsonage-house, or school, a mixed committee of the district should be holden, to ascertain the sufficiency of the proposed means, and the landlord should then fix upon the spot; that no protestants should be compelled to attend mass, witness catholic processions, or pay dues to the Romish priests; that they might form consistories and hold synods, but that no laws or ordinances framed at those meetings should be operative without the royal confirmation; that their authority over their own schools should also be subject to their sovereign's control; and that they might publish religious books, under the inspection of censors of their own appointment, who should, however, be responsible to the government for their official conduct. It was also decreed that they should be eligible to public offices, and even to a seat in the diet, equally with the Romanists.*

These grants were deemed, by the catholics, great *favours* and liberal *concessions;* but, by the protestants, they were considered as no more than natural *rights*. The Romish bigots. in some instances, counteracted the new ordinances, and prevented the immediate accomplishment of the patriotic intentions of the diet: but the court, and the catholics in general, were disposed to permit the execution of the decree.

The protestants of Bohemia were, at the same time, freed from all persecution and molestation, on the subject of religion. During a great part of the century, the Jews in that kingdom were more favoured by its catholic rulers, than were even the Christian sects: but the latter, at length, found an opportunity of emerging from their difficulties and depression.

When the revolution had broken out in France, the spirit of irreligion was more openly manifested in Germany, among the three denominations of Christians, than it had been at any time from the first establishment of the religion of Jesus in that country; and, being mingled with the desire of enjoying a greater portion of civil liberty, it prompted the people, in several states of the empire, to submit to the arms of France, soon after the war began to rage. When French fraternity had lost the charm of novelty, many repented of the blind forwardness with which they had accepted it: but, when the yoke was fixed upon their necks, it was too late to retract. In the ecclesiastical electorates, capricious varieties of opinion were substituted for the catholic creed; and, although religion was not absolutely neglected by all classes of people, either in the protestant or catholic states, the worship became less decorous and regular; the public service of God ceased, in a great measure, to be an object of devout attention.

CHAPTER IV.

History of the Church of England and its Dependencies, and also of the Protestant Sects in the British Dominions.

When the church of England had been rescued from danger by the seasonable exertions of the prince of Orange, and the free exercise of *particular* worship had been allowed by a wise and liberal parliament to those protestants who dissented from the *general* religion of the state, the defeat and depression of the catholics, and the removal of anxiety from the minds both of the orthodox and the sectaries, produced a degree of tranquillity which the church had not enjoyed from the time of the Reformation. The schism of the nonjurors, indeed, still subsisted at the beginning of the eighteenth century; the legality of the ecclesiastical government was boldly disputed by many zealots; and a spirited contest was carried on between the high-church and low-church factions, or the Tories and Whigs of the hierarchy. But the collisions of party were less vehement, and the animosity of disputants less bitter and malignant.

If Anne had reigned immediately after the Revolution, she would not have been so ready as king William to grant toleration to dissenters. She suspected them of aiming at the ruin of the church, while they professed only a wish for an unmolested indulgence of their peculiar opinions. But, as the legislature had thought proper to gratify them with the freedom to which they had long aspired, she resolved not to encroach upon their admitted claims, or offer the least violence to what she called their tender consciences. She wished, however, to prevent the practice of occasional conformity, by which not a few presbyterians and other dissenters procured employments intended only for the orthodox. They took the sacrament according to the established forms, to qualify themselves by law for particular offices, and then frequented the meeting-houses of non-conformists. The Tories frequently introduced a bill to restrain this interested duplicity. Thrice their views were baffled by the influence of the Whigs; but when, upon a renewed attempt, clauses were inserted for the security of the protestant succession and the confirmation of the act which tolerated nonconformity, the low church party suffered the bill to pass.

In the convocation, or clerical senate, the two parties occasionally disputed with eagerness; but the queen's ministers rather checked than promoted these debates, because they deemed it sufficient that the parliament should be the scene of contest. The literary war, on the subject of the claims and rights of the convocation, which had been carried on in the reign of William, did not cease amidst the discouragement of debates in that assembly: but it gradually declined; and the able work of Dr. Wake, archbishop of Canterbury, seemed triumphantly to close the controversy in favour of the Whigs. The Tories had maintained, that it was the indisputable right of the clergy, not only to meet in ordinary synods, but (as often as a new parliament met) to sit and vote in convocation; and that in this assembly they might deliberate upon ecclesiastical affairs, and agree to various resolutions, without the formality of a previous license. The opposite party referred all the acts of the church to the pleasure of the sovereign, without whose permission the clergy could not lawfully meet, debate, or enact

* Travel in Hungary, by Robert Townson, LL. D.

It is remarkable that the former of these factions, while they disputed the power of the temporal prince in religious affairs, recommended passive obedience on the part of the people, as what the governing power of the state might justly claim; and that the Whigs, on the other hand, while they promoted the authoritative interference of the crown in the government of the church, professed a desire of clipping, on other occasions, the wings of royalty.

The predications of the maxims and doctrines of Toryism by Sacheverel, a hot-headed divine, excited in parliament a flame which diffused itself through the kingdom. The Whig leaders imprudently fanned it, and, by impeaching a zealot, whose effusions might safely have been neglected, seriously injured their own interests. The sentence of the high court of peers seemed rather to be a triumph than a punishment; and the high-church party obtained a decisive advantage in the cabinet. The queen then indulged the clergy with a greater latitude of debate in convocation, than she had allowed them in the former part of her reign.

The church of Ireland was also agitated by the distinctions of Whig and Tory; but its tranquillity was not disturbed in any remarkable degree. The catholics still formed the great bulk of the nation: but power was in the hands of their adversaries, who, from principles of policy, and in the spirit of self defence, were determined to hold it with a vigorous grasp. The holders of benefices, however, in the wild and unfrequented parts of that island, found it difficult and even dangerous to collect tithes from the papists, who sometimes were guilty of acts of violence and outrage.

The presbyterian establishment in Scotland remained unimpaired under the sway of Anne: and its preservation was an essential article of the legislative union which dignified her reign. The episcopalians, however, were tolerated in that country; and a bill was enacted, in 1712, by the united parliament, in confirmation of the unrestrained freedom of their worship. Public chapels, which had not been allowed to them in the preceding reign, were now erected in many parts of North Britain; and the people, confiding in the protection of the *court*, were not afraid to dissent from the *kirk*.

These episcopalians, in general, were unfriendly to the Revolution, and to the succession of the house of Hanover; and, therefore, fell under the general suspicion of favouring the views of the queen's brother, the catholic claimant of the crown. When the elector of Hanover had ascended the British throne, this suspicion became stronger; and, during the rebellion that arose in the year 1715, those who had no concern in it were closely watched, and the ministers of their communion were restricted in their functions; with the exercise of which, however, they were soon re-indulged.

During the reign of that ruler, the church of England continued to flourish. The king, indeed, supported that party which did not bear the character of being particularly zealous for the ecclesiastical establishment; and we need not be surprised at his habitual regard for the Whigs, as they were the only cordial promoters of those statues and arrangements which paved his way to the throne. He encouraged those divines who recommended the principles of civil liberty, and who at the same time wished to subject the church to the state, and give the temporal prince a commanding height of religious authority; not such, however, as would enable him to oppress the church, but only to secure its welfare and tranquillity, in the midst of general toleration.

After the suppression of the rebellion, while the nation enjoyed general repose, the church was disturbed by the warm prosecution of a literary controversy. This dispute was occasioned by a sermon which the king (who heard it) ordered to be printed. Dr. Benjamin Hoadley, who had been honoured with a vote of the house of commons, requesting the crown to reward his services, as a friend of liberty and of the protestant settlement, was the preacher of this discourse, in which he delivered his sentiments on the subject of Christ's kingdom or church. He endeavoured to prove, that the true church did not require any other than spiritual sanctions; that it was not intended by its divine founder to be supported by political *encouragements*, or checked by political *discouragements;* that such interferences, on the part of the state, tended to give to the church a worldly character, not altogether consistent with genuine piety, and not favourable to pure or sublime devotion; and that the ecclesiastical establishment would flourish more under its own guidance, than under temporal direction. The kingdoms of this world, he said, could not suggest proper ideas of that government which ought to prevail, in a visible and sensible manner, in Christ's kingdom. The sanctions of Christ's laws, appointed by himself, were not the rewards of this world, not the offices or glories of this state, not the pains of imprisonment or of exile, or the smaller discouragements that belong to human society; these could not be the instruments of such a persuasion as would be acceptable to God. To "teach Christians that they must either profess, or be silent, against their own consciences, because of the authority of others over them, was to found that authority upon the ruins of sincerity and common honesty; to teach a doctrine which would have prevented the Reformation, and even the existence of the church of England." No power, repugnant to the supreme authority of Christ, could be justly claimed over the church by Christians, even of the highest rank. His supremacy, as legislator and judge, no temporal or human power ought to infringe or invalidate. These opinions were censured in convocation, as tending to produce disorder and anarchy in the church, and to prevent the due subserviency of that body to the state; and they were combated in print by the celebrated Sherlock and other divines. The dispute was denominated the Bangorian controversy; and, when it ceased, the same diversity of sentiment remained, which had before prevailed on the subject. Such is the frequent result of a literary dispute!

While the controversy was at its height, the

dissenters were gratified, in the session of 1718–9, by the introduction of a bill, calculated to relieve them from those tests to which the bishop of Bangor objected: but it did not pass in that favourable shape which it assumed at its first appearance; for it did not provide, as the sovereign wished, for the repeal of the sacramental test, although it annulled the acts against schism and occasional conformity.

The dissenters affirm, that tests of this kind are the remains of a persecuting spirit, and are therefore disgraceful to a government which professes to avoid persecution. When conscientious individuals, they say, are excluded, on account of their religious opinions, from those offices and preferments which are bestowed on their fellow-citizens, they do not enjoy the full rights of toleration. It is not sufficient that they are allowed to worship God in their own way, if they are debarred from the general advantages of that community with which they are connected. Their claims, we answer, might be admitted where no particular religion is established by law and authority, as preferable to all other creeds and systems: but, where an ecclesiastical establishment forms a part of the constitution, it is by no means unreasonable to exclude, from its advantages and emoluments, those who are unwilling to conform to it. It is the natural character of sects to be hostile to each other; and those who differ from the establishment cannot be expected to be its defenders or preservers. To guard against the intrusion of such men, it is ordained that conditions should be annexed to the acceptance of benefices; and, if the consciences of individuals should be too scrupulous to suffer them to accede to the terms, they ought rather to blame themselves than the government, for the want of preferment in that church to which they are not closely allied; or (to put the affair in another point of view) they may congratulate themselves on their disinterested piety. But tests, they say, only serve to make hypocrites; for many will be induced to conform outwardly, who secretly retain their supposed heresy: only good men, therefore, or the ingenuous and sincere professors of religion, are discountenanced and stigmatised. We answer, that it is not the wish of the rulers of the state to obtain merely exterior conformity: that is an accidental circumstance, arising from the interested views of the candidates for preferment; and there is surely less danger in having a few hypocritical intruders, than in opening the doors of the church to all who may choose to dissent from its doctrines; the majority of whom, though many of them may be pious and worthy men, would wish to overturn the prevailing system.

The utility of the test, as a barrier to the church, has influenced the greater part of the nobility, and also of the national representatives, to withstand all the efforts made by the dissenters for its annulment; and it is not very probable that the present generation will witness its removal. It has repeatedly resisted, in our times, all the eloquence of latitudinarian orators, and all the arts of presbyterian and independent sophists. The chief objectors to it would, perhaps, if their system should ever be predominant, recommend a stronger exclusion of all other religionists from power: such is the perverseness, such the selfishness of human nature!

The tolerant disposition of the king induced him to disapprove the violence of the Tories, who endeavoured to procure a new penal act against the Arians and Socinians, and all who might be guilty of blasphemy and profaneness. The Whigs strenuously opposed the bill; and it was not suffered to be added to the statutes of the realm. The same party checked the spirit of debate which agitated the ecclesiastical senate; and, from that time, the two houses of convocation have only met *pro formâ*, with every new parliament.

During the remainder of this reign, the church of England, and also that of Ireland, enjoyed tranquillity: but the increased liberty of the times encouraged a freedom of thinking, which led some bold spirits into a denial of Christianity and of all divine revelation. Anthony Collins was one of these assailants; and he rendered himself so obnoxious to the clergy, that they reviled him as an atheist. As he had attacked revelation under the government of a devout queen, it was not likely that he would refrain or desist when the sovereign (though not a freethinker) was less religiously disposed. He therefore again took up the pen, and, in 1724, published a Discourse of the Grounds and Reasons of the Christian Religion. Some able theologians strenuously defended the faith and system which he thus attacked; and his Scheme of Literal Prophecy likewise drew forth spirited replies and indignant animadversions. Bernard de Mandeville, an emigrant Dutch physician, also wrote, both in this and the succeeding reign, against Christianity. Dr. Matthew Tindal, a professor of the civil law, represented this religion as being coeval with the creation;—in other words, he controverted the credibility of Christ's mission; and, alleging the sufficiency of natural religion, denied the expediency of any revelation of the divine will. He even affected to think that such a communication was incompatible with the rights of man. This bold attack was repelled by the learning of the orthodox Waterland, and the ability of the virtuous though schismatical Foster.

We do not find that any new sects arose in this island under the government of the first George; but, in the long reign of his son, various instances of schism occurred, both in North and South Britain. To the former of these reigns may be assigned the formation of a religious *party*,* which, although it never became numerous, drew some distinguished men into its vortex. Mr. John Hutchinson, a pretender to philosophy, controverted the Newtonian system,† substituted a *plenum* for a *vacuum*, and ridiculed the laws of gravity. The true system of nature, he said, was to be found in the writings of Moses; and no philosophy

* As the followers of Hutchinson did not form a distinct church or society, and continued to belong to the church or body with which they were formerly connected, they did not so far give way to schism as to compose a sect.

† In a work entitled, "Moses' *Principia*," the first part of which appeared in 1724.

could be deemed correct, except that of the Hebrew Scriptures. With regard to the doctrine of the Trinity, he advanced a fanciful opinion, importing that the idea of three persons of one and the same essence, answered to fire, light, and spirit, the three grand agents in nature, or the three modifications of the same substance, namely, air. His opinions were eagerly espoused, and warmly recommended, by Mr. Julius Bate, whose zeal he rewarded by procuring him a benefice. Sixteen years after his death, his system was defended by Mr. George Horne, a young clergyman, whose merit afterwards elevated him to the episcopal dignity. Forbes, the Scottish judge, also wrote in its vindication; Mr. Romaine, the popular preacher, gave his assent to it; Dr. Wetherell, William Jones, and other divines not destitute of learning, regarded it as worthy of adoption and support. Bate and Spearman, the editors of Hutchinson's works, maintained, not (as some have interpreted the author's meaning) that the sun moves and the earth stands still, but that no scriptural passages, properly construed, are repugnant to the Copernican hypothesis respecting those parts of the universe.

A secession from the established church of Scotland took place in the year 1727, in consequence of the independent spirit of John Glas, who, disapproving every establishment of a *national* church, maintained that all churches ought only to be *congregational;* in other words, that no general church ought to be formed for a nation, but that each religious society in a kingdom or state should be self-constituted and controlled only by itself. For this and other opinions, he was suspended from his ministerial functions, and, for continued contumacy, he was deposed from the rank of minister, first by a provincial synod, and afterwards (in 1730) by the general assembly of the Scottish church. He persisted, however, in the propagation of his sentiments, both by preaching and writing, and formed several congregations, of which the most numerous was that of Dundee.*

While Mr. Glas, and those who adopted his opinions, were employed in strengthening their secession, some other divines, on different grounds, were meditating a retreat from the establishment. These ministers wished to maintain the national church in its original strictness; and, as they could not accomplish that object, they resolved to form new congregations. Supposed infringements of the constitution of the kirk had excited their strong disgust. They complained of the laws of patronage, and wished for a popular election of ministers: they alleged that the right of protest against the proceedings of the assembly had been invaded, and that the rulers of the kirk, beside acting arbitrarily, suffered its doctrines to be corrupted. Four ministers were suspended from their parochial functions, in 1733, for the freedom of their animadversions on these points; but the assembly reinstated them in the following year: yet, as the grievances of which they complained were not redressed, they refused to re-join the establishment. They strengthened their interest by considerable adjunctions of force, drawn from the ranks both of the clergy and laity, particularly after they had published a second *testimony* of the grounds of their secession. Being cited to appear before the assembly, and refusing to acknowledge its jurisdiction, they were debarred, in 1740, from all clerical functions in the kirk, and excluded from all emoluments connected with that church. It may be proper to mention, that Ebenezer Erskine, who had acted as minister at Stirling, was the chief of these seceders.*

When the seceders had formed three presbyteries, a division arose among them, in 1747, in consequence of an oath which some of them deemed inconsistent with the sentiments avowed in their *testimony.* It was the ordinary oath of a burgess, in support of the *true religion* established by law. We cannot, said one party, conscientiously honour with that appellation the establishment from which we have seceded; while the other members of the synod contended, that the oath might safely be taken, as the religion of the state was still the true faith, though many of its ostensible votaries had departed from its principles, or loosely professed it. The former, who were called *Anti-burghers,* prevailed on this occasion, and voted, that the oath was incompatible with the testimony. they even excommunicated the members by whom it was vindicated. This idle dispute long continued to keep the seceders in distinct synods: and, at the close of the century, the schism was not entirely healed, though the two parties were less hostile than they had been.

The secession of Mr. Glas was continued by Robert Sandeman, who, in 1757, published his opinions in a series of letters, which led to the establishment of several congregations in England, as well as in Scotland. The sect also extended itself to North America, particularly to New England. Its members were of opinion, that all who *found* the apostolic report concerning the death and resurrection of Christ *true in their minds*, possessed that *faith* from which *justification* resulted, even if they were the most sinful of mankind; that, though good works be not essential to justification, it is proper to observe the moral precepts which were inculcated in the times of the apostles; that brotherly love and social kindness ought strikingly to mark the demeanour of Christians; that such love however, ought not to preclude the excommunication and disgrace of an offending brother; and that, in this and other cases of deliberation, not merely a majority, but the whole congregation, ought to decide. They required the sacrament of the eucharist to be taken every week; and they encouraged a great frequency of prayer. They had *love-feasts*, or meetings of mutual hospitality, which were terminated with hymns and the kiss of charity; and, in the same spirit of fraternal affection, they inculcated the maxim of a community of goods.†

* Adams' Religious World Displayed, vol. iii. p. 170-6.

* Adams' Religious World Displayed, vol. iii. p. 193—6.

† Adam, vol. iii. p. 177—84.

In the same reign, a sect, which soon became far more numerous and flourishing than those now mentioned, arose in England, and spread over the British dominions. We have already remarked, that the animosities between the orthodox and the dissenters had gradually subsided after the Revolution; and we may add, that this diminution of rancour was more particularly observable after the accession of the Hanoverian family to the throne, when the principles of toleration were more fully established amidst the progress of free inquiry. At the same time, the clergy of the establishment seemed in general to sink into a lukewarmness and indifference which disgusted all but the worldly-minded pursuers of immediate interest. Infidelity also gained ground among the laity, and sneers at religion were beginning to be a part of the fashionable system.

This degeneracy was observed with sensations of horror by John and Charles Wesley, who were then students at the university of Oxford, and had contracted a serious turn of mind from the writings of William Law, the celebrated mystic. These devout brothers passed a great part of their time in religious conversation, in reflecting on the interesting contents of the Holy Scriptures, and in private prayer. They were joined by some other academics who were religiously disposed; and a sect which afterwards made an extraordinary progress, took its rise in the year 1729, deriving the appellation of *Methodists* from the regular distribution of their time, their orderly and composed demeanour, and the supposed purity of their religious principles. Mr. Hervey, the author of the Meditations, occasionally attended their meetings; and, in 1735, they were gladdened with the adjunction of a young and eloquent orator, named George Whitefield. In that year, the two Wesleys undertook a voyage to Georgia, to impart to the colonists the doctrine of *saving grace:* but their mission did not produce any extraordinary effect. When they had left the province, Mr. Whitefield undertook the task of chief missionary.

Pure, genuine, evangelical religion, or that which Mr. John Wesley considered as such, was at length* publicly preached by him, after his return to Great Britain, not in the churches of the metropolis or of the different counties, (for the incumbents would not suffer him to enter their pulpits,) but in the open air and in the fields. As souls might be saved even in this seemingly irregular way, it was far better, he said, so to preach, than not to preach at all. He soon drew many into his opinions, and propagated, with great success, the doctrine of salvation by faith. For his new society he instituted rules, not inexpedient or injudicious, recommending an orderly behaviour and an avoidance of dissipation and licentiousness. Meeting-houses were gradually erected by his followers, and, in defiance of the insults of the populace, and the sneers of the higher orders, methodism extended itself into all parts of England and Wales, made some progress in Scotland, and crossed the sea into Ireland.

A division of sentiment, between Wesley and Whitefield, resulted from those deliberations and reflections which occupied the mind of the latter, while he acted as a preacher beyond the Atlantic. He became more inclined to Calvinism than to Arminianism, to which the former was well affected. This difference, however, did not produce in their minds the bitterness of animosity. Each spoke favourably of the Christian piety of his *quandam* associate; and, if not cordial friends, they were not enemies to each other.

The opinions and the piety of Mr. Whitefield recommended him to the notice of a devout peeress, who appointed him her chaplain, and patronized him through life. This lady was Selina, countess dowager of Huntingdon, who liberally promoted the erection of meeting houses for the Calvinistic Methodists, and erected a college at Treveka (in Monmouthshire) for the instruction of future preachers. Happy in the idea and prospect of drawing sinners from the error of their way, and of diffusing an acquaintance with the Scriptures, as understood and explained by Mr. Whitefield and his associates, she disregarded the ridicule to which she was exposed by a taste so unusual among persons of rank, and prosecuted her religious career with inflexible perseverance.*

The proselytes of Whitefield were less numerous than those of Wesley, and their association was less compact. Their ministers and places of worship were respectively supported by the different congregations, not (like those of the Wesleyan sect) by a general fund. The former had not an annual court for the government of the whole body: but the latter had a regular session, under the name of a *Conference*, in which the affairs and circumstances of the confederacy were examined, funds provided, abuses corrected, and grievances redressed. This meeting was composed of preachers chosen by the assemblies of preachers of different *districts*, as representatives of the Methodist connexion, and of the superintendents of the *circuits* (or inferior divisions:) it was at first limited to one hundred of the senior itinerant predicators; but, in the sequel, all the preachers were permitted to assist, if they were so inclined, or had an opportunity of attending. At first, laymen were allowed to preach; but ministers were afterwards ordained for that purpose by the clerical heads of the society. It may here be observed, that Wesley and some of his associates had taken orders regularly in the church of England.

The same pious and indefatigable preacher, to counteract the misconceptions of the character of a Methodist, fully stated the "distinguishing marks" of his followers. Those marks, he said, were not to be found in "their opinions of any sort," in their words and phrases, or in any desire of being "distinguished by actions, customs, or usages, of an indifferent nature,

* In the year 1738.

* Between the sects thus formed, the chief points of difference are the following. The Whitefieldian or Calvinistic Methodists do not admit the possibility of attaining perfection in this life; but the followers of Wesley believe that it may be attained. The latter substitute imputed faith for imputed righteousness. They reject the doctrine of predestination, and also that of irresistible grace; both of which are maintained by the disciples of Whitefield and the followers of lady Huntingdon.

undetermined by the word of God;" nor did they lay the whole stress of religion upon any single part of it. But they were distinguished by having the love of God shed abroad in their hearts, by being always happy in God, ever resting on him, giving thanks for every thing, praying constantly with earnestness and fervour; by purifying their hearts from the lust of the flesh and of the eye, from envy and malice, from pride and petulance; by doing kind offices to neighbours and strangers, to friends and enemies; and by other fruits of a *living faith.* Nothing, he added, was required by St. Paul but the faith here mentioned. By that alone could any one be justified, or accounted righteous before God; and the remission of sins could only be obtained through the merits of Christ, not by the good works or supposed deserts of individuals. Holiness of heart and life would flow from such faith: but good deeds without it would be inoperative and nugatory. No man could produce it in himself, as it was the work of omnipotence. It was the free gift of God to those who were before "ungodly and unholy, and fit only for everlasting destruction." He who received it was born again, yet was not so perfectly regenerate, as to be fully sanctified; for there would still be some struggles between the old and the new man, which would not cease before the Holy Spirit had given to the zealous Christian "a new and clean heart." He would then attain the *acmē* of sanctification, and be qualified for the society of "just men made perfect."*

Thus did Mr. Wesley vindicate his opinions; and he continued to propagate them with zeal and success. He sometimes preached four times in one day, in places considerably distant from each other; and his zeal seemed so far to invigorate his frame, that he fainted not in his spiritual course. Not content with preaching, he promoted by writing, the system which he deemed most conformable to the will of God, the instructions of our Redeemer, and the suggestions of the Holy Spirit.

Mr. Whitefield's constitution did not preserve itself so long unbroken, or so well support the fatigue of preaching, as that of Mr. Wesley; for he died of a disorder of the lungs, in 1770, at the age of fifty-five years; whereas the life of Wesley was not closed before he had made some progress in his eighty-eighth year.†

Nearly at the same time with Mr. Wesley, died the countess of Huntingdon, who, although she admired the eloquence of Mr. Whitefield, and approved the fundamental principles of his system, organized a society that differed in some points from his sect, and which, indeed, deviated less from the church of England. Her seminary at Treveka, not being endowed, expired with her: but a new one quickly arose at Cheshunt, from which have issued some distinguished preachers.

A sect less obnoxious than the Methodists to the orthodox clergy, assumed the denomination of *United Brethren.* These were called Moravians by the public, and are said to have first appeared in England in the year 1728. Their rise and progress upon the continent we have already noticed. They were favoured with the patronage of some of our prelates, (particularly archbishop Potter) by whose recommendation they obtained a parliamentary recognition, in 1749, as composing an ancient protestant episcopal church. As their number increased, so did their zeal; and they meritoriously distinguished themselves by their eagerness for the propagation of Christianity among pagans and barbarians. A society was formed at London for this purpose; and missionaries were employed with success both in the eastern and western hemispheres. The Brethren were opposed in their views by numerous adversaries, who accused them of disseminating pernicious doctrines, and indulging in dissolute and immoral practices, particularly at their love-feasts: but they repelled these charges with effect, and acquired the esteem of unprejudiced observers of their conduct.

Near the close of the century, this sect had three provincial settlements in England, beside meeting-houses or chapels in London and some other towns. At the same time, the Brethren had six settlements in North America. The most flourishing was that of Bethlehem in Pennsylvania; an establishment which was distinguished by the moral respectability, decorous behaviour, and philanthropic spirit, of its members. They "studied (as we are informed by an English visitant of their settlement) to render their conduct strictly conformable to the principles of the Christian religion. They seemed to have only one wish at heart,—the propagation of the Gospel and the good of mankind." They were active and industrious; carried on manufactures of woollen and linen, and indeed practised all the necessary arts of life; and, at the same time, they did not neglect literary pursuits. Three of the largest houses in the town were respectively occupied, in 1797, by unmarried young men, young women, and widows, who were employed in various arts, and lived in a monastic or conventual mode. It may be added, that the savages are more amenable to conversion under the influence of arguments and persuasions offered by the Moravians, than from the endeavours of other votaries of Christianity.*

Amidst the progress of sectarian opinions, and particularly while the Methodists and Moravians were extending their influence, an able defender of the establishment rose into notice and reputation. This was William Warburton, a provincial clergyman (afterwards bishop of Glocester,) who, in a work which appeared in the year 1736, enforced the "necessity and equity of an established religion and a test-law, from the essence and end of civil society." In his next performance, he was less successful in point of argument. It was entitled "the Divine Legation of Moses demonstrated on the Principles of a Religious Deist, from the Omission of the Doctrine of a Future state of Rewards and Punishments, in the Jewish Dispensation." We do not dispute the divinity of the mission of that legislator, while we

* History of Religion, vol. iv.

† He died in March, 1791.

* Weld's Travels through the States of North America, in the years 1795, 1796, and 1797; letter xxxvii.

believe it to be sufficiently evident, that the doctrine in question was a part of the ancient Jewish creed. This work was answered by Dr. Middleton, Stebbing, and other divines, to whom Warburton replied with contemptuous acrimony. During the rebellion of the year 1745, he was one of the assailants of popery, and assisted in confirming the zeal of the protestant majority of the nation. He afterwards took part in the controversy occasioned by Dr. Middleton's Enquiry concerning the Miraculous Powers supposed to have subsisted in the Christian Church from the earliest Ages;* a dispute in which he was more orthodox than the ingenious author whom he opposed; who maintained, that miracles had ceased at the expiration of the apostolic age. Dr. Warburton also defended revealed religion with spirit against the infidel philosophy of lord Bolingbroke, the annunciation of whose unpublished works had alarmed the votaries of Christianity; and an answer from him to Hume's Natural History of Religion, roused into asperity the feelings of that artful sceptic.

The two free-thinkers whom we have here incidentally mentioned, call for more than a transient notice, in a history of that religion which they endeavoured to undermine and subvert. Bolingbroke was a man of great talents, an able orator, a polite scholar, and an interesting writer. As a statesman, however, he did not evince that wisdom which might have been expected from his abilities; and, as a philosopher, he so conducted his inquiries, as to persuade himself into a disbelief of the Christian revelation, while he outwardly supported that establishment which connected this religion with the state. By furnishing his friend, the bard of Twickenham, with the philosophical basis of the Essay on Man, he entailed upon that writer the suspicion either of being unfriendly to revelation, or of not fully comprehending the tendency of his own poem. Crousaz, a Swiss professor, reprobated the Essay as a system of fatality and naturalism; and, although it was vindicated by Warburton, the defence was not generally regarded as satisfactory. Pope, however, thought the attack sufficiently repelled, and thanked his clerical advocate for what he termed a clear and full answer to the charge.

Bolingbroke's chief attacks upon Christianity were comprehended in his posthumous works: These he ordered to be published;† and therefore he deserves the stigma of a propagator of impiety; a practice which he had condemned (in a private letter) as mischievously atrocious. As soon as they appeared, they were read with avidity; but they did not answer the expectations either of his friends or of the public in general. His reasoning was found to be feeble and inconclusive; and his weapon, instead of being the club of a giant, seemed merely to be the dart of a pigmy.

* Until the Reformation, it was the general opinion, that a miraculous power had continued in the church from the era of Christianity. It was afterwards maintained by protestants, that such a power did not extend beyond the first three centuries from that epoch; but the Romanists affirm, that it is still exercised by the saints of their church.

† The editor was David Mallet, the poet

David Hume possessed greater acuteness than the profane peer. His vanity would not suffer him to wait for his death before he should illuminate the world with his anti-religious writings; and he attacked Christianity with a degree of insiduous art, which seduced many readers into the paths of infidelity. He ridiculed the belief in miracles, and sneered at other parts of the Christian creed. Campbell and Adams took the field against him, as champions of the miraculous powers of the apostolic age; and other divines defended with zeal the general cause of orthodoxy. It was in consequence of his infidelity, that he was disappointed of a professorship of moral philosophy, which he wished to obtain; and, in the general assembly of the kirk, it was proposed that a vote of censure should pass against him for his attacks upon the religion of his country; but this was not deemed necessary by the majority. In the words of Bolingbroke, (applied to free-thinkers in general,) Hume was a pest of society, because he endeavoured to loosen its bands, and to remove at least one curb out of the mouth of that wild beast, man, who required many more curbs.

While infidelity spread on one hand, sectarianism or non-conformity increased on the other. The Baptists, Anabaptists, or Anti-pædo-baptists, were then gaining ground in this country. The *remonstrant* or *general* Baptists were openly joined, in 1747, by the learned but eccentric Whiston, who was of opinion that they were the best Christians in the kingdom, both in doctrine and practice, and "the only body of Christian people who rightly constituted their three orders of ecclesiastical governors, *bishops* [*angels* or *messengers*,] *presbyters*, and *deacons*." He recommended their *immersion* of *adults*, as the genuine practice of the apostolic age: he agreed with them in believing the *millennium;* and he adopted, with them, the idea of *hades*, or an "intermediate state and place between heaven and hell." He was pleased with their "abstaining from blood and things strangled," and with the practice of some of their congregations, of praying over the sick, and "anointing them with holy oil, upon the confession of their sins;" and, with many of those sectaries, he denied original sin. But he blamed them for dipping only once, instead of practising the *trine immersion;* for using wine undiluted with water in the sacrament (an abuse which, he said, had also crept into the foreign protestant churches;) and for requiring that such as had been baptized in infancy, or by sprinkling, should be re-baptized before they could be admitted into this sect.*

He afterwards endeavoured to form a union of the Baptists with the presbyterians and in-

* Memoirs of the Life of Mr. William Whiston, written by himself, p. 461—487.—Before this divine entered into the fraternity of Baptists, their ablest defender was Dr. John Gale, whose animadversions on Dr. Wall's History of Infant Baptism influenced James Foster to join the sect. This convert became an admired preacher and an esteemed writer; and his merit would have reflected honour upon any society.—We may here incidentally mention the growing connexion between the baptists and independents, the latter usually admitting the former into their communion.

dependents; and, with this view, he recommended and re-published some "heads of agreement assented to by the united ministers in and about London,* formerly called presbyterian and congregational." But all his efforts, and those of other divines in the same cause, were rendered abortive by the prejudices of some, the vanity of others, and the general want of a conciliatory spirit.

The *Calvinistic* or *particular* Baptists, who had little communication with the former class, augmented their number much more considerably than the remonstrant or Arminian division; but they had not in their sect so many respectable ministers as the other class could boast. Some congregations of both classes were also called *Sabbatarians*, from keeping their sabbath on Saturday.

With an exception of the time of Oliver Cromwell, when a Baptist church subsisted at Edinburgh, no traces of the sect have been discovered in Scotland before the year 1765, when a congregation was formed by Mr. Carmichael and Mr. Mac-Lean. The latter not only assisted the former in preaching, but wrote several vindications of *Believer-Baptism*, against the attacks of the advocates of *infant-sprinkling*. These ministers and their followers maintained, that, as only the baptism of believers could be justified by Scripture, infants, being unable to believe, ought not to be made partakers of that sacrament: yet, they thought, there was reason to conclude that children, recommended to Christ by the prayers of believing parents, would be saved, even without that holy ceremony. They admitted that mere baptism, without proofs of faith and spiritual conversion, would be insufficient to save adults. Faith, they said, would operate in that respect without good works; yet the effect of true faith and of God's grace would appear in the performance of just, virtuous, and benevolent acts.†

In the same division of this island, another party quitted the establishment,‡ and assumed the title of the *reformed Presbytery;* a less modest denomination than the *dissenting Presbytery*, an appellation which has also been given to these descendants of the old supporters of the solemn league and covenant. Persecuted in the reigns of the arbitrary brothers, Charles and James, the covenanters enjoyed tranquillity after the Revolution; but they were not satisfied with the religious arrangements of that period. They looked back with regret to the good old times, when the reformed faith was at its zenith in Scotland, and when the three kingdoms were united in the sacred bonds of the same pure religion. Lamenting the defection of the national rulers, and the majority of the people, from the true principles of the Reformation, a party of religious malcontents renounced all connexion with the *revolution kirk*, and, under the guidance of Mac-Millan and Nairn, formed a seceding presbytery. By these ministers, others were selected for the same functions; and the secession has been continued to the present time. Beside the congregations of this complexion in North Britain, there are several in Ireland, and some in North America. The members profess to follow the Scripture as their principal guide, and the ordinances of the Westminster assembly in the next place. They disapprove the high authority assumed by the state over the church of Christ, as the fruit of worldly policy, rather than a claim justified by the genuine spirit of religion. Yet they submit peaceably to the higher powers, and do not indulge in the clamours of sedition or the murmurs of disaffection.

Their worship is thus described by one of their own ministers:* "Public prayers, with the heart, and with the understanding also, and in a known tongue, but not in written or in humanly prescribed forms; singing psalms of divine inspiration, and these alone; reading and expounding the Scriptures; preaching and receiving the word; administering and receiving the sacraments of baptism and the Lord's supper; together with public fasting and thanksgiving; are considered by them as the divinely instituted ordinances of religious worship, while they reject all ceremonies of human invention."

While these reformers were slowly increasing their numbers, a more considerable sect, in the year 1752, departed from the establishment. Mr. Gillespie, having opposed the reception of a new minister, whose appointment was unpleasing to the majority of the inhabitants of Inverkeithing, was expelled from the church in which he officiated; but he soon found followers, who, like him, wished to throw the election of pastors into the hands of the people, and formed a congregation at Dunfermline. The *Presbytery of Relief*, in allusion to the desired relief from the arbitrary rigour of the laws of patronage, was the denomination assumed by this body of seceders. They were more liberal than the generality of presbyterians; for they were willing to admit into their communion all those who seemed worthy of being called Christians, however they might differ with regard to particular points. Their congregations continued to multiply; and, about the close of the century, above sixty places of worship belonged to the association.

Above twenty years after the formation of the Presbytery of Relief, the Berean† sect arose in Scotland. Mr. Barclay, who was its founder, represented a mere *belief* of the Gospel as producing an absolute certainty of salvation. "Faith in Christ," he said, "and an assurance of salvation through his merits, are inseparable, or rather the same." As this faith, he added, is the gift of God alone, so the individual to whom it is imparted is as conscious of possessing it as he is of his existence; and the assurance of it is "established, with the resurrection from the dead, upon the direct testimony of God, believed in the heart."

* In the year 1691.

† Adams' Religious World Displayed, vol. iii. p. 233, &c.

‡ In the year 1743.

* In an account of the Old Dissenters, sent to Mr Adam for insertion in his Religious World.

† So called from the Bereans of the apostolic age who "received the word with all readiness of mind (μετα πασης προθυμιας,) and searched the Scriptures daily."

This is, apparently, a confident and presumptuous statement of the nature of faith, and a *personal* application of *general* passages of Scripture. In the opinion of the Bereans, unbelief is the sin against the Holy Ghost, which has been pronounced unpardonable. They admit the most profligate characters into their society, if a belief of the Gospel be declared by the applicants; but these members, if they should afterwards disgrace themselves, are excluded from the Berean pale.

The leaders of these sects propagated their sentiments by the press, as well as in the pulpit; and hence frequent controversies arose. Among the religious disputes which have excited attention in the present reign, that which related to confessions may claim early mention. It was the opinion of many, both divines and laymen, that the freedom of conscience and of sentiment ought not to be so far obstructed, even in an established church, as to render an occasional disagreement in unessential points a ground of exclusion from the emoluments of that church; that, when the bulk of a nation agree in a reformed religion. precise and circumstantial confessions of faith are unnecessary; and that subscription to a variety of articles, not all closely connected or concordant, ought by no means to be enforced. Mr. Francis Blackburne, a respectable divine, maintained these points with ability in a work entitled "the Confessional,* or a full and free enquiry into the right, utility, edification, and success, of establishing systematic Confessions of faith and doctrine in Protestant Churches." Many pens were drawn against this work; and the propriety of subscription was strongly vindicated. The opposer of confessions did not resign the preferments which he had already obtained, but was so far conscientious as to reject the offer of an additional benefice. He had previously entered into a controversy respecting a state of happiness or misery between death and the resurrection, (a supposition which he did not consider as sufficienly countenanced by the Scriptures;) and he afterwards took part in the dispute with the catholics, in a manner which did not accord with his usual benignity and liberality of mind. He contended against the grant of toleration to those who were unwilling to allow it to others; but true generosity will prompt a person to do more for others than they will do for him; and it ought to be considered, that the catholics of that time were not so bigoted or intolerant as those of former periods.

By those members of the church who agreed with Mr. Blackburne on the subject of religious confessions, a petition was signed, and presented in 1772 to the house of commons. The Tory members strongly opposed the request of those whom they considered as latitudinarian religionists; and the assembly refused to relax the rigour of compulsory subscription. A similar application being made by the protestant dissenters, the commons agreed to a bill in their favour; which, however, the house of peers rejected. The catholic dissenters, six years afterwards, obtained indulgences for which they had long wished. They were permitted to meet publicly in chapels, keep schools, and hold landed property, on taking the oath of allegiance, and denying that the bishop of Rome had any temporal power or jurisdiction in Great Britain. The presbyterians and other protestant sects then renewed their request for a release from subscription and the legislature no longer refused compliance.

After a long interval, during which the catholics were distinguished by their peaceable behaviour, they were placed in the same predicament with the orthodox subjects of Great Britain, (except with regard to places and employments,) on disclaiming the intolerant spirit and sanguinary zeal of their church against supposed heretics.*

The catholics of Ireland were more favoured than those of Great Britain; for they were declared eligible to all posts and employments, except some of the highest under the crown, and were allowed to vote for parliamentary candidates. It may seem surprising, that they should be more gratified and indulged, in a country where their great superiority of number might make it hazardous to trust them with power, than in a kingdom where they formed a very small proportion of the community: but it was deemed a point of policy to conciliate the sect. When the union with Ireland took place, strong hopes were entertained, by the catholics, of the grant of every thing which they could desire: but the reigning prince repeatedly declared, that he could not conscientiously agree to their complete emancipation, which, he thought, would be repugnant to the clause in his coronation-oath, binding him to support the church, *as by law established*. Yet, if both houses of parliament should vote a bill for the gratification of the catholics, his assent to it might be vindicated, as those two assemblies, in concert with the sovereign, are allowed to make greater alterations than the mere grant of the remaining demands of a tolerated sect.

The doctrine of the Trinity, in which the church of England and the catholics agree, employed at various times the pens of controversial theologians. Some thought it incomprehensible; others laboured to explain it on rational principles; and some opposed it, as unsupported either by reason or by Scripture. After having sustained occasional and desultory attacks, it was exposed to a systematic assault from Dr. Joseph Priestley, who endeavoured to prove that it was not the opinion of the early Christians, and that it was introduced by artifice and imposture, in repugnance to repeated declarations both of the Old and New Testament.†

* Which first appeared in 1766.

* Those of South Britain in 1791, and those of Scotland in 1793.—In the time between those years, the penal laws against the Scottish episcopalians were abrogated, as the death of the pretender had induced them to acquiesce, with seeming cordiality, in the claims of the house of Hanover.

† In an Essay on Spirit, Anti-Trinitarian notions were boldly urged, in 1751, by a clergyman of the Irish establishment; and Dr. Clayton, bishop of Clogher, who had adopted it as his own work, afterwards proposed, to the peers of Ireland, the omission of the Athanasian and Nicene creeds in the service of the

Dr. Priestley was a man of considerable talents, of an ardent and active spirit, who wished at once to shine as a philosopher, a divine and a politician. He certainly extended our knowledge of air, and of other natural objects: but we are less indebted to him for his endeavours to enlighten mankind in theology or in the art of government. In politics, he was inclined to republicanism; in religion, he entertained various notions which are exploded by more erudite biblical scholars and more profound divines. Unawed by the terrors of the law, which denounced punishment against all who, in sermons or in writings, denied the Trinity, he gave new vigour to the Socinian doctrine, and maintained that Christ was a mere man, divinely commissioned indeed, but not God himself, or the son of God. He even went farther than Socinus, and affirmed that Jesus was only entitled to respect, not to adoration or worship, from the world which he so essentially served. He and his followers unwilling to be called Socinians, claimed the appellation of *Unitarians*, as they preferred the idea of one God to that doctrine which represented the Deity as consisting of three persons, equal in power and dignity. Mr. Lindsey warmly supported the same opinion; and he, as well as Dr. Disney, resigned a benefice, from a conscientious preference of the divine Unity to the Trinity. The number of Unitarians, from this time, rapidly increased; and they seemed to think themselves the only rational professors of religion, while the Trinitarians did not regard them as true Christians.

To avoid the terrors of the law, the Unitarians made an appeal to that tolerating spirit which, they hoped, would actuate the majority of the house of commons. They petitioned that assembly for the repeal of all penalties denounced against those who denied the Trinity; and Mr. Fox supported their pretensions with animated eloquence. But their request was not granted, because many of the members considered them as a dangerous set of men, and others thought it unnecessary to abrogate the law in question, as it was suffered by the lenity of the government to lie dormant.

Dr. Priestley and many of his Unitarian brethren maintained another doctrine, which excited strong opposition,—that of *materialism*. They asserted that the soul, though a sentient principle, was the mere result of an organized system of matter;* and that, consequently, death would extinguish all consciousness; but that a resurrection was still possible, and even probable.* This doctrine led to that of *necessity*, or the *necessary agency* of human beings, which this philosopher strenuously inculcated. It extended to the *mind* what was known to belong to *matter:* it represented the causes of volition and action, in the former, as equally decisive and irresistible with the impellants of the material world.† These opinions were combated by various writers, both in and out of the establishment; and the debated points are not yet decided; for the disputes of theologians are endless.

On one of these topics we may observe, that the properties of the soul are so essentially different from those of matter, as to produce a conviction (even if we had no revelation to guide us in our inquiries,) that these two parts of our composition are decidedly dissimilar, notwithstanding the connexion of one with the other, and the reciprocal influence of each. If the ideas of the materialists, however, be adopted, the resurrection (it would seem) will not be that which we are taught to expect, namely, that of *identity*, but the excitation of the spark of life in new frames. This is a very gloomy and discouraging doctrine, and one that no good man would be disposed to propagate.

The second opinion is represented by its advocates as the only mode of doing justice to the prescience and omniscience of the Deity. Whatever is done by any one, must, they say, have been fore-known and pre-determined by the Almighty: yet persons, they add, are not absolutely *compelled* to act as they do, although it be fated that they should so act; for they are still influenced by motives, and have therefore some freedom of choice, being unacquainted with the pre-determination of God respecting what they should do, or forbear to do. For instance, when a man has been guilty of robbery or murder, which his Creator knew that he would commit, these reasoners say, that he had the liberty of avoiding either of those crimes, but that God permitted him to incur this guilt, instead of preventing him by a particular exertion of providence. Some of these Necessitarians even boast, that their system is the only theory consistent with true morality; but, if *definite circumstances* (to use their ex-

church. The zeal of the prelate hastened his death; for, when he had renewed his attack upon the Trinity, he was menaced with a prosecution, the dread of which threw him into a nervous fever.

* Early in the century of which we are treating, Dr. Coward had propagated a similar doctrine; and his Grand Essay, as he styled his work upon this subject, was followed by Dodwell's "Epistolary Discourse, proving, from the Scriptures and the first fathers, that the soul is a principle naturally mortal, but immortalized actually by the pleasure of God, to punishment or reward, by its union with the divine baptismal spirit." Dr. Hartley afterwards discussed the same topic in his Essay on Man (published in 1749,) and referred thought, reflection, judgment, &c. to the laws of animal organization; thus endeavouring to invalidate the idea of a separate immaterial soul, while he seemed, in some parts of his work, to be inclined to adopt it. La Metherie and Helvetius more decidedly and avowedly maintained the doctrine of Materialism; and l'Homme Machine of the former was publicly burned in Holland. Priestley was chiefly influenced by the reasoning of Hartley, and also by that of Dr. Law, to adopt sentiments which exposed him to the imputation of infidelity and even of atheism.

* Not (said Priestley) from the light or evidence of nature, but from the authority of Scripture, and the example of Christ's resurrection.

† Priestley first imbibed his notions of necessity from Collins, who, in 1715, had published a Philosophical Inquiry into Human Liberty. Leibnitz had previously given to the world his Essays on the Goodness of God, the Freedom of Man, and the Origin of Evil, in which he vindicated God's permission of partial evil, according to the system of necessity, by contending that it would lead to general good; and, avoiding the predestinarian rigour of Calvin, made benevolence the chief attribute of the Deity So thought our ancestors, when they gave the name of *God* (that is, goodness in the abstract) to the Divine Being. See Dr. Maclaine's note [†] upon the progress of Arminianism, Cent. xvii. sect. ii. part ii chap. 3.

pressions) produce *definite volitions*, where will be the merit of a good action, or the demerit of a bad one? Their scheme detracts from the goodness, justice, and wisdom of the Deity, by holding him up to view as an encourager of evil, and as a punisher of those who, from fate or necessity, have fallen into wickedness or guilt. Others pretend, that, if the mind had a self-determining power, the world would be a scene of confusion, and the purposes of God might be defeated: for a self-governing mind, therefore, they substitute motives that cannot be effectually controlled or resisted. The supposed derangement of the plans of Providence is an absurb supposition, in the case of an omnipotent Creator; and the idea of irresistible impulse is repugnant to that obvious freedom which enables an individual to act from choice, and frequently to follow the suggestions of wild caprice.

Upon this and other points of metaphysical theology, arguments might be multiplied on both sides by the sophistry of disputation; but it is unnecessary to dwell on a subject in which absolute certainty cannot be attained by our limited faculties. A Thomas Aquinas or a Duns Scotus might spin out a long thread of argument upon such a topic; but, though they would amuse some, they would weary others, and give little instruction to any.

The Unitarians, in recent times, have found some artful and plausible vindicators of their doctrine; and they have been so elevated by their success in making proselytes, that they seem to expect the ultimate triumph of their creed. They assure themselves, that a great number of Christians who *profess* an adherence to the church of England, really *think* with them, but are deterred by motives of interest from an avowal of their opinions.

The majority of modern Unitarians affirm, that, as far as they can judge from Scripture, from which all Christians profess to deduce their doctrines, Christ had no existence before the time assigned for his human birth;* that he was not miraculously conceived; and that he is not God, nor was ever invested with a superhuman nature. But they allow, that he was chosen by the Creator of the world to be a medium of communication between him and fallen man, to teach truth and righteousness, and lead sinners to repentance and salvation; and that he obtained the favour of resurrection, as a reward for his obedience to the divine commands, without *atoning* (in the sense of the Trinitarians) for the sins of men by his sufferings and death. They consider the Holy Ghost not as a distinct person, but as a mere emanation of the Deity; and they are not even willing to allow, that it has any extraordinary influence or operation upon the mind or heart, so as to produce a disposition to piety. They differ from the Methodists in denying the necessity or utility of grace, and in earnestly recommending integrity, good works, and social kindness; and many of them agree with the Universalists, in thinking that the punishment of the most flagitious sinners will only be temporary, and that the whole human race will finally be "gathered unto Christ."

Some of the Unitarians entered into a controversy with the followers of Swedenborg, a Swedish baron, with whose ideas of the Trinity they were disgusted. This nobleman published *Arcana Cœlestia*, (Heavenly Secrets,) Angelic Wisdom, the True Christian Religion, a Treatise upon Heaven and Hell, and many other works. It may excite surprise, that a being, merely human, should pretend to know so much of heaven and hell, or presume to judge so confidently of the precise nature of both those *kingdoms*, as did baron Swedenborg: but our surprise will abate, when we reflect on the force of enthusiasm and the unfettered boldness of a wild imagination. The noble Swede fancied that all secrets respecting futurity had been disclosed to him, and that he was better enabled and qualified to lead an erring world into the way of truth, than any former or contemporary theologian. He affected to be guided by Scripture in his pursuits and researches; but he interpreted its hints according to his own fanciful ideas, and expanded its meaning to a conformity with his own visionary conceptions. He peopled the new Jerusalem at his pleasure, and regulated its polity by the whimsies of his eccentric brain. He framed a religious world with as much ease as the author of Utopia had formed a civil one; certainly with good intentions, but not always with the soundest judgment. Considering himself as commissioned to enlighten his fellow-creatures with the knowledge of every thing that concerned their essential and eternal interests, he published his religious code with the air of a dictator, and, as if he had been a new prophet, pretended to point out the promised land.

The writings of this enthusiastic nobleman did not at first produce the desired effect; but they gradually attracted notice, and at length so far operated as to make many converts. Congregations were formed upon his principles, and ministers were animated with a portion of his zeal. His chief doctrines were of the following conplexion. He asserted the divinity of Jesus Christ, in whose person, he thought, resided the whole Trinity: a point which he endeavoured to explain by comparing it with the human trinity. As every man, he said, consisted of soul, body, and operation, so the Trinity was formed by the Father, or soul, the Son, or divine humanity, and the Holy Ghost, or virtue proceeding from the two former. The redemption, he added, was not the mere fruit of the supposed death of Christ, considered as a sacrifice to the justice or wrath of God, or as an atonement for the sins of men, but consisted in the triumph obtained over Satan and other evil spirits, by the exertions of Jehovah, manifested in the flesh, and appearing in a state of glorified humanity. In substance, perhaps, there is no great difference between this and the ordinary doctrine of the Trinity.

Another doctrine, propagated by the baron, was that of man's co-operation with Christ. An inclination, he said, was requisite on the part of man (as a free agent,) to work out his own salvation, as it was unreasonable to suppose

* Those Unitarians who are of the Arian class admit the pre-existence of Christ.

that he was to remain in a state of indolence, or to neglect the duties of his station. We therefore ought so to exert ourselves, as if all our future hopes and prospects depended on our own efforts. Yet, as all our powers are the gifts of God, all the merit we are disposed to claim is not strictly our own, but must be referred to the adorable giver of all grace and virtue: it belongs to Christ, not to man.

The correspondence between spiritual and natural things formed the basis of Swedenborg's doctrine relative to the Scriptures. He affirmed that they were written with an eye to the natural world, so as to explain divine things by a comparison with those which are plain and obvious. Imagining that he had been favoured with the means of interpreting this correspondence, he was willing to impart, to the well disposed, the mode of obtaining this clue to scriptural truth and celestial wisdom.*

From the Scriptures, and from his own experience, he maintained the connexion between human beings and angels or spirits, by whose influence and aid the former were encouraged to think and act justly, and guided in the most interesting concerns. He did not, however, wish that the idea of this association should preclude a constant attention to holy writ, the grand source of wisdom and illumination.

In giving advice for the conduct of life, he inculcated the propriety of avoiding all sins and vices prohibited by the divine law, and of fulfilling every duty required by the laws of government and society. He also enjoined repentance as a necessary preparative to justification and acceptance with God.

* Mr. Adam, after remarking that "Some persons will be disposed to doubt the credibility" of baron Swedenborg's doctrines, "on the ground of the utter improbability, that a mortal man, during his residence in a material body, should have been permitted to enjoy open intercourse with the world of departed spirits, and instructed, during the uninterrupted period of twenty-seven years, in the internal sense of the Scriptures, hitherto undiscovered," ventures to observe, that "others (as appears from many respectable instances) will see nothing *improbable* in all this, referring the case to those extraordinary dispensations of the providence of an All-wise and All-Powerful Being, who, in all ages of the world, has been pleased to enlighten and instruct *chosen servants* concerning his will and kingdom." The latter opinion seems to be that of Mr. Adam himself; but we cannot wholly concur with him. As nothing is impossible with God, it is not *impossible* that such a communication of his *will* might take place; but that, we think, is the utmost extent to which a rational Christian can proceed in this argument. To see nothing *improbable* in it, argues a degree of superstitious credulity, which we should not have expected to find in a modern clergyman. What reason can we have to suppose that God would impart his will, by a supernatural medium, to a person who had no claim to such peculiarity of distinction, after the lapse of many ages from a similar revelation, and at a time when the most enlightened nations acquiesced in, and seemed satisfied with, the scriptural knowledge that they had already acquired? Is there any thing, in the intimations of Swedenborg, so much more important and material than the former treasure of divine wisdom, as to justify the belief of a new revelation? If we admit his *ipse dixit*, we may also believe the declaration of the Arabian legislator, who affirmed that he had received from heaven, by the angel Gabriel, the substance of the *koran;* or we may give credit to the legends and pretended miracles in the lives of the Romish saints; listen with implicit faith to the reveries of Jacob Behman, and regard the vaticinations of Joanna Southcott, as the prophetic effusions of unerring wisdom!

With regard to the resurrection, he declared it to be his opinion, that, as every one has a spiritual frame, enclosed in a material body, the former, after the death of the individual, would rise again, and dwell for ever with angels, or, in case of incorrigible depravity, with evil spirits.

The variations between these doctrines and those of the church of England, did not induce the baron's disciples and followers in general to desert the communion of that church; nor did all the presbyterians, or other dissenters, who adopted the Swedenborgian tenets, abandon the worship to which they were before attached. The orthodox ministers, however, seemed to consider them as fanatics; and the majority of the dissenters were not pleased with the doctrinal alterations of their respective creeds. Yet the votaries of the New Jerusalem gradually multiplied; and several men of ability entered into the association. Their preachers still have sufficient influence to draw other Christians within their pale, as well as to prevent their former communicants from renouncing the system.

Another sect, also, boasted of the spiritual joys of the New Jerusalem, but exhibited, in a stronger point of view, the leaven of fanaticism. A party of enthusiasts left England for America in 1774, and settled in the province of New York, where the society soon increased, and received the ludicrous denomination of *Shakers*, from the practice of *shaking* and dancing.* They affected to consider themselves as forming the only true church, and their preachers as possessing all the apostolic gifts. The wicked, they thought, would only be punished for a time, with an exception of those who should be so incorrigibly depraved as to fall from *their* church: for these miserable offenders, there would be no forgiveness. Baptism was not practised by these sectaries; nor did they celebrate the eucharist. They did not object to those sacramental ceremonies as improper in themselves, but alleged that they had been abolished in the apostolic times, and that they were particularly unnecessary in the present age, as the *new dispensation*, (at least with regard to their society) was beginning to take place. This was an allusion to the Millennium; in which period, they said, Christ would not appear personally, but only by his sainted votaries. Their leader was Anna Lee, who, they ridiculously pretended, was the woman mentioned by St. John as a great wonder.† The successors of this *elect lady* have been, they say, as perfect in their characters as she was, have enjoyed unreserved intercourse with departed spirits and with angels, and have possessed the power of imparting a plenitude of spiritual blessings to their disciples.‡

* These devotees, in their religious *exercises*, resemble the *Jumpers* of Wales, who thus testify their joy for spiritual blessings.

† "There appeared a woman clothed with the sun, and the moon under her feet, and upon her head a crown of twelve stars." *Revelations*, xii. 1.

‡ "Erskine's Sketches of Church-History.—The *Dunkers* of North America, (so called from their baptizing by immersion) formed a sect long before the Shakers, but never became so numerous as these religionists. In the year 1777, their number did not exceed 500. Their principal tenet is, that future

The Shakers chiefly confined themselves to New England and New York, scarcely making any proselytes in the other provinces of North America, from Lake Ontario to the frontiers of Florida. During the subjection of those provinces to the sway of Great Britain, the religion of the church of England prospered in a very inconsiderable degree among the colonial communities, in comparison with presbyterianism, or with the prevailing system of the independents: yet it gradually gained ground, as the people became more polished in their manners, and less infected with puritanical austerity. The prelate, to whose authority the Trans-Atlantic episcopalians then submitted, was the bishop of London: but, when the provinces rose to the dignity of an independent state, this spiritual connexion ceased with the political ties which had bound them to the mother country. As a new director of the headless church was deemed requisite, application was made to some English prelates for the canonical consecration of a bishop, who was to reside in the province of Connecticut. The divine upon whom the Americans fixed, was Dr. Seabury, who had been employed as a missionary by the society for the propagation of the Gospel.* The doubts and hesitation of the prelates of England, with regard to the mode of proceeding in this case, on account of the new predicament in which the provincials stood, induced the reverend stranger to apply to those of Scotland; and by them he was gratified, in the year 1784, with the episcopal honour and dignity. The parliament afterwards deliberated upon this affair, and enacted a bill which empowered either the primate or the archbishop of York to consecrate subjects of foreign states to the rank and office of bishop. In consequence of this statute, two clergymen, one from Philadelphia, the other from New York, were invested by the archbishop of Canterbury and some of his brethren, in 1787, with the episcopal character; and the sanction thus given to the views of the American episcopalians promoted the growth and respectability of their church. A convention of this church had already been holden at Philadelphia;† and, in that assembly, some alterations had been made in the liturgy and service of the church of England, and the thirty-nine articles were reduced to twenty. In a subsequent convention, several of these alterations were revoked, and all intentions of departing from our church in any essential point of doctrine, discipline, or worship, were disclaimed. From this time the number of Episcopalians continued to increase in the territories of the United States; so that, in the penultimate year of the century, fifty-two congregations of that description were reckoned in Connecticut, twenty-five in New-Jersey, and sixteen in the Massachusetts state, beside a considerable number in other parts of the republican territory. Seven bishops then presided over this church, and it boasted of a university and an academy at Philadelphia.

happiness can only be secured by penance and mortification. They deny the imputation of Adam's sin to his posterity, and the eternity of punishment for wickedness; hate war and violence, and protest against the practice of enslaving others. They allow marriage; and yet do not seem to entertain a high opinion of the sanctity of that union, as they compel those who have thus fallen into the snare of temptation to retire to a distant settlement.

* This society had been enabled, by the subscriptions and legacies of well-disposed Christians, to make considerable progress, not only in converting the American savages, but also in diffusing among the colonists the doctrines of the church of England.

† In the year 1785.

A small party or association, which may be thought worthy of some notice among the varied sects of the age, arose in England from the zeal of Joanna Southcott. This crafty or enthusiastic female offered herself to notice as a prophetess in the year 1792; and she soon met with friends and admirers. She pretended that she was influenced and tutored by the Holy Spirit, and that her unlimited obedience to that divine power had procured for her the signal honour of being commissioned to announce the approaching accomplishment of scriptural promises, the establishment of Christ's kingdom on the ruin of that of Satan, and the redemption of pious believers and penitent sinners from the effects of the fall of man. She intimated that various disasters and calamities would befall the nations, as warnings to a sinful world; but that these awful visitations would have less immediate effect upon other communities than upon the people of this favoured island, who enjoyed the benefit of her personal presence. This nation, she said, would have the good fortune to be the first redeemed from the bondage of sin and the tyranny of Satan, and would become an instrument in the hands of Providence for awakening the rest of the world to a lively sense of true religion.* Such a supposition is an instance of patriotic enthusiasm, rather than the fruit of just reasoning, or the dictate of a sound mind.

Another pretended prophet was a naval officer of the name of Brothers, who, for giving hints of the king's eventual dethronement, when he (the prophet) should be recognised as prince of the Hebrew nation, was apprehended as a seditious delinquent. Mr. Halhed, a senator of distinguished learning, but apparently not of sound judgment, vindicated the fanatical effusions of Brothers, and gravely advised the national representatives to peruse his writings, that they might have a chance of religious conversion. The officer was afterwards confined as a lunatic, and was thus deprived of an opportunity of forming a sect.

Of those who have faith in supposed prophecies, many (particularly the most sinful) may be more disposed to listen to the deliberate opinions of the Universalists, than to the reveries of Southcott or Brothers. From several passages of Scripture, alluding to the restitution of all things and the reconciliation of all to the Father by the blood of the cross, the celebrated Origen, and other divines in successive ages, inferred that redemption and salvation would be universal; that, if punishment should be inflicted upon sinners, it would be temporary; and that an eternity of happi-

* Sketch of the Denominations of the Christian World, by the Rev. John Evans, *the eleventh edition* p. 221–225.

ness would follow. They entertained the idea of *election*, in a sense which implied that some were chosen but merely as examples to others, and as the first-fruits of the harvest of salvation. Baxter had softened the rigours of Calvinism by admitting, that every one had a portion of grace, with which he might work out his own salvation; so that if he should not attain everlasting life, it would be his own fault. He gave name to a sect which so understood his meaning; but we now hear little of the *Baxterians*. The Universalists were, more positively and determinately, the advocates of fallen man.

A distinguished modern supporter of the doctrine of universal restoration was Mr. Elhanan Winchester, a native of North America, who visited Great Britain about the year 1787, with a view of disseminating his consolatory tenets.* He published a course of lectures which he had delivered with applause, upon the "Prophecies remaining to be fulfilled," and also Dialogues on Universal Restoration.

The Rellyan universalists may here be mentioned. They are the followers of Mr. James Relly, who entered into public life as an associate of Whitefield, but at length renounced his Calvinistic opinions, and preached salvation to all. He believed in "a resurrection to life, and a resurrection to condemnation." Believers only, he thought, would enjoy the former, and dwell with Christ in his kingdom of the *millennium;* but unbelievers, after being raised from death would be obliged to wait, in darkness and under wrath, the ultimate manifestation of the great Redeemer of the world.

These sectaries were stigmatised as *antinomians* by their adversaries; but, as they recommended morality and good works, they disclaimed the imputation. With regard to antinomianism, we may here observe, that it tends to encourage every species of immorality. It releases its votaries from the ties of moral honour, and the duties of social life. If respectable individuals belong to the sect, they were not rendered so by the tenets which they profess, but by the innate goodness of character, which the wild effusions of their ministers have not corrupted. Let piety and devotion be encouraged; but let not morality and rectitude be superseded by affected purity of religious zeal. Those sectaries who deride good works, are not good members of society; for they endeavour to loosen its bonds, and to invalidate its regulations. If we were not advocates for unlimited toleration, we should wish that the latitude of antinomianism might be restrained by public authority.

The antinomian system has been refuted by various writers; and, as it has not been (nor can be) defended with equal ability, it rarely makes the least impression upon men of sense. It is still professed, however, in some parts of Great Britain and of Germany. In 1761, one of its professors maintained, that prayers for the forgiveness of our sins are unnecessary; that repentance is not requisite; that no judgment will take place after this life, and no punishment will be inflicted; that Christ, by subduing the evil spirit, introduced universal righteousness, and thus redeemed all mankind from what would otherwise have been the effect of sin. Many antinomians, on the contrary, are rigid Calvinists, and, by their doctrine of partial, or indeed general, reprobation, endeavour to counteract the last mentioned opinion.

The different sects, beside their habitual eagerness to disseminate their particular notions among other classes of Christians, were in general well disposed to propagate Christianity among heathen tribes; and a few years before the century closed, the consideration of the benighted state of pagan ignorance, in which the inhabitants of the numerous islands of the Pacific Ocean were involved, prompted the friends of religion to form an extensive scheme of missionary exertion. Some clergymen of the establishment, and of almost every sect, concurred in the scheme: but it appears to have been devised and chiefly promoted by Calvinistic Methodists. When subscriptions had produced a sufficiency of pecuniary supplies for the commencement of the enterprise, a ship was freighted with every requisite, and sent out under the command of Mr. Wilson, who had as much zeal for the success of the mission, as any of the preachers that embarked with him. Religious colonies were formed at some of the Society and Friendly Islands: but difficulties and dangers obstructed the progress of conversion, and several of the missionaries perished amidst barbarian commotions. Many other adventurers, however, visited the Pacific with the same views, and new attempts were made to subdue the prejudices of the islanders, and bring them within the pale of Christianity.

While the missionaries of the first embarkation were thus engaged, Mr. Haldane, an opulent North Briton, on the rejection of a proposal which he had made to the government for instituting a mission in the East Indies, resolved to employ himself and others in a similar plan within the limits of this island. He therefore, in 1797, organized an association, which he called the "Society for propagating the Gospel at home." Itinerant preachers were deputed with this view; tabernacles were built, and seminaries established; and considerable success attended the well-meant undertaking. The members of this society and of the rising congregations were styled *New Independents*. Menaced with the vengeance of the kirk, they still prosecuted their object, and firmly asserted the irreproachable propriety of their conduct, and the commendable nature of their exertions. They reprobated all fixed national creeds and systems, all civil establishments of religion; and professed to regulate all church government and discipline by the rules of Scripture, not by human ordinances. They declared

* Dr. Chauncy, of Boston, was also a zealous advocate for this doctrine; whence the Universalists are sometimes called by his name. It was controverted by the president Edwards and his son; the latter of whom imputed to Chauncy a provisional retention of the scheme of *Destruction*, if the system of the Universalists should not be tenable. The abettors of the scheme alluded to, maintain that the wicked will neither be subjected to endless misery, nor be finally saved, but will be involved in total destruction

that the church had no head upon earth; yet they were willing to pay proper submission to the temporal sovereign.

Their efforts in the cause of what they considered as the true or evangelical religion, exposed them to the censures of the kirk; and a pastoral admonition* was issued against them by the general assembly; but they boldly continued their career, and extended their influence.

The New Independents were not the only persons who endeavoured to promote religious zeal. Some individuals of considerable talents, in England, also pursued that object, but in a different manner, and without recommending a secession from the establishment. The prevalent habit of moral preaching, and the want of religious fervour in persons of rank, and also in the middle class of society, had disgusted and shocked those Christians who were studiously attentive to the concerns of their souls and to the interests of genuine piety. Mr. Wilberforce, who had distinguished himself by his reiterated efforts for the abolition of the slave trade, and had acquired the reputation of an able and independent senator, surprised the public by appearing as a religious writer. He published in the year 1797, a "Practical View of the prevailing Religious System of Professed Christians, in the higher and middle classes in this country, contrasted with real Christianity." He enumerated the chief defects of the former of these systems, such as the want of adequate conceptions concerning our Redeemer and the Holy Spirit, or of sufficiently exalted ideas of the strictness of practical Christianity, the neglect of the peculiar doctrines of our religion, and the allowance of only a narrow and qualified jurisdiction to that which ought to embrace every object and influence every pursuit. He animadverted on the error of substituting amiable tempers and useful lives in the place of piety; a "great and desperate error," involving a "fatal distinction between morality and religion." The *particular good* arising from such lives, he said, might be more than counterbalanced by the *general evil*, as they tended to discourage "that principle (namely religion) which is the great operative spring of usefulness in the bulk of mankind." He therefore earnestly exhorted his countrymen to attend strictly to the doctrines and precepts of evangelical religion and vital Christianity, to look to Jesus, imitate the example of his blameless life, and surrender, unconditionally, their souls and bodies to the will and service of God. Undoubtedly, he added, the sincere Christian has a great work to perform, and his internal state is a continued scene of discipline and warfare; but pleasures of the purest kind attend his progress; and he is enlivened with the consciousness of well-meant endeavours, encouraged by the succours of divine grace, and animated by the hope of a blissful immortality. He may enjoy the innocent amusements of life, partake of the delights of social intercourse, open his heart to the calls of philanthropy, indulge the sensibilities of taste and genius, and cultivate his mind with the varieties of science.

Much praise is certainly due to the good intentions of this writer. Similar praise may be bestowed on a celebrated female who has laboured in the same cause—we mean Hannah More. In her "Strictures on the Modern System of Female Education, and view of the Principles and Conduct prevalent among Women of Rank and Fortune," she has given much good advice to the fair sex, and has properly censured the frivolity and dissipation of the age, and the relaxed morals of the higher classes.

* Dr. Haweis, speaking of the *admonition*, says, "Whoever is at the pains to examine facts, and the assertions in this philippic against the promoters of evangelical religion, will find *as many falsehoods as lines*." It breathes, indeed, a spirit of intolerance; but, in thus inveighing against it, the indignant divine incautiously deviates from that strict veracity which he recommends to others.

SKETCH OF THE ECCLESIASTICAL HISTORY OF THE NINETEENTH CENTURY.

CHAPTER I.

History of the Romish Church.

The corrupt state in which we left this church at the close of the last century, has not yielded to the influence of that superior light which has since illuminated the civilized world. The Romish bigots have still some remains of an intolerant spirit, and still resist the progress of free inquiry; yet even the catholic governments find it expedient to profess liberal principles, and to endure that boldness of dissent which they dare not punish and cannot effectually prevent.

After the death of the unfortunate pontiff, Pius VI., this church remained for eleven months without a head, while the cardinals, exiled from Rome, were dispersed over different countries. The pious zeal of the emperor of Germany at length prompted him to provide a remedy for this unsettled state of affairs, which seemed to reflect disgrace on those princes who professed a reverential regard for the catholic hierarchy. He desired the fugitive members of the sacred college to hold a conclave at Venice, which was then an Austrian dependency; and the cardinal di Chiaramonte, a native of Cesena, who had been raised by the late pope to the see of Imola, was advanced to the papal dignity.* This pontiff

* On the 14th of March, 1800.—The votes were

assumed the designation of Pius VII., and entered with alacrity upon the exercise of his spiritual functions, to which the advantages of temporal power were again annexed, when the Roman territory was recovered by the vigour of the allied arms.

When Napoleon had raised himself to the dignity of first consul or sovereign of France, he applied to the new pope for the purpose of a religious settlement. It was then stipulated that the 'catholic, apostolic, and Romish religion,' should be freely and publicly exercised in France; that a new division of dioceses should take place; that, as soon as the first consul should have nominated bishops, the pope should confer upon them the honour of canonical institution; that the prelates should appoint, for parochial ministers, such persons as the three consuls should approve; that no council or synod should meet without the consent of the government; and that no papal legate or nuncio should act, and no bull or brief be operative in France, unless the ruling power should sanction such interference. Ten archbishops, and fifty bishops, were assigned to the whole republic; and it was required that they should be natives of France, and have attained the age of thirty years. They were not to be very liberally remunerated for the due exercise of their functions, only 15,000 francs being promised to each of the former as an annual stipend, and 10,000 to each of the latter;* and the parochial priests were declared to be entitled only to 1500 or 1000 francs *per annum*.

While Napoleon allowed that the Romish faith should be the established religion of France, he did not mean to preclude himself or his eventual successors from the power of making such alterations as might be deemed expedient, either in doctrine or in discipline; for his great object was to be despotic both in religious and civil affairs, and to dictate the law in every branch of polity.

His power was now at its height; but he was not content without the acquisition of the imperial dignity; and, when he had obtained his wish from a servile and prostrate nation, he aspired to the honour of being anointed and crowned, in the most solemn and religious manner. Full of this idea, he applied to his friend, the pope, and requested his speedy attendance at Paris. Sensible of the expediency of compliance, Pius submitted with a good grace to a mandate which he had not the courage to resist, and prepared for a journey to France. Having convoked a secret council of cardinals, he congratulated his venerable brethren on the effect of the *concordat*, which had restored the true worship of God in France, and had seasonably checked the mischievous influence of impiety and profaneness: he applauded the zeal of that powerful prince who had promoted this change, and declared that he felt himself bound both by policy and gratitude to bestow the imperial crown on 'his dearest son in Christ.' When a prince earnestly desired the performance of a sacred ceremony, it was the duty of the head of the church (said the servile pope) to gratify him by impressing a religious character on the ties which bound him to his people; and an act of this kind would be rewarded with the divine benediction. Having given directions for the administration of public affairs (although, in a state which he knew not how to govern, no serious injury could result from his absence,) he presented himself at Paris in the autumn of the year 1804, and officiated at the imperial coronation, which, with all its splendour, did not strikingly excite the joy or enthusiasm of the people. He was treated by Napoleon with politeness and respect; but, if he had the honour or the feelings of a man, he could not be altogether pleased with his own conduct. He had given the force of religious sanction to the usurpation of an adventurer.

After his return to Rome, Pius gave a pompous account of the result of his journey. Even his appearance in France, he said, had been visibly beneficial to the cause of religion. An innumerable crowd followed him in every part of his progress, and his readiness to grant apostolical benediction gladdened the people, and invigorated their pious zeal. He reclaimed to their duty some bishops who had refused to submit to the *concordat*, and procured decrees for the augmentation of the revenues of the prelates, for the regular establishment of funds sufficient to defray the expenses of public worship, for the erection of theological seminaries, and for the revival of many religious societies, particularly the Priests of the Mission and the Daughters of Charity. He also obtained an edict, allowing to the bishops the full liberty of judging with regard to spiritual offences, and of punishing violations of the canonical laws. In return for these concessions (which, in all probability, were not carried into full effect,) he conferred on the archbishops of Paris and Rouen the highest dignity that he could grant, by presenting the cardinal's hat to each of those prelates.

The French had left to the pope scarcely any other pretence for interfering in their concerns, than that of granting canonical institution to those prelates whom their emperor might think proper to nominate: but with this shadow of honour his holiness was not so elate as to be particularly anxious for the performance of that ceremony. The applications made to him for that purpose were coolly disregarded; so that, in 1811, twenty-seven bishops waited for his confirmation of the imperial choice. Resenting his refusal, Napoleon declared that the *concordat* was at an end, and called a council of prelates to act in this case for the refractory pontiff. He hinted that the pope, if he

long divided between the cardinals Bellezoni and Mattei; but the election terminated in favour of the bishop of Imola, even though he was supposed to be more friendly to the French than to the Austrian interest.

That the character of the new pope was not very highly estimated, may be inferred,—yet not decisively,—from the satirical effusion of Pasquin, the unknown director, or perhaps only the follower, of the general opinion at Rome. The anagram of the pontiff's title was thus given: *Roma, china-ti*, that is, 'Rome, humble thyself.' The pun upon the word *Pax*, inserted by the order of Pius above his coat of arms, was still more severe: for the satirist hinted that those letters could only be meant for the initials of *Peggoire Assai X.*—'ten times worse.'

* That is, 625 pounds sterling to an archbishop, and two thirds of that sum to an inferior prelate.

would not conduct himself like a Frenchman, could not expect to retain any authority or influence in the great empire. This is not an unreasonable doctrine; for every state ought to have a peculiar director of its religious concerns, rather than have recourse on any occasion to a foreign priest.

Napoleon always pretended to be a friend to religion; and, in his own opinion, he did not forfeit that character, when (in the year 1809) he divested the pope of his temporal power: but, however justly he might argue in this case, he acted solely from motives of ambition. It suited his policy to adopt a line of argument which philosophers had used, by representing the possession of political power as inconsistent with the essence of religion, and injurious to the purity and sanctity of spiritual government. But the despot went still farther, and, by imprisoning the pontiff at Avignon, disunited him from the sacred college, prevented him from presiding in a grand ecclesiastical council, and impaired his authority and influence as a director of the conscience and a teacher of piety. Pius did not tamely bear the insults and injuries to which he was subjected. He protested, in a public declaration, against the outrageous violence and sacrilegious wickedness of Napoleon, and even ventured to excommunicate the daring oppressor; but it must be observed, that he evinced his moderation even in this act of apparent revenge; for he disclaimed all intention of exciting a revolt or an insurrection, declaring that the act was merely a spiritual censure, inflicted with a view of bringing the delinquent to a due sense of his error and a consequent reparation of his injustice. He indeed denied and condemned the assertion of some former pontiffs, that sovereigns might lawfully be deposed by the spiritual father of Christendom. If a national council had at any time voted the deposition of a prince, the pope (he said) might as justly confirm the sentence, if it suited his own ideas of policy or rectitude, as he might crown a legitimate prince, or consecrate a foreign prelate who had received his appointment from the ruling power in the state to which he belonged. This acknowledgement was a concession to the reforming spirit of modern times, and a proof of the decline of pontifical arrogance.

The idle thunder of excommunication only provoked the tyrant's derision, and the mode in which it was softened excited ridicule, while this treatment of the pontiff was considered by many catholics as a judgment upon him for having favoured and indulged an enemy of the church in the *concordat* and at the coronation.

Still affecting a high regard for religion and its ministers, the ruler of France concluded a new agreement with the pope, whom he unexpectedly gratified with the privilege of nomination to ten bishoprics, either in France or in Italy, allowing him also to exercise the pontificate in France, and in the kingdom which had been formed in the north of Italy, in the same manner in which his predecessors had acted: but the master of Rome was not yet so humbled by a reverse of fortune, as to be disposed to reinstate the pontiff in his temporal authority.

The ruin of Napoleon was at length the consequence of his wanton ambition. After his mad expedition to Russia, he was unable to withstand that powerful confederacy which, with the most determined zeal, was organized against him. Holland and the German states shook off his yoke,—and Rome reverted to its temporal and spiritual lord.

Adversity has been styled a teacher of wisdom; but the maxim was not verified by the conduct of the restored pontiff, who soon manifested his bigotry and imprudence, instead of displaying the enlightened policy of a wise prince. Not content with the resumption of ecclesiastical property, and the abolition of Napoleon's code in the Roman state, he re-ordained the observance of all the festivals, re-established the monastic orders, revived, in some degree, the inquisition, and reinstated the obnoxious society of the Jesuits. As an excuse for the last measure, he declared that the catholic world demanded, with an unanimous voice, the revival which he had ordered.* He therefore readily granted to Taddeo Barzozowski, 'general of the company of Jesus,' and his associates, all suitable and necessary powers for the admission of all who might be disposed to follow the rules prescribed by St. Ignatius of Loyola,—for the education of youth in the principles of the catholic faith and in good morals,—for hearing confessions, preaching the word of God, and administering the sacraments of the church. As this edict required funds for its execution, such property as had not been irrevocably transferred from the former association was assigned to the new fraternity, compensations were allowed for that which had been alienated, and subscriptions were requested from the opulent and the liberal.

Even if this impolitic conduct in religious affairs had been accompanied with the display of wisdom and justice in the civil and ordinary administration, it would not have been sufficiently redeemed from censure or complaint; but, when joined with general misgovernment, it tended only to convince the public of the pope's unfitness to be the ruler of a nation. Pius, however, proceeded in his course with little alteration and few concessions, considering himself as the worthy successor of St. Peter, and as a proper object of general regard and esteem.†

* We ought not to dispute the pope's veracity: but, as we know that the influence of the chief catholic powers constrained Ganganelli to dissolve the institution, we doubt whether the call for its re-establishment was either strong or unanimous.

† While we adopt the general impression which prevailed with regard to the political conduct and administration of this pontiff, we are bound to annex a different statement, given by a writer who boldly maintains the accuracy of his information.—"Pius (says M. Vieusseux) effected many useful improvements in the country over which he ruled. His impoverished finances, the inveterate habits of the people, the old forms and routine of church-government, his own scrupulous and gentle nature, and the prejudices of some of his advisers, prevented him from doing more. He enacted a law, however, compelling the proprietors of the large estates in the Campagna

After the deposition and banishment of Napoleon, the pope entertained the hope of some accession to his authority, as it was not to be supposed that Louis XVIII. would retain, unaltered, the ecclesiastical settlement which the usurper had framed; but, when a new compact was adjusted with France, in the year 1817, it was more calculated to augment and dignify the establishment, than to increase the influence of the supposed head of the church. Thirty-two new sees were ordered to be erected; but his holiness was to have no more concern with them than to grant canonical institution to such individuals as might be nominated by the king; and it was foreseen or understood that, if he should refuse to confirm the royal appointment, his majesty would not revoke it; for Louis, however pious and devout, was determined to support the independence of his kingdom against the high claims even of the spiritual father of Christendom.

The general state of religion in France, for a considerable time after the expulsion of Napoleon, was so inconsistent with true piety, that the respectable part of the priesthood seemed to apprehend its speedy extinction. Alarmed at this prospect, many churchmen, in different parts of the kingdom, undertook missions with a view of reclaiming the people. As a specimen of the mode in which these missions were conducted, we may observe, that, in the year 1819, nine ecclesiastics paraded the chief streets of Avignon, singing penitential psalms, and two of them, halting on a hill, preached to two divisions of the assembled multitude. On the following day, they visited the churches, and harangued overflowing congregations; and, for a week, their time was almost wholly employed in giving public or private instructions to the citizens, and in visiting the hospitals and prisons for the same purpose; and the second week was principally devoted to the consolation of those who came to confess their sins, and who, seeming to be penitent, received absolution and pardon. The baptismal vows were publicly renewed with pompous solemnity, and, in every church, while the Gospel was holden up to general view, all were required to swear that they would faithfully observe the precepts contained in that divine book. After the administration of all the sacraments of the church, a great cross was borne in magnificent procession, and erected on a terrace in holy triumph; and the mission was closed with appropriate and interesting discourses.

As these missions had only a partial effect the state of the church was represented as deplorable, in a letter which the bishops addressed to the pope. The ecclesiastical discipline, they said, was relaxed; many dioceses were so neglected by their lawful rulers, or so ill-governed, that the faithful wandered like sheep without shepherds; the enemies of the church took advantage of this weakness, to inflict severe wounds on the declining hierarchy; and the pious divines who endeavoured, by acting as itinerant preachers, to revive that religious spirit which had nearly become extinct, were treated with contempt or with insult. It was therefore highly expedient that some measures should be speedily taken to restore the dignity and influence of the church. Repeated deliberations on this subject in the French cabinet led to a royal ordinance for the erection of chapels of ease wherever they seemed to be requisite, for the immediate grant of pecuniary aid to the impoverished church, and for the general protection of that establishment. 'It was the duty of every state (said the leading minister on this occasion) to foster or to renew a religious spirit. To support religion was to support the unfortunate whom it consoles, to cherish that morality which it elevates, and that virtue which it creates and maintains.'

While these measures were operating to the relief of the established church, tranquillity was restored to the south of France. At Nismes and other towns, the protestants had for several years been most illiberally molested by the catholics, and in a great measure deprived of that toleration to which they were by law entitled. Some of them had been murdered on their way to the meetings of the electoral colleges, and, in defending their cause, two military officers of high rank had lost their lives. It was pretended that the court connived at these outrages, because the sufferers were more attached to Napoleon than to the house of Bourbon; but this was an unfounded allegation; for the king, though he did not in every point adhere to the charter which he had granted, was not disposed to violate its provisions in the case of the protestants. The ultra-royalists (as the friends of the old *regime* were styled) would probably have continued these persecutions to the present day, if Louis had not covered the descendants of the Huguenots with the broad mantle of toleration.

The pope, from the time of his restoration to the day of his death, was chiefly influenced by the counsels of cardinal Gonsalvi, who was a better governor both of the church and state than his master. Thus the pontiff became more popular in the decline of his life than he had been in the vigour of his age; and his death, which happened in the eighty-fourth year of his age and the twenty-fourth of his reign,* was not unlamented either by the clergy or the people.

The intrigues for the election of a new pope were conducted, on the part of the Italian cardinals, with great art and dexterity. They re-

di Roma, to cultivate all their lands, or give up, for a reasonable compensation, those which they could not bring into culture; he allowed rewards for the plantation of trees; he completed the *cadastro* of the Roman provinces, begun before his time, and fixed upon its basis the rate of a moderate land-tax, in lieu of the arbitrary contributions previously exacted; he abolished the unjust exemptions of the upper classes from proportional taxation; he enforced a rigid economy in the expenditure of his household, and in the charges of the public departments; he established manufactures of wool and cotton in the houses appropriated to the reception of the poor; he instituted an office for the registration of mortgages, and the security of loans; he withdrew from circulation the base and enormously-depreciated coin which had been issued in disordered times, and replaced it by standard money, at a great loss to his treasury; and he issued an edict, announcing a plan of legal and judicial reform, which, however, was imperfectly followed."

* On the 20th of August, 1823.

solved neither to be ruled by the French nor by the Austrian faction, and were intent upon the choice of a zealot, who would be disposed to assert and maintain the high prerogatives of the church. Cardinal Severoli, though not so violent in his disposition as some of the bigots wished, was one whose professed principles were agreeable to the party; and therefore, on one of the days of meeting, he had twenty-six votes. He might have had as many more as would have served his purpose, if the Austrian party had not, in the emperor's name, *excluded* him from the chance of appointment; for there are four potentates who are allowed to exercise that right. When the exclusion was announced to him, he seemed to bear it with fortitude; and he desired that the act might be registered to prevent the privilege from being exercised twice in the same conclave, as in that case one of his intimate friends might be rendered ineligible. The disappointment preyed on his spirits, and is said to have hastened his death.

On the morning after this rejection, the friends of Severoli requested him to name a fit candidate for the papal throne. He replied, that, if he had sufficient influence over the election, either the cardinal Annibale della Genga, or Gregorio, (an illegitimate son of Charles III. of Spain,) would be the next pontiff. The former was the determined enemy of Gonsalvi, and his election, which quickly followed the recommendation, demonstrated the prevalence of the bigoted party. He assumed the denomination of Leo XII., because one of his ancestors had received some feudal property from the tenth pope of that name.

Gonsalvi was now dismissed from power, and the chief adviser of the new pope was the cardinal della Somiglia, who, like his sovereign, had been a libertine in his youth and in his middle age. From the high-church principles and arbitrary policy of such men, no just government, no attention to the rights of the people, could be expected; and their subsequent conduct appears to have proved, that those who foreboded ill from their combination with the Jesuits, did not judge too harshly. Indeed, priests in general are not the best administrators of temporal power, and, when we say that they ought to be restricted to their spiritual duties, we mean no disrespect to their sacred order.

With all his bigotry, and all his zeal against reform, the present pontiff has treated the protestants in his dominions with a degree of mildness and complacency not expected from his rigid principles. He even allows a chapel at Rome for the exercise of their religion, being probably influenced by a regard for the British and other protestant governments, even while he thinks that the professors of this faith do not pursue that course which would give them a full assurance of salvation. He finds it expedient to make some concessions to the more enlightened spirit of the age, while his own mind is darkened by inveterate prejudices. He would wish to dictate, as his predecessors did, to all the princes of Christendom; but as he cannot influence them to the extent of his wishes, he is content to exhort without commanding. The prince whom he finds most devoted to him, is the French king (Charles X.,) who, in his late law against sacrilege, has imitated the pontifical rigour of the middle ages; but it does not appear that even this monarch is inclined to surrender, to the claims of the papacy, any of the prerogatives of the Gallican church.

The reigning pope has had the high honour of celebrating a Jubilee. It commenced on Christmas eve, in 1824, and a whole year from that time is considered as peculiarly sacred. The beginning of the ceremonial was a solemn procession to the sacred gate which leads to St. Peter's church. The magistrates of Rome, the chief citizens, the cross-bearers and other ecclesiastical attendants, the parochial clergy, the bishops and cardinals, and (last in order, though first in dignity) the holy father, with his *tiara* carried before him, advanced to the gate. As it did not open at the first blow which he gave to the wall with a silver hammer, he tried a second, saying, with an air of authority, 'I will enter thy house, O Lord.' An opening not being yet made, he struck the wall a third time, and, with the aid of workmen on the other side, a passage was opened for the anxious throng. Fragments of stone, thrown out in this operation, were eagerly picked up by the votaries of superstition, and the medals which had been left within the wall at the jubilee of the year 1800, were also seized by the scrambling devotees. The church was soon filled to an overflow: the pope set the example of singing and praying, and the thanksgiving service was performed amidst the united sounds of choral and martial music, enlivened by peals of bell-ringing. Similar scenes occurred at three other churches; and all the subjects of the state, as well as pilgrims who flocked from various countries, now hoped for a remission of their sins, a favour which may be purchased at the altars on moderate terms. Poor strangers it appears, obtain this indulgence *gratis;* and the pope sometimes condescends to grant it to them in person. He presides at the celebration of the most sacred service in the metropolitan church, and afterwards entertains the pilgrims at the Vatican palace with humble fare and spiritual conversation, and distributes silver medals among them, commemorative of the jubilee. But the usual place of resort, for these strangers, is the hospital of the *Pelegrini*, where they are treated with great respect, and even have their feet washed by some of the cardinals. In the course of the year which is thus dignified with peculiar sanctity, public amusements and diversions are prohibited: yet the idea of a jubilee ought not, we think, to 'impoverish the public stock of harmless pleasure.' Where a general fast is ordered, there may be some reason for a suspension of ordinary amusements; but, in the case of a joyful celebrity, the interdiction seems to be misplaced and inapplicable.

From the religious concerns of France and of Italy, we proceed to the survey of other catholic governments. In Spain, the pope's authority was not suffered to be free from control, as will appear from the following restrictions upon his representative. In 1803, the council of Castile, in admitting the archbishop of Nicea to the office of papal legate in the Spanish dominions, stated three remarkable exceptions to the authority claimed by that officer. One was, that he was not to have the power of visiting the patriarchal, metropolitan, or other churches, with a view to correction or reform; another was, that he was not to examine any individual, whether of a religious or civil character, who might be estranged from a particular community or institution, or in any way criminal; and the third imported, that he would not be allowed to receive appeals from the ordinary judges.

The pontifical authority was still more restricted after the usurpation of the Spanish throne by Napoleon's brother Joseph, who, while he declared that only the Romish religion should be allowed, left to his holiness a mere shadow of power, suppressed a considerable number of monasteries, and abolished the court of inquisition. But, as the continued efficacy of his regulations depended on the permanence of his power, (for they were not attended with the general assent of the nation,) it remained for the cortes to determine whether his ordinances should be exploded or confirmed. They decreed, in the year 1813, that the inquisition was injurious to religion and to the state; but, to gratify the bigots, they voted the erection of episcopal courts for the trial of heretics. They made various attempts for the reformation of abuses and the redress of grievances; but, amidst the prevalence of war and civil dissentions, they could not make great or effective progress in their schemes; and their acts were annulled by the tyranny of that prince whose throne they endeavoured to establish. Being released by Napoleon in 1814, Ferdinand re-entered Spain with those emotions of resentment which prompted him to reject the new constitution; and, by listening to the suggestions of priests, excited discontent and odium. He was even so attached to the old school of bigotry, that he concurred with the pope in the propriety of re-establishing the order of Jesuits, and commanded that all the colleges, houses, funds, and rents, which belonged to this fraternity at the time of the suppression, and had not been altogether alienated, should be quickly restored. Yet, in his other concerns with the court of Rome, he displayed a laudable spirit; for, when the papal nuncio required that the ancient oath of fidelity to the king and regard for his prerogative, exacted from every prelate on his consecration, should no longer be administered, he answered the unwarrantable demand by declaring, that no innovation should be made in that respect. This prince, indeed, though deficient in sense and judgment, is sufficiently disposed to defend his prerogative against papal encroachments and attacks. The king of Portugal is equally attached with Ferdinand to the Romish faith, and, at the same time, equally ready to resist the high claims of the pontiff.

All the Austrian prelates, except the archbishop of Olmutz, are nominated or appointed by the emperor; and, although the papal confirmation is afterwards accepted, it is not considered as absolutely necessary. As king of Hungary, the same prince appoints the prelates of the Latin and Greek churches; and those who are named immediately exercise their full jurisdiction before they receive the pope's confirmation of their appointments; for it is a settled point in these countries, that bishops hold their power directly from God. When the episcopal oath is taken, it is understood to imply only a canonical obedience to the pope, not derogating in the smallest degree from the rights of the emperor, or encroaching on the duties which the prelates, as subjects of the state, are expected to perform to the ruling power. This practice certainly tends to explode the idea of a double allegiance on the part of the Austrian subjects, whose sovereign, while he is an hereditary bigot to the Romish faith, is determined to secure his own authority from the encroachments of a foreign pontiff. By the *Placitum Regium*, no papal edicts or rescripts are allowed to have any force or operation without the express consent of the government; and no persons are even suffered to apply to his holiness with regard to any new act of devotion, or for any other purpose, without the emperor's permission.

The catholic zeal of the Bavarian government has in this century declined. Bigotry has in a great measure yielded to a sense of liberality, and the protestants are not only tolerated but encouraged. A new constitution, allowing a national assembly, has been conceded to the people, and a meliorated system, both in the church and state, consequently prevails.

In the catholic cantons of Switzerland, there is not a uniformity of religious regulation. The rulers of Fribourg, in 1815, renounced the right of appointing their bishop, leaving it to the uninfluenced judgment of the pope In the Grison territory (now a part of the Swiss republic,) the bishop of Coire is elected by the twenty-four canons of the establishment; but it appears that the pope is allowed to fill up the vacancies among these canons, alternately with the chapter itself. The same bishop promulgates the papal ordinances, without waiting for the sanction of the temporal power In the new canton of Tessin, the bishop of Como is appointed by the government; but the papal confirmation is deemed requisite for the establishment of his pretensions. In the Valais, four priests are proposed by the chapter to the diet for the episcopal dignity: of these, one is selected as the most unobjectionable candidate; the pontiff at first pretends to reject him, but soon after nominates the same person, as if no previous recommendation had been given. In those states which, before the year 1815, composed a part of the diocese of Constance, the prelates are chosen by the government; and his holiness is expected to confirm the appointment. Thus, on the prelate's death, in 1818, a new bishop was nominated by the grand duke of Baden, and, though the pope objected, he was obliged to yield to the spirit of that prince. In most of the cantons, no papal or episcopal ordinances except those which relate to an exemption from fasts, or other affairs of little moment, are suffered to operate without the consent of the civil power. With regard to the monasteries, it appears, that the election of the head depends, in some, upon the pope, and, in the rest, upon the bishops.

In the kingdom of Naples, the pope's authority is seriously checked by the spirit of the government, although the doctrines which he maintains are still professed by the people. No bulls, rescripts, or dispensations, are effective without the royal assent; and, in the appointment of bishops, the court justly assumes a paramount authority.

In speaking of Naples, our attention is called to a remarkable society, which was formed in the year 1812, while Murat (that is, the usurper Joachim) filled the throne of Ferdinand. We are induced to mention it, not for its chief object, which was evidently political, but because its members mingled a sense of religion with their general views, and professed a high regard for evangelical truth, declaring that their grand aim was to establish on that basis a system of freedom and justice. Our Redeemer, they said, was the victim of despotic tyranny; and it was therefore the duty of his votaries to use all their efforts for its extinction. The founders of this association were the friends of the exiled family; but many persons of different political principles were encouraged to join them; and, borrowing the symbol of their confederacy from the charcoal trade, they did not disdain the degrading appellation of *Carbonari*. The existence of such a society did not escape the vigilance of Murat, who took measures for the repression of its audacity; and, being thus endangered it was reduced to a comparatively small number; for the leaders dismissed a very considerable part of their force, and carried on their intrigues with greater caution and secrecy. After the death of Joachim, Ferdinand, the restored king, or rather his minister the prince of Canosa, instituted a new association as a counterpoise to the Carbonari; but this did not prevent the great increase of the latter, who now propagated their principles of reform over many parts of Europe. At length, in the year 1820, their intrigues produced a revolution in the Neapolitan kingdom; but it was easily suppressed by the operations of an Austrian army, and many of these malcontents were punished in various modes. The society then desisted from its machinations, and declined in to insignificance.

In Sicily, so feeble is the papal power, that it is treated with a freedom bordering on contempt; and the intercourse still maintained with the court of Rome is confined to the formality of procuring either patents for bishoprics, to be granted to those who are nominated by the king, or dispensations for spiritual wants, when the individuals who apply for them have received the royal permission. If these applications should be disregarded, the king, being (by an ancient grant) a legate of the holy see by birth, would, in all probability, order the prelate who acts for him in that capacity, and who presides in the spiritual courts, to accede to the different requests in the pope's name, like the English parliamentarians, who, when they opposed Charles I. in the field, pretended to act in his name.

In the grand duchy of Tuscany, after the laudable efforts of Leopold in opposition to papal encroachments, little remained to be done in the present century to establish the independence of the temporal sovereign. It appears, indeed, that the pope ostensibly supplies the vacancies in episcopal preferments; but the rule is, that the names and pretensions of four candidates are communicated to him by the Tuscan minister at Rome, who points out the one more particularly favoured by the grand duke; and with this recommendation his holiness feels himself obliged to comply. The ordinary benefices are conferred on such persons as are deemed by the king or the bishops the most deserving; and the pope's confirmation of any appointment of this kind is considered as absolutely unnecessary. The injunctions of the pontiff are allowed to have some influence in cases of conscience or of private penance; but, if the answers to these cases should affect in any way the civil state of the persons who have solicited the illuminations of his wisdom, the acceptance is noticed and sometimes punished as a misdemeanour.

Even the hereditary bigotry of the king of Sardinia does not render him a slave to the pope. He bestows the highest ecclesiastical preferments at his own discretion, and rejects such orders from Rome as relate to the external polity of the church. He indeed suffers appeals to be made from bishops or their judicial deputies to the pontiff, in those few causes which are still subject to the jurisdiction of an ecclesiastical tribunal; but these appeals are not actually transferred to Rome, unless each subject should have been thrice investigated, without a uniformity of decision, by pontifical delegates, chosen from the whole number of churchmen resident within the kingdom.

CHAPTER II.

History of the Greek Church, and of the Christian Communities in Asia and Africa.

When the Roman empire was divided into two great states, it could not be expected, either that a community of interest, or an entire coincidence of religion would long prevail. As adult persons, who have left their homes and formed new families, do not feel themselves bound to adhere invariably to the opinions or the practices of their parents, nations, when disjoined by mutual consent, gradually adopt new sentiments, both in religion and in politics: we cannot, therefore, be surprised on finding that the Greeks soon began to differ from their former friends and fellow-subjects. The occasional religious differences between them have been stated by our predecessor; they were not essentially important, but sufficient in the eyes of irritable theologians to justify a secession. The schism still subsists to such an extent, that there are many Greeks, especially in the Morea, who are more unwilling to be upon friendly terms with the members of the Latin church, than even with Moslems or pagans. These haters of their Christian brethren, we may conclude, are men of weak minds and illiberal dispositions; and the majority of the Hellenic race, we hope, are not so bigoted and intolerant, though they certainly do not harmonise with the Romanists. A respectable votary of the Greek church, we are informed, made a formal application to the pope in 1825, requesting his authoritative aid and support in the present contest, and holding out the prospect of a religious union: but it does not appear that he was authorised on this occasion by the leaders of the insurgent confederacy, or that they are disposed to sacrifice any point of doctrine or even of ceremonial practice for the insignificant assistance which they can derive from the feeble remains of power and influence, yet enjoyed by the head of the Romish church.

The contest to which we incidentally referred, did not arise from any new provocation, but from continued reflection upon the enormity of existing abuses. The Greeks, habituated to the most disgraceful slavery, seemed to submit with patience to the sway of the most brutal barbarians that ever obstructed the progress of humanity and civilization: but, when the Spaniards, Portuguese, and Neapolitans, had roused themselves from that torpor which was apparently inconsistent with the warmth of their dispositions, the descendants of an illustrious nation resolved to exert their energy for the recovery of their independence. They boldly took up arms in the year 1821, and soon formed a new government, which, unaided by the jealous and selfish powers of the continent, they are still defending against their savage oppressors. Without speculating on the probable event of the contest, we shall merely observe that they are entitled to encouragement and support from all the advocates of freedom, and all the professors of Christianity. But, say the abettors of arbitrary power, rebels ought rather to be punished than assisted. As a general rule, we admit that position; but we may venture to affirm, that an exception ought to be allowed in the case of the Greeks, the injured slaves of a government which is in itself an *anomaly* and an *outrage*.

The ministers of the church, in general, were among the promoters of the revolt, and many of them are even engaged in the military service, in which some have displayed great alertness and courage. The priests, also, in numerous instances, take part with the rest of the community in agricultural labours, and in the mechanic arts, and thus eke out their scanty incomes in a mode which detracts from the respect that would otherwise be paid to them.

The doctrines and ceremonies of this church do not appear to have been altered since the beginning of the century. The priests have continued their old course; the people have not called for any innovation; and, since the insurrection unfolded the banners of liberty, religion has been treated as a secondary concern.

Adverting to the state of the Greek church in one point of ceremonial observance, which also exhibits traits of national manners, we are induced to take notice of the celebration of Easter. This festival, being deemed the most important of all, is observed with great joy and respect. The termination of *fasting* necessarily leads to the idea of *feasting;* but devotional exercises and pompous ceremonies in the churches precede the general indulgence and merriment. All the inhabitants of the towns and villages, in holiday trim, or in their best apparel, sally forth to pay visits and to receive congratulations; and they salute each other on the cheek, saying at the same moment, "Christ has risen." Beside private rejoicings, firings from the batteries and discharges of small arms announce the prevailing joy; and, not content with putting powder into their muskets or pistols, they introduce bullets, not, we hope, with a malicious intent, but from the wantonness of joy. In the evening a grand ceremony takes place in the chief towns: all men who sustain public characters, after attending divine service in the principal church, meet in the street, and the members of the executive body, approaching the legislative subjects of the state, who are drawn up in a line, embrace them with an air of affection. On Easter Monday, the festivities are renewed. In the environs of the towns, while many of the women, dressed in a tasteful manner, are reclining on the grass, listening to the attractive sounds of the guitar and the flute, equestrian bands are scouring the plain, and hurling their javelins; other parties are engaged in the Romaic dance, while discharges of pistols add to the effect of the music; children, fancifully arrayed and crowned with flowers, sport around their delighted relatives and friends; and apparent joy and hilarity animate the scene. Yet there is no great degree of true piety or sincere devotion in this celebration of Easter;—not more, indeed, than we observe in the Christmas festivities of England, where few think of the religious origin of the general joy.

As the Russian ecclesiastical establishment scarcely differs in any respect from the mother-church, there is no occasion for the formality of descriptive remark. Ceremonies are more regarded both by the clergy and the laity than the dictates of sound morality. Prostrations before the pictures or figures of saints,—

——"Who never yet had being,
Or, being, ne'er were saints;"

pilgrimages over immense deserts to favourite chapels and shrines, and other marks of superstition, are the general substitutes for true piety. The majority of the priests are men of low birth and imperfect education, and many of them attend more to the length of their beards than to the propriety of setting a good example to their flocks.

The late emperor Alexander, while he followed the rules of the established church, tolerated all sects in the exercise of their respective modes of worship, but did not suffer them to make proselytes. It was on this ground that he banished the Jesuits from his dominions. If they had been content with teaching the elements of literature, he would have left them unmolested; but they endeavoured to seduce the youth into the pale of the Romish church. The same prince treated the Jews, and the Moslem and pagan tribes of his Asiatic empire, with mildness and forbearance, promoting without enforcing their conversion When he completed the reduction of Georgia under his yoke, he found the people already Christians; and, allured by his beneficent sway, they seemed more observant, than they had before been, of the ordinances of the Greek church. Over Armenia and Kurdistan he had some influence, because those countries seemed not to have any regular government; but he did not ostensibly direct either their religion or politics.

Directing our course to the neighbouring territory of Chaldæa, we meet with a numerous body of Christians. They inhabit the country on each side of the Tigris, and are said to amount to 500,000 persons. They form an unconquered state, and are so determined to resist all attempts for their subjugation, that they constantly bear weapons of defence, which they do not lay aside even when they assemble for public worship. Their ostensible ruler is a patriarch, who exercises both a spiritual and civil jurisdiction; but he is not invested with that arbitrary power which is so prevalent in Asia; for the government is, in effect, rather republican than monarchical. The most intelligent men in Chaldæa do not pretend to know either at what time, or by whom, Christianity was first preached in that country; but it is probable that Gregory, styled the Enlightener, whom the Armenians consider as the founder of their church, introduced the Gospel likewise among the ancestors of those tribes of which we are now speaking. Yet, as the majority of their number follow the opinions of Nestorius, they differ from the Armenians, who are Monophysites. They appear to be divided into two hostile parties,—namely, the Nestorians, who compose an independent church, and the converts to the Romish persuasion. Literature, at present, is at a very low ebb among them; and we need not wonder at this circumstance, when their neighbours, in every direction, are equally unenlightened, or still more ignorant.*

In Persia are found the remains of sects that have Christianity for the basis of their religion; but the superstructure is a miscellaneous kind of erection, not fully suited to the foundation. The Sabeans, near the Persian Gulf, have tenets and practices borrowed from the Jewish and Mohammedan systems; but, as they believe in the divinity of Christ, and the redemption and atonement, they are justly considered as Christians. The Sefis resemble our Quakers in their regard to moral duties, and their endeavours to subdue the violence of the passions.

In India the Christians are widely diffused, not only in consequence of the invigorated exertions of modern missionaries, but from the remains of ancient conversions. Some have thought that the Saads are Christians in their hearts, though not in their external professions: but it appears that they are still heathens. About 155 years ago, one Jogee Das declared, at Dahli and other places, that he had been commissioned by the divine pupil of the Supreme Being to deliver the people from the clouds of error, in which they had been long enveloped; and he soon found many who were willing to secede from the Hindoo idolatry, and to assist him in the propagation of his doctrines. These sectaries resemble the Quakers in the plainness of their dress and the simplicity of their manners, in the avoidance of frivolous amusements, in that opinion of the profaneness of an oath which does not exclude a strict regard to honour and truth, and in their detestation of war and violence. They believe in the immortality of the soul, and expect a day of final judgment. Many of those who have intercourse with our missionaries seem inclined to become Christians; but, even among these well-disposed men, conversions are yet uncommon.

In the territory of Canara we still find a large Christian community, sufficiently remarkable to claim our notice. It was from the settlement of Goa that the rays of evangelical light diffused their lustre over Canara; but at what time a Christian colony was first formed in this part of Southern India, cannot be ascertained. The influence of the Portuguese government not only conduced to the protection of the settlers, but procured for them the favour of princely patronage, so that they obtained from the rajahs of the country, grants of land and various privileges. They received occasional accessions of European devotees and of native converts from Goa, and, by their forcible persuasions, drew many of the inhabitants from the darkness of idolatry; and the establishment became so flourishing, that about 80,000 persons are said to have belonged to it at the time when Hyder Ali, the bold usurper of the throne of Maissour, attacked and subdued Canara.* They were terrified at the success of a Moslem conqueror; but he treated them with mildness and humanity, and confirmed their privileges. Far different was the conduct of his son Tippoo, who, although he found them ready to submit to his authority, pretended to suspect that, under the influence of Christian zeal, they would not long remain faithful subjects to a prince of his religion. He therefore insisted on their adoption of that system which he preferred, and, observing their reluctance, proceeded to acts of violence and outrage. He banished or imprisoned the priests; sent the greater part of their flocks to Seringapatam and other towns, to linger in poverty and wretchedness; destroyed the churches, and seized the lands. The fall of the tyrant, however, in 1799, revived the establishment. Those who had been compelled to renounce the Christian faith, were re-admitted into the church; many who had emigrated during the persecution returned into Canara; religious structures gradually arose in various parts; and, in 1818, the population was estimated at 21,800. Agriculture is the occupation of the majority of this number; and, in that and other employments, the industrious habits and orderly conduct of the people are eminently conspicuous.

The spiritual concerns of this community are conducted by about twenty-five priests, who receive instructions from the primate of Goa. The religion of the establishment is consequently that of the Romish church. The

* An account of the Chaldæan Christians, by the Rev. Dr. Robert Walsh.

* In the year 1767.

mass is solemnized in Latin, while the sermon and other parts of the service are delivered in the vernacular tongue. Images of our Redeemer, the Virgin Mary, and favourite saints, are exhibited in the churches, and receive humble adoration; but public processions are avoided, from an unwillingness to shock the prejudices of the Hindoos. There is no ecclesiastical tribunal in the province, and the only punishment inflicted by the church is that of excommunication, of which there are two species, one trifling, and the other not so severe as to preclude the exercise of kind and charitable offices toward the delinquent.

Other parts of India, as well as a part of Canara, have received the Gospel from catholic emissaries. A missionary, writing to a friend in the year 1806, represented the Romish places of worship as very numerous in Travancour; but he added, that, in most of them, mass was performed only once in two years. Notwithstanding this apparent neglect of exterior ordinances, he thought that above 1000 catholic missionaries were dispersed over India; but this, we apprehend, is an exaggeration. We know, however, that the protestant missionaries are very numerous, extending their labours in one direction from Lahor to Cape Comorin, and, in another, from the Persian frontier to China. The mission in the province of Bengal appears to be the most flourishing; and it is more regularly organized, in consequence of the establishment of an episcopal see and a college at Calcutta. The late Dr. Middleton laboured with great zeal for the diffusion both of Christianity and learning among the Hindoos; and his successor in the bishopric (Dr. Heber) is usefully employed in the promotion of the same objects.

The promoters of Christianity are not very successful in the Chinese empire. They are rarely suffered to penetrate into the interior parts of the country;* and, even at Canton, where the British influence is very considerable, they are viewed with an eye of jealousy, and checked in their benevolent purposes. In the hope of more auspicious times, they carry on their operations at Macao, and also at Malacca, where a college has been erected, in which are many Chinese students. The New Testament has been translated into the Chinese language; and copies have been gladly accepted by many of those emigrants who have transferred their industry and arts to the islands of the Indian ocean.

In Syria and the Holy Land, our missionaries are also actively engaged. They hold religious conversations with the natives of all persuasions, preach the pure word of God, distribute translations of the Scriptures and religious tracts, and establish schools. Their success is not equal to their wishes: yet they are not discouraged. If they convert few of the Jews or Moslems, they guide the members of the Greek and Latin churches into a better path in their religious journey. As the Druses are supposed by some antiquaries to be, in a great measure, the descendants of the crusaders of the middle ages, it might be expected that they would be disposed to listen to the exhortations of Christian preachers. Many of them certainly are so inclined; the reigning emir is said to be a Christian in his heart; and we are assured that the votaries of the Gospel in their country outnumber the followers of the Koran. However that may be, the Druses certainly live on more friendly terms with the Christians than the subjects of any other government in Western Asia.

In Egypt, the few Europeans who undertake the task of conversion are treated with mildness by the pasha who now rules over that country as an independent prince; but, though he is fond of European arts, he is not inclined to assist in the propagation of that faith which his hereditary prejudices teach him to reprobate, and the labours of the missionaries are counteracted by the efforts of itinerant Moslems, sent from a college at Cairo to enforce the doctrines of the pseudo-prophet.

The Abyssinians might be called a religious people, if we could depend on their professions of piety; but, when they make pompous boasts of their zeal, they speak more like Pharisees than lovers of truth. They are more attentive to forms and ceremonies than to the practice of true holiness and virtue; for their morality hangs loosely upon them, and their conduct is not sufficiently regulated by the laws of honour or by good principles. Their addiction to perjury is an odious trait in their characters; for they will frequently imprecate curses upon themselves if their assertions should be false, knowing at the same moment that they are wholly unfounded; and, when the king has sworn that he will pardon a delinquent, whom he afterwards wishes to punish, he says to his attendants, 'Take notice that I scrape this oath away from the tongue which pronounced it,'—making movements and gestures corresponding with his faithless declaration. They do not regard marriage as a religious obligation, and the priests therefore do not officiate on the occasion; and chastity is little regarded by either sex. They consider fasting as a strong proof of piety; but the priests, while they order the laity to fast about 190 days in a year, only practise that kind of forbearance for 70 days. At the end of each fast the chief priest entertains his brethren, who greedily devour the raw flesh of a cow, sing hymns, and drink some fermented liquor until they are stupified. With regard to the authority of the abuna or metropolitan, it does not appear that he has a great extent of power or patronage. Officers, who are not required to be priests, administer the revenues of the churches and monasteries, and determine spiritual causes,—an appeal to the king alone being permitted, if the decision should not give satisfaction.

CHAPTER III.

History of the Ecclesiastical Communities of the Lutherans and Calvinists.

THE Lutherans still bear the chief sway in the Swedish and Danish kingdoms. Their

* It is affirmed that, in the year 1815, the French missionaries and their converts had chapels at Fo-kein and other towns, but that a persecution arose against them, and ruined a concern which seemed to promise well.

zeal, however, is less fervent than it formerly was, and they are less arbitrary and intolerant. They begin to partake of the candour and liberality which are now more prevalent than even in the last century; they entertain more just sentiments of the right which all persons have to think for themselves in points of religion and of conscience; and they are more disposed to follow, in practice, that rational and well-founded axiom. Indeed, they now grant full toleration, from which even the Jews are not excluded. The addition of Norway to the kingdom of Sweden, in the year 1814, tended to infuse a more liberal spirit into the government. The easy acquisition of a new territory puts a prince into good humour, and he instantly becomes more mild and conciliatory: but, even before that event, it was ordained, in the new constitution which was promulgated in 1809, that no person should be harassed or called to an account for his religious opinions, unless it should clearly appear that his avowal of them, or the exercise of that religion to which they appertained, might be injurious to the state. This exception, it may be said, furnished a pretence for molesting the sectaries; yet the ordinance, we believe, was intended to convey a complete toleration.

The present Danish government is liberal and beneficent; and the king is as attentive to the interests of the church as to that of the state. Aware of the poverty of his clerical subjects in Iceland, he allows pensions to those who cannot procure a sufficiency of income from the limited bounty of their congregations; and he evinces his Christian zeal in the promotion of missionary undertakings.

In the kingdom of the Netherlands, formed in the year 1814, by the union of the seven United Provinces with those which the French had wrested from the hands of the Austrian emperor, the sovereign, though a Calvinist, granted to his new subjects an entire freedom of religious opinion and worship, and an equal share with the protestants in the representative government. This equality did not satisfy the prelates, who were of opinion that the Romish faith, followed for so many ages by the people of the Netherlands, entitled its professors to superior privileges: but the king, instead of adopting their suggestion, merely promised that every proposal connected with their religion should be submitted to the consideration of an executive committee, consisting of catholics. Since that time, they have occasionally vented their ill humour in complaints and remonstrances; but they cannot effectually resist the commanding influence of the protestants. In 1825, the king gratified them by the establishment of a seminary, in which candidates for the catholic ministry might acquire a sufficient fund of learning for the proper discharge of their sacred trust. With the same view, and in the same spirit of complacency, the college of Maynooth in Ireland is supported by the liberality of a protestant parliament.

In France, the protestants are chiefly Calvinists. With regard both to the French and German branches of that sect, it was stipulated, in the agreement between Napoleon and the pope, that a synod, composed of five consistorial churches, should regulate all religious and ecclesiastical concerns, but that its resolutions should be submitted to the rulers of the state for confirmation; and that the appointment of pastors should be subject to similar recognition or approbation. If the contributions of the different communities should be insufficient for the support of the officiating ministers, the government promised to increase the amount to a fair allowance. As the incorporation of a part of Germany with France had added a multitude of Lutherans to the state, it was provided by the same *concordat*, that their church should be regulated, under the authority of the consuls, by consistories both general and local, and by councils of inspection. The ministers of the Calvinist persuasion were to be educated at Geneva, and those of the Lutheran church at a peculiar seminary of their own religion. When the territories in which these protestants resided were withdrawn by the allied powers from the French yoke, in the year 1815, such regulations were made as softened the arbitrary clauses of the former compact, and yet left a controlling authority in the hands of the civil power.

The attachment of the elector (now king) of Saxony to the Romish faith did not induce the people of that country to relinquish their habitual regard for the Lutheran system; and therefore no catholic bishop is allowed to act or reside in that realm, except the king's confessor, to whom the pope grants the authority of an apostolic vicar. In Upper Lusatia, some dignitaries who form a *chapter*, elect a mitred dean, in the presence and with the approbation of an Austrian commissary; and, at Bautzen, there is a chapter which, though catholic, has a Lutheran president. In civil rights, the members of the two communions now stand upon an equal footing in Saxony. In the Hanoverian territories, the catholics were long subjected, by the Lutheran rulers of the state, to various restrictions. They were not allowed to carry the host publicly, or to have any processions; and, in points of ecclesiastical jurisdiction, they were obliged to have recourse to the odious authority of a Lutheran consistory. But more auspicious days at length dawned upon them; and they are now gratified with all the rights of citizens.

In the three electoral archbishoprics (Mentz, Cologne, and Treves,) which were incorporated with the Prussian monarchy by the congress of Vienna, it might be supposed that the catholics, forming the bulk of the population, would be treated with lenity and indulgence, if not highly favoured; and, in fact, they have greater privileges than their brethren who reside in other parts of the king's dominions. They have, at the court of Rome, an agent who promotes their interest, and encourages the pope to counteract the arbitrary spirit of Frederic. In Silesia, where the catholics form only a third part of the population of the capital, the king has suppressed some of their monasteries, and precluded all appeals to Rome. In East Prussia he suffers no Romish bishop to act, though the priests are retained; and, in Brandenburg and other provinces, he rules the sect with a high hand, yet not with oppressive tyranny. At the same time, he favours the Calvinists more than the Lutherans, but is so far rom suffering the former to molest the latter, that he would rather witness their union than their discord.

The increasing liberality of sentiment, in the present age, is strikingly evinced by the union of the Lutheran and Reformed churches in many of the German states. The grand duke of Nassau, being connected in marriage with a lady of the latter persuasion, and wishing to preclude religious differences among his children, resolved, as far as his influence could extend, to unite his family and his subjects in the same devotional forms and worship; and his laudable endeavours were crowned with success. In the grand duchy of Hesse and some other states the example was speedily followed; and the completion of three centuries from the first exertions of Luther in the cause of religious reform, furnished an appropriate day* for the first public celebration of the new union. To all liberal minded Christians this must have been a day of joy and of sincere congratulation. They recurred to the page of history for an elucidation of the dawn of religious reform: they reflected on the troubles and sufferings to which their ancestors were subjected in the progress of emancipation from the yoke of a corrupt church; and they now hailed with heart-felt satisfaction the union of those who, without differing on essential points, had long been unhappily divided.†

Notwithstanding these approaches to a union of sentiment, differences of religious opinion still subsist in various parts even of protestant Germany; for a uniform standard of thought cannot be expected to exist in any community. In those universities in which freedom of speech is in any degree allowed, the desire of political liberty appears to be accompanied with freethinking on the subject of religion. It is affirmed by professor Tholuck, that the university of Halle is the seat of infidelity, and that even some of the teachers of theology are infected with an anti-christian spirit. This hostility to the truth, he says, is still more prevalent at Weimar, where zealous Christians are discountenanced and persecuted: but he seems, in this instance, to have used the language of exaggeration. We admit that those who wish to be reformers in politics are in general equally desirous of what they call a reformation in religion; but the charge of infidelity is the common resource of intolerant bigots, who are offended even with such as differ from them in unimportant particulars, and stigmatize, as infidelity, that which is merely a sectarian difference of opinion.

Dissatisfied with the religious systems established in Germany, the baroness Krudener ventured to propose a reform. This lady, in her youth, was not strongly impressed with sentiments of piety. Her vivacity seemed to disdain all restrictions, and her morals were not pure or correct: but, in the progress of her studies, she at length met with the works of Stilling, a German enthusiast, whose effusions, operating upon the warmth of her disposition, excited in her mind a strong devotional spirit. When the sparks of her piety were kindled into a flame, she resolved to illuminate the world, as far as her abilities would allow, and began, in the year 1813, to propagate her opinions publicly at Heidelberg. In the following year she visited Paris, in the character of a religious reformer, and praved and preached at her hotel for the edification of the dissolute and depraved French; but, while she amused them by her eccentricity, she made no impression upon their minds. To Switzerland she afterwards directed her course, and preached in the open air to large congregations. She dwelt on the necessity of regeneration, and asserted the saving power of faith and grace, even without those works which are meritorious in the opinion of the world. She was consequently more severe in her denunciations against what the Methodists call sin, than against acts of worldly wickedness and guilt. She pretended to be convinced that her frequent and earnest prayers had so far secured the divine favour, as to give her that inspired and influential character which enabled her to reclaim thousands of sinners: but, by declaiming at the same time against some civil ordinances, she so displeased the rulers of several cantons, that they ordered her to quit the country. Retiring into the duchy of Baden, she assembled at her house the supposed friends of true religion, and boldly continued her career, until the magistrates stopped these irregular proceedings. She thus became sensible of the danger of defying the constituted authorities, and was more prudent and cautious in her subsequent conduct. She lived many years unmolested on an estate which she possessed near Riga, where, as well as in her other places of abode, she was idolized by the poor for her numerous acts of charity and beneficence. She died in the Crimea, in 1824, without the fame of having instituted a formal sect.

While a protestant lady of Germany thus asserted her pretensions to the honour of inspiration, a Romish fanatic of the same country seemed to think himself equally favoured with the divine aid. This was the prince Alexander Hohenlohe of Bamberg, who pretended that he could cure bodily disorders by prayers and devotional exercises; and several cases have been obtruded on the credulous part of the community, containing attestations, seemingly strong, of the providential grant of relief (at the precise time when the prince solemnized the mass and offered up prayers to Heaven) to persons in distant countries, whose friends had applied to him in the fulness of their faith and the fervour of their zeal.

Of the twenty-two cantons which now compose the Helsetic confederacy, six are attached to the protestant communion; and of these Bern is the most populous and flourishing. In six of the states, the catholics and protestants bear equal sway, while the other ten cantons follow the Romish system In these, a tolera-

* In the year 1817.

† Among the Bavarian protestants, this reconciliation was adjusted with particular formality in the year 1818. The united establishment received the appellation of the Protestant Evangelical Christian Church, and the holy scripture was declared to be the only basis of faith to which its members ought to adhere.

ting disposition usually prevails; but there has lately been an exception from that rule in the case of the Pays de Vaud. A new sect arose in this canton, or rather a number of persons resolved to commence a more methodical course of religious duties and devotional exercises, not supposing that their zeal in this respect could excite the displeasure of the ruling power. If they had restricted these marks of piety to their own families, the government would not have taken the least notice of their conduct; but their offence, it seems, consisted in propagating the same spirit among others, by inviting their friends to their houses to join in these acts of worship. It does not appear that they entertained any new opinions or heterodox notions; and therefore the great council of the canton had no sufficient ground of interference; nor ought it, indeed, to have interfered, even if the people had been heretically disposed; for, as belief depends on the unsophisticated mind, it ought never to be subjected to force or constraint. A minister of the Gospel, however, was accused, in the year 1824, of the *heinous crime* of having read and expounded a chapter of the Scriptures to four persons beside his own family, and condemned to banishment for three years by his arbitrary judges.* Other ministers were arraigned for similar conduct; but, when twenty-six clergymen petitioned the government to relax its rigour in cases of this kind, the prosecutions, we believe, were discontinued.

While the catholics sometimes transgressed the limits prescribed by the government, but (in the case which we have stated) without serious delinquency, the protestants occasionally deviated from the ordinary course of legitimate proceedings, and, in one case, disgraced their holy cause by sanguinary excesses. In a village of the canton of Zurich, the family and neighbours of a farmer, named John Peter, were infected with the superstitious folly of his daughter Margaret, who, having a tendency to devout enthusiasm, had been inflamed into absolute phrenzy by the effusions of itinerant preachers. So high was the opinion of her sanctity, that she was even supposed to have been favoured with celestial inspiration; and, by the influence which she thus obtained, she was enabled to hold religious assemblies, in which the most shameful extravagances and the most hideous enormities were practised. She maintained the necessity of waging perpetual war with Satan, to prevent him from triumphing over Jesus Christ, and recommended, as the most effectual mode of saving souls from the grasp of the restless fiend, either an act of self-sacrifice, or the infliction of mortal wounds on friends and relatives. At a meeting of her disciples, she attacked one of her brothers with such fury, that only the opportune aid of a female domestic saved him from death. Her sister then offered herself as a victim, and was beaten to death with an iron mallet by the cruel enthusiast and one of her mad friends. Her father did not actually witness these outrages; but he knew that she was perpetrating some enormity, and yet did not rush into the apartment to secure peace and order. He suffered the storm to rage, while he calmly pursued his ordinary occupations. Margaret's phrenzy was not yet cooled; and, while she sat on the bed on which remained the palpitating body of her sister, she began to strike herself with the mallet. Not satisfied with the vigour of her own arm, she desired a friend to use the instrument with fatal effect; but, suddenly thinking that crucifixion would be a more legitimate death, she insisted on suffering that species of torture. Some pieces of timber were then placed upon the bed in the form of a cross, and to these she was deliberately nailed, without seeming to feel any pain,—so great was her fortitude, and so determined her self-devotement. At length she said, 'Drive a nail into my heart, or split my head;' the latter part of the alternative was instantly executed, and a low moan announced her expiration. A judicial inquiry was made into these horrid acts; and Ursula Kundig, the most willing and ready agent in the work of murderous fanaticism, was sentenced to imprisonment and labour for sixteen years. Some of Margaret's male associates were deprived, for the rest of their lives, of their political rights; and her father's house, the scene of her folly and cruelty, was demolished. Her opinions and fancies were not immediately renounced by her votaries, some of whom pretended to believe that she would soon re-appear in the world.

The commanding number of protestants in Switzerland may be supposed to keep those of Piedmont in countenance; but the latter (we mean the Vaudois) have been so discouraged by the bigotry of the court and the Romish clergy, that they are reduced to a small number, not exceeding 20,000, who are under the spiritual direction of thirteen pastors. They preserve those tenets which they maintained on their original separation from the Romish church. 'We are called heretics by the members of that church (said their primate Peyrani to a late visitant of their secluded valleys;) but our church is founded on the durable rock of Christianity. We have adhered to the pure tenets of the apostolic age, and the Romanists have separated from us.'

In all the states of which we have been speaking, the Jews were at an early period mingled with the Christians, notwithstanding the rooted odium which subsisted between the humbled posterity of the ancient patriarchs and the triumphant adorers of the Messiah. Although the former may be thought to have no concern in a history of the church of Christ, it may not be altogether improper to take notice of the treatment which they have received in our time from the Christian governments. While the French revolution was in progress, Gregorie was the first who openly proposed that they should be rescued from the state of degradation to which they had long been subjected; and, as freedom was then (ostensibly at least) the order of the day, there was no pretence for withholding it from the Israelites

* Des Persecutions Religieuses dans le Canton de Vaud.—A similar case occurred in France in 1825. At the village of St. Etienne, one man, sixteen women, and two children, were apprehended for meeting at a private house to read the New Testament; and, for this alleged violation of the law, they were reprimanded by the magistrates and fined.

In consequence of this change of opinion, they were admitted into corporations, promoted to a variety of offices, obtained considerable rank in the army during Napoleon's sway, and were deemed not unfit to belong even to his celebrated Legion of Honour. It was pretended that he entertained the idea of re-establishing their power in Palestine; but, though he perhaps mentioned that wild scheme in a moment of rhodomontade, he had no intention of carrying it into effect. By his order, however, seventy-four deputies, representing the whole Jewish community in the French empire, met at Paris, in 1806, and gave satisfactory answers to various questions respecting their institutions and practices, and their ideas of the allegiance due to the government. In return they were assured by the emperor, that he would not only secure to them the free exercise of their religion, but the full enjoyment of the rights of French citizens. This meeting was followed by one of a more dignified character and a more religious nature,—even by the convocation of the grand Sanhedrim. The revival of an assembly which had so long been discontinued gladdened the hearts of the Jews. Those of Italy were requested to send deputies to it; and the Mosaic tribes of Germany readily concurred in the proposed reform. Their worship was re-organized at the meeting; their moral system was placed on a more sound basis; and their civil conduct was judiciously regulated.

In Germany, Lessing, the philosophic dramatist, was the first who publicly avowed himself a friend to the Jews; and, with a view to their rescue from degradation and contempt, he introduced upon the stage a worthy and respectable Jew, as Cumberland did at a later period in England. He also gave the hand of friendship to Mendelsohn (a youth of that despised race,) whose subsequent literary exertions tended to dispel the mists of prejudice, and promote the diffusion of just and liberal principles. Some distinguished statesmen espoused the same cause, and urged the rulers under whom they acted to extend equal protection to all classes of their subjects. Indeed, the loyal zeal of the Jews entitled them to the favourable opinion of the German princes; and, from some of these rulers, they received honourable testimonies of approbation, and, from the Prussian monarch, all the rights of citizens. These marks of regard gave them a degree of confidence which the zealous Christians construed into arrogance; and hence arose in some of the cities, loud clamours against them. The senate of Lubeck resolved to treat them as strangers or aliens, and prohibited them from carrying on any branch of trade within the limits of the city; and, in several other free towns, the obnoxious Israelites were assailed by the tumultuous fury of the populace. But the envoys of the chief German powers, assembled at Carlsbad, were so far from being disposed to countenance these unjustifiable proceedings, that they menaced the constituted authorities of those cities with signal marks of displeasure, if the Jews should not meet with that protection which they had a right to claim. This interposition was at once honourable to the great powers and effective in its result.

In Holland, long before the present age, the Jews enjoyed full toleration and complete protection. They increase rather than decline in number, and now compose a thirtieth part of the population. At Amsterdam they have many synagogues; but the most respectable congregation is that which, near the close of the last century, was formed by the secession of some German Jews from the old community.

In Poland, the Jews are highly favoured; and it has been remarked (by many visitants of that kingdom) that they have a greater appearance of consequence and dignity, than the Israelites who reside in any other country. They carry on the chief trade, and, except the nobles, they form the most opulent portion of the community.

In Great Britain, the Jews cannot expect to be encouraged, because it has been repeatedly declared, from the judicial bench, that Christianity is a part of the established and constitutional law of the realm; yet, with the exception of power and office, they have every reason to be satisfied with their lot. They have opportunities of acquiring opulence, and they well know that riches not only impart comfort, but promote influence. Even under the sway of Roman catholic princes and the tyranny of Moslem barbarians, they are not prevented from indulging in their favourite practice of pecuniary accumulation; and, if they are sometimes harassed and fleeced, they are not totally ruined.

CHAPTER IV.

History of the Church of England and its Dependencies, of the various Sects in the British Dominions, and of the Ecclesiastical Communities in the United States of America.

Our divines affect to consider the church of England as the best of all Christian establishments, because they belong to it; and many persons who have no interest in it, and who are therefore less prejudiced observers, entertain the same opinion. Yet there are some who venture to made one objection to the establishment, by alleging that the princely incomes of many of our prelates excite, in the public mind, suspicions of ambition and of selfishness, and that theological aspirants seek high preferments from motives of interest, much more than from views of piety. The primitive bishops, say these objectors, were content with the means of comfortable subsistence and of respectable appearance; luxury, parade, and ostentation, had no charms for them; they were meek and humble-minded, and aimed only at the propagation of religious sentiments in that mode which was most likely to render them efficacious. But many ages, they continue to observe, did not elapse before the prelates were corrupted by the flattery and submission of superstitious votaries, and by the increasing prosperity of the church; and they were then disposed to assume the lordly demeanour and high tone of the noble and the opulent. Even he who styled himself the "servant of the servants of God," gladly accept the grant of temporal sovereignty and of princely power, and, in his new capacity, acted more as the domineering potentate than as the father or friend of his people. Such conduct, in the opinion of these censors, did not tend to promote the prevalence of a proper sense of religion, which would have been more generally diffused, if the leading members of the clerical body had not raised themselves so highly above the ordinary state of society.

Without presuming to settle this dispute, which Mr. Burke triumphantly (as he thought) decided in favour of the prevailing system, we take this opportunity of remarking, that our church is apparently more pure, in point of doctrine, than any other Christian establishment, and that its discipline is liable to few or no objections. We also readily allow that the episcopal bench exhibits talent, erudition, and virtue, and that the inferior clergy are, in general, respectable; but, if their piety should be accompanied with greater zeal and earnestness, their exhortations and example would be more influential and edifying.

The state of our church, at the close of the last century, was as tranquil as it was flourishing. It was not agitated by such dissensions as had prevailed at the time when the convocation acted in some measure like a parliament; and it exhibited a dignified front and an air of boldness, which overawed the discontented part of the nation. The majesty of the fabric was supposed to contribute to the preservation of its strength; and, while the bishops, deans, and archdeacons, kept the inferior ranks of the clerical order in a state of due submission and ready obedience, the church militant bore the aspect of a formidable phalanx. It might reasonably have been concluded, that the conscientious spirit which induced the protestants to claim for themselves the full freedom of religious opinion, would have disposed them to tolerate every sect which demanded the same right; but it unfortunately happens, that both churchmen and politicians, when *out of* power, make pompous promises and plausible protestations, which they are not willing to remember when they are *in* power. Thus the champions of the church of England, when they had obtained a separate establishment by differing from *the pope*, would not quietly suffer any sectaries to differ from *them.* Even archbishop Cranmer, who was considered as very mild and humane, became a cruel persecutor, when poor and humble Christians ventured to differ from him; and queen Elizabeth, when she had subverted the Romish system in this country, put many persons to death for only asserting the same privileges which she claimed for herself and her supporters. The puritans also (when, under the appellation of Presbyterians, they gained the ascendency about the middle of the seventeenth century,) persecuted the adherents of the church of England with bitter animosity; and toleration did not properly exist in this country before the reign of king William III., who, while he studiously discountenanced the violent spirit and malignity of the *catholics*, admitted the *protestants* of every denomination to the free exercise of their religion. The catholics were not then entitled to such indulgence, because time had not then shown the increase of their humanity, or the melioration of their social feelings; and even now, when there is no reason to suppose that they would break out into the brutal fury of religious murder, even if they had the opportunity of authoritative exertion, we still say that they ought not to be trusted with *power*. They still cherish the zeal of conversion; they still brand us with the stigma of heresy; they still think that no one can be saved out of the pale of their church. They may say that we have no right to censure them for entertaining such an opinion; yet we have a right to exclude them from that establishment which they would wish to overturn, and from those emoluments in which, if they should eve gain their grand object, they would not allow us to participate. They, and also their puritanical opponents refused to tolerate when they ought to have been so inclined, and would still, we apprehend, be equalled bigoted; but the members of the church of England have derived lenity from the softening progress of time, and now make every concession that their adversaries can reasonably demand. They allow full protection and constitutional security, while they withhold the grant of that power which may be abused and misapplied.

This is the point which is still disputed between the advocates of the establishment on one hand, and the catholics and protestant dissenters on the other. The only ground of refusal, on the part of the former, is the danger that may be apprehended from that hostility which their opponents cannot fully disguise. Notwithstanding this ground of alarm, the leaders of the cabinet, in the year 1807, were advocates for the claims of the catholics. At a time when the rancorous hostility of a powerful enemy threatened the kingdom with serious danger, it became highly expedient to concentrate all the energy of the nation, and call forth the animated exertions of every class and of every sect. It was therefore proposed by the ministry, that the permission which had been granted to the Irish catholics to hold any rank in the army except the highest stations, should be extended to their brethren in Great Britain, and that persons of all religious persuasions should likewise be allowed to serve in the navy. When the scheme was communicated to the king, he reluctantly gave his assent to the introduction of a bill on the subject. Its provisions, on more deliberate consideration, were in some degree extended; and his majesty then not only made strong objections to it, but insisted on a written assurance from the ministers, that they would never again bring it forward. They properly refused to agree to a demand which they deemed (and which unquestionably was) irregular and unconstitutional, and retired from the public service. The dread of danger from too great concessions to a sect avowedly hostile to the protestant ascendency, spread from the throne among the people, and the cry of 'no popery' again prevailed, not merely because it was artfully raised by the partisans of the new ministry, but from the general unwillingness of the nation to favour an intolerant sect.

As it was supposed that the prince regent was not hostile to the claims of the catholics, their advocates brought forward the question in 1813, at a time when the zeal of the British nation against them seemed to be dormant. Mr. Grattan denied that they contended for power; they only desired (he said) the same civil rights and official qualifications which other citizens enjoyed. He adduced the instances of France and Hungary to prove, that even the bigotry of catholic governments allowed them to give more than mere toleration to the protestants; and this was an example which our parliament ought readily to follow with regard to the present claimants. In the bill which he introduced, it was proposed that they should be eligible to a seat in parliament, and might be appointed to any civil office whatever, except two or three of the highest employments, on taking a new oath against the pope's temporal power and pretended infallibility, and disavowing any intention of subverting or disturbing the protestant establishment, either in the church or the state. When the question was put on the parliamentary clause, it was rejected by a majority of four votes; and the bill, having thus lost its leading feature, was indignantly relinquished by those who had exerted their whole strength in its support. Even the catholics were not united in its favour; for the prelates of their sect, in Ireland, alleged that it would encroach on the due exercise of their functions, and on the spiritual jurisdiction of their supreme pastor, although this result was not contemplated by the framers of the bill.

For many years the inferior catholics seemed to treat with indifference the question of their *emancipation* (as the claim was styled by their leaders;) but they at length loudly called, more particularly those of Ireland, for the restoration of their rights, and it was resolved that every effort should be made to interest the parliament in their behalf. Sir Francis Burdett, in the year 1825, readily undertook the enforcement of what he conceived to be their just pretensions, and introduced a bill which obtained the support of the house of commons; but the peers, impressed with a sense of constitutional policy, rejected the bill by a majority of 48 votes. The disappointment did not discourage the bold sectaries. Although an association which they had formed for the more effectual prosecution of their grand object was suppressed by a specific statute, they declared that no obstacles which might be thrown in their way by the illiberality and malice of their adversaries should deter them from a renewal of their demands.

Among the protestant sects in Great Britain, the Presbyterians are considered as the most numerous class; the Independents are said to be the next in point of number; and the Baptists, or Anabaptists, are supposed to take the third place. The Methodists are rapidly increasing; and, indeed, their ministers in general are more earnest and zealous than the preachers among the other sects, and thus make a more powerful and permanent impression.

Amidst the multiplication of the votaries of *religion*, the followers of the *spirit* (we mean the Quakers) do not augment their number; we may rather say, that, for many years past, this has been a declining sect. Their more extensive concerns in trade, and the consequent increase of their connexions with worldly-minded men, and with the mass of the community, may have partly contributed to this effect; and, amidst the fondness for pleasure that pervades the nation, many of them may have imbibed a spirit of dissipation, which the grave elders of the fraternity have been unwilling to countenance. A philosophic reader may be induced to add, that the more enligh tened reflection of modern times must have had the principal effect in accelerating the decline of Quakerism. Whatever may be the *causes* of it, the *fact* is admitted by the *Friends* themselves. They still form, however, a respectable sect; and a summary view of the principles which they at the present time profess, may perhaps gratify the curious observer of sectarian varieties. They are of opinion, that God has imparted to all human beings, though in different degrees, a portion of his own *spirit*, without which it would be impossible for them to discern spiritual things, or even to understand the Scriptures. It is, they say, a primary and infallible guide; and, as those who encourage it are in their progress to salvation or redemption, it becomes also a *redeemer*. They consider redemption in two points of view; either as it is promoted by outward or inward means, or as it relates to past or future sins. Jesus Christ, by offering himself as a victim, effected the former redemption; but it is the spirit, or Christ within, which tends to produce the latter, by leading to regeneration and to the perfection of piety and virtue. Christ, they add, was *man*, because he became *incarnate;* and he was *divinity*, because he was the *word*. A resurrection, they think, will take place, though not of the body as it is. In the regulations of future punishment, guilt will not be imputed to any one on the ground of original sin, or the delinquency of Adam and Eve, but only for the actual commission of sin. Baptism and the eucharist are not essentials of Christianity as outward ordinances, but only as they are administered by the spirit. By this internal guide, persons of both sexes are qualified for the ministerial functions; and, like the primitive Christians, they ought to preach the Gospel gratuitously. No difference of religious opinion can be a just ground of obloquy or persecution. Evil ought not to be returned for evil; and not only all private violence, but all wars and public hostilities, ought to be avoided. The loss of life is not a proper punishment for any crime; the reformation of a delinquent ought to be the great object of jurisprudence. The laws ought not in any case to be forcibly resisted; and, even if the conscience should be offended by submitting to them, the penalties are to be patiently borne. Moral education ought to be the object of particular attention; and it is the duty of every religious community, not only to assist its poor members in point of bodily comfort, but to provide for the instruction of their children. The dignity of man requires, that his word should be equivalent to an oath, and the Scriptures, in the most positive manner, confirm this sentiment. Trade is not in itself degrading; but honesty, and a punctual adherence to engagements, are requisite for its prosecution, and such branches as may be attended with the moral detriment of the trader himself or of others, ought to be carefully avoided by every Christian.

These principles unquestionably exhibit the Quakers in the light of a moral sect; and those who are well acquainted with them will not deny their general claim to that character. They may also be regarded as a friendly community, if not distinguished by politeness of behaviour or elegance of manners. Shrewdness and good sense are frequently observed among them, though we cannot affirm that many of them are eminent for learning or erudition.

The Quakers, when their sect had been fully formed, were scarcely ever divided by doctrinal disputes; but, early in the present century, they began to be agitated by a spirit of dissension; and the committee of management, selected at one of the annual meetings, seemed willing to assume a degree of authority which the synod never intended to allow. One of the friends, in a spirited pamphlet, animadverted upon this arrogant conduct, and particularly censured the proceedings against Hannah Bernard, an itinerant expounder of Quakerism, who, for denying the Trinity, expressing her disbelief in miracles, and differing from the committee in other points, had been prohibited from preaching. William Matthews also took up the pen against the new dictators, whom he accused of having arbitrarily excommunicated him for such doctrinal variations as he was prepared to justify. Dissensions of this kind are occasionally renewed, without leading, however, to a violent explosion.

Although the Unitarians had been excused from the obligation of subscribing the thirty-nine articles, they were not satisfied while the act of king William hung over their heads, menacing them with penal inflictions, if they should deny the Trinity either in conversation or in writing; but from this state of apprehension they were relieved in the year 1813. Another ground of dissatisfaction still remained; for their marriages, like those of the catholics, were not considered as legal, when the ceremonies were merely accordant to their own ritual. They therefore repeatedly applied to the parliament for a redress of this grievance. On their last application, in 1825, they were alarmed at the declaration of the lord chancellor, that, however they might think themselves protected by statute law, they are yet liable to prosecution and punishment, by the common law of the land, for denying that doctrine which is an essential part of Christianity. They loudly complained of this insinuation, and declared that they would take the earliest opportunity of obviating its effects. The learned judge says that they are not Christians, as they deny the divinity of our Redeemer; and yet he connives at the toleration enjoyed by the Jews, the avowed enemies of every establishment which bears the impress of Christianity. He has uniformly opposed their efforts to procure an act of parliament for the solemnization of their marriages according to their own forms, and, in this pertinacity, he is supported by the majority of the peers, in defiance of the arguments and influence of his more liberal friend, the prime minister. There is no good reason for withholding so slight a favour, or (as the Unitarians would say) so just a claim.

A new association has been formed upon the same basis. The framers of this society were at first Universalists, and so far orthodox as to be Trinitarians; but a doubt arose in the mind of one of the members, whether the holy Trinity really existed, and, in the progress of deliberation, he convinced himself that the idea of the divine Unity was a more rational doctrine. By the plausibility of his arguments he drew others into his opinion; and, when the pastor of the flock pronounced it to be heretical, a secession was the natural result. The seceders publicly declared the motives and reasons of their conduct, and, as if they were at a loss for an ecclesiastical constitution, and had never before thought of such a subject, attentively studied the New Testament, with a view of ascertaining the nature and the laws of the primitive Christian church. The result of this inquiry was a conviction that the unity of the church was one of its principal characteristics; that the equality of its members distinguished the kingdom of Jesus from all political realms, and formed the true ground and security of Christian liberty; that this general equality ought not to prevent the appointment of elders and of deacons, who might preserve order in the establishment, and superintend its concerns; that not only these, but all the members of their society, had a right to teach and exhort, so as to preclude the necessity of appointing regular preachers; and that it was a sufficient ground of communion with their sect, to acknowledge the authority of Christ as a divine teacher, without regard to the various doctrines which have been engrafted upon that simple basis. They style themselves Free-thinking Christians, and appear to have made some progress in impressing others with their sentiments.

While these sectaries were extending their influence, a scheme of union was framed by the advocates of the same general principles. It was proposed, in the year 1825, that three partial societies should be united under the title of the British and Foreign Unitarian Association, which would be authorized to embrace every object and circumstance connected with the propagation of Unitarianism. The proposal was readily adopted; and, as many protestant dissenters had lately joined in the petitions presented to the parliament against the relief of the catholics, the assembly took this opportunity of expressing a 'thorough disavowal and disapprobation' of such conduct, and a determination to support every effort which might be made to 'break the chains imposed by interested or short-sighted policy upon the sacred rights of conscience.'

Some years before this concentration of Unitarian strength, a secession from the established church occurred, not perhaps very important, but at least entitled to our notice. Several ministers, who had been in the habit of conferring on religious topics, began to question the propriety of continuing in a state of external adherence to the church, when they entertained what they deemed reasonable objections to various parts of the ritual and the liturgy, and also disapproved the enforced dependence of the church (according to the present constitution) upon the temporal power. The baptismal service, they said, prescribed a ritual observance in lieu of a divine and spiritual operation: in the service appropriated to the dead, every one was styled a Christian, whereas many who were thus honoured were merely so in external profession; and the Athanasian creed was repugnant to that scriptural declaration which promised salvation to all who believed in Christ. They at length resolved to renounce the general assent which they had given at their ordination to the thirty-nine articles, the homilies, and the prayer book, while they readily acquiesced in particular clauses of those branches of our religious system; and, being conscientious men, they resigned their ecclesiastical preferments, which they considered as the wages of error, if not of iniquity. They then began to exercise their new ministry in the vicinity of Taunton; but, being considered as Antinomians, they were not so far respected as to be enabled to make great progress in the work of proselytism. They agreed with the Methodists in their opinion of *faith*, which alone, they thought, could produce a sinner's justification; and, when it was argued against them that they did not sufficiently inculcate the axiom of religious obedience, they alleged that their enforcement of the principle or the theory would lead to the requisite practice. They believed (as far as we can judge from the opinions of some individuals of their number) that Christ existed with God before the creation of the present world, and that he is the proper object of religious worship, the prophet, priest, and king of the church; and they leaned to the doctrine of election, without making it so prominent a part of their system as the rigid Calvinists do. With regard to the Trinity, they held a middle course between the orthodox clergy and the Unitarians. Some variations have occurred in their opinions since their original secession; but these are of little moment, and are such as might reasonably be expected from sectaries who have not framed a deliberate creed.

The reveries of Joanna Southcott we mentioned on a former occasion. She continued her delusions long after the commencement of this century, and not only retained her influence over her original followers, but drew many more into her train. A seal, bearing the initials of her name, which she pretended to have accidentally found when she was at work in her master's house, furnished her with a pretence for declaring that she was authorized by Providence to propagate a new revelation; and, in the midst of her spiritual avocations, she derived temporal advantage from the sale of sealed passports for the admission of the faithful into the celestial regions. Near the close of her life, in the year 1814, she impudently announced herself as the future mother (though a virgin) of the Shiloh promised in holy writ. Her followers now became still more numerous, and by their senseless liberality, presents were lavished upon the supposed object of divine favour, that the approaching birth might be celebrated with due splendour. The lady, however, died without enjoying the honour of being a mother. Many of her friends would not believe that she was actually dead, and fondly expected the speedy resuscitation of the spark of life: but, after an anxious suspense of four days, they resigned their hopes, and suffered her to be consigned, like an ordinary mortal, to the grave. Her chaplain then declared, that she had renounced, on her death-bed, the visions of her disordered brain; yet there are still, it is said, many who are not ashamed to own that they yet follow her opinions. It might have been supposed that her recantation would have put an end to the delusion: but, even in enlightened times, the most senseless fanaticism will occasionally take possession of weak heads and narrow minds.

Compared with the wild fanaticism of Joanna, the sentiments of Dr. Alexander Tilloch may even seem reasonable. He was a philosophical and scientific man, who differed in some respects from the established church. He and his friends assumed the denomination of Christian Dissenters, declaring, at the same time, that they were slaves to no sect, though it was supposed that they entertained opinions similar to those of the Sandemanians. They professed a determination of directing their conduct by the rules and injunctions of the Scriptures, and went so far in the formation of a sect as to appoint two elders for the administration of their spiritual concerns. The death of the philosopher, in the year 1825, probably dissolved the association; for we do not hear of its continuance.

An attempt to form a religious party at Coventry may here be mentioned, though its features are not so marked as to entitle it to the distinction of a new sect. The members call themselves Samaritans, and we hope that their philanthropy gives them a just claim to the honourable appellation. They resemble the Quakers in the plainness of their apparel, in their allowance of female preachers, and their abstinence from oaths; but they seem to lean more to the doctrines of the Methodists than to those of any other sect.

A zealot named Muloch lately endeavoured to create a sect, by exclaiming against the corruptions of Christianity, and proposing such a reform as would, in his opinion, render that religion much more efficacious and salutary than it now is. By drawing the people about him at Oxford, and exhorting them to adopt his opinions and advice, he exposed himself to an attack from the supporters of orthodoxy: but the riot had no serious consequences. In his conduct toward the members of his society, he has shown himself to be more influenced by the arbitrary and intemperate spirit of Knox than the conciliatory mildness of Melancthon.

Having thus treated of the established church, and also noticed the deliberate secessions from its rules and ordinances, we advert to missionary concerns, in which both the orthodox and the heterodox are disposed to concur. Missions had been occasionally undertaken before the current century; but it is only in our times that the attempts of British subjects with that view have assumed a regular and systematic form. The English, for ages, were very slow in the promotion of missionary labours. They thought more of their immediate concerns than of foreign undertakings, and were content with the secure enjoyment of their religion at home, without troubling themselves about the faith or the piety of the rest of the world. Desultory attempts, indeed, were occasionally made for the conversion of the slaves in our colonies, and also of the neighbouring savages; and, after the establishment of the Society for the propagation of the Gospel in Foreign Parts, either zealous and adventurous clergymen, or pious and well educated laymen, were regularly employed in that salutary work; yet their operations were conducted on a small scale, and the government did not add its energetic weight to the scheme, but merely suffered it to take its course under that nominal encouragement which it derived from a royal charter. A new ebullition of zeal, however, in this cause, appeared before the close of the last century, and it has so far increased in vigour, as to form one of the marked features of the age in which we live. The first *stimulus* in our time appears to have been given by a mechanic of the name of Carey, and John Thomas, an equally zealous Christian. The former, being strongly inclined to preach the Gospel, had solicited and obtained the honour of ordination among the Baptists; and, at a meeting of his brethren, he proposed a question relative to the practicability of an effective diffusion of evangelical truth among the pagan communities. As the other ministers concurred with him in the affirmative opinion, he went with his family to India, accompanied by his friend, who had already preached to the Hindoos in Bengal. They were afterwards joined by some other missionaries, but were checked in their pious operations by the British government, and therefore gladly took refuge in the Danish town of Serampore, where they opened a school, and converted some of the natives to Christianity. The marquis Wellesley at length allowed them to travel in those provinces which he governed; but this permission, far from being fully granted, was arbitrarily restricted. The missionaries, however, prosecuted their course without murmuring, and in some measure diminished the number of Pagans.

While Mr. Carey and his associates were thus employed, a scheme of conversion was formed, in the year 1800, on a grand and comprehensive plan, by the ministers and friends of the established church, and the institution was denominated the 'Church Missionary Society to Africa and the East,' with a proviso that the ostensible limitation of the efforts of its members and missionaries should not 'bind them to an exclusion of their attempts from any other unoccupied place, which might present a prospect of success to their labours.' The leaders of the society at first resolved that none but those who had received episcopal ordination should act on these occasions; but, when it was found difficult to procure a sufficient number of clerical missionaries, catechists were employed in the propagation of the Christian doctrines and the enforcement of salutary precepts. For the promotion of these objects, pecuniary contributions were earnestly solicited in all parts of the kingdom and of its dependencies; and even the smallest donations were thankfully accepted. During many years the produce was very inconsiderable, the zeal of the nation not being sufficiently awakened· yet the fund of the society continued to increase, and its income has enabled it to establish nine grand missions: these are extended over forty-two stations, comprehending 255 schools, in which about 1,350 adults and 11,500 children are instructed in religion and the elements of literature.* For the use of these pupils and other inhabitants of the country about these stations, the Scriptures have been printed in a great variety of languages, and useful tracts, composed in a familiar style, have been circulated. As a specimen of the effect of these pious labours, the growing civilization of the colony of Sierra Leone may be mentioned with pleasure. Two-thirds of its population consist of negroes, (rescued from the hands of base and infamous dealers in slaves,) the majority of whom, by the care and example of Christian instructors, have been so far civilized as to become quiet and friendly neighbours, industrious artisans and agriculturists, and devout frequenters of places of worship.

Other instances of missionary success may be drawn from many of the inhabited spots in

* To this institution, and other schemes calculated for religious purposes, the subjects of the British empire are now more liberal than they ever were before our time. For instance, in the year 1822, they contributed a sum nearly amounting to 352,000*l.*—a subscription far exceeding the revenues of some German principalities. The British and Foreign Bible Society received much more than a fourth part of this sum; the next receipts, in point of magnitude, accrued to the Society for promoting Christian Knowledge; the next, to the Church Missionary Institution; the London and Wesleyan Missionary Societies obtained the next proportion; the Society for the Propagation of the Gospel in Foreign Parts had a smaller, yet a considerable share; then came the Baptist Missionary Institution, and the Society for the Conversion of the Jews. The five societies which received the smallest sums were the following;—one which was established for the promotion of religious knowledge among the poor, one for the distribution of the Scriptures among seamen in the mercantile service, one for the diffusion of orthodox tracts, and Sunday School Society, and the Irish Society of London. This enumeration, though partial (for the list then published included thirty-one associations,) serves to evince the proportional interest taken by the public in these pious undertakings. Many might think that the Gospel Society deserved the most marked encouragement from the contributors; but we have no right to blame, in this instance, the exercise of private discretion. These associations undoubtedly reflect great credit on the country to which we belong; and we trust that the zeal by which they are fostered will not suffer any abatement.

the Pacific Ocean. In the Society Islands, in particular, a great change has taken place. The manners and deportment of the natives are comparatively civilized; their morals are much less depraved, and (says a reverend gentleman) a "system of idolatry has been annihilated, which was reared by treachery and crime, and had for ages, through the terrors which it inspired, kept the population in a state of abject wretchedness." The Scriptures have been translated into that language which, with little variation of dialect, is diffused over many clusters of islands in the wide extent of the Pacific; and, in various places, public meetings are annually holden by the chieftains, to deliberate on the most effectual means of propagating that religion which they consider as a great blessing, communicated to them by the servants of God and the friends of mankind.

As the success of these labours, however, appeared to be partial and limited, it was found expedient to quicken, at intervals, the zeal of the public. It was therefore stated, in a late address from the Society for the Propagation of Christian Knowledge, that the great increase of population in those territories to which its operations had been more particularly directed, rendered a considerable augmentation of the number of missionaries and school-masters necessary for the useful prosecution of its career, although these now exceeded 200 in the American colonies alone; that, 'with a view to the formation of a body of native clergy for the service of the colonies, the society had contributed largely to the support of the King's College (at Windsor in Nova Scotia,) by an annual grant and by the endowment of divinity scholarships and exhibitions;' that the directors of its funds had also made frequent grants toward the erection of churches in the infant settlements, and had been greatly instrumental in diffusing the national system of education over every part of the Trans-Atlantic colonies; and that another source of expenditure had been opened by the extended colonization of the southern parts of Africa and the interior of New Holland. Thus religious instruction and elementary learning were happily combined.

The systematic addition of the duty of the school-master to that of the missionary, arose from the zeal of the Rev. Dr. Bell, who, wishing to render ordinary scholarship more general, introduced a system of elementary education more comprehensive with regard to the number of pupils, and more rapid in its progress, than the ordinary mode of instruction. The supporters of the scheme boasted that 500 boys and girls might be taught to read and write, and to perform the common rules of arithmetic, sooner than fifty in the usual way. The plan chiefly consisted in simultaneous dictation to a large assemblage, and in the employment of a number of instructors gradually selected from the aggregate number of the pupils.

The scheme has an air of quackery; but it has been practised with such success, in the national schools of Great Britain, and in various parts of the continent, that there are more readers and writers than at any former period. It is now a prevailing wish that all the inhabitants of this, and every other country, should receive instruction in reading and writing: but the proposal has been condemned by some prejudiced men of the higher class of society, who pretend that the plebeian learners would thus sooner imbibe ideas of reform and false doctrines of every kind, or, from the pride of learning, would contract ideas too high for the stations which they might eventually fill. In reply to these objections we may remark, that principles of pretended reform may be taught to individuals who cannot read, and whose illiteracy will render them less able to detect the fallacies of the artful teacher; and, in the next place, that the instruction derivable by the poor from this plan, though useful, will not be of so elevated a kind as to inspire them with overweening pride or vanity, or give them a disgust to the meanness of ordinary occupations.

The labours of the missionaries in the West Indies were exposed to a serious check by the commotions which arose at Barbadoes in the year 1823. Apprehending that the parliament might be induced to put an end to slavery, and knowing that measures had been taken to repress the shameful tyranny of the planters, the leading men in that island exclaimed against the 'villanous African Society,' calumniated the characters of Mr. Wilberforce and his friends, and denounced vengeance against the Methodist missionaries, whom they accused of instigating the negroes and mulattoes to disaffection and sedition. The charge was ill-founded; yet many persons of reputed respectability encouraged the white rabble of Bridge-town to insult and harass the Methodists and their friends, and demolish their meeting houses. The chief preacher fled in consternation to the island of St. Vincent; those who remained at Barbadoes were not allowed to act as ministers, and no other missionaries were suffered to land. The parliament expressed its indignation at these outrages; but we do not find that any steps were taken for the punishment of the perpetrators. This forbearance excited strong animadversion when contrasted with the cruel treatment of the slaves in Demarara, many of whom, for an unwillingness to work, and for some riotous acts, were sacrificed, under the forms of justice, to the vindictive rage of the planters.

The late appointment of several bishops for the West Indies will, it is hoped, produce, by the influence of their examples and persuasions, a better spirit among the white population, and promote the conversion and enlightenment of the people of colour and the negroes. But it is necessary, for the due accomplishment of these desirable purposes, that the new prelates should be more active and zealous than those of Europe.

In the United States of North America, the episcopal appointments are still kept up, and the other religious communities and congregations are in that regular progress which proves that the nation is not ungodly, although the laws and government do not ordain or recognize, as in the European states, the superiority of a particular creed or mode of worship Hence there is no occasion for the grant or *toleration*, as that term implies an allowance, by the ruling power, of such doctrines, ceremonies, and practices, as are not exactly consonant with the established system. As no community predominates over another, all are equal in the eye of the law; the Episcopalians and Presbyterians, the Jews and Roman Catholics, the Moravians and Quakers, are perfectly on a level.

Among the more recent religious communities beyond the Atlantic, the Shakers seem to have excited the greatest degree of attention. Having mentioned their origin and their doctrines on a former occasion, we now state some particulars respecting their manners and conduct. Even while they disallow marriage, and do not permit a man to touch a woman on any occasion or pretence, they are assembled in families. The males and females occupy different apartments in the same house, and have separate tables, but meet occasionally for society and labour, as well as for religious service. They exercise all the useful arts and manufactures among themselves, without being indebted to persons of other persuasions for the least assistance. As far as they conveniently can, they have every thing in common; and, when new members are admitted, they are required to assign their property to the directors of the society for the general benefit. They profess to follow the advice of the apostle, "Let all things be done decently and in order." In one respect they appear to be disorderly; for, in the midst of their public worship, they sing and dance like maniacs: yet they have "method in their madness." Upon the whole, they form a quiet, inoffensive, and apparently virtuous community.

Another sect (if indeed a religious party in a country which has no established national creed can properly be called a *sect*) has arisen in North America; but it is little known, and not very prevalent. Mr. Rees, a Welsh clergyman, transported himself to America with the benevolent view of propagating Christianity in that form which he considered as the most pure and genuine, or rather in that way which would leave every one at liberty to follow his own opinion in points which were not essential, while he acknowledged Christ as his only head. He proposed that the society which should be instituted should be styled the Christian Church, and that no other guide than the New Testament should be allowed to its members; and a secondary part of his scheme was the propagation of the Gospel among the heathen communities. While he laboured to make religious converts, he endeavoured, with equal zeal, to put an end to the existence of slavery in the United States; but he did not, either in this or in his other pursuit, meet with that success which his good intentions deserved.

Thus we have taken a cursory survey of the state of Christianity, both in the eastern and western hemispheres, and its progress during the first quarter of the present century. Some progress it has unquestionably made, although its increase has not been so great as its zealous friends wished or expected. Its movements, depending on human agency, are necessarily slow; and, if no miracles should intervene, many ages may elapse, before the majority of the pagan nations, of the Jewish tribes, and of the followers of the Arabian pseudo-prophet, shall be numbered among the votaries of that system which we conscientiously follow and earnestly recommend. In the mean time, let Christians preserve their faith unimpaired, and exhibit, to unbelievers, impressive examples of piety and virtue.

CHRONOLOGICAL TABLES.

ADVERTISEMENT,

BY DR. MACLAINE.

THE following Tables have been compiled with much attention and pains from the best authors; and it is therefore hoped that they will be considered as an useful addition to Dr. Mosheim's work; and the more so, as they are not confined to the *persons* and *things* contained in it.

The dates, that are placed in the tables which contain the sovereign princes and popes are designed to mark the year of their decease.

As several of the *Ecclesiastical* and *Theological Writers*, mentioned in these Tables, deserve a place also among *profane authors*, on account of their philosophical, literary, or historical productions; so their names will be repeated in the two distinct heads that contain the learned men of each century.

It is farther to be observed, that the Romish church, even long before the time of the Reformation, looked upon many persons as *heretics*, whom we, on our principles, cannot consider in the same light, and whose doctrines really tended to promote that reformation in which we glory. I have therefore, in many places, added the words *real* or *reputed* after *heretics*, rather than seem to submit, in this point, to the decisions of a superstitious church.

CENTURY I.

SOVEREIGN PRINCES.

Roman Emperors:—A. D.—Augustus, 14. Tiberius, 37. Caligula, 41. Claudius, 54. Nero, 68. Galba, 69 Otho, 69. Vitellius, 70. Vespasian, 79. Titus, 81. Domitian, 96. Nerva, 98.

POPES, OR BISHOPS OF ROME.

The succession of the first bishops of Rome is a matter full of intricacy and obscurity.—We shall herein follow the learned bishop Pearson. Linus. Anacletus. Clement. Evaristus. Alexander. The dates of the deaths of the Roman pontiffs are not the same in the accounts of chronologists. Petau, Fleury, Pearson, Marcel, Pfaff, Bower, Lenglet, and others, differ frequently in this respect; and their differences sometimes are considerable. For example, the death of pope Anicetus is placed, by Petau and Lenglet, in the year 161, by Pearson and Pfaff in 162, by Fleury, Walch, and Bower, in 168. As it is impossible to reconcile these historians, and difficult often to decide which calculates best, we shall follow Pearson and Pfaff as the surest guides.

ECCLESIASTICAL AND THEOLOGICAL WRITERS.

The Evangelists and Apostles. The three Apostolic Fathers, Clement, Barnabas, Hermas. Philo, the Jew. Flavius Josephus. These are almost all the genuine ecclesiastical writers of the first century, whose works are now extant; for the supposed letter of Christ to Abgarus, the Gospels, Acts, Epistles, and Liturgies, that have (beside those which we esteem canonical) been attributed to the Apostles—as also the Epistles of Mary to Ignatius and others—the Acts of Pilate—the Epistles of Seneca to St. Paul, &c., must be considered as apocryphal and spurious. The works that bear the name of Dionysius the Areopagite, were forged in the fifth century.

HERETICS.

Dositheus. Simon Magus. The Gnostics, Cerinthus, Hymenæus, Philetus, who together with Demas and Diotrephes, are rather to be considered as apostates than as heretics. The Nicolaitans. Ebion. The Nazarenes. N. B. The Ebionites and Nazarenes, though generally placed by the learned in the first century, yet belong more properly to the second.

REMARKABLE EVENTS.

The tax of Augustus Cæsar. The birth of Christ. The offerings presented to Jesus Christ by the Wise Men from the East. The Four Passovers celebrated by Christ. John the Baptist beheaded. Christ's miracles, sufferings, death, resurrection, and ascension. The descent of the Holy Ghost. St. Stephen, the first Martyr. The conversion of St. Paul. Institution of *Agapæ*, or Feasts of Charity. Baptism is administered by immersion. Several Christian Churches founded. The first persecution under Nero. The oracles reduced to silence, a dubious, or rather a fabulous story. The destruction of Jerusalem. The accounts of a dispute between St. Peter and Simon the magician at Rome, and of the erection of a statue to the latter in that city, seem idle fictions. The second persecution of the Christians under Domitian. St. John thrown into a caldron of boiling oil, a doubtful story. The adventures of Apollonius Tyaneus.

PROFANE AUTHORS.

Titus Livius. Germanicus. Gratius. Ovid. Hyginus. Labeo. Valerius Maximus. Phædrus. Vertius Flaccus. Strabo. Dionysius of Alexandria. Seneca, the rhetorician. Seneca, the philosopher and poet. Velleius Paterculus. Cremutius. Isidore of Charax. Celsus, the physician. Massurius Sabinus. Didymus of Alexandria. Cocceius Nerva. Philo the Jew. Pomponius Mela. Columella. Remmius Palæmon. Votienus. Servilius Marcus. Annæus Cornutus. Lucan. Andromachus. Petronius. Persius. Epictetus. Dioscorides. Flavius Josephus. Silius Italicus. Valerius Flaccus. Pliny the Elder. Pliny the Younger. Asconius Pedianus. Plinius Valerianus. Juvenal. Martial. Statius. Frontinus. Quintilian. Dion Chrysostom. Tacitus. Phlegon. Apion. Trogus Pompeius. Athenodorus.

CENTURY II.

SOVEREIGN PRINCES.

Roman Emperors:—A. D.—Trajan, 117. Adrian, 138. Anton. Pius, 161. M. Antoninus, 180. L. Verus Commodus, 192. Pertinax, 193. Did. Julianus, 193. Niger, 194. Albinus 197.

POPES, OR BISHOPS OF ROME.

Xystus or Sixtus, 127. Telesphorus, 138. Hyginus, 150. Pius I., 153. Anicetus, 162. Soter, 1?2. Eleutherius, 185. Victor, 196.

ECCLESIASTICAL AND THEOLOGICAL WRITERS.

Ignatius of Antioch. Polycarp. Justin Martyr. Hegesippus. Theophilus of Antioch, the first who made use of the word Trinity to express the distinction of what divines call persons in the Godhead. The Christian church is very little obliged to him for his invention. The use of this and other unscriptural terms, to which men attach either no ideas, or false ones, has wounded charity and peace, without promoting truth and knowledge. It has produced heresies of the worst kind.—Melito. Tatian.* Papias. Claudius Apollinaris. Hermias. Athenagoras. Clemens Alexandrinus. Tertullian. Aquila. Theodotion. Symmachus. The unknown author of the Sibylline oracles. Irenæus. Polycrates. Dionysius of Corinth. Pantænus. Quadratus. Add to these several fragments of the writings of some of the principal heretics mentioned in the following table. These fragments are collected by Cotelerius Grabe, &c.

HERETICS.

Nazarenes. Gnostics. Cainites. Elxai. Saturninus. The Millenarians. Basilides. Isidore, the Son. Carpocrates and his followers. Marcellina and Epiphanes. Prodicus, the chief of the Adamites. Valentine and his followers. *Tatian supposed to be the chief of the Encratites, Hydroparastates, and Apotactics. Ptolomæus Secundus. Cerdo. Marcion. Florinus. The Docetæ, or Phantasiasts. The Melitonians. The Saccophori. Severians. Ophites. Artotyrites. Theodotus, the Tanner, chief of the Alogi. Montanus. Tertullian. Priscilla and Maximilla, who were called Montanists, Cataphryges and Pepuzians. The Sethites and Abelites. Heracleon. Bassus. Colarbasus. Blastus. Mark. The Valentinians. Bardesanes. Hermogenes. Apelles. Praxeas, the chief of the Patropassians, Seleucus and Hermias. Artemon.

REMARKABLE EVENTS, AND RELIGIOUS RITES AND INSTITUTIONS.

Third persecution under Trajan, mitigated by the intercession of Pliny, the Younger. Fourth persecution under Adrian. Fifth Persecution under Antoninus Pius, continued under Marcus Aurelius and Lucius Verus. Conversion of the Germans and Gauls, and (if we may give credit to Bede) of the Britons. The Thundering Legion—a dubious event. Insurrections of the Jews against the Romans. Sedition and slaughter of that people under the standards of Barcocheba, the false Messiah. The Jews are driven from Jerusalem. Horrible calumnies thrown out against the Christians by Lucian, Crescens, Celsus, and the Pagans in general. The perusal of the Sibylline Oracles prohibited by an imperial edict. Christian assemblies are held on Sundays, and other stated days, in private houses, and in the burying-places of Martyrs. Infant baptism and sponsors used in this century. Various festivals and fasts established. A distinction formed between bishops and presbyters, who, with the deacons and readers, are the only orders of ecclesiastics known in this century. The sign of the cross and anointing used. The custom of praying towards the East introduced.

PROFANE AUTHORS.

Arrian. Aulus Gellius. Plutarch. Florus. Celsus, the lawyer. Œnomaus Philo of Phœnicia. Ptolemy the astronomer and geographer. Salvius Julianus. Seutonius. Apollonius, the philosopher. Appian.

Fronto. Maximus Tyrius. Taurus Calvisius. Apuleius. Artemidorus. Lucian. Numenes. Pausanias. Polyænus. Sextus Empiricus. Athenæus. Julius Pollux. Diogenes Laertius. Gallienus. Ammonius Saccas. Priscus. Cephalion. Aristides. Hermogenes, who at the age of seventeen published his Rhetoric; at twenty, his Book on Ideas; and, at twenty-five, is said to have forgotten all that he had learned. Justin Martyr. Theophylus of Antioch. Chrysorus. Marcus Antoninus. Harpocration. Athenagoras. Celsus, the philosopher. Julinus Solinus. Plotinus. Papinian.

CENTURY III.

SOVEREIGN PRINCES.

Roman Emperors:—A. D.—Serverus, 211. Caracalla, 217. Geta, 212. Macrinus. 218. Heliogabalus, 222. Severus Alexander, 235. Maximin, 237. Gordian I. II., 237. Pupienus and Balbinus, 238. Gordian III., 244 Philip the Arabian, supposed to have been the first Christian emperor, 250. Decius, 252. Gallus and Volusianus, 253. Æmilianus, 253. Valerian, 259. Gallienus, 268. Claudius II., 270. Quintilius, 270. Aurelian, 275. Tacitus, 275. Florianus, 276. Probus, 282. Carus, 283. Carinus, 284. Numerianus, 284. Diocletian. Maximian.

POPES, OR BISHOPS OF ROME.

Zephyrinus, 219. Callistus, 224. Urban, 231. Pontianus, 235. Anterus, 236. Fabianus, 251. Cornelius, 254. A contest between him and Novatian Lucius, 256. Stephen, 258. Sixtus II., 259. Dionysius, 270 Felix, 275. Eutychianus, 283. Caius Marcellinus, 296.

ECCLESIASTICAL AND THEOLOGICAL WRITERS.

The author of the Acts of Perpetua and Felicitas. Minutius Felix. Hippolytus. Ammonius. Julius Africanus. Origen. Cyprian. Novatian. Gregory Thaum. Dionysius of Alexandria. Pamphilus. Anatolius. Arnobius Africanus. Commodianus. Archelaus. Lucianus. Hesychius. Methodius. Theognostus. Malchion. Paul of Samosata. Stephen, R. Pont. Eusebius, a deacon of Alexandria. Dionysius, R. Pont. Basilides, Bishop of Pentapolis. Victorinus. Prudentius.

HERETICS.

Adelphius. Aquilinus. Manes, the chief of the Manicheans. Hierax. Noetus. Sabellius. Beryllus. Paul of Samosata. Novatians. Patropassians. Arabians. Cathari. Valesians. Privatus. A schism between Stephen and Cyprian, concerning the re baptizing of heretics.

REMARKABLE EVENTS, AND RELIGIOUS RITES AND INSTITUTIONS.

Sixth Persecution under Severus, in which Leonidas, Irenæus, Victor, bishop of Rome, Perpetua, Felicitas, and others, suffer martyrdom. Seventh Persecution (after one under Maximin) under Decius, in which Fabianus, the Roman pontiff, Babylas, Alexander, and others, suffer martyrdom. Eighth Persecution under Valerian, in which those more illustrious martyrs, Cyprian, Lucius, Stephen I. Sixtus I. and Laurentius, suffer for the faith. Ninth Persecution under Diocletian, Maximian, Galerius, and Maximin, much more cruel than the preceding, and famous for the martyrdom of the Theban Legion, which however is a very dubious story. The Jewish Talmud and Targum composed in this century. The Jews are allowed to return into Palestine. Jewish schools erected at Babylon, Sora, and other places. Remarkable deaths of those who persecuted the Christians, related by Tertullian, Eusebius, and Lucius Cæcilius. Many illustrious men, and Roman senators, converted to Christianity. The origin of the monastic life derived from the austere manners of Paul the Theban, the first hermit. Diocletian assumes the name and honours due to Jupiter, and orders the people to worship him. Religious rites are greatly multiplied in this century; altars used; wax tapers employed. Public churches, called in Greek Κυριακα, built for the celebration of divine worship. The pagan mysteries injudiciously imitated in many respects by Christians. The tasting of milk and honey, previous to baptism, introduced. The person is anointed before and after that holy rite—receives a crown, and goes arrayed in white for some time after. The story of the seven sleepers of Ephesus, and the martyrdom of Ursula, and the 11,000 British Virgins, the principal fables invented in this century.

PROFANE AUTHORS.

Ælius Maurus. Oppian, the Poet. Quintus Seren. Sammonicus. Julius Africanus. Acolus. Dio Cassius. Ulpian. Ephorus. Censorinus. C. Curius Fortunatus. Herodian. Nicagoras. Amelius. Gentilianus. Erennius. Dexippus. Cassius Longinus. Julius Capitolinus. Ælius Lampridius. Trebellius Pollio. Porphyry. Ælius Spartianus. Flavius Vopiscus. M. Aurel. Olymp. Nemesianus. Alexander, a Greek philosopher. Philostratus. Julius Paulus. Sextus Pomponius. Herennius. Modestinus. Hermogenianus. Palladius Rutilius. Taurus Æmilianus. Justin. Julius Calphurnius. Arnobius.

CENTURY IV.

SOVEREIGN PRINCES.

Roman Emperors:—A. D.—Diocletian and Maximian abdicate the empire in the year 305. Galerius, 311. Constantius, 306. Constantine the Great, 337. His adversaries, Maximin, 313. Maxentius, 312. Licinius, 325. Constantine II., 338. Constantius, 361. Constans, 350. Julian, the Apostate, 363. Jovian, 364. Valentinian, 375. Valens, 378. Gratian, 383. Valentinian II., 392. Theodosius the Great, 395. The divisions of the Roman Empire into the Eastern and Western Empires. [*The Visigoths settle in Gaul and Spain about the end of this century.*] Athanaric, 382. Alaric.

POPES, OR BISHOPS OF ROME.

Marcellinus, 304. Marcellus, 309. Eusebius, 311. Melchiades, 313. Sylvester, 335. Mark, 336. Julius, 352. Liberius, 367. A schism between Liberius and Felix. Damasus, 384. A new schism between this pontiff and Ursinus. Siricius, 398.

ECCLESIASTICAL AND THEOLOGICAL WRITERS.

Lactantius Firm. Lucius Cæcilius. Dorotheus, bishop of Tyre. Eusebius, bishop of Cæsarea. Constantine the Great. Eustathius, bishop of Antioch. Commodianus. Alexander, bishop of Alexandria Juvencus. Athanasius, bishop of Alexandria. Antonius, who (with Paul the hermit) was the first institutor of the monastic life. Marcellus, bishop of Ancyra. Theodore, bishop of Heraclea. Julius, bishop of Rome. Jul. Firm. Maternus. Pachomius. Eusebius, bishop of Emessa. Serapion. Cyril, bishop of Jerusalem. Hilarius, bishop of Poictiers. Lucifer, bishop of Cagliari. Phœbadius, bishop of Agen. Eunomius. Zeno, bishop of Verona. Titus, bishop of Bostra. Damacus, bishop of Rome. Epiphanius, bishop of Salamis. Optatus, bishop of Milevi. Pacianus. Marius Victorinus. Liberius, bishop of Rome. Ephraim the Syrian. Didymus of Alex. Basil, bishop of Cæsarea. Gregory, bishop of Nazianzum. Gregory, bishop of Nyssa. Amphilochius, bishop of Iconium. Hegesippus. Apollinaris, Father and Son. Eusebius, bishop of Verceil. Diodore, bishop of Tarsus. Proba Falconia. The three Macarii. Ambrose. Jerome. Ruffinus. Philastrius. Paulinus, bishop of Nola. Augustin. John Chrysostom.

HERETICS, REAL OR REPUTED.

The Manichæans disguised under the denominations of Encratites, Apotactics, Saccophori, Hydroparastates, and Solitaries. Arius and his followers, who were divided into Eunomians, Semiarians, Eusebians, Homoiousians, Acacians, and Psathyrians. Photinus, Apollinaris, Father and Son. Macedonius. The Anthropomorphites. Priscillian. Andæus. The Messalians, or Euchites. Collyridians. Eustathians. Coluthus. Helvidius. Bonosus. Vigilantius. Three schisms of the Meletians, and Luciferians, and Donatists.

REMARKABLE EVENTS, AND RELIGIOUS RITES AND INSTITUTIONS.

The Tenth Persecution continued. The Athanasians or Orthodox persecuted by Constantius, who was an Arian, and by Valens, who ordered 80 of their deputies, all ecclesiastics, to be put on board of a ship, to which fire was set as soon as it had cleared the coast. The Christians persecuted by Sapor. The supposed conversion of Constantine the Great, by a vision representing a fiery cross in the air. First General council. It was held at Nice in 325. In it the opinions of Arius were condemned, and the popes declared merely equal in dignity to other Christian bishops. A second general council is held in the year 381, at Constantinople, in which the errors of Macedonius are condemned. Remarkable progress of the Christian religion among the Indians, Goths, Marcomanni, and Iberians. The famous donation of Constantine in favour of the Roman see—a mere fable. The miraculous defeat of Eugenius by Theodosius. Julian's attempt to invalidate the predictions of the prophets, by encouraging the Jews to rebuild the temple of Jerusalem, defeated by an earthquake and fiery eruption. See the learned bishop Warburton's interesting and ingenious work, entitled *Julian*. Theodosius the Great is obliged by Ambrose, bishop of Milan, to do public penance for the slaughter of the Thessalonians. The Eucharist was, during this century, administered in some places to infants and persons deceased. Something like the doctrine of Transubstantiation is maintained, and the ceremony of the elevation used in the celebration of the Eucharist. The council of Elvira in Spain, held in the year 305, not only solemnly forbids the adoration of pictures or images, but even prohibits the use of them. The use of incense and of the censer, with several other superstitious rites, introduced.—The churches are considered as externally holy, the saints are invoked, images used, and the Cross worshipped. The clerical order augmented by new ranks of ecclesiastics, such as archdeacons, country bishops, archbishops, metropolitans, exarchs, &c.

PROFANE AUTHORS.

Ælius Donatus. Servius. Helladius. Andronicus Nonius. Marcellus. Sext. Aurelius Victor. Maximus of Smyrna, who is supposed to have taught the emperor Julian magic. Oribases. Eutropius. Libanius. Ausonius. Pappus, the famous mathematician. Prudentius. Rufus Festus. Avienus. Themistius. Flavius Vegetius. Hierocles. Julian. Ammianus Marcellinus. Symmachus. Lactantius. Jamblichus. Ælius Lampridius. Eusebius of Cæsarea. Jul. Firmicus Maternus. Chalcidius. Pomponius. Festus Quirtus Curtius. Macrobius.

CENTURY V.

SOVEREIGN PRINCES.

Emperors of the West:—A. D.—Honorius, 423. Valentinian III., 455. Maximus, 455. Avitus, 456. Majorianus, 461. Severus, 465. Anthemius, 472. Olybrius, 472. Glycerius, deposed in 474. Julius Nepos, deposed in 475. Romulus Augustulus, who reigned till the 23d of August, when Odoacer took the title of king of Italy, and put an end to the western empire. *Kings of Italy:*—Odoacer, 493. Theodoric. *Emperors of the East:*—Arcadius, 408. Theodosius II., 450. Marcianus, 457. Leo I., 474. Leo II., 474. Zeno Isaur, 491. Anastasius. *Gothic Kings of Spain:*—Alaric, 411. Ataulphus, 415. Sigeric, 415. Vallia, 420. Theodoric, 451. Thorismond, 452. Theodoric II., 466. Euric, 484. Alaric II. *Kings of France:*—Pharamond, first king, 420. Clodion, 451. Meroveus, 456. Childeric, 481. Clovis I. *The Kings of the Vandals in Africa, where they settled in the year* 429. Genseric, 466. Huneric, 484. Gontamond, 496. Thrasamond. *Kings of England:*—Vortigern. Kingdom of Kent founded by Hengist the Saxon, in 457, and that of Sussex by Ælla, in 499.

POPES, OR BISHOPS OF ROME.

Anastasius, 402. Innocent, 417. Zosimus, 418. Boniface I., 423. A schism between this pope and Eulalius. Celestine I., 432. Sixtus III., 440. Leo the Great, 461. Hilarius, 467. Simplicius, 483. Felix III., 492. Gelasius, 496. Anastasius II., 498. Symmachus I. A schism between him and Laurentius

ECCLESIASTICAL AND THEOLOGICAL WRITERS.

Gaudentius, bishop of Bresse. Sulpicius Severus. Palladius. Heraclides. Innocentius. Polybius. Pelagius. Cœlestius. Theodore, bishop of Mopsuesta. Polychronius. Nonnus. Synesius. Isidore of Pelusium. Cyril of Alexandria. Orosius. Marius Mercator. Maximus, bishop of Turin. Theodoret. Cassian. Peter Chrysologus. Hilarius. Philostorgius. Vincent of Lerins. Socrates. Sozomenes. Leo the Great. Prosper. Idacius. Basil. Seleucus. Arnobius the Younger. Claudian Mamertus. Faustus. Felix, the Roman pontiff. Vigilius Tapsensis, supposed by some learned men to have been the author of what is commonly called the Athanasian Creed. Victor the African. Gennadius. Zosimus. Prosper. Sidonius Apollinar. Æneas Gaza.

HERETICS, REAL OR REPUTED.

Vigilantius. Pelagius, Cœlestius, Julian, authors of what is called the Pelagian Heresy. John Cassian Faustus. Gennadius, Vincent of Lerins, Semi-Pelagians. Nestorius. Theodoret. Theodore of Tarsus. Theodore of Mopsus. Nestorians. Eutyches. Dioscorus. The Acephali.—Monophysites.—Jacobites.—Armenians.—Theopaschites.—Predestinarians.—Cœlicolæ. Peter, the Fuller. Xenaias.

REMARKABLE EVENTS.

Foundation of the French monarchy by Pharamond, or rather by Clovis. An earthquake swallows up several cities in Palestine. A third General Council held at Ephesus, at which Nestorius was deposed, in the year 431. A fourth General Council held at Chalcedon against Eutyches in the year 451. Progress of Christianity among the Franks and Germans. The conversion of the Irish to the Christian faith attempted in vain by Palladius, but effected by St. Patrick, whose original name was Succathus, who arrived in Ireland in the year 432. Terrible persecutions carried on against the Christians in Britain, by the Picts, Scots, and Anglo-Saxons,—in Spain, Gaul, and Africa, by the Vandals—in Italy and Pannonia, by the Visigoths—in Africa, by the Donatists and Circumcellians—in Persia, by Isdegerdes—beside the particular persecutions carried on alternately against the Arians and Athanasians. The extinction of the western empire. The Theodosian Code drawn up. The city of Venice founded by the inhabitants of the adjacent coast, who fled from the incursions of the Barbarians. Felix III. bishop of Rome (whom Bower and others look upon as the second pope of that name) is excommunicated, and his name struck out of the diptychs, or sacred registers, by Acacius, bishop of Constantinople. Many ridiculous fables are invented during this century, such as the story of the vial of oil, brought from heaven by a pigeon at the baptism of Clovis—the vision of Attila, &c.

PROFANE AUTHORS.

Anienus. Martianus Capella. Claudian. Eunapius. Macrobius. Olympiodorus. Orosius. Peutinger. Rutilius Claudius. Numantianus. Servius Honoratus. Sidonius Apollinaris. Candidus, the Isaurian. Zosimus the historian. Idacius. Quintus, or Cointus. Priscus. Musæus. Proclus. Simplicius.

CENTURY VI.

SOVEREIGN PRINCES.

Kings of Italy:—A. D.—Theodoric, 526. Athalaric, 534. Amalasuntha, 534. Theodatus, 536. Vitiges, 540. Idebald, 541. Totila, 553. Teias, 554. *Emperors of the East:*—Anastasius, 518. Justin I., 527. Justinian, 565. Justin II., 578. Tiberius II., 586. Mauritius. *Gothic Kings of Spain:*—Alaric, 507. Gesalric, 512. Amalaric, 531. Theudis, 548. Theodegesil, 548. Agila, 552. Athanagilda, 567. Leuva, 568. Leuvigild, 585. Recared. These princes were masters also of Narbonne and Aquitaine. *Kings of England:*—The third Saxon kingdom is founded in England by Cerdic, in 519, and is called the kingdom of the West Saxons. The fourth, or that of the East Saxons, by Erchenwin, in 527. The fifth, that of Northumberland, by Ida, in 547. The sixth, that of the East Angles, by Uffa, in 573. The seventh, that of Mercia, by Crida, in 585. Thus was successively formed the Saxon Heptarchy. *Kings of France:*—Clovis I., 511. The kingdom is divided among his four sons, viz. Thierry, Metz, 534. Clodomir, Orleans, 534. Childebert, Paris, 558. Clotaire, Soisons, 562. A second division of the kingdom among the four sons of Clotaire I. viz. Cherebert, Paris, 566. Gontran, Orleans, 593. Chilperic, Soissons, 584. Sigebert, Metz, 575. *Kings of the Vandals in Africa:*—Thrasamond, 523. Hilderic, 530. Gilimer, defeated and taken prisoner by Belisarius, in the year 534. By this event Africa became again subject to the Emperors of the East. *Kings of the Lombards, who entered Italy in the year* 568. Alboinus, 571. Clephis, 573. Antharis, 590. Agilulph. *Exarchs of Ravenna:*—Lingonus. 583. Smaragdus, 588. Romanus, 598. Callinicus.

POPES, OR BISHOPS OF ROME.

Symmachus, 514. Hormisdas, 523. John I., 526. Felix IV., 529. Boniface II., 531. A schism between Boniface and Dioscorus. John II., 535. Agapetus I., 536. Sylverius, 540. A schism between Sylverius and Vigilius. Vigilius, 555. Pelagius I., 558. John III., 572. Benedict I., 577. Pelagius II., 590. Gregory I.

ECCLESIASTICAL AND THEOLOGICAL WRITERS.

Cæsarius, bishop of Arles. Fulgentius, bishop of Ruspa. Boethius. Timothy of Constantinople. Emidius. Severus. Cassiodorus. Procopius. Peter, the deacon. Maxentius, a Scythian monk. Dionysius, the Little. Fulgentius Ferrandus. Marcellinus. Zachary, the schoolman. Hesychius. Facundus Hemian. Pope Vigilius. Rusticus, a Roman deacon. Junilius. Victor of Capua. Primasius. Jornandes Liberatus. Victor, the African. Venantius Fortunatus. Anastasius of Mount Sinai, afterwards bishop of Antioch. John, the schoolman. Cosmas. Gildas. Leander. John of Constantinople. Columbanus. Leontius Byzant. Leontius of Cyprus. Gregory the Great. Isidore of Seville. Lucius Carinus. Proclus Diadochus.

HERETICS.

Deuterius. Severus, leader of the Acephali. Themistius, chief of the Agnoites, who maintained that Christ was ignorant of the day of judgment. Barsanians, or Semidulites, who maintained that Christ had suffered only in appearance. Jacob Zanzale, the chief of the Jacobites, or Monophysites. John Philopomus, the chief of the Tritheites. Damianists. Origenists. Corrupticolæ. Acœmetæ. The Arians Nestorians, Eutychians, and Pelagians, continued to raise troubles in the church.

REMARKABLE EVENTS.

Several nations converted to Christianity. The canon of the mass established by Gregory the Great The Benedictine Order founded. Forty Benedictine monks, with Augustine at their head, are sent into Britain by Gregory the Great, in the year 596; who convert Ethelbert, king of Kent, to the Christian faith The Ostrogothic kingdom is destroyed by Justinian, who becomes master of Italy. The Lombards invade Italy in the year 568, and erect a new kingdom at Ticinum. The Christians are persecuted in several places. The orthodox are oppressed by the emperor Anastasius, Thrasamond, king of the Vandals, Theodoric, king of the Ostrogoths, &c. Female convents are greatly multiplied in this century. Litanies introduced into the church of France. The Arians are driven out. Superstition of the Stylites introduced by Simeon, the head of that crazy sect, who spent his life on the top of a pillar, and foolishly imagined, that he would, by this trick, render himself agreeable to the Deity. The Romish writers say, he chose this lofty habitation (for the pillar was 36 cubits high) to avoid the multitude which crowded about him to see his miracles. The Christian æra is formed in this century by Dionysius the Little, who first began to reckon the course of time from the birth of Christ. The Justinian code, Pandect, Institutions, and Novels, collected and formed into a body. Antioch, that was destroyed by an earthquake, is rebuilt by Justinian. The fifth general council assembled at Constantinople in the year 553, under Justinian I. in which the Origenists and the Three Chapters were condemned.

LEARNED MEN, HISTORIANS, PHILOSOPHERS, AND POETS.

Justinian Boethius. Trebonian. Agathias, who continued the history composed by Procopius. Jornandes. Gregory of Tours. Marius, bishop of Avranches, an eminent historian. Menander, the historian. Stephen of Byzantium. Magn. Aurelius Cassiodorus. Dionysius the Little.

CENTURY VII.

SOVEREIGN PRINCES.

Emperors of the East:—A. D.—Mauritius, 602. Phocas, 610. Heraclius, 641. Constantine III., 641. Heracleonas, 642. Constans II., 668. Constantine IV., 685. Leontius, 698. Tiberius III., 703. Justinian II. *Kings of the Goths in Spain:*—Victeric. Gondemar. Sisebut, 621. Recared II., 621. Suinthila, 631. Sizenand, 636. Chintila, 640. Tulga, 642. Chindasuinthe, 649. Recesuinthe, 672. Vamba, 680. Ervige, 687. Egica. *Kings of France:*—Clotaire II., 628. Dagobert, 638. Sigebert II., 654. Clovis, 660. Clotaire III., 668. Childeric II., 673. Dagobert II., 679. Theodoric, 690. Clovis III., 695. Childebert III. The race of the weak kings begins with Theodoric III. and ends with Childeric III. *England:*—The Heptarchy. *Kings of the Lombards in Italy:*—Agilulph, 616. Adaloaldus, 626. Ariovaldus, 638. Rotharis, 653 Rodoald, 656. Aripert, 662. Gondipert, 662. Grimoald, 673. Garibald, 673. Bertharit, 689. Cunipert, 706. *Exarchs of Ravenna:*—Smaragdus, 610. John, 615. Eleutherius, 617. Isaac, 648. Theodore Calliopa, 649. Olympius, 650. Theodore Calliopa II., 686. Theodore, 687. John. Plato, 702.

POPES, OR BISHOPS OF ROME.

Gregory I., 604. Sabinianus, 605. Boniface III., 606. Boniface IV., 614. Deodatus, 617. Boniface V., 625. Honorius I., 630. Severinus I., 639. John IV., 641. Theodore I., 648. Martin I., 655. Eugenius I., 656. Vitalianus, 671. Adeodatus, 676. Domnus, 678. Agatho I., 682. Leo II., 684. Benedict II., 685. John V., 686. Conon, 687. Sergius I., 701. A schism occasioned by the pretensions of Theodore and Paschal.

ARCHBISHOPS OF CANTERBURY.

Augustine, first archbishop of Canterbury, was nominated to that high office in the year 597 by Gregory the Great, bishop of Rome, with the consent of Ethelbert, king of Kent: he died in the year 611, or, as some say, in 605. Laurence, 619. Melletus, 624. Justus, 634. Honorius, 653. Adeodatus, 664. Theodore, 690. Brithwald.

ECCLESIASTICAL AND THEOLOGICAL WRITERS.

John Philonus. John Malela. Hesychius of Jerusalem. Theophylact. Simocatta. Antiochus. Modestus. Cyrus of Alexandria. Jonas. Gallus. John Moschus. Andreas Damascenus. George Pisides. Eligius. The two Theodores. Paulus. The emperor Heraclius. Maximus Confucius. Theodore the monk. The emperor Constans II. Martin, bishop of Rome. Maurus of Ravenna. Anastasius, a monk—a Roman presb. Fructuosus. Peter, metropolitan of Nicomedia. Julian Pomerius. Agatho. John of Thessalonica. Cresconius. Ildefonsus. Marculph. John Climachus. Fortunatus Venant. Isidore of Seville, who composed Commentaries on the Historical Books of the Old Testament, and is acknowledged to have been the principal author of the famous Mosarabic Liturgy, which is the ancient Liturgy of Spain. Dorotheus. Sophronius, bishop of Jerusalem.

HERETICS, REAL OR REPUTED.

The ancient heresies were still in vigour during this century; to these were added the sects of the Paulicians and Monothelites.

REMARKABLE EVENTS.

An extraordinary progress is made in the conversion of the English. The archbishoprics of London and York are founded, with 12 bishoprics under the jurisdiction of each. The archbishopric of London is translated to Canterbury. The Gospel is propagated with success in Holland, Friseland and Germany. The schism, between the Greek and Latin churches, commences in this century. The rise of Mohammed, and the rapid progress of his religion, which is propagated by fire and sword. The Mohammedan æra, called the Hegira, commences with the year of Christ 622. The destruction of the Persian monarchy under the reign of Isdegerdes III. Boniface IV. receives from that odious tyrant Phocas (who was the great patron of the popes and the chief promoters of their grandeur) the famous Pantheon, which is converted into a church. Here Cybele was succeeded by the Virgin Mary, and the Pagan deities by Christian martyrs Idolatry still subsisted; but the objects of it were changed. Ina, king of the West Saxons, resigns his crown, and assumes the monastic habit in a convent at Rome. During the Heptarchy, many Saxon kings took the same religious turn. Pope Agatho discontinued the payment of the tribute which the see of Rome had been accustomed to pay the emperor at the election of its pontiff. The Sixth General council is held at Constantinople, under Constantine Pogonatus, against the Monothelites, in the year 680. The Seventh, which is looked upon by some as a kind of supplement to this, was held in the Trullus, under Justinian II. in the year 692, and is called Quinisextum.

PROFANE AUTHORS.

The author of the Alexandrian Chronicle. Isidore of Seville, who, beside his theological productions, composed a History of the Goths and Vandals, and a work entitled Etymologicon Scientiarum, in which he gives an account of the origin and nature of the different sciences. In this century commenced that long period of ignorance and darkness which remained until the light of the Reformation arose.

CENTURY VIII.

SOVEREIGN PRINCES.

Emperors of the East:—A. D.—Justinian II., 711. Philippicus, 713. Anastasius II., 714. Theodosius III., 716. Leo III. Isaur, 741. Constantine V. Copron, 775. Leo IV., 780. Constantine VI. Porphyr, 797. Irene. *Kings of the Visigoths in Spain:*—Egica, 701. Vitiza, 710. Roderic, the last king of the Goths, 713. *Kings of Leon and the Asturias:*—Pelagius, 737. Favila, 739. Alphonso, 757. Froila, 768 Aurelio, 774. Silo, 783. Mauregato, 789. Veremond, 791. Alphonso II. *Kings of France:*—Childebert III., 711. Dagobert III., 715. Chilperic II., 720. Theodoric IV., 736. Interregnum, from the year 737 to 743, during which time Carloman and Pepin, sons of Charles Martel, govern without the regal title. Childeric III. dethroned in 750. The last king of the first race. *Second race:*—Pepin, 768. Charlemagne. *England:*—The Heptarchy. *Kings of the Lombards in Italy:*—Luitpert, 704. Ragombert, 704. Aripert, 712. Ansprand, 712. Luitprand, 744. Rachis, 750. Aistulphus, 756. Desiderius, 773. The kingdom of the Lombards, which subsisted during the space of 206 years, was overturned by Charlemagne, who, having defeated Desiderius, caused himself to be crowned king of the Lombards, in the year 774. *Exarchs of Ravenna:*—Theophylact, 710. Jo. Procopius, 712. Paul, 729. Eutychius, 752. The Exarchate subsisted during the space of 185 years. It ended in the reign of Aistulphus, king of the Lombards, who reduced Ravenna, and added it to his dominions. But this prince was obliged by Pepin, king of France, to surrender the Exarchate, with all its territories, castles, &c. to be for ever held by Stephen III. and his successors in the see of Rome. This is the true foundation of the temporal grandeur of the popes.

POPES, OR BISHOPS OF ROME.

John VI., 705. John VII., 707. Sisinius, 708. Constantine, 714. Gregory II., 731. Gregory III., 741. Zachary, 752. Stephen II., 752. Stephen III., 757. Paul, 767. A schism between Paul and Theophylact. Stephen IV., 772. A schism between Constantine, Philip, and Stephen IV. Adrian, 797. Leo III.

ARCHBISHOPS OF CANTERBURY.

Brithwald, 731. Tatwin, 734. Nothelm, 741. Cuthbert, 758. Bregwin, 762. Lambert, 790. Athelard.

ECCLESIASTICAL AND THEOLOGICAL WRITERS.

Venerable Bede. John Damascenus. The anonymous author of a Book entitled, Ordo Romanus de Divinis Officiis, published in the Bibl. Patr. Charlemagne: see the Capitularia, published by Baluze at Paris, in 1677, and the Codex Carolinus, published at Ingolstadt, in 1634, by Gretzer. Ambrosius Authpertus. The popes Gregory I. Gregory II. and Adrian. Paul the Lombard. Paulinus, bishop of Aquileia. Alcuin, a native of England, and one of the principal instruments employed by Charlemagne for the restoration of learning. He is considered by M. Du-Pin as the person that first introduced polite literature into France; and it is to him that the universities of Paris, Tours, Soissons, &c. owe their origin. Felix, archbishop of Ravenna. Germanus, bishop of Constantinople. The unknown author of a book entitled, Liber Diurnus Pontificum Romanorum. Egbert, Archbishop of York. Bartholomew, a monk of Edessa, who refuted the Koran. Boniface, archbishop of Mentz, commonly called the Apostle of Germany. Anastasius, abbot in Palestine. Theophanes Aldhelm, bishop of Sherborne, under the heptarchy, and nephew to Ina, king of the West Saxons.

HERETICS, REAL OR REPUTED.

The Eutychians, Monothelites, and Jacobites, continue to propagate their doctrines. The Paulo-Johannists, who were so called from their leaders Paul and John, and embraced the pernicious errors of Valentine and Manes. The Agonoclites, a wrong headed set of people who prayed dancing. Adelbert. Felix, bishop of Urgel. Elipand, bishop of Toledo. Leo, the Isaurian, who destroyed the images in the churches, and was the chief of the Iconoclastes; and Clement, who preferred the decisions of Scripture to the decrees of councils; are reputed heretics by the church of Rome. Virgilius was also accused of heresy, by pope Zacharry, because he was a good mathematician, and believed the existence of Antipodes. Those who promoted the worship of images and relics in this century deserve much more justly the denomination of Heretics.

REMARKABLE EVENTS, AND RELIGIOUS RITES.

Rapid progress of the Saracens in Asia and Africa. The subversion of the kingdom of the Lombards and of the exarchate of Ravenna, the latter of which is granted to the see of Rome, by Pepin, king of France. Charlemagne adds to the grant of Pepin several provinces, though the titles and acts of this grant have not been produced by the Roman Catholic historians. The ceremony of kissing the pope's toe introduced. The Saxons, with Witekind, their monarch, converted to Christianity. The Christians persecuted by the Saracens, who massacred five hundred monks in the abbey of Lerins. The Saracens take possession of Spain. Controversy between the Greek and Latin churches, concerning the Holy Ghost's proceeding from the Son. The Germans converted by Boniface. The Gospel propagated in Hyrcania and Tartary. The right of election to the see of Rome conferred upon Charlemagne and his successors by pope Adrian, in a council of bishops assembled at Rome. The worship of images authorised by the second council of Nice in the year 787, which is improperly called the seventh general council. The reading of the epistles and gospels introduced into the service of the church. Solitary or private masses instituted. Churches built in honour of saints. Masses for the dead. Willebrod sent to convert the Frisons; he was the first bishop of Utrecht.

PROFANE AUTHORS.

Alcuin—see page 432. Bede. Fredegarius. John Damascenus. George Syncellus. Virgilius.

CENTURY IX.

SOVEREIGN PRINCES.

Emperors of the East:—A. D.—Irene, 802. Nicephorus, 811. Stauratius, 811. Michael Curopolites, 813 Leo Armen., 820. Michael Balb., 829. Theophilus, 842. Michael III., 867. Basil I. Macedo, 886. Leo VI. Philos. *Emperors of the West:*—The western empire was restored in the year 800, in favour of Charlemagne, who died in 814. Louis, the Debonnaire, 840. Lothaire, 855. Louis II., 875. Charles II. surnamed the Bald, 877. Louis III., 879. Carloman, 880. Charles III. deposed, 887. After the death of this prince, (who was the last king of France that was emperor) Germany and Italy were entirely separated from the French monarchy. Arnolph, 899. Louis IV. *Kings of Spain,* i. e. *of Leon and the Asturias:*—Alphonso the Chaste, 824. Ramiro, 851. Ordogno, 862. Alphonso III. *Kings of France:*—Charlemagne, 814. Louis the Debonnaire, 840. Charles the Bald, 877. Louis III., 879. Carloman, 884. Charles III., 888. Eudes, 889. Charles the Simple. *Kings of England:*—The Heptarchy finished by the union of the seven kingdoms under the government of Egbert. Egbert, 836. Ethelwolf, 857. Ethelbald, 860. Ethelbert, 866. Ethelred I., 871. Alfred the Great, 901. *Kings of Scotland:*—The history of Scotland is divided into four great periods. The first, which commences with Fergus I. 330 years before Christ, and contains a series of 68 kings, ending with Alpinus, in the year 823, is looked upon as entirely fabulous. We shall therefore begin this chronological list with the second period, which commences with Kenneth II. Kenneth II., 854. Donald V., 858. Constantine II., 874. Ethus, 875. Gregory, 893. Donald VI. *Kings of Sweden:*—The origin of this kingdom is covered with uncertainty and fables. Some historians reckon 36 kings before Biorno III., but it is with this prince that chronologers generally begin their series. Biorno III., 824. Brantamond, 827. Sivard, 842. Heroth, 856. Charles VI., 868. Biorno IV., 883. Ingo, or Ingeld, 891.

POPES, OR BISHOPS OF ROME.

Leo III., 816. Stephen V., 817. Paschal I., 824. Eugenius II., 827. A schism between Eugenius II. and Zizinnus. Valentine, 827. Gregory IV., 844. Sergius II., 847. Leo IV., 855. Pope Joan Bened. III., 858. A schism between Benedict and Anastasius. Nicolas I., 867. Adrian II., 872. John VIII., 882. Marinus I., 884. Adrian III., 885. Formosus, 897. A schism between him and Sergius. Boniface VI. 897. Stephen VII., 901. A schism between Stephen VII. John IX. Romanus I. and II. and Theodore III.

ARCHBISHOPS OF CANTERBURY.

Athelard, 806. Wulfred, 830. Theogild, 830. Celnoth, 871. Ethelred, 889. Plegmund.

ECCLESIASTICAL AND THEOLOGICAL WRITERS.

Nicephorus, patriarch of Constantinople. Amalarius, bishop of Treves. Theodore Studita. Agobard, archbishop of Lyons. Eginhard. Claudius. Clement, bishop of Turin. Jonas, bishop of Orleans. Freculph, bishop of Lysieux. Moses Barcepha. Phocius, patriarch of Constantinople. Theod. Abucara. Petrus Siculus. Nicetas David. Rabanus Maurus, archbishop of Mentz. Hilduin. Servatus Lupus. Drepanius Florus. Druthmar. Godeschalcus. Paschasius Radbert, the chief of the Transubstantiarians. Bertram or Ratram of Corby, who refuted the monstrous errors of Radbert, and was at the head of those who denied the corporal presence of Christ in the Eucharist. Haymo, bishop of Halberstadt. Walafridus Strabo. Hincmar, archbishop of Rheims. John Scot Erigena. Ansegisus. Florus, the deacon. Prudens, bishop of Troyes. Remy of Lyons. Nicolas. Adrian. John VIII. Pope. Anastasius, Bibl. Auxilius. Theodulph, bishop of Orleans. Smaragdus. Aldric, bishop of Mans. Ado of Vienna. Isidore Mercator, author of the False Decretals. Jesse, bishop of Amiens. Dungale. Halitgaire, bishop of Cambray. Amulo, archbishop of Lyons. Vandalbert. Angelome. Epiphanes, archbishop of Constantia, in the island of Cyprus. Regino. Abbo. William, the librarian. Pope Formosus. Pope Stephen. Methodus, who invented the Sclavonian characters, and made a translation of the Bible for the Bulgarians, which was used by the Russians. Alfred the Great, king of England, composed a Saxon Paraphrase on the Ecclesiastical History of Bede, a Saxon Version of Orosius, and a Saxon Psalter. The emperor Basil Maced. The emperor Leo, surnamed the Wise.

HERETICS, REAL OR REPUTED.

Paulicians, a branch of the Manicheans. Iconoclastes. Iconolatræ, or image worshippers. Prædestinarians. Adoptians. Transubstantiarians. Clement, bishop of Turin, who followed the sentiments of Felix of Urgel.

REMARKABLE EVENTS AND RELIGIOUS RITES.

The conversion of the Swedes, Danes, Saxons, Huns, Bohemians, Moravians, Sclavonians, Russians, Indians, and Bulgarians: by the last a controversy is occasioned between the Greek and Latin churches. The rise of transubstantiation and the sacrifice of the mass. The cause of Christianity suffers in the east under the Saracens, and in Europe under the Normans. The power of the pope increases; that of the bishops diminishes; and the emperors are divested of their ecclesiastical authority. The Decretals are forged, by which the popes extended the limits of their jurisdiction and authority. The fictitious relics of St. Mark, St. James, and St. Bartholomew, are imposed upon the credulity of the people. Monks and abbots now first employed in civil affairs, and called to the courts of princes. The festival of All-Saints is added, in this century, to the Latin calendar by Gregory IV. though some authors of note place this institution in the seventh century, and attribute it to Boniface IV. The superstitious festival of the Assumption of the Virgin Mary, instituted by the council of Mentz, and confirmed by pope Nicolas I. and afterwards by Leo X. The trial by cold water introduced by pope Eugenius II. though Le Brun, in his Histoire des Pratiques Superstitieses, endeavours to prove this ridiculous invention more ancient. The emperor Louis II. is obliged by the arrogant pontiff Nicolas I. to perform the functions of a groom, and hold the bridle of this pope's horse, while his pretended holiness was dismounting. The first Legends or Lives of the Saints appear in this century. The Apostles' Creed is sung in the churches.—Organs, bells, and vocal music, are introduced in many places.—Festivals multiplied. The order of St. Andrew, or the Knights of the Thistle in Scotland. Michael I. emperor of the East, abdicates the throne, and retires into a monastery, with his wife and six children. Photius, patriarch of Constantinople, excommunicates the pope. The canonization of saints introduced by Pope Leo II. The university of Oxford founded by Alfred. The sciences are cultivated among the Saracens, and, particularly encouraged by the khalif Al-Mamoun. Theophilus, from his abhorrence of images, banishes the painters out of the Eastern Empire. Harold, king of Denmark, is dethroned by his subjects, on account of his attachment to Christianity. The university of Paris founded.

PROFANE AUTHORS.

Photius. Smaragdud. Eginhard. Rabanus Maurus. Abbon. Herempert. Leon. Sergius. Methodius. Walafridus Strabo. John Scot Erigena. Alfred the Great, king of England. His Saxon version of Orosius was never published. Abon-Nabas, an Arabian poet. The khalif Al-Mamoun, an eminent mathematician and astronomer. N. B. Haroun, the father of this prince, sent to Charlemagne a striking clock, with springs and wheels, which was the first ever seen in France, and shows that, at this period, the arts were more cultivated in Asia than in Europe. Albategni, the mathematician. Albumasar, or Abou-Mashar, the Arabian astronomer.

CENTURY X.

SOVEREIGN PRINCES.

Emperors of the East:—A. D.—Leo, the philosopher, 911. Alexander, 912. Constantine VII. surnamed Porphyrogenitus, 959. Romanus Lecapenus took advantage of the youth of this prince, and seized the imperial throne, but was deposed by his son Stephen, and died in 948. Romanus, first or second son to Constantine VII., 963. Nicephorus Phoc., 970. John Zimisces, 975. Basil III. Constantine VIII. *Emperors of the West:*—Louis IV., 912. Conrad I., 919. Henry I. surnamed the Fowler, 936. Otho I., 9[illegible]. Otho II., 983. Otho III. *Kings of Spain*, i. e. *Leon and Asturias:*—Alphonso III. surnamed the Great, abdicates the crown in the year 910. Garcias, 913. Ordogno II., 923. Froila II., 924. Alphonso IV., 931. Ramiro II., 950. Ordogno III., 955. Ordogno IV., 956. Sanchez, the Fat, 967. Ramiro III., 982. Bermudo, called, by some, Veremond II., 999. Alphonso V. *Kings of France:*—Charles the Simple, 929. Ralph usurps the throne. Louis d'Outremer, 954. Lothaire II., 986. Louis the Idler, the last king of the line of Charlemagne, 987. *Third Race:*—Hugh Capet, 996. Robert. *Kings of England:*—A. D.—Edward, 925. Athelstan, 941. Edmund, 946. Edred, 955. Edwy, 959. Edgar, 975. Edward the Martyr, 979. Ethelred II. *Kings of Scotland:*—Donald VI., 903. Constantine III., 943. Malcolm I., 958. Indulf, 967. Duff, 972. Cullen, 976. Kenneth III., 994. Constantine IV., 995. Grime. *Kings of Sweden:*—Ingeld II. 907. Eric VI., 926. Eric VII., 940. Eric VIII., 980. Olaus II. the Tributary. The beginnings of the Danish monarchy are so fabulous that we shall begin with Harold, who died in 980. Sweyn. *Poland:*—Micislaus the first Christian duke, dies 999.

POPES, OR BISHOPS OF ROME.

John IX., 905. A schism between John IX. and Sergius. Benedict IV., 906. Leo V., 906. A schism between Leo V. and Christopher. Christopher, 907. A schism between Christopher and Sergius. Sergius III., 910. Anastasius III., 912. Lando, 913. John X., 928. Leo VI., 929. Stephen VIII., 931. John XI., 936. Leo VII., 939. Stephen IX., 943. Marinus II., 946. Agapetus II., 955. John XII., 964. A schism between John XII. and Leo. Leo VIII., 964. Benedict V., 965. John XIII., 972. Domnus II., 972. Benedict VI., 975. Boniface VII., 984. Benedict VII., 984. John XIV., 985. John XV., 985. John XVI., 996. Gregory V., 999. A schism between John and Gregory V. Sylvester II.

ARCHBISHOPS OF CANTERBURY.

Plegmund, 917. Athelm, 924. Wolfhelm, 934. Odo, 959. Dunstan, 988. Ethelgar, 989. Siricius, 994 Aluric, or Alfric.

ECCLESIASTICAL AND THEOLOGICAL WRITERS.

Simeon Metaphrastes. Leontius of Byzantium. Odo of Clugni. Ratherius, bishop of Verona and Liege. Hippolytus, the Theban. Odo, archbishop of Canterbury. Eutychius, patriarch of Alexandria. Said, patriarch of Alexandria. Flodoard. Joseph Genesius Atto, bishop of Verceil. Dunstan, archbishop of Canterbury. Luitprand, abbot of Fleury. Notger, bishop of Liege. Suidas. Roswida, a poetess. Edgar, king of England. Ælfridus. Heriger. Olympiodorus. Œcumenius. Odilo. Burchard. Valerius of Astorga in Spain. His Lives of the Fathers, very different from those that are published, are still in MS. in the library of Toledo. John Malela. Constantine Porphyrogenitus. John of Capua. Nicholas, patriarch of Constantinople. Gregory of Cæsarea. Epiphanes. Severus. Alfric, archbishop of Canterbury Pope Gerbert. Oswald. Sisinius. Hubald. Luitprand.

HERETICS, REAL OR REPUTED.

No new heresies were invented during this century. That of the Anthropomorphites was revived, and the greatest part of the others were continued. Thus we find Nestorians, Eutychians, Paulicians, Armenians, Anthropomorphites, and Manichæans. making a noise in this century.

REMARKABLE EVENTS AND RELIGIOUS RITES.

Irruption of the Huns into Germany, and of the Normans into France. The Danes invade England. The Moors enter Spain. The Hungarians, and several northern nations, are converted to Christianity. The pirate Rollo is made duke of Normandy, and embraces the Christian faith. The Polanders are converted to Christianity under Micislaus, in the year 965. The Christian religion is established in Moscovy, Denmark, and Norway. The plan of the holy war is formed in this century, by pope Sylvester II. The baptism of bells; the festival in remembrance of departed souls; the institution of the Rosary; and a multitude of superstitious rites, shocking to common sense, and an insult upon true religion, are introduced in this century. Fire-ordeal introduced. The Turks and Saracens united. The Danish war continues to convulse England. Feudal tenures begin to take place in France. The influence and power of the monks increase greatly in England. The kingdom of Italy is united by Otho to the German empire. Pope Boniface VII. is deposed and banished for his crimes. Arithmetical figures are brought from Arabia into Europe by the Saracens. The empire of Germany is rendered elective by Otho III.

PROFANE AUTHORS.

This century, by way of eminence, is styled the age of barbarism and ignorance. The greatest part of the ecclesiastical and theological authors mentioned above, were mean, ignorant, and trivial writers, and wrote upon mean and trivial subjects. At the head of the learned men of this age we must place Gerbert, otherwise known by the papal denomination of Sylvester II. This learned pontiff endeavoured to revive the drooping sciences; and the effects of his zeal were visible in this, but still more in the following century. Suidas. Geber, an Arabian chemist, celebrated by the learned Boerhaave. Constantine Porphyrogen. Mohammed Ebn Jaber Al-Batani, an Arabian astronomer. Razi, a celebrated Arabian chemist and physician. Leontius, one of the Byzantine historians. Joseph Genesius.

CENTURY XI.

SOVEREIGN PRINCES.

Emperors of the East:—A. D.—Basil III., 1025. Constantine VIII., 1028. Romanus II. Argyr., 1034 Michael IV. Paphl., 1041. Michael V. Calaphates, 1051. Constantine IX. Monomach, 1054. Theodora 1056. Michael VI. Strat., 1057. Isaac I. Comn. 1059. Constantine X. Ducas, 1067. Romanus III. Diogenes, 1071. Nicephorus II. Botoniates, 1081. Alexis I. Comnen. *Emperors of the West:*—Otho III., 1002. Henry II., 1024. Conrad II., 1039. Henry III., 1056. Henry IV. *Kings of Spain*, i. e. *of Leon and the Asturias:*—Alphonso V., 1027. Vermond III., 1037. *Kings of Leon and Castile united:*—Ferdinand I. surnamed the Great, 1065. Sancho II., 1073. Alphonso VI. *Kings of France:*—Robert, 1031. Henry I., 1060 Philip I. *Kings of England:*—Ethelred II., 1016. Edmond Ironside, 1017. Canute the Great, king of Denmark, 1035. Harold Harefoot, 1039. Hardicanute, 1041. Edward the Confessor, 1066. Harold, 1066 *Norman line:*—William the Conqueror, 1087. William Rufus, 1100. *Kings of Scotland:*—Grime, 1003 Malcolm II., 1033. Donald VII. by some called Duncan, 1040. Macbeth, 1057. Malcolm III., 1093. Donald VIII. dethroned, 1094. Duncan II., 1096. Donald again, 1097. *Kings of Sweden:*—Olaus II., 1019. Asmund, 1035. Asmundslem, 1041. Hakon, 1059. Stenchil, 1061. Ingo III., 1064. Alstan, 1080. Philip. *Kings of Denmark:*—Sweyn, 1014. Canute the Great, king of England, 1035. Hardicanute, 1041 Magnus, 1048. Sweyn II., 1074. Harold, 1076. St. Canute, 1085. Olaus, 1093. Eric II. *Kings of Poland:*—Boleslaus, first king, 1025. Micislaus, 1034. Interregnum. Casimir, 1058. Boleslaus II., 1081. Uladislaus. *Kings of Jerusalem:*—Godfrey, chosen king in 1099, dies in 1100. Baldwin I.

POPES, OR BISHOPS OF ROME.

Sylvester II., 1003. John XVII., 1003. John XVIII., 1009. Sergius IV., 1012. Benedict VIII., 1024. A schism between Gregory and Benedict. John XIX., 1033. Benedict IX., 1044. A schism between the two Johns and Benedict. Gregory VI., 1046. Clement II., 1048. Damasus II., 1049 Leo IX., 1054. Victor

II., 1057. Stephen X., 1059. Benedict X., 1059. Nicolas II., 1061. A schism between Nicolas and Benedict. Alexander II., 1073. A schism between Alexander and Cadalous. Gregory VII., 1086. A schism between Gregory and Guy, bishop of Ravenna. Victor III., 1088. Urban II., 1099.

ARCHBISHOPS OF CANTERBURY.

Aluric or Alfric, 1006. Elphegus, massacred by the Danes in 1012. Livingus, 1020. Agelnoth, 1038. Eadsius, 1050. Robert Gemeticensis, 1052. Stigand, deposed in 1070. Lanfranc, 1089. Anselm.

ECCLESIASTICAL AND THEOLOGICAL WRITERS.

Dithmar, bishop of Mersburg. Leo the Grammarian. Aimon. Fulpert, bishop of Chartres. Adelbold, bishop of Utrecht. Alexis, patriarch of Constantinople. Berno, of Augsburg. Ademar. The Brunos. Lanfranc, archbishop of Canterbury. Theophanes Cerameus. Nilus Doxopatrius. Michael Psellus. Michael Cerularius. Simeon the Younger. Theophylact, a Bulgarian. Cardinal Humbert. Petrus Damianus. Marianus Scotus. Anselm, archbishop of Canterbury. Ivo, bishop of Chartres. Hildebert, archbishop of Tours. Pope Gregory VII. Gerhard. Hugh of Breteuil. Berthold. Hermannus Contract. Peter, patriarch of Antioch. Glaber Radulphus. Deoduinus, bishop of Liege. Adelman. Nicetas Pectoratus. Leo of Bulgaria. Guitmund. Manasses, archbishop of Rheims. John, patriarch of Antioch. Sigefrid. Samon of Gaza. Samuel of Morocco, a converted Jew. John Xiphilin. Lambert. Adam of Bremen. John Curopalata. Benno of Ravenna. Nicholas of Methrone. Philip the Solitary. Othlon of Fulda. Tangmar. Guido Aretino. Eugesippus. A famous, but anonymous work, called Micrologus, appeared in this century. Dominic of Grado. Alberic. Osborn, a monk of Canterbury.

HERETICS, REAL OR REPUTED.

Berenger, famous for his opposition to the monstrous doctrine of transubstantiation **Roscelin, a Tritheite.** A sect of French Manichæans, condemned in the council of Orleans.

REMARKABLE EVENTS AND RELIGIOUS RITES.

The Crusades are carried on with all the enormities that usually attend a blind, extravagant, and inhuman zeal. Godfrey of Bouillon takes possession of Jerusalem in the year 1099. A contest between the emperors and popes, in which the latter discover a most arrogant and despotic spirit. The dignity of cardinal is first instituted in this century. The Moors are driven by degrees from several parts of Spain; hence arose the division of that country into so many little kingdoms. Matilda, daughter of Boniface, duke of Tuscany, leaves all her possessions to the church of Rome, in consequence of her passionate attachment to Hildebrand, otherwise known by the papal name of Gregory VII. with whom she lived in a licentious commerce. Sicily, Castile, Poland, and Hungary, are erected into kingdoms. The kingdom of Burgundy and Arles is transferred to the emperor Conrad II. by Rondolph king of Burgundy. Several of the popes are looked upon as magicians, as in these times of darkness, learning, and more especially philosophy and mathematics, were considered as magic. Investitures introduced in this century. Papal tyranny is nobly opposed by the emperors Henry I. II. and III. by William I. king of England, and other monarchs of that nation, by Philip, king of France, and by the British and German churches. Baptism is performed by triple immersion. The Sabbath Fasts introduced by Gregory VII. The Cistercian, Carthusian, and Whipping Orders, with many others, are founded in this century. The emperor Henry IV. goes barefooted to the insolent pontiff Gregory VII. at Canusium. and does homage to this spiritual tyrant in the most ignominious manner. The same emperor, however, besieges Rome soon after, and makes a noble stand against the pontiff. Domesday-book is compiled from a survey of all the estates in England. Jerusalem is taken by the Crusaders.

PROFANE AUTHORS.

Leo, the Grammarian. Adelbord. Michael Psellus. Anselm, archbishop of Canterbury. Guido Aretino, inventor of musical notes. Wippo. John Scylitzes. Avicenna, or Ebn Sina, an Arabian philosopher. Stephen, the first Christian king of Hungary. Alphes, a Jew. Josippon, or the false Josephus. Ferdousi a Persian Poet. Roscellin. John the philosopher. John Curopalata, one of the Byzantine historians

---

CENTURY XII.

SOVEREIGN PRINCES.

Emperors of the East:—A. D.—Alexis I. Comnen., 1118. John II. Comnen., 1143. Emanuel Comnen, 1180. Alexis II. Comnen., 1183. Andronicus Comnen., 1185. Isaac II. Ang., 1195. Alexis III. *Emperors of the West:*—Henry IV., 1106. Henry V., 1125. Lothaire II., 1138. Conrad III., 1152. Frederic I. surnamed Barbarossa, 1190. Henry VI., 1198. Philip. *Kings of Spain,* i. e. *of Leon and Castile:*—Alphonso VI., 1109. Alphonso VII., 1134. Alphonso VIII. 1157. Sancho III., 1158. Ferdinand II., 1175. Alphonso IX. *Kings of France:*—Philip I., 1108. Louis VI., surnamed the Gross, 1137. Louis VII. surnamed the Young 1180. Philip Aug. *Kings of England:*—Henry I., 1135. Stephen, 1154. Henry II., 189. Richard I., 1199. John. *Kings of Scotland:*—Edgar, 1106. Alexander, 1124. David, 1153. Mal colm IV., 1165. William. *Kings of Sweden:*—Philip, 1110. Ingo IV., 1129. Ragwald, 1140. Magnus, deposed in 1148. Suercher, 1160. Eric, the Holy, 1161. Charles VII., 1168. Canute, 1192. Suercher II *Kings of Denmark:*—Eric II., 1101. Nicolas, 1135. Eric III., 1138. Eric IV., 1147. Canute V., 1155 Sweyn III., 1157. Waldemar, 1182. Canute VI. *Kings of Poland:*—Uladislaus, 1102. Boleslaus III., 1139. Uladislaus II., 1146. Boleslaus IV., 1173. Micislaus, 1178. Casimir II., 1195. Lescus or Lecho V. *Kings of Jerusalem:*—Baldwin I., 1118. Baldwin II., 1131. Foulques or Fulk, 1141. Baldwin III., 1162. Almeric, 1173. Baldwin IV., 1185. Baldwin V., 1186. Guy of Lusignan. Jerusalem was retaken by the Infidels in 1187. Almeric from 1196 to 1205. *Kings of Portugal:*—Alphonso I. proclaimed king in 1139, dies in 1185. Sancho I.

POPES, OR BISHOPS OF ROME.

Pascal II., 1118. Anti-Popes. Clement, Albert, Theodore, and Maginulph. Gelasius II., 1119. Calistus II., 1124. Honorius II., 1130. Innocent II., 1143. Celestine II., 1144. Lucius II., 1145. Eugenius III., 1153. Anastasius IV., 1154. Adrian IV., 1159. Alexander III., 1181. Lucius III., 1185. Ur III., 1187. Gregory VIII., 1188. Clement III., 1191. Celestine III., 1199.

ARCHBISHOPS OF CANTERBURY.

Anselm, 1109. Ralph, 1122. William de Corboil, 1136. Theobald, 1161. Thomas Becket, 1170. Richard, 1183. Baldwin, 1191. Reginald Fitz-Jocelin, 1191. Hubert Fitz-Walter.

ECCLESIASTICAL AND THEOLOGICAL WRITERS.

Gilbert, abbot of Westminster. Guibert. Sigebert of Gembloura. Peter Alphonso. Odo of Orleans. Godfrey of Vendome. Rupert of Duitz. Baldric. Arnulph, bishop of Lisieux. Bernard of Clairva. Abelard. Athelred. Baldwin, archbishop of Canterbury. Euthymius Zigab. William of Malmesbury. John of Salisbury. Thomas Becket, archbishop of Canterbury. Gervase, a monk of Canterbury. Nicephorus of Brienne. Anselm, bishop of Havelberg. Jo. Zonaras. Mich. Glycas. Hugo Victorinus. Eadmerus. George Cedrenus. Peter, the Venerable. Honorius of Autun. Foucher. Alger. Gratian. Peter Lombard. Henry of Huntingdon. William, bishop of Rheims. Constantine Harmen. Orderic Vital Constantine Manass. Zacharias Chrysop. Peter of Blois. Peter Comestor. Peter de Cellus. Peter of Poictiers. John Cinnamus. John Beleth. Helmold. Gislebert, bishop of London. Stephen Harding, George Xiphilin. Alexan. Arist. Godfrey of Viterbo. Theod. Balsamon. Richard of St. Victor. William of Auxerre. Bruno of Asti. Simeon of Durham.

HERETICS, REAL OR REPUTED.

The Bogomiles and Catharists were a kind of Manichæans. The Pasaginians were a kind of Arians, who also discovered a strange attachment to the ceremonial law of Moses. Eon, a madman, rather than a heretic. The same thing may be said of Tranquillinus. As to Arnold of Brescia, the Petrobrussians, Henricians, Waldenses, and Apostolics, if allowance be made for some few points, they rather deserve the title of Reformers and Witnesses to the Truth, than that of Heretics. Peter Abelard and Gilbert de la Porree differed from the notions commonly received with respect to the Holy Trinity. The Albigenses, a branch of the Waldenses, are branded with the denomination of Manichæans.

REMARKABLE EVENTS AND RELIGIOUS RITES.

The Sclavonians and the inhabitants of the island of Rugen receive the light of the Gospel, and their example is followed by the Livonians and Finlanders. The state of affairs in Asiatic Tartary changes in favour of the Christians, by the elevation of Prester-John. The Crusade is renewed. The kingdom of Jerusalem is overturned, and the affairs of the Christians in Palestine decline. A third Crusade undertaken. The three famous military orders instituted, viz. The Knights of St. John of Jerusalem—The Knights Templars—The Teutonic Knights of St. Mary. The original MS. of the famous Pandect of Justinian is discovered in the ruins of Amalphi, or Melfi, when that city was taken by Lothaire II. in 1137, and this emperor makes a present of it to the city of Pisa, whose fleet had contributed, in a particular manner, to the success of the siege. The contest between the emperors and popes is renewed under Frederic Barbarossa and Adrian IV.—The insolence of the popes excessive. Becket, archbishop of Canterbury, assassinated before the altar, while he was at vespers in his cathedral. The scandalous traffic of indulgences begun by the bishops, and soon after monopolized by the popes. The Scholastic Theology, whose jargon did such mischief in the church, had its rise in this century. The seeds of the Reformation were sown, in this century, by the Waldenses, and other eminent men in England and France. Pope Paschal II. orders the Lord's supper to be administered only in one kind, and retrenches the cup. The Canon-law formed into a body, by Gratian. Academical degrees introduced in this century. Learning revives and is encouraged in the university of Cambridge. The pope declares war against Roger king of Sicily, who takes from his holiness Capua and Beneventum. The council of Clarendon held against Becket. The kings of England and France go to the Holy Land. Henry II. of England, being called by one of the Irish kings to assist him, takes possession of Ireland.

PROFANE AUTHORS.

Anselm of Leon. Vacarius. Leoninus, the supposed introducer of Latin rhymes. Roger Hoveden, John of Salisbury. William of Malmesbury. John Zonaras. George Cedrenus. John Cinnamus. Silvester Girald, bishop of St. David's. Godfrey of Viterbo. William of Newburgh, an English historian. Pelagius, bishop of Oviedo. John of Milan, author of the poem called Schola Salermitana. Robert Pullein an English cardinal. Abraham Eben-Ezra. John and Isaac Tzetzes. Henry of Huntingdon. Nicetas

Werner. Moses Maimonides. Anvari, a Persian astronomer. Portius Azo. Nestor, a Russian historian. Falcandus. Benjamin of Tudela, a Spanish Jew, whose Travels were translated by Baratier. Averroes or Ebn-Zohr. Eustathius, bishop of Thessalonica. Solomon Jarchi. Al-Hasen, an Arabian, who composed a large work on Optics. George Al-Makin, author of the History of the Saracens translated by Erpenias. Geoffrey of Monmouth.

CENTURY XIII.

SOVEREIGN PRINCES.

Emperors of the East:—A. D.—Alexis III. dethroned in 1203. Alexis IV. dethroned in 1204. Alexis Ducas, surnamed Murzurphle, 1204. *Latin Emperors of the East residing at Constantinople:*—Balduin I., 1205. Henry, 1216. Peter, 1221. Robert, 1229. Balduin II., 1259. *Greek Emperors residing at Nice:*—Theodore Lascaris, 1222. John Ducas III., 1255. Theodore Lascaris. 1259. John Lascaris IV., 1259. Michael Palæologus retakes Constantinople in the year 1261, and thus unites, in his person, the Latin and Greek empires; he dies in 1283. Andronicus II. *Emperors of the West:*—Philip, 1208. Otho IV., 1218. Frederic II., 1250. Civil wars and an interregnum, during which Conrad of Suabia, William count of Holland, Richard king of England, Alphonso of Spain, Ottocar of Bohemia, appear on the scene of action. Rodolphus of Hapsburg is elected emperor in 1273, and dies in 1291. Adolphus of Nassau, deposed in 1298. Albert I. *Kings of Spain,* i. e. *of Leon and Castile:*—Alphonso IX., 1214. Henry I., 1217. Ferdinand III., 1252. Alphonso X., 1284. Sancho IV., 1295. Ferdinand IV. *Kings of France:*—Philip Aug., 1223. Louis VIII., 1226. Louis IX. sainted, 1270. Philip III. the Hardy, 1285. Philip IV. the Fair. *Kings of England:*—John, 1216. Henry III., 1272. Edward I. *Kings of Scotland:*—William, 1214. Alexander II., 1249. Alexander III., 1285. Interregnum. John Baliol. *Kings of Sweden:*—Suercher II., 1211. Eric X., 1218. John I., 1222. Eric XI., 1250. Waldemar, 1276. Magnus, 1290. Birger. *Kings of Denmark:*—Canute VI., 1202. Waldemar II., 1241. Eric VI., 1250. Abel, 1252. Christopher, 1259. Eric VII., 1286. Eric VIII. *Kings of Poland:*—Lescus V., 1203. Uladislaus III., 1226. Boleslaus V., 1279. Lescus VI., 1289. Boleslaus, Henry, and Uladislaus, take the title of Governors. Premislaus, 1296. Uladislaus IV. deposed in 1300. Wenceslaus, king of Bohemia. *Kings of Portugal:*—Sancho I., 1212. Alphonso II., 1223 Sancho II., 1246. Alphonso III., 1279. Denis.

POPES, OR BISHOPS OF ROME.

Innocent III., 1216. Honorius III., 1226. Gregory IX., 1241. Celestine IV., 1243. Innocent IV., 1254. Alexander IV., 1261. Urban IV., 1264. Clement IV., 1268. Gregory X., 1276. Innocent V., 1276. Adrian V., 1276. John XX., 1277. Nicolas III., 1280. Martin IV., 1285. Honorius IV., 1288. Nicolas IV., 1292 Celestine V., 1294.

ARCHBISHOPS OF CANTERBURY.

Hub. Fitz-Walter, 1204. Stephen Langton, 1228. Richard Le Grand, 1231. St. Edmund, 1242. Boniface, 1270. Robert Kilwardby, 1278. John Peckham, 1291. Robert Winchesley.

ECCLESIASTICAL AND THEOLOGICAL WRITERS.

Joachim. John, bishop of Macedonia. Demetrius Chomatenus. Mark, patriarch of Alexandria. Malachy, archbishop of Armagh. Nicetas Choniata. François d'Assise. Alan de l'Isle. Jacobus de Vitriaco. Peter, the monk. Antony of Padua. Germanus. Cæsarius. William of Paris. Raymond of Pennafort. Alexander Hales. Edmund Rich, archbishop of Canterbury. Thomas of Spalatro. John Peckham, archbishop of Canterbury. Roger Bacon. Albert, the Great. Rob. Grossetete. Vincent de Beauvais. Robert of the Sorbonne. George Acropolita. Hugo de St. Caro. George Metochita. Guillaume de St. Amour. Nicephorus Blem. Thomas Aquinas. Bonaventura. Gilbert of Tournay. John of Paris, an opposer of transubstantiation and papal tyranny. John Beccus. Nicetus Acominatus. Theodore Lascaris. Arsenius. George Pachymer. George the Cyprian. Stephen Langton, archbishop of Canterbury. Robert Capito. Thomas Cantiprat. Richard Middleton. William Durand. Ægidius de Columna. Guil. Peraldus. Martin Polon. Raymond Martin. Jacob de Voragine. Guillaume de Seignelai, bishop of Auxerre. William of Auvergne, bishop of Paris. Henry of Ghent. Pope Boniface VIII.

HERETICS, REAL OR REPUTED.

The Waldenses. Nestorians. Jacobites. The Brethren and Sisters of the Free Spirit, otherwise called Beghards and Beguttes, Beghins and Turlupins. Amalric. Joachim. Wihelmina. The sect of the Apostles. John of Parma, author of the everlasting gospel. Flagellants. Circumcelliones.

REMARKABLE EVENTS AND RELIGIOUS RITES.

The Moslem religion triumphs over Christianity in China and the northern parts of Asia, by flattering the passions of voluptuous princes. A papal embassy is sent to the Tartars by Innocent IV. A fourth crusade is undertaken by the French and Venetians, who make themselves masters of Constantinople, with a design to restore the throne to Isaac Angelus, who had been dethroned by his brother Ducas. The emperor Isaac is put to death in a sedition, and his son Alexis strangled by Alexis Ducas, the ringleader of this faction. The crusaders take Constantinople a second time, dethrone Ducas, and elect Baldwin, count of Flanders, emperor of the Greeks. The empire of the Franks in the East, which had subsisted fifty-seven years, is overturned by Michael Palæologus. A fifth crusade, which is carried on by the confederate arms of Italy and Germany. The fleet of the crusaders ruined by the Saracens. The fifth crusade undertaken by Louis IX. who takes Damietta, but is afterwards reduced, with his army, to extremities; dies of the plague in a second crusade, and is canonized. The knights of the Teutonic Order, under the command of Herman de Saliza, conquer and convert to Christianity the Prussians, at the desire of Conrad. duke of Masovia. Christianity is propagated among the Arabians in Spain. The philosophy of Aristotle triumphs over all the systems that were in vogue before this century. The power of creating bishops, abbots, &c. is claimed by the Roman pontiffs, whose wealth and revenues are thereby greatly augmented. John, king of England, excommunicated by pope Innocent III. is guilty of the basest compliances, through his slavish fear of that insolent pontiff. The inquisition established in Narbonne Gaul, and committed to the direction of Dominic and his order, who treat the Waldenses, and other reputed heretics, with most inhuman cruelty. The adoration of the Host is introduced by Pope Honorius III. The Magna Charta is signed by king John and his barons on the 15th of June, at Runemede, near Windsor. A debate arises between the Dominicans and Franciscans concerning the immaculate conception of the Virgin Mary. Jubilees instituted by pope Boniface VIII. The Sicilian Vespers—when the French in Sicily, to the number of 8000, were massacred in one evening, at a signal given by John of Prochyta, a Sicilian nobleman. Conrad, duke of Suabia, and Frederic of Austria, beheaded at Naples by the counsel of pope Clement IV. The Jews are driven out of France by Louis IX. and all the copies of the Talmud, that could be found, are burned. The college of electors founded in the empire. The association of the Hans-Towns. The Dominicans, Franciscans, Servites, Mendicants, and the Hermits of St. Augustin, date the origin of their orders from this century. The fables concerning the removal of the chapel of Loretto; the vision of Sim. Stockius, the Wandering Jew, and St. Antony's obliging an ass to adore the sacrament, are invented about this time. The festivals of the Nativity of the blessed Virgin, and of the Holy Sacrament or Body of Christ, instituted. The rise of the house of Austria is referred to this century. Wales is conquered by Edward, and united to England. There is an uninterrupted succession of English parliaments from the year 1293.

PROFANE AUTHORS.

Roger Bacon, one of the great restorers of learning and philosophy. Saxo Grammaticus. Ralph de Diceto. Walter of Coventry. Alexander of Paris, the founder of French poetry. Villehardouin, an historian. Accursi of Florence. Kimchi, a Spanish Jew. Conrad de Lichtenau. John Holywood, called De Sacro Bosco, author of the Sphæra Mundi. Actuarius, a Greek physician. Rod. Ximenes, archbishop of Toledo. Michael Coniat, bishop of Athens. Ivel. Rigord, an historian. Pierre de Vignes Matthew Paris. Suffridus. Sozomen, author of the Universal Chronology, which is yet in MS. in the possession of the Regular Canons of Fesoli, near Florence. Barthol. Cotton, of Norwich; see Wharton's Anglia Sacra. Engelbert. Thomas Wicke, an English historian. Vitellio, a Polish mathematician. Albert the Great. Colonna, archbishop of Messina. Michael Scot, the translator of Aristotle. Gregory Abulfaragius. Foscari of Bologna. Alphonso, king of Castile. Cavalcanti of Florence. Dinus, a famous jurist. Marco Polo, a Venetian whose travels in China are curious. Francis Barberini, an Italian poet.

CENTURY XIV.

SOVEREIGN PRINCES.

Emperors of the East:—A. D.—Andronicus II., 1332. Andronicus, the Younger, 1341. John Cantacuzenus usurps the government under John Palæologus, and holds it till the year 1355. John VI. Palæol. 1390. Andronicus IV., 1392. Emanuel II. *Emperors of the West:*—Albert I., 1308. Henry VII. of Luxemburg, 1313. Louis V. Bav., 1347. Charles IV., 1378. Wenceslaus, 1406. *Kings of Spain*, i. e. *of Leon and Castile:*—Ferdinand IV., 1312. Alphonso XI., 1350. Pedro the Cruel, 1369. Henry II., 1379. John I., 1390. Henry III. *Kings of France:*—Philip the Fair, 1314. Louis X. Hutin, 1316. Philip V., 1321. Philip VI. of Valois, 1350. John, 1364. Charles V., 1380. Charles VI. *Kings of England:*—Edward I 1307. Edward II., 1327. Edward III., 1377. Richard II., 1399. Henry IV. *Kings of Scotland:*—John Baliol, 1306. Robert Bruce, 1329. David II., 1370. Robert II., 1390. Robert III. *Kings of Sweden:*—Birger, 1326. Magnus, 1363. Albert, defeated by Margaret queen of Denmark in 1387, dies in the year 1396. Margaret. *Sovereigns of Denmark:*—Eric VIII., 1321. Christopher II., 1333. Waldemar III., 1375. Olaus, 1387. Margaret. *Kings of Poland:*—Wenceslaus, 1305. Uladislaus reascends the throne, and dies in 1333. Casimir III. the last of the Piasts, 1370. Louis, king of Hungary, 1381. Interregnum. Uladislaus Jagellon, duke of Lithuania. *Kings of Portugal:*—Denis, 1325. Alphonso IV., 1357. Pedro, the Justiciary, 1367. Ferdinand, 1383. Interregnum. John I. *Ottoman Emperors:*—The ancient history of the Turks extends from the beginning of the seventh to the commencement of the fourteenth century. The modern commences about the beginning of the fourteenth century. Othman, 1327. Or Khan, 1359. Amurath, or Morad, 1389. Bajazet or Ba-yezid.

POPES, OR BISHOPS OF ROME.

Boniface VIII., 1303. Benedict XI., 1304. Clement V., 1314. John XXI., 1334. A schism between Peter and John. Benedict XII., 1342. Clement VI., 1352. Innocent VI., 1362. Urban V., 1372. A schism between Urban and Clement. Gregory XI., 1378. The death of Gregory XI. occasioned that violent schism which threw the western church into the utmost confusion. The church of Rome had two popes, one residing at Rome, the other at Avignon. *At Rome:*—Urban VI., 1389. Boniface IX. *At Avignon:*—Clement VII. not acknowledged, 1394. Benedict XIII.

ARCHBISHOPS OF CANTERBURY.

Robert Winchelsey, 1313. Walter Raynold, 1327. Simon Mepham, 1333. I. Stratford, 1348. Thomas Bradwardine, 1349. Simon Islip, 1365. Simon Langham, 1374. Simon Sudbury, 1381. W. Courtenay, 1396. Thomas Arundel

ECCLESIASTICAL AND THEOLOGICAL WRITERS.

Nicephorus Callistus. Raymond Lully. Matthæus Blastares. Greg. Acindynus. John Cantacuzenus. Nicephorus Greg. Duns Scotus. Andrew of Newcastle. Francis Mayron. Durand of St. Portian. Nicolas de Lyra. John Bacon. William Occam. Nicolas Trivet. Andrew Horne. Richard Bury. Walter Burley. Richard Hampole. Robert Holkot. Thomas Bradwardine, archbishop of Canterbury. John Wickliffe. Thomas Stubbs. John de Burgo. William Wolfort. The last thirteen all English authors Peter Aureolus. John Bassolis. Bernard Guido. Alvarus Pelagius. Theophanes, bishop of Nice. Philotheus. Antonius Andreas. Herveus Natalis. Thomas of Strasburg. Raynerius of Pisa. John of Fribourg. Pope Clement VI. Thomas Joysius. John of Naples. Albert of Padua. Michael Cesenas. Gregory Palamas. Andronicus. Peter of Duisburg. Ludolf Saxon. Cardinal Caietan. James of Viterbo. Cardinal Balde. George of Rimini. The popes Benedict XI. and XII. Gui of Perpignan. Nicolas Cabasilas, archbishop of Thessalonica. Richard, bishop of Armagh. Demetrius Cydonius. Petranch. Peter Berchorius. John Cyparissotes. Nicolas Oresme. Philip Ribot. Nilus Rhodius. Maximus Plan. John Taulerus. Greg. Palamas. Nic. Eymericus. John Rusbroch. Manuel Caleca. Catharine of Sienna. St. Bridget. Gerard of Zutphen. Pierre Ailli. Francis Zabarella. Marsigli of Padua, who wrote against the papal jurisdiction. Philippe de Mazieres. Jordan of Quedinburg. Barth. Albizi of Pisa, author of the famous book of the Conformities of St. Francis with Jesus Christ. Fabri, bishop of Chartres. Michael Anglianus. Raymond Jordan. Jac. de Theramo. Manuel Chrysoloras. Cardinal Francis Zabarella with many others, too numerous to mention.

HERETICS, REAL OR REPUTED.

Waldenses. Palamites, Hesychasts, and Quietists, three different names for one sect. Spiritual Franciscans. Ceccus Asculanus, who was burned at Florence by the Inquisition for making some experiments in mechanics that appeared miraculous to the vulgar. Beghards, and Beguines. As to the Cellites or Lollards, they cannot be deemed heretics. The followers of John Wickliffe deserve an eminent place, with their leader, in the list of Reformers. Nicolas of Calabria. Martin Gonsalvo. Bartold de Rorbach. The Dancers.

REMARKABLE EVENTS, AND RELIGIOUS RITES.

Fruitless attempts made to renew the crusades. Christianity encouraged in Tartary and China: but loses ground towards the end of this century. The Lithuanians and Jagello, their prince, converted to the Christian faith in the year 1386. Many of the Jews are compelled to receive the Gospel. Philosophy and Grecian literature are cultivated with zeal in this century. The disputes between the Realists and Nominalists revive. Philip the Fair, king of France, opposes with spirit the tyrannic pretensions of the pope to a temporal jurisdiction over kings and princes, and demands a general council to depose Boniface VIII. whom he accuses of heresy, simony, and several enormities. The papal authority declines. The residence of the popes removed to Avignon. The universities of Avignon, Perugia, Orleans, Angers, Florence, Cahors, Heidelberg, Prague, Perpignan, Cologne, Pavia, Cracow, Vienna, Orange, Sienna, Erfort, Geneva, founded. The rise of the great western schism, which destroyed the unity of the Latin church, and placed at its head two rival popes. John Wickliffe opposes the monks, whose licentiousness and ignorance were scandalous, and recommends the study of the Holy Scriptures. A warm contest arises among the Franciscans about the poverty of Christ and his Apostles. Another between the Scotists and Thomists, about the doctrines of their respective chiefs. Pope Clement V. orders the Jubilee which Boniface had appointed to be held in every hundredth year to be celebrated twice within that period. The Knights Templars are seized and imprisoned; the greatest part of them put to death, and their order suppressed. The Golden Bull, containing rules for the election of an emperor of Germany, and a precise account of the dignity and privileges of the electors, is issued by Charles IV. Clement VI. adds the country of Avignon to the papal territories. The emperor Henry VII dies, and is supposed by some authors to have been poisoned by a consecrated wafer, which he received at the sacrament, from the hands of Bernard Politian, a Dominican monk. This account is denied by authors of good credit. The matter, however, is still undecided. Gunpowder is invented by Schwartz, a monk. The mariner's compass is invented by John Gioia, or as others allege, by Flavio. The city of Rhodes is taken from the Saracens, in the year 1309, by the Knights Hospitalers, subsequently called the Knights of Malta. Timour extends his conquests in the East. The Bible is translated into French by the order of Charles V. The festival of the holy lance and nails that pierced Jesus Christ instituted by Clement V.—Such was this pontiff's arrogance, that once, while he was dining, he ordered Dandolo, the Venetian ambassador, to be chained under the table like a dog. The beginning of the Swiss Cantons. The emperor Louis of Bavaria, Philip the Fair, king of France, Edward III., king of England, who opposed the tyranny of the popes, may be looked upon as witnesses to the truth and preparers of the Reformation. To these we may add Duraud, Gerson, Olivus, who called the pope Anti-christ, and Wickliffe, who rejected transubstantiation, the sacrifice of the mass, the adoration of the host, purgatory, meritorious satisfactions by penance, auricular confession, the celibacy of the clergy, papal excommunications, the worship of images, of the Virgin and relics. The order of the Garter is instituted in England by Edward III.

PROFANE AUTHORS.

Dante, the principal restorer of philosophy and letters, and also one of the most sublime poets of modern times. Petrarca. Boccaccio. Chaucer. Matthew of Westminster. Nicolas Trivet. Nicephorus Gregoras, a compiler of the Byzantine History. Theodore Metochita. Guillaume de Nangis. historian. Henry Stero, historian. Dinus Mugellanus. Evrard, historian. Hayton, an Armenian historian. Albertino Mussato. Oderic de Forli. Leopold, bishop of Bamberg. Peter of Duisburg, an historian Albert of

Strasburg, an historian. Balaam of Calabria, master of Petrarch. Joinville. Peter de Apono, physician and astronomer. Marsigli of Padua, a famous lawyer. John Andre, an eminent jurist. Leontius Pilato one of the restorers of learning. Gentiles de Foligno. Ismael Abulfeda, an Arabian prince. Peter of Ferrara. Arnold of Villa-Nova. William Grisant, an English mathematician. Homodi of Milan. Albergotti of Arezzo. Philip of Leyden. Baldus de Ubaldis. Froissart, a French historian.

CENTURY XV.

SOVEREIGN PRINCES.

Emperors of the East:—A. D.—Emanuel II., 1425. John VI. Palæologus, 1448. Constantine Palæologus, so far down as the year 1453, when Constantinople was taken by Mohammed II. *Emperors of the West:*—Rupert or Robert, 1410. Jodocus not acknowledged. Sigismund, 1437. Albert II. of Austria, 1439. Frederic III., 1493. Maximilian I. *Kings of Spain, i. e. of Leon and Castile:*—Henry III., 1406. John II., 1454. Henry IV., 1474. Ferdinand, in right of Isabella. *Kings of France:*—Charles VI. Charles VII., 1461. Louis XI., 1483. Charles VIII., 1498. Louis XII. *Kings of England:*—Henry VI., 1413. Henry V. 1422. Henry VI. dethroned in 1461. Edward IV., 1483. Edward V., 1483. Richard III., 1485. Henry VIII. *Kings of Scotland:*—Robert III., 1406. James I., 1437. James II., 1460. James III., 1488. James IV. *Sovereigns of Sweden and Denmark:*—Margaret, 1412. Eric IX. deposed in 1438. Christopher III., 1448. Charles Canutson, 1471. An interregnum until the year 1483. John. *Kings of Poland:*—Uladislaus, Jag., 1434. Uladislaus, king of Hungary, 1444. An interregnum of three years. Casimir IV., 1492. John Albert. *Kings of Portugal:*—John I., 1433. Edward, 1438. Alphonso V., 1481. John II., 1495. Emmanuel the Great. *Ottoman Emperors:*—Ba-yezid, taken prisoner by Timour in 1402. Solyman, 1410. Mousa, 1413. Mohammed I., 1421. Morad II., 1451. Mohammed II. who takes Constantinople in 1453, and dies in 1481. Bayezid II. *Czars, or Emperors of Russia:*—There reigns, in the chronology of these princes, an uncommon degree of confusion, suitable to the barbarism of that nation. In the year 1732, they began to publish, at Petersburg, a series of their sovereigns, beginning with duke Ruric, who is supposed to have reigned in the ninth century. From that time downward, all is darkness and perplexity, until we come to the reign of John Basilowitz I. who, in the fifteenth century, shook off the yoke of the Tartars, and assumed first the title of Czar, after having conquered the kingdom of Casan. We therefore begin with this prince, and shall follow the chronology observed by the authors of the Modern Universal History, in their History of Russia. The reader may, however, consult the Tablettes Chronologiques de l'Histoire Universelle of Lenglet, who places this prince in the 16th century.* John Basilowitz.

POPES, OR BISHOPS OF ROME.

Boniface IX., 1404. Innocent VII., 1406. Gregory XII. deposed, 1409. Alexander V., 1410. John XXII. deposed, 1417. Martin V., 1431. Eugenius IV., 1447. A schism.—The council of Basil depose Eugenius, and elect Amadeus, first duke of Savoy, who assumes the title of Felix V. Eugenius, however, triumphs in the issue. Nicolas V., 1455. Calistus III., 1458. Pius II., 1464. Paul II., 1471. Sixtus IV., 1484. Innocent VIII., 1492. Alexander VI.

ARCHBISHOPS OF CANTERBURY.

Thomas Arundel, 1413. H. Chichele, 1443. John Stafford, 1452. John Kemp, 1453. Thomas Bouchier 1486. J. Morton, 1500.

ECCLESIASTICAL AND THEOLOGICAL WRITERS.

John Huss. Jerome of Prague. Paulus Anglicus. John Gerson. Herman de Petra. Theod. de Niem, bishop of Cambray. Tho. Valdensis. Pope Alexander V. John Capreolus. Peter de Ancharano. Nicolas de Clemangis. Theod. Urias. Alphons. Tostat. John, patriarch of Antioch. Mark of Ephesus Cardinal Bessarion. G. Scholarius. G. Gemistus. John de Turrecremata. George of Trapezond. John Capistran. Laurentius Valla. John of Segovia. Franc. de la Place. Reginald, bishop of St. Asaph. Antoninus, archbishop of Florence. Nicolas de Cusa, bishop of Brixen, and cardinal. Thomas a Kempis. Anton. de Rosellis. Rickel. Ducas. Bened. de Accoltis. Guill. d'Aoupelande. James Paradise, an English Carthusian. Æneas Sylvius Picolomini, or pope. Pius II. Lorenzo Justiniani. John Gobelin. Alphonso de Spina. Greg. of Heimburg. Theod. Lelio. Henry of Gorcum. I. Ant. Campanus. Alex. de Imola. Henry Harphius. J. Perez. P. de Natalibus. B. Platina. P. Niger. John de Wesalia. Hermol. Barbarus. Michael of Milan. Stephen Brulefer. Cardinal Andr. du St. Sixte. Savanarola. Marsilius Ficinus. John Tritheme. Picus, or Pico of Mirandula. Ant. de Lebrixa. Boussard. J. Reuchlin, otherwise called Capnio. Jovianus Pontanus. Nicolas Simonis. Claude de Seyssel. Simeon of Thessalonica. Gobelin Persona. Henry of Hesse. George Fhranza. Vincent Ferrieres. Julianus Cæsarinus. Nich. Tudeschus. Raymond de Sabunde, or Sebeyde. Catharine of Bologna. Gregorius Melissen. Marcus Eugenius. Sylvester Syropul. Ambrose, general of the Camaldolites. George Codinus. Onuphr. Panvinius. Gabriel Biel. John Nauclerus. John Nieder.

HERETICS, REAL OR REPUTED.

The Waldenses. The Wickliffites. The White Brethren. The men of understanding, who were headed by Ægidius Cantar, and William of Hildernissen. Picard, an Adamite. The following deserve rather the denomination of Reformers than Heretics, viz. John Huss, Jerome of Prague. Branches of the Hussites, the Calixtines. Orebites. Orphans. Taborites. Bohemian Brethren; also John Petit. John Wellus. Peter Osma. Matth. Grabon.

* He died in that century, but flourished chiefly in the fifteenth. —EDIT.

REMARKABLE EVENTS AND RELIGIOUS RITES.

The Moors and Jews are converted in Spain, by force. In the year 1492, Christopher Columbus opens a passage into America, by the discovery of the islands of Hispaniola, Cuba, and Jamaica. Constantinople taken by the Turks in the year 1453.—Letters flourish in Italy, under the protection of the house of Medici and the Neapolitan monarchs of the house of Arragon. The calamities of the Greeks under the Turkish government, conduce to the advancement of learning among the Latins. The council of Constance is assembled by the emperor Sigismond in the year 1414. John Huss, and Jerome of Prague, are committed to the flames, by a decree of that council. The council of Basil is opened in the year 1431, and in it the reformation of the church is attempted in vain. Horrible enormities are committed by the pope of this century, and more especially by Alexander VI. The council of Constance remove the sacramental cup from the laity, and declare it lawful to violate the most solemn engagements when made to heretics. The war of the Hussites in Bohemia. Institution of the Order of the Golden Fleece. The Moors and Jews driven out of Spain. The Massacre of Varna, in the year 1444. The order of Minimes instituted by Franc. de Paulo. Exploits of the Maid of Orleans. The art of printing with moveable wooden types, is invented by Coster at Haerlem; and the farther improvements of this admirable art are owing to Gensfleisch and Guttemberg, of Mentz, and Schœffer of Strasbourg. The universities of Leipsic, Louvaine, Fribourg, Rostock, Basil, Tubingen, Wurtzburg, Turin, Ingolstadt, St. Andrew's in Scotland, Poictiers, Glasgow, Gripswald in Pomerania, Pisa, Bourdeaux, Treves, Toledo, Upsal, Mentz, Copenhagen, founded in this century. The first book printed with types of Metal; which was the Vulgate Bible, published at Mentz in 1450: a second edition of the same book appeared at Mentz in 1642, and has been mistaken for the first. The famous Pragmatic Sanction established in France. The university of Caen in Normandy is founded by the English in the year 1437. The Portuguese sail, for the first time, to the East Indies under Vasquez de Gama. Maximilian divides the empire into six circles.

PROFANE AUTHORS.

Laurentius Valla, the great restorer of Latin elocution. Leonard Aretin. Gasparini. William Lyndewood. Alexander Chartier. Fr. Frezzi. Christina of Pisa. Paul de Castro. Poggio of Florence. John Fortescue, high chancellor of England. Theod. Gaza. Bart. Facio. Dluglossus, a Polish historian. R. Sanc. de Arevallo Chalcondylas. J. Savonarola. Marcilius Ficinus. John Picus de Mirandula. Marc. Coc. Sabellicus. Forestus. Ant. Bonfinius. Jovian. Pontanus. G. Gemistus. J. Alvarot. Guarini of Verona. J. Juv. des Ursins. Mass. Vegio. Flavio Bindo. J. Argyropulus. Dr. Thomas Linacre. The Strozzi. Bon. Monbritius. P. Callim. Esperiente. Jul. Pompon Lætus. Angelo. Politiano. Fulgosi. A. Urceus Codrus. Mich. Marullus. Oliver de la Marche. Caiado. Abrabanel. Calepin Rebel. Martial de Paris. Phil. de Comines. Al. Achillini. Scipio Carteromaco. John Baptista Porto. Aldus Manutius. Cherefeddin Ali, a Persian historian. Arabshah, an Arabian historian. J. Whethamsted. Ulug-beg, a Tartar prince. J. Braccelli. Palmieri. Villon, otherwise Corbueil. Muller, surnamed Regiomontanus. Calentius, a Latin poet. Dom. Calderini. Barth. Fontius. Enguerr. de Monstrelet. Andronicus of Thessalonica. Er. Philelphi. Alex. Imola. J. Ant. Campani. Nich. Perotti. Th. Littleton. Ant. of Palermo. Constant. Lascaris. A. Barbatius. Gobelin Persona. Bern. Justiniani. Dieb. Schilling. Ralph Agricola. I. Andreas. Alex. ab. Alexandro. G. Merula. M. M. Boiardo. A. Mancinelli. Rob. Gaguin. Bern. Corio. Garbr. Altilius. Gul. Caoursin. J. Nai. Al. Ranuccini. P Crinitus. Molines. Cettes. John Murmelius. Mark Musurus. Jason Mainus. Pandolfo Collenucio. R Langius. Pietro Cosimo. Abraham Zachut.

CENTURY XVI.

SOVEREIGN PRINCES.

Emperors:—A. D.—Maximilian I., 1519. Charles V. abdicates the empire in 1556, and dies in 1558. Ferdinand, 1564. Maximilian II., 1576. Rodolph II. *Kings of Spain:*—Ferdinand V. surnamed the Catholic, king of Arragon, in consequence of his marriage with Isabella, becomes king of Castile; and the kingdoms of Arragon and Castile remain united. Isabella died in 1504, and Ferdinand in 1516. Philip I. of Austria, 1506. Jane, 1516. Charles I. or V., 1558. Philip II., 1598. Philip III. N. B.—Philip II. seized Portugal, which remained in the possession of the kings of Spain until the year 1640. *Kings of France:*—Louis XII., 1515. Francis I., 1547. Henry II., 1559. Francis II., 1560. Charles IX., 1574. Henry III., 1589. Henry IV. *Kings of England:*—Henry VII., 1509. Henry VIII., 1547. Edward VI., 1553. Mary, 1558. Elizabeth. *Kings of Scotland:*—James IV., 1513. James V., 1542. Mary, beheaded in 1587. James VI. *Kings of Sweden and Denmark:*—John, 1513. Christiern II. deposed in 1522. Gustavus Ericson, 1560. N. B. Sweden is separated from Denmark under this prince. Eric deposed in 1568. John III., 1592. Sigismond, king of Poland, deposed in 1599. Charles IX. *Kings of Denmark:*—Christiern II. deposed in 1522. Frederic I., 1533. Christiern III., 1559. Frederic II., 1588. Christiern IV. *Kings of Poland:*—John Albert, 1501. Alexander, 1506. Sigismund I., 1548. Sigismund II., 1572. Henry of Anjou, until the year 1574. Stephen Bathori, 1587. Sigismond king of Sweden. *Kings of Portugal:*—Emanuel the Great, 1521. John III., 1557. Sebastian, 1578. Henry, Card. 1580. Portugal is reduced under the dominion of Spain by Philip II. *Ottoman Emperors:*—Ba-yezid II., 1512. Selim I., 1520. Solyman II., 1566. Selim II., 1574. Morad III., 1595. Mohammed III. *Czars of Muscovy:*—John Basilowitz, 1505. Basil Ivanowitz, who received from Maximilian I. the title of Emperor, 1533. John Basilowitz II., 1584. Theodore Ivanowitz, 1597. Boris Godenow. *Stadtholders of the United Provinces:*—William I. the glorious founder of their liberty, 1584. Maurice.

POPES, OR BISHOPS OF ROME

Alexander VI., 1503. Pius III., 1503. Julius II., 1513. Leo X., 1521. Adrian VI., 1523. Clement VII., 1534. Paul III., 1549. Julius III., 1555. Marcellus II., 1555. Paul IV., 1559. Pius IV. 1566. Pius V., 1572. Gregory XIII., 1585. Sixtus V., 1590. Urban VII., 1590. Gregory XIV., 1591. Innocent IX., 1592 Clement VIII.

ARCHBISHOPS OF CANTERBURY.

Henry Dean, 1504. W. Warham, 1532. Thomas Cranmer, 1555. Reginald Pole, 1558. Matthew Parker, 1575. Edmund Grindal, 1583. John Whitegift.

ECCLESIASTICAL AND THEOLOGICAL WRITERS.

John Sleidan. William Budæus. Desiderius Erasmus. Martin Luther. Ph. Melancthon. John Brentius. Martin Bucer. Ulric Zuingle. Peter Galatin. Fr. Ximenes. Thomas More. John Whitegift, archbishop of Canterbury. John Fisher. John Œcolampadius. And. Carolostadius, or Carlstadt. John Tiligius. James Faber. Matthew Flacius. John Calvin. Martin Chemnitz. James Andreas. David Chytræus. William Farel. Theodore Beza. Faustus Socinus. Bened. Arias Montanus. And. Osiander. Ægid. Hunnius. Melchior Canus. Polyc. Lyserus. George Wicellus. Cardinal Bellarmine. Stella. Crantzius. Thomas Illiricus. Jacob Ben-Chaim, who gave an edition of the Hebrew Bible. Sanderus. Isid. Clarius. John Major. Andrew Vega. Franc. Vatable. Cardinal Sadolet. Cardinal Cortesius. John Cochlæus. Alphons. Zamora. Vivaldi. J. Almain. Spagnoli. Aug. Dathus. Pope Adrian VI. Petro de Monte. Pope Leo X. Alb. Pighius. Henry VIII. king of England. Louis Vives. S. Pagninus. Leo de Castro. Matth. Ugonius. Cardinal Caietan. James Hoogstraat. Ambr. Catharini. John Faber. Ortuin Gratius. John Eckins. Leander Alberti. Nic. Serrarius. Pet. Canisius. Cæsar Baronius. Fran. Ribera. Pierre Pithou. Mich. Baius. W. Alan, English cardinal. Dr. John Colet. Mercator. Nic. Harpfield. Leunclavius. Molina. Salmeron. Maldonat. J. Natalis. J. P. Maffei. Cardinal Hosius. Jansenius. John Tillet. James Naclantus. De Vargas. Cardinal Seripand. And. Masius. Pope Paul IV. Widmanstadt. Cassander. Stapleton. Mercerus. F. Xavier. Ign. Loyola. Bishop Gardiner. Jer. Oleaster, with many others too numerous to mention. N. B. It is remarkable that, among the ecclesiastical writers of this century, there are above 55 who employed their labours in the exposition and illustration of the Scriptures; and this happy circumstance contributed, without doubt, to prepare the minds of many for the Reformation, and thus rendered its progress more rapid.

HERETICS, REAL OR REPUTED.

Schwenckfeld. Andr. Osiander. Stancarus. The Adiaphorists. Interimists. Agricola of Eisleben, the chief of the Antinomians. George Major. N. Amsdorf. The Synergists. M. Flacius. The Crypto-Calvinists. Anabaptists. Mennonites. Theoph. Paracelsus. Postellus. David Georgius. Franc. Pucius. Defid. Erasmus. Agrippa. Cassander and Wicelius. Conr. Vorstius. Sam. Huberus. Mich. Servetus. Valent. Gentilis. Lælius Socinus. Faustus Socinus. Quintin, the chief of the Libertines

REMARKABLE EVENTS AND RELIGIOUS RITES

The Reformation is introduced into Germany by Luther, in the year 1517; into France by Calvin about 1529; into Switzerland by Zuingle, in 1519. Henry VIII. of England, throws off the papal yoke, and becomes supreme head of the church. Edward VI. encourages the Reformation in England. The reign of queen Mary restores Popery, and exhibits a scene of barbarous persecution that shocks nature. The name of Protestants given to the Reformed at the Diet of Spire, in 1529. The league of Smalcald is formed in 1530. The Reformation introduced into Scotland by John Knox, about the year 1560; and into Ireland by George Brown, about the same time; into the United Provinces, about the year 1566. Gustavus Ericson introduces the Reformation into Sweden, by the ministry of Olaus Petri, in 1530. It was received in Denmark, in 1521. The Gospel is propagated by the papal missionaries in India, Japan, and China. The Jesuit order is founded, in 1540, by Ignatius Loyola. The famous council of Trent is assembled. The Pragmatic Sanction is abrogated by Leo X. and the Concordat substituted for it. Pope Julius III. bestows a cardinal's hat upon the keeper of his monkeys. The Inquisition is established at Rome by Paul IV. The war of the Peasants. The universities of Wittenberg, Francfort on the Oder, Alcala, Saragossa, Marpurg, Seville, Compostella, Oviedo, Grenada, Franeker, Strasbourg, Parma, Macerata, Tortosa, Coimbra, Konigsberg, Leyden, Florence, Rheims, Dillengen, Mexico, St. Domingo, Tarragona, Helmstadt, Altorf, Paderborn, Sigen, founded in this century. The treaty of Passau, in 1552. The Paris massacre of the protestants on St. Bartholomew's day. The republic of the United Provinces formed by the union of Utrecht. The edict of Nantes granted to the Protestants by Henry IV. of France.

PROFANE AUTHORS.

British Authors:—Sir Thomas More. Thomas Linacre. S. Purchas. Thomas Elliot. Hect. Boethius. J. Leland, the antiquary. Ed. Wotton. J. Christophorson. Cuth. Tonstal. R. Ascham. J. Kaye. Thomas Smith. George Buchanan. Alex. Arbuthnot. Sir Phil. Sidney. John Fox. Fr. Walsingham. Ed. Grant. Ed. Anderson. John Dee. Thomas Craig. G. Creighton. Ed. Brerewood. *French Authors:*—William Budæus, or Bude. Clement Marot. Fr. Rabelais. Ja. Dubois (Sylvius.) Pierre Gilles Or. Finee. Robert Etienne, or Stephens. P. Belon. William Morel. Adr. Turnebus. Ch. Du Moulin. Gilb. Cousin. Mich. de l'Hopital. L. Le Roy (Regius.) Hub. Languet, author of the Vindiciæ contra Tyrannos. Laur. Joubert. James Pelletier. Fr. Belleforest. M. A. Fr. Muret. P. Ronsard. J. Dorat. James Cujas. Fr. Hotoman. James Amyot. Mich. de Montagne. Mich. de Castelnau. P. Pithou. J. Bodin. Nic. Vignier. Bl. de Vigenere. Henri Etienne, commonly called Stephens. J. De Serres (Serranus.) Cl. Fauchet. J. Passerat. J. J. Boissard. P. Daniel d'Orleans. Francis Viete. Cardinal d'Ossat. Rob. Constantin. P. Morin. Jos. Just. Scaliger. Nic. Rapin. J. Papire. Masson. P. B. Brantome. St. Pasquier. *Italian Authors:*—Americo Vespucci. J. Jocondi of Verona, who discovered the Letters of Pliny. A. F. Grazzini. Leonicini, the translator of Galen. Pomponace M. A. Casanova. P. Gravina. Sannazarius. Machiavel. Vida. J. A. Lascaris. Alcyonius, translator of Aristotle. Ariosto. Bern. Maffei. Fr. Guicciardini. Cardinal Bembo. Cardinal Sadolet. And. Alciat. M. A. Flaminio d Imola. Lilius Giraldus. J. Fracastor. Polydore Virgil. M. A. Majoragio. P. Aretino. J. de la Casa. L. Alamanni. N. Tartaglia. Palingenius. Julius Cæsar Scaliger. Zanchius. Gab Faerno. Gab. Fallopius. J. Acronius. Lodovico Cornaro. Robertello. Palearius Onuph Panvini

Argentieri. J. Bar de Vignole. Paul Manutius. Jerome Cardan. A. Palladio. C. Sigonius. P. Victorius. Oct. Ferrari. James Zabarella. L. Guicciardini. A. de Costanzo. Torq. Tasso. Fr. Patritius or Patrizi. Ant. Riccoboni. G. Panciroli. And. Cesalpino. Natalis Comes. Aldrovandi. Gratiani B. Guarini. *Swiss Authors:*—Aur. Ph. Paracelus. Theod. Bibliander. Theod. Swinger. Isaac Casaubon. *German, Dutch, and Flemish Authors:*—J. Reuchlin. P. Mosellan. M. Aurogallus, who assisted Luther in the translation of the Bible. H. C. Agrippa. D. Erasmus of Rotterdam. Luscinius. Simon Grynæus. Adr. Barland of Zealand. Nic. Copernicus, a Prussian. J. Secundus of the Hague. J. Olaus Magnus. Peutinger. Paul Faglus. Sebastian Munster. G. Agricola. John Sleidan. Gasp. Bruschius. P. Lotichius. Conrad Gesner. G. Fabricius. A. Masius. Joach. Camerarius. Virgilius of Zuichem. Hubert Goltzius. John Sturmius. J. Sambuc. A. G. de Busbec. J. Leunclavius. G. Mercator. Læv. Torrentius. Raphelengius. Ortelius. Heurnius of Utrecht. Justus Lipsius. Paul Merula of Leyden. A. Gorlæus. Schonæus. Em. van Meteren. Dom. Baudius. *Danish Authors:*—Tycho Brahe, the astronomer. Nicolas Craig.

CENTURY XVII.

SOVEREIGN PRINCES.

Emperors:—A. D.—Rodolph II., 1612. Matthias, 1619. Ferdinand II., 1637. Ferdinand III., 1657. Leopold. *Kings of Spain:*—Philip III., 1621. Philip IV., 1665. (Portugal throws off the Spanish yoke, and recovers its independence, in the year 1640.) Charles II., 1700. *Sovereigns of France:*—Henry IV., 1610. Louis XIII., 1643. Louis XIV. *Sovereigns of England:*—Elizabeth, 1603. James I. (VI. of Scotland,) 1625. Charles I. beheaded in the year 1649. Cromwell usurps the government under the title of Lord Protector, and dies in 1658. Charles II., 1685. James II. abandons his kingdom in the year 1688, and dies in 1701. William III. and Mary, 1694. *Kings of Scotland:*—James VI., 1625. This prince and his successors were kings both of England and Scotland so far down as the year 1707, when these kingdoms were united into one monarchy. *Kings of Sweden:*—Charles IX., 1611. Gustavus Adolphus, 1632. Christina abdicates the crown in 1654, and dies in 1689. Charles Gustavus, 1660. Charles XI., 1697. Charles XII. *Kings of Denmark:*—Christiern IV., 1648. Frederic III., 1670. Christian V., 1699. Frederic IV. *Kings of Poland:*—Sigismond III., 1632. Uladislaus Sig., 1648. John Casimir, 1669. Michael I., 1674. John Sobieski, 1696. Frederic Augustus, elector of Saxony. *Kings of Portugal:*—John, duke of Braganza, chosen king in 1640, dies in 1656. Alphonso VI. dethroned in 1667. Pedro II. *Ottoman Emperors:*—Mohammed III., 1604. Ahmed I., 1617. Mustapha, 1617. Osman, 1622. Mustapha restored, 1623. Morad IV., 1640. Ibrahim, 1649. Mohammed IV., 1687. Solyman III., 1691. Ahmed II., 1695. Mustapha II. *Czars of Moscovy:*—Boric, 1605. Theodore Borissowitz, 1605. The false Demetrius, 1606. Basil Zuski, 1610. Demetrius II., 1610. Demetrius III., 1610. Uladislaus of Poland, 1613. Demetrius IV., 1613. Michael Theodorowitz, 1645. Alexis Michaelowitz, 1676. Theodore Alexiowitz, 1682. Ivan, or John, and Peter I. jointly. Ivan died in 1696. *Stadtholders of the United Provinces:*—Maurice, 1625. Frederic Henry, 1647. William II., 1650. The dignity of Stadtholder remains vacant during the space of 22 years.

POPES, OR BISHOPS OF ROME

Clement VIII., 1605. Leo XI., 1605. Paul V., 1621. Gregory XV., 1623. Urban VIII., 1644. Innocent X., 1655. Alexander VII., 1667. Clement IX., 1669. Clement X., 1676. Innocent XI., 1689. Alexander VIII., 1691. Innocent XII., 1700.

ARCHBISHOPS OF CANTERBURY.

Dr. J. Whitgift, 1604. Dr. R. Bancroft, 1610. Dr. George Abbot, 1633. Dr. W. Laud, 1645. Dr. W. Juxon, 1663. Dr. Gil. Sheldon, 1677. Dr. W. Sancroft, deprived in 1690, died 1693. Dr. John Tillotson, 1694. Dr. Thomas Tenison.

ECCLESIASTICAL AND THEOLOGICAL WRITERS.

Protestant Writers:—Archbishop Abbot. John Lightfoot. Matthew Poole. Bishop Pearson. Bishop Fell. Gataker. Bishop Ward. Owen. Edward Pocock. Dr. Goodwin. Dr. Manton. Richard Baxter. Dr. Calamy. Howe. Bates. Bishop Bull. Grew. Bishop Burnet. Jo. Forbes. J. Baxter. Archbishop Tillotson. Dr. Sherlock. Archbishop Wake. Chillingworth. Henry Hammond. Thomas Hyde. William Cave. Brian Walton. Drusius. Hospinian. Trigland. Ittigius. Fr. Spanheim. R. Cudworth. Ed. Stillingfleet. H. Prideaux. J. Locke. W. Lloyd, bishop of Worcester. J. Milton. St. Nye. Claude. Daille. J. Morin. Amyrault. Samuel and James Basnage. Jurieu. Benoit. Turretin. Elias Saurin. Morus. Le Cene. Mesterzat. Le Blanc. Arminius. Grotius. Episcopius. Curcellæus. Limborch. Sleidan. Coccelus. Voetius. Gomar. Lud. Capellus, or Louis Capel. S. Bochart. Gerhard. Hoe. Calixtus. G. and Fred. Heilbronner. Haffenreffer. Thummius. The Osianders. Musæus. Hutter. Hunnius, Guy and Nic. The Mentzers. Godfrey Olcarius. Fred. Baldwin. Alb. Grawer. Carpzovius. Tarnovius. J. and Paul John Asselman. Eilhart Luber. The Lysers. Michael Walter. Joach. Hildebrand. J. Val. Andreas. Solomon Glassius. Ab. Calovius. Theod. Hachspan. J. Hulseman. Jacob Weller. J. Conr. Danhauer. J. G. Dorschæus. John Arndt. Martin Geyer. Schertzer. Balthasar and John Meisner. Aug. Pfeiffer. Muller. H. and J. Just. Chr. Schomer. Sebast. Schmidt. Christ. Horsholt. Ph. Jac. Spener. G. Th. Mayer. Fred. Bechman. From Gerhard to Fred. Bechman inclusively all are Lutherans. *Roman Catholic Authors:*—Baronius. Bellarmine. Serrarius. Fevardentius. Possevin. Gretser. Combesis. Nat. Alexander. J. Sirmond. Petau. Cellot. Caussin. Renaud. Fra. Paolo. Pallavicini. Labbe. Maimbourg. Thomassin. Sfondrat. Aguirre. Henry Noris. D'Achery. Mabillon. Hardouin. Simon. Ruinart. Montfaucon. Galloni. Cornelius a Lapide. Bonfrere. Menard. Segenot. Bernard. Lamy. Bollandus. Henschen. Papebroch. Perron. Estius. Launoy. Tillemont. Godeau. Albaspinæus. Richelieu. Holstenius. Baluzius. Bona. Huet. Bossuet. Fenelon. Thiers. Du-Pin. Leo Allatius. Zaccagni. Cotelier. Filesac. Visconti. Molina. Arriaga. Rigault. Richer

Pererius. Mariana. Fr. Pithou. Fr. de Sales. M. de Calafio. Lessius. Pineda. C. Jansenius Bentivoglio. Sponde. Bzovius. H. de Valois. P. de Marca. Arnaud d'Andilly. Du Cange. Pascal. Du Boulay. A. Arnaud. Vavasseur. Neercassel. J. Le Maitre de Sacy. Pagi. Pezron. Gerberon. Quesnel. These are the most distinguished writers of the Romish church during this century.

HERETICS, REAL OR REPUTED.

The doctrine of the Jesuits, concerning philosophical sin, condemned by pope Alexander VIII. in 1690 The Probabilists (so the Jesuits were called from their odious doctrine of probability,) condemned by the Sorbonne. The Franciscans are judged heretics on account of their doctrine concerning the immaculate conception of the Virgin Mary. Jansenius, Quesnel, and Arnauld, as also Fenelon, Molinos, and the pietists, are condemned in France. Arminius, and his followers, the Universalists. Bekker, the Cartesian divines, Labadie. Bourignon, Poiret, Leehoff, and Claude Pajon, are regarded as heretics by the reformed churches in France and Holland. The Independents, Antinomians, Ranters, and Quakers, and among the latter, Fox, Barclay, Keith, and Penn, are looked upon in the same light. Add to these, Enthusiasts, and Fanatics of various kinds, such as Jacob Behmen, Valentine Weigel, Nic. Drabicius, Seidel Stifelius, and the Rosecrucians

---

REMARKABLE EVENTS AND RELIGIOUS RITES.

The congregation *de propaganda Fide*, founded at Rome in 1622, by pope Gregory XV. Christianity is propagated in the kingdoms of Siam, Tonquin, and Cochin-china, by the Jesuit missionaries. The thirty years' war breaks out. The Moors are driven out of Spain. The Protestants are persecuted in France. The Gunpowder Treason discovered in England. A rupture between pope Paul V. and the Venetians. The royal society is founded in the year 1662. A Jubilee is celebrated by pope Clement VIII. in the year 1600. In 1605, Maurice, landgrave of Hesse Cassel, introduces the reformed religion into Marpurg. Paul V. excommunicates the Venetians, whose cause is defended by Fra. Paolo. In the year 1606, Rodolph II. allows the Hungarians the free exercise of the Protestant religion, formerly granted by Ferdinand I. but abolished by his successor. In 1608, the Socinians publish their Catechism at Cracow. The Silesians, Moravians, and Bohemians, are allowed by Rodolph II. the free exercise of their religion in 1609. The Protestants form a confederacy at Heilbron, in 1610; and the Roman catholics form a league at Wurtzburg in opposition to it. The Bohemians choose Frederic V. elector Palatine, for their king, in order to maintain them in the free exercise of the Protestant religion;—but he is conquered, and they are forced to embrace popery. In 1625, the princes of Lower Saxony enter into a league with Christian IV. of Denmark, which concludes by the peace of Lubeck. Ferdinand II. publishes, in 1629, an edict, ordering the Protestants to surrender and restore all the ecclesiastical domains and possessions of which they had become masters after the pacification of Passau.—This edict is disobeyed. Gustavus Adolphus enters Germany. The peace of Munster and Osnabrug concluded, by which the three religions are tolerated in the empire. The synod of Dordrecht assembled in the year 1618. Henry IV. of France is assassinated by Ravaillac This event exposes the Protestants to new persecutions. The edict of Nantes is perfidiously revoked by Louis XIV. and the Protestants are treated with the utmost barbarity. A contest between Louis XIV. and pope Innocent XI., concerning the collation of benefices, and the privileges and pretensions of the crown during their vacancy. The French clergy, in a general assembly at St. Germain's, declare the pope's pretensions to temporalities null and void; place the authority of a general council above that of the pope, and maintain that his decisions are not infallible, unless they be attended with the consent of the church. The Irish massacre in 1641, in which above 40,000 (some say 150,000) Protestants are murdered. Charles I. king of England, beheaded in the year 1649. A sort of commonwealth introduced by Cromwell, under which episcopacy suffers, and the Presbyterians, or rather the Independents, flourish. Charles II. restored, and with him episcopacy re-established. The glorious Revolution renders memorable the year 1688. The Protestants are oppressed and persecuted in many places. Several false Messiahs discovered, particularly Sabbati Levi, who, to avoid death, embraces the Moslem faith. The universities of Lunden in Sweden, Giessen, Pampeluna, Saltzburg, Derpt in Livonia, Utrecht, Abo, Duisburg, Kiel in Holstein, Inspruck, Halle. The academies of Inscriptions and of Sciences founded at Paris.

PROFANE AUTHORS.

No century has been so fertile in authors as this before us. Their number amounts to above 850. We shall confine ourselves to those who were most eminent in each country. *In Great Britain and Ireland:*— Sir John Harrington. James Harrington. J. Pitt. R. Stanihurst. Sir Henry Saville. Thomas Hariot, the inventor of algebra. W. Camden. Nicolas Fuller. Benjamin Jonson. Shakespear, or Shakspeare. Henry Wotten. Thomas Lydiat. Joseph Hall, called the English Seneca. Lord Herbert of Cherbury. Thomas Gataker. W. Habington. Archbishop Usher. W. Harvey, who first discovered the circulation of the blood. Sir Ken. Digby. Sir James Ware. John Milton. Abraham Cowley. The Chancellor Clarendon. Sir Matthew Hale. Fr. Glisson. Thomas Stanley. Joseph Glanvil. Samuel Butler. Algernon Sidney. John Collins, mathematician. Robert Morison. William Dugdale. Ralph Cudworth. J. Rushworth. Robert Boyle. John Locke. W. Molyneux. Sir Paul Ricaut. H. Hody. Bishop Beverage. Sir Samuel Garth. Thomas Gale. John Philips. Bishop Sprat. Thomas Dempster. John Fletcher. Ph. Massinger. Edm. Gunter. Francis Bacon, lord Verulam. Thomas Ridley. John Speed. John Donne. Bishop Godwin, the annalist. Edward Coke. Thomas Randolph. Thomas Farnaby. John Napier, inventor of logarithms. G. Keating. John Greaves. Edward Simson. John Selden. William Burton. Richard Zouch. W Oughtred. B. Walton. P. Heylin. James Howel. Sir John Denham. Sir John Marsham. Bishop Wilkins. James Gregory. Thomas Willis. Bulst. Whitelocke. John Price. Isaac Barrow. Thomas Hobbes. Thomas Brown. Thomas Marshal. Edmund Castel. Thomas Otway. Ed. Waller. Dr. Sydenham. Anthony Wood. Ed. Bernard, professor of astronomy. Bishop Stillingfleet. William Bonner. John Dryden. John Wallis. John Ray. D. Gregory. M. Lister. Henry Dodwell. N. Grew. Sir H. Spelman. *French Authors:*—J. Aug. de Thou. Pineau. Gilot. Mornac. P. Matthieu. Du Vair. Fr. Pithou. J. Barclai. Savaron. Pr. Jeannin. Godefroi. Bergier. Le Mercier. Boulanger. Goulart. Malherbe. Marillac. N. and C. Le Bois. J. B. Le Menestrier. J. Bap. Duval. P. Haye du Chastelet. R. Des Cartes. N. Fab. de Peiresc. Henr. duc de Rohan. De Meziriac. J. Bourdelot. J. Guthieres. And. du Chesne. Louis Savot. Val. Conrart. Cardinal Richelieu. Rochemallet. Philip Monet. Nicholas Bourbon. Augustus Galland. J. F. Niceron. Edm. Merille. Samuel Petit. M. Mersenne Voiture. De Vaugelas. Ch. Justel. Did. Herault. J. Baudouin. P. du Puy. G and L. de St. Marthe. Denis Petau. G Fournior. Cl. Saumaise. G. Naude. N. Rigault J L. de Balzac. G. B. de Gramont.

Sarasin. D. Blondel. P. Gassendi. J. Bignon. C. H. Fabrot. L. Ch. Le Fevre. N. Perrot d'Ablancourt. N. Sanson. Briet. Tan. Le Fevre. La Mothe Vayer. Moliere. G. M. le Jay. Roberval. Rohault. H. and Adr. de Valois. F. H. d'Aubignac. J. Esprit. L. Moreri. Duc de Rochefoucault. R. le Bossu. F. E. de Mezeray. P. Corneille. Ed. Mariotte. J. Spon. G. d'Estrades. Charles and Perrault. P. Bayle. Vauban. Tournefort. Th. Corneille. Boileau. Ren. Rapin. Jean Doujat. Fr. Bernier. Ch. Du Fresne. Du Cange. Is. de Benserade. Thevenot. G. Menage. De St. Real. Pelisson. Bussy Rabutin. Ch. Patin. B. d'Herbelot. Cl. Lancelot. St. Evremond. Amelot de la Houssaye. Louis Cousin. F. S. Regn. Des Marais. A. Felibien. Jean de la Bruyere. Sim. Foucher. J. Domat. J. B. Santeuil. C. P. Richelet. P. J. d'Orleans. J. Racine. J. Barbeyrac. J. B. Morin. Baudrand Segrais. Chevreau. Charpentier. Bouhours. Marquis de l'Hopital. Vaillant. P. Silv. Regis. Theod Agrip. d'Aubigne. *Italian Authors:*—Prosper Alpini. B. Baldi. J. A. Magini. A. Morosini. Luc. Valeri. Paul Ben.. Davila. L. Pignoria. Salvador. Sanctorius. Thomas Campanella. Alexander Donato. Mascardi Galilei. Bentivoglio. Strozzi. Leo de Modena. Bonav. Cavalieri. Ev. Torricelli. J. V. Rossi. Fam. Strada. T. Galluzzi. Martini. Imperiali. Tomassini. Virgilio Malvezzi. Molinetti. Sert. Orsato. J. B. Nani. J. A. Borelli. Ricci. Oct. Ferrari. Bartalocci. M. Malpighi. Bellori. Viviani Bellini. Bocconi. Averani. Cassini. Magalotti. *Spanish and Portuguese Authors:*—Cervantes. Antonio de Ledesma. J. Mariana, the historian. Antonio Herrera, the historian. Aldrete, the antiquarian. Balbuena. J. L. de la Cerda. Lopez de Vega, the Spanish Homer. Nic. de Antonio. Balth. Gracian. Diego de Coutu. Jos. Texeira. Rod. Lobo. Eman. Faria e Sousa. Ant. Perez. Man. Alvarez. Pegase. *German, Dutch, Swiss, Swedish, &c. Authors:*—Pauw, Anatomy. Aiguillon. Emmius. Gruterus. Bertius. Andr. Schott. Martinius. Snellius of Leyden. James and Adrian Metius Cunæus. J. Meursius. Louis de Dieu. J. B. van Helmont. Hugo Grotius. Louis de Dieu. Erycius Puteanus Gasp. Barlæus. Van Hooft. Const. Imperator. Manasseh Ben-Israel. B. Varenius. Sanderus. Van der-Linden. J. Golius. Aitzema. Hœschelius. Ch. Helvicus. Melchior Adam. Cluverius. Hospinian. Rosinus. Buxtorf, father and son. Kepler. Goldast. Horstias. Sennert. Erasmus Schmidt. Alstedius. J. F. Gronovius. Meric Casaubon. Fr. Junius. Conringius. R. Heinsius. Noldius. H. Meibomius. Olaus Wormius. Jos. Arndius. J. G. Suicer. Wetstein. Gurtler. Thomasius. J. P. Pareus Hoffman. Scioppius. G. J. Vossius. Barthius. Freinsheim. Schrevelius. J. Gerard. Hornius. Et muller. Olaus Rudbeck. Bartholinus, father and son. Isaac Pontanus. Chr. Longomontanus. J. Rhodius. Bangius. Ad. Olearius. Graaf. Swammerdam. Ath. Kircher. Anna Maria Schurman. Ab. de Wicquefort. J. Kunckel. Ludolf. J. G. Grævius. Burchard de Volder. Varenius. Dodonæus. Otto Guerick, inventor of the air-pump. Morhoff. Isaac Vossius. Olaus Borrichius. G. Sagittarius. J. Tollius. Huygens. Pufendorff. Leusden. Wagenseil. Brockhuisen. Cellarius. Ezekiel Spanheim.

CENTURY XVIII.

SOVEREIGN PRINCES.

Emperors of Germany:—A. D.—Leopold, 1705. Joseph, 1711. Charles VI., 1740. Charles VII. (elector of Bavaria) 1745. Francis of Lorrain, 1765. Joseph II., 1790. Leopold II., 1792. Francis II. *Kings of Spain:*—Philip V. resigns the crown in 1724. Louis dies in 1724. Philip reascends the throne; and dies in 1746. Ferdinand VI., 1759. Charles III., 1788. Charles IV. *Kings of France:*—Louis XIV., 1715. Louis XV., 1774. Louis XVI. deposed in 1792 and beheaded in 1793. After several changes of government, Bonaparte became sovereign of France in 1799, under the denomination of first consul, for which he afterwards substituted the more dignified title of emperor. *Sovereigns of Great Britain:*—William III., 1702. Anne, 1714. George I., 1727. George II., 1760. George III. *Sovereigns of Sweden:*—Charles XII., 1718. Ulrica Eleonora, 1751. Frederic of Hesse Cassel. 1751. Adolphus of Holstein, 1771. Gustavus III.—assassinated in 1792. Gustavus IV. deposed by his uncle in 1809. *Kings of Denmark:*—Frederic IV., 1730. Christiern VI., 1746. Frederic V., 1766. Christiern VII. *Kings of Poland:*—Frederic Augustus, 1733. Stanislaus is twice elected, but abdicates the crown. Frederic Augustus II., 1764. Stanislaus, count Poniatowski, succeeds; but he is deposed by foreign powers in 1794, and the kingdom is dismembered. *Sovereigns of Portugal:*—Pedro II., 1706. John V., 1750. Joseph, 1777. Maria. *Turkish Emperors:*—Mustapha II., 1703. Ahmed III.—deposed in 1730. Mahmoud, 1754. Osman III., 1757. Mustapha III., 1774. Abdul-hamed, 1789. Selim III. *Russian Sovereigns:*—Peter the Great, 1725. Catharine I., 1727. Peter II., 1730. Anne, 1740. Ivan, or John—deposed in 1741, and assassinated in 1762. Elizabeth, 1762. Peter III. murdered in 1762. Catharine II., 1796. *Stadtholders of the United Provinces:*—William III., 1702. This dignity remained vacant for 45 years. William IV., 1751. William V. deposed by the French in 1795. *Kings of Prussia:*—Frederic I., 1713. Frederic William I., 1740. Frederic II., 1786. Frederic William II., 1797. Frederic William III. *Kings of Sardinia:*—Victor Amadeus I., 1730 Charles Emanuel, 1773. Victor II., 1796.

POPES, OR BISHOPS OF ROME.

Clement XI., 1721. Innocent XIII., 1724. Benedict XIII., 1730. Clement XII., 1740. Benedict XIV. 1758. Clement XIII., 1769. Clement XIV., 1774. Pius VI., 799. Pius VII.

ARCHBISHOPS OF CANTERBURY.

Dr. Thomas Tenison, 1715. Dr. William Wake, 1737. Dr. John Potter, 1747. Dr. Thomas Herring. 1757. Dr. Matthew Hutton, 1758. Dr. Thomas Secker, 1768. Dr. Frederic Cornwallis 1783. Dr. John Moore.

ECCLESIASTICAL AND THEOLOGICAL WRITERS.

N. B. In this list, only deceased authors are mentioned. *Protestant Writers:*—Sir Isaac Newton. Dr. Bentley. Archbishops Wake, Potter, and Secker. Bishops Hare, Cumberland, Atterbury, Berkeley, Butler, Benson, Smallridge, Sherlock, Conybeare, Warburton, Lowth, Hurd, Horsley, and Porteus. Wesley. Dr. Mill. Dr. Edwards. Dr. Whitby. Dr. Clarke. W. Whiston. Wollaston. The lord chancellor King

Dr. J. Leland. Dr. Derham. Jeremiah Seed. James Hervey. Balguy. Chapman. Dr. Jortin. Dr. Paley. Dr. Blair. Dr. Hickes. Abernethy. Dr. George Benson. Dr. Chandler. Dr. James Foster. Dr Watts. Dr. Doddridge. Dr. Taylor, of Norwich. Pierce. Hallet. Grove. Lardner. Dr. Priestley. *French, Swiss, German, and Dutch Writers:*—Abbadie. Pictet. James Saurin. Oudin. Ostervald. Jurieu. Turretin. Werenfels. Vitringa. Leydeiker. Marck. Braun. Jablonski. Mosheim. Witsius and Trigland of Leyden. Spener. Pecht. Mayer. Masius. Wandalinus. Wincler. Fabricius. Schmidt. Rechenberg. Ittigius. Seeligman. Loscher. Foertsch. Buddeus. Luthenius. Antonius. Franckius. Langius. Maius. Pritius. N. B. The twenty writers last mentioned are Lutherans. *Romish Authors:*—Gonsalez. Beaugendre. Papin. Van Espen. F. Lami. Pouget. Des-Marets. D. de St. Marthe Hyac. Serri. G. Helyot. F. Timoleon de Choisi. Huet. J. Martiany. Hure. Habert. Fleuri. Massillon. Eusebius Renaudot. Houdry. P. Constant. Baltus. P. de la Broue. G. Daniel. Hardouin J. J. Boileau. Marsollier. Garnier. Le Bœuf. Anselme. Joubert. Tournemine. Duguet. Longuerue. Le Quien. Longueval. Vertot. Gibert. Martenne. Boursier. Blondel. Montfaucon. C. de la Rue. Sabatier. Benoit. Colbert. Languet. Dantine. Houteville. Lenglet du-Fresnoi. Martin. Berruyer. De Caylus. Bon. Racine. Calmet. Cellier. Maran. Des-Champs. Morvan de Bellegarde. The popes Clement XI. Benedict XIII. and XIV Orsini. Muratori. Bianchini. Orsi. Tomasi. Banduri.

HERETICS, AND FREE THINKERS.

John Toland. Matthew Tindall. Ant. Collins. Thomas Woolston. Charles Blount. Thomas Chubb. Thomas Morgan. Bernard de Mandeville. Lord Bolingbroke, and others less worthy of notice. Among the sects of this century we may reckon the Herrenhutters, or Moravian ethren, and the followers of Swedenborg.

REMARKABLE EVENTS IN THE CHURCH.

The French Missionaries make many converts to popery in the eastern parts of the world; in the Carnatic, on the coast of Malabar, in China, &c. A great controversy is occasioned by the indulgence of the Jesuits towards the Chinese, in allowing them to retain the religious ceremonies of paganism. Protestant missionaries are sent to India by the English, Dutch, and Danes. The bull *Unigenitus*, issued by Clement XI. in 1713, condemns Quesnel's edition of the New Testament, and produces violent debates and divisions in the Gallican church, more especially between the Jesuits and the Jansenists. The latter endeavour to support their declining credit by fictitious miracles, said to be wrought at the tomb of the abbe Paris. The study of philosophy is placed on a new footing in Germany, by Leibnitz and Wolff; and their method of demonstration is transferred by some divines to theology. Christopher Matthew Pfaff, a very learned and respectable divine, forms a plan of reconciliation and union between the Lutheran and Reformed churches; the execution of which, however, is prevented by bigotry and party spirit. Sacheverel, an incendiary, who inveighs against civil and religious liberty, is impeached and censured. Lady Moyer founds a lecture for the defence of the Trinity. Dr. Bampton also establishes a lecture at Oxford, for the general defence of Christianity. The Protestant religion, and the blessings of civil liberty, are established in Great Britain by the accession of the house of Brunswick-Lunenburg to the throne. An attempt is made to assassinate Louis XV. by Damien, who is supposed (but not on sufficient grounds) to have been instigated by the Jesuits to that nefarious act. Louis suppresses the order of Jesuits in France, shuts their schools, and confiscates their revenues, in the year 1764. The kings of Portugal and Spain banish all Jesuits from their dominions. Pope Clement XIV. dissolves the order in 1773. A revolution breaks out in France in 1789; and, in its progress, the Gallican church is nearly annihilated; but Bonaparte restores catholicism. Pope Pius VI. is deposed by the French, and dies in exile, in 1799.

PROFANE AUTHORS.

Sir Isaac Newton. J. Flamsteed. J. Keill. Maclaurin. Bradley. Dr. Clarke. Dr. Bentley. Bishop Hare. Addison. Pope. Gay. Prior. Dr. Swift. Sir R. Steele. Dr. Arbuthnot. Dr. Friend. Dr. Mead. Dr. Woodward. Sir Hans Sloane. Sir Christopher Wren. Dr. Halley. Dr. Hutcheson, the metaphysician. Dr. Middleton. Dr. Berkeley, bishop of Cloyne. The lords Shaftsbury and Bolingbroke. Congreve. Wycherly. Sir John Vanbrugh. Lord Somers. Mrs. Cockburn. Nicholas and Thomas Rowe. Mrs. Rowe. Thompson. Dr. Young. Akenside. Armstrong. Collins. Gray. Lord Lyttleton. Glover. Goldsmith. Churchill. Cowper. Burns. Foote. Colman. The earl of Chesterfield. Horace, earl of Oxford. Sir William Blackstone. Hume. Robertson. Stuart. Gibbon. Burnet, or lord Monboddo. Home, or lord Kames. Sir William Jones. Harris. Dr. Johnson. Adam Smith. Burke. Richardson. Fielding. Smollett. Dr. Moore. Dr. William Hunter. John Hunter. Pott. Dr. Heberden. Sir John Pringle. Dr. Cullen. Dr. Brown. Dr. Darwin. Dr. Black. Stephen Hales. Henry Cavendish. Dr. Priestley. *French Authors:*—Malebranche. B. Lany. Lemery. Fenelon. Sauveur. P. de la Hire. Flechier. Le Vassor. J. F. Simon. Isaac de Larrey. J. F. Felibien. Andrew and Anne Dacier. Claudius and William de l'Isle. Renaudot. Tarteron. Huet. J. le Long. Boulainvilliers. Louis and John Boivin. Rapin de Thoyras. James Basnage. J. and P. L. Savary. Louis de Sacy. Du Resnel. N. L. de la Caille. B. de la Monnoye. The abbe Fraguier. Gabriel Daniel. G. J. du Verney. Valincourt. Geoffroy. De la Mothe. Joachim le Grand. Sanadon. Damon. Vertot. Catrou. Rouille. Beausobre. The abbe de la Bleterie. Niceron. De la Barre. Melon. De la Croze. Vanier. Montfaucon. Rollin. Longuerue. Banier. Cardinal Polignac. J. J. Rousseau. Du-Bois. Brumoy. Velley. Villaret. Bourget. Bignon. Goguet. Abbe de St. Pierre. Fontenelle. Du-Halde. De Moivre. Bougeant. Folard. Marquis de Puy-Segur. M. D'Argens. Abbe Des-Fountaines. Freret. Le Sage. The Fourmonts. Montesquieu. Mongault. Gabrielle du Chastelet. Des-Touches. Terrason. Caylus. Casp. de Real. Crevier. Marmontel. Reaumur. Du-Hamel. Le Gendre. Morabin. Helvetius. Maupertius. Condillac. D'Alembert. Voltaire. The Crebillons. Diderot. Condorcet. Clairault. Buffon. Lavosier. Bailly. Mirabeau. *Italian Authors:*—Poli. Magliabechi. Musitani. Battaglini. Gravina. Lancisi. Buonanni. Zanicheli. Fontanini. Micheli. Manfredi. Giannone. Muratori. Zeno. Maffei. Cardinals Quirini and Passionei. Buonamici. Cassini. Beccaria. Spalanzani. Metastasio. *Swiss Writers:*—D. and J. le Clerc Konig. Burlamaqui. Schenchzer. Crousaz. The Bernouillis. Euler. De Saussure. De Luc. Haller. Mallet. Sol. Gesner. *German Authors:*—Leibnitz. Wolff. Krosig. Kuster. Moller. J. A. Schmidt. Eccard. Mencke. Hubner. J. A. Fabricius. Neumann. Heineccius. C. Wormius. Keysler. Doppelmaier. Reiske. Werner. Pallas. Zimmermann. Herder. Gellert. Mendelsohn. Klopstock. Muller. *Dutch Writers:*—Adrian Reland. J. F. Gronovius. Cuper. Perizonius. Nieuwentyt. Noodt. Hartsoeker. Bynkershoek. Boerhaave. W. J. Gravesande. Schultens. Van

Loon. M schenbroek. Wesseling. Havercamp. Hemsterhuis. Nieuland. *Russian Writers:*—Prince Cherbatoff. Lomonosoff. Sum rokoff. *Danish and Swedish Authors:*—Baron Holberg. Fabricius. C. von Linne, or Linnæus. Si Torbern Bergman. Scheele.

CENTURY XIX.

SOVEREIGN PRINCES.

Emperor of Germany or of Austria:—A. D.—Francis II. *Kings of Spain:*—Charles IV. is deposed by Napoleon, 1808. Ferdinand VII. succeeds; but he is inveighled into France. Joseph Bonaparte usurps the throne, and reigns over a part of the kingdom, while the other parts are ruled by a council of state and the Cortes. In 1814, Ferdinand was liberated by the tyrant, and restored; and he still [in 1826] rules over a reluctant nation. *Sovereigns of Portugal:*—Maria, 1816. John VI., 1826. *Sovereigns of France:*—Bonaparte or the emperor Napoleon, reigned until the year 1814: he was then deposed and banished. In 1815, he regained his power, but lost it before the end of the year. Louis XVIII., 1824. Charles X. *King of Holland:*—Louis Bonaparte, from 1806 to 1810. *King of the Netherlands:*—William VI. prince of Orange. *King of Prussia:*—Frederic V. or Frederic William III. *Kings of Bavaria:*—Maximilian, 1824. Charles Louis. *King of Saxony:*—Frederic Augustus. *Kings of Wurtemberg:*—Frederic William, 1817. His son. *King of Hanover:*—George Augustus, also king of Great Britain. *Kings of Sweden:*—Gustavus IV. deposed in 1809. Charles XIII., 1818. Charles XIV. *Kings of Denmark:*—Christiern VII., 1808. Frederic VI. *Emperors of Russia:*—Paul, murdered in 1801. Alexander, 1825. Nicolas. *Emperors of Turkey:*—Selim III. dethroned in 1807. Mustapha IV. deposed in 1808. Mahmoud II. *Kings of Naples and Sicily:*—Ferdinand IV., 1824. Francis. *Kings of Sardinia:*—Charles Emanuel II. resigned, 1802. Victor III. resigned, 1821. Charles Felix.

POPES, OR BISHOPS OF ROME.

Pius VII., 1823. Leo XII.

ARCHBISHOPS OF CANTERBURY.

Dr. John Moore, 1805. Dr. Charles Manners Sutton.

ECCLESIASTICAL AND THEOLOGICAL WRITERS.

Dr. Richard Watson, bishop of Llandaff. Dr. George Horne, bishop of Norwich. Dr. Joseph White. Dr. Joshua Toulmin.

SECTARIES.

Joanna Southcott. The baroness von Krudener.

REMARKABLE EVENTS IN THE CHURCH.

Napoleon concludes a treaty with the pope, in 1801, for the adjustment of the religious concerns of France. The French seize the pope's territories, confine his holiness, and leave him only a shadow of power. In 1809, by the new constitution of Sweden, a full religious toleration is allowed. Recovering his authority in 1814, the pope annuls the French regulations at Rome, re-establishes the monastic orders, and revives the Society of Jesuits. By the union of the Austrian Netherlands with Holland, in 1814, the catholics lose their sway in the former country. In several of the German states, the Lutherans and Calvinists, in 1817 and 1818, enter into a union. In 1817, Louis XVIII. concludes a concordat with the pope. The year 1825 is marked, at Rome, by the solemnity of a Jubilee.

PROFANE AUTHORS.

Richard Porson, Greek professor at Cambridge. Lord Byron. Elizabeth Carter. Anna Seward. Dr. Erasmus Darwin. Dr. James Beattie. Richard Cumberland. Richard Brinsley Sheridan. John Horne Tooke. John Walcot. *French Writers:*—Madame de Stael. Madame Cottin. *German Authors:*—Klopstock. Schiller. Wieland. Kotzebue

INDEX.

THE END

www.ingramcontent.com/pod-product-compliance
Lightning Source LLC
LaVergne TN
LVHW020929110826
845150LV00004B/811
* 9 7 8 1 4 2 5 5 5 3 3 8 8 *